MODERN AMERICAN POETRY

*and*

MODERN BRITISH POETRY

## OTHER BOOKS BY LOUIS UNTERMEYER

*Poetry*

SELECTED POEMS AND PARODIES

FOOD AND DRINK

—AND OTHER POETS

*Tales*

CHIP: MY LIFE AND TIMES

THE DONKEY OF GOD

THE FAT OF THE CAT AND OTHER STORIES

THE LAST PIRATE

*Travel*

BLUE RHINE—BLACK FOREST

*Essays and Criticism*

AMERICAN POETRY SINCE 1900

THE FORMS OF POETRY

POETRY: ITS APPRECIATION AND ENJOYMENT

(*with Carter Davidson*)

*Critical Collections*

THE BOOK OF LIVING VERSE

AMERICAN POETRY FROM THE BEGINNING TO WHITMAN

MODERN AMERICAN POETRY

MODERN BRITISH POETRY

THIS SINGING WORLD

YESTERDAY AND TODAY

RAINBOW IN THE SKY

POEMS OF HEINRICH HEINE

*Novel*

MOSES

*A CRITICAL ANTHOLOGY*

# *Modern American Poetry*

# *Modern British Poetry*

## EDITED BY LOUIS UNTERMEYER

COMBINED EDITION

*Harcourt, Brace and Company, New York*

MODERN AMERICAN POETRY

COPYRIGHT, 1919, 1921, 1925, 1930, 1936, BY

HARCOURT, BRACE AND COMPANY, INC.


MODERN BRITISH POETRY

COPYRIGHT, 1920, 1925, 1930, 1936, BY

HARCOURT, BRACE AND COMPANY, INC.

PRINTED IN THE UNITED STATES OF AMERICA
BY QUINN & BODEN COMPANY, INC., RAHWAY, N. J.

## PUBLISHER'S NOTE

The latest revisions of *Modern American Poetry* and *Modern British Poetry* have been so detailed that a new combined edition of both volumes has been necessary. This new combined edition has been made because of the continued demand. It is not a selection from the two books, nor in any sense a condensation. The contents of both volumes appear exactly as printed in the latest revised editions. The two volumes are bound together and a blank colored page indicates where one ends and the other begins.

As before, the combined edition has been prepared to give the reader several advantages. For one thing, there is a physical advantage in having both books together. For another, the opportunities for rapid survey, intensive study, and comparison are greatly increased. Both books have been brought sharply up-to-date by extending the biographies and bibliographies, as well as by the inclusion of several of the younger and more experimental writers. The more important poets of the period are further emphasized by their increased groups of poems.

The prefaces of both volumes have been similarly increased, and a more thorough comparison of the poetry of the two English-writing and -speaking countries may be made through an examination of the separate introductions as well as of the individual poets. The space saved by eliminating almost ninety poets from both books has allowed the editor to concentrate on the outstanding personalities and their work.

In the American section there are now 784 poems by 107 poets; in the British section there are 820 poems by 115 poets. Thus this volume of 1203 pages includes 1604 poems by 222 poets, beginning with Christina Rossetti, in England, and Walt Whitman, in America, presenting a range of approximately a century in time and an unprecedented variety of forms, tendencies, and accomplishments.

# MODERN AMERICAN POETRY

## (Fifth Revised Edition)

# A FOREWORD

## To the Fifth Revised Edition

THIS revision of *Modern American Poetry* differs from the preceding editions in several ways. It contains more poems by the more important poets and emphasizes their contribution to the period. It presents longer poems, narrative and philosophical, as well as lyrical pieces. It begins with Walt Whitman, with whom modern American poetry may be said to have begun.

To make room for these additions, and to keep an already large book from becoming unwieldy, I have been compelled to omit some fifty authors from the earlier editions.

More than ever the aim has been to reflect the range and diversity of recent American poetry by making the compilation inclusive rather than exclusive. No group or "school" has been favored at the expense of another; the pages presume to record the pendulum-play of convention and revolt, concerning themselves with the poet's achievement rather than with his program. The object, in short, is to present something of a panorama in which outstanding figures assume logical prominence, but in which the valuable lesser ones are not lost.

It is here that the editor has his most serious misgivings. Never before have there been so many poets writing in America, never before has the verse been on such a level of competence. Even in the "depression years" poetry has not failed to be written, printed, and circulated with industry. In the fifteen years following 1920 more than one hundred magazines devoted themselves exclusively to the publication of verse, forty-five of them surviving in 1935. The historian of the period will have to begin with *Poetry: A Magazine of Verse* (the first as well as the best edited in the field), consider the experimental quarterlies *Smoke* and *Alcestis*, and run through *The Measure, The Fugitive, Voices, The Lyric, The American Poetry Journal*, all the way down to such strange ephemera as *Silhouette, Decimal, Embryo, Skyline, Fantasy, Parnassus, Star-Dust, Spirit, Troubadour, Kaleidoscope, The Rebel Poet*, to say nothing of the countless undergraduate publications such as *College Verse* and *Verse Craft*.

But the rapid multiplication of poetry magazines barely suggests the amount of verse annually produced in "these singing States." A rough calculation, based on figures from *The Publishers' Weekly*, indicates that in the twenty years covering the "renascence"—from 1912 to 1932—no fewer than four thousand American poets have published volumes in this country. This does not include pamphlets or anthologies or privately printed books which could not be catalogued, but ascertainable and (presumably) original volumes. . . . Four thousand poets! . . . But this number gives no idea of the armies of writers who have kept girding up their rhymes, whipping on their emotions, and bat-

tling for the crucial adjective. It is safe to say that for every poet fortunate
enough to emerge from the struggle with a volume to his credit, there were
ten (the number is probably nearer fifty) who were not so victorious and had
to content themselves with publication in magazines, in trade journals, in the
poetry corner and other columns of the local newspaper. Forty thousand poets,
then . . . But wait. It is fair to assume that there must be still at least ten
times as many who have chewed pencils, crumpled paper, cursed the inade-
quacy of the Rhyming Dictionary, and, somehow, got their lines to fit without
achieving the pleasure of print anywhere at all. Four hundred thousand—a
thorough search would probably double the figure—four hundred thousand
poets plying their difficult trade with desperately little hope and even less
chance of reward.

Selection of the ten or twenty "leading poets" is not so difficult. Everyone
will agree on the poets whose appearance is imperative in a collection of this
type. It is when one goes further and presumes to suggest the flux and fecundity of the period that differences of opinion are sure to follow. In the end
every editor is driven back upon that mixture of preference, prejudice, and
intuition known as personal taste—and it is only in rare instances that one can
escape the limitations imposed by one's temperament.

That inescapable personal factor also explains the manner of editing and
selection. That a poem has appeared in various anthologies is no proof that it
is a good poem. Nor (in spite of those opposed to anthologies) is such publication anything against it. A good poem remains a good poem, no matter how
often it is reprinted. On the other hand, it should be admitted that where the
choice has been between a much-quoted poem and one which has not been
handed on from one anthologist to another, I have—where both poems seemed
equally worthy—favored the less familiar example. Since this is a collection
which attempts to chart a period, I have included various examples of those
who have been dismissed as "mere experimenters," believing that experimentation is as vital a process of creation—and surely as significant a part of this
age—as the unvarying acceptance of tradition. This same spirit has also impelled
me to go to the other extreme, to reprint a small portion of that species which
lies between light verse and authentic poetry, believing again that no survey of
the period, no matter how casual, would be complete without the negro dialect of Paul Laurence Dunbar, the Hoosier accents of James Whitcomb Riley,
the light patter of Eugene Field, the metropolitan chuckles of Franklin P.
Adams, the Italian-American patois of T. A. Daly.

Besides the inclusion of Whitman other changes have been made in this
edition. The Preface, extended in 1930, has been enlarged considerably. The
paragraphs preceding the groups of poems have been amplified, the biographical and bibliographical data have been brought up to date, and the notes made
more critical than before. To compensate for the poets omitted a few of the
younger poets have been added, while the number of poems by the leading
poets has been noticeably increased.

One thing remains to be said. Although the notes as well as the number of
poems selected make the editor's preferences obvious, it should be added that
he has attempted to make each poet's group representative. To accomplish this,

not only the early but the most recent writing of the contemporaries appears here—some of it for the first time between covers. Wherever possible, the selections as well as the authors have been chronologically arranged; that is, the earlier work is placed at the beginning of each group, the later work following in approximately the order in which it was written. I am greatly indebted to most of the living poets, not only for invaluable data, but for their collaborative assistance: many of the following pages embody their choice of their own poems as well as the editor's preferences.

Finally, I am grateful to the many publishers who have, in every instance, displayed a generosity and coöperation without which the successive editions of this volume would not have been possible. This indebtedness is alphabetically acknowledged to the following firms, as holders of the copyrights:

THE ALCESTIS PRESS—for selections from *Ideas of Order* by Wallace Stevens, *The Mediterranean and Other Poems* by Allen Tate, and *Thirty-Six Poems* by Robert Penn Warren.

D. APPLETON-CENTURY COMPANY, INC.—for selections from *Going-to-the-Sun* and *Going-to-the-Stars* by Vachel Lindsay, *Merchants from Cathay* by William Rose Benét, and *War and Laughter* by James Oppenheim.

BOBBS-MERRILL COMPANY—for selections from the *Biographical Edition of The Complete Works of James Whitcomb Riley,* copyright 1913, reprinted by special permission of the publishers, and *A Cedar Box* by Robert Nathan.

A. AND C. BONI—for selections from *The Janitor's Boy and Other Poems, Lava Lane* and *The Singing Crow* by Nathalia Crane, *Tulips and Chimneys* by E. E. Cummings, *For Eager Lovers* by Genevieve Taggard, *Spring Thunder* and *Now the Sky* by Mark Van Doren.

THE BORZOI CHAPBOOKS (Alfred A. Knopf, Inc.)—for poems by Léonie Adams, Witter Bynner, and Louis Untermeyer.

NICHOLAS L. BROWN—for selections from *Blood of Things* by Alfred Kreymborg.

JONATHAN CAPE AND HARRISON SMITH, INC.—for selections from *Blue Juniata* by Malcolm Cowley.

COVICI, FRIEDE—for selections from *Chorus for Survival* by Horace Gregory.

COWARD-MCCANN, INC.—for selections from *Compass Rose* by Elizabeth J. Coatsworth and *Venus Invisible* by Nathalia Crane.

THE JOHN DAY COMPANY—for selections from *High Falcon* by Léonie Adams.

THE DIAL PRESS (Lincoln MacVeagh)—for selections from *Observations* by Marianne Moore.

DODD, MEAD & COMPANY—for selections from *Golden Fleece* by William Rose Benét, *Lyrics of Lowly Life* (Copyright 1896) and from *Lyrics of Love and Laughter* (Copyright 1903) by Paul Laurence Dunbar, all of which are used by permission of the publishers, Dodd, Mead and Company, Inc.

DOUBLEDAY, DORAN & COMPANY—for selections from *Man Possessed* and *Moons of Grandeur* by William Rose Benét, *Trees and Other Poems* by Joyce Kilmer, *In Other Words* and *Tobogganing on Parnassus* by Franklin P. Adams, *The Man with the Hoe* and *Lincoln and Other Poems* by Edwin Markham, *Trinc* by H. Phelps Putnam, *Tiger Joy* and *John Brown's Body* by Stephen Vincent Benét, and the selections from *Leaves of Grass* (Inclusive and Authorized Edition) by Walt Whitman.

E. P. DUTTON & COMPANY—for selections from *The Vale of Tempe* by Madison Cawein, and *Cry of Time* by Hazel Hall.

FABER AND FABER, LTD., London—for "Journey of the Magi," "Animula," and "A Song for Simeon" from *The Ariel Poems* by T. S. Eliot, with the permission of T. S. Eliot.

FARRAR & RINEHART, INC.—for the selection from *A Draft of XXX Cantos* by Ezra Pound.

FOUR SEAS COMPANY—for selections from *The Charnel Rose, The Jig of Forslin,* and *The House of Dust* by Conrad Aiken, and *Sour Grapes* by William Carlos Williams.

HARCOURT, BRACE AND COMPANY—for selections from *A Miscellany of American Poetry—1920; American Poetry—A Miscellany, 1922; American Poetry—A Miscellany, 1925* and *1927, The Book of the American Negro, Canzoni* and *Carmina* by T. A. Daly, *Less Lonely* by Alfred Kreymborg, *The Noise That Time Makes* and *Six Sides to a Man* by Merrill Moore, *Harlem Shadows* by Claude McKay, *Behind Dark Spaces* by Melville Cane, *Smoke and Steel, Slabs of the Sunburnt West* and *Good Morning America* by Carl Sandburg, *Challenge, The New Adam, Roast Leviathan, Burning Bush, Food and Drink,* and *Selected Poems and Parodies* by Louis Untermeyer, *Poems 1909-1925* and *Collected Poems* by T. S. Eliot.

HARPER & BROTHERS—for selections from *Earth Moods and Other Poems* by Hervey Allen, *Sunrise Trumpets* and *Cyclops' Eye* by Joseph Auslander, *Fables for the Frivolous* by Guy Wetmore Carryl, *Color* and *Copper Sun* by Countee Cullen, *Renascence* (Copyright 1917) by Edna St. Vincent Millay, *Second April* (Copyright 1921) by Edna St. Vincent Millay, *A Few Figs from Thistles* (Copyright 1922) by Edna St. Vincent Millay, *The Harp Weaver* (Copyright 1921, 1922, 1923) by Edna St. Vincent Millay, *The Buck in the Snow* (Copyright 1928) by Edna St. Vincent Millay, *Fatal Interview* (Copyright 1931) by Edna St. Vincent Millay, and *Wine from These Grapes* (Copyright 1934) by Edna St. Vincent Millay.

HARR WAGNER PUBLISHING COMPANY—for selections from *The Complete Poetical Works of Joaquin Miller.*

HENRY HOLT AND COMPANY—for selections from *A Boy's Will, North of Boston, Mountain Interval, New Hampshire, West-Running Brook* and *Collected Poems* by Robert Frost, *Chicago Poems* and *Cornhuskers* by Carl Sandburg, *The Box of God* by Lew Sarett, and *Selected Poems* by George Sterling.

HOUGHTON MIFFLIN COMPANY—The selections from *The Complete Poems of Thomas Bailey Aldrich, The Complete Works of Bret Harte, The Shoes That Danced* by Anna Hempstead Branch, *Grimm Tales Made Gay* by Guy Wetmore Carryl, *Sea Garden* by H. D., *The Tall Men* by Donald Davidson, *Preludes and Symphonies* by John Gould Fletcher, *A Roadside Harp* and *Happy Endings* by Louise Imogen Guiney, *Ballads* by John Hay, *Sword Blades and Poppy Seed, Men, Women and Ghosts, Pictures of the Floating World,* and *What's O'Clock* by Amy Lowell, *Streets in the Moon, New Found Land, Poems 1924-1933,* and *Panic* by Archibald MacLeish, *The Northeast Corner* by F. R. McCreary, *Poems and Poetic Dramas* by William Vaughn Moody, *Lyrics of Joy* by Frank Dempster Sherman,

*Poems* by Edward Rowland Sill, and the quotations from *Some Imagist Poets* are used by permission of, and by special arrangement with, HOUGHTON MIFFLIN COMPANY, the authorized publishers.

MITCHELL KENNERLEY—for selections from *Sonnets of a Portrait Painter* by Arthur Davison Ficke.

ALFRED A. KNOPF, INC.—for selections from *A Canticle of Pan* by Witter Bynner, *Advice* by Maxwell Bodenheim, *Verse* by Adelaide Crapsey, *Punch: The Immortal Liar* by Conrad Aiken, *Fine Clothes to the Jew* by Langston Hughes, *Asphalt and Other Poems* by Orrick Johns, *Mushrooms* by Alfred Kreymborg, *Songs for the New Age, Golden Bird,* and *The Sea* by James Oppenheim, *Lustra* by Ezra Pound, *Chills and Fever* and *Two Gentlemen in Bonds* by John Crowe Ransom, *Harmonium* by Wallace Stevens, *Travelling Standing Still* by Genevieve Taggard, *Nets to Catch the Wind, Black Armour, Trivial Breath, Angels and Earthly Creatures* and *Collected Poems* by Elinor Wylie, which are reprinted by permission of, and by special arrangement with, ALFRED A. KNOPF, INC.

THE LAURENTIAN PUBLISHERS—for the poem from *Motley Measures* by Bert Leston Taylor.

LITTLE, BROWN & COMPANY—for the selections from *The Complete Poems of Emily Dickinson, Further Poems by Emily Dickinson,* and *The Poems of Emily Dickinson, Centenary Edition,* edited by Martha Dickinson Bianchi and Alfred Leete Hampson, reprinted by permission of Little, Brown & Company.

THE LIVERIGHT COMPANY—for selections from *White Buildings, The Bridge,* and *Collected Poems* by Hart Crane, *Collected Poems* by H. D., *Personae* by Ezra Pound, and *Priapus and the Pool* by Conrad Aiken.

LONGMANS, GREEN AND COMPANY—for selections from *Stone Dust* by Frank Ernest Hill.

THE MACMILLAN COMPANY—for selections from *Poems* by Gladys Cromwell, *The Chinese Nightingale* by Vachel Lindsay, *Collected Poems* by Vachel Lindsay, *Spoon River Anthology* and *Songs and Satires* by Edgar Lee Masters, *The Quest* by John G. Neihardt, *The Man Against the Sky, Collected Poems* and *Dionysus in Doubt* by Edwin Arlington Robinson, *Rivers to the Sea, Love Songs, Flame and Shadow* and *Dark of the Moon* by Sara Teasdale, *Hesperides* by Ridgely Torrence and *Steep Ascent* by Jean Starr Untermeyer.

EDWIN MARKHAM—for selections from *The Man with the Hoe and Other Poems, Poems, The Shoes of Happiness and Other Poems,* and *New Poems,* published by Doubleday, Doran & Company and copyright by Edwin Markham, with whose permission, by special arrangement, the poems are reprinted.

EDNA ST. VINCENT MILLAY and her agents, Brandt & Brandt—for permission to reprint her poems which are copyright as follows: "God's World," and "Renascence," from *Renascence,* published by Harper & Brothers, copyright 1917, 1924, by Edna St. Vincent Millay. "The Pear Tree," copyright 1919 by Edna St. Vincent Millay. "Elegy," "The Poet and His Book," "Spring," "Passer Mortuus Est," and "Wild Swans," from *Second April,* published by Harper & Brothers, copyright 1921, 1924, by Edna St. Vincent Millay. "I Shall Go Back," "What Lips My Lips Have Kissed," "Pity Me Not," "Euclid Alone Has Looked on Beauty Bare," and "Departure" from *The Harp-Weaver and Other Poems,* published by Harper & Brothers, copyright 1920, 1921, 1922 and 1923 by

Edna St. Vincent Millay. "Sonnet to Gath," "On Hearing a Symphony of Beethoven," "The Cameo," and "Justice Denied in Massachusetts," from *The Buck in the Snow,* published by Harper & Brothers, copyright 1928 by Edna St. Vincent Millay. "Oh, Sleep Forever in the Latmian Cave" from *Fatal Interview,* published by Harper & Brothers, copyright 1931 by Edna St. Vincent Millay. "The Return" and "See Where Capella with Her Golden Kids" from *Wine from These Grapes,* copyright 1934 by Edna St. Vincent Millay.

ROBERT M. McBRIDE & COMPANY—for selections from *Those Not Elect* by Léonie Adams, *Body of This Death* by Louise Bogan, and *Youth Grows Old* by Robert Nathan.

THE MANAS PRESS (Claude Bragdon)—for selections from *Verse* by Adelaide Crapsey.

THE METROPOLITAN PRESS (Portland, Oregon)—for a poem from *The Mountain in the Sky* by Howard McKinley Corning.

MINTON, BALCH AND COMPANY—for selections from *Mr. Pope and Other Poems* by Allen Tate.

THE MODERN LIBRARY—for the selections by Robinson Jeffers originally published in *A Miscellany of American Poetry—1927* reprinted in *Roan Stallion, Tamar and Other Poems.*

JOHN P. MORTON & COMPANY—for selections from the poems of Madison Cawein.

THOMAS B. MOSHER—for selections from *A Quiet Road* and *A Wayside Lute* by Lizette Woodworth Reese.

THE OBJECTIVIST PRESS—for the selection from *Collected Poems* by William Carlos Williams.

ROBERT PACKARD & COMPANY—for the selection from *Bow of Burning Gold* by E. Merrill Root.

PAGAN PUBLISHING COMPANY—for selections from *Minna and Myself* by Maxwell Bodenheim.

RANDOM HOUSE—for selections from *Cawdor, Dear Judas and Other Poems, Thurso's Landing,* and *Solstice* by Robinson Jeffers. Also for the poems, copyright individually by the authors, from *The Poetry Quartos* by Robert Frost, E. A. Robinson, Conrad Aiken, William Rose Benét, and Elinor Wylie.

A. M. ROBERTSON—for selections from *The House of Orchids* by George Sterling.

NORMAN REMINGTON COMPANY—for selections from *Spicewood* and *Wild Cherry* by Lizette Woodworth Reese.

CHARLES SCRIBNER'S SONS—for selections from *Preludes for Memnon* and *Selected Poems* by Conrad Aiken, *Dark Summer* by Louise Bogan, *The Complete Works of Eugene Field, Poems of Sidney Lanier,* copyright 1884, 1891, 1916, by Mary D. Lanier, *The Crows* by David McCord, *The Children of the Night* and *Town Down the River* by Edwin Arlington Robinson, *Poems* (Revised Edition) by George Santayana, *Poems: 1928-1931* by Allen Tate, *Dust and Light* and *The Black Panther* by John Hall Wheelock, all of which are printed by permission of, and special arrangement with, Charles Scribner's Sons.

SHERMAN, FRENCH AND COMPANY—for selections from *The Human Fantasy* and *The Beloved Adventure* by John Hall Wheelock.

SMALL, MAYNARD & COMPANY—for selections from *Ballads of Lost Haven* by Bliss

Carman, *Along the Trail* by Richard Hovey, *Songs from Vagabondia* and *More Songs from Vagabondia* by Richard Hovey and Bliss Carman.

HARRISON SMITH & ROBERT HAAS, INC.—for a poem from *Dance of Fire* by Lola Ridge.

F. A. STOKES COMPANY—for selections from *War Is Kind* by Stephen Crane and *Grenstone Poems* by Witter Bynner.

STURGIS & WALTON COMPANY—for a selection from *Monday Morning* by James Oppenheim.

THE TROUTBECK PRESS (Amenia, New York)—for selections from *Dear Lovely Death* by Langston Hughes.

THE UNICORN PRESS—for a selection from *Lost Eden* by E. Merrill Root.

HAROLD VINAL, LTD.—for selections from *Hale's Pond* by James Whaler.

THE VIKING PRESS—for selections from *Boy in the Wind* and *The Flowering Stone* by George Dillon, *The Seventh Hill* by Robert Hillyer, *God's Trombones* by James Weldon Johnson, *The Vaunt of Man* by William Ellery Leonard, *The Ghetto* and *Sun-up* by Lola Ridge, *Under the Tree* by Elizabeth Madox Roberts, *Growing Pains* and *Dreams Out of Darkness* by Jean Starr Untermeyer, and *The Hesitant Heart* by Winifred Welles.

WASHBURN & THOMAS—for a poem from *Floodgate* by David McCord.

WYCKOFF & GELBER—for selections from *Hawaiian Hilltop* by Genevieve Taggard.

THE YALE UNIVERSITY PRESS—for selections from *Young Adventure* by Stephen Vincent Benét, *The Burglar of the Zodiac* by William Rose Benét, *Permit Me Voyage* by James Agee, and *Theory of Flight* by Muriel Rukeyser.

For those poems which have appeared in various publications but which have not yet been collected in volumes by their authors I am indebted to the following magazines:

THE AMERICAN MERCURY—for poems by Conrad Aiken, Robert Frost, Margaret Marks, Merrill Moore, and David McCord.

THE AMERICAN REVIEW—for poems by Robert Penn Warren and John Crowe Ransom.

THE AMERICAN POETRY JOURNAL—for a poem by Robert Hillyer.

THE ATLANTIC MONTHLY—for poems by Robert Hillyer and Lew Sarett.

THE NATION—for a poem by Mark Van Doren.

THE NEW REPUBLIC—for poems by Léonie Adams, George Dillon, John Crowe Ransom, Robert Penn Warren, and Winifred Welles.

THE NEW YORKER—for poems by Stephen Vincent Benét, Robert Hillyer, and Louis Untermeyer.

POETRY: A MAGAZINE OF VERSE—for poems by Countee Cullen, Howard McKinley Corning, Elizabeth Madox Roberts, and Robert Penn Warren.

THE SATURDAY REVIEW OF LITERATURE—for poems by Anna Hempstead Branch, Genevieve Taggard, Robert Frost, and Robinson Jeffers.

THE SOUTHERN REVIEW—for a poem by Robert Penn Warren.

THE VIRGINIA QUARTERLY REVIEW—for poems by Elizabeth Madox Roberts, Lizette Woodworth Reese and Melville Cane.

VOICES—for poems by F. R. McCreary and E. Merrill Root.
THE WESTMINSTER MAGAZINE—for a poem by John Gould Fletcher.
THE YALE REVIEW—for poems by Sara Teasdale and Melville Cane.

The introductory note to the group of poems by Walt Whitman is a revision of the paragraphs which first appeared in the editor's *American Poetry from the Beginning to Whitman* published in 1931.

For the use of poems in manuscript and poems not yet printed in any of their volumes I am indebted gratefully to Léonie Adams, James Agee, Conrad Aiken, Stephen Vincent Benét, Elizabeth Coatsworth, Melville Cane, T. S. Eliot, John Gould Fletcher, Robert Frost, Raymond Holden, Robert Hillyer, Robinson Jeffers, Margaret Marks, David McCord, Merrill Moore, Lizette Woodworth Reese, Elizabeth Madox Roberts, Wallace Stevens, Allen Tate, Mark Van Doren, Robert Penn Warren, and William Carlos Williams.

I must also record my thanks to Henry A. Stickney and William W. Mathewson for permission to reprint the poems of Trumbull Stickney; to Julian R. Hovey for permission to reprint poems by Richard Hovey; and to Ruth Hall for her assistance concerning certain poems by her sister Hazel Hall.

For many helpful suggestions during the preparation of the manuscript I am obligated to Kenneth A. Robinson, Dartmouth College; and Robert Hillyer, Harvard University. Finally I must gratefully acknowledge the unremitting labors of my wife, Esther Antin, in the combined rôles of secretary, critic, and collaborator.

# CONTENTS

# CONTENTS

# PREFACE

IT MAY be difficult, if not impossible, to determine the boundaries as well as the beginnings of "modernism," but only a few appraisers will deny that American literature became modern as well as American with the advent of Mark Twain, Herman Melville, and Walt Whitman. In the history of poetry the line may be drawn with a measure of certainty, and it is with the Civil War and the publication of the third edition of *Leaves of Grass* that modern American poetry is defined.

## AFTERMATH OF THE CIVIL WAR

The Civil War inspired volumes of indignant, military, religious, and patriotic verse without adding more than four or five memorable pieces to the anthologies; the conflict produced a vast quantity of poems but practically no important poetry. Its end marked the end of an epoch, political, social, and literary. The arts declined; the New England group began to disintegrate. The poets had overstrained and outsung themselves; it was a time of surrender and swan-songs. Unable to respond to the new forces of political nationalism and industrial reconstruction, the Brahmins (that famous group of intellectuals who had dominated literary America) withdrew into their libraries. Such poets as Longfellow, Bryant, Taylor, turned their eyes away from the native scene, rhapsodized endlessly about Europe, echoed the "parlor poetry" of England, or left creative writing altogether and occupied themselves with translations. "They had been borne into an era in which they had no part," writes Fred Lewis Pattee (*A History of American Literature Since 1870*), "and they contented themselves with reëchoings of the old music." For them poetry ceased to be a reflection of actuality, "an extension of experience." Within a period of six years, from 1867 to 1872, there appeared Longfellow's *Divina Commedia,* C. E. Norton's *Vita Nuova,* T. W. Parsons' *Inferno,* William Cullen Bryant's *Iliad* and *Odyssey,* and Bayard Taylor's *Faust.*

Suddenly the break came. America developed a national consciousness; the West discovered itself, and the East discovered the West. Grudgingly at first, the aristocratic leaders made way for a new expression; crude, jangling, vigorously democratic. The old order was changing with a vengeance. All the preceding writers—poets like Emerson, Lowell, Longfellow, Holmes—were not only products of the New England colleges, but typically "Boston gentlemen of the early Renaissance." To them the new men must have seemed like a regiment recruited from the ranks of vulgarity. Walt Whitman, Mark Twain, Bret Harte, John Hay, Joaquin Miller, Joel Chandler Harris, James Whitcomb Riley—these were men who had graduated from the farm, the frontier, the mine, the pilothouse, the printer's shop! For a while, the movement seemed of little consequence; the impact of Whitman and the Westerners was averted.

3

The poets of the transition, with a deliberate art, ignored the surge of a spontaneous national expression. They were even successful in holding it back. But it was gathering force.

## THE "POST-MORTEM" PERIOD

The nineteenth century, up to its last quarter, had been a period of new vistas and revolts: a period of protest and iconoclasm—the era of Shelley and Byron, the prophets of "liberty, equality and fraternity." It left no immediate heirs. In England, its successors by default were the lesser Victorians. In America, the intensity of men like Emerson and Whittier gave way to the pale romanticism and polite banter of the transition, or what might be called the "post-mortem," poets. "Much of our poetry," Thoreau wrote, "has the very best manners, but no character." These interim lyrists were frankly the singers of an indefinite reaction, reminiscently digging among the bones of a long-dead past. They burrowed and borrowed, half archeologists, half artisans, impelled not so much by the need of creation as recreation. They did not write poetry, they echoed it.

From 1866 to 1880 the United States was in a chaotic and frankly materialistic condition; it was full of political scandals, panics, frauds, malfeasance in high places. The moral fiber was flabby; the country was apathetic, corrupt and contented. As in all such periods of national unconcern, the artists turned from life altogether, preoccupying themselves with the by-products of art: with method and technique, with elaborate and artificial conceits, with facile ideas rather than fundamental ideals.

Bayard Taylor, Thomas Buchanan Read, Richard Henry Stoddard, Paul Hamilton Hayne, Thomas Bailey Aldrich—all of these authors, in an effort to escape a reality they could not express and did not even wish to understand, fled to a more congenial realm of fantasy. They took the easiest routes to a prim and academic Arcadia, to a cloying and devitalized Orient, to a mildly sensuous, "reconstructed" Greece. Their verse, confessing its own defeat, was cluttered with silk divans, Astrakhans, Vesuvian Bays, burning deserts, Assyrian temples, Spanish cloths of gold. Originality was as far from their thoughts as thinking itself; they followed wherever Keats, Shelley (in his lesser lyrics) and Tennyson seemed to lead them. However, not being explorers themselves, they ventured no further than their predecessors, but remained politely in the rear, repeating dulcetly what they had learned from their greater guides—pronouncing it with little variety but with a sentimental unction. In their desperate preoccupation with lures and legends overseas, they were not, except for the accident of birth, American at all; all of them owed much more to old England than to New England.

## WALT WHITMAN

Whitman, who was to influence future generations so profoundly in Europe as well as in America, had already appeared. The third edition of that stupendous volume, *Leaves of Grass,* had been printed in 1860. Almost immediately after, the publisher failed and the book passed out of public notice. But private scrutiny was keen. In 1865 a petty official discovered that Whitman was the author of the "notorious" *Leaves of Grass* and, in spite of Whitman's sacrifice in nursing hundreds of wounded soldiers, in spite of his many past services and his present poverty, the offending poet was dismissed from his clerkship in the Department of the Interior at Washington, D. C. Other reverses followed rapidly. But Whitman, broken in health and cheated by his exploiters, lived to see not only a seventh edition of his work published in 1881, but a complete collection printed in his seventy-third year (1892) in which the twelve poems of the experimental first edition had grown to nearly four hundred.

The influence of Whitman can scarcely be overestimated. It has touched every shore of letters, quickened every current of contemporary art. And yet, as late as 1900, Barrett Wendell in his *Literary History of America* could speak of Whitman's "eccentric insolence of phrase and temper," and, perturbed by the poet's increasing vogue across the Atlantic (Whitman had been hailed by men as eminent as Swinburne, Symonds, Rossetti), he was led to write such a preposterous sentence as "In temperament and style he was an exotic member of that sterile brotherhood which eagerly greeted him abroad."

Such a judgment would be impossible today. Whitman has been acclaimed by a great and growing public. He has been hailed as prophet, as pioneer, as rebel, as fiery humanist not only in America, but in England and throughout Europe. The whole scheme of *Leaves of Grass* is inclusive rather than exclusive; its form is elemental, dynamic, free.

Nor was it only in the relatively minor matter of form that Whitman became a poetic emancipator. He led the way toward a wider aspect of democracy; he took his readers out of fusty, lamp-lit libraries into the coarse sunlight and the buoyant air. He was, as Burroughs wrote, preëminently the poet of vista; his work had the power "to open doors and windows, to let down bars rather than to put them up, to dissolve forms, to escape narrow boundaries, to plant the reader on a hill rather than in a corner." He could do this because, first of all, he believed implicitly in life—in its physical as well as its spiritual manifestations; he sought to grasp existence as a whole, not rejecting the things that, to other minds, had seemed trivial or tawdry. The cosmic and the commonplace were synonymous to him; he declared he was part of elemental, primitive things and constantly identified himself with them. He transmuted, by the intensity of his emotion, material which had been hitherto regarded as too unpoetic for poetry. His long poem "Song of Myself" is a magnificent example. Here his "barbaric yawp," sounded "over the roofs of the world," is softened, time and again, to express a lyric ecstasy and naïf wonder.

I believe a leaf of grass is no less than the journeywork of the stars,
And the pismire is equally perfect, and a grain of sand, and the egg of the wren,
And the tree-toad is a chef-d'œuvre for the highest,
And the running blackberry would adorn the parlors of heaven,
And the narrowest hinge in my hand puts to scorn all machinery,
And the cow crunching with depress'd head surpasses any statue,
And a mouse is miracle enough to stagger sextillions of infidels!

It is this large naturalism, this affection for all that is homely and of the soil, that sets Whitman apart from his fellow craftsmen as our first distinctively American poet. This blend of familiarity and grandeur, this racy but religious mysticism animates all his work. It swings with tremendous vigor through "Crossing Brooklyn Ferry"; it sharpens the sturdy rhythms (and occasional rhymes) of the "Song of the Broad-Ax"; it beats sonorously through "Drum-Taps"; it whispers immortally through the "Memories of President Lincoln" (particularly that magnificent threnody "When Lilacs Last in the Dooryard Bloom'd"); it quickens the "Song of the Open Road" with what Tennyson called "the glory of going on," and lifts with a biblical solemnity "Out of the Cradle Endlessly Rocking."

Whitman did not scorn the past; no one was quicker than he to see its wealth and glories. But most of the older flowerings belonged to their own era; they were foreign to his country—transplanted, they did not flourish on this soil. What was original with many transatlantic poets was being merely aped by facile and unoriginal bards in these States; they seemed bent on transforming poetry into a pedant's stroll through Bulfinch's *Age of Fable*. Concerned only with the myths of other and older countries, they were blind to the living legends of their own. In his "Song of the Exposition" Whitman wrote not only his own *credo,* but uttered the manifesto of the new generation—especially in these lines:

Come, Muse, migrate from Greece and Ionia,
Cross out please those immensely overpaid accounts,
That matter of Troy and Achilles' wrath, and Aeneas', Odysseus' wanderings,
Placard "Removed" and "To Let" on the rocks of your snowy Parnassus, . . .
For know a better, fresher, busier sphere, a wide, untried domain awaits, demands
    you.

The final estimate of Whitman's work is yet to be written. Whitman's universality—and his inconsistencies—have defeated his commentators. To the craftsmen, Whitman's chief contribution was his form; hailing him as the father of the free verse movement, they placed their emphasis on his flexible sonority, his orchestral *timbre,* his tidal rhythms, his piling up of details into a symphonic structure. To the philosophers, he was the first of modern prophets; a rhapsodic mystic with a magnificently vulgar sense of democracy. To the psychologist, he was the most revealing of autobiographers; "whoever touches this book, touches a man," he wrote. To the lay reader, he was a protagonist of "the divine average"; celebrating himself—hearty, gross, noble, "sane and sensual to the core"—he celebrated humanity.

But it is Whitman's spirit, not his technique nor his subject-matter, which assures him permanence. It is the broad and resistless affirmation—Whitman's favorite term "democracy" is too special a word for it—which quickens everything he wrote and which so profoundly affected the spirit (not the letter) of subsequent writing. It is the spirit synthesized in the poem to a common prostitute: "Not till the sun excludes you do I exclude you." It is the quick recognition of the commonplace, the glorification of the unnoticed in a pismire and a grain of sand.

What the extent of this spirit is no one has determined. It is gross and sensual and, at the same time, tender and mystical; it calls for "life coarse and rank," yet it lifts appetite beyond life and death; it is as explosive as a teamster's oath and as grave as the Psalms which influenced it. Its ecstasy, even its exhibitionism, though flushed with a raw and rowdy exuberance, is filled with a calm "mortis'd in granite." It is, possibly, a too all-embracing love which intensifies whatever it touches, an over-vigorous optimism compared to which even Browning's seems anemic. But its indiscriminate acceptance is the very core of its faith, enclosing good and evil, beauty and ugliness in the mystic's circle of complete affirmation.

## EMILY DICKINSON

Contemporary with Whitman, though, as far as the records show, utterly unaware of him, that strange phenomenon, Emily Dickinson, lived and wrote her emblematic poetry. Only four of the poems now famous were published during her lifetime; she cared nothing for a public, less for publicity. It was not until forty years after her death that she was recognized as one of the most original of American poets and, in some ways, the most remarkable woman poet since Sappho. Her centenary, occurring in the same year as Christina Rossetti's, was signaled by salvos of appreciation and the inevitable comparisons with the Englishwoman born five days earlier than her Amherst contemporary. Both poets were born in 1830; both were strongly influenced by their fathers. Both were, in spite of every difference, puritan "beyond the blood." Both made "the great abnegation"—Christina because she could not face marriage, Emily because, it is assumed, the man she loved was married and she could face misery without him better than social tragedy with him. Here the personal similarities end. The poetic likenesses are more remote. True, both poets are linked by language, but even that tie cannot hold the two together long. They, themselves, would have been the first to repudiate the bond. Emily Dickinson would have been impatient with the round rhetoric of Christina Rossetti; much that the American wrote would have seemed reprehensible and, oftener than not, incomprehensible to the Englishwoman. As Christina grew older, her verse grew thinner and more repetitive; moments of vision were expanded into ever-lengthening sententiousness. After Emily weathered the crisis, her verse grew continually tighter, her divinations condensed until the few lines became telegraphic and these telegrams seemed not only self-addressed but written in code. Not that Christina lacked divination; in the magnificent "From Hearth to Home," in several of the austere sonnets, and in some fifteen lyrics she attained sheer illumination. What is more difficult, she communicated it. At her infrequent highest, Christina Rossetti breathed a clearer, calmer air than "the nun of Amherst." Hers was a cloistral faith, secure above time and a troubling universe. Rumor to the contrary, there was nothing nun-like about Emily Dickinson. If the episodes of her childhood (*vide* the *Life and Letters*) were not sufficient to prove it, the poetry is; the freedom of her spirit manifests itself in the audacity of her images, the wild leap of her epithets, the candor which extends from irreverent mischief to divine challenge. Sometimes elliptical, sometimes so concentrated as to be cryptic, hers is a poetry of continual surprise where metaphors turned to epigrams, epigrams to compact dramas, a poetry where playfulness and passion merged and were sublimated in pure thought.

Could anyone have failed to recognize this revelation at the outset? One supposes a few tense quatrains, a dozen syllables must have been sufficient to reveal the definiteness of her genius. "The authorities" disdained or forgot her. As late as 1914 *The New International Encyclopaedia* dismissed her life and work in ten lines, concluding "In thought her introspective lyrics are striking but are deficient in form." *The Encyclopaedia Britannica* seemed even less aware of her existence until 1926; the thirteenth edition contained only a mention, a cross-reference by way of comparison; her name did not appear in the Index. Yet her *Poems* (*First Series*) had appeared as early as 1890 and two subsequent collections had been published before 1896. In these volumes—as well as in *The Single Hound* (1915) and *Further Poems,* an amazing set of "newly discovered" verses published in 1929—Emily Dickinson anticipated not only her avowed disciples but a score of poets unaware of her influence. Quaintly, without propaganda, she fashioned her imagist etchings fifty years before Imagism became a slogan; her experiments in "slant" or "suspended" rhyme were far more radical than those of any exponent of assonance; her ungrammatical directness was more spontaneous than the painful dislocations of "the new primitives."

The evidence of this anticipating modernity is everywhere. Emily would have been the last to claim anything, particularly the claim of being a fore-runner, yet "Death's large democratic fingers" might well have prompted E. E. Cummings. MacLeish's *"Ars Poetica"* startles us by its abstraction:

> Poetry should not mean
> But be—

and Emily, sometime in the '70s, concludes:

> Beauty is not caused,
> It is.

Hodgson tells us "God loves an idle rainbow no less than laboring seas" and that "Reason has moons, but moons not hers lie mirrored on the sea, confounding her astronomers but, Oh, delighting me." And Emily (who knows how many years earlier?) was saying:

> The rainbow never tells me
> That gust and storm are by,
> Yet she is more convincing
> Than all philosophy.

Not that she despised philosophy. On the contrary, in the midst of her cakes and puddings and ice-creams, the family breadmaker (for Emily gloried in her housewifery) would turn to consider Bishop Berkeley. Intricately but with a final clarity, she expressed herself on the paradox of discipline:

Experience is the angled road
Preferred against the mind
By paradox, the mind itself
Presuming it to lead
Quite opposite. How complicate
The discipline of man,
Compelling him to choose himself
His pre-appointed plan.

Thus, and continuously, Emily would jot down the notes for her unco-ordinated autobiography. When that difficult work is synthesized, when some inspired arranger imposes an order on the more than twelve hundred poems—many of which are still unpublished—the differing versions of many of the lines and the contradictions of her various editors will be resolved. As early as 1891, one of them (Mabel Loomis Todd) wrote: "To what further rigorous pruning her verses would have been subjected had she published them herself, we cannot know. They should be regarded in many cases as merely the first strong and suggestive sketches of an artist, intended to be embodied at some time in the finished picture." Her manner of writing made it equally hazardous for her editors, some of whom erred by too much editing, some by a too literal following of spacing, punctuation and obvious mistakes. "In most of her poems, particularly the later ones, everything by way of punctuation was dis-carded, except numerous dashes; and all important words began with capitals."

Thus Emily Dickinson became a puzzle. Biographers supplied fresh con-fusions and misleading clues in a mistaken zeal for detection. As in life, the poet escaped them all. Much of her problem remains in the realm of the mysterious. She was like no other poet; her very "roughnesses" were individual. Time and again she skipped the expected rhyme, twisted the easy phrase, and put her indubitable mark on every line she wrote. Wholly underivative, her poetry was unique; her influence, negligible at first, is now incalculable.

## THE AWAKENING OF THE WEST

By 1870 the public had been surfeited with sugared conceits and fine-spun delicacies. For almost twelve years, Whitman had stormed at the squeamish overrefinements of the period, but comparatively few had listened. Yet an instinctive distaste for the prevailing affectations had been growing, and when the West began to express itself in the raw accents of Mark Twain and Bret Harte, the people turned to them with enthusiasm and no little relief. Mark Twain, a frustrated prose Whitman, revealed the romantic Mississippi and the vast mid-West; Bret Harte, beginning a new American fiction in 1868, ushered in the wild humor and wilder poetry of California. It is still a question whether Bret Harte or John Hay first discovered the literary importance of Pike County narratives. Twain was positive that Hay was the pioneer; docu-mentary evidence points to Harte. But it is indisputable that Harte developed—and even overdeveloped—the possibilities of his backgrounds, whereas Hay, after a few brilliant ballads, reverted to his early poetic ideals and turned to the production of studied, polished, and undistinguished verse. Lacking the gusto of Mark Twain or even the native accuracy of Hay, Bret Harte perfected a terse, dramatic idiom. Less exuberant than his compeers, he became more skillful in making his situations "effective"; he popularized dialect, sharpening his outlines and intensifying the edges of his prose. Harte's was an influence that found its echo in the Hoosier stories of Edward Eggleston and made so vivid an impress on nineteenth-century literature.

To the loose swagger of the West, two other men added their diverse contributions. Edward Rowland Sill, cut short just as his work was gaining headway and strength, brought to it a gentle radicalism, a calm and cultured honesty; Joaquin Miller, rushing to the other extreme, theatricalized and exaggerated all he touched. He shouted platitudes at the top of his voice. His lines boomed with the pomposity of a brass band; floods, fires, hurricanes, extravagantly blazing sunsets, Amazonian women, the thunder of a herd of buffaloes— all were unmercifully piled upon each other. And yet, even in its most blatant *fortissimo,* Miller's poetry occasionally captured the grandeur of his surroundings, the spread of the Sierras, the lavish energy of the Western world.

Now that the leadership of letters had passed from the East, all parts of the country began to try their voices. The West continued to hold its rugged supremacy; the tradition of Harte and Hay was followed (softened and sentimentalized) by Eugene Field and James Whitcomb Riley. In the South, Irwin Russell was pioneering in negro dialect (1875), Sidney Lanier fashioned his intricate harmonies (1879), and Madison Cawein began to create his tropical and overluxuriant lyrics. A few years later the first phase of the American renascence had passed.

### REACTION AND REVOLT IN THE '90S

The reaction set in at the beginning of the last decade of the nineteenth century. The passionate urge had spent itself, and in its place there remained nothing but imitation and gesticulation, the dumb-show of poetry. The poetasters wrote verse that was precise, scholarly, and patently echoed their literary loves. "In 1890," writes Percy H. Boynton, "the poetry-reading world was chiefly conscious of the passing of its leading singers for the last half-century. It was a period when they were recalling Emerson's 'Terminus' and Longfellow's 'Ultima Thule,' Whittier's 'A Lifetime,' Tennyson's 'Crossing the Bar,' and Browning's 'Asolando.'" . . . The poetry of this period (whether it is the fine-chiseled verse of John B. Tabb or the ornate delicacy of Richard Watson Gilder) reflects a kind of moribund resignation; it is dead because it detached itself from the actual world. But those who regarded poetry chiefly as a not too energetic indoor-exercise were not to rule unchallenged. Restlessness was in the air and revolt openly declared itself with the publication of *Songs from Vagabondia* (1894), *More Songs from Vagabondia* (1896) and *Last Songs from Vagabondia* (1900). No one could have been more surprised at the tremendous popularity of these care-free celebrations (the first of the three collections went through seven rapid editions) than the young authors, Richard

Hovey and Bliss Carman. For theirs was a revolt without a program, a headlong flight to escape—what? In the very first poem, Hovey voices their
manifesto:

> Off with the fetters
> That chafe and restrain!
> Off with the chain!
> Here Art and Letters,
> Music and Wine
> And Myrtle and Wanda,
> The winsome witches,
> Blithely combine.
> Here is Golconda,
> Here are the Indies,
> Here we are free—
> Free as the wind is,
> Free as the sea,
> Free!

Free for what? one asks doggedly. Hovey does not answer directly, but with
unflagging buoyancy, whipped up by scorn for the smug ones, he continues:

> I tell you that we,
> While you are smirking
> And lying and shirking
> Life's duty of duties,
> Honest sincerity,
> We are in verity
> Free!
> Free to rejoice
> In blisses and beauties!
> Free as the voice
> Of the wind as it passes!
> Free . . . *etc.*

Free, one concludes, to escape and dwell with Music and Wine, Myrtle and
Wanda, Art and Letters. Free, in short, to follow, with a more athletic energy,
the same ideals as the parlor-poets they gibed so relentlessly. But the new insurgence triumphed. It was the heartiness, the gypsy jollity, the rush of high
spirits that conquered. Readers of the *Vagabondia* books were swept along by
their speed faster than by their philosophy.

The enthusiastic acceptance of these new apostles of outdoor vigor was,
however, not as much of an accident as it seemed. On one side (the world of
art) the public was wearied by barren meditations set to tinkling music; on
the other (the world of action) it was faced by a staggering growth of ma-
terialism which it feared. Hovey, Carman and their imitators offered a swift
way out. But it was neither an effectual nor a permanent escape. The war
with Spain, the industrial turmoil, the growth of social consciousness and new
ideas of responsibility made America look for fresh valuations. Hovey began
to go deeper into himself and his age; in the mid-West, William Vaughn
Moody grappled with the problems of his times only to have his work cut

short by death in 1910. But these two were exceptions. In the main, it was another interval—two decades of appraisal and expectancy, of pause and preparation.

## INTERIM—1890-1912

This interval of about twenty years was notable for its effort to treat the spirit of the times with a cheerful evasiveness, a humorous unconcern. Its most representative craftsmen were, with four exceptions, the writers of light verse. These four exceptions were Richard Hovey, Bliss Carman, William Vaughn Moody and Edwin Markham.

Moody's power was the greatest, although it never reached its potentialities. In "An Ode in Time of Hesitation," he protested against turning the "new-world victories into gain" and painted American idealism on an idealistic canvas. In "The Quarry" he celebrated America's part in preventing the breaking up of China by the empires of Europe, an act accomplished by John Hay, poet and diplomat. In "On a Soldier Fallen in the Philippines," a dirge wrenched from the depths of his nature, Moody cried out against our own imperialists. It was the fulfillment of this earlier poem which found its climax in the lengthy Ode, with such lines as:

> Was it for this our fathers kept the law?
> This crown shall crown their struggle and their ruth?
> Are we the eagle nation Milton saw
> Mewing its mighty youth? . . .
> . . . O ye who lead
> Take heed!
> Blindness we may forgive, but baseness we will smite.

Early in 1899, the name of Edwin Markham flashed across the land when, out of San Francisco, rose the challenge of "The Man with the Hoe." This poem, which was once ecstatically called "the battle-cry of the next thousand years" (Joaquin Miller declared it contained "the whole Yosemite—the thunder, the might, the majesty"), caught up the passion for social justice that was waiting to be intensified in poetry. Markham summed up and spiritualized the unrest that was in the air; in the figure of one man with a hoe, he drew a picture of men in the mines, men in the sweatshop, men working without joy, without hope. To social consciousness he added social conscience. In a ringing if rhetorical blank verse, Markham crystallized the expression of outrage, the heated ferment of the period.

Inspiring as these examples were, they did not generate others of their kind; the field lay fallow for more than a decade. The lull was pronounced, the gathering storm remained inaudible.

## RENASCENCE—1913

Suddenly the "new" poetry burst upon the country with unexpected vigor and extraordinary variety. Moody and Markham were its immediate forerunners; Whitman its spiritual godfather. October, 1912, saw the first issue of

*Poetry: A Magazine of Verse,* a monthly that was to introduce the work of hitherto unknown poets, schools, and "movements." The magazine came at the very moment of the breaking of the storm. Flashes and rumblings had already been troubling the literary heavens; a few months later came the deluge! For four years the skies continued to discharge such strange and divergent phenomena as Ezra Pound's *Canzoni* and *Ripostes* (1912), Vachel Lindsay's *General William Booth Enters into Heaven* (1913), James Oppenheim's *Songs for the New Age* (1914), the first anthology of *The Imagists* (1914), *Challenge* (1914), Amy Lowell's *Sword Blades and Poppy Seed* (1914), Lindsay's *The Congo and Other Poems* (1914), Robert Frost's *North of Boston* (1914), Edgar Lee Masters' *Spoon River Anthology* (1915), John Gould Fletcher's *Irradiations* (1915), Conrad Aiken's *Turns and Movies* (1916), Edwin Arlington Robinson's *The Man Against the Sky* (1916), Carl Sandburg's *Chicago Poems* (1916). By 1917, the "new" poetry was ranked as "America's first national art"; its success was sweeping, its sales unprecedented. People who never before had read verse, turned to it and found they could not only read but relish it. They discovered that for the enjoyment of poetry it was no longer necessary to have at their elbows a dictionary of rare words and classical references; they were not required to be acquainted with Latin legendry and the minor love-affairs of the Greek divinities. Life was their glossary, not literature. The new work spoke to them in their own language. And it did more: it spoke to them of what they rarely had heard expressed; it was not only closer to their soil but nearer to their souls.

### EDWIN ARLINGTON ROBINSON

One reason why the new poetry achieved so sudden a success was its freedom from the traditionally stilted "poetic diction." Revolting strongly against the assumption that poetry must have a vocabulary of its own, the poets of the new era spoke in the oldest and most stirring tongue; they used a language that was the language not of the poetasters but of the people. In the tones of ordinary speech they rediscovered the strength, the dignity, the vital core of the commonplace.

Edwin Arlington Robinson had already been employing the sharp epithet, the direct and clarifying utterance which was to become part of our present technique. As early as 1897, in *The Children of the Night,* Robinson anticipated the brief characterizations and etched outlines of Masters' *Spoon River Anthology;* he stressed the psychological element with unerring artistry and sureness of touch. His sympathetic studies of men whose lives were, from a worldly standpoint, failures were a sharp reaction to the current high valuation on financial achievements, ruthless efficiency, and success at any cost. Ahead of his period, he had to wait until 1916, when a public prepared for him by the awakened interest in native poetry discovered *The Man Against the Sky* (1916) and the richness of Robinson at the same time. After that, his audience increased steadily. His Arthurian legends replaced Tennyson's, *Tristram* (1927), achieving a greater response than most successful novels. *Cavender's House* (1929), although a difficult and lengthy monologue, solidified his position; the Pulitzer Prize for Poetry was thrice awarded to him; and there was no longer any doubt as to the importance of his contribution to American literature. Death in 1935 found him at the peak of fame.

## EDGAR LEE MASTERS

Frost and Masters were the bright particular planets of 1915, although the star of the latter waned while the light of the former grew in magnitude. Yet Masters' most famous book ranks as a landmark. In it, Masters synthesized the small towns of the mid-West with a background unmistakably local and with implications that are universal. This amazing volume, in its curiosity and comprehensiveness, laid open a broad cross-section of whole communities. Beneath its surface tales and dramas, its condensation of grocery-store gossip, *Spoon River Anthology* was a great part of America in microcosm; it prepared the way for Sinclair Lewis' *Main Street* and the critical fiction of small-town life.

The success of the volume was sensational. In a few months, it went into edition after edition. Perhaps most readers passed over the larger issues (Masters' revelation of the sordid cheats and hypocrisies, his arraignment of dirty politics and dirtier chicanery) intent on seeing their neighbors pitilessly exposed. Yet had Masters dwelt only on the drab disillusion of the village, had he (as he was constantly in danger of doing) overemphasized the morbid and sensual episodes, he would have left only a spectacular and poorly balanced work. But the book ascends to a definite exaltation and ends on a plane of half-victorious idealism. Indigenous to its roots, it is stark, unflinching, unforgettable.

## ROBERT FROST

The same year that brought forth *Spoon River Anthology* saw the American edition of Frost's *North of Boston*. It was evident at once that the true poet of New England had arrived. Unlike his predecessors, Frost was never a poetic provincial—never parochial in the sense of America still being a literary parish of England. Frost was as native as the lonely farmhouses, the dusty blueberries, the isolated people, the dried-up brooks and mountain intervals that he described. Loving, above everything else, the beauty of the Fact, he shared, with Robinson and Masters, the determination to tell not merely the actual but the factual truth. But Frost, a less disillusioned though a more saddened poet, wore his rue and his realism with a difference. Where Robinson was definite, Frost diverged, going roundabout and, in his speculative wandering, covering a wider territory of thought. Where Masters was violent and hotly scornful, Frost was reticent and quietly sympathetic. Again where Masters, viewing the mêlée above the struggle, wrote *about* his characters, Frost was *of* his people. Where Robinson, in his more racy and reminiscent moods, often reflected New England, Frost *was* New England.

*North of Boston* was well described by the poet's own subtitle: "a book of people." In it one not only sees a countryside of people living out the intricate pattern of their lives, one catches them thinking out loud, one can hear the very tones of their voices. Here we have speech so arranged and translated that the speaker is heard on the printed page; any reader will be led by the kind and color of these words into reproducing the changing accents in which they are supposed to be uttered. It is this insistence that "all poetry is the reproduction of the tones of actual speech" which gives these poems, as well as the later lyrics, a quickly communicated emotional appeal. It endows them with the deepest power of which words are capable—the power to transmit significant sounds. These sounds, let in from the vernacular, are full of a robust, creative energy; they are compacted of the blood and bones of the people they speak for.

But Frost was by no means the dark naturalist that many suspected. Behind the mask of "grimness" which many critics fastened upon him, there is a continual elfin pucker; a whimsical smile, a half-disclosed raillery glints beneath his most somber monologues. The later *New Hampshire* (1923) and *West-Running Brook* (1928) proved his "other side"; Frost's lyrics are no less personal for being philosophical. Now it is obvious how Vergilian a spirit animated a passionate Puritan; his *Collected Poems* (1930) reveals him as one of the three great pastoral poets of all time. Nor is his greatness due to his self-limited choice of material; Frost's concrete facts are symbols of spiritual values. Through his very reticence as well as through his revelations one hears much more than the voice of New England.

## CARL SANDBURG

The great mid-West, that vast region of steel mills and slaughter-houses, of cornfields and prairies, of crowded cities and empty skies, spoke through Carl Sandburg. In Sandburg, industrial America found its voice: *Chicago Poems* (1916), *Cornhuskers* (1918), *Smoke and Steel* (1920) and *Good Morning, America* (1928) vibrate with the immense purring of dynamos, the rhythms of threshing arms, the gossip and laughter of construction gangs, the gigantic and tireless energy of the machine. Frankly indebted to Whitman, Sandburg's poems are less sweeping but more varied; musically his lines mark an advance. He sounds the extremes of the gamut; there are few poems in our language more violent than "To a Contemporary Bunkshooter," few lyrics as hushed and tender as "Cool Tombs."

Like Frost, Sandburg was true to *things*. But Frost was content with the inexhaustible fact and its spiritual implications; he never hoped to drain it all. Sandburg also fed on the fact, but it did not satisfy him. He had strange hungers; he hunted eagerly for the question behind, the answer beyond. The actual scene, to him, was a point of vivid and abrupt departure. Reality, far from being the earth on which he dwelt, was, for Sandburg, the ground he touched before rising; realism acted merely as a springboard from which this poet dove into a romantic mysticism. His later work, in fact, was almost too full of gnomic gestures.

When *Chicago Poems* first appeared, it was received with a disfavor ranging from hesitant patronization to the scornful jeers of the academicians. Sandburg was accused of verbal anarchy; of a failure to distinguish prose matter from poetic material; of uncouthness, vulgarity, assaults on the English language and a score of other crimes. In the face of those who even in *Good Morning, America* (1928) still see only a coarseness and distorted veritism in Sandburg, it cannot be said too often that he is brutal only when dealing with brutal things; that his "vulgarity" springs from love of life as a whole, not from affection for a drab or decorative part of it; that his bitterest invectives are the result of a disgust of shams. The strength of his hatred is exceeded by the challenge of his love.

### THE IMAGISTS AND AMY LOWELL

Sandburg established himself as the most daring user of American words—rude words ranging from the racy metaphors of the soil to the slang of the street. But long before this, the possibilities of a new vocabulary were being tested. As early as 1865, Whitman was saying, "We must have new words, new potentialities of speech—an American range of self-expression. . . . The new times, the new people need a tongue according, yes, and what is more, they will have such a tongue—will not be satisfied until it is evolved."

It is curious to think that one of the most effective agents to fulfill Whitman's prophecy and free modern poetry from an affected diction was that little band of preoccupied specialists, the Imagists. They were, for all their preciosity and occasional extravagances, liberators in the sense that their programs, pronouncements, and propaganda compelled their most dogged adversaries to acknowledge the integrity of their aims. Their restatement of old truths was one of the things which helped the new poetry out of a bog of rhetorical rubbish.

Ezra Pound was the first to gather the insurgents into a definite group. During the winter of 1913, he collected a number of poems illustrating the Imagist point of view, conceiving Imagism as a discriminating term like "lyricism," and had them printed in a volume: *Des Imagistes* (1914). A little later Pound withdrew from the clan. The rather queerly assorted group began to disintegrate, and Amy Lowell, then in England, brought some of the younger members together in three yearly anthologies (*Some Imagist Poets*) which appeared in 1915, 1916 and 1917. There were, in Miss Lowell's new grouping, three Englishmen (D. H. Lawrence, Richard Aldington, F. S. Flint), three Americans (H. D., John Gould Fletcher, Amy Lowell), and their creed, summed up in six statements,[1] was as follows:

1. To use the language of common speech, but to employ always the *exact* word, not the merely decorative word.

2. To create new rhythms—as the expression of new moods. We do not insist upon "free-verse" as the only method of writing poetry. . . . We do believe that the individuality of a poet may often be better expressed in free verse than in conventional forms.

3. To allow absolute freedom in the choice of subject.

4. To present an image (hence the name: "Imagist"). We are not a school of

---

[1] The stern injunction to "use no word which does not contribute to the presentation"—a Spartan injunction originating with Pound—was soon forgotten by Miss Lowell's "Amygists."

painters, but we believe that poetry should render particulars exactly and not deal in vague generalities, however magnificent and sonorous.

5. To produce poetry that is hard and clear, never blurred or indefinite.

6. Finally, most of us believe that concentration is the very essence of poetry.

It does not seem possible that these six obvious and almost platitudinous principles (which, incidentally, the Imagists often neglected in their poetry) could have evoked the storm of argument, fury, and downright vilification that broke as soon as the militant Miss Lowell began to champion them. Far from being revolutionary, these principles were not new; they were not even thought so by their sponsors. The Imagists themselves realized that they were restating ideals which had fallen into desuetude, and declared, "They are the essentials of all great poetry, indeed of all great literature." And yet many conservative critics, joined by the one hundred per cent reactionaries, rushed wildly to combat these "heresies"! They forgot that, in trying to protect the future from such lawlessness as "using the exact word," from "freedom in the choice of subject," from the importance of "concentration," they were actually attacking the highest traditions of their enshrined past.

The fracas succeeded in doing more good than the work of the Imagists themselves. H. D. removed herself from controversies and took up her residence in Switzerland, perfecting her delicate and exquisitely finished designs. John Gould Fletcher, a more vacillating expatriate, remained in London and continued to strengthen his gift through shifting his standards; his later and richer work was in complete opposition to the early pronouncements. Miss Lowell was left to carry on the battle single-handed, to defend the theories which, in practice, she was beginning to violate brilliantly. A most energetic and unflagging experimenter, the late Miss Lowell was amazing in her versatility. She wielded a controversial cudgel with one hand and, with the other, wrote Chaucerian stanzas, polyphonic prose, monologs in New England dialect, irregular *vers libre,* conservative couplets, myths from the Peruvian, translations from the French, echoes from the Japanese, re-creations of Indian folk-lore!

The work of the Imagists was done. Its members began to develop themselves by themselves. They had helped to swell the tide of realistic and romantic naturalism—a tide of which their contribution was merely one wave, a breaker that carried its impact far inshore.

### THE FREE VERSE FURORE

One of the tenets of the Imagists (the belief that the individuality of a poet may often be expressed better in free verse than in conventional forms) spread further than all the other articles of their faith. The ease of its fulfillment more than its apparent truth led hundreds who were not, in any sense, Imagist poets to adopt *vers libre* as their medium. The result was an inundation of footless— and often headless—writing; the little which was incisive and original was lost in heavy floods of merely loquacious "shredded prose." For fully six years there was produced an incalculable quantity of tiresome exhibitionism. Most of this verse was frankly bad. But so, the defenders of *vers libre* objected, are most sonnets. The fact, however, remains that the original exponents of free verse began to look with distrust on the dubious achievements of their camp-followers. H. D.'s chiseled lines, Amy Lowell's enameled pictures, Edgar Lee Masters' brusque epitaphs remain unusual examples of their genre. Other writers gave this amorphous medium a certain definiteness: John Gould Fletcher based his symphonic effects on free sweep and cadence instead of meter; Maxwell Bodenheim forced unions of unhappy nouns and pitiless adjectives without benefit of rhyme; Alfred Kreymborg accomplished a type of staccato whimsy in which no particular beat was perceptible. But the poets themselves, partly because of the wish to change, partly to show that they were not bound by a theory, began to turn back to orthodox patterns.

Amy Lowell's last work was largely in formal verse; her later rhymes and ballads relied greatly on the steady pace of iambics. Bodenheim and Fletcher employed more symmetrical structures; Masters returned to the blank verse of his youth. H. D., who was the one perfect Imagist, the surest artisan in unrhymed cadence, achieved delicate effects in interwoven rhyme. And Kreymborg, who surpassed them all in metrical eccentricities, whose lines were so brittle and elusive that melodic comments (performed by the poet on his mandolute) were required to fill out the elisions, finally turned to the creation of straightforward sonnets and simple couplets. Only Carl Sandburg was faithful to his experiments; he remained the most consistent as well as the most colorful user of free verse. In his fidelity to the loose rhythms, whether employed for thumbnail impressions or extended apostrophes, he was practically alone.

To what can we attribute the return of the prodigal *vers libertine?* To a reversion to orthodox type? Or a revulsion from mere novelty of expression? It seems more likely that, having passed through various phases of experimentation, these poets, like all other workers, desired to crystallize their idiom in some lasting shape. The chief fault with free verse was that it yielded too easily, and what the creator enjoys is the feel of a firm medium, a half-forbidding, half-pliant form. No real artist has failed to want—and work with—"the resisting mass."

## FOLK-RHYTHMS AND THE NEGRO

In a country that has not been mellowed by antiquity, that has not possessed songs for its peasantry or traditions for its singers, one cannot look for a wealth of folk-stuff. In the United States folk-poetry followed the path of the pioneer. At first these homely songs were mere adaptations and localized versions of English ballads and border minstrelsy, of which Cecil Sharp's *Folk Songs of the Appalachian Highlands* and the *Lonesome Tunes* recovered in the Kentucky mountains by Howard Brockway and Loraine Wyman are excellent examples. But a more definitely native spirit found expression in various sections of these States. In the West (during the Seventies) Bret Harte and John Hay celebrated, in their own accents, the rough miners, ranchers, steamboat pilots, the supposed descendants of the emigrants from Pike County,

Missouri. In the Middle West the desire for local color and music led to the popularity of James Whitcomb Riley's Hoosier ballads and the spirited jingles of Eugene Field. In the South the inspiration of the negro spirituals and ante bellum songs was utilized to good effect by Irwin Russell, Joel Chandler Harris and, later, by Paul Laurence Dunbar.

The Indian, a more ancient primitive, has remained as difficult to adopt poetically as he has been to assimilate ethnically. Nevertheless, in spite of the fact that the white and red races are worlds apart in sentiment, philosophy, and attitude to life, many gallant attempts were made to bring the spirit of the Indian into our literature. Natalie Curtis Burlin did excellent pioneering work in *The Indians' Book;* Mary Austin, in spite of a far-fetched theory and dubious conclusions, made an extended study of the matter in *The American Rhythm;* and *The Path on the Rainbow,* edited by George W. Cronyn in 1918, proved to be the best general collection on the subject available to the public. Among the individual workers in the field, other than those mentioned, praise was given to Constance Lindsay Skinner, Alice Corbin Henderson, and Witter Bynner.

Since the days of Dunbar, the Negro had made great strides in self-expression. American music—"classical" as well as popular—benefited from the strong insistence of African drums and the syncopated shuffling of the feet of slaves. Jazz itself became glorified; the intelligentsia claimed it as their own! In sociology the Negro, through men like W. E. Burghardt DuBois, Benjamin Brawley, Walter White, turned to be his own analyst. In poetry the results were mixed and uneven. But it became apparent that the Negro was beginning to free himself, not only from a sentimentality designed to please the whites, but from an attitude which was not so much race-conscious as self-conscious. He established his identity at the same time as his poetic integrity.

Beginning in about 1922, the Negro, so long despised as a creator, became a literary fashion. Several volumes of the stirring Spirituals were followed by collections of his secular songs, "blues," "mellows," work-ballads, etc. His ante bellum chants swept over post-war America and Europe; his primitive rhythms affected the most sophisticated of modern composers. James Weldon Johnson's pioneer anthology, *American Negro Poetry* (1922), was followed by Countee Cullen's *Caroling Dusk* (1927) and C. V. Calverton's *An Anthology of American Negro Literature* (1929). Appraisal set in almost simultaneously; a dozen tomes bristling with energy and research appeared, one of them (*American Negro Folk-Songs* by Newman I. White) containing over eight hundred songs divided into thirteen groups. These imposingly annotated collections, added to the more original work, made interest assume the proportions of a Revival. The Negro himself became suddenly articulate; his novels, essays, poems— many of them of unsuspected high caliber—were published everywhere. James Weldon Johnson, after a long career as propagandist, leapt into prominence with *God's Trombones,* seven negro sermons in verse; Claude McKay expressed a stern if over-violent spirit in verse and prose; Countee Cullen, Langston Hughes and Jean Toomer ranged from dulcet lyrics to hot "blues" and savage protests. For a while the Negro gained and suffered from being a craze. Then the cult passed; the genuine creations remained.

Meanwhile, scholars all over America were ransacking backwood and byway. South Carolina ballads, songs of Maine lumberjacks, ballads of men who worked in the woods of Wisconsin, songs of the "shanty-boy" of Michigan and Minnesota, original and derived folk-tunes of the South, cowboy songs from the West—into every State the recorders went, hot on the trail of the vanishing folk-idiom. The poets were not far behind. The tradition of Harte and Hay was carried on by such interpreters as Harry Herbert Knibbs and Edwin Ford Piper. The Kentucky Mountain region was interpreted by Elizabeth Madox Roberts and Roy Helton. The "white South" found expression through John Crowe Ransom, Allen Tate, Donald Davidson, Merrill Moore and Robert Penn Warren. A group of Oregon poets—Oluf Olsen, H. L. Davis, H. M. Corning—emerged in the late 1920s. But, of all who absorbed and approximated the spirit of folk-poetry, none made more striking or more indubitably American contributions than Vachel Lindsay of Springfield, Illinois.

### LINDSAY AND OPPENHEIM

Lindsay was essentially a people's poet. He did not hesitate to express himself in terms of the lowest common denominator; his fingers seemed alternately on his pen and the public pulse. Living near enough to the South to appreciate the Negroes' qualities without wishing to theatricalize them, Lindsay was tremendously influenced by the colorful suggestions, the fantastic superstitions, the revivalistic gusto, the half-savage Christianity and, above all, by the curiously syncopated music that once characterized the black man in America. In "The Congo," "John Brown" and the less extended "Simon Legree," the words roll with the solemnity of an exhortation, dance with a grotesque fervor, or snap, crackle, and leap with all the humorous rhythms of a piece of "ragtime." Lindsay caught the burly color and boisterous music of camp-meetings, minstrel shows, revival jubilees. He was an itinerant evangelist preaching the Gospel through a saxophone.

And Lindsay did more. He carried his democratic determinations further than any of his *confrères*. Dreaming of a great communal Art, he insisted that all villages should be centers of beauty, all citizens, artists. At heart a missionary even more than a minstrel, Lindsay often lost himself in his own doctrines. Worse, he frequently cheapened himself and caricatured his own gift by pandering to the vaudeville instinct, putting a noisy "punch" into everything, regardless of taste, artistry, or a sense of proportion. He was most impressive when purely fantastic (as in "The Ghosts of the Buffaloes," the shorter fancies, the series of metaphorical poems about the moon) or when a greater theme and a finer restraint unite (as in "The Eagle That Is Forgotten") to create a preaching that does not cease to be poetry.

Something of the same blend of prophet and poet was found in the work of James Oppenheim. Oppenheim, a throwback to the ancient Hebrew singers, rolled the music of the Psalms through his lines; his poetry, with its obvious reminders of Whitman, was biblical in its inflection, Oriental in its heat. It carried to the Western world the color of the East, adding the gift of prophecy to purpose. In books like *War and Laughter* and *Songs for the New Age* the race of god-breakers and god-makers spoke with a new voice; here, with analytic intensity, the old iconoclasm and still older worship were united.

## ELIOT AND HIS INFLUENCE

Two strongly opposed tendencies were noticeable for several years after 1915. The one was a use of the colloquial speech popularized by Sandburg, Lindsay, and Masters and heightened by Frost; the other was a striking departure from both the consistent conversational tone and the traditional "poetic" language to which such poets as E. A. Robinson and Edna St. Vincent Millay remained loyal. The abrupt break in idiom was brought about by T. S. Eliot, who brought it from France. Eliot, borrowing the method from Laforgue, Valéry, and Rimbaud, used the technique of the Symbolist school with such skill that he soon had a host of imitators on both sides of the Atlantic. Some were unable, some unwilling to follow Eliot's inner difficulties and despairs, but all were fascinated by his technical devices, and only a few were uninfluenced by them. The formula was, roughly, this: To reveal man in his complex relation to the universe the poet must show him not only concerned with the immensities but with the trivialities of daily life, with a sense of the past continually interrupting the present, and with swiftly contradictory moods disputing dream and action. This was, obviously, a difficult if not impossible program to achieve in any one poem or even a set of poems. It was, however, attempted and suggested by a variety of effects: by a rapid leaping from image to image with a minimum of "explanatory" metaphors; by a liberal use of discords, juxtaposing tense images and prosy statements, following lyrical passages with deliberate banalities; by the continual play of free association, in which one idea prompted a chain of others, accomplishing an emotional (or literary) progress, often gaining a new series of overtones, often sacrificing all continuity—Ezra Pound's *Cantos,* Crane's *The Bridge,* and Eliot's *The Waste Land* being the most famous examples of the mood "mixing memory and desire."

The method had its distinct advantages; it enlarged the gamut of poetic devices and permitted a greater sensitivity of expression. But it was abused by many and even its champions were aware of its limitations. "The substitution of emotional for logical sequence," wrote C. Day Lewis in *A Hope for Poetry,* "may finally be classed as one of the manifestations of the general distrust of logic and dethroning of reason brought about by the Great War." Such a poem as *The Waste Land,* though it helped shape a subtler poetic speech, made one aware of "the nervous exhaustion, the exaggerated self-consciousness, the pathetic gropings after the fragments of a shattered faith. . . . But in so doing it enlarged our conception of the field of poetic activity; as Eliot himself said, 'the essential advantage for a poet is not to have a beautiful world with which to deal; it is to be able to see beneath both beauty and ugliness; to see the boredom, and the horror, and the glory.'"

The earlier *Prufrock* and *Sweeney* series accomplished the purpose in an acrid light verse; Eliot's later ironies emphasized, with new bitterness, the hollowness of a life without purpose and without faith. Far from celebrating the feeble, Eliot satirized the futilitarians:

We are the hollow men
We are the stuffed men
Leaning together
Headpiece filled with straw. Alas!
Our dried voices, when
We whisper together
Are quiet and meaningless
As wind in dry grass
Or rats' feet over broken glass
In our dry cellar

Shape without form, shade without color,
Paralyzed force, gesture without motion—

But most of those so strongly influenced by Eliot—and by Eliot's influences—
captured nothing except his (and Jules Laforgue's) idiom. His abrupt allusiveness, his style at once coarse and subtle, his emotional acuteness, could be imitated but not captured; his unacknowledged disciples merely parodied the trick
of disassociation, the erudition without Eliot's wisdom, the gesture without (if
I may misquote) emotion. The results were inevitable: sterile intellectualism
at one extreme, infantile barbarism at the other.

However, to condemn an entire group because of the failures is unjust. The
younger poets (1920-1930), sometimes condemned as "a lost generation," matured in a period which afforded them no security nor dignity nor any sem-
blance of peace. Being sensitive, even over-sensitive recorders, they reflected the
doubt, the very discontinuity of the times. Little wonder theirs was a "literature
of nerves," little wonder their symbols were uncertain, their allusions private,
and their work often obscure to the point of unintelligibility. The clearest of
them maintained their individuality, though they demonstrated their limited
heritage; even the more prominent acknowledged the influence of Eliot. As in
England, where Stephen Spender, W. H. Auden, and C. Day Lewis were
affected by Eliot's technique, though not by his philosophy, so Eliot's experiments may be traced in the work of Archibald MacLeish, Conrad Aiken,
Horace Gregory, and the entire Nashville group.

### THE NEW BARBARISM

The common reader, confronted by the extremely "modernist" poet, was
unsure whether to claim his rights as reader, or turn altogether from what
seemed a communication that communicated nothing more intelligible than
the author's wish to be let alone. Robert Graves and Laura Riding in *A Survey
of Modernist Poetry* (1927) summarized the situation: "The bond between the
Victorian poet and his reader was at least an agreement between them of a
common, though not an original, sentiment. The meaning of a poem was
understood between them beforehand from the very title, and the persuasion
of the word-music was intended to keep the poem vibrating in the memory
long after it had been read. . . . The modernist poet does not have to issue a
program declaring his intentions toward the reader or to issue an announce-

ment of tactics. . . . The important part of poetry is now not the personality of the poet as embodied in a poem, but the personality of the poem itself; that is, its quality of independence from both the reader and the poet, once the poet has separated it from his personality by making it complete—a new and self-explanatory creature."

Sometimes these "self-explanatory creatures" explained; sometimes they did not. Often they exhibited nothing more specific than self-conscious snobbery. But the best of them, oppressed by the dead hand of the past, were effective in their revolt; they destroyed that semi-comatose condition which so often attends the reading of poetry and (being a criticism of bad poetry as well as of the reader) revealed new wit, new vitality, new signals of beauty beneath the surface oddities. Thus E. E. Cummings, a lyrical poet in spite of his eccentricities, wrote: "To create is first of all to destroy. . . . There is and can be no such thing as authentic art until the *bons trucs* (whereby we are taught to see and imitate on canvas and in stone and by words this so-called world) are entirely and thoroughly and perfectly annihilated by that vast and painful process of unthinking which may result in a minute bit of purely personal feeling. Which minute bit is art."

Thus we had the phenomenon of Gertrude Stein "destroying" the English language, attempting to create a speech in which words had only tonal and abstract values, and James Joyce, in his later work, breaking up and reconstructing syllables until they resembled a colorful game of anagrams. Between a literature of obscure scholasticism and experiments in "the vast and painful process of unthinking," the younger writers evolved a phase if not a philosophy of their own. Malcolm Cowley, expressing this for them, summarized it: "We ourselves have found that most of our philosophical difficulties can be solved not by philosophy itself, but by living on, by changing one's angle of approach, and often simply by changing one's place. The war, which carried many of our generation into strange countries, had a partly intellectual, partly emotional effect that is generally disregarded. It destroyed our sense of dull security and taught us to live from day to day. It gave us a thirst for action and adventure. It presented us with violent contrasts, with very simple tragedies, and so led us back toward the old themes of love and death."

### PROLETARIAN POETS AND MACLEISH

Much was written concerning an imminent proletarian school of poetry, but no one expressed in verse what such novelists as Robert Cantwell, Albert Halper, and James T. Farrell expressed in prose. *The New Masses* printed a quantity of proletarian free verse, but, of all the contributors to the group, Kenneth Fearing alone combined slang and a staccato rhetoric (not quite successfully) to satirize the cheap heroics and blatant miseries, the five-and-ten cent lives and tabloid minds of the industrial centers and a decaying system. Horace Gregory sounded the depths of social dissatisfaction with a subtlety that delighted the artists, but failed to move the masses. Langston Hughes concerned himself with the plight of the black workers. Clifford Odets seemed the most promising poet of revolt, but Odets' work was in the theater, where

*Awake and Sing, Till the Day I Die,* and *Waiting for Lefty* voiced the passion and poetry of the inarticulate. Lola Ridge remained the most intense as well as the most integrated of the revolutionaries, yet her work in *Firehead* and *Dance of Fire* was traditional in pattern, the peak of the latter volume being a sequence of mystical sonnets.

Much also had been expected from those who celebrated a "machine age poetry." In 1929 Hart Crane wrote, "Unless poetry can absorb the machine, i.e., *acclimatize* it as naturally and casually as trees, cattle, galleons, castles, and all other human associations of the past, then poetry has failed of its full contemporary function." This sentiment was echoed by many, but few Americans carried out the process of assimilating or "acclimatizing" the machine. Three young English poets—W. H. Auden, Stephen Spender, and C. Day Lewis— went further to justify Crane than any poet in this country. Crane himself almost accomplished it in *The Bridge,* but this ambitious poem failed in the end, partly because it lacked a culminating effect, partly because Crane was unable to solidify his mood and his material. MacKnight Black, hoping to communicate the spirit of Diesel engines and piston-rings in his *Machinery* and *Thrust at the Sky,* attempted unsuccessfully to unite new subject-matter and an old poetic vocabulary, merely romanticizing the mechanical objects. Others considered the wish to "express" the machine ill-advised and futile. For one thing, they maintained, the machine has been always with us without winning our affections; today it is no closer to man's emotions—and the stuff of poetry—than it was in the first days of the loom, the mill, the cotton-gin. For another, the machine has no fixed character; it changes too rapidly to become part of man's deeper experience.

It was a poet of the aristocratic tradition whose later work—particularly in *Frescoes for Mr. Rockefeller's City* and in *Panic*—symbolized the impasse of the current social system and its tragic consequences. This poet who made the deepest impression since the advent of Frost and Eliot was Archibald MacLeish. MacLeish took the Symbolist manner further and broke new ground; he adapted the Eliot-Laforgue technique, as well as the form of Pound's *Cantos* and Perse's *Anabase,* and extended it. He began tentatively enough with *The Pot of Earth,* enlarged the gamut in *Streets in the Moon,* and declared himself fully in *New Found Land* and *Conquistador,* an epic in little. Adding several devices of his own—notably a skillful interior rhyme and a suspended *terza rima*—MacLeish perfected a verse which is both firm and delicate, sinewy yet supple. His unusually flexible line was used with genuine, not theatrical, eloquence in the play *Panic,* produced in 1935, a play whose power was projected in living symbols, pointing the possible revival of the poetic drama and emphasizing the importance of MacLeish's style.

### THE NASHVILLE GROUP

In a preceding section mention was made of the spirit animating the new South. Apart from the short-lived Carolina local color school and the work of the previously considered Negro poets, the most important group centered about Vanderbilt University in Nashville, Tennessee. It originated in a body of teachers and students known as "The Fugitives," after their magazine which was published from April, 1922, to December, 1925. It was never explained what the fugitives were fleeing to escape, and it soon became apparent that there were differences of taste and temperament among the members. But a sense of their backgrounds, a sympathy beyond an ear for quaint localisms, bound them together. This unannounced expression of unity—a union of old dreams and new issues—was to develop into a controversy centering about Agrarianism, but it began with poetry and it was on poetry that the group maintained itself.

John Crowe Ransom was the stimulator if not the founder of the school. He guided its fortunes and, for a while, dictated (unconsciously perhaps) its program and style. That style was a curious fusion of the pedantic and the metaphysical, a fusion which even he, in his later poetry, failed to lift above a cryptic overelaboration. At his best—and no less than a dozen poems represent him at that enviable height—Ransom has a finesse and a flavor unlike any other poet; he is master of an urbane grace and a mockery which masks a teasing tenderness. His vocabulary and his highly original technique equip him to sound the depths with a light and almost nonchalant touch; there are times when he even accomplishes an integration of the sublime and the ridiculous.

Donald Davidson's style is less metaphysical and more emotional than Ransom's; his poems, particularly *The Tall Men,* reveal his concern with things rather than with abstractions. Originally influenced by Ransom and Eliot, Davidson found himself in his recreations and reveries of the War Between the States and, though he spent much of his energies teaching and reviewing, his longer poems have an almost epic breadth.

Allen Tate was the most unpredictable and belligerent of the group. Ten years younger than Ransom and five years younger than Davidson his energy was astonishing. He turned from poetry to biography, from biography to criticism, from criticism to controversy, from controversy back to poetry. Everything he did was achieved with distinction and despatch, everything except his poetry. His poetry continually called for revision—at least so it seemed to its author—and before he was forty Tate had published several versions of the same poems. Robert Penn Warren, born in 1905, the youngest of the group, is also the most fiery. Strong feeling forces itself through the simplest of his poems; pictorial verses, whose effect would ordinarily be merely visual, are surcharged with a plain-spoken force which seldom fails to communicate its excitement. Even the metaphysical conceit (a favorite device of "The Fugitives") achieves an unexpected intensity in his image-crowded lines. Merrill Moore, born in 1903, was the most fecund of the group, probably the most prolific of American poets. Before he was thirty he had composed so many sonnets—a rough calculation approximated the number at twenty thousand—that he had to resort to short-hand to get them down between his labors as instructor and psychiatrist. His poetry has both the charm and the handicap of improvisation; it suffers from its speed and the author's inability to review his errors or revise a single unfortunate phrase. But Moore's fluency results in many startling effects. Moreover, he has a particularly Southern humor—half grave, half grotesque—and he can make beauty out of banality, confronting the reader with wildness wrung from conversational small change.

The outstanding excellence of the Nashville group was its free use of the discord—juxtaposing the traditionally poetic and the common colloquial—and the establishment of a sharp-edged diction. In thought as well as technique it emphasized intelligence; it insisted on adult poetry as against the plethora of pretty, thoughtless, and immature verse written by adults. Its chief defect was a too frequent retreat into a remote classicism; with its metaphysical predilections the poetry sometimes became recondite and even incomprehensible. The stock of subjects grew low and, as John Gould Fletcher concluded in an otherwise sympathetic consideration of the school, "the 'Southern type' of poem tends to become distorted, fragmentary, obscure the more the poets speculate on the *intellectual* content as opposed to the emotional, or *sensible,* content of their subject matter." But the best of this poetry rose above its limitations and cleared a direction of its own.

### RANGE AND DIVERSITY: STEVENS TO JEFFERS

After 1920 lines divided, ran parallel; groups coalesced, split apart; many tendencies were in the air at one time. The difficult and re-creative "process of unthinking" often degenerated into mere thoughtlessness, a tendency glorified by the "Super-realists" and the editors of *transition*. Opposed to this the "classicism" of Eliot pointed in a contrary direction. Joined to a cool scholasticism, orderliness came to offset the loose writing and looser thinking of the free verse plethora. Founded on a definite esthetic, intellectual rather than emotional, much of the new work achieved a shapeliness in which thought restrained sentiment, in which conception and perception were skillfully balanced.

Language was being tested in a dozen different directions; where one poet tightened the forms, another loosened them. A new semi-cavalier grace warred with forthright declarations. Wallace Stevens, departing from a depiction of things—actually disputing the "thinginess" of literature—perfected an orchidaceous flowering of words from words, achieving a type of witty suggestion new to the period. The euphuistic distortions of Maxwell Bodenheim and the over-luxuriant figures of E. E. Cummings grew in the same lustrum as the austere, later lyrics of Sara Teasdale and the emotional directness of Edna St. Vincent Millay.

Of the younger men Horace Gregory and James Agee contributed striking work. Widely different though their poems were they had two characteristics in common: a combination of "high seriousness" and irony, and the ability to employ images straight from contemporary life.

An unprecedented vigor of language was brought into American poetry about 1926 by Robinson Jeffers. Jeffers successfully experimented with a peculiarly long line, whose strength matched the dark power of its author's philosophy. His technique derived from Whitman's, but his attitude was the antithesis of that over-emphatic affirmer's, and his images attained a strange pessimistic splendor. "The creatures of Jeffers's imagination," wrote Horace Gregory in *The New Mythology,* "strive, love, and die within a nightmare that is becoming known as the American consciousness, which is a poetic distortion of the American scene. They are manifestations of a civilization that seems child-ishly innocent and harmlessly insane." Never had the range of American verse been so extensive, and Jeffers strenuously helped to extend it.

### THE NEW LYRICISTS

The lyric note was bound to be affected. It, too, fluctuated to express the shift from convention to revolt, from decision to doubt, from a fixed form to an almost dissolving line. Conrad Aiken developed a peculiarly wavering music which, if often vague and repetitive, was capable of haunting effects, both in the early lyrics and the later somber preludes. David McCord alternated easily from the meditative to the whimsically mocking. Stephen Vincent Benét and William Rose Benét, brothers in blood and balladry, plundered modernity and antiquity for their fancies; the former, taking the Civil War for a background in *John Brown's Body,* constructed a many-voiced lyric of epic proportions. John Hall Wheelock luxuriated in leaping if somewhat determined affirma-tions. George Dillon, a singer in water-color, composed delicately patterned interrogations. The short lyrics of Robert Frost grew consistently in strength and suggestiveness.

The work of the women ranged from the outspoken to the involved. Two distinct influences governed many of them: Emily Dickinson and Lizette Woodworth Reese. The epigrammatic condensations of the former affected an entire generation with increasing force. The firm speech and sparse imagery of the latter won many away from the lush and cloying love-songs of the type enshrined in 1842 by Rufus W. Griswold in his waxwork *Gems from American Female Poets.* Edna St. Vincent Millay, in the later sonnets no less than in the early "Renascence," deepened an already impassioned note, increasing the ad-miration as well as the size of her audience. Sara Teasdale intensified a simple but flexible melodic line. Genevieve Taggard and Jean Starr Untermeyer lifted the ordinary round of woman's everyday into the extraordinary and, not sel-dom, into the ecstatic.

Others, refining their poetry of a too thickly human passion, turned to an elliptical metaphysics. The "mechanism of sensibility" brought them back to Crashaw, Vaughan, Webster, and Donne. One caught the overtones of the late Elizabethans in the accents of Louise Bogan, Léonie Adams, Hazel Hall, Elinor Wylie, among others. Elinor Wylie acknowledged the relationship implicitly, the title of her first volume (*Nets to Catch the Wind*) being taken from a poem by Webster, the title of her last (*Angels and Earthly Creatures*) from a sermon by Donne. But these poets did not depend too much on intellectual virtuosity and involuted images; their sensibility was their own. Less prodigal (and, it may be added, less passionate) than Donne and his followers, they reflected something of his order and his fiercely conceived beauty through temperaments essentially modern and feminine. Elinor Wylie, never "confusing the spiritual and the sen-sual either through false fear or false reverence," began with verbal brilliance and ended by celebrating the radiance of spirit and "the pure and valiant mind." Léonie Adams, a more withdrawn metaphysician, yielded her secret only to those who were already poets, though even the unlettered could sense the music and authority of her verse. Louise Bogan, pursued by the mutability of time, and Hazel Hall, haunted by the finality of death, outlined a poetry that was both sensuous and cerebral.

### EFFECTS OF THE CRISIS

The financial crash of October, 1929, was not immediately reflected in the poetry of the period. But by 1933 it was evident that a crisis had occurred in literature as well as in finance and government. The poets turned, tentatively enough, to a consideration of economic and social problems; some of them deserted poetry altogether. It is noteworthy that whereas the five years from 1913 to 1918 produced a dozen or more poets of national importance, not more than two or three new poets of any significance appeared between 1930 and 1935.

Poetry seemed to suffer a partial paralysis, unable to express the crisis except by negation. Yet, no matter what the conditions, man cannot remain inarticulate for long, and there were signs that the younger poets were grappling with the situation, deeply affected or momentarily silenced by the breakdown. It was not long before they attempted to express the universal bewilderment, doubtfully, even desperately. In this attempt they were following the example of their predecessors, trying to organize confusion and achieve a clarity, if not a solution. Theirs was a more difficult task. Values were distorted, standards questioned, the traditional responses were deadened. But the basic feelings, unbalanced, disturbed, and temporarily stunned, could not remain paralyzed. A few poets dared to sound the uncertain spirit of the times; and poetry, which refines all experience through the filter of the emotions, began to reassert itself.

### THE WIDER PANORAMA

The poets of the period answered the demands put upon them by a rapidly changing civilization. They reflected the paradoxical energy of the age and its sterility, its contradictory appetite for realism and fantasy, its skepticism and the faith submerged beneath doubtful searching. They sounded a range hitherto barely suggested in America, creating a poetry panoramic instead of parochial. Differing widely from most of their English fellow-craftsmen, they were far less hampered by the burdens of tradition or the necessity of casting them off. The temper of the times was for catholicity, for variety of thought and gesture. Both in the conventional and in the experimental modes, America became a literary melting-pot. The very variety of subject matter was in striking opposition to the thin, limited products of the "transition" poet. Geographically, the range was no less wide. New England ceased to be the one literary center; there was scarcely a village which could not boast a local laureate. As the country matured, the poets grew with it, springing up in most unlikely places, ready to celebrate urban miracles of stone and steel or gaunt prairie silences no less than the traditional scenes and emotions.

Evaluations and reappraisals followed. Poets turned critics, critics returned to poetry. The period was shrewdly analyzed by Conrad Aiken, Amy Lowell,

Edmund Wilson, Allen Tate, Malcolm Cowley, Horace Gregory, and by Yvor
Winters, whose practice fell short of his excellent theories.

It was as if submerged springs had suddenly burst through arid soil; instead
of one placid stream, there were a dozen rushing currents, a score of unsuspected freshets.

### THE NEW SPIRIT

Most of the poets represented in this collection found vigorous material in a
world of honest and often harsh reality. They learned to distinguish beauty
from prettiness; to wring loveliness out of squalor; to search for truth even
in the dark caves of the unconscious.

And with the acceptance of the material of everyday life, there came a further simplification: the use of the language of everyday speech. The stilted and
mouth-filling phrases were practically discarded in favor of an ordinary vocabulary. It would be hard to find a representative poet employing such awkward
and outworn contractions as *'twixt, 'mongst, ope';* such evidences of poor pad-
ding as *adown, did go, doth smile;* such dull rubber-stamps (*clichés* is the
French term) as *heavenly blue, roseate glow, golden hope, girlish grace, gentle
breeze, pearly dew, purple hills, sparkling eyes,* etc. The *peradventures, forsooths* and *mayhaps* have disappeared (one hopes) forever.

As the speech of the modern poet grew less elaborate, so did the patterns
embodying it. Not necessarily discarding rhyme, regular rhythm, or any of the
musical assets of the older poets, forms grew simpler; the intricate versification
gave way to lines that reflect or suggest the tones of animated and even exalted
speech.

One could go into minute particulars concerning the growth of an American
spirit in our literature and point out how many of the poets responded to
forces larger than their backgrounds. Such a course would be endless and un-
profitable. It is pertinent, however, to observe that, young as this nation may
be, it is already being supplied with the stuff of legends, ballads, and even
epics. Most of the modern singers turned to their own locale for indigenous
material. They turned impartially to mountain songs, city stories, semi-
mythical figures like John Brown and Paul Bunyan, transformed heroes (*vide*
the growth of a legendary Lincoln apart from the actual one), to the intricate
relation of men and machines. Believing not only in the uncertainties of
struggle but in the certainty of some sort of goal, they achieved, through
search and experiment, that order out of chaos which is poetry.

After a turning away from reality there was an almost complete return to
the substance of contemporary life. The defeatist attitude was no longer popular; by 1934 the philosophy of T. S. Eliot and Ezra Pound was considered old-
fashioned and suspect. It was once more held that the poet's place is to address
the public—and to speak not only to the people, but for them. The democratic
ideals—a new order, a disciplined vitality, a common understanding—were
courageously revived.

✦

In conclusion it must be repeated that though this collection claims to be
panoramic it is also critical. Detailed study of every corner of the field is,

therefore, impossible; the period being particularly rich in these so articulate States, many omissions were imperative. In extenuation the editor, maintaining that art itself is only a record of temperament and taste, pleads—as all editors must—*chacun à son gout*. He realizes that any gathering, no matter how voluminous, cannot be a summary but only an introduction to an epoch. The purpose of an anthology, he concludes dogmatically, is to stimulate interest rather than to satisfy curiosity. It is the provoking as well as the sharing of enjoyment, which, at the heart of the poet, is the very purpose of poetry.

L. U.

# Walt Whitman

WALT (ORIGINALLY WALTER) WHITMAN was born at West Hills, near Huntington, Long Island, May 31, 1819. His mother's people were hard-working Dutch Quakers, his maternal grandfather having been a Long Island horse-breeder. On his father's side he was descended from English Puritans who had farmed American soil for a century and a half.

Whitman's father was a less successful agrarian than his ancestors and, since he was a better carpenter than farmer, the elder Whitman moved his family to the then provincial suburb of Brooklyn. Here the country child grew into the town boy, was lifted up for a moment by Lafayette when the hero revisited America, was equally fascinated by his father's wood-smelling shop and the city streets, received his first sight of "fish-shaped Paumanok" which was to become his beloved Mannahatta, learned at least the rudiments of the three R's, and left school before his teens. At eleven he was already at work as an errand-boy. At twelve he became a "printer's devil." By the time he was fourteen he had learned the various fonts and began to set type in the composing-room of *The Long Island Star*. At seventeen, taking up residence in the more profitable metropolis, he was well on the road to being an itinerant printer-journalist. But New York was no Golconda for an uneducated, self-conscious youth and, after a few months, Whitman went back to Long Island.

There he remained until his twenty-second year, living with his numerous relations, intermittently teaching school, delivering papers, contributing "pieces" to *The Long Island Democrat*. In 1841 Whitman returned to Brooklyn and New York, writing sentimental fillers, novelettes, rhetorical and flabby verses, hack-work editorials for journals now forgotten. In 1842 he wrote a temperance tract, *Franklin Evans, or The Inebriate,* a mixture of campaign material and fourth-rate Dickens, a volume which Whitman later claimed was written for cash in three days. Blossoming out in frock coat and high hat, debonair, his beard smartly trimmed, Whitman at twenty-three was editor of *The Daily Aurora*. In the capacity of reporter-about-town, he promenaded lower Broadway, spent much time in the theaters, cultivated the opera, flirted impartially with street-corner politics and the *haut monde*. He was still Walter Whitman when, at the age of twenty-seven, he joined the *Brooklyn Eagle*.

Various biographers—Emory Holloway, in particular—have ferreted out Whitman's sketches and editorials of this period and, while there are occasional suggestions of the poet to come, most of them betray him as a fluent, even a prolific, journalist and nothing more. The style is alternately chatty and highfalutin; the ideas are undistinguished. At the end of two years, either because of his politics or his unsatisfactory articles, Whitman suddenly lost his editorial position and, with equal abruptness, received an offer from a stranger who was about to start an independent paper in New Orleans. Thereupon he left New York early in 1848 to become a special writer on the staff of the daily *Crescent.*

Whitman's few months in the South have led to much speculation. Emory Holloway concludes that New Orleans was the background for the poet's first love-affair and implies that his inamorata was one of the *demimonde,* probably a quadroon beauty. But this is sheer guess-work, barely supported by Whitman's later poetry where the wish often substitutes for the action. This much is evident: He and his younger brother Jeff enjoyed the more languorous tempo of the Creole culture; the "Paris of America" made him less priggish; his quickened perceptions took in the whole alphabet of sights and sounds, "not missing a letter from A to Izzard." His literary style, however, had not improved and, after three months, he was dismissed from the *Crescent,* possibly because of his careless, even puerile writing.

Returning to New York, Whitman immediately plunged into editing another paper. His failures as a journalist had not yet convinced him he was mistaking his career and in his thirtieth year he was in charge of the Brooklyn *Freeman.* This free-soil journal soon shifted its political course; Whitman was not agile enough to turn with it; and in September, 1849, he withdrew, "taking his flag with him." As a free-lance, he wrote for the New York *Evening Post* and the *Advertiser,* his contributions being chiefly articles—and badly over-written ones—on music. He "took up" art, gushed about Donizetti's "Favorita," became a metropolitan Bohemian. Meanwhile, finding he could not live by the pen alone, he helped his father and brothers build houses in Brooklyn. Meanwhile, also, he began to write the book which was to be his life-work.

It was at this time that Walter Whitman, the dandified journalist, disappeared and the Walt Whitman of tradition suddenly emerged. He was, one suspects, not unconscious of the tradition and, from the outset, used every means to foster it.

Whitman was now thirty-one; an entirely different apparition from the man who, in his late twenties, frequented the more fashionable lobbies. The once trim beard, streaked with premature gray, was now worn loose and prophetic; the well-tailored coat and spruce cane were discarded in favor of rough workman's clothes, high boots, a large felt hat and a red shirt with the collar nonchalantly—or carefully— opened wide enough to show red flannel underneath. He prepared several lectures on the democracy of art and delivered one at the Brooklyn Art Union in 1851, but found lecturing too tame. He consorted with ferry-men, bus-drivers and other "powerful, uneducated persons." The legend persists that, when one of the drivers was ill, Whitman took his route and drove the omnibus, shouting passages of Shakespeare up and down Broadway. Another legend—repeated by Holloway as a fact—pictures Whitman reading Epictetus to one of the boatmen and, afterwards, "cramming his own volume into the pocket of the sailor's monkey-jacket." These are Homeric gestures and one would like to believe them uncalculated. But even the most confirmed Whitman-worshiper must have his doubts. Subsequent actions add to the admirer's misgivings.

The first edition of *Leaves of Grass* was published in 1855. This epochal volume made its initial appearance as a poorly printed pamphlet of twelve poems brought out anonymously and bearing, instead of a signature, a portrait of the author with one hand in his pocket, one on his hip, the characteristic open shirt and a slouch hat rakishly tilted. One of the first copies of the pamphlet was sent to Ralph Waldo

Emerson, which—considering Whitman's indebtedness in spirit if not in form—was no more than proper. Within a fortnight, Emerson, overlooking the questionable taste of the frontispiece, and with something of the master's gratification on being hailed by an unknown but fervent disciple, wrote the famous letter of July 21, 1855, in which he hailed the young writer, concluding, "I give you joy of your free and brave thought. I have great joy in it. . . . I find the courage of treatment which so delights us, and which large perception only can inspire. I greet you at the beginning of a great career."

But Emerson's lavish praise (which Whitman, without waiting for permission, blazoned on the cover of his second edition) was not loud enough. Nor, was Whitman, despite the convictions contained in the lengthy prose preface, confident enough of his work; he sought to force public approval. In direct opposition to Emersonian standards and the spiritual ideals implied in his foreword, Whitman set about to cause a controversy, to inflame opinion by inflating himself. The task—considering the howls which greeted *Leaves of Grass*—was not difficult. It was—so defenders have insisted—the day of the anonymous review and "self-puffery" was not uncommon. But Whitman's offenses in this regard (and there were many of them) are inexcusable in view of the principles he professed. Two months after the first printing of *Leaves of Grass,* he caused one of a series of anonymous articles to be printed in the Brooklyn *Times* (September 29, 1855). In it—and the idiom is unmistakable—he wrote: "Very devilish to some, and very divine to some, will appear the poet of these new poems, these *Leaves of Grass:* an attempt, as they are, of a naïve, masculine, affectionate, contemplative, sensual, imperious person to cast into literature not only his own grit and arrogance, but his own flesh and form, undraped, regardless of models, regardless of modesty or law." There was much more in the same self-laudatory vein, stressing Whitman's unkempt virility, his firm attachment for loungers and the "free rasping talk of men," his refusal to associate with literary people or (forgetting his lecture programs) to appear on platforms, his lusty physiology "corroborating a rugged phrenology," not even forgetting to mention the fact that he "is always dressed freshly and clean in strong clothes—neck open, shirt-collar flat and broad." Other anonymous salutations announced that the author was "a fine brute," "the most masculine of beings," "one of the roughs, large, proud, affectionate, eating, drinking and breeding."

It requires little psychology to analyze what is so obvious an over-compensation. In these anonymous tributes to himself, Whitman revealed far more than he intended. None but a blinded devotee can fail to suspect a softness beneath the bluster; a psychic impotence poorly shielded by all the talk about fine brutishness, drinking and breeding, flinging his arms right and left, "drawing men and women to his close embrace, loving the clasp of their hands, the touch of their necks and breasts." The poet protests his maleness too vociferously.

Meanwhile, the second edition of *Leaves of Grass,* containing thirty-two instead of the original twelve poems (as well as the press notices written by himself) appeared in 1856. In the third edition (1860) the number of poems leaped to one hundred and fifty-seven. Then the Civil War made all other controversies negligible.

Whitman did not go to war, although his married brother George was one of the first to enlist. Holloway implies an idealistic motive; Harvey O'Higgins charges a cowardly Narcissism. In any case, Whitman refused to join the conflict and, only when George was reported missing, did he see at first hand what he had begun to sketch in "Drum-Taps." Finding his brother wounded in a camp on the Rappahannock, Whitman nursed him and remained in Washington, serving in the hospitals. He acted not only as wound-dresser but as good angel—"a bearded fairy godmother"—for the disabled men; he wrote their letters, brought them tobacco and ice-cream, read tales and poems, made life livelier and death easier for the sufferers. These ministrations, so freely given, gave him much in return: an intimacy with life in the raw which, for all his assertions, he had never seen so closely. No longer a spectator, he was a participant, and purgation as well as passion are manifest in the series of war-echoes, "Drum-Taps," and the uplifted "Memories of President Lincoln" with its immortal elegy "When Lilacs Last in the Dooryard Bloom'd." The end of the Civil War defined a new spirit in Whitman: the man and his poetry became one.

In 1864, through the pressure of friends, a minor clerkship in the Indian Bureau of the Interior Department was found for Whitman. But, though he was promoted, he did not hold the position long. His chief, Secretary James Harlan, once a Methodist preacher, had heard rumors of his subordinate's "immorality." Without stopping to consider the ethics of the situation, Harlan purloined Whitman's private copy of *Leaves of Grass* after closing-time, and fell afoul of the "Children of Adam" section. Nothing more was needed to prove the truth of the rumors and, without an hour's notice, Whitman was dismissed. A few friends rushed to his defense but Harlan, a sincere bigot, stuck to his resolve. William Douglas O'Connor, an Abolitionist author who was one of Whitman's staunchest admirers, issued a pamphlet not merely defending but glorifying Whitman, coining, for his title, the phrase "The Good Gray Poet"—a sobriquet which has outlasted all of O'Connor's works.

Affairs were at a low ebb. As a person, Whitman was stranded with no livelihood and little influence; as a poet he was repudiated by all but a small coterie at home and abroad. Eight years later, and seventeen years after the first edition of *Leaves of Grass* (in January, 1872), Whitman complained to Dowden, who had praised him unreservedly in England, "If you write again for publication about my books . . . I think it would be proper and even essential to include the important facts (for facts they are) that the *Leaves of Grass* and their author are contemptuously ignored by the recognized literary organs here in the United States, rejected by the publishing houses, the author turned out of a government clerkship and deprived of his means of support . . . solely on account of having written the book."

Transferred to the office of the Attorney General after his dismissal, Whitman remained there until 1873 when, on the night of February twenty-second, he was struck by paralysis. Whitman's mother, lying ill in his brother George's house, was spared the news of his attack. She died the following May and Whitman somehow rallied sufficiently to be at her bedside. For months after he could not use his limbs and—let the psychoanalysts make what they will of it—it is doubtful if he ever recovered from the effect of her death. Two years later, while arranging his prose writings for publication, he confided, "I occupy myself . . . still enveloped in thoughts of my dear Mother, the most perfect and magnetic character, the rarest combination of practical, moral and spiritual, and the least selfish, of all and any I have ever known—and by me O so much the most deeply loved."

At fifty-five Whitman was almost completely incapacitated. He did not suffer the daily agonies of Heine on his mattress grave, but confinement in Camden, where his mother had died and where his brother lived, was grueling enough. His solitude was alleviated by letters from abroad and the beginnings of recognition at home. Although he got out of doors a little, he could not walk any distance, and Edward Carpenter, John Burroughs, Richard Maurice Bucke (later one of Whitman's executors) and others made pilgrimages to his room in Mickle Street, near the railroad yards. There were intervals when his health improved sufficiently to permit small visits to New York and Boston, but by 1877, he was enfeebled and, in spite of friends, poverty-stricken. He was reduced to peddling his books from a basket in the streets of Philadelphia and Camden, and, although his brother George offered him a special place in the house he was building in Burlington, New Jersey, Whitman chose to stay where he was.

Whitman grew old with dignity and not without honor. In June, 1888, after a longer drive than usual, Whitman took cold. A new and more severe paralytic shock followed. For a time Whitman lost the power of speech. In 1890 he bought ground for his grave and planned an appropriately massive tomb. The following March he was wheeled over to Philadelphia—a move that meant much discomfort and actual suffering—to deliver a tribute to Lincoln. He was failing, but not rapidly. In 1891 a birthday dinner tendered by friends was served in his own rooms, a festive occasion, to judge from his own letter, at which Whitman drank champagne, speaking "a few words of honor and reverence for our Emerson, Bryant, Longfellow—dead—and then for Whittier and Tennyson, the boss of us all." That December Whitman contracted pneumonia "with complications" and knew he would not recover. Aided by Horace Traubel, the young Jewish Quaker who became the Boswell of his later days, he prefaced a final "deathbed edition" of *Leaves of Grass*. Death came toward the end of his seventy-third year, on March 26, 1892.

Analysis of Whitman's poetry is the more difficult because it presents a paradox— a paradox of which Whitman was not unaware. He knew his "barbaric yawp" was untranslatable, unconforming, impossible to transfix with a phrase or a theory. "I depart as air . . . If you want me again look for me under your boot-soles." The same contradictions which marked his personality are evident in his rhapsodies. *Leaves of Grass* sets out to be the manifesto of the ordinary man, "the divine average," yet it is doubtful if the ordinary man understands its rhetoric or, understanding, responds to it. No great common audience has rallied to Whitman's philosophy, no army of poets has followed his form. Few of the "powerful uneducated persons" for whom Whitman believed his book would be a "democratic Gospel" can appreciate, and fewer still can admire, his extraordinary mixture of self-adulation and impotence, abnormality and mysticism. The same contradictions which mark his personality are evident in his style. His work aims toward a simplification of speech— an American language experiment—yet its homeliness is not always racy. Sometimes it is mere flat statement, sometimes it is a grotesque combination of the colloquial and the grandiose. Sometimes, indeed, it is corrupted by linguistic bad taste and polyglot phrasing as naïvely absurd as "the tangl'd long-deferr'd éclaircissement of human life" . . . "See my cantabile—you Libertad!" "Exalté . . . the mighty earth-eidólon" . . . "These from me, O Democracy, to serve you, ma femme!" "No dainty dolce affetuoso I!"

Only Whitman's lack of ease and certainty in rhyme made him sacrifice its counterpoint for the looser cadence. Nor was his form as revolutionary as it seemed. Heine's "North Sea" cycles had been composed in "free," unrhymed rhythms and the sonorous strophes of the Old Testament were Whitman's avowed model. Whitman was the first to object to the charge that his work had "the freedom of formlessness." He did not even admit its irregularity. In one of the unsigned reviews of *Leaves of Grass* he explained, "His rhythm and *uniformity* he will conceal in the roots of his verses, not to be seen of themselves, but to break forth loosely as lilacs on a bush or take shapes compact as the shapes of melons." None can deny the music in this poetry which is capable of the widest orchestral effects. It is a music accomplished in a dozen ways—by the Hebraic "balance" brought to perfection in Job and the Psalms, by the long and extraordinarily flexible line suddenly whipped taut, by repetitions at the beginnings of lines and reiterations within the lines, by following his recitatives with a soaring aria. Thus, in the midst of the elaborate piling up in "Song of Myself" there are such sheer lyrical outbursts as the passages beginning "Press close, bare-bosomed night," "Smile, O voluptuous cool-breath'd earth," "The last scud of the day holds back for me," "A child said 'What is the grass?'" . . . "No counting of syllables," wrote Anne Gilchrist, "will reveal the mechanism of this music." But the music is there, now rising in gathering choirs of brasses, now falling to the rumor of a flute.

Mass and magnitude are the result. And rightly, for mass was the material. Unlike the cameo-cutting Aldrich and the polished Stedman, both of whom belittled him, Whitman was no lapidary. His aim was not to remodel or brighten a few high facets of existence; he sought to embody a universe in the rough. For him no aspect of life was trivial; every common, superficial cover was a cavern of rich and inexhaustible depths. A leaf of grass, with its tendrils twined about the core of earth, was no less than the journey-work of the stars; the cow, "crunching with depressed head," put Phidias to shame; the roadside running blackberry, seen with the eye of vision, was "fit to adorn the parlors of heaven." Nothing was mean; nothing was rejected. Whitman had read Blake, Dante, Shakespeare, Shelley; besides knowing his Bible, he was acquainted with the sacred books of the East and their reëxpression in Emerson. His transcendentalism was not a new thing; but the fusion of identity and impersonality, the union of the ego-driven self and the impartially moving universe was newly synthesized in his rhapsodies. His aim was inclusive—the lack of exclusiveness may be Whitman's chief defect—for though he celebrated the person in all his separateness, he added "the word democratic, the word *En-masse*." All was included in "the procreant urge of the world." Opposites merge into one: the unseen is proved by the seen; all goes onward and outward, nothing collapses. Light and dark, good and evil, body and soul do not merely emphasize but complete each other.

Whitman's insistence that the body was holy in all its manifestations caused a great deal of contemporary misunderstanding and developed into mysterious whisperings. His early commentators—Burroughs (whose estimates were dictated by Whitman), Carpenter, Bucke, Traubel—magnified his maleness, insisted too much on his normality, and generally misinterpreted him. As late as 1926 Emory Holloway made no effort to resolve the contradictions and, apart from an obscure hint or two, scarcely suggested that there was a split between Whitman's pronouncements and his nature. The split was actually a gulf. Whitman's preoccupation with the details of clothes—he was as fastidious about the way a workman's shirt should be worn as he once was about the set of a high hat—his rôle as nurse during the Civil War, his pathetic insistence that he was the father of six children, none of which ever appeared, and his avoidance of women make it clear that this "fine brute," this "most masculine of beings," was really an invert. Whitman's brother told Traubel that "Walt never fell in love. . . . He did not seem to affect the girls," and even Edward Carpenter concluded "there can be no doubt that his intimacies with men were much more numerous than with women." Not the least of his inconsistencies is Whitman's delusion that an "adhesive" love, the love of "comrades," was the basis on which a broader democracy would be built.

Whitman's "all-inclusive love" springs not only from his own pathological eccentricities, but from an undefined Pantheism. His very eagerness to express the whole cosmos often results in a chaotic pouring forth of prophecy and claptrap. For this reason Whitman should be read, not as one reads a book of lyrics, weighing and appraising individual stanzas, but as one reads an epic, letting the movement, the swelling volume, carry the lines along. It is only in the rare instances that we stop to remark the particularities—the extraordinarily graphic description of an old-time sea-fight in "Song of Myself," or images as breath-taking as "the indolent, sinking sun, burning, expanding the air" and "The hands of the sisters Death and Night incessantly softly wash again, and ever again, this soil'd world" and "Out of the cradle endlessly rocking; out of the mocking bird's throat, the musical shuttle . . ."

Here, framed in firm syllables, are large convictions, strong wants. Tenderness, not pretty sentiment, rises to new heights in the Lincoln elegies, in "Out of the Cradle Endlessly Rocking," in the superbly quiet "On the Beach at Night." There is, it is true, a degree of affectation here—affectation of nationalism and simplicity (referring to Six-month rather than to May, to Mannahatta rather than to New York); affectation of hybrid terms ("Me imperturbe!" "Camerado!" "I exposé," "Deliriate, thus preluding," "Allons! from all formules!" "How plenteous! how spiritual! how résumé!" etc.); affectations, always, of too insistent a strength. It is also true that we read Whitman in youth—as we read Swinburne—for intoxication, uncritically, contemptuous of reservations which maturity compels.

The contradictions resist complete synthesis. It is impossible to analyze Whitman's final significance to American social and cultural development; we can only record the greatness of his contribution. His windy optimism remains an emotional rather than a rational influence. His whole-heartedness, his large yea-saying, coming at a time of cautious skepticism, hesitancy and insecurity, is Whitman's gift not only to his period but to posterity.

Whitman's inconsistency, especially his paradox of democracy, continues to baffle the literary historians. In 1930, in the third volume of his monumental *Main Currents in American Thought* (the uncompleted volume entitled *The Beginnings of Critical Realism in America*) the late Vernon L. Parrington concludes that Whitman is the complete embodiment of Enlightenment—"the poet and prophet of a democracy that the America of the Gilded Age was daily betraying." Yet Parrington himself, though he sees Whitman as "the most deeply religious soul that American literature knows," sees also Whitman's failure as a prophet. "The great hopes on which he [Whitman] fed have been belied by after events—so his critics say; as the great hopes of the Enlightenment have been belied. Certainly in this welter of today, with science become the drab and slut of war and industrialism, with sterile money-slaves instead of men, Whitman's expansive hopes seem grotesque enough. Democracy may indeed be only a euphemism for the rulership of fools."

Yet the paradox must be grasped—or, at least, admitted—if one is to understand Whitman at all. Somehow the contradictions are resolved; somehow the prophet, the pamphleteer, and the poet achieve a unity if only through an intensification of the inner life: a liberal humanism. That Whitman was self-confounded is fairly obvious; he seems to have confused an ideal culture founded on quality with a merely quantitative conception of life. But his faith, romantic as it was resurgent, triumphed over his contradictions, actually imposed a sort of harmony upon them.

Thus Whitman rises above his defects. The reader forgets the lesser flaws, the lumbering failures. The illumined phrases burn clear; the pictures, once etched upon the imagination, are there to stay. Above all, the *effect* remains, an effect not reducible to phrases; a sense of released power, irresistible and benevolent, immense in affirmation. Beyond what Symonds called "delicate and evanescent moods of sensibility" is the communication of amplitudes. It expands the air.

Such poetry, whatever its lapses, has the stuff of permanence. It will persist not only because of its rebellious and compelling power, but because the poet has transcended his material. The personal contact is achieved, as Whitman knew it would be. "Who touches this book touches a man." Lascelles Abercrombie, a poet of an entirely different persuasion, said that Whitman created "out of the wealth of his experience that vividly personal figure which is surely one of the few supremely great things in modern poetry—the figure of himself." But his work was larger than the man. Whitman was not dilating his value when he claimed to contain multitudes. His book projects and creates them in a sphere nobler than our own. Employing words, he harnessed elements.

### I HEAR AMERICA SINGING

I hear America singing, the varied carols I hear,
Those of mechanics, each one singing his as it should be blithe and strong,
The carpenter singing his as he measures his plank or beam,
The mason singing his as he makes ready for work, or leaves off work,
The boatman singing what belongs to him in his boat, the deckhand singing on the
    steamboat deck,
The shoemaker singing as he sits on his bench, the hatter singing as he stands,
The wood-cutter's song, the plowboy's on his way in the morning, or at noon inter-
    mission or at sundown,
The delicious singing of the mother, or of the young wife at work, or of the girl
    sewing or washing,
Each singing what belongs to him or her and to none else,
The day what belongs to the day—at night the party of young fellows, robust,
    friendly,
Singing with open mouths their strong melodious songs.

## THE MUSE IN THE NEW WORLD

*(from "Song of the Exposition")*

Come, Muse, migrate from Greece and Ionia,
Cross out please those immensely overpaid accounts,
That matter of Troy and Achilles' wrath, and Aeneas', Odysseus' wanderings,
Placard "Removed" and "To Let" on the rocks of your snowy Parnassus,
Repeat at Jerusalem, place the notice high on Jaffa's gate and on Mount Moriah,
The same on the walls of your German, French and Spanish castles, and Italian
  collections,
For know a better, fresher, busier sphere, a wide, untried domain awaits, demands
  you.

Responsive to our summons,
Or rather to her long-nurs'd inclination,
Join'd with an irresistible, natural gravitation,
She comes! I hear the rustling of her gown,
I scent the odor of her breath's delicious fragrance,
I mark her step divine, her curious eyes a-turning, rolling,
Upon this very scene.
I say I see, my friends, if you do not, the illustrious émigré, (having it is true in her
  day, although the same, changed, journey'd considerable,)
Making directly for this rendezvous, vigorously clearing a path for herself, striding
  through the confusion,
By thud of machinery and shrill steam-whistle undismay'd,
Bluff'd not a bit by drain-pipe, gasometers, artificial fertilizers;
Smiling and pleas'd with palpable intent to stay,
She's here, install'd amid the kitchen-ware!

## RECORDERS AGES HENCE

Recorders ages hence,
Come, I will take you down underneath this impassive exterior, I will tell you
  what to say of me,
Publish my name and hang up my picture as that of the tenderest lover,
The friend the lover's portrait, of whom his friend his lover was fondest,
Who was not proud of his songs, but of the measureless ocean of love within him,
  and freely pour'd it forth,
Who often walk'd lonesome walks thinking of his dear friends, his lovers,
Who pensive away from one he lov'd often lay sleepless and dissatisfied at night,
Who knew too well the sick, sick dread lest the one he lov'd might secretly be
  indifferent to him,
Whose happiest days were far away through fields, in woods, on hills, he and
  another wandering hand in hand, they twain apart from other men,
Who oft as he saunter'd the streets curv'd with his arm the shoulder of his friend,
  while the arm of his friend rested upon him also.

### THE COMMONPLACE

The commonplace I sing;
How cheap is health! how cheap nobility!
Abstinence, no falsehood, no gluttony, lust;
The open air I sing, freedom, toleration,
(Take here the mainest lesson—less from books—less from the schools,)
The common day and night—the common earth and waters,
Your farm—your work, trade, occupation,
The democratic wisdom underneath, like solid ground for all.

### A NOISELESS PATIENT SPIDER

A noiseless patient spider,
I mark'd where on a little promontory it stood isolated,
Mark'd how to explore the vacant vast surrounding,
It launch'd forth filament, filament, filament, out of itself.
Ever unreeling them, ever tirelessly speeding them.

And you O my soul where you stand,
Surrounded, detached, in measureless oceans of space,
Ceaselessly musing, venturing, throwing, seeking the spheres to connect them.
Till the bridge you will need be form'd, till the ductile anchor hold,
Till the gossamer thread you fling catch somewhere, O my soul.

### TO A COMMON PROSTITUTE

Be composed—be at ease with me—I am Walt Whitman, liberal and lusty as Nature,
Not till the sun excludes you do I exclude you,
Not till the waters refuse to glisten for you and the leaves to rustle for you, do my
    words refuse to glisten and rustle for you.
My girl I appoint with you an appointment, and I charge you that you make prep-
    aration to be worthy to meet me,
And I charge you that you be patient and perfect till I come.

Till then I salute you with a significant look that you do not forget me.

### WHEN I HEARD THE LEARN'D ASTRONOMER

When I heard the learn'd astronomer,
When the proofs, the figures, were ranged in columns before me,
When I was shown the charts and diagrams, to add, divide, and measure them,
When I sitting heard the astronomer where he lectured with much applause in the
    lecture-room,
How soon unaccountable I became tired and sick,
Till rising and gliding out I wander'd off by myself,
In the mystical moist night-air, and from time to time,
Look'd up in perfect silence at the stars.

## RECONCILIATION

Word over all, beautiful as the sky,
Beautiful that war and all its deeds of carnage must in time be utterly lost,
That the hands of the sisters Death and Night incessantly softly wash again, and
    ever again, this soil'd world;
For my enemy is dead, a man divine as myself is dead,
I look where he lies white-faced and still in the coffin—I draw near,
Bend down and touch lightly with my lips the white face in the coffin.

## I HEAR IT WAS CHARGED AGAINST ME

I hear it was charged against me that I sought to destroy institutions,
But really I am neither for or against institutions,
(What indeed have I in common with them? or what with the destruction of them?)
Only I will establish in the Mannahatta and in every city of these States inland and
    seaboard,
And in the fields and woods, and above every keel little or large that dents the water,
Without edifices or rules or trustees or any argument,
The institution of the dear love of comrades.

## MANNAHATTA

I was asking for something specific and perfect for my city,
Whereupon lo! upsprang the aboriginal name.

Now I see what there is in a name, a word, liquid, sane, unruly, musical, self-
    sufficient,
I see that the word of my city is that word from of old,
Because I see that word nested in nests of water-bays, superb,
Rich, hemm'd thick all around with sailships and steamships, an island sixteen
    miles long, solid-founded,
Numberless crowded streets, high growths of iron, slender, strong, light, splendidly
    uprising toward clear skies,
Tides swift and ample, well-loved by me, toward sundown,
The flowing sea-currents, the little islands, larger adjoining islands, the heights, the
    villas,
The countless masts, the white shore-steamers, the lighters, the ferry-boats, the black
    sea-steamers well model'd,
The down-town streets, the jobbers' houses of business, the houses of business of the
    ship-merchants and money-brokers, the river-streets,
Immigrants arriving, fifteen thousand in a week,
The carts hauling goods, the manly race of drivers of horses, the brown-faced sailors,
The summer air, the bright sun shining, and the sailing clouds aloft,
The winter snows, the sleigh-bells, the broken ice in the river, passing along up or
    down with the flood-tide or ebb-tide,
The mechanics of the city, the masters, well-form'd, beautiful-faced, looking you
    straight in the eyes,
Trottoirs throng'd, vehicles, Broadway, the women, the shops and shows,

A million people—manners free and superb—open voices—hospitality—the most
     courageous and friendly young men,
City of hurried and sparkling waters! city of spires and masts!
City nested in bays! my city!

SONG OF MYSELF

1

I celebrate myself, and sing myself,
And what I assume you shall assume,
For every atom belonging to me as good belongs to you.

I loafe and invite my soul,
I learn and loafe at my ease observing a spear of summer grass.

My tongue, every atom of my blood, form'd from this soil, this air,
Born here of parents born here from parents the same, and their parents the same,
I, now thirty-seven years old in perfect health begin,
Hoping to cease not till death.
Creeds and schools in abeyance,
Retiring back a while sufficed at what they are, but never forgotten,
I harbor for good or bad, I permit to speak at every hazard,
Nature without check with original energy.

2

Houses and rooms are full of perfumes, the shelves are crowded with perfumes,
I breathe the fragrance myself and know it and like it,
The distillation would intoxicate me also, but I shall not let it.

The atmosphere is not a perfume, it has no taste of the distillation, it is odorless,
It is for my mouth forever, I am in love with it,
I will go to the bank by the wood and become undisguised and naked,
I am mad for it to be in contact with me.

The smoke of my own breath,
Echoes, ripples, buzz'd whispers, love-root, silk-thread, crotch and vine,
My respiration and inspiration, the beating of my heart, the passing of blood and
     air through my lungs,
The sniff of green leaves and dry leaves, and of the shore and dark-color'd sea-rocks,
     and of hay in the barn,
The sound of the belch'd words of my voice loos'd to the eddies of the wind,
A few light kisses, a few embraces, a reaching around of arms,
The play of shine and shade on the trees as the supple boughs wag,
The delight alone or in the rush of the streets, or along the fields and hill-sides,
The feeling of health, the full-moon trill, the song of me rising from bed and
     meeting the sun.
Have you reckon'd a thousand acres much? have you reckon'd the earth much?
Have you practic'd so long to learn to read?
Have you felt so proud to get at the meaning of poems?

Stop this day and night with me and you shall possess the origin of all poems,
You shall possess the good of the earth and sun, (there are millions of suns left,)
You shall no longer take things at second or third hand, nor look through the eyes
    of the dead, nor feed on the specters in books,
You shall not look through my eyes either, nor take things from me,
You shall listen to all sides and filter them from your self.

### 3

I have heard what the talkers were talking, the talk of the beginning and the end,
But I do not talk of the beginning or the end.

There was never any more inception than there is now,
Nor any more youth or age than there is now,
And will never be any more perfection than there is now,
Nor any more heaven or hell than there is now.

Urge and urge and urge,
Always the procreant urge of the world.
Out of the dimness opposite equals advance, always substance and increase, always
    sex,
Always a knit of identity, always distinction, always a breed of life.

To elaborate is no avail, learn'd and unlearn'd feel that it is so.

Sure as the most certain sure, plumb in the uprights, well center-tied, braced in the
    beams,
Stout as a horse, affectionate, haughty, electrical,
I and this mystery here we stand.
Clear and sweet is my soul, and clear and sweet is all that is not my soul.

Lack one lacks both, and the unseen is proved by the seen,
Till that becomes unseen and receives proof in its turn.

Showing the best and dividing it from the worst age vexes age,
Knowing the perfect fitness and equanimity of things, while they discuss I am silent,
    and go bathe and admire myself.

Welcome is every organ and attribute of me, and of any man hearty and clean,
Not an inch nor a particle of an inch is vile, and none shall be less familiar than
    the rest.

I am satisfied—I see, dance, laugh, sing;
As the hugging and loving bed-fellow sleeps at my side through the night, and
    withdraws at the peep of the day with stealthy tread,
Leaving me baskets cover'd with white towels swelling the house with their plenty,
Shall I postpone my acceptation and realization and scream at my eyes,
That they turn from gazing after and down the road,
And forthwith cipher and show to me a cent,
Exactly the value of one and exactly the value of two, and which is ahead?

4

Trippers and askers surround me,
People I meet, the effect upon me of my early life or the ward and city I live in,
    or the nation,
The latest dates, discoveries, inventions, societies, authors old and new,
My dinner, dress, associates, looks, compliments, dues,
The real or fancied indifference of some man or woman I love,
The sickness of one of my folks or of myself, or ill-doing or loss or lack of money,
    or depressions or exaltations,
Battles, the horrors of fratricidal war, the fever of doubtful news, the fitful events;
These come to me days and nights and go from me again,
But they are not the Me myself.

Apart from the pulling and hauling stands what I am,
Stands amused, complacent, compassionating, idle, unitary,
Looks down, is erect, or bends an arm on an impalpable certain rest,
Looking with side-curved head curious what will come next,
Both in and out of the game and watching and wondering at it.

Backward I see in my own days where I sweated through fog with linguists and
    contenders,
I have no mockings or arguments, I witness and wait.

5

I believe in you my soul, the other I am must not abase itself to you,
And you must not be abased to the other.

Loafe with me on the grass, loose the stop from your throat,
Not words, not music or rhyme I want, not custom or lecture, not even the best.
Only the lull I like, the hum of your valvèd voice.

✦

Swiftly arose and spread around me the peace and knowledge that pass all the
    argument of the earth,
And I know that the hand of God is the promise of my own,
And I know that the spirit of God is the brother of my own,
And that all the men ever born are also my brothers, and the women my sisters and
    lovers,
And that a kelson of the creation is love,
And limitless are leaves stiff or drooping in the fields,
And brown ants in the little wells beneath them,
And mossy scabs of the worm fence, heap'd stones, elder, mullein and poke-weed.

6

A child said, *What is the grass?* fetching it to me with full hands;
How could I answer the child? I do not know what it is any more than he.

I guess it must be the flag of my disposition, out of hopeful green stuff woven.

Or I guess it is the handkerchief of the Lord,
A scented gift and remembrancer designedly dropt,
Bearing the owner's name someway in the corner, that we may see and remark, and
   say *Whose?*

Or I guess the grass is itself a child, the produced babe of the vegetation.
Or I guess it is a uniform hieroglyphic,
And it means, Sprouting alike in broad zones and narrow zones,
Growing among black folks as among white,
Kanuck, Tuckahoe, Congressman, Cuff, I give them the same, I receive them the
   same.

And now it seems to me the beautiful uncut hair of graves,

Tenderly will I use you curling grass,
It may be you transpire from the breasts of young men,
It may be if I had known them I would have loved them,
It may be you are from old people, or from offspring taken soon out of their mothers'
   laps,
And here you are the mothers' laps.

This grass is very dark to be from the white heads of old mothers,
Darker than the colorless beards of old men,
Dark to come from under the faint red roofs of mouths.
O I perceive after all so many uttering tongues,
And I perceive they do not come from the roofs of mouths for nothing.
I wish I could translate the hints about the dead young men and women,
And the hints about old men and mothers, and the offspring taken soon out of their
   laps.

What do you think has become of the young and old men?
And what do you think has become of the women and children?

They are alive and well somewhere,
The smallest sprout shows there is really no death,
And if ever there was it led forward life, and does not wait at the end to arrest it,
And ceas'd the moment life appear'd.

All goes onward and outward, nothing collapses,
And to die is different from what anyone supposed, and luckier.

### 7

Has anyone supposed it lucky to be born?
I hasten to inform him or her it is just as lucky to die, and I know it.

I pass death with the dying and birth with the new-wash'd babe, and am not
   contain'd between my hat and boots,
And peruse manifold objects, no two alike and every one good,
The earth good and the stars good, and their adjuncts all good.

I am not an earth nor an adjunct of an earth,
I am the mate and companion of people, all just as immortal and fathomless as
     myself,
(They do not know how immortal, but I know.)
Every kind for itself and its own, for me mine male and female,
For me those that have been boys and that love women,
For me the man that is proud and feels how it stings to be slighted,
For me the sweet-heart and the old maid, for me mothers and the mothers of
     mothers,
For me lips that have smiled, eyes that have shed tears,
For me children and the begetters of children.

Undrape! you are not guilty to me, nor stale nor discarded,
I see through the broadcloth and gingham whether or no,
And am around, tenacious, acquisitive, tireless, and cannot be shaken away.

### 8

The little one sleeps in its cradle,
I lift the gauze and look a long time, and silently brush away flies with my hand.

The youngster and the red-faced girl turn aside up the bushy hill,
I peeringly view them from the top.

The suicide sprawls on the bloody floor of the bedroom,
I witness the corpse with its dabbled hair, I note where the pistol has fallen.

The blab of the pave, tires of carts, sluff of boot-soles, talk of the promenaders,
The heavy omnibus, the driver with his interrogating thumb, the clank of the shod
     horses on the granite floor,
The snow-sleighs, clinking, shouted jokes, pelts of snow-balls,
The hurrahs for popular favorites, the fury of rous'd mobs,
The flap of the curtain'd litter, a sick man inside borne to the hospital,
The meeting of enemies, the sudden oath, the blows and fall,
The excited crowd, the policeman with his star quickly working his passage to the
     center of the crowd,
The impassive stones that receive and return so many echoes,
What groans of over-fed or half-starv'd who fall sunstruck or in fits,
What exclamations of women taken suddenly who hurry home and give birth to
     babes,
What living and buried speech is always vibrating here, what howls restrain'd by
     decorum,
Arrests of criminals, slights, adulterous offers made, acceptances, rejections with
     convex lips,
I mind them or the show or resonance of them—I come and I depart.

### 9

The big doors of the country barn stand open and ready,
The dried grass of the harvest-time loads the slow-drawn wagon,
The clear light plays on the brown gray and green intertinged,
The armfuls are pack'd to the sagging mow.

I am there, I help, I came stretch'd atop of the load,
I felt its soft jolts, one leg reclined on the other,
I jump from the cross-beams and seize the clover and timothy,
And roll head over heels and tangle my hair full of wisps.

### 10

Alone far in the wilds and mountains I hunt,
Wandering amazed at my own lightness and glee,
In the late afternoon choosing a safe spot to pass the night,
Kindling a fire and broiling the fresh-kill'd game,
Falling asleep on the gather'd leaves with my dog and gun by my side.

The Yankee clipper is under her sky-sails, she cuts the sparkle and scud,
My eyes settle the land, I bend at her prow or shout joyously from the deck.

The boatmen and clam-diggers arose early and stopt for me,
I tuck'd my trowser-ends in my boots and went and had a good time;
You should have been with us that day round the chowder-kettle.

I saw the marriage of the trapper in the open air in the far west, the bride was a
      red girl,
Her father and his friends sat near cross-legged and dumbly smoking, they had
      moccasins to their feet and large thick blankets hanging from their shoulders,
On a bank lounged the trapper, he was drest mostly in skins, his luxuriant beard
      and curls protected his neck, he held his bride by the hand,
She had long eyelashes, her head was bare, her coarse straight locks descended upon
      her voluptuous limbs and reach'd to her feet.

The runaway slave came to my house and stopt outside,
I heard his motions crackling the twigs of the woodpile,
Through the swung half-door of the kitchen I saw him limpsy and weak,
And went where he sat on a log and led him in and assured him,
And brought water and fill'd a tub for his sweated body and bruis'd feet,
And gave him a room that enter'd from my own, and gave him some coarse clean
      clothes,
And remember perfectly well his revolving eyes and his awkwardness,
And remember putting plasters on the galls of his neck and ankles;
He staid with me a week before he was recuperated and pass'd north,
I had him sit next me at table, my fire-lock lean'd in the corner.

### 11

Twenty-eight young men bathe by the shore.
Twenty-eight young men and all so friendly;
Twenty-eight years of womanly life and all so lonesome.
She owns the fine house by the rise of the bank,
She hides handsome and richly drest aft the blinds of the window.

Which of the young men does she like the best?
Ah the homeliest of them is beautiful to her.

Where are you off to, lady? for I see you,
You splash in the water there, yet stay stock still in your room.

Dancing and laughing along the beach came the twenty-ninth bather,
The rest did not see her, but she saw them and loved them.

The beards of the young men glisten'd with wet, it ran from their long hair,
Little streams pass'd all over their bodies.

An unseen hand also pass'd over their bodies,
It descended tremblingly from their temples and ribs.

The young men float on their backs, their white bellies bulge to the sun, they do
    not ask who seizes fast to them,
They do not know who puffs and declines with pendant and bending arch,
They do not think whom they souse with spray.

### 14

The wild gander leads his flock through the cool night,
*Ya-honk* he says, and sounds it down to me like an invitation,
The pert may suppose it meaningless, but I listening close,
Find its purpose and place up there toward the wintry sky.

The sharp-hoof'd moose of the north, the cat on the house-sill, the chickadee, the
    prairie-dog,
The litter of the grunting sow as they tug at her teats,
The brood of the turkey-hen and she with her half-spread wings,
I see in them and myself the same old law.

The press of my foot to the earth springs a hundred affections,
They scorn the best I can do to relate them.

I am enamour'd of growing out-doors,
Of men that live among cattle or taste of the ocean or woods,
Of the builders and steerers of ships and the wielders of axes and mauls, and the
    drivers of horses,
I can eat and sleep with them week in and week out.

What is commonest, cheapest, nearest, easiest, is Me,
Me going in for my chances, spending for vast returns,
Adorning myself to bestow myself on the first that will take me,
Not asking the sky to come down to my good will,
Scattering it freely forever.

### 15

The pure contralto sings in the organ loft,
The carpenter dresses his plank, the tongue of his foreplane whistles its wild ascend-
    ing lisp,
The married and unmarried children ride home to their Thanksgiving dinner,
The pilot seizes the king-pin, he heaves down with a strong arm,
The mate stands braced in the whale-boat, lance and harpoon are ready,

The duck-shooter walks by silent and cautious stretches,

The deacons are ordain'd with cross'd hands at the altar,

The spinning-girl retreats and advances to the hum of the big wheel,

The farmer stops by the bars as he walks on a First-day loaf and looks at the oats and rye,

The lunatic is carried at last to the asylum a confirm'd case,

(He will never sleep any more as he did in the cot in his mother's bedroom;)

The jour printer with gray head and gaunt jaws works at his case,

He turns his quid of tobacco while his eyes blur with the manuscript;

The malform'd limbs are tied to the surgeon's table,

What is removed drops horribly in a pail;

The quadroon girl is sold at the auction-stand, the drunkard nods by the bar-room stove,

The machinist rolls up his sleeves, the policeman travels his beat, the gate-keeper marks who pass,

The young fellow drives the express-wagon, (I love him, though I do not know him;)

The half-breed straps on his light boots to compete in the race,

The western turkey-shooting draws old and young, some lean on their rifles, some sit on logs,

Out from the crowd steps the marksman, takes his position, levels his piece;

The groups of newly-come immigrants cover the wharf or levee,

As the woolly-pates hoe in the sugar-field, the overseer views them from his saddle,

The bugle calls in the ball-room, the gentlemen run for their partners, the dancers bow to each other,

The youth lies awake in the cedar-roof'd garret and harks to the musical rain,

The Wolverine sets traps on the creek that helps fill the Huron,

The squaw wrapt in her yellow-hemm'd cloth is offering moccasins and bead-bags for sale,

The connoisseur peers along the exhibition-gallery with half-shut eyes bent sideways,

As the deck-hands make fast the steamboat the plank is thrown for the shore-going passengers,

The young sister holds out the skein while the elder sister winds it off in a ball, and stops now and then for the knots,

The one-year wife is recovering and happy having a week ago borne her first child,

The clean-hair'd Yankee girl works with her sewing machine or in the factory or mill,

The paving-man leans on his two-handed rammer, the reporter's lead flies swiftly over the note-book, the sign-painter is lettering with blue and gold,

The canal boy trots on the tow-path, the book-keeper counts at his desk, the shoe-maker waxes his thread,

The conductor beats time for the band and all the performers follow him,

The child is baptized, the convert is making his first profession,

The regatta is spread on the bay, the race is begun, (how the white sails sparkle!)

The drover watching his drove sings out to them that would stray,

The peddler sweats with his pack on his back, (the purchaser higgling about the odd cent;)

The bride unrumples her white dress, the minute-hand of the clock moves slowly,

The opium-eater reclines with rigid head and just-open'd lips,

The prostitute draggles her shawl, her bonnet bobs on her tipsy and pimpled neck,

The crowd laugh at her blackguard oaths, the men jeer and wink to each other,
(Miserable! I do not laugh at your oaths nor jeer you;)
The President holding a cabinet council is surrounded by the great Secretaries,
On the piazza walk three matrons stately and friendly with twined arms,
The crew of the fish-smack pack repeated layers of halibut in the hold,
Coon-seekers go through the regions of the Red river or through those drain'd by
    the Tennessee, or through those of the Arkansas,
Torches shine in the dark that hangs on the Chattahooche or Altamahaw,
Patriarchs sit at supper with sons and grandsons and great grandsons around them,
In walls of adobie, in canvas tents, rest hunters and trappers after their day's sport,
The city sleeps and the country sleeps,
The living sleep for their time, the dead sleep for their time,
The old husband sleeps by his wife and the young husband sleeps by his wife;
And these tend inward to me, and I tend outward to them,
And such as it is to be of these more or less I am,
And of these one and all I weave the song of myself.

### 18

With music strong I come, with my cornets and my drums,
I play not marches for accepted victors only, I play marches for conquer'd and
    slain persons.

Have you heard that it was good to gain the day?
I also say it is good to fall, battles are lost in the same spirit in which they are won.

I beat and pound for the dead,
I blow through my embouchures my loudest and gayest for them.

Vivas to those who have fail'd!
And to those whose war-vessels sank in the sea!
And to those themselves who sank in the sea!
And to all generals that lost engagements, and all overcome heroes!
And the numberless unknown heroes equal to the greatest heroes known!

### 19

This is the meal equally set, this the meat for natural hunger,
It is for the wicked just the same as the righteous, I make appointments with all,
I will not have a single person slighted or left away,
The kept-woman, sponger, thief, are hereby invited,
There shall be no difference between them and the rest.

This is the press of a bashful hand, this the float and odor of hair,
This the touch of my lips to yours, this the murmur of yearning,
This the far-off depth and height reflecting my own face,
This the thoughtful merge of myself, and the outlet again.
Do you guess I have some intricate purpose?
Well I have, for the Fourth-month showers have, and the mica on the side of the
    rock has.

Do you take it I would astonish?
Does the daylight astonish? does the early redstart twittering through the woods?
Do I astonish more than they?

This hour I tell things in confidence,
I might not tell everybody, but I will tell you.

20

Who goes there? hankering, gross, mystical, nude;
How is it I extract strength from the beef I eat?

What is a man anyhow? what am I? what are you?

All I mark as my own you shall offset it with your own,
Else it were time lost listening to me.

I do not snivel that snivel the world over,
That months are vacuums and the ground but wallow and filth.

Whimpering and truckling fold with powders for invalids, conformity goes to the
    fourth-remov'd,
I wear my hat as I please indoors or out.

Why should I pray? why should I venerate and be ceremonious?

Having pried through the strata, analyzed to a hair, counsel'd with doctors and
    calculated close,
I find no sweeter fat than sticks to my own bones.

In all people I see myself, none more and not one a barleycorn less,
And the good or bad I say of myself I say of them.
I know I am solid and sound,
To me the converging objects of the universe perpetually flow,
All are written to me, and I must get what the writing means.

I know I am deathless,
I know this orbit of mine cannot be swept by a carpenter's compass,
I know I shall not pass like a child's carlacue cut with a burnt stick at night.

I know I am august,
I do not trouble my spirit to vindicate itself or be understood,
I see that the elementary laws never apologize,
(I reckon I behave no prouder than the level I plant my house by, after all.)

I exist as I am, that is enough,
If no other in the world be aware I sit content,
And if each and all be aware I sit content.

One world is aware and by far the largest to me, and that is myself,
And whether I come to my own today or in ten thousand or ten million years,
I can cheerfully take it now, or with equal cheerfulness I can wait.

My foothold is tenon'd and mortis'd in granite,
I laugh at what you call dissolution,
And I know the amplitude of time.

21

I am the poet of the Body and I am the poet of the Soul,
The pleasures of heaven are with me and the pains of hell are with me,
The first I graft and increase upon myself, the latter I translate into a new tongue.
I am the poet of the woman the same as the man,
And I say it is as great to be a woman as to be a man,
And I say there is nothing greater than the mother of men.

I chant the chant of dilation or pride,
We have had ducking and deprecating about enough,
I show that size is only development.

Have you outstript the rest? are you the President?
It is a trifle, they will more than arrive there every one, and still pass on.

I am he that walks with the tender and growing night,
I call to the earth and sea half-held by the night.

Press close bare-bosom'd night—press close magnetic nourishing night!
Night of south winds—night of the large few stars!
Still nodding night—mad naked summer night.

Smile O voluptuous cool-breath'd earth!
Earth of the slumbering and liquid trees!
Earth of departed sunset—earth of the mountains misty-topt!
Earth of the vitreous pour of the full moon just tinged with blue!
Earth of shine and dark mottling the tide of the river!
Earth of the limpid gray of clouds brighter and clearer for my sake!
Far-swooping elbow'd earth—rich apple-blossom'd earth!
Smile, for your lover comes.

Prodigal, you have given me love—therefore I to you give love!
O unspeakable passionate love.

22

You sea! I resign myself to you also—I guess what you mean,
I behold from the beach your crooked inviting fingers,
I believe you refuse to go back without feeling of me,
We must have a turn together, I undress, hurry me out of sight of the land,
Cushion me soft, rock me in billowy drowse,
Dash me with amorous wet, I can repay you.

Sea of stretch'd ground-swells,
Sea breathing broad and convulsive breaths,
Sea of the brine of life and of unshovel'd yet always-ready graves,
Howler and scooper of storms, capricious and dainty sea,
I am integral with you, I too am of one phase and of all phases.

Partaker of influx and efflux I, extoller of hate and conciliation,
Extoller of amies [1] and those that sleep in each other's arms.

[1] Friends, as distinguished from lovers.

I am he attesting sympathy,
(Shall I make my list of things in the house and skip the house that supports them?)

I am not the poet of goodness only, I do not decline to be the poet of wickedness also.

What blurt is this about virtue and about vice?
Evil propels me and reform of evil propels me, I stand indifferent,
My gait is no fault-finder's or rejecter's gait,
I moisten the roots of all that has grown.

Did you fear some scrofula out of the unflagging pregnancy?
Did you guess the celestial laws are yet to be work'd over and rectified?

I find one side a balance and the antipodal side a balance,
Soft doctrine as steady help as stable doctrine,
Thoughts and deeds of the present our rouse and early start.

This minute that comes to me over the past decillions,
There is no better than it and now.

What behaved well in the past or behaves well today is not such a wonder,
The wonder is always and always how there can be a mean man or an infidel.

### 25

Dazzling and tremendous how quick the sunrise would kill me,
If I could not now and always send sun-rise out of me.

We also ascend dazzling and tremendous as the sun,
We found our own O my soul in the calm and cool of the daybreak.

My voice goes after what my eyes cannot reach,
With the twirl of my tongue I encompass worlds and volumes of worlds.

Speech is the twin of my vision, it is unequal to measure itself,
It provokes me forever, it says sarcastically,
*Walt you contain enough, why don't you let it out then?*

Come now I will not be tantalized, you conceive too much of articulation,
Do you not know O speech how the buds beneath you are folded?
Waiting in gloom, protected by frost,
The dirt receding before my prophetical screams,
I underlying causes to balance them at last,
My knowledge my live parts, it keeping tally with the meaning of all things,
Happiness, (which whoever hears me let him or her set out in search of this day.)

My final merit I refuse you, I refuse putting from me what I really am,
Encompass worlds, but never try to encompass me,
I crowd your sleekest and best by simply looking toward you.

Writing and talking do not prove me,
I carry the plenum of proof and every thing else in my face,
With the hush of my lips I wholly confound the skeptic.

### 30

All truths wait in all things,
They neither hasten their own delivery nor resist it,
They do not need the obstetric forceps of the surgeon,
The insignificant is as big to me as any,
(What is less or more than a touch?)

Logic and sermons never convince,
The damp of the night drives deeper into my soul.

(Only what proves itself to every man and woman is so,
Only what nobody denies is so.)

A minute and a drop of me settle my brain,
I believe the soggy clods shall become lovers and lamps,
And a compend of compends is the meat of a man or woman,
And a summit and flower there is the feeling they have for each other,
And they are to branch boundlessly out of that lesson until it becomes omnific,
And until one and all shall delight us, and we them.

### 31

I believe a leaf of grass is no less than the journeywork of the stars,
And the pismire is equally perfect, and a grain of sand, and the egg of the wren,
And the tree-toad is a chef-d'œuvre for the highest,
And the running blackberry would adorn the parlors of heaven,
And the narrowest hinge in my hand puts to scorn all machinery,
And the cow crunching with depress'd head surpasses any statue,
And a mouse is miracle enough to stagger sextillions of infidels.

I find I incorporate gneiss, coal, long-threaded moss, fruits, grains, esculent roots,
And am stucco'd with quadrupeds and birds all over,
And have distanced what is behind me for good reasons,
But call any thing back again when I desire it.

In vain the speeding or shyness,
In vain the plutonic rocks send their old heat against my approach,
In vain the mastodon retreats beneath its own powder'd bones,
In vain objects stand leagues off and assume manifold shapes,
In vain the ocean settling in hollows and the great monsters lying low,
In vain the buzzard houses herself with the sky,
In vain the snake slides through the creepers and logs,
In vain the elk takes to the inner passes of the woods,
In vain the razor-bill'd auk sails far north to Labrador,
I follow quickly, I ascend to the nest in the fissure of the cliff.

### 32

I think I could turn and live with animals, they're so placid and self-contain'd,
I stand and look at them long and long.

They do not sweat and whine about their condition,
They do not lie awake in the dark and weep for their sins,

They do not make me sick discussing their duty to God,
Not one is dissatisfied, not one is demented with the mania of owning things,
Not one kneels to another, nor to his kind that lived thousands of years ago,
Not one is respectable or unhappy over the whole earth.

So they show their relations to me and I accept them,
They bring me tokens of myself, they evince them plainly in their possession.

I wonder where they get those tokens,
Did I pass that way huge times ago and negligently drop them?

Myself moving forward then and now and forever,
Gathering and showing more always and with velocity,
Infinite and omnigenous, and the like of these among them,
Not too exclusive toward the reachers of my remembrancers,
Picking out here one that I love, and now go with him on brotherly terms.

A gigantic beauty of a stallion, fresh and responsive to my caresses,
Head high in the forehead, wide between the ears,
Limbs glossy and supple, tail dusting the ground,
Eyes full of sparkling wickedness, ears finely cut, flexibly moving.
His nostrils dilate as my heels embrace him,
His well-built limbs tremble with pleasure as we race around and return.

I but use you a minute, then I resign you, stallion,
Why do I need your paces when I myself out-gallop them?
Even as I stand or sit passing faster than you.

### 35

Would you hear of an old-time sea-fight?
Would you learn who won by the light of the moon and stars?
List to the yarn, as my grandmother's father the sailor told it to me.

Our foe was no skulk in his ship I tell you, (said he,)
His was the surly English pluck, and there is no tougher or truer, and never was,
    and never will be;
Along the lower'd eve he came horribly raking us.

We closed with him, the yards entangled, the cannon touch'd,
My captain lash'd fast with his own hands.

We had receiv'd some eighteen pound shots under the water,
On our lower-gun-deck two large pieces had burst at the first fire, killing all around
    and blowing up overhead.

Fighting at sun-down, fighting at dark,
Ten o'clock at night, the full moon well up, our leaks on the gain, and five feet of
    water reported,
The master-at-arms loosing the prisoners confined in the afterhold to give them a
    chance for themselves.
The transit to and from the magazine is now stopt by the sentinels,
They see so many strange faces they do not know whom to trust.

Our frigate takes fire,
The other asks if we demand quarter?
If our colors are struck and the fighting done?

Now I laugh content, for I hear the voice of my little captain,
*We have not struck,* he composedly cries, *we have just begun our part of the fighting.*

Only three guns are in use,
One is directed by the captain himself against the enemy's mainmast,
Two well serv'd with grape and canister silence his musketry and clear his decks.

The tops alone second the fire of this little battery, especially the main-top,
They hold out bravely during the whole of the action.

Not a moment's cease.
The leaks gain fast on the pumps, the fire eats toward the powder-magazine.

One of the pumps has been shot away, it is generally thought we are sinking.

Serene stands the little captain,
He is not hurried, his voice is neither high nor low,
His eyes give more light to us than our battle-lanterns.

Toward twelve there in the beams of the moon they surrender to us.

### 36

Stretch'd and still lies the midnight,
Two great hulls motionless on the breast of the darkness,
Our vessel riddled and slowly sinking, preparations to pass to the one we have
    conquer'd,
The captain on the quarter-deck coldly giving his orders through a countenance
    white as a sheet,
Near by the corpse of the child that serv'd in the cabin,
The dead face of an old salt with long white hair and carefully curl'd whiskers,
The flames spite of all that can be done flickering aloft and below,
The husky voices of the two or three officers yet fit for duty,
Formless stacks of bodies and bodies by themselves, dabs of flesh upon the masts and
    spars,
Cut of cordage, dangle of rigging, slight shock of the soothe of waves,
Black and impassive guns, litter of powder-parcels, strong scent,
A few large stars overhead, silent and mournful shining,
Delicate sniffs of sea-breeze, smells of sedgy grass and fields by the shore, death-
    messages given in charge to survivors,
The hiss of the surgeon's knife, the gnawing teeth of his saw,
Wheeze, cluck, swash of falling blood, short wild scream, and long, dull, tapering
    groan,
These so, these irretrievable.

### 37

You laggards there on guard! look to your arms!
In at the conquer'd doors they crowd! I am possess'd!
Embody all presences outlaw'd or suffering,

See myself in prison shaped like another man,
And feel the dull intermitted pain.

For me the keepers of convicts shoulder their carbines and keep watch,
It is I let out in the morning and barr'd at night.
Not a mutineer walks handcuff'd to jail but I am handcuff'd to him and walk by
his side,
(I am less the jolly one there, and more the silent one with sweat on my twitching
lips.)

Not a youngster is taken for larceny but I go up too, and am tried and sentenced.

Not a cholera patient lies at the last gasp but I also lie at the last gasp,
My face is ash-color'd, my sinews gnarl, away from me people retreat.

Askers embody themselves in me and I am embodied in them,
I project my hat, sit shame-faced, and beg.

### 38

Enough! enough! enough!
Somehow I have been stunn'd. Stand back!
Give me a little time beyond my cuff'd head, slumbers, dreams, gaping,
I discover myself on the verge of a usual mistake.

That I could forget the mockers and insults!
That I could forget the trickling tears and the blows of the bludgeons and hammers!
That I could look with a separate look on my own crucifixion and bloody crowning!

I remember now,
I resume the overstaid fraction,
The grave of rock multiplies what has been confided to it, or to any graves,
Corpses rise, gashes heal, fastenings roll from me.

I troop forth replenish'd with supreme power, one of an average unending pro-
cession,
Inland and sea-coast we go, and pass all boundary lines,
Our swift ordinances on their way over the whole earth,
The blossoms we wear in our hats the growth of thousands of years.

### 40

Flaunt of the sunshine I need not your bask—lie over!
You light surfaces only, I force surfaces and depths also.

Earth! you seem to look for something at my hands,
Say, old top-knot, what do you want?

Behold, I do not give lectures or a little charity,
When I give I give myself.

You there, impotent, loose in the knees,
Open your scarf'd chops till I blow grit within you,

Spread your palms and lift the flaps of your pockets,
I am not to be denied, I compel, I have stores plenty and to spare,
And any thing I have I bestow.

I do not ask who you are, that is not important to me,
You can do nothing and be nothing but what I will infold you.

To cotton-field drudge or cleaner of privies I lean,
On his right cheek I put the family kiss,
And in my soul I swear I never will deny him.

To anyone dying, thither I speed and twist the knob of the door,
Turn the bed-clothes toward the foot of the bed,
Let the physician and the priest go home.

I seize the descending man and raise him with resistless will,
O despairer, here is my neck,
By God, you shall not go down! hang your whole weight upon me.

44

It is time to explain myself—let us stand up.

What is known I strip away,
I launch all men and women forward with me into the Unknown.

The clock indicates the moment—but what does eternity indicate?

We have thus far exhausted trillions of winters and summers,
There are trillions ahead, and trillions ahead of them.

Rise after rise bow the phantoms behind me,
Afar down I see the huge first Nothing, I know I was even there,
I waited unseen and always, and slept through the lethargic mist,
And took my time, and took no hurt from the fetid carbon.

Long I was hugg'd close—long and long.
Immense have been the preparations for me,
Faithful and friendly the arms that have help'd me.

Cycles ferried my cradle, rowing and rowing like cheerful boatmen,
For room to me stars kept aside in their own rings,
They sent influences to look after what was to hold me.

Before I was born out of my mother generations guided me,
My embryo has never been torpid, nothing could overlay it.

For it the nebula cohered to an orb,
The long slow strata piled to rest it on,
Vast vegetables gave it sustenance,
Monstrous sauroids transported it in their mouths and deposited it with care.

All forces have been steadily employ'd to complete and delight me,
Now on this spot I stand with my robust soul.

### 48

I have said that the soul is not more than the body,
And I have said that the body is not more than the soul,
And nothing, not God, is greater to one than one's self is,
And whoever walks a furlong without sympathy walks to his own funeral drest
  in his shroud,
And I or you pocketless of a dime may purchase the pick of the earth,
And to glance with an eye or show a bean in its pod confounds the learning of all
  times,
And there is no trade or employment but the young man following it may become
  a hero,
And there is no object so soft but it makes a hub for the wheel'd universe,
And I say to any man or woman, Let your soul stand cool and composed before a
  million universes.

And I say to mankind, Be not curious about God,
For I who am curious about each am not curious about God,
(No array of terms can say how much I am at peace about God and about death.)

I hear and behold God in every object, yet understand God not in the least,
Nor do I understand who there can be more wonderful than myself.

Why should I wish to see God better than this day?
I see something of God each hour of the twenty-four, and each moment then,
In the faces of men and women I see God, and in my own face in the glass,
I find letters from God dropt in the street, and every one is sign'd by God's name,
And I leave them where they are, for I know that wheresoe'er I go,
Others will punctually come for ever and ever.

### 49

And as to you Death, and you bitter hug of mortality, it is idle to try to alarm me.

To his work without flinching the accoucheur comes,
I see the elder-hand pressing receiving supporting,
I recline by the sills of the exquisite flexible doors,
And mark the outlet, and mark the relief and escape.
And as to you Corpse I think you are good manure, but that does not offend me,
I smell the white roses sweet-scented and growing,
I reach to the leafy lips, I reach to the polish'd breasts of melons.

And as to you Life I reckon you are the leavings of many deaths,
(No doubt I have died myself ten thousand times before.)

I hear you whispering there O stars of heaven,
O suns—O grass of graves—O perpetual transfers and promotions,
If you do not say any thing how can I say any thing?

Of the turbid pool that lies in the autumn forest,
Of the moon that descends the steeps of the soughing twilight,
Toss, sparkles of day and dusk—toss on the black stems that decay in the muck,
Toss to the moaning gibberish of the dry limbs.

I ascend from the moon, I ascend from the night,
I perceive that the ghastly glimmer is noonday sunbeams reflected,
And debouch to the steady and central from the offspring great or small.

### 50

There is that in me—I do not know what it is—but I know it is in me.

Wrench'd and sweaty—calm and cool then my body becomes,
I sleep—I sleep long.

I do not know it—it is without name—it is a word unsaid,
It is not in any dictionary, utterance, symbol.

Something it swings on more than the earth I swing on,
To it the creation is the friend whose embracing awakes me.
Perhaps I might tell more. Outlines! I plead for my brothers and sisters.
Do you see O my brothers and sisters?
It is not chaos or death—it is form, union, plan—it is eternal life—it is Happiness.

### 51

The past and present wilt—I have fill'd them, emptied them,
And proceed to fill my next fold of the future.

Listener up there! what have you to confide to me?
Look in my face while I snuff the sidle of evening,
(Talk honestly, no one else hears you, and I stay only a minute longer.)

Do I contradict myself?
Very well then I contradict myself,
(I am large, I contain multitudes.)

I concentrate toward them that are nigh, I wait on the door-slab.

Who has done his day's work? who will soonest be through with his supper?
Who wishes to walk with me?

Will you speak before I am gone? will you prove already too late?

### 52

The spotted hawk swoops by and accuses me, he complains of my gab and my
    loitering.

I too am not a bit tamed, I too am untranslatable,
I sound my barbaric yawp over the roofs of the world.

The last scud of day holds back for me,
It flings my likeness after the rest and true as **any on** the shadow'd wilds,
It coaxes me to the vapor and the dusk.
I depart as air, I shake my white locks at the runaway sun,
I effuse my flesh in eddies, and drift it in lacy jags.

I bequeath myself to the dirt to grow from the grass I love,
If you want me again look for me under your boot-soles.

You will hardly know who I am or what I mean,
But I shall be good health to you nevertheless,
And filter and fiber your blood.

Failing to fetch me at first keep encouraged,
Missing me one place search another,
I stop somewhere waiting for you.

## SONG OF THE OPEN ROAD

### (*Condensed*)

Afoot and light-hearted I take to the open road,
Healthy, free, the world before me,
The long brown path before me leading wherever I choose.

Henceforth I ask not good-fortune, I myself am good-fortune,
Henceforth I whimper no more, postpone no more, need nothing,
Done with indoor complaints, libraries, querulous criticisms,
Strong and content I travel the open road.

The earth, that is sufficient,
I do not want the constellations any nearer,
I know they are very well where they are,
I know they suffice for those who belong to them.

(Still here I carry my old delicious burdens,
I carry them, men and women, I carry them with me wherever I go,
I swear it is impossible for me to get rid of them,
I am fill'd with them, and I will fill them in return.)

You road I enter upon and look around, I believe you are not all that is here,
I believe that much unseen is also here.
Here the profound lesson of reception, nor preference nor denial,
The black with his woolly head, the felon, the diseas'd, the illiterate person, are not
     denied;
The birth, the hasting after the physician, the beggar's tramp, the drunkard's stag-
     ger, the laughing party of mechanics,
The escaped youth, the rich person's carriage, the fop, the eloping couple,
The early market-man, the hearse, the moving of furniture into the town, the return
     back from the town,

They pass, I also pass, any thing passes, none can be interdicted,
None but are accepted, none but shall be dear to me.

You air that serves me with breath to speak!
You objects that call from diffusion my meanings and give them shape!
You light that wraps me and all things in delicate equable showers!
You paths worn in the irregular hollows by the roadsides!
I believe you are latent with unseen existences, you are so dear to me.

I inhale great draughts of space,
The east and the west are mine, and the north and the south are mine.

I am larger, better than I thought,
I did not know I held so much goodness.

All seems beautiful to me,
I can repeat over to men and women, You have done such good to me I would do
     the same to you,
I will recruit for myself and you as I go,
I will scatter myself among men and women as I go,
I will toss a new gladness and roughness among them,
Whoever denies me it shall not trouble me,
Whoever accepts me he or she shall be blessed and shall bless me.

Allons! whoever you are come travel with me!
Traveling with me you find what never tires.

The earth never tires,
The earth is rude, silent, incomprehensible at first, Nature is rude and incompre-
     hensible at first,
Be not discouraged, keep on, there are divine things well envelop'd,
I swear to you there are divine things more beautiful than words can tell.

Allons! we must not stop here,
However sweet these laid-up stores, however convenient this dwelling we cannot
     remain here,
However shelter'd this port and however calm these waters we must not anchor
     here,
However welcome the hospitality that surrounds us we are permitted to receive it
     but a little while.

Allons! the inducements shall be greater,
We will sail pathless and wild seas,
We will go where winds blow, waves dash, and the Yankee clipper speeds by under
     full sail.

Allons! with power, liberty, the earth, the elements,
Health, defiance, gayety, self-esteem, curiosity;
Allons! from all formules!
From your formules, O bat-eyed and materialistic priests.

Allons! through struggles and wars!
The goal that was named cannot be countermanded.

Have the past struggles succeeded?
What has succeeded? yourself? your nation? Nature?
Now understand me well—it is provided in the essence of things that from any
    fruition of success, no matter what, shall come forth something to make a
    greater struggle necessary.

My call is the call of battle, I nourish active rebellion,
He going with me must go well arm'd,
He going with me goes often with spare diet, poverty, angry enemies, desertions.

Allons! the road is before us!
It is safe—I have tried it—my own feet have tried it well—be not detain'd!
Let the paper remain on the desk unwritten, and the book on the shelf unopen'd!
Let the tools remain in the workshop! let the money remain unearn'd!
Let the school stand! mind not the cry of the teacher!
Let the preacher preach in his pulpit! let the lawyer plead in the court, and the
    judge expound the law.

Camerado, I give you my hand!
I give you my love more precious than money,
I give you myself before preaching or law;
Will you give me yourself? will you come travel with me?
Shall we stick by each other as long as we live?

### THE BROAD-AX

*(from "Song of the Broad-Ax")*

Weapon shapely, naked, wan,
Head from the mother's bowels drawn,
Wooded flesh and metal bone, limb only one and lip only one,
 Gray-blue leaf by red-heat grown, helve produced from a little seed sown,
Resting the grass amid and upon,
To be lean'd and to lean on.

### ON THE BEACH AT NIGHT

On the beach at night,
Stands a child with her father,
Watching the east, the autumn sky.

Up through the darkness,
While ravening clouds, the burial clouds, in black masses spreading,
Lower sullen and fast athwart and down the sky,
Amid a transparent clear belt of ether yet left in the east,
Ascends large and calm the lord-star Jupiter,
And nigh at hand, only a very little above,
Swim the delicate sisters the Pleiades.

From the beach the child holding the hand of her father,
Those burial clouds that lower victorious soon to devour all,
Watching, silently weeps.

Weep not, child,
Weep not, my darling,
With these kisses let me remove your tears,
The ravening clouds shall not long be victorious;
They shall not long possess the sky, they devour the stars only in apparition,
Jupiter shall emerge, be patient, watch again another night, the Pleiades shall
    emerge,
They are immortal, all those stars both silvery and golden shall shine out again,
The great stars and the little ones shall shine out again, they endure,
The vast immortal suns and the long-enduring pensive moons shall again shine.

Then dearest child mournest thou only for Jupiter?
Considerest thou alone the burial of the stars?

Something there is,
(With my lips soothing thee, adding I whisper,
I give thee the first suggestion, the problem and indirection,)
Something there is more immortal even than the stars,
(Many the burials, many the days and nights, passing away,)
Something that shall endure longer even than lustrous Jupiter,
Longer than sun or any revolving satellite,
Or the radiant sisters the Pleiades.


### OUT OF THE CRADLE ENDLESSLY ROCKING

Out of the cradle endlessly rocking,
Out of the mocking-bird's throat, the musical shuttle,
Out of the Ninth-month midnight,
Over the sterile sands and the fields beyond where the child leaving his bed wan-
    der'd alone, bareheaded, barefoot,
Down from the shower'd halo,
Up from the mystic play of shadows twining and twisting as if they were alive,
Out from the patches of briers and blackberries,
From the memories of the bird that chanted to me,
From your memories sad brother, from the fitful risings and fallings I heard,
From under that yellow half-moon late-risen and swollen as if with tears,
From those beginning notes of yearning and love there in the mist,
From the thousand responses of my heart never to cease,
From the myriad thence-arous'd words,
From the word stronger and more delicious than any,
From such as now they start the scene revisiting,
As a flock, twittering, rising, or overhead passing,
Borne hither, ere all eludes me, hurriedly,
A man, yet by these tears a little boy again,
Throwing myself on the sand, confronting the waves,
I, chanter of pains and joys, uniter of here and hereafter,
Taking all hints to use them, but swiftly leaping beyond them,
A reminiscence sing.

Once Paumanok,
When the lilac-scent was in the air and Fifth-month grass was growing,
Up this seashore in some briers,
Two feather'd guests from Alabama, two together,
And their nest, and four light-green eggs spotted with brown,
And every day the he-bird to and fro near at hand,
And every day the she-bird crouch'd on her nest, silent, with bright eyes,
And every day I, a curious boy, never too close, never disturbing them,
Cautiously peering, absorbing, translating.

*Shine! shine! shine!*
*Pour down your warmth, great sun!*
*While we bask, we two together,*

*Two together!*
*Winds blow south, or winds blow north,*
*Day come white, or night come black,*
*Home, or rivers and mountains from home,*
*Singing all time, minding no time,*
*While we two keep together.*

Till of a sudden,
May-be kill'd, unknown to her mate,
One forenoon the she-bird crouch'd not on the nest,
Nor return'd that afternoon, nor the next,
Nor ever appear'd again.

And thenceforward all summer in the sound of the sea,
And at night under the full of the moon in calmer weather,
Over the hoarse surging of the sea,
Or flitting from brier to brier by day,
I saw, I heard at intervals the remaining one, the he-bird,
The solitary guest from Alabama.

*Blow! blow! blow!*
*Blow up sea-winds along Paumanok's shore;*
*I wait and I wait till you blow my mate to me.*

Yes, when the stars glisten'd,
All night long on the prong of a moss-scallop'd stake,
Down almost amid the slapping waves,
Sat the lone singer wonderful causing tears.

He call'd on his mate,
He pour'd forth the meanings which I of all men know.

Yes my brother I know,
The rest might not, but I have treasur'd every note,
For more than once dimly down to the beach gliding,
Silent, avoiding the moonbeams, blending myself with the shadows,
Recalling now the obscure shapes, the echoes, the sounds and sights after their sorts,

The white arms out in the breakers tirelessly tossing,
I, with bare feet, a child, the wind wafting my hair,
Listen'd long and long.

Listen'd to keep, to sing, now translating the notes,
Following you my brother.

*Soothe! soothe! soothe!*
*Close on its wave soothes the wave behind,*
*And again another behind embracing and lapping, every one close,*
*But my love soothes not me, not me.*
*Low hangs the moon, it rose late,*
*It is lagging—O I think it is heavy with love, with love.*

*O madly the sea pushes upon the land,*
*With love, with love.*

*O night! do I not see my love fluttering out among the breakers?*
*What is that little black thing I see there in the white?*

*Loud! loud! loud!*
*Loud I call to you, my love!*
*High and clear I shoot my voice over the waves,*
*Surely you must know who is here, is here,*
*You must know who I am, my love.*

*Low-hanging moon!*
*What is that dusky spot in your brown yellow?*
*O it is the shape, the shape of my mate!*
*O moon do not keep her from me any longer.*

*Land! land! O land!*
*Whichever way I turn, O I think you could give me my mate back again if you*
*    only would,*
*For I am almost sure I see her dimly whichever way I look.*

*O rising stars!*
*Perhaps the one I want so much will rise, will rise with some of you.*

*O throat! O trembling throat!*
*Sound clearer through the atmosphere!*
*Pierce the woods, the earth,*
*Somewhere listening to catch you must be the one I want.*

*Shake out carols!*
*Solitary here, the night's carols!*
*Carols of lonesome love! death's carols!*
*Carols under that lagging, yellow, waning moon!*
*O under that moon where she droops almost down into the sea!*
*O reckless despairing carols.*

*But soft! sink low!*
*Soft, let me just murmur,*
*And do you wait a moment you husky-nois'd sea,*
*For somewhere I believe I heard my mate responding to me,*
*So faint, I must be still, be still to listen,*
*But not altogether still, for then she might not come immediately to me.*

*Hither my love!*
*Here I am! here!*
*With this just-sustain'd note I announce myself to you,*
*This gentle call is for you my love, for you.*

*Do not be decoy'd elsewhere,*
*That is the whistle of the wind, it is not my voice,*
*That is the fluttering, the fluttering of the spray,*
*Those are the shadows of leaves.*
*O darkness! O in vain!*
*O I am very sick and sorrowful.*

*O brown halo in the sky near the moon, drooping upon the sea!*
*O troubled reflection in the sea!*
*O throat! O throbbing heart!*
*And I singing uselessly, uselessly all the night.*

*O past! O happy life! O songs of joy!*
*In the air, in the woods, over fields,*
*Loved! loved! loved! loved! loved!*
*But my mate no more, no more with me!*
*We two together no more.*

The aria sinking,
All else continuing, the stars shining,
The winds blowing, the notes of the bird continuous echoing,
With angry moans the fierce old mother incessantly moaning,
On the sands of Paumanok's shore gray and rustling,
The yellow half-moon enlarged, sagging down, drooping, the face of the sea almost
    touching,
Are you whispering it, and have been all the time, you sea waves?
Is that it from your liquid rims and wet sands?

Whereto answering, the sea,
Delaying not, hurrying not,
Whisper'd me through the night, and very plainly before daybreak,
Lisp'd to me the low and delicious word death,
And again death, death, death, death,
Hissing melodious, neither like the bird nor like my arous'd child's heart,
But edging near as privately for me rustling at my feet,
Creeping thence steadily up to my ears and laving me softly all over,
Death, death, death, death, death.

Which I do not forget,
But fuse the song of my dusky demon and brother,
That he sang to me in the moonlight on Paumanok's gray beach,
With the thousand responsive songs at random,
My own songs awaked from that hour,
And with them the key, the word up from the waves,
The word of the sweetest song and all songs,
That strong and delicious word which, creeping to my feet,
(Or like some old crone rocking the cradle, swathed in sweet garments, bending
    aside,)
The sea whisper'd me.

### COME UP FROM THE FIELDS FATHER

Come up from the fields father, here's a letter from our Pete,
And come to the front door mother, here's a letter from thy dear son.

Lo, 'tis autumn,
Lo, where the trees, deeper green, yellower and redder,
Cool and sweeten Ohio's villages with leaves fluttering in the moderate wind,
Where apples ripe in the orchards hang and grapes on the trellis'd vines
(Smell you the smell of the grapes on the vines?
Smell you the buckwheat where the bees were lately buzzing?)

Above all, lo, the sky so calm, so transparent after the rain, and with wondrous
    clouds,
Below too, all calm, all vital and beautiful, and the farm prospers well.

Down in the fields all prospers well,
But now from the fields come father, come at the daughter's call,
And come to the entry mother, to the front door come right away.

Fast as she can she hurries, something ominous, her steps trembling,
She does not tarry to smooth her hair nor adjust her cap.

Open the envelope quickly,
O this is not our son's writing, yet his name is sign'd,
O a strange hand writes for our dear son, O stricken mother's soul!
All swims before her eyes, flashes with black, she catches the main words only,
Sentences broken, *gunshot wound in the breast, cavalry skirmish, taken to hospital,*
*At present low, but will soon be better.*

Ah now the single figure to me,
Amid all teeming and wealthy Ohio with all its cities and farms,
Sickly white in the face and dull in the head, very faint,
By the jamb of a door leans.

*Grieve not so, dear mother,* (the just-grown daughter speaks through her sobs,
The little sisters huddle around speechless and dismay'd,)
*See, dearest mother, the letter says Pete will soon be better.*

Alas poor boy, he will never be better, (nor may-be needs to be better, that brave
    and simple soul,)

While they stand at home at the door he is dead already,
The only son is dead.

But the mother needs to be better,
She with thin form presently drest in black,
By day her meals untouch'd, then at night fitfully sleeping, often waking,
In the midnight waking, weeping, longing with one deep longing,
O that she might withdraw unnoticed, silent from life escape and withdraw,
To follow, to seek, to be with her dear dead son.

### WHEN LILACS LAST IN THE DOORYARD BLOOM'D[1]

#### 1

When lilacs last in the dooryard bloom'd,
And the great star early droop'd in the western sky in the night,
I mourn'd, and yet shall mourn with ever-returning spring.

Ever-returning spring, trinity sure to me you bring,
Lilac blooming perennial and drooping star in the west,
And thought of him I love.

#### 2

O powerful western fallen star!
O shades of night—O moody, tearful night!
O great star disappear'd—O the black murk that hides the star!
O cruel hands that hold me powerless—O helpless soul of me!
O harsh surrounding cloud that will not free my soul.

#### 3

In the dooryard fronting an old farm-house near the whitewash'd palings,
Stands the lilac-bush tall-growing with heart-shaped leaves of rich green,
With many a pointed blossom rising delicate, with the perfume strong I love,
With every leaf a miracle—and from this bush in the dooryard,
With delicate-color'd blossoms and heart-shaped leaves of rich green,
A sprig with its flower I break.

#### 4

In the swamp in secluded recesses,
A shy and hidden bird is warbling a song.

Solitary the thrush,
The hermit withdrawn to himself, avoiding the settlements,
Sings by himself a song.

Song of the bleeding throat,
Death's outlet song of life, (for well dear brother I know,
If thou wast not granted to sing thou would'st surely die.)

#### 5

Over the breast of the spring, the land, amid cities,
Amid lanes and through old woods, where lately the violets peep'd from the ground,
    spotting the gray débris,

---

[1] This, one of the noblest elegies in the language, and the rhymed stanzas that follow on the same theme, are part of a group which Whitman entitled "Memories of President Lincoln."

Amid the grass in the fields each side of the lanes, passing the endless grass,
Passing the yellow-spear'd wheat, every grain from its shroud in the dark-brown
　　fields uprisen,
Passing the apple-tree blows of white and pink in the orchards,
Carrying a corpse to where it shall rest in the grave,
Night and day journeys a coffin.

6

Coffin that passes through lanes and streets,
Through day and night with the great cloud darkening the land,
With the pomp of the inloop'd flags with the cities draped in black,
With the show of the States themselves as of crape-veil'd women standing,
With processions long and winding and the flambeaus of the night,
With the countless torches lit, with the silent sea of faces and the unbared heads,
With the waiting depot, the arriving coffin, and the somber faces,
With dirges through the night, with the thousand voices rising strong and solemn,
With all the mournful voices of the dirges pour'd around the coffin,
The dim-lit churches and the shuddering organs—where amid these you journey,
With the tolling tolling bells' perpetual clang,
Here, coffin that slowly passes,
I give you my sprig of lilac.

7

(Nor for you, for one alone,
Blossoms and branches green to coffins all I bring,
For fresh as the morning, thus would I chant a song for you O sane and sacred
　　death.

All over bouquets of roses,
O death, I cover you over with roses and early lilies,
But mostly and now the lilac that blooms the first,
Copious I break, I break the sprigs from the bushes,
With loaded arms I come, pouring for you,
For you and the coffins all of you O death.)

8

O western orb sailing the heaven,
Now I know what you must have meant as a month since I walk'd,
As I walk'd in silence the transparent shadowy night,
As I saw you had something to tell as you bent to me night after night,
As you droop'd from the sky low down as if to my side, (while the other stars all
　　look'd on,)
As we wander'd together the solemn night, (for something I know not what kept
　　me from sleep,)
As the night advanced, and I saw on the rim of the west how full you were of woe,
As I stood on the rising ground in the breeze in the cool transparent night,
As I watch'd where you pass'd and was lost in the netherward black of the night,
As my soul in its trouble dissatisfied sank, as where you sad orb,
Concluded, dropt in the night, and was gone.

9

Sing on there in the swamp,
O singer bashful and tender, I hear your notes, I hear your call,
I hear, I come presently, I understand you,

But a moment I linger, for the lustrous star has detain'd me,
The star my departing comrade holds and detains me.

### 10

O how shall I warble myself for the dead one there I loved?
And how shall I deck my song for the large sweet soul that has gone?
And what shall my perfume be for the grave of him I love?

Sea-winds blown from east and west,
Blown from the Eastern sea and blown from the Western sea, till there on the
    prairies meeting,
These and with these and the breath of my chant,
I'll perfume the grave of him I love.

### 11

O what shall I hang on the chamber walls?
And what shall the pictures be that I hang on the walls,
To adorn the burial-house of him I love?
Pictures of growing spring and farms and homes,
With the Fourth-month eve at sundown, and the gray smoke lucid and bright,
With floods of the yellow gold of the gorgeous, indolent, sinking sun, burning, ex-
    panding the air,
With the fresh sweet herbage under foot, and the pale green leaves of the trees
    prolific,
In the distance the flowing glaze, the breast of the river, with a wind-dapple here
    and there,
With ranging hills on the banks, with many a line against the sky, and shadows,
And the city at hand, with dwellings so dense, and stacks of chimneys,
And all the scenes of life and the workshops, and the workmen homeward returning.

### 12

Lo, body and soul—this land,
My own Manhattan with spires, and the sparkling and hurrying tides, and the ships,
The varied and ample land, the South and the North in the light, Ohio's shores
    and flashing Missouri,
And ever the far-spreading prairies cover'd with grass and corn.

Lo, the most excellent sun so calm and haughty,
The violet and purple morn with just-felt breezes,
The gentle soft-born measureless light,
The miracle spreading bathing all, the fulfill'd noon,
The coming eve delicious, the welcome night and the stars,
Over my cities shining all, enveloping man and land.

### 13

Sing on, sing on you gray-brown bird,
Sing from the swamps, the recesses, pour your chant from the bushes,
Limitless out of the dusk, out of the cedars and pines.
Sing on dearest brother, warble your reedy song,
Loud human song, with voice of uttermost woe.

O liquid and free and tender!
O wild and loose to my soul—O wondrous singer!
You only I hear—yet the star holds me, (but will soon depart,)
Yet the lilac with mastering odor holds me.

### 14

Now while I sat in the day and look'd forth,
In the close of the day with its light and the fields of spring, and the farmers pre-
    paring their crops,
In the large unconscious scenery of my land with its lakes and forests,
In the heavenly aerial beauty, (after the perturb'd winds and the storms,)
Under the arching heavens of the afternoon swift passing, and the voices of chil-
    dren and women,
The many-moving sea-tides, and I saw the ships how they sail'd,
And the summer approaching with richness, and the fields all busy with labor,
And the infinite separate houses, how they all went on, each with its meals and
    minutia of daily usages,
And the streets how their throbbings throbb'd, and the cities pent—lo, then and
    there,
Falling upon them all and among them all, enveloping me with the rest,
Appear'd the cloud, appear'd the long black trail,
And I knew death, its thought, and the sacred knowledge of death.

Then with the knowledge of death as walking one side of me,
And the thought of death close-walking the other side of me,
And I in the middle as with companions, and as holding the hands of companions,
I fled forth to the hiding receiving night that talks not,
Down to the shores of the water, the path by the swamp in the dimness,
To the solemn shadowy cedars and ghostly pines so still.

And the singer so shy to the rest receiv'd me,
The gray-brown bird I know receiv'd us comrades three,
And he sang the carol of death, and a verse for him I love.

From deep secluded recesses,
From the fragrant cedars and the ghostly pines so still,
Came the carol of the bird.

And the charm of the carol rapt me
As I held as if by their hands my comrades in the night,
And the voice of my spirit tallied the song of the bird.

*Come lovely and soothing death,*
*Undulate round the world, serenely arriving, arriving,*
*In the day, in the night, to all, to each,*
*Sooner or later delicate death.*

*Prais'd be the fathomless universe,*
*For life and joy, and for objects and knowledge curious,*
*And for love, sweet love—but praise! praise! praise!*
*For the sure-enwinding arms of cool-enfolding death.*

*Dark mother always gliding near with soft feet,*
*Have none chanted for thee a chant of fullest welcome?*
*Then I chant it for thee, I glorify thee above all,*
*I bring thee a song that when thou must indeed come, come unfalteringly.*

*Approach strong deliveress,*
*When it is so, when thou hast taken them I joyously sing the dead,*
*Lost in the loving floating ocean of thee,*
*Laved in the flood of thy bliss O death.*

*From me to thee glad serenades,*
*Dances for thee I propose saluting thee, adornments and feastings for thee,*
*And the sights of the open landscape and the high-spread sky are fitting,*
*And life and the fields, and the huge and thoughtful night.*

*The night in silence under many a star,*
*The ocean shore and the husky whispering wave whose voice I know,*
*And the soul turning to thee O vast and well-veil'd death,*
*And the body gratefully nestling close to thee.*

*Over the tree-tops I float thee a song,*
*Over the rising and sinking waves, over the myriad fields and the prairies wide,*
*Over the dense-pack'd cities all and the teeming wharves and ways,*
*I float this carol with joy, with joy to thee O death.*

### 15

To the tally of my soul,
Loud and strong kept up the gray-brown bird,
With pure deliberate notes spreading filling the night.

Loud in the pines and cedars dim,
Clear in the freshness moist and the swamp-perfume,
And I with my comrades there in the night.

While my sight that was bound in my eyes unclosed,
As to long panoramas of visions.

And I saw askant the armies,
I saw as in noiseless dreams hundreds of battle-flags,
Borne through the smoke of the battles and pierc'd with missiles I saw them,
And carried hither and yon through the smoke, and torn and bloody,
And at last but a few shreds left on the staffs, (and all in silence,)
And the staffs all splinter'd and broken.

I saw battle-corpses, myriads of them,
And the white skeletons of young men, I saw them,
I saw the débris and débris of all the slain soldiers of the war,
But I saw they were not as was thought,
They themselves were fully at rest, they suffer'd not,
The living remain'd and suffer'd, the mother suffer'd,
And the wife and the child and the musing comrade suffer'd,
And the armies that remain'd suffer'd.

### 16

Passing the visions, passing the night,
Passing, unloosing the hold of my comrades' hands,

Passing the song of the hermit bird and the tallying song of my soul,
Victorious song, death's outlet song, yet varying ever-altering song,
As low and wailing, yet clear the notes, rising and falling, flooding the night,
Sadly sinking and fainting, as warning and warning, and yet again bursting with
    joy,
Covering the earth and filling the spread of the heaven,
As that powerful psalm in the night I heard from recesses,
Passing, I leave thee lilac with heart-shaped leaves,
I leave thee there in the dooryard, blooming, returning with spring.

I cease from my song for thee,
From my gaze on thee in the west, fronting the west, communing with thee,
O comrade lustrous with silver face in the night.

Yet each to keep and all, retrievements out of the night,
The song, the wondrous chant of the gray-brown bird,
And the tallying chant, the echo arous'd in my soul,
With the lustrous and drooping star with the countenance full of woe,
With the holders holding my hand nearing the call of the bird,
Comrades mine and I in the midst, and their memory ever to keep, for the dead I
    loved so well,
For the sweetest, wisest soul of all my days and lands—and this for his dear sake,
Lilac and star and bird twined with the chant of my soul,
There in the fragrant pines and the cedars dusk and dim.


### O CAPTAIN! MY CAPTAIN!

O Captain! my Captain! our fearful trip is done,
The ship has weather'd every rack, the prize we sought is won,
The port is near, the bells I hear, the people all exulting,
While follow eyes the steady keel, the vessel grim and daring;
      But O heart! heart! heart!
        O the bleeding drops of red,
          Where on the deck my Captain lies,
          Fallen cold and dead.

O Captain! my Captain! rise up and hear the bells;
Rise up—for you the flag is flung—for you the bugle trills,
For you bouquets and ribbon'd wreaths—for you the shores a-crowding,
For you they call, the swaying mass, their eager faces turning;
      Here Captain! dear father!
        The arm beneath your head!
          It is some dream that on the deck,
          You've fallen cold and dead.

My Captain does not answer, his lips are pale and still,
My father does not feel my arm, he has no pulse nor will,
The ship is anchor'd safe and sound, its voyage closed and done,
From fearful trip the victor ship comes in with object won;
      Exult O shores, and ring O bells!
        But I with mournful tread,
          Walk the deck my Captain lies,
          Fallen cold and dead.

### AFTER THE SUPPER AND TALK

After the supper and talk—after the day is done,
As a friend from friends his final withdrawal prolonging,
Good-by and Good-by with emotional lips repeating,
(So hard for his hand to release those hands—no more will they meet,
No more for communion of sorrow and joy, of old and young,
A far-stretching journey awaits him, to return no more,)
Shunning, postponing severance—seeking to ward off the last word ever so little,
E'en at the exit-door turning—charges superfluous calling back—e'en as he descends
    the steps,
Something to eke out a minute additional—shadows of nightfall deepening,
Farewells, messages lessening—dimmer the forthgoer's visage and form,
Soon to be lost for aye in the darkness—loth, O so loth to depart!
Garrulous to the very last.

### THE LAST INVOCATION

At the last, tenderly,
From the walls of the powerful fortress'd house,
From the clasp of the knitted locks, from the keep of the well-closed doors,
Let me be wafted.

Let me glide noiselessly forth;
With the key of softness unlock the locks—with a whisper,
Set ope the doors O soul.

Tenderly—be not impatient,
(Strong is your hold O mortal flesh.
Strong is your hold O love.)

## Emily Dickinson

EMILY (ELIZABETH [1]) DICKINSON was born in Amherst, Massachusetts, December 10, 1830. Her life was, except for a circumstance which has caused much speculation and a controversy among her biographers, bare of outward event. She died in the house in which she was born; after she was twenty-six she rarely left it. Her childhood had the ordinary uneventful events common to other children in Amherst which at that time was so remote that, only a few years before, her mother's dower had been brought to the town by a team of oxen. Her family was not quite like other families; it was a distillation of all that was New England, a synthesis and refinement of its reticence and high thinking. A contemporary, Samuel G. Ward, commented shrewdly, "We came to this country to think our own thoughts with nobody to hinder. We conversed with our own souls till we lost the art of communicating with other people. . . . It was awfully high but awfully lonesome. . . . If

---

[1] Often given as "Norcross," which was not her middle name, but her sister Lavinia's.

the gift of articulateness was not denied, you had Channing, Emerson, Hawthorne, a stupendous example, and many others. Mostly, it was denied, and became a family fate. This is where Emily Dickinson comes in. She was the articulate inarticulate."

Emily Dickinson's father, Edward Dickinson, was a lawyer who was nominated for the office of Lieutenant Governor (which he declined) and one of the town's most influential men. Emily adored him. In the *Life and Letters of Emily Dickinson* Martha Dickinson Bianchi, Emily's niece, quotes her as saying, "If father is asleep on the sofa the house is full." At sixteen she formed a close friendship with a girl who visited Amherst and later married her brother Austin (the "sister Sue" of *The Single Hound*) and who disputed with Lavinia the belated honor of being Emily's confidante. At seventeen Emily entered South Hadley Female Seminary, disliked it intensely, grew homesick, rebelled at the extremities of its Puritanism and, on one occasion, packed her bags and took the stage home. From eighteen to twenty-three she was, according to her first biographer, "a social creature in the highest sense."

When she was twenty-three she spent some weeks in Washington with her father who was in Congress for two terms. On the return to Amherst Emily visited in Philadelphia and met the Reverend Charles Wadsworth—a meeting which, according to one of her biographers, determined not only the course of her life but the character of her poetry. As late as 1929 Mme. Bianchi (Sue's daughter) wrote, "Even now, after the many slow years she has been removed from us in the body, her spirit hinders the baring of that chapter which has been so universally misunderstood." Nothing could have done more to further the misunderstanding; it provoked speculation, inspired the very gossip it purported to evade, and placed the emphasis on a puzzle rather than on the poetry.

But this was part of a posthumous wrangle from which Emily Dickinson was mercifully spared. The known facts are these: After 1856 she immured herself in the family mansion. She was rarely seen even in the house except as a figure vanishing ghostily down a corridor; she loved music, but refused to come in the parlor where it was played, and remained seated, out of view, in the hall. She developed certain idiosyncrasies: was an indefatigable letter-writer but had a congenital prejudice against addressing her notes and got others to do this for her; invariably dressed in white, but refused to be "fitted," her sister performing this task for her; sent perennial roots and cookies with cryptic lines to neighbors and even to children, and became, in short, the village oddity. She died of Bright's disease, May 15, 1886, in her fifty-sixth year.

Thus the flat physical data of the woman. The poet made her appearance only after her death. During her lifetime four of her poems had been published—through no desire of her own. She never cared to see her emotions in print; "she habitually concealed her mind, like her person, from all but a very few friends," wrote Higginson. Even more deeply than Heine she might have cried, *"Aus meinen grossen Schmerzen mach ich die kleinen Lieder"*—and these brief, almost telegraphic revelations tucked away in boxes and hidden in bureau drawers have outlasted the more pretentious writing of a century. After Emily's death her executors were amazed at the amount of material which she had left. More than twelve hundred poems were unearthed, of which many are still unpublished. "Sister Sue" had written a tribute to Emily in the town paper, but it was upon Lavinia that the burden fell. Lavinia assumed it. She knew her limitations, but she knew, or at least surmised, the greatness of which she was guardian. She called upon her friends Mabel Loomis Todd and Thomas Wentworth Higginson. Mrs. Todd began to copy the poems, and not only to copy but to edit them, for Emily usually appended a list of alternative words and it was Mrs. Todd who had to decide which word should appear as Emily's choice. In November, 1890, the first volume of the *Poems of Emily Dickinson* appeared with an introduction by Thomas Wentworth Higginson. It has been supposed that these spontaneous illuminations, so different from the politely prepared verse of the day, fell on barren ground. The opposite is true. Though there were many scoffers and parodists, critics were not slow to see the essential quality—a Blake-like purity combined with a most un-Puritan pertness— readers responded, and six editions were printed in as many weeks. A year later *Poems of Emily Dickinson—Second Series (1891)* appeared, again edited by Mabel Loomis Todd and Thomas Wentworth Higginson. In 1893 the first *Letters of Emily Dickinson* was edited by Mrs. Todd, incorporated by Mme. Bianchi in her later volume, and revised and enlarged in 1931, the original two volumes being an invaluable mine of source material. In 1896 Mrs. Todd alone was responsible for *Poems—Third Series.*

The public taste changed; for thirty years little was heard of Emily Dickinson; her *Letters* went out of print, the publishers thought so little of them that they did not even renew the copyright. The "authorities" contained only slighting references to her or none at all. One of the encyclopedias (*The New International*) decided that her lyrics were "striking, but deficient in form"; the *Britannica,* as late as 1926, failed to mention her name except as a cross-reference, omitting her entirely in the Index.

In 1914 Mme. Bianchi prepared a further volume, *The Single Hound,* but, though the reception was cordial, it was by no means overwhelming. An occasional article appeared, showing the poet's "lack of control" or, beneath a cover of condescension, ridiculing her "hit-or-miss grammar, sterile rhythms, and appalling rhymes." A devotee here and there defended the quaint charm of her use of assonance and half-rhyming vowels. Her audience grew, but gradually. Suddenly, in 1924, Emily Dickinson became a figure of international importance. Almost forty years after her death her name became a poetic shibboleth when in one year there were published Martha Dickinson Bianchi's *The Life and Letters of Emily Dickinson,* the first collected *Complete Poems* (a misnomer as it turned out to be), and the first English compilation, *Selected Poems of Emily Dickinson,* edited with a penetrating preface by Conrad Aiken.

The enthusiasm attending the triple appearance was unprecedented. Martin Armstrong, the English poet, said, "Mr. Aiken calls Emily Dickinson's poetry 'perhaps the finest by a woman in the Enlish language.' I quarrel only with his 'perhaps.'" Nor were other plaudits less vociferous. "A feminine Blake," "an epigrammatic Walt Whitman," "a New England mystic," were a few of the characterizations fastened upon her. Other appraisals sought to "interpret" her involved but seldom obscure verses in the light of the "mystery" of her life. But "The Amherst Nun" would have repudiated the amateur psychoanalysts as vigorously as she, whose verses and letters brim with mischievous fancy, would have laughed at their epithets.

In 1929 there was published another generous collection of "undiscovered" or "withheld" poems, *Further Poems of Emily Dickinson,* edited by Martha Dickinson

Bianchi and Alfred Leete Hampson. There were one hundred and seventy-six hitherto unpublished pieces, and their clear beauty as well as mysterious appearance, all too vaguely explained, caused something of a furore. The excitement increased in 1930, the centenary of Emily Dickinson's birth. A new volume, *Unpublished Poems by Emily Dickinson,* appeared toward the end of 1935.

In the centenary year three new biographies appeared: *Emily Dickinson: The Human Background* by Josephine Pollitt, *The Life and Mind of Emily Dickinson* by Genevieve Taggard, and *Emily Dickinson: Friend and Neighbor* by Macgregor Jenkins. Jenkins' little book concerned itself chiefly with his boyhood memories; it was amiable and undistinguished. It was with the two other full-size volumes that interpretation grew fabulous and legend-making ran amok. Had someone written a dispassionate authoritative life immediately after Emily Dickinson's death this could not have happened; had Mme. Bianchi been more explicit it could have been avoided. But Mme. Bianchi chose to tell a vague story vaguely and helped swell the growing flood of conjecture. She spread the now familiar tale of Emily's "lover" in her chapter "The End of Peace." Mme. Bianchi told of the "fateful" visit to Philadelphia, of an encounter with a man already married—rumor had not scrupled to repeat the name of the Reverend Charles Wadsworth—of Emily's refusal to deviate from "her high sense of duty" and be "the inevitable destruction of another woman's life," of a precipitate flight back to Amherst, of a pursuit by the reckless lover, of a last agonized abnegation, denying herself not only to her lover but to the world. In *Emily Dickinson Face to Face* (1932) Mme. Bianchi amplified the account, became more specific, and supplied further valuable details, proving among other things that Emily's "dissonant" rhymes were not accidental but calculated.

The other two biographies betrayed far wilder attempts to supply "the missing chapter" and identify the man who prompted the love poems. Josephine Pollitt seized upon a scrap of a letter written by Higginson, and concluded that Emily's secret lover was Edward Bissell Hunt, the husband of the talented author Helen Hunt (Jackson), who happened to be Emily's closest friend. This theory was used as the basis of a drama, *Brittle Heaven,* by Frederick J. Pohl and Vincent York, produced in 1934, a more theatrical if less literary structure than Susan Glaspell's earlier *Alison's House,* a play based on the posthumous publication of the poems, which won the Pulitzer Prize for 1932.

Genevieve Taggard in her sensitive though over-written study discovered an undergraduate who "conditioned" Emily and her work. He was George Gould, one of the *Indicator* staff at Amherst College, and Miss Taggard believes Emily was engaged to him but that her father, a fire-breathing patriarch, opposed the union in true Old Testament New England style; whereupon Emily refused the young man, dressed in white, and dismissed him from her life—except for a prolonged secret correspondence, which has never been discovered—forever.

All the theories are possible. But there are others equally plausible. It might be suggested that there was no love story at all—none, that is, in the sense of a mutual *rapport*. It was an age of rhetoric. Male friends wrote effusively to each other; Emily herself used the word "love" indiscriminately. Whoever it was that captured Emily's regard may have been quite unconscious of it. He may have been impressed—and a bit puzzled—by the girl's crisp rejoinders, but he probably soon forgot the plain girl with her fancy phrases. It may have been nothing to him; to Emily it was All.

This, too, is conjecture. And all of it tends to belittle the poetry by a probing of the person; so lengthy a concern about the "mystery" in Emily's life obscures the mastery of her work. For mastery it is. The seal of genius, that unmistakable insignia, is on everything she wrote. Here is that inimitable idiom, playful yet profound; here are the rapid ascent of images and the sudden swoop of immensities, the keen epithet that cuts to the deepest layer of consciousness, and the paradox on whose point innumerable angels dance. She is Blake one moment, Vaughan the next, then Jonathan Edwards, and herself all the time. Emotion, idea, and words are not marshaled in their usual order; they spring simultaneously, inevitably, one including the other. Here is the effect—never the affectation—of emotion and its enveloping phrase.

More fully than her biographers Emily Dickinson told the secret of her love, her first rebellious impulse, her inner denial, her resignation, her assured waiting for reunion in Eternity. There is little to add except meaningless names and irrelevant street numbers.

> I took one draught of life,
> I'll tell you what I paid,
> Precisely an existence—
> The market-price, they said.
>
> They weighed me dust by dust,
> They balanced film with film,
> Then handed me my being's worth—
> A single dram of Heaven.

The poetry of Emily Dickinson courts criticism and defies it. (An interesting discussion of her syntactical peculiarities, *A Study of Unusual Verb Constructions in the Poems of Emily Dickinson* by Grace B. Sherrer, may be found in the quarterly *American Literature* for March, 1935.) That her verses were sometimes erratic, half-done, and thrown off in the heat of creation is self-evident. But, in the great majority of her poems, the leap of thought is so daring, the gaps so provocative, that passages which, in a smaller spirit, would be merely pretty or audacious conceits become snatches of revelation. Is it a flippancy or an anguished cry when, robbed by Life, she stands "a beggar before the door of God," and confronts Him with "Burglar, banker, father!" Is it anything less than Olympian satire when, asking God to accept "the supreme iniquity," she declares:

> We apologize to Thee
> For Thine own duplicity.

Beauty, Love, Justice—these were no abstractions to her, but entities, weights and measures, which the architect had failed to use perfectly. She sought the Builder not to commend but to question Him. Emily argued, upbraided, accused Creation; she recognized an angel only when she wrestled with him. Paradox was her native element.

Her gnomic imagery was tremendous in implication, and her range is far greater than a first reading reveals. Although the poet often indulged herself by retreating into a style cryptic and wayward, her tiny quatrains are lavish with huge ideas and almost overpowering figures. She speaks of music as "the silver strife"; she sees the railway train "lap the miles and lick the valleys up"; she speaks ironically of splitting the lark to find the music "bulb after bulb in silver rolled"; she pictures the thunder crumbling "like a stuff" while the lightning "skipped like mice"; she glimpses evening as "the house-wife in the west" sweeping the sunset "with many colored brooms"; she asks "who laid the rainbow piers." Pondering on the power of words, she meditates:

> Could mortal lip divine
>     The undeveloped freight
> Of a delivered syllable,
>     'Twould crumble with the weight.

Her lightest phrases bear the accent of finality. Without striving to be clever she achieves one startling epigram after another; no poet ever existed with a more aphoristic mind. "Denial is the only fact received by the denied." "At leisure is the soul that gets a staggering blow." "Renunciation is the choosing against itself." "Longing is like the seed that wrestles in the ground."

Her letters, sometimes marred with affectations, have an unpredictable way of turning about their subject; they combine the impish with the mystical; they announce tremendous things in an offhand tone of voice. Few definitions of poetry give us the sense of poetry as sharply as her informal:

"If I read a book and it makes my whole body so cold no fire can ever warm me, I know it is poetry. If I feel physically as if the top of my head were taken off, I know this is poetry. These are the only ways I know it."

Are there no reservations? In the midst of her telegraphic concisions—all sparks and flashes—does one never miss the long line, the sustained breath? She lived in metaphor, and the terse luxuriance of her figures—the impulse to point every adjective—has had an unhappy effect on most of her admirers, an effect of pretty artifice. Worse still is her habit of acting coy among the immensities. She is overfond of playing the spoiled, "old-fashioned, naughty child"—a little girl who sits in the lap of Deity and tweaks His beard and asks God coyly to lift her over the stile, an imperious child for whose success guns should be fired at sea, for a glimpse of whom saints should run to windows and seraphs swing their snowy hats. The impulse to pirouette before the mirror of her soul has already had its result in hundreds of young "female poets" (Griswold's phrase) who, lacking their model's intensities, have succeeded only in being verbally arresting and "cute."

A critical appraisal does not have to be a condemnatory one, but it must steer a course between the early ridicule and the present unreserved adulation. The undoubted charm does not necessarily extend to errors in grammar, nor does the taut, uncanny rightness of her epithets disguise her frequent failure to differentiate between inspiration and whim. Can one, need one, applaud all the eccentricities, the familiarities, the pertnesses? Banter may be refreshing, but is archness with God always delightful? And what is one to say of that more reprehensible spinsterly failing, archness to children?

And yet it is a tough and poetry-resisting soul which does not eventually succumb to her rhetoric, irregularities and all. Her vivacity covers self-consciousness and carries off her contradictions. Her swift condensations—surpassed by no writer of any age—win the most reluctant. One gasps at the way she packs huge ideas into an explosive quatrain (a living poet has called her verse "uncombusted meteors") fascinated by an utterance so paradoxical, so seemingly naïve, so actually metaphysical. She may annoy us with her self-indulgent waywardness, but illumination is never far off; out of a smooth, even sentimental sky, comes a crackling telegram from God and, tucked in a phrase, the "imperial thunderbolt that scalps your naked soul."

The obvious defects and quaint irregularities have been accepted; they even have a charm of their own. The brilliance of her imagery blinds us to her overfrequent coyness and the overstressed self-pity which could allow the poet to call herself "Empress of Calvary." The consistency of her imperfections is, in itself, a kind of perfection. Her personal magic—a kind of super-observation—lives in such phrases as a dog's "belated feet, like intermittent plush," a humming bird whose flight is "a route of evanescence, a resonance of emerald," an engine "neighing like Boanerges," a mushroom whose whole career "is shorter than a snake's delay," the wind "tapping like a tired man."

What else, then, matters? Whatever the provocation, all that remains is the poetry. The much-sought but still unknown inspirer of the love poems may have been Wadsworth or Gould or Hunt—or Legion—but it is not he who is immortalized in her book; it is Emily. Though there are evocations of the vanished lover, we are never made to see him, hear him, realize his being, whereas we have (in the same poems) a complete projection of Emily, her heart, soul, and housekeeping, her books, birds, and influences, her bodily postures, tricks of thought, even her way of crossing the room and reading a letter.

Denied a public, even of one, Emily perfected her imperfections in secret. Lacking the partner, she played her game with herself. Yet, when all the biographies are considered and contrasted, possibly the most successful game was the one she played on the world. A solitary recluse who had the world in her garden; an escapist who summoned infinity with the trick of a forefinger and the crook of her mind. It is doubtful if, in spite of her geographical isolation, there was ever a less lonely woman. She who contained a universe did not need the world. Everything, whether seen or imagined, lived for her in full immediacy; all, she knew, existed only in thought. "Captivity's consciousness," she said, "so's liberty." In that rich and nimble consciousness she was always at home—and always free.

## I TASTE A LIQUOR NEVER BREWED

I taste a liquor never brewed,
From tankards scooped in pearl;
Not all the vats upon the Rhine
Yield such an alcohol!

Inebriate of air am I,
And debauchee of dew,
Reeling, through endless summer days,
From inns of molten blue.

When landlords turn the drunken bee
Out of the foxglove's door,
When butterflies renounce their drams,
I shall but drink the more!

Till seraphs swing their snowy hats,
And saints to windows run,
To see the little tippler
Leaning against the sun!

## A BIRD CAME DOWN THE WALK

A bird came down the walk:
He did not know I saw;
He bit an angle-worm in halves
And ate the fellow, raw.

And then he drank a dew
From a convenient grass,
And then hopped sidewise to the wall
To let a beetle pass.

He glanced with rapid eyes
That hurried all abroad,—
They looked like frightened beads, I thought
He stirred his velvet head

Like one in danger; cautious,
I offered him a crumb,
And he unrolled his feathers
And rowed him softer home

Than oars divide the ocean,
Too silver for a seam,
Or butterflies, off banks of noon,
Leap, plashless, as they swim.

### ELYSIUM IS AS FAR

Elysium is as far as to
The very nearest room,
If in that room a friend await
Felicity or doom.

What fortitude the soul contains,
That it can so endure
The accent of a coming foot,
The opening of a door.

### I NEVER SAW A MOOR

I never saw a moor,
I never saw the sea;
Yet know I how the heather looks,
And what a wave must be.

I never spoke with God,
Nor visited in Heaven;
Yet certain am I of the spot
As if the chart were given.

### I NEVER LOST AS MUCH

I never lost as much but twice,
And that was in the sod;
Twice have I stood a beggar
Before the door of God!

Angels, twice descending,
Reimbursed my store.
Burglar, banker, father,
I am poor once more!

### INDIAN SUMMER

These are the days when birds come back
A very few, a bird or two,
To take a backward look.

These are the days when skies put on
The old, old sophistries of June,—
A blue and gold mistake.

Oh, fraud that cannot cheat the bee,
Almost thy plausibility
Induces my belief,

Till ranks of seeds their witness bear,
And softly through the altered air
Hurries a timid leaf!

Oh, sacrament of summer days,
Oh, last communion in the haze,
Permit a child to join,

Thy sacred emblems to partake,
Thy consecrated bread to break,
Taste thine immortal wine!

### I DIED FOR BEAUTY

I died for beauty, but was scarce
Adjusted in the tomb,
When one who died for truth was lain
In an adjoining room.

He questioned softly why I failed?
"For beauty," I replied.
"And I for truth,—the two are one;
We brethren are," he said.

And so, as kinsmen met a night,
We talked between the rooms,
Until the moss had reached our lips
And covered up our names.

### THE SKY IS LOW

The sky is low, the clouds are mean,
A traveling flake of snow
Across a barn or through a rut
Debates if it will go.

A narrow wind complains all day
How someone treated him.
Nature, like us, is sometimes caught
Without her diadem.

### MYSTERIES

The murmur of a bee
A witchcraft yieldeth me.
If any ask me why,
'Twere easier to die
Than tell.

The red upon the hill
Taketh away my will;
If anybody sneer,
Take care, for God is here,
That's all.

The breaking of the day
Addeth to my degree;
If any ask me how,
Artist, who drew me so,
Must tell!

### I LIKE TO SEE IT LAP THE MILES

I like to see it lap the miles,
And lick the valleys up,
And stop to feed itself at tanks;
And then, prodigious, step

Around a pile of mountains,
And, supercilious, peer
In shanties by the sides of roads;
And then a quarry pare

To fit its sides, and crawl between,
Complaining all the while
In horrid, hooting stanza;
Then chase itself down hill

And neigh like Boanerges;
Then, punctual as a star,
Stop—docile and omnipotent—
At its own stable door.

### THE SOUL SELECTS

The soul selects her own society,
Then shuts the door;

On her divine majority
Obtrude no more.

Unmoved, she notes the chariots pausing
At her low gate;
Unmoved, an emperor is kneeling
Upon her mat.

I've known her from an ample nation
Choose one;
Then close the valves of her attention
Like stone.

### MY LIFE CLOSED TWICE BEFORE ITS CLOSE

My life closed twice before its close;
It yet remains to see
If Immortality unveil
A third event to me,

So huge, so hopeless to conceive,
As these that twice befell.
Parting is all we know of heaven,
And all we need of hell.

### THE HEART ASKS PLEASURE FIRST

The heart asks pleasure first;
And then, excuse from pain;
And then, those little anodynes
That deaden suffering;

And then, to go to sleep;
And then, if it should be
The will of its Inquisitor,
The liberty to die.

### I CANNOT LIVE WITH YOU

I cannot live with you.
It would be life,
And life is over there
Behind the shelf

The sexton keeps the key to,
Putting up
Our life, his porcelain,
Like a cup

Discarded of the housewife,
Quaint or broken;
A newer Sèvres pleases,
Old ones crack.

I could not die with you,
For one must wait
To shut the other's gaze down,
You could not.

And I, could I stand by
And see you freeze,
Without my right of frost,
Death's privilege?

Nor could I rise with you,
Because your face
Would put out Jesus',
That new grace

Grow plain and foreign
On my homesick eye,
Except that you, than he
Shone closer by.

They'd judge us—how?
For you served Heaven, you know,
Or sought to;
I could not,

Because you saturated sight,
And I had no more eyes
For sordid excellence
As Paradise.

And were you lost, I would be,
Though my name
Rang loudest
On the heavenly fame.

And were you saved,
And I condemned to be
Where you were not,
That self were hell to me.

So we must keep apart,
You there, I here,
With just the door ajar
That oceans are,
And prayer,
And that pale sustenance,
Despair!

## OF COURSE I PRAYED

Of course I prayed—
And did God care?
He cared as much as
On the air
A bird had stamped her foot
And cried "Give me!"

My reason, life,
I had not had, but for yourself.
'Twere better charity
To leave me in the atom's tomb,
Merry and nought and gay and numb,
Than this smart misery.

## THERE IS NO FRIGATE LIKE
## A BOOK

There is no frigate like a book
   To take us lands away,
Nor any coursers like a page
   Of prancing poetry.
This traverse may the poorest take
   Without oppress of toll;
How frugal is the chariot
   That bears a human soul!

## I HAD BEEN HUNGRY ALL
## THE YEARS

I had been hungry all the years;
My noon had come to dine;
I, trembling, drew the table near,
And touched the curious wine.

'Twas this on tables I had seen,
When turning, hungry, lone,
I looked in windows, for the wealth
I could not hope to own.

I did not know the ample bread;
'Twas so unlike the crumb
The birds and I had often shared
In Nature's dining-room.

The plenty hurt me, 'twas so new,—
Myself felt ill and odd,
As berry of a mountain bush
Transplanted to the road.

Nor was I hungry; so I found
That hunger was a way
Of persons outside windows,
The entering takes away.

## I HEARD A FLY BUZZ WHEN
### I DIED

I heard a fly buzz when I died;
  The stillness round my form
Was like the stillness in the air
  Between the heaves of storm.

The eyes beside had wrung them dry,
  And breaths were gathering sure
For that last onset, when the king
  Be witnessed in his power.

I willed my keepsakes, signed away
  What portion of me I
Could make assignable,—and then
  There interposed a fly,

With blue, uncertain, stumbling buzz,
  Between the light and me;
And then the windows failed, and then
  I could not see to see.

## THERE'S A CERTAIN SLANT
### OF LIGHT

There's a certain slant of light,
On winter afternoons,
That oppresses, like the weight
Of cathedral tunes.

Heavenly hurt it gives us;
We can find no scar,
But internal difference
Where the meanings are.

None may teach it anything,
'Tis the seal, despair,—
An imperial affliction
Sent us of the air.

When it comes, the landscape listens,
Shadows hold their breath;
When it goes, 'tis like the distance
On the look of death.

## I MEASURE EVERY GRIEF I MEET

I measure every grief I meet
  With analytic eyes;
I wonder if it weighs like mine,
  Or has an easier size.

I wonder if they bore it long,
  Or did it just begin?
I could not tell the date of mine,
  It feels so old a pain.

I wonder if it hurts to live,
  And if they have to try,
And whether, could they choose between,
  They would not rather die.

I wonder if when years have piled—
  Some thousands—on the cause
Of early hurt, if such a lapse
  Could give them any pause;

Or would they go on aching still
  Through centuries above,
Enlightened to a larger pain
  By contrast with the love.

The grieved are many, I am told;
  The reason deeper lies,—
Death is but one and comes but once,
  And only nails the eyes.

There's grief of want, and grief of cold,—
  A sort they call "despair";
There's banishment from native eyes,
  In sight of native air.

And though I may not guess the kind
  Correctly, yet to me
A piercing comfort it affords
  In passing Calvary,

To note the fashions of the cross,
  Of those that stand alone,
Still fascinated to presume
  That some are like my own.

## THE BRAIN IS WIDER THAN
### THE SKY

The brain is wider than the sky,
  For, put them side by side,

The one the other will include
  With ease, and you beside.

The brain is deeper than the sea,
  For, hold them, blue to blue,
The one the other will absorb,
  As sponges, buckets do.

The brain is just the weight of God,
  For, lift them, pound for pound,
And they will differ, if they do,
  As syllable from sound.

### BRING ME THE SUNSET
### IN A CUP

Bring me the sunset in a cup,
Reckon the morning's flagons up,
  And say how many dew;
Tell me how far the morning leaps,
Tell me what time the weaver sleeps
  Who spun the breadths of blue!

Write me how many notes there be
In the new robin's ecstasy
  Among astonished boughs;
How many trips the tortoise makes,
How many cups the bee partakes,—
  The debauchee of dews!

Also, who laid the rainbow's piers,
Also, who leads the docile spheres
  By withes of supple blue?
Whose fingers string the stalactite,
Who counts the wampum of the night,
  To see that none is due?

Who built this little Alban house
And shut the windows down so close
  My spirit cannot see?
Who'll let me out some gala day,
With implements to fly away,
  Passing pomposity?

### THE TINT I CANNOT TAKE
### IS BEST

  The tint I cannot take is best,
  The color too remote
  That I could show it in bazaar
  A guinea at a sight—

The fine impalpable array
That swaggers on the eye
Like Cleopatra's company
Repeated in the sky—

The moments of dominion
That happen on the Soul
And leave it with a discontent
Too exquisite to tell—

The eager look on landscapes
As if they just repressed
Some secret that was pushing,
Like chariots, in the breast—

The pleading of the Summer,
That other prank of snow
That covers mystery with tulle
For fear the squirrels know—

Their graspless manners mock us,
Until the cheated eye
Shuts arrogantly in the grave,
Another way to see.

### I DREADED THAT FIRST ROBIN SO

I dreaded that first robin so,
But he is mastered now,
And I'm accustomed to him grown,—
He hurts a little, though.

I thought if I could only live
Till that first shout got by,
Not all pianos in the woods
Had power to mangle me.

I dared not meet the daffodils,
For fear their yellow gown
Would pierce me with a fashion
So foreign to my own.

I wished the grass would hurry,
So when 'twas time to see,
He'd be too tall, the tallest one
Could stretch to look at me.

I could not bear the bees should come,
I wished they'd stay away
In those dim countries where they go:
What word had they for me?

They're here, though; not a creature failed,
No blossom stayed away
In gentle deference to me,
A Queen of Calvary.

Each one salutes me as he goes,
And I my childish plumes
Lift, in bereaved acknowledgment
Of their unthinking drums.

## AFTER GREAT PAIN A FORMAL
## FEELING COMES

After great pain a formal feeling comes—
The nerves sit ceremonious like tombs;
The stiff heart questions—was it He that
  bore?
And yesterday—or centuries before?

The feet mechanical go round
A wooden way,
Of ground or air of Ought,
Regardless grown;
A quartz contentment like a stone.

This is the hour of lead
Remembered if outlived
As freezing persons recollect
The snow—
First chill, then stupor, then
The letting go.

## A CEMETERY

This quiet Dust was Gentlemen and Ladies,
  And Lads and Girls;
Was laughter and ability and sighing,
  And frocks and curls.

This passive place a Summer's nimble man-
  sion,
  Where Bloom and Bees
Fulfilled their Oriental Circuit,
  Then ceased like these.

## AMPLE MAKE THIS BED

Ample make this bed,
Make this bed with awe;
In it wait till judgment break
Excellent and fair.

Be its mattress straight,
Be its pillow round;
Let no sunrise' yellow noise
Interrupt this ground.

## ALTHOUGH I PUT AWAY
## HIS LIFE

Although I put away his life,
An ornament too grand
For forehead low as mine to wear,
This might have been the hand

That sowed the flowers he preferred,
Or smoothed a homely pain,
Or pushed a pebble from his path,
Or played his chosen tune

On lute the least, the latest,
But just his ear could know
That whatsoe'er delighted it
I never would let go.

The foot to bear his errand
A little boot I know
Would leap abroad like antelope
With just the grant to do.

His weariest commandment
A sweeter to obey
Than "Hide and Seek," or skip to flutes,
Or all day chase the bee.

Your servant, Sir, will weary,
The surgeon will not come,
The world will have its own to do,
The dust will vex your fame.

The cold will force your tightest door
Some February day,
But say my apron bring the sticks
To make your cottage gay,

That I may take that promise
To Paradise with me—
To teach the angels avarice
Your kiss first taught to me!

## THE WORLD FEELS DUSTY

The world feels dusty
When we stop to die;
We want the dew then,
Honors taste dry.

Flags vex a dying face,
But the least fan
Stirred by a friend's hand
Cools like the rain.

Mine be the ministry
When thy thirst comes,
Dews of thyself to fetch
And holy balms.

### LIGHTLY STEPPED A YELLOW STAR

Lightly stepped a yellow star
To its lofty place,
Loosed the Moon her silver hat
From her lustral face.
All of evening softly lit
As an astral hall—
"Father," I observed to Heaven,
"You are punctual!"

### GO NOT TOO NEAR A HOUSE OF ROSE

Go not too near a house of rose,
The depredation of a breeze

Or inundation of a dew
Alarm its walls away;
Nor try to tie the butterfly;
Nor climb the bars of ecstasy.
In insecurity to lie
Is joy's insuring quality.

### I RECKON, WHEN I COUNT AT ALL

I reckon, when I count at all,
First Poets—then the Sun—
Then Summer—then the Heaven of God—
And then the list is done.
But looking back—the first so seems
To comprehend the whole—
The others look a needless show,
So I write Poets—All.
Their summer lasts a solid year,
They can afford a sun
The East would deem extravagant,
And if the final Heaven
Be beautiful as they disclose
To those who trust in them,
It is too difficult a grace
To justify the dream.

# *Thomas Bailey Aldrich*

THOMAS BAILEY ALDRICH was born November 11, 1836, at Portsmouth, New Hampshire, where he spent most of the sixteen years which he has recorded in that delightful memoir, *The Story of a Bad Boy* (1869). After a brief clerkship, he became junior literary critic of *The Evening Mirror* at nineteen, publishing his first book (*The Bells*), an immature collection of echoes, at the same time. From 1855 to 1866 he held various journalistic positions, associating himself with the leading metropolitan *literati*. Nathaniel Willis, Bayard Taylor, Edmund Clarence Stedman, William Winter were his intimates, and their influence reënforced the inherent artificiality of Aldrich's tastes. Abetted by his associates he chose the "flicker rather than the flame"; he praised Stedman but despised Whitman, he worshiped Longfellow and belittled Poe, imitated Willis and could see nothing in Emily Dickinson except her "infelicities."

Although Aldrich mingled with the New York group, he was not part of it; he longed for the more rarefied intellectual atmosphere of New England and when, in 1866, Osgood offered him the editorship of *Every Saturday*, published in Boston, Aldrich accepted with alacrity. A few years later he became editor of *The Atlantic*

*Monthly,* holding that position from 1881 to 1890. In the meanwhile *The Ballad of Babie Bell* (1858), an incredibly banal and insincere piece of work, and *Pampinea and Other Poems* (1861) had appeared, bearing practically no relation to their times. Other volumes followed; *Complete Poems* being first issued in 1882, and in 1898 Aldrich made a comprehensive revision of all the poems he cared to preserve.

Aldrich's work falls into two sharply divided classes. The first half is full of over-loaded phrase-making, fervid extravagances. The reader sinks beneath clouds of damask, azure, emerald, pearl and gold; he is drowned in a sea of musk, aloes, tiger-lilies, spice, soft music, orchids, attar-breathing dusks. There is no real air in these verses; it is Nature as conceived by a poet reading the Arabian Nights in a hot-house. In company with Stoddard and Taylor, Aldrich dwelt in a literary Orientalism (Stoddard's *Book of the East* followed fast upon Taylor's *Poems of the Orient*) and Aldrich's *Cloth of Gold* was suffused with similar "vanilla-flavored adjectives and patchouli-scented participles," to quote Holmes.

The other phase of Aldrich's art is more human in appeal and surer in artistry. He learned to sharpen his images, to fashion his smallest lyrics with a well-bred *finesse.* "In the little steel engravings that are the best expressions of his peculiar talent," writes Percy H. Boynton, "there is a fine simplicity; but it is the simplicity of an accomplished woman of the world rather than of a village maid." Although Aldrich bitterly resented the charge that he was a maker of tiny perfections, a carver of cherry-stones, those poems of his which have the best chance of permanence are some of the epigrams, the short lyrics and a few of the sonnets, passionless in tone but graceful in design.

Aldrich died in his seventy-first year in 1907.

### MEMORY

My mind lets go a thousand things,
Like dates of wars and deaths of kings,
And yet recalls the very hour—
'Twas noon by yonder village tower,
And on the last blue moon in May—
The wind came briskly up this way,
Crisping the brook beside the road;
Then, pausing here, set down its load
Of pine-scents, and shook listlessly
Two petals from that wild-rose tree.

### ENAMORED ARCHITECT OF AIRY RHYME

Enamored architect of airy rhyme,
Build as thou wilt, heed not what each man says.
Good souls, but innocent of dreamers' ways,
Will come, and marvel why thou wastest time;
Others, beholding how thy turrets climb
'Twixt theirs and heaven, will hate thee all thy days;
But most beware of those who come to praise.
O wondersmith, O worker in sublime

And heaven-sent dreams, let art be all in all;
Build as thou wilt, unspoiled by praise or blame,
Build as thou wilt, and as thy light is given;
Then, if at last the airy structure fall,
Dissolve, and vanish—take thyself no shame.
They fail, and they alone, who have not striven.

### IDENTITY

Somewhere—in desolate wind-swept space—
  In Twilight-land—in No-man's land—
Two hurrying Shapes met face to face,
  And bade each other stand.

"And who are you?" cried one agape,
  Shuddering in the gloaming light.
"I know not," said the second Shape,
  "I only died last night!"

### HEREDITY

A soldier of the Cromwell stamp,
With sword and psalm-book by his side,
At home alike in church and camp:
Austere he lived, and smileless died.

But she, a creature soft and fine—
From Spain, some say, some say from France
Within her veins leapt blood like wine—
She led her Roundhead lord a dance!

In Grantham church they lie asleep;
Just where, the verger may not know.
Strange that two hundred years should keep
The old ancestral fires aglow!

In me these two have met again;
To each my nature owes a part:
To one, the cool and reasoning brain;
To one, the quick, unreasoning heart.

# John Hay

JOHN HAY was born October 8, 1838, in Salem, Indiana, graduated from Brown
University in 1858 and was admitted to the Illinois bar a few years later. At
nineteen, when he went back to Warsaw, the little Mississippi town where he had
lived as a boy, he dreamed only of being a poet—a poet, it must be added, of the
pleasantly conventional, transition type. But the Civil War was to disturb his mild
fantasies. He went to the front and saw active service under General Hunter. He
became private secretary to Lincoln, then major and assistant adjutant-general under
General Gilmore, then a colonel by brevet, then secretary of the Legation at Paris,
*chargé d'affaires* at Vienna and Secretary of Legation at Madrid.

His few vivid *Pike County Ballads* came more as a happy accident than as a
deliberate creative effort. When Hay returned from Spain in 1870, bringing with
him his *Castilian Days,* he still had visions of becoming an orthodox lyric poet. But
he found everyone reading Bret Harte's short stories and the new expression of the
rude West. He speculated upon the possibility of doing something similar, translating
the characters into poetry. The result was the six racy ballads in a vein utterly different from everything Hay wrote before or after. The poet-politician seems to have
regarded this series somewhat in the nature of light, extempore verse, belonging to a
far lower plane than his serious publications; he talked about them reluctantly; he
even hoped that these "diversions" would be forgotten. It is difficult to say whether
this regret grew because Hay, loving the refinements of culture, at heart hated any

suggestion of vulgarity, or because of a basic lack of courage—Hay having published his novel of labor unrest in the early 80's (*The Breadwinners*) anonymously.

The fact remains, his rhymes of Pike County have survived all his more "classical" lines. They served for a time as a fresh influence; they remain a creative accomplishment. "Banty Tim" is quoted not only for its own sake, but as an interesting anticipation of Kipling's "Gunga Din"; "Jim Bludso" was the first of a long line of dramatic "recitations."

Hay was in politics all the later part of his life, ranking as one of the most brilliant Secretaries of State the country has ever had. Under President Hayes he was ambassador to Great Britain. In collaboration with J. G. Nicolay he wrote a most authoritative and vivid life of Lincoln, a biography which was unequaled until Carl Sandburg's volumes. He died in 1905.

### JIM BLUDSO

#### OF THE PRAIRIE BELLE

all, no! I can't tell whar he lives,
Becase he don't live, you see;
astways, he's got out of the habit
Of livin' like you and me.
har have you been for the last three year
That you haven't heard folks tell
ow Jimmy Bludso passed in his checks
The night of the Prairie Belle?

e warn't no saint,—them engineers
Is all pretty much alike,—
e wife in Natchez-under-the-Hill
And another one here, in Pike;
keerless man in his talk was Jim,
And an awkward hand in a row,
t he never flunked, and he never lied,—
I reckon he never knowed how.

d this was all the religion he had:
To treat his engine well;
ver be passed on the river;
To mind the pilot's bell;
d if ever the Prairie Belle took fire,
A thousand times he swore,
'd hold her nozzle agin the bank
Till the last soul got ashore.

boats has their day on the Mississip,
And her day come at last,—
e Movastar was a better boat,
But the Belle she *wouldn't* be passed.
d so she came tearin' along that night—
The oldest craft on the line—
ith a nigger squat on her safety-valve,
And her furnace crammed, rosin and pine.

The fire bust out as she clar'd the bar,
And burnt a hole in the night,
And quick as a flash she turned and made
For that willer-bank on the right.
Thar was runnin' and cussin', but Jim yelled out,
Over all the infernal roar,
"I'll hold her nozzle agin the bank
Till the last galoot's ashore."

Through the hot, black breath of the burnin' boat
Jim Bludso's voice was heard,
And they all had trust in his cussedness,
And knowed he would keep his word.
And, sure's you're born, they all got off
Afore the smokestacks fell,—
And Bludso's ghost went up alone
In the smoke of the Prairie Belle.

He warn't no saint,—but at jedgement
I'd run my chance with Jim,
'Longside of some pious gentlemen
That wouldn't shook hands with him.
He seen his duty, a dead-sure thing,—
And went for it thar and then;
And Christ ain't a-goin' to be too hard
On a man that died for men.

### BANTY TIM

*(Remarks of Sergeant Tilmon Joy to the White Man's Committee of Spunky Point, Illinois)*

I reckon I git your drift, gents,—
You 'low the boy sha'n't stay;

This is a white man's country;
  You're Dimocrats, you say;
And whereas, and seein', and wherefore,
  The times bein' all out o' j'int,
The nigger has got to mosey
  From the limits o' Spunky P'int!

Let's reason the thing a minute:
  I'm an old-fashioned Dimocrat too,
Though I laid my politics out o' the way
  For to keep till the war was through.
But I come back here, allowin'
  To vote as I used to do,
Though it gravels me like the devil to train
  Along o' sich fools as you.

Now dog my cats ef I kin see,
  In all the light of the day,
What you've got to do with the question
  Ef Tim shill go or stay.
And furder than that I give notice,
  Ef one of you tetches the boy,
He kin check his trunks to a warmer clime
  Than he'll find in Illanoy.

Why, blame your hearts, jest hear me!
  You know that ungodly day
When our left struck Vicksburg Heights,
  how ripped
And torn and tattered we lay.
When the rest retreated I stayed behind,
  Fur reasons sufficient to me,—

With a rib caved in, and a leg on a strike,
  I sprawled on that damned glacee.

Lord! how the hot sun went for us,
  And br'iled and blistered and burned!
How the Rebel bullets whizzed round us
  When a cuss in his death-grip turned!
Till along toward dusk I seen a thing
  I couldn't believe for a spell:
That nigger—that Tim—was a-crawlin'
  me
  Through that fire-proof, gilt-edged hell!

The Rebels seen him as quick as me,
  And the bullets buzzed like bees;
But he jumped for me, and shouldered me,
  Though a shot brought him once to l
  knees;
But he staggered up, and packed me off,
  With a dozen stumbles and falls,
Till safe in our lines he drapped us both,
  His black hide riddled with balls.

So, my gentle gazelles, thar's my answer,
  And here stays Banty Tim:
He trumped Death's ace for me that day,
  And I'm not goin' back on him!
You may rezoloot till the cows come home,
  But ef one of you tetches the boy,
He'll wrastle his hash tonight in hell,
  Or my name's not Tilmon Joy!

## Bret Harte

Francis bret harte was born August 25, 1839, at Albany, New York. (In certain quarters doubt is thrown on the date of his birth. One or two sources maintain that a compositor, upsetting a 6, made the "correct" date, 1836, "wrongly" 1839. However, practically all the encyclopedias and biographies agree upon 1839 as authentic.) His childhood was spent in various cities of the East. Late in 1853 his widowed mother went to California with a party of relatives, and two months later, when he was fifteen, Bret Harte and his sister followed. During the next few years he was engaged in school-teaching, typesetting, politics, mining and journalism, becoming editor of *The Overland Monthly* in San Francisco in 1868.

Harte's fame came suddenly. Late in the Sixties he had written a burlesque in rhyme of two Western gamblers trying to fleece a guileless Chinaman who claimed to know nothing about cards, but who, it turned out, was scarcely as innocent as he appeared. Harte, in the midst of writing serious poetry, had put the verses aside as too crude and trifling for publication. Some time later, just as *The Overland Monthly* was going to press, it was discovered that the form was one page short. Having nothing else on hand, Harte had these rhymes set up. Instead of passing unnoticed, the poem was quoted everywhere; it swept the West and captivated the East. When *The Luck of Roaring Camp* followed, Harte became not only a national but an international figure. England acclaimed him and *The Atlantic Monthly* paid him $10,000 to write for a year in his Pike County vein.

*East and West Poems* appeared in 1871; in 1872 Harte published an enlarged *Poetical Works* including many earlier pieces. His scores of short stories represent Harte at his best; "M'liss," "Tennessee's Partner," "The Outcast of Poker Flat"— these are the work of a lesser, transplanted Dickens. His novels are of minor importance; they are carelessly constructed, theatrically conceived.

His serious poetry has many of the faults of his prose. A melodramatic crudeness alternates with an equally exaggerated sentimentalism; even those verses not in dialect (like "What the Bullet Sang") suffer from defects of emphasis. But the occasional verse will remain to delight readers who rarely glance at Harte's other work except for documentation.

In 1872 Harte, encouraged by his success, returned to his native East; in 1878 he went to Germany as consul at Crefeld. Two years later he was transferred to Scotland and, after five years there, went to London, where he remained the rest of his life. Harte's later period remains mysteriously shrouded. He never came back to America, not even for a visit; he ceased to correspond with his family; he separated himself from all the most intimate associations of his early life. He died, suddenly, at Camberley, England, May 6, 1902.

### "JIM"

Say there! P'r'aps
Some on you chaps
    Might know Jim Wild?
Well,—no offense:
Thar ain't no sense
    In gittin' riled!

Jim was my chum
    Up on the Bar:
That's why I come
    Down from up yar,
Lookin' for Jim.
Thank ye, sir! *You*
Ain't of that crew,—
    Blest if you are!

Money? Not much:
    That ain't my kind;
I ain't no such.
    Rum? I don't mind,
Seein' it's you.

Well, this yer Jim,—
Did you know him?
Jes' 'bout your size;
Same kind of eyes;—
Well, that is strange:
    Why, it's two year
    Since he came here,
Sick, for a change.

Well, here's to us:
        Eh?
The h—— you say!
        Dead?
That little cuss?

What makes you star',
You over thar?
Can't a man drop
's glass in yer shop
But you must r'ar?
    It wouldn't take
    D—d much to break
You and your bar.

Dead!
Poor—little—Jim!
Why, thar was me,
Jones, and Bob Lee,
Harry and Ben,—
No-account men:
Then to take *him!*

Well, thar—Good-by.
No more, sir—I—
        Eh?
What's that you say?
Why, dern it!—sho'—
No? Yes! By Joe!
        Sold!
Sold! Why, you limb.
You ornery,
    Derned, old,
Long-legged Jim.


### PLAIN LANGUAGE FROM TRUTHFUL JAMES

*(Table Mountain, 1870)*

Which I wish to remark,
    And my language is plain,
That for ways that are dark
    And for tricks that are vain,
The heathen Chinee is peculiar,
    Which the same I would rise to explain.

Ah Sin was his name;
    And I shall not deny,
In regard to the same,
    What that name might imply;
But his smile it was pensive and childlike,
    As I frequent remarked to Bill Nye.

It was August the third,
    And quite soft was the skies;
Which it might be inferred
    That Ah Sin was likewise;
Yet he played it that day upon William
And me in a way I despise.

Which we had a small game,
    And Ah Sin took a hand:
It was Euchre. The same
    He did not understand;
But he smiled as he sat by the table,
    With a smile that was childlike and bland.

Yet the cards they were stocked
    In a way that I grieve,
And my feelings were shocked
    At the state of Nye's sleeve,
Which was stuffed full of aces and bowers
    And the same with intent to deceive.

But the hands that were played
    By that heathen Chinee,
And the points that he made,
    Were quite frightful to see,—
Till at last he put down a right bower,
    Which the same Nye had dealt unto me!

Then I looked up at Nye,
    And he gazed upon me;
And he rose with a sigh,
    And said, "Can this be?
We are ruined by Chinese cheap labor,"—
    And he went for that heathen Chinee.

In the scene that ensued
    I did not take a hand,
But the floor it was strewed
    Like the leaves on the strand
With the cards that Ah Sin had been hiding,
    In the game "he did not understand."

In his sleeves, which were long,
    He has twenty-four packs,—
Which was coming it strong,
    Yet I state but the facts;
And we found on his nails, which were taper,
    What is frequent in tapers,—that's wax.

Which is why I remark,
    And my language is plain,
That for ways that are dark
    And for tricks that are vain,
The heathen Chinee is peculiar,—
    Which the same I am free to maintain.


### WHAT THE BULLET SANG

O joy of creation,
    To be!
O rapture, to fly
    And be free!
Be the battle lost or won,
Though the smoke shall hide the sun,
I shall find my love, the one
    Born for me!

I shall know him where he stands
  All alone,
With the power in his hands
  Not o'erthrown;
I shall know him by his face,
By his godlike front and grace;
I shall hold him for a space
  All my own!

It is he—O my love!
  So bold!
It is I—all thy love
  Foretold!
It is I—O love, what bliss!
Dost thou answer to my kiss?
O sweetheart! what is this
  Lieth there so cold?

### THE AGED STRANGER

*(An Incident of the Civil War)*

I was with Grant"—the stranger said;
Said the farmer, "Say no more,
But rest thee here at my cottage porch,
  For thy feet are weary and sore."

I was with Grant"—the stranger said;
Said the farmer, "Nay, no more.

I prithee sit at my frugal board,
  And eat of my humble store.

"How fares my boy,—my soldier boy,
  Of the old Ninth Army Corps?
I warrant he bore him gallantly
  In the smoke and the battle's roar!"

"I know him not," said the aged man,
  "And, as I remarked before,
I was with Grant"—"Nay, nay, I know,"
  Said the farmer, "say no more.

"He fell in battle,—I see, alas!
  Thou'dst smooth these tidings o'er.
Nay, speak the truth, whatever it be,
  Though it rend my bosom's core."

"I cannot tell," said the aged man,
  "And should have remarked before,
That I was with Grant,—in Illinois,—
  Three years before the war."

Then the farmer spake him never a word,
  But beat with his fist full sore
That aged man, who had worked for Grant
  Three years before the war.

## Joaquin Miller

JOAQUIN MILLER was, as he desired to be, a mysterious figure. The date of his birth is conjectural; even his name is a matter of doubt. However, from recent evidence—particularly the researches of Frank R. Reade—it seems safe to say that his name was originally Cincinnatus Hiner Miller: Cincinnatus, according to his brother, "for a certain Roman General (!) and mother named him Hiner for Dr. Hiner, who brought him into the world." Although Joaquin Miller claimed that his middle name was "Heine" and that his mother named him Heine because of her love for the German poet, there is proof that Miller adopted the Heine *after* he had heard of the author of *Buch der Lieder*. The date of his birth is also disputed. March tenth seems to be the favored day assigned to his entry into the world and, although 1839 has been advanced as the latest "definite" date, most biographers choose 1841 as the year in which Miller was born.

A few facts are indisputable. Miller was of mixed Dutch and Scotch stock, his father's father having been killed at Fort Meigs in the War of 1812. As Miller himself wrote (and this particular bit of biography has stood the scrutiny of his more exact commentators), "My cradle was a covered wagon, pointed west. I was born in a covered wagon, I am told, at or about the time it crossed the line dividing Indiana from Ohio." When Miller was twelve, his family left the mid-West with "two big heavily laden wagons, with eight yoke of oxen to each, a carriage and two horses for mother and baby sister, and a single horse for the three boys to ride." The distance covered in their cross-country exodus (they took a roundabout route to Oregon) was nearly three thousand miles and the time consumed was more than seven months.

At fifteen we find Miller living with the Indians as one of them; in 1859 (at the age of eighteen) he attends a mission-school "college" in Eugene, Oregon; between 1860 and 1865 he is express-messenger, editor of a pacifist newspaper that is suppressed for opposing the Civil War, lawyer and, occasionally, a poet. He holds a minor judgeship from 1866 to 1870.

His first book (*Specimens*) appears in 1868, his second (*Joaquin et al.,* from which he took his name) in 1869. No response—not even from "the bards of San Francisco Bay" to whom he had dedicated the latter volume. He is chagrined, discouraged, angry. He resolves to quit America, to go to the land that has always been the nursing-ground of poets. "Three months later, September 1, 1870, I was kneeling at the grave of Burns. I really expected to die there in the land of my fathers." He arrives in London, unheralded, unknown. He takes his manuscripts to one publisher after another with the same negative result. Finally, with a pioneer desperation, he prints privately one hundred copies of his *Pacific Poems,* sending them out for review. The result is a sensation; the reversal of Miller's fortunes is one of the most startling in all literature. The reviews are a series of superlatives, the personal tributes still more fervid. Miller becomes famous overnight. He is fêted, lauded, lionized; he is ranked as an equal of Browning, given a dinner by the Pre-Raphaelites, acclaimed as "the great interpreter of America," "the Byron of Oregon!"

His dramatic success in England is easily explained. He brought to the calm air of literary London a breath of the great winds of the plain. The more he exaggerated his crashing effects, the louder he roared, the better the English public liked it. When he entered Victorian parlors in his velvet jacket, hip-boots and flowing hair, childhood visions of the "wild and woolly Westerner" were realized and the very bombast of his work was glorified as "typically American."

And yet, for all his overstressed muscularity, Miller is strangely lacking in creative energy. His whipped-up rhetoric cannot disguise the essential weakness of his verse. It is, in spite of a certain breeziness and a few magnificent descriptions of cañons and mountain-chains, feeble, full of cheap heroics, atrocious taste, impossible men and women. One or two individual poems, like "Crossing the Plains," "The Yukon," and parts of his apostrophes to the Sierras, the Pacific Ocean and the Missouri River may live; the rest seem doomed to extinction.

From 1872 to 1876 Miller traveled in Europe and the Holy Land, and, although he speaks of being in Egypt in 1879, there is good ground for believing this to be another romantic exaggeration. At all events, he built a log cabin in Washington in 1883, after spending some time in Boston and New York. After being married for the third time, he returned to California in 1885. In 1886 he bought "The Hights" and tried to found an experimental Greek Academy for aspiring writers. He died there, after a determinedly picturesque life, in sight of the Golden Gate in 1913.

## BY THE PACIFIC OCEAN

Here room and kingly silence keep
Companionship in state austere;
The dignity of death is here,
The large, lone vastness of the deep.
Here toil has pitched his camp to rest:
The west is banked against the west.

Above yon gleaming skies of gold
The lone imperial peak is seen;
While gathered at his feet in green
Ten thousand foresters are told.
And all so still! so still the air
That duty drops the web of care.

Beneath the sunset's golden sheaves
The awful deep walks with the deep,
Where silent sea-doves slip and sweep,
And commerce keeps her loom and weaves.
The dead red men refuse to rest;
Their ghosts illume my lurid West.

## CROSSING THE PLAINS

What great yoked brutes with briskets low,
With wrinkled necks like buffalo,
With round, brown, liquid, pleading eyes,
That turn'd so slow and sad to you.
That shone like love's eyes soft with tears,
That seem'd to plead, and make replies,
The while they bow'd their necks and drew
The creaking load; and looked at you.
Their sable briskets swept the ground,
Their cloven feet kept solemn sound.

Two sullen bullocks led the line,
Their great eyes shining bright like wine;
Two sullen captive kings were they,
That had in time held herds at bay,
And even now they crush'd the sod
With stolid sense of majesty,
And stately stepp'd and stately trod,
As if 'twere something still to be
Kings even in captivity.

## FROM "BYRON"

In men whom men condemn as ill
I find so much of goodness still,
In men whom men pronounce divine
I find so much of sin and blot,
I do not dare to draw a line
Between the two, where God has not.

## THE ARCTIC MOON

### (from "The Yukon")

The moon resumed all heaven now,
She shepherded the stars below
Along her wide, white steeps of snow,
Nor stooped nor rested, where or how.
She bared her full white breast, she dared
The sun to show his face again.
She seemed to know no change, she kept
Carousal constantly, nor slept,
Nor turned aside a breath, nor spared
The fearful meaning, the mad pain,
The weary eyes, the poor dazed brain,
That came at last to feel, to see
The dread, dead touch of lunacy.

How loud the silence! Oh, how loud!
How more than beautiful the shroud
Of dead Light in the moon-mad north
When great torch-tipping stars stand forth
Above the black, slow-moving pall
As at some fearful funeral!

The moon blares as mad trumpets blare
To marshaled warriors long and loud;
The cobalt blue knows not a cloud,
But, oh, beware that moon, beware
Her ghostly, graveyard, moon-mad stare!
Beware white silence more than white!
Beware the five-horned starry rune;
Beware the groaning gorge below;
Beware the wide, white world of snow,
Where trees hang white as hooded nun—
No thing not white, not one, not one!
But most beware that mad white moon.

# Edward Rowland Sill

EDWARD ROWLAND SILL was born at Windsor, Connecticut, in 1841. In 1861 he was graduated from Yale and shortly thereafter his poor health compelled him to go West. After various unsuccessful experiments, he drifted into teaching, first in the high schools in Ohio, later in the English department of the University of California. His uncertain physical condition added to his mental insecurity. Unable to ally himself either with the conservative forces whom he hated or with the radicals whom he distrusted, Sill became an uncomfortable solitary; half rebellious, half resigned. During the last decade of his life, his brooding seriousness was less pronounced, a lighter irony took the place of dark reflections. Although Sill remains among the minor poets both in scope and style, a few of his poems (such as "The Fool's Prayer" and "Opportunity") have established themselves securely.

*The Hermitage,* his first volume, was published in 1867, a later edition (including later poems) appearing in 1889. His two posthumous books are *Poems* (1887) and *Hermione and Other Poems* (1899). A volume of his prose "essays in literature and education" was published in 1900. His later and little known work deserved—and deserves—a wider audience. It established a serenity that was not without flashes of spirit, a gravity compounded with quiet wit.

Sill died, after bringing something of the Eastern culture and "finish" to the West, in 1887.

### OPPORTUNITY

This I beheld, or dreamed it in a dream:—
There spread a cloud of dust along a plain;
And underneath the cloud, or in it, raged
A furious battle, and men yelled, and swords
Shocked upon swords and shields. A prince's banner
Wavered, then staggered backward, hemmed by foes.
A craven hung along the battle's edge,
And thought, "Had I a sword of keener steel—
That blue blade that the king's son bears,—but this
Blunt thing—!" he snapt, and flung it from his hand,
And lowering crept away and left the field.
Then came the king's son, wounded, sore bestead,
And weaponless, and saw the broken sword,
Hilt-buried in the dry and trodden sand,
And ran and snatched it, and with battle-shout
Lifted afresh he hewed his enemy down,
And saved a great cause that heroic day.

### THE FOOL'S PRAYER

The royal feast was done; the King
    Sought some new sport to banish care,
And to his jester cried: "Sir Fool,
    Kneel now, and make for us a prayer!"

The jester doffed his cap and bells,
　And stood the mocking court before;
They could not see the bitter smile
　Behind the painted grin he wore.

He bowed his head, and bent his knee
　Upon the monarch's silken stool;
His pleading voice arose: "O Lord,
　Be merciful to me, a fool!

" 'Tis not by guilt the onward sweep
　Of truth and right, O Lord, we stay;
'Tis by our follies that so long
　We hold the earth from heaven away.

"These clumsy feet, still in the mire,
　Go crushing blossoms without end;
These hard, well-meaning hands we thrust
　Among the heart-strings of a friend.

"The ill-timed truth we might have kept—
　Who knows how sharp it pierced and stung?
The word we had not sense to say—
　Who knows how grandly it had rung?

"Our faults no tenderness should ask,
　The chastening stripes must cleanse them all;
But for our blunders—oh, in shame
　Before the eyes of heaven we fall.

"Earth bears no balsam for mistakes;
　Men crown the knave, and scourge the tool
That did his will; but Thou, O Lord,
　Be merciful to me, a fool!"

The room was hushed; in silence rose
　The King, and sought his gardens cool,
And walked apart, and murmured low,
　"Be merciful to me, a fool!"

# Sidney Lanier

SIDNEY LANIER was born at Macon, Georgia, February 3, 1842. His was a family
of musicians (Lanier himself was a skillful performer on various instruments),
and it is not surprising that his verse emphasizes—even overstresses—the influence
of music on poetry. He attended Oglethorpe College, graduating at the age of eighteen (1860), and, a year later, volunteered as a private in the Confederate army. After
several months' imprisonment (he had been captured while acting as signal officer

on a blockade-runner), Lanier was released in February, 1865, returning from Point Lookout to Georgia on foot, accompanied only by his flute. His physical health, never the most robust, had been further impaired by his incarceration, and he was already suffering from tuberculosis. The rest of his life was spent in an unequal struggle against it.

He was now only twenty-three years old and the problem of choosing a vocation was complicated by his marriage in 1867. He spent five years in the study and practice of law, during which time he wrote comparatively little verse. But the law could not hold him; he felt premonitions of death and realized he must devote his talents to art before it was too late. He was fortunate enough to obtain a position as flautist with the Peabody Symphony Orchestra in 1873 in Baltimore, where he had free access to the music and literature he craved. Here he wrote all his best poetry. In 1879, he was made lecturer on English in Johns Hopkins University, and it was for his courses there that he wrote his chief prose work, a brilliant if inconclusive study, *The Science of English Verse*. Besides his poetry, he wrote several books for boys, the two most popular being *The Boys' Froissart* (1878) and *The Boys' King Arthur* (1880).

Lanier's poetry suffers from his all too frequent theorizing, his too-conscious effort to bring verse over into the province of pure music. He thought almost entirely in terms of musical form. His main theory that English verse has for its essential basis not *accent* but a strict musical *quantity* is a wholly erroneous conclusion, possible only to one who could write "whatever turn I have for art is purely musical—poetry being with me a mere tangent into which I shoot." Lanier is at his best in his ballads, although a few of his lyrics have a similar spontaneity. In spite of novel schemes of rhythm and stanza-structure, much of his work is marred by strained effects, literary conceits (especially his use of pseudo-Shakespearean images) and a kind of verse that approaches mere pattern-making. But such a ballad as the "Song of the Chattahoochee," lyrics like "Night and Day," and parts of the symphonic "Hymns of the Marshes" have won a place in American literature. His triumphs over the exigencies of disease and his accomplishments in two arts were the result of undefeated spirit, a bravery that dazzled his commentators, who confused the attainments of courage with those of creation.

A comprehensive collection of Lanier's verse was first issued in 1906: *Collected Poems of Sidney Lanier,* edited by his wife, with a memorial by William Hayes Ward. It includes not only the poet's well-known musical experiments, but the rarely printed dialect verses and all that remains of "The Jacquerie."

Lanier died, a victim of his disease, in the mountains of North Carolina, September 7, 1881.

SONG OF THE CHATTAHOOCHEE

Out of the hills of Habersham,
  Down the valleys of Hall,
I hurry amain to reach the plain,
Run the rapid and leap the fall,
Split at the rock and together again,
Accept my bed, or narrow or wide,
And flee from folly on every side

With a lover's pain to attain the plain
  Far from the hills of Habersham,
  Far from the valleys of Hall.

All down the hills of Habersham,
  All through the valleys of Hall,
The rushes cried *Abide, abide,*
The willful waterweeds held me thrall,
The laving laurel turned my tide,

ie ferns and the fondling grass said *Stay*,
ie dewberry dipped for to work delay,
id the little reeds sighed *Abide, abide,*
*Here in the hills of Habersham,*
*Here in the valleys of Hall.*

High o'er the hills of Habersham,
Veiling the valleys of Hall,
ie hickory told me manifold
ir tales of shade, the poplar tall
rought me her shadowy self to hold,
ie chestnut, the oak, the walnut, the pine,
verleaning, with flickering meaning and
    sign,
id, *Pass not, so cold, these manifold*
*Deep shades of the hills of Habersham,*
*These glades in the valleys of Hall.*

And oft in the hills of Habersham,
And oft in the valleys of Hall,
he white quartz shone, and the smooth
    brook-stone
id bar me of passage with friendly brawl,
nd many a luminous jewel lone
-Crystals clear or acloud with mist,
ıby, garnet and amethyst—
ade lures with the lights of streaming stone
In the clefts of the hills of Habersham,
In the beds of the valleys of Hall.

But oh, not the hills of Habersham,
And oh, not the valleys of Hall

Avail: I am fain for to water the plain.
Downward the voices of Duty call—
Downward, to toil and be mixed with the
    main,
The dry fields burn, and the mills are to
    turn,
And a myriad flowers mortally yearn,
And the lordly main from beyond the plain
    Calls o'er the hills of Habersham,
    Calls through the valleys of Hall.

## NIGHT AND DAY

The innocent, sweet Day is dead.
Dark Night hath slain her in her bed.
O, Moors are as fierce to kill as to wed!
    —Put out the light, said he.

A sweeter light than ever rayed
From star of heaven or eye of maid
Has vanished in the unknown Shade
    —She's dead, she's dead, said he.

Now, in a wild, sad after-mood
The tawny Night sits still to brood
Upon the dawn-time when he wooed
    —I would she lived, said he.

Star-memories of happier times,
Of loving deeds and lovers' rhymes,
Throng forth in silvery pantomimes.
    —Come back, O Day! said he.

## FROM "THE MARSHES OF GLYNN"

Inward and outward to northward and southward the beach-lines linger and curl
As a silver-wrought garment clings to and follows the firm sweet limbs of a girl.
Vanishing, swerving, evermore curving again into sight,
Softly the sand-beach wavers away to a dim gray looping of light.
And what if behind me to westward the wall of the woods stands high?
The world lies east: how ample, the marsh and the sea and the sky!

A league and a league of marsh-grass, waist-high, broad in the blade,
Green, and all of a height, and unflecked with a light or a shade,
Stretch leisurely off, in a pleasant plain,
To the terminal blue of the main.

Ye marshes, how candid and simple and nothing-withholding and free
Ye publish yourselves to the sky and offer yourselves to the sea!
Tolerant plains, that suffer the sea and the rains and the sun,
Ye spread and span like the catholic man who hath mightily won

God out of knowledge and good out of infinite pain
And sight out of blindness and purity out of a stain.

As the marsh-hen secretly builds on the watery sod,
Behold I will build me a nest on the greatness of God:
I will fly in the greatness of God as the marsh-hen flies
In the freedom that fills all the space 'twixt the marsh and the skies:
By so many roots as the marsh-grass sends in the sod
I will heartily lay me a-hold on the greatness of God:
Oh, like to the greatness of God is the greatness within
The range of the marshes, the liberal marshes of Glynn.

And the sea lends large, as the marsh: lo, out of his plenty the sea
Pours fast: full soon the time of the flood-tide must be:
Look how the grace of the sea doth go
About and about through the intricate channels that flow
    Here and there,
        Everywhere,
Till his waters have flooded the uttermost creeks and the low-lying lanes,
And the marsh is meshed with a million veins,
That like as with rosy and silvery essences flow
In the rose-and-silver evening glow.

      Farewell, my lord Sun!
The creeks overflow: a thousand rivulets run
'Twixt the roots of the sod; the blades of the marsh-grass stir;
Passeth a hurrying sound of wings that westward whirr;
Passeth, and all is still; and the currents cease to run;
And the sea and the marsh are one.
How still the plains of the waters be!
The tide in his ecstasy.
The tide is at his highest height:
      And it is night.

And now from the Vast of the Lord will the waters of sleep
Roll in on the souls of men,
But who will reveal to our waking ken
The forms that swim and the shapes that creep
      Under the waters of sleep?
And I would I could know what swimmeth below when the tide comes in
On the length and breadth of the marvelous marshes of Glynn.

SONG FOR "THE JACQUERIE"

    The hound was cuffed, the hound was kicked,
    O' the ears was cropped, o' the tail was nicked,
(*All.*)        Oo-hoo-o, *howled the hound.*
    The hound into his kennel crept;
    He rarely wept, he never slept.
    His mouth he always open kept
      Licking his bitter wound,
        The hound,
(*All.*)        U-lu-lo, *howled the hound.*

A star upon his kennel shone
That showed the hound a meat-bare bone.
(*All.*)        O hungry was the hound!
The hound had but a churlish wit.
He seized the bone, he crunched, he bit.
"An thou wert Master, I had slit
        Thy throat with a huge wound,"
            Quo' hound.
(*All.*)        O, angry was the hound.

The star in castle-window shone,
The Master lay abed, alone.
(*All.*)        Oh ho, why not? quo' hound.
He leapt, he seized the throat, he tore
The Master, head from neck, to floor,
And rolled the head i' the kennel door,
        And fled and salved his wound,
            Good hound!
(*All.*)        U-lu-lo, *howled the hound.*

### A BALLAD OF THE TREES AND THE MASTER

Into the woods my Master went,
Clean forspent, forspent.
Into the woods my Master came,
Forspent with love and shame.
But the olives they were not blind to Him,
The little gray leaves were kind to Him:
The thorn-tree had a mind to Him
When into the woods He came.

Out of the woods my Master went,
And He was well content.
Out of the woods my Master came,
Content with death and shame.
When Death and Shame would woo Him last,
From under the trees they drew Him last:
'Twas on a tree they slew Him—last
When out of the woods He came.

## James Whitcomb Riley

JAMES WHITCOMB RILEY, possibly the most widely read native poet of his day, was
born October 7, 1849, in Greenfield, Indiana, a small town twenty miles from
Indianapolis, where he spent his later years. Contrary to popular belief, Riley was
not, as many have gathered from his bucolic poems, a struggling child of the soil;
his father was a lawyer in comfortable circumstances, and Riley was given not only
a good education, but was prepared for the law. His temperament, however, craved

something more adventurous. At eighteen he shut the pages of Blackstone, slipped out of the office and joined a traveling troupe of actors who sold patent medicines during the intermissions. Riley's functions were varied: he beat the bass-drum, painted their flaring banners, wrote local versions of old songs, coached the actors and, when occasion arose, took part in the performance himself.

Even before this time, Riley had begun to send verses to the newspapers, young experiments, bits of homely sentiment, simple snatches and elaborate hoaxes—the poem "Leonainie," published over the initials "E. A. P.," being accepted in many quarters as a newly discovered poem by Poe. In 1882, when he was on the staff of the Indianapolis *Journal,* he began printing the series of dialect poems which he claimed were by a rude and unlettered farmer, one "Benj. F. Johnson, of Boone, the Hoosier poet." A collection of these rustic verses appeared, in 1883, as *The Ole Swimmin' Hole,* and Riley leaped into widespread popularity.

Other collections followed rapidly: *Afterwhiles* (1887), *Old-Fashioned Roses* (1888), *Pipes o' Pan at Zekesbury* (1889), *Rhymes of Childhood* (1890). All met an instant response; Riley endeared himself, by his homely idiom and his ingenuity, to a countryful of readers, adolescent and adult.

But Riley's simplicity is seldom as artless as it seems. Time and again, one can watch him trading wantonly on the emotions of his unsophisticated readers. He sees them about to smile—and broadens the point of his joke; he observes them on the point of tears—and pulls out the sobbing *tremolo* stop. In many respects he is patently the most artificial of those poets who claim to give us the stuff of the soil. He is the poet of obtrusive sentiment rather than of quiet convictions, the poet of lulling assurance, of philosophies that never disturb his readers, of sweet truisms rather than searching truths. His influence has given rise to an entire school of "cheerful philosophy" versifiers; its lowest ebb may be seen in the newspaper columns of the "A Smile a Day" variety and the syndicated syrup of Edgar A. Guest.

That work of his which may endure will survive because of the personal flavor that Riley often gave it. Such poems as "When the Frost Is on the Punkin," and "The Raggedy Man," seem part of American folk-literature; "Little Orphant Annie" was read wherever there was a schoolhouse or, for that matter, a nursery.

Riley died in his little house in Lockerbie Street, Indianapolis, July 22, 1916.

### WHEN THE FROST IS ON THE PUNKIN

When the frost is on the punkin and the fodder's in the shock,
And you hear the kyouck and gobble of the struttin' turkey-cock,
And the clackin' of the guineys, and the cluckin' of the hens,
And the rooster's hallylooer as he tiptoes on the fence;
O, it's then the time a feller is a-feelin' at his best,
With the risin' sun to greet him from a night of peaceful rest,
As he leaves the house, bareheaded, and goes out to feed the stock,
When the frost is on the punkin and the fodder's in the shock.

They's something kindo' harty-like about the atmusfere
When the heat of summer's over and the coolin' fall is here—
Of course we miss the flowers, and the blossoms on the trees,
And the mumble of the hummin'-birds and buzzin' of the bees;

But the air's so appetizin'; and the landscape through the haze
Of a crisp and sunny morning of the airly autumn days
Is a pictur' that no painter has the colorin' to mock—
When the frost is on the punkin and the fodder's in the shock.

The husky, rusty russel of the tossels of the corn,
And the raspin' of the tangled leaves as golden as the morn;
The stubble in the furries—kindo' lonesome-like, but still
A-preachin' sermuns to us of the barns they growed to fill;
The strawstack in the medder, and the reaper in the shed;
The hosses in theyr stalls below—the clover overhead!—
O, it sets my hart a-clickin' like the tickin' of a clock,
When the frost is on the punkin and the fodder's in the shock.

Then your apples all is gethered, and the ones a feller keeps
Is poured around the cellar-floor in red and yaller heaps;
And your cider-makin's over, and your wimmern-folks is through
With theyr mince and apple-butter, and theyr souse and sausage too! . . .
I don't know how to tell it—but ef such a thing could be
As the angels wantin' boardin', and they'd call around on *me*—
I'd want to 'commodate 'em—all the whole-indurin' flock—
When the frost is on the punkin and the fodder's in the shock.

### A PARTING GUEST

What delightful hosts are they—
    Life and Love!
Lingeringly I turn away,
    This late hour, yet glad enough
They have not withheld from me
    Their high hospitality.
So, with face lit with delight
    And all gratitude, I stay
    Yet to press their hands and say,
"Thanks.—So fine a time! Good night."

# Eugene Field

Although Eugene Field was born September 2, 1850, in St. Louis, Missouri, his work belongs to the literature of the West. Colorado and the Rocky Mountain region claimed him as their own and Field never repudiated the allegiance; he even called most of his poetry "Western Verse."

Field's area of education embraced New England, Missouri, and what European territory he could cover in six months. At twenty-three he became a reporter on the St. Louis *Evening Journal;* the rest of his life was given, with a dogged devotion, to journalism. Driven by the demands of his unique daily columns (those on the Denver *Tribune* [1881-1883] and the Chicago *Daily News* [1883-1895] were widely copied), Field first capitalized and then standardized his high spirits, his erudition, his whimsicality, his fondness for children. He wrote so often with his tongue in his cheek that it is difficult to say where true sentiment stops and where exaggerated sentimentality begins. "Field," says Fred Lewis Pattee, in his detailed study of *American Literature Since 1870,* "more than any other writer of the period, illustrates the way the old type of literary scholar was to be modified and changed by the newspaper. Every scrap of Field's voluminous product was written for immediate newspaper consumption. . . . He was a pioneer in a peculiar province: he stands for the journalization of literature, a process that, if carried to its logical extreme, will make of the man of letters a mere newspaper reporter."

Though Field was overrated by his confrères, some of his child lyrics, his homely philosophic ballads (in the vein which Harte and Riley popularized) and his burlesques won him, for the time, a conspicuous place. Readers of all tastes found much to delight them in *A Little Book of Western Verse* (1889), *With Trumpet and Drum* (1892), *A Second Book of Verse* (1893) and those remarkable versions (and perversions) of Horace, *Echoes from the Sabine Farm* (1893), written in collaboration with his equally adroit though practically unknown brother, Roswell M. Field. A complete one-volume edition of his verse was issued in 1910.

Field died in Chicago, Illinois, November 4, 1895.

### OUR TWO OPINIONS

Us two wuz boys when we fell out,—
　Nigh to the age uv my youngest now;
Don't rec'lect what 'twuz about,
　Some small deeff'rence, I'll allow.
Lived next neighbors twenty years,
　A-hatin' each other, me 'nd Jim,—
He havin' *his* opinyin uv *me,*
　'Nd *I* havin' *my* opinyin uv *him.*

Grew up together 'nd wouldn't speak,
　Courted sisters, 'nd marr'd 'em, too;
'Tended same meetin'-house oncet a week,
　A-hatin' each other through 'nd through!
But when Abe Linkern asked the West
　F'r soldiers, we answered,—me 'nd Jim,—
*He* havin' *his* opinyin uv *me,*
　'Nd *I* havin' *my* opinyin uv *him.*

But down in Tennessee one night
　Ther' wuz sound uv firin' fur away,
'Nd the sergeant allowed ther'd be a fight
　With the Johnnie Rebs some time nex'
　　day;
'Nd as I wuz thinkin' uv Lizzie 'nd home
　Jim stood afore me, long 'nd slim,—
*He* havin' *his* opinyin uv *me,*
　'Nd *I* havin' *my* opinyin uv *him.*

Seemed like we knew there wuz goin' to
　Serious trouble f'r me 'nd him;
Us two shuck hands, did Jim 'nd me,
　But never a word from me or Jim!
He went *his* way 'nd *I* went *mine,*
　'Nd into the battle's roar went we,—
*I* havin' *my* opinyin uv *Jim,*
　'Nd *he* havin' *his* opinyin uv *me.*

Jim never came back from the war again,
　But I hain't forgot that last, last night
When, waitin' f'r orders, us two men
　Made up 'nd shuck hands, afore the fig
'Nd after it all, it's soothin' to know
　That here I be 'nd younder's Jim,—
*He* havin' *his* opinyin uv *me,*
　'Nd *I* havin' *my* opinyin uv *him.*

### LITTLE BOY BLUE

The little toy dog is covered with dust,
　But sturdy and staunch he stands;
The little toy soldier is red with rust,
　And his musket molds in his hands.
Time was when the little toy dog was ne
　And the soldier was passing fair;
And that was the time when our Little B
　Blue
　Kissed them and put them there.

Now don't you go till I come," he said,
"And don't you make any noise!"
, toddling off to his trundle bed,
He dreamt of the pretty toys;
nd, as he was dreaming, an angel song
Awakened our Little Boy Blue—
h! the years are many, the years are
   long,
But the little toy friends are true!

Aye, faithful to Little Boy Blue they stand,
   Each in the same old place,
Awaiting the touch of a little hand,
   The smile of a little face;
And they wonder, as waiting the long years
   through
   In the dust of that little chair,
What has become of our Little Boy Blue,
   Since he kissed them and put them there.

## SEEIN' THINGS

I ain't afraid uv snakes or toads, or bugs or worms or mice,
An' things 'at girls are skeered uv I think are awful nice!
I'm pretty brave I guess; an' yet I hate to go to bed,
For, when I'm tucked up warm an' snug an' when my prayers are said,
Mother tells me "Happy Dreams" an' takes away the light,
An' leaves me lyin' all alone an' seein' things at night!

Sometimes they're in the corner, sometimes they're by the door,
Sometimes they're all a-standin' in the middle uv the floor;
Sometimes they are a-sittin' down, sometimes they're walkin' round
So softly and so creepy-like they never make a sound!
Sometimes they are as black as ink, an' other times they're white—
But color ain't no difference when you see things at night!

Once, when I licked a feller 'at had just moved on our street,
An' father sent me up to bed without a bite to eat,
I woke up in the dark an' saw things standin' in a row,
A-lookin' at me cross-eyed an' p'intin' at me—*so!*
Oh, my! I wuz so skeered 'at time I never slep' a mite—
It's almost alluz when I'm bad I see things at night!

Lucky thing I ain't a girl or I'd be skeered to death!
Bein' I'm a boy, I duck my head an' hold my breath.
An' I am, oh *so* sorry I'm a naughty boy, an' then
I promise to be better an' I say my prayers again!
Gran'ma tells me that's the only way to make it right
When a feller has been wicked an' sees things at night!

An' so when other naughty boys would coax me into sin,
I try to skwush the Tempter's voice 'at urges me within;
An' when they's pie for supper, or cakes 'at's big an' nice,
I want to—but I do not pass my plate f'r them things twice!
No, ruther let Starvation wipe me slowly out o' sight
Than I should keep a-livin' on an' seein' things at night!

# Edwin Markham

EDWIN MARKHAM was born in Oregon City, Oregon, April 23, 1852, the youngest son of pioneer parents. His father died before he reached his fifth year and in 1857 he was taken by his mother to a wild valley in the Suisun Hills in central California. Here he grew to young manhood: farming, broncho-riding, laboring on a cattle ranch, educating himself in the primitive country schools. At eighteen he determined to be a teacher and entered the State Normal School at San José.

Since childhood, Markham had been writing verses of no extraordinary merit, one of his earliest pieces being a Byronic echo (*A Dream of Chaos*) full of the high-sounding fustian of the period. Several years before he uttered his famous challenge, Markham was writing poems of protest, insurrectionary in theme but conventional in effect. Suddenly, in 1899, a sense of outrage at the inequality of human struggle voiced itself in the sonorous poem, "The Man with the Hoe." Inspired by Millet's painting, Markham made the bowed, broken French peasant a symbol of the poverty-stricken toiler in all lands—his was a protest not against toil but the exploitation of labor. "The Yeoman is the landed and well-to-do farmer," says Markham, "you need shed no tears for him. But here in the Millet picture is his opposite—the Hoeman; the landless workman of the world."

The success of the poem upon its appearance in the San Francisco *Examiner* (January 15, 1899) was instantaneous. The lines appeared in every part of the globe; they were quoted and copied in every walk of life, in the literary and the labor world. The same year of its publication, it was incorporated in Markham's first volume, *The Man with the Hoe and Other Poems* (1899). Two years later, his almost equally well known poem was published. The same passion that fired Markham to champion the great common workers equipped him to write of the great Commoner in *Lincoln, and Other Poems* (1901). His later volumes are a descent, melodious but scarcely remarkable. They have the rhetoric without the resonance of the forerunners. Never reaching the heights, there are, nevertheless, moments of dignity in *The Shoes of Happiness* (1914), *The Gates of Paradise* (1920), and *New Poems: Eighty Songs at Eighty* (1932), published with a nice appropriateness on the poet's eightieth birthday. Many of the quatrains are memorable epigrams.

Markham came East in 1901, where he has lived ever since, making his home on Staten Island, New York, compiling and lecturing.

### OUTWITTED.

He drew a circle that shut me out—
Heretic, rebel, a thing to flout.
But Love and I had the wit to win:
We drew a circle that took him in!

## THE MAN WITH THE HOE[1]

*(Written after seeing Millet's world-famous painting)*

Bowed by the weight of centuries he leans
Upon his hoe and gazes on the ground,
The emptiness of ages in his face,
And on his back the burden of the world.
Who made him dead to rapture and despair,
A thing that grieves not and that never hopes,
Stolid and stunned, a brother to the ox?
Who loosened and let down this brutal jaw?
Whose was the hand that slanted back this brow?
Whose breath blew out the light within this brain?

Is this the Thing the Lord God made and gave
To have dominion over sea and land;
To trace the stars and search the heavens for power;
To feel the passion of Eternity?
Is this the dream He dreamed who shaped the suns
And marked their ways upon the ancient deep?
Down all the caverns of Hell to their last gulf
There is no shape more terrible than this—
More tongued with censure of the world's blind greed—
More filled with signs and portents for the soul—
More packt with danger to the universe.

What gulfs between him and the seraphim!
Slave of the wheel of labor, what to him
Are Plato and the swing of Pleiades?
What the long reaches of the peaks of song,
The rift of dawn, the reddening of the rose?
Through this dread shape the suffering ages look;
Time's tragedy is in that aching stoop;
Through this dread shape humanity betrayed,
Plundered, profaned, and disinherited,
Cries protest to the Judges of the World,
A protest that is also prophecy.

O masters, lords and rulers in all lands,
Is this the handiwork you give to God,
This monstrous thing distorted and soul-quenched?
How will you ever straighten up this shape;
Touch it again with immortality;
Give back the upward looking and the light;
Rebuild in it the music and the dream;
Make right the immemorial infamies,
Perfidious wrongs, immedicable woes?

O masters, lords and rulers in all lands,
How will the Future reckon with this man?

[1] Revised version, 1920. Copyright by Edwin Markham.

How answer his brute question in that hour
When whirlwinds of rebellion shake all shores?
How will it be with kingdoms and with kings—
With those who shaped him to the thing he is—
When this dumb terror shall rise to judge the world,
After the silence of the centuries?

### THE AVENGERS

The laws are the secret avengers,
And they rule above all lands;
They come on wool-soft sandals,
But they strike with iron hands.

### THE THIRD WONDER

"Two things," said Kant, "fill me with breathless awe:
The starry heaven and the moral law."
I know a thing more awful and obscure—
The long, long patience of the plundered poor.

### PREPAREDNESS

For all your days prepare,
And meet them ever alike:
When you are the anvil, bear—
When you are the hammer, strike.

### LINCOLN, THE MAN OF THE PEOPLE

When the Norn Mother saw the Whirlwind Hour
Greatening and darkening as it hurried on,
She left the Heaven of Heroes and came down
To make a man to meet the mortal need.
She took the tried clay of the common road—
Clay warm yet with the genial heat of earth,
Dasht through it all a strain of prophecy;
Tempered the heap with thrill of human tears;
Then mixt a laughter with the serious stuff.
Into the shape she breathed a flame to light
That tender, tragic, ever-changing face;
And laid on him a sense of the Mystic Powers,
Moving—all husht—behind the mortal veil.
Here was a man to hold against the world,
A man to match the mountains and the sea.

The color of the ground was in him, the red earth;
The smack and tang of elemental things:
The rectitude and patience of the cliff;
The good-will of the rain that loves all leaves;

The friendly welcome of the wayside well;
The courage of the bird that dares the sea;
The gladness of the wind that shakes the corn;
The pity of the snow that hides all scars;
The secrecy of streams that make their way
Under the mountain to the rifted rock;
The tolerance and equity of light
That gives as freely to the shrinking flower
As to the great oak flaring to the wind—
To the grave's low hill as to the Matterhorn
That shoulders out the sky. Sprung from the West,
He drank the valorous youth of a new world.
The strength of virgin forests braced his mind,
The hush of spacious prairies stilled his soul.
His words were oaks in acorns; and his thoughts
Were roots that firmly gript the granite truth.

Up from log cabin to the Capitol,
One fire was on his spirit, one resolve—
To send the keen ax to the root of wrong,
Clearing a free way for the feet of God,
The eyes of conscience testing every stroke,
To make his deed the measure of a man.
He built the rail-pile as he built the State,
Pouring his splendid strength through every blow:
The grip that swung the ax in Illinois
Was on the pen that set a people free.

So came the Captain with the mighty heart.
And when the judgment thunders split the house,
Wrenching the rafters from their ancient rest,
He held the ridgepole up, and spiked again
The rafters of the Home. He held his place—
Held the long purpose like a growing tree—
Held on through blame and faltered not at praise.
And when he fell in whirlwind, he went down
As when a lordly cedar, green with boughs,
Goes down with a great shout upon the hills,
And leaves a lonesome place against the sky.

# Charles E. S. Wood

CHARLES ERSKINE SCOTT WOOD was born at Erie, Pennsylvania, February 20, 1852, educated at the United States Military Academy (1874) and Columbia, where he received the degrees of Ph.B. and LL.B. in 1883. Wood served in the United States Army for almost ten years, acting as lieutenant in various campaigns against the Indians during 1877-8. He was admitted to the bar in 1884, practiced at Portland, Oregon, and retired in 1919.

In 1901 he published *A Book of Tales, Being Myths of the North American Indians*. In 1904, his symbolic *A Masque of Love* appeared. His finest work, however, was *The Poet in the Desert* (1915), a pageant of protest from which the first two quoted excerpts are taken. The volume itself is one long poem, a rhapsodic dialogue between Truth and a poet. The central theme might be termed the manhood of humanity, and about this leading *motif* Wood has woven a set of graphic variations. A disgust of tyranny, a challenge to injustice, a celebration of bastards—these may be the motive power prompting the poet; what results, however, has not merely the ring of passion but is a controlled assembling of sharply drawn pictures.

In 1918 a limited number of privately printed copies of *Maia* appeared. *Maia* is a sonnet sequence of the seasons with numerous interjections by the author and a few interpolations by Sara Bard Field, to whom is credited the form of the volume. *Heavenly Discourses,* which had originally appeared in *The Masses,* caused more discussion upon republication in 1927, Wood being compared to Voltaire, Paine and Mark Twain. *The Poet in the Desert* was reissued in a popular form in 1928.

## SUNRISE

### (from "The Poet in the Desert")

The lean coyote, prowler of the night,
Slips to his rocky fastnesses.
Jack-rabbits noiselessly shuttle among the sage-brush,
And, from the castellated cliffs,
Rock-ravens launch their proud black sails upon the day.
The wild horses troop back to their pastures.
The poplar-trees watch beside the irrigation-ditches.
Orioles, whose nests sway in the cotton-wood trees by the ditch-side, begin to twitter.
All shy things, breathless, watch
The thin white skirts of dawn,
The dancer of the sky,
Who trips daintily down the mountain-side
Emptying her crystal chalice. . . .
And a red-bird, dipped in sunrise, cracks from a poplar's top
His exultant whip above a silver world.

## THE DESERT

She is a nun, withdrawing behind her veil;
Gray, mysterious, meditative, unapproachable.
Her body is tawny with the eagerness of the Sun
And her eyes are pools which shine in deep canyons.
She is a beautiful swart woman
With opals at her throat,
Rubies at her wrists
And topaz about her ankles.
Her breasts are like the evening and the day stars.

She sits upon her throne of light, proud and silent,
Indifferent to wooers.

The Sun is her servitor, the stars her attendants,
Running before her.
She sings a song unto her own ears,
Solitary but sufficient:
The song of her being.
She is a naked dancer, dancing upon
A pavement of porphyry and pearl,
Dazzling, so that the eyes must be shaded.
She wears the stars upon her bosom
And braids her hair with the constellations.

### FIRST SNOW

The cows are bawling in the mountains.
The snowflakes fall.
They are leaving the pools and pebbled fountains;
Troubled, they bawl.
They are winding down the mountain's shoulders
Through the open pines,
Through wild rose thickets and the granite bowlders
In broken lines.
Each calf trots close beside its mother
And so they go,
Bawling and calling to one another
About the snow.

## Lizette Woodworth Reese

LIZETTE WOODWORTH REESE was born January 9, 1856, in Waverly, Baltimore County, Maryland, of mixed English and German stock. After receiving an education chiefly in private schools she taught English at the Western High School in Baltimore, where she lived. After many years of service, she retired in 1921. In 1923, the alumni of the High School where she had taught for a score of years, together with the teachers and pupils, presented the school with a bronze tablet inscribed with her poem, "Tears," one of the most famous sonnets written by an American.

At first glance, Miss Reese's work seems merely a continuation of the traditional strain; some of her critics decried her poetry as being English rather than American. But it was natural that her verse should sound a note which has been the dominant one in English pastoral poetry from Wordsworth to Housman. Nor was Miss Reese's inheritance alone responsible for this. The country around Baltimore, every tree and path of which Miss Reese knew intimately, was settled by the English and had the shape and color of counties like Sussex and Buckinghamshire.

Miss Reese's first book, *A Branch of May* (1887), had an undercurrent of intensity beneath its quiet contours. Few of its readers in the Nineties would have dreamed that this straightforward undidactic speech would pave the way for the direct songs of Sara Teasdale and Edna St. Vincent Millay. In a period of sugared sentiment and lace valentine lyrics, Miss Reese's crisp lines were a generation ahead of the times and were consequently appreciated only for their pictorial if somewhat prim felicities. *A Handful of Lavender* (1891), *A Quiet Road* (1896), and *A Wayside Lute* (1909) established an artistry which, for all its seemingly old-fashioned elegance, is as spontaneous as it is skillful. Here are no verbal tricks, no false postures; here is a simple record which is, somehow, never banal. "This poetry of hers," writes Mary Colum, "will persist, not because the author was cleverer or more original than other writers, but because in some way her nerves were more subtle in response to the kinds of life and experiences that came her way."

From 1909 to 1920 there was a silence. During these ten years, Miss Reese wrote little, and published less. Suddenly her work appeared again, more concise than ever. *Spicewood* was published in 1920; *Wild Cherry* in 1923; a generous *Selected Poems* in 1926; *Little Henrietta* in 1927, the poet's seventy-second year; *A Victorian Village,* her reminiscences of a changing world, in 1929.

*White April* (1930) and *Pastures* (1933), published in the poet's seventy-eighth year, are as fresh as anything she wrote in her youth. The limitations are obvious, but they are the limitations which marked her from the beginning: a preoccupation with the surprise of spring, the inevitable changes of love, the unchanging heart of nature. Individual poems make romance out of the commonplace, juxtaposing the minute with the momentous, and, while the poems lack singularity, the verve is unmistakable.

These volumes, like the earlier ones, reveal the qualities which influenced a generation of women poets. In her late seventies, writing like a young girl, the poet sings of lilacs in Old York Lane, of thorn trees and blackberry rain, of Judas-blossoms and daffodils, of spring ecstasy and lost love, of a dead lady in her garden, and Mary at the manger. But there is always something personal, always something which makes the very repetitions take on a light which is fresh and clear. At least a dozen of her brief songs and lyrical sonnets have found a niche in American literature. Hers is a singing that is not dependent on a fashion.

Lizette Reese died, after a brief illness a few weeks before her eightieth birthday, December 17, 1935.

### TEARS

When I consider Life and its few years—
A wisp of fog betwixt us and the sun;
A call to battle, and the battle done
Ere the last echo dies within our ears;
A rose choked in the grass; an hour of fears;
The gusts that past a darkening shore do beat;
The burst of music down an unlistening street,—
I wonder at the idleness of tears.

Ye old, old dead, and ye of yesternight,
Chieftains, and bards, and keepers of the sheep,
By every cup of sorrow that you had,
Loose me from tears, and make me see aright
How each hath back what once he stayed to weep:
Homer his sight, David his little lad!

## SPICEWOOD

The spicewood burns along the gray, spent sky,
In moist unchimneyed places, in a wind,
That whips it all before, and all behind,
Into one thick, rude flame, now low, now high.
It is the first, the homeliest thing of all—
At sight of it, that lad that by it fares,
Whistles afresh his foolish, town-caught airs—
A thing so honey-colored and so tall!

It is as though the young Year, ere he pass
To the white riot of the cherry tree,
Would fain accustom us, or here, or there,
To his new sudden ways with bough and grass,
So starts with what is humble, plain to see,
And all familiar as a cup, a chair.

### SPRING ECSTASY

Oh, let me run and hide,
  Let me run straight to God;
The weather is so mad with white
  From sky down to the clod!

If but one thing were so,
  Lilac, or thorn out there,
It would not be, indeed,
  So hard to bear.

The weather has gone mad with white;
  The cloud, the highway touch.
White lilac is enough;
  White thorn too much!

### OWNERSHIP

Love not a loveliness too much,
For it may turn and clutch you so,
That you be less than any serf,
And at its nodding go.

Be master; otherwise you grow
Too small, too humble, like to one
Long dispossessed, who stares through tears
At his lost house across the sun.

Wild carrot in an old field here,
Or steeple choked with music there,
Possess, as part of what is yours;
Thus prove yourself the heir.

Your barony is sky and land,
From morning's start to the night's close
Bend to your need Orion's hounds,
Or the small fagot of a rose.

### A PURITAN LADY

Wild Carthage held her, Rome,
  Sidon. She stared to tears
Tall, golden Helen, wearying
  Behind the Trojan spears.

Towered Antwerp knew her well;
  She wore her quiet gown
In some hushed house in Oxford grass,
  Or lane in Salem town.

Humble and high in one,
  Cool, certain, different,
She lasts; scarce saint, yet half a child,
  As hard, as innocent.

What grave, long afternoons,
  What caged airs round her blown,
Stripped her of humor, left her bare
  As cloud, or wayside stone?

Made her as clear a thing,
  In this slack world as plain
As a white flower on a grave,
  Or sleet sharp at a pane?

## A FLOWER OF MULLEIN

I am too near, too clear a thing for you,
A flower of mullein in a crack of wall,
The villagers half-see, or not at all;
Part of the weather, like the wind or dew.
You·love to pluck the different, and find
Stuff for your joy in cloudy loveliness;
You love to fumble at a door, and guess
At some strange happening that may wait behind.
Yet life is full of tricks, and it is plain,
That men drift back to some worn field or roof,
To grip at comfort in a room, a stair;
To warm themselves at some flower down a lane:
You, too, may long, grown tired of the aloof,
For the sweet surety of the common air.

## MIRACLE

Who is in love with loveliness,
    Need not shake with cold;
For he may tear a star in two,
    And frock himself in gold.

Who holds her first within his heart,
    In certain favor goes;
If his roof tumbles, he may find
    Harbor in a rose.

## WILD CHERRY

Why make your lodging here in this spent lane,
Where but an old man, with his sheep each day,
Twice through the forgotten grass goes by your way,
Half sees you there, and not once looks again?
For you are of the very ribs of spring,
And should have many lovers, who have none.
In silver cloaks, in hushed troops down the sun
Should they draw near, oh, strange and lovely thing!
Beauty has no set weather, no sure place;
Her careful pageantries are here as there,
With nothing lost. And soon, some lad may start—
A strayed Mayer in this unremembered space—
At your tall white, and know you very fair,
Let all else go to roof within your heart.

## OLD SAUL

I cannot think of any word
To make it plain to you,
How white a thing the hawthorn bush
That delicately blew

Within a crook of Tinges Lane;
Each May Day there it stood;
And lit a flame of loveliness
For the small neighborhood.

So fragile-white a thing it was,
I cannot make it plain.
Or the sweet fumbling of the bees,
Like the break in a rain.

Old Saul lived near. And this his life:—
To cobble for his bread;
To mourn a tall son lost at sea;
A daughter worse than dead.

And so, in place of all his lack,
He set the hawthorn-tree;
Made it his wealth, his mirth, his god,
His Zion to touch and see.

Born English he. Down Tinges Lane
His lad's years came and went,
He saw out there behind his thorn,
A hundred thorns of Kent.

At lovers slipping through the dusk,
He shook a lover's head;
Grudged them each flower. It was too white
For any but the dead.

Once on a blurred, wet, silver day,
He said to two or three:
"Folks, when I go, pluck yonder bloom,
That I may take with me."

But it was winter when he went,
The road wind-wrenched and torn;
They laid upon his coffin lid
A wreath made all of thorn.

### WOMEN

Some women herd such little things—a box
Oval and glossy, in its gilt and red,
Or squares of satin, or a high, dark bed—
But when love comes, they drive to it all their flocks;
Yield up their crooks; take little; gain for fold
And pasture each a small, forgotten grave.
When they are gone, then lesser women crave
And squander their sad hoards; their shepherds' gold.

Some gather life like faggots in a wood,
And crouch its blaze, without a thought at all
Past warming their pinched selves to the last spark.
And women as a whole are swift and good,
In humor scarce, their measure being small;
They plunge and leap, yet somehow miss the dark.

### SURETY

How do I know that you will come again?
I judge you by imperishable things
Like crab-trees rosy as the cloaks of kings,
That twice a year blow down the same tall lane.
I dare the silence in the house, each place
Without you, as a stalk of leaf, the wrong
The neighbors do you in their talk, the song
Beaten out of bells, and dusk, and a great space.
Nothing can tear the spring from out the year,
Or love from out the heart. Both hands have I
Filled with crab-bloom November as in May.
Is bloom to bough than you to me more dear?
Has the old trick of flowering been put by?
You will come back, you will come back and stay.

### CROWS

Earth is raw with this one note,
  This tattered making of a song,
Narrowed down to a crow's throat,
  Above the willow-trees that throng

The crooking field from end to end.
  Fixed as the sun, the grave, this sound;
Of what the weather has to spend
  As much a part as sky or ground.

The primal yellow of that flower,
  The tansy making August plain;

And the stored wildness of this hour
  It sucks up like a bitter rain.

Miss it we would, were it not here,
  Simple as water, rough as spring,
It hurls us at the point of spear,
  Back to some naked, early thing.

Listen now. As with a hoof
  It stamps an image on the gust;
Chimney by chimney a lost roof
  Starts for a moment from its dust.

# Frank Dempster Sherman

FRANK DEMPSTER SHERMAN was born at Peekskill, New York, May 6, 1860. He entered Columbia University in 1879, where, after graduation and a subsequent instructorship, he was made adjunct professor in 1891 and Professor of Graphics in 1904. He held the latter position until his death, which occurred September 19, 1916.

  Besides being a writer of airy lyrics and epigrammatic quatrains, Sherman was an enthusiastic genealogist and a designer (especially of book-plates) of no little skill.

As a poet, his gift was essentially that of a writer of light verse—fragrant, fragile, yet seldom too sentimental. Pleasant is the word for it, a pleasantness perfumed with wit.

Sherman never wearied of the little lyric; even the titles of his volumes are instances of his penchant for the brief snatch of song: *Madrigals and Catches* (1887), *Lyrics for a Lute* (1890), *Little-Folk Lyrics* (1892), *Lyrics of Joy* (1904). A sumptuous collected edition of his poems was published, with an Introduction by Clinton Scollard, in 1917.

### AT MIDNIGHT

, yonder, the belfry tower
That gleams in the moon's pale light—
is it a ghostly flower
That dreams in the silent night?

sten and hear the chime
Go quavering over the town,
d out of this flower of Time
Twelve petals are wafted down.

### BACCHUS

Listen to the tawny thief,
Hid beneath the waxen leaf,
Growling at his fairy host,
Bidding her with angry boast
Fill his cup with wine distilled
From the dew the dawn has spilled:
Stored away in golden casks
Is the precious draught he asks.

Who,—who makes this mimic din
In this mimic meadow inn,
Sings in such a drowsy note,
Wears a golden-belted coat;

Loiters in the dainty room
Of this tavern of perfume;
Dares to linger at the cup
Till the yellow sun is up?

Bacchus 'tis, come back again
To the busy haunts of men;
Garlanded and gayly dressed,
Bands of gold about his breast;
Straying from his paradise,
Having pinions angel-wise,—
'Tis the honey-bee, who goes
Reveling within a rose!

### TWO QUATRAINS

#### IVY

Upon the walls the graceful Ivy climbs
  And wraps with green the ancient ruin gray:
Romance it is, and these her leafy rhymes
  Writ on the granite page of yesterday.

#### DAWN

Out of the scabbard of the night
  By God's hand drawn,
Flashes his shining sword of light,
  And lo—the dawn!

## Louise Imogen Guiney

LOUISE IMOGEN GUINEY was born in Boston, Massachusetts, in 1861. Although she attended Elmhurst Academy in Providence, most of her studying was with private tutors. In 1901 she went to England, where she lived until her death.

Traditional in form and feeling, Miss Guiney's work has a distinctly personal vigor; even her earliest collections, *Songs at the Start* (1884) and *The White Sail and Other Poems* (1887), are not without individuality. Her two most characteristic volumes are *A Roadside Harp* (1893) and *Patrins* (1897). *Happy Ending* appeared in 1909, and was reissued with additional poems in 1927.

Though much of her work is poeticizing rather than poetry, there is no mistaking the high seriousness of her aim. Responding to the influence of the Cavalier poets whom she greatly admired, her best lines beat with a galloping courage. Aware of the poet's mission, she held her pen "in trust to Art, not serving shame or lust"; a militant faith was the very keynote of her writing. Contemporary life affected her but little; even her peasant songs ("In Leinster" for example) have a remoteness which escapes the impact of the present. Still, she was not a literary escapist; a mystic with vitality, her verse was vigorous even when she was most spiritual. "The Kings" and "The Wild Ride" are assured of a place as long as American anthologies are made.

Miss Guiney died at Chipping-Campden, near Oxford, England, November 3, 1920.

### THE KINGS

A man said unto his Angel:
  "My spirits are fallen low,
And I cannot carry this battle:
  O brother! where might I go?"

"The terrible Kings are on me
  With spears that are deadly bright;
Against me so from the cradle
  Do fate and my fathers fight."

Then said to the man his Angel:
  "Thou wavering, witless soul,
Back to the ranks! What matter
  To win or lose the whole,

"As judged by the little judges
  Who hearken not well, nor see?
Not thus, by the outer issue,
  The Wise shall interpret thee.

"Thy will is the sovereign measure
  And only event of things:

The puniest heart, defying,
  Were stronger than all these Kings.

"Though out of the past they gather,
  Mind's Doubt, and Bodily Pain,
And pallid Thirst of the Spirit
  That is kin to the other twain.

"And Grief, in a cloud of banners,
  And ringleted Vain Desires,
And Vice, with the spoils upon him
  Of thee and thy beaten sires,—

"While Kings of eternal evil
  Yet darken the hills about,
Thy part is with broken saber
  To rise on the last redoubt;

"To fear not sensible failure,
  Nor covet the game at all,
But fighting, fighting, fighting,
  Die, driven against the wall!"

### THE WILD RIDE

*I hear in my heart, I hear in its ominous pulses,*
*All day, on the road, the hoofs of invisible horses,*
*All night, from their stalls, the importunate pawing and neighing.*

Let cowards and laggards fall back! But alert to the saddle
Weatherworn and abreast, go men of our galloping legion,
With a stirrup-cup each to the lily of women that loves him.

The trail is through dolor and dread, over crags and morasses;
There are shapes by the way, there are things that appal or entice us;
What odds? We are Knights of the Grail, we are vowed to the riding.

Thought's self is a vanishing wing, and joy is a cobweb,
And friendship a flower in the dust, and glory a sunbeam:
Not here is our prize, nor, alas! after these our pursuing.

A dipping of plumes, a tear, a shake of the bridle,
A passing salute to this world and her pitiful beauty;
We hurry with never a word in the track of our fathers.

*I hear in my heart, I hear in its ominous pulses,*
*All day, on the road, the hoofs of invisible horses,*
*All night, from their stalls, the importunate pawing and neighing.*

We spur to a land of no name, outracing the storm-wind;
We leap to the infinite dark like sparks from the anvil.
Thou leadest, O God! All's well with Thy troopers that follow.

## *Bliss Carman*

(William) Bliss Carman was born in Fredericton, New Brunswick, Canada, April 15, 1861, of a long line of United Empire Loyalists who withdrew from Connecticut at the time of the Revolutionary War. Carman was educated at the University of New Brunswick (1879-81), at Edinburgh (1882-3), and Harvard (1886-8). He took up his residence in the United States about 1889.

In 1893, Carman issued his first book, *Low Tide on Grand Pré: A Book of Lyrics.* From the outset, it was evident that Carman possessed lyrical power: the ability to interpret the external world through personal intensity. A buoyancy, new to American literature, made his *camaraderie* with Nature frankly pagan in contrast to the moralizing tributes of his contemporaries. This freshness and whimsy made Carman the natural collaborator for Richard Hovey, and when their first joint *Songs from Vagabondia* appeared in 1894 Carman's fame was established. Even so devout a poet as Francis Thompson was enthusiastic about the book's irresponsibility: "These snatches," wrote Thompson, "have the spirit of a gypsy Omar Khayyám. They have always careless verve and often careless felicity; they are masculine and rough as roving songs should be."

Although the three *Vagabondia* collections contain Carman's best poems, several of his other volumes (he published over twenty of them) vibrate with something of the same pulse. A physical gayety rises from *Ballads of Lost Haven* (1897), *From the Book of Myths* (1902) and *Songs of the Sea Children* (1904), songs for the open road, the windy beach, the mountaintop.

Carman also wrote several volumes of essays and, in conjunction with Mary Perry King, devised poem-dances (*Daughters of Dawn,* 1913), suggesting Vachel Lindsay's later poem-games. Although the strength is diluted and the music thinned in the later collections, such as *April Airs* (1916) and *Wild Garden* (1929), some of the old magic persists; the spell is over-familiar but it is not quite powerless.

Carman died in June, 1929, at New Canaan, Connecticut, and was buried in his native province of New Brunswick.

## A VAGABOND SONG

There is something in the autumn that is native to my blood—
Touch of manner, hint of mood;
And my heart is like a rhyme,
With the yellow and the purple and the crimson keeping time.

The scarlet of the maples can shake me like a cry
Of bugles going by.
And my lonely spirit thrills
To see the frosty asters like a smoke upon the hills.

There is something in October sets the gypsy blood astir;
We must rise and follow her,
When from every hill of flame
She calls and calls each vagabond by name.

## THE GRAVEDIGGER

Oh, the shambling sea is a sexton old,
And well his work is done.
With an equal grave for lord and knave,
He buries them every one.

Then hoy and rip, with a rolling hip,
He makes for the nearest shore;
And God, who sent him a thousand ship,
Will send him a thousand more;

But some he'll save for a bleaching grave,
And shoulder them in to shore,—
Shoulder them in, shoulder them in,
Shoulder them in to shore.

Oh, the ships of Greece and the ships of Tyre
Went out, and where are they?
In the port they made, they are delayed
With the ships of yesterday.

He followed the ships of England far,
As the ships of long ago;
And the ships of France they led him a dance,
But he laid them all arow.

Oh, a loafing, idle lubber to him
Is the sexton of the town;

For sure and swift, with a guiding lift,
He shovels the dead men down.

But though he delves so fierce and grim,
His honest graves are wide,
As well they know who sleep below
The dredge of the deepest tide.

Oh, he works with a rollicking stave at
And loud is the chorus skirled;
With the burly rote of his rumbling throa
He batters it down the world.

He learned it once in his father's house,
Where the ballads of eld were sung;
And merry enough is the burden rough,
But no man knows the tongue.

Oh, fair, they say, was his bride to see,
And willful she must have been,
That she could bide at his gruesome side
When the first red dawn came in.

And sweet, they say, is her kiss to those
She greets to his border home;
And softer than sleep her hand's first sw
That beckons, and they come.

h, crooked is he, but strong enough
o handle the tallest mast;
rom the royal barque to the slaver dark,
e buries them all at last.

hen hoy and rip, with a rolling hip,
e makes for the nearest shore;
nd God, who sent him a thousand ship,
'ill send him a thousand more;
ut some he'll save for a bleaching grave,
nd shoulder them in to shore,—
houlder them in, shoulder them in,
oulder them in to shore.

### HEM AND HAW

em and Haw were the sons of sin,
reated to shally and shirk;
em lay 'round and Haw looked on
hile God did all the work.

em was foggy, and Haw was a prig,
r both had the dull, dull mind;
nd whenever they found a thing to do,
ey yammered and went it blind.

em was the father of bigots and bores;
s the sands of the sea were they.
nd Haw was the father of all the tribe
ho criticize today.

t God was an artist from the first,
nd knew what he was about;

While over his shoulder sneered these two,
And advised him to rub it out.

They prophesied ruin ere man was made;
"Such folly must surely fail!"
And when he was done, "Do you think, my
  Lord,
He's better without a tail?"

And still in the honest working world,
With posture and hint and smirk,
These sons of the devil are standing by
While man does all the work.

They balk endeavor and baffle reform,
In the sacred name of law;
And over the quavering voice of Hem
Is the droning voice of Haw.

### DAISIES

Over the shoulders and slopes of the dune
I saw the white daisies go down to the sea,
A host in the sunshine, an army in June,
The people God sends us to set our hearts
  free.

The bobolinks rallied them up from the dell,
The orioles whistled them out of the wood;
And all of their singing was, "Earth, it is
  well!"
And all of their dancing was, "Life, thou art
  good!"

# George Santayana

GEORGE SANTAYANA was born in Madrid, Spain, December 16, 1863, came to the United States at the age of nine, and was educated at Harvard, where later he became instructor of philosophy the same year he received his Ph.D. This was in 1889. From 1889 to 1912 he remained at Harvard, becoming not merely one of the most noted professors in the history of the University, but one of the most notable minds in America. In 1914, he went abroad; since then he has been living in France, in England and in Italy.

Santayana's first work was in verse, *Sonnets and Poems* (1894). It is a wise seriousness which is here proclaimed, although the idiom is as traditional as the figures are orthodox. *The Sense of Beauty* (1896), and *The Life of Reason* (1905), a study of the phases of human progress in five volumes, received far more attention than

Santayana's verse. In the interval he achieved fame as a philosopher, and it was with an almost apologetic air that Santayana prefaced his collected *Poems* which, after a process of revision, appeared in 1923. "Of impassioned tenderness or Dionysiac frenzy I have nothing, nor even of that magic and pregnancy of phrase—really the creation of a fresh idiom—which marks the high lights of poetry. Even if my temperament had been naturally warmer, the fact that the English language (and I can write no other with assurance) was not my mother-tongue would of itself preclude any inspired use of it on my part; its roots do not quite reach to my center. I never drank in in childhood the homely cadences and ditties which in pure spontaneous poetry set the essential key."

Yet, as Santayana himself maintained later on, the thoughts which prompted his verses could not have been transcribed in any other form. If the prosody is worn somewhat thin, it is because the poet-philosopher chose the classic mold in the belief that the innate freedom of poets to hazard new forms does not abolish the freedom to attempt the old ones. The moralizing is personal, even the rhetoric is justified. "Here is the hand of an apprentice, but of an apprentice in a great school."

The tradition has, even in these experimental days, its defenders. One of the most persuasive of them, Robert Hillyer, writes, "In the shrewd, though perhaps too deprecatory, preface to his *Collected Poems,* George Santayana builds up the case for what is sometimes called the rhetorical style. He affirms the validity of the traditional, even the conventional, mode—not to the exclusion of more experimental patterns but as equally defensible with the newer forms. Such is his statement; his implication is clearly in favor of tradition. 'To say that what was good once is good no longer is to give too much importance to chronology. Esthetic fashions may change, losing as much beauty at one end as they gain at the other, but innate taste continues to recognize its affinities, however remote, and need never change.' His poetry shows both the virtues and the defects inherent in such standards. Some of the sonnets are among the finest in the language; the 'Athletic Ode,' on the other hand, is a set piece wherein half-backs and Greek deities quite naturally eye each other askance.

"Mr. Santayana's output in verse has not been large. Besides the sonnets and odes, he composed an epic drama, *Lucifer,* which deserves study for the frequent magnificence of its style and the intricacy of its thought. But for the common reader, the sonnets will be most easily acceptable. Many modern readers are as dogmatic in their rejection of the traditional style as professors are supposed to be in their rejection of the new. But if our ears and minds are not wholly closed to dignity and sumptuousness of phrasing, we shall not hesitate to place Mr. Santayana's sequence among the greatest in our literature. Had he composed it two or three hundred years ago no one would quibble; but that a contemporary should insist on Parnassus is almost as shocking as a preference for old Bohemia over new Czecho-Slovakia. Mr. Santayana is definitely behind the times. Perhaps he is also ahead of them."

Not even the most casual appraisal of Santayana's contribution to the period can be complete without a tribute to his prose. At seventy-two he made his début as novelist with *The Last Puritan* (1936). The quality of Santayana's thinking is heightened by his style, a style which is both firm and flexible, the gift of one of the unquestionable masters of English prose.

### AS IN THE MIDST OF BATTLE THERE IS ROOM

As in the midst of battle there is room
For thoughts of love, and in foul sin for mirth;
As gossips whisper of a trinket's worth
Spied by the death-bed's flickering candle-gloom;
As in the crevices of Caesar's tomb
The sweet herbs flourish on a little earth:
So in this great disaster of our birth
We can be happy, and forget our doom.
For morning, with a ray of tenderest joy
Gilding the iron heaven, hides the truth,
And evening gently woos us to employ
Our grief in idle catches. Such is youth;
Till from that summer's trance we wake, to find
Despair before us, vanity behind.

### AFTER GRAY VIGILS, SUNSHINE IN THE HEART

After gray vigils, sunshine in the heart;
After long fasting on the journey, food;
After sharp thirst, a draught of perfect good
To flood the soul, and heal her ancient smart.
Joy of my sorrow, never can we part;
Thou broodest o'er me in the haunted wood,
And with new music fill'st the solitude
By but so sweetly being what thou art.
He who hath made thee perfect, makes me blest.
O fiery minister, on mighty wings
Bear me, great love, to mine eternal rest.
Heaven it is to be at peace with things;
Come chaos now, and in a whirlwind's rings
Engulf the planets. I have seen the best.

### ON THE DEATH OF A METAPHYSICIAN

Unhappy dreamer, who outwinged in flight
The pleasant region of the things I love,
And soared beyond the sunshine, and above
The golden cornfields and the dear and bright
Warmth of the hearth,—blasphemer of delight,
Was your proud bosom not at peace with Jove,
That you sought, thankless for his guarded grove,
The empty horror of abysmal night?

Ah, the thin air is cold above the moon!
I stood and saw you fall, befooled in death,
As, in your numbèd spirit's fatal swoon,
You cried you were a god, or were to be;
I heard with feeble moan your boastful breath
Bubble from depths of the Icarian sea.

### THE RUSTIC AT THE PLAY

Our youth is like a rustic at the play
That cries aloud in simple-hearted fear,
Curses the villain, shudders at the fray,
And weeps before the maiden's wreathèd bier.
Yet once familiar with the changeful show,
He starts no longer at a brandished knife,
But, his heart chastened at the sight of woe,
Ponders the mirrored sorrows of his life.
So tutored too, I watch the moving art
Of all this magic and impassioned pain
That tells the story of the human heart
In a false instance, such as poets feign;
I smile, and keep within the parchment furled
That prompts the passions of this strutting world.

### O WORLD, THOU CHOOSEST NOT THE BETTER PART

O world, thou choosest not the better part!
It is not wisdom to be only wise,
And on the inward vision close the eyes,
But it is wisdom to believe the heart.
Columbus found a world, and had no chart
Save one that faith deciphered in the skies;
To trust the soul's invincible surmise
Was all his science and his only art.
Our knowledge is a torch of smoky pine
That lights the pathway but one step ahead
Across a void of mystery and dread.
Bid, then, the tender light of faith to shine
By which alone the mortal heart is led
Unto the thinking of the thought divine.

# Richard Hovey

RICHARD HOVEY was born May 4, 1864, at Normal, Illinois, and graduated from Dartmouth in 1885. After leaving college, he became, in rapid succession, theologian, actor, journalist, lecturer, professor of English literature at Barnard, poet and dramatist.

His first volume, *The Laurel: An Ode* (1889), betrayed the over-musical influence of Lanier but gave promise of that extraordinary facility which often brought Hovey perilously close to mere technique. His exuberant virility found its outlet in the series of poems published in collaboration with Bliss Carman: the three volumes of *Songs from Vagabondia* (1894, 1896, 1900). Here he let himself go completely; nothing remained sober or static. His lines flung themselves across the page; danced with intoxicating abandon; shouted, laughed, and carried off the reader in a gale of high spirits. The famous *Stein Song* is an interlude in the midst of a far finer poem that, with its flavor of Whitman, begins:

> I said in my heart, "I am sick of four walls and a ceiling.
> I have need of the sky.
> I have business with the grass.
> I will up and get me away where the hawk is wheeling,
> Low and high,
> And the slow clouds go by.
> I will get me away to the waters that glass
> The clouds as they pass. . . ."

Hovey's attitude to his art was expressed in his own words concerning the poet: "It is not his mission," wrote Hovey in the *Dartmouth Magazine,* "to write elegant canzonettas for the delectation of the *dilettanti,* but to comfort the sorrowful and hearten the despairing, to champion the oppressed and declare to humanity its in-alienable rights, to lay open to the world the heart of man—all its heights and depths, all its glooms and glories, to reveal the beauty in things and breathe into his fellows a love of it." This too conscious awareness of the poet's "mission" marred Hovey's work; responding to a program, he frequently overstressed his ringing enthusiasm, and strained his muscularity. But his power was as unflagging as his energy was persuasive.

Some of Hovey's best work was accomplished without shouting. The little known "Contemporaries" showed how well he could handle double portraiture, antedating the psycho-philosophical delineations of E. A. Robinson. As he grew older, Hovey became dissatisfied with the wanderlusty motif and its panacea of open roads and youthful comradeship. His subjects grew larger, his symbols were less obvious and not confined to "something potent brimming through the earth." The work on which he was engaged at the time of his death is significant; *Launcelot and Guene-vere: A Poem in Five Dramas,* exemplary in its restrained force.

Although the varied lyrics in *Songs from Vagabondia* are the heartiest examples of Hovey, a representative collection of his riper work may be found in *Along the Trail* (1898). Hovey was slow to mature; this volume, in conjunction with the un-completed *Taliesin: A Masque,* shows his later, more intensive power. The mood reflected is spiritual rather than physical; the note is high but never shrill. Besides the later work, *Along the Trail* contains "Spring" and the stirring "Comrades" in full.

Hovey died, during his thirty-sixth year, in New York, February 24, 1900.

### AT THE CROSSROADS

ou to the left and I to the right,
or the ways of men must sever—
nd it well may be for a day and a night,
nd it well may be forever.
ut whether we meet or whether we part
or our ways are past our knowing),
  pledge from the heart to its fellow
heart
n the ways we all are going!

Here's luck!
For we know not where we are going.

Whether we win or whether we lose
With the hands that life is dealing,
It is not we nor the ways we choose
But the fall of the cards that's sealing.
There's a fate in love and a fate in fight,
And the best of us all go under—
And whether we're wrong or whether we're
  right,

We win, sometimes, to our wonder.
Here's luck!
That we may not yet go under!

With a steady swing and an open brow
We have tramped the ways together,
But we're clasping hands at the crossroads
     now
In the Fiend's own night for weather;
And whether we bleed or whether we smile
In the leagues that lie before us
The ways of life are many a mile
And the dark of Fate is o'er us.
Here's luck!
And a cheer for the dark before us!

You to the left and I to the right,
For the ways of men must sever,
And it well may be for a day and a night
And it well may be forever!
But whether we live or whether we die
(For the end is past our knowing),
Here's two frank hearts and the open sky,
Be a fair or an ill wind blowing!
*Here's luck!*
In the teeth of all winds blowing.

### UNMANIFEST DESTINY[1]

To what new fates, my country, far
     And unforeseen of foe or friend,

Beneath what unexpected star
     Compelled to what unchosen end,

Across the sea that knows no beach,
     The Admiral of Nations guides
Thy blind obedient keels to reach
     The harbor where thy future rides!

The guns that spoke at Lexington
     Knew not that God was planning then
The trumpet word of Jefferson
     To bugle forth the rights of men.

To them that wept and cursed Bull Run,
     What was it but despair and shame?
Who saw behind the cloud the sun?
     Who knew that God was in the flame?

Had not defeat upon defeat,
     Disaster on disaster come,
The slave's emancipated feet
     Had never marched behind the drum.

There is a Hand that bends our deeds
     To mightier issues than we planned;
Each son that triumphs, each that bleeds,
     My country, serves Its dark command.

I do not know beneath what sky
     Nor on what seas shall be thy fate;
I only know it shall be high,
     I only know it shall be great.

### LOVE IN THE WINDS

When I am standing on a mountain crest,
Or hold the tiller in the dashing spray,
My love of you leaps foaming in my breast,
Shouts with the winds and sweeps to their foray.
My heart bounds with the horses of the sea
And plunges in the wild ride of the night,
Flaunts in the teeth of tempest the large glee
That rides out Fate and welcomes gods to fight.

Ho, love, I laugh aloud for love of you,
Glad that our love is fellow to rough weather,—
No fretful orchid hothoused from the dew,
But hale and hardy as the highland heather,
     Rejoicing in the wind that stings and thrills,
     Comrade of ocean, playmate of the hills.

---

[1] The phrase "manifest destiny," which came into usage during the Spanish-American War, was meant to indicate America's paternal (or, as the opposing faction claimed, imperialistic) mission. Hovey was one who denied any but unselfish motives to the conduct of his country.

## COMRADES

Comrades, pour the wine tonight,
　For the parting is with dawn.
Oh, the clink of cups together,
　With the daylight coming on!
　　Greet the morn
　　With a double horn,
When strong men drink together!

Comrades, gird your swords tonight,
　For the battle is with dawn.
Oh, the clash of shields together,
　With the triumph coming on!
　　Greet the foe
　　And lay him low,
When strong men fight together.

Comrades, watch the tides tonight,
　For the sailing is with dawn.
Oh, to face the spray together,
　With the tempest coming on!
　　Greet the Sea
　　With a shout of glee,
When strong men roam together.

Comrades, give a cheer tonight,
　For the dying is with dawn.
Oh, to meet the stars together,
　With the silence coming on!
　　Greet the end
　　As a friend a friend,
When strong men die together.


## CONTEMPORARIES

"A barbered woman's man,"—yes, so
He seemed to me a twelvemonth since;
And so he may be—let it go—
Admit his flaws—we need not wince
To find our noblest not all great.
What of it? He is still the prince,
And we the pages of his state.

The world applauds his words; his fame
Is noised wherever knowledge be;
Even the trader hears his name,
As one far inland hears the sea;
The lady quotes him to the beau
Across the cup of Russian tea;
They know him and they do not know.

I know him. In the nascent years
Men's eyes shall see him as one crowned;
His voice shall gather in their ears
With each new age prophetic sound;
And you and I and all the rest,
Whose brows today are laurel-bound,
Shall be but plumes upon his crest.

A year ago this man was poor,—
This Alfred whom the nations praise;
He stood a beggar at my door
For one mere word to help him raise
From fainting limbs and shoulders bent
The burden of the weary days;
And I withheld it—and he went.

I knew him then, as I know now,
Our largest heart, our loftiest mind;
Yet for the curls upon his brow
And for his lisp, I could not find
The helping word, the cheering touch.
Ah, to be just, as well as kind,—
It costs so little and so much!

It seemed unmanly in my sight
That he, whose spirit was so strong
To lead the blind world to the light,
Should look so like the mincing throng
Who advertise the tailor's art.
It angered me—I did him wrong—
I grudged my groat and shut my heart.

I might have been the prophet's friend,
Helped him who is to help the world!
Now, when the striving is at end,
The reek-stained battle-banners furled,
And the age hears its muster-call,
Then I, because his hair was curled,
I shall have lost my chance—that's all.


## A STEIN SONG

### (from "Spring")

Give a rouse, then, in the Maytime
　For a life that knows no fear!

Turn night-time into daytime
  With the sunlight of good cheer!
    For it's always fair weather
    When good fellows get together,
With a stein on the table and a good song ringing clear.

When the wind comes up from Cuba,
  And the birds are on the wing,
And our hearts are patting juba
  To the banjo of the spring,
    Then it's no wonder whether
    The boys will get together,
With a stein on the table and a cheer for everything.

For we're all frank-and-twenty
  When the spring is in the air;
And we've faith and hope a-plenty,
  And we've life and love to spare:
    And it's birds of a feather
    When we all get together,
With a stein on the table and a heart without a care.

For we know the world is glorious,
  And the goal a golden thing,
And that God is not censorious
  When his children have their fling;
    And life slips its tether
    When the boys get together,
With a stein on the table in the fellowship of spring.

# Madison Cawein

Madison (JULIUS) CAWEIN was born in Louisville, Kentucky, in 1865, and spent most of his life in the state of his birth. He wrote an enormous quantity of verse, publishing more than twenty volumes of pleasant, but seldom distinguished, poetry. *Lyrics and Idyls* (1890) and *Vale of Tempe* (1905) contain his most characteristic stanzas, packed with the lush love of Nature that led certain admirers to call him (and, one must admit, the alliteration was tempting) "the Keats of Kentucky."

Cawein's work divides itself into two distinct veins. In the realistic one he dealt with the scenes and incidents of his mountain environment: the sag of an old house in the hills, the echoes of a feud, rumblings of the Ku Klux Klan, the ghastly details of a lynching. In his other mood (the one which unfortunately possessed him the greater part of the time) he spent page after page romanticizing Nature, gilding his already painted lilies, polishing his thinly plated artificialities until the base metal showed through. He pictured all outdoors with painstaking detail; and yet it is somehow unreal, prettified, remote. With irritating frequency, he tries to transport his audience to a literary Fairyland; but the reader is quickly wearied by the almost interminable procession of gnomes, nixies, elves, dryads, sprites, fays and fauns—be they ever so lyrical.

In spite of Cawein's too profuse lyricism, several of his pieces will doubtless remain, though it is not likely that the survivors will be the sugared sweetmeats by which his champions (including William Dean Howells) set such store. Those which show signs of life are those in which the poet's fancy is natural, restrained rather than urged to the limits of literary imagination.

Cawein died in Kentucky in 1914. His twenty volumes desperately need winnowing; a selected one-volume edition might lead to a new appraisal. It is doubtful whether, with a few exceptions, any poetry ever belonged more definitely to the "literature of escape," most of it having been written during the nineteen years while Cawein was employed as cashier in a Kentucky gambling house.

### SNOW

The moon, like a round device
On a shadowy shield of war,
Hangs white in a heaven of ice
With a solitary star.

The wind has sunk to a sigh,
And the waters are stern with frost;
And gray, in the eastern sky,
The last snow-cloud is lost.

White fields, that are winter-starved,
Black woods, that are winter-fraught,
Cold, harsh as a face death-carved
With the iron of some black thought.

### THE MAN HUNT

The woods stretch wild to the mountain side,
And the brush is deep where a man may hide.

They have brought the bloodhounds up again
To the roadside rock where they found the slain.

They have brought the bloodhounds up, and they
Have taken the trail to the mountain way.

Three times they circled the trail and crossed,
And thrice they found it and thrice they lost.

Now straight through the pines and the underbrush
They follow the scent through the forest's hush.

And their deep-mouthed bay is a pulse of fear
In the heart of the wood that the man must hear.

The man who crouches among the trees
From the stern-faced men that follow these.

A huddle of rocks that the ooze has mossed—
And the trail of the hunted again is lost.

An upturned pebble; a bit of ground
A heel has trampled—the trail is found.

And the woods reëcho the bloodhounds' bay
As again they take to the mountain way.

A rock; a ribbon of road; a ledge,
With a pine-tree clutching its crumbling edge.

A pine, that the lightning long since clave,
Whose huge roots hollow a ragged cave.

A shout; a curse; and a face aghast,
And the human quarry is laired at last.

The human quarry, with clay-clogged hair
And eyes of terror, who waits them there;

That glares and crouches and rising then
Hurls clods and curses at dogs and men.

Until the blow of a gun-butt lays
Him stunned and bleeding upon his face.

A rope, a prayer, and an oak-tree near.
And a score of hands to swing him clear.

A grim black thing for the setting sun
And the moon and the stars to look upon.

### THE WINDS

Those hewers of the clouds, the Winds,—that lair
At the four compass-points,—are out tonight;
I hear their sandals trample on the height,
I hear their voices trumpet through the air:
Builders of storm, God's workmen, now they bear
Up the steep stair of sky, on backs of might,
Huge tempest bulks, while—sweat that blinds their sight—
The rain is shaken from tumultuous hair:
Now, sweepers of the firmament, they broom
Like gathered dust, the rolling mists along
Heaven's floors of sapphire; all the beautiful blue
Of skyey corridor and celestial room—
Preparing, with large laughter and loud song,
For the white moon and stars to wander through.

### DESERTED

The old house leans upon a tree
  Like some old man upon a staff:
The night wind in its ancient porch
  Sounds like a hollow laugh.

The heaven is wrapped in flying clouds
  As grandeur cloaks itself in gray:
The starlight flitting in and out,
  Glints like a lanthorn ray.

The dark is full of whispers. Now
  A fox-hound howls: and through the night,
Like some old ghost from out its grave,
  The moon comes misty white.

# *William Vaughn Moody*

WILLIAM VAUGHN MOODY was born in Spencer, Indiana, July 8, 1869, and was educated at Harvard. After graduation, he spent the remaining eighteen years of his life in travel and intensive study—he taught, for eight years, at the University of Chicago—his death coming at the very height of his creative power.

*The Masque of Judgment,* his first work, was published in 1900. A richer and more representative collection appeared the year following; in *Poems* (1901) Moody effected that mingling of challenging lyricism and spiritual philosophy which became more and more insistent. Throughout his career, and particularly in such lines as the hotly expostulating "On a Soldier Fallen in the Philippines" and the uncompleted "The Death of Eve," Moody successfully achieved the union of poet and preacher. "Gloucester Moors" was an outcry against the few exploiting the many; "The Quarry" and "An Ode in Time of Hesitation" were impassioned and prophetic. His last extended works were little read; their too crowded details and difficult diction prevented them from becoming popular. Further, Moody did not offer a happy solution of life as was attempted by the vague socialism of Markham or the reckless optimism of Hovey; he maintained, rather, that men's spirits were "plagued, impatient things, all dream and unaccountable desire." Creation, he felt, was moving toward some far end, but he never presumed to know the goal, he would not even declare of our destiny: "I only know it shall be great." Man, to Moody, must make himself greater before he could claim to be the object of great purposes.

Moody's prose play *The Great Divide* (1907) was extremely successful when produced by Henry Miller. *The Faith Healer* (1909), another play in prose, because of its more exalted tone, did not win the favor of the theater-going public. A complete edition of *The Poems and Poetic Dramas of William Vaughn Moody* was published in 1912 in two volumes.

In the summer of 1909 Moody was stricken with the illness from which he never recovered. Had he lived he might well have become one of the major poets of his country. He died in October, 1910.

## PANDORA'S SONG

### (from "The Fire-Bringer")

I stood within the heart of God;
It seemed a place that I had known:
(I was blood-sister to the clod,
Blood-brother to the stone.)

I found my love and labor there,
My house, my raiment, meat and wine,
My ancient rage, my old despair,—
Yea, all things that were mine.

I saw the spring and summer pass,
The trees grow bare, and winter come;
All was the same as once it was
Upon my hills at home.

Then suddenly in my own heart
I felt God walk and gaze about;
He spoke; his words seemed held apart
With gladness and with doubt.

"Here is my meat and wine," He said,
"My love, my toil, my ancient care;
Here is my cloak, my book, my bed,
And here my old despair.

"Here are my seasons: winter, spring,
Summer the same, and autumn spills
The fruits I look for; everything
As on my heavenly hills."

## GLOUCESTER MOORS

A mile behind is Gloucester town
Where the fishing fleets put in,
A mile ahead the land dips down
And the woods and farms begin.
Here where the moors stretch free
In the high blue afternoon,
Are the marching sun and talking sea,
And the racing winds that wheel and flee
On the flying heels of June.

Jill-o'er-the-ground is purple blue,
Blue is the quaker-maid,

The wild geranium holds its dew
Long in the bowlder's shade.
Wax-red hangs the cup
From the huckleberry boughs,
In barberry bells the gray moths sup,
Or where the choke-cherry lifts high up
Sweet bowls for their carouse.

Over the shelf of the sandy cove
Beach-peas blossom late.
By copse and cliff the swallows rove
Each calling to his mate.
Seaward the sea-gulls go,
And the land-birds all are here:
That green-gold flash was a vireo,
And yonder flame where the marsh-flag
  grow
Was a scarlet tanager.

This earth is not the steadfast place
We landsmen build upon;
From deep to deep she varies pace,
And while she comes is gone.
Beneath my feet I feel
Her smooth bulk heave and dip;
With velvet plunge and soft upreel
She swings and steadies to her keel
Like a gallant, gallant ship.

These summer clouds she sets for sail,
The sun is her masthead light,
She tows the moon like a pinnace frail
Where her phosphor wake churns bright.
Now hid, now looming clear,
On the face of the dangerous blue
The star fleets tack and wheel and veer,
But on, but on does the old earth steer
As if her port she knew.

God, dear God! Does she know her port,
Though she goes so far about?
Or blind astray, does she make her sport
To brazen and chance it out?
I watched when her captains passed:
She were better captainless.
Men in the cabin, before the mast,
But some were reckless and some aghast,
And some sat gorged at mess.

By her battened hatch I leaned and caught
sounds from the noisome hold,—
Cursing and sighing of souls distraught
And cries too sad to be told.
Then I strove to go down and see;
But they said, "Thou art not of us!"
I turned to those on the deck with me
And cried, "Give help!" But they said, "Let
  be:
Our ship sails faster thus."

Ill-o'er-the-ground is purple blue,
Blue is the quaker-maid,
The alder-clump where the brook comes
  through
Breeds cresses in its shade.
To be out of the moiling street
With its swelter and its sin!
Who has given to me this sweet,
And given my brother dust to eat?
And when will his wage come in?

Scattering wide or blown in ranks,
Yellow and white and brown,
Boats and boats from the fishing banks
Come home to Gloucester town.
There is cash to purse and spend,
There are wives to be embraced,
Hearts to borrow and hearts to lend,
And hearts to take and keep to the end,—
O little sails, make haste!

But thou, vast outbound ship of souls,
What harbor town for thee?
What shapes, when thy arriving tolls,
Shall crowd the banks to see?
Shall all the happy shipmates then
Stand singing brotherly?
Or shall a haggard ruthless few
Warp her over and bring her to,
While the many broken souls of men
Fester down in the slaver's pen,
And nothing to say or do?

## ROAD-HYMN FOR THE START

Leave the early bells at chime,
Leave the kindled hearth to blaze,
Leave the trellised panes where children linger out the waking-time,
Leave the forms of sons and fathers trudging through the misty ways,
Leave the sounds of mothers taking up their sweet, laborious days.

Pass them by! even while our soul
Yearns to them with keen distress.
Unto them a part is given; we will strive to see the whole.
Dear shall be the banquet table where their singing spirits press;
Dearer be our sacred hunger, and our pilgrim loneliness.

We have felt the ancient swaying
Of the earth before the sun,
On the darkened marge of midnight heard sidereal rivers playing;
Rash it was to bathe our souls there, but we plunged and all was done.
That is lives and lives behind us—lo, our journey is begun!

Careless where our face is set,
Let us take the open way,
What we are no tongue has told us: Errand-goers who forget?
Soldiers heedless of their harry? Pilgrim people gone astray?
We have heard a voice cry "Wander!" That was all we heard it say.

Ask no more: 'Tis much, 'tis much!
Down the road the day-star calls;
Touched with change in the wide heavens, like a leaf the frost winds touch,

Flames the failing moon a moment, ere it shrivels white and falls;
Hid aloft, a wild throat holdeth sweet and sweeter intervals.

Leave him still to ease in song
Half his little heart's unrest:
Speech is his, but we may journey toward the life for which we long.
God, who gives the bird its anguish, maketh nothing manifest,
But upon our lifted foreheads pours the boon of endless quest.

### FROM "JETSAM"

Once at a simple turning of the way
I met God walking; and although the dawn
Was large behind Him, and the morning stars
Circled and sang about his face as birds
About the fieldward morning cottager,
My coward heart said faintly, "Let us haste!
Day grows and it is far to market-town."
Once where I lay in darkness after fight,
Sore smitten, thrilled a little thread of song
Searching and searching all my muffled sense
Until it shook sweet pangs through all my blood,
And I beheld one globed in ghostly fire
Singing, star-strong, her golden canticle;
And her mouth sang, "The hosts of Hate roll past,
A dance of dust-motes in the sliding sun;
Love's battle comes on the wide wings of storm,
From east to west one legion! Wilt thou strive?"
Then, since the splendor of her sword-bright gaze
Was heavy on me with yearning and with scorn,
My sick heart muttered, "Yea, the little strife,
Yet see, the grievous wounds! I fain would sleep."

O heart, shalt thou not once be strong to go
Where all sweet throats are calling, once be brave
To slake with deed thy dumbness? Let us go
The path her singing face looms low to point,
Pendulous, blanched with longing, shedding flames
Of silver on the brown grope of the flood;
For all my spirit's soilure is put by
And all my body's soilure, lacking now
But the last lustral sacrament of death
To make me clean for those near-searching eyes
That question yonder whether all be well,
And pause a little ere they dare rejoice.

Question and be thou answered, passionate face!
For I am worthy, worthy now at last
After so long unworth; strong now at last
To give myself to beauty and be saved.

ON A SOLDIER FALLEN IN THE PHILIPPINES[1]

Streets of the roaring town,
Hush for him; hush, be still!
He comes, who was stricken down
Doing the word of our will.
Hush! Let him have his state.
Give him his soldier's crown,
The grists of trade can wait
Their grinding at the mill.
But he cannot wait for his honor, now the trumpet has been blown.
Wreathe pride now for his granite brow, lay love on his breast of stone.

Toll! Let the great bells toll
Till the clashing air is dim,
Did we wrong this parted soul?
We will make it up to him.
Toll! Let him never guess
What work we sent him to.
Laurel, laurel, yes.
He did what we bade him do.
Praise, and never a whispered hint but the fight he fought was good;
Never a word that the blood on his sword was his country's own heart's-blood.

A flag for a soldier's bier
Who dies that his land may live;
O banners, banners here,
That he doubt not nor misgive!
That he heed not from the tomb
The evil days draw near
When the nation robed in gloom
With its faithless past shall strive.
Let him never dream that his bullet's scream went wide of its island mark,
Home to the heart of his darling land where she stumbled and sinned in the dark.

# George Sterling

GEORGE STERLING was born at Sag Harbor, New York, December 1, 1869, and educated at various private schools in the Eastern States. He moved to the Far West about 1895 and lived in California until, discouraged and dipsomaniac, he met death by his own hand in 1926.

Of Sterling's ten volumes of poetry, *The Testimony of the Suns* (1903), *A Wine of Wizardry* (1908) and *The House of Orchids and Other Poems* (1911) are the most characteristic. Ambrose Bierce was the first to hail Sterling with what now

[1] Compare the point of view expressed in Hovey's "Unmanifest Destiny" on page 128. This poem was likewise written at the time of the Spanish-American War.

seems extravagant praise; he declared that *A Wine of Wizardry* contained some of the greatest lines in English poetry.

As the titles of Sterling's volumes indicate, this is poetry of a flamboyant and rhetorical type, of luxuriant sentences and emotions declared in "the grand manner." Yet Sterling added vigor to his ornate tropes. He was not always hurling suns about, sweeping the skies with orchids, strange gods and exotic stars. His extravagances, partly temperamental, partly climatic, are Californian—as he intended them to be. He was not at ease when attempting to curb his grandiose periods; but a few of his simpler verses, though not in his most familiar vein, show what Sterling might have accomplished with more discipline. The least memorable poems are not without a redeeming line.

A comprehensive *Selected Poems* was published in 1923.

### THE BLACK VULTURE

Aloof upon the day's immeasured dome,
    He holds unshared the silence of the sky.
    Far down his bleak, relentless eyes descry
The eagle's empire and the falcon's home—
Far down, the galleons of sunset roam;
    His hazards on the sea of morning lie;
    Serene, he hears the broken tempest sigh
Where cold sierras gleam like scattered foam.

And least of all he holds the human swarm—
    Unwitting now that envious men prepare
    To make their dream and its fulfillment one,
When, poised above the caldrons of the storm,
    Their hearts, contemptuous of death, shall dare
    His roads between the thunder and the sun.

### THE MASTER MARINER

My grandsire sailed three years from home
  And slew unmoved the sounding whale:
Here on a windless beach I roam
  And watch far out the hardy sail.

The lions of the surf that cry
  Upon this lion-colored shore
On reefs of midnight met his eye:
  He knew their fangs as I their roar.

My grandsire sailed uncharted seas,
  And toll of all their leagues he took:
I scan the shallow bays at ease,
  And tell their colors in a book.

The anchor-chains his music made
  And wind in shrouds and running-gear:

The thrush at dawn beguiles my glade,
  And once, 'tis said, I woke to hear.

My grandsire in his ample fist
  The long harpoon upheld to men:
Behold obedient to my wrist
  A gray gull's-feather for my pen!

Upon my grandsire's leathern cheek
  Five zones their bitter bronze had set:
Some day their hazards I will seek,
  I promise me at times. Not yet.

I think my grandsire now would turn
  A mild but speculative eye
On me, my pen and its concern,
  Then gaze again to sea—and sigh.

## THE NIGHT OF GODS

Their mouths have drunken the eternal wine—
The draught that Baal in oblivion sips.
Unseen about their courts the adder slips,
Unheard the sucklings of the leopard whine;
The toad has found a resting-place divine,
And bloats in stupor between Ammon's lips.
O Carthage and the unreturning ships,
The fallen pinnacle, the shifting Sign!

Lo! when I hear from voiceless court and fane
Time's adoration of eternity,—
The cry of kingdoms past and gods undone,—
I stand as one whose feet at noontide gain
A lonely shore; who feels his soul set free,
And hears the blind sea chanting to the sun.

## *Edwin Arlington Robinson*

EDWIN ARLINGTON ROBINSON was born December 22, 1869, in the village of Head Tide, Maine. When he was still a child, the Robinson family moved to the near-by town of Gardiner, which figures in Robinson's poetry as "Tilbury Town." In 1891 he entered Harvard College, but left in 1893. A little collection of verse (*The Torrent and the Night Before*) was privately printed in 1896 and the following year much of it was incorporated with other work in *The Children of the Night* (1897).

Somewhat later, Robinson was struggling in various capacities to make a living in New York, five years passing before the publication of *Captain Craig* (1902). This richly detailed narrative, recalling Browning's method, increased Robinson's audience, and his work was brought to the attention of Theodore Roosevelt (then President of the United States), who became interested in the poet, at the time earning a living as an inspector in the New York Subway, then in course of construction. In 1904, President Roosevelt offered him a clerkship in the New York Custom House. Robinson held this position from 1905 to 1910, leaving it the same year which marked the appearance of his volume, *The Town Down the River*. Robinson's three books, up to this time, showed his clean, firmly drawn quality, but, in spite of their excellences, they seem little more than a succession of preludes for the dynamic volume that was to establish him in the first rank of American poets. *The Man Against the Sky,* in many ways Robinson's fullest and most penetrating work, appeared in 1916. This was followed by *The Three Taverns* (1920), a less arresting but equally concentrated, many voiced collection of poems.

In all these books there is manifest a searching for the light beyond illusion. But Robinson's transcendentalism is no mere emotional escape; his temper subjects the slightest phrase to critical analysis, his intuitions are supported—or scrutinized—by a vigorous intellectuality. Purely as a psychological portrait painter, Robinson has given American literature an entire gallery of memorable figures: Richard Cory, who "glittered when he walked," gnawing his dark heart while he fluttered pulses with his apparent good fortune; Miniver Cheevy, frustrate dreamer, sighing "for what was not"; Aaron Stark, the miser with eyes "like little dollars in the dark"; the nameless mother in "The Gift of God," transmuting her mediocrity of a son into a shining demigod; Bewick Finzer, the wreck of wealth, coming for his pittance, "familiar as an old mistake, and futile as regret," Luke Havergal, Cliff Klingenhagen, Reuben Bright, Annandale, the tippling Mr. Flood—they persist in the mind more vividly than most living people. Such sympathetic illuminations reveal Robinson's sensitive power, especially in his projection of the apparent failures of life. Indeed, much of Robinson's work seems a protest, a criticism by implication, of that type of standardized success which so much of the world worships. Frustration and defeat are like an organ-point heard below the varying music of his verse; failure is almost glorified in his pages.

Technically, Robinson is as precise as he is dexterous. He is, in company with Frost, a master of the slowly diminished ending. But he is capable of cadences as rich as that which ends "The Gift of God," as pungent as the climax of "Calvary," as brilliantly fanciful as the sestet of his sonnet, "The Sheaves," as muted but sustained as the finale of "Eros Turannos" which might have been composed by a more controlled Swinburne.

There is never a false image or a blurred line in any of these verses which, while adhering to the strictest models and executed according to traditional forms, are always fresh and surprising. It is interesting to observe how the smoothness of his rhymes, playing against the hard outlines of his verse, emphasizes the epigrammatic strength of poems like "The Gift of God," that magnificent modern ballad "John Gorham," "For a Dead Lady," and "The Master," one of the finest evocations of Lincoln which is, at the same time, a bitter commentary on the commercialism of the times and the "shopman's test of age and worth."

Robinson's blank verse is scarcely less individual. It is astringent, personal, packed with the instant. In "Ben Jonson Entertains a Man from Stratford" we have the clearest and most human portrait of Shakespeare ever attempted; the lines run as fluently as good conversation, as inevitably as a perfect melody. In his reanimations of the Arthurian legends, *Merlin* (1917), *Launcelot* (1920), *Tristram* (1927), Robinson, shaming the tea-table idyls of Tennyson, has colored the tale with somber reflections of the collapse of old orders, the darkness of an age in ashes.

*Avon's Harvest,* which the author has called "a dime novel in verse," a study of a fear-haunted, hate-driven man, appeared in 1921. In the same year the Macmillan Company issued his *Collected Poems,* which received the Pulitzer Prize for 1921 and which was enlarged in 1929. Subsequent volumes strengthened his admirers' convictions and disproved any fears that Robinson might have "written himself out." *Roman Bartholow* (1923) is a single poem of almost two hundred pages; a dramatic and introspective narrative in blank verse. *The Man Who Died Twice* (1924), which was awarded the Pulitzer Prize for that year, is likewise one long poem: a tale which is a cross between a grotesque recital and inspired metaphysics. Curiously enough, the mixture is one of Robinson's greatest triumphs; none of his portraits, either miniatures or full-length canvases, has given us a profounder insight of a tortured soul than this of Fernando Nash, "the king who lost his crown before he had it."

*Dionysus in Doubt* (1925) begins and ends with a caustic arraignment of our mechanistic civilization, and is primarily a scornful and carefully premeditated condemnation of the Eighteenth Amendment, an attack which never descends to polemics or political diatribe. Robinson's ironic accents lift every phrase above the argumentative matter; the darkest of his doubts are illumined by "the salvage of a smile." Besides two other longish poems, this volume includes eighteen sonnets which again display Robinson's supremacy in the form. Time and again, he packs huge scenes into fourteen lines; if sonnets can assume the proportion of dramatic narratives, Robinson's have achieved the almost impossible feat.

Possibly the fact that Robinson had already won the Pulitzer Prize twice, possibly the increasing interest of his work may have accounted for his increased audience. Not even his most enthusiastic admirers awaited the reception accorded to *Tristram* (1927). Adopted by the most prominent book-club as its "book-of-the-month," awarded unstinted praise and the Pulitzer Prize for the third time, it outsold most "best-selling" novels. This was something of a phenomenon, for *Tristram* was not only a single poem of over forty thousand words, it was Robinson's most intricate and knotted work. But it was no mere problem in involution; Robinson, as though reacting against the charge of Puritanism, abandoned himself to a drama passionate and headlong.

*Cavender's House* (1929) was scarcely less esteemed. Formerly regarded as a poet's poet, the later volumes established Robinson in popular favor, no matter from what epoch he chose his theme. *Tristram* was medieval, *Cavender's House* was modern. Like *Avon's Harvest* and *Roman Bartholow,* the latter was melodrama glorified, but sharper and tenser than its predecessors. Both renewed the inevitable—and false—comparisons. Robinson's manner was likened to Browning's, his matter (particularly in the Arthurian tales) to Tennyson's. The comparison to Browning, though superficial and inaccurate, is at least comprehensible. The author of *Merlin,* like the author of *Sordello,* delights in subtly psychological portraiture, in the half-withheld inner drama, in the shift of suspensions and nuances of tension. But where Browning is forthright, Robinson is tangential; where Browning is lavish with imagery and flaring interjections, Robinson is sparse in metaphor and so economic with words that almost every phrase seems twisted and wrung of everything except its essential meaning. But the principal dissimilarity lies in their *Weltanschauung;* here they are diametrically opposed. Where Browning regards the universe compact of sweetness and light, Robinson observes a scheme whose chief components are bitterness and blight; the realm where "God's in his heaven, all's right with the world" becomes (as in the significantly entitled *The Man Against the Sky*) a place where

> He may go forward like a stoic Roman
> Where pangs and terrors in his pathway lie—
> Or, seizing the swift logic of a woman,
> Curse God and die.

Although Robinson was accused of holding consistently a negative attitude toward life, his poetry reveals a restless, uncertain, but persistent search for moral values. This quest—and questioning—of ultimates runs through his work as it ran through an age no longer satisfied with arid skepticism. It is significant that the same year which disclosed Eliot turning to a faith beyond intellect showed Robinson driving past reason to find

> . . . There must be God; or if not God, a purpose and a law.

The conclusion of his sonnet to Crabbe might well be applied to him:

> Whether or not we read him, we can feel
> From time to time the vigor of his name
> Against us like a finger for the shame
> And emptiness of what our souls reveal
> In books that are as altars where we kneel
> To consecrate the flicker, not the flame.

After 1928 Robinson's poetry tended to become repetitious and prolix. Writing for an income and fearing the future, he felt it incumbent upon him to write an annual volume. Each year for seven years, until the very month of his death, he planned and issued a narrative poem in which personal as well as physical fatigue was increasingly evident. *The Glory of the Nightingales* (1930) is a melancholy tragedy which suffers from dryness of thought and atrophy of emotion. *Matthias at the Door* (1931) is another gloomy study which exhibits the author's narrowing limitations—the dark, deliberate idiom spoken indiscriminately by all the characters, the lack of life in any of the *dramatis personae* who function only as disembodied intellects in a state of continually painful thought, and a sense of hopeless defeatism. *Nicodemus* (1932) attempts to revive earlier spirits, but the summoned Annandale, Ponce de Leon, and Toussaint L'Ouverture are little more than garrulous ghosts. *Talifer* (1933) is far better, the happiest and most teasing of Robinson's longer poems, an unexpected blend of wisdom and wicked irony. *Amaranth* (1934) is another nightmare narrative of deluded failures and dream-ridden mediocrities. Unfortunately the poem, for all its dramatic possibilities, is wholly without drama, and it is difficult to tell whether Robinson is sympathizing with his lost shadows or satirizing them. The theme of frustration is continued in the posthumous *King Jasper* (1935) which was introduced with a shrewd analysis of "new ways of being new" by Robert Frost; unfortunately *King Jasper* is an involved and dubious allegory.

Subsequent to 1911 Robinson lived most of his summers at Peterborough, New Hampshire, at the MacDowell Colony, of which he was the unofficial but acknowledged presiding genius. He divided his winters between New York and Boston until ill health forced him to forego travel of any sort. His last winter in Boston was full of suffering, chiefly due to a growth in the pancreas, and when he was taken to the New York Hospital he was in a pitifully weakened condition. It was impossible to operate successfully and he died there April 6, 1935.

Upon his death there were the inevitable belated tributes to an unhappy poet and a lonely man. The most eloquent of them was Robinson Jeffers' spontaneous response. "I cannot speak of E. A. Robinson's work," wrote Jeffers. "Better critics than I have praised its qualities, and will again. Let me notice instead the debt we owe him for the qualities of his life; for the dignity with which he wore his fame, for the example of his reticence and steady concentration, for the single-mindedness with which he followed his own sense of direction, unbewildered and undiverted. . . . We are grateful that he was not what they call 'a good showman,' but gave himself to his work, not to his audience, and would have preferred complete failure to any success with the least taint of charlatanry." It was this undeviating integrity which carried him through his difficulties, the very integrity which made him turn out too much work in return for the small income he received and won him the admiration of all his contemporaries, irrespective of their preferences or poetic affiliations.

## MINIVER CHEEVY

Miniver Cheevy, child of scorn,
  Grew lean while he assailed the seasons;
He wept that he was ever born,
  And he had reasons.

Miniver loved the days of old
  When swords were bright and steeds were
    prancing;
The vision of a warrior bold
  Would set him dancing.

Miniver sighed for what was not,
  And dreamed, and rested from his labors;
He dreamed of Thebes and Camelot,
  And Priam's neighbors.

Miniver mourned the ripe renown
  That made so many a name so fragrant;
He mourned Romance, now on the town,
  And Art, a vagrant.

Miniver loved the Medici,
  Albeit he had never seen one;
He would have sinned incessantly
  Could he have been one.

Miniver cursed the commonplace
  And eyed a khaki suit with loathing;
He missed the medieval grace
  Of iron clothing.

Miniver scorned the gold he sought,
  But sore annoyed was he without it;
Miniver thought, and thought, and thought,
  And thought about it.

Miniver Cheevy, born too late,
  Scratched his head and kept on thinking;
Miniver coughed, and called it fate,
  And kept on drinking.

## CLIFF KLINGENHAGEN

Cliff Klingenhagen had me in to dine
With him one day; and after soup and meat,
And all the other things there were to eat,
Cliff took two glasses and filled one with wine
And one with wormwood. Then, without a sign
For me to choose at all, he took the draught
Of bitterness himself, and lightly quaffed
It off, and said the other one was mine.

And when I asked him what the deuce he meant
By doing that, he only looked at me
And grinned, and said it was a way of his.
And though I know the fellow, I have spent
Long time a-wondering when I shall be
As happy as Cliff Klingenhagen is.

### THE HOUSE ON THE HILL

They are all gone away,
　The House is shut and still,
There is nothing more to say.

Through broken walls and gray
　The winds blow bleak and shrill;
They are all gone away.

Nor is there one today
　To speak them good or ill:
There is nothing more to say.

Why is it then we stray
　Around that sunken sill?
They are all gone away,

And our poor fancy-play
　For them is wasted skill:
There is nothing more to say.

There is ruin and decay
　In the House on the Hill:
They are all gone away,
There is nothing more to say.

### AN OLD STORY

Strange that I did not know him then,
　That friend of mine.
I did not even show him then
　One friendly sign;

But cursed him for the ways he had
　To make me see
My envy of the praise he had
　For praising me.

I would have rid the earth of him
　Once, in my pride.
I never knew the worth of him
　Until he died.

### RICHARD CORY

Whenever Richard Cory went down town,
　We people on the pavement looked at him:
He was a gentleman from sole to crown,
　Clean favored, and imperially slim.

And he was always quietly arrayed,
　And he was always human when he talked;
But still he fluttered pulses when he said,
　"Good-morning," and he glittered when he walked.

And he was rich—yes, richer than a king—
　And admirably schooled in every grace:
In fine, we thought that he was everything
　To make us wish that we were in his place.

So on we worked, and waited for the light,
　And went without the meat, and cursed the bread;
And Richard Cory, one calm summer night,
　Went home and put a bullet through his head.

### BEWICK FINZER

Time was when his half million drew
　The breath of six per cent;
But soon the worm of what-was-not
　Fed hard on his content;
And something crumbled in his brain
　When his half million went.

Time passed, and filled along with his
　The place of many more;
Time came, and hardly one of us
　Had credence to restore,
From what appeared one day, the man
　Whom we had known before.

The broken voice, the withered neck,
　The coat worn out with care,

he cleanliness of indigence,
  The brilliance of despair,
he fond imponderable dreams
  Of affluence,—all were there.

oor Finzer, with his dreams and schemes,
  Fares hard now in the race,
Vith heart and eye that have a task
  When he looks in the face

Of one who might so easily
  Have been in Finzer's place.

He comes unfailing for the loan
  We give and then forget;
He comes, and probably for years
  Will he be coming yet,—
Familiar as an old mistake,
  And futile as regret.

## REUBEN BRIGHT

Because he was a butcher and thereby
Did earn an honest living (and did right)
I would not have you think that Reuben Bright
Was any more a brute than you or I;
For when they told him that his wife must die,
He stared at them and shook with grief and fright,
And cried like a great baby half that night,
And made the women cry to see him cry.

And after she was dead, and he had paid
The singers and the sexton and the rest,
He packed a lot of things that she had made
Most mournfully away in an old chest
Of hers, and put some chopped-up cedar boughs
In with them, and tore down the slaughter-house.

## FOR A DEAD LADY

No more with overflowing light
Shall fill the eyes that now are faded,
Nor shall another's fringe with night
Their woman-hidden world as they did.
No more shall quiver down the days
The flowing wonder of her ways,
Whereof no language may requite
The shifting and the many-shaded.

The grace, divine, definitive,
Clings only as a faint forestalling;
The laugh that love could not forgive
s hushed, and answers to no calling;

The forehead and the little ears
Have gone where Saturn keeps the years;
The breast where roses could not live
Has done with rising and with falling.

The beauty, shattered by the laws
That have creation in their keeping,
No longer trembles at applause,
Or over children that are sleeping;
And we who delve in beauty's lore
Know all that we have known before
Of what inexorable cause
Makes Time so vicious in his reaping.

## CALVARY

Friendless and faint, with martyred steps and slow,
Faint for the flesh, but for the spirit free,
Stung by the mob that came to see the show,
The Master toiled along to Calvary;
We gibed him, as he went, with houndish glee,
Till his dimmed eyes for us did overflow;

We cursed his vengeless hands thrice wretchedly,—
And this was nineteen hundred years ago.
But after nineteen hundred years the shame
Still clings, and we have not made good the loss
That outraged faith has entered in his name.
Ah, when shall come love's courage to be strong!
Tell me, O Lord—tell me, O Lord, how long
Are we to keep Christ writhing on the cross!

## VICKERY'S MOUNTAIN

Blue in the west the mountain stands,
  And through the long twilight
Vickery sits with folded hands,
  And Vickery's eyes are bright.

Bright, for he knows what no man else
  On earth as yet may know:
There's a golden word that he never tells,
  And a gift that he will not show.

He dreams of honor and wealth and fame,
  He smiles, and well he may;
For to Vickery once a sick man came
  Who did not go away.

The day before the day to be,
  "Vickery," said the guest,
"You know as you live what's left of me—
  And you shall know the rest.

"You know as you live that I have come
  To what we call the end.
No doubt you have found me troublesome,
  But you've also found a friend;

"For we shall give and you shall take
  The gold that is in view;
The mountain there and I shall make
  A golden man of you.

"And you shall leave a friend behind
  Who neither frets nor feels;
And you shall move among your kind
  With hundreds at your heels.

"Now this I have written here
  Tells all that need be told;
So, Vickery, take the way that's clear,
  And be a man of gold."

Vickery turned his eyes again
  To the far mountain-side,
And wept a tear for worthy men
  Defeated and defied.

Since then a crafty score of years
  Have come, and they have gone;
But Vickery counts no lost arrears:
  He lingers and lives on.

Blue in the west the mountain stands,
  Familiar as a face,
Blue, but Vickery knows what sands
  Are golden at its base.

He dreams and lives upon the day
  When he shall walk with kings.
Vickery smiles—and well he may:
  The life-caged linnet sings.

Vickery thinks the time will come
  To go for what is his;
But hovering, unseen hands at home
  Will hold him where he is.

There's a golden word that he never tells
  And a gift that he will not show.
All to be given to someone else—
  And Vickery shall not know.

## TOO MUCH COFFEE

Together in infinite shade
  They defy the invincible dawn:
The Measure that never was made,
  The Line that never was drawn.

## THE MASTER

(*Lincoln. Supposed to have been written no*
  *long after the Civil War*)

A flying word from here and there
Had sown the name at which we sneered,
But soon the name was everywhere,
To be reviled and then revered:

A presence to be loved and feared,
We cannot hide it, or deny
That we, the gentlemen who jeered,
May be forgotten by and by.

He came when days were perilous
And hearts of men were sore beguiled;
And having made his note of us,
He pondered and was reconciled.
Was ever master yet so mild
As he, and so untamable?
We doubted, even when he smiled,
Not knowing what he knew so well.

He knew that undeceiving fate
Would shame us whom he served unsought;
He knew that he must wince and wait—
The jest of those for whom he fought;
He knew devoutly what he thought
Of us and of our ridicule;
He knew that we must all be taught
Like little children in a school.

We gave a glamour to the task
That he encountered and saw through,
But little of us did he ask,
And little did we ever do.
And what appears if we review
The season when we railed and chaffed?
It is the face of one who knew
That we were learning while we laughed.

The face that in our vision feels
Again the venom that we flung,
Transfigured to the world reveals
The vigilance to which we clung.
Shrewd, hallowed, harassed, and among
The mysteries that are untold,
The face we see was never young,
Nor could it ever have been old.

For he, to whom we had applied
Our shopman's test of age and worth,
Was elemental when he died,
As he was ancient at his birth:
The saddest among kings of earth,
Bowed with a galling crown, this man
Met rancor with a cryptic mirth,
Laconic—and Olympian.

The love, the grandeur, and the fame
Are bounded by the world alone;
The calm, the smoldering, and the flame
Of awful patience were his own:
With him they are forever flown
Past all our fond self-shadowings,
Wherewith we cumber the Unknown
As with inept Icarian wings.

For we were not as other men:
'Twas ours to soar and his to see.
But we are coming down again,
And we shall come down pleasantly;
Nor shall we longer disagree
On what it is to be sublime,
But flourish in our perigee
And have one Titan at a time.

## MR. FLOOD'S PARTY

Old Eben Flood, climbing alone one night
Over the hill between the town below
And the forsaken upland hermitage
That held as much as he should ever know
On earth again of home, paused warily.
The road was his with not a native near;
And Eben, having leisure, said aloud,
For no man else in Tilbury Town to hear:

"Well, Mr. Flood, we have the harvest moon
Again, and we may not have many more;
The bird is on the wing, the poet says,
And you and I have said it here before.
Drink to the bird." He raised up to the light
The jug that he had gone so far to fill,

And answered huskily: "Well, Mr. Flood,
Since you propose it, I believe I will."

Alone, as if enduring to the end
A valiant armor of scarred hopes outworn,
He stood there in the middle of the road
Like Roland's ghost winding a silent horn.
Below him, in the town among the trees,
Where friends of other days had honored him,
A phantom salutation of the dead
Rang thinly till old Eben's eyes were dim.

Then, as a mother lays her sleeping child
Down tenderly, fearing it may awake,
He set the jug down slowly at his feet
With trembling care, knowing that most things break;
And only when assured that on firm earth
It stood, as the uncertain lives of men
Assuredly did not, he paced away,
And with his hand extended paused again:

"Well, Mr. Flood, we have not met like this
In a long time; and many a change has come
To both of us, I fear, since last it was
We had a drop together. Welcome home!"
Convivially returning with himself,
Again he raised the jug up to the light;
And with an acquiescent quaver said:
"Well, Mr. Flood, if you insist, I might.

"Only a very little, Mr. Flood—
For auld lang syne. No more, sir; that will do."
So, for the time, apparently it did,
And Eben evidently thought so too;
For soon amid the silver loneliness
Of night he lifted up his voice and sang,
Secure, with only two moons listening,
Until the whole harmonious landscape rang—

"For auld lang syne." The weary throat gave out,
The last word wavered; and the song being done,
He raised again the jug regretfully
And shook his head, and was again alone.
There was not much that was ahead of him,
And there was nothing in the town below—
Where strangers would have shut the many doors
That many friends had opened long ago.

### GEORGE CRABBE

Give him the darkest inch your shelf allows,
Hide him in lonely garrets, if you will,—

But his hard, human pulse is throbbing still
With the sure strength that fearless truth endows.
In spite of all fine science disavows,
Of his plain excellence and stubborn skill
There yet remains what fashion cannot kill,
Though years have thinned the laurel from his brows.

Whether or not we read him, we can feel
From time to time the vigor of his name
Against us like a finger for the shame
And emptiness of what our souls reveal
In books that are as altars where we kneel
To consecrate the flicker, not the flame.

### LUKE HAVERGAL

Go to the western gate, Luke Havergal,
There where the vines cling crimson on the wall,
And in the twilight wait for what will come.
The leaves will whisper there of her, and some,
Like flying words, will strike you as they fall;
But go, and if you listen, she will call.
Go to the western gate, Luke Havergal—
Luke Havergal.

No, there is not a dawn in eastern skies
To rift the fiery night that's in your eyes;
But there, where western glooms are gathering,
The dark will end the dark, if anything:
God slays himself with every leaf that flies,
And hell is more than half of paradise.
No, there is not a dawn in eastern skies—
In eastern skies.

Out of a grave I come to tell you this,
Out of a grave I come to quench the kiss
That flames upon your forehead with a glow
That blinds you to the way that you must go.
Yes, there is yet one way to where she is,
Bitter, but one that faith may never miss.
Out of a grave I come to tell you this—
To tell you this.

There is the western gate, Luke Havergal,
There are the crimson leaves upon the wall.
Go, for the winds are tearing them away,—
Nor think to riddle the dead words they say,
Nor any more to feel them as they fall;
But go, and if you trust her she will call.
There is the western gate, Luke Havergal—
Luke Havergal.

### JOHN GORHAM

"Tell me what you're doing over here, John Gorham,
 Sighing hard and seeming to be sorry when you're not;
 Make me laugh or let me go now, for long faces in the moonlight
 Are a sign for me to say again a word that you forgot."—

"I'm over here to tell you what the moon already
 May have said or maybe shouted ever since a year ago;
 I'm over here to tell you what you are, Jane Wayland,
 And to make you rather sorry, I should say, for being so."—

"Tell me what you're saying to me now, John Gorham,
 Or you'll never see as much of me as ribbons any more;
 I'll vanish in as many ways as I have toes and fingers,
 And you'll not follow far for one where flocks have been before."—

"I'm sorry now you never saw the flocks, Jane Wayland,
 But you're the one to make of them as many as you need.
 And then about the vanishing: It's I who mean to vanish;
 And when I'm here no longer you'll be done with me indeed."—

"That's a way to tell me what I am, John Gorham!
 How am I to know myself until I make you smile?
 Try to look as if the moon were making faces at you,
 And a little more as if you meant to stay a little while."—

"You are what it is that over rose-blown gardens
 Makes a pretty flutter for a season in the sun;
 You are what it is that with a mouse, Jane Wayland,
 Catches him and lets him go and eats him up for fun."—

"Sure I never took you for a mouse, John Gorham;
 All you say is easy, but so far from being true,
 That I wish you wouldn't ever be again the one to think so;
 For it isn't cats and butterflies that I would be to you."—

"All your little animals are in one picture—
 One I've had before me since a year ago tonight;
 And the picture where they live will be of you, Jane Wayland,
 Till you find a way to kill them or to keep them out of sight."—

"Won't you ever see me as I am, John Gorham,
 Leaving out the foolishness and all I never meant?
 Somewhere in me there's a woman, if you know the way to find her.
 Will you like me any better if I prove it and repent?"—

"I doubt if I shall ever have the time, Jane Wayland;
 And I dare say all this moonlight lying round us might as well
 Fall for nothing on the shards of broken urns that are forgotten,
 As on two that have no longer much of anything to tell."

### HOW ANNANDALE WENT OUT

"They called it Annandale—and I was there
To flourish, to find words, and to attend:
Liar, physician, hypocrite, and friend,
I watched him; and the sight was not so fair
As one or two that I have seen elsewhere:
An apparatus not for me to mend—
A wreck, with hell between him and the end,
Remained of Annandale; and I was there.

"I knew the ruin as I knew the man;
So put the two together, if you can,
Remembering the worst you know of me.
Now view yourself as I was, on the spot,
With a slight kind of engine. Do you see?
Like this . . . You wouldn't hang me? I thought not."

### THE FIELD OF GLORY

ar shook the land where Levi dwelt,
d fired the dismal wrath he felt,
at such a doom was ever wrought
his, to toil while others fought;
toil, to dream—and still to dream,
ith one day barren as another;
consummate, as it would seem,
e dry despair of his old mother.

off one afternoon began
e sound of man destroying man;
d Levi, sick with nameless rage,
ndemned again his heritage,
d sighed for scars that might have come,
d would, if once he could have sundered
ose harsh, inhering claims of home
at held him while he cursed and wondered.

other day, and then there came,
ugh, bloody, ribald, hungry, lame,
yet themselves, to Levi's door,
o remnants of the day before.
ey laughed at him and what he sought;
ey jeered him and his painful acre;
Levi knew that they had fought,
d left their manners to their Maker.

That night, for the grim widow's ears,
With hopes that hid themselves in fears,
He told of arms, and fiery deeds,
Whereat one leaps the while he reads,
And said he'd be no more a clown,
While others drew the breath of battle.
The mother looked him up and down,
And laughed—a scant laugh with a rattle.

She told him what she found to tell,
And Levi listened, and heard well
Some admonitions of a voice
That left him no cause to rejoice.—
He sought a friend, and found the stars,
And prayed aloud that they should aid him;
But they said not a word of wars,
Or of a reason why God made him.

And who's of this or that estate
We do not wholly calculate,
When baffling shades that shift and cling
Are not without their glimmering;
When even Levi, tired of faith,
Beloved of none, forgot by many,
Dismissed as an inferior wraith,
Reborn may be as great as any.

### THE CLERKS

I did not think that I should find them there
When I came back again; but there they stood,
As in the days they dreamed of when young blood
Was in their cheeks and women called them fair.
Be sure they met me with an ancient air,—
And yes, there was a shop-worn brotherhood
About them; but the men were just as good,
And just as human as they ever were.

And you that ache so much to be sublime,
And you that feed yourselves with your descent,
What comes of all your visions and your fears?
Poets and kings are but the clerks of Time,
Tiering the same dull webs of discontent,
Clipping the same sad alnage of the years.

### THE DARK HILLS

Dark hills at evening in the west,
Where sunset hovers like a sound
Of golden horns that sang to rest
Old bones of warriors under ground,
Far now from all the bannered ways
Where flash the legions of the sun,
You fade—as if the last of days
Were fading and all wars were done.

### EROS TURANNOS

She fears him, and will always ask
  What fated her to choose him;
She meets in his engaging mask
  All reasons to refuse him;
But what she meets and what she fears
Are less than are the downward years,
Drawn slowly to the foamless weirs
  Of age, were she to lose him.

Between a blurred sagacity
  That once had power to sound him,
And Love, that will not let him be
  The Judas that she found him,
Her pride assuages her almost,
As if it were alone the cost.
He sees that he will not be lost,
  And waits and looks around him.

A sense of ocean and old trees
  Envelops and allures him;

Tradition, touching all he sees,
  Beguiles and reassures him;
And all her doubts of what he says
Are dimmed with what she knows of days
Till even prejudice delays
  And fades, and she secures him.

The falling leaf inaugurates
  The reign of her confusion;
The pounding wave reverberates
  The dirge of her illusion;
And home, where passion lived and died,
Becomes a place where she can hide,
While all the town and harbor-side
  Vibrate with her seclusion.

We tell you, tapping on our brows,
  The story as it should be,
As if the story of a house
  Were told, or ever could be;
We'll have no kindly veil between
Her visions and those we have seen,—
As if we guessed what hers have been,
  Or what they are or would be.

Meanwhile we do no harm; for they
  That with a god have striven,
Not hearing much of what we say,
  Take what the god has given;
Though like waves breaking it may be,
Or like a changed familiar tree,
Or like a stairway to the sea
  Where down the blind are driven.

### THE SHEAVES

Where long the shadows of the wind had rolled,
Green wheat was yielding to the change assigned;
And as by some vast magic undivined
The world was turning slowly into gold.
Like nothing that was ever bought or sold
It waited there, the body and the mind;
And with a mighty meaning of a kind
That tells the more the more it is not told.

So in a land where all days are not fair,
Fair days went on till on another day
A thousand golden sheaves were lying there,
Shining and still, but not for long to stay—
As if a thousand girls with golden hair
Might rise from where they slept and go away.

### BEN JONSON ENTERTAINS A MAN FROM STRATFORD

You are a friend then, as I make it out,
Of our man Shakespeare, who alone of us
Will put an ass's head in Fairyland
As he would add a shilling to more shillings,
All most harmonious—and out of his
Miraculous inviolable increase
Fills Ilion, Rome, or any town you like
Of olden time with timeless Englishmen;
And I must wonder what you think of him—
All you down there where your small Avon flows
By Stratford, and where you're an Alderman.
Some, for a guess, would have him riding back
To be a farrier there, or say a dyer;
Or maybe one of your adept surveyors;
Or like enough the wizard of all tanners.
Not you—no fear of that; for I discern
In you a kindling of the flame that saves—
The nimble element, the true caloric;
I see it, and was told of it, moreover,
By our discriminate friend himself, no other.
Had you been one of the sad average,
As he would have it—meaning, as I take it,
The sinew and the solvent of our Island,
You'd not be buying beer for this Terpander's
Approved and estimated friend Ben Jonson;
He'd never foist it as a part of his
Contingent entertainment of a townsman
While he goes off rehearsing, as he must,
If he shall ever be the Duke of Stratford.
And my words are no shadow on your town—

Far from it; for one town's like another
As all are unlike London. Oh, he knows it—
And there's the Stratford in him; he denies it,
And there's the Shakespeare in him. So, God help him!

I tell him he needs Greek; but neither God
Nor Greek will help him. Nothing will help that man.
You see the fates have given him so much,
He must have all or perish—or look out
Of London, where he sees too many lords.
They're part of half what ails him: I suppose
There's nothing fouler down among the demons
Than what it is he feels when he remembers
The dust and sweat and ointment of his calling
With his lords looking on and laughing at him.
King as he is, he can't be king *de facto*,
And that's as well, because he wouldn't like it;
He'd frame a lower rating of men then
Than he has now; and after that would come
An abdication or an apoplexy.
He can't be king, not even king of Stratford—
Though half the world, if not the whole of it,
May crown him with a crown that fits no king
Save Lord Apollo's homesick emissary:
Not there on Avon, or on any stream
Where Naiads and their white arms are no more
Shall he find home again. It's all too bad.
But there's a comfort, for he'll have that House—
The best you ever saw; and he'll be there
Anon, as you're an Alderman. Good God!
He makes me lie awake o' nights and laugh.

And you have known him from his origin,
You tell me; and a most uncommon urchin
He must have been to the few seeing ones—
A trifle terrifying, I dare say,
Discovering a world with his man's eyes,
Quite as another lad might see some finches,
If he looked hard and had an eye for Nature.
But this one had his eyes and their foretelling,
And he had you to fare with, and what else?
He must have had a father and a mother—
In fact I've heard him say so—and a dog,
As a boy should, I venture; and the dog,
Most likely, was the only man who knew him.
A dog, for all I know, is what he needs
As much as anything right here today,
To counsel him about his disillusions,
Old aches, and parturitions of what's coming—
A dog of orders, an emeritus,
To wag his tail at him when he comes home,

And then to put his paws up on his knees
And say, "For God's sake, what's it all about?"

I don't know whether he needs a dog or not—
Or what he needs. I tell him he needs Greek;
I'll talk of rules and Aristotle with him,
And if his tongue's at home he'll say to that,
"I have your word that Aristotle knows,
And you mine that I don't know Aristotle."
He's all at odds with all the unities,
And what's yet worse it doesn't seem to matter;
He treads along through Time's old wilderness
As if the tramp of all the centuries
Had left no roads—and there are none, for him;
He doesn't see them, even with those eyes—
And that's a pity, or I say it is.
Accordingly we have him as we have him—
Going his way, the way that he goes best,
A pleasant animal with no great noise
Or nonsense anywhere to set him off—
Save only divers and inclement devils
Have made of late his heart their dwelling-place.
A flame half ready to fly out sometimes
At some annoyance may be fanned up in him,
But soon it falls, and when it falls goes out;
He knows how little room there is in there
For crude and futile animosities,
And how much for the joy of being whole,
And how much for long sorrow and old pain.
On our side there are some who may be given
To grow old wondering what he thinks of us
And some above us, who are, in his eyes,
Above himself—and that's quite right and English.
Yet here we smile, or disappoint the gods
Who made it so; the gods have always eyes
To see men scratch; and they see one down here
Who itches, manor-bitten, to the bone,
Albeit he knows himself—yes, yes, he knows—
The lord of more than England and of more
Than all the seas of England in all time
Shall ever wash. D'ye wonder that I laugh?
He sees me, and he doesn't seem to care;
And why the devil should he? I can't tell you.
I'll meet him out alone of a bright Sunday,
Trim, rather spruce, and quite the gentleman.
"What, ho, my lord!" say I. He doesn't hear me;
Wherefore I have to pause and look at him.
He's not enormous, but one looks at him.
A little on the round if you insist,
For now, God save the mark, he's growing old;
He's five and forty, and to hear him talk

These days you'd call him eighty; then you'd add
More years to that. He's old enough to be
The father of a world, and so he is.
"Ben, you're a scholar, what's the time of day?"
Says he; and there shines out of him again
An aged light that has no age or station—
The mystery that's his—a mischievous
Half-mad serenity that laughs at fame
For being won so easy, and at friends
Who laugh at him for what he wants the most,
And for his dukedom down in Warwickshire;—
By which you see we're all a little jealous. . . .
Poor Greene! I fear the color of his name
Was even as that of his ascending soul;
And he was one where there are many others—
Some scrivening to the end against their fate,
Their puppets all in ink and all to die there;
And some with hands that once would shade an eye
That scanned Euripides and Aeschylus
Will reach by this time for a pot-house mop
To slush their first and last of royalties.
Poor devils! and they all play to his hand;
For so it was in Athens and old Rome.
But that's not here or there; I've wandered off.
Greene does it, or I'm careful. Where's that boy?

Yes, he'll go back to Stratford. And we'll miss him?
Dear sir, there'll be no London here without him.
We'll all be riding, one of these fine days,
Down there to see him—and his wife won't like us;
And then we'll think of what he never said
Of women—which, if taken all in all
With what he did say, would buy many horses.
Though ·nowadays he's not so much for women.
"So few of them," he says, "are worth the guessing."
But there's a worm at work when he says that,
And while he says it one feels in the air
A deal of circumambient hocus-pocus.
They've had him dancing till his toes were tender,
And he can feel 'em now, come chilly rains.
There's no long cry for going into it,
However, and we don't know much about it.
But you in Stratford, like most here in London,
Have more now in the *Sonnets* than you paid for;
He's put one there with all her poison on,
To make a singing fiction of a shadow
That's in his life a fact, and always will be.
But she's no care of ours, though Time, I fear,
Will have a more reverberant ado
About her than about another one
Who seems to have decoyed him, married him,

And sent him scuttling on his way to London—
With much already learned, and more to learn,
And more to follow. Lord! how I see him now,
Pretending, maybe trying, to be like us.
Whatever he may have meant, we never had him;
He failed us, or escaped, or what you will—
And there was that about him (God knows what—
We'd flayed another had he tried it on us)
That made as many of us as had wits
More fond of all his easy distances
Than one another's noise and clap-your-shoulder.
But think you not, my friend, he'd never talk!
Talk? He was eldritch at it; and we listened—
Thereby acquiring much we knew before
About ourselves, and hitherto had held
Irrelevant, or not prime to the purpose.
And there were some, of course, and there be now,
Disordered and reduced amazedly
To resignation by the mystic seal
Of young finality the gods had laid
On everything that made him a young demon;
And one or two shot looks at him already
As he had been their executioner;
And once or twice he was, not knowing it—
Or knowing, being sorry for poor clay
And saying nothing . . . Yet, for all his engines,
You'll meet a thousand of an afternoon
Who strut and sun themselves and see around 'em
A world made out of more that has a reason
Than his, I swear, that he sees here today;
Though he may scarcely give a Fool an exit
But we mark how he sees in everything
A law that, given that we flout it once too often,
Brings fire and iron down on our naked heads.
To me it looks as if the power that made him,
For fear of giving all things to one creature,
Left out the first—faith, innocence, illusion,
Whatever 'tis that keeps us out o' Bedlam—
And thereby, for his too consuming vision,
Empowered him out of nature; though to see him,
You'd never guess what's going on inside him.
He'll break out some day like a keg of ale
With too much independent frenzy in it;
And all for cellaring what he knows won't keep,
And what he'd best forget—but that he can't.
You'll have it, and have more than I'm foretelling;
And there'll be such a roaring at the Globe
As never stunned the bleeding gladiators.
He'll have to change the color of its hair
A bit, for now he calls it Cleopatra.
Black hair would never do for Cleopatra.

But you and I are not yet two old women,
And you're a man of office. What he does
Is more to you than how it is he does it—
And that's what the Lord God has never told him.
They work together, and the Devil helps 'em;
They do it of a morning, or if not,
They do it of a night; in which event
He's peevish of a morning. He seems old;
He's not the proper stomach or the sleep—
And they're two sovran agents to conserve him
Against the fiery art that has no mercy
But what's in that prodigious grand new House.
I gather something happening in his boyhood
Fulfilled him with a boy's determination
To make all Stratford 'ware of him. Well, well,
I hope at last he'll have his joy of it,
And all his pigs and sheep and bellowing beeves,
And frogs and owls and unicorns, moreover,
Be less than hell to his attendant ears.
Oh, past a doubt we'll all go down to see him.

He may be wise. With London two days off,
Down there some wind of heaven may yet revive him,
But there's no quickening breath from anywhere
Shall make of him again the young poised faun
From Warwickshire, who'd made, it seems, already
A legend of himself before I came
To blink before the last of his first lightning.
Whatever there be, there'll be no more of that;
The coming on of his old monster Time
Has made him a still man; and he has dreams
Were fair to think on once, and all found hollow.
He knows how much of what men paint themselves
Would blister in the light of what they are;
He sees how much of what was great now shares
An eminence transformed and ordinary;
He knows too much of what the world has hushed
In others, to be loud now for himself;
He knows now at what height low enemies
May reach his heart, and high friends let him fall;
But what not even such as he may know
Bedevils him the worst: his lark may sing
At heaven's gate how he will, and for as long
As joy may listen, but *he* sees no gate,
Save one whereat the spent clay waits a little
Before the churchyard has it, and the worm.

Not long ago, late in an afternoon,
I came on him unseen down Lambeth way,
And on my life I was afear'd of him:
He gloomed and mumbled like a soul from Tophet,

His hands behind him and his head bent solemn.
"What is it now," said I, "another woman?"
That made him sorry for me, and he smiled.
"No, Ben," he mused; "it's Nothing. It's all Nothing.
We come, we go; and when we're done, we're done;
Spiders and flies—we're mostly one or t'other—
We come, we go; and when we're done, we're done."
"By God, you sing that song as if you knew it!"
Said I, by way of cheering him; "what ails ye?"
"I think I must have come down here to think,"
Says he to that, and pulls his little beard;
"Your fly will serve as well as anybody,
And what's his hour? He flies, and flies, and flies,
And in his fly's mind has a brave appearance;
And then your spider gets him in her net,
And eats him out, and hangs him up to dry.
That's Nature, the kind mother of us all.
And then your slattern housemaid swings her broom,
And where's your spider? And that's Nature, also.
It's Nature, and it's Nothing. It's all Nothing.
It's all a world where bugs and emperors
Go singularly back to the same dust,
Each in his time; and the old, ordered stars
That sang together, Ben, will sing the same
Old stave tomorrow."

          When he talks like that,
There's nothing for a human man to do
But lead him to some grateful nook like this
Where we be now, and there to make him drink.
He'll drink, for love of me, and then be sick;
A sad sign always in a man of parts,
And always very ominous. The great
Should be as large in liquor as in love—
And our great friend is not so large in either:
One disaffects him, and the other fails him;
Whatso he drinks that has an antic in it,
He's wondering what's to pay in his insides;
And while his eyes are on the Cyprian
He's fribbling all the time with that damned House.
We laugh here at his thrift, but after all
It may be thrift that saves him from the devil;
God gave it, anyhow—and we'll suppose
He knew the compound of His handiwork.
Today the clouds are with him, but anon
He'll out of 'em enough to shake the tree
Of life itself and bring down fruit unheard-of—
And, throwing in the bruised and whole together,
Prepare a wine to make us drunk with wonder;
And if he live, there'll be a sunset spell

Thrown over him as over a glassed lake
That yesterday was all a black wild water.

God send he live to give us, if no more,
What now's a-rampage in him, and exhibit,
With a decent half-allegiance to the ages
An earnest of at least a casual eye
Turned once on what he owes to Gutenberg,
And to the fealty of more centuries
Than are as yet a picture in our vision.
"There's time enough—I'll do it when I'm old,
And we're immortal men," he says to that;
And then he says to me, "Ben, what's 'immortal'?
Think you by any force of ordination
It may be nothing of a sort more noisy
Than a small oblivion of component ashes
That of a dream-addicted world was once
A moving atomy much like your friend here?"
Nothing will help that man. To make him laugh
I said then he was a mad mountebank—
And by the Lord I nearer made him cry.
I could have eat an eft then, on my knees,
Tails, claws, and all of him; for I had stung
The king of men, who had no sting for me,
And I had hurt him in his memories;
And I say now, as I shall say again,
I love the man this side idolatry.
He'll do it when he's old, he says. I wonder.
He may not be so ancient as all that.
For such as he the thing that is to do
Will do itself—but there's a reckoning;
The sessions that are now too much his own,
The roiling inward of a still outside,
The churning out of all those blood-fed lines,
The nights of many schemes and little sleep,
The full brain hammered hot with too much thinking,
The vexed heart over-worn with too much aching—
This weary jangling of conjoined affairs
Made out of elements that have no end,
And all confused at once, I understand,
Is not what makes a man to live forever.
O, no, not now! He'll not be going now:
There'll be time yet for God knows what explosions
Before he goes. He'll stay awhile. Just wait:
Just wait a year or two for Cleopatra,
For she's to be a balsam and a comfort;
And that's not all a jape of mine now, either.
For granted once the old way of Apollo
Sings in a man, he may then, if he's able,
Strike unafraid whatever strings he will
Upon the last and wildest of new lyres;
Nor out of his new magic, though it hymn

The shrieks of dungeoned hell, shall he create
A madness or a gloom to shut quite out
A cleaving daylight, and a last great calm
Triumphant over shipwreck and all storms.
He might have given Aristotle creeps,
But surely would have given him his *katharsis*.
He'll not be going yet. There's too much yet
Unsung within the man. But when he goes,
I'd stake ye coin o' the realm his only care
For a phantom world he sounded and found wanting
Will be a portion here, a portion there,
Of this or that thing or some other thing
That has a patent and intrinsical
Equivalence in those egregious shillings.
And yet he knows, God help him! Tell me, now,
If ever there was anything let loose
On earth by gods or devils heretofore
Like this mad, careful, proud, indifferent Shakespeare!
Where was it, if it ever was? By heaven,
'Twas never yet in Rhodes or Pergamon—
In Thebes or Nineveh, a thing like this!
No thing like this was ever out of England;
And that he knows. I wonder if he cares.
Perhaps he does. . . . O Lord, that House in Stratford!

## NEW ENGLAND

Here where the wind is always north-north-east
And children learn to walk on frozen toes,
Wonder begets an envy of all those
Who boil elsewhere with such a lyric yeast
Of love that you will hear them at a feast
Where demons would appeal for some repose,
Still clamoring where the chalice overflows
And crying wildest who have drunk the least.

Passion is here a soilure of the wits,
We're told, and Love a cross for them to bear;
Joy shivers in the corner where she knits
And Conscience always has the rocking-chair,
Cheerful as when she tortured into fits
The first cat that was ever killed by Care.

## THE GIFT OF GOD

Blessed with a joy that only she
Of all alive shall ever know,
She wears a proud humility
For what it was that willed it so,—
That her degree should be so great
Among the favored of the Lord

That she may scarcely bear the weight
Of her bewildering reward.

As one apart, immune, alone,
Or featured for the shining ones,
And like to none that she has known
Of other women's other sons,—

The firm fruition of her need,
He shines anointed; and he blurs
Her vision, till it seems indeed
A sacrilege to call him hers.

She fears a little for so much
Of what is best, and hardly dares
To think of him as one to touch
With aches, indignities, and cares;
She sees him rather at the goal,
Still shining; and her dream foretells
The proper shining of a soul
Where nothing ordinary dwells.

Perchance a canvass of the town
Would find him far from flags and shouts,
And leave him only the renown
Of many smiles and many doubts;
Perchance the crude and common tongue
Would havoc strangely with his worth;

But she, with innocence unwrung,
Would read his name around the earth.

And others, knowing how this youth
Would shine, if love could make him gr
When caught and tortured for the truth
Would only writhe and hesitate;
While she, arranging for his days
What centuries could not fulfill,
Transmutes him with her faith and pra
And has him shining where she will.

She crowns him with her gratefulness,
And says again that life is good;
And should the gift of God be less
In him than in her motherhood,
His fame, though vague, will not be sm
As upward through her dream he fares,
Half clouded with a crimson fall
Of roses thrown on marble stairs.

## THE PRODIGAL SON

You are not merry, brother. Why not laugh,
As I do, and acclaim the fatted calf?
For, unless ways are changing here at home,
You might not have it if I had not come.
And were I not a thing for you and me
To execrate in anguish, you would be
As indigent a stranger to surprise,
I fear, as I was once, and as unwise.
Brother, believe as I do, it is best
For you that I'm again in the old nest—
Draggled, I grant you, but your brother still,
Full of good wine, good viands, and good will.
You will thank God, some day, that I returned,
And may be singing for what you have learned,
Some other day; and one day you may find
Yourself a little nearer to mankind.
And having hated me till you are tired,
You will begin to see, as if inspired,
It was fate's way of educating us.
Remembering then when you were venomous,
You will be glad enough that I am gone,
But you will know more of what's going on;
For you will see more of what makes it go,
And in more ways than are for you to know.
We are so different when we are dead,
That you, alive, may weep for what you said;
And I, the ghost of one you could not save,
May find you planting lentils on my grave.

# Edgar Lee Masters

EDGAR LEE MASTERS was born at Garnett, Kansas, August 23, 1869, of Puritan and pioneering stock. When he was still a boy, the family moved to Illinois, where, after desultory schooling, he studied law in his father's office at Lewiston. For a year he practiced with his father and then went to Chicago, where he became a successful attorney.

Before going to Chicago, Masters had composed a quantity of rhymed verse in traditional forms on traditional themes; by the time he was twenty-four he had written about four hundred poems, revealing the result of wide reading and betraying the influence of Poe, Keats, Shelley, and Swinburne. His work, previous to the publication of *Spoon River Anthology,* was derivative and undistinguished. In 1895 he wrote a blank verse play on Benedict Arnold. In 1898 he published *A Book of Verses,* a selection of some sixty of the early four hundred. In 1902 *Maximilian,* another blank verse play, appeared, causing no more comment than the others. Nothing daunted, Masters published several volumes in rapid succession (three books of poetry appearing, under various pseudonyms, between 1905 and 1912), *The New Star Chamber and Other Essays* (1904), *Blood of the Prophets* (1905), *Althea,* a play (1907), *The Trifler,* another play (1908).

In 1914, Masters, at the suggestion of his friend, William Marion Reedy, turned from his preoccupation with classic subjects and began to draw upon the life he knew for those concise records which made him famous. Taking as his model *The Greek Anthology,* which Reedy had pressed upon him, Masters evolved *Spoon River Anthology,* that astonishing assemblage of over two hundred self-inscribed epitaphs, in which the dead of a Middle Western town are supposed to have written the truth about themselves. Through these frank revelations, many of them interrelated, the village is re-created for us; it lives again with all its intrigues, hypocrisies, feuds, martyrdoms and occasional exaltations. The monotony of existence in a drab township, the defeat of ideals, the struggle toward higher goals are synthesized in these crowded pages. All moods and all manner of voices are heard here—even Masters', who explains the reason for his medium and the selection of his form through "Petit, the Poet."

The success of the volume was extraordinary. With every new attack (and its frankness continued to make fresh enemies) its readers increased; it was imitated, parodied, reviled as "a piece of yellow journalism"; hailed as "an American Comédie Humaine." Finally, after the storm of controversy, it has taken its place as a landmark in American literature.

With *Spoon River Anthology* Masters arrived—and left. He went back to his first rhetorical style, resurrecting many of his earlier trifles, reprinting dull echoes of Tennyson, imitations of Shelley, archaic paraphrases in the manner of Swinburne. Yet though none of Masters' subsequent volumes can be compared to his masterpiece, all of them contain passages of the same straightforwardness and the stubborn searching that intensified his best-known characterizations.

*Songs and Satires* (1916) includes the startling "All Life in a Life" and the gravely moving "Silence." *The Great Valley* (1917) is packed with echoes and a growing dependence on Browning. In *Toward the Gulf* (1918), the Browning influence predominates, although there are such splendid monologues as "The World Saver," "St. Deseret" and "Front the Ages with a Smile." *Starved Rock* (1919), *Domesday Book* (1920) and *The New Spoon River* (1924) are, like all Masters' later books, queerly assembled mixtures of good, bad, and derivative verse in which, though the aim is cosmic, the language is pretentious and prosy. These volumes prepared us for the novels which, in their mixture of sharp concept and dull writing, were as uneven as his verse. *The Fate of the Jury* (1929) is a continuation of *Domesday Book* with its mechanics suggested by *The Ring and the Book,* large in outline, feeble in detail. *Godbey* (1931) is a dramatic poem containing six thousand lines of rhymed verse with a few sharply projected ideas, an occasionally vivid scene, and literally thousands of pedestrian couplets given over to debate and diatribe. The book is a jumble of pseudo-philosophy and pseudo-science, of endocrines and gastropods, in which the author of the vivid *Spoon River Anthology* loses his readers not only because he is dogmatic but because he is dull.

*Invisible Landscapes* (1935) contains several ambitious poems devoted to varying manifestations of Nature, but they are impressive chiefly in length. One has only to compare Masters' "Hymn to Earth" with Elinor Wylie's poem of the same title to realize the difference between clairvoyance and doggedness.

Yet for all his windiness and borrowings, in spite of his repetitions and disillusions, Masters' work is a continual if irritable quest for some key to the mystery of truth and mastery of life. And there is always that milestone, the original *Spoon River Anthology.*

### PETIT, THE POET

Seeds in a dry pod, tick, tick, tick,
Tick, tick, tick, like mites in a quarrel—
Faint iambics that the full breeze wakens—
But the pine tree makes a symphony thereof.
Triolets, villanelles, rondels, rondeaus.
Ballades by the score with the same old thought:
The snows and the roses of yesterday are vanished;
And what is love but a rose that fades?
Life all around me here in the village:
Tragedy, comedy, valor and truth,
Courage, constancy, heroism, failure—
All in the loom, and, oh, what patterns!
Woodlands, meadows, streams and rivers—
Blind to all of it all my life long.
Triolets, villanelles, rondels, rondeaus,
Seeds in a dry pod, tick, tick, tick,
Tick, tick, tick, what little iambics,
While Homer and Whitman roared in the pines!

### LUCINDA MATLOCK

I went to the dances at Chandlerville,
And played snap-out at Winchester.
One time we changed partners,

Driving home in the moonlight of middle June,
And then I found Davis.
We were married and lived together for seventy years,
Enjoying, working, raising the twelve children,
Eight of whom we lost
Ere I had reached the age of sixty.
I spun, I wove, I kept the house, I nursed the sick,
I made the garden, and for holiday
Rambled over the fields where sang the larks,
And by Spoon River gathering many a shell,
And many a flower and medicinal weed—
Shouting to the wooded hills, singing to the green valleys.
At ninety-six I had lived enough, that is all,
And passed to a sweet repose.
What is this I hear of sorrow and weariness,
Anger, discontent and drooping hopes?
Degenerate sons and daughters,
Life is too strong for you—
It takes life to love Life.

### ANNE RUTLEDGE

Out of me unworthy and unknown
The vibrations of deathless music:
"With malice toward none, with charity for all."
Out of me the forgiveness of millions toward millions,
And the beneficent face of a nation
Shining with justice and truth.
I am Anne Rutledge who sleep beneath these weeds,
Beloved in life of Abraham Lincoln,
Wedded to him, not through union,
But through separation.
Bloom forever, O Republic,
From the dust of my bosom!

### SILENCE

I have known the silence of the stars and of the sea,
And the silence of the city when it pauses,
And the silence of a man and a maid,
And the silence for which music alone finds the word,
And the silence of the woods before the winds of spring begin,
And the silence of the sick
When their eyes roam about the room.
And I ask: For the depths
Of what use is language?
A beast of the field moans a few times
When death takes its young.
And we are voiceless in the presence of realities—
We cannot speak.

A curious boy asks an old soldier
Sitting in front of the grocery store,
"How did you lose your leg?"
And the old soldier is struck with silence,
Or his mind flies away
Because he cannot concentrate it on Gettysburg.
It comes back jocosely
And he says, "A bear bit it off."
And the boy wonders, while the old soldier
Dumbly, feebly lives over
The flashes of guns, the thunder of cannon,
The shrieks of the slain,
And himself lying on the ground,
And the hospital surgeons, the knives,
And the long days in bed.
But if he could describe it all
He would be an artist.
But if he were an artist there would be deeper wounds
Which he could not describe.

There is the silence of a great hatred,
And the silence of a great love,
And the silence of a deep peace of mind,
And the silence of an embittered friendship,
There is the silence of a spiritual crisis,
Through which your soul, exquisitely tortured,
Comes with visions not to be uttered
Into a realm of higher life.
And the silence of the gods who understand each other without speech,
There is the silence of defeat.
There is the silence of those unjustly punished;
And the silence of the dying whose hand
Suddenly grips yours.
There is the silence between father and son,
When the father cannot explain his life,
Even though he be misunderstood for it.

There is the silence that comes between husband and wife.
There is the silence of those who have failed;
And the vast silence that covers
Broken nations and vanquished leaders.
There is the silence of Lincoln,
Thinking of the poverty of his youth.
And the silence of Napoleon
After Waterloo.
And the silence of Jeanne d'Arc
Saying amid the flames, "Blessèd Jesus"—
Revealing in two words all sorrow, all hope.
And there is the silence of age,
Too full of wisdom for the tongue to utter it
In words intelligible to those who have not lived
The great range of life.

And there is the silence of the dead.
If we who are in life cannot speak
Of profound experiences,
Why do you marvel that the dead
Do not tell you of death?
Their silence shall be interpreted
As we approach them.

# Stephen Crane

STEPHEN CRANE, whose literary career was one of the most meteoric in American letters, was born in Newark, New Jersey, November 1, 1871. After taking a partial course at Lafayette College, he entered journalism at sixteen and, until the time of his death, was a reporter and writer of newspaper sketches. When he died prematurely, at the age of thirty, he had ten printed volumes to his credit, two more announced for publication, and two others which were appearing serially.

Crane's most famous novel, *The Red Badge of Courage* (1895), was a *tour de force,* written when he was twenty-two years old. What is even more astonishing is the fact that this detailed description of blood and battlefields was written by a civilian far from the scene of conflict. *The Atlantic Monthly* pronounced it "great enough to set a new fashion in literature"; H. G. Wells, speaking of its influence in England, said Crane was "the first expression of the opening mind of a new period . . . a record of intensity beyond all precedent."

Crane's other books, although less powerful than *The Red Badge of Courage,* are scarcely less vivid. *The Open Boat* (1898) and *The Monster* (1899) are full of an intuitive wisdom and a passionate sensitivity that caused Wells to exclaim, "The man who can call these 'brilliant fragments' would reproach Rodin for not 'completing' his fragments."

At various periods in Crane's brief career, he experimented in verse, seeking to find new effects in unrhymed lines, a new acuteness of symbol and vision. The results were embodied in two volumes of unusual poetry—*The Black Riders* (1895) and *War Is Kind* (1899), lines that strangely anticipated the Imagists and the elliptical free verse that followed fifteen years later. Acidulous and biting, these concisions were unappreciated in his day; Crane's suggestive verse has not yet received its due in an age which employs its very technique. But it was forty years before Emily Dickinson won her rightful audience, and a quarter of a century passed before a publisher risked a *Complete Works of Stephen Crane*. It was not until 1930 that a *Collected Poems* appeared.

Besides novels, short stories and poems, Crane was writing, at the time of his death, descriptions of the world's great battles for *Lippincott's Magazine;* his droll *Whilomville Stories* for boys were appearing in *Harper's Monthly,* and he was beginning a series of similar stories for girls. It is more than probable that this feverish energy of production aggravated the illness that caused Crane's death. He reached his refuge in the Black Forest only to die at the journey's end, June 5, 1900.

## I SAW A MAN

I saw a man pursuing the horizon;
Round and round they sped.
I was disturbed at this;
I accosted the man.
"It is futile," I said,
"You can never—"
"You lie," he cried,
And ran on.

## THE WAYFARER

The wayfarer,
Perceiving the pathway to truth,
Was struck with astonishment.
It was thickly grown with weeds.
"Ha," he said,
"I see that no one has passed here
In a long time."
Later he saw that each weed
Was a singular knife.
"Well," he mumbled at last,
"Doubtless there are other roads."

## HYMN

A slant of sun on dull brown walls,
A forgotten sky of bashful blue.

Toward God a mighty hymn,
A song of collisions and cries,
Rumbling wheels, hoof-beats, bells,
Welcomes, farewells, love-calls, final moans,
Voices of joy, idiocy, warning, despair,
The unknown appeals of brutes,
The chanting of flowers,
The screams of cut trees,
The senseless babble of hens and wise men—
A cluttered incoherency that says to the stars:
"O God, save us!"

## THE BLADES OF GRASS

In Heaven,
Some little blades of grass
Stood before God.
"What did you do?"
Then all save one of the little blades
Began eagerly to relate
The merits of their lives.

This one stayed a small way behind,
Ashamed.

Presently, God said,
"And what did you do?"
The little blade answered, "Oh, my Lord
Memory is bitter to me,
For, if I did good deeds,
I know not of them."
Then God, in all his splendor,
Arose from his throne.
"Oh, best little blade of grass!" he said.

## THE BOOK OF WISDOM

I met a seer.
He held in his hands
The book of wisdom.
"Sir," I addressed him,
"Let me read."
"Child—" he began.
"Sir," I said,
"Think not that I am a child,
For already I know much
Of that which you hold;
Aye, much."

He smiled.
Then he opened the book
And held it before me.
Strange that I should have grown so sud
denly blind.

## THE CANDID MAN

Forth went the candid man
And spoke freely to the wind—
When he looked about him he was in a fa
strange country.

Forth went the candid man
And spoke freely to the stars—
Yellow light tore sight from his eyes.

"My good fool," said a learned bystander,
"Your operations are mad."

"You are too candid," cried the candid ma
And when his stick left the head of th
learned bystander
It was two sticks.

### THE HEART

In the desert
I saw a creature, naked, bestial,
Who, squatting upon the ground,
Held his heart in his hands,

And ate of it.
I said, "Is it good, friend?"
"It is bitter—bitter," he answered;
"But I like it
Because it is bitter,
And because it is my heart."

## Edwin Ford Piper

EDWIN FORD PIPER was born at Auburn, Nebraska, February 8, 1871, and literally grew up in the saddle. In 1893 he entered the University of Nebraska, from which he received an A.B. in 1897 and an A.M. in 1900. He studied at Harvard (1903-4), was one of the editors of *The Kiote* (a magazine published from 1898 to 1902 in Lincoln, Nebraska), and, since 1905, has been a professor of English at the State University of Iowa.

Piper's *Barbed Wire and Other Poems* (1918) is saturated with the color of his environment. His later poems are equally vivid and racy. "Sweetgrass Range" (with its acknowledged debt to Burns' "Rattlin' Roarin' Willie") and "Bindlestiff" are fresh evidences of this author's creative interest in ballads and folk-lore.

### BINDLESTIFF

*Oh, the lives of men, lives of men,*
  *In pattern-molds be run;*
*But there's you, and me, and Bindlestiff—*
  *And remember Mary's Son.*

At dawn the hedges and the wheel-ruts ran
Into brightening sky. The grass bent low
With shimmering dew, and many a late wild rose
Unrolled the petals from its odorous heart
While birds held tuneful gossip. Suddenly,
Each bubbling trill and whistle hid away
As from a hawk; the fragrant silence heard
Only the loving stir of little leaves;
Then a man's baritone broke roughly in:

*I've gnawed my crust of moldy bread,*
  *Skimmed my mulligan stew;*
*Laid beneath the barren hedge—*
  *Sleety night-winds blew.*

*Slanting rain chills my bones,*
  *Sun bakes my skin;*
*Rocky road for my limping feet,*
  *Door where I can't go in.*

Above the hedgerow floated filmy smoke
From the hidden singer's fire. Once more the voice:

> I used to burn the mules with the whip
>     When I worked on the grading gang;
> But the boss was a crook and he docked my pay—
>     Some day that boss will hang.

> I used to live in a six by nine,
>     Try to save my dough—
> It's a bellyful of the chaff of life,
>     Feet that up and go.

The mesh of leafy branches rustled loud,
Into the road slid Bindlestiff. You've seen
The like of the traveler: gaunt humanity
In stained and broken coat, with untrimmed hedge
Of rusty beard and curling sunburnt hair;
His hat, once white, a dull uncertain cone;
His leathery hands and cheeks, his bright blue eyes
That always see new faces and strange dogs;
His mouth that laughs at life and at himself.

> Sometimes they shut you up in jail—
>     Dark, and a filthy cell;
> I hope the fellows built them jails
>     Find 'em down in hell.

> But up above, you can sleep outdoors—
>     Feed you like a king;
> You never have to saw no wood,
>     Only job is sing.

The tones came mellower, as unevenly
The tramp limped off trailing the hobo song:

> Good-by, farewell to Omaha,
>     K. C., and Denver, too;
> Put my foot on the flying freight,
>     Going to ride her through.

Bindlestiff topped a hillock, against the sky
Showed stick and bundle with his extra shoes
Jauntily dangling. Bird to bird once more
Made low sweet answer; in the wild rose cups
The bee found yellow meal; all softly moved
The white and purple morning-glory bells
As on the gently rustling hedgetop leaves
The sun's face rested. Bindlestiff was gone.

> Oh, the lives of men, lives of men,
>     In pattern-molds be run;
> But there's you, and me, and Bindlestiff—
>     And remember Mary's Son.

### SWEETGRASS RANGE

Come sell your pony, cowboy—
    Sell your pony to me;
Braided bridle and your puncher saddle,
    And spend your money free.

"If I should sell my pony,
    And ride the range no more,
Nail up my hat and my silver spurs
    Above my shanty door;

"And let my door stand open wide
    To the snow and the rain and sun;
And bury me under the green sweetgrass
    Where you hear the river run."

As I came down the sweetgrass range
    And by the cabin door,
I heard a singing in the early dusk
    Along the river shore;

I heard a singing to the early stars,
    And the tune of a pony's feet.
The joy of the riding singer
    I never shall forget.

## T. A. Daly

THOMAS AUGUSTINE DALY was born in Philadelphia, Pennsylvania, May 28, 1871. He attended Villanova College and Fordham University, leaving there at the end of his sophomore year to become a newspaper man. Since 1891 he has been with various Philadelphia journals, writing reviews, editorials, travel-notes and, chiefly, running the columns in which his verse originally appeared.

*Canzoni* (1906) and *Carmina* (1909) contain the best known of Daly's varied dialect verse. Although he has written in half a dozen different idioms including "straight" English (*vide Songs of Wedlock*, 1916), his half-humorous, half-pathetic interpretations of the Irish and Italian immigrants are his *forte*. "Mia Carlotta" and "Between Two Loves" rank with the best dialect rhyming of the period; "The Song of the Thrush," though less laugh-provoking, is a more personal communication.

Seldom descending to caricature, Daly exhibits the foibles of his characters without exploiting them; even the lightest passages in *McAroni Ballads* (1919) are done with delicacy and a not too sentimental appreciation. Less popular than Riley or Dunbar, Daly is more skillful and versatile than either; his range and quality are comparable to Field's.

### THE SONG OF THE THRUSH

Ah! the May was grand this mornin'!
Shure, how could I feel forlorn in
Such a land, when tree and flower tossed their kisses to the breeze?
Could an Irish heart be quiet
While the Spring was runnin' riot,
An' the birds of free America were singin' in the trees?
In the songs that they were singin'
No familiar note was ringin',
But I strove to imitate them an' I whistled like a lad.
Oh, my heart was warm to love them
For the very newness of them—
For the ould songs that they helped me to forget—an' I was glad.

So I mocked the feathered choir
To my hungry heart's desire,
An' I gloried in the comradeship that made their joy my own.
Till a new note sounded, stillin'
All the rest. A thrush was trillin'!
Ah, the thrush I left behind me in the fields about Athlone!
Where, upon the whitethorn swayin',
He was minstrel of the Mayin',
In my days of love an' laughter that the years have laid at rest;
Here again his notes were ringin'!
But I'd lost the heart for singin'—
Ah, the song I could not answer was the one I knew the best.


### MIA CARLOTTA

Giuseppe, da barber, ees greata for "mash,"
He gotta da bigga, da blacka mustache,
Good clo'es an' good styla an' playnta good cash.

W'enevra Giuseppe ees walk on da street,
Da people dey talka, "how nobby! how neat!
How softa da handa, how smalla da feet."

He raisa hees hat an' he shaka hees curls,
An' smila weeth teetha so shiny like pearls;
O! many da heart of da seely young girls
He gotta.
Yes, playnta he gotta—
But notta
Carlotta!

Giuseppe, da barber, he maka da eye,
An' lika da steam engine puffa an' sigh,
For catcha Carlotta w'en she ees go by.

Carlotta she walka weeth nose in da air,
An' look through Giuseppe weeth far-away stare,
As eef she no see dere ees som'body dere.

Giuseppe, da barber, he gotta da cash,
He gotta da clo'es an' da bigga mustache,
He gotta da seely young girls for da "mash,"
But notta—
You bat my life, notta—
Carlotta.
I gotta!

### BETWEEN TWO LOVES

I gotta lov' for Angela,
I lov' Carlotta, too.
I no can marry both o' dem,
So w'at I gonna do?

O! Angela ees pretta girl,
She gotta hair so black, so curl,
An' teeth so white as anytheeng.
An' O! she gotta voice to seeng,
Dat mak' your hearta feel eet must
Jump up an' dance or eet weel bust.
An' alla time she seeng, her eyes
Dey smila like Italia's skies,
An' makin' flirtin' looks at you—
But dat ees all w'at she can do.

Carlotta ees no gotta song,
But she ees twice so big an' strong
As Angela, an' she no look
So beautiful—but she can cook.
You oughta see her carry wood!
I tal you w'at, eet do you good.
When she ees be som'body's wife
She worka hard, you bat my life!
She never gattin' tired, too—
But dat ees all w'at she can do.

O! my! I weesh dat Angela
Was strong for carry wood,
Or else Carlotta gotta song
An' looka pretta good.
I gotta lov' for Angela,
I lov' Carlotta, too.
I no can marry both o' dem,
So w'at I gonna do?

## James Weldon Johnson

JAMES WELDON JOHNSON was born in Jacksonville, Florida, June 17, 1871. He was educated at Atlanta University and at Columbia University, where he received his A.M. He was principal of the colored high school in Jacksonville, was admitted to the Florida bar in 1897, and in 1901 removed to New York City, where he collaborated with his brother J. Rosamond Johnson in writing for vaudeville and the light opera stage. He served seven years as United States Consul in Venezuela and Nicaragua, became secretary of the National Association for Advancement of Colored People, and occupied the chair of Creative Literature at Fisk University. His version of the libretto of *Goyescas* was produced at the Metropolitan Opera House in 1915. He divides his time between Nashville, Tennessee, and his summer home at Great Barrington, Massachusetts.

His first book of verse *Fifty Years and Other Poems* (1918) contains much that is meretricious and facile; but, half buried in the midst of clichés, there is not only the humor but the stern pathos characteristic of the Negro as singer. This quality was pronounced in *God's Trombones* (1927), Johnson's richest book of poems. The volume consists of seven Negro sermons in verse, done after the manner of the old Negro plantation sermons. In these poems the folk-stuff is used much as a composer might use folk-themes in writing a larger musical composition. "The Creation" and "Go Down, Death," in particular are large in conception; sonorous, strongly rhythmical free verse, reflecting the unctuous periods, the uninhibited imagery of the plantation preacher. They and, in a lesser degree, the other poems in *God's Trombones,* are a rambling mixture of Biblical and tropical figures, but always an artistically governed expression.

*Saint Peter Relates an Incident of the Resurrection Day* (privately distributed in 1930 and re-issued, with other poems, for general circulation in 1935) is a stirring expression in which irony masks a sense of outrage. Johnson was at work on the manuscript of a book when he picked up a newspaper and read that the government was sending to France a contingent of Gold Star mothers whose soldier sons were buried there, but that the Negro Gold Star mothers would not be allowed to sail on the ship with the white mothers. He threw the manuscript he was writing aside and did not take it up until he had finished the long satirical poem.

Among Johnson's other work are the novel *The Autobiography of an Ex-Colored Man* (1912, republished in 1927), *Black Manhattan* (1930), the story of the Negro in New York, and the eloquent autobiography *Along this Way* (1933). He also collaborated with his brother in the two collections of American Negro Spirituals in 1925 and 1926 and edited *The Book of American Negro Poetry.*

THE CREATION

(*A Negro Sermon*)

And God stepped out on space,
And He looked around and said,
*"I'm lonely—*
*I'll make me a world."*

And far as the eye of God could see
Darkness covered everything,
Blacker than a hundred midnights
Down in a cypress swamp.

Then God smiled,
And the light broke,
And the darkness rolled up on one side,
And the light stood shining on the other,
And God said, *"That's good!"*

Then God reached out and took the light in His hands,
And God rolled the light around in His hands,
Until He made the sun;
And He set that sun a-blazing in the heavens.
And the light that was left from making the sun
God gathered up in a shining ball
And flung against the darkness,
Spangling the night with the moon and stars.
Then down between
The darkness and the light
He hurled the world;
And God said, *"That's good!"*

Then God himself stepped down—
And the sun was on His right hand,
And the moon was on His left;
The stars were clustered about His head,
And the earth was under His feet.
And God walked, and where He trod
His footsteps hollowed the valleys out
And bulged the mountains up.

Then He stopped and looked and saw
That the earth was hot and barren.
So God stepped over to the edge of the world
And He spat out the seven seas;
He batted His eyes, and the lightnings flashed;
He clapped His hands, and the thunders rolled;
And the waters above the earth came down,
The cooling waters came down.

Then the green grass sprouted,
And the little red flowers blossomed,
The pine-tree pointed his finger to the sky,
And the oak spread out his arms;
The lakes cuddled down in the hollows of the ground,
And the rivers ran down to the sea;
And God smiled again,
And the rainbow appeared,
And curled itself around His shoulder.

Then God raised His arm and He waved His hand
Over the sea and over the land,
And He said, *"Bring forth! Bring forth!"*
And quicker than God could drop His hand,
Fishes and fowls
And beasts and birds
Swam the rivers and the seas,
Roamed the forests and the woods,
And split the air with their wings,
And God said, *"That's good!"*

Then God walked around
And God looked around
On all that He had made.
He looked at His sun,
And He looked at His moon,
And He looked at His little stars;
He looked on His world
With all its living things,
And God said, *"I'm lonely still."*

Then God sat down
On the side of a hill where He could think;
By a deep, wide river He sat down;
With His head in His hands,
God thought and thought,
Till He thought, *"I'll make me a man!"*

Up from the bed of the river
God scooped the clay;
And by the bank of the river
He kneeled Him down;
And there the great God Almighty,
Who lit the sun and fixed it in the sky,
Who flung the stars to the most far corner of the night,
Who rounded the earth in the middle of His hand—
This Great God,
Like a mammy bending over her baby,
Kneeled down in the dust
Toiling over a lump of clay
Till He shaped it in His own image;
Then into it He blew the breath of life,
And man became a living soul.
Amen. Amen.

# Paul Laurence Dunbar

PAUL LAURENCE DUNBAR was born in 1872 at Dayton, Ohio, the son of Negro slaves. He was, before and after he began to write his verse, an elevator-boy. He tried newspaper work unsuccessfully and, in 1899, was given a position in the Library of Congress at Washington, D. C.

Although Dunbar wrote several volumes of short stories and two novels, he was most at home in his verse. Even here, his best work is not those "literary English" pieces by which he set such store, but the racy rhymes written in Negro dialect, alternately tender and mocking. Dunbar's first collection, *Lyrics of Lowly Life* (1896), contains many of his most characteristic poems. In an introduction, in which mention was made of the octoroon Dumas and the great Russian poet Pushkin, who was a mulatto, William Dean Howells wrote, "So far as I could remember, Paul Dunbar was the first man of pure African blood and of American civilization to feel the Negro life esthetically and express it lyrically. . . . His brilliant and unique achievement was to have studied the American Negro objectively, and to have represented him as he found him—with humor, with sympathy, and yet with what the reader must instinctively feel to be entire truthfulness." Dunbar was the precursor of those Negro poets who, turning away from sentimentality, genuinely expressed the Negro.

*Lyrics of the Hearthside* (1899) and *Lyrics of Love and Laughter* (1903) are two other volumes full of folk-stuff. Though the final *Lyrics of Sunshine and Shadow* (1905) is less original, being crowded with echoes of all kinds of poetry from the songs of Robert Burns to the childhood rhymes of J. W. Riley, it contains a few of Dunbar's least known but keenest interpretations.

Dunbar died in his birthplace, Dayton, Ohio, February 10, 1916.

## THE TURNING OF THE BABIES IN THE BED

Woman's sho' a cur'ous critter, an' dey ain't no doubtin' dat.
She's a mess o' funny capahs f'om huh slippahs to huh hat.
Ef yo' tries to un'erstan' huh, an' yo' fails, des' up an' say:
"D' ain't a bit o' use to try to un'erstan' a woman's way."

I don' mean to be complainin', but I's jes' a-settin' down
Some o' my own obserwations, w'en I cas' my eye eroun'.
Ef yo' ax me fu' to prove it, I ken do it mighty fine,
Fu' dey ain't no bettah 'zample den dis ve'y wife o' mine.

In de ve'y hea't o' midnight, w'en I's sleepin' good an' soun',
I kin hyeah a so't o' rustlin' an' somebody movin' 'roun'.
An' I say, "Lize, whut yo' doin'?" But she frown an' shek huh haid,
"Hesh yo' mouf, I's only tu'nin' of de chillun in de bed.

"Don' yo' know a chile gits restless, layin' all de night one way?
An' yo' got to kind o' 'range him sev'al times befo' de day?
So de little necks won't worry, an' de little backs won't break;
Don' yo' t'ink 'cause chillun's chillun dey haint got no pain an' ache,"

So she shakes 'em, an' she twists 'em, an' she tu'ns 'em 'roun' erbout,
'Twell I don' see how de chillun evah keeps f'om hollahin' out.
Den she lif's 'em up head down'ards, so's dey won't git livah-grown,
But dey snoozes des' ez peaceful ez a liza'd on a stone.

W'en hit's mos' nigh time fu' wakin' on de dawn o' jedgement day,
Seems lak I kin hyeah ol' Gab'iel lay his trumpet down an' say,
"Who dat walkin' 'roun' so easy, down on earf ermong de dead?"—
'Twill be Lizy up a-tu'nin' of de chillun in de bed.

## A COQUETTE CONQUERED

Yes, my ha't's ez ha'd ez stone—
Go 'way, Sam, an' lemme 'lone.
No; I ain't gwine change my min';
Ain't gwine ma'y you—nuffin' de kin'.

Phiny loves you true an' deah?
Go ma'y Phiny; whut I keer?
Oh, you needn't mou'n an' cry—
I don't keer how soon you die.

Got a present! What you got?
Somef'n fu' de pan er pot!
Huh! Yo' sass do sholy beat—
Think I don't git 'nough to eat?

Whut's dat un'neaf yo' coat?
Looks des lak a little shoat.
'Tain't no possum? Bless de Lamb!
Yes, it is, you rascal, Sam!

Gin it to me; whut you say?
Ain't you sma't! Oh, go 'way!
Possum do look mighty nice;
But you ax too big a price.

Tell me, is you talkin' true,
Dat's de gal's whut ma'ies you?
Come back, Sam; now whah's you gwine?
Co'se you knows dat possum's mine!

## DISCOVERED

Seen you down at chu'ch las' night,
  Nevah min', Miss Lucy.
What I mean? Oh, dat's all right,
  Nevah min', Miss Lucy.
You was sma't ez sma't could be,
But you couldn't hide f'om me.
Ain't I got two eyes to see!
  Nevah min', Miss Lucy.

Guess you thought you's awful keen;
  Nevah min', Miss Lucy.
Evahthing you done, I seen;
  Nevah min', Miss Lucy.
Seen him tek yo' ahm jes' so,
When he got outside de do'—
Oh, I know dat man's yo' beau!
  Nevah min', Miss Lucy.

Say now, honey, wa'd he say?—
  Nevah min', Miss Lucy.
Keep yo' secrets—dat's yo' way—
  Nevah min', Miss Lucy.
Won't tell me, an' I'm yo' pal!
I'm gwine tell his othah gal,—
Know huh, too; huh name is Sal.
  Nevah min', Miss Lucy.

# Guy Wetmore Carryl

GUY WETMORE CARRYL, son of Charles Edward Carryl, author of *Davy and the Goblin* and *The Admiral's Caravan*, was born in New York City, March 4, 1873. He was graduated from Columbia University in 1895, was editor of *Munsey's Magazine*, 1895-6, and, during the time he lived abroad (from 1897 to 1902), was the foreign representative of various American publications.

As a writer of prose he was received with no little acclaim; his stories, *The Transgression of Andrew Vane* (1902) and *Zut and Other Parisians* (1903), held the attention of a restless reading public. But it was as a writer of light verse that Carryl became preëminent. Inheriting a remarkable technical gift from his father, young Carryl soon surpassed him as well as other rivals in the field of brilliantly rhymed, adroitly turned burlesques.

Although he wrote several serious poems which were collected in the posthumously published *The Garden of Years* (1904), Carryl's most characteristic work is to be found in his perversions of the parables of Aesop, *Fables for the Frivolous* (1898); the topsy-turvy interpretations of nursery rhymes, *Mother Goose for Grownups* (1900); and the fantastic variations on fairy tales in *Grimm Tales Made Gay* (1903)—all of them with a surprising (and punning) Moral attached. Even those who scorn the gymnastics of most light verse usually succumb to the ease with which Carryl overcomes seemingly impossible hazards in the rhyme-leaping fable of the fox and the raven or the appalling pun-juggling in the new version of Puss-in-Boots. He lacked only a Sullivan—and a sense of satire—to be called the Gilbert of America.

This extraordinary versifier died, before reaching the height of his power, at the age of thirty-one, in the summer of 1904.

#### HOW JACK FOUND THAT BEANS MAY GO BACK ON A CHAP

Without the slightest basis
For hypochondriasis
   A widow had forebodings which a cloud around her flung,
And with expression cynical
For half the day a clinical
   Thermometer she held beneath her tongue.

Whene'er she read the papers
She suffered from the vapors,
   At every tale of malady or accident she'd groan;
In every new and smart disease,
From housemaid's knee to heart disease,
   She recognized the symptoms as her own!

She had a yearning chronic
To try each novel tonic,
   Elixir, panacea, lotion, opiate, and balm;
And from a homeopathist
Would change to an hydropathist,
   And back again, with stupefying calm!

She was nervous, cataleptic,
And anemic, and dyspeptic:
   Though not convinced of apoplexy, yet she had her fears.
She dwelt with force fanatical
Upon a twinge rheumatical,
   And said she had a buzzing in her ears!

Now all of this bemoaning
And this grumbling and this groaning
   The mind of Jack, her son and heir, unconscionably bored.
His heart completely hardening,
He gave his time to gardening,
   For raising beans was something he adored.

Each hour in accents morbid
This limp maternal bore bid
   Her callous son affectionate and lachrymose good-bys.
She never granted Jack a day
Without some long "Alackaday!"
   Accompanied by rolling of the eyes.

But Jack, no panic showing,
Just watched his beanstalk growing,
   And twined with tender fingers the tendrils up the pole.
At all her words funereal
He smiled a smile ethereal,
   Or sighed an absent-minded "Bless my soul!"

That hollow-hearted creature
Would never change a feature:
   No tear bedimmed his eye, however touching was her talk.
She never fussed or flurried him,
The only thing that worried him
   Was when no bean-pods grew upon the stalk!

But then he wabbled loosely
His head, and wept profusely,
   And, taking out his handkerchief to mop away his tears,
Exclaimed: "It hasn't got any!"
He found this blow to botany
   Was sadder than were all his mother's fears.

*The Moral* is that gardeners pine
Whene'er no pods adorn the vine.
Of all sad words experience gleans
The saddest are: "It *might* have beans."
   (I did not make this up myself:
   'Twas in a book upon my shelf.
   It's witty, but I don't deny
   It's rather Whittier than I!)

### THE SYCOPHANTIC FOX AND THE GULLIBLE RAVEN

   A raven sat upon a tree,
      And not a word he spoke, for
   His beak contained a piece of Brie,
      Or, maybe, it was Roquefort.
         We'll make it any kind you please—
         At all events it was a cheese.

Beneath the tree's umbrageous limb
  A hungry fox sat smiling;
He saw the raven watching him,
  And spoke in words beguiling:
    *"J'admire,"* said he, *"ton beau plumage,"*
    (The which was simply persiflage).

Two things there are, no doubt you know,
  To which a fox is used:
A rooster that is bound to crow,
  A crow that's bound to roost;
    And whichsoever he espies
    He tells the most unblushing lies.

"Sweet foul," he said, "I understand
  You're more than merely natty,
I hear you sing to beat the band
  And Adelina Patti.
    Pray render with your liquid tongue
    A bit from 'Götterdämmerung.' "

This subtle speech was aimed to please
  The crow, and it succeeded;
He thought no bird in all the trees
  Could sing as well as he did.
    In flattery completely doused,
    He gave the "Jewel Song" from "Faust."

But gravitation's law, of course,
  As Isaac Newton showed it,
Exerted on the cheese its force,
  And elsewhere soon bestowed it.
    In fact, there is no need to tell
    What happened when to earth it fell.

I blush to add that when the bird
  Took in the situation
He said one brief, emphatic word,
  Unfit for publication.
    The fox was greatly startled, but
    He only sighed and answered "Tut."

*The Moral* is: A fox is bound
  To be a shameless sinner.
And also: When the cheese comes round
  You know it's after dinner.
    But (what is only known to few)
    The fox is after dinner, too.

## HOW A CAT WAS ANNOYED AND A POET WAS BOOTED

A poet had a cat.
There was nothing odd in that—

(I *might* make a little pun about the *Mews!*)
But what is really more
Remarkable, she wore
   A pair of pointed patent-leather shoes.
    And I doubt me greatly whether
      You have heard the like of that:
    Pointed shoes of patent-leather
      On a cat!

His time he used to pass
Writing sonnets, on the grass—
   (I *might* say something good on *pen* and *sward!*)
While the cat sat near at hand,
Trying hard to understand
   The poems he occasionally roared.
    (I myself possess a feline,
      But when poetry I roar
    He is sure to make a bee-line
      For the door.)

The poet, cent by cent,
All his patrimony spent—
   (I *might* tell how he went from *verse* to *worse!*)
Till the cat was sure she could,
By advising, do him good.
   So addressed him in a manner that was terse:
    "We are bound toward the scuppers,
      And the time has come to act,
    Or we'll both be on our uppers
      For a fact!"

On her boot she fixed her eye,
But the boot made no reply—
   (I *might* say: "Couldn't speak to save its *sole!*")
And the foolish bard, instead
Of responding, only read
   A verse that wasn't bad upon the whole.
    And it pleased the cat so greatly,
      Though she knew not what it meant,
    That I'll quote approximately
      How it went:—

"If I should live to be
The last leaf upon the tree"—
   (I *might* put in: "I think I'd just as *leaf!*")
"Let them smile, as I do now,
At the old forsaken bough"—
   Well, he'd plagiarized it bodily, in brief!
    But that cat of simple breeding
      Couldn't read the lines between,
    So she took it to a leading
      Magazine.

She was jarred and very sore
When they showed her to the door.
  (I *might* hit off the *door* that was a *jar!*)
To the spot she swift returned
Where the poet sighed and yearned,
  And she told him that he'd gone a little far.
    "Your performance with this rhyme has
      Made me absolutely sick,"
    She remarked. "I think the time has
      Come to kick!"

I could fill up half the page
With descriptions of her rage—
  (I *might* say that she went a bit *too fur!*)
When he smiled and murmured: "Shoo!"
"There is one thing I can do!"
  She answered with a wrathful kind of purr.
    "You may shoe me, an it suit you,
      But I feel my conscience bid
    Me, as tit for tat, to boot you!"
      (Which she did.)

*The Moral* of the plot
(Though I say it, as should not!)
  Is: An editor is difficult to suit.
But again there're other times
When the man who fashions rhymes
  Is a rascal, and a bully one to boot!

# *Trumbull Stickney*

(Joseph) Trumbull Stickney was born June 20, 1874, at Geneva, Switzerland, of New England parents. In 1891 he entered Harvard and was graduated with high classical honors in 1895. Immediately thereafter, he went abroad, studying at the Sorbonne and Collège de France for seven years. The University of Paris gave him the Doctorat ès Lettres, never before conferred on an American, for two scholarly theses in 1903, the critic Masqueray pronouncing his *"Les Sentences dans la Poesie Grecque"* one of the best modern studies of Hellenic literature. A few months later he returned to America, where he became instructor of Greek at Harvard University. Here his work was suddenly interrupted by death, caused by a tumor on the brain, and he died at the age of thirty, October 11, 1904.

One year after his death, his friends, George Cabot Lodge, John Ellerton Lodge and William Vaughn Moody, edited his posthumous *Poems* (1905), a small and wholly forgotten volume, *Dramatic Verses,* having appeared in 1902. Stickney seems to have found no wider circle of readers than his restricted intimate one. The collections of the period have no record of him; Stedman's voluminous anthology does not even mention his name. Yet there can be no question but that Stickney was a representative poet of his generation, worthy to stand beside Moody, whose point of view as well as his rhetoric he shared. There is a note, however, in Stickney's poetry wholly unlike Moody's, a preoccupation with death that relates him—in spirit at least—to the later Jeffers. He spoke of divinely learning to suffer loneliness; his, he wrote, were the "wise denials."

### LIVE BLINDLY AND UPON THE HOUR

Live blindly and upon the hour. The Lord,
Who was the Future, died full long ago.
Knowledge which is the Past is folly. Go,
Poor child, and be not to thyself abhorred.
Around thine earth sun-winged winds do blow
And planets roll; a meteor draws his sword;
The rainbow breaks his seven-colored chord
And the long strips of river-silver flow:
Awake! Give thyself to the lovely hours.
Drinking their lips, catch thou the dream in flight
About their fragile hairs' aërial gold.
Thou art divine, thou livest,—as of old
Apollo springing naked to the light,
And all his island shivered into flowers.

### IN THE PAST

There lies a somnolent lake
Under a noiseless sky,
Where never the mornings break
Nor the evenings die.

Mad flakes of color
Whirl on its even face
Iridescent and streaked with pallor;
And, warding the silent place,

The rocks rise sheer and gray
From the sedgeless brink to the sky
Dull-lit with the light of pale half-day
Thro' a void space and dry.

And the hours lag dead in the air
With a sense of coming eternity
To the heart of the lonely boatman there:
That boatman am I,

I, in my lonely boat,
A waif on the somnolent lake,
Watching the colors creep and float
With the sinuous track of a snake.

Now I lean o'er the side
And lazy shades in the water see,
Lapped in the sweep of a sluggish tide
Crawled in from the living sea;

And next I fix mine eyes,
So long that the heart declines,
On the changeless face of the open skies
Where no star shines;

And now to the rocks I turn,
To the rocks, around
That lie like walls of a circling urn
Wherein lie bound

The waters that feel my powerless streng
And meet my homeless oar
Laboring over their ashen length
Never to find a shore.

But the gleam still skims
At times on the somnolent lake,
And a light there is that swims
With the whirl of a snake;

And tho' dead be the hours in the air,
And dayless the sky,
The heart is alive of the boatman there:
That boatman am I.

### AGE IN YOUTH

From far she's come, and very old,
And very soiled with wandering.
The dust of seasons she has brought
Unbidden to this field of Spring.

She's halted at the log-barred gate.
The May-day waits, a tangled spill
Of light that weaves and moves along
The daisied margin of the hill,

Where Nature bares her bridal heart,
And on her snowy soul the sun
Languors desirously and dull,
An amorous pale vermilion.

She's halted, propped her rigid arms,
With dead big eyes she drinks the west;
The brown rags hang like clotted dust
About her, save her withered breast.

A very soilure of a dream
Runs in the furrows of her brow,
And with a crazy voice she croons
An ugly catch of long ago.

But look! Along the molten sky
There runs strange havoc of the sun.
"What a strange sight this is," she says,
"I'll cross the field, I'll follow on."

The bars are falling from the gate.
The meshes of the meadow yield;
And trudging sunsetward she draws
A journey thro' the daisy field.

The daisies shudder at her hem.
Her dry face laughs with flowery light;
An aureole lifts her soiled gray hair:
"I'll on," she says, "to see this sight."

In the rude math her torn shoe mows
Juices of trod grass and crushed stalk
Mix with a soiled and earthy dew,
With smear of petals gray as chalk.

The Spring grows sour along her track;
The winy airs of amethyst
Turn acid. "Just beyond the ledge,"
She says, "I'll see the sun at rest."

And to the tremor of her croon,
Her old, old catch of long ago,
The newest daisies of the grass
She shreds and passes on below. . . .

The sun is gone where nothing is
And the black-bladed shadows war.
She came and passed, she passed along
That wet, black curve of scimitar.

In vain the flower-lifting morn
With golden fingers to uprear;
The weak Spring here shall pause awhile:
This is a scar upon the year.

### ALONE ON LYKAION

Alone on Lykaion since man hath been
Stand on the height two columns, where at
    rest
Two eagles hewn of gold sit looking East
Forever; and the sun goes up between.
Far down around the mountain's oval green
An order keeps the falling stones abreast.
Below within the chaos last and least
A river like a curl of light is seen.
Beyond the river lies the even sea,
Beyond the sea another ghost of sky,—
O God, support the sickness of my eye
Lest the far space and long antiquity
Suck out my heart, and on this awful ground
The great wind kill my little shell with
    sound.

## Anna Hempstead Branch

ANNA HEMPSTEAD BRANCH was born at New London, Connecticut. She was graduated from Smith College in 1897 and has devoted herself to literature and
social service, mostly in New York.

Her two chief volumes, *The Shoes That Danced* (1905) and *Rose of the Wind*

(1910), reveal the lyrist, but they show a singer who is less fanciful than philosophic. Often, indeed, Miss Branch weighs down her simple melodies with intellectuality; more often, she attains a high level of lyricism. Her lines are admirably condensed; rich in personal as well as poetic value, they maintain a high and austere level. A typical poem is "The Monk in the Kitchen," which, with its spiritual loveliness and verbal felicity, is a celebration of cleanness that gives order an almost mystical nobility and recalls George Herbert.

Although nothing she has ever written has attained the popularity of her shorter works, "Nimrod" has an epic sweep, a large movement which, within the greater curve, contains moments of exalted imagery. The deeply religious feeling implicit governs the author as person no less than as poet, for Miss Branch had given a great part of her life to settlement work at Christadora House on New York's East Side. "To a Dog" is more direct than is Miss Branch's wont; "The Monk in the Kitchen" is no less straightforward, though its metaphysics make it seem less forthright.

## THE MONK IN THE KITCHEN

### I

Order is a lovely thing;
On disarray it lays its wing,
Teaching simplicity to sing.
It has a meek and lowly grace,
Quiet as a nun's face.
Lo—I will have thee in this place!
Tranquil well of deep delight,
All things that shine through thee appear
As stones through water, sweetly clear.
Thou clarity,
That with angelic charity
Revealest beauty where thou art,
Spread thyself like a clean pool.
Then all the things that in thee are,
Shall seem more spiritual and fair,
Reflection from serener air—
Sunken shapes of many a star
In the high heavens set afar.

### II

Ye stolid, homely, visible things,
Above you all brood glorious wings
Of your deep entities, set high,
Like slow moons in a hidden sky.
But you, their likenesses, are spent
Upon another element.
Truly ye are but seemings—
The shadowy cast-off gleamings
Of bright solidities. Ye seem
Soft as water, vague as dream;
Image, cast in a shifting stream.

### III

What are ye?
I know not.
Brazen pan and iron pot,
Yellow brick and gray flagstone
That my feet have trod upon—
Ye seem to me
Vessels of bright mystery
For ye do bear a shape, and so
Though ye were made by man, I know
An inner Spirit also made,
And ye his breathings have obeyed.

### IV

Shape, the strong and awful Spirit,
Laid his ancient hand on you.
He waste chaos doth inherit;
He can alter and subdue.
Verily, he doth lift up
Matter, like a sacred cup.
Into deep substance he reached, and lo
Where ye were not, ye were; and so
Out of useless nothing, ye
Groaned and laughed and came to be,
And I use you, as I can,
Wonderful uses, made for man,
Iron pot and brazen pan.

### V

What are ye?
I know not;
Nor what I really do
When I move and govern you.
There is no small work unto God.
He required of us greatness;
Of his least creature

high angelic nature,
ature superb and bright completeness.
e sets to us no humble duty.
ch act that he would have us do
haloed round with strangest beauty;
rrific deeds and cosmic tasks
: his plainest child he asks.
hen I polish the brazen pan
ear a creature laugh afar
the gardens of a star,
id from his burning presence run
aming wheels of many a sun.
hoever makes a thing more bright,
e is an angel of all light.
hen I cleanse this earthen floor
y spirit leaps to see
ight garments trailing over it,
cleanness made by me.
rger of all men's thoughts and ways,
ith labor do I sound Thy praise,
y work is done for Thee.
hoever makes a thing more bright,
e is an angel of all light.
erefore let me spread abroad
e beautiful cleanness of my God.

### VI

One time in the cool of dawn
Angels came and worked with me.
The air was soft with many a wing.
They laughed amid my solitude
And cast bright looks on everything.
Sweetly of me did they ask
That they might do my common task.
And all were beautiful—but one
With garments whiter than the sun
Had such a face
Of deep, remembered grace;
That when I saw I cried—"Thou art
The great Blood-Brother of my heart.
Where have I seen thee?"—And he said,
"When we were dancing round God's throne,
How often thou art there.
Beauties from thy hands have flown
Like white doves wheeling in mid-air.
Nay—thy soul remembers not?
Work on, and cleanse thy iron pot."

### VII

What are we? I know not.

## WHILE LOVELINESS GOES BY

Sometimes when all the world seems gray and dun
And nothing beautiful, a voice will cry,
"Look out, look out! Angels are drawing nigh!"
Then my slow burdens leave me one by one,
And swiftly does my heart arise and run
Even like a child while loveliness goes by—
And common folk seem children of the sky,
And common things seem shapèd of the sun,
Oh, pitiful! that I who love them, must
So soon perceive their shining garments fade!
And slowly, slowly, from my eyes of trust
Their flaming banners sink into a shade!
While this earth's sunshine seems the golden dust
Slow settling from that radiant cavalcade.

## TO A DOG

### I

If there is no God for thee
Then there is no God for me,

If He sees not when you share
With the poor your frugal fare,

Does not see you at a grave,
Every instinct bred to save;

As if you were the only one
Believing in a resurrection;

When you wait, as lovers do,
Watching till your friend comes true;

Does not reverence when you take
Angry words for love's sweet sake;

If his eye does not approve
All your faith and pain and love;

If the heart of justice fail
And is for you of no avail;

If there is no heaven for thee
Then there is no heaven for me.

II

If the Lord they tell us of
Died for men yet loves not love,

If from out His Paradise
He shuts the innocent and wise,

The gay, obedient, simple, good,
The docile ones, of friendly mood,

Those who die to save a friend
Heavenly faithful to the end;

If there is no cross for thee
Then there is no cross for me.

III

If its boughs reach not so high
That they bowed star and sky,

If its roots are not so sound
That they cleave the heavy ground,

If it thrills not through all Nature
Plunged through every living creature,

If its leaves do not enmesh
Every bit of groaning flesh,

If it strike no mighty spur
Through fang and claw and tooth and fu

Piercing tree and earth and stone,
Then indeed I stand alone.

Nothing less than this can save
Me, from out my fleshly grave,

Me, in whom such jungles are
Where the beasts go out to war.

If there is no God for thee
Then there is no God for me.

# Amy Lowell

AMY LOWELL was born in Brookline, Massachusetts, February 9, 1874, of a long line of noted publicists and poets; the first colonist (a Percival Lowell) arrived in Newburyport in 1637. James Russell Lowell was a cousin of her grandfather; Abbott Lawrence, her mother's father, was minister to England; Percival Lowell, the astronomer who charted the conjectural canals on Mars, was a brother; and Abbott Lawrence Lowell, her other brother, was president of Harvard University.

Miss Lowell obtained her early education through private tuition and travel abroad. These European journeys were the background upon which much of Miss Lowell's later work was unconsciously woven; her visits to France, Egypt, Turkey, and Greece bore fruit, many years later, in the exotic colors of her verse. As a young girl, she had vague aspirations toward being a writer; but it was not until 1902, when she was twenty-eight years old, that she definitely determined to be a poet. For eight years she served a rigorous apprenticeship, reading the classics of all schools, studying the technique of verse, but never attempting to publish a line. In 1910 her first verse was printed in *The Atlantic Monthly;* two years later her first book appeared.

This volume, *A Dome of Many-colored Glass* (1912), was a strangely unpromising first book. Subject and treatment were conventional; the influence of Keats and

Tennyson was evident; the tone was soft and sentimental, without a trace of personality. It was a queer prologue to the vivid *Sword Blades and Poppy Seed* (1914), which marked not only an extraordinary advance but a new individuality. This second volume contained many poems written in the usual forms, a score of pictorial pieces illustrating Miss Lowell's identification with the Imagists, and, possibly most important from a technical standpoint, the first appearance in English of "polyphonic prose." Of this extremely flexible form, Miss Lowell, in an essay on John Gould Fletcher, wrote, " 'Polyphonic' means 'many-voiced,' and the form is so-called because it makes use of the 'voices' of poetry, namely: meter, *vers libre,* assonance, alliteration, rhyme and return. It employs every form of rhythm, even prose rhythm at times." By this time Miss Lowell had "captured" the Imagist movement from Ezra Pound, had reorganized it, and, by her belligerent championing of *vers libre,* freedom of choice of subject, and other seeming innovations, had made poetry a fighting word.

It was because of her experiments in form and technique that Miss Lowell first attracted attention and is still best known. But, beneath a preoccupation with theories and novelty of utterance, there was the skilled story-teller, who revivified history with creative excitement. *Men, Women and Ghosts* (1916) brims with this contagious vitality; it is richer in variety than its predecessors, swifter in movement. It is, in common with all of Miss Lowell's work, best in its portrayal of colors and sounds, of physical perceptions rather than the reactions of inner experience. She is, pre-eminently, the poet of the external world; her visual effects are as "hard and clear" as the most uncompromising Imagist could desire. The colors with which her works are studded seem like bits of bright enamel; every leaf and flower has a lacquered brilliance. To compensate for the lack of the spirit's warmth, Miss Lowell feverishly agitates all she touches; nothing remains quiescent. Whether she writes about a fruit shop, or a flower-garden, or a string quartet, or a Japanese print—everything flashes, leaps, startles, and burns with dynamic, almost savage, speed. Motion too often takes the place of emotion.

In *Can Grande's Castle* (1918) Miss Lowell achieves a broader line; the teller of stories, the bizarre decorator, and the experimenter finally fuse. The poems in this volume are only four in number—four polyphonic prose-poems of unusual length, extraordinarily varied in their sense of amplitude and time. *Pictures of the Floating World* (1919) which followed is, in many ways, Miss Lowell's most personal revelation. Although there are pages devoted to the merely dazzling and grotesque, most of the poems are in a quieter key.

*Legends* (1921) is closely related to *Can Grande's Castle;* eleven stories are placed against seven different backgrounds. The first poem must be rated among Miss Lowell's most dazzling achievements: a *tour de force* with colors as strange and metallic as the scene it pictures. The next years were devoted to her Keats researches.

Besides Miss Lowell's original poetry, she undertook many studies in foreign literatures; she made the English versions of the poems translated from the Chinese by Florence Ayscough in the vivid *Fir-Flower Tablets* (1921). She also wrote two volumes of critical essays: *Six French Poets* (1915) and *Tendencies in Modern American Poetry* (1917), valuable aids to the student of contemporary literature. Two years after its publication she acknowledged the authorship of the anonymous *A Critical Fable* (1922), a modern sequel to James Russell Lowell's *A Fable for Critics.*

Her monumental *John Keats,* an exhaustive biography and analysis of the poet in two volumes, appeared early in 1925.

For years Miss Lowell had been suffering from ill health; she had been operated upon several times, but her general condition, as well as her continual desire to work, nullified the effects of the operations. In April, 1925, her condition became worse; she was forced to cancel a projected lecture trip through England and to cease all work. She died as the result of a paralytic stroke on May 12, 1925. Her death occasioned nation-wide tributes; the very journals which had ridiculed her during her life were loud in praise: it was agreed that hers was one of the most daring and picturesque figures in contemporary literature. Like all pioneers, she was the target of scorn and hostility; but, unlike most innovators, she lived to see her experiments rise from the limbo of ridicule to a definite place in their period.

Three posthumous volumes appeared at yearly intervals immediately after her death: *What's O'Clock* (1925) which was awarded the Pulitzer Prize for that year, *East Wind* (1926), and *Ballads for Sale* (1927). The first was arranged by the poet herself and includes such poems as "Meeting-House Hill" and "Lilacs" which are tart and native; the second is a set of dialect and highly overdramatized New England narratives; the third is a miscellaneous collection. Her qualities are epitomized in these three books and the fact that they show no particular advance upon the earlier "Patterns" is significant. Her brilliance, her command of the lacquered phrase and the glazed figure, her pyrotechnique which causes words to bloom and burst at the same moment as though issuing from firework flower-pots, her restless excitement provoking inanimate objects to a furious life of their own—these were characteristics recognizable from the first. In some of the new poems, the juxtaposition of the thing observed and the thing imagined ("Meeting-House Hill" is a particularly vivid example) is more than ordinarily surprising, but one is prepared for the verve and alacrity of upspringing colors, for the purposeful shifting and distortion of surfaces like the clash of planes in an agitated canvas. Perhaps the most important of the posthumous poems are the expressive and personal "Lilacs," "Evelyn Ray," a virtuoso piece in couplets, and "The Sisters," a shrewd commentary on the "queer lot of women who write poetry," particularly her "spiritual relations" Sappho, Mrs. Browning, and Emily Dickinson.

At the end of "The Sisters" the poet confesses that, in spite of her admiration for the Greek poet, the Englishwoman, and the American genius, none of the three has any word for her. They were, first of all, deeply emotional poets; Miss Lowell was not at home among the emotions. She triumphed in the visual world, in the reflection of reflections, in capturing the minute disturbances of light and movement. It has been said that, though a poet, she failed as a humanist, that she never touched deep feelings because she never knew where to look for them. This—contradicted by such poems as "Patterns," "Madonna of the Evening Flowers" and the ecstatic "In Excelsis"—is true in the sense that passion was not this poet's domain nor, except in a few instances, her concern. Color and *finesse* were her preoccupations, and her many volumes testify to a continually adroit craftsmanship.

Amy Lowell, storm-center, Imagist, strategist, poet, and personality, is shown in her vigorous many-sidedness in the comprehensive, if uncritical, biography *Amy Lowell* (1935) by S. Foster Damon.

### A LADY

You are beautiful and faded,
Like an old opera tune
Played upon a harpsichord;
Or like the sun-flooded silks
Of an eighteenth-century boudoir.
In your eyes
Smolder the fallen roses of outlived minutes,
And the perfume of your soul
Is vague and suffusing,
With the pungence of sealed spice-jars.
Your half-tones delight me,
And I grow mad with gazing
At your blent colors.

My vigor is a new-minted penny,
Which I cast at your feet.
Gather it up from the dust
That its sparkle may amuse you.

### SOLITAIRE

When night drifts along the streets of the city,
And sifts down between the uneven roofs,
My mind begins to peek and peer.
It plays at ball in odd, blue Chinese gardens,
And shakes wrought dice-cups in Pagan temples
Amid the broken flutings of white pillars.
It dances with purple and yellow crocuses in its hair,
And its feet shine as they flutter over drenched grasses.
How light and laughing my mind is,
When all good folk have put out their bedroom candles,
And the city is still.

### PATTERNS

I walk down the garden-paths,
And all the daffodils
Are blowing, and the bright blue squills.
I walk down the patterned garden-paths
In my stiff, brocaded gown.
With my powdered hair and jeweled fan,
I too am a rare
Pattern. As I wander down
The garden-paths.

My dress is richly figured,
And the train
Makes a pink and silver stain
On the gravel, and the thrift

Of the borders.
Just a plate of current fashion,
Tripping by in high-heeled, ribboned shoes.
Not a softness anywhere about me,
Only whalebone and brocade.
And I sink on a seat in the shade
Of a lime tree. For my passion
Wars against the stiff brocade.
The daffodils and squills
Flutter in the breeze
As they please.
And I weep;
For the lime-tree is in blossom
And one small flower has dropped upon my bosom.

And the plashing of waterdrops
In the marble fountain
Comes down the garden-paths.
The dripping never stops.
Underneath my stiffened gown
Is the softness of a woman bathing in a marble basin,
A basin in the midst of hedges grown
So thick, she cannot see her lover hiding,
But she guesses he is near,
And the sliding of the water
Seems the stroking of a dear
Hand upon her.
What is Summer in a fine brocaded gown!
I should like to see it lying in a heap upon the ground.
All the pink and silver crumpled up on the ground.

I would be the pink and silver as I ran along the paths,
And he would stumble after,
Bewildered by my laughter.
I should see the sun flashing from his sword-hilt and the buckles on his shoes.
I would choose
To lead him in a maze along the patterned paths,
A bright and laughing maze for my heavy-booted lover.
Till he caught me in the shade,
And the buttons of his waistcoat bruised my body as he clasped me,
Aching, melting, unafraid.
With the shadows of the leaves and the sundrops,
And the plopping of the waterdrops,
All about us in the open afternoon—
I am very like to swoon
With the weight of this brocade,
For the sun sifts through the shade.

Underneath the fallen blossom
In my bosom
Is a letter I have hid.
It was brought to me this morning by a rider from the Duke.

"Madam, we regret to inform you that Lord Hartwell
Died in action Thursday se'nnight."
As I read it in the white, morning sunlight,
The letters squirmed like snakes.
"Any answer, Madam," said my footman.
"No," I told him.
"See that the messenger takes some refreshment.
No, no answer."
And I walked into the garden,
Up and down the patterned paths,
In my stiff, correct brocade.
The blue and yellow flowers stood up proudly in the sun,
Each one.
I stood upright too,
Held rigid to the pattern
By the stiffness of my gown;
Up and down I walked,
Up and down.

In a month he would have been my husband.
In a month, here, underneath this lime,
We would have broke the pattern;
He for me, and I for him,
He as Colonel, I as Lady,
On this shady seat.
He had a whim
That sunlight carried blessing.
And I answered, "It shall be as you have said."
Now he is dead.

In Summer and in Winter I shall walk
Up and down
The patterned garden-paths
In my stiff, brocaded gown.
The squills and daffodils
Will give place to pillared roses, and to asters, and to snow.
I shall go
Up and down
In my gown.
Gorgeously arrayed,
Boned and stayed.
And the softness of my body will be guarded from embrace
By each button, hook, and lace.
For the man who should loose me is dead,
Fighting with the Duke in Flanders,
In a pattern called a war.
Christ! What are patterns for?

### WIND AND SILVER

Greatly shining,
The Autumn moon floats in the thin sky;
And the fish-ponds shake their backs and flash their dragon scales
As she passes over them.


### NIGHT CLOUDS

The white mares of the moon rush along the sky
Beating their golden hoofs upon the glass Heavens;
The white mares of the moon are all standing on their hind legs
Pawing at the green porcelain doors of the remote Heavens.
Fly, mares!
Strain your utmost,
Scatter the milky dust of stars,
Or the tiger sun will leap upon you and destroy you
With one lick of his vermilion tongue.


### FREE FANTASIA ON JAPANESE THEMES

All the afternoon there has been a chirping of birds,
And the sun lies warm and still on the western sides of swollen branches,
There is no wind;
Even the little twigs at the ends of the branches do not move,
And the needles of the pines are solid
Bands of inarticulated blackness
Against the blue-white sky,
Still, but alert;
And my heart is still and alert,
Passive with sunshine,
Avid of adventure.

I would experience new emotions,
Submit to strange enchantments,
Bend to influences
Bizarre, exotic,
Fresh with burgeoning.
I would climb a sacred mountain
Struggle with other pilgrims up a steep path through pine-trees,
Above to the smooth, treeless slopes,
And prostrate myself before a painted shrine,
Beating my hands upon the hot earth,
Quieting my eyes upon the distant sparkle
Of the faint spring sea.

I would recline upon a balcony
In purple curving folds of silk,
And my dress should be silvered with a pattern
Of butterflies and swallows,
And the black band of my *obi*
Should flash with gold circular threads,

And glitter when I moved.
I would lean against the railing
While you sang to me of wars
Past and to come—
Sang, and played the samisen.
Perhaps I would beat a little hand drum
In time to your singing;
Perhaps I would only watch the play of light
Upon the hilt of your two swords.

I would sit in a covered boat,
Rocking slowly to the narrow waves of a river,
While above us, an arc of moving lanterns,
Curved a bridge,
A hiss of gold
Blooming out of darkness,
Rockets exploded,
And died in a soft dripping of colored stars.
We would float between the high trestles,
And drift away from other boats,
Until the rockets flared soundless,
And their falling stars hung silent in the sky,
Like wistaria clusters above the ancient entrance of a temple.

I would anything
Rather than this cold paper;
With outside, the quiet sun on the sides of burgeoning branches,
And inside, only my books.

## A DECADE

When you came, you were like red wine and honey,
And the taste of you burnt my mouth with its sweetness.
Now you are like morning bread,
Smooth and pleasant.
I hardly taste you at all, for I know your savor;
But I am completely nourished.

## MADONNA OF THE EVENING FLOWERS

All day long I have been working,
Now I am tired.
I call: "Where are you?"
But there is only the oak tree rustling in the wind.
The house is very quiet,
The sun shines in on your books,
On your scissors and thimble just put down,
But you are not there.

Suddenly I am lonely:
Where are you?
I go about searching.

Then I see you,
Standing under a spire of pale blue larkspur,
With a basket of roses on your arm.
You are cool, like silver,
And you smile.

I think the Canterbury bells are playing little tunes,
You tell me that the peonies need spraying,
That the columbines have overrun all bounds,.
That the pyrus japonica should be cut back and rounded.
You tell me these things.
But I look at you, heart of silver,
White heart-flame of polished silver,
Burning beneath the blue steeples of the larkspur,
And I long to kneel instantly at your feet,
While all about us peal the loud, sweet *Te Deums* of the Canterbury bells.

### EVELYN RAY

No decent man will cross a field
Laid down to hay, until its yield

Is cut and cocked, yet there was the track
Going in from the lane and none coming back.

But that was afterwards; before,
The field was smooth as a sea off shore

On a shimmering afternoon, waist-high
With bent, and red top, and timothy.

Lush with oat grass and tall fescue,
And the purple green of Kentucky blue;

A noble meadow, so broad each way
It took three good scythes to mow in a day.

Just where the field broke into a wood
A knotted old catalpa stood,

And in the old catalpa-tree
A cat-bird sang immoderately.

The sky above him was round and big
And its center seemed just over his twig.

The earth below him was fresh and fair,
With the sun's long fingers everywhere.

The cat-bird perched where a great leaf hung,
And the great leaf tilted, and flickered, and swung.

The cat-bird sang with a piercing glee
Up in the sun-specked catalpa-tree.

He sang so loud and he sang so long
That his ears were drowned in his own sweet song.

But the little peering leaves of grass
Shook and sundered to let them pass,

To let them pass, the men who heard
Nothing the grass said, nothing the bird.

Each man was still as a shining stone,
Each man's head was a buzzing bone

Wherein two words screeched in and out
Like a grinding saw with its turn about:

"Evelyn Ray," each stone man said,
And the words cut back and forth through his head,
And each of them wondered if he were dead.

The cat-bird sang with his head cocked up
Gazing into the sky's blue cup.

The grasses waved back into place,
The sun's long fingers stroked each face,

Each grim, cold face that saw no sun.
And the feet led the faces on and on.

They stopped beside the catalpa-tree,
Said one stone face to the other: "See!"

The other face had nothing to say,
Its lips were frozen on "Evelyn Ray."

They laid their hats in the tall green grass
Where the crickets and grasshoppers pass and pass.

They hung their coats in the crotch of a pine
And paced five feet in an even line.

They measured five paces either way,
And the saws in their heads screeched "Evelyn Ray."

The cat-bird sang so loud and clear
He heard nothing at all, there was nothing to hear.

Even the swish of long legs pushing
Through grass had ceased, there was only the hushing

Of a windless wind in the daisy tops,
And the jar stalks make when a grasshopper hops.

Every now and then a bee boomed over
The black-eyed Susans in search of clover,

And crickets shrilled as crickets do:
One—two. One—two.

The cat-bird sang with his head in the air,
And the sun's bright fingers poked here and there,

Past leaf, and branch, and needle, and cone.
But the stone men stood like men of stone.

Each man lifted a dull stone hand
And his fingers felt like weaving sand,

And his feet seemed standing on a ball
Which tossed and turned in a waterfall.

Each man heard a shot somewhere
Dropping out of the distant air.

But the screaming saws no longer said
"Evelyn Ray," for the men were dead.

✦

I often think of Evelyn Ray.
What did she do, what did she say?
Did she ever chance to pass that way?

I remember it as a lovely spot
Where a cat-bird sang. When he heard the shot,
Did he fly away? I have quite forgot.

When I went there last, he was singing again
Through a little fleeting, misty rain,
And pine-cones lay where they had lain.

This is the tale as I heard it when
I was young from a man who was threescore and ten.
A lady of clay and two stone men.

A pretty problem is here, no doubt,
If you have a fancy to work it out:
What happens to stone when clay is about?

Muse upon it as long as you will,
I think myself it will baffle your skill,
And your answer will be what mine is—nil.

But every sunny Summer's day
I am teased with the thought of Evelyn Ray,
Poor little image of painted clay.
And Heigh-o! I say.
What if there be a judgment-day?

What if all religions be true,
And Gabriel's trumpet blow for you
And blow for them—what will you do?

Evelyn Ray, will you rise alone?
Or will your lovers of dull gray stone
Pace beside you through the wan

Twilight of that bitter day
To be judged as stone and judged as clay,
And no one to say the judgment nay?

Better be nothing, Evelyn Ray,
A handful of buttercups that sway
In the wind for a children's holiday.

For earth to earth is the best we know,
Where the good blind worms push to and fro
Turning us into the seeds which grow,

And lovers and ladies are dead indeed,
Lost in the sap of a flower seed.
Is this, think you, a sorry creed?

Well, be it so, for the world is wide
And opinions jostle on every side.
What has always been hidden will always hide.

And every year when the fields are high
With oat grass, and red top, and timothy,
I know that a creed is the shell of a lie.

Peace be with you, Evelyn Ray,
And to your lovers, if so it may,
For earth made stone and earth made clay.

### THE TAXI

When I go away from you
The world beats dead
Like a slackened drum.
I call out for you against the jutted stars
And shout into the ridges of the wind.
Streets coming fast,
One after the other,

Wedge you away from me,
And the lamps of the city prick my eyes
So that I can no longer see your face.
Why should I leave you,
To wound myself upon the sharp edges of the night?


IN EXCELSIS

You—you
Your shadow is sunlight on a plate of silver;
Your footsteps, the seeding-place of lilies;
Your hands moving, a chime of bells across a windless air.

The movement of your hands is the long, golden running of light from a rising sun;
It is the hopping of birds upon a garden-path.

As the perfume of jonquils, you come forth in the morning.
Young horses are not more sudden than your thought,
Your words are bees about a pear-tree,
Your fancies are the gold-and-black striped wasps buzzing among red apples.
I drink your lips,
I eat the whiteness of your hands and feet.
My mouth is open,
As a new jar I am empty and open.
Like white water are you who fill the cup of my mouth,
Like a brook of water thronged with lilies.

You are frozen as the clouds,
You are far and sweet as the high clouds.
I dare reach to you,
I dare touch the rim of your brightness.
I leap beyond the winds,
I cry and shout,
For my throat is keen as a sword
Sharpened on a hone of ivory.
My throat sings the joy of my eyes,
The rushing gladness of my love.

How has the rainbow fallen upon my heart?
How have I snared the seas to lie in my fingers
And caught the sky to be a cover for my head?
How have you come to dwell with me,
Compassing me with the four circles of your mystic lightness,
So that I say "Glory! Glory!" and bow before you
As to a shrine?

Do I tease myself that morning is morning and a day after?
Do I think the air a condescension,
The earth a politeness,
Heaven a boon deserving thanks?
So you—air—earth—heaven—

I do not thank you,
I take you,
I live.
And those things which I say in consequence
Are rubies mortised in a gate of stone.

## MEETING-HOUSE HILL

I must be mad, or very tired,
When the curve of a blue bay beyond a railroad track
Is shrill and sweet to me like the sudden springing of a tune,
And the sight of a white church above thin trees in a city square
Amazes my eyes as though it were the Parthenon.
Clear, reticent, superbly final,
With the pillars of its portico refined to a cautious elegance,
It dominates the weak trees,
And the shot of its spire
Is cool and candid,
Rising into an unresisting sky.

Strange meeting-house
Pausing a moment upon a squalid hill-top.
I watch the spire sweeping the sky,
I am dizzy with the movement of the sky;
I might be watching a mast
With its royals set full
Straining before a two-reef breeze.
I might be sighting a tea-clipper,
Tacking into the blue bay,
Just back from Canton
With her hold full of green and blue porcelain
And a Chinese coolie leaning over the rail
Gazing at the white spire
With dull, sea-spent eyes.

## LILACS

Lilacs,
False blue,
White,
Purple,
Color of lilac,
Your great puffs of flowers
Are everywhere in this my New England.
Among your heart-shaped leaves
Orange orioles hop like music-box birds and sing
Their little weak soft songs;
In the crooks of your branches
The bright eyes of song sparrows sitting on spotted eggs
Peer restlessly through the light and shadow
Of all Springs.

Lilacs in dooryards
Holding quiet conversations with an early moon;
Lilacs watching a deserted house
Settling sideways into the grass of an old road;
Lilacs, wind-beaten, staggering under a lopsided shock of bloom
Above a cellar dug into a hill.
You are everywhere.
You were everywhere.
You tapped the window when the preacher preached his sermon,
And ran along the road beside the boy going to school.
You stood by pasture-bars to give the cows good milking,
You persuaded the housewife that her dish-pan was of silver
And her husband an image of pure gold.
You flaunted the fragrance of your blossoms
Through the wide doors of Custom Houses—
You, and sandalwood, and tea,
Charging the noses of quill-driving clerks
When a ship was in from China.
You called to them: "Goose-quill men, goose-quill men,
May is a month for flitting,"
Until they writhed on their high stools
And wrote poetry on their letter-sheets behind the propped-up ledgers.
Paradoxical New England clerks,
Writing inventories in ledgers, reading the "Song of Solomon" at night,
So many verses before bedtime,
Because it was the Bible.
The dead fed you
Amid the slant stones of graveyards.
Pale ghosts who planted you
Came in the night time
And let their thin hair blow through your clustered stems.
You are of the green sea,
And of the stone hills which reach a long distance.
You are of elm-shaded streets with little shops where they sell kites and marbles,
You are of great parks where everyone walks and nobody is at home.
You cover the blind sides of greenhouses
And lean over the top to say a hurry-word through the glass
To your friends, the grapes, inside.

Lilacs,
False blue,
White,
Purple,
Color of lilac,
You have forgotten your Eastern origin,
The veiled women with eyes like panthers,
The swollen, aggressive turbans of jeweled Pashas.
Now you are a very decent flower,
A reticent flower,
A curiously clear-cut, candid flower,
Standing beside clean doorways,

Friendly to a house-cat and a pair of spectacles,
Making poetry out of a bit of moonlight
And a hundred or two sharp blossoms.

Maine knows you,
Has for years and years;
New Hampshire knows you,
And Massachusetts
And Vermont.
Cape Cod starts you along the beaches to Rhode Island;
Connecticut takes you from a river to the sea.
You are brighter than apples,
Sweeter than tulips,
You are the great flood of our souls
Bursting above the leaf-shapes of our hearts,
You are the smell of all Summers,
The love of wives and children,
The recollection of the gardens of little children,
You are State Houses and Charters
And the familiar treading of the foot to and fro on a road it knows.
May is lilac here in New England,
May is a thrush singing "Sun up!" on a tip-top ash-tree,
May is white clouds behind pine-trees
Puffed out and marching upon a blue sky.
May is a green as no other,
May is much sun through small leaves,
May is soft earth,
And apple-blossoms,
And windows open to a South wind.
May is a full light wind of lilac
From Canada to Narragansett Bay.

Lilacs,
False blue,
White,
Purple,
Color of lilac,
Heart-leaves of lilac all over New England,
Roots of lilac under all the soil of New England,
Lilac in me because I am New England,
Because my roots are in it,
Because my leaves are of it,
Because my flowers are for it,
Because it is my country
And I speak to it of itself
And sing of it with my own voice
Since certainly it is mine.

THE SISTERS

Taking us by and large, we're a queer lot
We women who write poetry. And when you think
How few of us there've been, it's queerer still.
I wonder what it is that makes us do it,
Singles us out to scribble down, man-wise,
The fragments of ourselves. Why are we
Already mother-creatures, double-bearing,
With matrices in body and in brain?
I rather think that there is just the reason
We are so sparse a kind of human being;
The strength of forty thousand Atlases
Is needed for our every-day concerns.
There's Sapho, now I wonder what was Sapho.
I know a single slender thing about her:
That, loving, she was like a burning birch-tree
All tall and glittering fire, and that she wrote
Like the same fire caught up to Heaven and held there,
A frozen blaze before it broke and fell.
Ah, me! I wish I could have talked to Sapho,
Surprised her reticences by flinging mine
Into the wind. This tossing off of garments
Which cloud the soul is none too easy doing
With us today. But still I think with Sapho
One might accomplish it, were she in the mood
To bare her loveliness of words and tell
The reasons, as she possibly conceived them,
Of why they are so lovely. Just to know
How she came at them, just to watch
The crisp sea sunshine playing on her hair,
And listen, thinking all the while 'twas she
Who spoke and that we two were sisters
Of a strange, isolated little family.
And she is Sapho—Sapho—not Miss or Mrs.,
A leaping fire we call so for convenience.
But Mrs. Browning—who would ever think
Of such presumption as to call her "Ba."
Which draws the perfect line between sea-cliffs
And a close-shuttered room in Wimpole Street.
Sapho could fly her impulses like bright
Balloons tip-tilting to a morning air
And write about it. Mrs. Browning's heart
Was squeezed in stiff conventions. So she lay
Stretched out upon a sofa, reading Greek
And speculating, as I must suppose,
In just this way on Sapho; all the need,
The huge, imperious need of loving, crushed
Within the body she believed so sick.
And it was sick, poor lady, because words
Are merely simulacra after deeds

Have wrought a pattern; when they take the place
Of actions they breed a poisonous miasma
Which, though it leave the brain, eats up the body.
So Mrs. Browning, aloof and delicate,
Lay still upon her sofa, all her strength
Going to uphold her over-topping brain.
It seems miraculous, but she escaped
To freedom and another motherhood
Than that of poems. She was a very woman
And needed both.
                           If I had gone to call,
Would Wimpole Street have been the kindlier place,
Or Casa Guidi, in which to have met her?
I am a little doubtful of that meeting,
For Queen Victoria was very young and strong
And all-pervading in her apogee
At just that time. If we had stuck to poetry,
Sternly refusing to be drawn off by mesmerism
Or Roman revolutions, it might have done.
For, after all, she is another sister,
But always, I rather think, an older sister
And not herself so curious a technician
As to admit newfangled modes of writing—
"Except, of course, in Robert, and that is neither
Here nor there for Robert is a genius."
I do not like the turn this dream is taking,
Since I am very fond of Mrs. Browning
And very much indeed should like to hear her
Graciously asking me to call her "Ba."
But then the Devil of Verisimilitude
Creeps in and forces me to know she wouldn't.
Convention again, and how it chafes my nerves,
For we are such a little family
Of singing sisters, and as if I didn't know
What those years felt like tied down to the sofa.
Confound Victoria, and the slimy inhibitions
She loosed on all us Anglo-Saxon creatures!
Suppose there hadn't been a Robert Browning,
No "Sonnets from the Portuguese" would have been written.
They are the first of all her poems to be,
One might say, fertilized. For, after all,
A poet is flesh and blood as well as brain;
And Mrs. Browning, as I said before,
Was very, very woman. Well, there are two
Of us, and vastly unlike that's for certain.
Unlike at least until we tear the veils
Away which commonly gird souls. I scarcely think
Mrs. Browning would have approved the process
In spite of what had surely been relief;
For speaking souls must always want to speak
Even when bat-eyed, narrow-minded Queens

Set prudishness to keep the keys of impulse.
Then do the frowning Gods invent new banes
And make the need of sofas. But Sapho was dead
And I, and others, not yet peeped above
The edge of possibility. So that's an end
To speculating over tea-time talks
Beyond the movement of pentameters
With Mrs. Browning.
                                        But I go dreaming on,
In love with these my spiritual relations.
I rather think I see myself walk up
A flight of wooden steps and ring a bell
And send a card in to Miss Dickinson.
Yet that's a very silly way to do.
I should have taken the dream twist-ends about
And climbed over the fence and found her deep
Engrossed in the doings of a humming-bird
Among nasturtiums. Not having expected strangers,
She might forget to think me one, and holding up
A finger say quite casually: "Take care.
Don't frighten him, he's only just begun."
"Now this," I well believe I should have thought,
"Is even better than Sapho. With Emily
You're really here, or never anywhere at all
In range of mind." Wherefore, having begun
In the strict center, we could slowly progress
To various circumferences, as we pleased.
About the naked majesty of God.

Good-by, my sisters, all of you are great,
And all of you are marvelously strange,
And none of you has any word for me.
I cannot write like you, I cannot think
In terms of Pagan or of Christian now.
I only hope that possibly some day
Some other woman with an itch for writing
May turn to me as I have turned to you
And chat with me a brief few minutes. How
We lie, we poets! It is three good hours
I have been dreaming. Has it seemed so long
To you? And yet I thank you for the time,
Although you leave me sad and self-distrustful,
For older sisters are very sobering things.
Put on your cloaks, my dears, the motor's waiting.
No, you have not seemed strange to me, but near,
Frightfully near, and rather terrifying.
I understand you all, for in myself—
Is that presumption? Yet indeed it's true—
We are one family. And still my answer
Will not be any one of yours, I see.
Well, never mind that now. Good night! Good night!

# Ridgely Torrence

(Frederic) Ridgely Torrence was born at Xenia, Ohio, November 27, 1875, and was educated at Miami and Princeton University. For several years he was librarian of the Astor Library in New York City (1897-1901), later assuming an editorial position on the *Cosmopolitan Magazine*. He was, for several years, poetry editor of *The New Republic*.

His first volume, *The House of a Hundred Lights* (1900), bears the grave sub-title "A Psalm of Experience after Reading a Couplet of Bidpai." It is a whimsical hodge-podge of philosophy, love lyrics, artlessness and impudence.

Not until a quarter of a century later did Torrence publish his second volume of verse. In the meantime, poems of his had attracted attention upon their appearance in magazines and a few of his lyrics had been quoted so often that they were fa-miliar to those who had never heard of Torrence's other work. Torrence had re-mained in the peculiar position of one whose best verse was not only unprocurable, but unprinted. *Hesperides* (1925) remedied this strange circumstance. Like his first volume, this is not a large book, but these one hundred pages contain definite and distinguished poetry. In *Hesperides* one finds the magnificent "Eye-Witness," a most original treatment of the theme of Christ's second coming, the purely lyrical "The Singers in a Cloud" and that brief epic, "The Bird and the Tree" which is as famous as it is stirring.

Between Torrence's earliest and most recent volume, three of his plays were pub-lished: *El Dorado* (1903), *Abelard and Héloise* (1907), and *Granny Maumee, The Rider of Dreams, Simon the Cyrenian* (1917). The last group, being three plays for a Negro theater, contains the best of Torrence's dramatic writing. He has caught here, particularly in *Granny Maumee* and *The Rider of Dreams,* something of that high color which the Negro himself has begun to articulate.

## THE BIRD AND THE TREE

Blackbird, blackbird in the cage,
There's something wrong tonight.
Far off the sheriff's footfall dies,
The minutes crawl like last year's flies
Between the bars, and like an age
The hours are long tonight.

The sky is like a heavy lid
Out here beyond the door tonight.
What's that? A mutter down the street.
What's that? The sound of yells and feet.
For what you didn't do or did
You'll pay the score tonight.

No use to reek with reddened sweat,
No use to whimper and to sweat.
They've got the rope; they've got the guns,
They've got the courage and the guns;

An' that's the reason why tonight
No use to ask them any more.
They'll fire the answer through the door—
You're out to die tonight.

There where the lonely cross-road lies,
There is no place to make replies;
But silence, inch by inch, is there,
And the right limb for a lynch is there;
And a lean daw waits for both your eyes,
Blackbird.

Perhaps you'll meet again some place.
Look for the mask upon the face;
That's the way you'll know them there—
A white mask to hide the face.
And you can halt and show them there
The things that they are deaf to now,
And they can tell you what they meant—

To wash the blood with blood. But how
If you are innocent?

Blackbird singer, blackbird mute,
They choked the seed you might have found.
Out of a thorny field you go—
For you it may be better so—
And leave the sowers of the ground
To eat the harvest of the fruit,
Blackbird.

### THE SON

#### (Southern Ohio Market Town)

I heard an old farm-wife,
Selling some barley,

Mingle her life with life
And the name "Charley."

Saying: "The crop's all in,
We're about through now;
Long nights will soon begin,
We're just us two now.

"Twelve bushels at sixty cents,
It's all I carried—
He sickened making fence;
He was to be married—

"It feels like frost was near—
His hair was curly.
The spring was late that year,
But the harvest early."

# Robert Frost

Aｌｔｈｏｕｇｈ known as the chief interpreter of New England, Robert (Lee) Frost
was born in San Francisco, California, March 26, 1875. His father, born in
New Hampshire, taught school, edited a paper, entered politics, and moved to San
Francisco where his "copperhead" sympathy with the South led him to christen his
son Robert Lee. Frost's mother, after the death of her husband, supported herself
and her children by teaching school; bringing the family back East to the towns
and hills where, for eight generations, his forefathers had lived and where, much
later, Frost was to uphold the tradition by lecturing, accepting an "idle professor-
ship" ("being a sort of poetic radiator") at Amherst, and buying farms in Vermont.
After graduating from the high school at Lawrence, Massachusetts, in 1892, Frost
entered Dartmouth College, where he remained only a few months. The routine of
study was too much for him and he decided to earn his living and became a bobbin-
boy in one of the mills at Lawrence. He had already begun to write poetry; a few
of his verses had appeared in The Independent. But the strange, soil-flavored quality
which even then distinguished his lines was not relished by the editors, and the
very magazines to which he sent poems that today are famous rejected his verse
with unanimity. For twenty years Frost continued to write his highly characteristic
work in spite of the discouraging apathy, and for twenty years the poet remained
unknown.

In 1897, two years after his marriage, Frost moved his family to Cambridge,
Massachusetts, entering Harvard in a final determination to achieve culture. This
time he followed the curriculum for two years, but at the end of that dry period he
stopped trying to learn and started to teach. (Curiously enough, though Frost made
light of and even ridiculed his scholarship, his marks in Greek and the classical
studies were always exceptionally high.) For three years he followed the family tradition and taught school in New England; he also made shoes, edited a weekly

paper, and in 1900 became a farmer at Derry, New Hampshire. During the next eleven years Frost labored to wrest a living from stubborn hills with scant success. Loneliness claimed him for its own; the rocks refused to give him a living; the literary world continued to remain oblivious of his existence. Frost sought a change of environment and, after a few years' teaching at Derry and Plymouth, New Hampshire, sold his farm and, with his wife and four children, sailed for England in September, 1912.

For the first time in his life, Frost moved in a literary world. Groups merged, dissolved and separated overnight; controversy and creation were in the air. A friendship was established with the poets Abercrombie, Brooke and Gibson, a close intimacy with Edward Thomas. Here Frost wrote most of his longer narratives, took his lyrics to a publisher with few hopes, went back to the suburban town of Beaconsfield and turned to other matters. A few months later *A Boy's Will* (1913) was published and Frost was recognized at once as one of the authentic voices of modern poetry.

*A Boy's Will* is seemingly subjective; in spite of certain reminiscences of Browning it is no set of derivations. In *A Boy's Will* Frost is not yet completely in possession of his own idiom; but the *timbre* is recognizably his. No one but Frost could have written "Reluctance" or "The Tuft of Flowers." Wholly lyrical, this volume, lacking the concentrated emotion of his subsequent works, is a significant introduction to the following book, which became an international classic. Early in 1914, Frost leased a small place in Gloucestershire; in the spring of the same year, *North of Boston* (1914), one of the most intensely American books ever printed, was published in England. (See Preface.) This is, as he has called it, a "book of people." And it is more than that—it is a book of backgrounds as living and dramatic as the people they overshadow. Frost vivifies a stone wall, an empty cottage, a grindstone, a mountain, a forgotten wood-pile left

> To warm the frozen swamp as best it could
> With the slow, smokeless burning of decay.

*North of Boston,* like its successor, contains much of the finest poetry of our time. Rich in its actualities, richer in its spiritual values, every line moves with the double force of observation and implication. The very first poem in the book illustrates this power of character and symbolism. Although Frost is not arguing for anything in particular, one senses here something more than the enemies of walls. In "Mending Wall," we see two elemental and opposed forces. "Something there is that doesn't love a wall," insists the seeker after causes; "Good fences make good neighbors," doggedly replies the literal-minded lover of tradition. Here, beneath the whimsical turns and pungency of expression, we have the essence of nationalism versus the internationalist: the struggle, though the poet would be the last to prod the point, between blind obedience to custom and questioning iconoclasm.

So with all of Frost's characters. Like the worn-out incompetent in "The Death of the Hired Man" (one of the finest *genre* pictures of our time), or the autobiographical country boy climbing "black branches up a snow-white trunk toward heaven" in "Birches," or the positive, tight-lipped old lady in "The Black Cottage," or the headlong but laconic Brown of "Brown's Descent," his people are always amplified through the poet's circumlocutory but precise psychology. They remain close to their soil. Frost's monologs and dramatic idyls, written in a conversational blank verse, establish the connection between the vernacular and the language of literature; they remain rooted in realism. But Frost is never a photographic realist. "There are," he once said, "two types of realist—the one who offers a good deal of dirt with his potato to show that it is a real one; and the one who is satisfied with the potato brushed clean. I'm inclined to be the second kind. . . . To me, the thing that art does for life is to clean it, to strip it to form."

In March, 1915, Frost came back to America—to a hill outside of Franconia, New Hampshire. *North of Boston* had been reprinted in the United States and its author, who had left the country an unknown writer, returned to find himself famous. Honors were awarded to him; within ten years one university after another conferred degrees upon him who was unwilling to graduate from any of them; he became "professor in residence" at Amherst. His lectures (actually glorified philosophic speculations) were notable, although he permitted only one of them, *Education by Poetry* (1930), which Frost called "a meditative monologue," to be reduced to print.

*Mountain Interval,* containing some of Frost's most characteristic poems ("Birches," and "An Old Man's Winter Night" are typical), appeared in 1916. The idiom is the same as in the earlier volumes, but the notes are more varied, the lyrics intensified, the assurance is stronger. The subtle variations of the tones of speech find their sympathetic reporter here; the lines disclose delicate shades of emphasis in the way they present an entire scene by giving only a significant detail. Altogether natural, yet fanciful no less than realistic, this poetry escapes labels, "but," Frost once said, with a suspicion of a twinkle, "if I must be classified as a poet, I might be called a Synecdochist; for I prefer the synecdoche in poetry—that figure of speech in which we use a part for the whole."

*New Hampshire* (1923), which was awarded the Pulitzer Prize for the best volume of poetry published in 1923, synthesizes Frost's qualities: it combines the stark unity of *North of Boston* and the diffused geniality of *Mountain Interval.* If one thing predominates, it is a feeling of quiet classicism; the poet has lowered his voice but not the strength of his convictions. To say, as was said, that Frost gives us a poetry "without the delight of the senses, without the glow of warm feeling" is—particularly when faced with *New Hampshire*—to utter an absurdity. Frost, in spite of a superficial underemphasis, does not hesitate to declare his close affection. Such poems as "Two Look at Two," with its tremendous wave of love, "To Earthward," with its unreserved intensity, even the brilliantly condensed "Fire and Ice," with its candidly registered passion—all these brim with a physical radiance, with the very delight and pain of the senses. Nor is the fanciful by-play, the sly banter so characteristic of this poet, absent from the volume. Who but Frost could put so whimsical an accent in the farewell to an orchard entitled "Good-by and Keep Cold"; who but he could summon, with so few strokes, the frightened colt "with one forefoot on the wall, the other curled at his breast" in "The Runaway"? The very scheme of *New Hampshire* is an extended whimsicality: he offers the contents of the volume as a series of explanatory notes (and grace notes) to the title poem, which is supposed to be the book's *raison d'être.* The long poems (the "notes") rank with the narrative monologs in *North of Boston;* the "grace notes" contain not merely Frost's finest lines but some of the most haunting lyrics ever written by an American. Such a poem as "Stopping by Woods on a Snowy Evening" once in the mind of a reader will never leave it. Had Frost written nothing but these thirty "grace notes" his place in poetry would be assured. A revised *Selected Poems* (revised in 1928 and 1935) and a rearranged *Collected Poems* (1930) which again won the Pulitzer Prize, confirmed the conclusions; the unpretentious bucolics had become contemporary classics.

It has been said that Frost's work suffers from an exclusiveness, and even his most ardent admirers would be willing to admit that his is not an indiscriminately inclusive passion like Whitman's. But Frost loves what he loves with a fierce attachment, a tenderness fixed beyond a more easily transferred regard. His devotion to the intimacies of earth is, even more than Wordsworth's, rich, almost inordinate in its fidelity; what his emotion (or his poetry) may lack in windy range, is trebly compensated for by its untroubled depths.

This is more true than ever of *West-Running Brook* (1928) which was hailed with loud—and misleading—enthusiasm. No contemporary poet received more praise than Frost, and none was more praised for the wrong attributes. As late as 1928, most of the critics were surprised that the writer identified with the long monologs in *North of Boston* should turn to lyrics, forgetting that Frost's first volume (written in the 1890's and published twenty years later) was wholly and insistently lyrical. One reviewer, echoing the false platitude concerning New England bleakness, applauded Frost's almost colorless reticence, his "preference for black and white." Another made the discovery that "where he was formerly content to limn a landscape . . . here the emphasis is primarily the poet's emotion." A more understanding consideration of Frost's poetry would have instructed the critics. They would have seen that no volumes have ever been less black and white, no poetry so delicately shaded. The so-called inhibitions disappear upon rereading. Frost's poems are only superficially reticent; actually they are profound and personal revelations. Frost has never been "content to limn a landscape." He cannot suggest a character or a countryside without informing the subject with his own philosophy, a philosophy whose bantering accents cannot hide a moral earnestness. Beyond the fact ("the dearest dream that labor knows"), beyond the tone of voice, which is— at least technically—the poet's first concern, there is that ardent and unifying emotion which is Frost's peculiar quality and his essential spirit. Nothing could prove it more fully than the title-poem with its seemingly casual but actually cosmic philosophy. Such poetry, with its genius for suggestive understatement, establishes Frost among the first of contemporary writers and places him with the very best of American poets past or present. It is not the technique nor even the thought, but the essence which finally convinces; the reader is fortified by Frost's serenity, strengthened by his strength.

*West-Running Brook* is a reflection and restatement of all that has gone before. The autobiographical references are a little more outspoken; Amy Lowell's assertion that "there is no poem which has San Francisco as a background nor which seems to owe its inception to the author's early life" is answered again and again by poems which are packed with the poet's youth. Thus a student will learn that the presumably "late" poem entitled "On Going Unnoticed" was written as early as 1901; the poem "Bereft" was conceived about 1893; and "Once by the Pacific" is half-humorously dated "as of about 1880"—at which time the poet was exactly six years old.

In *West-Running Brook* and the subsequent memorable lyrics Frost maintains his
rôle of half-earnest synecdochist. Here, again, offering the part for the whole, he re-
establishes the force of suggestion and reaffirms his conviction: "All that an artist
needs is samples." Parsimony is achieved in every one of the new poems. It sharpens
the ruminating accents of "Tree at My Window," fastens the epigrammatic irony of
"The Peaceful Shepherd," quickens the somber power of "Bereft" and "Once by
the Pacific," points the teasing play of "The Bear." It is, parenthetically, interesting
to observe how Frost's poetry answers the charge that he is unremittingly grave;
poems as late as "The Egg and the Machine" and as early as "Brown's Descent"
have not only that talk-flavored tone which he cherishes but a humor pungent and
broad. The ripe repose, the banked passions, the nicely blended tenderness and
humor are everywhere. Here neighborliness is universalized and localism is a province of humanity. But beneath all is the individual to whom, as G. R. Elliott points
out, the "eternal mystery" is "eternal appetite under eternal control." The rich play
of the serious mind is emphasized by the later "Two Tramps in Mud-Time," and
the self-revealing "A Leaf-Treader" and "Desert Places."

Growth? Change? A new note? The answers may be found in the *Collected
Poems* and in two lines of one of Frost's first poems, a premonitory couplet written
before 1900:

> They would not find me changed from him they knew,
> Only more sure of all I thought was true.

No reviewer has written, no critic will write, a better summary.

### THE PASTURE

I'm going out to clean the pasture spring;
I'll only stop to rake the leaves away
(And wait to watch the water clear, I may):
I shan't be gone long.—You come too.

I'm going out to fetch the little calf
That's standing by the mother. It's so young,
It totters when she licks it with her tongue.
I shan't be gone long.—You come too.

### THE TUFT OF FLOWERS

I went to turn the grass once after one
Who mowed it in the dew before the sun.

The dew was gone that made his blade so keen
Before I came to view the leveled scene.

I looked for him behind an isle of trees;
I listened for his whetstone on the breeze.

But he had gone his way, the grass all mown,
And I must be, as he had been,—alone,

"As all must be," I said within my heart,
"Whether they work together or apart."

But as I said it, swift there passed me by
On noiseless wing a bewildered butterfly,

Seeking with memories grown dim over night
Some resting flower of yesterday's delight.

And once I marked his flight go round and round,
As where some flower lay withering on the ground.

And then he flew as far as eye could see,
And then on tremulous wing came back to me.

I thought of questions that have no reply,
And would have turned to toss the grass to dry;

But he turned first, and led my eye to look
At a tall tuft of flowers beside a brook,

A leaping tongue of bloom the scythe had spared
Beside a reedy brook the scythe had bared.

I left my place to know them by their name,
Finding them butterfly-weed when I came.

The mower in the dew had loved them thus,
By leaving them to flourish, not for us,

Nor yet to draw one thought of ours to him,
But from sheer morning gladness at the brim.

The butterfly and I had lit upon,
Nevertheless, a message from the dawn,

That made me hear the wakening birds around,
And hear his long scythe whispering to the ground,

And feel a spirit kindred to my own;
So that henceforth I worked no more alone;

But glad with him, I worked as with his aid,
And weary, sought at noon with him the shade;

And dreaming, as it were, held brotherly speech
With one whose thought I had not hoped to reach.

"Men work together," I told him from the heart,
"Whether they work together or apart."

## RELUCTANCE

Out through the fields and the woods
   And over the walls I have wended;
I have climbed the hills of view
   And looked at the world, and descended;
I have come by the highway home,
   And lo, it is ended.

The leaves are all dead on the ground,
   Save those that the oak is keeping
To ravel them one by one
   And let them go scraping and creeping
Out over the crusted snow,
   When others are sleeping.

And the dead leaves lie huddled and still,
   No longer blown hither and thither;
The last lone aster is gone;
   The flowers of the witch-hazel wither;
The heart is still aching to seek,
   But the feet question "Whither?"

Ah, when to the heart of man
   Was it ever less than a treason
To go with the drift of things
   To yield with a grace to reason,
And bow and accept the end
   Of a love or a season?

## MENDING WALL

Something there is that doesn't love a wall,
That sends the frozen-ground-swell under it,
And spills the upper bowlders in the sun;
And makes gaps even two can pass abreast.
The work of hunters is another thing:
I have come after them and made repair
Where they have left not one stone on a stone,
But they would have the rabbit out of hiding,
To please the yelping dogs. The gaps I mean,
No one has seen them made or heard them made,
But at spring mending-time we find them there.
I let my neighbor know beyond the hill;
And on a day we meet to walk the line
And set the wall between us once again.
We keep the wall between us as we go.
To each the bowlders that have fallen to each.
And some are loaves and some so nearly balls
We have to use a spell to make them balance:
"Stay where you are until our backs are turned!"

We wear our fingers rough with handling them.
Oh, just another kind of outdoor game,
One on a side. It comes to little more:
There where it is we do not need the wall:
He is all pine and I am apple-orchard.
My apple trees will never get across
And eat the cones under his pines, I tell him.
He only says, "Good fences make good neighbors."
Spring is the mischief in me, and I wonder
If I could put a notion in his head:
"*Why* do they make good neighbors? Isn't it
Where there are cows? But here there are no cows.
Before I built a wall I'd ask to know
What I was walling in or walling out,
And to whom I was like to give offense.
Something there is that doesn't love a wall,
That wants it down!" I could say "elves" to him,
But it's not elves exactly, and I'd rather
He said it for himself. I see him there,
Bringing a stone grasped firmly by the top
In each hand, like an old-stone savage armed.
He moves in darkness, as it seems to me,
Not of woods only and the shade of trees.
He will not go behind his father's saying,
And he likes having thought of it so well
He says again, "Good fences make good neighbors."

## THE COW IN APPLE-TIME

Something inspires the only cow of late
To make no more of a wall than an open gate,
And think no more of wall-builders than fools.
Her face is flecked with pomace and she drools
A cider sirup. Having tasted fruit,
She scorns a pasture withering to the root.
She runs from tree to tree where lie and sweeten
The windfalls spiked with stubble and worm-eaten.
She leaves them bitten when she has to fly.
She bellows on a knoll against the sky.
Her udder shrivels and the milk goes dry.

## THE DEATH OF THE HIRED MAN

Mary sat musing on the lamp-flame at the table
Waiting for Warren. When she heard his step,
She ran on tip-toe down the darkened passage
To meet him in the doorway with the news
And put him on his guard. "Silas is back."
She pushed him outward with her through the door
And shut it after her. "Be kind," she said.

She took the market things from Warren's arms
And set them on the porch, then drew him down
To sit beside her on the wooden steps.
"When was I ever anything but kind to him?
But I'll not have the fellow back," he said.
"I told him so last haying, didn't I?
'If he left then,' I said, 'that ended it.'
What good is he? Who else will harbor him
At his age for the little he can do?
What help he is there's no depending on.
Off he goes always when I need him most.
'He thinks he ought to earn a little pay,
Enough at least to buy tobacco with,
So he won't have to beg and be beholden.'
'All right,' I say, 'I can't afford to pay
Any fixed wages, though I wish I could.'
'Someone else can.' 'Then someone else will have to.'
I shouldn't mind his bettering himself
If that was what it was. You can be certain,
When he begins like that, there's someone at him
Trying to coax him off with pocket-money,—
In haying time, when any help is scarce.
In winter he comes back to us. I'm done."

"Sh! not so loud: he'll hear you," Mary said.

"I want him to: he'll have to soon or late."

"He's worn out. He's asleep beside the stove.
When I came up from Rowe's I found him here,
Huddled against the barn-door fast asleep,
A miserable sight, and frightening, too—
You needn't smile—I didn't recognize him—
I wasn't looking for him—and he's changed.
Wait till you see."

                    "Where did you say he'd been?"

"He didn't say. I dragged him to the house,
And gave him tea and tried to make him smoke.
I tried to make him talk about his travels,
Nothing would do: he just kept nodding off."

"What did he say? Did he say anything?"

"But little."

          "Anything? Mary, confess
He said he'd come to ditch the meadow for me."

"Warren!"

"But did he? I just want to know."

"Of course he did. What would you have him say?
Surely you wouldn't grudge the poor old man
Some humble way to save his self-respect.
He added, if you really care to know,
He meant to clear the upper pasture, too.
That sounds like something you have heard before?
Warren, I wish you could have heard the way
He jumbled everything. I stopped to look
Two or three times—he made me feel so queer—
To see if he was talking in his sleep.
He ran on Harold Wilson—you remember—
The boy you had in haying four years since.
He's finished school, and teaching in his college.
Silas declares you'll have to get him back.
He says they two will make a team for work:
Between them they will lay this farm as smooth!
The way he mixed that in with other things.
He thinks young Wilson a likely lad, though daft
On education—you know how they fought
All through July under the blazing sun,
Silas up on the cart to build the load,
Harold along beside to pitch it on."

"Yes, I took care to keep well out of earshot."

"Well, those days trouble Silas like a dream.
You wouldn't think they would. How some things linger!
Harold's young college boy's assurance piqued him.
After so many years he still keeps finding
Good arguments he sees he might have used.
I sympathize. I know just how it feels
To think of the right thing to say too late.
Harold's associated in his mind with Latin.
He asked me what I thought of Harold's saying
He studied Latin like the violin
Because he liked it—that an argument!
He said he couldn't make the boy believe
He could find water with a hazel prong—
Which showed how much good school had ever done him.
He wanted to go over that. But most of all
He thinks if he could have another chance
To teach him how to build a load of hay—"

"I know, that's Silas' one accomplishment.
He bundles every forkful in its place,
And tags and numbers it for future reference,
So he can find and easily dislodge it
In the unloading. Silas does that well.
He takes it out in bunches like birds' nests.

You never see him standing on the hay
He's trying to lift, straining to lift himself."

"He thinks if he could teach him that, he'd be
Some good perhaps to someone in the world.
He hates to see a boy the fool of books.
Poor Silas, so concerned for other folk,
And nothing to look backward to with pride,
And nothing to look forward to with hope,
So now and never any different."

Part of a moon was falling down the west,
Dragging the whole sky with it to the hills.
Its light poured softly in her lap. She saw
And spread her apron to it. She put out her hand
Among the harp-like morning-glory strings,
Taut with the dew from garden bed to eaves,
As if she played unheard the tenderness
That wrought on him beside her in the night.
"Warren," she said, "he has come home to die:
You needn't be afraid he'll leave you this time."

"Home," he mocked gently.

                              "Yes, what else but home?
It all depends on what you mean by home.
Of course he's nothing to us, any more
Than was the hound that came a stranger to us
Out of the woods, worn out upon the trail."

"Home is the place where, when you have to go there,
They have to take you in."

                              "I should have called it
Something you somehow haven't to deserve."

Warren leaned out and took a step or two,
Picked up a little stick, and brought it back
And broke it in his hand and tossed it by.
"Silas has better claim on us, you think,
Than on his brother? Thirteen little miles
As the road winds would bring him to his door.
Silas has walked that far no doubt today.
Why didn't he go there? His brother's rich,
A somebody—director in the bank."

"He never told us that."

                              "We know it though."

"I think his brother ought to help, of course.
I'll see to that if there is need. He ought of right

To take him in, and might be willing to—
He may be better than appearances.
But have some pity on Silas. Do you think
If he'd had any pride in claiming kin
Or anything he looked for from his brother,
He'd keep so still about him all this time?"

"I wonder what's between them."

       "I can tell you.
Silas is what he is—we wouldn't mind him—
But just the kind that kinsfolk can't abide.
He never did a thing so very bad.
He don't know why he isn't quite as good
As anyone. He won't be made ashamed
To please his brother, worthless though he is."

"I can't think Si ever hurt anyone."

"No, but he hurt my heart the way he lay
And rolled his old head on that sharp-edged chair-back.
He wouldn't let me put him on the lounge.
You must go in and see what you can do.
I made the bed up for him there tonight.
You'll be surprised at him—how much he's broken.
His working days are done; I'm sure of it."

"I'd not be in a hurry to say that."

"I haven't been. Go, look, see for yourself.
But, Warren, please remember how it is:
He's come to help you ditch the meadow.
He has a plan. You mustn't laugh at him.
He may not speak of it, and then he may.
I'll sit and see if that small sailing cloud
Will hit or miss the moon."

      It hit the moon.
Then there were three there, making a dim row,
The moon, the little silver cloud, and she.

Warren returned—too soon, it seemed to her,
Slipped to her side, caught up her hand and waited.

"Warren?" she questioned.

      "Dead," was all he answered.

### AFTER APPLE-PICKING

My long two-pointed ladder's sticking through a tree
Toward heaven still,
And there's a barrel that I didn't fill
Beside it, and there may be two or three
Apples I didn't pick upon some bough.
But I am done with apple-picking now.
Essence of winter sleep is on the night,
The scent of apples: I am drowsing off.
I cannot rub the strangeness from my sight
I got from looking through a pane of glass
I skimmed this morning from the drinking trough
And held against the world of hoary grass.
It melted, and I let it fall and break.
But I was well
Upon my way to sleep before it fell,
And I could tell
What form my dreaming was about to take.
Magnified apples appear and disappear,
Stem-end and blossom-end,
And every fleck of russet showing clear.
My instep arch not only keeps the ache,
It keeps the pressure of a ladder-round.
I feel the ladder sway as the boughs bend.
And I keep hearing from the cellar bin
The rumbling sound
Of load on load of apples coming in.
For I have had too much
Of apple-picking: I am overtired
Of the great harvest I myself desired.
There were ten thousand fruit to touch,
Cherish in hand, lift down, and not let fall.
For all
That struck the earth,
No matter if not bruised or spiked with stubble,
Went surely to the cider-apple heap
As of no worth.
One can see what will trouble
This sleep of mine, whatever sleep it is.
Were he not gone,
The woodchuck could say whether it's like his
Long sleep, as I describe its coming on,
Or just some human sleep.

### AN OLD MAN'S WINTER NIGHT

All out of doors looked darkly in at him
Through the thin frost, almost in separate stars,
That gathers on the pane in empty rooms.
What kept his eyes from giving back the gaze

Was the lamp tilted near them in his hand.
What kept him from remembering what it was
That brought him to that creaking room was age.
He stood with barrels round him—at a loss.
And having scared the cellar under him
In clomping there, he scared it once again
In clomping off; and scared the outer night,
Which has its sounds, familiar, like the roar
Of trees and crack of branches, common things,
But nothing so like beating on a box.
A light he was to no one but himself
Where now he sat, concerned with he knew what;
A quiet light, and then not even that.
He consigned to the moon, such as she was,
So late-arising, to the broken moon
As better than the sun in any case
For such a charge, his snow upon the roof,
His icicles along the wall to keep;
And slept. The log that shifted with a jolt
Once in the stove, disturbed him and he shifted,
And eased his heavy breathing, but still slept.
One aged man—one man—can't fill a house,
A farm, a countryside, or if he can,
It's thus he does it of a winter night.

## BIRCHES

When I see birches bend to left and right
Across the line of straighter darker trees,
I like to think some boy's been swinging them.
But swinging doesn't bend them down to stay.
Ice-storms do that. Often you must have seen them
Loaded with ice a sunny winter morning
After a rain. They click upon themselves
As the breeze rises, and turn many-colored
As the stir cracks and crazes their enamel.
Soon the sun's warmth makes them shed crystal shells
Shattering and avalanching on the snow-crust—
Such heaps of broken glass to sweep away
You'd think the inner dome of heaven had fallen.
They are dragged to the withered bracken by the load,
And they seem not to break; though once they are bowed
So low for long, they never right themselves:
You may see their trunks arching in the woods
Years afterwards, trailing their leaves on the ground
Like girls on hands and knees that throw their hair
Before them over their heads to dry in the sun.
But I was going to say when Truth broke in
With all her matter-of-fact about the ice-storm
I should prefer to have some boy bend them
As he went out and in to fetch the cows—

Some boy too far from town to learn baseball,
Whose only play was what he found himself,
Summer or winter, and could play alone.
One by one he subdued his father's trees
By riding them down over and over again
Until he took the stiffness out of them,
And not one but hung limp, not one was left
For him to conquer. He learned all there was
To learn about not launching out too soon
And so not carrying the tree away
Clear to the ground. He always kept his poise
To the top branches, climbing carefully
With the same pains you use to fill a cup
Up to the brim, and even above the brim.
Then he flung outward, feet first, with a swish,
Kicking his way down through the air to the ground.

So was I once myself a swinger of birches;
And so I dream of going back to be.
It's when I'm weary of considerations,
And life is too much like a pathless wood
Where your face burns and tickles with the cobwebs
Broken across it, and one eye is weeping
From a twig's having lashed across it open.
I'd like to get away from earth awhile
And then come back to it and begin over.
May no fate willfully misunderstand me
And half grant what I wish and snatch me away
Not to return. Earth's the right place for love:
I don't know where it's likely to go better.
I'd like to go by climbing a birch tree,
And climb black branches up a snow-white trunk
*Toward* heaven, till the tree could bear no more,
But dipped its top and set me down again.
That would be good both going and coming back.
One could do worse than be a swinger of birches.

BROWN'S DESCENT

OR, THE WILLY-NILLY SLIDE

Brown lived at such a lofty farm
  That everyone for miles could see
His lantern when he did his chores
  In winter after half-past three.

And many must have seen him make
  His wild descent from there one night,
'Cross lots, 'cross walls, 'cross everything,
  Describing rings of lantern light.

Between the house and barn the gale
  Got him by something he had on

And blew him out on the icy crust
  That cased the world, and he was gone!

Walls were all buried, trees were few:
  He saw no stay unless he stove
A hole in somewhere with his heel.
  But though repeatedly he strove

And stamped and said things to himself,
  And sometimes something seemed to yield
He gained no foothold, but pursued
  His journey down from field to field.

metimes he came with arms outspread
Like wings revolving in the scene
pon his longer axis, and
With no small dignity of mien.

ster or slower as he chanced,
Sitting or standing as he chose,
cording as he feared to risk
His neck, or thought to spare his clothes,

e never let the lantern drop.
And some exclaimed who saw afar
ne figure he described with it,
"I wonder what those signals are

rown makes at such an hour of night!
He's celebrating something strange.
wonder if he's sold his farm,
Or been made Master of the Grange."

e reeled, he lurched, he bobbed, he checked;
He fell and made the lantern rattle
ut saved the light from going out).
So half-way down he fought the battle

credulous of his own bad luck.
And then becoming reconciled
everything, he gave it up
And came down like a coasting child.

Jell—I—be—" that was all he said,
As standing in the river road,

He looked back up the slippery slope
(Two miles it was) to his abode.

Sometimes as an authority
On motor-cars, I'm asked if I
Should say our stock was petered out,
And this is my sincere reply:

Yankees are what they always were.
Don't think Brown ever gave up hope
Of getting home again because
He couldn't climb that slippery slope;

Or even thought of standing there
Until the January thaw
Should take the polish off the crust.
He bowed with grace to natural law,

And then went round it on his feet,
After the manner of our stock;
Not much concerned for those to whom,
At that particular time o'clock,

It must have looked as if the course
He steered was really straight away
From that which he was headed for—
Not much concerned for them, I say,

But now he snapped his eyes three times;
Then shook his lantern, saying, "Ile's
'Bout out!" and took the long way home
By road, a matter of several miles.

### THE RUNAWAY

Once when the snow of the year was beginning to fall,
We stopped by a mountain pasture to say, "Whose colt?"
A little Morgan had one forefoot on the wall,
The other curled at his breast. He dipped his head
And snorted to us. And then he had to bolt.
We heard the miniature thunder where he fled,
And we saw him, or thought we saw him, dim and gray,
Like a shadow against the curtain of falling flakes.
"I think the little fellow's afraid of the snow.
He isn't winter-broken. It isn't play
With the little fellow at all. He's running away.
I doubt if even his mother could tell him, 'Sakes,
It's only weather.' He'd think she didn't know!
Where is his mother? He can't be out alone."
And now he comes again with a clatter of stone
And mounts the wall again with whited eyes

And all his tail that isn't hair up straight.
He shudders his coat as if to throw off flies.
"Whoever it is that leaves him out so late,
When other creatures have gone to stall and bin,
Ought to be told to come and take him in."

### TO EARTHWARD

Love at the lips was touch
As sweet as I could bear;
And once that seemed too much;
I lived on air

That crossed me from sweet things,
The flow of—was it musk
From hidden grapevine springs
Down hill at dusk?

I had the swirl and ache
From sprays of honeysuckle
That when they're gathered shake
Dew on the knuckle.

I craved strong sweets, but those
Seemed strong when I was young;
The petal of the rose
It was that stung.

Now no joy but lacks salt
That is not dashed with pain
And weariness and fault;
I crave the stain

Of tears, the aftermark
Of almost too much love,
The sweet of bitter bark
And burning clove.

When stiff and sore and scarred
I take away my hand
From leaning on it hard
In grass and sand,

The hurt is not enough:
I long for weight and strength
To feel the earth as rough
To all my length.

### FIRE AND ICE

Some say the world will end in fire,
Some say in ice.
From what I've tasted of desire
I hold with those who favor fire.
But if it had to perish twice,
I think I know enough of hate
To say that for destruction ice
Is also great
And would suffice.

### TWO LOOK AT TWO

Love and forgetting might have carried them
A little further up the mountain side
With night so near, but not much further up.
They must have halted soon in any case
With thoughts of the path back, how rough it was
With rock and washout, and unsafe in darkness;
When they were halted by a tumbled wall
With barbed-wire binding. They stood facing this,
Spending what onward impulse they still had
In one last look the way they must not go,
On up the failing path, where, if a stone
Or earthslide moved at night, it moved itself;
No footstep moved it. "This is all," they sighed,
"Good-night to woods." But not so; there was more.
A doe from round a spruce stood looking at them
Across the wall as near the wall as they.

She saw them in their field, they her in hers.
The difficulty of seeing what stood still,
Like some up-ended bowlder split in two,
Was in her clouded eyes: they saw no fear there.
She seemed to think that two thus they were safe.
Then, as if they were something that, though strange,
She could not trouble her mind with too long,
She sighed and passed unscared along the wall.
"*This,* then, is all. What more is there to ask?"
But no, not yet. A snort to bid them wait.
A buck from round the spruce stood looking at them
Across the wall, as near the wall as they.
This was an antlered buck of lusty nostril.
Not the same doe come back into her place.
He viewed them quizzically with jerks of head,
As if to ask, "Why don't you make some motion?
Or give some sign of life? Because you can't.
I doubt if you're as living as you look."
Thus till he had them almost feeling dared
To stretch a proffering hand—and a spell-breaking.
Then he too passed unscared along the wall.
Two had seen two, whichever side you spoke from.
"This *must* be all." It was all. Still they stood,
A great wave from it going over them,
As if the earth in one unlooked-for favor
Had made them certain earth returned their love.

### A SKY PAIR

#### CANIS MAJOR

The Great Overdog,
That heavenly beast
With a star in one eye,
Gives a leap in the East.

He dances upright
All the way to the West,
And never once drops
On his forefeet to rest.

I'm a poor Underdog;
But tonight I will bark,
With the Great Overdog
That romps through the dark.

#### THE PEACEFUL SHEPHERD

If heaven were to do again,
And on the pasture bars
I leaned to line the figures in
Between the dotted stars,

I should be tempted to forget,
I think, the Crown of Rule,
The Scales of Trade, the Cross of Faith,
As hardly worth renewal.

For these have governed in our lives,
And see how men have warred!
The Cross, the Crown, the Scales, may all
As well have been the Sword.

#### BEREFT

Where had I heard this wind before
Change like this to a deeper roar?
What would it take my standing there for,
Holding open a restive door,
Looking down hill to a frothy shore?
Summer was past and day was past.
Somber clouds on the West were massed.
Out in the porch's sagging floor
Leaves got up in a coil and hissed,
Blindly struck at my knee and missed.
Something sinister in the tone

Told me my secret must be known:
Word I was in the house alone
Somehow must have gotten abroad;
Word I was in my life alone;
Word I had no one left but God.

### TREE AT MY WINDOW

Tree at my window, window tree,
My sash is lowered when night comes on;
But let there never be curtain drawn
Between you and me.

Vague dream-head lifted out of the ground,
And thing next most diffuse to cloud,

Not all your light tongues talking aloud
Could be profound.

But, tree, I have seen you taken and tosse
And if you have seen me when I slept,
You have seen me when I was taken an
    swept
And all but lost.

That day she put our heads together,
Fate had her imagination about her,
Your head so much concerned with outer,
Mine with inner, weather.

### WEST-RUNNING BROOK

"Fred, where is north?"
                                "North? North is there, my love.
The brook runs west."
                                "West-running Brook then call it."
(West-running Brook men call it to this day.)
"What does it think it's doing running west
When all the other country brooks flow east
To reach the ocean? It must be the brook
Can trust itself to go by contraries
The way I can with you—and you with me—
Because we're—we're—I don't know what we are.
What are we?"
                                "Young or new?"
                                                "We must be something.
We've said we two. Let's change that to we three.
As you and I are married to each other,
We'll both be married to the brook. We'll build
Our bridge across it, and the bridge shall be
Our arm thrown over it asleep beside it.
Look, look, it's waving to us with a wave
To let us know it hears me."
                                                "Why, my dear,
That wave's been standing off this jut of shore—"
(The black stream, catching on a sunken rock,
Flung backward on itself in one white wave,
And the white water rode the black forever,
Not gaining but not losing, like a bird
While feathers from the struggle of whose breast
Flecked the dark stream and flecked the darker pool
Below the point, and were at last driven wrinkled
In a white scarf against the far shore alders.)
"That wave's been standing off this jut of shore

Ever since rivers, I was going to say,
Were made in heaven. It wasn't waved to us."

"It wasn't, yet it was. If not to you
It was to me—in an annunciation."

"Oh, if you take it off to lady-land,
As 'twere the country of the Amazons
. We men must see you to the confines of
And leave you there, ourselves forbid to enter,—
It is your brook! I have no more to say."

"Yes, you have, too. Go on. You thought of something."

"Speaking of contraries, see how the brook
In that white wave runs counter to itself.
It is from that in water we were from
Long, long before we were from any creature.
Here we, in our impatience of the steps,
Get back to the beginning of beginnings,
The stream of everything that runs away.
Some say existence like a Pirouot
And Pirouette, forever in one place,
Stands still and dances, but it runs away,
It seriously, sadly, runs away
To fill the abyss' void with emptiness.
It flows beside us in this water brook,
But it flows over us. It flows between us
To separate us for a panic moment.
It flows between us, over us, and *with* us.
And it is time, strength, tone, light, life and love
And even substance lapsing unsubstantial;
The universal cataract of death
That spends to nothingness—and unresisted,
Save by some strange resistance in itself,
Not just a swerving, but a throwing back,
As if regret were in it and were sacred.
It has this throwing backward on itself
So that the fall of most of it is always
Raising a little, sending up a little.
Our life runs down in sending up the clock.
The brook runs down in sending up our life.
The sun runs down in sending up the brook.
And there is something sending up the sun.
It is this backward motion toward the source,
Against the stream, that most we see ourselves in,
The tribute of the current to the source.
It is from this in nature we are from.
It is most us."
　　　　　"Today will be the day

You said so."
                    "No, today will be the day
You said the brook was called West-running Brook."

"Today will be the day of what we both said."


### ONCE BY THE PACIFIC

The shattered water made a misty din,
Great waves looked over others coming in,
And thought of doing something to the shore
That water never did to land before.
The clouds were low and hairy in the skies
Like locks blown forward in the gleam of eyes.
You could not tell, and yet it looked as if
The sand was lucky in being backed by cliff,
The cliff in being backed by continent.
It looked as if a night of dark intent
Was coming, and not only a night, an age.
Someone had better be prepared for rage.
There would be more than ocean water broken
Before God's last *Put out the light* was spoken.


### THE BEAR

The bear puts both arms around the tree above her
And draws it down as if it were a lover
And its choke-cherries lips to kiss good-by,
Then lets it snap back upright in the sky.
Her next step rocks a bowlder on the wall
(She's making her cross-country in the fall.)
Her great weight creaks the barbed-wire in its staples
As she flings over and off down through the maples,
Leaving on one wire tooth a lock of hair.
Such is the uncaged progress of the bear.
The world has room to make a bear feel free;
The universe seems cramped to you and me.
Man acts more like a poor bear in a cage
That all day fights a nervous inward rage,
His mood rejecting all his mind suggests.
He paces back and forth and never rests
The toe-nail click and shuffle of his feet,
The telescope at one end of his beat,
And at the other end the microscope,
Two instruments of nearly equal hope,
And in conjunction giving quite a spread.
Or if he rests from scientific tread,
'Tis only to sit back and sway his head
Through ninety odd degrees of arc, it seems,
Between two metaphysical extremes.

He sits back on his fundamental butt
With lifted snout and eyes (if any) shut,
(He almost looks religious but he's not),
And back and forth he sways from cheek to cheek,
At one extreme agreeing with one Greek,
At the other agreeing with another Greek
Which may be thought, but only so to speak.
A baggy figure, equally pathetic
When sedentary and when peripatetic.

### SAND DUNES

Sea waves are green and wet,
But up from where they die
Rise others vaster yet,
And those are brown and dry.

They are the sea made land
To come at the fisher town,
And bury in solid sand
The men she could not drown.

She may know cove and cape,
But she does not know mankind
If by any change of shape
She hopes to cut off mind.

Men left her a ship to sink;
They can leave her a hut as well,
And be but more free to think
For the one more cast-off shell.

### THE LOVELY SHALL BE CHOOSERS

The Voice said, "Hurl her down!"

The Voices, "How far down?"

"Seven levels of the world."

"How much time have we?"

"Take twenty years.
She would refuse love safe with wealth and honor.
The Lovely shall be choosers, shall they?
Then let them choose!"

"Then we shall let her choose?"

"Yes, let her choose.
Take up the task beyond her choosing."

Invisible hands crowded on her shoulder
In readiness to weigh upon her.

But she stood straight still,
In broad round ear-rings, gold and jet with pearls,
And broad round suchlike brooch,
Her cheeks high colored,
Proud and the pride of friends.

The Voice asked, "You can let her choose?"

"Yes, we can let her and still triumph."

"Do it by joys. And leave her always blameless.
Be her first joy her wedding,
That though a wedding,
Is yet—well, something *they* know, he and she.
And after that her next joy
That though she grieves, her grief is secret:
Those friends know nothing of her grief to make it shameful.
Her third joy that though now they cannot help but know,
They move in pleasure too far off
To think much or much care.
Give her a child at either knee for fourth joy
To tell once and once only, for them never to forget,
How once she walked in brightness,
And make them see in the winter firelight.
But give her friends, for them she dares not tell
For their foregone incredulousness.
And be her next joy this:
Her never having deigned to tell them.
Make her among the humblest even
Seem to them less than they are.
Hopeless of being known for what she has been,
Failing of being loved for what she is,
Give her the comfort for her sixth of knowing
She fails from strangeness to a way of life
She came to from too high too late to learn.
Then send some *one* with eye to see
And wonder at her where she is
And words to wonder in her hearing how she came there,
But without time to stay and hear her story.
Be her last joy her heart's going out to this one
So that she almost speaks.

You know them—seven in all."

"Trust us," the Voices said.

### THE EGG AND THE MACHINE

He gave the solid rail a hateful kick.
From far away there came an answering tick;
And then another tick. He knew the code:
His hate had roused an engine up the road.

He wished when he had had the track alone
He had attacked it with a club or stone
And bent some rail wide open like a switch
So as to wreck the engine in the ditch.
Too late, though, now to throw it down the bank;
Its click was rising to a nearer clank.
Here it came breasting like a horse in skirts.
(He stood well back for fear of scalding squirts.)
Then for a moment there was only size,
Confusion, and a roar that drowned the cries
He raised against the gods in the machine.
Then once again the sand-bank lay serene.
The traveler's eye picked up a turtle trail,
Between the dotted feet a streak of tail,
And followed it to where he made out vague,
But certain signs of buried turtle egg;
And probing with one finger not too rough,
He found suspicious sand, and sure enough
The pocket of a little turtle mine.
If there was one egg in it, there were nine,
Torpedo-like, with shell of gritty leather
All packed in sand to wait the trump together.
"You'd better not disturb me any more,"
He told the distance. "I am armed for war.
The next machine that has the power to pass
Will get this plasm in its goggle glass."

## STOPPING BY WOODS ON A SNOWY EVENING

Whose woods these are I think I know.
His house is in the village though;
He will not see me stopping here
To watch his woods fill up with snow.

My little horse must think it queer
To stop without a farmhouse near
Between the woods and frozen lake
The darkest evening of the year.

He gives his harness bells a shake
To ask if there is some mistake.
The only other sound's the sweep
Of easy wind and downy flake.

The woods are lovely, dark and deep,
But I have promises to keep,
And miles to go before I sleep,
And miles to go before I sleep.

## NOTHING GOLD CAN STAY

Nature's first green is gold,
Her hardest hue to hold.
Her early leaf's a flower;
But only so an hour.
Then leaf subsides to leaf.
So Eden sank to grief,
So dawn goes down to day.
Nothing gold can stay.

## THE ROAD NOT TAKEN

Two roads diverged in a yellow wood,
And sorry I could not travel both
And be one traveler, long I stood
And looked down one as far as I could
To where it bent in the undergrowth;

Then took the other, as just as fair,
And having perhaps the better claim,
Because it was grassy and wanted wear;
Though as for that the passing there
Had worn them really about the same,

And both that morning equally lay
In leaves no step had trodden black.
Oh, I kept the first for another day!
Yet knowing how way leads on to way,
I doubted if I should ever come back.

I shall be telling this with a sigh
Somewhere ages and ages hence:
Two roads diverged in a wood, and I—
I took the one less traveled by,
And that has made all the difference.

### A LEAF-TREADER

I have been treading on leaves all day until I am autumn-tired.
God knows all the color and form of leaves I have trodden on and mired.
Perhaps I have put forth too much strength and been too fierce from fear.
I have safely trodden under foot the leaves of another year.

All summer long they were overhead more lifted up than I;
To come to their final place in earth they had to pass me by.
All summer long I thought I heard them threatening under their breath,
And when they came it seemed with a will to carry me with them to death.

They spoke to the fugitive in my heart as if it were leaves to leaf;
They tapped at my eyelids and touched my lips with an invitation to grief.
But it was no reason I had to go because they had to go.
Now up, my knee, to keep on top of another year of snow.

### LOST IN HEAVEN

The clouds, the source of rain, one stormy night
Offered an opening to the source of dew,
Which I accepted with impatient sight,
Looking for my old sky-marks in the blue.

But stars were scarce in that part of the sky,
And no two were of the same constellation—
No one was bright enough to identify.
So 'twas with not ungrateful consternation,

Seeing myself well lost once more, I sighed,
"Where, where in heaven am I? But don't tell me,"
I warned the clouds, "by opening me wide!
Let's let my heavenly lostness overwhelm me."

### DESERT PLACES

Snow falling and night falling fast, oh, fast
In a field I looked into going past,
And the ground almost covered smooth in snow,
But a few weeds and stubble showing last.

The woods around it have it—it is theirs.
All animals are smothered in their lairs.
I am too absent-spirited to count:
The loneliness includes me unawares.

And lonely as it is, that loneliness
Will be more lonely ere it will be less,
A blanker whiteness of benighted snow,
With no expression—nothing to express.

They cannot scare me with their empty spaces
Between stars—on stars void of human races.
I have it in me so much nearer home
To scare myself with my own desert places.

## TWO TRAMPS IN MUD-TIME

ut of the mud two strangers came
nd caught me splitting wood in the yard.
nd one of them put me off my aim
y hailing cheerily "Hit them hard!"
knew pretty well why he dropped behind
nd let the other go on a way.
knew pretty well what he had in mind:
e wanted to take my job for pay.

ood blocks of beech it was I split,
s large around as the chopping-block;
nd every piece I squarely hit
ell splinterless as a cloven rock.
he blows that a life of self-control
ares to strike for the common good
hat day, giving a loose to my soul,
spent on the unimportant wood.

he sun was warm but the wind was chill.
ou know how it is with an April day:
Vhen the sun is out and the wind is still,
ou're one month on in the middle of May.
ut if you so much as dare to speak,
 cloud comes over the sunlit arch,
 wind comes off a frozen peak,
nd you're two months back in the middle
 of March.

 bluebird comes tenderly up to alight
nd fronts the wind to unruffle a plume,
lis song so pitched as not to excite
 single flower as yet to bloom.
 is snowing a flake: and he half knew
Vinter was only playing possum.
xcept in color he isn't blue,
ut he wouldn't advise a thing to blossom.

he water for which we may have to look
 summertime with a witching-wand,
 every wheelrut's now a brook,

In every print of a hoof a pond.
Be glad of water, but don't forget
The lurking frost in the earth beneath
That will steal forth after the sun is set
And show on the water its crystal teeth.

The time when most I loved my task
These two must make me love it more
By coming with what they came to ask.
You'd think I never had felt before
The weight of an ax head poised aloft,
The grip on earth of outspread feet,
The life of muscles rocking soft
And smooth and moist in vernal heat.

Out of the woods two hulking tramps
(From sleeping God knows where last night
But not long since in the lumber camps).
They thought all chopping was theirs of
    right.
Men of the woods and lumber-jacks,
They judged me by their appropriate tool.
Except as a fellow handled an ax,
They had no way of knowing a fool.

Nothing on either side was said.
They knew they had but to stay their stay
And all their logic would fill my head:
As that I had no right to play
With what was another man's work for gain.
My right might be love but theirs was need.
And where the two exist in twain
Theirs was the better right—agreed.

But yield who will to their separation,
My object in life is to unite
My avocation and my vocation
As my two eyes make one in sight.
Only where love and need are one,
And the work is play for mortal stakes,
Is the deed ever really done
For Heaven and the future's sakes.

# *William Ellery Leonard*

WILLIAM ELLERY LEONARD was born in Plainfield, New Jersey, January 25, 1876. He received his A.M. at Harvard in 1899 and completed his studies at the Universities of Göttingen and Bonn. After traveling for several years throughout Europe, he became a teacher and has been professor of English in the University of Wisconsin since 1906.

*The Vaunt of Man* (1912) is a characteristic volume. Traditional in form and material, it is anything but conservative in spirit. Leonard's fervor speaks in the simplest of his quatrains and sonnets. This protesting passion is given an even wider sweep in *The Lynching Bee and Other Poems* (1920).

*Tutankhamen and After* (1924) is an ambitious attempt to picture the continuity of man's life in three pages, but in spite of a few felicitous lines the title-poem is prosy. It was a grave injustice to claim this as Leonard's "most representative volume." That distinction must be claimed by *Two Lives,* which was privately issued in 1923 and publicly offered in 1925. Reminiscent of Richard Dehmel's *Zwei Menschen,* this chain of sonnets compresses an intensity in which the effect of the cumulative drama is far greater than that of any single poem.

*The Locomotive God* (1927) is a strange document written in autobiographical prose. It is the narrative of a student and poet who ends as a neurotic confined by an unusual phobia within a few blocks' radius of his home. Disproportionate in its concern with trifles, painful as analysis of fevered imagination, the book has a personal interest beyond the case history.

*A Son of Earth* (1929) is composed of selections from Leonard's previous poetry with the exception of his translations and *Two Lives.* It, too, was arranged autobiographically "with reference to activities, aims, influences, crises." This larger collection suffers the same defects as *Two Lives;* its sincerity is compelling, its candor unreserved, but only a few pages could be offered as examples of poetry *per se.* *A Son of Earth* contains page after page of inversions and pomposities incredibly preserved; one can understand the youth that luxuriated in such *clichés* as "golden fee," "slumbering aeons," "shadowy woodlands," "white nymphs," "brazen trumpets," "immemorial tides," but it is hard to credit a maturity that proudly reprints them. Rhetoric aside, there is wisdom here and wit, a malicious sparkle in the revised fables grouped under "Aesop and Hyssop."

Besides his original poetry, Leonard has published several volumes of translations of Beowulf, Empedocles and Lucretius.

### THE IMAGE OF DELIGHT

O how came I that loved stars, moon, and flame,
And unimaginable wind and sea,
All inner shrines and temples of the free,
Legends and hopes and golden books of fame;
I that upon the mountain carved my name
With cliffs and clouds and eagles over me,

O how came I to stoop to loving thee—
I that had never stooped before to shame?

O 'twas not thee! Too eager of a white
Far beauty and a voice to answer mine,
Myself I built an image of delight,
Which all one purple day I deemed divine—
And when it vanished in the fiery night,
I lost not thee, nor any shape of thine.

### TO THE VICTOR

Man's mind is larger than his brow of tears;
This hour is not my all of time; this place
My all of earth; nor this obscene disgrace
My all of life; and thy complacent sneers
Shall not pronounce my doom to my compeers
While the Hereafter lights me in the face,
And from the Past, as from the mountain's base,
Rise, as I rise, the long tumultuous cheers.
And who slays me must overcome a world:
Heroes at arms, and virgins who became
Mothers of children, prophecy and song;
Walls of old cities with their flags unfurled;
Peaks, headlands, ocean and its isles of fame—
And sun and moon and all that made me strong!

# Carl Sandburg

CARL (AUGUST) SANDBURG was born of Swedish stock at Galesburg, Illinois, January 6, 1878. His schooling was haphazard; at thirteen he went to work on a milk wagon. During the next six years he was, in rapid succession, porter in a barber shop, scene-shifter in a cheap theater, truck-handler in a brickyard, turner-apprentice in a pottery, dish-washer in Denver and Omaha hotels, harvest hand in Kansas wheatfields. These tasks equipped him, as no amount of learning could have done, to be the laureate of industrial America. When war with Spain was declared in 1898, Sandburg, avid for fresh adventure, enlisted in Company C, Sixth Illinois Volunteers.

On his return from the campaign in Porto Rico, Sandburg entered Lombard College in Galesburg and, for the first time, began to think in terms of literature. After leaving college, where he had been captain of the basket-ball team as well as editor-in-chief of the college paper, Sandburg did all manner of things to earn a living. He was advertising manager for a department store and worked as district organizer for the Social-Democratic party of Wisconsin. He became salesman, pamphleteer, newspaperman.

In 1904 Sandburg published the proverbial "slender sheaf," a tiny pamphlet of twenty-two poems, uneven in quality, but strangely like the work of the mature

Sandburg in feeling. What is more, these experiments anticipated the inflection of
the later poems, with their spiritual kinship to Henley and Whitman; several of
these early experiments (with the exception of the rhymed verses) might be placed,
without seeming incongruous, in the later collections. The idiom of *Smoke and
Steel* (1920) is more intensified, but it is the same idiom as that of "Milville" (1903),
which begins:

Down in southern New Jersey they make glass.
By day and by night, the fires burn on in Milville and bid the sand let in the light.

Meanwhile the newspaperman was struggling to keep the poet alive. Until he
was thirty-six years old Sandburg was unknown to the literary world. In 1914 a
group of his poems appeared in *Poetry: A Magazine of Verse;* during the same year
one of the group (the now famous "Chicago") was awarded the Levinson prize of
two hundred dollars. A little more than a year later his first real book was published, and Sandburg "arrived."

*Chicago Poems* (1916) is full of ferment; it seethes with loose energy. If Frost
is an intellectual aristocrat, Sandburg might be termed an emotional democrat. Sandburg's speech is simple and powerful; he uses slang as freely as his predecessors used
the now archaic tongue of their times. Never has the American vulgate been used
with such artistry and effect. Immediately cries of protest were heard: Sandburg was
coarse and brutal; his work ugly and distorted; his language unrefined, unfit for
poetry. His detractors forgot that Sandburg was brutal only to condemn brutality;
that beneath his toughness, he was one of the tenderest of living poets; that, when
he used colloquialisms and a richly metaphorical slang, he was searching for new
poetic values in "limber, lasting, fierce words"—unconsciously answering Whitman
who asked, "Do you suppose the liberties and brawn of These States have to do
only with delicate lady-words? With gloved gentleman-words?"

*Cornhuskers* (1918) is another step forward; it is as sweeping as its forerunner
and more sensitive. The gain in power and restraint is evident in the very first poem,
a wide-swept vision of the prairie. Here is something of the surge of a Norse saga;
*Cornhuskers* is keen with a salty vigor, a sympathy for all that is splendid and terrible in Nature. But the raw violence is restrained to the point of half-withheld mysticism. There are, in this volume, dozens of those delicate perceptions of beauty that
must astonish those who think that Sandburg can write only a big-fisted, rough-
neck sort of poetry. As Sandburg has sounded some of the most *fortissimo* notes in
modern poetry, he has also breathed some of its softest phrases. "Cool Tombs," one
of the most poignant lyrics of our times, moves with a low music; "Grass" whispers
as quietly as the earlier "Fog" stole in on stealthy, cat feet.

*Smoke and Steel* (1920) is the synthesis of its predecessors. In this collection,
Sandburg has fused mood, accent and image. Whether the poet evokes the spirit of
a jazz-band or, having had the radiance (the "flash crimson"), prays to touch life
at its other extreme, this volume is not so vociferous as it is assured. Smoke-belching
chimneys are here, quarries and great bowlders of iron-ribbed rock; here are titanic
visions: the dreams of men and machinery. And silence is here—the silence of sleeping tenements and sun-soaked cornfields.

*Slabs of the Sunburnt West* (1923) is a fresh fusing: here in quick succession are
the sardonic invectives of "And So Today," the rhapsody of "The Windy City" (an

amplification of the early "Chicago"), and the panoramic title-poem. Although the book's chief exhibit is the amplitude of its longer poems, there are a few brevities (such as "Upstream") which have the vigor of a jubilant cry. Sandburg is still tempted to talk at the top of his voice, to bang the table and hurl his loudest epithets into the teeth of his opponents. But often he goes to the other extreme; he is likely to leave his material soft and loose instead of solidifying his emotions. There are times when the poet seems unsure whether or not he can furnish more than a clew to the half-realized wisps of his imagination. But though his meaning may not always be clear, there is no mistaking the power of his feeling nor the curious cadences of his music.

*Good Morning, America* (1928) is characteristically Sandburg at his best and worst. There are passages which are hopelessly enigmatic, passages which are only inflations of commonplace ideas. On the other hand, there are pages which are remarkable experiments in suspension, pages sensitive with a beauty delicately perceived. The thirty-eight "Tentative (First Model) Definitions of Poetry" with which the volume is prefaced are footnotes as well as prologues to his work in general, and the purely descriptive pieces are among his finest. Incidentally, the volume shows how far Sandburg has gone in critical esteem since the time when his *Chicago Poems* was openly derided, the title poem of *Good Morning, America,* having been read as a Phi Beta Kappa poem at Harvard. Here, too, one is impressed by Sandburg's hatred of war; Sandburg was one of the first American poets to express the growing protests in "A. E. F." and other poems.

Besides his poetry, Sandburg has written three volumes of imaginative and, if one can conceive of such a thing, humorously mystical tales for children: *Rootabaga Stories* (1922), *Rootabaga Pigeons* (1923) and *Potato Face* (1930), the last being— so the poet and publisher insist—tales for adults of all ages. A collection of the Rootabaga stories was illustrated by Peggy Bacon in 1929. Eight years were spent traveling and studying documents for his vitalized *Abraham Lincoln: The Prairie Years* (1926), and assembling material for his collection of native folk-tunes *The American Songbag* (1927), a massive and revealing folio of words, music, and accompaniments to two hundred and eighty songs, more than one hundred of them never in print until Sandburg's ear and notebook gathered them from pioneer grandmothers, work-gangs, railroad men, hoboes, convicts, cowboys, mountain people, and others who sing "because they must." Another ten years prepared him to write *Abraham Lincoln: The War Years,* the four volumes constituting the most extensive modern presentation of Lincoln and his times.

In 1924 the poet perfected a unique lecture—part recital, part singing of American folk-tunes, part "circus," as he describes it—which he continued to give throughout the country. Accompanied by his guitar, Sandburg brought new values to the reading of poetry. His low-toned footnotes were full of philosophic asides. Speaking of realism and romanticism, he once told the following fable: "There was a man who did not find in his house all he desired. One day he came in to find his wife working with a workbasket full of bright silk threads. He caught up a handful. He held them tight for a moment. Then he opened his hand. The threads became hundreds of brilliant butterflies flying joyfully about the room. The man watched them. Then he opened his hand, gathered them all in, tightened his hold. They became silk threads; he returned them to the workbasket. . . . And if you can believe that," Sandburg concluded with the ghost of a smile, "you are a romanticist."

Sandburg lives most of the year at Harbert, Michigan, overlooking Lake Michigan from a hilltop where on clear nights may be seen across the lake the Lindbergh beacon on a Chicago skyscraper, "circling the sky with a white spike of light."

## TEN DEFINITIONS OF POETRY

1 Poetry is a projection across silence of cadences arranged to break that silence with definite intentions of echoes, syllables, wave lengths.

2 Poetry is the journal of a sea animal living on land, wanting to fly the air.

3 Poetry is a series of explanations of life, fading off into horizons too swift for explanations.

4 Poetry is a search for syllables to shoot at the barriers of the unknown and the unknowable.

5 Poetry is a theorem of a yellow-silk handkerchief knotted with riddles, sealed in a balloon tied to the tail of a kite flying in a white wind against a blue sky in spring.

6 Poetry is the silence and speech between a wet struggling root of a flower and a sunlit blossom of that flower.

7 Poetry is the harnessing of the paradox of earth cradling life and then entombing it.

8 Poetry is a phantom script telling how rainbows are made and why they go away.

9 Poetry is the synthesis of hyacinths and biscuits.

10 Poetry is the opening and closing of a door, leaving those who look through to guess about what is seen during a moment.

## CHICAGO

Hog Butcher for the World,
Tool Maker, Stacker of Wheat,
Player with Railroads and the Nation's Freight Handler;
Stormy, husky, brawling,
City of the Big Shoulders:
They tell me you are wicked and I believe them, for I have seen your painted women under the gas lamps luring the farm boys.
And they tell me you are crooked and I answer: Yes, it is true I have seen the gunman kill and go free to kill again.
And they tell me you are brutal and my reply is: On the faces of women and children I have seen the marks of wanton hunger.
And having answered so I turn once more to those who sneer at this my city, and I give them back the sneer and say to them:
Come and show me another city with lifted head singing so proud to be alive and coarse and strong and cunning.

Flinging magnetic curses amid the toil of piling job on job, here is a tall bold
    slugger set vivid against the little soft cities;
Fierce as a dog with tongue lapping for action, cunning as a savage pitted against
    the wilderness,
        Bareheaded,
        Shoveling,
        Wrecking,
        Planning,
        Building, breaking, rebuilding.
Under the smoke, dust all over his mouth, laughing with white teeth,
Under the terrible burden of destiny laughing as a young man laughs,
Laughing even as an ignorant fighter laughs who has never lost a battle,
Bragging and laughing that under his wrist is the pulse, and under his ribs the
    heart of the people,
                    Laughing!
Laughing the stormy, husky, brawling laughter of Youth, half-naked, sweating,
    proud to be Hog Butcher, Tool Maker, Stacker of Wheat, Player with Railroads
    and Freight Handler to the Nation.

### FOG

The fog comes
on little cat feet.
It sits looking
over harbor and city
on silent haunches
and then moves on.

### GRASS

Pile the bodies high at Austerlitz and Waterloo.
Shovel them under and let me work—
    I am the grass; I cover all.

And pile them high at Gettysburg
And pile them high at Ypres and Verdun.
Shovel them under and let me work.
Two years, ten years, and passengers ask the conductor:
    What place is this?
    Where are we now?

    I am the grass.
    Let me work.

### COOL TOMBS

When Abraham Lincoln was shoveled into the tombs, he forgot the copperheads
    and the assassin . . . in the dust, in the cool tombs.

And Ulysses Grant lost all thought of con men and Wall Street, cash and collateral
    turned ashes . . . in the dust, in the cool tombs.

Pocahontas' body, lovely as a poplar, sweet as a red haw in November or a pawpaw in May, did she wonder? does she remember? . . . in the dust, in the cool tombs?

Take any streetful of people buying clothes and groceries, cheering a hero or throwing confetti and blowing tin horns . . . tell me if the lovers are losers . . . tell me if any get more than the lovers . . . in the dust . . . in the cool tombs.

### NOCTURNE IN A DESERTED BRICKYARD

Stuff of the moon
Runs on the lapping sand
Out to the longest shadows.
Under the curving willows,
And round the creep of the wave line,
Fluxions of yellow and dusk on the waters
Make a wide dreaming pansy of an old pond in the night.

### LIMITED

I am riding on a limited express, one of the crack trains of the nation.
Hurtling across the prairie into blue haze and dark air go fifteen all-steel coaches holding a thousand people.
(All the coaches shall be scrap and rust and all the men and women laughing in the diners and sleepers shall pass to ashes.)
I ask a man in the smoker where he is going and he answers: "Omaha."

### FOUR PRELUDES ON PLAYTHINGS OF THE WIND

*"The Past Is a Bucket of Ashes."*

1

The woman named Tomorrow
sits with a hairpin in her teeth
and takes her time
and does her hair the way she wants it
and fastens at last the last braid and coil
and puts the hairpin where it belongs
and turns and drawls: Well, what of it?
My grandmother, Yesterday, is gone.
What of it? Let the dead be dead.

2

The doors were cedar
and the panel strips of gold
and the girls were golden girls
and the panels read and the girls chanted:
We are the greatest city,
and the greatest nation:
nothing like us ever was.

The doors are twisted on broken hinges,
Sheets of rain swish through on the wind
  where the golden girls ran and the panels read:
  We are the greatest city,
  the greatest nation,
  nothing like us ever was.

3

It has happened before.
Strong men put up a city and got
  a nation together,
And paid singers to sing and women
  to warble: We are the greatest city,
   the greatest nation,
   nothing like us ever was.

And while the singers sang
and the strong men listened
and paid the singers well,
  there were rats and lizards who listened
  . . . and the only listeners left now
  . . . are . . . the rats . . . and the lizards.
  And there are black crows
  crying, "Caw, caw,"
  bringing mud and sticks
  building a nest
  over the words carved
  on the doors where the panels were cedar
  and the strips on the panels were gold
  and the golden girls came singing:
   We are the greatest city,
   the greatest nation:
   nothing like us ever was.

The only singers now are crows crying, "Caw, caw,"
And the sheets of rain whine in the wind and doorways.
And the only listeners now are . . . the rats . . . and the lizards.

4

The feet of the rats
scribble on the doorsills;
the hieroglyphs of the rat footprints
chatter the pedigrees of the rats
and babble of the blood
and gabble of the breed
of the grandfathers and the great-grandfathers
of the rats.

And the wind shifts
and the dust on a doorsill shifts
and even the writing of the rat footprints
tells us nothing, nothing at all

about the greatest city, the greatest nation
where the strong men listened
and the women warbled: Nothing like us ever was.

## A. E. F.

There will be a rusty gun on the wall, sweetheart,
The rifle grooves curling with flakes of rust.
A spider will make a silver string nest in the darkest, warmest corner of it.
The trigger and the range-finder, they too will be rusty.
And no hands will polish the gun, and it will hang on the wall.
Forefingers and thumbs will point absently and casually toward it.
It will be spoken among half-forgotten, wished-to-be-forgotten things.
They will tell the spider: Go on, you're doing good work.

## PRAYERS OF STEEL

Lay me on an anvil, O God.
Beat me and hammer me into a crowbar.
Let me pry loose old walls;
Let me lift and loosen old foundations.

Lay me on an anvil, O God.
Beat me and hammer me into a steel spike.
Drive me into the girders that hold a skyscraper together.
Take red-hot rivets and fasten me into the central girders.
Let me be the great nail holding a skyscraper through blue nights into white stars.

## JAZZ FANTASIA

Drum on your drums, batter on your banjos, sob on the long cool winding saxo-
    phones. Go to it, O jazzmen.

Sling your knuckles on the bottoms of the happy tin pans, let your trombones ooze,
    and go husha-husha-hush with the slippery sandpaper.

Moan like an autumn wind high in the lonesome treetops, moan soft like you
    wanted somebody terrible, cry like a racing car slipping away from a motor-
    cycle-cop, bang-bang! you jazzmen, bang altogether drums, traps, banjos, horns,
    tin cans—make two people fight on the top of a stairway and scratch each
    other's eyes in a clinch tumbling down the stairs.

Can the rough stuff . . . Now a Mississippi steamboat pushes up the night river
    with a hoo-hoo-hoo-oo . . . and the green lanterns calling to the high soft
    stars . . . a red moon rides on the humps of the low river hills. . . . Go to
    it, O jazzmen.

## BLUE ISLAND INTERSECTION

Six street-ends come together here.
They feed people and wagons into the center.

In and out all day horses with thoughts of nose-bags,
Men with shovels, women with baskets and baby buggies.
Six ends of streets and no sleep for them all day.
The people and wagons come and go, out and in.
Triangles of banks and drug stores watch.
The policemen whistle, the trolley cars bump:
Wheels, wheels, feet, feet, all day.

In the false dawn where the chickens blink
And the east shakes a lazy baby toe at tomorrow,
And the east fixes a pink half-eye this way,
In the time when only one milk wagon crosses
These three streets, these six street-ends
It is the sleep time and they rest.
The triangle banks and drug stores rest.
The policeman is gone, his star and gun sleep.
The owl car blutters along in a sleep-walk.

## FROM "SMOKE AND STEEL"

Smoke of the fields in spring is one,
Smoke of the leaves in autumn another.
Smoke of a steel-mill roof or a battleship funnel,
They all go up in a line with a smokestack,
Or they twist . . . in the slow twist . . . of the wind.

If the north wind comes they run to the south.
If the west wind comes they run to the east.
 By this sign
 all smokes
 know each other.
Smoke of the fields in spring and leaves in autumn,
Smoke of the finished steel, chilled and blue,
By the oath of work they swear: "I know you."

Hunted and hissed from the center
Deep down long ago when God made us over,
Deep down are the cinders we came from—
You and I and our heads of smoke.

✦

Some of the smokes God dropped on the job
Cross on the sky and count our years
And sing in the secrets of our numbers;
Sing their dawns and sing their evenings,
Sing an old log-fire song:
 You may put the damper up,
 You may put the damper down,
 The smoke goes up the chimney just the same.

Smoke of a city sunset skyline,
Smoke of a country dusk horizon—
    They cross on the sky and count our years.

✦

Smoke of a brick-red dust
    Winds on a spiral
    Out of the stacks
For a hidden and glimpsing moon.
This, said the bar-iron shed to the blooming mill,
This is the slang of coal and steel.
The day-gang hands it to the night-gang,
The night-gang hands it back.

Stammer at the slang of this—
Let us understand half of it.
    In the rolling mills and sheet mills,
    In the harr and boom of the blast fires,
    The smoke changes its shadow
    And men change their shadow;
    A nigger, a wop, a bohunk changes.

    A bar of steel—it is only
Smoke at the heart of it, smoke and the blood of a man.
A runner of fire ran in it, ran out, ran somewhere else,
And left smoke and the blood of a man
And the finished steel, chilled and blue.

So fire runs in, runs out, runs somewhere else again,
And the bar of steel is a gun, a wheel, a nail, a shovel,
A rudder under the sea, a steering-gear in the sky;
And always dark in the heart and through it,
    Smoke and the blood of a man.
Pittsburgh, Youngstown, Gary, they make their steel with men.

In the blood of men and the ink of chimneys
The smoke nights write their oaths:
Smoke into steel and blood into steel;
Homestead, Braddock, Birmingham, they make their steel with men.
Smoke and blood is the mix of steel. . . .

## LOSERS

If I should pass the tomb of Jonah
I would stop there and sit for a while;
Because I was swallowed one time deep in the dark
And came out alive after all.

If I pass the burial spot of Nero
I shall say to the wind, "Well, well!"—

I who have fiddled in a world on fire,
I who have done so many stunts not worth the doing.

I am looking for the grave of Sinbad too.
I want to shake his ghost-hand and say,
"Neither of us died very early, did we?"

And the last sleeping-place of Nebuchadnezzar—
When I arrive there I shall tell the wind:
"You ate grass; I have eaten crow—
Who is better off now or next year?"

Jack Cade, John Brown, Jesse James,
There too I could sit down and stop for a while.
I think I could tell their headstones:
"God, let me remember all good losers."

I could ask people to throw ashes on their heads
In the name of that sergeant at Belleau Woods,
Walking into the drumfires, calling his men,
"Come on, you . . . Do you want to live forever?"

## WIND SONG

Long ago I learned how to sleep,
In an old apple orchard where the wind swept by counting its money and throwing
   it away,
In a wind-gaunt orchard where the limbs forked out and listened or never listened
   at all,
In a passel of trees where the branches trapped the wind into whistling, "Who, who
   are you?"
I slept with my head in an elbow on a summer afternoon and there I took a sleep
   lesson.
There I went away saying: I know why they sleep, I know how they trap the tricky
   winds.
Long ago I learned how to listen to the singing wind and how to forget and how
   to hear the deep whine,
Slapping and lapsing under the day blue and the night stars:
                    Who, who are you?

                    Who can ever forget
                    listening to the wind go by
                    counting its money
                    and throwing it away?

## PRIMER LESSON

Look out how you use proud words.
When you let proud words go, it is not easy to call them back.
They wear long boots, hard boots; they walk off proud; they can't hear you calling—
Look out how you use proud words.

### BROKEN-FACE GARGOYLES

All I can give you is broken-face gargoyles.
It is too early to sing and dance at funerals,
Though I can whisper to you I am looking for an undertaker humming a lullaby
and throwing his feet in a swift and mystic buck-and-wing, now you see it and
now you don't.

Fish to swim a pool in your garden flashing a speckled silver,
A basket of wine-saps filling your room with flame-dark for your eyes and the tang
of valley orchards for your nose,
Such a beautiful pail of fish, such a beautiful peck of apples, I cannot bring you
now.
It is too early and I am not footloose yet.

I shall come in the night when I come with a hammer and saw.
I shall come near your window, where you look out when your eyes open in the
morning,
And there I shall slam together bird-houses and bird-baths for wing-loose wrens
and hummers to live in, birds with yellow wing tips to blur and buzz soft all
summer.

So I shall make little fool homes with doors, always open doors for all and each to
run away when they want to.
I shall come just like that even though now it is early and I am not yet footloose,
Even though I am still looking for an undertaker with a raw, wind-bitten face and
a dance in his feet.
I make a date with you (put it down) for six o'clock in the evening a thousand
years from now.

All I can give you now is broken-face gargoyles.
All I can give you now is a double gorilla head with two fish mouths and four eagle
eyes hooked on a street wall, spouting water and looking two ways to the ends
of the street for the new people, the young strangers, coming, coming, always
coming.

It is early.
I shall yet be footloose.


### FLASH CRIMSON

I shall cry God to give me a broken foot.

I shall ask for a scar and a slashed nose.

I shall take the last and the worst.

I shall be eaten by gray creepers in a bunkhouse where no runners of the sun come
and no dogs live.

And yet—of all "and yets" this is the bronze strongest—

I shall keep one thing better than all else; there is the blue steel of a great star of early evening in it; it lives longer than a broken foot or any scar.

The broken foot goes to a hole dug with a shovel or the bone of a nose may whiten on a hilltop—and yet—"and yet"—

There is one crimson pinch of ashes left after all; and none of the shifting winds that whip the grass and none of the pounding rains that beat the dust know how to touch or find the flash of this crimson.

I cry to God to give me a broken foot, a scar, or a lousy death.

I who have seen the flash of this crimson, I ask God for the last and worst.

### EARLY LYNCHING

Two Christs were at Golgotha.
One took the vinegar, another looked on.
One was on the cross, another in the mob.
One had the nails in his hands, another the stiff fingers holding a hammer driving nails.
There were many more Christs at Golgotha, many more thief pals, many many more in the mob howling the Judean equivalent of "Kill Him! Kill Him!"
The Christ they killed, the Christ they didn't kill, those were the two at Golgotha.

Pity, pity, the bones of these broken ankles.
Pity, pity, the slimp of these broken wrists
The mother's arms are strong to the last.
She holds him and counts the heart drips.

The smell of the slums was on him,
Wrongs of the slums lit his eyes.
Songs of the slums wove in his voice
The haters of the slums hated his slum heart.

The leaves of a mountain tree,
Leaves with a spinning star shook in them,
Rocks with a song of water, water, over them,
Hawks with an eye for death any time, any time,
The smell and the sway of these were on his sleeves, were in his nostrils, his words.

The slum man they killed, the mountain man lives on.

### PRECIOUS MOMENTS

Bright vocabularies are transient as rainbows.
Speech requires blood and air to make it.
Before the word comes off the end of the tongue,
While the diaphragms of flesh negotiate the word,
In the moment of doom when the word forms
It is born, alive, registering an imprint—

Afterward it is a mummy, a dry fact, done and gone,
The warning holds yet: Speak now or forever hold your peace.
*Ecce homo* had meanings: Behold the man! Look at him!
    Dying he lives and speaks!

## MOIST MOON PEOPLE

The moon is able to command the valley tonight.
The green mist shall go a-roaming, the white river shall go a-roaming.
Yet the moon shall be commanding, the moon shall take a high stand on the sky.

When the cats crept up the gullies,
And the goats fed at the rim a-laughing,
When the spiders swept their rooms in the burr oaks,
And the katydids first searched for this year's accordions,
And the crickets began a-looking for last year's concertinas—

I was there, I saw that hour, I know God had grand intentions about it.
If not, why did the moon command the valley, the green mist and white river go
    a-roaming, and the moon by itself take so high a stand on the sky?

If God and I alone saw it, the show was worth putting on,
Yet I remember others were there, Amos and Priscilla, Axel and Hulda, Hank and
    Jo, Big Charley and Little Morningstar.
They were all there; the clock ticks spoke with castanet clicks.

## BUNDLES

I have thought of beaches, fields,
Tears, laughter.

I have thought of homes put up—
And blown away.

I have thought of meetings and for
Every meeting a good-by.

I have thought of stars going alone,
Orioles in pairs, sunsets in blundering
Wistful deaths.

I have wanted to let go and cross over
To a next star, a last star.

I have asked to be left a few tears
And some laughter.

## UPSTREAM

The strong men keep coming on,
They go down shot, hanged, sick, broken.

They live on fighting, singing, lucky as plungers.
The strong mothers pulling them on . . .
The strong mothers pulling them from a dark sea, a great prairie, a long mountain.
Call hallelujah, call amen, call deep thanks.
The strong men keep coming on.

### SUNSETS

here are sunsets who whisper a good-by.
is a short dusk and a way for stars.
rairie and sea rim they go level and even,
nd the sleep is easy.

There are sunsets who dance good-by.
They fling scarves half to the arc,
To the arc then and over the arc.
Ribbons at the ears, sashes at the hips,
Dancing, dancing good-by. And here sleep
Tosses a little with dreams.

### ELEPHANTS ARE DIFFERENT TO DIFFERENT PEOPLE

Wilson and Pilcer and Snack stood before the zoo elephant.

Wilson said, "What is its name? Is it from Asia or Africa? Who feeds it? Is it a he or a she? How old is it? Do they have twins? How much does it cost to feed? How much does it weigh? If it dies how much will another one cost? If it dies what will they use the bones, the fat, and the hide for? What use is it besides to look at?"

Pilcer didn't have any questions; he was murmuring to himself, "It's a house by itself, walls and windows, the ears came from tall cornfields, by God; the architect of those legs was a workman, by God; he stands like a bridge out across deep water; the face is sad and the eyes are kind; I know elephants are good to babies."

Snack looked up and down and at last said to himself, "He's a tough son-of-a-gun outside and I'll bet he's got a strong heart, I'll bet he's strong as a copper-riveted boiler inside."

They didn't put up any arguments.
They didn't throw anything in each other's faces.
Three men saw the elephant three ways
And let it go at that.
They didn't spoil a sunny Sunday afternoon;
"Sunday comes only once a week," they told each other.

### FOR YOU

he peace of great doors be for you.
ait at the knobs, at the panel oblongs;
ait for the great hinges.

he peace of great churches be for you,
here the players of loft pipe-organs
ractice old lovely fragments, alone.

he peace of great books be for you,
ains of pressed clover leaves on pages,
leach of the light of years held in leather.

he peace of great prairies be for you.
isten among windplayers in cornfields,
he wind learning over its oldest music.

The peace of great seas be for you.
Wait on a hook of land, a rock footing
For you, wait in the salt wash.

The peace of great mountains be for you,
The sleep and the eyesight of eagles,
Sheet mist shadows and the long look across.

The peace of great hearts be for you,
Valves of the blood of the sun,
Pumps of the strongest wants we cry.

The peace of great silhouettes be for you,
Shadow dancers alive in your blood now,
Alive and crying, "Let us out, let us out."

The peace of great changes be for you.
Whispers, oh beginners in the hills.
Tumble, oh cubs—tomorrow belongs to you.

The peace of great loves be for you.
Rain, soak these roots; wind, shatter the dry
   rot.
Bars of sunlight, grips of the earth; hug these.

The peace of great ghosts be for you,
Phantoms of night-gray eyes, ready to go
To the fog-star dumps, to the fire-whi
   doors.

Yes, the peace of great phantoms be for yo
Phantom iron men, mothers of bronze,
Keepers of the lean clean breeds.

## *Adelaide Crapsey*

Adelaide crapsey, daughter of the famous minister, Algernon S. Crapsey, was
born, September 9, 1878, in Rochester, New York, where she spent her childhood. She entered Vassar College in 1897, graduating with the class of 1901. Two
years after graduation she began work as a teacher of History and Literature, in
Kemper Hall, Kenosha, Wisconsin, where she had attended preparatory school. In
1905 she went abroad, studying archeology in Rome. After her return she tried again
to teach, but her failing health compelled her to discontinue, and though she became
instructor in Poetics at Smith College in 1911 the burden was too great for her.

Prior to this time she had written little verse, her chief work being an analysis of
English metrics, an investigation (which she never finished) of problems in verse
structure. In 1913, after her breakdown, she began to write her precise and sometimes poignant lines; most of her tiny volume was composed during the last few
months of her life. She was particularly happy in her brief "Cinquains," a form
which she originated. These five-line stanzas in the strictest possible pattern (the
lines having, respectively, two, four, six, eight and two syllables) doubtless owe
something to the Japanese *hokku,* but Adelaide Crapsey saturated them with her
own fragile loveliness.

"Her death," writes Claude Bragdon, who was not only her friend but her first
publisher, "was tragic. Full of the desire of life she was forced to go, leaving her
work all unfinished. Her last year was spent in exile at Saranac. From her window
she looked down on the graveyard—'Trudeau's Garden,' she called it, with grim-gay
irony. Here, forbidden the work her metrical study entailed, these poems grew—
flowers of a battlefield of the spirit." She died at Saranac Lake, New York, on October 8, 1914.

Her small volume *Verse* appeared in 1915, and a part of the unfinished *Study in
English Metrics* was posthumously published in 1918. A second edition of *Verse*
with a few additional poems appeared in 1922. An unconscious Imagist, she gave
fragility a firmness which saved the smallest of her designs from preciosity.

FIVE CINQUAINS

NOVEMBER NIGHT

Listen . . .
With faint dry sound,
Like steps of passing ghosts,

The leaves, frost-crisp'd, break from the tre
And fall.

SUSANNA AND THE ELDERS

"Why do
You thus devise

Evil against her?" "For that
She is beautiful, delicate.
Therefore."

### TRIAD

These be
Three silent things:
The falling snow . . . the hour
Before the dawn . . . the mouth of one
Just dead.

### NIAGARA

(*Seen on a night in November*)

How frail
Above the bulk
Of crashing water hangs,
Autumnal, evanescent, wan,
The moon.

### THE WARNING

Just now,
Out of the strange
Still dusk . . . as strange, as still . . .
A white moth flew. Why am I grown
So cold?

### ON SEEING WEATHER-BEATEN TREES

it as plainly in our living shown,
slant and twist, which way the wind hath
blown?

### VENDOR'S SONG

y songs to sell, good sir!
I pray you buy.
ere's one will win a lady's tears,
Here's one will make her gay,
ere's one will charm your true love true
Forever and a day;
ood sir, I pray you buy!

Oh, no, he will not buy.

My songs to sell, sweet maid!
I pray you buy.
This one will teach you Lilith's lore,
And this what Helen knew,
And this will keep your gold hair gold,
And this your blue eyes blue;
Sweet maid, I pray you buy!

Oh, no, she will not buy.

If I'd as much money as I could tell,
I never would cry my songs to sell.
I never would cry my songs to sell.

### THE LONELY DEATH

In the cold I will rise, I will bathe
In waters of ice; myself
Will shiver and shrive myself,
Alone in the dawn, and anoint
Forehead and feet and hands;
I will shutter the windows from light,
I will place in their sockets the four
Tall candles and set them a-flame
In the gray of the dawn; and myself
Will lay myself straight in my bed,
And draw the sheet up under my chin.

### SONG

I make my shroud, but no one knows—
So shimmering fine it is and fair,
With stitches set in even rows.
I make my shroud, but no one knows.

In door-way where the lilac blows,
Humming a little wandering air,
I make my shroud and no one knows,
So shimmering fine it is and fair.

## *Vachel Lindsay*

(Nicholas) Vachel Lindsay was born in Springfield, Illinois, November 10, 1879. His home for many years was next door to the executive mansion of the State of Illinois; from the window where Lindsay did most of his writing, he saw governors come and go, including the martyred John P. Altgeld, whom he has celebrated in one of his finest poems. He graduated from the Springfield High School, attended Hiram College (1897-1900), studied at the Art Institute at Chicago (1900-3) and at the New York School of Art (1904). After two years of lecturing and settlement work, he took the first of his long tramps, walking through Florida, Georgia, and the Carolinas, preaching "the gospel of beauty," and formulating his unique plans for a communal art. During the following five years, Lindsay made several of these trips, traveling as a combination missionary and minstrel. Like a true revivalist, he attempted to wake a response to beauty, distributing a little pamphlet entitled "Rhymes to Be Traded for Bread."

Lindsay began to create more poetry to reach the public—all of his verse was written in his rôle of apostle. He was, primarily, a rhyming John the Baptist singing to convert the heathen, to stimulate and encourage the half-hearted dreams that hide and are smothered in sordid villages and townships. But the great audiences he was endeavoring to reach did not hear him, even though his collection *General William Booth Enters Into Heaven* (1913) struck many a loud and racy note.

Lindsay broadened his effects, developed the chant, and, the following year, published his *The Congo and Other Poems* (1914), an infectious blend of rhyme, religion, and rag-time. In the title-poem and, in a lesser degree, the three companion chants, Lindsay struck his most powerful—and most popular—vein. When intoned in Lindsay's resonant baritone, it gave people that primitive joy in syncopated sound that is at the very base of song. In these experiments in breaking down the barriers between poetry and music, Lindsay (obviously infected by the echolalia of Poe's "Bells") tried to create what he called a "Higher Vaudeville" imagination, carrying the form back to the old Greek precedent where every line was half-spoken, half-sung.

Lindsay's innovation succeeded at once. The novelty, the speed, the clatter, forced the attention of people who had never paid the slightest heed to the poet's quieter verses. Men heard the *sounds* of hurtling America in these lines even when they were deaf to its spirit. They failed to see that, beneath the noise of "The Kallyope Yell" and "The Santa Fé Trail," Lindsay was partly an admirer, partly an ironical critic of the shrieking energy of these states. By his effort to win the enemy over, Lindsay had persuaded the proverbially tired business man to listen at last. But, in overstressing the vaudeville features, there arose the danger of Lindsay the poet being lost in Lindsay the entertainer. The sympathetic celebration of Negro spirits and psychology (seen at their best in "The Congo," "John Brown" and "Simon Legree") degenerated into the crude buffooneries of "The Daniel Jazz" and "The Blacksmith's Serenade." The three bracketed poems, and a few others, are certain of a place in the history of American poetry.

Lindsay's earnestness, keyed up by an exuberant fancy, saved him. *The Chinese*

*Nightingale* (1917) begins with the most whimsical extended rhymes Lindsay ever devised. This title-poem, with its air of free improvisation, is his finest piece of sheer texture. And if the subsequent *The Golden Whales of California* (1920) is less distinctive, it is principally because the author has written too much and too speedily to be self-critical. It is his peculiar appraisal of loveliness, the rollicking high spirits joined to a stubborn evangelism, that makes Lindsay so representative a product of his environment.

*Collected Poems* (1923) is a complete and almost cruel exhibit of Lindsay's best and worst. Inflated stanzas alternate with some of the most charming children's poetry of the times; the set of fanciful Moon Poems would be enough to keep Lindsay's name alive. That Lindsay had lost whatever faculty of self-appraisal he may have possessed is evidenced by page after page of crudities; verses are propelled by nothing more than physical energy whipping up a trivial idea. What mars so much of this writing is Lindsay's attempt to give every wisp of fancy a cosmic or at least a national significance. Thus that intoxicating chant "The Ghosts of the Buffaloes" appears in the later edition with an unfortunate appendage, an irrelevant hortatory appeal beginning, "Would I might rouse the Lincoln in you all!" But, in spite of the fact that the poet suffered from a complex of undiscriminating patriotism, a curious hero-worship which makes him link Woodrow Wilson with Socrates, his very catholicity was representative of a great part of his country. Johnny Appleseed and John L. Sullivan, Daniel Boone and William Jennings Bryan, Andrew Jackson and P. T. Barnum—such figures were the symbols of his motley America. They were not merely heroes but demi-gods. They typified the incongruous blend of high idealism and childish fantasy, of beauty and ballyhoo which made America resemble (to Lindsay) a County Fair—

> every soul resident
> In the earth's one circus tent.

It was a combination that made the United States "the golden dream" created by pioneers and baseball players, Presidents and movie-queens. Nuances of thought or expression were forgotten; exuberance, uncontrolled by taste or reason, triumphed. *Going-to-the-Sun* (1923), *Going-to-the-Stars* (1926), and *The Candle in the Cabin* (1927), illustrated with Lindsay's characteristic and flowery drawings, contain some charming and almost girlish verses, but followed each other in too rapid succession and betray Lindsay's uncritical loquacity. His prose is far better than the later verse. *The Litany of Washington Street* (1929), described as "a kind of Washington's birthday, Lincoln's birthday, Whitman's birthday, Jefferson's birthday book," is a set of Fourth of July orations on an idealized Main Street stretching from Connecticut to Calcutta.

Much of Lindsay will die; he will not live as either a prophet or a politician. But the vitality which impels the best of his galloping meters will persist; his innocent wildness of imagination, outlasting his naïve programs, will charm even those to whom his declamations are no longer a novelty. His gospel is no less original for being preached through a saxophone.

Besides his original poetry, Lindsay has embodied his experiences and meditations on the road in two prose volumes, *A Handy Guide for Beggars* (1916) and *Adventures While Preaching the Gospel of Beauty* (1914), as well as an enthusiastic study of the "silent drama," *The Art of the Moving Picture* (1915). A curious document, half rhapsody, half visionary novel, entitled *The Golden Book of Springfield,* appeared in 1920.

Lindsay traded on his surplus energy. Some of it went into private games, such as the establishment of each individual's "personal hieroglyphics," some into grandiose but futile schemes, most into lecturing. For more than twenty years he ranged the country, exciting his audiences and exhausting himself. After fifty the strain was too much for him. He collapsed at the beginning of his fifty-third year just as his work was taking a new turn. He died December 4, 1931. Edgar Lee Masters in *Vachel Lindsay: A Poet in America* (1935) implies that Lindsay killed himself after being broken by poverty and misunderstanding, and states explicitly that his tragedy was due to flagging vitality and to "that weakness which resulted from the magnitude of the dream, leaving no strength to execute the plan."

### THE CONGO

#### (*A Study of the Negro Race*)

#### I. THEIR BASIC SAVAGERY

| | |
|---|---|
| Fat black bucks in a wine-barrel room, | |
| Barrel-house kings, with feet unstable, | |
| Sagged and reeled and pounded on the table, | *A deep rolling* |
| Pounded on the table, | *bass.* |
| Beat an empty barrel with the handle of a broom, | |
| Hard as they were able, | |
| Boom, boom, BOOM, | |
| With a silk umbrella and the handle of a broom, | |
| Boomlay, boomlay, boomlay, BOOM. | |
| | |
| THEN I had religion, THEN I had a vision. | |
| I could not turn from their revel in derision. | |
| THEN I SAW THE CONGO, CREEPING THROUGH THE BLACK, | *More deliberate.* |
| CUTTING THROUGH THE JUNGLE WITH A GOLDEN TRACK. | *Solemnly chanted.* |
| | |
| Then along that riverbank | |
| A thousand miles | |
| Tattooed cannibals danced in files; | |
| Then I heard the boom of the blood-lust song | |
| And a thigh-bone beating on a tin-pan gong. | *A rapidly piling* |
| And "BLOOD" screamed the whistles and the fifes of the warriors, | *climax of speed* |
| "BLOOD" screamed the skull-faced, lean witch-doctors, | *and racket.* |
| "Whirl ye the deadly voo-doo rattle, | |
| Harry the uplands, | |
| Steal all the cattle, | |
| Rattle-rattle, rattle-rattle, | |
| Bing! | |
| Boomlay, boomlay, boomlay, BOOM," | |
| A roaring, epic, rag-time tune | *With a philo-* |
| From the mouth of the Congo | *sophic pause.* |
| To the Mountains of the Moon. | |

Death is an Elephant,                          *Shrilly and with a*
Torch-eyed and horrible,                        *heavily accented*
Foam-flanked and terrible.                      *meter.*
Boom, steal the pygmies,
Boom, kill the Arabs,
Boom, kill the white men,
Hoo, Hoo, Hoo.                                  *Like the wind in*
Listen to the yell of Leopold's ghost           *the chimney.*
Burning in Hell for his hand-maimed host.
Hear how the demons chuckle and yell
Cutting his hands off, down in Hell.
Listen to the creepy proclamation,
Blown through the lairs of the forest-nation,
Blown past the white-ants' hill of clay,
Blown past the marsh where the butterflies play:—
"Be careful what you do,
Or Mumbo-Jumbo, God of the Congo,              *All the o sounds*
And all of the other                           *very golden.*
Gods of the Congo,                             *Heavy accents*
                                               *very heavy.*
Mumbo-Jumbo will hoo-doo you,                  *Light accents*
Mumbo-Jumbo will hoo-doo you,                  *very light. Last*
Mumbo-Jumbo will hoo-doo you."                 *line whispered.*

### II. Their Irrepressible High Spirits

Wild crap-shooters with a whoop and a call      *Rather shrill*
Danced the juba in their gambling-hall          *and high.*
And laughed fit to kill, and shook the town,
And guyed the policemen and laughed them down
With a boomlay, boomlay, boomlay, Boom. . . .
Then I saw the Congo, creeping through the black, *Read exactly as*
Cutting through the jungle with a golden track.   *in first section.*
A negro fairyland swung into view,              *Lay emphasis on*
A minstrel river                                *the delicate ideas.*
Where dreams come true.                         *Keep as light-*
                                                *footed as possible.*
The ebony palace soared on high
Through the blossoming trees to the evening sky,
The inlaid porches and casements shone
With gold and ivory and elephant-bone.
And the black crowd laughed till their sides were sore
At the baboon butler in the agate door,
And the well-known tunes of the parrot band
That trilled on the bushes of that magic land.
A troupe of skull-faced witch-men came         *With pomposity.*
Through the agate doorway in suits of flame,
Yes, long-tailed coats with a gold-leaf crust
And hats that were covered with diamond-dust.
And the crowd in the court gave a whoop and a call
And danced the juba from wall to wall.
But the witch-men suddenly stilled the throng  *With a great*
With a stern cold glare, and a stern old song:— *deliberation and*
"Mumbo-Jumbo will hoo-doo you." . . .          *ghostliness.*

Just then from the doorway, as fat as shotes,
Came the cake-walk princes in their long red coats,
Shoes with a patent leather shine,
And tall silk hats that were red as wine.
And they pranced with their butterfly partners there,
Coal-black maidens with pearls in their hair,
Knee-skirts trimmed with the jessamine sweet,
And bells on their ankles and little black feet.
And the couples railed at the chant and the frown
Of the witch-men lean, and laughed them down.
(O rare was the revel, and well worth while
That made those glowering witch-men smile).

*With overwhelm-
ing assurance,
good cheer, and
pomp.*

*With growing
speed and
sharply marked
dance-rhythm.*

The cake-walk royalty then began
To walk for a cake that was tall as a man
To the tune of "Boomlay, boomlay, Boom,"
While the witch-men laughed, with a sinister air,
And sang with the scalawags prancing there:—
"Walk with care, walk with care,
Or Mumbo-Jumbo, God of the Congo,
And all of the other
Gods of the Congo,
Mumbo-Jumbo will hoo-doo you.
Beware, beware, walk with care,
Boomlay, boomlay, boomlay, boom.
Boomlay, boomlay, boomlay, boom,
Boomlay, boomlay, boomlay, boom,
Boomlay, boomlay, boomlay,
Boom."
O rare was the revel, and well worth while
That made those glowering witch-men smile.

*With a touch of
negro dialect,
and
as rapidly as
possible toward
the end.*

*Slow philo-
sophic calm.*

### III. The Hope of Their Religion

A good old negro in the slums of the town
Preached at a sister for her velvet gown.
Howled at a brother for his low-down ways,
His prowling, guzzling, sneak-thief days.
Beat on the Bible till he wore it out,
Starting the jubilee revival shout.
And some had visions, as they stood on chairs,
And sang of Jacob, and the golden stairs.
And they all repented, a thousand strong,
From their stupor and savagery and sin and wrong
And slammed their hymn books till they shook the room
With "Glory, glory, glory,"
And "Boom, boom, Boom."
Then I saw the Congo, creeping through the black,
Cutting through the jungle with a golden track.
And the gray sky opened like a new-rent veil
And showed the Apostles with their coats of mail.
In bright white steel they were seated round

*Heavy bass.
With a literal
imitation of
camp-meeting
racket, and
trance.*

*Exactly as in
the first section.*

And their fire-eyes watched where the Congo wound.
And the twelve Apostles, from their thrones on high,
Thrilled all the forest with their heavenly cry:—
"Mumbo-Jumbo will die in the jungle;
Never again will he hoo-doo you,
Never again will he hoo-doo you."

*Sung to the tune
of "Hark, ten
thousand harps
and voices."*

Then along that river, a thousand miles
The vine-snared trees fell down in files.
Pioneer angels cleared the way
For a Congo paradise, for babes at play,
For sacred capitals, for temples clean.
Gone were the skull-faced witch-men lean.
There, where the wild ghost-gods had wailed
A million boats of the angels sailed
With oars of silver, and prows of blue
And silken pennants that the sun shone through.
'Twas a land transfigured, 'twas a new creation.
Oh, a singing wind swept the negro nation
And on through the backwoods clearing flew:—
"Mumbo-Jumbo is dead in the jungle.
Never again will he hoo-doo you.
Never again will he hoo-doo you."

*With growing
deliberation
and joy.*

*In a rather
high key—as
delicately as
possible.*

*To the tune of
"Hark, ten
thousand harps
and voices."*

Redeemed were the forests, the beasts and the men,
And only the vulture dared again
By the far, lone mountains of the moon
To cry, in the silence, the Congo tune:—
"Mumbo-Jumbo will hoo-doo you,
Mumbo . . . Jumbo . . . will . . . hoo-doo . . . you."

*Dying off into
a penetrating,
terrified whisper.*

## TO A GOLDEN-HAIRED GIRL IN A LOUISIANA TOWN

You are a sunrise,
If a star should rise instead of the sun.
You are a moonrise,
If a star should come in the place of the moon.
You are the Spring;
If a face should bloom instead of an apple-bough.
You are my love,
If your heart is as kind
As your young eyes now.

## GENERAL WILLIAM BOOTH ENTERS INTO HEAVEN

(To be sung to the tune of "The Blood of the Lamb" with indicated instruments)

I

*(Bass drum beaten loudly.)*
Booth led boldly with his big brass drum—
(Are you washed in the blood of the Lamb?)
The Saints smiled gravely and they said: "He's come."

(Are you washed in the blood of the Lamb?)
Walking lepers followed, rank on rank,
Lurching bravos from the ditches dank,
Drabs from the alleyways and drug fiends pale—
Minds still passion-ridden, soul-powers frail:—
Vermin-eaten saints with moldy breath,
Unwashed legions with the ways of Death—
(Are you washed in the blood of the Lamb?)

    *(Banjos.)*
Every slum had sent its half-a-score
The round world over. (Booth had groaned for more.)
Every banner that the wide world flies
Bloomed with glory and transcendent dyes.
Big-voiced lasses made their banjos bang,
Tranced, fanatical they shrieked and sang:—
"Are you washed in the blood of the Lamb?"
Hallelujah! It was queer to see
Bull-necked convicts with that land make free.
Loons with trumpets blowed a blare, blare, blare
On, on upward thro' the golden air!
(Are you washed in the blood of the Lamb?)

II
    *(Bass drum slower and softer.)*
Booth died blind and still by faith he trod,
Eyes still dazzled by the ways of God.
Booth led boldly, and he looked the chief,
Eagle countenance in sharp relief,
Beard a-flying, air of high command
Unabated in that holy land.

    *(Sweet flute music.)*
Jesus came from out the court-house door,
Stretched his hands above the passing poor.
Booth saw not, but led his queer ones there
Round and round the mighty court-house square.
Yet in an instant all that blear review
Marched on spotless, clad in raiment new.
The lame were straightened, withered limbs uncurled
And blind eyes opened on a new, sweet world.

    *(Bass drum louder.)*
Drabs and vixens in a flash made whole!
Gone was the weasel-head, the snout, the jowl!
Sages and sibyls now, and athletes clean,
Rulers of empires, and of forests green!

    *(Grand chorus of all instruments. Tambourines to the foreground.)*
The hosts were sandaled, and their wings were fire!
(Are you washed in the blood of the Lamb?)
But their noise played havoc with the angel-choir.

(Are you washed in the blood of the Lamb?)
Oh, shout Salvation! It was good to see
Kings and Princes by the Lamb set free.
The banjos rattled and the tambourines
Jing-jing-jingled in the hands of Queens.

(*Reverently sung, no instruments.*)
And when Booth halted by the curb for prayer
He saw his Master thro' the flag-filled air.
Christ came gently with a robe and crown
For Booth the soldier, while the throng knelt down.
He saw King Jesus. They were face to face,
And he knelt a-weeping in that holy place.
Are you washed in the blood of the Lamb?

### THE EAGLE THAT IS FORGOTTEN

(*John P. Altgeld. Born December 30, 1847; died March 12, 1902*)

Sleep softly . . . eagle forgotten . . . under the stone.
Time has its way with you there, and the clay has its own.
"We have buried him now," thought your foes, and in secret rejoiced.
They made a brave show of their mourning, their hatred unvoiced,
They had snarled at you, barked at you, foamed at you, day after day,
Now you were ended. They praised you, . . . and laid you away.

The others that mourned you in silence and terror and truth,
The widow bereft of her pittance, the boy without youth,
The mocked and the scorned and the wounded, the lame and the poor
That should have remembered forever, . . . remember no more.

Where are those lovers of yours, on what name do they call
The lost, that in armies wept over your funeral pall?
They call on the names of a hundred high-valiant ones,
A hundred white eagles have risen, the sons of your sons,
The zeal in their wings is a zeal that your dreaming began
The valor that wore out your soul in the service of man.

Sleep softly, . . . eagle forgotten, . . . under the stone,
Time has its way with you there, and the clay has its own.
Sleep on, O brave-hearted, O wise man, that kindled the flame—
To live in mankind is far more than to live in a name,
To live in mankind, far, far more . . . than to live in a name.

### THE GHOSTS OF THE BUFFALOES

Last night at black midnight I woke with a cry,
The windows were shaking, there was thunder on high,
The floor was atremble, the door was ajar,
White fires, crimson fires, shone from afar.

I rushed to the dooryard. The city was gone.
My home was a hut without orchard or lawn.
It was mud-smear and logs near a whispering stream,
Nothing else built by man could I see in my dream . . .

Then . . .
Ghost-kings came headlong, row upon row,
Gods of the Indians, torches aglow.
They mounted the bear and the elk and the deer,
And eagles gigantic, agèd and sere,
They rode long-horn cattle, they cried "A-la-la."
They lifted the knife, the bow, and the spear,
They lifted ghost-torches from dead fires below,
The midnight made grand with the cry "A-la-la."
The midnight made grand with a red-god charge,
A red-god show,
A red-god show,
"A-la-la, a-la-la, a-la-la, a-la-la."

With bodies like bronze, and terrible eyes
Came the rank and the file, with catamount cries,
Gibbering, yipping, with hollow-skull clacks,
Riding white bronchos with skeleton backs,
Scalp-hunters, beaded and spangled and bad,
Naked and lustful and foaming and mad,
Flashing primeval demoniac scorn,
Blood-thirst and pomp amid darkness reborn,
Power and glory that sleep in the grass
While the winds and the snows and the great rains pass.
They crossed the gray river, thousands abreast,
They rode out in infinite lines to the west,
Tide upon tide of strange fury and foam,
Spirits and wraiths, the blue was their home,
The sky was their goal where the star-flags are furled,
And on past those far golden splendors they whirled.
They burned to dim meteors, lost in the deep,
And I turned in dazed wonder, thinking of sleep.

And the wind crept by
Alone, unkempt, unsatisfied,
The wind cried and cried—
Muttered of massacres long past,
Buffaloes in shambles vast . . .
An owl said, "Hark, what is a-wing?"
I heard a cricket caroling,
I heard a cricket caroling,
I heard a cricket caroling.

Then . . .
Snuffing the lightning that crashed from on high
Rose royal old buffaloes, row upon row.
The lords of the prairie came galloping by.

And I cried in my heart "A-la-la, a-la-la.
A red-god show,
A red-god show,
A-la-la, a-la-la, a-la-la."
Buffaloes, buffaloes, thousands abreast,
A scourge and amazement, they swept to the west.
With black bobbing noses, with red rolling tongues,
Coughing forth steam from their leather-wrapped lungs,
Cows with their calves, bulls big and vain,
Goring the laggards, shaking the mane,
Stamping flint feet, flashing moon eyes,
Pompous and owlish, shaggy and wise.

Like sea-cliffs and caves resounded their ranks
With shoulders like waves, and undulant flanks.
Tide upon tide of strange fury and foam,
Spirits and wraiths, the blue was their home,
The sky was their goal where the star-flags are furled,
And on past those far golden splendors they whirled.
They burned to dim meteors, lost in the deep,
And I turned in dazed wonder, thinking of sleep.

I heard a cricket's cymbals play,
A scarecrow lightly flapped his rags,
And a pan that hung by his shoulder rang,
Rattled and thumped in a listless way,
And now the wind in the chimney sang,
The wind in the chimney,
The wind in the chimney,
The wind in the chimney,
Seemed to say:—
"Dream, boy, dream,
If you anywise can.
To dream is the work
Of beast or man.
Life is the west-going dream-storm's breath,
Life is a dream, the sigh of the skies,
The breath of the stars, that nod on their pillows
With their golden hair mussed over their eyes."
The locust played on his musical wing,
Sang to his mate of love's delight.
I heard the whippoorwill's soft fret.
I heard a cricket caroling,
I heard a cricket caroling,
I heard a cricket say: "Good-night, good-night,
Good-night, good-night, . . . good-night."

### THE TRAVELER

The moon's a devil jester
Who makes himself too free.

The rascal is not always
Where he appears to be.
Sometimes he is in my heart—
Sometimes he is in the sea;
Then tides are in my heart,
And tides are in the sea.

O traveler, abiding not
Where he pretends to be!

### A NEGRO SERMON: — SIMON LEGREE

Legree's big house was white and green.
His cotton-fields were the best to be seen.
He had strong horses and opulent cattle,
And bloodhounds bold, with chains that would rattle.
His garret was full of curious things:
Books of magic, bags of gold,
And rabbits' feet on long twine strings,
*But he went down to the Devil.*

Legree, he sported a brass-buttoned coat,
A snake-skin necktie, a blood-red shirt.
Legree, he had a beard like a goat,
And a thick hairy neck, and eyes like dirt.
His puffed-out cheeks were fish-belly white,
He had great long teeth, and an appetite.
He ate raw meat, 'most every meal,
And rolled his eyes till the cat would squeal.
His fist was an enormous size
To mash poor niggers that told him lies:
He was surely a witch-man in disguise.
*But he went down to the Devil.*

He wore hip-boots, and would wade all day
To capture his slaves that had fled away.
*But he went down to the Devil.*
He beat poor Uncle Tom to death
Who prayed for Legree with his last breath.
Then Uncle Tom to Eva flew,
To the high sanctoriums bright and new;
And Simon Legree stared up beneath,
And cracked his heels, and ground his teeth:
*And went down to the Devil.*
He crossed the yard in the storm and gloom;
He went into his grand front room.
He said, "I killed him, and I don't care."
He kicked a hound, he gave a swear;
He tightened his belt, he took a lamp,
Went down cellar to the webs and damp.

There in the middle of the moldy floor
He heaved up a slab; he found a door—
*And went down to the Devil.*

His lamp blew out, but his eyes burned bright.
Simon Legree stepped down all night—
*Down, down to the Devil.*
Simon Legree he reached the place,
He saw one half of the human race,
He saw the Devil on a wide green throne,
Gnawing the meat from a big ham-bone,
And he said to Mister Devil:
    "I see that you have much to eat—
    A red ham-bone is surely sweet.
    I see that you have lion's feet;
    I see your frame is fat and fine,
    I see you drink your poison wine—
    Blood and burning turpentine."

And the Devil said to Simon Legree:
    "I like your style, so wicked and free.
    Come sit and share my throne with me,
    And let us bark and revel."
And there they sit and gnash their teeth,
And each one wears a hop-vine wreath.
They are matching pennies and shooting craps,
They are playing poker and taking naps.
And old Legree is fat and fine:
He eats the fire, he drinks the wine—
Blood and burning turpentine—
    *Down, down with the Devil;*
    *Down, down with the Devil;*
    *Down, down with the Devil.*

## JOHN BROWN

(To be sung by a leader and chorus, the leader singing the body of the poem, while the chorus interrupts with the question)

I've been to Palestine.
    *What did you see in Palestine?*
I saw the ark of Noah—
It was made of pitch and pine.
I saw old Father Noah
Asleep beneath his vine.
I saw Shem, Ham and Japhet
Standing in a line.
I saw the tower of Babel
In the gorgeous sunrise shine—
By a weeping willow tree
Beside the Dead Sea.

I've been to Palestine.
    *What did you see in Palestine?*
I saw abominations
And Gadarene swine.
I saw the sinful Canaanites
Upon the shewbread dine,
And spoil the temple vessels
And drink the temple wine.
I saw Lot's wife, a pillar of salt
Standing in the brine—
By a weeping willow tree
Beside the Dead Sea.

I've been to Palestine.
    *What did you see in Palestine?*
Cedars on Mount Lebanon,
Gold in Ophir's mine,

And a wicked generation
Seeking for a sign,
And Baal's howling worshipers
Their god with leaves entwine.
And . . .
I saw the war-horse ramping
And shake his forelock fine—
By a weeping willow tree
Beside the Dead Sea.

I've been to Palestine.
           *What did you see in Palestine?*
Old John Brown.
Old John Brown.
I saw his gracious wife
Dressed in a homespun gown.
I saw his seven sons
Before his feet bow down.
And he marched with his seven sons,
His wagons and goods and guns,
To his campfire by the sea,
By the waves of Galilee.

I've been to Palestine.
           *What did you see in Palestine?*
I saw the harp and psalt'ry
Played for Old John Brown.
I heard the ram's horn blow,
Blow for Old John Brown.
I saw the Bulls of Bashan—
They cheered for Old John Brown.
I saw the big Behemoth—
He cheered for Old John Brown.
I saw the big Leviathan—
He cheered for Old John Brown.
I saw the Angel Gabriel
Great power to him assign.
I saw him fight the Canaanites
And set God's Israel free.
I saw him when the war was done
In his rustic chair recline—
By his campfire by the sea
By the waves of Galilee.

I've been to Palestine.
           *What did you see in Palestine?*
Old John Brown.
Old John Brown.
And there he sits

To judge the world.
His hunting-dogs
At his feet are curled.
His eyes half-closed,
But John Brown sees
The ends of the earth,
The Day of Doom.
And his shot-gun lies
Across his knees—
Old John Brown,
Old John Brown.

### THE DOVE OF NEW SNOW

I give you a house of snow,
I give you the flag of the wind above it,
I give you snow-bushes
In a long row,
I give you a snow-dove,
And ask you
To love it.

The snow-dove flies in
At the snow-house window,
He is a ghost
And he casts no shadow.
His cry is the cry of love
From the meadow,
The meadow of snow where he walked in
   glow,
The glittering, angelic meadow.

### THE FLOWER-FED BUFFALOES

The flower-fed buffaloes of the spring
In the days of long ago,
Ranged where the locomotives sing
And the prairie flowers lie low;
The tossing, blooming, perfumed grass
Is swept away by wheat,
Wheels and wheels and wheels spin by
In the spring that still is sweet.
But the flower-fed buffaloes of the spring
Left us long ago.
They gore no more, they bellow no more,
They trundle around the hills no more:—
With the Blackfeet lying low,
With the Pawnees lying low.

### ABRAHAM LINCOLN WALKS AT MIDNIGHT
#### (*In Springfield, Illinois*)

It is portentous, and a thing of state
That here at midnight, in our little town
A mourning figure walks, and will not rest,
Near the old court-house pacing up and down,

Or by his homestead, or in shadowed yards
He lingers where his children used to play,
Or through the market, on the well-worn stones
He stalks until the dawn-stars burn away.

A bronzed, lank man! His suit of ancient black,
A famous high top-hat and plain worn shawl
Make him the quaint great figure that men love,
The prairie-lawyer, master of us all.

He cannot sleep upon his hillside now.
He is among us:—as in times before!
And we who toss and lie awake for long,
Breathe deep, and start, to see him pass the door.

His head is bowed. He thinks of men and kings.
Yea, when the sick world cries, how can he sleep?
Too many peasants fight, they know not why;
Too many homesteads in black terror weep.

The sins of all the war-lords burn his heart.
He sees the dreadnaughts scouring every main.
He carries on his shawl-wrapped shoulders now
The bitterness, the folly and the pain.

He cannot rest until a spirit-dawn
Shall come;—the shining hope of Europe free:
A league of sober folk, the workers' earth,
Bringing long peace to Cornland, Alp and Sea.

It breaks his heart that kings must murder still,
That all his hours of travail here for men
Seem yet in vain. And who will bring white peace
That he may sleep upon his hill again?

### WHEN LINCOLN CAME TO SPRINGFIELD

When Lincoln came to Springfield,
  In the ancient days,
Queer were the streets and sketchy,
  And he was in a maze.

Leaving log cabins behind him.
  For the mud streets of this place,
Sorrow for Anne Rutledge
  Burned in his face.

He threw his muddy saddle bags
  On Joshua Speed's floor,

He took off his old hat,
  He looked around the store.

He shook his long hair
  On his bison-head,
He sat down on the counter,
  "Speed, I've moved," he said.


NANCY HANKS, MOTHER OF
ABRAHAM LINCOLN

*"Out of the eater came forth meat; and out of the
strong came forth sweetness." Judges 14 : 14*

A sweet girl graduate, lean as a fawn,
The very whimsy of time,
Read her class upon Commencement Day—
A trembling filigree rhyme.
The pansy that blooms on the window sill,
Blooms in exactly the proper place;
And she nodded just like a pansy there,
And her poem was all about bowers and
  showers,
Sugary streamlet and mossy rill,
All about daisies on dale and hill—
And she was the mother of Buffalo Bill.

Another girl, a cloud-drift sort,
Dreamlit, moonlit, marble-white,
Light-footed saint on the pilgrim shore,
The best since New England fairies began,
Was the mother of Barnum, the circus man.

A girl from Missouri, snippy and vain,
As frothy a miss as any you know,
A wren, a toy, a pink silk bow,
The belle of the choir, she drove insane
Missouri deacons and all the sleek,
Her utter tomfoolery made men weak,
Till they could not stand and they could ɪ
  speak.
Oh, queen of fifteen and sixteen,
Missouri sweetened beneath her reign—
And she was the mother of bad Mark Twaɪ

Not always are lions born of lions,
Roosevelt sprang from a palace of lace;
On the other hand is the dizzy truth:
Not always is beauty born of beauty.
Some treasures wait in a hidden place.
All over the world were thousands of bell
In far-off eighteen hundred and nine,
Girls of fifteen, girls of twenty,
Their mammas dressed them up a-plenty
Each garter was bright, each stocking fine,
But for all their innocent devices,
Their cheeks of fruit and their eyes of wiɪ
And each voluptuous design,
And all soft glories that we trace
In Europe's palaces of lace,
A girl who slept in dust and sorrow,
Nancy Hanks, in a lost cabin,
Nancy Hanks had the loveliest face!


WILD CATS

Here, as it were, in the heart of roaring Rome,
Here as far as men may get from the soil,
Here where political lords
Are proud of oil,
Oil in their skins,
Oil in their robber wells,
Where money and stone and orations are combined,
Here in Washington, D. C.,
Here where sins are refined and over-refined,
Here where they ape the very walls of Rome,
The temples and pillars of Imperial Rome,
We think of the time the wild cats kept awake
Our little camp, and filled our hearts with fright,
When porcupine and bear-cub stirred the brake,
And the friendliest wind seemed cold and impolite.
We think of our terror through the camp-fire night,
Of how we hoped to kiss the earth aright,

In spite of fear, and hoped not all in vain,
Of how we hoped for wild days, clean with power,
Of how we sought the fine log-cabin hour,
Of how we thought to rule
By leading men to a lone log-cabin school.
We think of our pioneer American pride,
Our high defiance that has not yet died,
Here, as it were, in the heart of roaring Rome,
In Washington, D. C.
Where they ape the very walls of Rome.


## THE APPLE-BARREL OF JOHNNY APPLESEED

On the mountain peak, called "Going-To-The-Sun,"
I saw gray Johnny Appleseed at prayer
Just as the sunset made the old earth fair.
Then darkness came; in an instant, like great smoke,
The sun fell down as though its great hoops broke
And dark rich apples, poured from the dim flame
Where the sun set, came rolling toward the peak,
A storm of fruit, a mighty cider-reek,
The perfume of the orchards of the world,
From apple-shadows: red and russet domes
That turned to clouds of glory and strange homes
Above the mountain tops for cloud-born souls:—
Reproofs for men who build the world like moles,
Models for men, if they would build the world
As Johnny Appleseed would have it done—
Praying, and reading the books of Swedenborg
On the mountain top called "Going-To-The-Sun."


## THE VOYAGE

What is my mast? A pen.
What are my sails? Ten crescent moons.
What is my sea? A bottle of ink.
Where do I go? To heaven again.
What do I eat? The amaranth flower,
While the winds through the jungles think old tunes.
I eat that flower with ivory spoons
While the winds through the jungles play old tunes;
The songs the angels used to sing
When heaven was not old autumn, but spring—
The bold, old songs of heaven and spring.


## THE CHINESE NIGHTINGALE

### (*A Song in Chinese Tapestries*)

"How, how," he said. "Friend Chang," I said,
"San Francisco sleeps as the dead—

Ended license, lust and play:
Why do you iron the night away?
Your big clock speaks with a deadly sound,
With a tick and a wail till dawn comes round,
While the monster shadows glower and creep,
What can be better for man than sleep?"

"I will tell you a secret," Chang replied;
"My breast with vision is satisfied,
And I see green trees and fluttering wings,
And my deathless bird from Shanghai sings."
Then he lit five firecrackers in a pan,
"Pop, pop," said the firecrackers, "cra-cra-crack."
He lit a joss stick long and black.
Then the proud gray joss in the corner stirred;
On his wrist appeared a gray small bird,
And this was the song of the gray small bird:
"Where is the princess, loved forever,
Who made Chang first of the kings of men?"

And the joss in the corner stirred again;
And the carved dog, curled in his arms, awoke,
Barked forth a smoke-cloud that whirled and broke.
It piled in a maze round the ironing-place,
And there on the snowy table wide
Stood a Chinese lady of high degree,
With a scornful, witching, tea-rose face. . . .
Yet she put away all form and pride,
And laid her glimmering veil aside
With a childlike smile for Chang and me.

The walls fell back, night was aflower,
The table gleamed in a moonlit bower,
While Chang, with a countenance carved of stone,
Ironed and ironed, all alone.
And thus she sang to the busy man Chang:
"Have you forgotten . . .
Deep in the ages, long, long ago,
I was your sweetheart, there on the sand—
Storm-worn beach of the Chinese land?
We sold our grain in the peacock town—
Built on the edge of the sea-sands brown—
Built on the edge of the sea-sands brown. . . .
When all the world was drinking blood
From the skulls of men and bulls
And all the world had swords and clubs of stone,
We drank our tea in China beneath the sacred spice-trees,
And heard the curled waves of the harbor moan.
And this gray bird, in Love's first spring,
With a bright-bronze breast and a bronze-brown wing,
Captured the world with his caroling.

Do you remember, ages after,
At last the world we were born to own?
You were the heir of the yellow throne—
The world was the field of the Chinese man
And we were the pride of the Sons of Han?
We copied deep books and we carved in jade,
And wove blue silks in the mulberry shade. . . ."

"I remember, I remember
That Spring came on forever,
That Spring came on forever,"
Said the Chinese nightingale.

My heart was filled with marvel and dream,
Though I saw the western street-lamps gleam,
Though dawn was bringing the western day,
Though Chang was a laundryman ironing away. . . .
Mingled there with the streets and alleys,
The railroad-yard and the clock-tower bright,
Demon clouds crossed ancient valleys;
Across wide lotus-ponds of light
I marked a giant firefly's flight.

And the lady, rosy-red,
Flourished her fan, her shimmering fan,
Stretched her hand toward Chang, and said:
"Do you remember,
Ages after,
Our palace of heart-red stone?
Do you remember
The little doll-faced children
With their lanterns full of moon-fire,
That came from all the empire
Honoring the throne?—
The loveliest fête and carnival
Our world had ever known?
The sages sat about us
With their heads bowed in their beards,
With proper meditation on the sight.
Confucius was not born;
We lived in those great days
Confucius later said were lived aright. . . .
And this gray bird, on that day of spring,
With a bright-bronze breast and a bronze-brown wing,
Captured the world with his caroling.
Late at night his tune was spent.
Peasants,
Sages,
Children,
Homeward went,
And then the bronze bird sang for you and me.

We walked alone. Our hearts were high and free.
I had a silvery name, I had a silvery name,
I had a silvery name—do you remember
The name you cried beside the tumbling sea?"

Chang turned not to the lady slim—
He bent to his work, ironing away;
But she was arch, and knowing and glowing,
For the bird on his shoulder spoke for him.

"Darling . . . darling . . . darling . . . darling . . ."
Said the Chinese nightingale.

The great gray joss on the rustic shelf,
Rakish and shrewd, with his collar awry,
Sang impolitely, as though by himself,
Drowning with his bellowing the nightingale's cry:
"Back through a hundred, hundred years
Hear the waves as they climb the piers,
Hear the howl of the silver seas,
Hear the thunder.
Hear the gongs of holy China
How the waves and tunes combine
In a rhythmic clashing wonder,
Incantation old and fine:
    'Dragons, dragons, Chinese dragons,
    Red firecrackers, and green firecrackers
    And dragons, dragons, Chinese dragons.'"

Then the lady, rosy-red,
Turned to her lover Chang and said:
"Dare you forget that turquoise dawn
When we stood in our mist-hung velvet lawn,
And worked a spell this great joss taught
Till a God of the Dragons was charmed and caught?
From the flag high over our palace home
He flew to our feet in rainbow-foam—
A king of beauty and tempest and thunder
Panting to tear our sorrows asunder.
A dragon of fair adventure and wonder.
We mounted the back of that royal slave
With thoughts of desire that were noble and grave.
We swam down the shore to the dragon-mountains,
We whirled to the peaks and the fiery fountains.
To our secret ivory house we were borne.
We looked down the wonderful wind-filled regions
Where the dragons darted in glimmering legions.
Right by my breast the nightingale sang;
The old rhymes rang in the sunlit mist
That we this hour regain—
Song-fire for the brain.

When my hands and my hair and my feet you kissed,
When you cried for your heart's new pain,
What was my name in the dragon-mist,
In the rings of the rainbowed rain?"

"Sorrow and love, glory and love,"
Sang the Chinese nightingale,
"Sorrow and love, glory and love,"
Said the Chinese nightingale.

And now the joss broke in with his song:
"Dying ember, bird of Chang,
Soul of Chang, do you remember?—
Ere you returned to the shining harbor
There were pirates by ten thousand
Descended on the town
In vessels mountain-high and red and brown,
Moon-ships that climbed the storms and cut the skies.
On their prows were painted terrible bright eyes.
But I was then a wizard and a scholar and a priest;
I stood upon the sand;
With lifted hand I looked upon them
And sunk their vessels with my wizard eyes,
And the stately lacquer-gate made safe again.
Deep, deep below the bay, the seaweed and the spray,
Embalmed in amber every pirate lies,
Embalmed in amber every pirate lies."

Then this did the noble lady say:
"Bird, do you dream of our home-coming day
When you flew like a courier on before
From the dragon-peak to our palace-door,
And we drove the steed in your singing path—
The ramping dragon of laughter and wrath:
And found our city all aglow,
And knighted this joss that decked it so?
There were golden fishes in the purple river
And silver fishes and rainbow fishes.
There were golden junks in the laughing river,
And silver junks and rainbow junks:
There were golden lilies by the bay and river,
And silver lilies and tiger-lilies,
And tinkling wind-bells in the gardens of the town
By the black-lacquer gate
Where walked in state
The kind king Chang
And his sweetheart mate. . . .
With his flag-born dragon
And his crown of pearl . . . and . . . jade,
And his nightingale reigning in the mulberry shade,
And sailors and soldiers on the sea-sands brown,
And priests who bowed them down to your song—

By the city called Han, the peacock town,
By the city called Han, the nightingale town,
The nightingale town."

Then sang the bird, so strangely gay,
Fluttering, fluttering, ghostly and gray,
A vague, unraveling, final tune,
Like a long unwinding silk cocoon;
Sang as though for the soul of him
Who ironed away in that bower dim:—
  "I have forgotten
  Your dragons great,
   Merry and mad and friendly and bold.
Dim is your proud lost palace-gate.
I vaguely know
There were heroes of old,
Troubles more than the heart could hold,
There were wolves in the woods
Yet lambs in the fold,
Nests in the top of the almond tree. . . .
The evergreen tree . . . and the mulberry tree. . . .
Life and hurry and joy forgotten,
Years and years I but half-remember . . .
Man is a torch, then ashes soon,
May and June, then dead December,
Dead December, then again June.
Who shall end my dream's confusion?
Life is a loom, weaving illusion. . . .
I remember, I remember
There were ghostly veils and laces. . . .
In the shadowy bowery places. . . .
With lovers' ardent faces
Bending to one another,
Speaking each his part.
They infinitely echo
In the red cave of my heart.
'Sweetheart, sweetheart, sweetheart,'
They said to one another.
They spoke, I think, of perils past.
They spoke, I think, of peace at last.
One thing I remember:
Spring came on forever,
Spring came on forever,"
Said the Chinese nightingale.

# Melville Cane

M ELVILLE CANE was born April 15, 1879, at Plattsburg, New York. He was educated at Columbia Grammar School, received his A.B. at Columbia in 1900, LL.B. in 1903. At Columbia he was editor-in-chief of the Literary Monthly; he wrote the lyrics of the Varsity operetta, the music of which was supplied by John Erskine. While still in college he contributed light verse to *Puck, Judge,* and the more sedate *Century* and was a reporter on the *New York Evening Post.* Upon graduation he engaged in the practice of law, specializing in the law of copyright and the theater.

After an interval of twenty years, he resumed writing and turned to a wholly unforeseen expression. *January Garden* (1926) is the antithesis of the light verse of Cane's youth; it is sensitive and unequivocally serious. Most of the volume is in a free verse whose contours are shaped by introspection. A somber cast may have accounted for the sparse enthusiasm with which it was received, but it is more difficult to account for failure to recognize the delicacy of the pictorial effects.

Cane's *Behind Dark Spaces* (1930) is less impressionistic, but what it loses in suggestion it gains in sharpness. Mixing "pure" and "suspended" rhyme, his tone-color has grown richer; concentrating on instead of writing around the object, he has developed power without resorting to force. Since 1934 Cane has written in a new genre, a type of poetry which blends seriousness and *vers de société* with a nice balance.

### SNOW TOWARD EVENING

Suddenly the sky turned gray,
The day,
Which had been bitter and chill,
Grew soft and still.
Quietly
From some invisible blossoming tree
Millions of petals cool and white
Drifted and blew,
Lifted and flew,
Fell with the falling night.

### TREE IN DECEMBER

Frost has sealed
The still December field.
Over fern and furrow,
Over the quickening
Within each meadowy acre,
Frost, invisibly thorough,
Spreads its thickening
Stiffening lacquer.

Above the field, beneath a sky
Heavy with snow stirring to fly,

A tree stands alone,
Bare of fruit, leaves gone
Bleak as stone.

Once, on a similar glazed
Field, on a similar tree,
Dead as the eye could see,
The first man, dazed
In the first December, grimly gazed,
Never having seen
The miracle of recurring green,
The shining spectacle of rebirth
Rising out of frozen earth.

Snow fell and all about
Covered earth, and him with doubt.
More chill grew the air
And his mute despair.

Leaves that April had uncurled
Now were blown dust in the world,
Apples mellowing sweet and sound
Now were icy rot in the ground;
Roses August sunned in bloom
Now were less than lost perfume.

Had he seen the final hour
Of fruit and leaf and flower?
Had the last bird taken wing,
Nevermore to sing?
Never to fly in the light of another spring?

The man trembled with cold, with dread,
Thinking of all things dead
And his own earthen bed.

Trembling, he grew aware
Of a new quiet in the air;
Snow had ceased;
A ray came faintly through;
The wavering slit of blue
Vaguely increased.

Trembling, the first man gazed
At the glazed
And glittering tree,
Dead as the eye could see.

Whence came the sight
To read the sign aright?
The hint,—
The glad intimation, flashing:
"Wintry rains
Are blood in the veins;
Under snows and binding sleets
Locked roots live, a heart still beats"?

From what impalpable breath
Issued the faith,
The inner cry: "This is not death"?

### DAWN HAS YET TO RIPPLE IN

What is this that I have heard?
Scurrying rat or stirring bird?
Scratching in the wall of sleep?
Twitching on the eaves of sleep?
I can hear it working close
Through a space along the house,
Through a space obscure and thin.
Night is swiftly running out,
Dawn has yet to ripple in,
Dawn has yet to clear the doubt,
Rat within or bird without.

### HYMN TO NIGHT

Now it grows dark.
Red goes
Out of the rose;
Out of the lawn
Green's withdrawn;
Each buttercup now yields
Its gold from blurring fields;
Larkspur and sky surrender
Blue wonder.

We were dark within, we relied
For our strength on the nourishing sun;
Now it is under and gone.
Now, as the light grows duller,
We, who had flourished on color,
Stand, in the ever-deepening shade,
Bereft, dismayed.

We were dark within, it was death
We saw, we had never seen
Within the dark, we had never known
The spark, the vital breath.
If only we had known
That black is neither loss nor lack
But holds the essential seed
Of mortal hope and need!

Now sheltering dusk,
Shepherd of color and light for dawns un-
ending,
Tends the holy task.

Praise be to black, the benign,
No longer malign,
Prolonger of days!
Praise the preserver of shine,
The keeper of blaze!

Praise Night,
Forever praise
Savior Night,
Who surely stays
The arm of time,
Who guards the flame,
Who hoards the light.

Praised be the Night.

# *Franklin P. Adams*

FRANKLIN PIERCE ADAMS, better known to the readers of his column as F. P. A., was born in Chicago, Illinois, November 15, 1881. He attended the University of Michigan (1899-1900) and, after a brief career as insurance agent, plunged into journalism. Adams had already been an ardent contributor to B. L. T.'s "A Line o' Type or Two" and, in 1903, he began conducting a column of his own on the Chicago *Journal*. Late in 1904, he came to New York, running his section on *The Evening Mail* until 1914, when he started "The Conning Tower" for the New York *Tribune*, transferring it some years later to the New York *World* and, later still, to the New York *Herald Tribune*.

Adams is the author of several volumes of a light verse that is unusually skillful. *Tobogganing on Parnassus* (1909), *In Other Words* (1912), *By and Large* (1914), *Weights and Measures* (1917), *Something Else Again* (1920), and *So There* (1923), reveal a spirit which is essentially one of mockery. These contain impudent—and faithful—paraphrases of Horace and Propertius, last-line twists *à la* O. Henry (with whom Adams wrote a comic opera that never reached New York), and a healthy satire that runs sharply through the smooth lines. The best of his later work is in *Christopher Columbus* (1930) and that modern metropolitan chronicle *The Diary of Our Own Samuel Pepys* (1935), which is a prose portrait of himself and a period.

### THE RICH MAN

The rich man has his motor-car,
　　His country and his town estate.
He smokes a fifty-cent cigar
　　And jeers at Fate.

He frivols through the livelong day,
　　He knows not Poverty, her pinch.
His lot seems light, his heart seems gay;
　　He has a cinch.

Yet though my lamp burns low and dim,
　　Though I must slave for livelihood—
Think you that I would change with him?
　　You bet I would!

### THOSE TWO BOYS

When Bill was a lad he was terribly bad.
　　He worried his parents a lot;
He'd lie and he'd swear and pull little girls' hair;
　　His boyhood was naught but a blot.

At play and in school he would fracture each rule—
　　In mischief from autumn to spring;

And the villagers knew when to manhood he grew
  He would never amount to a thing.

When Jim was a child he was not very wild;
  He was known as a good little boy;
He was honest and bright and the teacher's delight—
  To his mother and father a joy.

All the neighbors were sure that his virtue'd endure,
  That his life would be free of a spot;
They were certain that Jim had a great head on him
  And that Jim would amount to a lot.

And Jim grew to manhood and honor and fame
  And bears a good name;
While Bill is shut up in a dark prison cell—
  You never can tell.


# John G. Neihardt

JOHN GNEISENAU NEIHARDT was born in Sharpsburg, Illinois, January 8, 1881. He completed a scientific course at Nebraska Normal College in 1897 and lived among the Omaha Indians for six years (1901-7), studying their customs, characteristics, and legends.

Although he had already published two books, *A Bundle of Myrrh* (1908) was his first volume to attract notice. It was full of enthusiastic, insistent virility—a quality which was extended (and overemphasized) in *Man-Song* (1909). Neihardt found a new restraint in *The Stranger at the Gate* (1911), the best of the lyrics from these three volumes appearing in *The Quest* (1916).

Neihardt meanwhile had been going deeper into folk-lore, the results of which appeared in *The Song of Hugh Glass* (1915), *The Song of Three Friends* (1919), *The Song of the Indian Wars* (1926). In 1920 the second of these divided the annual prize offered by the Poetry Society with Gladys Cromwell's *Poems*. These three of Neihardt's are detailed long poems, part of a projected epic series celebrating the winning of the West by the pioneers. What prevents these volumes from fulfilling the breadth at which they aim is the disparity between the author's story and his style. Legend and locution are joined without being united; essentially racy narratives are recited in an archaic, incongruous speech. Yet, in spite of a rhetoric that considers prairies and trappers in terms of "Ilion," "Iseult," "Clotho," the "dim far shore of Styx," Neihardt has achieved his effects with no little skill. Dramatic and dignified, his works are American in conception if not in execution.

*The Song of the Messiah* (1935), the most vivid as well as the most symbolic of the cycle, was the fourth of the series to be published although it will stand as the fifth and final volume.

## WHEN I AM DEAD

When I am dead and nervous hands have thrust
My body downward into careless dust;
I think the grave cannot suffice to hold
My spirit prisoned in the sunless mold!
Some subtle memory of you shall be
A resurrection of the life of me.
Yea, I shall be, because I love you so,
The speechless spirit of all things that grow.
You shall not touch a flower but it shall be
Like a caress upon the cheek of me.
I shall be patient in the common grass
That I may feel your footfall when you pass.
I shall be kind as rain and pure as dew,
A loving spirit 'round the life of you.
When your soft cheeks by perfumed winds are fanned,
'Twill be my kiss—and you will understand.
But when some sultry, storm-bleared sun has set,
*I will be lightning if you dare forget!*

## CRY OF THE PEOPLE

Tremble before thy chattels,
Lords of the scheme of things!
Fighters of all earth's battles,
Ours is the might of kings!
Guided by seers and sages,
The world's heart-beat for a drum,
Snapping the chains of ages,
Out of the night we come!

Lend us no ear that pities!
Offer no almoner's hand!
Alms for the builders of cities!
When will you understand?
Down with your pride of birth
And your golden gods of trade!
A man is worth to his mother, Earth,
All that a man has made!

We are the workers and makers.
We are no longer dumb!
Tremble, O Shirkers and Takers!
Sweeping the earth—we come!

Ranked in the world-wide dawn,
Marching into the day!
*The night is gone and the sword is drawn
And the scabbard is thrown away!*

## LET ME LIVE OUT MY YEARS

Let me live out my years in heat of blood!
Let me die drunken with the dreamer's wine!
Let me not see this soul-house built of mud
Go toppling to the dust—a vacant shrine.

Let me go quickly, like a candle light
Snuffed out just at the heyday of its glow.
Give me high noon—and let it then be night!
Thus would I go.

And grant that when I face the grisly Thing,
My song may trumpet down the gray Per-
  haps.
Let me be as a tune-swept fiddlestring
That feels the Master Melody—and snaps!

# *Witter Bynner*

WITTER BYNNER was born in Brooklyn, New York, August 10, 1881. He was graduated from Harvard in 1902 and was assistant editor of various periodicals as well as adviser to publishers. He spent much of his time lecturing on poetry, traveling in the Orient and studying the American Indian. He lives most of the year in Santa Fé, New Mexico.

*Young Harvard* (1907), the first of Bynner's volumes, was, as the name implies, a celebration of his *Alma Mater. The New World* (1915) is a far more ambitious effort. In this extended poem, Bynner sought—almost too determinedly—to translate the ideals of democracy into verse. Neither of these volumes displays its author's gifts at their best, for Bynner is, first of all, a lyric poet. *Grenstone Poems* (1917) and *A Canticle of Pan* (1920) reveal a natural singing voice. Bynner harmonizes in many keys; transposing, modulating, and shifting from one tonality to another. This very ease is his handicap, for Bynner's facility leads him not only to write too much, but in too many different styles. Many of his poems seem like sounding-boards that echo the tones of every poet except the composer of them. Instead of a fusion of gifts we have, too often, as in *Caravan* (1925), only a confusion.

When Bynner is least dexterous he is most ingratiating. When he does not try to echo the whole gamut of modern poetry from the lyrics of A. E. Housman to the attenuated epigrams of Ezra Pound, he can strike his own note with clarity. Even in *The Beloved Stranger* (1919), where the borrowed accents of his *alter ego* are only too apparent, one is arrested by lines of charm and fluency.

Under the pseudonym "Emanuel Morgan" Bynner was co-author with Arthur Davison Ficke (writing under the name of "Anne Knish") of *Spectra* (1916). *Spectra* was a serious burlesque of some of the extreme manifestations of modern poetic tendencies—a hoax that deceived many of the radical propagandists as well as most of the conservative critics.

A volume in collaboration with Kiang Kang-Hu, *The Jade Mountain* (1929), included three hundred translations of poems of the T'ang Dynasty. *Indian Earth* (1929) summons the effect rather than the rhythms of the buffalo dance at Santo Domingo, the rain invocation at Cochiti and the Shalako dance-dramas in a technique as delicate as the brush-strokes used to evoke the shifting scene.

*Eden Tree* (1931) is Bynner's own synthesis of himself and his work viewed in retrospect at fifty. It is his most distinguished and also his most disquieting book, being not so much a philosophy as a confession. The tone is a troubled one, the approach is by way of fantasy running into phantasmagoria; but the mood between clear perception and cloudy consciousness is skillfully maintained. *Guest Book* (1935) is a lighter volume, a series of seventy sonnets which "portray" contemporary persons with more rhetoric than accuracy. The complimentary poems are not deeply registered and the satirical ones are not sharp enough to be effective caricatures. Bynner, as host, is too tactful a recorder; the real poet is in *Eden Tree*.

## GRASS-TOPS

hat bird are you in the grass-tops?
ur poise is enough of an answer,
ith your wing-tips like up-curving fingers
 the slow-moving hands of a dancer . . .

d what is so nameless as beauty,
hich poets, who give it a name,
e only unnaming forever?—
ntent, though it go, that it came.

## VOICES

O there were lights and laughter
 And the motions to and fro
Of people as they enter
 And people as they go . . .

And there were many voices
 Vying at the feast,
But mostly I remember
 Yours—who spoke the least.

## A FARMER REMEMBERS LINCOLN

"Lincoln?—
Well, I was in the old Second Maine,
The first regiment in Washington from the Pine Tree State.
Of course I didn't get the butt of the clip;
We was there for guardin' Washington—
We was all green.

"I ain't never ben to the theayter in my life—
I didn't know how to behave.
I ain't never ben since.
I can see as plain as my hat the box where he sat in
When he was shot.
I can tell you, sir, there was a panic
When we found our President was in the shape he was in!
Never saw a soldier in the world but what liked him.

"Yes, sir. His looks was kind o' hard to forget.
He was a spare man,
An old farmer.
Everything was all right, you know,
But he wasn't a smooth-appearin' man at all—
Not in no ways;
Thin-faced, long-necked,
And a swellin' kind of a thick lip like.

"And he was a jolly old fellow—always cheerful;
He wasn't so high but the boys could talk to him their own ways.
While I was servin' at the Hospital
He'd come in and say, 'You look nice in here,'
Praise us up, you know.
And he'd bend over and talk to the boys—
And he'd talk so good to 'em—so close—
That's why I call him a farmer.
I don't mean that everything about him wasn't all right, you understand,
It's just—well, I was a farmer—
And he was my neighbor, anybody's neighbor.
I guess even you young folks would 'a' liked him."

### TRAIN-MATES

Outside hove Shasta, snowy height on height,
A glory; but a negligible sight,
For you had often seen a mountain-peak
But not my paper. So we came to speak . . .
A smoke, a smile,—a good way to commence
The comfortable exchange of difference!
You a young engineer, five feet eleven,
Forty-five chest, with football in your heaven,
Liking a road-bed newly built and clean,
Your fingers hot to cut away the green
Of brush and flowers that bring beside a track
The kind of beauty steel lines ought to lack,—
And I a poet, wistful of my betters,
Reading George Meredith's high-hearted letters,
Joining betweenwhiles in the mingled speech
Of a drummer, circus-man, and parson, each
Absorbing to himself—as I to me
And you to you—a glad identity!

After a time, when others went away,
A curious kinship made us choose to stay,
Which I could tell you now; but at the time
You thought of baseball teams and I of rhyme,
Until we found that we were college men
And smoked more easily and smiled again;
And I from Cambridge cried, the poet still:
"I know your fine Greek theater on the hill
At Berkeley!" With your happy Grecian head
Upraised, "I never saw the place," you said—
"Once I was free of class, I always went
Out to the field."

                              Young engineer, you meant
As fair a tribute to the better part
As ever I did. Beauty of the heart
Is evident in temples. But it breathes
Alive where athletes quicken curly wreaths,
Which are the lovelier because they die.
You are a poet quite as much as I,
Though differences appear in what we do,
And I an athlete quite as much as you.
Because you half-surmise my quarter-mile
And I your quatrain, we could greet and smile.
Who knows but we shall look again and find
The circus-man and drummer, not behind
But leading in our visible estate—
As discus-thrower and as laureate?

### THE SINGING HUNTSMAN

ɪe huntswoman-moon was my mother,
ɪd the song-man, Apollo, my sire;
ɪd I know either trick like the other,
ɪe trick of the bow and the lyre.

ɪd when beauty darts by me or lingers,
hen it opens or folds its wing,
ɪ bow and on lyre are my fingers,
ɪd I shoot, and I sing.

### AGAINST THE COLD

ɪtumn is only winter in disguise,
summer-skeleton in scarlet cover.

Now is no spring nor summer in the skies
Nor early song of nightingale or plover.
Bones are the fingers now that touch the grass
And turn the edge of timothy and clover;
Bones are the feet that on the highway pass
And tread the weeds and turn the gravel over.
Bear backward, then, within the warming walls
Of stone or wood or clay, no more a rover
Beside the meadowlands and waterfalls
But an abashed and reverential lover—
And build of better stuff than spring, the old
Unceasing fortitude against the cold.

## James Oppenheim

JAMES OPPENHEIM was born in St. Paul, Minnesota, May 24, 1882. Two years later his family moved to New York City, where he lived most of his life. After a public school education, he took special courses at Columbia University (1901-3) and engaged in settlement work, acting in the capacity of assistant head worker of the Hudson Guild Settlement, and superintendent of the Hebrew Technical School for Girls (1904-7). His studies and experiences on the lower East Side of New York furnished material for his first book of short stories, *Doctor Rast* (1909).

Oppenheim's initial venture as a poet, *Monday Morning and Other Poems* (1909), was imitative and experimental. In spite of its obvious indebtedness to Whitman, most of the verses are in formal meters and regular (though ragged) rhyme. Beauty is sought, but seldom captured here; the message is coughed out between bursts of eloquence and fits of stammering.

*Songs for the New Age* (1914) made Oppenheim his own liberator. The speech, echoing the Whitmanic sonority, develops a music that is strangely Biblical and yet native. It is the expression of an ancient people reacting to modernity, of a race in solution. This volume, like all of Oppenheim's subsequent work, is analysis in terms of poetry; a slow searching beneath the musical surface attempts to diagnose the tortured soul of man and the twisted times he lives in. The old Isaiah note, with a new introspection, rises out of such poems as "The Slave," "We Dead," "Tasting the Earth"; the music and imagery of the Psalms are heard in "The Flocks," and "The Runner in the Skies."

*War and Laughter* (1916) holds much of its predecessor's fervor. The Semitic blend of delight and disillusion—that quality which hates the world for its hypocrisies and loves it in spite of them—is revealed in "Greed," in the ironic "Report on the Planet Earth" and the affirmative "Laughter."

*The Book of Self* (1917) is an imperfect fusion. Oppenheim's preoccupation with analytical psychology mars the effect of the long passages which contain flashes of clairvoyance. Most of it reads like *Leaves of Grass* translated by Freud. *The Solitary* (1919) is a stride forward; its major section, a long symbolic poem called "The Sea," breathes the same note that was the burden of the earlier books: "We are flesh on the way to godhood."

*The Mystic Warrior* (1921) is an autobiography in free verse. It is a chronicle of inhibition, the effort of an artist to find himself and freedom in a rigid, mechanistic environment. Oppenheim's studies and practice in psychoanalysis are, again, somewhat too evident in this volume; the chief figure emerges as a weak and groping stumbler towards immensities, a figure lost between self-contempt and over-reaching egotism. *Golden Bird* (1923) is a return to Oppenheim's less personal mysticism. It suffers from loquacity and a curious "yearning back," but some of the poems (such as "Hebrews") rise from a rather cloying catalog of perished beauty.

*The Sea,* Oppenheim's most comprehensive volume, was published in 1923. It includes the best of all his previous books of poetry with the addition of several "connecting" verses.

Besides his poetry, Oppenheim has published several volumes of short stories, five novels, and two poetic plays. During 1916-17 he was editor of that provoking but short-lived magazine, *The Seven Arts.* Later he tried hack-work; he prepared a "popular" handbook on psychoanalysis and another, *American Types* (1931), of a similar nature. He died, after a severe illness, August 4, 1932.

### THE SLAVE

They set the slave free, striking off his chains . . .
Then he was as much of a slave as ever.

He was still chained to servility,
He was still manacled to indolence and sloth,
He was still bound by fear and superstition,
By ignorance, suspicion, and savagery . . .
His slavery was not in the chains,
But in himself. . . .

They can only set free men free . . .
And there is no need of that:
Free men set themselves free.

### THE RUNNER IN THE SKIES

Who is the runner in the skies,
With her blowing scarf of stars,
And our Earth and sun hovering like bees about her blossoming heart?
Her feet are on the winds, where space is deep,
Her eyes are nebulous and veiled;
She hurries through the night to a far lover . . .

### THE LINCOLN CHILD

Clearing in the forest,
In the wild Kentucky forest,
And the stars, wintry stars strewn above!
O Night that is the starriest
Since Earth began to roll—
For a Soul
Is born out of Love!
Mother love, father love, love of Eternal God—
Stars have pushed aside to let him through—
Through heaven's sun-sown deeps
One sparkling ray of God
Strikes the clod—
(And while an angel-host through wood and clearing sweeps!)
Born in the wild
The Child—
Naked, ruddy, new,
Wakes with the piteous human cry and at the mother-heart sleeps.

To the mother wild berries and honey,
To the father awe without end,
To the child a swaddling of flannel—
And a dawn rolls sharp and sunny
And the skies of winter bend
To see the first sweet word penned
In the godliest human annal.

Frail Mother of the Wilderness,
How strange the world shines in
And the cabin becomes chapel
And the baby lies secure—
Sweet Mother of the Wilderness,
New worlds for you begin,
You have tasted of the apple
That giveth wisdom sure. . . .

Soon in the wide wilderness,
On a branch blown over a creek,
Up a trail of the wild coon,
In a lair of the wild bee,
The rugged boy, by danger's stress,
Learnt the speech the wild things speak,
Learnt the Earth's eternal tune
Of strife-engendered harmony—
Went to school where Life itself was master,
Went to church where Earth was minister—
And in Danger and Disaster
Felt his future manhood stir!

All about him the land,
Eastern cities, Western prairie,
Wild, immeasurable, grand;
But he was lost where blossomy boughs make airy
Bowers in the forest, and the sand
Makes brook-water a clear mirror that gives back
Green branches and trunks black
And clouds across the heavens lightly fanned.
Yet all the Future dreams, eager to waken,
Within that woodland soul—
And the bough of boy has only to be shaken
That the fruit drop whereby this Earth shall roll
A little nearer God than ever before.
Little recks he of war,
Of national millions waiting on his word—
Dreams still the Event unstirred
In the heart of the boy, the little babe of the wild—
But the years hurry and the tide of the sea
Of Time flows fast and ebbs, and he, even he,
Must leave the wilderness, the wood-haunts wild.
Soon shall the cyclone of Humanity
Tearing through Earth suck up this little child
And whirl him to the top, where he shall be
Riding the storm-column in the lightning-stroke,
Calm at the peak, while down below worlds rage,
And Earth goes out in blood and battle-smoke,
And leaves him with the Sun—an epoch and an age!

And lo, as he grew ugly, gaunt,
And gnarled his way into a man,
What wisdom came to feed his want,
What worlds came near to let him scan!
And as he fathomed through and through
Our dark and sorry human scheme,
He knew what Shakespeare never knew,
What Dante never dared to dream—
That Men are one
Beneath the sun,
And before God are equal souls—
This truth was his,
And this it is
That round him such a glory rolls—
For not alone he knew it as a truth,
He made it of his blood, and of his brain—
He crowned it on the day when piteous Booth
Sent a whole land to weeping with world pain—
When a black cloud blotted the sun
And men stopped in the streets to sob,
To think Old Abe was dead.
Dead, and the day's work still undone,
Dead, and war's ruining heart athrob,

And earth with fields of carnage freshly spread—
Millions died fighting,
But in this man we mourned
Those millions, and one other—
And the States today uniting,
North and South,
East and West,
Speak with a people's mouth
A rhapsody of rest
To him our beloved best,
Our big, gaunt, homely brother—
Our huge Atlantic coast-storm in a shawl,
Our cyclone in a smile—our President,
Who knew and loved us all
With love more eloquent
Than his own words—with Love that in real deeds was spent. . . .

O living God, O Thou who living art,
And real, and near, draw, as at that babe's birth,
Into our souls and sanctify our Earth—
Let down Thy strength that we endure
Mighty and pure
As mothers and fathers of our own Lincoln-child—
Make us more wise, more true, more strong, more mild,
That we may day by day
Rear this wild blossom through its soft petals of clay;
That hour by hour
We may endow it with more human power
Than is our own—
That it may reach the goal
Our Lincoln long has shown!
O Child, flesh of our flesh, bone of our bone,
Soul torn from out our Soul!
May you be great, and pure, and beautiful—
A Soul to search this world
To be a father, brother, comrade, son,
A toiler powerful;
A man whose toil is done
One with God's Law above:
Work wrought through Love!

### NIGHT NOTE

A little moon was restless in Eternity
And, shivering beneath the stars,
Dropped in the hiding arms of the western hill.
Night's discord ceased:
The visible universe moved in an endless rhythm:
The wheel of the heavens turned to the pulse of a cricket in the grass.

### TASTING THE EARTH

In a dark hour, tasting the Earth.

As I lay on my couch in the muffled night, and the rain lashed my window,
And my forsaken heart would give me no rest, no pause and no peace,
Though I turned my face far from the wailing of my bereavement. . . .
Then I said: I will eat of this sorrow to its last shred,
I will take it unto me utterly,
I will see if I be not strong enough to contain it. . . .
What do I fear? Discomfort?
How can it hurt me, this bitterness?

The miracle, then!
Turning toward it, and giving up to it,
I found it deeper than my own self. . . .
O dark great mother-globe so close beneath me . . .
It was she with her inexhaustible grief,
Ages of blood-drenched jungles, and the smoking of craters, and the roar of
     tempests,
And moan of the forsaken seas,
It was she with the hills beginning to walk in the shapes of the dark-hearted
     animals,
It was she risen, dashing away tears and praying to dumb skies, in the pomp-
     crumbling tragedy of man . . .
It was she, container of all griefs, and the buried dust of broken hearts,
Cry of the christs and the lovers and the child-stripped mothers,
And ambition gone down to defeat, and the battle overborne,
And the dreams that have no waking. . . .

My heart became her ancient heart:
On the food of the strong I fed, on dark strange life itself:
Wisdom-giving and somber with the unremitting love of ages. . . .
There was dank soil in my mouth,
And bitter sea on my lips,
In a dark hour, tasting the Earth.

### HEBREWS

I come of a mighty race . . . I come of a very mighty race . . .
Adam was a mighty man, and Noah a captain of the moving waters,
Moses was a stern and splendid king, yea, so was Moses . . .
Give me more songs like David's to shake my throat to the pit of the belly,
And let me roll in the Isaiah thunder . . .
Ho! the mightiest of our young men was born under a star in midwinter . . .
His name is written on the sun and it is frosted on the moon . . .
Earth breathes him like an eternal spring; he is a second sky over the Earth.

Mighty race! mighty race!—my flesh, my flesh
Is a cup of song,
Is a well in Asia . . .

I go about with a dark heart where the Ages sit in a divine thunder . . .
My blood is cymbal-clashed and the anklets of the dancers tinkle there . . .
Harp and psaltery, harp and psaltery make drunk my spirit . . .
I am of the terrible people, I am of the strange Hebrews . . .
Amongst the swarms fixed like the rooted stars, my folk is a streaming Comet,
The Wanderer of Eternity, the eternal Wandering Jew . . .

Ho! we have turned against the mightiest of our young men
And in that denial we have taken on the Christ,
And the two thieves beside the Christ,
And the Magdalen at the feet of the Christ,
And the Judas with thirty silver pieces selling the Christ,
And our twenty centuries in Europe have the shape of a Cross
On which we have hung in disaster and glory . . .

Mighty race! mighty race!—my flesh, my flesh
Is a cup of song,
Is a well in Asia.


# Lola Ridge

L OLA RIDGE was born in Dublin, Ireland, leaving there in infancy and spending her
childhood in Sydney, Australia. After living some years in New Zealand, she returned to Australia to study art. In 1907, she came to the United States, and supported herself for three years by writing fiction for popular magazines. She stopped
this work only, as she says, "because I found I would have to do so if I wished to
survive as an artist." For several years she earned her living in a variety of ways—
as organizer for an educational movement, as advertisement writer, as illustrator,
artist's model, factory-worker. In 1918, *The New Republic* published her long poem,
"The Ghetto," and Miss Ridge, until then totally unknown, became the "discovery"
of the year.

Her volume, *The Ghetto and Other Poems* (1918), contains one poem that is
brilliant, several that are powerful, and none that is mediocre. The title-poem is its
pinnacle; it is a poem of the city, of its sodden brutalities, its sudden beauties. Swift
figures shine from these lines, like barbaric colors leaping out of darkness; images
are surprising but never strained; confusion is given clarity. In the other poems—
especially in "The Song of Iron," "Faces" and the poignant portrait "Marie"—the
same dignity is maintained, though with somewhat less magic.

*Sun-Up* (1920) and *Red Flag* (1924) are less integrated, more frankly experimental. But the same vibrancy and restrained power that distinguished her first book
are manifest here. Her delineations are sensitive, her phrases vivid yet natural. In
spite of an overuse of similes, she accomplishes the maximum in effect with a minimum of effort.

*Firehead* (1929) is a narrative poem, the time and scene of which are the day of
the Crucifixion. Making John, Peter and the two Marys interpret the significance of
the event, Miss Ridge has written a poem of depth and urgent penetration. If

anything, the effort is too grandiose; the reader loses sight of the central figure in a bright cloud of metaphors. Phrases rise, not from the core of the tragedy, but from the prodded literary mind; the Passion is lost in a panorama. And yet there is a finality in *Firehead* beyond the finality of phrase. Passages move in and out of the large design taking possession of the imagination, passages that are music visualized and "time made audible."

In *Dance of Fire* (1935) her gift of unusual but accurate image, her undeviating integrity, and her passion for social justice are fused and concentrated in the clean fire which she celebrates. Miss Ridge is a revolutionary in a technical as well as a spiritual sense; yet it is a curious thing that, whereas her first published work was wholly in free verse, *Dance of Fire* is cast almost entirely in regular patterns, the peak of the volume being the three-part section "Via Ignis," a series of twenty-eight sonnets. These sonnets reveal a discipline which makes them worthy to stand with the best sonnet cycles produced in this period.

### PASSAGES FROM "THE GHETTO"

Old Sodos no longer makes saddles.
He has forgotten how . . .
Time spins like a crazy dial in his brain,
And night by night
I see the love-gesture of his arm
In its green-greasy coat-sleeve
Circling the Book,
And the candles gleaming starkly
On the blotched-paper whiteness of his face,
Like a miswritten psalm . . .
Night by night
I hear his lifted praise,
Like a broken whinnying
Before the Lord's shut gate.

✦

Lights go out
And the stark trunks of the factories
Melt into the drawn darkness,
Sheathing like a seamless garment.

And mothers take home their babies,
Waxen and delicately curled,
Like little potted flowers closed under the stars. . . .

Lights go out . . .
And colors rush together,
Fusing and floating away.
Pale worn gold like the settings of old jewels . . .
Mauve, exquisite, tremulous, and luminous purples,
And burning spires in aureoles of light
Like shimmering auras.
They are covering up the pushcarts . . .

Now all have gone save an old man with mirrors—
Little oval mirrors like tiny pools.
He shuffles up a darkened street
And the moon burnishes his mirrors till they shine like phosphorus. . . .
The moon like a skull,
Staring out of eyeless sockets at the old men trundling home the pushcarts.

✦

A sallow dawn is in the sky
As I enter my little green room.
Without, the frail moon,
Worn to a silvery tissue,
Throws a faint glamor on the roofs,
And down the shadowy spires
Lights tip-toe out . . .
Softly as when lovers close street doors.

Out of the Battery
A little wind
Stirs idly—as an arm
Trails over a boat's side in dalliance—
Rippling the smooth dead surface of the heat,
And Hester Street,
Like a forlorn woman over-borne
By many babies at her teats,
Turns on her trampled bed to meet the day.

## FACES

late snow beats
With cold white fists upon the tenements—
Hurriedly drawing blinds and shutters,
Like tall old slatterns
Pulling aprons about their heads.

Lights slanting out of Mott Street
Gibber out,
Or dribble through bar-room slits,
Anonymous shapes
Conniving behind shuttered panes
Caper and disappear . . .
Where the Bowery
Is throbbing like a fistula
Back of her ice-scabbed fronts.

Livid faces
Glimmer in furtive doorways,
Or spill out of the black pockets of alleys,
Smears of faces like muddied beads,
Making a ghastly rosary
The night mumbles over

And the snow with its devilish and silken
        whisper . . .
Patrolling arcs
Blowing shrill blasts over the Bread Line
Stalk them as they pass,
Silent as though accouched of the darkness,
And the wind noses among them,
    Like a skunk
That roots about the heart . . .

Colder:
And the Elevated slams upon the silence
Like a ponderous door.
Then all is still again,
Save for the wind fumbling over
The emptily swaying faces—
The wind rummaging
Like an old Jew . . .

Faces in glimmering rows . . .
(No sign of the abject life—
Not even a blasphemy . . .)
But the spindle legs keep time
To a limping rhythm,

And the shadows twitch upon the snow
    Convulsively—
As though death played
With some ungainly dolls.

### NEW ORLEANS

Do you remember
Honey-melon moon
Dripping thick sweet light
Where Canal Street saunters off by herself
    among quiet trees?
And the faint decayed patchouli—
Fragrance of New Orleans . . .
New Orleans,
Like a dead tube rose
Upheld in the warm air . . .
Miraculously whole.

### WIND IN THE ALLEYS

Wind, rising in the alleys,
My spirit lifts in you like a banner
    streaming free of hot walls.
You are full of unshaped dreams . . .
You are laden with beginnings . . .
There is hope in you . . . not sweet . . .
    acrid as blood in the mouth.
Come into my tossing dust
Scattering the peace of old deaths,
Wind rising out of the alleys
Carrying stuff of flame.

### MARIE

Marie's face is a weathered sign
To the palace of gliding cars
Over the bend where the trolley dips:
A dime for a wired rose,
Nickel-a-ride to the zig-zag stars,
And then men in elegant clothes,

That feed you on cardboard ships,
And the sea-floats so fine!—
Like a green and gorgeous bubble
God blew out of his lips.

When Marie carries down the stair
The ritual of her face,
Your greeting takes her unaware,
And her glance is timid-bold
As a dog's unsure of its place.
With that hair, of the rubbed-off gold
Of a wedding-ring worn to a thread,
In a halo about the head,
And those luminous eyes in their rims
    paint,
She looks a bedizened saint.

But when the worn moon, like a face st
    beautiful,
Wavers above the Battery,
And light comes in, mauve-gray,
Squeezing through shutters of furnish
    rooms
Till only corners hold spots of darkness—
As a tablecloth its purple stains
When a festival is ended—
Then Marie creeps into the house.

The paint is lonesome on her cheek.
The paint is gone from off her mouth
That curls back loosely away from her teet
She pushes slackly at the dawn
That crawls upon the yellow blind,
And enters like an aimless moth
Whose dim wings hover and alight
Upon the blurred face of the clock,
Or on the pallor of her feet—
Or anything that's white.
Until dispersed upon the sheet,
All limp, her waxen body lies
In its delinquent grace,
Like a warm bent candle
That flares about its place.

### APRIL OF OUR DESIRE

Is not this April of our brief desire
That stirs the robins to a twittering
But waste vibration of some vaster spring
Which moves the void to utterance. This fire
Once babbled on our hills (that have forgot
Their fiery accents) when the earth was cleft

And flooding in her canyons, raging hot,
Ere this intricate, fair design was left.

Long, long before strange creatures overhead
Cast wheeling shadows on the desert, wings
Flamed from out the mountains; radiant things,
That stood erect upon each blazing rim
Of horned horizons, shone like seraphim
And shook the earth with their enormous tread.


# *Arthur Davison Ficke*

ARTHUR DAVISON FICKE was born in Davenport, Iowa, November 10, 1883. He received his A.B. at Harvard, studied for the law and was admitted to the bar in 1908. In 1919, after two years' service in France, he gave up his law practice and devoted himself to literature exclusively.

Ficke is the author of eleven volumes of verse, the most representative of which are *Sonnets of a Portrait Painter* (1914), *The Man on the Hilltop* (1915) and *An April Elegy* (1917). In these the author succeeded in combininig clarity of vision with an intensified seriousness, especially in the sonnets and shorter poems.

Having been an expert collector and student of Japanese prints, Ficke has written two books on this theme. His intellectual equipment is reënforced by a gift of satire. Writing under the pseudonym "Anne Knish," he was one of the co-authors (with Witter Bynner) of *Spectra* (1916), which, caricaturing some of the wilder outgrowths of the new poetry, was taken seriously by a majority of the critics and proved to be a brilliant hoax.

*Out of Silence and Other Poems* (1924) and *Mountain Against Mountain* (1929) are records of a romanticist's effort to escape a world he half understands and wholly fears. The poet—at least so his poems assure us—is "homesick in modernity." Even the earth's beauty hurts; loveliness does not fulfill him, he is frustrated by it. Nevertheless, the foretold failure of his "secret, impossible hopes" does not prevent him from wringing an occasional if too protracted poignance from his defeat.


## PORTRAIT OF AN OLD WOMAN

he limps with halting painful pace,
Stops, wavers and creeps on again;
ers up with dim and questioning face,
Void of desire or doubt or pain.

er cheeks hang gray in waxen folds
Wherein there stirs no blood at all.
hand, like bundled cornstalks, holds
The tatters of a faded shawl.

here was a breast, sunk bones she clasps;
A knot jerks where were woman-hips;

A ropy throat sends writhing gasps
Up to the tight line of her lips.

Here strong the city's pomp is poured . . .
She stands, unhuman, bleak, aghast:
An empty temple of the Lord
From which the jocund Lord has passed.

He has builded him another house,
Whenceforth his flame, renewed and bright,
Shines stark upon these weathered brows
Abandoned to the final night.

### THE THREE SISTERS

Gone are the three, those sisters rare
   With wonder-lips and eyes ashine.
One was wise and one was fair,
   And one was mine.

Ye mourners, weave for the sleeping hair
   Of only two your ivy vine.
For one was wise and one was fair,
   But one was mine.

### SONNET

There are strange shadows fostered of the moon,
More numerous than the clear-cut shade of day. . . .
Go forth, when all the leaves whisper of June,
Into the dusk of swooping bats at play;
Or go into that late November dusk
When hills take on the noble lines of death,
And on the air the faint, astringent musk
Of rotting leaves pours vaguely troubling breath.
Then shall you see shadows whereof the sun,
Knows nothing—aye, a thousand shadows there
Shall leap and flicker and stir and stay and run,
Like petrels of the changing foul or fair;
Like ghosts of twilight, of the moon, of him
Whose homeland lies past each horizon's rim.

### LEAF-MOVEMENT

From its thin branch high in the autumn wind
The yellow leaf now sails in upward flight;
Hovers at top-slope; then, a whirling bright
Eddy of motion, sinks. The storm behind
With gusts and veering tyrannies would uphold
Even as it downward beats this gorgeous thing
Which like an angel's lost and shattered wing
Against the gray sky sweeps its broken gold.
Another eddy, desperate or in mirth,
Brings it to rest here on the crackled earth
Where men can see it better than on the bough.
What quite preposterous irony of wind's will
Touches it where it lies, golden and still,
And once more lifts it vainly heavenward now!

# Wallace Stevens

WALLACE STEVENS, born in Pennsylvania, educated there and at Harvard, devoting himself to legal work in Hartford, Connecticut, is a poet of peculiar reticences. His attitude to his work is, in itself, significant. Although most of it appeared in the two best known poetry magazines of the period, *Others* and *Poetry: A Magazine of Verse,* as early as 1913, it was not until ten years later that Stevens' first book, *Harmonium* (1923), appeared.

The most casual reading of this volume discloses that Stevens is a stylist of unusual delicacy. Even the least sympathetic reader must be struck by the poet's hypersensitive and ingenious imagination. It is a curiously ambiguous world which Stevens paints: a world of merging half-lights, of finicking shadows, of disembodied emotions. Even this last word is an exaggeration, for emotion itself seems absent from the brightly colored segments of the poet's designs.

Considered as a painter, Stevens is one of the most original impressionists of the times. He is fond of little blocks of color, verbal mosaics in which syllables are used as pigments. Little related to any human struggle, the content of *Harmonium* progresses toward a sort of "absolute" poetry which, depending on tone rather than on passion, aims to flower in an air of pure estheticism. His very titles—which deliberately add to the reader's confusion by having little or no connection with most of the poems—betray this quality: "Hymn from a Watermelon Pavilion," "The Paltry Nude Starts on a Spring Voyage," "Frogs Eat Butterflies, Snakes Eat Frogs, Hogs Eat Snakes, Men Eat Hogs." Such poems have much for the eye, something for the ear, but little for that central hunger which is at the core of all the senses.

> Chieftain Iffucan of Azcan in caftan
> Of tan with henna hackles, halt!

Thus Stevens begins his "Bantam in Pine-Woods" and his pleasure in playing with sounds must be evident to the most perplexed reader. Like Williams, to whose *Collected Poems* Stevens furnished an introduction, Stevens is interested in things chiefly from their "unreal" aspect. He is, nevertheless, in his very attitude to realism, romantic. A romantic poet nowadays, says Stevens, "happens to be one who still dwells in an ivory tower, but who insists that life there would be intolerable except for the fact that one has, from the top, such an exceptional view of the public dump and the advertising signs. . . . He is the hermit who dwells alone with the sun and moon, and insists on taking a rotten newspaper." That is why Stevens can write of "The Worms at Heaven's Gate" with no disrespect to Shakespeare, make a study in esthetics of the contents of a cab, and entitle a poem on death ("the finale of seem") "The Emperor of Ice-Cream."

"Sunday Morning" and "Sea Surface Full of Clouds" are curious blends of disintegrated fantasy and fictitious reality. Superficially obscure, these poems are highly selective in choice of allusions, inner harmonies and special luxuriance of sound; they foliate in a mid-region where the esthetic instinct encroaches on the reasoning intellect. "Thirteen Ways of Looking at a Blackbird" and "Domination of Black" have a delicacy of design which suggests the Chinese; "Peter Quince at the

Clavier" and the exquisite "To the One of Fictive Music" (Stevens' most obviously musical moment) reveal a distinction which places "this auditor of insects, this lutanist of fleas" as one who has perfected a kind of poetry which is, for all its limitations, a strangely hermetic art.

After a twelve years' silence Stevens published *Ideas of Order* (1935) in a strictly limited edition. The format of the book and its private publication emphasized the limitation as well as the elegance of the contents. Here, as in *Harmonium,* Stevens seldom writes poetry about the *Ding an sich* but almost always about the overtones which the thing creates in his mind; here even the candid surface quickly gives off cryptic colors, and emotional scenes are recorded in a deft but elusive phrase. This poet's province is the real in terms of the unreal; his forte is unpredictability. Often enough a poem refuses to yield a meaning, but "Academic Discourse at Havana" and "The Idea of Order at Key West" surrender themselves in an almost pure music. Stevens may be a puzzling poet, but he seldom lacks piquancy and his lines are seldom without wit and a fastidious provocation.

## PETER QUINCE AT THE CLAVIER

### I

Just as my fingers on these keys
Make music, so the self-same sounds
On my spirit make a music, too.

Music is feeling, then, not sound;
And thus it is that what I feel,
Here in this room, desiring you,

Thinking of your blue-shadowed silk,
Is music. It is like the strain
Waked in the elders by Susanna:

Of a green evening, clear and warm,
She bathed in her still garden, while
The red-eyed elders, watching, felt

The basses of their beings throb
In witching chords, and their thin blood
Pulse pizzicati of Hosanna.

### II

In the green water, clear and warm,
Susanna lay,
She searched
The touch of springs,
And found
Concealed imaginings.
She sighed,
For so much melody.

Upon the bank, she stood
In the cool

Of spent emotions.
She felt, among the leaves,
The dew
Of old devotions.

She walked upon the grass,
Still quavering.
The winds were like her maids
On timid feet,
Fetching her woven scarves,
Yet wavering.

A breath upon her hand
Muted the night.
She turned—
A cymbal crashed,
And roaring horns.

### III

Soon, with a noise like tambourines,
Came her attendant Byzantines.

They wondered why Susanna cried
Against the elders by her side;

And as they whispered, the refrain
Was like a willow swept by rain.

Anon, their lamps' uplifted flame
Revealed Susanna and her shame.

And then, the simpering Byzantines
Fled, with a noise like tambourines.

IV

eauty is momentary in the mind—
he fitful tracing of a portal;
ut in the flesh it is immortal.

he body dies; the body's beauty lives.
o evenings die, in their green going,
wave, interminably flowing.
o gardens die, their meek breath scenting

The cowl of Winter, done repenting.
So maidens die, to the auroral
Celebration of a maiden's choral.

Susanna's music touched the bawdy strings
Of those white elders; but, escaping,
Left only Death's ironic scraping.
Now, in its immortality, it plays
On the clear viol of her memory,
And makes a constant sacrament of praise.

### TO THE ONE OF FICTIVE MUSIC

Sister and mother and diviner love,
And of the sisterhood of the living dead
Most near, most clear, and of the clearest bloom,
And of the fragrant mothers the most dear
And queen, and of diviner love the day
And flame and summer and sweet fire, no thread
Of cloudy silver sprinkles in your gown
Its venom of renown, and on your head
No crown is simpler than the simple hair.

Now, of the music summoned by the birth
That separates us from the wind and sea,
Yet leaves us in them, until earth becomes,
By being so much of the things we are,
Gross effigy and simulacrum, none
Gives motion to perfection more serene
Than yours, out of our imperfections wrought,
Most rare, or ever of more kindred air
In the laborious weaving that you wear.

For so retentive of themselves are men
That music is intensest which proclaims
The near, the clear, and vaunts the clearest bloom,
And of all vigils musing the obscure,
That apprehends the most which sees and names,
As in your name, an image that is sure,
Among the arrant spices of the sun,
O bough and bush and scented vine, in whom
We give ourselves our likest issuance.

Yet not too like, yet not so like to be
Too near, too clear, saving a little to endow
Our feigning with the strange unlike, whence springs
The difference that heavenly pity brings.
For this, musician, in your girdle fixed
Bear other perfumes. On your pale head wear
A band entwining, set with fatal stones.
Unreal, give back to us what once you gave:
The imagination that we spurned and crave.

SUNDAY MORNING

I

Complacencies of the peignoir, and late
Coffee and oranges in a sunny chair,
And the green freedom of a cockatoo
Upon a rug, mingle to dissipate
The holy hush of ancient sacrifice.
She dreams a little, and she feels the dark
Encroachment of that old catastrophe,
As a calm darkens among water-lights.
The pungent oranges and bright green wings
Seem things in some procession of the dead,
Winding across wide water, without sound.
The day is like wide water, without sound,
Stilled for the passing of her dreaming feet
Over the seas, to silent Palestine,
Dominion of the blood and sepulcher.

II

She hears, upon that water without sound,
A voice that cries: "The tomb in Palestine
Is not the porch of spirits lingering;
It is the grave of Jesus, where He lay."
We live in an old chaos of the sun,
Or old dependency of day and night,
Or island solitude, unsponsored, free,
Of that wide water, inescapable.
Deer walk upon our mountains, and the quail
Whistle about us their spontaneous cries;
Sweet berries ripen in the wilderness;
And in the isolation of the sky,
At evening, casual flocks of pigeons make
Ambiguous undulations as they sink,
Downward to darkness, on extended wings.

III

She says: "I am content when wakened birds,
Before they fly, test the reality
Of misty fields, by their sweet questionings;
But when the birds are gone, and their warm fields
Return no more, where, then, is paradise?"
There is not any haunt of prophecy,
Nor any old chimera of the grave,
Neither the golden underground, nor isle
Melodious, where spirits gat them home,
Nor visionary South, nor cloudy palm
Remote on heaven's hill, that has endured
As April's green endures; or will endure
Like her remembrance of awakened birds,
Or her desire for June and evening, tipped
By consummation of the swallow's wings.

### IV

She says, "But in contentment I still feel
The need of some imperishable bliss."
Death is the mother of beauty; hence from her,
Alone, shall come fulfillment to our dreams
And our desires. Although she strews the leaves
Of sure obliteration on our paths—
The path sick sorrow took, the many paths
Where triumph rang its brassy phrase, or love
Whispered a little out of tenderness—
She makes the willow shiver in the sun
For maidens who were wont to sit and gaze
Upon the grass, relinquished to their feet.
She causes boys to bring sweet-smelling pears
And plums in ponderous piles. The maidens taste
And stray impassioned in the littering leaves.

### V

Supple and turbulent, a ring of men
Shall chant in orgy on a summer morn
Their boisterous devotion to the sun—
Not as a god, but as a god might be,
Naked among them, like a savage source.
Their chant shall be a chant of paradise,
Out of their blood, returning to the sky;
And in their chant shall enter, voice by voice,
The windy lake wherein their lord delights,
The trees, like seraphim, and echoing hills,
That choir among themselves long afterward.
They shall know well the heavenly fellowship
Of men that perish and of summer morn—
And whence they came and whither they shall go,
The dew upon their feet shall manifest.

### DOMINATION OF BLACK

At night, by the fire,
The colors of the bushes
And of the fallen leaves,
Repeating themselves,
Turned in the room,
Like the leaves themselves
Turning in the wind.
Yes: but the color of the heavy hemlocks
Came striding.
And I remembered the cry of the peacocks.

The colors of their tails
Were like the leaves themselves
Turning in the wind,
In the twilight wind.

They swept over the room;
Just as they flew from the boughs of the hemlocks
Down to the ground.
I heard them cry—the peacocks.
Was it a cry against the twilight
Or against the leaves themselves
Turning in the wind,
Turning as the flames
Turned in the fire,
Turning as the tails of the peacocks
Turned in the loud fire,
Loud as the hemlocks
Full of the cry of the peacocks?
Or was it a cry against the hemlocks?

Out of the window,
I saw how the planets gathered
Like the leaves themselves
Turning in the wind.
I saw how the night came,
Came striding like the color of the heavy hemlocks.
I felt afraid.
And I remembered the cry of the peacocks.

## SEA SURFACE FULL OF CLOUDS

### I

In that November off Tehuantepec,
The slopping of the sea grew still one night
And in the morning summer hued the deck

And made one think of rosy chocolate
And gilt umbrellas. Paradisal green
Gave suavity to the perplexed machine

Of ocean, which like limpid water lay.
Who, then, in that ambrosial latitude
Out of the light evolved the moving blooms,

Who, then, evolved the sea-blooms from the clouds
Diffusing balm in that Pacific calm?
C'était mon enfant, mon bijou, mon âme.

The sea-clouds whitened far below the calm
And moved, as blooms move, in the swimming green
And in its watery radiance, while the hue

Of heaven in an antique reflection rolled
Round those flotillas. And sometimes the sea
Poured brilliant iris on the glistening blue.

## II

In that November off Tehuantepec
The slopping of the sea grew still one night.
At breakfast jelly yellow streaked the deck

And made one think of chop-house chocolate
And sham umbrellas. And a sham-like green
Capped summer-seeming on the tense machine

Of ocean, which in sinister flatness lay.
Who, then, beheld the rising of the clouds
That strode submerged in that malevolent sheen,

Who saw the mortal massives of the blooms
Of water moving on the water-floor?
*C'était mon frère du ciel, ma vie, mon or.*

The gongs rang loudly as the windy blooms
Hoo-hooed it in the darkened ocean-blooms.
The gongs grew still. And then blue heaven spread

Its crystalline pendentives on the sea
And the macabre of the water-glooms.
In an enormous undulation fled.

## III

In that November off Tehuantepec,
The slopping of the sea grew still one night,
And a pale silver patterned on the deck

Made one think of porcelain chocolate
And pied umbrellas. An uncertain green,
Piano-polished, held the tranced machine

Of ocean, as a prelude holds and holds.
Who, seeing silver petals of white blooms
Unfolding in the water, feeling sure

Of the milk within the saltiest spurge, heard, then,
The sea unfolding in the sunken clouds?
*Oh! C'était mon extase et mon amour.*

So deeply sunken were they that the shrouds,
The shrouding shadows, made the petals black
Until the rolling heaven made them blue,

A blue beyond the rainy hyacinth,
And smiting the crevasses of the leaves
Deluged the ocean with a sapphire hue.

IV

In that November off Tehuantepec
The night-long slopping of the sea grew still.
A mallow morning dozed upon the deck

And made one think of musky chocolate
And frail umbrellas. A too-fluent green
Suggested malice in the dry machine

Of ocean, pondering dank stratagem.
Who then beheld the figures of the clouds,
Like blooms secluded in the thick marine?

Like blooms? Like damasks that were shaken off
From the loosed girdles in the spangling must.
*C'était ma foi, la nonchalance divine.*

The nakedness would rise and suddenly turn
Salt masks of beard and mouths of bellowing,
Would— But more suddenly the heaven rolled

Its bluest sea-clouds in the thinking green
And the nakedness became the broadest blooms,
Mile-mallows that a mallow sun cajoled.

V

In that November off Tehuantepec
Night stilled the slopping of the sea. The day
Came, bowing and voluble, upon the deck,

Good clown. . . . One thought of Chinese chocolate
And large umbrellas. And a motley green
Followed the drift of the obese machine

Of ocean, perfected in indolence.
What pistache one, ingenious and droll,
Beheld the sovereign clouds as jugglery

And the sea as turquoise-turbaned Sambo, neat
At tossing saucers—cloudy-conjuring sea?
*C'était mon esprit batard, l'ignominie.*

The sovereign clouds came clustering. The conch
Of loyal conjuration trumped. The wind
Of green blooms turning crisped the motley hue

To clearing opalescence. Then the sea
And heaven rolled as one and from the two
Came fresh transfigurings of freshest blue.

### ANNUAL GAIETY

In the morning in the blue snow
The catholic sun, its majesty,
Pinks and pinks the ice-hard melanchole.

Wherefore those prayers to the moon?
Or is it that alligators lie
Along the edges of your eye
Basking in desert Florida?

Père Guzz, in heaven, thumb your lyre
And chant the January fire
And joy of snow and snow.

### HOMUNCULUS ET LA BELLE ETOILE

In the sea, Biscayne, there prinks
The young emerald, evening star,
Good light for drunkards, poets, widows,
And ladies soon to be married.

By this light the salty fishes
Arch in the sea like tree-branches,
Going in many directions
Up and down.

This light conducts
The thoughts of drunkards, the feelings
Of widows and trembling ladies,
The movements of fishes.

How pleasant an existence it is
That this emerald charms philosophers,
Until they become thoughtlessly willing
To bathe their hearts in later moonlight,

Knowing that they can bring back thought
In the night that is still to be silent,
Reflecting this thing and that,
Before they sleep!

It is better that, as scholars,
They should think hard in the dark cuffs
Of voluminous cloaks,
And shave their heads and bodies.

It might well be that their mistress
Is no gaunt fugitive phantom.
She might, after all, be a wanton,
Abundantly beautiful, eager,

Fecund,
From whose being by starlight, on sea-coast,
The innermost good of their seeking
Might come in the simplest of speech.

It is a good light, then, for those
That know the ultimate Plato,
Tranquilizing with this jewel
The torments of confusion.

### TWO FIGURES IN DENSE VIOLET LIGHT

I had as lief be embraced by the porter at the hotel
As to get no more from the moonlight
Than your moist hand.

Be the voice of night and Florida in my ear.
Use dusky words and dusky images.
Darken your speech.

Speak, even, as if I did not hear you speaking,
But spoke for you perfectly in my thoughts,
Conceiving words,

As the night conceives the sea-sounds in silence,
And out of their droning sibilants makes
A serenade.

Say, puerile, that the buzzards crouch on the ridge-pole
And sleep with one eye watching the stars fall
Below Key West.

Say that the palms are clear in a total blue,
Are clear and are obscure; that it is night;
That the moon shines.

### GALLANT CHATEAU

Is it bad to have come here
And to have found the bed empty?

One might have found tragic hair,
Bitter eyes, hands hostile and cold.

There might have been a light on a book
Lighting a pitiless verse or two.

There might have been the immense solitude
Of the wind upon the curtains.

Pitiless verse? A few words tuned
And tuned and tuned and tuned.

It is good. The bed is empty,
The curtains are stiff and prim and still.

### THE IDEA OF ORDER AT KEY WEST

She sang beyond the genius of the sea.
The water never formed to mind or voice,
Like a body wholly body, fluttering
Its empty sleeves; and yet its mimic motion
Made constant cry, caused constantly a cry,
That was not ours although we understood,
Inhuman, of the veritable ocean.

The sea was not a mask. No more was she.
The song and water were not medleyed sound,
Even if what she sang was what she heard,
Since what she sang she uttered word by word.
It may be that in all her phrases stirred
The grinding water and the gasping wind;
But it was she and not the sea we heard.

For she was the maker of the song she sang.
The ever-hooded, tragic-gestured sea
Was merely a place by which she walked to sing.
Whose spirit is this? we said, because we knew
It was the spirit that we sought and knew
That we should ask this often as she sang.

If it was only the dark voice of the sea
That rose, or even colored by many waves;

If it was only the outer voice of sky
And cloud, of the sunken coral water-walled,
However clear, it would have been deep air,
The heaving speech of air, a summer sound
Repeated in a summer without end
And sound alone. But it was more than that,
More even than her voice, and ours, among
The meaningless plungings of water and the wind,
Theatrical distances, bronze shadows heaped
On high horizons, mountainous atmospheres
Of sky and sea.

                It was her voice that made
The sky acutest at its vanishing.
She measured to the hour its solitude.
She was the single artificer of the world
In which she sang. And when she sang, the sea,
Whatever self it had, became the self
That was her song, for she was maker. Then we,
As we beheld her striding there alone,
Knew that there never was a world for her
Except the one she sang and, singing, made.

Ramon Fernandez, tell me, if you know,
Why, when the singing ended and we turned
Toward the town, tell why the glassy lights,
The lights in the fishing boats at anchor there,
As the night descended, tilting in the air,
Mastered the night and portioned out the sea,
Fixing emblazoned zones and fiery poles,
Arranging, deepening, enchanting night.

Oh! Blessed rage for order, pale Ramon,
The maker's rage to order words of the sea,
Words of the fragrant portals, dimly-starred,
And of ourselves and of our origins,
In ghostlier demarcations, keener sounds.

# William Carlos Williams

WILLIAM CARLOS WILLIAMS was born in Rutherford, New Jersey, September 17, 1883, the son of Raquel Ellen Rose Hoheb, born at Mayaguez, Porto Rico, and William George Williams, born in Birmingham, England. Williams was educated at Horace Mann High School, New York, at Geneva, Switzerland, and graduated in medicine at the University of Pennsylvania in 1906. After studying abroad, he returned in 1910 and took up his practice in Rutherford, where he has lived ever since.

As Williams is of mixed Dutch, Jewish and Basque extraction, some have affected to find these mingled strains in his work. Be this as it may, Williams is one of the most interesting of the "left wing" of poetic expressionists. *The Tempers,* following an immature *Poems* (1909), was published in London in 1913, a tiny four-inch book which reveals nothing more unusual than youthful uncertainty. *Al Que Quiere* (1917) strikes a more decisive experimental note. From the mocking directions for a funeral which Williams has entitled "Tract" to the more extended "History," Williams achieves a purposely distorted intensification of figure. In *Kora in Hell* (1921) and *Sour Grapes* (1922) Williams seems to be wavering between sharp experiment and the mere exhibition of eccentricities. On one page he paints the scrupulous arrangement of "Queen-Ann's-Lace"; on the next he offers, with cheerful indiscrimination, the flat absurdity of "Complete Destruction."

Although it is difficult to accept Williams in his uncritical entirety, it is ridiculous to reject him, as so many have done, in toto. Even his wildest records, even the uncontrolled stammerings of the unconscious in *Spring and All* (1923), have an esthetic purpose. Those who have been quick to accuse Williams of charlatanry are those who have never ventured any farther than his disorganized moments and have not glimpsed the strong color and delicate movement of such poems as "Peace on Earth," "Daisy," "Metric Figure" and "Dawn."

Two prose works, *In the American Grain* (1925) and *A Voyage to Pagany* (1928), carry over Williams' stylized distinctiveness into a new *genre* of critical creation.

*Collected Poems 1921-1931,* published in 1934, proves again that Williams is an "original" and an "inventor." His way of looking at things old and new, colorful or commonplace, is quite his own. "The man," writes Wallace Stevens, who furnished the Preface, "has spent his life in rejecting the accepted sense of things. His passion for the anti-poetic is a blood passion and not a passion for the ink-pot. Something of the unreal is necessary to fecundate the real; something of the sentimental is necessary to fecundate the anti-poetic. . . . One might run through these pages and point out how often the essential poetry is the result of the conjunction of the unreal and the real, the sentimental and the anti-poetic, the constant interaction of two opposites. This seems to define Williams and his poetry." It also seems to define Wallace Stevens and his own poetry.

### METRIC FIGURE

There is a bird in the poplars—
It is the sun!
The leaves are little yellow fish
Swimming in the river;
The bird skims above them—
Day is on his wings.
Phoenix!
It is he that is making
The great gleam among the poplars.
It is his singing
Outshines the noise
Of leaves clashing in the wind.

### PEACE ON EARTH

The Archer is wake!
The Swan is flying!
Gold against blue
An Arrow is lying.
There is hunting in heaven—
Sleep safe till tomorrow.

The Bears are abroad!
The Eagle is screaming!
Gold against blue
Their eyes are gleaming!
Sleep!
Sleep safe till tomorrow.

The Sisters lie
With their arms intertwining;
Gold against blue
Their hair is shining!
The Serpent writhes!
Orion is listening!
Gold against blue
His sword is glistening!
Sleep!
There is hunting in heaven—
Sleep safe till tomorrow.

### DAWN

Ecstatic bird songs pound
the hollow vastness of the sky
with metallic clinkings—
beating color up into it
at a far edge,—beating it, beating it
with rising, triumphant ardor,—
stirring it into warmth,
quickening in it a spreading change,—
bursting wildly against it as
dividing the horizon, a heavy sun
lifts himself—is lifted—
bit by bit above the edge
of things,—runs free at last
out into the open—! lumbering
glorified in full release upward—

songs cease.

### POEM

By the road to the contagious hospital,
under the surge of the blue
mottled clouds driven from the
northeast—cold wind. Beyond, the
waste of broad, muddy fields,
brown with dried weeds, standing and fallen,

patches of standing water,
the scattering of tall trees.

All along the road the reddish,
purplish, forked, upstanding, twiggy
stuff of brushes and small trees
with dead, brown leaves under them
leafless vines—

Lifeless in appearance, sluggish,
dazed spring approaches—

They enter the new world naked,
cold, uncertain of all
save that they enter. All about them
the cold, familiar wind—

Now the grass, tomorrow
the stiff curl of wild-carrot leaf.

One by one objects are defined—
It quickens: clarity, outline of leaf,

But now the stark dignity of
entrance— Still, the profound change
has come upon them; rooted, they
grip down and begin to awaken.

### JANUARY

Again I reply to the triple winds
running chromatic fifths of derision
outside my window:

Play louder.
You will not succeed. I am
bound more to my sentences
the more you batter at me
to follow you.

And the wind,
as before, fingers perfectly
its derisive music.

### QUEEN-ANN'S-LACE

Her body is not so white as
anemone petals nor so smooth—nor
so remote a thing. It is a field
of the wild carrot taking
the field by force; the grass
does not raise above it.
Here is no question of whiteness,
white as can be, with a purple mole
at the center of each flower.
Each flower is a hand's span
of her whiteness. Wherever
his hand has lain there is
a tiny purple blemish. Each part
is a blossom under his touch
to which the fibers of her being
stem one by one, each to its end,
until the whole field is a
white desire, empty, a single stem,

a cluster, flower by flower,
a pious wish to whiteness gone over—
or nothing.

### DAISY

The dayseye hugging the earth
in August, ha! Spring is
gone down in purple,
weeds stand high in the corn,
the rainbeaten furrow
is clotted with sorrel
and crabgrass, the
branch is black under
the heavy mass of the leaves—
The sun is upon a
slender green stem
ribbed lengthwise.
He lies on his back—
it is a woman also—
he regards his former
majesty and
round the yellow center,
split and creviced and done into
minute flowerheads, he sends out
his twenty rays—a little
and the wind is among them
to grow cool there!

One turns the thing over
in his hand and looks
at it from the rear: brownedged,
green and pointed scales
armor his yellow.
But turn and turn,

the crisp petals remain
brief, translucent, greenfastened,
barely touching at the edges:
blades of limpid seashell.

### ON GAY WALLPAPER

The green-blue ground
is ruled with silver lines
to say the sun is shining

And on this mural sea
of grass or dreams lie flowers
or baskets of desires

Heaven knows what they are
between cerulean shapes
laid regularly round

Mat roses and tridentate
leaves of gold
threes, threes and threes

Three roses and three stems
the basket floating
standing in the horns of blue

Repeated to the ceiling
to the windows
where the day

Blows in
the scalloped curtains to
the sound of rain.

## Alfred Kreymborg

ALFRED KREYMBORG was born in New York City, December 10, 1883. His education was spasmodic, his childhood was spent beneath the roar of the elevated
trains. At ten he was an expert chess player. Later, he became a bookkeeper and
demonstrator of mechanical player-pianos; from seventeen to twenty-five he supported
himself by teaching chess and playing exhibition games. His passion, however, was
not mathematics but music. He dreamed of extending the borders of poetry into
the realms of tonic art, experimented with new systems of notation, technicalities of
rhythm. At thirty, he began to turn to the theater as a medium.

In 1914, he organized that group of radical poets which, half-deprecatingly, half-defiantly, called itself "Others." (He edited the three anthologies of their work published in 1916, 1917, and 1919.) Meanwhile he had been working on a technique that was an attempt to rid poetry of its too frequent wordiness. *Mushrooms* (1916) was the first collection in this vein. Here Kreymborg continually sought for simplification, cutting away at his lines until they assumed an almost naked expression. Often he overdid his effects, attaining nothing more than a false ingenuousness, a sophisticated simplicity.

*Blood of Things* (1920) is, for all the surface oddities, the work not only of an apt conjurer but a serious thinker. Humor is in these pages, but it is humor lifted. Here, in spite of what seems a persistence of occasional affectations, is a rich and sensitive imagination.

*Puppet Plays,* with a preface by Gordon Craig, appeared in 1923. Although in its predetermination to preserve an open-eyed wonder, Kreymborg's marionette-like emotions are often too doll-charming or too doll-tragic, these miniature dramas are appealing and witty. However, nothing which Kreymborg had written up to this time had prepared his readers for the volume which appeared a few months later. *Less Lonely* (1923) is partly in the idiom which the poet has made his own, but most of the volume is in the shape of conventional verse; there are even thirty orthodox sonnets excellently constructed. These simple formalities stood him in good stead in *Funnybone Alley* (1927) which combined quaint prose with city jingles for children. Kreymborg's belated love of the sonnet was, unfortunately, not reciprocated. *The Lost Sail* (1928) is a loose journal in which the sonnets suffer from long drawn-out casualness. The technique is clumsy, the presentation inadequate; worse still, the sentimental note struck tentatively in the early poems is sounded by all the instruments *con amore. Manhattan Men* (1929) is a compromise between Kreymborg's first and later manners.

Kreymborg confesses to being "guilty" of several premature novels and, during intervals between the founding of various experimental magazines, many prose sketches. *Troubadour* (1925) is his winning autobiography.

As a chronicler, Kreymborg is not at all the fantastic recorder one might expect. *Our Singing Strength* (1929) is a sober categorical outline of American poetry from Colonial times with over-personal emphasis on the contemporary scene, and *Lyric America* (1932) is a fairly orthodox compilation.

### OLD MANUSCRIPT

The sky
is that beautiful old parchment
in which the sun
and the moon
keep their diary.
To read it all,
one must be a linguist
more learned than Father Wisdom;
and a visionary
more clairvoyant than Mother Dream.
But to feel it,
one must be an apostle:

one who is more than intimate
in having been, always,
the only confidant—
like the earth
or the sea.

### DAWNS

I have come
from pride
all the way up to humility
This day-to-night.
The hill

was more terrible
than ever before.
This is the top;
there is the tall, slim tree.
It isn't bent; it doesn't lean;
It is only looking back.
At dawn,
under that tree,
still another me of mine
was buried.
Waiting for me to come again,
humorously solicitous
of what I bring next,
it looks down.

## IMPROVISATION

Wind:
Why do you play
that long beautiful adagio,
that archaic air,
tonight.
Will it never end?
Or is it the beginning,
some prelude you seek?

Is it a tale you strum?
*Yesterday, yesterday*—
Have you no more for us?

Wind:
Play on.
There is nor hope
nor mutiny
in you.

## PEASANT

It's the mixture of peasantry
    makes him so slow.
He waggles his head
    before he speaks,
like a cow
    before she crops.
He bends to the habit
    of dragging his feet
    up under him,
like a measuring-worm:

some of his forefathers,
stooped over books,
ruled short straight lines
under two rows of figures
to keep their thin savings
from sifting to the floor.
Should you strike him
    with a question,
he will blink twice or thrice
    and roll his head about,
like an owl
    in the pin-pricks
    of a dawn he cannot see.
There is mighty little flesh
    about his bones,
there is no gusto
    in his stride:
he seems to wait
    for the blow on the buttocks
    that will drive him
    another step forward—
    step forward to what?
There is no land,
    no house,
    no barn,
he has ever owned;
he sits uncomfortable
    on chairs
    you might invite him to:
if you did,
    he'd keep his hat in hand
    against the moment
    when some silent pause
    for which he hearkens
    with his ear to one side
    bids him move on—
    move on where?
It doesn't matter.
He has learned
    to shrug his shoulders,
    so he'll shrug his shoulders now:
caterpillars do it
    when they're halted by a stick.
Is there a sky overhead?—
    a hope worth flying to?—
Birds may know about it,
    but it's birds
    that birds descend from.

CROCUS

When trees have lost remembrance of the leaves
that spring bequeaths to summer, autumn weaves
and loosens mournfully—this dirge, to whom
does it belong—who treads the hidden loom?

When peaks are overwhelmed with snow and ice,
and clouds with crêpe bedeck and shroud the skies—
nor any sun or moon or star, it seems,
can wedge a path of light through such black dreams—

All motion cold, and dead all trace thereof:
What sudden shock below, or spark above,
starts torrents raging down till rivers surge—
that aid the first small crocus to emerge?

The earth will turn and spin and fairly soar,
that couldn't move a tortoise-foot before—
and planets permeate the atmosphere
till misery depart and mystery clear!—

And yet, so insignificant a hearse?—
who gave it the endurance so to brave
such elements?—shove winter down a grave?—
and then lead on again the universe?

# Sara Teasdale

Sara teasdale was born August 8, 1884, in St. Louis, Missouri, and educated there. After leaving school she traveled in Europe and the Near East. In 1916 she moved to New York City with her husband Ernst Filsinger. After her divorce, she lived in seclusion, and ill health emphasized her unhappiness. She was found, drowned in the bath of her New York apartment, January 28, 1933.

Her first book was a slight volume, *Sonnets to Duse* (1907), which gave little promise of the lyricism to follow. *Helen of Troy and Other Poems* (1911) contains hints of that delicate craftsmanship which this poet brought to such a pitch. The six opening monologues are written in a blank verse as musical as many of her lyrics. At times her quatrains suffer from too conscious a cleverness; the dexterity with which Miss Teasdale turns a phrase or twists her last line is frequently too obtrusive to be unreservedly enjoyable. Moreover, they seem written in a mood of predetermined and too picturesque romance, the mood of languishing roses, silken balconies, moonlight on guitars, and abstract kisses for unreal Colins.

*Rivers to the Sea* (1915) emphasizes a new skill and a greater restraint. The volume contains at least a dozen unforgettable snatches, lyrics in which the words seem to fall into place without art or effort. Seldom employing metaphor or striking imagery, almost bare of ornament, these poems have the touch of folk-song. Theirs is an artlessness that is something more than art.

*Love Songs* (1917) is a collection of Miss Teasdale's previous melodies for the *viola d'amore* together with several in which the turns are no longer obviously unexpected. Maturity is evident in the poet's rejection of many of her facile stanzas and her choice of firmer material.

*Flame and Shadow* (1920; revised edition, published in England, in 1924) is the ripest of her books. Here the emotion is fuller and deeper; an almost mystic radiance plays from these verses. Technically, also, this volume marks Miss Teasdale's greatest advance. The words are chosen with a keener sense of their actual as well as their musical values; the rhythms are more subtle and varied; the line moves with a greater naturalness. Beneath the symbolism of poems like "Water-Lilies," "The Long Hill," and "Let It Be Forgotten," one is conscious of a finer artistry, a more flexible speech that is all the lovelier for its slight (and logical) irregularities.

After *Flame and Shadow* Miss Teasdale's theme became somewhat autumnal. Though never funereal, the songs are preoccupied with the coming of age, the gathering of night, the mutability of things. *Dark of the Moon* (1926) is more thoughtful than any other previous verse. It is, as the title indicates, even more somber. If the movement is slower it is a no less delicate music that moves under the surface rhythms. "Wisdom," "The Solitary," "The Flight" may not be the most popular poems that Miss Teasdale has written, but they must be numbered among her best. Hers is a disillusion without cynicism; her proud acceptance of life's darker aspects adds new dignity to the old lyricism.

*Strange Victory* (1933) is Sara Teasdale's posthumous memorial to a world she never quite despised yet never wholly trusted. The poems are sad yet not sentimental. Though death overshadows the book there is never the querulous cry of frustration nor the melodrama of dying. As in the later lyrics the lines are direct, the emotion unwhipped; the beauty is in the restraint, the careful selection, the compression into the essential spirit, into a last serenity. It is an irony that as her admirers grew less voluble her work increased in value.

Besides her own books, Miss Teasdale had compiled an anthology, *The Answering Voice* (1917), comprising one hundred love lyrics by women, and a collection for children, *Rainbow Gold* (1922).

### NIGHT SONG AT AMALFI

I asked the heaven of stars
   What I should give my love—
It answered me with silence,
   Silence above.

I asked the darkened sea
   Down where the fishermen go—
It answered me with silence,
   Silence below.

Oh, I could give him weeping,
   Or I could give him song—

But how can I give silence
   My whole life long?

### SPRING NIGHT

The park is filled with night and fog,
   The veils are drawn about the world,
The drowsy lights along the paths
   Are dim and pearled.

Gold and gleaming the empty streets,
   Gold and gleaming the misty lake,
The mirrored lights like sunken swords,
   Glimmer and shake.

Oh, is it not enough to be  
Here with this beauty over me?  
My throat should ache with praise, and I  
Should kneel in joy beneath the sky.  
O beauty, are you not enough?  
Why am I crying after love  
With youth, a singing voice, and eyes  
To take earth's wonder with surprise?

Why have I put off my pride,  
Why am I unsatisfied,—  
I, for whom the pensive night  
Binds her cloudy hair with light,—  
I, for whom all beauty burns  
Like incense in a million urns?  
O beauty, are you not enough?  
Why am I crying after love?

### I SHALL NOT CARE

When I am dead and over me bright April  
    Shakes out her rain-drenched hair,  
Though you should lean above me broken-hearted,  
    I shall not care.

I shall have peace, as leafy trees are peaceful  
    When rain bends down the bough;  
And I shall be more silent and cold-hearted  
    Than you are now.

### THE LONG HILL

I must have passed the crest a while ago  
    And now I am going down—  
Strange to have crossed the crest and not to know,  
    But the brambles were always catching the hem of my gown.

All the morning I thought how proud I should be  
    To stand there straight as a queen,  
Wrapped in the wind and the sun with the world under me—  
    But the air was dull, there was little I could have seen.

It was nearly level along the beaten track  
    And the brambles caught in my gown—  
But it's no use now to think of turning back,  
    The rest of the way will be only going down.

### WATER-LILIES

If you have forgotten water-lilies floating  
    On a dark lake among mountains in the afternoon shade,  
If you have forgotten their wet, sleepy fragrance,  
    Then you can return and not be afraid.

But if you remember, then turn away forever  
    To the plains and the prairies where pools are far apart,  
There you will not come at dusk on closing water-lilies,  
    And the shadow of mountains will not fall on your heart.

## LET IT BE FORGOTTEN

Let it be forgotten, as a flower is forgotten,
  Forgotten as a fire that once was singing gold,
Let it be forgotten for ever and ever,
  Time is a kind friend, he will make us old.

If anyone asks, say it was forgotten
  Long and long ago,
As a flower, as a fire, as a hushed footfall
  In a long-forgotten snow.

## WISDOM

It was a night of early spring,
  The winter-sleep was scarcely broken;
Around us shadows and the wind
  Listened for what was never spoken.

Though half a score of years are gone,
  Spring comes as sharply now as then—
But if we had it all to do
  It would be done the same again.

It was a spring that never came;
  But we have lived enough to know
That what we never have, remains;
  It is the things we have that go.

## THE SOLITARY

My heart has grown rich with the passing of years,
  I have less need now than when I was young
To share myself with every comer,
  Or shape my thoughts into words with my tongue.

It is one to me that they come or go
  If I have myself and the drive of my will,
And strength to climb on a summer night
  And watch the stars swarm over the hill.

Let them think I love them more than I do,
  Let them think I care, though I go alone,
If it lifts their pride, what is it to me,
  Who am self-complete as a flower or a stone?

## THE CRYSTAL GAZER

I shall gather myself into myself again,
  I shall take my scattered selves and make them one,
I shall fuse them into a polished crystal ball
  Where I can see the moon and the flashing sun.

I shall sit like a sibyl, hour after hour intent,
   Watching the future come and the present go—
And the little shifting pictures of people rushing
   In tiny self-importance to and fro.

## APPRAISAL

Never think she loves him wholly,
Never believe her love is blind,
All his faults are locked securely
In a closet of her mind;
All his indecisions folded
Like old flags that time has faded,
Limp and streaked with rain,
And his cautiousness like garments
Frayed and thin, with many a stain—
Let them be, oh, let them be,
There is treasure to outweigh them,
His proud will that sharply stirred,
Climbs as surely as the tide,
Senses strained too taut to sleep,
Gentleness to beast and bird,
Humor flickering hushed and wide
As the moon on moving water,
And a tenderness too deep
To be gathered in a word.

## ON THE SOUTH DOWNS

Over the downs there were birds flying,
   Far off glittered the sea,
And toward the north the weald of Sussex
   Lay like a kingdom under me.

I was happier than the larks
   That nest on the downs and sing to the
   sky—
Over the downs the birds flying
   Were not so happy as I.

It was not you, though you were near,
   Though you were good to hear and see;
It was not earth, it was not heaven,
   It was myself that sang in me.

## AUGUST NIGHT

On a midsummer night, on a night that was eerie with stars,
   In a wood too deep for a single star to look through,
You led down a path whose turnings you knew in the darkness,
   But the scent of the dew-dripping cedars was all that I knew.

I drank of the darkness, I was fed with the honey of fragrance,
   I was glad of my life, the drawing of breath was sweet;
I heard your voice, you said, "Look down, see the glow-worm!"
   It was there before me, a small star white at my feet.

We watched while it brightened as though it were breathed on and burning,
   This tiny creature moving over earth's floor—
" 'L'amor che move il sole e l'altre stelle,' "
   You said, and no more.

## EFFIGY OF A NUN

### (Sixteenth Century)

Infinite gentleness, infinite irony
   Are in this face with fast-sealed eyes,
And round this mouth that learned in loneliness
   How useless their wisdom is to the wise.

In her nun's habit carved, patiently, lovingly,
· By one who knew the ways of womankind,
This woman's face still keeps, in its cold wistful calm,
    All of the subtle pride of her mind.

These long patrician hands, clasping the crucifix,
    Show she had weighed the world, her will was set;
These pale curved lips of hers, holding their hidden smile
    Once having made their choice, knew no regret.

She was of those who hoard their own thoughts carefully,
    Feeling them far too dear to give away,
Content to look at life with the high, insolent
    Air of an audience watching a play.

If she was curious, if she was passionate
    She must have told herself that love was great,
But that the lacking it might be as great a thing
    If she held fast to it, challenging fate.

She who so loved herself and her own warring thoughts,
    Watching their humorous, tragic rebound,
In her thick habit's fold, sleeping, sleeping,
    Is she amused at dreams she has found?

Infinite tenderness, infinite irony
    Are hidden forever in her closed eyes,
Who must have learned too well in her long loneliness
    How empty wisdom is, even to the wise.

### THE FLIGHT

We are two eagles
Flying together,
Under the heavens,
Over the mountains,
Stretched on the wind.
Sunlight heartens us,
Blind snow baffles us,
Clouds wheel after us,
Raveled and thinned.

We are like eagles;
But when Death harries us,
Human and humbled
When one of us goes,
Let the other follow—
Let the flight be ended,
Let the fire blacken,
Let the book close.

# Elizabeth Madox Roberts

ELIZABETH MADOX ROBERTS was born in 1885, at Perryville, near Springfield, Kentucky, and attended the University of Chicago, where she received her Ph.B. in 1921. Except when obliged to travel for health or warmth, she lives in the Salt River country of Kentucky, twenty-eight miles from Harrodsburg, old Fort Harrod, the first settlement in the state.

As an undergraduate she won the local Fiske Prize with a group of poems which later appeared in *Poetry: A Magazine of Verse.* An amplification of these verses appeared as *Under the Tree* (1922) and critics were quick to recognize the unusually fresh accents in this first volume. *Under the Tree* spoke directly to the young, for it was written, not so much for children, but as a sensitive child might write. The observation is precise, the reflections are candidly clear, the humor delicate, never simpering or archly beribboned. Here is a simplicity which is straightforward without being shrill or mincing. The verse is graceful where grace commands the gesture, but Miss Roberts' unforced *naïveté* allows her to be gauche whenever awkwardness is natural.

After this volume Miss Roberts returned to her native state, and spent much of her time studying the archaic English speech still spoken in the remote parts of Kentucky. "Orpheus," although written later than her first book, is a highly interesting use of her early idiom, localizing as well as vitalizing the old myth. "Stranger" is more definitely indigenous; it has something of the flavor of the *Lonesome Tunes* collected by Howard Brockway and Loraine Wyman. Concerning this poem, Miss Roberts writes, "In these verses I have used material from the old ballads—or suggestions from them, material which may be found abundantly in Kentucky, together with modern syncopation and a refrain designed to call up banjo notes." "A Ballet Song of Mary," which won the John Reed Memorial Prize in *Poetry* (1928), is an "artificial" piece—using the adjective in the best sense—founded on ancient archaic words and uses. Here, as in her prose, Miss Roberts writes with an ear always tuned to local phrase and feeling.

In 1925 Miss Roberts turned to the prose for which she has been so widely celebrated. *The Time of Man* (1926), one of the most moving novels of the period, is an epic of the Appalachians in which every chapter has the effect of a poem. *My Heart and My Flesh* (1927), a darker and more difficult exploration, discloses less local and more universal regions of the spirit. *Jingling in the Wind* (1928) is a less successful experiment, a light farce which tries but fails to be a satire on industrial civilization. All three are characterized by a lyrical charm and an inscrutability which set Miss Roberts apart from the competent writers of easy fiction.

*The Great Meadow* (1930) is an exploration of the material uncovered in her first novel. Placed in the Kentucky meadow-lands against the heroic backgrounds of early American history, it is a pioneering panorama. Native to the least grass-blade, it is much more than a narrative of the soil; it is a widening saga of the men and women who imposed themselves and their pattern on the unshaped wilderness. Thus *The Great Meadow* acts both as the preparation for and the rich completion of *The Time of Man.* A novel *He Sent Forth a Raven* (1935) combines her early individual diction with the later restrained mysticism, a combination that is curiously lilting and intense.

## THE SKY

I saw a shadow on the ground
And heard a bluejay going by;
A shadow went across the ground,
And I looked up and saw the sky.

It hung up on the poplar tree,
But while I looked it did not stay;
It gave a tiny sort of jerk
And moved a little bit away.

And farther on and farther on
It moved and never seemed to stop.
I think it must be tied with chains
And something pulls it from the top.

It never has come down again,
And every time I look to see,
The sky is always slipping back
And getting far away from me.

## CHRISTMAS MORNING

If Bethlehem were here today,
Or this were very long ago,
There wouldn't be a winter time
Nor any cold or snow.

I'd run out through the garden gate,
And down along the pasture walk;
And off beside the cattle barns
I'd hear a kind of gentle talk.

I'd move the heavy iron chain
And pull away the wooden pin;
I'd push the door a little bit
And tiptoe very softly in.

The pigeons and the yellow hens
And all the cows would stand away;
Their eyes would open wide to see
A lady in the manger hay,
If this were very long ago
And Bethlehem were here today.

And Mother held my hand and smiled—
I mean the lady would—and she

Would take the woolly blankets off
Her little boy so I could see.

His shut-up eyes would be asleep,
And he would look just like our John,
And he would be all crumpled too,
And have a pinkish color on.

I'd watch his breath go in and out.
His little clothes would all be white.
I'd slip my finger in his hand
To feel how he could hold it tight.

And she would smile and say, "Take care,"
The mother, Mary, would, "Take care";
And I would kiss his little hand
And touch his hair.

While Mary put the blankets back
The gentle talk would soon begin.
And when I'd tiptoe softly out
I'd meet the wise men going in.

## ORPHEUS

He could sing sweetly on a string.
He'd make the music curve around;
He'd make it tremble through the woods
And all the trees would leave the ground.

The tunes would walk on steps of air,
For in his hand a wire would sing;
The songs would fly like wild quick geese—
He could play sweetly on a string.

✦

If Orpheus would come today,
Our trees would lean far out to hear,
And they would stretch limb after limb;
Then the ellum trees would leave the groun
And the sycamores would follow him.

And the poplar tree and the locust tree
And the coffeeberry tree would come
And all the rows of osage thorns,
And then the little twisted plum.

e'd lead them off across the hill.
hey'd flow like water toward his feet.
e'd walk through fields and turn in roads;
e'd bring them down our street.

id he'd go by the blacksmith shop,
id one would say, "Now who are these?—
vonder who that fellow is,
id where he's going with the trees!"

'o the sawmill, likely," one would say,
)h, yes, the sawmill, I should think."
id then he'd cut the horse's hoof
id hammers would go *clink* and *clink*.

✦

 could play sweetly on a wire.
id he would lean down near his lyre
 hear its songs unfold and wind,

And it would reach up toward his ear
To hear the music in his mind.

And when the road turned by the kiln,
Then Orpheus would happen to see
The little plum and the sycamore
And the poplar tree and the chinaberry tree,

And all the rows of osage thorns—
When he happened once to look—
He'd see them coming after him . . .
Three birches, and he'd see the oak.

And he would lead them back again.
He'd bring each one to its own ground.
He'd bring each to its growing-place
And set them back with sound and sound.

He'd fit them in with whispered chords,
And tap them down with humming words.

## STRANGER

When Polly lived back in the old deep woods,
Sing, sing, sing and howdy, howdy-o!
Nobody ever went by her door,
Tum a-tum tum and danky, danky-o!

Valentine worked all day in the brush,
He grubbed out stumps and he chopped with his ax,
He chopped a clear road up out of the branch;
Their wheels made all the tracks.

And all they could see out doors were the trees,
And all the night they could hear the wolves go;
But one cold time when the dark came on
A man's voice said, "Hello, there, hello!"

He stood away by the black oak tree
When they opened the door in the halfway light;
He stood away by the buttonwood stump,
And Valentine said, "Won't you stay all night?"

He sat by the fire and warmed his bones.
He had something hidden down deep in a sack,
And Polly watched close while she baked her pones;
He felt of it once when she turned her back—
Polly had a fear of his sack.

Nobody lived this way or there,
And the night came down and the woods came dark,
A thin man sat by the fire that night,
And the cabin pane was one red spark.

He took the something out of his sack,
When the candle dimmed and the logs fell low,
It was something dark, as Polly could see,
Sing, sing, sing and howdy, howdy-o!

He held it up against his chest,
And the logs came bright with a fresh new glow,
And it was a fiddle that was on his breast,
Tum tum-a tum and danky, danky-o!

He played one tune and one tune more;
He played five tunes all in a long row.
The logs never heard any songs before.
Sing, sing, sing and howdy, howdy-o!

The tunes lay down like drowsy cats;
They tumbled over rocks where the waterfalls go;
They twinkled in the sun like little June gnats;
Tum a-tum tum and danky dee-o!

The stumps stood back in Valentine's mind;
The wolves went back so Polly couldn't see;
She forgot how they howled and forgot how they whined.
Tum tum a-tum and danky-dee!

The tunes flew by like wild quick geese,
Sing, sing, sing and howdy howdy-o!
And Polly said, "That's a right good piece."
Tum tum tum and danky danky-o!
Tum a-tum tum and danky dee-o!

### A BALLET SONG OF MARY

Her smock was of the holland fine,
Skinkled with colors three;
Her shawl was of the velvet blue,
The Queen of Galilee.

Her hair was yellow like the wax,
Like the silken floss fine-spun;
The girdle for her golden cloak
Was all in gold bedone.

She sat her down in her own bower place
And dressed herself her hair.
Her gold kemb in her braid she laid,
And a sound fell on the door.

He came within her own bower room
"Hail, Mary, hail!" says he;
"A goodly grace is on your head,
For the Lord is now with thee."

She folded down her little white hands
When Gabriel spoke again.
She set her shawl, the corners right,
For ceremony then.

"And the God will overshadow thee
And bring a holy sweven.
Fear not, fear not," then Gabriel said,
"It's the God of the good high heaven.

"And what must be born it will heal th
    sick;
It will make a goodly lear;
It will fettle men for christentie
And to keep holy gear."

Then up then rose this little maid
When Gabriel's word was said,
And out of the bower she ran in haste,
And out of the hall she is sped.

She is running far to Zachary's house—
"Is this the way?" says she.

little maid in haste," they said,
.as gone to the hills of Judee."


.d what will be born it will ope their eyes;
will hearten men in their stear;
will fettle men for christentie
d to have holy gear.


will scourge with a thong when those
nake gain
ere a humble man should be;
will cast the witches from out of his saule
d drown them into the sea.

It will give men drink from the horn of the
    wind,
And give men meat from the song of a bird;
Their cloak they will get from the sheen of
    the grass,
And a roof from a singin' word.

And when they come to the Brig o' Dread,
And they cry, "I fall! I'm afear!"
It will close their eyes and give them sleep
To heal them outen their lonesome cheer,
When they come to the Brig o' Dread.

### WOODCOCK OF THE IVORY BEAK

Bough of the plane tree, where is the clear-beaked bird
That was promised? When I walked here, now, I heard
A swift cry in my own voice lifted in laughter—absurd
Mock at a crow—crying under the glee-wrung word,
Saying, "Where?" Saying, "When?" Saying, "Will it be? Here?
The woodcock of the ivory bill? Will it be? Where?"

Old winds that blew deep chaos down through the valley,
Moan-haunted, sob-tossèd, shudder and shackle, rout and rally,
Where? Did you toss a feather and bend plume a cold May early
Morning, when the ivory bill shone, song lifted, pearly
Clear on the rose-stippled, blue-shadowed trunk of the plane tree?
Oh, woodcock of the ivory beak, I came here to see . . .


# Elinor Wylie

ELINOR (HOYT) WYLIE was born September 7, 1885, in Somerville, New Jersey, but she was, as she often protested, of pure Pennsylvania stock. The family was a literary one and it was soon evident that Elinor, the first born, was a prodigy. The facts of her life, if not the inner conflicts and personal sufferings, have been recorded by Nancy Hoyt, her younger sister, in *Elinor Wylie: The Portrait of an Unknown Woman* (1935), and, though the biography might have been fuller and franker without diminishing the poet's stature, it is invaluable source material. On both sides Elinor Wylie traced her ancestry back through old American families. A grandfather was Governor of Pennsylvania; her father, at the age of thirty-six, was Assistant Attorney-General under McKinley, later Solicitor General during Theodore Roosevelt's administration.

Elinor Hoyt's youth was spent in Washington, D. C. At eighteen she attended a life-class at the Corcoran Museum of Art, composing poems in secret, and wavering between painting and writing as a possible career. Shortly after her "coming-out party" there was a youthful romance and, disappointed because it was inconclusive, Elinor "rushed off and, without the knowledge of her parents, became engaged to a nice-looking and well-born young suitor with a bad temper," Philip Hichborn, son of an admiral. A son was born of the union, but the marriage was an unhappy one. Three years after, when scarcely twenty-four, she eloped with Horace Wylie, unable to obtain a divorce, disrupting the social circles in which she had conducted herself so primly. Elinor and Horace Wylie lived in England, where they were married some years later, until the World War forced them to return to America. It was in England that her first work was published, a tiny book of forty-three pages entitled *Incidental Numbers* (1912), privately printed and unsigned. It is a tentative collection and Elinor was so sensitive about its "incredible immaturity" that she pleaded with the few who knew of its existence never to refer to it until after her death. But she had no reason to be ashamed of it. ("I think the juvenilia superior to the rest," she wrote to the editor many years later.) Much of it is manifestly immature, since most of it was written in her early twenties and the rest was the product of her teens. Yet her characteristic touch—the firm thought matched by the firmly molded line—is already suggested, especially in such poems as "The Knight Fallen on Evil Days," anticipating the later beautifully knit sonnets, and "Pegasus Lost," a strangely ironic fantasy written at seventeen.

She returned to America in the summer of 1916, and lived in Boston and in Mount Desert, Maine. Her poems began to appear in the magazines; she moved to Washington, where she met various friends of her brother Henry, including William Rose Benét. In 1921 her first "real" volume, *Nets to Catch the Wind,* appeared. Three years later she was a famous person, the author of two volumes of poems and an extraordinary first novel (*Jennifer Lorn*), married to William Rose Benét, and part of the literary life of New York.

*Nets to Catch the Wind* impresses immediately because of its brilliance. The brilliance is one which, at first, seems to sparkle without burning. In several of the poems the author achieves a frigid ecstasy; emotion is not absent from her lines, but too frequently it seems a passion frozen at its source. It is the brilliance of moonlight coruscating on a plain of ice. But if Mrs. Wylie seldom allows her verses to grow agitated, she never permits them to remain dull. As a technician, she is always admirable; in "August" the sense of heat is conveyed by tropic luxuriance and contrast; in "The Eagle and the Mole" she lifts didacticism to a proud level. Her auditory effects are scarcely less remarkable; never has snow-silence been more unerringly communicated than in "Velvet Shoes."

*Black Armour* (1923) exhibits Mrs. Wylie's keenness against a mellower background. The beauty evoked in this volume no longer has "the hard heart of a child." The intellect has grown more fiery, the mood has grown warmer, and the craftsmanship is more dazzling than ever. This devotee of severe elegance has perfected an accent which is clipped and patrician; she varies the perfect modulation with rhymes that are delightfully acrid and unique departures which never fail of success. Mrs. Wylie, it is evident from the very titles of her volumes, had read the metaphysicans; Donne, Webster, and Eliot found a voice in her lines. She felt

> "behind a carnal mesh,
> The clean bones crying in the flesh."

Possibly the most obvious and arresting feature of her work is the variety of her gifts. She reached from the nimble dexterity of a rondo like "Peregrine" to the introspective poignance of "Self Portrait," from the fanciful "Escape" to the grave mockery of "Let No Charitable Hope." But a greater unfoldment was to come.

*Trivial Breath* (1928) is the work of a poet in transition. At times the craftsman is uppermost; at times the creative genius. A preoccupation with her material obscures the half-uttered wisdom. Many of the verses, steeped in literature, pay homage to the letter; a smaller number, less absorbed in shaping an immaculate phrase, do reverence to the spirit. Mrs. Wylie recognized the danger of her own exquisiteness, of a style where elegance was too often a richly embroidered cloak draped upon a neat triviality. In "Minotaur" she admonished herself:

> Go study to disdain
> The frail, the overfine
> That tapers to a line
> Knotted about the brain.

Her distrust of the "overfine" deepened; she became more influenced by the fiery spirit of Shelley; her prose grew less mannered and more searching; her poetry attained a new richness. While in England during the summer of 1928 she wrote, with almost breathless haste but with calm certainty, the verses which compose her posthumous volume. In the autumn she returned to America; suffering from high blood pressure and partial paralysis, she began to arrange her final work. The day before she died she decided on the order of the poems, affixed the motto from Donne, and got the manuscript ready for the printer. She died December 16, 1928.

*Angels and Earthly Creatures* (1929) is the sublimation of all her gifts. Here are the cunningly poised and polished syllables, here are the old concerns with freezing silvers, frail china, and pearly monotones, but here is a quality which lifts them high above themselves. Still indebted to the Jacobean metaphysicians, the poet transcends her influences and develops a highly personal mysticism. To say that her emotion is governed and disciplined is not to say that *Angels and Earthly Creatures* suffers from a lack of emotion. On the contrary, the sequence of nineteen sonnets has the spontaneity of a passionate improvisation, of something close to abandonment. The other poems share this intensity. "This Corruptible" is both visionary and philosophic; "O Virtuous Light" deals with that piercing clarity, the intuition which disturbs the senses, threatens reason and, "begotten of itself," unreconciled to ordinary experience, is "not a light by which to live." The other poems are scarcely less uplifted, finding their summit in "Hymn to Earth," which is possibly the deepest of her poems and one which is certain to endure. It was, as it happened, a clear premonition; it remains a noble valedictory. She could go no further. She had perfected her technique; without discarding her idiom, her spirit reached toward a final expression. She had suddenly attained the emotional stature of a great poet.

A sumptuous *Collected Poems of Elinor Wylie* was published in 1932, containing, with the exception of the booklet issued in England, her four books of poems as well as a section of forty-eight poems hitherto uncollected. Some of the posthumous verse had never seen print; others published in magazines—notably "Golden Bough" and "The Pebble"—may be ranked among the poet's ripest utterances. "The Pebble" is significant not only as a fine piece of craftsmanship but as a revealing bit of spiritual autobiography.

Though more mannered than her verse, her prose was scarcely less accomplished. *Jennifer Lorn* (1923), subtitled "A Sedate Extravaganza," *The Venetian Glass Nephew* (1925), and *The Orphan Angel* (1926) adroitly juggle a harlequin style, even when it is least appropriate to the matter. *Mr. Hodge and Mr. Hazard* is a somewhat more serious and ironic allegory. Differing widely from each other in plot, ranging from macabre artifice to an apocryphal legend of Shelley *redivivus* in America, the manipulation of these novels is always deft and the iridescent phrasing is the product of an unusually "jeweled" brain. An omnibus volume *Collected Prose of Elinor Wylie* (1933) includes the four novels besides ten uncollected short stories and essays introduced by William Rose Benét in the section "Fugitive Prose." Although one must admire the fine-spun filigree of *Jennifer Lorn* and the delicate diablerie of *The Venetian Glass Nephew,* even the height of her prose cannot match the peaks attained by such poems as "This Corruptible," "Hymn to Earth" and "O Virtuous Light."

For it was as a poet that Elinor Wylie was most at home in the world, and it is as a poet that she will be remembered. Whether she spins a web of words to catch an elusive whimsicality, or satirizes herself, or plunges from the fragmentary to the profound, every line bears her authentic stamp. The intellectual versatility is eventually reënforced by spiritual strength, insuring permanence to work which "preserves a shape utterly its own."

### THE EAGLE AND THE MOLE

Avoid the reeking herd,
Shun the polluted flock,
Live like that stoic bird,
The eagle of the rock.

The huddled warmth of crowds
Begets and fosters hate;
He keeps, above the clouds,
His cliff inviolate.

When flocks are folded warm,
And herds to shelter run,
He sails above the storm,
He stares into the sun.

If in the eagle's track
Your sinews cannot leap,
Avoid the lathered pack,
Turn from the steaming sheep.

If you would keep your soul
From spotted sight or sound,
Live like the velvet mole;
Go burrow underground.

And there hold intercourse
With roots of trees and stones,
With rivers at their source,
And disembodied bones.

### THE KNIGHT FALLEN ON EVIL DAYS

God send the Devil is a gentleman,
Else had I none amongst mine enemies!
O what uncouth and cruel times are these
In which the unlettered Boor and Artisan,
The snarling Priest and smirking Lawyer can
Spit filthy enmity at whom they please—
At one, returned from spilling overseas
The Princely blood of foes Olympian.

Apothecaries curse me, who of late
Was cursed by Kings for slaughtering French lords!
Friendless and loverless is my estate,
Yet God be praised that Hell at least affords
An adversary worthy of my hate,
With whom the Angels deigned to measure swords!

### PEGASUS LOST

And there I found a gray and ancient ass,
With dull glazed stare, and stubborn wrinkled smile,
Sardonic, mocking my wide-eyed amaze.
A clumsy hulking form in that white place
At odds with the small stable, cleanly, Greek,
The marble manger and the golden oats.
With loathing hands I felt the ass's side,
Solidly real and hairy to the touch.
Then knew I that I dreamed not, but saw truth;
And knowing, wished I still might hope I dreamed.
The door stood wide, I went into the air.
The day was blue and filled with rushing wind,
A day to ride high in the heavens and taste
The glory of the gods who tread the stars.
Up in the mighty purity I saw
A flashing shape that gladly sprang aloft—
My little Pegasus, like a far white bird
Seeking sun-regions, never to return.
Silently then I turned my steps about,
Entered the stable, saddled the slow ass;
Then on its back I journeyed dustily
Between sun-wilted hedgerows into town.

### MADMAN'S SONG

Better to see your cheek grown hollow,
Better to see your temple worn,
Than to forget to follow, follow,
After the sound of a silver horn.

Better to bind your brow with willow
And follow, follow until you die,
Than to sleep with your head on a golden pillow,
Nor lift it up when the hunt goes by.

Better to see your cheek grown sallow
And your hair grown gray, so soon, so soon,
Than to forget to hallo, hallo,
After the milk-white hounds of the moon.

### SANCTUARY

This is the bricklayer; hear the thud
Of his heavy load dumped down on stone.
His lustrous bricks are brighter than blood,
His smoking mortar whiter than bone.

Set each sharp-edged, fire-bitten brick
Straight by the plumb-line's shivering length;
Make my marvelous wall so thick
Dead nor living may shake its strength.

Full as a crystal cup with drink
Is my cell with dreams, and quiet, and cool. . . .
Stop, old man! You must leave a chink;
How can I breathe? *You can't, you fool!*

### VELVET SHOES

Let us walk in the white snow
    In a soundless space;
With footsteps quiet and slow,
    At a tranquil pace,
    Under veils of white lace.

I shall go shod in silk,
    And you in wool,
White as a white cow's milk,
    More beautiful
    Than the breast of a gull.

We shall walk through the still town
    In a windless peace;
We shall step upon white down,
    Upon silver fleece,
    Upon softer than these.

We shall walk in velvet shoes:
    Wherever we go

Silence will fall like dews
    On white silence below.
    We shall walk in the snow.

### ESCAPE

When foxes eat the last gold grape,
And the last white antelope is killed,
I shall stop fighting and escape
Into a little house I'll build.

But first I'll shrink to fairy size,
With a whisper no one understands,
Making blind moons of all your eyes,
And muddy roads of all your hands.

And you may grope for me in vain
In hollows under the mangrove root,
Or where, in apple-scented rain,
The silver wasp-nests hang like fruit.

### GOLDEN BOUGH

These lovely groves of fountain-trees that shake
    A burning spray against autumnal cool,
Descend again in molten drops to make
    The rutted path a river and a pool.

They rise in silence, fall in quietude,
    Lie still as looking-glass to every sense;
Only their lion-color in the wood
    Roars to miraculous heat and turbulence.

### AUGUST

Why should this Negro insolently stride
Down the red noonday on such noiseless feet?
Piled in his barrow, tawnier than wheat,
Lie heaps of smoldering daisies, somber-eyed,
Their copper petals shriveled up with pride,
Hot with a superfluity of heat,
Like a great brazier borne along the street
By captive leopards, black and burning pied.

Are there no water-lilies, smooth as cream,
With long stems dripping crystal? Are there none
Like those white lilies, luminous and cool,
Plucked from some hemlock-darkened northern stream
By fair-haired swimmers, diving where the sun
Scarce warms the surface of the deepest pool?

### PURITAN SONNET

Down to the Puritan marrow of my bones
There's something in this richness that I hate.
I love the look, austere, immaculate,
Of landscapes drawn in pearly monotones.
There's something in my very blood that owns
Bare hills, cold silver on a sky of slate,
A thread of water, churned to milky spate
Streaming through slanted pastures fenced with stones.

I love those skies, thin blue or snowy gray,
Those fields sparse-planted, rendering meager sheaves;
That spring, briefer than apple-blossom's breath,
Summer, so much too beautiful to stay,
Swift autumn, like a bonfire of leaves,
And sleepy winter, like the sleep of death.

### NEBUCHADNEZZAR

My body is weary to death of my mischievous brain;
I am weary forever and ever of being brave;
Therefore I crouch on my knees while the cool white rain
Curves the clover over my head like a wave.

The stem and the frosty seed of the grass are ripe;
I have devoured their strength; I have drunk them deep;
And the dandelion is gall in a thin green pipe,
But the clover is honey and sun and the smell of sleep.

### LET NO CHARITABLE HOPE

Now let no charitable hope
Confuse my mind with images
Of eagle and of antelope;
I am in nature none of these.

I was, being human, born alone;
I am, being woman, hard beset;
I live by squeezing from a stone
The little nourishment I get.

In masks outrageous and austere
The years go by in single file;
But none has merited my fear,
And none has quite escaped my smile.

### CONFESSION OF FAITH

I lack the braver mind
That dares to find
The lover friend, and kind.

I fear him to the bone;
I lie alone
By the beloved one,

And, breathless for suspense,
Erect defense
Against love's violence

Whose silences portend
A bloody end
For lover never friend.

But, in default of faith,
In futile breath,
I dream no ill of Death.

### "DESOLATION IS A DELICATE THING"

Sorrow lay upon my breast more heavily than winter clay
Lying ponderable upon the unmoving bosom of the dead;
Yet it was dissolved like a thin snowfall; it was softly withered away;
Presently like a single drop of dew it had trembled and fled.

This sorrow, which seemed heavier than a shovelful of loam,
Was gone like water, like a web of delicate frost;
It was silent and vanishing like smoke; it was scattered like foam;
Though my mind should desire to preserve it, nevertheless it is lost.

This sorrow was not like sorrow; it was shining and brief;
Even as I waked and was aware of its going, it was past and gone;
It was not earth; it was no more than a light leaf,
Or a snowflake in spring, which perishes upon stone.

This sorrow was small and vulnerable and short-lived;
It was neither earth nor stone; it was silver snow
Fallen from heaven, perhaps; it has not survived
An hour of the sun; it is sad it should be so.

This sorrow, which I believed a gravestone over my heart,
Is gone like a cloud; it eluded me as I woke;
Its crystal dust is suddenly broken and blown apart;
It was not my heart; it was this poor sorrow alone which broke.


## PETER AND JOHN

Twelve good friends
Walked under the leaves
Binding the ends
Of the barley sheaves.

Peter and John
Lay down to sleep
Pillowed upon
A haymaker's heap.

John and Peter
Lay down to dream.
The air was sweeter
Than honey and cream.

Peter was bred
In the salty cold.
His hair was red
And his eyes were gold.

John had a mouth
Like a wing bent down.
His brow was smooth
And his eyes were brown.

Peter to slumber
Sank like a stone,
Of all their number
The bravest one.

John more slowly
Composed himself,
Young and holy
Among the Twelve.

John as he slept
Cried out in grief,
Turned and wept
On the golden leaf:

"Peter, Peter,
Stretch me your hand
Across the glitter
Of the harvest land!

"Peter, Peter,
Give me a sign!
This was a bitter
Dream of mine,—

"Bitter as aloes
It parched my tongue.
Upon the gallows
My life was hung.

"Sharp it seemed
As a bloody sword.
Peter, I dreamed
I was Christ the Lord!"

Peter turned
To holy Saint John:
His body burned
In the falling sun.

In the falling sun
He burned like flame:
"John, Saint John,
I have dreamed the same!

"My bones were hung
On an elder tree;
Bells were rung
Over Galilee.

"A silver penny
Sealed each of my eyes.
Many and many
A cock crew thrice."

When Peter's word
Was spoken and done,
"Were you Christ the Lord
In your dream?" said John.

"No," said the other,
"That I was not.
I was our brother
Iscariot."

## FULL MOON

My bands of silk and miniver
Momently grew heavier;
The black gauze was beggarly thin;
The ermine muffled mouth and chin;
I could not suck the moonlight in.

Harlequin in lozenges
Of love and hate, I walked in these
Striped and ragged rigmaroles;
Along the pavement my footsoles
Trod warily on living coals.·

Shouldering the thoughts I loathed,
In their corrupt disguises clothed,
Mortality I could not tear
From my ribs, to leave them bare
Ivory in silver air.

There I walked and there I raged;
The spiritual savage caged
Within my skeleton, raged afresh
To feel, behind a carnal mesh,
The clean bones crying in the flesh.

## EPITAPH

For this she starred her eyes with salt
And scooped her temples thin,
Until her face shone pure of fault
From the forehead to the chin.

In coldest crucible of pain
Her shrinking flesh was fired
And smoothed into a finer grain
To make it more desired.

Pain left her lips more clear than glass;
It colored and cooled her hand.
She lay a field of scented grass
Yielded as pasture land.

For this her loveliness was curved
And carved as silver is:
For this she was brave: but she deserved
A better grave than this.

## BIRTHDAY SONNET

Take home Thy prodigal child, O Lord of Hosts!
Protect the sacred from the secular danger;
Advise her, that Thou never needst avenge her;
Marry her mind neither to man's nor ghost's
Nor holier domination's, if the costs
Of such commingling should transport or change her;
Defend her from familiar and stranger,
And earth's and air's contagions and rusts.

Instruct her strictly to preserve Thy gift
And alter not its grain in atom sort;
Angels may wed her to their ultimate hurt
And men embrace a specter in a shift
So that no drop of the pure spirit fall
Into the dust; defend Thy prodigal.

## O VIRTUOUS LIGHT

A private madness has prevailed
Over the pure and valiant mind;
The instrument of reason failed
And the star-gazing eyes struck blind.

Sudden excess of light has wrought
Confusion in the secret place
Where the slow miracles of thought
Take shape through patience into grace.

Mysterious as steel and flint
The birth of this destructive spark
Whose inward growth has power to print
Strange suns upon the natural dark.

O break the walls of sense in half
And make the spirit fugitive!
This light begotten of itself
Is not a light by which to live!

The fire of farthing tallow dips
Dispels the menace of the skies
So it illuminate the lips
And enter the discerning eyes.

O virtuous light, if thou be man's
Or matter of the meteor stone,
Prevail against this radiance
Which is engendered of its own!

## THE PEBBLE

If any have a stone to shy,
Let him be David and not I;
The lovely shepherd, brave and vain,
Who has a maggot in the brain,
Which, since the brain is bold and pliant,
Takes the proportions of a giant.
Alas, my legendary fate!
Who sometimes rage, but never hate.
Long, long before the pebble flieth
I see a virtue in Goliath;

Yea, in the Philistine his face,
A touching majesty and grace;
Then like the lights of evening shine
The features of the Philistine
Until my spirit faints to see
The beauty of my enemy.
If any have a stone to fling
Let him be a shepherd-king,
Who is himself so beautiful
He may detest the gross and dull
With holy rage and heavenly pride
To make a pebble sanctified
And feather its course with wings of scorn.
But, from the day that I was born
Until like corn I bow to the sickle,
I am in hatred false and fickle.
I am most cruel to anyone
Who hates me with devotion;
I will not freeze, I will not burn;
I make his heart a poor return
For all the passion that he spends
In swearing we shall never be friends;
For all the pains his passion spent
In hatred I am impotent;
The sad perversity of my mind
Sees in him my kin and kind.
Alas, my shameful heritage,
False in hate and fickle in rage!
Alas, to lack the power to loathe!
I like them each; I love them both;
Philistine and shepherd-king
They strike the pebble from my sling;
My heart grows cold, my spirit grows faint;
Behold, a hero and a saint
Where appeared, a moment since,
A giant and a heathen prince;
And I am bound and given over
To be no better than a lover,
Alas, who strove as a holy rebel!
They have broke my sling and stole my
    pebble:
If any have a stone to throw
It is not I, ever or now.

## SONNET FROM "ONE PERSON"

I hereby swear that to uphold your house
I would lay my bones in quick destroying lime
Or turn my flesh to timber for all time;
Cut down my womanhood; lop off the boughs

Of that perpetual ecstasy that grows
From the heart's core; condemn it as a crime
If it be broader than a beam, or climb
Above the stature that your roof allows.

I am not the hearthstone nor the cornerstone
Within this noble fabric you have builded;
Not by my beauty was its cornice gilded;
Not on my courage were its arches thrown:
My lord, adjudge my strength, and set me where
I bear a little more than I can bear.

### THIS CORRUPTIBLE

The Body, long oppressed
And pierced, then prayed for rest
(Being but apprenticed to the other Powers);
And kneeling in that place
Implored the thrust of grace
Which makes the dust lie level with the flowers.

Then did that fellowship
Of three, the Body strip;
Beheld his wounds, and none among them mortal;
The Mind severe and cool;
The Heart still half a fool;
The fine-spun Soul, a beam of sun can startle.

These three, a thousand years
Had made adventurers
Amid all villainies the earth can offer,
Applied them to resolve
From the universal gulph
What pangs the poor material flesh may suffer.

"This is a pretty pass;
To hear the growing grass
Complain; the clay cry out to be translated;
Will not this grosser stuff
Receive reward enough
If stabled after laboring, and baited?"

Thus spoke the Mind in scorn.
The Heart, which had outworn
The Body, and was weary of its fashion,
Preferring to be dressed
In skin of bird or beast,
Replied more softly, in a feigned compassion.

"Anatomy most strange
Crying to chop and change;

Inferior copy of a higher image;
While I, the noble guest,
Sick of your second-best
Sigh for embroidered archangelic plumage:

"For shame, thou fustian cloak!"
And then the Spirit spoke;
Within the void it swung securely tethered
By strings composed of cloud;
It spoke both low and loud
Above a storm no lesser star had weathered.

"O lodging for the night!
O house of my delight!
O lovely hovel builded for my pleasure!
Dear tenement of clay
Endure another day
As coffin sweetly fitted to my measure.

"Take Heart and call to Mind
Although we are unkind;
Although we steal your shelter, strength, and clothing;
'Tis you who shall escape
In some enchanting shape
Or be dissolved to elemental nothing.

"You, the unlucky slave,
Are the lily on the grave;
The wave that runs above the bones a-whitening;
You are the new-mown grass;
And the wheaten bread of the Mass;
And the fabric of the rain, and the lightning.

"If one of us elect
To leave the poor suspect
Imperfect bosom of the earth our parent;
And from the world avert
The Spirit of the Heart
Upon a further and essential errand;

"His chain he cannot slough
Nor cast his substance off;
He bears himself upon his flying shoulder;
The Heart, infirm and dull;
The Mind, in any skull;
Are captive still, and wearier and colder.

" 'Tis you who are the ghost,
Disintegrated, lost;
The burden shed; the dead who need not bear it;
O grain of God in power,
Endure another hour!
It is but for an hour," said the Spirit.

HYMN TO EARTH

Farewell, incomparable element,
Whence man arose, where he shall not return;
And hail, imperfect urn
Of his last ashes, and his firstborn fruit;
Farewell, the long pursuit,
And all the adventures of his discontent;
The voyages which sent
His heart averse from home:
Metal of clay, permit him that he come
To thy slow-burning fire as to a hearth;
Accept him as a particle of earth.

Fire, being divided from the other three,
It lives removed, or secret at the core;
Most subtle of the four,
When air flies not, nor water flows,
It disembodied goes,
Being light, elixir of the first decree,
More volatile than he;
With strength and power to pass
Through space, where never his least atom was:
He has no part in it, save as his eyes
Have drawn its emanation from the skies.

A wingless creature heavier than air,
He is rejected of its quintessence;
Coming and going hence,
In the twin minutes of his birth and death,
He may inhale as breath,
As breath relinquish heaven's atmosphere,
Yet in it have no share,
Nor can survive therein
Where its outer edge is filtered pure and thin:
It doth but lend its crystal to his lungs
For his early crying, and his final songs.

The element of water has denied
Its child; it is no more his element;
It never will relent;
Its silver harvests are more sparsely given
Than the rewards of heaven,
And he shall drink cold comfort at its side:
The water is too wide:
The seamew and the gull
Feather a nest made soft and pitiful
Upon its foam; he has not any part
In the long swell of sorrow at its heart.

Hail and farewell, beloved element,
Whence he departed, and his parent once;
See where thy spirit runs
Which for so long hath had the moon to wife;
Shall this support his life
Until the arches of the waves be bent
And grow shallow and spent?
Wisely it cast him forth
With his dead weight of burdens nothing worth,
Leaving him, for the universal years,
A little seawater to make his tears.

Hail, element of earth, receive thy own,
And cherish, at thy charitable breast,
This man, this mongrel beast:
He plows the sand, and, at his hardest need,
He sows himself for seed;
He plows the furrow, and in this lies down
Before the corn is grown;
Between the apple bloom
And the ripe apple is sufficient room
In time, and matter, to consume his love
And make him parcel of a cypress grove.

Receive him as thy lover for an hour
Who will not weary, by a longer stay,
The kind embrace of clay;
Even within thine arms he is dispersed
To nothing, as at first;
The air flings downward from its four-quartered tower
Him whom the flames devour;
At the full tide, at the flood,
The sea is mingled with his salty blood:
The traveler dust, although the dust be vile,
Sleeps as thy lover for a little while.

# Gladys Cromwell

GLADYS CROMWELL was born November 28, 1885, in New York City. She was educated in New York private schools and lived abroad a great deal. "Her life," writes Anne Dunn, "was little indented by outer events, being wholly of the mind and spirit." She was most at home in the world within herself, sensitive and —to the final, tragic degree—self-effacing.

In January, 1918, Gladys and Dorothea, her twin-sister, enrolled in the Canteen Service of the Red Cross, sailed for France and were stationed at Châlons. Both girls worked unremittingly for eight months. It was only at the end of their desperate labors that they gave way to hopelessness, believing their efforts futile and the whole world desolate. Signs of a mental breakdown occur in their diaries as early as October. "After the armistice," writes Anne Dunn in her biographical note which serves as an epilogue to Gladys Cromwell's *Poems,* "they showed symptoms of nervous prostration; but years of self-control and consideration for others made them conceal the black horror in which they lived, the agony through which they saw a world which, they felt, contained no refuge for beauty or quiet thought. And when, on their way home, they jumped from the deck of the *Lorraine* it was in response to a vision that promised them fulfillment and peace." After their death, which occurred January 19, 1919, the French Government awarded the two sisters the Croix de Guerre.

*Gates of Utterance* (1915) has something more than the usual "promise." But the best of Miss Cromwell's work can be found in her posthumously published *Poems* (1919), which, in 1920, received the yearly prize offered by the Poetry Society of America, dividing the honor with Neihardt's *The Song of Three Friends.* Gladys Cromwell's most significant poems betray that attitude to life which was at the heart of her tragedy—a mixture of fascination and fear. Her lines, never mediocre, are introspective and taut with serious concern. A few of her delicate songs tremble on the verge of something great just beyond the power of achievement.

### THE CROWNING GIFT

I have had courage to accuse;
And a fine wit that could upbraid;
And a nice cunning that could bruise;
And a shrewd wisdom, unafraid
Of what weak mortals fear to lose.

I have had virtue to despise
The sophistry of pious fools;
I have had firmness to chastise;
And intellect to make me rules
To estimate and exorcise.

I have had knowledge to be true;
My faith could obstacles remove;
But now my frailty I endue.
I would have courage now to love,
And lay aside the strength I knew.

### THE MOULD

No doubt this active will,
So bravely steeped in sun,
This will has vanquished death
And foiled oblivion.

But this indifferent clay,
This fine, experienced hand
So quiet, and these thoughts
That all unfinished stand,

Feel death as though it were
A shadowy caress;
And win and wear a frail
Archaic wistfulness.

## Ezra Pound

Ezra (LOOMIS) POUND was born at Hailey, Idaho, October 30, 1885, and entered the University of Pennsylvania at the age of fifteen. At sixteen, unbeknown to the faculty, he began studying comparative literature; before he was seventeen (in 1902) he enrolled as special student "to avoid irrelevant subjects." He continued the process at Hamilton College (1903-5) and from 1905 to 1907 was "Instructor with professorial functions" at the University of Pennsylvania. His next move brought him to Crawfordsville, Indiana—"'the Athens of the West,' a town with literary traditions, Lew Wallace having died there." Pound was dismissed from Wabash College after four months—"all accusations," he says, "having been ultimately refuted save that of being 'the Latin Quarter type.'"

Though a born educator, actually burning to teach, Pound was compelled to seek less academic circles. In 1908 he landed in Gibraltar with eighty dollars and lived on the interest for some time. The same year found him for the first time in Italy, which was to become his future home. *A Lume Spento* (1908) was printed in Venice. A few months later he was established in London, where he lived until 1920. Convinced of the aridity of England, he crossed over to Paris, from which, after four years, he moved to Rapallo, on the Italian Riviera, where he has lived since 1924.

Shortly after Pound's arrival in London he published *Personae* (1909), a work which, though small, contains some of his most arresting verse.

Although the young American was a total stranger to the English literary world, his book made a definite impression on critics of all shades and tastes. Edward Thomas, one of the most cautious appraisers, wrote, "The beauty of it is the beauty of passion, sincerity and intensity, not of beautiful words and images and suggestions. . . . The thought dominates the words and is greater than they are." Another critic (Scott James) placed the chief emphasis on Pound's metrical innovations, saying, "At first the whole thing may seem to be mere madness and rhetoric, a vain exhibition of force and passion without beauty. But as we read on, these curious meters seem to have a law and order of their own."

*Exultations* (1909) was printed in the autumn of the same year that saw the appearance of *Personae*. It was received with even greater cordiality; a new force and freedom were manifest in such poems as "Sestina: Altaforte," "Ballad of the Goodly Fere," and the stark "Ballad for Gloom." Both books were republished in a single volume, with other poems, as *Personae,* in 1926.

In these books there is evident Pound's erudition—a familiarity with medieval literature, Provençal singers, Troubadour ballads—an erudition which, later, was to degenerate into pedantry. Too often Pound seemed to become theory-logged, to sink himself in an intellectual Sargasso Sea, to be more the archeologist than the artist. *Canzoni* (1911) and *Ripostes* (1912) contain much that is sharp and living; they also contain the germs of desiccation and decay. Pound began to scatter his talents; to start movements which he quickly discarded for new ones; to spend himself in poetic propaganda for the Vorticists and others; to give more and more time to translation (*The Sonnets of Guido Cavalcanti* appeared in 1912) and arrangements from the Chinese (*Cathay,* paraphrased from the notes of Ernest Fenollosa, was issued in 1915); to lay the chief stress on technique, shades of color, verbal *nuances*. The result was a lassitude of the creative faculties, an impoverishment of emotion. In the later books, Pound seemed to suffer from a decadence which appraises the values in life chiefly as esthetic values.

*Lustra* appeared in 1916. In this collection, as in the preceding volumes, Pound struggled with his influences; accents of Swinburne, Browning, Lionel Johnson, and Yeats mingled with those of the Provençal poets. From his immediate predecessors Pound learned the value of "verse as speech" while, as Eliot has pointed out, from the more antiquarian studies Pound was learning the importance of "speech as song." It was not until *Hugh Selwyn Mauberley* (1920) and the *Cantos* that Pound integrated his own inflection, form, and philosophy.

The *Cantos,* as yet unfinished, must be recognized as Pound's chief work. The poem (for the *Cantos* are parts of a loosely connected *major opus*) when and if completed will comprise about one hundred "chapters." So far forty-one cantos have been published: *Cantos I-XVI* in 1925; *XVII-XXVII* in 1928; *A Draft of XXX Cantos* in 1930; *Eleven New Cantos: XXXI to XLI* in 1934. Complex in tone, bewildering in their shiftings of time and space, of many languages and multiple accents, the *Cantos* are easier to grasp in theory than in practice. Only a scholar versed in many cultures can pretend to follow the digressions, the obscure references, the self-interrupted narratives, comments, myths, legends, imprecations, jokes, the whole curious ambivalence which worships and destroys the poetic tradition in the same movement. Yet the scheme of the *Cantos* is reasoned and even formal: Pound is attempting to write a Human Comedy in several dimensions and many voices, using the repetitions of history as recurring leitmotifs. The structure is intended to be fugual (with subject, response, and counter-subject) and Pound, who has written music as well as words, has conceived the work on a huge scale. It juxtaposes the jargon of the modern world with disrupted quotations and a vast, even violent, scholasticism.

Critical opinion of the *Cantos* was sharply divided. To many the indicated pattern was a masterpiece of obfuscation, a jig-saw puzzle with the important pieces missing. "About the poems," wrote Edward Fitzgerald, "there hangs a dismal mist of unresolved confusion. Through that mist we can see fact, but fact historically stated, enlivened in no way by either a creative or a critical process." Some found it a garble of literature and nothing else, composed of scraps from newspapers, oddments from documents difficult of access, and the minor classics, all piled upon each other without an original idea or an experience outside of print. To others it was a modern Gospel. "One of the three great works of poetry of our time," wrote Allen Tate. Ford Madox Ford's enthusiasm was even less guarded. "The first words you have to say about the *Cantos,*" said Ford, "is: Their extraordinary beauty . . . They form an unparalleled history of a world seen from those shores which are the home of our civilization." John Crowe Ransom's estimate was more temperate. He concluded, "Mr. Pound, in his capacity of guide to literature, never wearies of telling us about the troubadour songs of Provence, which he reveres. He lays down the law that, the further the poem goes from its original character of song, the more dubious is its estate. But what if we apply that canon to the *Cantos?* The result is that we find ourselves sometimes admiring in Mr. Pound's poetry an effect of brilliance and nearly always missing the effect of poetry."

Whatever differences arose concerning the finality of Pound's performance, none could dispute the power of his influence. The accent of the *Cantos* can be traced through Eliot's *The Waste Land,* Hart Crane's *The Bridge,* and MacLeish's longer poems, particularly his *Conquistador.* Moreover, any attempt to do justice to Pound must take account of the chronology of his work in relation to others. He invented the term "Imagism" and organized the Imagist school long before the ensuing period of exploitation. He published *Cathay* in 1915, and rendered *Certain Noble Plays of Japan from the Fenollosa Manuscripts,* anticipating the flood of Chinese and Japanese translations that, soon after, inundated the country. He "placed" Tagore as literary artist, not as messiah, and saw the Bengalese poet become a cult. He fought for the musician George Antheil; wrote a study of Gaudier Brzeska, when that sculptor was unknown; created a controversy by his Provençal paraphrases, expanded his Italian studies into *The Poems of Guido Cavalcanti* (1930). As early as 1922 he established the proportion between Flaubert and James Joyce when the author of *Ulysses* was an unfamiliar name. Years later Joyce acknowledged the indebtedness: "Nothing could be more true than to say we all owe a great deal to him—I, surely, most of all." William Butler Yeats changed the idiom of his romantic lyrics to the conversational tone of his later poetry largely because of his admiration for Pound's condensations. Eliot wrote a laudatory introduction to Pound's *Selected Poems* (1928), which Eliot edited with his friend's assistance, affirming that the *Cantos* are "the only poem of some length by any of my contemporaries that I can read with enjoyment and admiration."

Besides his poetry Pound wrote, translated, and edited more than fourteen volumes of prose, the most characteristic being *A B C of Reading* (1934), an exposition of a critical method; *Make it New* (1935), which is a deceptive title since all but one of the essays appeared in *Pavannes and Divisions* (1918) and *Instigations* (1920); and the little known *Imaginary Letters*.

Too special to achieve permanence, too erudite to become popular, Pound's contribution to the period should not be underestimated. He was a pioneer in the new forms; he fought dullness wherever he encountered it; he experimented in a poetic speech which was alive and essentially his own, an idiom far more lively than his subject matter. "If a man succeeds in producing work which has a new direction he will twist the road for all who come after him," wrote Archibald MacLeish, acknowledging his indebtedness. "A new technique may open to poetry a whole world from which it has been previously excluded, or a new tone may profoundly alter the relation of the poet to *any* world." This new tone and technique helped broaden a path recognized by a few and unacknowledged by many more who followed the trail nonchalantly, unconscious of who had blazed it. Much of Pound's art is difficult, much of it is poetry in pantomime, but even the dumb-show gestures and the difficulties are significant. Pound's own self-estimate must be appreciated

> . . . seeing he had been born
> In a half-savage country, out of date;
> Bent resolutely on wringing lilies from the acorn . . .

One must also remember, by way of quotation and conclusion, that, in spite of a twisted pedantry and a dependence on the literary life, he strove

> . . . to resuscitate the dead art
> Of poetry; to maintain "the sublime"
> In the old sense.

Whether he survives as poet or influence, critic or creator, his importance must be acknowledged.

### AN IMMORALITY

> Sing we for love and idleness,
> Naught else is worth the having.

Though I have been in many a land,
There is naught else in living.

And I would rather have my sweet,
Though rose-leaves die of grieving,

Than do high deeds in Hungary
To pass all men's believing.


### A VIRGINAL

No, no! Go from me. I have left her lately.
I will not spoil my sheath with lesser brightness,
For my surrounding air has a new lightness;
Slight are her arms, yet they have bound me straitly
And left me cloaked as with a gauze of ether;
As with sweet leaves; as with a subtle clearness.
Oh, I have picked up magic in her nearness
To sheathe me half in half the things that sheathe her.

No, no! Go from me. I have still the flavor,
Soft as spring wind that's come from birchen bowers.
Green come the shoots, aye April in the branches,
As winter's wound with her sleight hand she staunches,
Hath of the trees a likeness of the savor:
As white their bark, so white this lady's hours.


### BALLAD FOR GLOOM

For God, our God is a gallant foe
That playeth behind the veil.

I have loved my God as a child at heart
That seeketh deep bosoms for rest,
I have loved my God as a maid to man—
But lo, this thing is best:

To love your God as a gallant foe that plays behind the veil;
To meet your God as the night winds meet beyond Arcturus' pale.

I have played with God for a woman,
I have staked with my God for truth,
I have lost to my God as a man, clear-eyed—
   His dice be not of ruth.

For I am made as a naked blade,
   But hear ye this thing in sooth:

Who loseth to God as man to man
   Shall win at the turn of the game.
I have drawn my blade where the lightnings meet

But the ending is the same:
Who loseth to God as the sword blades lose
Shall win at the end of the game.

For God, our God is a gallant foe that playeth behind the veil.
Whom God deigns not to overthrow hath need of triple mail.

### GREEK EPIGRAM

Day and night are never weary,
Nor yet is God of creating
For day and night their torch-bearers
The aube and the crepuscule.

So, when I weary of praising the dawn and
the sunset,
Let me be no more counted among the im-
mortals;
But number me amid the wearying ones,
Let me be a man as the herd,
And as the slave that is given in barter.

### BALLAD OF THE GOODLY FERE [1]

*(Simon Zelotes speaketh it somewhile after
the Crucifixion)*

Ha' we lost the goodliest fere o' all
For the priests and the gallows tree?
Aye, lover he was of brawny men,
O' ships and the open sea.

When they came wi' a host to take Our Man
His smile was good to see,
"First let these go!" quo' our Goodly Fere,
"Or I'll see ye damned," says he.

Aye, he sent us out through the crossed high
spears,
And the scorn of his laugh rang free,
"Why took ye not me when I walked about
Alone in the town?" says he.

Oh we drank his "Hale" in the good red
wine
When we last made company,
No capon priest was the Goodly Fere
But a man o' men was he.

I ha' seen him drive a hundred men
Wi' a bundle o' cords swung free,

[1] Fere = Mate, Companion.

When they took the high and holy house
For their pawn and treasury.

They'll no get him a' in a book I think
Though they write it cunningly;
No mouse of the scrolls was the Goodly
Fere
But aye loved the open sea.

If they think they ha' snared our Goodly Fere
They are fools to the last degree.
"I'll go to the feast," quo' our Goodly Fere,
"Though I go to the gallows tree."

"Ye ha' seen me heal the lame and the blind,
And wake the dead," says he,
"Ye shall see one thing to master all:
'Tis how a brave man dies on the tree."

A son of God was the Goodly Fere
That bade us his brothers be.
I ha' seen him cow a thousand men.
I ha' seen him upon the tree.

He cried no cry when they drave the nails
And the blood gushed hot and free,
The hounds of the crimson sky gave tongue
But never a cry cried he.

I ha' seen him cow a thousand men
On the hills o' Galilee,
They whined as he walked out calm between,
Wi' his eyes like the gray o' the sea.

Like the sea that brooks no voyaging
With the winds unleashed and free,
Like the sea that he cowed at Gennesaret
Wi' twey words spoke' suddenly.

A master of men was the Goodly Fere,
A mate of the wind and sea,
If they think they ha' slain our Goodly Fere
They are fools eternally.

I ha' seen him eat o' the honey-comb
Sin' they nailed him to the tree.

### A GIRL

The tree has entered my hands,
The sap has ascended my arms,
The tree has grown in my breast
Downward,
The branches grow out of me, like arms.

Tree you are,
Moss you are,
You are violets with wind above them.
A child—so high—you are;
And all this is folly to the world.

### IN A STATION OF THE METRO

The apparition of these faces in the crowd;
Petals on a wet, black bough.

### DANCE FIGURE

(*For the Marriage in Cana of Galilee*)

Dark eyed,
O woman of my dreams,
Ivory sandaled,
There is none like thee among the dancers,
None with swift feet.

I have not found thee in the tents,
In the broken darkness.
I have not found thee at the well-head
Among the women with pitchers.
Thine arms are as a young sapling under the bark;
Thy face as a river with lights.

White as an almond are thy shoulders;
As new almonds stripped from the husk.
They guard thee not with eunuchs;
Not with bars of copper.

Gilt turquoise and silver are in the place of thy rest.
A brown robe with threads of gold woven in patterns hast thou gathered about thee,
O Nathat-Ikanaie, "Tree-at-the-river."

As a rillet among the sedge are thy hands upon me;
Thy fingers a frosted stream.

Thy maidens are white like pebbles;
Their music about thee!

There is none like thee among the dancers;
None with swift feet.

### ΔΩΡΙΑ

Be in me as the eternal moods
        of the bleak wind, and not
    As transient things are—
        gayety of flowers.

> Have me in the strong loneliness
>                     of sunless cliffs
> And of gray waters.
>                     Let the gods speak softly of us
> In days hereafter,
>                     the shadowy flowers of Orcus
> Remember thee.

### SILET

When I behold how black, immortal ink
Drips from my deathless pen—ah, well-away!
Why should we stop at all for what I think?
There is enough in what I chance to say.

It is enough that we once came together;
What is the use of setting it to rime?
When it is autumn do we get spring weather,
Or gather may of harsh northwindish time?

It is enough that we once came together;
What if the wind have turned against the rain?
It is enough that we once came together;
Time has seen this, and will not turn again.

And who are we, who know that last intent,
To plague tomorrow with a testament!

### PORTRAIT D'UNE FEMME[1]

Your mind and you are our Sargasso Sea,
London has swept about you this score years
And bright ships left you this or that in fee:
Ideas, old gossip, oddments of all things,
Strange spars of knowledge and dimmed wares of price.
Great minds have sought you—lacking someone else.
You have been second always. Tragical?
No. You preferred it to the usual thing:
One dull man, dulling and uxorious,
One average mind—with one thought less, each year.
Oh, you are patient. I have seen you sit
Hours, where something might have floated up.
And now you pay one. Yes, you richly pay.
You are a person of some interest, one comes to you
And takes strange gain away:
Trophies fished up; some curious suggestion;
Fact that leads nowhere; and a tale for two,
Pregnant with mandrakes, or with something else
That might prove useful and yet never proves,
That never fits a corner or shows use,

[1] Compare the poem on the same theme on page 425.

Or finds its hour upon the loom of days:
The tarnished, gaudy, wonderful old work;
Idols, and ambergris and rare inlays.
These are your riches, your great store; and yet
For all this sea-hoard of deciduous things,
Strange woods half sodden, and new brighter stuff:
In the slow float of differing light and deep,
No! there is nothing! In the whole and all,
Nothing that's quite your own.

                                  Yet this is you.

### THE RETURN

See, they return; ah see the tentative
Movements, and the slow feet,
The trouble in the pace and the
       uncertain
Wavering!

See, they return, one, and by one,
With fear, as half-awakened;
As if the snow should hesitate
And murmur in the wind,
       and half turn back;
These were the "Wing'd-with-Awe,"
       Inviolable.

Gods of the wingèd shoe!
With them the silver hounds,
       sniffing the trace of air!

Haie! Haie!
    These were the swift to harry;
These were the keen-scented;
These were the souls of blood.

Slow on the leash,
       pallid the leash-men!

### ENVOI

Go, dumb-born book,
Tell her that sang me once that song of
   Lawes:
Hadst thou but song
As thou hast subjects known,
Then were there cause in thee that should
   condone
Even my faults that heavy upon me lie,
And build her glories their longevity.

Tell her that sheds
Such treasure in the air,
Recking naught else but that her graces give
Life to the moment,
I would bid them live
As roses might, in magic amber laid,
Red overwrought with orange and all made
One substance and one color
Braving time.

Tell her that goes
With song upon her lips
But sings not out the song, nor knows
The maker of it, some other mouth,
May be as fair as hers,
Might, in new ages, gain her worshipers,
When our two dusts with Waller's shall be
   laid,
Siftings on siftings in oblivion,
Till change hath broken down
All things save Beauty alone.

### THE REST

O helpless few in my country,
O remnant enslaved!

Artists broken against her,
Astray, lost in the villages,
Mistrusted, spoken-against,

Lovers of beauty, starved,
Thwarted with systems,
Helpless against the control;

You who cannot wear yourselves out
By persisting to successes,
You who can only speak,
Who cannot steel yourselves into reiteration;

You of the finer sense,
Broken against false knowledge,
You who can know at first hand,
Hated, shut in, mistrusted:

Take thought:
I have weathered the storm,
I have beaten out my exile.

## ITÉ

Go, my songs, seek your praise from the young and from the intolerant,
Move among the lovers of perfection alone.
Seek ever to stand in the hard Sophoclean light
And take your wounds from it gladly.

## CANTO I

And then went down to the ship,
Set keel to breakers, forth on the godly sea, and
We set up mast and sail on that swart ship,
Bore sheep aboard her, and our bodies also
Heavy with weeping, and winds from sternward
Bore us out onward with bellying canvas,
Circe's this craft, the trim-coifed goddess.
Then sat we amidships, wind jamming the tiller,
Thus with stretched sail, we went over sea till day's end.
Sun to his slumber, shadows o'er all the ocean,
Came we then to the bounds of deepest water,
To the Kimmerian lands, and peopled cities
Covered with close-webbed mist, unpierced ever
With glitter of sun-ray
Nor with stars stretched, nor looking back from heaven
Swartest night stretched over wretched men there.
The ocean flowing backward, came we then to the place
Aforesaid by Circe.
Here did they rites, Perimedes and Eurylochus,
And drawing sword from my hip
I dug the ell-square pitkin;
Poured we libations unto each the dead,
First mead and then sweet wine, water mixed with white flour.
Then prayed I many a prayer to the sickly death's-heads;
As set in Ithaca, sterile bulls of the best
For sacrifice, heaping the pyre with goods,
A sheep to Tiresias only, black and a bell-sheep.
Dark blood flowed in the fosse,
Souls out of Erebus, cadaverous dead, of brides
Of youths and of the old who had borne much;
Souls stained with recent tears, girls tender,
Men many, mauled with bronze lance heads,
Battle spoil, bearing yet dreary arms,
These many crowded about me; with shouting,
Pallor upon me, cried to my men for more beasts;
Slaughtered the herds, sheep slain of bronze;

Poured ointment, cried to the gods,
To Pluto the strong, and praised Proserpine;
Unsheathed the narrow sword,
I sat to keep off the impetuous impotent dead,
Till I should hear Tiresias.
But first Elpenor came, our friend Elpenor,
Unburied, cast on the wide earth,
Limbs that we left in the house of Circe,
Unwept, unwrapped in sepulcher, since toils urged other.
Pitiful spirit. And I cried in hurried speech:
"Elpenor, how art thou come to this dark coast?
"Cam'st thou afoot, outstripping seamen?"
           And he in heavy speech:
"Ill fate and abundant wine. I slept in Circe's ingle.
"Going down the long ladder unguarded,
"I fell against the buttress,
"Shattered the nape-nerve, the soul sought Avernus.
"But thou, O King, I bid remember me, unwept, unburied,
"Heap up mine arms, be tomb by sea-board, and inscribed:
"*'A man of no fortune and with a name to come.'*
"And set my oar up, that I swung mid fellows."

And Anticlea came, whom I beat off, and then Tiresias Theban,
Holding his golden wand, knew me, and spoke first:
"A second time? why? man of ill star,
"Facing the sunless dead and this joyless region?
"Stand from the fosse, leave me my bloody bever
"For soothsay."
           And I stepped back,
And he strong with the blood, said then: "Odysseus
"Shalt return through spiteful Neptune, over dark seas,
"Lose all companions." And then Anticlea came.
Lie quiet Divus. I mean that is Andreas Divus,
In officina Wecheli, 1538, out of Homer.
And he sailed, by Sirens and thence outward and away
And unto Circe.
           Venerandam,
In the Cretan's phrase, with the golden crown, Aphrodite,
Cypri munimenta sortita est, mirthful, oricalchi, with golden
Girdles and breast bands, thou with dark eyelids
Bearing the golden bough of Argicida.

# *Louis Untermeyer*

LOUIS UNTERMEYER was born October 1, 1885, in New York City, where he lived, except for brief intervals, until 1923. His schooling was fitful and erratic; he liked to boast that he was the least educated writer in America. He attended the De Witt Clinton High School, but his failure to comprehend the essentials of geometry prevented him from graduating, and the halls of colleges were unknown to him until he became an occasional lecturer. In youth his one ambition was to be a composer. At sixteen he appeared as a semi-professional pianist; at seventeen he entered his father's jewelry manufacturing establishment. For nearly twenty years he commuted to Newark, New Jersey, being advanced from designer to factory manager and vice-president. In 1923 he retired and, after two years of study abroad, returned to America to devote himself entirely to literature. In 1928 he achieved a lifelong desire, acquiring a farm, a trout-stream, and half a mountain of sugar-maples in the Adirondacks, where he lives when he is not traveling and lecturing.

It is difficult for the present compiler to consider this writer as severely as he deserves, the editor not having attained toward the poet that Olympian detachment which is the goal of criticism. However, it is evident that his work is divided into four kinds: his poetry, his parodies, his translations, and his critical prose. His initial volume of verse, *First Love* (1911), was a sequence of some seventy lyrics in which the influences of Heine and Housman were not only obvious but crippling. It is significant that when his *Selected Poems* appeared in 1935 just three of the seventy poems were included, and two of the three were self-satirizing.

It was with *Challenge* that the author first declared himself with any sort of integrity. Although the ghost of Henley haunts many of these pages, and the volume would benefit greatly by a few less "urges" and "surges," poems like "Prayer," and "Caliban in the Coal Mines" showed "a fresh and lyrical sympathy with the modern world. . . . His vision" (thus *The Boston Transcript*) "is a social vision, his spirit a passionately energized command of the forces of justice." *Challenge* was succeeded by *These Times* (1917), an "interval" book which, lacking the unity of its predecessor, sought, though it did not attain, larger horizons. The *New Adam* (1920) is more of a unit; "a frank expression of the modern poet's conception of love, this new Adam, caught in the eternal struggle of the flesh, is the child of a complex and analytical age."

*Roast Leviathan* (1923) was the most luxuriant of his volumes. The American critics found it too exuberant, but the English reviewers praised "the lavish use of interior rhyme and assonance, brilliant as an Oriental tapestry." "On every subject he treats," wrote Edwin Muir, "he gives opulent measure, an opulence within the reach of nobody in contemporary verse but himself." In *Burning Bush* (1928) the key is quieter, the tone surer. The author is still playing with variations in pattern and new devices in rhyme, but he has discarded almost entirely the over-muscular adjectives and heaven-storming epithets which marred his earlier work. "The restraint and suggestion," wrote Herbert S. Gorman, "the push of emotion that wholly impregnates but which is semi-obscured, the clear comprehension and unstressed technique prove that he has realized his complete maturity in poetry." *Food and Drink* (1932) is a further progress, presenting a fusion of observation and imagination rather than the determined exercise of ingenuity. Many of the poems (notably "Food and Drink" and "Last Words Before Winter") experiment in the masking of serious, even solemn, emotion in a light tone of voice. "It reveals the author as a total personality," concluded *The Boston Transcript,* "in a way that his other books have never done."

Four volumes of his parodies appeared: *The Younger Quire* (1911), a burlesque of an anthology; *—and Other Poets* (1917), chiefly distinguished by the set of Mother

Goose rhymes "rewritten" by contemporary poets; *Including Horace* (1919), paraphrases of the Latin lyricist as various classic and modern poets might have rendered him; and *Heavens* (1922), which, after gently mocking his confrères, waved a farewell to the field of parody. The four books were combined in *Collected Parodies* (1926), which the author, with great self-restraint, refrained from calling "Parodies Regained."

His interests in German backgrounds and literature were manifested in *Poems of Heinrich Heine* (1917, revised edition 1923); a translation of Ernst Toller's *Masse Mensch,* produced by the Theatre Guild in 1924; and *Blue Rhine—Black Forest* (1930), an informal guide and day-book.

Beginning with an adaptation of Gottfried Keller's Swiss stories (published under the title *The Fat of the Cat*) the author alternately wrote volumes of prose and poetry. The best of his fiction, he insists, is *Moses* (1928), miscalled a novel. Actually the work is a combination of historical reconstruction and poetic fantasia full of speculations that caused much controversy among the literalists. Other fictional work included *The Donkey of God* (1932), written for a young audience, which won the Italian Enit Award in 1934 for the best recent book on Italy written in any language by a non-Italian, and *The Last Pirate* (1934), in which the author presumed to do for Gilbert and Sullivan what the Lambs had done for Shakespeare.

A book of essays, *The New Era in American Poetry* (1919), was amplified and shaped into a more balanced set of twenty subdivided chapters as *American Poetry Since 1900* (1923). The critical anthologies *Modern American Poetry* and *Modern British Poetry* were revised and enlarged several times since their original publication in 1919 and 1920, and used as textbooks in the universities. A companion volume *American Poetry from the Beginning to Whitman* (1931) attempted a comprehensive and drastic reappraisal of native poetry from 1620 to 1880. One third of the volume was devoted to early American ballads and folk-songs.

Besides these critical compilations the editor prepared several anthologies with a minimum of prefatory or interpretive matter: *The Book of Living Verse* (1932), the widest in scope, ranging from the thirteenth century to the twentieth; *Yesterday and Today* (1927), a "comparative" collection of the present and the immediate past; *This Singing World* (1923), a selection of modern verse for a not too elderly audience; *This Singing World for Younger Readers* (1926); and *Rainbow in the Sky* (1935) for still younger people. These volumes were adopted in high schools and junior colleges, as was *The Forms of Poetry* (1926), a "pocket dictionary of verse."

A collaboration with David and Clara Mannes resulted in *New Songs for New Voices* (1928), in which the editor made his first (and last) public appearance as composer; *Poetry: Its Appreciation and Enjoyment* (1934), written with Carter Davidson, is a cross between a treatise and a textbook. His *Selected Poems and Parodies* (1935), the most representative showing of his original and satirical work, appeared on his fiftieth birthday. This volume, said William Rose Benét handsomely, "entitles him to occupy the place of a Heine in American poetry."

Besides admitting himself the author of these too numerous volumes the editor furnished introductions to some dozen other works; helped conduct *The Liberator, The Seven Arts,* and *Paper Books;* became Poetry Editor of *The American Mercury* in 1935; and wrote the articles on contemporary American poetry for the *Encyclopaedia Britannica.*

### PRAYER

od, though this life is but a wraith,
Although we know not what we use,
though we grope with little faith,
Give me the heart to fight—and lose.

er insurgent let me be,
Make me more daring than devout;
om sleek contentment keep me free,
And fill me with a buoyant doubt.

en my eyes to visions girt
With beauty, and with wonder lit—
t let me always see the dirt,
And all that spawn and die in it.

en my ears to music; let
Me thrill with Spring's first flutes and
    drums—
t never let me dare forget
The bitter ballads of the slums.

om compromise and things half-done,
Keep me, with stern and stubborn pride.
d when, at last, the fight is won,
God, keep me still unsatisfied.

### CALIBAN IN THE COAL MINES

od, we don't like to complain;
We know that the mine is no lark.
t—there's the pools from the rain;
But—there's the cold and the dark.

od, You don't know what it is—
You, in Your well-lighted sky—
atching the meteors whizz;
Warm, with a sun always by.

od, if You had but the moon
Stuck in Your cap for a lamp,
en You'd tire of it soon,
Down in the dark and the damp.

othing but blackness above
And nothing that moves but the cars. . . .
od, if You wish for our love,
Fling us a handful of stars!

### AT THE BOTTOM OF THE WELL

Something befell
    Young Adam Hope,

Who had a well
    For a telescope

In which the stars
    Came crystal-clear,
Brighter than Mars
    Or Jupiter,

Till Adam scarcely
    Looked at the sky,
Strewn so sparsely,
    Stretched so high.

Night after night,
    The neighbors tell,
He put out the light,
    He stole to the well.

To that dark funnel
    He came to pray,
"If only the sun'll
    Stay away,

"And nothing occurs
    Until I finish,
One of those stars
    Will forget to vanish.

"And when that late one
    Loafs and lingers,
I'll catch a great one
    With my fingers."

Adam's aim
    Grew fixed and stronger.
Then one night came
    That lasted longer

Than nights should last
    By natural law;
And when it passed
    The neighbors saw

Something that glistened
    Deep in the well.
They looked; they listened;
    They could not tell

The tale's conclusion.
    At the end of the rope
Was it truth or illusion,
    Or Adam Hope?

### THE DARK CHAMBER

The brain forgets, but the blood will remember.
  There, when the play of sense is over,
The last, low spark in the darkest chamber
  Will hold all there is of love and lover.

The war of words, the life-long quarrel
  Of self against self will resolve into nothing;
Less than the chain of berry-red coral
  Crying against the dead black of her clothing.

What has the brain that it hopes to last longer?
  The blood will take from forgotten violence,
The groping, the break of her voice in anger.
  There will be left only color and silence.

These will remain, these will go searching
  Your veins for life when the flame of life smolders:
The night that you two saw the mountains marching
  Up against dawn with the stars on their shoulders—

The jetting poplars' arrested fountains
  As you drew her under them, easing her pain—
The notes, not the words, of a half-finished sentence—
  The music, the silence. . . . These will remain.


### SCARCELY SPRING

Nothing is real. The world has lost its edges;
The sky, uncovered, is the one thing clear.
The earth is little more than atmosphere
Where yesterday were rocks and naked ridges.
Nothing is fixed. Tentative rain dislodges
Green upon green or lifts a coral spear
That breaks in blossom, and the hills appear
Too frail to be the stony fruit of ages.

Nothing will keep. Even the heavens waver.
Young larks, whose first thought is to cry aloud,
Have spent their bubble notes. And here or there
A few slow-hearted boys and girls discover
A moon as unsubstantial as a cloud
Painted by air on washed and watery air.


### OBITUARY

There was the world that Jackson always found
In sleep, a heaven of crime and lusty vices,
Where, swaggering in various disguises,
He killed, he conquered, and was always crowned.

And then there was the world where he was downed
By every small delay and hourly crisis;
A niggling world of customers and prices,
And reckoning the pennies to the pound.

Now who shall toll the bell for Jackson Kirke,
Who never lived his dream, nor here nor there.
Surely no demon warming to his work,
For Jackson nightly offered up his prayer;
And who on earth will ever heed a clerk
Dangling, twixt heaven and hell, in pitiless air.

### TRANSFIGURED SWAN

start—
nd the rich dart
lossoms in the unripened heart.

t last
here is no rest
or the long-locked and over-rounded breast.

o blood
ains the ecstatic moment, but a flood
f mounting gratitude.

nd the one choice
f a delivered voice
to rejoice.

f the disdains,
he frozen dreams, the unresponsive pains,
lothing remains.

nd of the wound,
Videning and unbound,
here is no sound.

raise, only praise,
xtends the throat, invents a hundred ways
o lift the swelling phrase.

ill, like an overtone of prayer, the long
choes are everywhere,
nd the loose air
stretched and strong.

lothing remains but song.

### JERUSALEM DELIVERED

King David Hotel, Jerusalem, offers Tea Dances
Vednesday and Saturday, Aperitif Concerts every
inday, and Cocktail Parties in the Winter
arden.—*Adv. in the Palestine News.*

Miriam, strike your cymbal,
     Young David, add your voice;
Once more the tribes are nimble,
     Once more the Jews rejoice.

Beneath the flowering mango
     Where peace and perfume drip,
Solomon does the tango
     And Sheba shakes a hip.

Rebekah trots with Aaron,
     Deborah treads the earth,
Fresh as the Rose of Sharon
     With evening gowns by Worth.

Susannah meets the Elders
     With an increased regard;
Pounds, dollars, marks, and guilders
     Receive their due reward.

Jerusalem the Golden,
     With milk and honey blest,
Revive the rapt and olden
     Ardor within each breast;

Add Gilead to Gomorrah;
     Fling torches through the dark;
Dancing before the Torah,
     With cocktails at the Ark!

### ON THE EVE OF NEW WARS

Man,
Do not despair;
You can surpass, with but a little care,
Nature's malevolent plan.

True,
The lion wreaks
His lust upon the lamb; talons and beaks
Sharpen on doves. But you,

Lord
Of earth and air,
Can flourish nonchalantly everywhere
Bomb, bayonet, gas and sword.

You,
Only you, can find
A formula for killing your own kind
With a fine phrase or two.

Clear
A great path abroad!
Strike down your brother for the love of God.
Prove you are master here.

### LONG FEUD

Where, without bloodshed, can there be
A more relentless enmity
Than the long feud fought silently

Between man and the growing grass.
Man's the aggressor, for he has
Weapons to humble and harass

The impudent spears that charge upon
His sacred privacy of lawn.
He mows them down, and they are gone

Only to lie in wait, although
He builds above and digs below
Where never a root would dare to go.

His are the triumphs till the day
There's no more grass to cut away
And, weary of labor, weary of play,

Having exhausted every whim,
He stretches out each conquering limb.
And then the small grass covers him.

### BURNING BUSH

And suddenly the flowing night stands still
    And the loose air grows tense and small;
Runners of flame from nowhere rise and fill
    The narrowest veins, till all

The martyrdom of fire is not enough
    For bodies eager to be doomed;
Burning in one long agony of love,
    Burning but not consumed.

And the last white blaze leaps from our being's core
    And flesh, too shaken to rejoice,
Cries out till quiet, vaster than before,
    Speaks in the still, small voice.

### UNREASONING HEART

Here in a world whose heaven is powder-white,
Where, cased in glass, the branches bear a weight
Too light for leaves and far too cold for flowers,
Nothing disturbs these alabaster floors.
The black stream does not move; it is a vein
Of onyx cropping out, a metal vine
Twisted and thrown away. There is no sound.
Blankets of snow, curtains of snow-flake sand
Bury the footsteps of the one man here.
Here, where the world has died, away from her,
Here for the fevered mind too long harassed
Is wintry silence, cooling space and rest.

Waves of a soundless music rise to lift
The unburied thing that lived and even laughed.
And, as a broken life can be made whole
By looking at the slant of one long hill,
In this eternity of peace, the heart
Forgetting all forgets that it can hurt.

And yet, does even the weariest heart want peace?
Back to the fever, the intemperate pace,
Back to the ruthless word, the headlong deed
(Fearing that passion stilled is passion dead)
The worn heart hungers. Forever unappeased,
Forever self-persuaded, self-opposed,
It turns away from each escape, to pine
For the old wars and victories of pain;
Embracing all that reason hopes to leave,
With no less hurt and even greater love.
As though to cry, "Here I belong—I must!
Here is the place where I have suffered most."

## FOOD AND DRINK

Why has our poetry eschewed
The rapture and response of food?
What hymns are sung, what prayers are said
For home-made miracles of bread?
Since what we love has always found
Expression in enduring sound,
Music and verse should be competing
To match the transient joy of eating.
There should be present in our songs
As many tastes as there are tongues;
There should be humbly celebrated
The passion that is never sated.

Let us begin it with the first
Distinction of a conscious thirst
When the collusion of the vine
Lifted water into wine.
Let us give thanks before we turn
To other things of less concern
For all the poetry of the table:
Clams that parade their silent fable;
Lobsters that have a rock for stable;
Red-faced tomatoes ample as
A countryman's full-bosomed lass;
Plain-spoken turnips; honest beets;
The carnal gusto of red meats;
The wood-fire pungence of smoked ham;
The insipidity of lamb;
Young veal that's smooth as natural silk;
The lavish motherliness of milk;

Sweet-sour carp, beloved by Jews;
Pot luck simplicity of stews;
Crabs, juiciest of Nature's jokes;
The deep reserve of artichokes;
Mushrooms, whose taste is texture, loath
To tell of their mysterious growth;
Quick, mealy comfort glowing in
A baked potato's crackled skin;
The morning promise, hailed by man,
Of bacon crisping in the pan;
The sage compound of *Hasenpfeffer*
With dumplings born of flour and zephyr;
Spinach whose spirit is the soil;
Anchovies glorified in oil;
Corn that is roasted in the ash;
The eternal compromise of hash;
The slow-gold nectar maples yield;
Pale honey tasting of the field
Where every clover is Hymettus;
The cooling sanity of lettuce,
And every other herbal green
Whose touch is calm, whose heart is clean;
Succulent bean-sprouts; bamboo-shoots;
The sapid catalogue of fruits:
Plebeian apple; caustic grape;
Quinces that have no gift for shape;
Dull plums that mind their own affairs;
Incurably bland and blunted pears;
Fantastic passion-fruit; frank lemons
With acid tongues as sharp as women's;
Exotic loquats; sly persimmons;

White currants; amber-fleshed sultanas
(Miniature and sweetened mannas);
Expansive peaches; suave bananas;
Oranges ripening in crates;
Tight-bodied figs; sun-wrinkled dates;
Melons that have their own vagaries;
The bright astringency of berries;
Pepper, whose satire stings and cuts;
The pointless persiflage of nuts;
Sauces of complex mysteries;
Proverbial parsnips; muscular cheese;
Innocent eggs that scorn disguises;
Languid molasses; burning spices
In kitchen-oracles to Isis;
Thick sauerkraut's fat-bellied savor;
Anything with a chocolate flavor;
Deep generosity of pies;
Rich puddings bursting to surprise;
The smug monotony of rice;
Raisins that doze in cinnamon buns;
Kentucky biscuits, Scottish scones;
Venison steaks that smack of cloisters;
Goose-liver for the soul that roisters;
Reticent prawn; Lucullan oysters;
Sausages, fragrant link on link. . . .

The vast ambrosias of drink:
Tea, that domestic mandarin;
Bucolic cider; loose-lipped gin;
Coffee, extract of common sense,
Purgative of the night's pretense;
Cocoa's prim nursery; the male
Companionship of crusty ale;
Cognac as oily as a ferret;
The faintly iron thrust of claret;
Episcopal port, aged and austere;
Rebellious must of grape; the clear,
Bluff confraternity of beer—

All these are good, all are a part
Of man's imperative needs that start
Not in the palate but the heart.
Thus fat and fiber, root and leaf,
Become quick fuel and slow grief.
These, through the chemistry of blood,
Sustain his hungering manhood,
Fulfilling passion, ripening pain;
Steel in his bone, fire at his brain.
So, until man abjures the meats
Terrestrial, and impermanent sweets,
Growing beyond the thing he eats,

Let us be thankful for the good
Beauty and benison of food;
Let us join chiming vowel with vowel
To rhapsodize fish, flesh and fowl;
And let us thank God in our songs
There are as many tastes as tongues!

### LAST WORDS BEFORE WINTER

*All my sheep*
*Gather in a heap,*
*For I spy the woolly, woolly wolf.*

Farewell, my flocks,
Farewell. But let me find you
Safe in your stall and barn and box
With your winter's tale behind you.

Farewell, my cattle (both).
I leave you just as loath
As though you were a hundred head,
Instead
Of two-and-a-half.
(Two cows and a calf.)

Farewell, my apple-trees;
You have learned what it is to freeze,
With the drift on your knees.
But, oh, beware
Those first kind days, the snare
Of the too promising air,
The cost
Of over-sudden trust—
And then the killing frost.

Farewell, belovéd acres;
I leave you in the hands
Of one whose earliest enterprise was land
Your Maker's.

Yard, hutch, and house, farewell.
It is for you to tell
How you withstood the great white wo
   whose fell
Is softer than a lambkin's, but whose brea
Is death.
Farewell, hoof, claw, and wing,
Finned, furred, and feathered thing,
Till Spring—

*All my sheep*
*Gather in a heap,*
*For I spy the woolly, woolly wolf.*

## FIRST WORDS BEFORE SPRING

Snow-beaten, winter-bound, all that I see
Stare back at me with neither sight nor sound,
Like once profound but care-forgotten passions,
Lost in despair.
Oh, dear possessions,
Now more than ever you must be
All that we lack: the new-leafed tree;
The first home-coming bird; the word
That robins have been heard and trilliums found;
The warm blue rain; the old pain stirred
With the rich wound, the harrowing of the ground.

For this is February, when the frost
Strikes at the cellared roots and, overnight,
Wrings the last apple's heart and all is lost;
When nothing sings or cares for our delight,
And nothing dares, not mouse nor mink nor mole,
Nor even groundhog, hugging fast his hole,
Too weak to cast a shadow.
                     Speak, my soul,
Speak for courageous color, for the bud
That breaks in snow. Speak quickly for the flood
Of meadow-music every morning when
One world awakes the other.
                     Rise, unroll
The flicker's rousing drum. Speak for the wren,
Even for the frog, the bullfinch of the fen.

For this is February fill-dike, this the still
Eternity of nothings, when the will
Is wasted, and the starving-greedy eyes
Look to the skies, like any rustic miser,
Only for snow, the poor man's fertilizer.

Confess
That the bleak heart asks more, asks nothing less
Than all. Out of this emptiness
Speak for the word made flesh, the world made whole;
For brave, and weak, and grave, and droll,
Speak, my soul!

# John Gould Fletcher

JOHN GOULD FLETCHER was born at Little Rock, Arkansas, January 3, 1886. He was educated at Harvard (1903-7) and, after spending several years in Massachusetts, moved to England, where he lived for fifteen years. In 1933 he returned to America, to the family home in Little Rock.

In 1913 Fletcher published five books of poems which he has referred to as "his literary wild oats," five small collections of experimental and faintly interesting verse. In 1914, shortly after the publication of his *Fire and Wine* (one of the early quintet), Fletcher joined the Imagists. With H. D. and Amy Lowell he became one of the leaders of this interesting movement and his contributions were among the outstanding features of the three anthologies which furnish so illuminating a record of the esthetics of the period. Coincident with the first appearance of *Some Imagist Poets,* Fletcher discarded his previous style and emerged as a decidedly less conservative and far more arresting poet with *Irradiations—Sand and Spray* (1915). This volume is full of an extraordinary fancy; imagination riots through it, though it is sometimes a bloodless and bodiless imagination. It is crowded—even overcrowded—with shifting subtleties; a brilliant, haphazard series of improvisations.

In the following book, *Goblins and Pagodas* (1916), Fletcher carries his unrelated harmonies much further. Color dominates him; the ambitious set of eleven "color symphonies" is an elaborate design in which tone and thought are summoned by color-associations, sometimes closely related, sometimes far-fetched. "It contains," says Conrad Aiken in his appreciative chapter on Fletcher in *Scepticisms,* "little of the emotion which relates to the daily life of men and women. . . . It is a sort of absolute poetry, a poetry of detached waver and brilliance, a beautiful flowering of language alone—a parthenogenesis, as if language were fertilized by itself rather than by thought or feeling. Remove the magic of phrase and sound and there is nothing left: no thread of continuity, no thought, no story, no emotion. But the magic of phrase and sound is powerful, and it takes one into a fantastic world."

In 1917 Fletcher again began to change in spirit as well as style. Emotion declared itself with surprising candor. After having appeared in the three Imagist anthologies, he sought for depths rather than surfaces; his "Lincoln" accomplished a closer relation to humanity. A moving mysticism speaks from *The Tree of Life* (1918); the more obviously native *Granite and Breakers* (1921) and *Parables* (1925) contain a prophetic note new to this poet. Though less arresting than the ones by which he is best known, the later poems reach depths which the preceding verses never attained. Although the unconscious often dictates Fletcher's fantasies, a calm music dominates them. A grave, subdued lyricism moves through *The Black Rock* (1928) and *Branches of Adam* (1926), in which the philosophy is akin to Nietzsche's while the motto might well be Blake's "How is it we have walked through fire, and yet are not consumed?" Never a popular poet, Fletcher gains—and suffers—from his original and fluctuating power. He is the poet held in a state of flux.

*XXIV Elegies* (1935) is a work which took Fletcher twenty years to write; the poems, one for each hour of the twenty-four, having been composed between 1914 and 1934. The dignified tone and depth of feeling are communicated throughout.

There are, as there would be in a work of this character, many tedious passages, and an American poet in the twentieth century might have spared himself an elegy on "Tristan in Brittany" and an "Elegy on Tintern Abbey." But he atones for these lapses in the "Elegy on the Building of the Washington Bridge," "Elegy on the Jewish People," "Elegy in a Civil War Cemetery," and by the general accent, an inflection which uses the grand manner but restrains the rhetoric, holding the ecstatic material within the bounds of experience.

Besides his quality as poet Fletcher ranks high as a translator from the French, having made the English versions of *The Dance over Fire and Water* (by Elie Faure) in 1926 and *The Reveries of a Solitary* (by J. J. Rousseau) in 1927. *The Two Frontiers* (1930) is a speculative but highly serious consideration—a sort of prophetic historical essay—regarding the parallels and contrasts of America and Russia.

FROM "IRRADIATIONS"

I

Over the roof-tops race the shadows of clouds;
Like horses the shadows of clouds charge down the street.

Whirlpools of purple and gold,
Winds from the mountains of cinnabar,
Lacquered mandarin moments, palanquins swaying and balancing
Amid vermilion pavilions, against the jade balustrades,
Glint of the glittering wings of dragon-flies in the light:
Silver filaments, golden flakes settling downwards,
Rippling, quivering flutters, repulse and surrender,
The sun broidered upon the rain,
The rain rustling with the sun.

Over the roof-tops race the shadows of clouds;
Like horses the shadows of clouds charge down the street.

II

Flickering of incessant rain
On flashing pavements:
Sudden scurry of umbrellas:
Bending, recurved blossoms of the storm.

The winds come clanging and clattering
From long white highroads whipping in ribbons up summits:
They strew upon the city gusty wafts of apple-blossom,
And the rustling of innumerable translucent leaves.

Uneven tinkling, the lazy rain
Dripping from the eaves.

III

The trees, like great jade elephants,
Chained, stamp and shake 'neath the gadflies of the breeze;
The trees lunge and plunge, unruly elephants:
The clouds are their crimson howdah-canopies,

The sunlight glints like the golden robe of a Shah.
Would I were tossed on the wrinkled backs of those trees.

### IV

O seeded grass, you army of little men
Crawling up the long slope with quivering, quick blades of steel:
You who storm millions of graves, tiny green tentacles of Earth,
Interlace yourselves tightly over my heart,
And do not let me go:
For I would lie here forever and watch with one eye
The pilgrimaging ants in your dull, savage jungles,
The while with the other I see the stiff lines of the slope
Break in mid-air, a wave surprisingly arrested,—
And above them, wavering, dancing, bodiless, colorless, unreal,
The long thin lazy fingers of the heat.

### V

The morning is clean and blue and the wind blows up the clouds:
Now my thoughts gathered from afar
Once again in their patched armor, with rusty plumes and blunted swords,
Move out to war.

Smoking our morning pipes we shall ride two and two
Through the woods,
For our old cause keeps us together,
And our hatred is so precious not death or defeat can break it.

God willing, we shall this day meet that old enemy
Who has given us so many a good beating.
Thank God we have a cause worth fighting for,
And a cause worth losing and a good song to sing.

## GREEN SYMPHONY

### I

The glittering leaves of the rhododendrons
Balance and vibrate in the cool air;
While in the sky above them
White clouds chase each other.

Like scampering rabbits,
Flashes of sunlight sweep the lawn;
They fling in passing
Patterns of shadow,
Golden and green.

With long cascades of laughter,
The mating birds dart and swoop to the turf:
'Mid their mad trillings
Glints the gay sun behind the trees.

Down there are deep blue lakes:
Orange blossom droops in the water.
In the tower of the winds
All the bells are set adrift:
Jingling
ᵀor the dawn.

Thin fluttering streamers
Of breeze lash through the swaying boughs,
Palely expectant
The earth receives the slanting rain.

The glittering leaves of the rhododendron
Are shaken like blue-green blades of grass,
Flickering, cracking, falling:
Splintering in a million fragments.

The wind runs laughing up the slope
Stripping off handfuls of wet green leaves,
To fling in people's faces.
Wallowing on the daisy-powdered turf,
Clutching at the sunlight,
Cavorting in the shadow.

Like baroque pearls,
Like cloudy emeralds,
The clouds and the trees clash together;
Whirling and swirling,
In the tumult
Of the spring,
And the wind.

II

The trees splash the sky with their fingers,
A restless green rout of stars.

With whirling movement
They swing their boughs
About their stems:
Planes on planes of light and shadow
Pass among them,
Opening fanlike to fall.

The trees are like a sea;
Tossing,
Trembling,
Roaring,
Wallowing,
Darting their long green flickering fronds up at the sky,
Spotted with white blossom-spray.

The trees are roofs:
Hollow caverns of cool blue shadow,
Solemn arches
In the afternoons.
The whole vast horizon
In terrace beyond terrace,
Pinnacle above pinnacle,
Lifts to the sky
Serrated ranks of green on green.

They caress the roofs with their fingers,
They sprawl about the river to look into it;
Up the hill they come
Gesticulating challenge:
They cower together
In dark valleys;
They yearn out over the fields.

Enameled domes
Tumble upon the grass,
Crashing in ruin,
Quiet at last.

The trees lash the sky with their leaves,
Uneasily shaking their dark green manes.

### III

Far let the voices of the mad wild birds be calling me,
I will abide in this forest of pines.

When the wind blows
Battling through the forest,
I hear it distantly,
The crash of a perpetual sea.

When the rain falls,
I watch the silver spears slanting downwards
From pale river-pools of sky,
Enclosed in dark fronds.

When the sun shines,
I weave together distant branches till they enclose mighty circles,
I sway to the movement of hooded summits,
I swim leisurely in deep blue seas of air.

I hug the smooth bark of stately red pillars
And with cones carefully scattered
I mark the progression of dark dial-shadows
Flung diagonally downwards through the afternoon.

This turf is not like turf:
It is a smooth dry carpet of velvet,
Embroidered with brown patterns of needles and cones.
These trees are not like trees:
They are innumerable feathery pagoda-umbrellas,
Stiffly ungracious to the wind,
Teetering on red-lacquered stems.

In the evening I listen to the winds' lisping,
While the conflagrations of the sunset flicker and clash behind me,
Flamboyant crenellations of glory amid the charred ebony boles.

In the night the fiery nightingales
Shall clash and trill through the silence:
Like the voices of mermaids crying
From the sea.

Long ago has the moon whelmed this uncompleted temple.
Stars swim like gold fish far above the black arches.

Far let the timid feet of dawn fly to catch me:
I will abide in this forest of pines:
For I have unveiled naked beauty,
And the things that she whispered to me in the darkness,
Are buried deep in my heart.

Now let the black tops of the pine-trees break like a spent wave,
Against the gray sky:
These are tombs and temples and altars sun-kindled for me.

### LONDON NIGHTFALL

I saw the shapes that stood upon the clouds:
And they were tiger-breasted, shot with light,
And all of them, lifting long trumpets together,
Blew over the city, for the night to come.
Down in the street, we floundered in the mud;
Above, in endless files, gold angels came
And stood upon the clouds, and blew their horns
For night.

Like a wet petal crumpled,
Twilight fell soddenly on the weary city;
The 'buses lurched and groaned,
The shops put up their doors.

But skywards, far aloft,
The angels, vanishing, waved broad plumes of gold,
Summoning spirits from a thousand hills
To pour the thick night out upon the earth.

### THE SKATERS

Black swallows swooping or gliding
In a flurry of entangled loops and curves;
The skaters skim over the frozen river.
And the grinding click of their skates as they impinge upon the surface,
Is like the brushing together of thin wing-tips of silver.

### LINCOLN

#### I

Like a gaunt, scraggly pine
Which lifts its head above the mournful sandhills;
And patiently, through dull years of bitter silence,
Untended and uncared for, begins to grow.

Ungainly, laboring, huge,
The wind of the north has twisted and gnarled its branches;
Yet in the heat of midsummer days, when thunder-clouds ring the horizon,
A nation of men shall rest beneath its shade.

And it shall protect them all,
Hold everyone safe there, watching aloof in silence;
Until at last one mad stray bolt from the zenith
Shall strike it in an instant down to earth.

#### II

There was a darkness in this man; an immense and hollow darkness,
Of which we may not speak, nor share with him, nor enter;
A darkness through which strong roots stretched downwards into the earth
Towards old things;
Towards the herdman-kings who walked the earth and spoke with God,
Towards the wanderers who sought for they knew not what, and found their goal
    at last;
Towards the men who waited, only waited patiently when all seemed lost,
Many bitter winters of defeat;
Down to the granite of patience
These roots swept, knotted fibrous roots, prying, piercing, seeking,
And drew from the living rock and the living waters about it
The red sap to carry upwards to the sun.

Not proud, but humble,
Only to serve and pass on, to endure to the end through service;
For the ax is laid at the root of the trees, and all that bring not forth good fruit
Shall be cut down on the day to come and cast into the fire.

#### III

There is silence abroad in the land today,
And in the hearts of men, a deep and anxious silence;
And, because we are still at last, those bronze lips slowly open,
Those hollow and weary eyes take on a gleam of light.

Slowly a patient, firm-syllabled voice cuts through the endless silence
Like laboring oxen that drag a plow through the chaos of rude clay-fields:
"I went forward as the light goes forward in early spring,
But there were also many things which I left behind.

"Tombs that were quiet;
One, of a mother, whose brief light went out in the darkness,
One, of a loved one, the snow on whose grave is long falling,
One, only of a child, but it was mine.

"Have you forgot your graves? Go, question them in anguish,
Listen long to their unstirred lips. From your hostages to silence,
Learn there is no life without death, no dawn without sun-setting,
No victory but to Him who has given all."

IV

The clamor of cannon dies down, the furnace-mouth of the battle is silent.
The midwinter sun dips and descends, the earth takes on afresh its bright colors.
But he whom we mocked and obeyed not, he whom we scorned and mistrusted,
He has descended, like a god, to his rest.

Over the uproar of cities,
Over the million intricate threads of life wavering and crossing,
In the midst of problems we know not, tangling, perplexing, ensnaring,
Rises one white tomb alone.
Beam over it, stars.
Wrap it round, stripes—stripes red for the pain that he bore for you—
Enfold it forever, O flag, rent, soiled, but repaired through your anguish;
Long as you keep him there safe, the nations shall bow to your law.

Strew over him flowers:
Blue forget-me-nots from the north, and the bright pink arbutus
From the east, and from the west rich orange blossoms,
But from the heart of the land take the passion-flower;

Rayed, violet, dim,
With the nails that pierced, the cross that he bore and the circlet,
And beside it there lay also one lonely snow-white magnolia,
Bitter for remembrance of the healing which has passed.

A REBEL

Tie a bandage over his eyes,
And at his feet
Let rifles drearily patter
Their death-prayers of defeat.

Throw a blanket over his body,
It need no longer stir;
Truth will but stand the stronger
For all who died for her.

Now he has broken through
To his own secret place;
Which, if we dared to do,
We would have no power left to look on that dead face.

### BEFORE OLYMPUS

Across the sky run streaks of white light, aching;
Across the earth the chattering grass is sprawling;
Across the sea roll troubled gleams awaking,
Across the steeps dark broken shapes are crawling.

We have been scourged with youth, a rod in pickle
To cut the hide from our own hearts. We know
The tree of life is also cursed. We heed
The silent laughter of gray gods of time.

We do not seek the lithe and brittle music
Of swords and flame. We have no more desire
For glory or contempt. The moment flies
Past us, and shouting carries its echo on.

The clank of wheels and pumps, the screech of levers
No longer now afflicts our inmost bearing;
The old wise nightingales have longer ears,
They sing the blooming of wild immortelles.

And through the desolation of great cities
As in a madhouse we go peering where
Black butterflies flit about a carcass. Words
Gallop about the sky. The earth broods like a stone.

Heaven is a blank news-sheet fixed and trembling
Between the knees of God. The grass runs crawling.
The waves of the sea their laughter are dissembling,
But who will reap them when our scythes are falling?

### ADVENT

I have no more gold;
I spent it all on foolish songs,
Gold I cannot give to you.

Incense, too, I burned
To the great idols of this world;
I must come with empty hands.

Myrrh I lost
In that darker sepulcher
Where another Christ
Died for man in vain.—

I can only give myself,
I have nothing left but this.
Naked I wait, naked I fall
Into Your Hands, Your Hands.


THE BIRTH OF LUCIFER

Helpless is God in struggling with that star
  Which in derision makes His light less dim;
The evening bids the morning from afar
  To rise and conquer Him;

After nine hours of night the sun, expiring,
  Breaks the dark vessel that it fills; and then
Erect against the noon it stands, desiring
  This transience, making us both Gods and men:

Life seeks again its dark and secret places,
  Where under the sunset's leveled sword, it keeps
Its rest until rekindled in new faces,
  Old worlds awake from their too dreamless sleep.


A NEW HEAVEN

We have our hopes and fears that flout us,
We have our illusions, changeless through the years;
We have our dreams of rest after long struggle,
After our toil is finished, folded hands.
But for those who have fallen in battle,
What Heaven can there be?

Heaven is full of those who can remember
The ebbing-out of life that slowly lingered
At the dark doors of pain;
Heaven is full of those who dropped their burden
At last through weariness;
But these the War has taken
Remember naught but their own exultant youth
Filling their hearts with unaccomplished dreams:
The trumpet-call—then the swift searing darkness
Stilling the proud sad song.

How will these enter in
Our old dull Heaven?
Where we seek only to drowse at ease, unthinking,
Since we are safe at last.
Safe? For these souls who faced a thousand dangers,
And found sly Death that robbed them of their chance,
Ere it befell?
Safe—can a Heaven which is safe and painless,
Ever be Heaven to them?

Somewhere amid the clouds there is the home of thunder;
Thunder is naught to them,
It is a ball, a heavy plaything
They may kick hither and thither with their feet.
Lightning is but a toy—the flaming stars
Are endless camp-fire lights;
And for the silence of eternity,
They too on out-post duty, often heard it speak.

We have the dreams of our fat lives that lead us
To waste our lives;
We have the false hope we are serving others
When it is but ourselves we serve;
Yet these who have never lived, and whose sole service
Was but to die too soon,
Perhaps somewhere are making a new Heaven
Filled with the divine despair and joy this dead earth never knew.

### AD MAJOREM HOMINIS GLORIAM

In the summit of my head
Pride and wrath their pain have shed;

In my heart's fierce furnace-fire
Knowledge struggles with desire:

At the bottom of my heart,
Love and pity sleep apart.

Wherefore should my hells be high,
And my heavens below my eye?

Why should I, who earthfixed dwell,
Sink to heaven, rise to hell?

### THE LOFTY HOUSE

Go not into the lofty house;
Nor pass the pillared portico that, tall,
Looks over all;
Unless you wish to rouse
The dead. They will be ready when you call.
Thin hands will touch worn chair-backs and
    sad eyes
Look on you long without the least surprise.
Go not into the lofty house, at Spring or Fall.
For ghosts are happiest left
About their own affairs;
Why should you trouble these, so long bereft
Of all but loss, with loss that is not theirs?
Go not into the house, I say;
Let the pale pillars still untroubled rear
Their light against the moons that shifting,
    play
Against the pediment. Let windows peer
Or remain blank, close-shuttered. Let the
    mouse
Gnaw the old trunks in the dark attic stored.
For God's sake do not go into the house,
Unless you share a past still undeplored.

# William Rose Benét

WILLIAM ROSE BENÉT was born at Fort Hamilton, New York Harbor, February 2, 1886. He was educated at Albany Academy and graduated from Yale in 1907. After various experiences as freelance writer, publisher's reader, magazine editor, and second lieutenant in the U. S. Air Service, Benét became Associate Editor of the New York Post's *Literary Review* in 1920. He resigned in 1924 to become one of the founders and editors of *The Saturday Review of Literature*.

The outstanding feature of Benét's verse is its extraordinary versatility; an Oriental imagination runs through his pages. Like the title-poem of his first volume, *Merchants from Cathay* (1913), Benét's volumes vibrate with a vigorous music; they are full of the sonorous stuff that one rolls out crossing wintry fields or tramping a road alone. But Benét's charm is not confined to the lift and swing of rollicking choruses. *The Falconer of God* (1914), *The Great White Wall* (1916) and *The Burglar of the Zodiac* (1918) contain decorations bold as they are brilliant; they ring with a strange and spicy music evoked from seemingly casual words. His scope is wide, although he is most at home in fancies which glow with a half-lurid, half-humorous reflection of the grotesque. There are times indeed when Benét seems to be forcing his ingenuity. The poet frequently lets his fantastic Pegasus run away with him, and what started out to be a gallop among the stars ends in a scraping of shins on the pavement. But he is saved by an acrobatic dexterity even when his energy betrays him. *Perpetual Light* (1919), a memorial to his first wife, is, naturally, a more subdued collection.

*Moons of Grandeur* (1920) represents an appreciable development of Benét's whimsical gift; a combination of Eastern phantasy and Western vigor. Even more arresting are those poems which appeared subsequent to this volume. A firmer line, a cooler condensation may be found in *Man Possessed* (1927), a selection of the best of the previous volumes with many new poems. "Whale" is a particularly brilliant example; "The Horse Thief" is one of the most fanciful and one of the most popular of American ballads; "Jesse James" rocks with high spirits and the true balladist's gusto; "Inscription for a Mirror in a Deserted Dwelling," written during the life of his second wife, Elinor Wylie, reflects the poet who wrote it and the poet to whom it was written, while "Sagacity" is a tribute to her memory. *Golden Fleece* (1935) is a more critical selection of Benét's poems with the addition of several new verses, many of them in an unexpectedly light vein.

Besides his verse, the older Benét is the author of two novels and several tales for children, the editor (with Henry Seidel Canby and John Drinkwater) of *Twentieth Century Poetry* (1929), and *Fifty Poets* (1932), an "auto-anthology" in which fifty American poets chose their own best, or favorite, poems. He also prepared the literary history for *Adventures in English Literature,* a textbook published in 1931.

## MERCHANTS FROM CATHAY

*How that*
*They came.*
Their heels slapped their bumping mules; their fat chaps glowed.
   Glory unto Mary, each seemed to wear a crown!
Like sunset their robes were on the wide, white road:
   So we saw those mad merchants come dusting into town!

*Of their*
*Beasts,*
Two paunchy beasts they rode on and two they drove before.
   May the Saints all help us, the tiger-stripes they had!
And the panniers upon them swelled full of stuffs and ore!
   The square buzzed and jostled at a sight so mad.

*And their*
*Boast,*
They bawled in their beards, and their turbans they wried.
   They stopped by the stalls with curvetting and clatter.
As bronze as the bracken their necks and faces dyed—
   And a stave they sat singing, to tell us of the matter.

*With its*
*Burthen*

"*For your silks, to Sugarmago! For your dyes, to Isfahan!*
   *Weird fruits from the Isle o' Lamaree.*
     *But for magic merchandise,*
     *For treasure-trove and spice,*
*Here's a catch and a carol to the great, grand Chan,*
   *The King of all the Kings across the sea!*

*And*
*Chorus.*

"*Here's a catch and a carol to the great, grand Chan;*
*For we won through the deserts to his sunset barbican;*
*And the mountains of his palace no Titan's reach may span*
   *Where he wields his seignorie!*

*A first*
*Stave*
*Fearsome,*

"Red-as-blood skins of panthers, so bright against the sun
   On the walls of the halls where his pillared state is set
They daze with a blaze no man may look upon.
   And with conduits of beverage those floors run wet.

*And a second*
*Right hard*
*To stomach*

"His wives stiff with riches, they sit before him there.
   Bird and beast at his feast make song and clapping cheer.
And jugglers and enchanters, all walking on the air,
   Make fall eclipse and thunder—make moons and suns appear!

*And a third,*
*Which is a*
*Laughable*
*Thing.*

"Once the Chan, by his enemies sore-prest, and sorely spent,
   Lay, so they say, in a thicket 'neath a tree
Where the howl of an owl vexed his foes from their intent:
   Then that fowl for a holy bird of reverence made he!

*We gape to*
*Hear them end,*

"*A catch and a carol to the great, grand Chan!*
*Pastmasters of disasters, our desert caravan*
*Won through all peril to his sunset barbican,*
   *Where he wields his seignorie!*
*And crowns he gave us! We end where we began:*
*A catch and a carol to the great, grand Chan!*
   *The King of all the Kings across the sea!*"

*And are in*
*Terror,*

Those mad, antic Merchants! . . . Their stripèd beasts did beat
   The market-square suddenly with hooves of beaten gold!
The ground yawned gaping and flamed beneath our feet!
   They plunged to Pits Abysmal with their wealth untold!

*And dread*
*it is*
*Devil's Work!*

And some say the Chan himself in anger dealt the stroke—
For sharing of his secrets with silly, common folk:
But Holy, Blessed Mary, preserve us as you may
Lest once more those mad Merchants come chanting from Cathay!

### NIGHT

Let the night keep
What the night takes,
Sighs buried deep,
Ancient heart-aches,
Groans of the lover,
Tears of the lost;

Let day discover not
All the night cost!

Let the night keep
Love's burning bliss,
Drowned in deep sleep
Whisper and kiss,

Thoughts like white flowers
In hedges of May;
Let such deep hours not
Fade with the day!

Monarch is night
Of all eldest things,
Pain and affright,
Rapturous wings;
Night the crown, night the sword
Lifted to smite.
Kneel to your overlord,
Children of night!

### THE FAWN IN THE SNOW

The brown-dappled fawn
Bereft of the doe
Shivers in blue shadow
Of the glaring snow,

His whole world bright
As a jewel, and hard,
Diamond white,
Turquoise barred.

The trees are black,
Their needles gold,
Their boughs crack
In the keen cold.

The brown-dappled fawn
Bereft of the doe
Trembles and shudders
At the bright snow.

The air whets
The warm throat,
The frost frets
At the smooth coat.

Brown agate eyes
Opened round
Agonize
At the cold ground,

At the cold heaven
Enameled pale,
At the earth shriven
By the snowy gale,

At magic glitter
Burning to blind,
At beauty bitter
As an almond rind.

Fawn, fawn,
Seek for your south,
For kind dawn
With her cool mouth,

For green sod
With gold and blue
Dappled, as God
Has dappled you, . . .

The shivering fawn
Paws at the snow.
South and dawn
Lie below;

Richness and mirth,
Dearth forgiven,
A happy earth,
A warm heaven.

The sleet streams;
The snow flies;
The fawn dreams
With wide brown eyes.

### WHALE

*Rain, with a silver flail;*
 *Sun, with a golden ball;*
*Ocean, wherein the whale*
 *Swims minnow-small;*

*I heard the whale rejoice*
 *And cynic sharks attend;*
*He cried with a purple voice,*
 *"The Lord is my Friend!"*

"With flanged and battering tail,
 With huge and dark baleen,
He said, 'Let there be Whale
 In the Cold and Green!'

"He gave me a water-spout,
 A side like a harbor wall;
The Lord from cloud looked out
 And planned it all.

With glittering crown atilt
  He leaned on a glittering rail;
He said, 'Where Sky is spilt,
  Let there be Whale.'

"Tier upon tier of wings
  Blushed and blanched and bowed;
Phalanxed fiery things
  Cried in the cloud;

"Million-eyed was the mirk
  At the plan not understood;
But the Lord looked on His work
  And saw it was good.

"He gave me marvelous girth
  For the curve of back and breast,
And a tiny eye of mirth
  To hide His jest.

"He made me a floating hill,
  A plunging deep-sea mine.
This was the Lord's will;
  The Lord is Divine.

"I magnify His name
  In earthquake and eclipse,
In weltering molten flame
  And wrecks of ships,

"In waves that lick the moon;
  I, the plow of the sea!
I am the Lord's boon;
  The Lord made me!"

The sharks barked from beneath,
  As the whale rollicked and roared,
"Yes, and our grinning teeth,
  Was it not the Lord?"

Then questions pattered like hail
  From fishes large and small.
"The Lord is mighty," said Whale,
  "The Lord made all!"

"His is a mammoth jest
  Life may never betray;
He has laid it up in His breast
  Till Judgment Day;

"But high when combers foam
  And tower their last of all,
My power shall haul you home
  Through Heaven wall.

"A trumpet then in the gates,
  To the ramps a thundering drum,
I shall lead you where He waits
  For His Whale to come.

"Where His cloudy seat is placed
  On high in an empty dome,
I shall trail the Ocean abased
  In chains of foam,

"Unwieldy, squattering dread.
  Where the blazing cohorts stand
At last I shall lift my head
  As it feels His hand.

"Then wings with a million eyes
  Before mine eyes shall quail:
'Look you, all Paradise,
  I was His Whale!'"

*I heard the Whale rejoice,*
  *As he splayed the waves to a fan:*
"And the Lord shall say with His Voice,
  *'Leviathan!'*

"The Lord shall say with His Tongue,
  'Now let all Heaven give hail
To my Jest when I was young,
  To my very Whale.'"

*Then the Whale careered in the Sea,*
  *He floundered with flailing tail;*
*Flourished and rollicked he,*
  "Aha! Mine Empery!"
For the Lord said, 'Let Whale Be!'
  And there Was Whale!"

### THE HORSE THIEF

There he moved, cropping the grass at the purple canyon's lip.
  His mane was mixed with the moonlight that silvered his snow-white side,
For the moon sailed out of a cloud with the wake of a spectral ship.
  I crouched and I crawled on my belly, my lariat coil looped wide.

Dimly and dark the mesas broke on the starry sky.
  A pall covered every color of their gorgeous glory at noon.
I smelt the yucca and mesquite, and stifled my heart's quick cry,
  And wormed and crawled on my belly to where he moved against the moon!

Some Moorish barb was that mustang's sire. His lines were beyond all wonder.
  From the prick of his ears to the flow of his tail he ached in my throat and eyes.
Steel and velvet grace! As the prophet says, God had "clothed his neck with thunder."
  Oh, marvelous with the drifting cloud he drifted across the skies!

And then I was near at hand—crouched, and balanced, and cast the coil;
  And the moon was smothered in cloud, and the rope through my hands with a rip!
But somehow I gripped and clung, with the blood in my brain a-boil,—
  With a turn round the rugged tree-stump there on the purple canyon's lip.

Right into the stars he reared aloft, his red eye rolling and raging.
  He whirled and sunfished and lashed, and rocked the earth to thunder and flame.
He squealed like a regular devil horse. I was haggard and spent and aging—
  Roped clean, but almost storming clear, his fury too fierce to tame.

And I cursed myself for a tenderfoot moon-dazzled to play the part,
  But I was doubly desperate then, with the posse pulled out from town,
Or I'd never have tried it. I only knew I must get a mount and a start.
  The filly had snapped her foreleg short. I had had to shoot her down.

So there he struggled and strangled, and I snubbed him around the tree.
  Nearer, a little nearer—hoofs planted, and lolling tongue—
Till a sudden slack pitched me backward. He reared right on top of me.
  Mother of God—that moment! He missed me . . . and up I swung.

Somehow, gone daft completely and clawing a bunch of his mane,
  As he stumbled and tripped in the lariat, there I was—up and astride
And cursing for seven counties! And the mustang? *Just insane!*
  Crack-bang! went the rope; we cannoned off the tree—then—gods, that ride!

A rocket—that's all, a rocket! I dug with my teeth and nails.
  Why, we never hit even the high spots (though I hardly remember things),
But I heard a monstrous booming like a thunder of flapping sails
  When he spread—well, *call* me a liar!—when he spread those wings, those wings!

So white that my eyes were blinded, thick-feathered and wide unfurled,
  They beat the air into billows. We sailed, and the earth was gone.
Canyon and desert and mesa withered below, with the world.
  And then I knew that mustang; for I—was Bellerophon!

Yes, glad as the Greek, and mounted on a horse of the elder gods,
  With never a magic bridle or a fountain-mirror nigh!
*My chaps and spurs and holster must have looked it?* What's the odds?
  I'd a leg over lightning and thunder, careering across the sky!

And forever streaming before me, fanning my forehead cool,
  Flowed a mane of molten silver; and just before my thighs
(As I gripped his velvet-muscled ribs, while I cursed myself for a fool),
  The steady pulse of those pinions—their wonderful fall and rise!

The bandanna I bought in Bowie blew loose and whipped from my neck.
  My shirt was stuck to my shoulders and ribboning out behind.
The stars were dancing, wheeling and glancing, dipping with smirk and beck.
  The clouds were flowing, dusking and glowing. We rode a roaring wind.

We soared through the silver starlight to knock at the planets' gates.
  New shimmering constellations came whirling into our ken.
Red stars and green and golden swung out of the void that waits
  For man's great last adventure. The Signs took shape—and then

I knew the lines of that Centaur the moment I saw him come!
  The musical box of the heavens all round us rolled to a tune
That tinkled and chimed and trilled with silver sounds that struck you dumb,
  As if some archangel were grinding out the music of the moon.

Melody-drunk on the Milky Way, as we swept and soared hilarious,
  Full in our pathway, sudden he stood—the Centaur of the Stars,
Flashing from head and hoofs and breast! I knew him for Sagittarius.
  He reared, and bent and drew his bow. He crouched as a boxer spars.

Flung back on his haunches, weird he loomed—then leapt—and the dim void
    lightened.
  Old White Wings shied and swerved aside, and fled from the splendor-shod.
Through a flashing welter of worlds we charged. I knew why my horse was
    frightened.
  He *had* two faces—a dog's and a man's—that Babylonian god!

Also, he followed us real as fear. Ping! went an arrow past.
  My broncho buck-jumped, humping high. We plunged . . . I guess that's all!
I lay on the purple canyon's lip, when I opened my eyes at last—
  Stiff and sore and my head like a drum, but I broke no bones in the fall.

So you know—and now you may string me up. Such was the way you caught me.
  Thank you for letting me tell it straight, though you never could greatly care.
For I took a horse that wasn't mine! . . . But there's one the heavens brought me,
  And I'll hang right happy, because I know he is waiting for me up there.

From creamy muzzle to cannon-bone, by God, he's a peerless wonder!
  He is steel and velvet and furnace-fire, and death's supremest prize,
And never again shall be roped on earth that neck that is "clothed with thunder. . . ."
  String me up, Dave! Go dig my grave! *I rode him across the skies!*

### BRAZEN TONGUE

Quick in spite I said unkind
Words that should have struck me blind.
Flatly on my eardrums rung
The raucous echoes of my tongue.

Burnished bees in an iron hive
Seemed my wits, and scarce alive
I sat with elbows on my knees
Sick with silence like disease.

Slowly through the solid floor
I sank, till there was nothing more
Than a grease-spot of me there
Shadowed by the upright chair.

O last night I lay awake
Parrying darkness for your sake,
Like an armory glittered bright
The lilied hours of our delight!

O this morning I intended
All the virtues this has ended,

Golden as a new-coined planet!
Now I wither into granite.

Tongue, you are a tongue of fire,
Shriveling like a white-hot wire,
Blackening like a dragon's breath
Flower-fluttering fields with death.

Tongue, you are a tongue of brass
In the jawbone of an ass,
Slaying what was most divine,—
Not the reeking Philistine.

So, she dug me from my quarry;
Came and said that she was sorry;
Sprinkled me with words like myrrh;
So I sat and stared at her;

And so I climb the burning mountain
And sit beside the lava fountain,
And, white with ashes, wonder why
In the devil I am I.

### JESSE JAMES

#### (*A Design in Red and Yellow for a Nickel Library*)

Jesse James was a two-gun man,
    (*Roll on, Missouri!*)
Strong-arm chief of an outlaw clan,
    (*From Kansas to Illinois!*)
He twirled an old Colt forty-five;
    (*Roll on, Missouri!*)
They never took Jesse James alive.
    (*Roll, Missouri, roll!*)

Jesse James was King of the Wes';
    (*Cataracts in the Missouri!*)
He'd a di'mon' heart in his lef' breas';
    (*Brown Missouri rolls!*)
He'd a fire in his heart no hurt could stifle;
    (*Thunder, Missouri!*)
Lion eyes an' a Winchester rifle.
    (*Missouri, roll down!*)

Jesse James rode a pinto hawse;
Come at night to a water-cawse;
Tetched with the rowel that pinto's flank;
She sprung the torrent from bank to bank.

Jesse rode through a sleepin' town;
Looked the moonlit street both up an' down;

Crack-crack-crack, the street ran flames
An' a great voice cried, "I'm Jesse James!"

Hawse an' afoot they're after Jess!
    *(Roll on, Missouri!)*
Spurrin' an' spurrin'—but he's gone Wes'.
    *(Brown Missouri rolls!)*
He was ten foot tall when he stood in his boots;
    *(Lightnin' like the Missouri!)*
More'n a match fer sich galoots.
    *(Roll, Missouri, roll!)*

Jesse James rode outa the sage;
Roun' the rocks come the swayin' stage;
Straddlin' the road a giant stan's
An' a great voice bellers, "Throw up yer han's!"

Jesse raked in the di'mon' rings,
The big gold watches an' the yuther things;
Jesse divvied 'em then an' thar
With a cryin' child had lost her mar.

They're creepin'; they're crawlin'; they're stalkin' Jess;
    *(Roll on, Missouri!)*
They's a rumor he's gone much further Wes';
    *(Roll, Missouri, roll!)*
They's word of a cayuse hitched to the bars
    *(Ruddy clouds on Missouri!)*
Of a golden sunset that busts into stars.
    *(Missouri, roll down!)*

Jesse James rode hell fer leather;
He was a hawse an' a man together;
In a cave in a mountain high up in air
He lived with a rattlesnake, a wolf, an' a bear.

Jesse's heart was as sof' as a woman;
Fer guts an' stren'th he was sooper-human;
He could put six shots through a woodpecker's eye
And take in one swaller a gallon o' rye.

They sought him here an' they sought him there,
    *(Roll on, Missouri!)*
But he strides by night through the ways of the air;
    *(Brown Missouri rolls!)*
They say he was took an' they say he is dead,
    *(Thunder, Missouri!)*
But he ain't—he's a sunset overhead!
    *(Missouri down to the sea!)*

Jesse James was a Hercules.
When he went through the woods he tore up the trees.
When he went on the plains he smoked the groun'
An' the hull lan' shuddered fer miles aroun'.

Jesse James wore a red bandanner
That waved on the breeze like the Star Spangled Banner;
In seven states he cut up dadoes.
He's gone with the buffler an' the desperadoes.

Yes, Jesse James was a two-gun man
    *(Roll on, Missouri!)*
The same as when this song began;
    *(From Kansas to Illinois!)*
An' when you see a sunset bust into flames
    *(Lightnin' like the Missouri!)*
Or a thunderstorm blaze—that's Jesse James!
    *(Hear that Missouri roll!)*

### ETERNAL MASCULINE

Neither will I put myself forward as others may do,
Neither, if you wish me to flatter, will I flatter you;
I will look at you grimly, and so you will know I am true.

Neither when all do agree and lout low and salute,
And you are beguiled by the tree and devout for the fruit,
Will I seem to be aught but the following eyes of a brute.

I will stand to one side and sip of my hellebore wine,
I will snarl and deride the antics and airs of the swine;
You will glance in your pride, but I will deny you a sign.

I will squint at the moon and be peaceful because I am dead,
I will whistle a tune and be glad of the harshness I said.
*O you will come soon, when the stars are a mist overhead!*

You will come, with eyes fierce; you will act a defiant surprise.
Quick lightings will pierce to our hearts from the pain in our eyes,
Standing strained and averse, with the trembling of love that defies.

And then I will know, by the heartbreaking turn of your head,
My madness brought low in a hell that is spared to the dead.
The upas will grow from the poisonous words that I said;

From under its shade out to where like a statue you stand,
Without wish to evade, I will reach, I will cry with my hand,
With my spirit dismayed, with my eyes and my mouth full of sand. . . .

### INSCRIPTION FOR A MIRROR IN A DESERTED DWELLING

Set silver cone to tulip flame!
The mantel mirror floats with night
Reflecting still green watery light.
The sconces glimmer. If she came
Like silence through the shadowy wall
Where walls are wading in the moon
The dark would tremble back to June.
So faintly now the moonbeams fall,
So soft this silence, that the verge
Of speech is reached. Remote and pale
As through some faint viridian veil
The lovely lineaments emerge,
The clearly amber eyes, the tint
Of pearl and faintest rose, the hair

To lacquered light, a silken snare
Of devious bronze, the tiny dint
With which her maker mocked the years
Beneath her lip imprinting praise.
Dim flower of desecrating days,
The old reflection, strange with tears,
Is gazing out upon the gloom,
Is widening eyes to find the light
In reminiscence, in the night
Of this foregone, forgotten room.

And you, the watcher, with your eyes
As wide as hers in dark distress,
Who never knew her loveliness
But guess through glass her shadowy guise,
For you around the glass I trace
This secret writing, that will burn
Like witch-fire should her shade return
To haunt you with that wistful face.

At least no gesturing figures pass;
Here is no tragic immanence
Of all the scenes of small events
That pantomimed before the glass.
No bliss, no passion, no despair,
No other actor lingers now;
The moonlight on a lifted brow
Is all,—the eyes so wide aware
Of clouds that pass with stars, and suns,
Of mystery that pales the cheek,
Of all the heart could never speak,
Of joy and pain so vivid once,
That ceased with music and the lights,
Dimming to darkness and repose. . . .
Lean then and kiss that ghostly rose
That was her face, this night of nights,—
And know the vision fled indeed,
The mirror's surface smooth and cold,
The words unbreathed, the tale untold,
The past unpiteous to your need!

## SAGACITY

We knew so much; when her beautiful eyes could lighten,
Her beautiful laughter follow our phrase;
Or the gaze go hard with pain, the lips tighten,
On the bitterer days.
Oh, ours was all knowing then, all generous displaying.
Such wisdom we had to show!
And now there is merely silence, silence, silence saying
All we did not know.

# Hazel Hall

Hazel hall was born February 7, 1886, in St. Paul, Minnesota, but as a small child was taken to Portland, Oregon, where she remained the rest of her life. Either from the effects of scarlet fever or as the result of a fall, she was unable to walk after she was twelve years old. She never complained. As Ruth Hall, her sister, wrote in a letter to the editor, "The word 'invalid' was anathema in her ears. Although she was forced to spend her days in a wheel chair, she possessed a rare abundance of health, which enabled her to know life concretely, as a satisfaction for her senses, even though it might remain an abstract sorrow for her mind. She lived life thoroughly, admiring its complexities, with a fine relish for the irony which gave a bitter-sweet taste to the whole."

*Curtains,* her first volume, which appeared in 1921, is, in the main, a book of charming rather than arresting lyrics; it is evident from the poems that her needle was not only a means of support but a refuge for the poet. The fact that she herself could never walk made her extraordinarily sensitive to the tramp or shuffle of feet; her mind seemed filled with the thought of men marching eternally about the earth. And so her second book, *Walkers* (1923), is filled with the wonder of mere pedestrian life, of a boy whacking a stick against a wall, of couples passing at dusk, of feet half-sinking in snow, of children's heels flashing in the sun.

Her third volume, *Cry of Time* (1929), upon which she was at work at the time of her death, contains her finest writing and the poems by which she probably will be remembered longest. These later poems have the appeal of the first two books with an emotional depth which the early volumes barely suggested.

Although Hazel Hall was in sound health until a few weeks before her death, she seemed to have a premonition that the end was near before she became critically ill. She died May 11, 1924. The last two poems which she wrote were "Slow Death" and "Riddle," both of which appeared a fortnight after her death.

### FLIGHT

A bird may curve across the sky—
A feather of dusk, a streak of song;
And save a space and a bird to fly
There may be nothing all day long.

Flying through a cloud-made place
A bird may tangle east and west,
Maddened with going, crushing space
With the arrow of its breast.

Though never wind nor motion bring
It back again from indefinite lands,
The thin blue shadow of its wing
May cross and cross above your hands.

### ANY WOMAN

When there is nothing left but darkness
And the day is like a leaf
Fallen onto sodden grasses,
You have earned a subtle grief.

Never let them take it from you,
Never let them come and say:
Night is made of black gauze; moonlight
Blows the filmy dark away.

You have a right to know the thickness
Of the night upon your face,
To feel the inky blue of nothing
Drift like ashes out of space.

You have a right to lift your fingers
And stare in pity at your hands

That are the exquisite frail mirrors
Of all the mind misunderstands.

Your hand, potent in portrayal,
Falls of its own weight to rest
In a quiet curve of sorrow
On the beating of your breast.

### HERE COMES THE THIEF

Here comes the thief
Men nickname Time,
Oh, hide you, leaf,
And hide you, rhyme.
Leaf, he would take you
And leave you rust.
Rhyme, he would flake you
With spotted dust.
Scurry to cover,
Delicate maid
And serious lover.
Girl, bind the braid
Of your burning hair;
He has an eye
For the lusciously fair
Who passes by.
O lover, hide—
Who comes to plunder
Has the crafty stride
Of unheard thunder.
Quick—lest he snatch,
In his grave need,
And sift and match,
Then sow like seed

Your love's sweet grief
On the backward air,
With the rhyme and the leaf
And the maiden's hair.

### SLOW DEATH

You need no other death than this
  Slow death that wears your heart away;
It is enough, the death that is
  Your every night, your every day.

It is enough, the sun that slants
Across your breast, heavy as steel,

Leaving the rust of radiance
  To shape a wound that will not heal.

Enough, the crystal at your lips,
  Wasting you even as it lies—
Vibrant there before it slips
  Away, torn from your mouth like cries.

There will be now, as fumes from wood,
  A passing, yet no new death's care.
You will know only the frustrate mood
  Of breath tarnished to color of air.

# Jean Starr Untermeyer

JEAN STARR was born at Zanesville, Ohio, May 13, 1886, and educated at the Putnam Seminary in the city of her birth. At sixteen she came to New York City, pursuing special studies at Columbia. She married Louis Untermeyer in 1907, divorced in 1933.

Growing Pains (1918) is a thin book of thirty-four poems, the result of eight years' slow and critical creation. This highly selective process did much to bring the volume up to an unusual level; a severity of standards maintains the poet on an austere plane. Perfection is a passion with her; the first poem in the book ("Clay Hills") declares it with almost intolerant definiteness.

Acutely self-analytical, there is a stern, uncompromising relentlessness toward her introspections; these poems are, as she explains in her title-poem—

> No songs for an idle lute,
> No pretty tunes of coddled ills,
> But the bare chart of my growing pains.

A sharp color sense, a surprising whimsicality, a translation of the ordinary in terms of the unexplored illumine such poems as "Sinfonia Domestica," "Clothes," and the much-quoted "Autumn," a celebration of domesticity which might be described as a housekeeper's paean. In the last named Mrs. Untermeyer has reproduced her early environment with bright pungency; "Verhaeren's Flemish genre pictures are no better," writes Amy Lowell. Several of her purely pictorial poems establish a swift kinship between the most romantic and most prosaic objects. The tiny "Moonrise" is an example; so is "High Tide," that, in one extended metaphor, turns the mere fact of a physical law into an arresting fancy.

Dreams Out of Darkness (1921) is a ripening of this author's power with a richer musical undercurrent. An increase of melody is manifest on every page, possibly most striking in "Lake Song," which, beneath its symbolism, is one of the few notable unrhymed lyrics of the period. The form of this poetry is, as Joseph Freeman has written, "distinguished not only by the clear qualities of chiseled marble, not only by a music so melodious that some of her free verse pieces have to be read two or three times before their lack of rhyme becomes noticeable, but also by its intellectual fluidity." Amy Lowell, amplifying this theme, concludes, "After all, beautiful as Mrs. Untermeyer's forms often are, it is her thoughts that make the book. This is the very heart of a woman, naked and serious, beautiful and un-ashamed."

Her training as a musician (she made her début as a *Liedersinger* in Vienna and London in 1924) added to her equipment as translator of the "official" life of *Franz Schubert* by Oscar Bie in 1928.

*Steep Ascent* (1927) marks this poet's spiritual as well as poetic climax. The dominant note, as might have been foreseen, is ethical, but there is no reliance on mere religiosity. Hers is a spirit whose essential quality other poets were quick to recognize. "Here," wrote Mary Sinton Leitch, "is no sorrow feigned for purposes of art, sorrow that gazes on itself to see what expression of despair best becomes it. Here is ruggedness of scarred, enduring granite and sincerity hardly to be sur-passed." "What is most remarkable about Jean Starr Untermeyer," wrote Edmund Wilson, "is the peculiar shading and force of her style. I believe that hers is clas-sically Hebraic. She has always seemed to me one of the few writers who have suc-cessfully preserved in a modern language something of the authentic austerity of Jewish literature."

The poems in *Wingèd Child* (1936)—two of which are reprinted in these pages— have a new serenity, even a sly humor; they do not proceed, as did many of the others, from struggle, but from assurance. The pitch is lower but no less vibrant; the note of rigorous austerity is softened and the forms are more varied. The early *vers libriste* gives way to the later formalist, even the "dissonant" rhymes of "Dew on a Dusty Heart" being cast in a sonnet.

### HIGH TIDE

I edged back against the night.
The sea growled assault on the wave-bitten shore.
And the breakers,
Like young and impatient hounds,
Sprang with rough joy on the shrinking sand.
Sprang—but were drawn back slowly
With a long, relentless pull,
Whimpering, into the dark.

Then I saw who held them captive;
And I saw how they were bound
With a broad and quivering leash of light,
Held by the moon,
As, calm and unsmiling,
She walked the deep fields of the sky.

AUTUMN

*(To My Mother)*

How memory cuts away the years,
And how clean the picture comes
Of autumn days, brisk and busy;
Charged with keen sunshine.
And you, stirred with activity,
The spirit of those energetic days.

There was our back-yard,
So plain and stripped of green,
With even the weeds carefully pulled away
From the crooked red bricks that made the walk,
And the earth on either side so black.

Autumn and dead leaves burning in the sharp air.
And winter comforts coming in like a pageant.
I shall not forget them:—
Great jars pompous with the raw green of pickles,
Standing in a solemn row across the back of the porch,
Exhaling the pungent dill;
And in the very center of the yard,
You, tending the great catsup kettle of gleaming copper,
Where fat, red tomatoes bobbed up and down
Like jolly monks in a drunken dance.
And there were bland banks of cabbages that came by the wagon-load,
Soon to be cut into delicate ribbons
Only to be crushed by the heavy, wooden stompers.
Such feathery whiteness—to come to kraut!
And after, there were grapes that hid their brightness under a gray dust,
Then gushed thrilling, purple blood over the fire;
And enameled crab-apples that tricked with their fragrance
But were bitter to taste.
And there were spicy plums and ill-shaped quinces,
And long string beans floating in pans of clear water
Like slim, green fishes.
And there was fish itself,
Salted, silver herring from the city. . . .

And you moved among these mysteries,
Absorbed and smiling and sure;
Stirring, tasting, measuring,
With the precision of a ritual.
I like to think of you in your years of power—
You, now so shaken and so powerless—
High priestess of your home.

### CLAY HILLS

It is easy to mold the yielding clay.
And many shapes grow into beauty
Under the facile hand.
But forms of clay are lightly broken;
They will lie shattered and forgotten in a dingy corner.

Yet underneath the slipping clay
Is rock . . .
I would rather work in stubborn rock
All the years of my life,
And make one strong thing
And set it in a high, clean place,
To recall the granite strength of my desire.

### SINFONIA DOMESTICA

When the white wave of a glory that is hardly I
　Breaks through my mind and washes it clean,
I know at last the meaning of my ecstasy,
　And know at last my wish and what it can mean.

To have sped out of life that night—to have vanished
　Not as a vision, but as something touched, yet grown
Radiant as the moonlight, circling my naked shoulder;
　Wrapped in a dream of beauty, longed for, but never known.

For how with our daily converse, even the sweet sharing
　Of thoughts, of food, of home, of common life,
How shall I be that glory, that last desire
　For which men struggle? Is Romance in a wife?

Must I bend a heart that is bowed to breaking
　With a frustration, inevitable and slow,
And bank my flame to a low hearth fire, believing
　You will come for warmth and life to its tempered glow?

Shall I mold my hope anew, to one of service,
　And tell my uneasy soul, "Behold, this is good"?
And meet you (if we do meet), even at Heaven's threshold,
　With ewer and basin, with clothing and with food?

### LAKE SONG

The lapping of lake water
Is like the weeping of women,
The weeping of ancient women
Who grieved without rebellion.

The lake falls over the shore
Like tears on their curven bosoms.
Here is languid, luxurious wailing;
The wailing of kings' daughters.

So do we ever cry,
A soft, unmutinous crying,
When we know ourselves each a princess
Locked fast within her tower.

The lapping of lake water
Is like the weeping of women,
The fertile tears of women
That water the dreams of men.

## BIRTHDAY

Now the beautiful business of summer is over,
Earth wraps herself in a bright, leaf-patterned shawl.
The hives cement the prodigal juice of the clover
And spendthrift gold is hoarded in bin and stall.
Beyond the wind-crisped hedge the cornstalks hover;
The pumpkin lies by the wall.

October's the heir of the year, and you, my lover,
October's darling, the first to come at her call,
May claim and hold what your wandering eyes discover
On jeweled hills that tempt a reluctant fall;
Blest by the fired earth, while skies above her
Spill golden peace over all.

## COUNTRY OF NO LACK

A lilac ribbon is unbound,
A band of gradual rose untied,
And lo, the glowing book of day
Is opened on the mountainside.

What curves salute, what colors sound
From this so-rich-illumined scroll,
For whose perusal one need pay
Only a just delight as toll.

The brook's clean silver set in stones
Is balanced by the silver sheen
Of clean-stripped logs, which in a field
Seem floating down a river of green.

Furze are not flowers, but the tones
Of sunlight that a bird has sung,
And broken purples but the yield
Of hoarded twilights, meadow-flung.

Against a heaven's faithful blue,
A fadeless forest lifts its pines,
From shadows deepening into black
A slim and shadowy road inclines.

Upon the printed air, how true
Stand lizard, lake and leaf, page-still.
Here in the country of no lack,
What care can move, what grief can chill

## ONE KIND OF HUMILITY

Shall we say heaven is not heaven
Since golden stairs are rugged and uneven

Or that no light illuminates a star
That swings in other regions than we ar

Deny with soured breath enduring God
Because we cling so rankly to the sod?

ɔ. Cleanse with weeping, fasting and with
prayer.
aise God. Look starward. Mount the stair!

### DEW ON A DUSTY HEART

If come into this world again I must
And take unto myself another form,
Oh, let it be unblemished by a mist
Of imperfections or the line infirm.

And let it shapen to a secret wish
Untouched, untinctured, even by a dram
Of earthiness; nor let the fretted wash
Of passion fray the fine-immaculate dream.

Oh, let me come back as a melody
New as the air it takes, no taint of ill
To halt such lovely flying as birds do
Going from infinite nought to infinite all.
Giving to dusty hearts that lag at even
The dewy rest they dream of and call heaven.

# H. D.

HILDA DOOLITTLE was born September 10, 1886, at Bethlehem, Pennsylvania. When she was still a child, her father became Director of the Flower Observatory and the family moved to a suburb in the outskirts of Philadelphia. Hilda Doolittle attended a private school in West Philadelphia; entered Bryn Mawr College in 1904; and went abroad, for what was intended to be a short sojourn, in 1911. After a visit to Italy and France she came to London, joined Ezra Pound, and helped to organize the Imagists. She married one of the original group, Richard Aldington, the English poet and novelist, whom she later divorced. Her work (signed "H. D.") began to appear in a few magazines and its unusual quality was recognized at once. Remaining for a while in London, she became one of the leaders of the movement, creating through a chiseled verse her flawless evocations of Greek poetry and sculpture. In 1920 she made a long-deferred visit to America, settling on the Californian coast, returning the following year to England. Since 1921 H. D. has lived in London and in a small town in Switzerland on the shore of Lake Geneva.

Her first collection, *Sea Garden,* appeared in 1916; an interval of five years elapsed before the publication of her second volume, *Hymen,* which was printed simultaneously in England and America in 1921. These volumes showed H. D. as the most important of her group. She was the only one who steadfastly held to the letter as well as the spirit of its *credo.* She was, in fact, the only true Imagist. Her poems are like a set of Tanagra figurines. Here, at first glance, the effect is chilling— beauty seems held in a frozen gesture. But it is in this very fixation of light, color and emotion that she achieves intensity. What at first seemed static becomes fluent; the arrested moment glows with a quivering tension.

Observe the poem entitled "Heat." Here, in the fewest possible words, is something beyond the description of heat—here is the effect of it. In these lines one feels the weight and solidity of a midsummer afternoon. So in "The Islands" a propulsion of feeling hurries forward the syllables balancing on light and dark vowels, and what might have been only a list of antique names becomes an outcry. Her efforts to draw the contemporary world are less happy. H. D. is best in her reflections of clear-cut loveliness in a quietly pagan world; in most of her moods, she seems less a modern writer than an inspired anachronism.

*Heliodora and Other Poems* appeared in 1924. So much had already been written concerning the form of H. D.'s poetry that it was no longer necessary to expatiate on the unique features of her metric. Even those least impressed by the program of the Imagists readily conceded her exquisite if oversubtle flavor, the stripped purity of her line, the precision of her epithets. But the most apparent feature of *Heliodora* —even more noticeable than its beauties of form—is its intensity. A freely declared passion radiates from lines which are at once ecstatic and austere. Even the most casual reading must convince one that this poet is not, as she first seemed to us, a Greek statue faintly flushed with life, a delightful but detached relic of another world. This is a woman responsive to color and pain, aroused by loveliness, shocked by betrayal, affected by all those manifestations which are too old to be timely, too fresh to be "antique."

Practically all of H. D.'s previous volumes were assembled in *Collected Poems* (1925) which contains not only her original work but the spirited translations from the Odyssey and her flexible expansions of fragmentary phrases of Sappho. A play, *Hippolytus Temporizes,* appeared in 1927. In the later works it is interesting to trace the tightening of form, the approximation of more regular structure, even the introduction of half-candid, half-concealed rhyme.

*Red Roses for Bronze* (1932) stresses the note of personal emotion, the emotion of love once requited but now unreturned. The poetry is more weighted than before and less dependent on its decorations; sometimes its direct appeal is compelling, sometimes it relies on platitudes of passion and rings hollow. At their best the poems combine the skill of the early Imagist with the strength of the mature poet.

H. D.'s prose is somewhat more derivative, bearing overtones of Gertrude Stein, but it rises above its influences. *Palimpsest* (1926) and *Hedylus* (1928) embody a poet's prose, the former a triptych of interrelated tragedies, actual and intuitive.

### OREAD

Whirl up, sea—
Whirl your pointed pines.
Splash your great pines
On our rocks.
Hurl your green over us—
Cover us with your pools of fir.

### PEAR TREE

Silver dust
lifted from the earth,
higher than my arms reach,
you have mounted.
O silver,
higher than my arms reach
you front us with great mass;
no flower ever opened
so staunch a white leaf,
no flower ever parted silver
from such rare silver;

O white pear,
your flower-tufts,
thick on the branch,
bring summer and ripe fruits
in their purple hearts.

### HEAT

O wind, rend open the heat,
cut apart the heat,
rend it to tatters.

Fruit cannot drop
through this thick air—
fruit cannot fall into heat
that presses up and blunts
the points of pears
and rounds the grapes.

Cut through the heat—
plow through it,

turning it on either side
of your path.

## ORCHARD

I saw the first pear
as it fell—
the honey-seeking, golden-banded,
the yellow swarm,
was not more fleet than I,
(spare us from loveliness!)
and I fell prostrate,
crying:
you have flayed us with your blossoms,
spare us the beauty
of fruit-trees!

The honey-seeking
paused not;
the air thundered their song,
and I alone was prostrate.

O rough-hewn
god of the orchard,
I bring you an offering—
do you, alone unbeautiful,
son of the god,
spare us from loveliness:

these fallen hazel-nuts,
stripped late of their green sheaths,
grapes, red-purple,
their berries
dripping with wine;
pomegranates already broken,
and shrunken figs,
and quinces untouched,
I bring you as offering.

## SONG

You are as gold
as the half-ripe grain
that merges to gold again,
as white as the white rain
that beats through
the half-opened flowers
of the great flower tufts
thick on the black limbs
of an Illyrian apple bough.

Can honey distill such fragrance
as your bright hair—
for your face is as fair as rain;
yet as rain that lies clear
on white honey-comb
lends radiance to the white wax,
so your hair on your brow
casts light for a shadow.

## FROM "LET ZEUS RECORD"

Stars wheel in purple, yours is not so rare
as Hesperus, nor yet so great a star
as bright Aldebaran or Sirius,
nor yet the stained and brilliant one of War;

stars turn in purple, glorious to the sight;
yours is not gracious as the Pleiads are,
nor as Orion's sapphires, luminous;

yet disenchanted, cold, imperious face,
when all the others, blighted, reel and fall,
your star, steel-set, keeps lone and frigid tryst
to freighted ships baffled in wind and blast.

## LAIS

Let her who walks in Paphos
take the glass,
let Paphos take the mirror
and the work of frosted fruit,
gold apples set
with silver apple-leaf,
white leaf of silver
wrought with vein of gilt.

Let Paphos lift the mirror;
let her look
into the polished center of the disk.
Let Paphos take the mirror:
did she press
flowerlet of flame-flower
to the lustrous white
of the white forehead?
Did the dark veins beat
a deeper purple
than the wine-deep tint
of the dark flower?

Did she deck black hair,
one evening, with the winter-white

flower of the winter-berry?
Did she look (reft of her lover)
at a face gone white
under the chaplet
of white virgin-breath?

Lais, exultant, tyrannizing Greece,
Lais who kept her lovers in the porch,
lover on lover waiting
(but to creep
where the robe brushed the threshold
where still sleeps Lais),
so she creeps, Lais,
to lay her mirror at the feet
of her who reigns in Paphos.

Lais has left her mirror,
for she sees no longer in its depth
the Lais' self
that laughed exultant,
tyrannizing Greece.

Lais has left her mirror,
for she weeps no longer,
finding in its depth
a face, but other
than dark flame and white
feature of perfect marble.

*Lais has left her mirror*
*(so one wrote)*
*to her who reigns in Paphos;*
*Lais who laughed a tyrant over Greece,*
*Lais who turned the lovers from the porch,*
*that swarm for whom now*
*Lais has no use;*
*Lais is now no lover of the glass,*
*seeing no more the face as once it was,*
*wishing to see that face and finding this.*

FROM "HALCYON"

("*Bird—loved of sea-men*")

I'm not here,
everything's vague, blurred everywhere,
then you are blown
into a room;

the sea comes where a carpet
laid red and purple,

and where the edge showed marble
there is sea-weed;

sedge breaks the wall
where the couch stands,
the hands of strange people,
twisting tassel and fringe

of rich cloth, become clear;
I understand the people,
they aren't hateful but dear;
over all

a shrill wind, clear sky;
O why, why, why
am I fretful, insecure,
why am I vague, unsure

until you are blown,
unexpected, small, quaint, unnoticeable,
a gray gull
into a room.

SONGS FROM CYPRUS

I

Gather for festival
bright weed and purple shell;
make on the holy sand
pattern as one might make
who tread with rose-red heel
a measure
pleasureful;

such as those songs we made
in rose and myrtle shade
where rose and myrtle fell
(shell-petal or rose-shell)
on just such holy sand;
ah, the song
musical;

give me white rose and red;
find me in citron glade
citron of precious weight,
spread gold before her feet,
ah, weave the citron flower;
hail, goddess
beautiful.

## II

Where is the nightingale,
in what myrrh-wood and dim?
ah, let the night come black,
for we would conjure back
all that enchanted him,
  *all that enchanted him.*

Where is the bird of fire?
in what packed hedge of rose?
in what roofed ledge of flower?
no other creature knows
what magic lurks within,
  *what magic lurks within.*

Bird, bird, bird, bird, we cry,
hear, pity us in pain;
hearts break in the sunlight,
hearts break in daylight rain,
only night heals again,
  *only night heals again.*

### HOLY SATYR

Most holy Satyr,
like a goat,
with horns and hooves
to match thy coat
of russet brown,
I make leaf-circlets
and a crown of honey-flowers
for thy throat;
where the amber petals
drip to ivory,
I cut and slip
each stiffened petal
in the rift
of carven petal;
honey horn
has wed the bright
virgin petal of the white
flower cluster: lip to lip
let them whisper,
let them lilt, quivering.

Most holy Satyr,
like a goat,
hear this our song,
accept our leaves,
love-offering,

return our hymn,
like echo fling
a sweet song,
answering note for note.

### THE ISLANDS

#### I

What are the islands to me,
what is Greece,
what is Rhodes, Samos, Chios,
what is Paros facing west,
what is Crete?

What is Samothrace,
rising like a ship,
what is Imbros rending the storm-waves
with its breast?

What is Naxos, Paros, Milos,
what the circle about Lycia,
what the Cyclades'
white necklace?

What is Greece—
Sparta, rising like a rock,
Thebes, Athens,
what is Corinth?

What is Euboia
with its island violets,
what is Euboia, spread with grass,
set with swift shoals,
what is Crete?

What are the islands to me,
what is Greece?

#### II

What can love of land give to me
that you have not—
what do the tall Spartans know,
and gentler Attic folk?

What has Sparta and her women
more than this?

What are the islands to me
if you are lost—
what is Naxos, Tinos, Andros,

and Delos, the clasp
of the white necklace?

### III

What can love of land give to me
that you have not,
what can love of strife break in me
that you have not?

Though Sparta enter Athens,
Thebes wrack Sparta,
each changes as water,
salt, rising to wreak terror
and falling back.

### IV

"What has love of land given to you
that I have not?"

I have questioned Tyrians
where they sat
on the black ships,
weighted with rich stuffs;
I have asked the Greeks
from the white ships,
and Greeks from ships whose hulks
lay on the wet sand, scarlet
with great beaks.
I have asked bright Tyrians
and tall Greeks—
"what has love of land given you?"
And they answered—"peace."

### V

But Beauty is set apart,
beauty is cast by the sea,
a barren rock,
beauty is set about
with wrecks of ships,
upon our coast, death keeps
the shallows—death waits
clutching toward us
from the deeps.

Beauty is set apart;
the winds that slash its beach,
swirl the coarse sand
upward toward the rocks.

Beauty is set apart
from the islands
and from Greece.

### VI

In my garden
the winds have beaten
the ripe lilies;
in my garden, the salt
has wilted the first flakes
of young narcissus,
and the lesser hyacinth,
and the salt has crept
under the leaves of the white hyacinth.

In my garden,
even the wind-flowers lie flat,
broken by the wind at last.

### VII

What are the islands to me
if you are lost,
what is Paros to me
if your eyes draw back,
what is Milos
if you take fright of beauty,
terrible, tortuous, isolated,
a barren rock?

What is Rhodes, Crete,
what is Paros facing west,
what, white Imbros?

What are the islands to me
if you hesitate,
what is Greece if you draw back
from the terror
and cold splendor of song
and its bleak sacrifice?

### HELEN

All Greece hates
the still eyes in the white face,
the luster as of olives
where she stands,
and the white hands.

All Greece reviles
the wan face when she smiles,
hating it deeper still
when it grows wan and white,
remembering past enchantments
and past ills.

Greece sees unmoved,
God's daughter, born of love,

the beauty of cool feet
and slenderest knees,
could love indeed the maid,
only if she were laid,
white ash amid funereal cypresses.

### LETHE

Nor skin nor hide nor fleece
    Shall cover you,
Nor curtain of crimson nor fine
Shelter of cedar-wood be over you,
    Nor the fir-tree
    Nor the pine.

Nor sight of whin nor gorse
    Nor river-yew,
    Nor fragrance of flowering bush,
Nor wailing of reed-bird to waken you.
    Nor of linnet
    Nor of thrush.

Nor word nor touch nor sight
    Of lover, you
Shall long through the night but for this:
The roll of the full tide to cover you
    Without question,
    Without kiss.

## John Hall Wheelock

JOHN HALL WHEELOCK was born at Far Rockaway, Long Island, in 1886. He was graduated from Harvard, receiving his B.A. in 1908, and finished his studies at the Universities of Göttingen and Berlin, 1908-10.

Wheelock's first book is, in many respects, his best. *The Human Fantasy* (1911) sings with the voice of youth—youth vibrantly, even vociferously, in love with existence. Rhapsodic and obviously influenced by Whitman and Henley, these lines beat bravely; headlong ecstasy rises from pages whose refrain is "Splendid it is to live and glorious to die." *The Beloved Adventure* (1912) is less powerful, but scarcely less passionate. Lyric after lyric moves by its athletic affirmation.

Wheelock's subsequent volumes are less individualized. *Love and Liberation* (1913) and *Dust and Light* (1919) are long dilutions of the earlier strain. The music is still here, but most of the vigor has gone. Wheelock has allowed himself to be exploited by his own fluency and the result is lyrical monotony. Yet vast stretches of two hundred and thirty unvaried love-songs cannot bury a dozen vivid poems which lie, half-concealed, in a waste of verbiage.

*The Black Panther* (1922) furnishes additional proof that though Wheelock's star may have waned it did not die. In this volume the poet's gift assumes greater dignity; the flashing athleticism has matured into a steady fervor. With the exception of a few innocuous songs, there is revealed a graver music than Wheelock has accomplished. In the longer poems, most effectively in "Earth," he expresses the paradox of conflict and consent: the philosophy of the single Consciousness which reconciles terror and tenderness, murder and laughter, dawn and destruction—"Life, the dreadful, the magnificent."

*The Bright Doom* (1927), the smallest of Wheelock's volumes, is full of his best and worst. No poem is bad; no poem is quite good enough. The total effect is of desperate sincerity lost in foggy generalities, genuine poetry floundering in a wash of rhetoric. The early verse, less notable in idea, is more persuasive in image, more winning as music.

### SUNDAY EVENING IN THE COMMON

Look—on the topmost branches of the world
  The blossoms of the myriad stars are thick;
  Over the huddled rows of stone and brick,
A few, sad wisps of empty smoke are curled
  Like ghosts, languid and sick.

One breathless moment now the city's moaning
  Fades, and the endless streets seem vague and dim;
  There is no sound around the whole world's rim,
Save in the distance a small band is droning
  Some desolate old hymn.

Van Wyck, how often have we been together
  When this same moment made all mysteries clear;
  —The infinite stars that brood above us here,
And the gray city in the soft June weather,
  So tawdry and so dear!

### TRIUMPH OF LOVE

I shake my hair in the wind of morning
  For the joy within me that knows no bounds,
I echo backward the vibrant beauty
  Wherewith heaven's hollow lute resounds.

I shed my song on the feet of all men,
  On the feet of all shed out like wine,
On the whole and the hurt I shed my bounty,
  The beauty within me that is not mine.

Turn not away from my song, nor scorn me,
  Who bear the secret that holds the sky
And the stars together, but know within me
  There speaks another more wise than I.

Nor spurn me here from your heart, to hate me!
  Yet hate me here if you will—not so
Myself you hate, but the Love within me
  That loves you, whether you would or no.

Here love returns with love to the lover,
  And beauty unto the heart thereof,
And hatred unto the heart of the hater,
  Whether he would or no, with love!

## NIRVANA

ep on, I lie at heaven's high oriels,
Over the stars that murmur as they go
Lighting your lattice-window far below;
d every star some of the glory spells
Whereof I know.

ave forgotten you long, long ago,
Like the sweet silver singing of thin bells
nished, or music fading faint and low.
Sleep on, I lie at heaven's high oriels,
ho loved you so.

## LOVE AND LIBERATION

Lift your arms to the stars
And give an immortal shout;
Not all the veils of darkness
Can put your beauty out!

You are armed with love, with love,
Nor all the powers of Fate
Can touch you with a spear,
Nor all the hands of hate.

What of good and evil,
Hell and Heaven above—
Trample them with love!
Ride over them with love!

## EARTH

Grasshopper, your fairy song
And my poem alike belong
To the dark and silent earth
From which all poetry has birth.
All we say and all we sing
Is but as the murmuring
Of that drowsy heart of hers
When from her deep dream she stirs:
If we sorrow, or rejoice,
You and I are but her voice.

Deftly does the dust express
In mind her hidden loveliness,
And from her cool silence stream
The cricket's cry and Dante's dream;
For the earth that breeds the trees
Breeds cities too, and symphonies.
Equally her beauty flows
Into a savior, or a rose—

Looks down in dream, and from above
Smiles at herself in Jesus' love.
Christ's love and Homer's art
Are but the workings of her heart;
Through Leonardo's hand she seeks
Herself, and through Beethoven speaks
In holy thunderings around
The awful message of the ground.

The serene and humble mold
Does in herself all selves enfold—
Kingdoms, destinies, and creeds,
Great dreams, and dauntless deeds,
Science that metes the firmament,
The high, inflexible intent
Of one for many sacrificed—
Plato's brain, the heart of Christ;
All love, all legend, and all lore
Are in the dust forevermore.

Even as the growing grass,
Up from the soil religions pass,
And the field that bears the rye
Bears parables and prophecy.
Out of the earth the poem grows
Like the lily, or the rose;
And all man is, or yet may be,
Is but herself in agony
Toiling up the steep ascent
Toward the complete accomplishment
When all dust shall be, the whole
Universe, one conscious soul.

Yea, the quiet and cool sod
Bears in her breast the dream of God.
If you would know what earth is, scan
The intricate, proud heart of man,
Which is the earth articulate,
And learn how holy and how great,
How limitless and how profound
Is the nature of the ground—
How without terror or demur
We may entrust ourselves to her
When we are wearied out and lay
Our faces in the common clay.

For she is pity, she is love,
All wisdom, she, all thoughts that move
About her everlasting breast
Till she gathers them to rest:
All tenderness of all the ages,
Seraphic secrets of the sages,

Vision and hope of all the seers,
All prayer, all anguish, and all tears
Are but the dust that from her dream
Awakes, and knows herself supreme—
Are but earth, when she reveals
All that her secret heart conceals
Down in the dark and silent loam,
Which is ourselves, asleep, at home.
Yea, and this, my poem, too,
Is part of her as dust and dew,
Wherein herself she doth declare
Through my lips, and say her prayer.

### THIS QUIET DUST

Here in my curving hands I cup
This quiet dust; I lift it up.

Here is the mother of all thought;
Of this the shining heavens are wrough
The laughing lips, the feet that rove,
The face, the body, that you love:
Mere dust, no more, yet nothing less,
And this has suffered consciousness,
Passion, and terror, this again
Shall suffer passion, death, and pain.

For, as all flesh must die, so all,
Now dust, shall live. 'Tis natural;
Yet hardly do I understand—
Here in the hollow of my hand
A bit of God Himself I keep,
Between two vigils fallen asleep.

# *Joyce Kilmer*

(Alfred) Joyce Kilmer was born at New Brunswick, New Jersey, December 6, 1886. He attended Rutgers College and received his A.B. from Columbia in 1906. After leaving Columbia he became, in rapid succession, instructor of Latin at Morristown High School, editor of a journal for horsemen, book salesman, bookreviewer, lexicographer, interviewer and socialist.

After Kilmer became converted to Catholicism his conception of the church was the Church Militant. "His thought," writes his biographer, Robert Cortes Holliday, "dwelt continually on warrior-saints. . . . As he saw it, there was no question as to his duty." In 1917 Kilmer joined the Officers' Reserve Training Corps, but he soon resigned from this. In less than three weeks after America entered the World War, he enlisted as a private in the Seventh Regiment, National Guard, New York. Shortly before the regiment left New York for Spartanburg, South Carolina, Kilmer was transferred at his own request to the 165th Infantry. In spite of his avowed militancy, Kilmer was "a poet trying to be a soldier"; he made no effort to glorify war; his one hope was to wring some spiritual satisfaction out of the brutality.

On July 28, 1918, the five-day battle for the mastery of the heights beyond the river Ourcq was begun. Two days later Kilmer was killed in action.

Death came before the poet had developed or even matured his gifts. His first volume, *Summer of Love* (1911), is wholly imitative; it is full of reflections of a dozen other sources, "a broken bundle of mirrors." *Trees and Other Poems* (1914) contains the title-poem by which Kilmer is best known and, though various influences are still strong (one cannot miss the borrowed accents of Patmore, Belloc, Chesterton, Housman and—*vide* "Martin"—E. A. Robinson), a refreshing candor brightens the lines. *Main Street and Other Poems* (1917) is less derivative; the simplicity is less self-conscious though the note struck is a familiar one.

Besides his own poetry, Kilmer edited a selection of *Verses* by Hilaire Belloc (1916) and *Dreams and Images,* an anthology of Catholic poets (1917).

### TREES

I think that I shall never see
A poem lovely as a tree.

A tree whose hungry mouth is prest
Against the sweet earth's flowing breast;

A tree that looks at God all day,
And lifts her leafy arms to pray;

A tree that may in summer wear
A nest of robins in her hair;

Upon whose bosom snow has lain;
Who intimately lives with rain.

Poems are made by fools like me,
But only God can make a tree.

### MARTIN

When I am tired of earnest men,
  Intense and keen and sharp and clever,
Pursuing fame with brush or pen
  Or counting metal disks forever,
Then from the halls of shadowland
  Beyond the trackless purple sea
Old Martin's ghost comes back to stand
  Beside my desk and talk to me.

Still on his delicate pale face
  A quizzical thin smile is showing,

His cheeks are wrinkled like fine lace,
  His kind blue eyes are gay and glowing.
He wears a brilliant-hued cravat,
  A suit to match his soft gray hair,
A rakish stick, a knowing hat,
  A manner blithe and debonair.

How good that he who always knew
  That being lovely was a duty,
Should have gold halls to wander through
  And should himself inhabit beauty.
How like his old unselfish way
  To leave those halls of splendid mirth
And comfort those condemned to stay
  Upon the bleak and somber earth.

Some people ask: What cruel chance
  Made Martin's life so sad a story?
Martin? Why, he exhaled romance
  And wore an overcoat of glory.
A fleck of sunlight in the street,
  A horse, a book, a girl who smiled,—
Such visions made each moment sweet
  For this receptive, ancient child.

Because it was old Martin's lot
  To be, not make, a decoration,
Shall we then scorn him, having not
  His genius of appreciation?
Rich joy and love he got and gave;
  His heart was merry as his dress.
Pile laurel wreaths upon his grave
  Who did not gain, but was, success.

## Roy Helton

ROY (ADDISON) HELTON was born at Washington, D. C., in 1886 and graduated from the University of Pennsylvania in 1908. He studied art—and found he was color-blind. He spent two years at inventions—and found he had no business sense. After a few more experiments he became a schoolmaster in West Philadelphia and at the Penn Charter School in Germantown.

Helton's first volume, *Youth's Pilgrimage* (1915), is a strange, mystical affair, full of vague symbolism and purple patches. *Outcasts in Beulah Land* (1918) is entirely different in theme and treatment. This is a much starker verse, direct and sharp in its effect.

Helton became intimately connected with primitive backgrounds, spending a great part of his time in the mountains of South Carolina and Kentucky. His later verse in *Lonesome Water* (1930) shows the influence of this intimacy. Its spirit creeps into his fanciful prose, *The Early Adventures of Peacham Grew* (1925), a story which unites quaintness and tragedy in a delicate chronicle of boyhood. Strangeness of another sort fills *Nitchie Tilley* (1934), a later novel.

"Old Christmas Morning" is obviously a Kentucky Mountain dialogue in which, not so obviously, Helton has introduced an element rare in modern verse. Told with the directness of an old ballad, this drama of the night twelve days after the universally celebrated Christmas unfolds a ghost story in which the surprise is heightened by the skillful suspensions. "Lonesome Water" is a direct communication in the vernacular. Asked to furnish a glossary, Helton wrote, "It is true that the ballads need footnotes, a living abomination. Yet to suppress the living tongue would be still worse. I have tried to use only the common and most general mountain words, despising that preciosity of folk-talk dug out and patched together which is now a fashion. . . . *Sang:* a universal Southernmountain word for Gin Seng wherever the weed is grown or picked. *Trace:* a trail or footpath. *Pretties:* any sort of toy or decoration. *Uses:* lives."

### OLD CHRISTMAS MORNING

#### (*A Kentucky Mountain Ballad*)

"Where are you coming from, Lomey Carter,
   So airly over the snow?
And what's them pretties you got in your hand,
   And where you aiming to go?

"Step in, Honey: Old Christmas morning
   I ain't got nothing much;
Maybe a bite of sweetness and corn bread,
   A little ham meat and such.

"But come in, Honey! Sally Anne Barton's
   Hungering after your face.
Wait till I light my candle up:
   Set down! There's your old place.

"Now where you been so airly this morning?"

   *"Graveyard, Sally Anne.*
*Up by the trace in the salt lick meadows*
   *Where Taulbe kilt my man."*

"Taulbe ain't to home this morning . . .
   I can't scratch up a light:
Dampness gets on the heads of the matches;
   But I'll blow up the embers bright."

*"Needn't trouble. I won't be stopping:*
*Going a long ways still."*

"You didn't see nothing, Lomey Carter,
Up on the graveyard hill?"

*"What should I see there, Sally Anne Barton?"*
"Well, sperits do walk last night."

*"There were an elder bush a-blooming*
*While the moon still give some light."*

"Yes, elder bushes, they bloom, Old Christmas,
And critters kneel down in their straw.
Anything else up in the graveyard?"

*"One thing more I saw:*
*I saw my man with his head all bleeding*
*Where Taulbe's shot went through."*
"What did he say?"
*"He stooped and kissed me."*
"What did he say to you?"

*"Said, Lord Jesus forguv your Taulbe;*
*But he told me another word;*
*He said it soft when he stooped and kissed me.*
*That were the last I heard."*

"Taulbe ain't to home this morning."
*"I know that, Sally Anne,*
*For I kilt him, coming down through the meadow*
*Where Taulbe kilt my man.*

*"I met him upon the meadow trace*
*When the moon were fainting fast,*
*And I had my dead man's rifle gun*
*And kilt him as he come past."*

"But I heard two shots."
*"'Twas his was second:*
*He shot me 'fore he died:*
*You'll find us at daybreak, Sally Anne Barton:*
*I'm laying there dead at his side."*

## LONESOME WATER

Drank lonesome water:
Warn't but a tad then
Up in a laurel thick
Digging for sang;
Came on a place where

The stones were hollow,
Something below them
Tinkled and rang.

Dug whar I heard it
Drippling below me:

Should a knowed better,
Should a been wise;
Leant down and drank it,
Clutching and gripping
The over hung cliv
With the ferns in my eyes.

Tasted of heart leaf
And that smells the sweetest,
Pawpaw and spice bush
And wild brier rose;
Must a been counting
The heels of the spruce pines,
And neighboring round
Whar angelica grows.

I'd drunk lonesome water,
I knowed in a minute:
Never larnt nothing
From then till today:
Nothing worth larning

Nothing worth knowing,
I'm bound to the hills
And I can't get away.

Mean sort of dried up old
Ground-hoggy fellow,
Laying out cold here
Watching the sky;
Pore as a hipporwill,
Bent like a grass blade;
Counting up stars
Till they count too high.

I know whar the gray foxes
Uses up yander:
Know what will cure you
Of tisic and chills,
But I never been way from here,
Never got going;
I've drunk lonesome water.
I'm bound to the hills.

## Orrick Johns

ORRICK JOHNS was born in St. Louis, Missouri, in 1887. He schooled himself to be an advertising copy writer, and kept his creative work as an avocation.

*Asphalt and Other Poems* (1917) is a queer mixture. Cheap stanzas crowd against lines of singular beauty; poor dialect verse elbows lyrics that are without a false note. The same incongruity is evident in *Black Branches* (1920), where much that is strained and artificial mingles with poetry that is spontaneous. At his best, notably in the refreshing "Country Rhymes," Johns is a true singer, a lyricist of no small stature.

Although Johns' long poem "Second Avenue" won the first prize offered by the editor of *The Lyric Year* (1912), the anthology which first brought to light Edna St. Vincent Millay's "Renascence," his more representative work is entirely in the short measure. *Wild Plum* (1926) assembles the best of his lyrics, which are not without searching moments. The simplicities are genuine and such songs as "The Interpreter," "Little Things" and "Wild Plum" are not easily forgotten.

### THE INTERPRETER

In the very early morning when the light was low
She got all together and she went like snow,
Like snow in the springtime on a sunny hill,
And we were only frightened and can't think still.

We can't think quite that the katydids and frogs
And the little crying chickens and the little grunting hogs,
And the other living things that she spoke for to us
Have nothing more to tell her since it happened thus.

She never is around for anyone to touch,
But of ecstasy and longing she too knew much . . .
And always when anyone has time to call his own
She will come and be beside him as quiet as a stone.

## LITTLE THINGS

There's nothing very beautiful and nothing very gay
About the rush of faces in the town by day;
But a light tan cow in a pale green mead,
That is very beautiful, beautiful indeed . . .
And the soft March wind and the low March mist
Are better than kisses in a dark street kissed . . .
The fragrance of the forest when it wakes at dawn,
The fragrance of a trim green village lawn,
The hearing of the murmur of the rain at play—
These things are beautiful, beautiful as day!
And I shan't stand waiting for love or scorn
When the feast is laid for a day new-born . . .
Oh, better let the little things I loved when little
Return when the heart finds the great things brittle;
And better is a temple made of bark and thong
Than a tall stone temple that may stand too long.

## DILEMMA

What though the moon should come
  With a blinding glow,
And the stars have a game
  On the wood's edge. . . .
A man would have to still
  Cut and weed and sow,
And lay a white line
  When he plants a hedge.

What though God
  With a great sound of rain
Came to talk of violets
  And things people do. . . .
I would have to labor
  And dig with my brain
Still to get a truth
  Out of all words new.

## WILD PLUM

They are unholy who are born
  To love wild plum at night,
Who once have passed it on a road
  Glimmering and white.

It is as though the darkness had
  Speech of silver words,
Or as though a cloud of stars
  Perched like ghostly birds.

They are unpitied from their birth
  And homeless in men's sight,
Who love, better than the earth,
  Wild plum at night.

## Marianne Moore

M ARIANNE MOORE was born in St. Louis, Missouri, November 15, 1887. She received her B.A. from Bryn Mawr College in 1909; taught stenography at the United States Indian school at Carlisle, Pennsylvania, from 1911 to 1915; was an assistant in the Hudson Park Branch of the New York Public Library, and editor of *The Dial* from 1925 to its demise in 1929.

Her verse was first published in *The Egoist* (London) in 1915 and, although her unusual lines attracted immediate attention, an inherent reticence kept her from submitting a collection to any publisher. It was not until 1921 that a few of her friends "pirated" her work and so, without her coöperation, *Poems* was published in that year by *The Egoist Press*. Three years later she received the Dial Award of two thousand dollars for "distinguished service to American letters." Her *Observations* (1924), a volume including the earlier poems as well as the more recent ones, appeared at the same time.

Miss Moore's work is frankly puzzling, not only to the disinterested reader, but to the student of modern poetry. Although her early verses present no difficulties, her more characteristic lines seem to erect a barrier of jagged clauses, barbed quotations and suspicious structures between herself and her audience. It has been asserted, and the editor shares this opinion, that Miss Moore's highly intellectualized dissertations are actually part of the domain of criticism rather than of poetry, and that her creations are in the latter division chiefly because of the physical pattern of her lines. Her studies are usually scornful and sophisticated, filled with statements which seem to be seeking their prose origins: a sort of witty and ironic geometry. Her satires are in a new *genre* and her observations are both precise and fantastic—she sees zebras "supreme in their abnormality," elephants "with their fog-colored skins."

*Selected Poems,* published in 1935, with an introduction by T. S. Eliot, accentuates the problems presented by her work. There can be no doubt about Miss Moore's wit or the incision of her ideas. Her language has a curious bite, and the phrasing is both exact and unusual. The lizard is "a nervous naked sword on little feet," the elephant "black earth preceded by a tendril," the snake has "hypodermic teeth." But readers are more likely to be irritated by Mr. Eliot's claims for Miss Moore than persuaded by them. He insists that such a pattern as:

> an
> injured fan . . .
> the
> turquoise sea

is a commendable innovation, and he finds such a distortion as:

> al-
> ways has been—at the antipodes from the init-
>     ial great truths. Part of it was crawling, part of it
> was about to crawl, the rest
>     was torpid in its lair. In the short-legged, fit-
> ful advance. . . .

is not only admirable but a fine example of *light* rhyme—and of this "light rhyme Miss Moore is the greatest living master." To the average, even to the sensitive, ear such a pattern is the very opposite of light rhyme; with its jig-saw arrangement and false emphasis, it is merely a heavy-handed and distorted design.

The mind of this poet is highly sensitized; it is both musing and microscopic; it is crammed with a vast amount of reading—there are fifteen pages of "Notes" which refer, among other things, to the Diary of Tolstoi, Lafcadio Hearn's *Talks to Writers,* the letters of Robert Browning, Ditmar's *Strange Animals I Have Known,* Baxter's *The Saints' Everlasting Rest,* and the *Illustrated London News.* Her pages are studded with quotations from these sources, and it is often impossible to see the poem because of the quotations. Such complex allusiveness, as in the case of Eliot's own poetry, leads to obscurity, and the accumulation of detail is at the expense of clarity. The variety of subjects and swiftness of juxtapositions do not compensate for the lack of any compelling emotion. Too often there is a dependence on literary sources, an impoverishment of the creative imagination, and one feels one is listening to an astringent essayist with a passion for textbooks and a perverted taste for rhyme.

### A TALISMAN

Under a splintered mast,
torn from the ship and cast
    near her hull,

a stumbling shepherd found,
embedded in the ground,
    a sea-gull

of lapis lazuli,
a scarab of the sea,
    with wings spread—

curling its coral feet,
parting its beak to greet
    men long dead.

### THAT HARP YOU PLAY SO WELL

O David, if I had
Your power, I should be glad—
    In harping, with the sling,
    In patient reasoning!

Blake, Homer, Job, and you,
Have made old wine-skins new.
    Your energies have wrought
    Stout continents of thought.

But, David, if the heart
Be brass, what boots the art
    Of exorcising wrong,
    Of harping to a song?

The scepter and the ring
And every royal thing
    Will fail. Grief's lustiness
    Must cure the harp's distress.


### TO A STEAM ROLLER

The illustration
is nothing to you without the application.
    You lack half wit. You crush all the particles down
        into close conformity, and then walk back and forth on them.

Sparkling chips of rock
are crushed down to the level of the parent block.
    Were not "impersonal judgment in esthetic
        matters, a metaphysical impossibility," you

might fairly achieve
it. As for butterflies, I can hardly conceive
    of one's attending upon you; but to question
    the congruence of the complement is vain, if it exists.


### ENGLAND

with its baby rivers and little towns, each with its abbey or its cathedral;
    with voices—one voice perhaps, echoing through the transept—the
criterion of suitability and convenience: and Italy with its equal
    shores—contriving an epicureanism from which the grossness has been

extracted: and Greece with its goats and its gourds, the nest of modified illusions:
    and France, the "chrysalis of the nocturnal butterfly" in
whose products, mystery of construction diverts one from what was originally one's
    object—substance at the core: and the East with its snails, its emotional

shorthand and jade cockroaches, its rock crystal and its imperturbability,
    all of museum quality: and America where there
is the little old ramshackle victoria in the south, where cigars are smoked on the
    street in the north; where there are no proof readers, no silkworms, no digressions;

the wild man's land; grass-less, links-less, language-less country—in which letters
        are written
not in Spanish, not in Greek, not in Latin, not in shorthand,
but in plain American which cats and dogs can read! The letter "a" in psalm and
        calm when
    pronounced with the sound of "a" in candle, is very noticeable but

why should continents of misapprehension have to be accounted for by the
    fact? Does it follow that because there are poisonous toadstools
which resemble mushrooms, both are dangerous? In the case of mettlesomeness
        which may be
    mistaken for appetite, of heat which may appear to be haste, no con-

clusions may be drawn. To have misapprehended the matter, is to have confessed
  that one has not looked far enough. The sublimated wisdom
of China, Egyptian discernment, the cataclysmic torrent of emotion compressed
  in the verbs of the Hebrew language, the books of the man who is able

to say, "I envy nobody but him and him only, who catches more fish than
  I do,"—the flower and fruit of all that noted superi-
ority—should one not have stumbled upon it in America, must one imagine
  that it is not there? It has never been confined to one locality.


### THE FISH

Wade
through black jade
    Of the crow-blue mussel shells, one
        keeps
        adjusting the ash heaps;
    opening and shutting itself like

an
injured fan.
    The barnacles which encrust the
        side
        of the wave, cannot hide
    there for the submerged shafts of the

sun,
split like spun
    glass, move themselves with spotlight swift-
        ness
        into the crevices—
    in and out, illuminating

the
turquoise sea
    of bodies. The water drives a
        wedge
        of iron through the iron edge
    of the cliff, whereupon the stars,

pink
rice grains, ink
    bespattered jelly-fish, crabs like
        green
        lilies and submarine
    toadstools, slide each on the other.

All
external
    marks of abuse are present on
        this
        defiant edifice—
    all the physical features of

ac-
cident—lack
   of cornice, dynamite grooves, burns
     and
      hatchet strokes, these things stand
   out on it; the chasm side is

dead.
Repeated
   evidence has proved that it can
     live
     on what cannot revive
   its youth. The sea grows old in it.

## *Robinson Jeffers*

ROBINSON JEFFERS' condensed autobiography runs as follows: "Born in Pittsburgh in 1887; my parents carried me about Europe a good deal. Of the first visit I remember three things—a pocketful of snails loosed on the walls of a kindergarten in Zürich, paintings of Keats and Shelley hanging side by side somewhere in London, and Arthur's Seat, the hill about Edinburgh. When I was fifteen I was brought home. Next year my family moved to California and I graduated at eighteen from Occidental College, Los Angeles. After that, desultory years at the University of Southern California, University of Zürich, Medical School in Los Angeles, University of Washington, but with faint interest. I wasn't deeply interested in anything but poetry. I married Una Call Kuster in 1913. We were going to England in the autumn of 1914. But the August news turned us to this village of Carmel instead; and when the stagecoach topped the hill from Monterey, and we looked down through pines and sea-fogs on Carmel Bay, it was evident that we had come without knowing it to our inevitable place." There, on the ocean's edge, Jeffers has lived ever since, identifying himself with the Californian rocks and headlands.

*Flagons and Apples* (1912) was Jeffers' undistinguished first volume; it was followed by *Californians* (1916), a scarcely more original book. In 1925 *Tamar and Other Poems* was brought out by a small printer and caused an overnight sensation. It was reprinted the following year, with the addition of new work, as *Roan Stallion, Tamar and Other Poems* (1926). This, it was evident at once, was masculine poetry, stark, even terrible in its intensities. Whatever defects this verse has—and it must be confessed that Jeffers piles on his catastrophes with little humor and less restraint—there is no denying its elemental power. He combines two almost contrary types of strength: the impetuous American and the stoic Greek.

*The Women at Point Sur* (1927) shows how easily Jeffers can swing the long line, how suddenly his phrases soar from the tawdry into the terrible, how boldly he can lift a language which, in the hands of most poets, would be nothing more than wild rhetoric.

*Cawdor* (1928) again reveals Jeffers turning away from gentle themes to almost unbearable ones. The long poem is a continuation of the bewilderment announced in the preceding volumes. Jeffers himself says, "I think of *Cawdor* as making a third with *Tamar* and *The Women at Point Sur;* but as if in *Tamar* human affairs had been seen looking westward against the ocean; in *Point Sur* looking upward, minimized to ridicule against the stars; in *Cawdor* looking eastward, against the earth, reclaiming a little dignity from that association. . . . Where not only generations but races drizzle away so fast, one wonders the more urgently what it is for, and whether this beautiful earth is amused or sorry at the procession of her possessors." There are also a number of shorter poems, not actually subversive but, continues Jeffers, "the mere common sense of our predicament as passionate bits of earth and water." . . . The setting of *Cawdor* is monstrous, the symbols excessive, the speech of his characters unreal; yet the backgrounds are not much more tragic than Jeffers' own weird Carmel coast and his people move in an atmosphere larger if more forbidding than reality. As in his other work, exaggerations of lust and violence outdo each other; but these, which in a lesser man would be absurd, are compelling because of the sheer force behind them and the malefic universe they imply.

This force is not only inherent in Jeffers' extraordinary language, but in his demonic search for ultimates. He disdains the illusions by which man makes life endurable: love, nature, the mind—these are all self-destructive and useless. Quiet is empty denial and peace a forlorn hope. Death seems the one freedom, "the huge gift," but annihilation itself, he realizes, is impossible. There is left only despair— and this is the cry beneath Jeffers' strength. The longing for oblivion explains his wild dreams, bloodshot landscapes, inhuman crimes, incests, brutalities, nightmare-struggles where life "drinks her defeat and devours her famine for food."

Thus he celebrates "the charm of the dark," enlarges on passions turned inward and men "all matted in one mesh"; he sings a frustrated *Dies Irae* to unresponding Nothingness. Therefore the things he loves best are rocks, black cypresses, depths of ocean, granite mountains—things that have their being without ambition, without hope, without consciousness.

But negation alone cannot explain the poet's dark persuasiveness. To Jeffers consciousness is the great curse of mankind; unconsciousness is the desirable state of nature. That man can never know such unconsciousness is what compels Jeffers' anguish and dictates his most impassioned lines. Impassioned they are, whatever one may think of the philosophy that prompts them, and an examination of Jeffers' utterance discloses a strange phenomenon: This poet preaches the gospel of Nothingness with an exuberant liveliness. He mourns, with inconsistent vigor, "the broken balance, the hopeless prostration of the earth under men's hands." His Jesus (in *Dear Judas*) is only an extension of the fanatically possessive Barclay (in *The Women at Point Sur*); even mystical passion becomes a high-pitched turbulence and love a last despair.

Thus Jeffers is in danger of emotional abandonment. His dramas are too often conditioned not by the exigencies of the situation nor by the demands of his characters, but by Jeffers' inverted violences. The chaos is self-generated; the didacticism no less didactic for being nullifying and uncontrolled; the imagination is too often disturbed by intellectual hysteria.

*Dear Judas* (1929) is composed of two long and a few short poems, the two longer ones bearing a relation to each other in the contrasted aspects of love, the shorter ones condensing Jeffers' philosophy into some of his finest moments. Like his other work, *Dear Judas* exhibits Jeffers projecting blind and bewildering Nature, misconceiving man as a "spectral episode." Here again is energy threshing in meaninglessness; here is force in need of a faith.

*Thurso's Landing* (1932) consists of one long poem and several highly characteristic shorter ones. The title-poem must rank among Jeffers' most important creations—a poem in which sheer power and eloquence triumph above black and unrelieved melodrama. Here again the *dramatis personae* are nakedly symbols of tortured humanity, "all compelled, all unhappy, all helpless." The idea dominating the book is the *idée fixe* which runs through all of Jeffers' volumes: Life is horrible. Love, as we practice it, is inverted and incestuous; not one self-adoring man in a million expresses outward-going passion. Death is the beautiful capricious savior, "the gay child with the gypsy eyes." Civilization is a transient sickness. Were the world free of this botch of humanity, this walking disease of consciousness, it would be a cleaner place, one in which the noble, impersonal elements would be at home. In a few thousand years this may well happen, and life will no longer be a torture for the living. Meanwhile our nature, "ignoble in its quiet times, mean in its pleasures, slavish in the mass" can, in its stricken moments, occasionally "shine terribly against the dark magnificence of things." Meanwhile we can learn from hawks and headlands; we can learn to bear; we can endure. Sometimes the philosophy is implicit in the action of Jeffers' characters; sometimes it is explicit, and the poet steps out of the drama to say:

> . . . No life
> Ought to be thought important in the weave of the world, whatever it may show of
>     courage or endured pain.
> It owns no other manner of shining but to bear pain; for pleasure is too little, our
>     inhuman God is too great, thought is too lost.

The shorter poems in *Give Your Heart to the Hawks* (1934) and *Solstice* (1935), like those in the preceding volumes, are Jeffers at his most characteristic; condensation forces his pessimism into a rhythm that is both long and compact, like a tightly coiled spring. Several of the finest appeared in the 1927 issue of *A Miscellany of American Poetry* and were added to the popular edition of *Roan Stallion, Tamar and Other Poems,* brought out by The Modern Library in 1935. This excellent reprint also contains an introduction by the author which is a valuable piece of self-appraisal, especially in its estimate of "originality." "It seemed to me," says Jeffers, "that Mallarmé and his followers, renouncing intelligibility in order to concentrate the music of poetry, had turned off the road into a narrowing lane. Their successors could only make further renunciations; ideas had gone, now meter had gone, imagery would have to go; then recognizable emotions would have to go; perhaps at last even words might have to go or give up their meaning, nothing be left but musical syllables. Every advance required the elimination of some aspect of reality, and what could it profit me to know the direction of modern poetry if I did not like the direction? It was too much like putting out your eyes to cultivate the sense of hearing, or cutting off the right hand to develop the left. These austerities were not for me; originality by amputation was too painful for me."

Three years after distressing himself about "originality" Jeffers began to write *Tamar,* the work which was one of the most original of his generation. Superficially, because of his loose musical line, Jeffers seems to resemble Whitman, but his spirit is the very opposite of that rude yea-sayer. Where Whitman loses himself in all-embracing affirmations, Jeffers loses himself—and the world—in all-inclusive negations. The Californian poet turns against the sense of love which upheld Whitman and which he upheld; until man can "love outwardly," love of man, to Jeffers, is only "the trap that catches noblest spirits, that caught—they say—God, when he walked on earth." It was, however, not so much Jeffers' negations to which the critics objected as to his abnormal themes. This was the more curious since, beneath his preoccupations with abnormality, the poet implied a definite morality. Jeffers explained this element of his work in a letter which leaves no doubt of his intentions: "In *Tamar* a little and in *The Women at Point Sur* consciously and definitely, incest is symbolized racial introversion: man regarding man exclusively—founding his values, desires, a picture of the universe, all on his own humanity. . . . The tendency to romanticize unmoral freedom leads to destruction—often of the individual but always of the social organism. One of the intentions of *Point Sur* was to indicate the destruction and strip everything but its natural ugliness from the unmorality." Love that "turns inward" is thus shown as the opposite of love; chaotic, evil, not only self- but all-destructive. The two long poems in *Solstice* emphasize this. The title-poem is the story of Medea transplanted to the Californian coast; "At the Birth of an Age" is half drama, half parable, with self-frustration as its theme.

Yet if Jeffers feeds on destruction and terror he is not sickened but sustained by it. His poetry communicates with force if not with power that stormy vigor. It never falters, but sweeps on, cumulative and irresistible. His epithets are almost always exact, his occasional metaphors as inevitable as "the leopard-footed evening," "she moved sighing, like a loose fire"; a hawk's wing "trails like a banner in defeat." He muses on "the lame feet of salvation," sees "Orion strung in the throat of the valley like a lamp-lighted bridge," hears "the stars blow long pipings of light." In his shorter poems, as well as in the longer and more elaborated work, Jeffers sounds a new music. He achieves a startling paradox: he sings death with such fervor that his bitter darkness shines more vividly than most surrounding sweetness and light.

Here one must, somehow, separate the idea and its expression, remembering that the poem transcends the experience or the personality that prompted it. It is especially necessary in this work, for between Jeffers the philosopher and Jeffers the poet there is a significant dichotomy. The philosophy is negative, repetitious, dismal. The poetry, even when bitterest, is positive as any creative expression must be; it is varied in movement and color; it vibrates with a reckless fecundity. It is like nothing else of which we can boast; it is continually breaking through its own pattern to dangerous and unfathomed depths. This is not a work to be enjoyed without sacrificing that sense of ease dear to the casual reader; it is doubtful if, in the common sense, it can be "enjoyed" at all. But here is an undeviating, full-throated poetry, remarkable in sheer drive and harrowing drama, a poetry we may never love but one we cannot forget.

### COMPENSATION

> Solitude that unmakes me one of men
> In snow-white hands brings singular recompense,
> Evening me with kindlier natures when
> On the needled pinewood the cold dews condense

About the hour of Rigel fallen from heaven
In wintertime, or when the long night tides
Sigh blindly from the sand-dune backward driven,
Or when on stormwings of the northwind rides
The foamscud with the cormorants, or when passes
A horse or dog with brown affectionate eyes,
Or autumn frosts are pricked by earliest grasses,
Or whirring from her covert a quail flies.
Why, even in humanity, beauty and good
Show from the mountainside of solitude.

### AGE IN PROSPECT

Praise youth's hot blood if you will, I think that happiness
Rather consists in having lived clear through
Youth and hot blood, on to the wintrier hemisphere
Where one has time to wait and to remember.

Youth and hot blood are beautiful, so is peacefulness.
Youth had some islands in it, but age is indeed
An island and a peak; age has infirmities,
Not few, but youth is all one fever.

To look around and to love in his appearances,
Though a little calmly, the universal God's
Beauty is better I think than to lip eagerly
The mother's breast or another woman's.

And there is no possession more sure than memory's;
But if I reach that gray island, that peak,
My hope is still to possess with eyes the homeliness
Of ancient loves, ocean and mountains,

And meditate the sea-mouth of mortality
And the fountain six feet down with a quieter thirst
Than now I feel for old age; a creature progressively
Thirsty for life will be for death too.

### ANTE MORTEM

It is likely enough that lions and scorpions
Guard the end; life never was bonded to be endurable nor the act of dying
Unpainful; the brain burning too often
Earns, though it held itself detached from the object, often a burnt age.
No matter, I shall not shorten it by hand.
Incapable of body or unmoved of brain is no evil, one always went envying
The quietness of stones. But if the striped blossom
Insanity spread lewd splendors and lightning terrors at the end of the forest;
Or intolerable pain work its known miracle,
Exile the monarch soul, set a sick monkey in the office . . . remember me
Entire and balanced when I was younger,
And could lift stones, and comprehend in the praises the cruelties of life.

### POST MORTEM

Happy people die whole, they are all dissolved in a moment, they have had what
    they wanted,
No hard gifts; the unhappy
Linger a space, but pain is a thing that is glad to be forgotten; but one who has
    given
His heart to a cause or a country,
His ghost may spaniel it a while, disconsolate to watch it. I was wondering how
    long the spirit
That sheds this verse will remain
When the nostrils are nipped, when the brain rots in its vault or bubbles in the
    violence of fire
To be ash in metal. I was thinking
Some stalks of the wood whose roots I married to the earth of this place will stand
    five centuries;
I held the roots in my hand,
The stems of the trees between two fingers; how many remote generations of
    women
Will drink joy from men's loins,
And dragged from between the thighs of what mothers will giggle at my ghost
    when it curses the axmen,
Gray impotent voice on the sea-wind,
When the last trunk falls? The women's abundance will have built roofs over all
    this foreland;
Will have buried the rock foundations
I laid here: the women's exuberance will canker and fail in its time and like clouds
    the houses
Unframe, the granite of the prime
Stand from the heaps: come storm and wash clean: the plaster is all run to the sea
    and the steel
All rusted; the foreland resumes
The form we loved when we saw it. Though one at the end of the age and far off
    from this place
Should meet my presence in a poem,
The ghost would not care but be here, long sunset shadow in the seams of the
    granite, and forgotten
The flesh, a spirit for the stone.

### NOON

The pure air trembles, O pitiless God,
The air aches with flame on these gaunt rocks
Over the flat sea's face, the forest
Shakes in gales of piercing light.

But the altars are behind and higher
Where the great hills raise naked heads,
Pale antagonists in the reverberance
Of the pure air and the pitiless God.

On the domed skull of every hill
Who stand blazing with spread vans,
The arms uplifted, the eyes in ecstasy?

What wine has the God drunk, to sing
Violently in heaven, what wine his worshipers
Whose silence blazes? The light that is over
Light, the terror of noon, the eyes
That the eagles die at, have thrown down
Me and my pride, here I lie naked
In a hollow of the shadowless rocks,
Full of the God, having drunk fire.


## CLOUDS OF EVENING

Enormous cloud-mountains that form over Point Lobos and into the sunset,
Figures of fire on the walls of tonight's storm,
Foam of gold in gorges of fire, and the great file of warrior angels:
Dreams gathering in the curdled brain of the earth—
The sky the brain-vault—on the threshold of sleep: poor earth, you, like your
      children
By inordinate desires tortured, make dreams?
Storms more enormous, wars nobler, more toppling mountains, more jeweled waters,
      more free
Fires on impossible headlands . . . as a poor girl
Wishing her lover taller and more desirous, and herself maned with gold,
Dreams the world right, in the cold bed, about dawn.
Dreams are beautiful; the slaves of form are beautiful also; I have grown to believe
A stone is a better pillow than many visions.


## TO THE STONE-CUTTERS

Stone-cutters fighting time with marble, you foredefeated
Challengers of oblivion,
Eat cynical earnings, knowing rock splits, records fall down,
The square-limbed Roman letters
Scale in the thaws, wear in the rain. The poet as well
Builds his monument mockingly;
For man will be blotted out, the blithe earth die, the brave sun
Die blind, his heart blackening:
Yet stones have stood for a thousand years, and pained thoughts found
The honey peace in old poems.


## GALE IN APRIL

Intense and terrible beauty, how has our race with the frail naked nerves,
So little a craft swum down from its far launching?
Why now, only because the northwest blows and the headed grass billows,
Great seas jagging the west and on the granite

Blanching, the vessel is brimmed, this dancing play of the world is too much
passion.
A gale in April so overfilling the spirit,
Though his ribs were thick as the earth's, arches of mountain, how shall one dare
to live,
Though his blood were like the earth's rivers and his flesh iron,
How shall one dare to live? One is born strong, how do the weak endure it?
The strong lean upon death as on a rock,
After eighty years there is shelter and the naked nerves shall be covered with deep
quietness.
O beauty of things, go on, go on, O torture
Of intense joy, I have lasted out my time, I have thanked God and finished,
Roots of millennial trees fold me in the darkness,
Northwest winds shake their tops, not to the root, not to the root, I have
passed
From beauty to the other beauty, peace, the night splendor.

### APOLOGY FOR BAD DREAMS

#### I

In the purple light, heavy with redwood, the slopes drop seaward,
Headlong convexities of forest, drawn in together to the steep ravine. Below, on the
sea-cliff,
A lonely clearing; a little field of corn by the streamside; a roof under spared trees.
Then the ocean
Like a great stone someone has cut to a sharp edge and polished to shining. Beyond
it, the fountain
And furnace of incredible light flowing up from the sunk sun. In the little clear-
ing a woman
Was punishing a horse; she had tied the halter to a sapling at the edge of the wood;
but when the great whip
Clung to the flanks the creature kicked so hard she feared he would snap the
halter; she called from the house
The young man her son; who fetched a chain tie-rope, they working together
Noosed the small rusty links round the horse's tongue
And tied him by the swollen tongue to the tree.
Seen from this height they are shrunk to insect size,
Out of all human relation. You cannot distinguish
The blood dripping from where the chain is fastened,
The beast shuddering; but the thrust neck and the legs
Far apart. You can see the whip fall on the flanks. . . .
The gesture of the arm. You cannot see the face of the woman.
The enormous light beats up out of the west across the cloud-bars of the trade-wind.
The ocean
Darkens, the high clouds brighten, the hills darken together. Unbridled and un-
believable beauty
Covers the evening world . . . not covers, grows apparent out of it, as Venus down
there grows out
From the lit sky. What said the prophet? "I create good: and I create evil: I am
the Lord."

## II

This coast crying out for tragedy like all beautiful places,
(The quiet ones ask for quieter suffering; but here the granite cliff the gaunt
    cypresses' crown
Demands what victim? The dykes of red lava and black what Titan? The hills
    like pointed flames
Beyond Soberanes, the terrible peaks of the bare hills under the sun, what im-
    molation?)
This coast crying out for tragedy like all beautiful places: and like the passionate
    spirit of humanity
Pain for its bread: God's, many victims', the painful deaths, the horrible trans-
    figurements: I said in my heart,
"Better invent than suffer: imagine victims
Lest your own flesh be chosen the agonist, or you
Martyr some creature to the beauty of the place." And I said,
"Burn sacrifices once a year to magic
Horror away from the house, this little house here
You have built over the ocean with your own hands
Beside the standing bowlders: for what are we,
The beast that walks upright, with speaking lips
And little hair, to think we should always be fed,
Sheltered, intact, and self-controlled? We sooner more liable
Than the other animals. Pain and terror, the insanities of desire; not accidents, but
    essential,
And crowd up from the core." I imagined victims for those wolves, I made the
    phantoms to follow.
They have hunted the phantoms and missed the house. It is not good to forget over
    what gulls the spirit
Of the beauty of humanity, the petal of a lost flower blown seaward by the night-
    wind, floats to its quietness.

## III

Bowlders blunted like an old bear's teeth break up from the headland; below them
All the soil is thick with shells, the tide-rock feasts of a dead people.
Here the granite flanks are scarred with ancient fire, the ghosts of the tribe
Crouch in the nights beside the ghost of a fire, they try to remember the sunlight,
Light has died out of their skies. These have paid something for the future
Luck of the country, while we living keep old griefs in memory: though God's
Envy is not a likely fountain of ruin, to forget evil calls down
Sudden reminders from the cloud: remembered deaths be our redeemers;
Imagined victims our salvation: white as the half moon at midnight
Someone flamelike passed me, saying, "I am Tamar Cauldwell, I have my desire,"
Then the voice of the sea returned, when she had gone by, the stars to their towers.
. . . Beautiful country, burn again, Point Pinos down to the Sur Rivers
Burn as before with bitter wonders, land and ocean and the Carmel water.

## IV

He brays humanity in a mortar to bring the savor
From the bruised root: a man having bad dreams, who invents victims, is only the
    ape of that God.
He washes it out with tears and many waters, calcines it with fire in the red
    crucible,

Deforms it, makes it horrible to itself: the spirit flies out and stands naked, he sees
    the spirit.
He takes it in the naked ecstasy; it breaks in his hand, the atom is broken, the
    power that massed it
Cries to the power that moves the stars, "I have come home to myself, behold me.
I bruised myself in the flint mortar and burnt me
In the red shell, I tortured myself, I flew forth,
Stood naked of myself and broke me in fragments,
And here am I moving the stars that are me."
I have seen these ways of God: I know of no reason
For fire and change and torture and the old returnings.
He being sufficient might be still. I think they admit no reason; they are the ways
    of my love.
Unmeasured power, incredible passion, enormous craft: no thought apparent but
    burns darkly
Smothered with its own smoke in the human brain-vault: no thought outside: a
    certain measure in phenomena:
The fountains of the boiling stars, the flowers on the foreland, the ever-returning
    roses of dawn.

## PROMISE OF PEACE

    The heads of strong old age are beautiful
    Beyond all grace of youth. They have strange quiet,
    Integrity, health, soundness, to the full
    They've dealt with life and been attempered by it.
    A young man must not sleep; his years are war
    Civil and foreign but the former's worse;
    But the old can breathe in safety now that they are
    Forgetting what youth meant, the being perverse,
    Running the fool's gauntlet and being cut
    By the whips of the five senses. As for me,
    If I should wish to live long it were but
    To trade those fevers for tranquillity,
    Thinking, though that's entire and sweet in the grave
    How shall the dead taste the deep treasure they have?

## BIRTH-DUES

Joy is a trick in the air; pleasure is merely contemptible, the dangled
Carrot the ass follows to market or precipice;
But limitary pain—the rock under the tower and the hewn coping
That takes thunder at the head of the turret—
Terrible and real. Therefore a mindless dervish carving himself
With knives will seem to have conquered the world.

The world's God is treacherous and full of unreason; a torturer, but also
The only foundation and the only fountain.
Who fights him eats his own flesh and perishes of hunger; who hides in the grave
To escape him is dead; who enters the Indian
Recession to escape him is dead; who falls in love with the God is washed clean
Of death desired and of death dreaded.

He has joy, but joy is a trick in the air; and pleasure, but pleasure is contemptible;
And peace; and is based on solider than pain.
He has broken boundaries a little and that will estrange him; he is monstrous, but
    not
To the measure of the God. . . . But I having told you—
However I suppose that few in the world have energy to hear effectively—
Have paid my birth-dues; am quits with the people.

## SUMMER HOLIDAY

When the sun shouts and people abound
One thinks there were the ages of stone and the age of bronze
And the iron age; iron the unstable metal;
Steel made of iron, unstable as his mother; the towered-up cities
Will be stains of rust on mounds of plaster.
Roots will not pierce the heaps for a time, kind rains will cure them,
Then nothing will remain of the iron age
And all these people but a thigh-bone or so, a poem
Stuck in the world's thought, splinters of glass
In the rubbish dumps, a concrete dam far off in the mountain. . . .

## CREDO

My friend from Asia has powers and magic, he plucks a blue leaf from the young
    blue-gum
And gazing upon it, gathering and quieting
The God in his mind, creates an ocean more real than the ocean, the salt, the actual
Appalling presence, the power of the waters.
He believes that nothing is real except as we make it.
                                            I humbler have found in my blood
Bred west of Caucasus a harder mysticism.
Multitude stands in my mind but I think that the ocean in the bone vault is only
The bone vault's ocean: out there is the ocean's;
The water is the water, the cliff is the rock, come shocks and flashes of reality. The
    mind
Passes, the eye closes, the spirit is a passage;
The beauty of things was born before eyes and sufficient to itself; the heart-breaking
    beauty
Will remain when there is no heart to break for it.

## PELICANS

Four pelicans went over the house,
Sculled their worn oars over the courtyard: I saw that ungainliness
Magnifies the idea of strength.
A lifting gale of sea-gulls followed them; slim yachts of the element,
Natural growths of the sky, no wonder
Light wings to leave sea; but those grave weights toil, and are powerful,
And the wings torn with old storms remember
The cone that the oldest redwood dropped from, the tilting of continents,

The dinosaur's day, the lift of new sea-lines.
The omnisecular spirit keeps the old with the new also.
Nothing at all has suffered erasure.
There is life not of our time. He calls ungainly bodies
As beautiful as the grace of horses.
He is weary of nothing; he watches air-planes; he watches pelicans.

### LOVE THE WILD SWAN

"I hate my verses, every line, every word,
Oh pale and brittle pencils ever to try
One grass-blade's curve, or the throat of one bird
That clings to twig, ruffled against white sky.
Oh cracked and twilight mirrors ever to catch
One color, one glinting flash, of the splendor of things.
Unlucky hunter, Oh bullets of wax,
The lion beauty, the wild-swan wings, the storm of the wings."
—This wild swan of a world is no hunter's game.
Better bullets than yours would miss the white breast,
Better mirrors than yours would crack in the flame.
Does it matter whether you hate your . . . self? At least
Love your eyes that can see, your mind that can
Hear the music, the thunder of the wings. Love the wild swan.

### NIGHT

The ebb slips from the rock, the sunken
Tide-rocks lift streaming shoulders
Out of the slack, the slow west
Sombering its torch; a ship's light
Shows faintly, far out,
Over the weight of the prone ocean
On the low cloud.

Over the dark mountain, over the dark pinewood,
Down the long dark valley along the shrunken river,
Returns the splendor without rays, the shining shadow,
Peace-bringer, the matrix of all shining and quieter of shining.
Where the shore widens on the bay she opens dark wings
And the ocean accepts her glory. O soul worshipful of her
You, like the ocean, have grave depths where she dwells always,
And the film of waves above that takes the sun takes also
Her, with more love. The sun-lovers have a blond favorite,
A father of lights and noises, wars, weeping and laughter,
Hot labor, lust and delight and the other blemishes.
    Quietness
Flows from her deeper fountain; and he will die; and she is immortal.

Far off from here the slender
Flocks of the mountain forest

Move among stems like towers
Of the old redwoods to the stream,
No twig crackling; dip shy
Wild muzzles into the mountain water
Among the dark ferns.

O passionately at peace you being secure will pardon
The blasphemies of glowworms, the lamp in my tower, the fretfulness
Of cities, the crescents of the planets, the pride of the stars.
This August night in a rift of cloud Antares reddens,
The great one, the ancient torch, a lord among lost children,
The earth's orbit doubled would not girdle his greatness, one fire
Globed, out of grasp of the mind enormous; but to you
        O Night
What? Not a spark? What flicker of a spark in the faint far glimmer
Of a lost fire dying in the desert, dim coals of a sand-pit the Bedouins
Wandered from at dawn. . . . Ah singing prayer to what gulfs tempted
Suddenly are you more lost? To us the near-hand mountain
Be a measure of height, the tide-worn cliff at the sea-gate a measure of continuance.

The tide, moving the night's
Vastness with lonely voices,
Turns, the deep dark-shining
Pacific leans on the land,
Feeling his cold strength
To the outmost margins: you Night will resume
The stars in your time.

O passionately at peace when will that tide draw shoreward,
Truly the spouting fountains of light, Antares, Arcturus,
Tire of their flow, they sing one song but they think silence.
The striding winter-giant Orion shines, and dreams darkness.
And life, the flicker of men and moths and the wolf on the hill,
Though furious for continuance, passionately feeding, passionately
Remaking itself upon its mates, remembers deep inward
The calm mother, the quietness of the womb and the egg,
The primal and the latter silences: dear Night it is memory
Prophesies, prophecy that remembers, the charm of the dark.
And I and my people, we are willing to love the four-score years
Heartily; but as a sailor loves the sea, when the helm is for harbor.

Have men's minds changed,
Or the rock hidden in the deep of the waters of the soul
Broken the surface? A few centuries
Gone by, was none dared not to people
The darkness beyond the stars with harps and habitations.
But now, dear is the truth. Life is grown sweeter and lonelier,
And death is no evil.

## SHINE, PERISHING REPUBLIC

While this America settles in the mold of its vulgarity, heavily thickening to empire,
And protest, only a bubble in the molten mass, pops and sighs out, and the mass
  hardens,

I sadly smiling remember that the flower fades to make fruit, the fruit rots to make
  earth.
Out of the mother; and through the spring exultances, ripeness and decadence; and
  home to the mother.

You make haste on decay: not blameworthy; life is good, be it stubbornly long or
  suddenly
A mortal splendor: meteors are not needed less than mountains: shine, perishing
  republic.

But for my children, I would have them keep their distance from the thickening
  center; corruption
Never has been compulsory, when the cities lie at the monster's feet there are left
  the mountains.

And boys, be in nothing so moderate as in love of man, a clever servant, insufferable
  master.
There is the trap that catches noblest spirits, that caught—they say—God, when he
  walked on earth.

## DIVINELY SUPERFLUOUS BEAUTY

The storm-dances of gulls, the barking game of seals,
Over and under the ocean . . .
Divinely superfluous beauty
Rules the games, presides over destinies, makes trees grow
And hills tower, waves fall.
The incredible beauty of joy
Stars with fire the joining of lips, O let our loves too
Be joined, there is not a maiden
Burns and thirsts for love
More than my blood for you, by the shore of seals while the wings
Weave like a web in the air
Divinely superfluous beauty.

## HURT HAWKS

The broken pillar of the wing jags from the clotted shoulder,
The wing trails like a banner in defeat,
No more to use the sky forever but live with famine
And pain a few days: cat nor coyote
Will shorten the week of waiting for death, there is game without talons.

He stands under the oak-bush and waits
The lame feet of salvation; at night he remembers freedom

And flies in a dream, the dawns ruin it.
He is strong and pain is worse to the strong, incapacity is worse.
The curs of the day come and torment him
At distance, no one but death the redeemer will humble that head,
The intrepid readiness, the terrible eyes.
The wild God of the world is sometimes merciful to those
That ask mercy, not often to the arrogant.
You do not know him, you communal people, or you have forgotten him;
Intemperate and savage, the hawk remembers him;
Beautiful and wild, the hawks, and men that are dying remember him.

✦

I'd sooner, except the penalties, kill a man than a hawk; but the great redtail
Had nothing left but unable misery
From the bone too shattered for mending, the wing that trailed under his talons
    when he moved.
We had fed him six weeks, I gave him freedom,
He wandered over the foreland hill and returned in the evening, asking for death,
Not like a beggar, still eyed with the old
Implacable arrogance. I gave him the lead gift in the twilight.
                                                    What fell was relaxed,
Owl-downy, soft feminine feathers; but what
Soared: the fierce rush: the night-herons by the flooded river cried fear at its rising
Before it was quite unsheathed from reality.

# Frank Ernest Hill

FRANK ERNEST HILL was born in San Jose, California, October 29, 1888. He graduated from Stanford University, taught at the University of Illinois, Stanford University and Columbia Extension. During the War, he went into the Air Service, and
after a brief experience with the Curtiss Aeroplane and Motor Corporation, engaged
in journalism, publishing, and teaching. In collaboration with Joseph Auslander, he
wrote *The Wingèd Horse* (1927), which is a story rather than a criticism of poetry,
and edited *The Wingèd Horse Anthology* (1929). His translation of *The Canterbury Tales* (1935), containing all the metrical tales unexpurgated, is the best modern rendering, being highly readable and authoritative.

*Stone Dust* (1928) is a volume which presents the clash between the mechanical
and creative forces in modern civilization. Neither scorning nor sentimentalizing
the machine, Hill appraises it in terms of inner as well as outer experience. "Upper
Air," "Wing Harbor," and the three other aeroplane poems are verses—possibly the
first—by one who has known flying intimately; they transcend physical sensation,
registering effects on spirit. The two longer poems, of which "Earth and Air" is the
better, pierce through the material with clear vision. It is interesting to compare
"Earth and Air"—particularly its point of view—with Elinor Wylie's "Hymn to
Earth."

## EARTH AND AIR

### I

Earth is the tower of granite, the floor of loam,
The grass that seeds, the sheep that fatten for men,
Shapes that are beaten in fire or built in wall,
The plow preparing the soil to be born again;
The crystal well, the gold of the honeycomb,
The hands that pattern with wool or hide or clay;
Earth is the wain, the sickle, the sledge, the stall—
    Earth is our yesterday.

### II

Air is the thrust of steam and burning gas,
The spark men take from the foam of a falling stream,
The word of the first sea caught on the last of the seven,
Ships with the speed of a dream made more than dream;
The throb of steel in a cage of steel and glass,
Iron fingers at smooth and gleaming play,
Air is the wings of men on the sea of heaven—
    Air is today.

### III

Earth is the suck of men, their loaf and their healing;
With earth they are poor but sapful, driven but strong;
Air is a high, thin world where their eyes grow weaker,
Their round breasts flatten, their cheeks fall white and long.
Air is a shifting floor and a viewless ceiling,
Genii building and wrecking and building again,
It is a half-heard magic speech from a hidden speaker
    Sounding through light and rain.

### IV

Men with the vision of air went planning and building;
They dreamed of slaves of iron and wrought their slaves;
They envied the wind and the eagle and spread their wings
Above the shadow of sinking woods and waves.
Men made little suns for the midnight's gilding,
Bridged with their wires the bridgeless gap of seas;
They dulled the teeth of winter, they turned the stings
    And withering of disease—

### V

Men with the dream of air have climbed to their vision,
But now they are faint for the meat of a day gone by;
The steeds of the sun race on in a golden madness,
The hurtling drivers are pale in the height of the sky.
Some say: "Hard Fate in a wrath and a great derision
Has laid the tools of gods in the hands of men;
Can dust breed stars? Can tears be distilled to gladness?
    Let us go to earth again!"

### VI

But the many hear not, the millions follow their dreaming
Driving their iron cattle on stone or steel,
Flying their iron hawks on an airy ocean,
Bearing children that play with the spark and the wheel.
They will never turn from swiftness and silver gleaming
Or the sense that he who has taken in wheel or rod
The staff of gods and the magic of god-like motion
    Himself shall become a god.

### VII

Perhaps they will come again to the sun and the bough,
The wind and the clod that once were their strife and their fare;
They will take not of olden beauty or olden toil;
They will only come back to earth when earth is air:
When they girdle peaks with their pavements and send their plow
Like a whirl of wind, and store their snow and their sun,
And sow where the strength they have sifted into the soil
    Yields five instead of one.

### VIII

Look back, then, you who had love for earth and regret her,
And mourn a change that harries your hill and sky;
For men are turned from the peace of the scythe and candle;
Their eyes are fierce for the bright and the swift and the high.
They have wrecked a world for the leaping dream of a better,
And gone from peace toward a peace beyond a war,
They have mounted untrodden stairs to a key and a handle
    That open a door.

### UPPER AIR

High, pale, imperial places of slow cloud
And windless wells of sunlit silence. . . . Sense
Of some aware, half-scornful Permanence
Past which we flow like water that is loud
A moment on the granite. Nothing here
Beats with the pulse that beat in us below;
That was a flame; this is the soul of snow
Immortalized in moveless atmosphere.

Yet we shall brood upon this haunt of wings
When love, like perfume washed away in rain,
Dies on the years. Still we shall come again,
Seeking the clouds as we have sought the sea,
Asking the peace of these immortal things
That will not mix with our mortality.

# *T. S. Eliot*

THOMAS STEARNS ELIOT was born in St. Louis, Missouri, September 26, 1888. He received his A.B. at Harvard, 1909, and his A.M., 1910. Subsequently, he studied at the Sorbonne and at Merton College, Oxford, becoming a teacher and lecturer in London, where he has lived (although he no longer teaches) since 1914. He was, for a while, assistant editor of *The Egoist* and is at present the leading spirit of *The Criterion,* a magazine which he helped to found, and a director of the publishing firm Faber and Faber.

*Prufrock* appeared in England in 1917. An American edition, including a number of other verses, was published under the title *Poems* in 1920. It was hailed, reviled, applauded, misunderstood, and imitated. There were indeed many imitators, particularly in England, where the younger men, rebounding from Georgian affectations, seized upon Eliot's disillusioned subtleties as a new gospel. Most of them patterned their lines upon the now famous "Sweeney" model, and by 1922 Eliot was one of the most discussed and disputed of living American poets. This volume, *Poems,* contains two sharply differentiated though related idioms. The more arresting and, therefore, the more copied evocations are the impressionistic sets of quatrains that compose "Sweeney Among the Nightingales," "Sweeney Erect," "The Hippopotamus" (that stinging whimsicality), "Mr. Eliot's Sunday Morning Service." It is a witty if recondite inflection which is heard beneath the muffled allusions; the edged lines crackle with observations as shrewd as "the snarled and yelping seas," "this oval O cropped out with teeth," "laughter tinkling among the teacups," "the damp souls of housemaids." Occasionally Eliot's wit takes on a darker intensity, as when, speaking of Donne's struggle to transcend the senses, he writes:

> He knew the anguish of the marrow,
> The ague of the skeleton;
> No contact possible to flesh
> Allayed the fever of the bone.

But there is another phase of Eliot, one that is disclosed in "The Love Song of J. Alfred Prufrock," the "Portrait of a Lady," and "La Figlia Che Piange," in which picture, philosophy and music are surprisingly blended. "The Love Song of J. Alfred Prufrock," written while Eliot was still at Harvard, is a minor masterpiece; nothing in recent poetry (if we forget Laforgue and the other French poets to whom Eliot is manifestly indebted), nothing in English at least, has communicated so great a sense of ambiguous hurt and general frustration. More condensed and equally precise in its hyperesthetic delicacy is the "Portrait of a Lady," that analytical study of the feminine dilettante, the faded votary of dimly lit studios— a baffled *précieuse* diffusing small talk and boredom. In these poems as well as the succeeding one, Eliot becomes the laureate of nostalgia, of a dwindling and futile *Wehmut.*

More important than Eliot's philosophy was his technique. It was a fascinating mixture of statement and suggestion, of passion and wit, of fact and symbol, and it was the first extended use in English of the Symbolist method. That method, as

Edmund Wilson declared in his valuable study *Axel's Castle,* was the result of an anti-scientific, romantic escapism; it consisted chiefly in approximating the "indefiniteness of music," mingling "the grand and prosaic manners," and, generally, avoiding plain statements in favor of intimations. Instead of seeking the "jewel-like phrase" with its finality of definition, the Symbolists attempted to communicate "states of feeling." Eliot carried the method further by communicating—or at least registering—states of feeling that were complicated and highly personal. To accomplish this he employed a complex verse, combining trivial and tawdry pictures with traditionally poetic subject-matter, linking the banalities of conversation to rich rhetoric, and interrupting the present with flash-backs of the past. This method, not unfamiliar to students of the films, made for a nervous disintegration; the rapid and, seemingly, unrelated images, the discordant metaphors achieved an emotional response at the expense of a logical progression. But logic was not the objective. The reader was carried on by the rapidity of suggestions, by the swiftly accumulating ideas and echoes, chiefly by the play of free association.

The play of free association is given full scope in Eliot's longest poem. *The Waste Land* (1922) is Eliot's attempt to sound his favorite theme—the disillusion-frustration motif—on a major scale. The publication of this forty-page poem caused an outburst so violent and prolonged that the echoes of the controversy hung in the air for several years. On the one hand it was dismissed as "an impudent hoax," "filthy bedlam raving"; on the other it was exalted as "the greatest document of our day, showing the starvation of our entire civilization." Both estimates are, of course, absurd; *The Waste Land* is neither "erudite gibberish" nor is it "a great work, with one triumph after another." It is, in essence, a set of mangled, difficult and (in spite of the arbitrary program of unification) separate failures and successes. If its pages are splintered with broken phrases and distorted pictures, one must remember that Eliot is attempting to portray disintegration itself. Its dependence on associations in other literatures makes it seem like an anthology of assimilations; its jumble of quotations (without inverted commas) from thirty-one sources gives the entire structure the look of a piece of literary carpentry done by a scholarly joiner. But certain passages are quick with poignance; several episodes are unforgettably etched. Clive Bell wrote, "The despairing tone which pervades Eliot's poetry is not, it seems to me, so much the despair of disillusionment as the morbidity of *The Yellow Book*." But, having quoted Bell, in derogation I should let him add, "But how the man can write! And the experience, if it be small, is perfectly digested and assimilated; it has gone into the blood and bones of his work. By his choice of words, by his forging of phrases, by his twisting, stretching and snapping of rhythms, Eliot can make out of his narrow vision things of perpetual beauty."

Critics were chiefly occupied with the subject-matter of *The Waste Land,* and many of the lesser writers imitated it. For a while it was fashionable to be defeatist, to rationalize, in non-rational sequences, lengthy and erudite evasions of reality. A few younger poets, however, paid far more attention to the technique than to the theme. They scorned Eliot's withdrawal into Anglo-Catholicism, but they admired—and imitated—his power of suggestion. In England W. H. Auden, Stephen Spender, and C. Day Lewis acknowledged his influence; in America his poetry affected the work of Conrad Aiken, Archibald MacLeish, and Horace Gregory, among others.

In his turn, Eliot was strongly influenced by his "ancestors" in France. Reviewing Peter Quennell's *Baudelaire and the Symbolists* in 1930 he refers to Arthur Symons' *Symbolist Movement in Literature,* saying, "I myself owe Mr. Symons a great debt. But for having read his book I should not, in the year 1908, have heard of Laforgue and Rimbaud; I should probably not have begun to read Verlaine; and but for reading Verlaine, I should not have heard of Corbière. So the Symons book is one of those which have affected the course of my life." But, as Edmund Wilson points out, though Eliot's main theme (the inferiority of the present to the past) is found in Laforgue and the other Romantics, though the idea of juxtaposing many literatures and a medley of idioms was suggested by Pound, "yet Eliot manages to be most effective precisely where he might be expected to be least original—he succeeds in conveying his meanings, in communicating his emotions, in spite of all his learning or mysterious allusions, and whether we understand them or not. . . . He has been able to lend even to the rhythms, to the words themselves, of his great predecessors a new music and a new meaning." Opposed to this there is Gerard Manley Hopkins' critical aphorism: "Echoes are a disease of education, literature is full of them, but they remain a disease, an evil." The very "mottoes" or epigraphs are intended not only to comment upon the poems which they introduce, but to amplify their suggestiveness. "The Love Song of J. Alfred Prufrock" is prefaced by a quotation from Dante emphasizing the repressed Prufrock's ultra-fastidious and isolated spirit; "Burbank with a Baedeker" is set off by the preceding jumble of phrases from Shakespeare, Browning, and Henry James referring to Venice; the quotation "Mistah Kurtz—he dead" from Conrad's *Heart of Darkness* intensifies the sense of loss and emptiness rising from the lines which follow—as F. O. Matthiessen remarks, it "epitomizes in a sentence the very tone of blasphemous hopelessness which issues from 'The Hollow Men.'"

Since *The Waste Land* Eliot's occasional poems (such as "A Song for Simeon," "Animula," and "Marina") are, except for a few, obscure in construction and religious in sentiment. By 1934 the erstwhile radical experimenter had progressed so far in orthodoxy that he wrote a pageant, *The Rock,* for a church fund, "blessed by a bishop and attended by Royalty." The later poems emphasized the author's evasions and his distrust of a world which had nothing stronger to lean on than despair or the church. Even his admirers revolted from the implications. "Reading Eliot's new poems," wrote Malcolm Cowley, "was like excavating buried cities at the edge of the Syrian desert; they were full of imposing temples and perfectly proportioned statues of the gods, but there was nothing in the streets that breathed." The more academic Henry Newbolt complained, "It is a lamentable thing to hear so despairing a voice in the hour of our anxiety. But it is still more lamentable that the assurance of our hopelessness should be conveyed to us in so trivial a manner. These contrasts should be crushing, but they are too clever for that; these ironies should be tragic, but they are hardly more than jeers." What Newbolt failed to see was Eliot's intention, which was not to console but rather to condemn. Newbolt was likewise in error in assuming that all Eliot's ironies were conveyed in a trivial manner and that when they were so conveyed, they were not less but more tragic because of their seeming flippancy of utterance. This essential seriousness was fortified by the publication of *For Lancelot Andrewes* (1929), the general point of view being that of a "classicist in literature, royalist in politics, and Anglo-Catholic in religion." The volume as a whole is a complete, disproof of the charge of cynical unconcern; here is no jeering detachment. Eliot insists not only on the necessity of ideas but on the need of ideals, saying explicitly, in an essay pointing out the deficiencies of the Humanism of Irving Babbitt, "If you mean a spiritual and intellectual coördination on a high level, then it is doubtful whether civilization can endure without religion, and religion without a church." The later poems, with hitherto unpublished verses, were assembled in *Collected Poems* (1936).

Besides his poetry Eliot has published several volumes of criticism and interpretation since *The Sacred Wood,* which appeared in 1921. The best of these were assembled in *Selected Essays 1917-1932* and which, with most of *The Sacred Wood* and *For Lancelot Andrewes,* includes the excellent series on the Elizabethan dramatists, the "Homage to John Dryden," and all of his introduction to Dante. *The Use of Poetry,* a set of spirited chapters which, somehow, evades a professed principle, was published in 1933; *After Strange Gods,* a "primer of modern heresy," in 1934. These volumes established Eliot as the most provocative and perhaps the most important critic of literature now writing in English. Wholly unlike his verse, sometimes academic, sometimes marred by fantastic theories, Eliot's criticism is persuasive and backed by authority. Though his writing lacks bulk, it does not lack profundity. Intensified by learning, sharpened by original apprehensions, his work has exercised an incalculable influence on his times.

*Murder in the Cathedral* (1935), a dramatization of the murder of Thomas Becket in 1170, was written for production at the Canterbury Festival in 1935. The language is surprisingly lucid, the action straightforward, and the poetry almost wholly free of the obliquity and harsh juxtapositions with which Eliot influenced a whole movement. Instead of a confusion of private references and literary allusions the verse has a simple unity, and the choruses are not only skillfully balanced but eloquent.

For a comprehensive, though uncritical, résumé of the poet's work the reader should examine *The Achievement of T. S. Eliot* (1935) by F. O. Matthiessen.

LA FIGLIA CHE PIANGE

*O quam te memorem virgo . . .*

Stand on the highest pavement of the stair—
Lean on a garden urn—
Weave, weave the sunlight in your hair—
Clasp your flowers to you with a pained surprise—
Fling them to the ground and turn
With a fugitive resentment in your eyes:
But weave, weave the sunlight in your hair.

So I would have had him leave,
So I would have had her stand and grieve,
So he would have left
As the soul leaves the body torn and bruised,
As the mind deserts the body it has used.

I should find
Some way incomparably light and deft,
Some way we both should understand,
Simple and faithless as a smile and shake of the hand.

She turned away, but with the autumn weather
Compelled my imagination many days,
Many days and many hours:
Her hair over her arms and her arms full of flowers,
And I wonder how they should have been together!
I should have lost a gesture and a pose.
Sometimes these cogitations still amaze
The troubled midnight and the noon's repose.


THE LOVE SONG OF J. ALFRED PRUFROCK

> *S'io credesse che mia risposta fosse*
> *A persona che mai tornasse al mondo,*
> *Questa fiamma staria senza piu scosse.*
> *Ma percioche giammai di questo fondo*
> *Non torno vivo alcun, s'i'odo il vero,*
> *Senza tema d'infamia ti rispondo.*

Let us go then, you and I,
When the evening is spread out against the sky
Like a patient etherized upon a table;
Let us go, through certain half-deserted streets,
The muttering retreats
Of restless nights in one-night cheap hotels
And sawdust restaurants with oyster-shells:
Streets that follow like a tedious argument
Of insidious intent
To lead you to an overwhelming question. . . .
Oh, do not ask, "What is it?"
Let us go and make our visit.

In the room the women come and go
Talking of Michelangelo.

The yellow fog that rubs its back upon the window-panes,
The yellow smoke that rubs its muzzle on the window-panes,
Licked its tongue into the corners of the evening,
Lingered upon the pools that stand in drains,
Let fall upon its back the soot that falls from chimneys,
Slipped by the terrace, made a sudden leap,
And seeing that it was a soft October night,
Curled once about the house, and fell asleep.

And indeed there will be time
For the yellow smoke that slides along the street,
Rubbing its back upon the window-panes;
There will be time, there will be time

To prepare a face to meet the faces that you meet;
There will be time to murder and create,
And time for all the works and days of hands
That lift and drop a question on your plate;
Time for you and time for me,
And time yet for a hundred indecisions,
And for a hundred visions and revisions,
Before the taking of a toast and tea.

In the room the women come and go
Talking of Michelangelo.

And indeed there will be time
To wonder, "Do I dare?" and, "Do I dare?"
Time to turn back and descend the stair,
With a bald spot in the middle of my hair—
(They will say: "How his hair is growing thin!")
My morning coat, my collar mounting firmly to the chin,
My necktie rich and modest, but asserted by a simple pin–
(They will say: "But how his arms and legs are thin!")
Do I dare
Disturb the universe?
In a minute there is time
For decisions and revisions which a minute will reverse.

For I have known them all already, known them all:
Have known the evenings, mornings, afternoons,
I have measured out my life with coffee spoons;
I know the voices dying with a dying fall
Beneath the music from a farther room.
     So how should I presume?

And I have known the eyes already, known them all—
The eyes that fix you in a formulated phrase,
And when I am formulated, sprawling on a pin,
When I am pinned and wriggling on the wall,
Then how should I begin
To spit out all the butt-ends of my days and ways?
     And how should I presume?

And I have known the arms already, known them all—
Arms that are braceleted and white and bare
(But in the lamplight, downed with light brown hair!)
Is it perfume from a dress
That makes me so digress?
Arms that lie along a table, or wrap about a shawl.
     And should I then presume?
     And how should I begin?

Shall I say, I have gone at dusk through narrow streets
And watched the smoke that rises from the pipes
Of lonely men in shirt-sleeves, leaning out of windows? . . .

I should have been a pair of ragged claws
Scuttling across the floors of silent seas.

✦

And the afternoon, the evening, sleeps so peacefully!
Smoothed by long fingers,
Asleep . . . tired . . . or it malingers,
Stretched on the floor, here beside you and me.
Should I, after tea and cakes and ices,
Have the strength to force the moment to its crisis?
But though I have wept and fasted, wept and prayed,
Though I have seen my head (grown slightly bald) brought in upon a platter,
I am no prophet—and here's no great matter;
I have seen the moment of my greatness flicker,
And I have seen the eternal Footman hold my coat, and snicker,
And in short, I was afraid.

And would it have been worth it, after all,
After the cups, the marmalade, the tea,
Among the porcelain, among some talk of you and me,
Would it have been worth while,
To have bitten off the matter with a smile,
To have squeezed the universe into a ball
To roll it toward some overwhelming question,
To say: "I am Lazarus, come from the dead,
Come back to tell you all, I shall tell you all"—
If one, settling a pillow by her head,
        Should say: "That is not what I meant at all;
        That is not it, at all."

And would it have been worth it, after all,
Would it have been worth while,
After the sunsets and the dooryards and the sprinkled streets,
After the novels, after the teacups, after the skirts that trail along the floor—
And this, and so much more?—
It is impossible to say just what I mean!
But as if a magic lantern threw the nerves in patterns on a screen:
Would it have been worth while
If one, settling a pillow or throwing off a shawl,
And turning toward the window, should say:
        "That is not it at all,
        That is not what I meant, at all."

✦

No! I am not Prince Hamlet, nor was meant to be;
Am an attendant lord, one that will do
To swell a progress, start a scene or two,
Advise the prince; no doubt, an easy tool,

Deferential, glad to be of use,
Politic, cautious, and meticulous;
Full of high sentence, but a bit obtuse;
At times, indeed, almost ridiculous—
Almost, at times, the Fool.

I grow old. . . . I grow old. . . .
I shall wear the bottoms of my trousers rolled.

Shall I part my hair behind? Do I dare to eat a peach?
I shall wear white flannel trousers, and walk upon the beach.
I have heard the mermaids singing, each to each.

I do not think that they will sing to me.

I have seen them riding seaward on the waves
Combing the white hair of the waves blown back
When the wind blows the water white and black.

We have lingered in the chambers of the sea
By sea-girls wreathed with seaweed red and brown
Till human voices wake us, and we drown.


### MORNING AT THE WINDOW

They are rattling breakfast plates in basement kitchens,
And along the trampled edges of the street
I am aware of the damp souls of housemaids
Sprouting despondently at area gates.

The brown waves of fog toss up to me
Twisted faces from the bottom of the street,
And tear from a passer-by with muddy skirts
An aimless smile that hovers in the air
And vanishes along the level of the roofs.


### PRELUDE

The winter evening settles down
With smells of steaks in passageways.
Six o'clock.
The burnt-out ends of smoky days.
And now a gusty shower wraps
The grimy scraps
Of withered leaves about his feet
And newspapers from vacant lots;
The showers beat
On broken blinds and chimney pots,
And at the corner of the street
A lonely cab-horse steams and stamps.
And then the lighting of the lamps.

## PORTRAIT OF A LADY[1]

### I

Among the smoke and fog of a December afternoon
You have the scene arrange itself—as it will seem to do—
With "I have saved this afternoon for you";
And four wax candles in the darkened room,
Four rings of light upon the ceiling overhead,
And atmosphere of Juliet's tomb
Prepared for all the things to be said, or left unsaid.
We have been, let us say, to hear the latest Pole
Transmit the Preludes, through his hair and finger-tips.
"So intimate, this Chopin, that I think his soul
Should be resurrected only among friends
Some two or three, who will not touch the bloom
That is rubbed and questioned in the concert room."
—And so the conversation slips
Among velleities and carefully caught regrets
Through attenuated tones of violins
Mingled with remote cornets
And begins.
"You do not know how much they mean to me, my friends,
And how, how rare and strange it is, to find
In a life composed so much, so much of odds and ends
(For indeed I do not love it . . . you knew? You are not blind!
How keen you are!)
To find a friend who has these qualities,
Who has, and gives
Those qualities upon which friendship lives.
How much it means that I say this to you—
Without these friendships—life, what *cauchemar!*"
Among the windings of the violins
And the ariettes
Of cracked cornets
Inside my brain a dull tom-tom begins
Absurdly hammering a prelude of its own,
Capricious monotone
That is at least one definite "false note."
—Let us take the air, in a tobacco trance,
Admire the monuments,
Discuss the late events,
Correct our watches by the public clocks,
Then sit for half an hour and drink our bocks.

### II

Now that lilacs are in bloom
She has a bowl of lilacs in her room
And twists one in her fingers while she talks.
"Ah, my friend, you do not know, you do not know

[1] Compare the poem by Ezra Pound on the same theme on page 341.

What life is, you should hold it in your hands";
(Slowly twisting the lilac stalks)
"You let it flow from you, you let it flow,
And youth is cruel, and has no remorse
And smiles at situations which it cannot see."

I smile, of course,
And go on drinking tea.
"Yet with these April sunsets, that somehow recall
My buried life, and Paris in the Spring,
I feel immeasurably at peace, and find the world
To be wonderful and youthful, after all."

The voice returns like the insistent out-of-tune
Of a broken violin on an August afternoon:
"I am always sure that you understand
My feelings, always sure that you feel,
Sure that across the gulf you reach your hand.
You are invulnerable, you have no Achilles' heel.
You will go on, and when you have prevailed
You can say: at this point many a one has failed.

"But what have I, but what have I, my friend,
To give you, what can you receive from me?
Only the friendship and the sympathy
Of one about to reach her journey's end.
I shall sit here, serving tea to friends. . . ."

I take my hat: how can I make a cowardly amends
For what she has said to me?

You will see me any morning in the park
Reading the comics and the sporting page.
Particularly I remark
An English countess goes upon the stage.
A Greek was murdered at a Polish dance.
Another bank defaulter has confessed.
I keep my countenance,
I remain self-possessed
Except when a street piano, mechanical and tired,
Reiterates some worn-out common song
With the smell of hyacinths across the garden,
Recalling things that other people have desired.
Are these ideas right or wrong?

III

The October night comes down; returning as before
Except for a slight sensation of being ill at ease
I mount the stairs and turn the handle of the door
And feel as if I had mounted on my hands and knees.

"And so you are going abroad; and when do you return?
But that's a useless question.
You hardly know when you are coming back;
You will find so much to learn."
My smile falls heavily among the bric-à-brac.

"Perhaps you can write to me."
My self-possession flares up for a second;
*This* is as I had reckoned.
"I have been wondering frequently of late
(But our beginnings never know our ends!)
Why we have not developed into friends."
I feel like one who smiles, and turning shall remark
Suddenly, his expression in a glass.
My self-possession gutters; we are really in the dark.

"For everybody said so, all our friends,
They all were sure our feelings would relate
So closely! I myself can hardly understand.
We must leave it now to fate.
You will write, at any rate.
Perhaps it is not too late.
I shall sit here, serving tea to friends."

And I must borrow every changing shape
To find expression . . . dance, dance
Like a dancing bear,
Cry like a parrot, chatter like an ape. . . .
Let us take the air, in a tobacco trance—
Well! and what if she should die some afternoon,
Afternoon gray and smoky, evening yellow and rose;
Should die and leave me sitting pen in hand
With the smoke coming down above the housetops;
Doubtful, for quite a while
Not knowing what to feel or if I understand
Or whether wise or foolish, tardy or too soon . . .
Would she not have the advantage, after all?
This music is successful with a "dying fall"
Now that we talk of dying—
And should I have the right to smile?

## CONVERSATION GALANTE

I observe: "Our sentimental friend, the moon!
Or possibly (fantastic, I confess)
It may be Prester John's balloon
Or an old battered lantern hung aloft
To light poor travelers to their distress."
     She then: "How you digress!"

And I then: "Someone frames upon the keys
That exquisite nocturne, with which we explain

The night and moonshine; music which we seize
To body forth our vacuity."
        She then: "Does this refer to me?"
        "Oh, no, it is I who am inane.

"You, madam, are the eternal humorist,
The eternal enemy of the absolute,
Giving our vagrant moods the slightest twist!
With your air indifferent and imperious
At a stroke our mad poetics to confute—"
        And—"Are we then so serious?"

### GERONTION

*Thou hast nor youth nor age
But as it were an after dinner sleep
Dreaming of both.*

Here I am, an old man in a dry month,
Being read to by a boy, waiting for rain.
I was neither at the hot gates
Nor fought in the warm rain
Nor knee deep in the salt marsh, heaving a cutlass,
Bitten by flies, fought.
My house is a decayed house,
And the Jew squats on the window sill, the owner,
Spawned in some estaminet of Antwerp,
Blistered in Brussels, patched and peeled in London.
The goat coughs at night in the field overhead;
Rocks, moss, stonecrop, iron, merds.
The woman keeps the kitchen, makes tea,
Sneezes at evening, poking the peevish gutter.

                                        I an old man,
A dull head among windy spaces.

Signs are taken for wonders. "We would see a sign":
The word within a word, unable to speak a word,
Swaddled with darkness. In the juvescence of the year
Came Christ the tiger

In depraved May, dogwood and chestnut, flowering judas,
To be eaten, to be divided, to be drunk
Among whispers; by Mr. Silvero
With caressing hands, at Limoges
Who walked all night in the next room;
By Hakagawa, bowing among the Titians;
By Madame de Tornquist, in the dark room
Shifting the candles; Fräulein von Kulp
Who turned in the hall, one hand on the door. Vacant shuttles

Weave the wind. I have no ghosts,
An old man in a draughty house
Under a windy knob.
After such knowledge, what forgiveness? Think now
History has many cunning passages, contrived corridors
And issues, deceives with whispering ambitions,
Guides us by vanities. Think now
She gives when our attention is distracted
And what she gives, gives with such supple confusions
That the giving famishes the craving. Gives too late
What's not believed in, or if still believed,
In memory only, reconsidered passion. Gives too soon
Into weak hands, what's thought can be dispensed with
Till the refusal propagates a fear. Think
Neither fear nor courage saves us. Unnatural vices
Are fathered by our heroism. Virtues
Are forced upon us by our impudent crimes.
These tears are shaken from the wrath-bearing tree.

The tiger springs in the new year. Us he devours. Think at last
We have not reached conclusion, when I
Stiffen in a rented house. Think at last
I have not made this show purposelessly
And it is not by any concitation
Of the backward devils.
I would meet you upon this honestly.
I that was near your heart was removed therefrom
To lose beauty in terror, terror in inquisition.
I have lost my passion: why should I need to keep it
Since what is kept must be adulterated?
I have lost my sight, smell, hearing, taste and touch:
How should I use it for your closer contact?

These with a thousand small deliberations
Protract the profit of their chilled delirium,
Excite the membrane, when the sense has cooled,
With pungent sauces, multiply variety
In a wilderness of mirrors. What will the spider do,
Suspend its operations, will the weevil
Delay? De Bailhache, Fresca, Mrs. Cammel, whirled
Beyond the circuit of the shuddering Bear
In fractured atoms. Gull against the wind, in the windy straits
Of Belle Isle, or running on the Horn,
White feathers in the snow, the Gulf claims,
And an old man driven by the Trades
To a sleepy corner.

            Tenants of the house,
Thoughts of a dry brain in a dry season.

## RHAPSODY ON A WINDY NIGHT

Twelve o'clock.
Along the reaches of the street
Held in a lunar synthesis,
Whispering lunar incantations
Dissolve the floors of memory
And all its clear relations,
Its divisions and precisions,
Every street lamp that I pass
Beats like a fatalistic drum,
And through the spaces of the dark
Midnight shakes the memory
As a madman shakes a dead geranium.

Half-past one,
The street-lamp sputtered,
The street-lamp muttered,
The street-lamp said, "Regard that woman
Who hesitates toward you in the light of the
    door
Which opens on her like a grin.
You see the border of her dress
Is torn and stained with sand,
And you see the corner of her eye
Twists like a crooked pin."

The memory throws up high and dry
A crowd of twisted things;
A twisted branch upon the beach
Eaten smooth, and polished
As if the world gave up
The secret of its skeleton,
Stiff and white.
A broken spring in a factory yard,
Rust that clings to the form that the strength
    has left
Hard and curled and ready to snap.

Half-past two,
The street-lamp said,
"Remark the cat which flattens itself in the
    gutter,
Slips out its tongue
And devours a morsel of rancid butter."
So the hand of the child, automatic,
Slipped out and pocketed a toy that was run-
    ning along the quay.
I could see nothing behind that child's eye.
I have seen eyes in the street
Trying to peer through lighted shutters,

And a crab one afternoon in a pool,
An old crab with barnacles on his back,
Gripped the end of a stick which I held
    him.

Half-past three,
The lamp sputtered,
The lamp muttered in the dark.
The lamp hummed:
"Regard the moon,
La lune ne garde aucune rancune,
She winks a feeble eye,
She smiles into corners.
She smooths the hair of the grass.
The moon has lost her memory.
A washed-out smallpox cracks her face,
Her hand twists a paper rose,
That smells of dust and eau de Cologne,
She is alone
With all the old nocturnal smells
That cross and cross her brain."
The reminiscence comes
Of sunless dry geraniums
And dust of crevices,
Smells of chestnuts in the streets,
And female smells in shuttered rooms,
And cigarettes in corridors
And cocktail smells in bars.

The lamp said,
"Four o'clock,
Here is the number on the door.
Memory!
You have the key,
The little lamp spreads a ring on the stair,
Mount.
The bed is open; the tooth-brush hangs on
    the wall,
Put your shoes at the door, sleep, prepare for
    life."

The last twist of the knife.

## SWEENEY AMONG THE
## NIGHTINGALES

Apeneck Sweeney spreads his knees
Letting his arms hang down to laugh,
The zebra stripes along his jaw
Swelling to maculate giraffe.

The circles of the stormy moon
Slide westward toward the River Plate,
Death and the Raven drift above
And Sweeney guards the hornèd gate.

Gloomy Orion and The Dog
Are veiled; and hushed the shrunken seas;
The person in the Spanish cape
Tries to sit on Sweeney's knees;

Slips and pulls the table cloth,
Overturns a coffee-cup,
Reorganized upon the floor
She yawns and draws a stocking up;

The silent man in mocha brown
Sprawls at the window-sill and gapes;
The waiter brings in oranges
Bananas figs and hothouse grapes;

The silent vertebrate in brown
Contracts and concentrates, withdraws;
Rachel *née* Rabinovitch
Tears at the grapes with murderous paws;

She and the lady in the cape
Are suspect, thought to be in league;
Therefore the man with heavy eyes
Declines the gambit, shows fatigue,

Leaves the room and reappears
Outside the window, leaning in,
Branches of wistaria
Circumscribe a golden grin;

The host with someone indistinct
Converses at the door apart,
The nightingales are singing near
The Convent of the Sacred Heart,

And sang within the bloody wood
When Agamemnon cried aloud,
And let their liquid siftings fall
To stain the stiff dishonored shroud.

## BURBANK WITH A BAEDEKER:
### BLEISTEIN WITH A CIGAR

*Tra-la-la-la-la-la-laire—nil nisi divinum stabile est;
caetera fumus—the gondola stopped, the old palace
was there, how charming its gray and pink—goats
and monkeys, with such hair too!—so the countess
passed on until she came through the little park,
where Niobe presented her with a cabinet, and so
departed.*

Burbank crossed a little bridge
    Descending at a small hotel;
Princess Volupine arrived,
    They were together, and he fell.

Defunctive music under sea
    Passed seaward with the passing bell
Slowly: the God Hercules
    Had left him, that had loved him well.

The horses, under the axletree
    Beat up the dawn from Istria
With even feet. Her shuttered barge
    Burned on the water all the day.

But this or such was Bleistein's way:
    A saggy bending of the knees
And elbows, with the palms turned out,
    Chicago Semite Viennese.

A lusterless protrusive eye
    Stares from the protozoic slime
At a perspective of Canaletto.
    The smoky candle end of time

Declines. On the Rialto once.
    The rats are underneath the piles.
The Jew is underneath the lot.
    Money in furs. The boatman smiles,

Princess Volupine extends
    A meager, blue-nailed, phthisic hand
To climb the waterstair. Lights, lights,
    She entertains Sir Ferdinand

Klein. Who clipped the lion's wings
    And flea'd his rump and pared his claws?
Thought Burbank, meditating on
    Time's ruins, and the seven laws.

### THE HOLLOW MEN

*Mistah Kurtz—he dead.*
            *A penny for the Old Guy*

I

We are the hollow men
We are the stuffed men
Leaning together
Headpiece filled with straw. Alas!
Our dried voices, when
We whisper together
Are quiet and meaningless
As wind in dry grass

Or rats' feet over broken glass
In our dry cellar

Shape without form, shade without color,
Paralyzed force, gesture without motion;

Those who have crossed
With direct eyes, to death's other Kingdom
Remember us—if at all—not as lost
Violent souls, but only
As the hollow men
The stuffed men.

## II

Eyes I dare not meet in dreams
In death's dream kingdom
These do not appear:
There, the eyes are
Sunlight on a broken column
There, is a tree swinging
And voices are
In the wind's singing
More distant and more solemn
Than a fading star.

Let me be no nearer
In death's dream kingdom
Let me also wear
Such deliberate disguises
Rat's coat, crowskin, crossed staves
In a field
Behaving as the wind behaves
No nearer—

Not that final meeting
In the twilight kingdom

## III

This is the dead land
This is cactus land
Here the stony images
Are raised, here they receive
The supplication of a dead man's hand
Under the twinkle of a fading star.

Is it like this
In death's other kingdom
Waking alone
At the hour when we are
Trembling with tenderness
Lips that would kiss
From prayers to broken stone.

## IV

The eyes are not here
There are no eyes here

In this valley of dying stars
In this hollow valley
This broken jaw of our lost kingdoms

In this last of meeting places
We grope together
And avoid speech
Gathered on this beach of the tumid river

Sightless, unless
The eyes reappear
As the perpetual star
Multifoliate rose
Of death's twilight kingdom
The hope only
Of empty men.

## V

*Here we go round the prickly pear*
*Prickly pear prickly pear*
*Here we go round the prickly pear*
*At five o'clock in the morning.*

Between the idea
And the reality
Between the motion
And the act
Falls the Shadow

                    *For Thine is the Kingdom*

Between the conception
And the creation
Between the emotion
And the response
Falls the Shadow

                         *Life is very long*

Between the desire
And the spasm
Between the potency
And the existence
Between the essence
And the descent
Falls the Shadow

                    *For Thine is the Kingdom*

For Thine is
Life is
For Thine is the

*This is the way the world ends*
*This is the way the world ends*
*This is the way the world ends*
*Not with a bang but a whimper.*

ANIMULA

"Issues from the hand of God, the simple soul"
To a flat world of changing lights and noise,
To light, dark, dry or damp, chilly or warm;
Moving between the legs of tables and of chairs,
Rising or falling, grasping at kisses and toys,
Advancing boldly, sudden to take alarm,
Retreating to the corner of arm and knee,
Eager to be reassured, taking pleasure
In the fragrant brilliance of the Christmas tree,
Pleasure in the wind, the sunlight and the sea;
Studies the sunlit pattern on the floor
And running stags around a silver tray;
Confounds the actual and the fanciful,
Content with playing-cards and kings and queens,
What the fairies do and what the servants say.
The heavy burden of the growing soul
Perplexes and offends more, day by day;
Week by week, offends and perplexes more
With the imperatives of "is and seems"
And may and may not, desire and control.
The pain of living and the drug of dreams
Curl up the small soul in the window seat
Behind the *Encyclopaedia Britannica*.
Issues from the hand of time the simple soul
Irresolute and selfish, misshapen, lame,
Unable to fare forward or retreat,
Fearing the warm reality, the offered good,
Denying the importunity of the blood,
Shadow of its own shadows, specter in its own gloom,
Leaving disordered papers in a dusty room;
Living first in the silence after the viaticum.

Pray for Guiterriez, avid of speed and power,
For Boudin, blown to pieces,
For this one who made a great fortune,
And that one who went his own way.
Pray for Floret, by the boarhound slain between the yew trees,
Pray for us now and at the hour of our birth.

A SONG FOR SIMEON

Lord, the Roman hyacinths are blooming in bowls and
The winter sun creeps by the snow hills;
The stubborn season has made stand.
My life is light, waiting for the death wind,
Like a feather on the back of my hand.
Dust in sunlight and memory in corners
Wait for the wind that chills towards the dead land.

Grant us thy peace.
I have walked many years in this city,
Kept faith and fast, provided for the poor,
Have given and taken honor and ease.
There went never any rejected from my door.
Who shall remember my house, where shall live my children's children
When the time of sorrow is come?
They will take to the goat's path, and the fox's home,
Fleeing from the foreign faces and the foreign swords.

Before the time of cords and scourges and lamentation
Grant us thy peace.
Before the stations of the mountain of desolation,
Before the certain hour of maternal sorrow,
Now at this birth season of decease,
Let the Infant, the still unspeaking and unspoken Word,
Grant Israel's consolation
To one who has eighty years and no tomorrow.

According to thy word.
They shall praise Thee and suffer in every generation
With glory and derision,
Light upon light, mounting the saints' stair.
Not for me the martyrdom, the ecstasy of thought and prayer,
Not for me the ultimate vision.
Grant me thy peace.
(And a sword shall pierce thy heart,
Thine also.)
I am tired with my own life and the lives of those after me,
I am dying in my own death and the deaths of those after me.
Let thy servant depart,
Having seen thy salvation.

## JOURNEY OF THE MAGI

"A cold coming we had of it,
Just the worst time of the year
For a journey, and such a long journey:
The ways deep and the weather sharp,
The very dead of winter."
And the camels galled, sore-footed, refractory,
Lying down in the melting snow.
There were times we regretted
The summer palaces on slopes, the terraces,
And the silken girls bringing sherbet.
Then the camel men cursing and grumbling
And running away, and wanting their liquor and women,
And the night-fires going out, and the lack of shelters,
And the cities hostile and the towns unfriendly
And the villages dirty and charging high prices:
A hard time we had of it.

At the end we preferred to travel all night,
Sleeping in snatches,
With the voices singing in our ears, saying
That this was all folly.

Then at dawn we came down to a temperate valley,
Wet, below the snow line, smelling of vegetation;
With a running stream and a water-mill beating the darkness,
And three trees on the low sky,
And an old white horse galloped away in the meadow.
Then we came to a tavern with vine-leaves over the lintel,
Six hands at an open door dicing for pieces of silver,
And feet kicking the empty wine-skins.
But there was no information, and so we continued
And arriving at evening, not a moment too soon
Finding the place; it was (you may say) satisfactory.

All this was a long time ago, I remember,
And I would do it again, but set down
This set down
This: were we led all that way for
Birth or Death? There was a Birth, certainly,
We had evidence and no doubt. I had seen birth and death,
But had thought they were different; this Birth was
Hard and bitter agony for us, like Death, our death.
We returned to our places, these Kingdoms,
But no longer at ease here, in the old dispensation,
With an alien people clutching their gods.
I should be glad of another death.

## John Crowe Ransom

JOHN CROWE RANSOM was born in Pulaski, Tennessee, April 30, 1888, of Scotch-Irish descent. Pulaski, so Ransom states, is otherwise distinguished as being the County Seat of Giles County, the birthplace of Sam Davis, the Confederate martyr, and of the Ku Klux Klan. (Ransom's own great-uncle took part in the foundation of the latter.) Ransom, the son of a local minister, was educated in his own state and abroad: he received his B.A. at Vanderbilt University in 1909, his B.A. at Oxford in 1923. At the latter he was Rhodes Scholar from Tennessee, taking the "Greats" (classical) course. He has taught at Vanderbilt since 1914, except for two years during which he was with the A.E.F. He was the chief instigator and one of the founders of *The Fugitive,* that bravely experimental journal which did much to disprove Mencken's contention that the "solid South" was a vast "Sahara of the Beaux Arts."

*Poems About God* appeared in 1919, a raw first book with a tang of bitter humor. Here was no southern gentleman's proverbial courtliness, no unctuous and mincing gallantry; here was a bristling acerbity blurted in a strong if uncertain utterance. The lines range from the roughly powerful (reminding one of a coarser Robert Frost) to the surprisingly banal. During the five-year interval between *Poems About God* and his next volume, Ransom's poetry underwent an almost complete change. Little of the crudeness remains in *Chills and Fever,* by all odds the most distinguished volume of poetry published in 1924. Ransom, it was evident, reacted from the callow simplicities and the tradition of Wonder in words of one syllable; his verse is definitely for mature minds willing not only to allow a mature poet his mixed modes but willing to follow them. It is, at first glance, a curiously involved speech which Ransom uses to clothe his semi-whimsical, semi-ironic philosophy. But beneath his precise circumlocutions one is made aware of an extraordinarily sensitive lyricist. What adds zest to his verses is the mocking gravity of his speech—a gravity which is sometimes exaggerated to the verge of parody, if a philosopher can achieve that dubious art.

Ransom strikes his note with a sureness that is almost defiant. He is witty, but his wit is strengthened by passion; he turns from dialectical fencing to sudden emotion. Surprise is his forte; he can weave patterns that are, at one time, fanciful and learned. His account of a small boy's walk in deep woods ("First Travels of Max") is as fine a macabre piece as anything achieved by Amy Lowell. He can draw portraits of dream-lost mediocrities as sympathetically as Robinson, "Tom, Tom, the Piper's Son" being a second cousin to "Miniver Cheevy" and "Bewick Finzer." He can sound the mordant brasses in "Captain Carpenter," the muted violins in "Here Lies a Lady" and the prophetic trumpets in "Spiel of the Three Mountebanks" with equal precision. "Parting Without a Sequel" is memorable in its combination of emotion and mockery. "Piazza Piece" is, perhaps, the most characteristic of these poems; in a sonnet balanced as a lyric Ransom has revitalized—and localized—the old theme of Death and the Lady.

Such music, half soothing, half stinging, is new in our poetry; the modulations are strange, the cadences charming in their slight irregularities. Ransom knows how to employ the unresolved suspension; he delights in pairing such slant rhymes as "drunkard-conquered," "little-scuttle," "ready-study." But it is not merely the free use of dissonance and assonance which distinguishes his poems; it is what he does with these properties. "Antique Harvesters" breathes the very quixotic spirit of the old South and the Southron's devotion to that spirit; "Lady Lost" is a perfect harmonizing of teasing and tenderness; "Janet Waking" uncannily mingles sympathy and mock pathos.

*Two Gentlemen in Bonds* (1927) has the fresh combination of cavalier grace and surprising savagery uttered in a precise softness of speech. But the surprise is not only occasioned by his tempo which is both nervous and drawling. As Mark Van Doren wrote, "He has been at pains to salt his rhymes and pepper his diction with fresh, realistic words; he has wrenched his cadences to fit his wayward thought; he has written with an original and almost acid gayety."

Yet, for all of Ransom's variety, in spite of his ability to play equally well in the spangles of harlequin and the graver habit of *Kapellmeister,* this Southerner will never be a popular poet. His is too elegant a speech to meet with general favor; his vocabulary is meticulous to the point of being overelaborate, his utterance is often so finical as to seem pedantic. The fact that a great part of this particularity is not affectation, but a scholar's gentle mockery, will not save him from the disapproval or the neglect of the public which dreads polysyllabic poets. Nor can one blame the common reader. Several of Ransom's poems lose themselves in ellipses and remote allusions, a few are so rarefied as to be unintelligible without footnotes and a chart of cross-references. His later work is both a growth and a departure. Such poems as "Prelude to an Evening," with its overtones of domestic worry, and "Painting: a Head" are a far cry from the philosophic-fanciful tone of "Here Lies a Lady." In this more difficult poetry Ransom seems to be hesitating between a veiled romanticism and an almost abstract intellectuality.

Nevertheless, even in a facile, overproductive age, there can be no doubt that these crisp narratives and teasing lyrics will, in spite of their idiom, find their niche. It will be neither a mean nor a long neglected one. Ransom has already received recognition beyond the borders of patriotic poetry societies. In 1924 the Hogarth Press (London) published *Grace After Meat,* an assembling of ten poems from *Poems About God* and the same number from *Chills and Fever.* It was sponsored by T. S. Eliot and introduced by Robert Graves, who ended his foreword by saying, "Ransom is doing for his own state what Frost has done for New England, Vachel Lindsay for his Middle West, Carl Sandburg for Chicago. Such poets are the forerunners of a national American school that will one day produce a synthesis of all regional contributions." One does not have to echo all the English writer's prophecy to accord Ransom his distinct autochthonous place nor to acknowledge that his influence has spread beyond the Nashville group he so strongly affected.

### BELLS FOR JOHN WHITESIDES' DAUGHTER

There was such speed in her little body,
And such lightness in her footfall,
It is no wonder that her brown study
Astonishes us all.

Her wars were bruited in our high window.
We looked among orchard trees and beyond,
Where she took arms against her shadow,
Or harried unto the pond

The lazy geese, like a snow cloud
Dripping their snow on the green grass,
Tricking and stopping, sleepy and proud,
Who cried in goose, Alas,

For the tireless heart within the little
Lady with rod that made them rise
From their noon apple-dreams, and scuttle
Goose-fashion under the skies!

But now go the bells, and we are ready;
In one house we are sternly stopped
To say we are vexed at her brown study,
Lying so primly propped.

LADY LOST

This morning, there flew up the lane
A timid lady-bird to our bird-bath
And eyed her image dolefully as death;
This afternoon, knocked on our windowpane
To be let in from the rain.

And when I caught her eye
She looked aside, but at the clapping thunder
And sight of the whole earth blazing up like tinder
Looked in on us again most miserably,
Indeed as if she would cry.

So I will go out into the park and say,
"Who has lost a delicate brown-eyed lady
In the West End Section? Or has anybody
Injured some fine woman in some dark way,
Last night or yesterday?

"Let the owner come and claim possession,
No questions will be asked. But stroke her gently
With loving words, and she will evidently
Resume her full soft-haired white-breasted fashion,
And her right home and her right passion."

BLUE GIRLS

Twirling your blue skirts, traveling the sward
Under the towers of your seminary,
Go listen to your teachers old and contrary
Without believing a word.

Tie the white fillets then about your lustrous hair
And think no more of what will come to pass
Than bluebirds that go walking on the grass
And chattering on the air.

Practice your beauty, blue girls, before it fail;
And I will cry with my loud lips and publish
Beauty which all our power shall never establish,
It is so frail.

For I could tell you a story which is true:
I know a lady with a terrible tongue,
Blear eyes fallen from blue,
All her perfections tarnished—and yet it is not long
Since she was lovelier than any of you.

## HERE LIES A LADY

Here lies a lady of beauty and high degree.
Of chills and fever she died, of fever and chills,
The delight of her husband, her aunts, an infant of three,
And of medicos marveling sweetly on her ills.

For either she burned, and her confident eyes would blaze,
And her fingers fly in a manner to puzzle their heads—
What was she making? Why, nothing; she sat in a maze
Of old scraps of laces, snipped into curious shreds—

Or this would pass, and the light of her fire decline
Till she lay discouraged and cold as a thin stalk white and blown,
And would not open her eyes, to kisses, to wine.
The sixth of these states was her last; the cold settled down.

Sweet ladies, long may ye bloom, and toughly I hope ye may thole,
But was she not lucky? In flowers and lace and mourning,
In love and great honor we bade God rest her soul
After six little spaces of chill, and six of burning.

## JANET WAKING

Beautifully Janet slept
Till it was deeply morning. She woke then
And thought about her dainty-feathered hen,
To see how it had kept.

One kiss she gave her mother,
Only a small one gave she to her daddy
Who would have kissed each curl of his shining baby;
No kiss at all for her brother.

"Old Chucky, Old Chucky!" she cried,
Running on little pink feet upon the grass
To Chucky's house, and listening. But alas,
Her Chucky had died.

It was a transmogrifying bee
Came droning down on Chucky's old bald head
And sat and put the poison. It scarcely bled,
But how exceedingly

And purply did the knot
Swell with the venom and communicate
Its rigor! Now the poor comb stood up straight
But Chucky did not.

So there was Janet
Kneeling on the wet grass, crying her brown hen

(Translated far beyond the daughters of men)
To rise and walk upon it.

And weeping fast as she had breath
Janet implored us, "Wake her from her sleep!"
And would not be instructed in how deep
Was the forgetful kingdom of death.

## SPIEL OF THE THREE
## MOUNTEBANKS

THE SWARTHY ONE—
  Villagers who gather round,
  This is Fides, my lean hound.
  Bring your bristled village curs
  To try his fang and tooth, sweet sirs:
  He will rend them, he is savage,
  Thinking nothing but to ravage,
  Nor with cudgel, fire, rope,
  May ye control my misanthrope;
  He would tear the moon in the sky
  And fly at Heaven, could he fly.
  And for his ravening without cease
  I have had of him no peace.
  Only once I bared the knife
  To quit my devil of his life,
  But listen, how I heard him say,
  "Think you I shall die today?
  Since your mother cursed and died,
  I am keeping at your side,
  We are firmly knit together,
  Two ends tugging at one tether,
  And you shall see when I shall die
  That you are mortal even as I."
  Bring your stoutest-hearted curs
  If ye would risk him, gentle sirs.

THE THICK ONE—
  Countrymen, here's a noble frame,
  Humphrey is my elephant's name.
  When my father's back was bent
  Under steep impediment,
  Humphrey came to my possession,
  With patient strength for all his passion.
  Have ye a mountain to remove?
  It is Humphrey's dearest love.
  Pile his burden to the skies,
  Loose a pestilence of flies,
  Foot him in the quick morass
  Where no laden beast can pass:

He will staunch his weariless back
And march unswerving on the track.
Have ye seen a back so wide,
Such impenetrable hide?
Nor think ye by this Humphrey hill
Prince Hamlet bare his fardels ill?
Myself I like it not for us
To wear beneath an incubus;
I take offense, but in no rage
May I dispose my heritage;
Though in good time the vast and tough
Shall sink and totter soon enough.
So pile your population up:
They are a drop in Humphrey's cup;
Add all your curses to his pack
To make one straw for Humphrey's back.

THE PALE ONE—
  If ye remark how poor I am,
  Come, citizens, behold my lamb!
  Have ye a lion, ounce, or scourge,
  Or any beast of dainty gorge?
  Agnus lays his tender youth
  Between the very enemy's mouth,
  And though he sniff his delicate meat,
  He may not bruise that flesh nor eat,
  He may not rend him limb from limb,
  If Agnus do but bleat on him.
  Fierce was my youth, but like a dream
  I saw a temple, and a stream,
  And where I knelt and washed my sore,
  This infant lamb stood on the shore,
  He mounted with me from the river.
  And still he cries, as brave as ever,
  "Lay me down by the lion's side
  To match my frailty with his pride;
  Fain would I welter in my blood
  To teach these lions true lionhood."
  So daily Agnus would be slain
  But daily is denied again,
  And still the hungry lions range
  While Agnus waits upon a change;

Only the coursing lions die
And in their deserts mortify.
So bring us lion, leopard, bear,

To try of Agnus without fear,
And ye less gentle than I am,
Come, be instructed of my Lamb.


### FIRST TRAVELS OF MAX

As hath been, lo, these many generations,
The best of the Van Vroomans was the youngest;
And even he, in a chevroned sailor's blouse
And tawny curls far from subdued to the cap,
Had slapped old Katie and betaken himself
From games for children. That was because they told
Him never, never to set a wicked foot
Into Fool's Forest, where the devil dwelt.

"Become Saint Michael's sword!" said Max to the stick,
And to the stone, "Be a brand-new revolver!"
Then Max was glad that he had armed so wisely,
As darker grew the wood, and shrill with silence.
All good fairies were helpless here; at night
Whipped in an inch of their lives; weeping, forbidden
To play with strange scared truant little boys
Who didn't belong there. Snakes were allowed there
And lizards and adders—people of age and evil
That lay on their bellies and whispered—no bird nor rabbit.
There were more rotten trees than there were sound ones;
In that wood, timber was degenerate
And rotted almost faster than it grew.
There were no flowers nor apples; too much age.
The only innocent thing in there was Max,
And even he had cursed his little sisters.

The little black tarn rose up almost in his face—
It was as black and sudden as the pit
The Adversary digs in the bowels of earth;
Bubbles were on it, breath of the black beast
(Formed like a spider, white bag for entrails)
Who took that sort of blackness to inhabit
And dangle after bad men in Fool's Forest.
"Must they be bad?" said casuistical Max.
"Mightn't a good boy who stopped saying his prayers
Be allowed to slip into the spider's fingers?"
Max raised his sword—but what can swords do
Against the Prince of the Dark? Max sheathed his point
And crept around the pool.

In the middle of the wood was a Red Witch.
Max half expected her. He never expected
To find a witch's house so dirty and foolish,
A witch with a wide bosom yellow as butter,
Or a witch combing so many obscene things

From her black hair into her scarlet lap.
He never believed there would attempt to sing
The one that taught the rats to squeal and Bashan's
Bull to bellow.

"Littlest and last Van Vrooman, do you come too?"
She knew him, it appeared, would know him better,
The scarlet hulk of hell with a fat bosom,
Pirouetting at the bottom of the forest.
Certainly Max had come, but he was going,
Unequal contests never being commanded
On young knights only armed in innocency.
"When I am a grown man I will come here
And cut your head off!" That was very well;
Not a true heart beating in Christendom
Could have said more, but that for the present would do.
Max went straight home; and nothing chilled him more
Than the company kept him by the witch's laugh
And the witch's song, and the creeping of his flesh.

Max is more firmly domiciliated.
A great house is Van Vrooman, a green slope
South to the sun do the great ones inhabit
And a few children play on the lawn with the nurse.
Max has returned to his play, and you may find him,
His famous curls unsmoothed, if you will call
Where the Van Vroomans live, the tribe Van Vrooman
Live there, at least, when any are at home.

### ANTIQUE HARVESTERS

*(Scene: Of the Mississippi the bank sinister, and of the
Ohio the bank sinister)*

Tawny are the leaves turned, but they still hold.
It is the harvest; what shall this land produce?
A meager hill of kernels, a runnel of juice.
Declension looks from our land, it is old.
Therefore let us assemble, dry, gray, spare,
And mild as yellow air.

"I hear the creak of a raven's funeral wing."
The young men would be joying in the song
Of passionate birds; their memories are not long.
What is it thus rehearsed in sable? "Nothing."
Trust not but the old endure, and shall be older
Than the scornful beholder.

We pluck the spindling ears and gather the corn.
One spot has special yield? "On this spot stood
Heroes and drenched it with their only blood."
And talk meets talk, as echoes from the horn

Of the hunter—echoes are the old men's arts
Ample are the chambers of their hearts.

Here come the hunters, keepers of a rite.
The horn, the hounds, the lank mares coursing by
Under quaint archetypes of chivalry;
And the fox, lovely ritualist, in flight
Offering his unearthly ghost to quarry;
And the fields, themselves to harry.

Resume, harvesters. The treasure is full bronze
Which you will garner for the Lady, and the moon
Could tinge it no yellower than does this noon;
But the gray will quench it shortly—the fields, men, stones.
Pluck fast, dreamers; prove as you rumble slowly
Not less than men, not wholly.

Bare the arm too, dainty youths, bend the knees
Under bronze burdens. And by an autumn tone
As by a gray, as by a green, you will have known
Your famous Lady's image; for so have these.
And if one say that easily will your hands
More prosper in other lands,

Angry as wasp-music be your cry then:
"Forsake the Proud Lady, of the heart of fire,
The look of snow, to the praise of a dwindled choir,
Song of degenerate specters that were men?
The sons of the fathers shall keep her, worthy of
What these have done in love."

True, it is said of our Lady, she ageth.
But see, if you peep shrewdly, she hath not stooped;
Take no thought of her servitors that have drooped,
For we are nothing; and if one talk of death—
Why, the ribs of the earth subsist frail as a breath
If but God wearieth.

### PIAZZA PIECE

—I am a gentleman in a dustcoat trying
To make you hear. Your ears are soft and small
And listen to an old man not at all;
They want the young men's whispering and sighing.
But see the roses on your trellis dying
And hear the spectral singing of the moon—
For I must have my lovely lady soon.
I am a gentleman in a dustcoat trying.

—I am a lady young in beauty waiting
Until my truelove comes, and then we kiss.
But what gray man among the vines is this

Whose words are dry and faint as in a dream?
Back from my trellis, sir, before I scream!
I am a lady young in beauty waiting.

### CAPTAIN CARPENTER

Captain Carpenter rose up in his prime
Put on his pistols and went riding out
But had got wellnigh nowhere at that time
Till he fell in with ladies in a rout.

It was a pretty lady and all her train
That played with him so sweetly but before
An hour she'd taken a sword with all her main
And twined him of his nose for evermore.

Captain Carpenter mounted up one day
And rode straightway into a stranger rogue
That looked unchristian but be that as it may
The Captain did not wait upon prologue.

But drew upon him out of his great heart
The other swung against him with a club
And cracked his two legs at the shinny part
And let him roll and stick like any tub.

Captain Carpenter rode many a time
From male and female took he sundry harms
He met the wife of Satan crying "I'm
The she-wolf bids you shall bear no more arms."

Their strokes and counters whistled in the wind
I wish he had delivered half his blows
But where she should have made off like a hind
The bitch bit off his arms at the elbows.

And Captain Carpenter parted with his ears
To a black devil that used him in this wise
O jesus ere his threescore and ten years
Another had plucked out his sweet blue eyes.

Captain Carpenter got up on his roan
And sallied from the gate in hell's despite
I heard him asking in the grimmest tone
If any enemy yet there was to fight?

"To any adversary it is fame
If he risk to be wounded by my tongue
Or burnt in two beneath my red heart's flame
Such are the perils he is cast among.

"But if he can he has a pretty choice
From an anatomy with little to lose
Whether he cut my tongue and take my voice
Or whether it be my round red heart he choose."

It was the neatest knave that ever was seen
Stepping in perfume from his lady's bower
Who at this word put in his merry mien
And fell on Captain Carpenter like a tower.

I would not knock old fellows in the dust
But there lay Captain Carpenter on his back
His weapons were the old heart in his bust
And a blade shook between rotten teeth alack.

The rogue in scarlet and gray soon knew his mind
He wished to get his trophy and depart;
With gentle apology and touch refined
He pierced him and produced the Captain's heart.

God's mercy rest on Captain Carpenter now
I thought him Sirs an honest gentleman
Citizen husband soldier and scholar enow
Let jangling kites eat of him if they can.

But God's deep curses follow after those
That shore him of his goodly nose and ears
His legs and strong arms at the two elbows
And eyes that had not watered seventy years.

The curse of hell upon the sleek upstart
Who got the Captain finally on his back
And took the red red vitals of his heart
And made the kites to whet their beaks clack clack.

### OLD MAN PONDERED

Three times he crossed our way where with me went
One who is fair and gentle, and it was strange,
But not once glancing did his vision range
Wayward on me, or my most innocent,
But strictly watched his own predicament.
How are old spirits so dead? His eye seemed true
As mine, he walked by it, it was as blue,
How came it monstered in its fixed intent?

But I will venture how. In his long years
Close-watched and dangerous, many a bright-barbed hate
Burning had smote against the optic gate
To enter and destroy. But the quick gears

Blinked shut the aperture. Else those grim leers
Had won to the inner chamber where sat Hope
To spin and pray, and made her misanthrope,
And bled her courage with a thousand spears.

Thus hate and scorn. And he must guard as well
Against alluring love, whose mild engine
Was perilous too for the lone sitter-in,
So hard consented to her little cell;
The tenderest looks vainly upon him fell,
Of dearest company, lest one light arrow
Be sharpened with a most immortal sorrow.
So had he kept his mansion shut of hell.

Firm and upright he walked for one so old,
Thrice-pondered; and I dare not prophesy
What age must bring me; for I look round bold
And seek my enemies out; and leave untold
The sideway watery dog's-glances I
Send fawning on you, thinking you will not scold.


## PARTING, WITHOUT A SEQUEL

She has finished and sealed the letter
At last, which he so richly has deserved,
With characters venomous and hatefully curved,
And nothing could be better.

But even as she gave it,
Saying to the blue-capped functioner of doom,
"Into his hands," she hoped the leering groom
Might somewhere lose and leave it.

Then all the blood
Forsook the face. She was too pale for tears,
Observing the ruin of her younger years.
She went and stood

Under her father's vaunting oak
Who kept his peace in wind and sun, and glistened
Stoical in the rain; to whom she listened
If he spoke.

And now the agitation of the rain
Rasped his sere leaves, and he talked low and gentle,
Reproaching the wan daughter by the lintel;
Ceasing, and beginning again.

Away went the messenger's bicycle,
His serpent's track went up the hill forever.
And all the time she stood there hot as fever
And cold as any icicle.

## PRELUDE TO AN EVENING

Do not enforce the tired wolf
Dragging his infected wound homeward
To sit tonight with the warm children
Naming the pretty kings of France.

The images of the invaded mind
Being as monsters in the dreams
Of your most brief enchanted headful,
Suppose a miracle of confusion:

That dreamed and undreamt become each
  other
And mix the night and day of your mind;
And it does not matter your twice crying
From mouth unbeautied against the pillow

To avert the gun of the same old soldier;
For cry, cock-crow, or the iron bell
Can crack the sleep-sense of outrage,
Annihilate phantoms who were nothing.

But now, by our perverse supposal,
There is a drift of fog on your mornings;
You in your peignoir, dainty at your orange
  cup,
Feel poising round the sunny room

Invisible evil, deprived and bold.
All day the clock will metronome
Your gallant fear; the needles clicking,
The heels detonating the stair's cavern.

Freshening the water in the blue bowls
For the buckberries, with not all your love,
You shall be listening for the low wind,
The warning sibilance of pines.

You like a waning moon, and I accusing
Our too banded Eumenides,
While you pronounce Noes wanderingly
And smooth the heads of the hungry chil-
  dren.

## PAINTING: A HEAD

By dark severance the apparition head
Smiles from the air a capital on no
Column or a Platonic perhaps head
On a canvas sky depending from nothing;

Stirs up an old illusion of grandeur
By tickling the instinct of heads to be
Absolute and to try decapitation
And to play truant from the body bush;

But too happy and beautiful for those sorts
Of head (homekeeping heads are happiest)
Discovers maybe thirty unwidowed years
Of not dishonoring the faithful stem;

Is nameless and has authored for the evil
Historian headhunters neither book
Nor state and is therefore distinct from tart
Heads with crowns and guilty gallery heads;

So that the extravagant device of art
Unhousing by abstraction this once head
Was capital irony by a loving hand
That knew the no treason of a head like this;

Makes repentance in an unlovely head
For vinegar disparagement of flesh
Till, the hurt flesh recusing, the hard egg
Is shrunken to its own deathlike surface;

And an image thus: the body bears the head
(So hardly one they terribly are two)
Feeds and obeys and unto please what end?
Not to the glory of tyrant head but to

The increase of body. Beauty is of body.
The flesh contouring shallowly on a head
Is a rock-garden needing body's love
And best bodiness to colorify

The big blue birds sitting and sea-shell flats
And caves and on the iron acropolis
To spread the hyacinthine hair and rear
The olive garden for the nightingales.

# *Lew Sarett*

L EW SARETT was born May 16, 1888, in Chicago, Illinois, and reared in the state of Michigan and in the Lake Superior country. He was educated at Beloit and the University of Illinois, receiving his LL.B. at the latter institution in 1916. However, he never practiced law because, as he says, "foot-loose adventures in the woods ruined me for any confining work." After sixteen he spent much of his life in the Rocky Mountains and in the Canadian North; for eight years he worked intermittently as woodsman and guide in that region. He has been a United States Ranger and still spends several months of each year in the remote districts of the National Parks. In this nomadic life on the frontiers of America he has lived much of the time with Indians and backwoods folk; thus he has come to understand the bush country, the voyageur, and the aborigine.

Sarett's first volume, *Many Many Moons,* appeared in 1920. It is, as he calls it, a book of wilderness poems, poems which endeavor to capture the peculiar influence of Indian thought as well as nature in its wilder aspects. His long and impressionistic monolog, "The Box of God," was awarded the Levinson prize (offered through *Poetry*) for 1921. It became the title poem of a subsequent volume, *The Box of God* (1922), a collection which expresses a sort of primitive pantheism; even the lyrics echo the wood sounds and scenes which are familiar to the Indian, even though it is not the Indian himself who speaks. Here are flute notes as well as the rattle of dried gourds and the dull insistence of the tom-tom.

Sarett's more recent lyrics show a wider range; there is social significance in such verses as "Feud," which is intensified by a passion personal as well as racial. *Slow Smoke* (1925) and *Wings Against the Moon* (1931) reveal an increase in technique and a wider outlook upon life.

### IRON-WIND DANCES

Over and under
The shaking sky,
The war-drums thunder
When I dance by!—
Ho! a warrior proud,
I dance on a cloud,
For my ax shall feel
The enemy reel;
My heart shall thrill
To a bloody kill,—
Ten Sioux dead
Split open of head!—
Look! to the West!—
The sky-line drips,—
Blood from the breast!
Blood from the lips!
Ho! when I dance by,

The war-drums thunder
Over and under
The shaking sky.
Beat, beat on the drums,
For the Thunderbird comes.
                    Wuh!
                    Wuh!


### FEUD

Poor wayworn creature! Oh, sorely harried deer,
    What drove you, quivering like a poplar-blade,
To refuge with my herd? What holds you here
    Within my meadow, broken and afraid?

Tilting your nose to tainted air, you thrill
    And freeze to wailing wolves! Fear you the sound
Of the coyotes eager for a tender kill?
    Or yet the baying of the hunter's hound?

Let fall your anguish, harried one, and rest;
    Bed yourself down among your kin, my cattle;
Sleep unperturbed. No spoiler shall molest
    You here this night, for I shall wage your battle.

There was a day when coyotes in a pack,
    Wolves of another hue, another breed,
With Christ upon their lips, set out to track
    Me down and drop me, for my blood, my creed.

Oh, hunted creature, once I knew the thud
    Of padded feet that put you into flight,
The bugle-cry, suffused with lust for blood,
    That trembled in the silver bell of night.

I knew your frenzied rocky run, the burst
    Of lungs, the rivers of fire in every vein;
I knew your foaming lip, your boundless thirst,
    The rain of molten-hammering in your brain.

Abide with me, then, against the wolves' return,
    For I shall carry on the feud for you;
And it shall be, to me, of small concern
    If the wolf-hearts walk on four soft feet or two.

Oh, let them come! And I shall burn their flanks
    With a blast of hell to end their revelry,
And whistle molten silver through their ranks,
    Laughing—one round for you, and one for me.

### TO A WILD GOOSE OVER DECOYS

O lonely trumpeter, coasting down the sky,
Like a winter leaf blown from the bur-oak tree
By whipping winds, and flapping silverly
Against the sun,—I know your lonely cry.

I know the worn wild heart that bends your flight
And circles you above this beckoning lake,
Eager of neck, to find the honking drake
Who speaks of reedy refuge for the night.

I know the sudden rapture that you fling
In answer to our friendly gander's call—
Halloo! Beware decoys!—or you will fall
With a silver bullet whistling in your wing.

Beat on your weary flight across the blue!
Beware, O traveler, of our gabbling geese!
Beware this weedy counterfeit of peace!—
Oh, I was once a passing bird like you.

## Conrad Aiken

CONRAD (POTTER) AIKEN was born at Savannah, Georgia, August 5, 1889. He attended Harvard, was chosen class poet during his senior year, received his A.B. in 1912, traveled extensively for three years, and since then devoted all his time to literature, living at South Yarmouth, Massachusetts, until 1921. In that year he moved his family to England; a few years later he bought a house on the Sussex coast at Rye. After a brief return to Massachusetts in 1928 Aiken remained in England except for occasional visits to America.

The outstanding feature of Aiken's work is its rapid adaptability and its slow growth. His first volume, *Earth Triumphant and Other Tales in Verse* (1914), is the Keats tradition crossed, paraphrased, and vulgarized by Masefield. *Turns and Movies* (1916) is a complete change; Masefield is exchanged for Masters. But in the less conspicuous half of this book Aiken begins to speak with his true voice. Here he is the natural musician, playing with new rhythms, haunting cadences. *The Jig of Forslin* (1916) is an elaboration of his method. In this volume Aiken goes back to the narrative—or rather, to a series of loosely connected stories—and, reënforced by studies in analytical psychology, explores "the process of vicarious wish fulfillment by which civilized man enriches his circumscribed life."

*Nocturne of Remembered Spring* (1917), *The Charnel Rose* (1918) and *The House of Dust* (1920) are packed with a tired but often beautiful music. Even though it is enlivened by injections of T. S. Eliot's conversational idiom, the effect is frequently misty and monotonous. Rain seems to fall persistently through these volumes; dust blows down the street; the shadows blur; everything dissolves in a wash of boredom and forgetfulness. Even the poignance seems on the point of falling asleep.

Often Aiken loses himself in this watery welter of language. In trying to create a closer *liaison* between poetry and music, he places so much importance on the rise and fall of syllables that his very excess of melody defeats his purpose. His verse, thus, gains greatly on the sensuous side, but loses, in its murmuring indefiniteness, that vitality of speech which is the very blood of poetry. It is a subaqueous music, strangely like the magic of Debussy.

This weakening overinsistence on sound does not prevent Aiken from attaining many exquisite effects. Primarily, a lyric poet, he condenses an emotion in a few lines; some of his best moments are these "lapses" into tune. The music of the "Morning Song from 'Senlin'" (in *The Charnel Rose*) is rich with subtleties of rhythm. But it is much more than a lyrical movement. Beneath the flow and flexibility of these lines there is a delightful whimsicality, a summoning of those immensities that loom behind the casual moments of everyday.

*Punch: The Immortal Liar* (1921) is an almost complete *volte face*. After it seemed established that Aiken's gift was limited to the twitching of overrefined nerves, to a too ready response to gloomy subconsciousness, the poet strikes out toward a naked directness. Dazzling though the first half of this work is, it is the second part which attains the heights. Here Punch, stripped of his mask of braggadocio, is revealed as the solitary, frustrated dreamer; a pitiful puppet floundering in a net he cannot see; jerked and gesticulating without knowledge of the strings which direct him—a symbol, in short, of man as marionette. This second part of *Punch* contains, not only Aiken's most delicate exposition of the inhibited soul, but some of the finest lyrics he has produced. Whatever the theme, the musician is triumphant.

*Priapus and the Pool* (1922) is preponderantly lyrical, containing twenty-five songs, several of which are as moving as those of any contemporary American singer. The succeeding volume, *The Pilgrimage of Festus* (1923), returns to the symphonic form; beneath its imaginative outlines it is an extended essay in epistemology. Festus is the lineal descendant of Aiken's own Senlin and a not distant relative of Ibsen's Peer Gynt. A revised and enlarged edition of *Priapus and the Pool* appeared in 1925.

Aiken, the keenest critic of his own poetry, has been quick to see its limitations as well as its potentialities. In a self-analysis in which he confessed that his verse has groped continually toward symphonic arrangement, Aiken wrote, "Here I give myself away as being in quest of a sort of absolute poetry, a poetry in which the intention is not so much to arouse an emotion, or to persuade of a reality, as to employ such emotion or sense of reality (tangentially struck) with the same cool detachment with which a composer employs notes or chords."

Here we are at the heart of the contradiction: the paradox that, though Aiken is undoubtedly one of the most musical of living poets, he is one of the least popular. An audience that prefers its emotion outright, that craves a palpable reality, resents (or, worse, ignores) the nuance "tangentially struck." The emphasis on overtone and implication creates, too often, an obscure pantomime; it is, as Aiken himself was quick to see, "a prestidigitation in which the juggler's bottles or balls are a little too apt, unfortunately, to be altogether invisible." What is even more obvious, an audience is quick to sense the performer's uncertainty. This—until the most recent work—has been Aiken's undoing. He has fancied himself as a symphonist when he was, preëminently, a lyricist, albeit a lyricist neither pure nor simple. More than any contemporary, except T. S. Eliot, who seems to have learned several tricks in dissonance from Aiken, he has evolved a subtly subjective poetry which flows as smoothly, as surprisingly, as the stream of the subconscious. He has given formlessness a form, has brought tortured self-analysis to a pitch of pure poetry, and (whether in the suspensions of the famous "Morning Song from 'Senlin' " or the more certain modulations of "Tetélestai") he has registered an immediacy of anguish. Aiken's growth in tonal surety must be evident to all but the tone-deaf. "The Road" is more than a compelling dream-picture; in it Aiken contradicts his own credo and participates in the struggle of humanity. "At a Concert of Music" and "Annihilation" bring the earlier modulations to a perfect cadence.

This musical advance is cumulatively established by the *Selected Poems* (1929), which won the Pulitzer Prize for that year, *John Deth and Other Poems* (1930), and *Landscape West of Eden* (1933). All these deal with sets of symbols and dream pictures in a limbo of fantasy. *John Deth* is one of the most curious poems Aiken has written, and the lyrics which follow it ("Annihilation," "The Quarrel," "At a Concert of Music," with others) are among his completely successful pieces, something which cannot be said for *The Coming Forth by Day of Osiris Jones* (1931).

The music of such meditative lyrics is pitched lower in the somber "preludes" which began preoccupying Aiken before 1930 and of which he has written a hundred or more. Sixty-three of these were published in *Preludes for Memnon* (1931) and, though Memnon typified the sun, these poems seem chiefly addressed to darkness. The mood is disconsolate, the tone languorous to lugubrious. Most of the book suggests that abstract and "absolute" poetry to which Aiken has so often tuned his muted instruments, yet several of the individual poems ("This is not you?" "So, in the evening to the simple cloister," "But how it came from earth," "One star fell and another as we walked") are rich in movement and emotional intensity.

Besides his poetry, Aiken has written a host of reviews, some of them containing extraordinarily sensitive criticism. *Scepticisms* (1919) is a provocative and valuable set of studies. His anthologies—*Modern American Poets* (1922) and *American Poetry, 1671-1928*—suffer from Aiken's predilection for experimental and abstract verse, but are far superior to the ordinary compilation. He edited the first *Selected Poems of Emily Dickinson* which appeared in England in 1924. In that year his prose began to attract attention. *Bring! Bring!* (1925) and *Costumes by Eros* (1928) are collections of introspective short stories in a successful if not altogether new genre. *Blue Voyage* (1927) is less influenced, a novel closely woven and strangely unresolved; *Great Circle* (1933) is a tense study in psychopathological maladjustment, a theme which Aiken employs with skill and extraordinary effect; *King Coffin* (1935), a novel, is a brilliant study of a paranoiac and his "perfect" crime.

BREAD AND MUSIC

Music I heard with you was more than music,
And bread I broke with you was more than bread;
Now that I am without you, all is desolate;
All that was once so beautiful is dead.

Your hands once touched this table and this silver,
And I have seen your fingers hold this glass.
These things do not remember you, belovèd,
And yet your touch upon them will not pass.

For it was in my heart you moved among them,
And blessed them with your hands and with your eyes;
And in my heart they will remember always,—
They knew you once, O beautiful and wise.

MIRACLES

Twilight is spacious, near things in it seem far,
And distant things seem near.
Now in the green west hangs a yellow star.
And now across old waters you may hear
The profound gloom of bells among still trees,
Like a rolling of huge bowlders beneath seas.

Silent as thought in evening contemplation
Weaves the bat under the gathering stars.
Silent as dew, we seek new incarnation,
Meditate new avatars.
In a clear dusk like this
Mary climbed up the hill to seek her son,
To lower him down from the cross, and kiss
The mauve wounds, every one.

Men with wings
In the dusk walked softly after her.
She did not see them, but may have felt
The winnowed air around her stir;
She did not see them, but may have known
Why her son's body was light as a little stone.
She may have guessed that other hands were there
Moving the watchful air.

Now, unless persuaded by searching music
Which suddenly opens the portals of the mind,
We guess no angels,
And are contented to be blind.
Let us blow silver horns in the twilight,
And lift our hearts to the yellow star in the green,
To find perhaps, if, while the dew is rising,
Clear things may not be seen.

MORNING SONG FROM "SENLIN"

It is morning, Senlin says, and in the morning
When the light drips through the shutters like the dew,

I arise, I face the sunrise,
And do the things my fathers learned to do.
Stars in the purple dusk above the rooftops
Pale in a saffron mist and seem to die,
And I myself on a swiftly tilting planet
Stand before a glass and tie my tie.

Vine-leaves tap my window,
Dew-drops sing to the garden stones,
The robin chirps in the chinaberry tree
Repeating three clear tones.

It is morning. I stand by the mirror
And tie my tie once more.
While waves far off in a pale rose twilight
Crash on a white sand shore.
I stand by a mirror and comb my hair:
How small and white my face!—
The green earth tilts through a sphere of air
And bathes in a flame of space.
There are houses hanging above the stars
And stars hung under a sea . . .
And a sun far off in a shell of silence
Dapples my walls for me. . . .

It is morning, Senlin says, and in the morning
Should I not pause in the light to remember God?
Upright and firm I stand on a star unstable,
He is immense and lonely as a cloud.
I will dedicate this moment before my mirror
To him alone, for him I will comb my hair.
Accept these humble offerings, clouds of silence!
I will think of you as I descend the stair.

Vine-leaves tap my window,
The snail-track shines on the stones;
Dew-drops flash from the chinaberry tree
Repeating two clear tones.

It is morning, I awake from a bed of silence,
Shining I rise from the starless waters of sleep.
The walls are about me still as in the evening,
I am the same, and the same name still I keep.
The earth revolves with me, yet makes no motion,
The stars pale silently in a coral sky.
In a whistling void I stand before my mirror,
Unconcerned, and tie my tie.

There are horses neighing on far-off hills
Tossing their long white manes,
And mountains flash in the rose-white dusk,
Their shoulders black with rains. . . .

It is morning, I stand by the mirror
And surprise my soul once more;
The blue air rushes above my ceiling,
There are suns beneath my floor. . . .

. . . It is morning, Senlin says, I ascend from darkness
And depart on the winds of space for I·know not where;
My watch is wound, a key is in my pocket,
And the sky is darkened as I descend the stair.
There are shadows across the windows, clouds in heaven,
And a god among the stars; and I will go
Thinking of him as I might think of daybreak
And humming a tune I know. . . .

Vine-leaves tap at the window,
Dew-drops sing to the garden stones,
The robin chirps in the chinaberry tree
Repeating three clear tones.


### THE ROOM

Through that window—all else being extinct
Except itself and me—I saw the struggle
Of darkness against darkness. Within the room
It turned and turned, dived downward. Then I saw
How order might—if chaos wished—become:
And saw the darkness crush upon itself,
Contracting powerfully; it was as if
It killed itself, slowly: and with much pain.
Pain. The scene was pain, and nothing but pain.
What else, when chaos draws all forces inward
To shape a single leaf? . . .
                              For the leaf came
Alone and shining in the empty room;
After a while the twig shot downward from it;
And from the twig a bough; and then the trunk,
Massive and coarse; and last the one black root.
The black root cracked the walls. Boughs burst the window:
The great tree took possession.
                              Tree of trees!
Remember (when time comes) how chaos died
To shape the shining leaf. Then turn, have courage,
Wrap arms and roots together, be convulsed
With grief, and bring back chaos out of shape.
I will be watching then as I watch now.
I will praise darkness now, but then the leaf.

THE PUPPET DREAMS

(*from "Punch: The Immortal Liar"*)

Sheba, now let down your hair,
And play upon it with your hands,
While girls from Tal and Mozambique
Parade before in sarabands,—

Play him songs inaudible
With white hands braceleted and slim,
Or shake your hair and let it fall
And softly darken him.

Cling to him, while cymbals far
Are sweetly smitten in the dusk,
And maenads, under a haughty star,
Break the white rose for its musk:

Cling to him, and with your lips
Feed his heart on crumbs of fire
That shall, perpetually, delight
But never slay desire!

✦

Open a window on the world
With all its sorrow, and then
When he has heard that sound a space,
Close it fast again. . . .

Sweet will it be, lapped round with ease
And music-troubled air,
To hear for a moment on the wind
A sound of far despair:

And then, to turn to lights again,
And fingers soft on strings,
While Sheba slips her bracelets off
And spreads her arms and sings. . . .

Sweet will it be, to hear far off
That gusty sound of pain,
And to remember, far away,
A world of death and rain:

And then, to close the window fast,
And laugh, and clap soft hands,
While girls from Tal and Mozambique
Parade in sarabands. . . .

Close now the window! Close it well!
That slow lament of pain
Was but the dissonance that makes
Dull music sweet again.

✦

There is a fountain in a wood
Where wavering lies a moon:
It plays to the slowly falling leaves
A sleepy tune.

. . . The peach-trees lean upon a wall
Of gold and ivory:
The peacock spreads his tail, the leaves
Fall silently. . . .

There, amid silken sounds and wine
And music idly broken,
The drowsy god observes his world
With no word spoken.

Arcturus, rise! Orion, fall! . . .
The white-winged stars obey. . . .
Or else he greets his Fellow-God;
And there, in the dusk, they play

A game of chess with stars for pawns
And a silver moon for queen:
Immeasurable as clouds, above
A chess-board world they lean

And thrust their hands amid their beards,
And utter words profound
That shake the star-swung firmament
With a fateful sound! . . .

. . . The peach-trees lean upon a wall
Of gold and ivory;
The peacock spreads his tail; the leaves
Fall silently. . . .

PORTRAIT OF A GIRL

This is the shape of the leaf, and this of the flower,
And this the pale bole of the tree
Which watches its bough in a pool of unwavering water
In a land we never shall see.

The thrush on the bough is silent, the dew falls softly,
In the evening is hardly a sound. . . .
And the three beautiful pilgrims who come here together
Touch lightly the dust of the ground.

Touch it with feet that trouble the dust but as wings do,
Come shyly together, are still,
Like dancers who wait in a pause of the music, for music
The exquisite silence to fill . . .

This is the thought of the first, and this of the second,
And this the grave thought of the third:
"Linger we thus for a moment, palely expectant,
And silence will end, and the bird

"Sing the pure phrase, sweet phrase, clear phrase in the twilight
To fill the blue bell of the world;
And we, who on music so leaflike have drifted together,
Leaflike apart shall be whirled

"Into what but the beauty of silence, silence forever? . . ."
. . . This is the shape of the tree,
And the flower and the leaf, and the three pale beautiful pilgrims:
This is what you are to me.

### AND IN THE HANGING GARDENS—

And in the hanging gardens there is rain
From midnight until one, striking the leaves
And bells of flowers, and stroking boles of planes,
And drawing slow arpeggios over pools
And stretching strings of sound from eaves to ferns.
The princess reads. The knave of diamonds sleeps.
The king is drunk, and flings a golden goblet
Down from the turret window (curtained with rain)
Into the lilacs.
　　　　　　And at one o'clock
The vulcan under the garden wakes and beats
The gong upon his anvil. Then the rain
Ceases, but gently ceases, dripping still,
And sound of falling water fills the dark
As leaves grow bold and upright, and as eaves
Part with water. The princess turns the page
Beside the candle, and between two braids
Of golden hair. And reads: "From there I went
Northward a journey of four days, and came
To a wild village in the hills, where none
Was living save the vulture and the rat
And one old man who laughed but could not speak.
The roofs were fallen in, the well grown over
With weed. And it was here my father died.

Then eight days further, bearing slightly west,
The cold wind blowing sand against our faces,
The food tasting of sand. And as we stood
By the dry rock that marks the highest point
My brother said: 'Not too late is it yet
To turn, remembering home.' And we were silent
Thinking of home." The princess shuts her eyes
And feels the tears forming beneath her eyelids
And opens them, and tears fall on the page.
The knave of diamonds in the darkened room
Throws off his covers, sleeps, and snores again.
The king goes slowly down the turret stairs
To find the goblet.
               And at two o'clock
The vulcan in his smithy underground
Under the hanging gardens, where the drip
Of rain among the clematis and ivy
Still falls from sipping flower to purple flower
Smites twice his anvil, and the murmur comes
Among the roots and vines. The princess reads:
"As I am sick, and cannot write you more,
And have not long to live, I give this letter
To him, my brother, who will bear it south
And tell you how I died. Ask how it was,
There in the northern desert, where the grass
Was withered, and the horses, all but one,
Perished . . ." The princess drops her golden head
Upon the page between her two white arms
And golden braids. The knave of diamonds wakes
And at his window in the darkened room
Watches the lilacs tossing, where the king
Seeks for the goblet.
              And at three o'clock
The moon inflames the lilac heads, and thrice
The vulcan, in his root-bound smithy, clangs
His anvil; and the sounds creep softly up
Among the vines and walls. The moon is round,
Round as a shield above the turret top.
The princess blows her candle out, and weeps
In the pale room, where scent of lilacs comes,
Weeping, with hands across her eyelids, thinking
Of withered grass, withered by sandy wind.
The knave of diamonds, in his darkened room,
Holds in his hands a key, and softly steps
Along the corridor, and slides the key
Into the door that guards her. Meanwhile, slowly,
The king, with raindrops on his beard and hands,
And dripping sleeves, climbs up the turret stairs,
Holding the goblet upright in one hand;
And pauses on the midmost step to taste
One drop of wine wherewith wild rain has mixed.

THE ROAD

Three then came forward out of darkness, one
An old man bearded, his old eyes red with weeping,
A peasant, with hard hands. "Come now," he said,
"And see the Road, for which our people die.
Twelve miles of road we've made, a little only,
Westward winding. Of human blood and stone
We build; and in a thousand years will come
Beyond the hills to sea."
                                    I went with them,
Taking a lantern, which upon their faces
Showed years and grief; and in a time we came
To the wild road which wound among wild hills
Westward; and so along this road we stopped,
Silent, thinking of all the dead men there
Compounded with sad clay. Slowly we moved:
For they were old and weak, had given all
Their life to build this twelve poor miles of road,
Muddy, under the rain. And in my hand,
Turning the lantern here or there, I saw
Deep holes of water where the raindrop splashed,
And rainfilled footprints in the grass, and heaps
Of broken stone, and rusted spades and picks,
And helves of axes. And the old man spoke,
Holding my wrist: "Three hundred years it took
To build these miles of road: three hundred years;
And human lives unnumbered. But the day
Will come when it is done." Then spoke another,
One not so old, but old, whose face was wrinkled:
"And when it comes, our people will all sing
For joy, passing from east to west, or west
To east, returning, with the light behind them;
All meeting in the road and singing there."
And the third said: "The road will be their life;
A heritage of blood. Grief will be in it,
And beauty out of grief. And I can see
How all the women's faces will be bright.
In that time, laughing, they will remember us.
Blow out your lantern now, for day is coming."

My lantern blown out, in a little while
We climbed in long light up a hill, where climbed
The dwindling road, and ended in a field.
Peasants were working in the field, bowed down
With unrewarded work and grief and years
Of pain. And as we passed them, one man fell
Into a furrow that was bright with water
And gave a cry that was half cry, half song—
"The road . . . the road . . . the road . . ." And all then fell

Upon their knees and sang.
                          We four passed on
Over the hills, to westward. . . . Then I felt
How tears ran down my face, tears without end,
And knew that all my life henceforth was weeping,
Weeping, thinking of human grief, and human
Endeavor fruitless in a world of pain.
And when I held my hands up they were old;
I knew my face would not be young again.


### ANNIHILATION

While the blue noon above us arches
And the poplar sheds disconsolate leaves,
Tell me again why love bewitches
And what love gives.

Is it the trembling finger that traces
The eyebrow's curve, the curve of the cheek?
The mouth that quivers, while the hand caresses,
But cannot speak?

No, not these, not in these is hidden
The secret, more than in other things:
Not only the touch of a hand can gladden
Till the blood sings.

It is the leaf that falls between us,
The bell that murmurs, the shadows that move,
The autumnal sunlight that fades upon us,
These things are love.

It is the "No, let us sit here longer,"
The "Wait till tomorrow," the "Once I knew"—
These trifles, said as you touch my finger
And the clock strikes two.

The world is intricate, and we are nothing.
It is the complex world of grass,
The twig on the path, a look of loathing,
Feelings that pass—

These are the secret; and I could hate you
When, as I lean for another kiss,
I see in your eyes that I do not meet you,
And that love is this.

Rock meeting rock can know love better
Than eyes that stare or lips that touch.
All that we know in love is bitter,
And it is not much.

### THE QUARREL

Suddenly, after the quarrel, while we waited,
Disheartened, silent, with downcast looks, nor stirred
Eyelid nor finger, hopeless both, yet hoping
Against all hope to unsay the sundering word:

While all the room's stillness deepened, deepened about us,
And each of us crept his thought's way to discover
How, with as little sound as the fall of a leaf,
The shadow had fallen, and lover quarreled with lover;

And while, in the quiet, I marveled—alas, alas—
At your deep beauty, your tragic beauty, torn
As the pale flower is torn by the wanton sparrow—
This beauty, pitied and loved, and now forsworn;

It was then, when the instant darkened to its darkest,—
When faith was lost with hope, and the rain conspired
To strike its gray arpeggios against our heartstrings,—
When love no longer dared, and scarcely desired:

It was then that suddenly, in the neighbor's room,
The music started: that brave quartette of strings
Breaking out of the stillness, as out of our stillness,
Like the indomitable heart of life that sings

When all is lost; and startled from our sorrow,
Tranced from our grief by that diviner grief,
We raised remembering eyes, each looked at other,
Blinded with tears of joy; and another leaf

Fell silently as that first; and in the instant
The shadow had gone, our quarrel became absurd;
And we rose, to the angelic voices of the music,
And I touched your hand, and we kissed, without a word.

### AT A CONCERT OF MUSIC

Be still, while the music rises about us: the deep enchantment
   Towers, like a forest of singing leaves and birds,
Built for an instant by the heart's troubled beating,
   Beyond all power of words.

And while you are silent, listening, I escape you,
   And I run, by a secret path, through that bright wood
To another time, forgotten, and another woman,
   And another mood.

Then, too, the music's pure algebra of enchantment
   Wrought all about us a bird-voice-haunted grove.

Then, too, I escaped, as now, to an earlier moment
  And a brighter love.

Alas! Can I never have peace in the shining instant?
  The hard bright crystal of being, in time and space?
Must I always touch, in the moment, a remembered moment,
  A remembered face?

Absolve me: I would adore you, had I the secret,
  With all this music's power, for yourself alone:
I would try to answer, in the world's chaotic symphony,
  Your one clear tone:

But alas, alas, being everything you are nothing;
  The history of all my life is in your face;
And all I can grasp is an earlier, more haunted moment,
  And a happier place.

## TETÉLESTAI

### I

How shall we praise the magnificence of the dead,
The great man humbled, the haughty brought to dust?
Is there a horn we should not blow as proudly
For the meanest of us all, who creeps his days,
Guarding his heart from blows, to die obscurely?
I am no king, have laid no kingdoms waste,
Taken no princes captive, led no triumphs
Of weeping women through long walls of trumpets;
Say rather, I am no one, or an atom;
Say rather, two great gods, in a vault of starlight,
Play ponderingly at chess, and at the game's end
One of the pieces, shaken, falls to the floor
And runs to the darkest corner; and that piece
Forgotten there, left motionless, is I. . . .
Say that I have no name, no gifts, no power,
Am only one of millions, mostly silent;
One who came with eyes and hands and a heart,
Looked on beauty, and loved it, and left it,
Say that the fates of time and space obscured me,
Led me a thousand ways to pain, bemused me,
Wrapped me in ugliness; and like great spiders
Dispatched me at their leisure. . . . Well, what then?
Should I not hear, as I lie down in dust,
The horns of glory blowing above my burial?

### II

Morning and evening opened and closed above me:
Houses were built above me; trees let fall
Yellowing leaves upon me, hands of ghosts;
Rain has showered its arrows of silver upon me

Seeking my heart; winds have roared and tossed me;
Music in long blue waves of sound has borne me
A helpless weed to shores of unthought silence;
Time, above me, within me, crashed its gongs
Of terrible warning, sifting the dust of death;
And here I lie. Blow now your horns of glory
Harshly over my flesh, you trees, you waters!
You stars and suns, Canopus, Deneb, Rigel,
Let me, as I lie down, here in this dust,
Hear, far off, your whispered salutation!
Roar now above my decaying flesh, you winds,
Whirl out your earth-scents over this body, tell me
Of ferns and stagnant pools, wild roses, hillsides!
Anoint me, rain, let crash your silver arrows
On this hard flesh! I am the one who named you,
I lived in you, and now I die in you.
I your son, your daughter, treader of music,
Lie, broken, conquered. . . . Let me not fall in silence.

### III

I, the restless one; the circler of circles;
Herdsman and roper of stars, who could not capture
The secret of self; I who was tyrant to weaklings,
Striker of children; destroyer of women; corrupter
Of innocent dreamers, and laugher at beauty; I,
Too easily brought to tears and weakness by music,
Baffled and broken by love, the helpless beholder
Of the war in my heart, of desire with desire, the struggle
Of hatred with love, terror with hunger; I
Who laughed without knowing the cause of my laughter, who grew
Without wishing to grow, a servant to my own body;
Loved without reason the laughter and flesh of a woman,
Enduring such torments to find her! I who at last
Grow weaker, struggle more feebly, relent in my purpose,
Choose for my triumph an easier end, look backward
At earlier conquests; or, caught in the web, cry out
In a sudden and empty despair, "Tetélestai!"
Pity me, now! I, who was arrogant, beg you!
Tell me, as I lie down, that I was courageous.
Blow horns of victory now, as I reel and am vanquished.
Shatter the sky with trumpets above my grave.

### IV

. . . Look! this flesh how it crumbles to dust and is blown!
These bones, how they grind in the granite of frost and are nothing!
This skull, how it yawns for a flicker of time in the darkness,
Yet laughs not and sees not! It is crushed by a hammer of sunlight,
And the hands are destroyed. . . . Press down through the leaves of the jasmine,
Dig through the interlaced roots—nevermore will you find me;
I was no better than dust, yet you cannot replace me. . . .
Take the soft dust in your hand—does it stir: does it sing?

Has it lips and a heart? Does it open its eyes to the sun?
Does it run, does it dream, does it burn with a secret, or tremble
In terror of death? Or ache with tremendous decisions? . . .
Listen! . . . It says: "I lean by the river. The willows
Are yellowed with bud. White clouds roar up from the south
And darken the ripples; but they cannot darken my heart,
Nor the face like a star in my heart! . . . Rain falls on the water
And pelts it, and rings it with silver. The willow trees glisten,
The sparrow chirps under the eaves; but the face in my heart
Is a secret of music. . . . I wait in the rain and am silent."
Listen again! . . . It says: "I have worked, I am tired,
The pencil dulls in my hand; I see through the window
Walls upon walls of windows with faces behind them,
Smoke floating up to the sky, an ascension of sea-gulls.
I am tired. I have struggled in vain, my decision was fruitless,
Why then do I wait? with darkness, so easy, at hand! . . .
But tomorrow, perhaps. . . . I will wait and endure till tomorrow!" . . .
Or again: "It is dark. The decision is made. I am vanquished
By terror of life. The walls mount slowly about me
In coldness. I had not the courage. I was forsaken.
I cried out, was answered by silence . . . Tetélestai! . . ."

V

Hear how it babbles!—Blow the dust out of your hand,
With its voices and visions, tread on it, forget it, turn homeward
With dreams in your brain. . . . This, then, is the humble, the nameless,—
The lover, the husband and father, the struggler with shadows,
The one who went down under shoutings of chaos, the weakling
Who cried his "forsaken!" like Christ on the darkening hilltop! . . .
This, then, is the one who implores, as he dwindles to silence,
A fanfare of glory. . . . And which of us dares to deny him?

### WHEN THE TREE BARES

When the tree bares, the music of it changes:
Hard and keen is the sound, long and mournful;
Pale are the poplar boughs in the evening light
Above my house, against a slate-cold cloud.
When the house ages and the tenants leave it,
Crickets sing in the tall grass by the threshold;
Spider, by the cold mantel, hangs his web.
Here, in a hundred years from that clear season
When first I came here, bearing lights and music,
To this old ghostly house my ghost will come,—
Pause in the half-light, turn by the poplar, glide
Above tall grasses through the broken door.
Who will say that he saw—or the dusk deceived him—
A mist with hands of mist blow down from the tree
And open the door and enter and close it after?
Who will say that he saw, as midnight struck
Its tremulous golden twelve, a light in the window,

And first heard music, as of an old piano,
Music remote, as if it came from the earth,
Far down; and then, in the quiet, eager voices?
". . . Houses grow old and die, houses have ghosts.
Once in a hundred years we return, old house,
And live once more." . . . And then the ancient answer,
In a voice not human, but more like the creak of boards
Or a rattle of panes in the wind—"Not as the owner,
But as a guest you come, to fires not lit
By hands of yours. . . . Through these long-silent chambers
Move slowly, turn, return, and bring once more
Your lights and music. It will be good to talk."

## ONE STAR FELL AND ANOTHER

One star fell and another as we walked.
Lifting his hand toward the west, he said—
—How prodigal that sky is of its stars!
They fall and fall, and still the sky is sky.
Two more have gone, but heaven is heaven still.

Then let us not be precious of our thought,
Nor of our words, nor hoard them up as though
We thought our minds a heaven which might change
And lose its virtue when the word had fallen.
Let us be prodigal, as heaven is;
Lose what we lose, and give what we may give,—
Ourselves are still the same. Lost you a planet—?
Is Saturn gone? Then let him take his rings
Into the Limbo of forgotten things.

O little foplings of the pride of mind,
Who wrap the phrase in lavender, and keep it
In order to display it: and you, who save our loves
As if we had not worlds of love enough—!

Let us be reckless of our words and worlds,
And spend them freely as the tree his leaves;
And give them where the giving is most blest.
What should we save them for,—a night of frost? . . .
All lost for nothing, and ourselves a ghost.

## BUT HOW IT CAME FROM EARTH

But how it came from earth this little white
this waxen edge this that is sharp and white
this that is mortal and bright the petals bent
and all so curved as if for lovers meant
and why the earth unfolded in this shape
as coldly as words from the warm mouth escape

Or what it is that made the blood so speak
or what it was it wanted that made this
breath of curled air this hyacinth this word
this that is deeply seen profoundly heard
miracle of quick device
from fire and ice

Or why the snail puts out a horn to see
or the brave heart puts up a hand to take
or why the mind, as if to agonize,
will close, a century ahead, its eyes—
a hundred years put on the clock
its own mortality to mock—

Christ come, Confucius come, and tell us why
the mind delights before its death to die
embracing nothing as a lover might
in a terrific ecstasy of night—
and tell us why the hyacinth is sprung
from the world's dull tongue.

Did death so dream of life, is this its dream?
Does the rock think of flowers in its sleep?
Then words and flowers are only thoughts of stone
unconscious of the joy it thinks upon;
and we ourselves are only the rock's words
stammered in a dark dream of men and birds.

### PRELUDE VI

This is not you? These phrases are not you?
That pomegranate of verses was not you?
The green bright leaf not you, nor the gold fruit
Burning amongst the leaves,—hot fruit of gold,—
Nor bird, nor bough, nor bole, nor heaven's blue? . . .
Alas, dear woman, I have sung in vain.

Let me dishevel then once more the leaves
Of Cupid's bright thesaurus, and there find
The word of words, the crimson seed of seeds,
The aureate sound of sounds; and out of this
Conceive once more your beauty, and in terms
Your feminine keen eye will not disdain.

For this is you: on April page it is,
Again on June, and once more on December;
On August page I find it twice; and March
Chronicles it in footnote; and July
Asserts it roundly. Thus, from page to page,
I find you many times in many terms.

It is a snowflake, which is like a star,
And melts upon the hand; it is a cobweb,
Shot with silver, that from the golden lip
Of April's dandelion hangs to the grass;
It is a raindrop,—of tremendous worth,—
Which slides the whole length of a lilac leaf. . . .

This is not you? These symbols are not you?
Not snowflake, cobweb, raindrop? . . . Woman, woman,
You are too literal, too strict with me.
What would you have? Some simple copper coin—
I love you, you are lovely, I adore you?
Or (better still) dumb silence, and a look?

No, no, this will not do; I am not one
For whom these silences are sovereign;
The pauses in the music are not music,
Although they make the music what it is.
Therefore I thumb once more the god's thesaurus,
For phrase and praise, and find it all for you.

It is a star which might be thought a snowflake,
Lost in a twinkling; it is a dandelion
Shrouded with silver brightness; it is a leaf
Which lets the raindrop go, but keeps its light. . . .
It is the purple veining in the white
That makes the pure throat of the iris pure. . . .

Yet you would have me say your hair is Helen's,—
Your gait angelic; while I turn from these
To the vast pages of that manuscript
On which the stars are stars, the world a world;
And there I find you written down, between
Arcturus and a primrose and the sea.

### CLOISTER

So, in the evening, to the simple cloister:
This place of boughs, where sounds of water, softly,
Lap on the stones. And this is what you are:
Here, in this dusty room, to which you climb
By four steep flights of stairs. The door is closed:
The furies of the city howl behind you:
The last bell plunges rock-like to the sea:
The horns of taxis wail in vain. You come
Once more, at evening, to this simple cloister;
Hushed by the quiet walls, you stand at peace.

What ferns of thought are these, the cool and green,
Dripping with moisture, that festoon these walls?
What water-lights are these, whose pallid rings
Dance with the leaves, or speckle the pale stones?

What spring is this, that bubbles the cold sand,
Urging the sluggish grains of white and gold? . . .
Peace. The delicious silence throngs with ghosts
Of wingèd sound and shadow. These are you.

Now in the evening, in the simple cloister,
You stand and wait; you stand and listen, waiting
For wingèd sounds, and wingèd silences,
And long-remembered shadows. Here the rock
Lets down its vine of many-colored flowers:
Waiting for you, or waiting for the lizard
To move his lifted claw, or shift his eye
Quick as a jewel. Here the lizard waits
For the slow snake to slide among cold leaves.
And, on the bough that arches the deep pool,
Lapped in a sound of water, the brown thrush
Waits, too, and listens, till his silence makes
Silence as deep as song. And time becomes
A timeless crystal, an eternity,
In which the gone and coming are at peace.

What bird is this, whose silence fills the trees
With rich delight? What leaves and boughs are these,
What lizard, and what snake? . . . The bird is gone:
And while you wait, another comes and goes,—
Another and another; yet your eye,
Although it has not moved, can scarcely say
If birds have come and gone,—so quick, so brief,—
Or if the thrush who waits there is the same. . . .
The snake and lizard change, yet are the same:
The flowers, many-colored, on the vine,
Open and close their multitude of stars,—
Yet are the same. . . . And all these things are you.

Thus, in the evening, in the simple cloister,
Eternity adds ring to ring, the darker
Beyond the brighter; and your silence fills
With such a world of worlds,—so still, so deep,—
As never voice could speak, whether it were
The ocean's or the bird's. The night comes on:
You wait and listen, in the darkened room,
To all these ghosts of change. And they are you

# Hervey Allen

HERVEY ALLEN (WILLIAM HERVEY ALLEN, JR.) was born December 8, 1889, in Pittsburgh, Pennsylvania. He received his early education in the city of his birth, attended the U. S. Naval Academy, but resigned before graduating; received his B.S. in Economics at Pittsburgh in 1915, and took special courses at Harvard 1921-1922. He saw military service as Second Lieutenant of Infantry on the Mexican border in 1916 and as First Lieutenant with the A.E.F. in France, where he was seriously wounded in August, 1918. Returning to America that year, he drifted South. From 1919 to 1924 he lived in Charleston, South Carolina, and while there wrote *Carolina Chansons* (1922) in collaboration with DuBose Heyward. With Heyward he founded The Poetry Society of South Carolina and assisted in awakening interest in poetry through the South. He wrote *Anthony Adverse* during five years in Bermuda, after which he returned to America.

*Wampum and Old Gold* (1921) and *The Bride of Huitzil* (1922) are Allen's two early volumes of verse; the most distinguished feature of the former is a war ballad, "The Blindman." *Earth Moods and Other Poems* (1925) is a more arresting presentation. This collection displays Allen as more than a local poet. The major part of the volume is devoted to long poems which attempt to express the evolutionary struggle from nebulous matter to man. The treatment is half epical, half legendary, and though as yet Allen's aim exceeds his grasp, there is a definiteness of execution in such poems as "The Saga of Lief the Lucky" and "Funeral at High Tide." The "other poems" are shorter and more compactly colored; "Gargantuana" and "Whim Alley" being particularly effective examples of Allen's ability to make decorations which do not suffer from picturesque affectations.

*New Legends* (1929) is the outcome of five years' research and immersion in the Bermuda Islands. It is divided into three parts, the keenest being the sections entitled "Legends" and "Lines on the Imagination." At present Allen stands at the crossroads: he has the possibilities of being either a lyricist, a writer of ambitious epics, or a successful novelist.

*Israfel: The Life and Times of Edgar Allan Poe* (1926) is a remarkable work of research and re-creation. This work of faithful biography furnishes an excellent complement to the psychoanalytical study of Poe by Joseph Wood Krutch. *Anthony Adverse* (1933), a picaresque novel of more than twelve hundred pages that turned out to be one of the greatest successes of the period, caused a revival in romantic fiction.

### WHIM ALLEY

Whim Alley once led into Danger Court
Loud with the raucous talk of cockatoos,
Where bearded Jews a-squat in alcove shops
Sat waiting like royal falcons in a mews.
Softly as rain the voweled Portuguese
Fell from their red-ripe lips with eastern news
Of galleons whose names were melodies—
Softly—between the shrieks of cockatoos.

Who cared for royal navigation laws
In Danger Court—for what the Soldan said—
Or papal lines between the east and west?
Abram out-Shylocked Isaac with applause,
And clutched the sweated doubloons to his chest,
Whose late lamented owners were scarce dead.
For there were smugglers' bargains to be made
Where leaping arches looped along the walls,
While sunlight smoldered down the long arcade
And dizened into flame on Spanish shawls,
And what the sequin brought in Louis d'or
Was news,—and rumors passed from Trebizond,
While Rachel clinked brass anklets in a door
With a straight glimpse of blue sea just beyond.
Dark sailors passed with tang of wine and tar,
And merchants with wide hats and wider fringes,
And two black Sambos smoked the same cigar
Upon a chest with three locks and five hinges.
Vanished in air! Those arches roof a cow,
To parrots' rings the frowsy hens resort;
Whim Alley leads to less than nothing now,
And only shadows dwell in Danger Court.

### GARGANTUANA

Gargantuan ranges of blue-dappled hills
Roll down titanic coasts of cobalt shires,
While inland dreams a sunstruck city's ghost,
Streaked with the level scarfs from temple fires.
Down, down the hills a bull-voiced waterfall
Plunges from cloudy cliffs that climb so high,
It echoes like an organ from a hall
Of stairs that wind into the windy sky.
And there are monstrous footprints in the sand
That twist up rusty roadways red as snakes
Onto an upland paved with level floors
Of copper water stagnant in iron lakes.
And hooded peaks vault into clouded wonder
From whence the island's voice rolls out to sea,
Reverberating words of blatant thunder,
Dull as a demon's glee.
Its hills sequester meadows walled with fire,
On which like evil prayers the sphinxes lie,
With flame-like plumes that bloom upon their wings,
While red clouds wither by—
The roc has made his nest among the cliffs,
And in the evening from a mountain's dome,
Remote as thought, there blurs the sound of drums
That call the giants home.

## James Whaler

JAMES WHALER was born May 5, 1889, in Wilmington, Delaware. His parents came from Maryland and Pennsylvania with no city backgrounds anywhere until the family reached Wilmington. Young Whaler attended the Wilmington Friends' School and graduated from Princeton University, from which he received a doctor's degree for a work on Miltonic simile. Paying hard for his education, he worked in many capacities until he became head of a Nature Study class at the Minnesota State Teachers' College and then Instructor of English at Goucher College, Baltimore.

His first impulse to write poetry came when he found himself in the depths of the Maine woods in 1922, but Whaler was thirty-eight before his first book, *Hale's Pond* (1927), was published. The volume attracted little notice; beyond two or three perfunctory reviews, there was no critical consideration of the six long narratives comprising this strange work. But though few copies of the book were sold, rumors of its quality seemed to spread by grapevine telegraph; here a surprised critic and there an unprofessional enthusiast spoke up for the coiled vigor of "Runaway," "Jordan," "Monsieur Pipereau." This was New England with a difference. Purporting to be the poetry of the Maine woods, it was the very antithesis of the *plein-air*-afoot-through-the-great-outdoors sort of verse to which the Wanderlust school had accustomed us. Instead of pedestrian platitudes, here were ideas as novel as their idiom; instead of dilutions of sentiment, here were emotional and verbal richness.

This luxuriance, at first commendable, is Whaler's chief handicap for it leads him to pile figure upon figure, pack word against word until his line becomes congested. So, too, his utterance, strained to its emotional capacity, tends to be pitched an octave too high. But Whaler might well be calling attention to a kind of Yankee we have forgotten. Understatement is characteristic of one type of New Englander; there is another—and as genuine a type—who, when he speaks, speaks too loudly with the abrupt release of long suppressions. The very knots and congestions, as well as the intense key of Whaler's verse, result from an endeavor to express the person who, when he talks, cries out his thought and who, when a poet, is likely to forget restraint. Whaler's faults are the faults of excess, not those of insufficiency, and, though here and there he shows the danger of knowing the woods too well, his men and women come first. He can—and does—draw the fine line between the incidental and the inevitable.

In varying degrees, all the long poems exhibit this power to seize on the significant-trivial, none better than "Monsieur Pipereau." In some ways this poem is the author's chief triumph, for here, without preamble or apology, Whaler calmly rewrites one of the world's most popular poems. "Monsieur Pipereau" is, plot for plot, detail for detail, Browning's "Pied Piper of Hamelin" translated to a lumber-camp in Maine. But instead of being overcome by the comparison, the reader forgets the American's audacity, even—after the first page or two—forgets the original. All he recognizes, all he remembers is the opulence and vitality of narration, the easy naturalizing of the supernatural.

"Runaway" and "Jordan" are no less remarkable. Though the former has moments of confused mysticism, the descriptions are keen, the concentrations are always surprising and accurate. This is a verse familiar in scene yet strange in spite of the homely speech. Following Wordsworth's pronouncement, it reaffirms the contention that poetry can talk as well as sing.

### THE POND

#### (*from "Runaway"*)

Shadowed in midnight green,
Wedging her belly down a wide ravine,
Pinned by birch-silver to a bed of umber,
Her splay-claws lax, vibrating with her slumber,
No moon to bathe her eyes
And wake her, warn her that a storm would rise,—
Hale's Pond I felt before me in an hour
By thick black scents of fish and fern and flower.
I rested on the "Dock"—
Two split logs slapping at a foundered rock
Where lichen-paint dripped into lily-wire;
Here often had I dived through June's wet fire,
Here often had I crawled a chill ooze-bed,
With frog-palms, trout-eyes, chest ribbed round with lead.

For Father, when he had a cider-bout,
And in the shame of it, would send me out
To weed—then dive instead, and shout and swim
Till sun-slope and the black cows' milking-hymn!
Was I not muskrat, water-snake, raccoon?
Was I not dragon-fly and diving loon?
Polliwog, dreaming under lily-pads?
Victor of song in frog-olympiads?
Crawfish investigating runes of stone?
Minnow of sucking glass and glassy bone?
I flamed a water-beetle's fat vermilion,
I joined the water-striders' cool cotillion;
I made my body calamus for thin
Silk fish to nibble at me, toe to chin;
And once, while I was floating like a mink,
Straight in my face a doe looked down to drink!
I saw my soul burn in her golden eyes,
Globed among ecstasies!
I caught her breath above a pickerel-bloom:
It was black plum and russet-mild mushroom.
But best of all, eyes fish-wide, six feet under,
Breasting the veil between two worlds asunder,
I measured the immeasurable caress,
The moving-calm, fin-naked gentleness
Of sunlight, and I heard an ocean boom
Afar, and my soul's treasure disentomb.

### MONSIEUR PIPEREAU

The worst camp-life man ever lived? That season
Up near Seboomook. Couldn't been worse. The reason?
RATS! Big enough rats to circumcise wildcats,
Sociable, devastating democrats,
Under the bunkhouse, up above the ceiling,
Under the cook-room, and forever squealing
Under the stables, through the manger-racks,
Round every bale of hay in herds and packs,
Under manure-piles, sawdust, shingles, sacks,
Kegs, harness, grease-pots, axle-trees, ropes, jacks,
Under our blankets, under our very backs,
Until that whole camp looked like maniacs!
For days big Simmons couldn't use his head:
Rats bit him in the neck one night in bed.
Nadeau got out his rosary and prayed
Currying his horses, he was so afraid;
And once I even saw him make his mare
Kneel down beside him in the straw for prayer.
Rogers, the foreman, had them send us traps
From Bangor: cages with invisible snaps
And flaps to hold a dozen, traps of steel
Whose center-plates would crash at a grasshopper's heel:
Flat-traps of maple, circle-traps of wire,
Traps built to serve mankind and to inspire,—
We had a hundred and seven traps all told;
And every brand of poison-mixture sold.
Ever study rats?—You'll take them by surprise
Once—no! not even once! No trap, how wise
Or simple, fools a rat in his right mind!
First day, caught ten—the deaf and dumb and blind;
And the first night six more—the sick and lean;
And next day none—making in all sixteen.
"Five cents per head!" Rogers announced that night.
Vainly imagining we could strike the light
Of inspiration, were there bounty to it,—
Lord! we'd have paid him ten per head to do it!
One way was left: rifles with powder and lead:
Shooting them from the rafters overhead
By lantern-glow; but almost all objected—
Preferring rats to one shot misdirected;
And when a bullet killed a laying-fowl
Of Mrs. Grove's, our cook, we heard a howl
That went into the food she fed us. RATS!
As it grew cold they took to shoes and hats.
I woke one morning minus watch and vest:
Some rat's idea to improve his nest.

Now Rogers and his wife, and Mrs. Grove
Her sister, had a cabin—with its drove

Of rats—all separate from ours. One night
We brought him final word we'd lost the fight,  .
Would have to quit, and asked to draw our pay.
But Rogers said: "Boys, hold it one more day.
I share this hell you're in that's worse than war.
We got 'em bad here too—just one day more!
Haven't talked much, but I've a large surprise
For this whole camp tomorrow. Shine your eyes
To see dead rats tomorrow—dead ones!—do y'hear?
Listen to what our Super writes: 'Monsieur
Bernard de Pipereau from Canada,
Expert in shrews, rats, mice, et cetera,
Will reach Seboomook Thursday. As to fee,
No more than forty for his guarantee.
Tom Rogers, hold the men! Write, let us know.'
Well, what are you grinning at? This Pipereau
Is known in Brunswick.—Men, we are in luck!
That's right, stay on one day, and if the ruck
Of these eternal varmints ain't in hell
By Saturday, then, by God! I'll pull the bell
To quit! But if that Canadian's what I say,
Then holiday
On me at Joe's, and pay goes on the same!"
Even while he argued, up the window-frame
Inside—behind him—slouched a long slick rat.
Big Simmons nearly cried. "We don't want that,"
Said nervous Nadeau. "Ain't we had enough
Holidays every night? Another bluff!"
Yet Rogers spoke so meek and fair and certain
You never had found the devil himself deserting.
"Of course you doubt me, boys, but that's not odd—
Doubt—honest doubt's the noblest work of God!"
"Yes, but a rat ain't!" wheezed old Shorty Myer,
Who set all laughing, as we slipped back sprier,
To dream in ratland one more day and night.

Next noon, accoutered as a wizard might
From Lapland if a parliament of witches
Had sent to Maine for heaps of flesh and riches,
The doctor came that Rogers promised—just
Floated to camp through arches of snow-dust,
And, galloping to messhouse, on a long
Stallion that snorted an Icelandic song,
He reined up in the center of a ring
Of men. We hailed him as our saviour-king.
But not till Tom came running with a grin,
Would he slide from the saddle and go in,
Leaving his horse in a long muzzle of steam
Snapping a drift with vicious teeth of cream.
Rogers came round and introduced.

"The boys—
Be pleased to meet the boys."
                                        "Ah! rat annoys
Such beeg, beeg men! I show you how you kill."
We sat down on the dinner-benches, still
Sizing the stranger up, some not through eating;
And other men came in, looked, passed no greeting,
For something strange was in the air: the oak
Logs on the hearth seemed damp and turned to smoke.

"The devil for looks!" said Shorty Myer low.
"He'd give a porcupine the vertigo!"
Nose long and thin, and eyes that never saw
The thing outside without its inside flaw.
Hair long and thin, ears long, cheeks thin and taper,
With the complexion of last year's newspaper;
Long thin mustaches and some spears of thin
Long bristles reddish-gray from a long chin.
That Frenchman's eyes wheeled round and hypnotized us:
Oh, there's no miracle would have surprised us
More than the thing he did! He sent a bench
Of men to the other end; and, like the French,
Talked with his elbows till he cleared a corner;
Then bows and squats before us like a mourner,
And, with long hands as stiff as cant-dog hooks,
He pulls a board away, and looks and looks
At two small rat-holes, motioning us be still:
I tell you not a body moved a gill.
Even Mrs. Grove held up her pan of beans
Steaming, but felt no heat or weight.—Such scenes
We think we dream in.—*Wee, wee-wee, hsts-hsts,
Hsts-hsts, wee-wee!* and, like ventriloquists,
He whistled so that cries were overhead,
Were underfoot, came from a box of bread.
Now feet were heard to patter under bench
And table; and the men began to blench.
He made a sound like tuning-forks from June
Mosquitoes, till that winter afternoon
Turned for the moment green, the snow was gone,
And birds began to whistle through the dawn.
We saw no longer human lips and teeth
On him who charmed those vermin underneath:
The motion of the music in his face
Made all his body tremble, and displace
The human by a beast—or worse than that:
The men close by him shrunk away,—a RAT!
And then he threw his brown coat round him like
A tent; his lightning-fingers gave a strike,
A shake, and, with a little laugh of French,
He tossed a dead rat to an empty bench.

The stable-kid began to cry hurrah,
But Pipereau turned black, and waved his claw,—
Seemed to congeal poor Joey's underjaw.
But Mrs. Grove, the pan pressed to her heart,
Murmured to Mrs. Rogers: "Ain't he smart!"
Close by the other hole once more he drew;
Whistling, he spread his coat for number two,
Flipped him to death with two invisible pinches,
And tossed him to Rogers,—a beast of eighteen inches
From tooth to tail-tip—longer than the first:
Tom Rogers grabbed the tails of both and cursed,
And pitched them to the fireplace nose in,
To test if they were real or he was dozing.

The Frenchman stood full height and said, "Plentee!
You have plentee and clevair rats—oui, oui!"
Then Rogers asked his terms. Quarter per head—
These first two free. Or, one gross sum instead,
And we'd be cured of rats in a day and night.
"One hundred dollars and I do it right!"
The price turned Rogers pale. "That is a great
Pile in this country, friend. It's not the rate
Named in this letter from my Company!—
*No more than forty for his guarantee.*"
"*Correct!* One hundred is ze lowest price
To kill or drife away all rats and mice;
But forty more—I *guarantee* you, men:
Zey leafe to *leafe,* and never come again!"
Tom whispered with his wife. . . . "That's reasonable,
Doctor," he said. "There's not an obstacle
To hinder here: we'll follow all you say
If you can rid our camp in a night and day."

✦

John Heald came hobbling from the cook-house. "Yep!
Rats have resigned! All night he made 'em step!"

"Ah, ah! Ze good time wiz ze boys?" Outside
Tom's cabin Pipereau left his horse untied.
Then as they talked within we boys leaned to.
"How, doctor, can you *prove* your job is through?
Suppose when you're gone tonight we find rats still?—
We've lost one hundred forty! What *proof* will
We ask? This: we take twenty buttered rolls,
And with them plug up twenty cook-room holes;
Take twenty squares of cheese, and lay a square
On every mess-room bench and table and chair.
The air's not cold outside—all hands can wait
Till seven o'clock. Then we'll inspect the bait."
"Eh bien! Oui, oui!"

At once the thing was done.
The Frenchman, bundled like a skeleton,
Wove round and round the camp a savage, quick
Canter that showed his horse knew every trick.
For two sharp hours he rode, while Rogers walked
Among his men around a fire and talked.
The moon was near the full, the woods were deep
With ghostly lights like any sick man's sleep.
John Heald, on crutches, shook his beard in two
Telling us what he saw that Frenchman do
When he looked through a keyhole. "Had a pipe,"
He said, "thin as the leg-bone of a snipe—
And on that pipe he trilled in graveyard pitch
The damnedest tunes! They would have laid a witch!
I *saw* them tunes! Brown smoke—that snaked a way
Down every chink and hole where rats can stay!
God help what falls into that Frenchman's clutches!
You think I dreamt, Tom! Never! Took up crutches
At twelve o'clock, and hobbled toward the barn,
Where, through a hole, what did I see, by darn!
But that horse eating in the moonlight there
Live rats as if it was a regular fare!
Live rats! I tell you not a one was dead
Until that stallion grabbed it by its head!
That pipe's peculiar music has such force
It sends those rats all racing for the horse,
Greedy to gaze into that horse's eye!
I saw them coming one by one—to die!
Endless processions—two and sometimes three
Rat-giants at once would stand up patiently
Waiting to catch that horse's eye! And they
Would mew like kittens playing in the hay.
Once Pipereau came in—I am no liar!—
And, Tom, those two rats you threw in the fire?
He brought 'em alive and well, to feed that horse!
It must have been the brute's five-hundredth course!
And then that Frenchman drew a rat-skin bag
Out of the saddle somewhere: such a swag!
Oh, such a swag! Gold coins and ruby globes!
Diamonds of folded fires like folded robes!
And little images of glowworm light—
I left off looking, I shook so for fright:
I'd only strength to make my bunk-room, lock
The door, and listen for the crowing cock.
I don't see how those women dared to serve
Meals to that rat!—They beat us men for nerve!
Oh, I forgot to tell about some stuff
I saw him take—" But Rogers cried, "Enough!
An interesting dream, John, that will keep!
See here, it's seven! It's business now, not sleep!"

And Pipereau was waiting with a yawn,
And a laughing wink that all our rats were gone.
He held the pail to pick up rolls and cheese
While Tom preceded, swinging lantern and keys.
Back they came arguing.
                          "I tell you flat,
Doctor, you haven't killed us *every* rat!
You saw me lay the bait—but here's nineteen,
No more than nineteen rolls! And you saw clean
White squares of cheese I cut: but these lack three
Of making twenty! And the rest, you see,
Are all gnawed through! And at my very door
An apple's gone that you saw there before! . . .
By contract, must I pay you anything
At all?—Here, take this forty, covering
All rats you killed and all you might have killed
Had you but had more time—or been more skilled."
The Frenchman clenched the bills and ground his teeth.
Jabbering a lightning lingo underneath
His chest, that shivered in the furs he wore;
And from the *dieu's* he blew I guessed he swore.
He leaped so quick upon the stallion that
We jumped, imagining a bloody rat!
He leaped so arrowy we thought he strode
The great moon that had risen from the road;
And the free stallion, treading clouds of snow,
Cut sharp that moon into a cameo,
While all was silent but our hearts, that shook.
Tom cried, "I'm through forever with that crook!"
We ate in silence.

                    Never was there bliss
Like ours that night! Oh, never night like this
In Rogers' camp! Dreamless and oathless—ratless!
No one to wake and find a wardrobe hatless,
Bootless or shoeless! Night so overpowering
Peaceful I woke while yet the moon was towering.
There lay the men like innocents new-born,
Some barely breathing, others blowing horn
Or bowing violins of wood and silk.
Not since these men had quit their mothers' milk
Was such content. I lit a pipe to think,
And walked out to the shed to get a drink,
When in the moonlight I could see Nadeau
Standing outside the doorway in the snow.
"Just like a nursery, ain't it!"
                                  "God, it's that!
But didn't you hear some time ago a cat?" . . .
"It's just from listening to John Heald's words
Last night, Nadeau; but John dreams dreams—and lies.
The plague is over! Frenchy takes the prize!

He's galloped to the moon with all his rats!"
We both turned in and slept like autocrats.

Of all days for calamity—Sunday! Black
Sunday it was in Rogers' almanac!
We boys awoke that morning with a shout
Of bliss: the rats were banished without doubt!—
Each of us glowing like a god of Rome,
Or like the wandering boy that's welcomed home.
Thermometer ten above,—just comfortable
To renovate our camp from stove to stall.
Now business first on Sundays was to shave
Or bathe, or both—but to do both was brave;
Yet every man this morning called for tub
And water, till we looked a swimming-club.
What if a wind had crossed the rising sun,
And flakes as round as quarters had begun
To quilt the roofs with whiter wool?—I say
Paradise gave up its morning to our day.

Well, I was raking off my beard for fair
At McIlvenny's mirror, and the air
Was being lit with hymns from twenty faces,
Nadeau's fine tenor up above the basses
In his pet lullaby, "Fair Infidel,"
And all were starving for the breakfast-bell,—
When on a sudden every note went flat!
I dropped my razor, nervous as a cat.
Someone was hollering in Rogers' house!
We opened doors to hear him.
                            "Cook's heraus!"
Called Al Lemure. Then Rogers burst in—hat
And coat off, bald head blue with cold. "That rat!
That French rat, boys!"
                        Well, late that night before,
His wife and Mrs. Grove unlocked their door,
All clad for travel—furs and gloves and hoods,—
Ran from the moonlight into the deep woods,
And up behind that Frenchman on that horse
They were now flying.—"God knows what their course!
Though you could still see footprints where they ran,
This new snow covers up that Frenchman's plan!
It's Pipereau's witchcraft—that rat Pipereau!—
And eight hours' start in all this world of snow!"

"Boys!" cried big Simmons, "is there road or trail,
Mountain or pond or stream or swamp or swale
Round here but we know better 'n a love-letter?
Wherever Tom's wife is I say we get her!"
"And bring the cook back too!" cried Al Lemure.

Well, up and down and round Moosehead we sure
Did spread the tidings of that Pipereau.
Some went to Greenville, Rogers through the snow
Drove clear to Foxcroft, and till Wednesday night,
As we'd agreed, we trailed that Frenchman's flight.
Whatever were the footprints, all led south,
Or we'd have mushed it to the St. Lawrence mouth.
Tom tried the law; but lawyers urged, of course,
One hundred dollars for a quick divorce.
Oh, Maine is broad, but Canada is broader:
That Frenchman, once he loped across the border,
Could have set sail to Lapland with his riches,
Or galloped there between a brace of witches.
Neither his wife nor cook Tom saw again,
Nor Pipereau, though trailed by many men.

Hear to the end: there's still a funeral;
For when Tom lost his wife, that was not all.
By Wednesday night we were too fagged to pull
Boots from our feet or speak a syllable.
Staggered and haggard like a wreck of drunks,
We fell, with no undressing, on our bunks,
Wind-broken dogs from shoeing through that snow—
And neither Frenchman, wife, nor cook to show.
And yet one comfort mightily surpassed
Our toil: we had a ratless camp at last!—
Oh, think of coming home to sleep, sleep, sleep
Without one prayer to God our souls to keep!
With such a hope one man can fight like ten;
Eagles can harbor in the heart of a wren.
Pure slumber to the muscles of my hair,
I fell to dreaming I had shot a bear,
When a volcano's voice shook through my head:
"Rats! Rats! *Rats!* RATS!—They're back!—They're on your bed!"
The moon burnt frosty through the panes of glass,
Annealing rafters to a milky brass,
Daubed everywhere with shadows big as cats—
RATS!
Tremendous teams and troupes of acrobats,
Chewing on harness and on leather puttees,
On snow-shoe straps as if it were on cheese.
I saw their eyes like little jeweled moons
Arching from rope to rope in glad festoons.
And under-floor I heard the pattering pests,—
The old full families squealing in their nests.
Wherever ear could listen there was gnawing
And clawing and pawing and chawing and wild seesawing.
A trunk that held my only Sunday suit
Was being investigated by one brute;
Two more I watched climb out of Mac's new shoes;
Nowhere in sight but they were working in twos

Where there'd been one before that Frenchman came.
Mac, with his gun out now, was taking aim.
"You'll wake up Rogers, Mac; don't waste your shell!"
Flump! The anatomies of dead rats fell
Over a dozen bunks—and then the room was hell!
The rats took cover while the lead kept flying;—
No use if Rogers had come pacifying;
The boys let powder loose at every hole
And shadow where they saw that Frenchman's soul.
At length ten minutes' peace, then hordes on hordes
Came swarming back to the same beams and boards.
We shot the roof into a sieve for snow
To cover up the flesh of rats below;
We shook that roof into a storm of flakes
Which melted on the bunks in crimson lakes.
A blizzard underneath the moon was that!
A battlefield of wild-man versus rat!
And all that night Tom Rogers stayed away,
But we'd hear bullets fired and ricochet
Inside his cabin, and we wished him well:
We knew his heaven, like ours, had turned to hell.

If, near Seboomook, on a rise of loose
Green bowlders and a single stand of spruce
And pine, you stumble on a ruined camp,
Find bits of bone around a broken lamp,
And shingles made of little holes,—begone!
Unless you are a wizard or a faun,
Oh, crave no harbor here for any night!
For in one hour of the fall of light
You will see life that Pharaoh did not see,
You will arise and shake—and you will flee
To cast your couch with dews and moss and rocks,
Lonelier than a woodrat, lonelier than a fox.

## Claude McKay

CLAUDE MC KAY was born in Jamaica, West Indies, in 1889. He had, as he says, "no education" except what instruction he received from his brother. For a while he was in the service of the Kingston Constabulary. He came to the United States in 1912 and studied agriculture at Kansas State College. After leaving school McKay tried to earn his living with varying success on Pullman cars, in kitchens, as a menial in hotels. Meanwhile, he had been writing, and some of his more belligerent verse had attracted the attention of a few literary radicals. In 1920 he became connected with *The Liberator* and, shortly thereafter, was made associate editor.

*Songs of Jamaica,* his first immature volume, was published while McKay was still in Jamaica; his second and more characteristic *Spring in New Hampshire* was published by Grant Richards in London in 1920. The best of both volumes with many more recent poems appear in *Harlem Shadows* (1922), with an introduction by Max Eastman. Here the pure-blooded Negro speaks with a boldness in curious contrast to the sentimental dialect verse which used to be affected by most of his race. His melodies are instinctive, the naked force of his invectives is deep.

*Home to Harlem* (1928) and *Banjo* (1929), subtitled "A Story Without a Plot," are novels in which realism and impressionism project·vivid character studies against foreign and native backgrounds.

### IF WE MUST DIE

If we must die—let it not be like hogs
Hunted and penned in an inglorious spot,
While round us bark the mad and hungry dogs,
Making their mock at our accursed lot.
If we must die—oh, let us nobly die,
So that our precious blood may not be shed
In vain; then even the monsters we defy
Shall be constrained to honor us though dead!

Oh, kinsmen! We must meet the common foe;
Though far outnumbered, let us still be brave,
And for their thousand blows deal one death-blow!
What though before us lies· the open grave?
Like men we'll face the murderous, cowardly pack,
Pressed to the wall, dying, but—fighting back!

### THE HARLEM DANCER

Applauding youths laughed with young prostitutes
And watched her perfect, half-clothed body sway;
Her voice was like the sound of blended flutes
Blown by black players upon a picnic day.
She sang and danced on gracefully and calm,
The light gauze hanging loose about her form;
To me she seemed a proudly-swaying palm
Grown lovelier for passing through a storm.
Upon her swarthy neck black, shiny curls
Profusely fell; and, tossing coins in praise,
The wine-flushed, bold-eyed boys, and even the girls,
Devoured her with their eager, passionate gaze;
But looking at her falsely-smiling face,
I knew her self was not in that strange place.

## Edna St. Vincent Millay

Eᴅɴᴀ sᴛ. ᴠɪɴᴄᴇɴᴛ ᴍɪʟʟᴀʏ was born February 22, 1892, in Rockland, Maine. After a childhood spent in her native State, she attended Vassar College, from which she was graduated in 1917. Coming to New York, she supported herself by writing short stories under various pseudonyms (*Distressing Dialogues,* 1924, published under the name of "Nancy Boyd"), translating songs, acting with the Provincetown Players in the capacity of playwright and performer. After her marriage to Eugen Boissevain, she moved to a farm in the Berkshires, which she leaves only to travel and deliver occasional readings.

Her first long poem, "Renascence," was the outstanding feature of *The Lyric Year* (1912), an anthology which revealed many new names. "Renascence" was written when Miss Millay was scarcely nineteen; it remains one of the most remarkable poems of this generation. Beginning like a casual aimless rhyme, it proceeds, with calm lucidity, to a set of climaxes. It is as if a child had, in the midst of ingenuousness, uttered some terrific truth. The cumulative power of this poem is surpassed only by its passages of individual beauty.

*Renascence,* Miss Millay's first volume, was published in 1917. It sounds, at intervals, the same passion as its title poem; here is a hunger for beauty so intense that no delight can appease it. Such poems as "God's World" and a few of the unnamed sonnets, capturing the breathless awe of "Renascence" in a smaller compass, vibrate with similar rapture.

*A Few Figs from Thistles* (originally published in 1920 and revised several times since then), although one of Miss Millay's most popular collections, is her least commendable performance. In many of the self-conscious flippancies, Miss Millay has exchanged her poetic birthright for a mess of cleverness. There are a few poems which are worthy of her calling, but the greater part of this volume smirks with a facile sophistication, admiring its own pertly cynical pirouettes. These heel-and-toe exercises are even less graceful in the later work where, it was maliciously said, they suffered from falling archness.

*Second April* (1921) is a return to the triumph of her first book. In spite of certain lapses in which the poet seems to have adopted a fixed simper, *Second April* expresses that passion for identification with all of life which few poets in her generation have surpassed; she has made ecstasy articulate and almost tangible. A new note, new at least for this singer, creeps into the lyrics, the note of gravity; here is dignity, almost an austerity, of emotion. In her inversions and archaic epithets, her "forsooths" and "alacks," Miss Millay seems to be a belated Elizabethan; she uses locutions which ordinarily have a false and affected ring. Far from marring her work, these antique accents suit the light banter of "The Bean-Stalk," as well as the intensity of "The Poet and His Book," the much quoted "Passer Mortuus Est," and the unforgettable "Elegy."

Three plays were published in 1921: *Two Slatterns and a King,* "a moral interlude" in adroit couplets, *The Lamp and the Bell,* a five-act drama which is a strange composite of native speech and Shakespearean echoes, and *Aria Da Capo,* a one-act play which, for all its brevity, is a profound satire on war and war-makers. A juvenile effort, *The Princess Marries the Page,* was exhumed from undergraduate days and published in 1932.

*The Harp-Weaver and Other Poems* (1924) wears its author's heart on its sleeve; often, in fact, that responsive organ is displayed as a shining bauble, a decoration tricked with frayed ribbons. But here Miss Millay begins to wear her heart with a difference. Rarely now is she narcissistic or consciously arch; she speaks with a disillusion that contains more than a tinge of bitterness. Love, she announces, sometimes with a wry wistfulness, sometimes with a proud scorn, is not enough. If, she tells us, it is hard never to attain one's desires, it is even more painful to have them fulfilled. This change of key makes *The Harp-Weaver and Other Poems* Miss Millay's most uneven collection. The title-poem, which was awarded the Pulitzer Prize for Poetry in 1922, barely saves itself from sentimentality. But the twenty-two sonnets which comprise Part Four of this book are not only representative of Miss Millay's best, but are among the finest modern examples of the form.

In spite of ill-health, Miss Millay devoted the summer of 1926 to a work which had been contracted for. In Santa Fe, she completed *The King's Henchman,* the libretto of an opera composed by Deems Taylor, which was produced at the Metropolitan Opera House early in 1927. Occasional poems had appeared in magazines, betraying that though her verse was still quick with homely facts of people and seasons, the gay impudence was no longer there; that she now loved what she loved not with variability nor desperation but with nostalgia. *The Buck in the Snow and Other Poems* (1928) is pitched in the key of loss. The heel-and-toe insouciance has disappeared; a new and more somber poet emerges from these pages. The happy vibrations of her early work have lengthened to a music that no longer celebrates eager dawn or headlong day but is tuned to the beginning of evening. Never has Miss Millay plucked so insistently on the autumnal string; never has she been so preoccupied with the water darkening, with the ceaseless "action of waves and the action of sorrow," with the lonely self, and the going down of "the sun that will not rise again." This is not to imply that the poet has become detached; Miss Millay's ecstasies are never abstract in the essential way that those of Léonie Adams are. Her metaphysics of passion remain personal; she is still too much in love with lost love, with the shards of the broken pot, with the memory of a world forgotten, with the spirit of persecution, and the minutiae of unrelinquishing mortal mind. The mood is rarely anything but subjective and self-perturbed. Even so general a poem on death as "Morituris" proceeds from an undignified fear, a "shrieking to the south and clutching at the north."

Exception, however, must be made in the case of a small part of the volume, especially the group which brings the book to its ascending close. The seven sonnets in *The Buck in the Snow* overcome the limitations of the poet as well as the limitations of the form. In "Sonnet to Gath" she has fashioned an irony far removed from impertinence; in "On Hearing a Symphony of Beethoven" she achieves the impossible, writing that rarest of things, a successful poem on a symphony, and holding, in fourteen lines, the music, the orchestra, the audience, and the triumphant catharsis which is Beethoven. Rising above its almost fatal first line, it turns inversions and generalities into a victory over rhetoric.

*Fatal Interview* (1931), a set of fifty-two love sonnets, was hailed with superlatives. Reviewers strained to outcry each other by comparing the sequence to Mrs. Browning's, Rossetti's, Sidney's, Petrarch's, Shakespeare's, mostly in Miss Millay's favor. Genevieve Taggard wrote, "Immortality is here defined, served and achieved." Only a few voices registered a minority opinion. Theodore Morrison objected that "the sonnets give the air of being manufactured, of being wondrously clever, an extraordinary simulation rather than the true substance of poetry," and a reviewer in the *London Times* flatly asserted that "the sequence as a whole is rather verbally than truly impassioned. . . . We admire the rhetoric but find little real feeling to which to respond. It is always at the pitch of romantic extravagance."

While this may be true of the sequence as a whole, several of the sonnets escape the strictures and rise above the overelaboration which makes most of them seem determined, if brilliant, exercises. Standing clear of the calculated conceits, such sonnets as the ones beginning "Love is not all," "Well, I have lost you," and the concluding "Oh, sleep forever in the Latmian cave," are not only ingenious in detail but admirably unified. They prove once more Miss Millay's control of her material and complete mastery of the form.

*Wine from These Grapes* (1934) betrays, in spite of its author's craftsmanship, the same reliance on rhetoric which marred *Fatal Interview*. Here, too, the emotion is sometimes inflated, the poem stretched beyond its capacity. There is, moreover, a certain magisterial utterance heard in the books published after 1924 which is suspiciously portentous, even pretentious. But here, as in the other volumes, the extremes are obvious. Here, in the midst of much that is strained and theatrical, are such quiet and gravely spoken finalities as "The Return," "How Naked, How Without a Wall," and "See Where Capella with Her Golden Kids," which synthesizes the spirit of the concluding group of sonnets "Epitaph for the Race of Man." *Wine from These Grapes* is, technically, Miss Millay's most uncertain volume; philosophically, it is her most mature one. Here the poet turns from prettiness and the pangs of romantic love, concerning herself with the unhappy, bewildered, self-torturing human spirit. The legendary Miss Millay, the feminine Byron of the early 1920s, worshiped by a thousand imitators, has become the larger being in her resignation. Critics of the future will be quick to discern the exaggeration, unevenness, and variety of Miss Millay's gifts; they will not fail to find, beyond the literary aptitude, the notes of authority.

## RENASCENCE

All I could see from where I stood
Was three long mountains and a wood;
I turned and looked another way,
And saw three islands in a bay.
So with my eyes I traced the line
Of the horizon, thin and fine,
Straight around till I was come
Back to where I'd started from;
And all I saw from where I stood
Was three long mountains and a wood.
Over these things I could not see;
These were the things that bounded me;
And I could touch them with my hand,
Almost, I thought, from where I stand.

And all at once things seemed so small
My breath came short, and scarce at all.
But, sure, the sky is big, I said;
Miles and miles above my head;
So here upon my back I'll lie
And look my fill into the sky.
And so I looked, and, after all,
The sky was not so very tall.
The sky, I said, must somewhere stop,
And—sure enough!—I see the top!
The sky, I thought, is not so grand;
I 'most could touch it with my hand!
And, reaching up my hand to try,
I screamed to feel it touch the sky.

I screamed, and—lo!—Infinity
Came down and settled over me;

Forced back my scream into my chest,
Bent back my arm upon my breast,
And, pressing of the Undefined
The definition on my mind,
Held up before my eyes a glass
Through which my shrinking sight did pass
Until it seemed I must behold
Immensity made manifold;
Whispered to me a word whose sound
Deafened the air for worlds around,
And brought unmuffled to my ears
The gossiping of friendly spheres,
The creaking of the tented sky,
The ticking of Eternity.

I saw and heard, and knew at last
The How and Why of all things, past,
And present, and forevermore.
The universe, cleft to the core,
Lay open to my probing sense
That, sickening, I would fain pluck thence
But could not,—nay! But needs must suck
At the great wound, and could not pluck
My lips away till I had drawn
All venom out.—Ah, fearful pawn!
For my omniscience I paid toll
In infinite remorse of soul.
All sin was of my sinning, all
Atoning mine, and mine the gall
Of all regret. Mine was the weight
Of every brooded wrong, the hate
That stood behind each envious thrust,
Mine every greed, mine every lust.
And all the while for every grief,
Each suffering, I craved relief
With individual desire,—
Craved all in vain! And felt fierce fire
About a thousand people crawl;
Perished with each,—then mourned for all!
A man was starving in Capri;
He moved his eyes and looked at me;
I felt his gaze, I heard his moan,
And knew his hunger as my own.
I saw at sea a great fog-bank
Between two ships that struck and sank;
A thousand screams the heavens smote;
And every scream tore through my throat;
No hurt I did not feel, no death
That was not mine; mine each last breath
That, crying, met an answering cry
From the compassion that was I.

All suffering mine, and mine its rod;
Mine, pity like the pity of God.
Ah, awful weight! Infinity
Pressed down upon the finite me!
My anguished spirit, like a bird,
Beating against my lips I heard;
Yet lay the weight so close about
There was no room for it without.
And so beneath the weight lay I
And suffered death, but could not die.

Long had I lain thus, craving death,
When quietly the earth beneath
Gave way, and inch by inch, so great
At last had grown the crushing weight,
Into the earth I sank till I
Full six feet under ground did lie,
And sank no more,—there is no weight
Can follow here, however great.
From off my breast I felt it roll,
And as it went my tortured soul
Burst forth and fled in such a gust
That all about me swirled the dust.

Deep in the earth I rested now;
Cool is its hand upon the brow
And soft its breast beneath the head
Of one who is so gladly dead.
And all at once, and over all,
The pitying rain began to fall.
I lay and heard each pattering hoof
Upon my lowly, thatchèd roof.
And seemed to love the sound far more
Than ever I had done before.
For rain it hath a friendly sound
To one who's six feet underground;
And scarce the friendly voice or face:
A grave is such a quiet place.

The rain, I said, is kind to come
And speak to me in my new home.
I would I were alive again
To kiss the fingers of the rain,
To drink into my eyes the shine
Of every slanting silver line,
To catch the freshened, fragrant breeze
From drenched and dripping apple-trees.
For soon the shower will be done,
And then the broad face of the sun
Will laugh above the rain-soaked earth
Until the world with answering mirth

Shakes joyously, and each round drop
Rolls, twinkling, from its grass-blade top.
How can I bear it; buried here,
While overhead the sky grows clear
And blue again after the storm?
O, multi-colored, multiform,
Belovèd beauty over me,
That I shall never, never see
Again! Spring-silver, autumn-gold,
That I shall never more behold!
Sleeping your myriad magics through,
Close-sepulchered away from you!
O God, I cried, give me new birth,
And put me back upon the earth!
Upset each cloud's gigantic gourd
And let the heavy rain, down-poured
In one big torrent, set me free,
Washing my grave away from me!

I ceased; and, through the breathless hush
That answered me, the far-off rush
Of herald wings came whispering
Like music down the vibrant string
Of my ascending prayer, and—crash!
Before the wild wind's whistling lash
The startled storm-clouds reared on high
And plunged in terror down the sky,
And the big rain in one black wave
Fell from the sky and struck my grave.

I know not how such things can be,
I only know there came to me
A fragrance such as never clings
To aught save happy living things;
A sound as of some joyous elf
Singing sweet songs to please himself,
And, through and over everything,
A sense of glad awakening.
The grass, a tip-toe at my ear,
Whispering to me I could hear;
I felt the rain's cool finger-tips
Brushed tenderly across my lips,
Laid gently on my sealèd sight,
And all at once the heavy night
Fell from my eyes and I could see,—
A drenched and dripping apple-tree,
A last long line of silver rain,
A sky grown clear and blue again.
And as I looked a quickening gust
Of wind blew up to me and thrust

Into my face a miracle
Of orchard-breath, and with the smell,—
I know not how such things can be!—
I breathed my soul back into me.

Ah! Up then from the ground sprang I
And hailed the earth with such a cry
As is not heard save from a man
Who has been dead and lives again.
About the trees my arms I wound;
Like one gone mad I hugged the ground;
I raised my quivering arms on high;
I laughed and laughed into the sky,
Till at my throat a strangling sob
Caught fiercely, and a great heart-throb
Sent instant tears into my eyes;
O God, I cried, no dark disguise
Can e'er hereafter hide from me
Thy radiant identity!
Thou canst not move across the grass
But my quick eyes will see Thee pass,
Nor speak, however silently,
But my hushed voice will answer Thee.
I know the path that tells Thy way
Through the cool eve of every day;
God, I can push the grass apart
And lay my finger on Thy heart!

The world stands out on either side
No wider than the heart is wide;
Above the world is stretched the sky,—
No higher than the soul is high.
The heart can push the sea and land
Farther away on either hand;
The soul can split the sky in two,
And let the face of God shine through.
But East and West will pinch the heart
That cannot keep them pushed apart;
And he whose soul is flat—the sky
Will cave in on him by and by.

THE PEAR TREE

In this squalid, dirty dooryard,
    Where the chickens scratch and run,
White, incredible, the pear tree
    Stands apart and takes the sun,

Mindful of the eyes upon it,
    Vain of its new holiness,
Like the waste-man's little daughter
    In her first communion dress.

## GOD'S WORLD

O world, I cannot hold thee close enough!
    Thy winds, thy wide gray skies!
    Thy mists that roll and rise!
Thy woods, this autumn day, that ache and sag
And all but cry with color! That gaunt crag
To crush! To lift the lean of that black bluff!
World, world, I cannot get thee close enough!

Long have I known a glory in it all,
    But never knew I this;
    Here such a passion is
As stretcheth me apart. Lord, I do fear
Thou'st made the world too beautiful this year.
My soul is all but out of me,—let fall
No burning leaf; prithee, let no bird call.

## WILD SWANS

I looked in my heart while the wild swans went over;—
    And what did I see I had not seen before?
    Only a question less or a question more;
Nothing to match the flight of wild birds flying.
Tiresome heart, forever living and dying!
    House without air! I leave you and lock your door!
Wild swans, come over the town, come over
The town again, trailing your legs and crying!

## THE POET AND HIS BOOK

*Down, you mongrel, Death!*
  *Back into your kennel!*
*I have stolen breath*
  *In a stalk of fennel!*
*You shall scratch and you shall whine*
  *Many a night, and you shall worry*
  *Many a bone, before you bury*
*One sweet bone of mine!*

When shall I be dead?
  When my flesh is withered,
And above my head
  Yellow pollen gathered
All the empty afternoon?
  When sweet lovers pause and wonder
  Who am I that lie thereunder,
Hidden from the moon?

This my personal death?—
  That my lungs be failing
To inhale the breath
  Others are exhaling?
This my subtle spirit's end?—
  Ah, when the thawed winter splashes
  Over these chance dust and ashes,
Weep not me, my friend!

Me, by no means dead
  In that hour, but surely
When this book, unread,
  Rots to earth obscurely,
And no more to any breast,
  Close against the clamorous swelling
  Of the thing there is no telling,
Are these pages pressed!

When this book is mold,
  And a book of many
Waiting to be sold
  For a casual penny,
In a little open case,
  In a street unclean and cluttered,

Where a heavy mud is spattered
From the passing drays,

Stranger, pause and look;
  From the dust of ages
Lift this little book,
  Turn the tattered pages,
Read me, do not let me die!
  Search the fading letters, finding
  Steadfast in the broken binding
All that once was I!

When these veins are weeds,
  When these hollowed sockets
Watch the rooty seeds
  Bursting down like rockets,
And surmise the spring again,
  Or, remote in that black cupboard,
  Watch the pink worms writhing upward
At the smell of rain,

Boys and girls that lie
  Whispering in the hedges,
Do not let me die,
  Mix me in your pledges;
Boys and girls that slowly walk
  In the woods, and weep, and quarrel,
  Staring past the pink wild laurel,
Mix me with your talk.

Do not let me die!
  Farmers at your raking,
When the sun is high,
  While the hay is making,
When, along the stubble strewn,
  Withering on their stalks uneaten,
  Strawberries turn dark and sweeten
In the lapse of noon;

Shepherds on the hills,
  In the pastures, drowsing
To the tinkling bells
  Of the brown sheep browsing;
Sailors crying through the storm;
  Scholars at your study; hunters
  Lost amid the whirling winter's
Whiteness uniform;

Men that long for sleep;
  Men that wake and revel;—
If an old song leap
  To your senses' level
At such moments, may it be
  Sometimes, though a moment only,

Some forgotten, quaint and homely
Vehicle of me!

Women at your toil,
  Women at your leisure
Till the kettle boil,
  Snatch of me your pleasure,
Where the broom-straw marks the leaf;
  Women quiet with your weeping
  Lest you wake a workman sleeping,
Mix me with your grief!

Boys and girls that steal
  From the shocking laughter
Of the old, to kneel
  By a dripping rafter
Under the discolored eaves,
  Out of trunks with hingeless covers
  Lifting tales of saint and lovers,
Travelers, goblins, thieves,

Suns that shine by night,
  Mountains made from valleys,—
Bear me to the light,
  Flat upon your bellies
By the webby window lie,
  Where the little flies are crawling,—
  Read me, margin me with scrawling,
Do not let me die!

*Sexton, ply your trade!*
  *In a shower of gravel*
*Stamp upon your spade!*
  *Many a rose shall ravel,*
*Many a metal wreath shall rust*
  *In the rain, and I go singing*
  *Through the lots where you are flinging*
*Yellow clay on dust!*

## SPRING

To what purpose, April, do you return again?
Beauty is not enough.
You can no longer quiet me with the redness
Of little leaves opening stickily.
I know what I know.
The sun is hot on my neck as I observe
The spikes of the crocus.
The smell of the earth is good.
It is apparent that there is no death.
But what does that signify?
Not only under ground are the brains of men
Eaten by maggots.

Life in itself
Is nothing,
An empty cup, a flight of uncarpeted stairs,
It is not enough that yearly, down this hill,
April
Comes like an idiot, babbling and strewing
    flowers.

### PASSER MORTUUS EST

Death devours all lovely things;
    Lesbia with her sparrow

Shares the darkness,—presently
    Every bed is narrow.

Unremembered as old rain
    Dries the sheer libation,
And the little petulant hand
    Is an annotation.

After all, my erstwhile dear,
    My no longer cherished,
Need we say it was not love,
    Now that love has perished?

### WHAT LIPS MY LIPS HAVE KISSED

What lips my lips have kissed, and where, and why,
I have forgotten, and what arms have lain
Under my head till morning; but the rain
Is full of ghosts tonight, that tap and sigh
Upon the glass and listen for reply;
And in my heart there stirs a quiet pain
For unremembered lads that not again
Will turn to me at midnight with a cry.

Thus in the winter stands the lonely tree,
Nor knows what birds have vanished one by one,
Yet knows its boughs more silent than before:
I cannot say what loves have come and gone;
I only know that summer sang in me
A little while, that in me sings no more.

### PITY ME NOT

Pity me not because the light of day
At close of day no longer walks the sky;
Pity me not for beauties passed away
From field and thicket as the year goes by;
Pity me not the waning of the moon,
Nor that the ebbing tide goes out to sea,
Nor that a man's desire is hushed so soon,
And you no longer look with love on me.

This have I known always: love is no more
Than the wide blossom which the wind assails;
Than the great tide that treads the shifting shore,
Strewing fresh wreckage gathered in the gales.
Pity me that the heart is slow to learn
What the swift mind beholds at every turn.

### DEPARTURE

It's little I care what path I take,
   And where it leads it's little I care;
But out of this house, lest my heart break,
   I must go, and off somewhere.

It's little I know what's in my heart,
   What's in my mind it's little I know,
But there's that in me must up and start,
   And it's little I care where my feet go.

I wish I could walk for a day and a night,
   And find me at dawn in a desolate place
With never the rut of a road in sight,
   Nor the roof of a house, nor the eyes of a face.

I wish I could walk till my blood should spout,
   And drop me, never to stir again,
On a shore that is wide, for the tide is out,
   And the weedy rocks are bare to the rain.

But dump or dock, where the path I take
   Brings up, it's little enough I care;
And it's little I'd mind the fuss they'll make,
   Huddled dead in a ditch somewhere.

*"Is something the matter, dear," she said,*
   *"That you sit at your work so silently?"*
*"No, mother, no, 'twas a knot in my thread.*
   *There goes the kettle, I'll make the tea."*

### I SHALL GO BACK

I shall go back again to the bleak shore
And build a little shanty on the sand
In such a way that the extremest band
Of brittle seaweed will escape my door
But by a yard or two, and nevermore
Shall I return to take you by the hand;
I shall be gone to what I understand
And happier than I ever was before.

The love that stood a moment in your eyes,
The words that lay a moment on your tongue,
Are one with all that in a moment dies,
A little under-said and over-sung;
But I shall find the sullen rocks and skies
Unchanged from what they were when I was
   young.

### ELEGY

Let them bury your big eyes
In the secret earth securely,
Your thin fingers, and your fair,
Soft, indefinite-colored hair,—
All of these in some way, surely,
From the secret earth shall rise.
Not for these I sit and stare,
Broken and bereft completely;
Your young flesh that sat so neatly
On your little bones will sweetly
Blossom in the air.

But your voice,—never the rushing
Of a river underground,
Not the rising of the wind
In the trees before the rain,

Not the woodcock's watery call,
Not the note the white-throat utters,
Not the feet of children pushing
Yellow leaves along the gutters
In the blue and bitter fall,
Shall content my musing mind
For the beauty of that sound
That in no new way at all
Ever will be heard again.

Sweetly through the sappy stalk
Of the vigorous weed,

Holding all it held before,
Cherished by the faithful sun,
On and on eternally
Shall your altered fluid run,
Bud and bloom and go to seed;
But your singing days are done;
But the music of your talk
Never shall the chemistry
Of the secret earth restore.
All your lovely words are spoken.
Once the ivory box is broken,
Beats the golden bird no more.

### JUSTICE DENIED IN MASSACHUSETTS[1]

Let us abandon then our gardens and go home
And sit in the sitting-room.
Shall the larkspur blossom or the corn grow under this cloud?
Sour to the fruitful seed
Is the cold earth under this cloud,
Fostering quack and weed, we have marched upon but cannot conquer;
We have bent the blades of our hoes against the stalks of them.

Let us go home, and sit in the sitting-room.
Not in our day
Shall the cloud go over and the sun rise as before,
Beneficent upon us
Out of the glittering bay,
And the warm winds be blown inward from the sea
Moving the blades of corn
With a peaceful sound.
Forlorn, forlorn,
Stands the blue hay-rack by the empty mow.
And the petals drop to the ground,
Leaving the tree unfruited.
The sun that warmed our stooping backs and withered the weed uprooted—
We shall not feel it again.
We shall die in darkness, and be buried in the rain.

What from the splendid dead
We have inherited—
Furrows sweet to the grain, and the weed subdued—
See now the slug and the mildew plunder.
Evil does overwhelm
The larkspur and the corn;
We have seen them go under.

Let us sit here, sit still,
Here in the sitting-room until we die;
At the step of Death on the walk, rise and go;

---

[1] Written after the final decision in the Sacco-Vanzetti case.

Leaving to our children's children this beautiful doorway,
And this elm,
And a blighted earth to till
With a broken hoe.


### EUCLID ALONE HAS LOOKED ON BEAUTY BARE

Euclid alone has looked on Beauty bare.
Let all who prate of Beauty hold their peace,
And lay them prone upon the earth and cease
To ponder on themselves, the while they stare
At nothing, intricately drawn nowhere
In shapes of shifting lineage; let geese
Gabble and hiss, but heroes seek release
From dusty bondage into luminous air.

O blinding hour, O holy, terrible day,
When first the shaft into his vision shone
Of light anatomized! Euclid alone
Has looked on Beauty bare. Fortunate they
Who, though once only and then but far away,
Have heard her massive sandal set on stone.


### ON HEARING A SYMPHONY OF BEETHOVEN

Sweet sounds, oh, beautiful music, do not cease!
Reject me not into the world again.
With you alone is excellence and peace,
Mankind made plausible, his purpose plain.
Enchanted in your air benign and shrewd,
With limbs a-sprawl and empty faces pale,
The spiteful and the stingy and the rude
Sleep like the scullions in the fairy-tale.
This moment is the best the world can give:
The tranquil blossom on the tortured stem.
Reject me not, sweet sounds! oh, let me live,
Till Doom espy my towers and scatter them,
A city spell-bound under the aging sun.
Music my rampart, and my only one.


### SONNET TO GATH

Country of hunchbacks!—where the strong, straight spine
Jeered at by crooked children, makes his way
Through by-streets at the kindest hour of day,
Till he deplore his stature, and incline
To measure manhood with a gibbous line;
Till out of loneliness, being flawed with clay,
He stoop into his neighbor's house and say,
"Your roof is low for me—the fault is mine."

Dust in an urn long since, dispersed and dead
Is great Apollo; and the happier he;
Since who amongst you all would lift a head
At a god's radiance on the mean door-tree,
Saving to run and hide your dates and bread,
And cluck your children in about your knee?


### THE CAMEO

Forever over now, forever, forever gone
That day. Clear and diminished like a scene
Carven in cameo, the lighthouse, and the cove between
The sandy cliffs, and the boat drawn up on the beach;
And the long skirt of a lady innocent and young,
Her hand resting on her bosom, her head hung;
And the figure of a man in earnest speech.

Clear and diminished like a scene cut in cameo
The lighthouse, and the boat on the beach, and the two shapes
Of the woman and the man; lost like the lost day
Are the words that passed, and the pain,—discarded, cut away
From the stone, as from the memory the heat of the tears escapes.

O troubled forms, O early love unfortunate and hard,
Time has estranged you into a jewel cold and pure;
From the action of the waves and from the action of sorrow forever secure,
White against a ruddy cliff you stand, chalcedony on sard.


### OH, SLEEP FOREVER IN THE LATMIAN CAVE

Oh, sleep forever in the Latmian cave,
Mortal Endymion, darling of the Moon!
Her silver garments by the senseless wave
Shouldered and dropped and on the shingle strewn,
Her fluttering hand against her forehead pressed,
Her scattered looks that trouble all the sky,
Her rapid footsteps running down the west—
Of all her altered state, oblivious lie!
Whom earthen you, by deathless lips adored,
Wild-eyed and stammering to the grasses thrust,
And deep into her crystal body poured
The hot and sorrowful sweetness of the dust:
Whereof she wanders mad, being all unfit
For mortal love, that might not die of it.


### SEE WHERE CAPELLA WITH HER GOLDEN KIDS

See where Capella with her golden kids
Grazes the slope between the east and north?
Thus when the builders of the pyramids
Flung down their tools at nightfall and poured forth

Homeward to supper and a poor man's bed,
Shortening the road with friendly jest and slur,
The risen She-Goat showing blue and red
Climbed the clear dusk, and three stars followed her.
Safe in their linen and their spices lie
The kings of Egypt; even as long ago
Under these constellations, with long eye
And scented limbs they slept, and feared no foe.
Their will was law; their will was not to die.
And so they had their way; or nearly so.

### THE RETURN

Earth does not understand her child,
    Who from the loud gregarious town
Returns, depleted and defiled,
    To the still woods, to fling him down.

Earth cannot count the sons she bore:
    The wounded lynx, the wounded man
Come trailing blood unto her door;
    She shelters both as best she can.

But she is early up and out,
    To trim the year or strip its bones;
She has no time to stand about
    Talking of him in undertones

Who has no aim but to forget,
    Be left in peace, be lying thus
For days, for years, for centuries yet,
    Unshaven and anonymous;

Who, marked for failure, dulled by grief,
    Has traded in his wife and friend
For this warm ledge, this alder leaf:
    Comfort that does not comprehend.

# Maxwell Bodenheim

MAXWELL BODENHEIM was born at Natchez, Mississippi, May 26, 1892. His education, with the exception of grammar school training, was achieved under the guidance of the U. S. Army, in which he served an enlistment of three years, beginning in 1910. For a while he studied law and art in Chicago, but his mind turned to literature. In 1918 his first volume appeared and even those who were puzzled or repelled by Bodenheim's complex idiom were forced to recognize its individuality.

*Minna and Myself* (1918) reveals, first of all, this poet's sensitivity to words. Words, under his hands, have unexpected growths; placid nouns and sober adjectives bear fantastic fruit. Sometimes he packs his metaphors so close that they become inextricably confused. Sometimes he spins his fantasies so thin that the cord of coherence snaps and the poem frays into unpatterned ravelings.

In *Advice* (1920) Bodenheim's manner—and his mannerisms—are intensified. There is scarcely a phrase that is not tricked out with more ornaments than it can bear; whole poems sink beneath the weight of profuse decorations, although there is evidence of the ironic imagination which dominates his subsequent work.

*Introducing Irony* (1922) and *Against This Age* (1923) allow the sardonic impulse to dictate its harshest accents. The communication is more involved than ever: the expression of an acrobatic mind that juggles a dozen mixed metaphors, balancing itself meanwhile upon the knives of emotion with a mordant grimace. *The Sardonic Arm* (1923) shows an author acrid, grotesque, verbally dandified—but seldom unintelligible. Even when Bodenheim writes in the spirit of resentment self-confessed in *Against This Age,* he has something to say which the reader, provoked though he may be by the author's supercilious disdain, might listen to with profit. It is, nevertheless, still true that Bodenheim too often writes in the rôle of literary ring-master, cracking his savage whip over cowering adjectives and recalcitrant adverbs, compelling them to leap in unwilling pairs over the fantastically piled barriers of his imagination.

In *The King of Spain and Other Poems* (1928) Bodenheim continues to exercise his invectives. Yet, in spite of the egotism of the notes which precede and follow many of the poems, the work is sharp and unhackneyed. It is obvious that no such language has ever been spoken as the conversation detailed in his volumes; not his characters but the author himself does all the talking; and it is he, a breathlessly sardonic euphuist, who leaps desperately from one image to another. But the images themselves are glittering, and in the realm of the whimsical-grotesque, Bodenheim's footing is sure; his is a nimble if disturbing transilience.

An effort to please popular taste, *Bringing Jazz* (1930), lived up neither to its title nor to its author's reputation for the unusual.

Bodenheim is also the author of several novels, *Crazy Man* (1924), *Replenishing Jessica* (1925), and *Sixty Seconds* (1929) being the most successful as well as the most self-revealing.

### POET TO HIS LOVE

An old silver church in a forest
Is my love for you.
The trees around it
Are words that I have stolen from your heart.
An old silver bell, the last smile you gave,
Hangs at the top of my church.
It rings only when you come through the forest
And stand beside it.
And then it has no need for ringing,
For your voice takes its place.

### OLD AGE

In me is a little painted square
Bordered by old shops with gaudy awnings.
And before the shops sit smoking, open-bloused old men,
Drinking sunlight.
The old men are my thoughts;
And I come to them each evening, in a creaking cart,
And quietly unload supplies.
We fill slim pipes and chat
And inhale scents from pale flowers in the center of the square. . . .
Strong men, tinkling women, and dripping, squealing children
Stroll past us, or into the shops.
They greet the shopkeepers and touch their hats or foreheads to me. . . .
Some evening I shall not return to my people.

### DEATH

I shall walk down the road;
I shall turn and feel upon my feet
The kisses of Death, like scented rain.
For Death is a black slave with little silver birds
Perched in a sleeping wreath upon his head.
He will tell me, his voice like jewels
Dropped into a satin bag,
How he has tip-toed after me down the road,
His heart made a dark whirlpool with longing for me.
Then he will graze me with his hands,
And I shall be one of the sleeping, silver birds
Between the cold waves of his hair, as he tip-toes on.

### HILL-SIDE TREE

Like a drowsy, rain-browned saint,
You squat, and sometimes your voice,
In which the wind takes no part,
Is like mists of music wedding each other.
A drunken, odor-laced peddler is the morning wind.
He brings you golden-scarfed cities
Whose voices are swirls of bells burdened with summer;
And maidens whose hearts are galloping princes.
And you raise your branches to the sky,
With a whisper that holds the smile you cannot shape.

### FACTORY GIRL

Why are your eyes like dry brown flower-pods,
Still, gripped by the memory of lost petals?
I feel that if I touched them
They would crumble to falling brown dust

And you would stand with blindness revealed.
Yet you would not shrink, for your life
Has been long since memorized,
And eyes would only melt out against its high walls.
Besides, in the making of boxes
Sprinkled with crude forget-me-nots,
One is curiously blessed if one's eyes are dead.

### ADVICE TO A BLUE-BIRD

Who can make a delicate adventure
Of walking on the ground?
Who can make grass-blades
Arcades for pertly careless straying?
You alone, who skim against these leaves,
Turning all desire into light whips
Molded by your deep blue wing-tips,
You who shrill your unconcern
Into the sternly antique sky.
You to whom all things
Hold an equal kiss of touch.

Mincing, wanton blue-bird,
Grimace at the hoofs of passing men.
You alone can lose yourself
Within a sky, and rob it of its blue!

## Archibald MacLeish

ARCHIBALD MAC LEISH was born in Glencoe, northern Illinois, May 7, 1892. The son of a Scotch merchant and a Connecticut clergyman's daughter, he spent his boyhood on the lake shore, was educated in the public schools of his native town, a Connecticut preparatory school, Yale University, and Harvard Law School. He served in the Field Artillery in France during the War, became a lawyer in Boston and gave up the practice of law for literature, living in the Berkshires during the summer and in Paris during the winter. After his return to America, he spent most of the year in New York, where he became one of the editors of Fortune.

MacLeish's first volume, Tower of Ivory (1917), gave few hints of the original talent that was revealed in The Happy Marriage (1924), The Pot of Earth (1925) and the curious Nobodaddy (1925). There are influences apparent in all of these. The Happy Marriage owes not a little to Conrad Aiken and E. A. Robinson; The Pot of Earth relies on T. S. Eliot's structure as well as his free use of dissonance and peculiar juxtapositions. But MacLeish has something to say which is quite his own, something about man's uncertain place in the Unknown and, in these volumes, he is learning how to say it.

In Streets in the Moon (1926) the complete poet emerges. Here his subject-matter, conceived in amplitude, conveys an unusual "sense of infinity." But it is his idiom even more than his theme which makes MacLeish an important modern poet. He can, by the skillful use of repetition, achieve new effects in harmony, he can prompt a new beat in even so old a form as the sonnet, *vide* "The End of the World." "Ars Poetica" is more than an extension of poetic language; beneath its successful experiments in timing, interior rhyme and suspension, it says a number of pointed and profound things which have nothing to do with timeliness and changing tastes. The tone of these verses may be as new as this generation; the spirit which moves beneath them is as old as the sung phrase and the unspoken word.

*The Hamlet of A. MacLeish* (1928) is clearer in pattern and suppler in power than any of his other long poems. Its blemishes are those of confirmed modernity. Speaking of its author, Conrad Aiken says, "He is a kind of slave of tradition, with the difference that the traditions which enslave him are contemporary ones." MacLeish has not completely thrown off the influence of Eliot and various modern French poets, but his conceptions are so much his own that no one could mistake the originality of his design. In *The Hamlet of A. MacLeish,* the poet has plunged deeper into himself. The half-conscious breaks through; remote associations, shifting allusions, disordered griefs, phantasms, fag-ends of memories float up. By overtone and undercurrent, the reader is led to identify himself—as the author has done—with the eternal Hamlet, that conglomeration of lover, poet, procrastinator, ranter, doer, and doubter.

*New Found Land* (1930) contains only fourteen poems, yet some of MacLeish's richest verses are in this small book. The mood is elegiac, but the melancholy is provocative rather than lulling. The perceptions are unusually keen, the images highly charged, and the tone throughout is not only uplifted but noble. Some of MacLeish's critics made much of his nostalgia for the past, forgetting that no poet (no person, in fact) is free of it, and what distinguishes the poet is not his subject-matter but the way in which he employs his material. No one could question the distinction of "You, Andrew Marvell," that beautiful and uncanny exercise in suspension, one of the finest poems of the period, "Immortal Autumn," with its classical overtones, "Epistle to be Left in the Earth," and others. In these poems—as in "Memorial Rain," which says more about War than any poetry since Owen's and Sassoon's—the style is elliptical but the figures are concrete; without strain or exaggeration MacLeish uses ordinary language to suggest extraordinary sensations and abstractions. Here, too, MacLeish is shown to be one of the most resourceful technicians of an experimental age; he employs all the approved forms and invents several of his own; extends the gamut of rhyme through dissonance and consonance to half-rhyme ("thin-continues," "sun-running," "dish-official," "star-harbor," etc.), rhyming consonants and unrhyming vowels ("lake-like," "vine-vane," "west-waste," etc.), and concealed internal rhyme.

*Conquistador* (1932) employs these effects on a wider scale for a larger purpose. Certain reviewers referred to the poem as being "loosely ductile" and "unrhymed." *Conquistador* happens to be highly formal, the form being nothing "looser" than terza rima. The rhyming trios, however, are unorthodox since MacLeish varies full rhyme with assonance ("market-carpenter-arsenal," "things-wind-insolent," etc.) and suspension. But it is not only in technique that *Conquistador* displays the poet's maturity; in accent and spirit it is a rich fulfillment of MacLeish's gifts. Richness of color, extension of musical devices, and a mastery of the long breath combine to produce the most accomplished saga-poem of the generation. Founded on Bernal Diaz's *True History of the Conquest of New Spain* and influenced by the accent of Pound's *Cantos,* especially Canto I, the narrative proceeds swiftly from one vivid detail to another. Sometimes the tale is disrupted as the aged narrator, "unused to the combing of words clean of the wool," confuses time and events; yet even here the poem does not lose but gains in movement, like the swift progression of a vivid dream. Everything contributes to the vitality of this movement, most of all Mac-Leish's vocabulary. *Conquistador,* in spite of being cast in the key of reminiscence, is a record of life in action; and this parade of fighting and feasting, of blood, song, and quick surrenders is tuned to words that live and leap no less actively. No modern writer has used the device of Anglo-Saxon alliteration so amazingly as MacLeish; we have to go back to *The Seafarer* to find narration so stripped in phrase, so speeded in close-packed measures. The poem as a whole is a triumph in sonorous lines and sustained power. *Conquistador* was awarded the Pulitzer Prize in 1933.

*Poems 1924-1933,* which definitely established MacLeish, contains several new poems besides the best of those previously published, experiments further in stylistic subtleties, and proves that MacLeish is one of the most consistently interesting and one of the most important poets of his time. In "Frescoes for Mr. Rockefeller's City" he rids himself of the Eliot-Pound rhetoric, devotes himself to contemporary subjects, and sounds a simple "nobility of emotion."

*Panic* (1935), even less preoccupied with esthetic questions, is wholly concerned with timely problems. *Panic* is a play in flexible verse, which caused no little controversy when it was produced in New York. Neither the reactionaries nor the revolutionists were cheered by it, for MacLeish refused to join either camp, but none could dispute the eloquence of the mass choruses, the drive behind the dissolving scenes, and the universality of the passion which marked *Panic* as a significant revival of the poetic drama. If no one was "converted" by the tragedy, no one was unmoved by it. It was a non-partisan attempt to express the personal responsibility and individual tragedy of man, in which MacLeish showed that, though he "suffered the universal qualms," he was unable to accept any of the current panaceas.

In spite of his achievements in technique, it is neither the novel form nor the phrase-making which distinguishes MacLeish. It is the discipline which he imposes on the flow of suggestions, on the very chaos of the unconscious; it is his orderly employment of material almost too fluent to fix, which has made him both the target and the envy of his fellow-poets.

ARS POETICA

A poem should be palpable and mute
As a globed fruit

Dumb
As old medallions to the thumb

Silent as the sleeve-worn stone
Of casement ledges where the moss has
  grown—

A poem should be wordless
As the flight of birds

✦

A poem should be motionless in time
As the moon climbs

Leaving, as the moon releases
Twig by twig the night-entangled trees,

Leaving, as the moon behind the winter
  leaves,
Memory by memory the mind—

A poem should be motionless in time
As the moon climbs

      ✦

A poem should be equal to:
Not true

For all the history of grief
An empty doorway and a maple leaf

For love
The leaning grasses and two lights above the
  sea—

A poem should not mean
But be.

### PROLOGUE

These alternate nights and days, these seasons
Somehow fail to convince me. It seems
I have the sense of infinity!

(In your dreams, O crew of Columbus,
O listeners over the sea
For the surf that breaks upon Nothing—)

Once I was waked by nightingales in the
  garden.
I thought, What time is it? I thought,
Time—Is it Time still?—Now is it Time?

(Tell me your dreams, O sailors:
Tell me, in sleep did you climb
The tall masts, and before you—)

At night the stillness of old trees
Is a leaning over, and the inertness
Of hills is a kind of waiting.

(In sleep, in a dream, did you see
The world's end? Did the water
Break—and no shore— Did you see?)

Strange faces come through the streets to me
Like messengers: and I have been warned
By the moving slowly of hands at a window.

O, I have the sense of infinity—
But the world, sailors, is round.
They say there is no end to it.

### IN MY THIRTIETH YEAR

And I have come upon this place
  By lost ways, by a nod, by words,
By faces, by the old man's face
  At Morlaix lifted to the birds,

By hands upon the tablecloth
  At Aldebori's, by the thin
Child's hands that opened to the moth
  And let the flutter of the moonlight in,

By hands, by voices, by the voice
  Of Mrs. Husman on the stair,
By Margaret's "If we had the choice
  To choose or not—" through her thick hair,

By voices, by the creak and fall
  Of footsteps on the upper floor,
By silence waiting in the hall
  Between the door-bell and the door,

By words, by voices, a lost way—
  And here above the chimney stack
The unknown constellations sway—
  And by what way shall I go back?

### MEMORIAL RAIN

Ambassador Puser the ambassador
Reminds himself in French, felicitous tongue,
What these (young men no longer) lie here for
In rows that once, and somewhere else, were young—

    All night in Brussels the wind had tugged at my door:
    I had heard the wind at my door and the trees strung
    Taut, and to me who had never been before
    In that country it was a strange wind blowing

Steadily, stiffening the walls, the floor,
The roof of my room. I had not slept for knowing
He too, dead, was a stranger in that land
And felt beneath the earth in the wind's flowing
A tightening of roots and would not understand,
Remembering lake winds in Illinois,
That strange wind. I had felt his bones in the sand
Listening.

         —Reflects that these enjoy
Their country's gratitude, that deep repose,
That peace no pain can break, no hurt destroy,
That rest, that sleep—

         At Ghent the wind rose.
There was a smell of rain and a heavy drag
Of wind in the hedges but not as the wind blows
Over fresh water when the waves lag
Foaming and the willows huddle and it will rain:
I felt him waiting.

         —Indicates the flag
Which (may he say) enisles in Flanders' plain
This little field these happy, happy dead
Have made America—

         In the ripe grain
The wind coiled glistening, darted, fled,
Dragging its heavy body: at Waereghem
The wind coiled in the grass above his head:
Waiting—listening—

         —Dedicates to them
This earth their bones have hallowed, this last gift
A grateful country—

         Under the dry grass stem
The words are blurred, are thickened, the words sift
Confused by the rasp of the wind, by the thin grating
Of ants under the grass, the minute shift
And tumble of dusty sand separating
From dusty sand. The roots of the grass strain,
Tighten, the earth is rigid, waits—he is waiting—

And suddenly, and all at once, the rain!

The people scatter, they run into houses, the wind
Is trampled under the rain, shakes free, is again
Trampled. The rain gathers, running in thinned
Spurts of water that ravel in the dry sand
Seeping into the sand under the grass roots, seeping
Between cracked boards to the bones of a clenched hand:
The earth relaxes, loosens; he is sleeping,
He rests, he is quiet, he sleeps in a strange land.

WEATHER

The northeast wind was the wind off the lake
Blowing the oak leaves pale side out like
Aspen: blowing the sound of the surf far
Inland over the fences: blowing for
Miles over smell of earth the alien
Lake smell.
        The southwest wind was thunder on
Afternoon: you saw the wind first in the vine
Over the side porch and the weather vane
Whirled on the barn and the doors slammed all together.
After the rain in the grass we used to gather
Wind-fallen cold white apples.
           The west
Wind was the August wind, the wind over waste
Valleys over the waterless plains where still
Were skulls of buffalo, where in the sand stale
Dung lay of wild cattle. The west wind blew
Day after day as the winds on the plains blow
Burning the grass, turning the leaves brown, filling
Noon with the bronze of cicadas, far out falling
Dark on the colorless water, the lake where not
Waves were nor movement.
            The north wind was at night
When no leaves and the husk on the oak stirs
Only nor birds then. The north wind was stars
Over the whole sky and snow in the ways
And snow on the sand where in summer the water was . . .
North here is the sea and westward the sea
And south the Tyrrhenian sea where the hills saw
Once the long oars and the helmsman. But here to me
The winds blow as always they blew in my
Country,
      the winds blow out of Illinois,
Out of Missouri, out of Michigan. I know
The northeast wind: I know how the trees look—
The northeast wind is the wind over the lake
Blowing the oak leaves pale side out. . . .

IMMORTAL AUTUMN

I speak this poem now with grave and level voice
In praise of autumn of the far-horn-winding fall
I praise the flower-barren fields the clouds the tall
Unanswering branches where the wind makes sullen noise

I praise the fall it is the human season now
No more the foreign sun does meddle at our earth
Enforce the green and thaw the frozen soil to birth
Nor winter yet weigh all with silence the pine bough

But now in autumn with the black and outcast crows
Share we the spacious world the whispering year is gone
There is more room to live now the once secret dawn
Comes late by daylight and the dark unguarded goes

Between the mutinous brave burning of the leaves
And winter's covering of our hearts with his deep snow
We are alone there are no evening birds we know
The naked moon the tame stars circle at our eaves

It is the human season on this sterile air
Do words outcarry breath the sound goes on and on
I hear a dead man's cry from autumn long since gone

I cry to you beyond this bitter air.

## YOU, ANDREW MARVELL

And here face down beneath the sun
And here upon earth's noonward height
To feel the always coming on
The always rising of the night

To feel creep up the curving east
The earthly chill of dusk and slow
Upon those under lands the vast
And ever-climbing shadow grow

And strange at Ecbatan the trees
Take leaf by leaf the evening strange
The flooding dark about their knees
The mountains over Persia change

And now at Kermanshah the gate
Dark empty and the withered grass
And through the twilight now the late
Few travelers in the westward pass

And Baghdad darken and the bridge
Across the silent river gone

And through Arabia the edge
Of evening widen and steal on

And deepen on Palmyra's street
The wheel rut in the ruined stone
And Lebanon fade out and Crete
High through the clouds and overblown

And over Sicily the air
Still flashing with the landward gulls
And loom and slowly disappear
The sails above the shadowy hulls

And Spain go under and the shore
Of Africa the gilded sand
And evening vanish and no more
The low pale light across that land

Nor now the long light on the sea—

And here face downward in the sun
To feel how swift how secretly
The shadow of the night comes on . . .

## THE END OF THE WORLD

Quite unexpectedly as Vasserot
The armless ambidextrian was lighting
A match between his great and second toe
And Ralph the lion was engaged in biting
The neck of Madame Sossman while the drum
Pointed, and Teeny was about to cough
In waltz-time swinging Jocko by the thumb—
Quite unexpectedly the top blew off:

And there, there overhead, there, there, hung over
Those thousands of white faces, those dazed eyes,
There in the starless dark, the poise, the hover,
There with vast wings across the canceled skies,
There in the sudden blackness, the black pall
Of nothing, nothing, nothing—nothing at all.

### THE TOO-LATE BORN

We too, we too, descending once again
The hills of our own land, we too have heard
Far off— Ah, que ce cor a longue haleine—
The horn of Roland in the passages of Spain,
The first, the second blast, the failing third,
And with the third turned back and climbed once more
The steep road southward, and heard faint the sound
Of swords, of horses, the disastrous war,
And crossed the dark defile at last, and found
At Roncevaux upon the darkening plain
The dead against the dead and on the silent ground
The silent slain—

### EPISTLE TO BE LEFT IN THE EARTH

. . . It is colder now
                        there are many stars
                                        we are drifting
North by the Great Bear
                        the leaves are falling
The water is stone in the scooped rocks
                                        to southward
Red sun gray air
                the crows are
Slow on their crooked wings
                                the jays have left us
Long since we passed the flares of Orion
Each man believes in his heart he will die
Many have written last thoughts and last letters
None know if our deaths are now or forever
None know if this wandering earth will be found

We lie down and the snow covers our garments
I pray you
                you (if any open this writing)
Make in your mouths the words that were our names
I will tell you all we have learned
                                I will tell you everything
The earth is round
                        there are springs under the orchards
The loam cuts with a blunt knife
                                beware of

Elms in thunder
                    the lights in the sky are stars
We think they do not see
                            we think also
The trees do not know nor the leaves of the grasses
                                                    hear us
The birds too are ignorant
                            Do not listen
Do not stand at dark in the open windows
We before you have heard this
                                they are voices
They are not words at all but the wind rising
Also none among us has seen God
(. . . We have thought often
The flaws of sun in the late and driving weather
Pointed to one tree but it was not so)
As for the nights I warn you the nights are dangerous
The wind changes at night and the dreams come

It is very cold
                    there are strange stars near Arcturus

Voices are crying an unknown name in the sky

### BURYING GROUND BY THE TIES

*(from "Frescoes for Mr. Rockefeller's City")*

Ayee! Ai! This is heavy earth on our shoulders:
There were none of us born to be buried in this earth:
Niggers we were Portuguese Magyars Polacks:

We were born to another look of the sky certainly:
Now we lie here in the river pastures:
We lie in the mowings under the thick turf:

We hear the earth and the all-day rasp of the grasshoppers:
It was we laid the steel on this land from ocean to ocean:
It was we (if you know) put the U. P. through the passes

Bringing her down into Laramie full load
Eighteen mile on the granite anticlinal
Forty-three foot to the mile and the grade holding:

It was we did it: hunkies of our kind:
It was we dug the caved-in holes for the cold water:
It was we built the gully spurs and the freight sidings:

Who would do it but we and the Irishmen bossing us?
It was all foreign-born men there were in this country:
It was Scotsmen Englishmen Chinese Squareheads Austrians . . .

Ayee! but there's weight to the earth under it:
Not for this did we come out—to be lying here
Nameless under the ties in the clay cuts:

There's nothing good in the world but the rich will buy it:
Everything sticks to the grease of a gold note—
Even a continent—even a new sky!

Do not pity us much for the strange grass over us:
We laid the steel to the stone stock of these mountains:
The place of our graves is marked by the telegraph poles!

It was not to lie in the bottoms we came out
And the trains going over us here in the dry hollows . . .

### PANIC

*(from "Panic")*

#### AN OLD MAN

Slowly the thing comes.
There are many signs: there are furnaces
Dead now that were burning
Thirty years in a town—
Never dark: there are foundries—
Fires drawn: trestles
Silent. The swifts nest in
Stacks that for generations
Flowed smoke. The patience of
Hawks is over the cities:
They circle in clean light where the
Smoke last year frightened them.

#### A WOMAN

The gears turn: twitter: are
Still now. The sound dies.
From the east with the sun's rising
Daily are fewer whistles:
Many mornings listening
One less or two.

#### A YOUNG MAN

The thing comes pursuing us
Creeping as death creeps in an
Old man: as sleep comes:
Leaving on one hill—
On the stand—the stalks silver—
Corn rotted in ear:
Leaving on land nearest us
Wagons abandoned: milk cows
Slaughtered for no sickness:
Rigs rusting at pit-heads:

Pumps frozen: switches
Green with the rain: the oil
Thickened: scale in boilers—
Good gear all of it:
Sound metal: faultless:
Idle now: never manned.

#### A GIRL

Men in the dusk—and they stand there
Letting the girls go by with the
Sweet scent: silent:
Leaning heavily: bent to the
Painted signs on the fences—
They that in other times
Calling after us climbed by the
Steep stair for the sight of a
Girl's knee delighting her.

#### A MAN

From what ill and what enemy
Armless shall we defend the
Evening—the night hours?

#### A MAN

No eyes of ours have
Ever knowing beheld it.
It comes not with the bells
Arousing towns: racing with
Smoke—with the wind's haste—
The tallest houses toppled.

#### A MAN

Comes not from the hospitals—
Odor of scattered lime—
Night burials climbing the
Empty streets by the markets.

A MAN

Not with the shot: with the barking of
Dogs before color of dawn—
The whistle over the lawn—the
Running footfalls stumbling.

A WOMAN

Nevertheless it comes.
Men die: houses
Fall among kitchen flowers.
Families scatter. Children
Wander the roads building of
Broken boxes shelter.
A land of great wealth and the
Old hungry: the young
Starving—but not with hunger.
None have beheld this enemy.
What arms can defend the
Evening—the night hours—
When fear: faceless: devours us?

A WOMAN

Blight—not on the grain!
Drouth—not in the springs!
Rot—not from the rain!

A MAN

What shadow hidden or
Unseen hand in our midst
Ceaselessly touches our faces?

FINAL CHORUS

(from "Panic")

AN OLD WOMAN (exultantly)

Bellies bitter with drinking the
Weak tears do you fear the
Fall of the walls and the sky
High over you shining there?

A MAN (exultantly)

Mouths bitter with hate and the
Aching of tears have you tasted the
New water that springs in the
Hollow of thirst in your fingers?

A MAN (exultantly)

Eyes blind with the sleet and the
Freezing of night have you seen how the
Wind's in the rising East and the
Mountains of morning increasing?

A WOMAN

The roof's fallen! The sun
Stands on the sky with his wonder.

A WOMAN

The wind—the wind's in the house!

A WOMAN

The walls open arousing us!

A MAN

Wildly as swollen river the
Dark will of the world
Flooded on rock rushes
Raving—bearing the brush down:
Breaking from ancient banks.
Cities are buried. The man
Drowns in his door who opposes it.

VOICES

Follow!

Give!

Go with the
Rushing of time in us!

Make of the
Silence of fate a trumpet!
Make of the time a drum!

March!

Shout!

A MAN

Run with the
Marching men: with the thunder of
Thousand heels on the earth—
Making of mortal burden a
Banner to shout and to break in the
Blazing of sunlight and shaken there!

VOICES

Take it!

Be taken!

The trumpet of
Time in our ears and the brazen and
Breaking shout of our days!

MANY VOICES

Man's fate is a drum!

# Winifred Welles

WINIFRED WELLES was born at Norwich Town, Connecticut, January 26, 1893, and educated in the vicinity of her home.

Her delicately fashioned lyrics are the feature of *The Hesitant Heart* (1920). This first volume, so appropriately named, has an unabashed tenderness which never grows maudlin and a wistful questioning that never forgets to sing.

For a while Miss Welles was one of the editors of *The Measure* in which some of her best verse appeared. *This Delicate Love* (1929) and *Blossoming Antlers* (1933) show that her standards have reached a more complete craftsmanship; the lines have grown surer and keener edged. "Actual Willow" and "Harvest Dust" are typical of her later work, slender in substance but firm in line. She paints life as a miniaturist, with adroit precision and scrupulous detail.

*Skipping Along Alone* (1931) is a book of verses for children written with a little too much emphasis on the prettily poetic. Miss Welles skips on a confident toe—light, if too determinedly fantastic—the whole book being a shade overfanciful.

*A Spectacle for Scholars* (1935) consists of four narratives, each of which concerns a New England eccentric. There is wit here as well as whimsicality and a touch of the bizarre. But Miss Welles is not the mistress of the macabre which Sylvia Warner is. She lacks Miss Warner's combination of the demure and the diabolic; she has something of the Englishwoman's precision and delicacy, but none of her power. Nevertheless, though Miss Welles' narratives suffer from weak spots and uncertain finales, one reads them for the grace of thought and the dexterity with which the thought is turned.

### FROM A CHINESE VASE

Roaming the lonely garden, he and I
Pursue each other to the fountain's brim,
And there grow quiet—woman and butterfly—
The frail clouds beckon me, the flowers tempt him.

My thoughts are rose-like, beautiful and bright,
Folded precise as petals are, and wings
Uplift my dreaming suddenly in flight,
And fill my soul with jagged colorings.

The waters tangle like a woman's hair
Above the dim reflection of a face—
He thinks those are his own lips laughing there,
His own breasts curving under silk and lace.

How shall we know our real selves, he and I,
Which is the woman, which the butterfly?

### LOVE SONG FROM NEW ENGLAND

In every solemn tree the wind
    Has rung a little lonesome bell,
As sweet and clear, as cool and kind
    As my voice bidding you farewell.

This is an hour that gods have loved
    To snatch with bare, bright hands and hold.
Mine, with a gesture, gray and gloved,
    Dismiss it from me in the cold.

Closely as some dark-shuttered house
    I keep my light. How should you know,
That, as you turn beneath brown boughs,
    My heart is breaking in the snow?

### ACTUAL WILLOW

Once when I looked at willows, I would say,
    "Thin-fingered women are underneath that hair!"
Or, at the close of a quieter day,
    A flock of tall birds would seem standing there
On single legs, heads tucked in for the night
    Under gray-green plumage—
                                    "Willow, willow is the note
If roots turn claws, and boughs go up in flight!"
    Or, "A river-woman with a long white throat
Will come if I call 'Willow!'"
                                    So I would say
    When I looked at willows once— But today,
The actual willow, the fact of a tree
    Seems fanciful and beautiful enough for me.

### HARVEST DUST

The road is burnt to dust, like more dust meadow rue
    Smokes in the meadow. Berries are balanced to fall
At a cowbell's echo. Apples will soon be over, nothing is left to do
    For the trees but to crook their elbows on the wall.

In the farmhouse doorway a woman husking corn
    Droops to where, softer than children's hair, a yellow heap
Of the silk fondles her hand. Under her eyes her face is as worn
    As the stone steps where she sits and has fallen asleep.

What is it all for? Why must the earth crack
    Over and over beneath this searing breath?
Only that apples be amber and berries black,
    And women content and wearied unto death.

# *Elizabeth J. Coatsworth*

ELIZABETH J. COATSWORTH was born in 1893 in Buffalo, New York. After extended travels she returned to America, where she divides her time between a cottage in Maine and an old house overlooking the harbor of Hingham, Massachusetts. She married Henry Beston, author of *Outermost House* and other books, in 1929.

Miss Coatsworth made her début with *Fox Footprints* (1921), a group of images and studies in the Oriental mood. Coming at a time when the country was surfeited with adaptations from the Chinese and paraphrases from the Japanese, Miss Coatsworth's volume was treated merely as another set of echoes. But, beneath the exotic influences, there was a vein of fresh imagery, a native fancy no more Eastern than Miss Coatsworth's own spirit.

*Atlas and Beyond* (1924) was a far more original piece of work. Although it, too, finds its subjects over-seas, there is nothing of the usual travel-book flavor in any poem; the section entitled "Italy" is particularly delightful because of its mixture of grace and irony.

*Compass Rose* (1929), her best work, has, as the title suggests, something of that mixture of accuracy and fancy, of explicit direction and charming vagueness characteristic of the old animated maps. As a rhyming explorer, Miss Coatsworth must be numbered among the more observant mariners. She is one for whom the fact is but the beginning of the story; to observation she adds imagination, and so brings home an unusually colorful report. Not that her level is always serene; she falters just when she is about to attain the heights. Miss Coatsworth frequently announces a theme of prime significance, but fails to develop it. When the poet is least ambitious she is most successful. Her imaginative ballads are pointed and persuasive; her practiced hand strikes the notes squarely, running bright scales with ease and even with brilliance. She sounds the ironically braggart in "Announcement," the mysteriously macabre in "A Lady Comes to an Inn," the muffled heroic in "Daniel Webster's Horses." But it is in the animal poems that she is happiest and seems most herself. In "The Old Mare," "The Circus-Postered Barn," "The Bad Kittens," "On a Night of Snow" she mingles humor, pity, and a faint satire. These are poems to which the reader is likely to turn for more than their gravely uttered whimsicality.

Miss Coatsworth recently developed a charming vein in her books for young people, prose fantasies liberally interspersed with verse. *The Cat that Went to Heaven* (1930) and *Away Goes Sally* (1934) are perhaps the most winning.

### ANNOUNCEMENT

Let it be understood that I am Don Juan Gomez!
My blood is pure blood from the proudest blood of Spain,
And I own hills and valleys beyond a long day's riding,
And heavy lies the silver upon my bridle rein.

Let it be understood that I am Don Juan Gomez!
My saddle cloth is fringed with scalps of Indians I have slain,

And when I see a girl and knock upon her shutter,
Though it be dawn or dark, I need not knock again.

Let it be understood that I am Don Juan Gomez!
Only in prayer to bend the knee and bow the head I deign;
And when I pray the saints go hurrying to the Virgin,
And cry, "Don Juan is praying, and must not pray in vain!"

### THE OLD MARE

Gray despair
Was on the old mare,
Grass turned bitter,
Sky a-glare,
And gnats like thoughts,
And thoughts like gnats,
Everywhere.

Her underlip
Hung pendulous wide,
Her ears twitched back,
Her dusty hide
Heaved with her heavy breathing
And her eyes rolled ominously
To one side.

The mule colt lay
In trampled grass,
Slick-tailed, long-eared,
Bespeaking the ass
Carried so long in her body,
Born in travail and sweat—
Alien, alas.

But staggering
To unsteady feet
The mule colt fumbles
An unknown teat;
And the old mare relaxes and sighs,
Finding any motherhood
Most sweet.

### DANIEL WEBSTER'S HORSES

If when the wind blows
Rattling the trees,

Clicking like skeletons'
Elbows and knees,

You hear along the road
Three horses pass—
Do not go near the dark
Cold window-glass.

If when the first snow lies
Whiter than bones
You see the mark of hoofs
Cut to the stones,

Hoofs of three horses
Going abreast—
Turn about, turn about,
A closed door is best!

Upright in the earth
Under the sod
They buried three horses
Bridled and shod,

Daniel Webster's horses—
He said as he grew old,
"Flesh, I loved riding,
Shall I not love it, cold?

"Shall I not love to ride
Bone astride bone,
When the cold wind blows
And snow covers stone?

"Bury them on their feet
With bridle and bit.
They were fine horses—
See their shoes fit."

### THE CIRCUS-POSTERED BARN

When Dobbin and Robin, unharnessed from the plow,
Stamp smoking to their stalls,

They pass beneath white horses with long manes
Shining upon the walls,
White horses airily leaping through great hoops
Along applauding tracks
Or carrying princesses in rosy tights
Upon their backs.

And Daisy, Madge and Buttercup
Raise their soft eyes,
Where through the darkness of the web-hung stable
Hippopotami arise,
Shaking the water from their enormous shoulders
Floundering in savage mud,
Showing those muzzles huge enough to ponder
An epic cud.

And Tom beside a rat-hole in the boarding
Meets the still stare
Of eyes fiercer than his eyes and a large lithe body
Above him there—
Despondent grow the inmates of the barnyard;
Not one achieves
The super-powers of those super-mammals
Beneath the eaves!

## PRETTY FUTILITY

Pretty Futility
Always declares
There's nothing so good
As a basket of pears,

Nothing so tranquil,
Nothing so sweet,
As eating ripe pears
In the quiet of heat.

She straightens her ruffles,
She smiles as she swings,
And when she has eaten
Futility sings.

## ON A NIGHT OF SNOW

Cat, if you go outdoors you must walk in the snow.
You will come back with little white shoes on your feet,
Little white slippers of snow that have heels of sleet.
Stay by the fire, my Cat. Lie still, do not go.
See how the flames are leaping and hissing low,
I will bring you a saucer of milk like a marguerite,

So white and so smooth, so spherical and so sweet—
Stay with me, Cat. Out-doors the wild winds blow.

Out-doors the wild winds blow, Mistress, and dark is the night.
Strange voices cry in the trees, intoning strange lore,
And more than cats move, lit by our eyes' green light,
On silent feet where the meadow grasses hang hoar—
Mistress, there are portents abroad of magic and might,
And things that are yet to be done. Open the door!

### A LADY COMES TO AN INN

Three strange men came to the inn,
One was a black man pocked and thin,
One was brown with a silver knife,
And one brought with him a beautiful wife.

That lovely woman had hair as pale
As French champagne or finest ale,
That lovely woman was long and slim
As a young white birch or a maple limb.

Her face was like cream, her mouth was a rose,
What language she spoke nobody knows,
But sometimes she'd scream like a cockatoo
And swear wonderful oaths that nobody knew.

Her great silk skirts like a silver bell
Down to her little bronze slippers fell,
And her low-cut gown showed a dove on its nest
In blue tattooing across her breast.

Nobody learned the lady's name
Nor the marvelous land from which they came,
But no one in all the countryside
Has forgotten those men and that beautiful bride.

## Donald Davidson

Donald Davidson was born August 18, 1893, in Campbellsville, Tennessee, was educated in his native state, and received his B.A. and M.A. degrees at Vanderbilt University. The son of a schoolteacher, he has taught, first in high schools and later at Vanderbilt University. He was one of the group which founded *The Fugitive,* that provocative little monthly which put Nashville on the literary map; in his turn he acted as editor of that magazine, and, later, as literary editor of the *Nashville Tennesseean.*

His first volume, *An Outland Piper,* was published in 1924. The diversity of its contents discloses, beneath a certain amount of echoing, a surplus of poetic energy. Although it is evident that Davidson is still "emerging," a fresh voice rises from the verses, even the most derivative.

*The Tall Men* (1927) is a work on a much larger canvas than anything previously attempted by Davidson. It testifies to an interesting phenomenon: that the Tennessee group was not at all "South-conscious" while it was publishing *The Fugitive,* but became very much so immediately upon the demise of its organ. This sectional consciousness may be seen in Ransom's later essays, in Tate's *Stonewall Jackson,* in Davidson's own belligerent prose. This consciousness mounted to a passion, a passion unfortunately without followers. The Tennesseean group was concerned with a crisis gathering through the South: the division between those intent on agrarianizing perished backgrounds and those who favor a "new South," a South obviously dominated by the North. *The Tall Men* is an expansion of this dichotomy in which Davidson (in a framework derived from Eliot on one hand and Masters on the other) contrasts the Tennessee of the hunters and soldiers with the Tennessee of the Buick-drivers. "Fire on Belmont Street," perhaps Davidson's finest poem, which was the Southern Prize Poem for 1926 and which acts as Epilogue, synthesizes *The Tall Men,* Davidson having built up, as Stephen Vincent Benét wrote, "A people, a State, a passage of time, and one man's mind." In the section entitled "Geography of the Brain," there is an eloquent section beginning:

> I have come a long way, I tell you. I am attended
> (The brain is attended here) by motley splendors:
> Dust of battles, creak of wagons, vows
> Rotting like antique lace; the smiles of women
> Broken like glass; the tales of old men blown
> From rheumy beards on the vague wind; silk gowns
> Crumbling in attics; ruffled shirts on bones
> Of gentlemen in forgotten graves; rifles,
> Hunting-shirts, Bibles, looms, and desperate
> Flags uncrowned.

Here is projected the nostalgia which haunts one part of this poet's work. Here also is a proof that he has come a long way.

Since 1930 Davidson has been chiefly occupied with the Agrarian movement, helping to direct its controversies and prepare its symposiums. His point of view is particularly revealed in *I'll Take My Stand.*

### CROSS SECTION OF A LANDSCAPE

> Here is the ice that girdles joyless ocean;
> Water girdling a sphere of quiet slime;
> Under it rock that has no light or motion
> Save from the twirl, the eternal pantomime.
>
> Under the rock is fire that dies by inches
> Over the slag and ash of old decay.
> Finally, what? The mathematician pinches
> Space to a point, in his ponderable way.

But when I was a boy I searched from pole to pole
Of a gaudy globe, a rainbow-colored ball,
Peeled the cover, unraveled the shiny whole
And was vexed to find at center nothing at all.


### SPOKEN AT A CASTLE GATE

Before you touch the bolt that locks this gate
Be warned. There's no return where you are going.
A sword is tinder at the touch of fate
And crumbles in a way beyond your knowing.

Something I've heard, but something less I tell.
An old man knows, advises; young men smile,
Blow slug-horns, chink a latch, or clank a bell.
I've watched a many a one this weary while.

You can hear the nightingales, I won't deny.
They always sing for eager souls like you,
Perched on their boughs of possibility,
Most vaguely heard and still more vaguely true.

And they are more, perhaps, than mere tradition.
They must exist, though none come back to say
How they are feathered, or what rare nutrition
Keeps them piping their sad peculiar lay.

Gardens there are, and Queens, no doubt, a-walking,
White blooms adrift on gold and marvelous hair.
Young men in murmurous dreams have heard them talking,
Leaped up, like you, and entered . . . vanished . . . where?

For all I know, the castle's just a dream,
A shadow piled to mask a dangerous ledge,
A fantasy blown from devils' lungs in steam,
Made permanent here, just on a chasm's edge,

Where you will plunge, forever, ever falling,
For infinite days and nights, a dark lump whirled
That hears or thinks it hears an old voice calling
Beyond the stars that cluster near this world;

A voice that follows you past endless night,
Familiar, yet not quite half-known or named,
The last and sorry remnant of delight
That you lived for, pursued, and touched, and claimed,

Even as you touch the bolt that locks this gate,
Smiling, with patience such as fits old men
Who prophesy. Ah, yes, what you create
Perhaps you'll find,—but never come back again.

### FIRE ON BELMONT STREET

*(Epilogue to "The Tall Men")*

He was a worthy citizen of the town.
"Where is the fire?" he babbled as he ran.
"The fire! The fire!" spat between pursy breaths.
He dropped his question, stuck his gross right hand
Against his watch-chain, ran, and stared, and sobbed,
*Out Belmont Street? My God, that's where I live!*
Stumbling with slow fat feet and tragic breath
While roaring sirens passed upon the wind.
And then I heard (what laughter!) blobs of heels
Pecking the night with hurry. Poor staccato,
Dragging a million feeble stumps across
The easy pavements while the flames went up,
Gobbling the roofs and sky. Beneath was earth.
Steady against all shouting, ground was waiting
Forever subtle, old. But walls dissolved
And houses quaked with Fire until I could
Endure no more, but ran, as clamorous
As all the plump mad mob, shouting like them:
"The fire," I cried. What fire? No gables burn,
Nor is that redness some unusual dawn
Sprawled against moonrise, nor a dragon's breath
Spurted from some old sewer you forgot,
Nor ghosts of the Red Men that your fathers knew,
Come back with devil-medicine to bombard
Your bungalows. Choctaw and Cherokee
Lie where the spitting Decherd rifles planted
Under the Tennessee grass, their tired bones.
The fire! What fire? Why, God has come alive
To damn you all, or else the smoke and soot
Have turned back to live coals again for shame
On this gray city, blinded, soiled, and kicked
By fat blind fools. The city's burning up?
Why, good! Then let her burn!
                                But I'll say more,
Remembering other odds, a narrow place,
A shock of arms, a cry of gables burning,
And there were gathered in that long grim room
Of warriors sixty who called Hnaef their lord,
Who saw the gray wolf creeping in the wood
And heard the grind of linden shields afar;
Surrounded were, yet held the door and died
While the strange light of swords and helmets made
The place like day.
                        But who will stand tonight,
Holding this other door against the press
Of brazen muscles? Who can conquer wheels

Gigantically rolled with mass of iron
Against frail human fingers? Who can quench
The white-hot fury of the tameless atoms
Bursting the secret jungle of their cells?
Oh, who can stay or ever chain the dull
Gnaw of the fiery smoke, eternally settling
Into the beating heart? There is no fire?
Only, perhaps, the breath of a Southern wind
That I have known too well in many a summer,
Drying the pulse, stopping the weary pulse,
Blowing the faint blood back in the curdled veins
Till there is no way to think of what might be
Better or worse. Yet maybe it were better
Climbing the tallest hill to cry at night:
"Citizens, awake! Fire is upon you, fire
That will not rest, invisible fire that feeds
On your quick brains, your beds, your homes, your steeples,
Fire in your sons' veins and in your daughters',
Fire like a dream of Hell in all your world.
Rush out into the night, take nothing with you,
Only your naked selves, your naked hearts.
Fly from the wrath of fire to the hills
Where water is and the slow peace of time."

There is a place where beech-trees droop their boughs
Down-slanting, and where the dark cedars grow
With stubborn roots threading the lichened rocks.
There the smooth limestone benches, rubbed
By warm primeval streams, yet hold the crystal
Forms of dead life. There on a summer's evening
The screech-owl quavers and unseen July-flies
Trill their thin songs. And there my father said,
Pointing a low mound out to me, "My son,
Stand on this Indian's grave and plainly ask,
*Indian, what did you die for?* And he'll say,
Nothing!"
                So was it! So it is!
What did you die for? Nothing, indeed nothing!
The seed of the white man grows on Indian graves,
Waxing in steel and stone, nursing the fire
That eats and blackens till he has no life
But in the fire that eats him. White man, remember,
Brother, remember Hnaef and his sixty warriors
Greedy for battle-joy. Remember the rifles
Talking men's talk into Tennessee darkness
And the long-haired hunters watching the Tennessee hills
In the land of big rivers for something.

### APPLE AND MOLE

For a heavy long time on the long green bough
Hangs the apple of a summer that is shaken
From its flat hot road to its apple-topped hill
With the scraping of a mole that would awaken.

He is under the turf of the long green meadow,
Snuffling under grass and lusty clover
With a sure blunt snout and capable paws
Up the long green slope past the beeches and the haws,
For the summer must be shaken and over.

It's a heavy long time that an apple must hang.
He is butting out a path; he is shoveling a furrow,
Till the tree will be a-quiver, feeling mole at the root,
It is tall, it is green, but he will burrow,

Till the root will be sapless and the twig will be dry,
And the long green bough will be shaken.
The apple is too old, it has worms at the core,
And the long green summer will be green no more.
The apple will fall and not awaken.

# F. R. McCreary

F. (FREDERICK) R. MC CREARY was born in Hartford, Connecticut, September 18, 1893, and was educated at the Hartford public schools and Syracuse University. Between 1915 and 1919 McCreary worked at a dozen different occupations from grave-digging to advertising. He neglects the details, saying, "I must admit that I dislike those writers who have had all the plebeian odd jobs that I have—'the pick and shovel poets,' 'Verses by a Postman,' 'The Minstrel of the Cornfields,' etc.— and using it all for publicity."

McCreary made his first definite impression with "Before Winter," a rhapsodic but unrhetorical poem which appeared in *Voices*. It is one of the high moments in his volume, *The Northeast Corner* (1925), a splendidly illuminating set of images bound by an emotional unity. There is not a figure in this too little known poem which is hackneyed nor a single metaphor that is strained. It is a sure, deep-pitched voice which rises from such imaginative lines.

### BEFORE WINTER

Long ago
The thunder went talking itself back to the dark hills,
Long ago
The green rows of peas went marching to a tiger lily sunset

While the crickets were sharpening their sickles
For the last of the late August moon.
Now hydrangea breasts hang full and low
To nourish more tenderly
Whatever of sunshine,
And the smell of bruised apples rises from the long rotted grass.

Those who come from the fields
Come with their arms overflowing,
And there sounds from the ripe barns
The restless paw of heavy hoofs,
As the smoky wind and the dusk
Go stabling the horses of summer.

Did autumn come with white lips
Sucking at a black beach where no one could listen?
Did she come in a moment neither night time nor day
Whirling red laughter about her,
Long ribbons of ivy leaves, crimson?
Did you see her a gray-shawled woman of the twilight
Seated in a crotch of the hills,
Supping from a half-empty cup?
Or was she a mother, goldenrod tucked in her hair,
Singing to a sunflower poking his head through the corn?
O whoever she is
And however she came
I love her.

I looked hours and hours
Into long golden wells of Indian summer.
I saw my face at the bottom
And staring, remembering,
I suddenly left them
To look at the moon.

For autumn is the sound of a door softly closing at dusk,
Of an old man's voice
Counting over and again
The bushels he stores in the cellar,
The hush of a mother telling herself and her fire,
"Sarah, Thomas and Kate,
These are my children."

Then the curves of a scythe handle tempted my hands.
I grasped them,
And eagerly
I reaped for the last time.
April, June, and August,
I took what was left
And tied it in bundles for the winter.

The dark mistress of fall
Stands in her bare feet by the barn door
Holding a sickle in her hands.
I have helped her gather red apples,
Filling her apron,
And to slit the throats of fat swine;
I have helped her find the hoes and the rakes
And stacked them in a corner with the plow.
So she stands smiling,
Watching the swirl of the smoke mist,
The slow fall of leaves and the night.

I have helped her, but now I must turn from her, whispering,
"Mothers, knit and knit,
As you watch from your windows
The way of your children, their arms full of leaves,
Swaddling the rose bushes.
Barns, hunch your backs to the north,
For your lady is going with her sickle
To beat on the cool door of the snow wind.
Pools, swallow all the stars that you can,
For the ice will come
And cover you over."

September, October, and November,
They are fearless,
So now while the smolder of leaves in the ditches
With tongues of flame and fire
Utter words of autumn prayer,
Let you, my neighbor, and I,
Go through the silence of the tented evening corn.
Let us light a fire at the edge of the fields and the woodside,
And let us stand round it, watching the leap of the shadows,
Saying over and over to ourselves,
"This is our mother, our sky mother autumn,
Who brings shadows and death all about us,
Who fills our hearts with the glory of dying
And soothes us with the promise of snow."
We thrust our hands into the memory of the night
And grasping the hands of our earth fathers, earth mothers,
They who were loyal,
We stand till the last flare and flicker yields to the darkness,
And the darkness is peace.

### SINCE CHRISTMAS

These evenings since the Child was born
Strange shadows nudge the roadside thorn,
Strange lanterns light old windows up
Where alien mouths have come to sup.

Since Christmas time when God touched man,
When the ice reached deep and the snow began,
The weathercock at twilight feels
A strange wind snatch at his golden heels.

The fences tramp the fields all night
To keep the winter whole and white,
• But round each door at dawn's grim stare
Are tracks of doubt that have trespassed there.

Now the young men watch the new flame climb
From candles fat with unburned time,
But the old men listen with twitching cheeks
Each time the uneasy wind-vane speaks.

# Robert Nathan

ROBERT NATHAN was born in New York City, January 2, 1894. He was educated
at private schools there and in Switzerland. He completed his studies at Harvard, and returned to live in the city of his birth.

His first book, *Peter Kindred* (1919), was a mildly interesting novel which was
succeeded by the far more original *Autumn* in 1921. The delicately tinted prose as
well as the interpolated rhymes revealed the fact that Nathan was a poet in disguise,
so it was no shock to his admirers when *Youth Grows Old,* a collection of verses,
appeared within a few months after his successful prose. Although there is variety
in these fifty pages, it is the mood of restrained melancholy which Nathan best reproduces. But even the lightest of his stanzas is saved from sentimentality by an
ironically lifted eyebrow. As a sequence *Youth Grows Old* (1922) suffers from
being pitched in too low a key; as individual songs there is no denying the charm of
the lyrics, manifestly the work of one who is a composer as well as an author.

*The Puppet Master* (1923), *Jonah* (1925), *The Bishop's Wife* (1928) continue the
strain of gentle resignation spiced with satire. *Road of Ages* (1934) is a far more
ambitious novel, in which the irony deepens on a larger canvas than any Nathan
had hitherto attempted, although many readers preferred the lighter *One More
Spring* (1933).

*A Cedar Box* (1929) lacks force and its few pages proceed at a gait that is overleisurely. Nathan is not a modernist; there are no experiments or departures here.
There is, on the other hand, a little sadness, a little shrugging whimsicality, and not
a little wisdom. "Gentle" is the adjective most often applied to his books, but the
connotations are misleading. Nathan is gentle as a surgeon is gentle, as an analyst
is gentle when depths are being probed. More original sonnets have been written
by poets of his generation; but, unconcerned with originality, Nathan restates traditional themes and, by the serenity of his utterance, accomplishes that delightful
miracle which lifts platitude into poetry. "There is a peace that I have made my
own," he writes, and that half-tired, half-triumphant peacefulness emanates from
all his work. *Selected Poems* (1935) contains the best of Nathan's verse.

### AT THE SYMPHONY

#### (*César Franck, D Minor*)

The 'cellos, setting forth apart,
Grumbled and sang, and so the day
From the low beaches of my heart
Turned in tranquillity away.

And over weariness and doubt
Rose up the horns like bellied sails,
Like canvas of the soul flung out
To rising and orchestral gales;

Passed on and left irresolute
The ebony, the silver throat . . .

Low over clarinet and flute
Hung heaven upon a single note.

### WHEN IN THE CROWD I SUDDENLY BEHOLD

When in the crowd I suddenly behold
  Your small, proud head, so like a queen for grace,
Bearing its weight of spun and twisted gold
  Like an old crown on an imperial face;
When through the chime of gossip and the cries,
  I meet your glance, amused, serene, and bright
With some small secret, and behold your eyes
  Leap into laughter and immediate light,
Then as a bird might hear repeated over
  (His own song done) the same familiar part
From distant boughs and from the absent lover,
  And with that single beauty fill his heart,
I hear all other sounds, all other words,
Dwindle to silence like the sound of birds.

### I RIDE THE GREAT BLACK HORSES OF MY HEART

I ride the great black horses of my heart
  With reins of steel across their flying hair;
So slow are they to halt, so swift to start,
  The stormy-breasted stallions of despair.
Dark as the night and fretful as the air,
  Fleeter than hounds that go with bellies thinned—
My wrists of all their strength have none to spare
  When those black hunters lean upon the wind.
What if the sudden thunder of their feet
  Wakes like a dream some farmer from his rest?

Dreams had I too, farmer, before these fleet
 Steeds of the night had broken from their nest.
Their weary flanks are green and white with foam.
Sleep, brother, sleep; I bring my horses home.


### BECAUSE MY GRIEF SEEMS QUIET AND APART

Because my grief seems quiet and apart,
 Think not for such a reason it is less.
True sorrow makes a silence in the heart,
 Joy has its friends, but grief its loneliness.
The wound that tears too readily to confess,
 Can mended be, by fortune or by art,
But there are woes no medicine can dress,
 As there are wounds that from the spirit start.
So do not wonder that I do not weep,
 Or say my anguish is too little shown.
There is a quiet here, there is a sleep,
 There is a peace that I have made my own.
Man by himself goes down into the deep,
 Certain and unbefriended, and alone.


# *Mark Van Doren*

Mark van doren was born at Hope, Illinois, June 13, 1894, and was educated at the University of Illinois and at Columbia. He taught English at Columbia, and became literary editor of *The Nation*. Since 1920 he has lived in New York except for the part of the year that he spends on his farm in Cornwall, Connecticut.

Besides his verses, he has published four volumes of criticism. *Henry David Thoreau, A Critical Study* (1916) and *The Poetry of John Dryden* (1920) are the best of his analytical appraisals. He took upon himself the huge labor of editing *An Anthology of World Poetry* (1928), which assembles the world's best poetry in the best English versions, and compiled *American Poets 1630-1930* (1932) and *The Oxford Book of American Prose* (1932). A novel called *The Transients* (1935) succeeded only in puzzling most of its readers.

*Spring Thunder and Other Poems* appeared in 1924. A glance through its pages reveals that Van Doren has been influenced by Robert Frost. He, too, writes of homely bucolic things: of water wheels which need mending, a mountain house in December, the coming of alfalfa, river snow, and dry meadows. His emotion, like Frost's, is restrained. But if neither his subjects nor his point of view is particularly individualized, his mellowness is his own, and the spirit which moves beneath the contours of his verse personifies even the simplest of his quatrains.

*Now the Sky* (1928) reveals Van Doren as a more metaphysical poet. He is still concerned with ferns, dark barns, deserted hollows, but he grows more and more preoccupied with "the crumbling away of former bright edges of courage and causeless decay." He sits in a circle of maples, feeling the cosmic pulse, wondering how long men have watched Arcturus, hearing waves "of an old awareness," underground wisdom—and so "to the sun again, and the fever of learning." Van Doren's material is ordinary enough and his method needs no prolonged analysis. But his touch is fine and his sensibility pronounced.

*Jonathan Gentry* (1933) is an impressive chronicle of five generations, interspersed with lyrics. It is a narrative poem which just misses being a great work, chiefly because of its author's facility.

*A Winter Diary* (1935) is Van Doren's richest volume, even though the book represents an alternation of tradition and technical experiment. The title poem is a genre picture in precise heroic couplets; the following group is a sequence of Shakespearean sonnets, complete to the slightest Elizabethan conceit; the lyrics range from the most formal designs to unexpected arrangements, from the inevitable pairings of vowels to consonance, even to lyrics with no rhyme at all. Apart from their novelty, the lyrics represent Van Doren at his best; no reader can fail to appreciate the delicate music of such poems as "Always Evening," "Report of Angels," and "This Amber Sunstream" which ends:

> Another hour and nothing will be here.
> Even upon themselves the eyes will close.
> Nor will this bulk, withdrawing, die outdoors
> In night, that from another silence flows.
> No living man in any western room
> But sits at amber sunset round a tomb.

The title-poem is the finest sustained piece of writing Van Doren has accomplished. It is nearly twelve hundred lines long, yet there is not one forced nor flat couplet. It is rich in accurate observation, spiced with wit, and sensitive to the least detail of daily life on a northern winter farm. For sympathetic landscape and portrait painting there has been nothing like it in American poetry since Whittier's "Snow Bound."

## FORMER BARN LOT

Once there was a fence here,
　And the grass came and tried—
Leaning from the pasture—
　To get inside.

But colt feet trampled it,
　Turning it brown;
Until the farmer moved
　And the fence fell down;

Then any bird saw,
　Under the wire,
Grass nibbling inward
　Like green fire.

## IMMORTAL

The last thin acre of stalks that stood
　Was never the end of the wheat.
Always something fled to the wood
　As if the field had feet.

In front of the sickle something rose—
　Mouse, or weasel, or hare;
We struck and struck, but our worst blows
　Dangled in the air.

Nothing could touch the little soul
　Of the grain. It ran to cover,
And nobody knew in what warm hole
　It slept till the winter was over,

And early seeds lay cold in the ground.
  Then—but nobody saw—
It burrowed back with never a sound,
  And awoke the thaw.

### THE PULSE

One thing is sure
When most are not:
That there is cold,
That there is hot,

That winter stars
Are swollen blue
And that bright summer
Bulges too—

Getting the same
Black sky with child;
And both are big,
And both are wild.

There is no error
In the frost;
With warmth away
No warmth is lost;

Waves are coming
Of a time
That has been written
In slow rhyme:

Hot and cold,
And cold and hot—
All things may fail,
But this one not.

Though hate and love
And mercy cease,
Under the rippling
Vapor-fleece

Of earth goes warmth
Pursuing cold
And neither is young,
And neither is old.

### THE DISTANT RUNNERS

*Six great horses of Spain, set free after his death
by De Soto's men, ran West and restored to America
the wild race lost there some thousands of years ago.*
                                            —*A legend.*

Ferdinand De Soto lies
Soft again in river mud.
Birds again, as on the day
Of his descending, rise and go
Straightly West, and do not know
Of feet beneath that faintly thud.

If I were there in other time,
Between the proper sky and stream;
If I were there and saw the six
Abandoned manes, and ran along,
I could sing the fetlock song
That now is chilled within a dream.

Ferdinand De Soto, sleeping
In the river, never heard
Four-and-twenty Spanish hooves
Fling off their iron and cut the green,
Leaving circles new and clean
While overhead the wing-tips whirred.

Neither I nor any walker
By the Mississippi now
Can see the dozen nostrils open
Half in pain for death of men—
But half in gladness, neighing then
As loud as loping would allow.

On they rippled, tail and back,
A prairie day, and swallows knew
A dark, uneven current there.
But not a sound came up the wind,
And toward the night their shadow thinned
Before the black that flooded through.

If I were there to bend and look,
The sky would know them as they sped
And turn to see. But I am here,
And they are far, and time is old.
Within my dream the grass is cold;
The legs are locked; the sky is dead.

### THE ESCAPE

Going from us at last,
He gave himself forever
Unto the mudded nest,
Unto the dog and the beaver.

Sick of the way we stood,
He pondered upon flying,

Or envied the triple thud
Of horses' hooves; whose neighing

Came to him sweeter than talk,
Whereof he too was tired.
No silences now he broke,
No emptiness explored.

Going from us, he never
Sent one syllable home.
We called him wild; but the plover
Watched him, and was tame.

### THE WHISPERER

Be extra careful by this door,
No least, least sound, she said.
It is my brother Oliver's,
And he would strike you dead.

Come on. It is the top step now,
And carpet all the way.
But wide enough for only one,
Unless you carry me.

I love your face as hot as this.
Put me down, though, and creep.

My father! He would strangle you,
I think, like any sheep.

Now take me up again, again;
We're at the landing post.
You hear her saying Hush, and Hush?
It is my mother's ghost.

She would have loved you, loving me.
She had a voice as fine—
I love you more for such a kiss,
And here is mine, is mine.

And one for her—O, quick, the door!
I cannot bear it so.
The vestibule, and out—for now
Who passes that would know?

Here we could stand all night and let
Strange people smile and stare.
But you must go, and I must lie
Alone up there, up there.

Remember? But I understand.
More with a kiss is said.
And do not mind it if I cry,
Passing my mother's bed.

## Raymond Holden

RAYMOND HOLDEN was born in New York City in 1894 and educated at Princeton. He was, after several years of free-lancing, managing editor of *Travel Magazine* from 1923 to 1925, and on the staff of *The New Yorker* and *Fortune*.

His first volume, *Granite and Alabaster* (1922), is full of intellectual strength; even the lyrics have philosophic undertones. His poetry accomplishes a fusion of the scientific fact and its romantic associations, of the thing seen and the thing imagined. It is New England which Holden projects in this volume—a world of questioning skies and ghostly retrospects, of brooding uncertainties and somber speculations. This "wind-walled quietness," this freighting of lyrics with oblique philosophy, recalls the work of Robert Frost, to whom Holden is obviously indebted. There are moments when it is Frost's rather than Holden's voice which is heard in these poems. But, except for half a dozen pages, Holden maintains himself even when he is most under the spell of his teacher. His intonation falters, but not his intensity.

The work which Holden has published subsequent to *Granite and Alabaster* is not reminiscent of Frost. The ideas as well as the technique are tenser and he has shaken himself free of idiomatic mimicry. "Winter Among the Days," "Geese in the Running Water," and "Dead Morning," combine cool projection with warm sensuousness. "Dead Morning" is as strange and powerful a love-poem as has been written in this generation; "Proud, Unhoped-For Light," a still later poem, has the same personal outcry beneath objective reticence.

Besides his poetry, Holden has written prose of no mean value. Turning biographer he published *Abraham Lincoln* (1929) which, though not to be compared with Sandburg's work, is interesting for Holden's picture of the frontier-politician period and the slow growth of the man into the myth. He is also the author of two detective novels written under a pseudonym and a penetrating novel, *Chance Has a Whip* (1935).

### DEAD MORNING

When sleep, the supposed guardian,
That had its hands upon my eyes,
Dissolved in moistened light and ran
Among the grasses, water-wise,
I saw above my head a sun
And near me, in a breathless oak,
Two bitter crows and on a stone
A third, wing-deep in silver smoke.
I suddenly knew that this was death
And burial in bodiless air,
And that I should not feel your breath
Against my throat, nor have your hair
Pile at my cheek its sea-sweet smell,
Nor have your body's dolphin length
Balance its curve against my strength.
I knew that I had waked in hell.

### GEESE IN THE RUNNING WATER

The geese in the running water, among the snowy stones,
Matching their feet with the geese in the mirror brook,
Stand preening, ruffling the feathers that grow on their hollow bones,
And a man stares from the field with the slowness of sleep in his look.

The arm of the rising dawn, flung over the eastern cloud,
The coming of day which none were sure would come back,
Caught in the eddies among the wide feet of the proud,
Spreads its deep change of light on the changing shallow of black.

The grave, web-footed birds look down at their images,
At the five white-breasted geese left in the ebb of the shadow.
Time that was hurrying over is torn by the crowns of the trees
And thrown to the ground at the feet of the man who crosses the meadow.

## WINTER AMONG THE DAYS

O flavorless white hour
That like a drift of snow
Has cold tongues to devour
The warmth of mind we know,
How shall man take his rest
Between your surfaces?
Blood goes thin in the breast
And pride is on its knees.
He must lie, taking tally,
On an unfriendly bed,
Of days continually
Leaping with hoof and head,
Falling with many a bleat
Back to their level flock
As if their heart-shaped feet
Could shake the iron rock.
This winter-crackled doze
Watching ram after ewe
Is all the sleep man knows,
The sleep that must renew

The mind which like a hand
Holds the mere body hung
Upon another land
Older than this, yet young.

## LIGHT THE LAMP EARLY

Wide flocks of narrow birds have fled
The glaze of frost-embittered air.
On burrows where the woodchucks sleep
The curled and colored leaves are deep.
The worm winds in the fallen pear.
The ewe that bore the lamb lies dead.

Light the lamp early. Billow breath
Festoons with fog the chilly pane.
Ladder the lighted hearth with logs,
That, as dreams ruffle sleeping dogs,
Warmth in this room may help maintain
This precious life, this twitch in death.

## PROUD, UNHOPED-FOR LIGHT

"Because, because," the sound of the hard road said
Stepping up into my brain as I went downhill.
But it was only a sound that shook in my head
And the tongue of my mouth let the cold bright air be still.

Out of the pasture, rotten with apples, the cows
Swung their smooth necks, moving as if they swam.
The breath of the thin light parted the apple boughs
And ruffled the flanks of the filly and her dam.

There was no answer to be spoken and no need
To cry out through the quietness to ask and protest.
The proud, unhoped-for light, without fear or heed,
Eager and kind, lay down with the heart in my breast.

# Jean Toomer

JEAN TOOMER was born in 1894, in Washington, D. C., received his education in the public schools, taught for a time, and made his first impression as a writer in the more experimental magazines.

Cane (1923) is a rhapsodic volume, which, in spite of traces of Sherwood Anderson and the distinct influence of Waldo Frank, reveals a discriminating idiom.

Toomer is especially adept in effects of repetition and balance, as is evident in so subtle a lyric as "Song of the Son" and the more formal "Georgia Dusk." Even his prose has this balanced rise and fall; a short story, "Fern"—reprinted in Calverton's *An Anthology of American Negro Literature* (1929)—is not merely an intensified narrative but a prose lyric.

### GEORGIA DUSK

The sky, lazily disdaining to pursue
　　The setting sun, too indolent to hold
　　A lengthened tournament for flashing gold,
Passively darkens for night's barbecue.

A feast of moon and men and barking hounds,
　　An orgy for some genius of the South
　　With blood-hot eyes and cane-lipped scented mouth,
Surprised in making folk-songs from soul sounds.

The sawmill blows its whistle, buzz-saws stop,
　　And silence breaks the bud of knoll and hill,
　　Soft settling pollen where plowed lands fulfill
Their early promises of bumper crop.

Smoke from the pyramidal sawdust pile
　　Curls up, blue ghosts of trees, tarrying low
　　Where only chips and stumps are left to show
The solid proof of former domicile.

Meanwhile, the men, with vestiges of pomp,
　　Race memories of king and caravan,
　　High-priests, an ostrich, and a juju-man,
Go singing through the footpaths of the swamp.

Their voices rise . . . the pine trees are guitars,
　　Strumming, pine-needles fall like sheets of rain . . .
　　Their voices rise . . . the chorus of the cane
Or caroling a vesper to the stars . . .

O singers, resinous and soft your songs
　　Above the sacred whisper of the pines,
　　Give virgin lips to cornfield concubines,
Bring dreams of Christ to dusky cane-lipped throngs.

### SONG OF THE SON

Pour, O pour that parting soul in song,
O pour it in the sawdust glow of night,
Into the velvet pine-smoke air tonight,
And let the valley carry it along,
And let the valley carry it along.

O land and soil, red soil and sweet-gum tree,
So scant of grass, so profligate of pines,
Now just before an epoch's sun declines,
Thy son, in time, I have returned to thee,
Thy son, I have, in time, returned to thee.

In time, for though the sun is setting on
A song-lit race of slaves, it has not set;
Though late, O soil, it is not too late yet
To catch thy plaintive soul, leaving, soon gone,
Leaving, to catch thy plaintive soul soon gone.

O Negro slaves, dark purple ripened plums,
Squeezed, and bursting in the pine-wood air,
Passing, before they stripped the old tree bare
One plum was saved for me, one seed becomes

An everlasting song, a singing tree,
Caroling softly souls of slavery,
What they were, and what they are to me,
Caroling softly souls of slavery.

# E. E. Cummings

E. E. (EDWARD ESTLIN) CUMMINGS, born in Cambridge, Massachusetts, in 1894, first attracted considerable attention by his curiously punctuated and even more strangely spaced poems in *The Dial*. What was most pronounced in his experiments was an eccentricity of pattern intended to accentuate a startling idiom. Because of these superficial oddities, Cummings was soon attacked by the orthodox as a literary nihilist and hailed by his misled admirers as a new leader of "the left wing." Cummings received, in fact, almost every sort of criticism except a detached one. His book on Russia, *Eimi* (1933), proved him to be anything but a revolutionist.

An unpartisan appraisal reveals several facts. First, Cummings is no more radical than any poetic experimenter who, attempting certain verbal effects, commits errors in emphasis and proportion. His preoccupation with typographical design has often tricked him; much of his work suffers because of his distortions, and that part of it which succeeds is successful in spite of, and not because of, its form. Second, he seems utterly incapable of self-criticism; his work, whether in an eruptive or quiet vein, has both the verve and the brashness of adolescence. It is evident that Cummings is extremely fecund, and so it is not strange that his first book, *Tulips and Chimneys* (1923), is a jumble of imaginative exuberance, cool precision, and archaic affectations. His is a mind which is, in quick succession, lyrical, fantastic, grotesque, pathetic, savage. His distorted punctuation is significant of esthetic immaturity. The breaking up of words which have an integrity only as long as they are joined, and the denoting of the first person singular with a small i fail to achieve either emphasis or modesty. In destroying what are usually essentially simple patterns, Cummings is likely to provoke the reader to nothing more than irritation. As has been implied, beneath his surface eccentricities which are responsible for his notoriety, Cummings' emotions are not at all bizarre; often they are actually banal. Unstrangled by the malformed calligrams adapted from Apollinaire, one detects a clean and distinct voice. Cummings is, after all, not so far from orthodoxy; his couplets remain couplets, even though he wedges white paper between them, and his appealingly youthful catalog of his lady's charms loses nothing by appearing in a form as regular as Villon's.

Above all, this poet exhibits a genuine gift of fresh imagination. His is undoubtedly a rhetorical language, but the rhetoric of Cummings has sometimes as fine a swing as any since Swinburne. It would be a pity if the annoyance caused by Cummings' visual disorganizations were to render the reader deaf to phrases as persuasive as, "Thy fingers make early flowers of all things," "The bulge and nuzzle of the sea," "Thy mouth is a chord of crimson music," "Thy forehead is a flight of flowers," "In the street of the sky night walks scattering poems," "Thoughts more white than wool," "Spring comes—the lean and definite houses are troubled," "The sea through her blind miles of crumbling silence."

*The Enormous Room* (1922), which preceded the poetry, is a novel, a brilliantly realized study of character against an intensified background of the War. Except for a few passages, it is orthodox in form.

Cummings' first volume of poetry was succeeded by *XLI Poems* (1925), the privately printed *&* (1925)—the sections of which were properly divided into A, N, and D—and *is 5* (1926), evidently so-called since this is volume five of Cummings' works. These, and his phantasmagoric play *him,* may, as Laura Riding and Robert Graves declare in *A Survey of Modernist Poetry,* "be considered conveniently to illustrate the divorce of advanced contemporary poetry from the common-sense standards of ordinary intelligence" and that "his only fault is that he has tried to do two things at once: to remain loyal to the requirements of the poetic mind for clearness, and to get the ordinary reading public to call the result 'poetry.'" It is to be suspected, however, that Cummings is little concerned with "the ordinary reading public" and cares more for his own pleasure in the mixing of grave and piquant. This mixture is the principal component of all his writing. Whatever the surface differences, whether the piece is a brusque satire or an involved drama, there is the same serious intent disguised by jig-saw typography, the same school-boy nose-thumbing interrupting a romantic and unashamed tenderness.

The mixture continues in maturity. In *No Thanks* (1935) there is again the sensitive commentator and the ornery boy, the skillful draughtsman and the leg-pulling cheapjack, the theorist, the lyric poet, and the clown. Often Cummings tries to be all these creatures at one time, often in the same poem. The result at forty is scarcely edifying. Here are, once more, the little eccentricities we have come to expect of the author—the purposeful mis-spellings, the cutely disrupted syllables, the nose-thumbing exhibitionism, the interpolation of a comma or a parenthesis or an arbitrary capital in the middle of an unimportant word, the dismemberment of a passage and its *disjecta membra* strewn over the page. And there are—as there always are in Cummings' volumes—a few unaffected lyrics; an almost sentimental tenderness is not quite elbowed out by the grimaces.

## WHEN GOD LETS MY BODY BE

when god lets my body be

From each brave eye shall sprout a tree
fruit that dangles therefrom

the purpled world will dance upon
Between my lips which did sing

a rose shall beget the spring
that maidens whom passion wastes

will lay between their little breasts
My strong fingers beneath the snow

into strenuous birds shall go
my love walking in the grass

their wings will touch with her face
and all the while shall my heart be

With the bulge and nuzzle of the sea

## SUNSET

stinging
gold swarms
upon the spires
silver
            chants the litanies the
great bells are ringing with rose
the lewd fat bells
                    and a tall

wind
is dragging
the
sea

with

dream

-S

## IMPRESSION—IV

the hours rise up putting off stars and it is
dawn
into the street of the sky light walks scattering poems

on earth a candle is
extinguished      the city
wakes
with a song upon her
mouth having death in her eyes

and it is dawn
the world
goes forth to murder dreams. . . .

i see in the street where strong
men are digging bread
and i see the brutal faces of
people contented hideous hopeless cruel happy

and it is day,

in the mirror
i see a frail
man
dreaming
dreams
dreams in the mirror

and it
is dusk        on earth

a candle is lighted
and it is dark.
the people are in their houses
the frail man is in his bed
the city

sleeps with death upon her mouth having a song in her eyes
the hours descend,
putting on stars. . . .

in the street of the sky night walks scattering poems

LA GUERRE

I

the bigness of cannon
is skillful,

but i have seen
death's clever enormous voice
which hides in a fragility
of poppies. . . .

i say that sometimes
on these long talkative animals
are laid fists of huger silence

I have seen all the silence
filled with vivid noiseless boys

at Roupy
i have seen
between barrages,

the night utter ripe unspeaking girls.

II

O sweet spontaneous
earth how often have
the
doting
        fingers of
prurient philosophers pinched
and
poked
thee
, has the naughty thumb
of science prodded
thy

beauty            , how
often have the religions taken
thee upon their scraggy knees
squeezing and

buffeting thee that thou mightest conceive
gods
        (but
true
to the incomparable
couch of death thy
rhythmic
lover

        thou answerest

them only with
                spring)

CHANSON INNOCENT

in Just-
spring        when the world is mud-
luscious the little
lame baloonman

whistles        far        and wee
and eddieandbill come
running from marbles and
piracies and it's
spring

when the world is puddle-wonderful

the queer
old baloonman whistles
far        and        wee

and bettyandisbel come dancing
from hop-scotch and jump-rope and

it's
spring
and
    the
       goat-footed

baloonman      whistles
far
and
wee

## ALWAYS BEFORE YOUR VOICE

Always before your voice my soul
half-beautiful and wholly droll
is as some smooth and awkward foal,
whereof young moons begin
the newness of his skin,

so of my stupid sincere youth
the exquisite failure uncouth
discovers a trembling and smooth
Unstrength, against the strong
silences of your song;

or as a single lamb whose sheen
of full unsheared fleece is mean
beside its lovelier friends, between
your thoughts more white than wool
My thought is sorrowful;

but my heart smote in trembling thirds
of anguish quivers to your words,
As to a flight of thirty birds
shakes with a thickening fright
the sudden fooled light.

It is the autumn of a year:
When the thin air is stooped with fear,
across the harvest whitely peer
empty of surprise
death's faultless eyes

whose hand my folded soul shall know
while on faint hills do frailly go
The peaceful terrors of the snow,
and before your dead face
which sleeps, a dream shall pass)

and these my days their sounds and flowers
Fall in a pride of petaled hours,
like flowers at the feet of mowers
whose bodies strong with love
through meadows hugely move.

yet what am i that such and such
mysteries very simply touch
me, whose heart-wholeness overmuch
Expects of your hair pale,
a terror musical?

while in an earthless hour my fond
soul seriously yearns beyond
this fern of sunset frond on frond
opening in a rare
Slowness of gloried air. . . .

The flute of morning stilled in noon—
noon the implacable bassoon—
now Twilight seeks the thrill of moon,
washed with a wild and thin
despair of violin.

## SONG

Thy fingers make early flowers of
all things.
thy hair mostly the hours love:
a smoothness which
sings, saying
(though love be a day)
do not fear, we will go amaying.

thy whitest feet crisply are straying.
Always
thy moist eyes are at kisses playing,
whose strangeness much
says; singing
(though love be a day)
for which girl art thou flowers bringing?

To be thy lips is a sweet thing
and small.
Death, thee i call rich beyond wishing
if this thou catch,
else missing.
(though love be a day
and life be nothing, it shall not stop kissing).

PORTRAIT

Buffalo Bill's
defunct
          who used to
          ride a watersmooth-silver
                                        stallion
and break onetwothreefourfive pigeonsjustlikethat
                                                            Jesus
he was a handsome man
                              and what i want to know is
how do you like your blueeyed boy
Mister Death


SONNET

a wind has blown the rain away and blown
the sky away and all the leaves away,
and the trees stand. I think i too have known
autumn too long

                    (and what have you to say,
wind wind wind—did you love somebody
and have you the petal of somewhere in your heart
pinched from dumb summer?
                                        O crazy daddy
of death dance cruelly for us and start

the last leaf whirling in the final brain
of air!) Let us as we have seen see
doom's integration . . . a wind has blown the rain

away and the leaves and the sky and the
trees stand:
                    the trees stand. The trees,
suddenly wait against the moon's face.


# H. Phelps Putnam

H. PHELPS PUTNAM was born in Boston, Massachusetts, in 1894. After the usual
public school education, he attended Phillips Exeter Academy and Yale College. Reacting from academic education, he worked in an Arizona copper mine, in
Washington as a government historian, in the importing business in New York,
and as an editorial assistant in Boston. In 1923, he left the latter position to spend
the year in Provence. Returning to America, he endeavored to make a serious profession out of what was a serious avocation, his first book, *Trinc,* appearing in 1927.

*Trinc* is sharply divided by its two sections. The first ("Green Wine") is straightforward and lyrical, a set of frankly youthful reactions. The second half ("Brandy") is built about an impressionistic structure in which myth and modernity combine. The symbols used by Phelps are archaic, but the expression is distinctly of the moment. His method is similarly contradictory, being alternately oblique and abruptly four-square. Thus his chief effect is achieved by esthetic shock, a device which Phelps frequently overdoes.

> "I travel brokenly, and I shall know,
> With Hermes and the alchemists—but, hell,
> What use is it talking that way to you?
> Hard-boiled, unbroken egg, what can you care
> For the enfolded passion of the Rose?"

Such incongruities are thrown across his pages until his transitions seem like the mere turn of a trick. But if, as Allen Tate wrote, "his attitude springs, in part, from the current romanticism of the 'hard-boiled,' the main feature of which is the worship of the crude, the barbaric, the 'un-intellectual,'" his Bill Williams, Hasbrouck, Jack Chance are figures in a new cosmogony. These heroes, presenting a latter-day scorn of the intelligence, are usually drunk (*Trinc,* according to Panurge, being "a Panomphean Word, signifying Drink") and always rugged; nevertheless—again by the contradiction of the author's spirit—their disintegrated sensitivities move in an undoubted atmosphere of poetry.

"Ballad of a Strange Thing" is such a poem. Translating Daphne from Thessaly to the township of Pollard Mill and Apollo into a bawdy harvester, Putnam accomplishes something more than surprise. In what is one of the most interesting of contemporary ballads, he makes an old myth immediate and gives backwoods America a nimbus of antique legend.

*The Five Seasons* (1933) is a philosophical-narrative poem in which the central figure struggles to find a basis for action. It is a not wholly successful but extremely interesting study of cross-purposes.

### BALLAD OF A STRANGE THING[1]

His name was Chance, Jack Chance, he said,
And that his family was dead.
He was a lucid fool, his eyes
Were cool and he beyond surprise.
Into the township Pollard Mill
He came in autumn alone one day,
Loafing along those roads which still,
Though dying in the grass, report
That lumber-sledges went that way.
He came idly and in our town
He raised a flight of birds, a brown
And silver flock, and underneath
Their wings were tinged with gold; his breath

[1] It is interesting to compare this treatment of a myth with Elizabeth Madox Roberts' use of a similar theme in "Orpheus," page 316.

Blew and the birds dipped and rose
As if they surely lived which were
But lies of the calm sorcerer.

Autumn came bringing free
Melancholy, but to me
Brought Jack, when I was sitting there
In the open barn door-way where
The sun moved in and I could get,
Drifting by, the sound and smell
Of late bees and of mignonette
From the dying garden by the wall,
And hear the thin defeated bell
Of distant time, and see the tall
Elms beyond the orchard slopes
Rising improbably, like hopes
Swaying above the mind, and I
Was sitting there and he came by.

Under his hat I saw his eyes
Measuring without disguise
The ripeness of my house,
And measuring myself, and he
Turned in, approached and spoke to me.
He had decided undismayed
This was the place for Chance, and I
The boy for him; and so he stayed.

And then the days moved gravely by,
Time drowned in fluent clarity
Flowing between him and me,
Who only lay along the walls
Unashamed of indolence, and heard
The dusty harvesters' harsh calls
To sweating teams, loading the sheaves
On the steep withered fields—their care
Was none of ours; or reasoned there
Where the mill-pond burned with leaves
And rustled at the dam, on those
Stark thoughts that rose
Out of cool spoken words, or we
Loafing in the arbor ate
Slowly the warm grapes, the rusty
Creaking swallows skimmed
The long ridgepoles, the day grew late
Easily, and dimmed.

At night we made a fire to mark
A spot of mirth against the dark,
There in a pasture which lay high
On the nearness of the sky.
Other countrymen would come,
Young farmers, farmers' men, and sons,
One after one they learned to come
And laugh with Chance and tap the old
Keg of cider, acrid gold,
Which we had borne carefully
Out of the cellar where it lay,
Drowsing wickedly it lay
Waiting for us to set free
Its vigor and its treachery.
Then Jack would sing his bawdy songs:
That old ballad which belongs
To timelessness, *The Bastard King,*
Or *Doctor Tanner,* or *Mademoiselle,*
Or *Lil* who died of lechering.
She died with her boots on, as they tell,
With a champion lad between her knees.
Or he would sometimes please,

If drinking brought delusion near,
To tell corrosive tales, the mere
Garments of lies, the cunning kind
Which echo somewhat in the mind,
And then they go, and you are more
Dull and baffled than before.

There went by then, in such a way,
Serene October; the last day
Came and the night was newly cold.
But the fire was high and the old
Cider burned within and we,
A dozen foolish farmers, kept
Alive the late hilarity
Of autumn, and the township slept.
Then Chance arose from where he sat
Against the keg and cocked his hat
Sideways and, walking slow around
The fire, said—"I have always found
Nothing new among much change;
But this I tell you now is strange:

It was at noon, the hour of sleep
For those who use their nights
In the deluding piracy
Of shadowy delights.

And so I slept, above the bank
Above the River Still,
Under an oak, the least of two
That rose under the hill.

But a sound crept through my nerves
And I woke and I could hear
Feet running fast and close,
Down the hill and near,

Then stop; and heard a noise like sobs
And stood up quietly
And peering saw that a breathless girl
Was clutching the other tree.

And then a man came following,
Loping leisurely,
And when he stood beside her said,
'I knew you would wait for me.'

And then she turned at bay; she was
Astonishingly rare,
A young ascetic fury she
Was something almost strange to me
With her honey fallen hair.

Yes—and have waited even too long,
Before now, to be glad,
Watching your insolence too long—
Oh, you were the gorgeous lad
With your dark lovely face and all
The women you have had.

I have seen the rabbits follow you
Unasked and eagerly;
O ladies, you should see him now,
Begging a kiss of me.'

She ceased, and we all three were still
While he admired her,
And I kept hidden watching them,
For I have that character.

He did not mock her when he spoke,
Where do they get these dull
Flash melodramas in their skulls?
And such a dainty skull.

Listen, I keep no list of names
For vanity; and I
Dislike the names and odors and ways
Of women; I am shy
Of their domestic wills; and I
Am tired of the melting lie.

But there you are—and sometimes love
Is more than remembered skill.'
'Love,' she said, 'is the rust which ate
The clean rancor of my will.'

He raised his quiet hand to touch
Her hair, but she
Turned sharply down the bank and he
Now followed instantly.

And there below the godly stream
Was whispering in its beard,
And she cried, 'Save me, River Still!'
Then stepped and disappeared.

Well—so far nothing strange;
But after that the queer
Began, and I have seen these things,
And I, the bastard son of change,
Would dare to call them queer.

I saw the girl had gone entirely,
And in her place a dry
Shivering graceful sheath of reeds
Sprang up, suddenly high;

And that he, following so close
That her hair was in his face,
Clutched and had no girl but had
Sharp reeds in his embrace.

He stepped back, looking at his hands
All laced with blood; a spike
Broke short and stood between his ribs
Most murderous like.

This feller was not eager now,
But only dazed,
And pulled the wet spike from his side,
Fumbling and amazed.

He stooped slowly to bathe his hands,
Then from his pocket drew
A folded knife and cut one reed,
Murmuring, 'This will do.

Sometimes there's music in these girls,
Sometimes,' and sitting then
He made a whistle which he tried
And changed and tried again.

He blew five even notes and stopped,
But the sound rippled away
Slowly, as if a sweet clang came
From the leaves and hummed away.

And then there came along the bank
A black majestic goat
With yellow eyes and gilded horns
And a white beard at its throat.

The goat lay down before his feet
Respectfully, dipping its head,
And the man laughed and, 'Can this be
A messenger?' he said.

And played again and now more wild
And cloudily intricate,
And the goat arose and danced like one
Hieratic and sedate.

And that is all," said Chance, and then
He said, "So long," and walked away
Casually, as if the night were day.
And we jumped up calling, and then
Stood silent for over us coldly fell
Five piercing notes, each like a spark;
We stood there stiffly and immersed,

Hearing laughter in the dark,
Until I spoke, being the first,
"We had better go home now to bed;
We have drunk too much," I said.

Thereafter the rains beat down
The autumn, the drenched leaves came down
From the black trees, choking the ditches,
And over the sea came sons-of-bitches
With a hollow quarrel, the talking rats
Of England and of Europe slithered
Down the hawsers, doffed their hats
And squealed; and the plague spread and
    came,
Taking the cleanly name
Of honor for its strange device,
Even to our town; the conscript lice
Played soldiers over Pollard Mill
And pitched their camp on the River Still;
But no more Jack, and we were more
Dull and baffled than before.

### ABOUT WOMEN

Fair golden thoughts and lovely words—
Away, away from her they call,
For women are the silly birds,
And perching on a sunny wall

They chirp the answer and the all;
They hold for true all futile things—
Life, death, and even love—they fall
To dreaming over jeweled rings.

Their bodies are uncouthly made,
And heavy swollen like a pear,
And yet their conquered, undismayed
And childish lovers call them fair.
Their honor fills them full of care,
Their honor that is nothingness,
The mystery of empty air,
The veil of vain delightfulness.

Their subtleties are thin and pale,
Their hearts betray them in their eyes:
They are a simple flute, and frail,
With triple stops for playing lies.
These poor machines of life are wise
To scorn the metaphysic glow,
The careless game that laughs and dies,
The heady grace they cannot know.

Well, give them kisses, scatter flowers,
And whisper that you cannot stay;
We shall have clarity and hours
Which women shall not take away.

## Genevieve Taggard

GENEVIEVE TAGGARD was born November 28, 1894, on an apple farm at Waitsburg,
Washington. At the age of two she was taken by her parents to Hawaii, where
she remained, with one brief interval, for the next eighteen years. She attended the
University of California, edited the college literary magazine, and graduated in 1919.
Two years later, in New York, with a group of other poets, she helped found *The
Measure,* that journal of poetry which was particularly hospitable to the modern
lyric. She taught at Bennington College, in Vermont, beginning in 1931 and, be-
ginning in 1935, at Sarah Lawrence College.

Her first volume, *For Eager Lovers,* was published in 1922. In spite of the banal
title, Miss Taggard's lines are unaffected and her general statements have almost
personal definiteness. It is always a sensitive artist speaking through such melodies
as "The Enamel Girl," and "With Child." *Hawaiian Hilltop,* a leaflet of poems
about her childhood in the tropics, was published in 1923. It proved that Miss Taggard was at her best in the more extended lyric; such a poem as "Solar Myth" is
more vivid, more richly delineated than most of her shorter melodies.

*Words for the Chisel* (1926) was notable for the long narrative "Poppy Juice" which opened the volume. Less comment was accorded the finer lyrics in which Miss Taggard had acquired a style subtle and colloquial. No poet could be more self-critical than was Miss Taggard, for two years later she made a selection from her previously published volumes and, after ten years' work, retained exactly twenty-eight poems for *Travelling Standing Still* (1928). The title is more fortunate than the one immediately preceding it in date of publication, for Miss Taggard's manner is far from stony. There is, it is true, a hardness here, but it is the tensity of emotion, not the toughness of a metallic technique. Such poems as "With Child" and "Dilemma of the Elm" proceed from experiences which are common and yet freshly observed.

*Not Mine to Finish* (1934) is as inconclusive as its title. It is a curious mixture, or, rather, a contradiction of moods, styles, and effects; part of it proceeds from Miss Taggard's natural lyrical gift, part from the strain of her recent (and poetically unconvincing) conversion to communism. Such a poem as "Try Tropic" is both sensuous and scrupulous; many of the other verses are either careless or shrill. The poet seems unhappily split, shifting, as Louise Bogan wrote, "between the high romantic desire to be struck dead by delight and the high revolutionary ambition to write songs for the people."

*Circumference,* a collection exhibiting "varieties of metaphysical verse" from Donne to E. E. Cummings, was edited by Miss Taggard and published in a distinguished format in 1930. She is also author of *The Life and Mind of Emily Dickinson* (1930), a sensitive if somewhat too fanciful combination of biography and speculation.

### WITH CHILD

Now I am slow and placid, fond of sun,
Like a sleek beast, or a worn one:
No slim and languid girl—not glad
With the windy trip I once had,
But velvet-footed, musing of my own,
Torpid, mellow, stupid as a stone.

You cleft me with your beauty's pulse, and
    now
Your pulse has taken body. Care not how
The old grace goes, how heavy I am grown,
Big with this loneliness, how you alone
Ponder our love. Touch my feet and feel
How earth tingles, teeming at my heel!
Earth's urge, not mine—my little death, not
    hers;
And the pure beauty yearns and stirs.

It does not heed our ecstasies, it turns
With secrets of its own, its own concerns,
Toward a windy world of its own, toward
    stark

And solitary places. In the dark,
Defiant even now, it tugs and moans
To be untangled from these mother's bones

### THE ENAMEL GIRL

Fearful of beauty, I always went
Timidly indifferent:

Dainty, hesitant, taking in
Just what was tiniest and thin;

Careful not to care
For burning beauty in blue air;

Wanting what my hand could touch—
That not too much;

Looking not to left or right
On a honey-silent night;

Fond of arts and trinkets, if
Imperishable and stiff.

They never played me false, nor fell
Into fine dust. They lasted well.

They lasted till you came, and then
When you went, sufficed again.

But for you, they had been quite
All I needed for my sight.

You faded. I never knew
How to unfold as flowers do,

Or how to nourish anything
To make it grow. I wound a wing

With one caress; with one kiss
Break most fragile ecstasies . . .

Now terror touches me when I
Dream I am touching a butterfly.

### SOLAR MYTH

(Maui, the dutiful son and great hero, yields to
his mother's entreaty and adjusts the center of the
universe to her convenience. The days are too short
for drying tapa. He is persuaded to slow down the
speed of the spider-sun with a lasso of sisal rope.)

The golden spider of the sky
Leaped from the crater's rim;
And all the winds of morning rose
And spread, and followed him.

The circle of the day swept out,
His vast and splendid path;
The purple sea spumed in the west
His humid evening bath.

Thrice twenty mighty legs he had,
And over earth there passed
Shadows daily whipping by,
Faster, faster, fast . . .

For daily did he wax more swift,
And daily did he run
The span of heaven to the sea,
A lusty, rebel sun.

Then Maui's mother came to him
With weight of household woes:
"I cannot get my tapa dry
Before the daylight goes.

"Mornings I rise and spread with care
My tapa on the grass;

Evenings I gather it again,
A damp and sodden mass."

Then Maui rose and climbed at night
The mountain. Dim and deep
Within the crater's bowl he saw
The sprawling sun asleep.

He looped his ropes, the mighty man,
He whirled his sisal cords;
They whistled like a hurricane
And cut the air like swords.

Up sprang the spider. Maui hurled
His lasso after him.
The spider fled. Great Maui stood
Firm on the mountain-rim.

The spider dipped and swerved and pulled
But struggle as he might,
Around one-half his whirl of legs
The sisal ropes cut tight.

He broke them off, the mighty man,
He dropped them in the sea,
Where there had once been sixty legs
There now were thirty-three.

Maui counted them, and took
The pathway home; and came
Back to his mother, brooding,—strode
Like a lost man, and lame.

The tarnished spider of the sky
Limped slowly over heaven,
And with his going mourned and moaned
The missing twenty-seven.

On with a hollow voice he mourned,
Poured out his hollow woe;
Over each day the sound of him
Bellowing, went below.

Maui saw the gulls swarm up
And scream and settle on
The carcass of the limping thing
That once had been the sun.

But still he thought at length to have
His mother satisfied.
"Can't you put back his legs again
Now all my tapa's dried?"

The days are long and dull," she said,
I loved to see them skim." . . .
Vearily the old sun shook
'he black birds off of him.

## DOOMSDAY MORNING

)eaf to God, who calls and walks
Jntil the earth aches with his tread
ummoning the sulky dead,
Ve'll wedge and stiffen under rocks
)r be mistaken for a stone,
.nd signal as children do, "Lie low,"
Vait and wait for God to go.

'he risen will think we slumber on
ike slug-a-beds. When they have gone
'rouped up before the Judgment Throne
Ve in the vacant earth, alone,—
bandoned by ambitious souls,
.nd deaf to God, who calls and walks
ike an engine overhead
)riving the disheveled dead,—
Ve will rise and crack the ground,
ear the roots and heave the rocks,
nd billow the surface where God walks,
nd God will listen to the sound
.nd know that lovers are below
Vorking havoc, till they creep
'ogether, from their sundered sleep.

'hen end, world! Let your final darkness
 fall!
nd God may call . . . and call . . . and
 call.

## TRY TROPIC

*n the Properties of Nature for Healing an
Illness*

'ry tropic for your balm,
 ry storm,
 nd after storm, calm.
 ry snow of heaven, heavy, soft, and slow,
 rilliant and warm.
 Iothing will help, and nothing do much
 harm.

)rink iron from rare springs; follow the sun;
 o far

To get the beam of some medicinal star;
Or in your anguish run
The gauntlet of all zones to an ultimate one.
Fever and chill
Punish you still,
Earth has no zone to work against your will.

Burn in the jeweled desert with the toad.
Catch lace
In evening mist across your haunted face;
Or walk in upper air the slanted road.
It will not lift that load;
Nor will large seas undo your subtle ill.

Nothing can cure and nothing kill
What ails your eyes, what cuts your pulse in
 two,
And not kill you.

## DILEMMA OF THE ELM

In summer elms are made for me.
 I walk ignoring them and they
Ignore my walking in a way
I like in any elegant tree.

Fountain of the elm is shape
For something I have felt and said. . . .
In winter to hear the lonely scrape
Of rooty branches overhead

Should make me only half believe
An elm had ever a frond of green—
Faced by the absence of a leaf
Forget the fair elms I have seen.

(A wiry fountain, black upon
The little landscape, pale-blue with snow—
Elm of my summer, obscurely gone
To leave me another elm to know.)

Instead, I paint it with my thought,
Not knowing, hardly, that I do;
The elm comes back I had forgot
I see it green, absurdly new,

Grotesquely growing in the snow.
In winter an elm's a double tree;
In winter all elms trouble me.

But in summer elms are made for me.
I can ignore the way they grow.

# E. Merrill Root

E. MERRILL ROOT was born in Baltimore, Maryland, in 1895. He spent most of his life, however, in New England, attending Amherst College, where he studied under Robert Frost. He was one of the editors of *The Measure,* a teacher and lecturer at Earlham College, Richmond, Indiana.

Lost Eden (1927) and *Bow of Burning Gold* (1929) betray, even in their titles, Root's mixture of influences. His verse, forthright and self-declared, sometimes suffers from its own downrightness, emerging from what is evidently a transitional period. But his protests are spontaneous, and from an avowedly romantic vision he reaches toward a poetry that has breadth. His descriptions are particularly rich; his poetry, writes Genevieve Taggard, "is often like the paintings of Rousseau—his animals rise up in the midst of thick blades of plants. He achieves what few moderns even try to achieve: the difficult welding of being and intellect."

## SCRUB OAK

I am like a scrub oak tree:
Granite is good earth for me.
I am small—but very tough:
Rock, for me, is food enough.
Elms may lift their pebbled towers
Higher, and the October flowers
Of the maples flush and blaze
Brighter than my sober phase;
But I hold my steadfast bronze
Leaves when they are skeletons.

Also in the summer I,
All that earth can do, defy:
Barren ledge and burning earth
Are foundation of my mirth.
There my silver-shaggy boughs
Feed the wildwood deer, not cows;
And that pert and furry flame—
The red-squirrel—in mad game
Runs across my leafy hills
For his emerald domiciles.
Oven-bird and loud towhee
Have a strong green shield in me,
Bravely held against the sun.
Under my low bosses run
Fragrant gloss and dainty twine
Of wintergreen and partridge-vine.
And (while I turn the sun's shock)
Spring's lusty burnished partridge-cock
Beats his wings until they drum
Love's superb exordium.

Rock below and sun above—
Such is the harsh life I love;
Sun above and rock below—
Still I bud, and leaf, and grow:
Like little Jack in the old tale
I fight my giants—and prevail.

In serenity I fashion
With quiet power and quiet passion
Stalwart, loving-intricate
Cups to hold the glossy freight
Of the future's forests shut
In the brown joke of a nut.

Ice storms come, and ice storms go;
Fire's crimson rivers flow
Flooding with their tidal waves
My green homely architraves:
Quietly I rise again
Over violence or chicane—
Defying from the deeper granite
The skin-diseases of the planet.

Listen to a scrub oak tree
Speaking his philosophy:
"Rock and sun and sand are good
Always to a brave man's mood:
Build on waste and desolation
Your green towers of affirmation;
If no God or man be fed,
Offer deer their emerald bread;
Tho you shield no man or maid,
Give the little rabbits shade!"

## PRETTY POLLY

An agile noisy jungle flower he flies
Where monkeys pelt fierce peccaries with nuts;
And alligators lurk for chance supplies
'Neath river villages of tree-top huts.

When the Brazilian sun—a red-hot drum—
Rises, he screams a challenge with gold beak
To tell the jungle that the day is come;
Then preens each crimson feather with a tweak.

Fed with Andean milk, the Amazon
Glitters between the forests where he dines;
He gathers golden fruit or lunches on
The lustrous berries of vanilla vines.

He shouts at pythons looped like harmless boughs,
Or the poor sleepy sloths that scarcely move;
He ruffles plumes and utters lyric vows
To tell some pretty parrot-flirt his love.

And he will guard, a brilliant sentinel,
The hollow nest where in a round warm egg
His son lies prisoner in a quiet cell,
Waiting his scarlet wing, his golden leg.

And when the sun, like some red armadillo,
Burrows into the West and birds must doze,
Cushioned all night upon an airy pillow
The parrot sleeps—except his gripping toes.

But someday it may be a Caliban
Will capture him and sell him to a cage
In our gray North, and make brass bars the span
Of one who had a jungle heritage.

*Bird of bronze lyrics once, who blazed and flew,*
*He will become a thing of solemn folly*
*To please old maids or yokels at a zoo:*
*He'll ask for crackers and say, "Pretty Polly!"*


# Robert Hillyer

ROBERT (SILLIMAN) HILLYER was born in East Orange, New Jersey, June 3, 1895. He attended Kent School and Harvard College. After graduating from the latter, he was an ambulance driver with the French army from 1917 to 1919, was at Copenhagen as Fellow of the American-Scandinavian foundation in 1921, and since that time has been Assistant Professor of English at Trinity College (from which he received the honorary degree of A.M.), and Associate Professor of English at Harvard.

Hillyer's first book was as innocuous as its title, *Sonnets and Other Lyrics* (1917), following which came six volumes of varying merit. Hillyer's seventh, entitled with an appropriateness suspiciously like a pun *The Seventh Hill* (1928), is his best. On the surface the verse seems to lack that sense of discovery which distinguishes poetry from versification. But this is only because Hillyer's technique and idiom are traditional. His experiences, if not unique, are significant and his utterance, though full of foreign and unmistakable accents, has unmistakable authority. Possibly because there is nothing local in his subject-matter or treatment, Hillyer's work found more favor in England than in America. *The Halt in the Garden* (1925) had a foreword by Arthur Machen and elicited high praise from Middleton Murry.

Though the contours of this poetry are delicate to the point of elegance, the spirit upholding them has a sustaining strength. "Prothalamion," which is the peak of the volume, is typical. Upon a theme which has done duty since the beginning of art, in a form which is uncompromisingly classical, Hillyer has constructed twenty-six stanzas, not one of which falls below a high seriousness.

*The Collected Verse of Robert Hillyer* (1933) confirms the praise of those critics who found Hillyer's poetry traditional in form but animated with feeling and "colored by something from within." It received the Pulitzer Prize in 1934, and the award drew attention to the longer poems as well as to the shorter lyrics. One of his most recent works, "Variations on a Theme," reveals (as Hillyer wrote of Santayana) "dignity and sumptuousness of phrasing" and sureness of technique. In the version printed here, the last section (the recapitulation) has been omitted.

Besides his verse Hillyer has published one book of prose, *Riverhead* (1931), a cross between a novel and a spiritual autobiography, the work of a poet throughout.

### AS ONE WHO BEARS BENEATH HIS NEIGHBOR'S ROOF

As one who bears beneath his neighbor's roof
Some thrust that staggers his unready wit
And brooding through the night on such reproof
Too late conceives the apt reply to it,
So all our life is but an afterthought,
A puzzle solved long past the time of need,
And tardy wisdom that one failure bought
Finds no occasion to be used in deed.

Fate harries us; we answer not a word,
Or answering too late, we waste our breath;
Not even a belated quip is heard
From those who bore the final taunt of death;
And thus the Jester parries all retort:
His jest eternal, and our lives so short.

### PASTORAL

So soft in the hemlock wood
The phoenix sang his lullaby,
Shepherds drowsed where they stood,
Slumber felled each passerby,
And lovers at their first caress
Slept in virgin loneliness.

Not for mortal eye to see
Naked life arise from embers;
Only the dark hemlock tree
Evergreen itself, remembers
How the Word came into being,
No man hearing, no man seeing.

From the taut bow of sleep
Shoots the phoenix toward the day,
Shepherds wake and call their sheep,
Wanderers go on their way.
Unaware how death went by,
Lovers under the hemlocks lie.

### PROTHALAMION

#### (Second Section)

he hills turn hugely in their sleep
Vith sound of grinding rock and soil
Vhile down their granite shoulders leap
he waterbrooks in white turmoil.
he vigil of Good Friday done,
Our second spring ascends the height;
he earth turns southward toward the sun,
And trees which guard the pascal door,
a leaf once more,
Once more are murmurous with strange delight.

or now is the world's Eastertide,
And born that they may die again
Arise from death the gods who died.
Osiris, slender as young grain,
Comes back to Isis; the shy lad
Adonis wakens by the stream;
And Jesus, innocently clad
a samite, walks beneath the trees,
Half ill-at-ease
hat Judas and the Cross were but a dream.

And thou art she whom I have seen
Always, but never understood,

In broken shrines festooned with green,
In twilight chapels of the wood;
Or on the hills a shepherdess
Walked with the sun full on her face,
And though her body and her dress
Appareled her in meek disguise,
I dropped my eyes,
For still I knew the goddess by her pace.

I know thee now in morning light
Though thou art wrought of flesh and blood,
And though the mother of the night
Resumes at dawn her maidenhood;
And though love severed with his knife
The girdle of the million years
And yielded to importunate life
The toll she asks of those who still
Would journey, till
They pass her known and visible frontiers.

The children from beyond the sun
Come bounding down the hillside grass,
And in the joyous rout is one
Who smiles and will not let us pass.
He stands, the fairest of them all,
And in his loveliness I trace
Thy loveliness. His light footfall
Bends not the grass he treads upon;
But he is gone
Before my eyes have feasted on his face.

Let him go back beyond the air;
This spring is ours, it is not his;
Those eager lips would take their share
Of love's yet undiminished kiss.
Fairer than he, as young, as gay,
As much a child, forget all things,
All but this transitory day
Of love, all things but love, and give
Thy fugitive
Delights to me who fly but with thy wings.

In undulant desire we merge,
On tides of light we sport and rest;
We swerve up from the deeper surge
To hover on the trembling crest
Of joy, and when the wave has passed,
Then smooth is the swing to the abyss
Of quietness, where with a last
Eye-darkening smile, we say farewell
Until the spell
Shall be renewed. Forget all things but this.

No grass-blade bends, no shadow stirs;
Love mounted high, slumber is deep;
Deep is the spring beneath the firs,
A sweet and lonely place for sleep.
And waking, we shall cool our flesh
In depths so clear they seem as air;
Twofold in beauty, thou refresh
Thy body in that water, bright
With muted light,
And brighter still for thy reflection there.

While I along the bank shall find
The flowers that opened with the day
Still dew-drenched, and with these entwined
New fronds of fern or darker bay.
Or pausing in a shaft of sun
That strikes across the mottled glade
Watch thee too long, beloved one,
Watch thee with eyes grown big with tears
Because the years
Suddenly spoke and made my heart afraid.

Giver of immortality—
That was thy name within the shrine—
The Mighty Mother, Star of the Sea,
All syllables of love were thine
To wear as lesser women wear
The garlands of their fragile spring;

Why then within my heart this fear
Of time? why then amid the shout
Of life, this doubt
That clouds the new sun like an outspread
    wing?

We must not to a foe like time
Yield up our present. Take my hand
And up the morning we shall climb
Until the wooded valley land
Lies all beneath us in the drowse
Of love's meridial aftermath;
The trellis of entwining boughs
Trembles in the great joy of green,
But does not screen
The comfortable glimpse of homeward path.

We will not to our ancient foe
Yield all this happiness; it lies
Shielded from sickle and from snow
And all the menace of the skies.
At night I shall watch over thee,
The future safe beneath thy breast,
And after autumn there shall be
Dayspring, when for each other's sake
We shall awake
And follow Love beyond the unknown west.

### NIGHT PIECE

There is always the sound of falling water here;
By day, blended with birdsong and windy leaves,
By night, the only sound, steady and clear
Through the darkness and half-heard through sleepers' dreams.
Here in the mottled shadow of glades, the deer,
Unstartled, waits until the walker is near,
Then with a silent bound, without effort is gone,
While the sound of falling water goes on and on.

Those are not stars reflected in the lake,
They are shadows of stars that were there aeons ago;
When you walk by these waters at night, you must forsake
All you have known of time; you are timeless, alone,
The mystery almost revealed, like the breath you take
In the summer dawn before the world is awake,
Or the last breath, when the spirit beyond recalling
Goes forth to the sound of water for ever falling.

Swift as deer, half-thoughts in the summer mind
Flash with their hints of happiness and are gone;
In the dark waters of ourselves we find

No stars but shadows of stars which memory lost.
Dark are the waters under the bridge we crossed,
And the sound of their falling knows neither end nor start.
Frail are your stars, deep are your waters, mind;
And the sound of falling water troubles my heart.

### VARIATIONS ON A THEME

#### I

You walk up a deep roadbed to a hilltop,
The trees are splintered and the sun is gray,
Shells rip the cheese-cloth air, and curling gas
That smells of death, out of the lungs of death
Breathes, it is like the sap of slaughtered poplars
Rancid with spring, it is like the breath of old men
Who have been dead a long time but still breathe.
Shell by shell you note the approaching range,
Methodical,—no doubt after a graph
Devised by the professors in Berlin,
And thus defeated by its own precision.
A scattered fire might, by a random chance,
Drape you like garlands on a broken tree,
But this! it is to laugh. You need not wince
Or fling yourself face down in mud until—
Well, until then! By God, they broke the rules;
That nearly got you. You must telegraph
Berlin and file complaints with the professors.
Euclid was wrong. The parallels have met.
But you're all right, stop jabbering the Lord's Prayer,
Since it was answered, and go on with Mozart,
G-minor Symphony, the second movement.
And now with Mozart playing in your skull
Tread daintily among the rats and shell-holes,
Pick your way up the hill between the fragments
Of men and horses, let the blue gas curl.
Listen, that pizzicato on the 'cellos.
Lovelier always with the increasing beauty
Of spring, which to an adolescent rapture
Yields not one half its glories, saving all
For those whose spring finds winter in their hearts.
Plucked strings are louder, if you listen for them,
Than shells exploding, and dead suns are brighter
Than Very lights or fear. Death is no rampart
From which, methodical, the fusillades
Of hidden foes come nearer and yet nearer
Until you gauge their range and duck. It is
Not as you think it, not dead breath of poplars;
It is a chance that after sundry warnings
Plotted methodically by distant science,
The shell will miss you, and you will arrive

Up on the hillcrest after lonely walking,
The sun grown splendid for the sunset glory
Hanging above a land ruined but quiet,
And friends whose voices waken you from nightmare,
Singing amid your tangled strands of Mozart:
"The Armistice! We have signed the truce with Death!"

## II

"What! you were in the war! I'd never guess it
Reading your books. What a strange man you are.
Think of dear Brooke and Seeger and Joyce Kilmer,—
Of course, they all met heroes' deaths,—but still
How can experiences so profound
Have failed to leave one comma on your verses?"
"Bird droppings, madam, are not punctuation,
However fair the bird, you do but join
The illimitable clamor of bad causes
Which deafen poetry. I must confess
Though born an Anglo-Catholic, I am
Lazy but not a skeptic, and although
Romantically I take the side of kings
I am no Royalist, and neither am I
Enamored of Moscow, for within her streets
I find not even so faint a trace of verse
As metric crowsfeet in the bloodstained snow.
These causes! You will find ten thousand of them
If you read Gibbon. The damned things are dead.
Search Shakspere and prepare for me a list
Of his outpourings on the Spanish menace
With rhetoric reserved for the Armada."
"But first, Shakspere was not aboard that flagship
Of Effingham's; and second, you're not Shakspere."
"True! True, and thirdly, there is a landscape
Where green Connecticut shrouds Massachusetts
In haze on haze on hills falling away,
Like lovely lies obscuring ugly fact.
I fear—to use geography as figure—
I am Connecticut. I face the ocean,
Yet of its turmoils hear but far-off surf;
I face the mountains yet climb never to them;
I face the mills of booming Massachusetts
Yet do not sweat nor jingle coin in pocket;
I face New York and let her lights be distant,
As seasonable shifts on pine and oak
Show the sun changing after winter solstice.
I listen always in my mind to music
That sings away my worries and the world."

## III

However much you love your wife, your child,
Time will divide you, and however much

You love yourself, time will divide you also
Into the many parts you have forgotten.
It is triumphant that the mortal man
Remembering so many deaths, can still
Sing in the twilight and take heart at dawn
And lift his cup and say: You, my beloved.
Surely beyond that moment's apprehension,
Beyond his conscious thought, beyond the depths
Of his unconscious where the false Messiahs
Bungle amid the delicate corals, and blow
Foul-smelling bubbles to the surface world
And signal with dream-cables: Watch my breath!
Surely beyond thought and all pseudo-science
Of the mind's last profundities, where Faith
Alone is Sea King, surely the soul dwells,
Timeless, immortal, alert to songs of earth
And knowing that when he says: You, my beloved,
Echoes start out and ring the golden spheres
To meet in perfect circles beyond space
And there to find again the voice they sprang from.
This is good physics, you who disbelieve
Acknowledge that your voice has also started
Motion throughout the Universe, and never
Though you should chase it through Paolo's whirlwind
Shall you catch up with it. You'd eat your words
But cannot, while throughout resounding space
The syllables of love clap laughing hands.
Whatever starts in time cannot be stopped.
Wherefore lift up your hearts all you that love
Gravely as well as passionately; wherefore
Take heed, you wastrels of the sacred word.
For time bequeaths her patience to eternity
Wherein so many ages beyond counting
Have poured what seemed immense and what was lost
In immensity and found in new dimensions.
However much you love your wife, your child,
Time will divide you, and beyond division
Eternity echoes: "You, you my beloved."

# Howard McKinley Corning

HOWARD MC KINLEY CORNING was born October 23, 1896, on a farm a few miles west of Lincoln, Nebraska. He spent the years of his youth in Ohio, but his schooling there was limited on account of ill-health. In 1919 his family journeyed to "the epic greenland of Oregon," where he took up his residence on Mount Tabor on the edge of Portland. It was here that he became a florist by vocation, raised prize poultry, and composed most of his verse.

His first volume, *These People* (1926), placed Corning as the leader of the group of young Oregon poets, a group which expressed itself through the work of H. L. Davis (whose "Primapara" received one of the prizes awarded by *Poetry: A Magazine of Verse*), Borghild Lee, Charles Oluf Olsen, Ethel Romig Fuller. Corning's equipment was greater than those of his fellows. Strangely enough, though *These People* was strongly local and Western in character, it was not without its foreign— and New England—influences. The inflection of E. A. Robinson directs though it does not dominate Corning's periods; in the subsequent poems the bantering metaphysics of Robert Frost are apparent. These lift Corning's preoccupations above a too rigid reporting and save him from a tendency to fall into monotonous reflections of monotony.

*The Mountain in the Sky* (1930) fulfills the promise of Corning's first book. The faults are accentual and not basic; the substance of his work is solid; its competence and sincerity are confirmed.

### PRUNING VINES

In February, when the sap's below
The inattentive earth, I take my shears
And prune away the too-audacious years.
It's grapes I want, and not mere leafy show.
I trim the trailing year's growth to a span,
With only laterals intact for crop;
A snip or two and I know where to stop
To bring a harvest where my hooks began.
It takes some fortitude to cut a vine
Half into dead ends for the cloying mold,
Where growth takes profit as the shears take hold,
Cutting the heart a little . . . as I cut mine.
But since it's grapes I want, I understand
How to rebuke the heart to fill the hand.

### AUTUMN BIRD

In autumn pastures where a bird had flown
I sought behind the curtains of the wind.
It wasn't any bird that I had known.
I followed it to leave my heart alone.

What bird it was it swiftly interlined
The meadow fence, and lo,
It left me thinking that my eyes were blind
Losing a bird so quickly, undefined.

It may have been that autumn's waning glow
Had seared my sight. It may have been that kind
Of bird that is less bird than hint of snow.
Perhaps it was the autumn I saw go.

## FAREWELL TO FIELDS

Farewell; the dark is falling on the wind.
Far off the lights of slumber lift and wane.
From harvest fields our hands are gone; the kind
Last grace is rain.

The little ends of stubble will not miss
Our feet, astride; but drinking at the stem
Be cool without a need, so kind is this
That covers them.

Then farewell; let them drink. Let sleep
Be outward bound for us, though deep the bed.
We, who were the hands to sow and reap,
We have been fed.

## THE MEADOW BROOK RUNS OVER

Whatever intentions
The brook had at first,
It broke its dimensions:
The meadow immersed.

The blade stood up silver,
The flower wore pearl
The bee could not pilfer
Nor warm wind uncurl.

A temporal sea
To the lark and the plover,
The sky looked to be
As under as over.

The oak stood a dwarf.
The water-skate ran his
Prow from the wharf
Of the clover-side crannies.

A month, and new flowers
Will never say here
Lay water for hours . . .
So heaven draws near,

Antiphonal, seen
A seasonless season;
Then lost in-between
The dream and the reason.

## Louise Bogan

LOUISE BOGAN was born in Livermore Falls, Maine, August 11, 1897, and was educated in country schools through New England and at the Girls' Latin School in Boston. Except for a year in Vienna and another in Santa Fé, she has lived in New York State since 1919.

*Body of This Death* (1923) is one of the most brilliant first books of the period. The accent is not new; we have already heard it more crisply in Elinor Wylie's precise syllables. But if Miss Bogan lacks her forerunner's dazzling craftsmanship, she achieves effects not unworthy of her subtlety. There are less than thirty poems in her volume and only two of them cover more than a page. Yet every stanza gives evidence of a mind which is as sensitized as the eye is sharp, an intellect which, for all its burden of thought, expresses itself best in the lyric. The longer blank verse is only moderately interesting compared with such a vivid screen as "Decoration" or so cool and chiseled a piece as "Statue and Birds." Few of her contemporaries have surpassed the finesse of these—few indeed have equaled it—while the bright contempt of "Women" and the frozen imagery in "Medusa" seem destined for more than contemporary applause.

*Dark Summer* (1929) emphasizes the impression made by her first volume. The technique, no longer so scintillating, is simpler; the accents, deep, bell-like, vesperal, are more her own. The metaphysical note has strengthened, the beat of measured blood has become more pronounced. "Simple Autumnal" and "Come, Break with Time" suggest Léonie Adams without implying indebtedness. Miss Bogan's poems, rooted in observation, rich in implication, are swiftly intuitive and her spirit has confirmed her intuitions.

Sometimes her spare definiteness reminds one of the later Yeats; sometimes the slow pace of her measures is too consciously thickened. But, mostly, mood and measure join to preserve her accurate quality.

### MEDUSA

I had come to the house, in a cave of trees,
Facing a sheer sky.
Everything moved,—a bell hung ready to strike,
Sun and reflection wheeled by.

When the bare eyes were before me
And the hissing hair,
Held up at a window, seen through a door.
The stiff bald eyes, the serpents on the forehead
Formed in the air.

This is a dead scene forever now.
Nothing will ever stir.
The end will never brighten it more than this,
Nor the rain blur.

The water will always fall, and will not fall,
And the tipped bell make no sound.
The grass will always be growing for hay
Deep on the ground.

And I shall stand here like a shadow
Under the great balanced day,
My eyes on the yellow dust that was lifting in the wind,
And does not drift away.

### WOMEN

Women have no wilderness in them,
They are provident instead,
Content in the tight hot cell of their hearts
To eat dusty bread.

They do not see cattle cropping red winter grass,
They do not hear
Snow water going down under culverts
Shallow and clear.

They wait, when they should turn to journeys,
They stiffen, when they should bend.
They use against themselves that benevolence
To which no man is friend.

They cannot think of so many crops to a field
Or of clean wood cleft by an ax.
Their love is an eager meaninglessness
Too tense, or too lax.

They hear in every whisper that speaks to them
A shout and a cry.
As like as not, when they take life over their door-sills
They should let it go by.

### DECORATION

A macaw preens upon a branch outspread
With jewelry of seed. He's deaf and mute.
The sky behind him splits like gorgeous fruit
And claw-like leaves clutch light till it has bled.
The raw diagonal bounty of his wings
Scrapes on the eye color too chafed. He beats
A flattered tail out against gauzy heats;
He has the frustrate look of cheated kings.
And all the simple evening passes by:
A gillyflower spans its little height
And lovers with their mouths press out their grief.
The bird fans wide his striped regality
Prismatic, while against a sky breath-white
A crystal tree lets fall a crystal leaf.

### STATUE AND BIRDS

Here, in the withered arbor, like the arrested wind,
Straight sides, carven knees,
Stands the statue, with hands flung out in alarm
Or remonstrances.

Over the lintel sway the woven bracts of the vine
In a pattern of angles.
The quill of the fountain falters, woods rake on the sky
Their brusque tangles.

The birds walk by slowly, circling the marble girl,
The golden quails,

The pheasants closed up in their arrowy wings,
Dragging their sharp tails.

The inquietudes of the sap and of the blood are spent.
What is forsaken will rest.
But her heel is lifted,—she would flee,—the whistle of the birds
Fails on her breast.


### THE ALCHEMIST

I burned my life that I might find
A passion wholly of the mind,
Thought divorced from eye and bone,
Ecstasy come to breath alone.
I broke my life to seek relief
From the flawed light of love and grief.

With mounting beat the utter fire
Charred existence and desire.
It died low, ceased its sudden thresh.
I had found unmysterious flesh—
Not the mind's avid substance—still
Passionate beyond the will.


### SIMPLE AUTUMNAL

The measured blood beats out the year's delay.
The tearless eyes and heart forbidden grief,
Watch the burned, restless, but abiding leaf,
The brighter branches arming the bright day.

The cone, the curving fruit should fall away,
The vine-stem crumble, ripe grain know its sheaf.
Bonded to time, fires should have done, be brief,
But, serfs to sleep, they glitter and they stay.

Because not last nor first, grief in its prime
Wakes in the day, and knows of life's intent.
Anguish would break the seal set over time
And bring the baskets where the bough is bent.

Full seasons come, yet filled trees keep the sky,
And never scent the ground where they will lie.


### CASSANDRA

To me, one silly task is like another.
I bare the shambling tricks of lust and pride.
This flesh will never give a child its mother,—
Song, like a wing, tears through my breast, my side,

And madness chooses out my voice again,
Again. I am the chosen no hand saves:
The shrieking heaven lifted over men,
Not the dumb earth, wherein they set their graves.

### COME, BREAK WITH TIME

Come, break with time,
You who were lorded
By a clock's chime
So ill afforded.
If time is allayed
Be not afraid.

*I shall break, if I will.*
Break, since you must.
Time has its fill,
Sated with dust.
Long the clock's hand
Burned like a brand.

Take the rocks' speed
And earth's heavy measure.
Let buried seed
Drain out time's pleasure,
Take time's decrees.
Come, cruel ease.

# Joseph Auslander

JOSEPH AUSLANDER was born in Philadelphia, Pennsylvania, October 19, 1897. He attended St. Catherine's School in Philadelphia, the Eastern District High School in Brooklyn, Harvard University, and The Sorbonne. In 1922 he became a teacher at Harvard and in 1924 his first volume, *Sunrise Trumpets,* appeared with a foreword by Padraic Colum.

The outstanding feature of *Sunrise Trumpets* is its technique. Auslander is an adroit fashioner of polished phrases, of smoothly slipping terms of speech. The music which he employs is wholly traditional; he disdains none of the older properties no matter how often they have been repeated. But, if Auslander is a promiscuous lover rather than a critical connoisseur of words, his romantic and, it may be suspected, rather conscious intoxication scatters a profusion of arresting epithets and images. He hears a cricket "stitching the dark edge of dawn," a cock "rapping in four rickety words his challenge to the sluggard," a bell which "jargons like water dripping in a well." If his verse seems to force the emotion rather than to allow the emotion to direct it, one remembers poems like "Interval," "Dawn at the Rain's Edge," and bits of illumination like "the hawk-dark trees," "water torturing through frozen snow," "the sulky gradual querulous content of chickens puffed and blinky in the sun," "lone gulls blown about the sky," "the bronze rumor of bees." •

Auslander's chief fault is his straining after effects which are not so much dramatic as theatrical. Verbal felicity becomes a coddled facility, and the simplest of objects is described with excess. There is something extraordinarily comic about picturing a cow in the pasture in such terms as

> . . . fragrantly plunging
> Down at the web-washed grass and the golden clover
> Wrenching sideways to get the full tingle. . . .
> Crushing a murmurous afternoon of late lush August to wine!

*Cyclop's Eye* (1926) has sharper edges. The poet, though still inclined to over-decorate, is less determined to make his strings quiver with a continual *vibrato*. He seeks for toughness and sometimes, as in "Knockout" and "Steel," attains it. *Letters to Women* (1929) is not so fortunate. Although some of the stanzas are shrewd, the book errs on the side of adulation and affectation. The author of these missives seems to have been so overcome by his subjects that he degenerates into the confused softness from which he had almost shaken himself free. He indulges in orgies of words—of words about words—and (in the "Letter to Elinor Wylie" for example) ties himself up in phrases and metaphors as hopelessly mixed as:

> O restless heart! O deft and ravenous brain
>   Whose diamond arithmetic devoured
> Confusion—only to be lost again
>   After the stringent epithet had flowered!

When Auslander is not so preoccupied with overloading the strange or saccharine epithet his verse has more quality. *Hell in Harness* (1929) is an unsuccessful over-compensation. Attempting the brusque savagery of Joseph Moncure March's *The Set-Up* and *The Wild Party,* Auslander's exaggerations are as glaring in his strained patois as in his abuse of precious words.

*No Traveller Returns* (1935) suffers from the same affectations which marred Auslander's earlier volumes. Here, however, the romantic lyricist is at war with himself; he wages an inconclusive struggle against his desire to prettify his objects. He would like to become one of the prophetic poets, but he is tricked by an ineradicable impulse to rely on the frayed trappings of the poetic stock-room, on a blurred composite pattern of April willows, bees, sea-gulls, mist,

> Weaving verses out of wind and rain
> And mist and buds and early morning.

This is a pity, for there is a genuine lyricist here. He can turn from light songs to the darkness of a deep human experience; he has a fine command of rhythms. In spite of a determinedly lush tone and an impulse to write too much poetry about poetry, the poet has something to say. Moreover, his taste, essentially sound when considering the poetry of the past and unconcerned with himself, is proved by *The Wingèd Horse* (1927) and *The Wingèd Horse Anthology* (1929), both of which were compiled in collaboration with Frank Ernest Hill.

### INTERVAL

Water pulls nervously whispering satin across cool roots, cold stones;
   And a bird balances his soul on a song flash, a desperate outcry:
These are the minor chords, the monotones;
   This the undefeated gesture against an armored sky.

The moment is metal; the sun crawling over it is a fly
   Head down on a bronze ceiling; the hot stillness drones:
And you go sliding through green sea shafts and I
   Am an old mountain warming his tired bones.

### ULYSSES IN AUTUMN

I, who knew Circe, have come back
To sink a furrow in the loam;
Left twilights bellowing and black
For the soft glow of home:
To hear instead of a guttural sea
The needles of Penelope.

Still in my heart the Trojan sack
Hisses; and Helen's beauty goes
Glimmering. . . . And I have come back
To drink the stale cup of repose—
I, who knew Circe, and the wine
That turns men grunting into swine.

Can I forget Achilles? Fly
For ever from Calypso's guile?
The roaring red pit of that Eye
Drown in some domestic smile?
Cluck at a sweaty plow, who led
The white-flanked stallions of Diomed?

No, for these nerves are iron yet,
And in these veins, this caverned breast,

Echoes the howling parapet;
The trumpets will not let me rest. . . .
Think you Odysseus drowses so
Who still can bend the terrible bow.

The lotus voices call my blood
Implacable and rumorous:
All night there drums a ghostly thud
Of feet. . . . O young Telemachus,
Plead with your mother to release
My spirit fevered for the Fleece!

The trees are straining in the storm,
Spattering gold; and from the sea
The old tang creeps between the warm
Breath of her lovely flesh and me:
Each dank leaf dripping down in fire
Fuels the dream of Troy and Tyre.

I know it will be some little thing
Like wild geese in a streaming wedge
Severely beautiful; a string
Of bird-prints on the water's edge
That suddenly shall crack galley whips
And hurl me headlong to the ships!

### DAWN AT THE RAIN'S EDGE

The drowsy, friendly, comfortable creak
   Of axles arguing and wet spokes gleaming,
When old empty tumbrels blunder dreaming, too sleepy to speak,
   Blunder down the road in the rain dreaming.

And the house-lights rub at the shining dripping shadows
   Over the windows; through the drenched silver willows; everywhere:
In the sulphurous fluctuant marsh this side the steaming meadows
   Where black weeds trouble the moon's drowned hair.

There is a sudden fuss of draggled feathers and the swing
   Of winds in a hissing burst of raindrops; then a cry

Of color at the hill's rim; a strange bright glimmering;
And a lark talking madness in some corner of the sky.

### TOUCH

I hear a cricket at my window sill
    Stitching the dark edge of the dawn; and now
    The climbing siren of a distant cow
Rouses the sun over the eastern hill.

A cock is rapping in four rickety words
    His challenge to the sluggard; and a bell
    Jargons like water dripping in a well;
And dew is in the throats of all the birds.

I need but outstretched hands and I embrace
    The luxury of leaves: yet, while I lean
    On their long coolness, I can feel the keen
Light of your fingers drift across my face!

### ELEGY

Fled is the swiftness of all the white-footed ones
Who had a great cry in them and the wrath of speed:
They are no more among us; they and their sons
Are dead indeed.

So the river mews twist in long loops over the river,
Wheeling and shifting with the wind's and the tide's shift,
And pass in a black night—and nothing is left but a shiver
To show they were swift.

Whenever I hear a gull's throat throb in a fog,
Watch the owl's velvet swoop, the high hawk's lonely paces,
I think of the heels of him who lies like a log
And his friends under turf and the rain creeping down on their faces

And my heart goes sick and the hell in my heart could break
To the edge of my eyes for the mates I shall not be knowing
Anywhere now though the ice booms loud in the lake
And the geese honk north again and the heron's going.

## David McCord

DAVID (THOMPSON WATSON) MCCORD was born in New York City, November 15,
1897. His ancestry is Colonial, "brick end." He looks with some pride on his
maternal forebears, particularly on Dr. John Morgan, First Surgeon-General, under
Washington, of the Revolutionary Army, and discoverer of pus, though, as he says,

"I don't see how anybody could have missed it." He has lived at both extremes of the continent; he went to private schools on Long Island and public schools in Oregon. He entered Harvard in 1917; went to Plattsburg, where he was Second Lieutenant in the Field Artillery; returned to college, where he specialized in physics and mathematics, planning to be an engineer, and graduated from Harvard in 1921, taking an A.M. in literature the following year.

After graduating he traveled extensively and worked at different occupations, the most important being his critical reviews, musical and dramatic, under H. T. Parker, for *The Boston Transcript*. This determined McCord's career as a writer. After his thirtieth year he alternated with ease and growing distinction between prose and poetry, between poetry and verse. *Oddly Enough* (1926) is a volume of characteristic essays. *Oxford Nearly Visited* (1929) and *Bay Window Ballads* (1935) are dexterous light verse which (especially in "Sonnets to Baedeker") attempt to graft American freedom on English form. *Floodgate* (1927) is composed of serious poetry, as is *The Crows* (1934), a far more important volume.

With *The Crows* a writer of delicate verse and distinguished prose emerges definitely as a poet. Perhaps McCord's outstanding "difference" is his blending of two tones: he not only combines but fuses light verse and pronounced poetry. Themes which another might develop into portentous effects are nimbly varied and played with a supple hand.

This unusual blend of grace and gravity is sounded in the untitled prelude which begins "If I should find, in the dark mind," in the introductory "Hyladae," in the group of eight poems "To a Child," in the whimsical "Moment in Marmalade," and the concise "Themis." Such poems are proof of McCord's dexterity and his cool disposal of rhymes. Sometimes he forgets to preserve that balance between the unexpected and the inevitable which is the perfection of rhyme. In the excess pleasure he derives from the pairing of hitherto unmated words he sometimes lapses into cleverness; in his too easy triumphs over the recalcitrant rhyme the technician achieves nothing nobler than preciosity. But these are infrequent flaws, and they do not apply at all to the title-poem and "A Bucket of Bees," the two high notes of the volume. The first is a monologue of a city-dweller remembering the guarded fields and windward knolls of his youth, the wet beginnings of Spring, recalled by the querulous talk—"the cool critical catarrh"—of crows flying over the town. "A Bucket of Bees" lacks the integration of the title-poem—its colloquial asides echo the tone of Frost and the opening lines recall Eliot and MacLeish—but the material is wholly McCord's, and the poem, gathering force as it proceeds, expresses a complete personality. The lines abound with verbal vigor, communicating authority without pomposity, strength without strain, a boy's remembered fancies mingled with a mature philosophy.

A collection of his delightful verse for children is still to be published.

THE CROWS

I

This morning, when I heard the crows
Blaming the rows

Of city houses, blaming the noise,
I knew no boys
Were chasing them from field to tree to field,
Or that the sentry, his sharp eye peeled
For danger from the farm,
Had spread wings and alarm,
And the whole flock, suddenly mutinous,
Gone flying over us.
There was no field nor acre
Which the proud city-maker
Had not dug to houses, set in stone,
Or scraped to the brown bone.
There was no traffic here
For crows this time of year
If not in summer when geranium pots
Flower the standard lots.
It must have been the spring that drew them by.
Lying in bed I didn't see them fly
In querulous talk
Above the sparrowed walk:
I only heard them cawing as you hear
Them in the longbow of the year,
When the dead chestnut breaks upon the hill,
And the dark woods come darker still
Because the light is younger where it shows
The clearest meadow and the blackest crows.

## II

They were not come to stay.
Crows never caw that way,
Trailing the sound behind them as if scare
Pursued them down the altitudes of air,
Except to say once more:
March is outside the door
Flaming some old desire
As man turns uneasily from his fire.
March in the sky, least in the ground, that is:
The city is not his
Who looks for blades on brick
And the cold dead to quick.
On heavy wing
                    they cleared us
                              in a file
Of wise old ministers who never smile.
Perhaps we seemed to them
Another theorem
Of parallels and planes
For corbel brains.
Perhaps they saw in smoke
The substituting oak,

And the last windward knoll
In calculus of coal.
We were the writhen horn
Above the wasting corn,
We were the western pass
To the deep eastern grass;
Perhaps they said:
                    the landfall of great seas,
Or to be feared, or to be tried as trees.
Lying in bed, I didn't hear it all:
They had to wake me through a city wall
With still the same cool critical catarrh
That I have heard afar
In greening wood or yellowing grain,
And knew that I should die just not to hear again.

### III

Whatever it meant, they never came to rest.
Their going (as I guessed)
Had more the text of migratory souls
Than wings for other springs
                            and other goals.
We were too much a fact or too unreal
To break the steel,
The bullet-heart, that drove
Home to the meadow and the maple grove.
I might have tried to strip the cloudy dawn
From the right sky to see where they had gone,
As one will follow geese
Disturbing the mind's peace;
But I preferred the lack
Of their long day flown slowly into night
And the last crow blinding from my sight,
Black into black.
It was enough that I should hear by name
Mention of the spring before it came;
Rumor, which is all a city has
Of the seed's own grievance to be grass.
March, April, goes . . .
I heard the crows
Who less than man or bird
Beg the impending word.
I saw the raven head,
Questioning
            (from my bed)
Searching horizons still
Over the dusty sill,
Leaving between two thoughts one consolate sign
Of what, too, once was mine.

OF RED IN SPRING

The maple's bloom is red,
There's red in early spring;
Winter, we know, is dead,
And dead's the final thing.

Autumn, we saw, was done
Whose smoke is chilled to ash;
But still the red comes on,
And still the mountains flash.

Who lit these kindling flares,
Since winter stood between,
To take us unawares
Who thought the spring was green?

A BUCKET OF BEES

So the wind blew all that night,
Bringing the rain, and the rain
Brought back Vermont, tomorrow,
A tendril, a twig, a package of the young spring green.
And it blew in the five blade needles of the pine,
On the hard leaf of the oak,
On farmers' ground still littoral with the red swamp maple.
It blew now
Blowing under the window, blowing the night
Across a cool lax harbor of the mind.
Whatever woke you woke
The great swell solo manual of the rain,
Filling the pipes with silver,
And the wind blew steadily improving noise.
And all that night the rain
Brought back the flower, grass, the headlands in the gulf,
The silent growing round the edge of barns,
The longer days,
The slack,
The disinfection of the spring.

I was too young to remember,
But even then malaria and quinine split
The nerves on edge already. Fever
Burned at the roots of eagerness and faith.
*It's dark. It's hot. I'm hot.*
The world was wrong as upside down, and lightning
Flashed from a cold sky whenever you went out.
The people talked too loud,
They were always going,
The cereals they gave you tasted black.
*It's dark. I'm hot!*

One night was full of dreams and empty corners,
And down the well without the fireman's pole.
*It's dark. I'm burning!*
So,
When a storm blew up along the coast,
As it always did in summer,
The door slammed and the rain came in the window sharp,
But never cool.
The voices down the hall died out.
*I want a drink!*
And what we match with solving intellect
Shouted for terror.
*Why?*
Or were you gone?

In the morning we all went for a long walk
On a country road in shining pools of water,
And I remembered remembering another storm.
The air was fine now,
And a warm sun worrying April out of March.
We saw what the wind had done: Where it snapped the ends
Of branches it should have snapped the year they died:
Old leaves blown out to new and leafless places.
Someone, we said, was raking in our woods
And ran away. But that was talk,
Though I could swear it so.
Most of the pools had sky in them, like mirrors
In an old room smiling to themselves;
Or some had trees and clouds, and some were cloudy,
Scored by the breeze that touched too near the ground.
Wearing stout shoes won't mean you won't get muddy;
But you don't mind it then, and just a step
In the clear water is stepping in the sky.
You break the image, and I'll argue
One blue splinter fastens to the sole.
    We walked on half an hour until the road
Managed it better where there was more view,
More cloud, less water. Round the bend
We could see just where a tree had fallen,
But not (and we were sorry) across our path.
It had gone left and down hill, or the way
The wind went. Down, we said,
And still, why should it break?
It broke off close. An oak.
Why not? The stump is rotten.
Well, if it's rotten it was done to die.
It's not just hollow.
Why not? I found a flying
Squirrel in one once, but you won't find one now.
No, I've found something better. Look in here!
Bees!

Honey! There
In the shell
(Like an old dugout at Ticonderoga)
Terraces and tiers of wax.
How many bees!
All anxious, crawling,
Tentative with cold,
Sensing
Disaster at the back of so much light.

If you had asked me once
Where the great world was:
Its limits, heart, earth, sky,
And all that is,
I should have said, 'The Garden'
Which was home, my universe,
Life bounden, A to Z.
   That's aster now, to zinnia, I find;
But flowers grew beyond their names, as gardens
Grow beyond the sunshine, as the birds
Fly beyond singing and our empty sight.
   Someone had planted it before me, sowing
Color with one hand, with the other scent.
And color mixed with color,
Smell with smell:
The apple blossom at the jonquil stem,
And lavender upon the wane of thyme.
   Flowers don't move, they said, but they were wrong.
Stirring the roots with water, the rainy soil
Raised to the bud their capillary powers,
And then one morning in another May
The winds shook out new blossoms, and they sailed
Into the dendron sea of I'll forget.
   The winds do that, but summer wears the tidy
Rhythm of standing still and bending down.
The humming bird, whose tongue has split a needle,
Darts from the white and voluntary bell,
Savors the rose, and sucks the bindweed dry.
His small obstructionist, the bee, climbs down
The little chalice, opening style and anther,
Bagged with the pollen, drunken of his find.
   If you had asked me once, I should have said:
Flower to flower, summer to summer, over
And over, living and dying,
Live and dead.

Back at the house we found a bucket
To put the bees in, and the lid
To keep them there until we found a hive.
Some of them were dead, we thought,

And some half frozen. None
(I thought) would do much stinging soon.
I used the canvas country gloves
That smelled of zwieback, and the bees were taken.
One of them climbed up inside my sleeve.
He acted for the others: Mind us, now.
I pinched him at the elbow and got burned,
But that was all. We killed the cripples.
I hate to kill a bee.
There was no queen,
Or else we couldn't find her.
                              That was odd.
   To put the broken honey in a pan,
We had to take the tree-dust with it too;
Cutting it loose there with a knife, and shaking
A bee or another off from the under side.
Professional store honey comes in squares,
As though the bees bled antiseptic flowers,
But this was some
The Greeks found once in Thessaly; or bears
In plunder, say as lucky as our own.
You try it with a finger when the spring
Is in the blood, and sorrow at the bone.
The little well, the hexagon of wax,
Interns a thimble of the blossom gone,
The wild bright summer stolen as the birds
Sang, and a man put whetstone to his scythe.
   The bucket had a heat now of itself,
But we must set it carefully near the stove.
The bees would want their strength,
And need it more,
To start again in a new hive,
Captive, with another queen.
                              They'd come
To life a month too soon: a little
Seething knot, explosive in the hand,
And the ground dead cold outside. . . .
   So wait till morning.
There was no wind that night:
The bees swarmed dark above the pillow,
Threatening, in a fashion, as I dreamed.

It was exciting then to see the city:
You went up in the morning on a train,
Played in a toyshop, had éclairs and chocolate,
Saw the great stores by holding to a hand,
And woke up with the brakeman shouting. . . .
Now you were going there forever. Monday
Was the last good-by.
                      Good-by, green fields,

Gray stone, tall trees, wet leaves;
Good-by, hill, brook, white fence;
                              take care, good-by.
Monday was the last day, and the farm
Looked very small and lonely, and inside
The rooms could empty with us standing talking.
    There were so many things we might have done:
The meadow lark had eggs,
                              but making butter
Needed cream of the cold crocks in the dark.
Why were they cutting down the pleasant wood?
Why on a Sunday?
With the right light, now, and very careful,
You could just see the trout swirl in the well.
Monday was the last day:
                              but the turtle
Walked in the yard the figures nineteen hundred.
    Silence follows sound, and the green forest
Follows the countryman and heels him down.
When all is said, we know the number *Vale!*
Wave us good-by: A century tomorrow
Shatters the still steeled waters of what is now.


There was a man who raised bees for the queen:
Her Majesty, long, wiry-legged, worth money.
He raised them on a roof up-town, but social
With blue dust, the soots of inland air.
The roof was flat, the hives stood in a row
From left to right in urban draft or weather,
And didn't wear the name of apiary:
But to the bees they seemed the size of home.
Down stairs a clack of men, the strain of wheels,
Or presses run by night, made cheap with sound
A counterfeit of August in the grasses.
Other buildings, windows, smoke, brick towers,
Higher, and deadly in a prison scheme,
Robbed the shrill colony of dawn and dusk.
That was a bee tree in a bonded wood,
A company whose stocks were liquid gold.
    We took the bucket in, the morning after,
Like a skilled workman starting with his lunch.
"These are the bees," we said, "the pioneers;
They don't know cities, but they do a flower—
Cockscomb and a honeysuckle vine.
You keep them here and tell them this is theirs.
Give them the ablest town queen of the roof.
You want new blood, and bees' blood if it's wild
Runs like a gypsy's in the swelt of summer."
    He put them in, and shutting down the lid
He shut the anger of that stormy day

Into a cubic foot of bee-black night.
"I guess they'll keep," he said. "They're better off,
They'll get more room than back in hollow stumps.
I tell you, son, I've got some workers here
Have been commuting longer than your dad;
They fly way out, up country now, that's where.
Taste the first drop, and I can name the field.
It's wicked what these animals can do.
They'll come straight down that single shaft of sun,
Straight as an arrow, yes, a whole lot straighter,
Their furry legs all tangled up with pollen.
The bread of life was good clean Christian flour,
But I've a notion beebread is the stuff
With finer spirit; leastwise there's a strength
And beauty to it for an evil city,
As if the bees went after more than clover
And brought us home free particles of God."

The bee goes out to flower
And the mind
Returns to youth his fountains or the slain.
Between us and the truce of foreign hills
Each day renews but life renewed before.
Cut down the clover, cut the heart-strings too!
The bee will find the blossom while the snath
Is sickling at the stem, and we shall hear
The heartbeats dying even as our death,
But not too soon.                    Life borders on the joy
Of joyful things.
If we grow old, it is not with our age
But with our youth: the hive too full,
The soul too mattered with divine content.
I take the red lance of the westering sun
And break my shield upon it: who shall say
I am not victor? only that the wound
Heals not, and that I fall again.
    O lovely land and ancient upright wood,
Call home thy servant, the conscriptive bee.
His life is thine, his work; the geometric field
An humble hire for fertilizing flowers.
Call home the child, whose credulous first hours
Burn at the heart of living, and surprise
The better reason with unbidden truth.
Call home the man. He will not come.
But in the closing dark his eyes may sometime
Circle the lost last rim of his own world:
"I walked there once. What turned my face away?"

### THE SPIDER

Now with a clean thread
Of a single span,
Softly he has spread
His silken fan

That shrub and thorn enclose
By the dead well,
Sweet where the sunning rose
Binds in a spell

The bee, the butterfly,
All foolish wings
That open at the sigh
Of lineal springs.

And there, against the day's
Delicious draft,
He carries in old ways
His cunning craft:

Dropping along the cool
Invisible track,
A spider with a spool
Upon his back;

And eyes, like garnets, filled
With bright desire
For bodies better stilled
In candle fire.

A lord within the cone
Of his domain,
He reckons from his throne
The shriveled slain:

A bottle fly, the moth
Who tried to pass
The filter of his cloth
And found it glass.

### A DOUBLE STAR

Under one star, now, or under two?
We can't be wrong if we choose them both
For a binary light is more than true
When it's twice itself—on the skyman's oath

And choosing a star of double strength,
As half to follow and half to share,
No matter the square of the light-year length
It will fall on the road with a beam to spare

Two stars, two people: alike or not,
An orbit in common has much to show
In the darkest night of the brightest spot,
And the eyes to see, and the way to go.

### OUT OF NOVEMBER: SPEAKING FOR ONE

Selves of myself, these waning days,
We meet more often than we used:
You find the late November haze
Too good for ghosts I once refused.

What is it you have come to tell?
I have no adequate replies.
It was not easy to dispel
What now is hard to recognize.

Why should you come? I being weak
In naming new things from the lost:
If you know better angels, speak!
Your world is failing with the frost.

O I shall wake some morning, cold
And wondering half what I'm to say.
My other selves, you'll be too old,
And I'll have no new ghosts to lay.

## Stephen Vincent Benét

STEPHEN VINCENT BENÉT, the younger brother of William Rose Benét, was born at Bethlehem, Pennsylvania, in July, 1898. He was educated in various parts of the country, and graduated from Yale in 1919.

At seventeen he published a small book containing six dramatic portraits, *Five Men and Pompey* (1915), a remarkable set of monologues which, in spite of distinct traces of Browning and Kipling, was little short of astounding, coming from a schoolboy. In Benét's next volume, *Young Adventure* (1918), published before he was twenty, one hears something more than the speech of an infant prodigy; the precocious facility has developed into a keen and individual vigor. *Heavens and Earth* (1920) charts a greater imaginative sweep. Like his brother, the younger Benét is at his best in the decoratively grotesque; his fancy exults in running the scales between the whimsically bizarre and the lightly diabolic.

For a while Stephen Benét was too prolific to be self-critical. He published several novels (the best of which are *Jean Huguenot* and *Spanish Bayonet*), collaborated on two plays which flickered a few nights in New York, and, unconsciously perhaps, began imitating his contemporaries. *King David,* published in book form a few months after it won *The Nation's* poetry prize for 1923, is less Benét than usual; it seems unjust that at least half the prize for this poem was not awarded to Vachel Lindsay. *Tiger Joy* (1925) betrays haste; the poet allows his rhymes to dictate and often to blur the course of his imagery. But though *Tiger Joy* is padded out with negligible verse, it contains "The Golden Corpse," a splendid octave of sonnets, "The Mountain Whippoorwill" and "The Ballad of William Sycamore," two vigorous and thoroughly American ballads.

Stephen Benét's faculty for ballad-making stood him in good stead when he came to reconstruct the Civil War period in *John Brown's Body* (1928). With this work, the author, hitherto known only to a small circle, leaped into instant popularity. Within a few months, the book had reached more than one hundred thousand people, and Benét had proved that a long narrative poem if skillfully blended could hold attention as easily as a novel. It was awarded the Pulitzer Prize the year following its publication.

The weakness of *John Brown's Body* is in the treatment. Although his canvas is epical, the author sacrifices the unity of the epic by abruptly changing meters, by a cinematographic switching from one character to another, by interluding his narrative with lyrics, ballads, elegies and even prose. Nor, in this intermingling, has he perfected a style of his own; the long cadences of Sandburg and the jingling beat of Lindsay occur throughout. It is, frankly, a work of assimilation rather than creation. Yet its virtues compensate for its defects. The historical events have been more powerfully projected by others, the battle-pictures are inferior to the fictional episodes—the forgotten George Parsons Lathrop has done better in "Keenan's Charge" —but the composite is so new, the issues so impartially treated, that the struggle takes on a vitality barely suggested by orthodox histories. Benét's achievement of showing the war through its impact on a large number of *dramatis personae*—of Jake Diefer, who sees the war in terms of his Pennsylvania farmland, of Spade, the runaway slave, of Breckenridge, the Tennessee mountaineer, of Connecticut-born Jack Ellyat—is no small triumph. If Benét sacrifices unity, he gains speed, sudden interest and the nervous contrasts which are continually stimulating. If no single passage contains that unanalyzable but unmistakable quality which permeates great poetry, the originality of the work, the vigor of its portraits, the interpolated lyrics, and the unflagging pace reveal an unusually rich talent.

With his wife Rosemary, Benét wrote *A Book of Americans* (1933), a set of fifty-six verses about famous pilgrims, pioneers, and presidents, obviously designed for uncritical young readers.

## RAIN AFTER A VAUDEVILLE SHOW

The last pose flickered, failed. The screen's dead white
Glared in a sudden flooding of harsh light
Stabbing the eyes; and as I stumbled out
The curtains rose. A fat girl with a pout
And legs like hams, began to sing "His Mother."
Gusts of bad air rose in a choking smother;
Smoke, the wet steam of clothes, the stench of plush,
Powder, cheap perfume, mingled in a rush.
I stepped into the lobby—and stood still,
Struck dumb by sudden beauty, body and will.
Cleanness and rapture—excellence made plain—
The storming, thrashing arrows of the rain!
Pouring and dripping on the roofs and rods,
Smelling of woods and hills and fresh-turned sods,
Black on the sidewalks, gray in the far sky,
Crashing on thirsty panes, on gutters dry,
Hurrying the crowd to shelter, making fair
The streets, the houses, and the heat-soaked air,—
Merciful, holy, charging, sweeping, flashing,
It smote the soul with a most iron clashing!
Like dragons' eyes the street-lamps suddenly gleamed,
Yellow and round and dim-low globes of flame.
And, scarce-perceived, the clouds' tall banners streamed.
Out of the petty wars, the daily shame,
Beauty strove suddenly, and rose, and flowered. . . .
I gripped my coat and plunged where awnings lowered.
Made one with hissing blackness, caught, embraced,
By splendor and by striving and swift haste—
Spring coming in with thunderings and strife—
I stamped the ground in the strong joy of life!

## WINGED MAN

The moon, a sweeping scimitar, dipped in the stormy straits,
The dawn, a crimson cataract, burst through the eastern gates,
The cliffs were robed in scarlet, the sands were cinnabar,
Where first two men spread wings for flight and dared the hawk afar.

There stands the cunning workman, the crafty, past all praise,
The man who chained the Minotaur, the man who built the Maze.
His young son is beside him and the boy's face is a light,
A light of dawn and wonder and of valor infinite.

Their great vans beat the cloven air, like eagles they mount up,
Motes in the wine of morning, specks in a crystal cup,
And lest his wings should melt apace old Daedalus flies low,
But Icarus beats up, beats up, he goes where lightnings go,

He cares no more for warnings, he rushes through the sky,
Braving the crags of ether, daring the gods on high,
Black 'gainst the crimson sunset, gold over cloudy snows,
With all Adventure in his heart the first winged man arose.

Dropping gold, dropping gold, where the mists of morning rolled,
On he kept his way undaunted, though his breaths were stabs of cold,
Through the mystery of dawning that no mortal may behold.

Now he shouts, now he sings in the rapture of his wings,
And his great heart burns intenser with the strength of his desire,
As he circles like a swallow, wheeling, flaming, gyre on gyre.

Gazing straight at the sun, half his pilgrimage is done,
And he staggers for a moment, hurries on, reels backward, swerves
In a rain of scattered feathers as he falls in broken curves.

Icarus, Icarus, though the end is piteous,
Yet forever, yea forever, we shall see thee rising thus,
See the first supernal glory, not the ruin hideous.

You were Man, you who ran farther than our eyes can scan,
Man absurd, gigantic, eager for impossible Romance,
Overthrowing all Hell's legions with one warped and broken lance.

On the highest steeps of Space he will have his dwelling-place
In those far, terrific regions where the cold comes down like Death
Gleams the red glint of his pinions, smokes the vapor of his breath.

Floating downward, very clear, still the echoes reach the ear
Of a little tune he whistles and a little song he sings,
Mounting, mounting still, triumphant, on his torn and broken wings!

## THE BALLAD OF WILLIAM SYCAMORE

### (1790-1871)

My father, he was a mountaineer,
His fist was a knotty hammer;
He was quick on his feet as a running deer,
And he spoke with a Yankee stammer.

My mother, she was merry and brave,
And so she came to her labor,
With a tall green fir for her doctor grave
And a stream for her comforting neighbor.

And some are wrapped in the linen fine,
And some like a godling's scion;
But I was cradled on twigs of pine
In the skin of a mountain lion.

And some remember a white, starched lap
And a ewer with silver handles;
But I remember a coonskin cap
And the smell of bayberry candles.

The cabin logs, with the bark still rough,
And my mother who laughed at trifles,
And the tall, lank visitors, brown as snuff,
With their long, straight squirrel-rifles.

I can hear them dance, like a foggy song,
Through the deepest one of my slumbers,
The fiddle squeaking the boots along
And my father calling the numbers.

The quick feet shaking the puncheon-floor,
The fiddle squeaking and squealing,
Till the dried herbs rattled above the door
And the dust went up to the ceiling.

There are children lucky from dawn till dusk,
But never a child so lucky!
For I cut my teeth on "Money Musk"
In the Bloody Ground of Kentucky!

When I grew tall as the Indian corn,
My father had little to lend me,
But he gave me his great, old powder-horn
And his woodsman's skill to befriend me.

With a leather shirt to cover my back,
And a redskin nose to unravel
Each forest sign, I carried my pack
As far as a scout could travel.

Till I lost my boyhood and found my wife,
A girl like a Salem clipper!
A woman straight as a hunting-knife
With eyes as bright as the Dipper!

We cleared our camp where the buffalo feed,
Unheard-of streams were our flagons;
And I sowed my sons like apple-seed
On the trail of the Western wagons.

They were right, tight boys, never sulky or
    slow,
A fruitful, a goodly muster.
The eldest died at the Alamo.
The youngest fell with Custer.

The letter that told it burned my hand.
Yet we smiled and said, "So be it!"
But I could not live when they fenced the
    land,
For it broke my heart to see it.

I saddled a red, unbroken colt
And rode him into the day there;
And he threw me down like a thunderbolt
And rolled on me as I lay there.

The hunter's whistle hummed in my ear
As the city-men tried to move me,
And I died in my boots like a pioneer
With the whole wide sky above me.

Now I lie in the heart of the fat, black soil,
Like the seed of a prairie-thistle;
It has washed my bones with honey and oil
And picked them clean as a whistle.

And my youth returns, like the rains of
    Spring,
And my sons, like the wild-geese flying;
And I lie and hear the meadow-lark sing
And have much content in my dying.

Go play with the towns you have built of
    blocks
The towns where you would have bound me!
I sleep in my earth like a tired fox,
And my buffalo have found me.

### LOVE CAME BY FROM THE RIVERSMOKE

*(from "John Brown's Body")*

Love came by from the riversmoke,
    When the leaves were fresh on the tree,
But I cut my heart on the blackjack oak
    Before they fell on me.

The leaves are green in the early spring,
    They are brown as linsey now,
I did not ask for a wedding-ring
    From the wind in the bending bough.

Fall lightly, lightly, leaves of the wild,
    Fall lightly on my care,
I am not the first to go with child
    Because of the blowing air.

I am not the first nor yet the last
    To watch a goosefeather sky,
And wonder what will come of the blast
    And the name to call it by.

Snow down, snow down, you whitefeather
    bird,
    Snow down, you winter storm,
Where the good girls sleep with a gospel
    word
    To keep their honor warm.

The good girls sleep in their modesty,
    The bad girls sleep in their shame,
But I must sleep in a hollow tree
    Till my child can have a name.

I will not ask for the wheel and thread
    To spin the labor plain,
Or the scissors hidden under the bed
    To cut the bearing-pain.

will not ask for the prayer in church
  Or the preacher saying the prayer,
But I will ask the shivering birch
  To hold its arms in the air.

Cold and cold and cold again,
  Cold in the blackjack limb,
The winds in the sky for his sponsor-men
  And a bird to christen him.

Now listen to me, you Tennessee corn,
  And listen to my word,

This is the first child ever born
  That was christened by a bird.

He's going to act like a hound let loose
  When he comes from the blackjack tree,
And he's going to walk in proud shoes
  All over Tennessee.

I'll feed him milk out of my own breast
  And call him Whistling Jack.
And his dad'll bring him a partridge nest,
  As soon as his dad comes back.

## SONG OF THE RIDERS

### (from "John Brown's Body")

The years ride out from the world like couriers gone to a throne
That is too far for treaty, or, as it may be, too proud;
The years marked with a star, the years that are skin and bone.
The years ride into the night like envoys sent to a cloud.

Perhaps they dismount at last, by some iron ring in the skies,
Dismount and tie their stallions and walk with an armored tread
Where an outlaw queen of the air receives strange embassies
Under a tree of wisdom between the quick and the dead.

Perhaps they are merely gone, as the white foam flies from the bit,
But the sparkling noise of their riding is ever in our ears.—
The men who came to the maze without foreknowledge of it,
The losers and the finders, under the riding years.

They pass, and the finders lose, the losers find for a space.
There are love and hate and delusion and all the tricks of the maze.
There are always losers and finders. There is no abiding place
And the years are unreturning. But, here and there, there were days.

Days when the sun so shone that the statue gave its cry
And a bird shook wings or a woman walked with a certain mirth,
When the staff struck out a spring from the leaves that had long been dry,
And the plow as before moved on from the hilltop, but its share had opened the
    earth.

So the bird is caught for an instant, and so the bird escapes.
The years are not halted by it. The losers and finders wait.
The years move on toward the sunset, the tall far-trafficking shapes,
Each with a bag of news to lay at a ghostly gate.

Riders shaking the heart with the hoofs that will not cease,
Will you never lie stretched in marble, the hands crossed over the breast,
Some with hounds at your feet to show that you passed in peace,
And some with your feet on lions? It is time that you were at rest.

1935

All night they marched, the infantrymen under pack,
But the hands gripping the rifles were naked bone
And the hollow pits of the eyes stared, vacant and black,
When the moonlight shone.

The gas mask lay like a blot on the empty chest,
The slanting helmets were spattered with rust and mold,
But they burrowed the hill for the machine-gun nest
As they had of old.

And the guns rolled, and the tanks, but there was no sound,
Never the gasp or rustle of living men
Where the skeletons strung their wire on disputed ground. . . .
I knew them, then.

"It is seventeen years," I cried. "You must come no more.
We know your names. We know that you are the dead.
Must you march forever from France and the last, blind war?"
*"Fool! From the next!"* they said.

# Horace Gregory

Horace Gregory was born April 10, 1898, in Milwaukee, Wisconsin, of English, Irish, and German descent. He attended the Milwaukee School of Fine Arts and, after a year of study under a tutor, went to the German English Academy, and then to the University of Wisconsin, from which he graduated in 1923. Then came six years of free lance writing, chiefly book-reviewing, in New York, where he married Marya Zaturenska, the poet. He has been on the English faculty at Sarah Lawrence College since 1933.

Gregory at first was entirely under the spell of the classics; after reading Byron, he turned to Landor, Pope, and Dryden. At college his interests became completely Latinized, and, though he dropped his classicism after seeing the tenements and poverty-ridden alleys of the sodden Chelsea section of Whitman's "glorious Manna-hatta," enough persisted so that he translated *The Poems of Catullus* (1931), rendering them, however, in the American idiom. There was a "first" book of traditional lyrics which Gregory destroyed upon his arrival in New York; a few years later he published *Chelsea Rooming House*.

*Chelsea Rooming House* (1930) is a half-detached, half-indignant work; a set of monologues dramatizing the lives of those crowded into the slums of New York's lower west side. Its observation is keen to the point of penetration; its sense of sympathy is surpassed only by the faintly restrained sense of outrage. There is no doubt about Gregory's social sentiments nor his political preferences, but he does not resort to polemics or propaganda. He persuades the reader by the integrity of his poetry. *No Retreat* (1933) is a more lyrical collection. Such poems as "Poems for My Daughter" and "Good Friday" owe something to T. S. Eliot's juxtaposition of the classic-rhetorical and the sharply colloquial tone, but the basic music is Gregory's, and "Valediction to My Contemporaries" is both biographically and esthetically authentic. The Levinson prize offered by *Poetry: A Magazine of Verse* was awarded to Gregory in 1934 because of this work.

*Chorus for Survival* appeared in 1935. This, with the two preceding volumes, affords the opportunity for summary. We have now a fairly rounded picture of the poet still young, but well out of his apprenticeship; experimental but almost, if not entirely, free of his influences. We see him as something of a modern realist and something of an abstracted metaphysician; a man intensely aware of the irrational world about him and determined, somehow, to impose an order, if not reason, upon it; a poet who seizes upon the least consequential figures as symbols charged with significance and who brings a firm personality to bear upon the impersonal event.

*Chorus for Survival* is the most frankly personal of Gregory's volumes. The intense self-participation is declared in the eloquent "Prologue," which is a sort of Prothalamion—1935 Model, with its nervous music. It lifts itself vividly in the poignant "Ask no return," nostalgically in the poems recalling his youth by the Great Lakes, symbolically in the fourteenth section in which Emerson figures to point an American panorama, gravely in the concluding lines "For you, my son." Some may object to a certain obscurity of utterance, a confusion of image and effect. But such obscurity (where it exists) is not willful. Nor does it proceed from a desire to overcompensate for a paucity of the imagination. The images crowd upon Gregory with such force that his mind leaps from one to the other, taking the ellipses in his stride —and the reader is sometimes unable to take the leap with him. As in Hopkins' poetry, and, more recently, in much of Stephen Spender's and some of C. Day Lewis', the rapid progress from image to image, the very tension during that transit, frequently results in obscurity. But, as Lewis says in his "A Hope for Poetry," if the reader will allow the images "to cohabit in his mind for a little, he will find that the contact is made, a spark thrown off which illuminates the whole situation." The appeal may be tangential, or circuitous, or highly associative, but it is there. Even those who find the passages difficult will not fail to appreciate the excellent use of a "heightened" common speech and the finely sensitized music.

Besides his poetry, Gregory has written *Pilgrim of the Apocalypse,* an important critical study of D. H. Lawrence, his symbols and his significance.

POEMS FOR MY DAUGHTER

Tell her I love
             she will remember me
always, for she
is of my tissues made;
                      she will remember
these streets where the moon's shade
falls and my shadow mingles
with shadows sprung
from a midnight tree.

Tell her I love that I
am neither in earth nor sky,
stone nor cloud,
but only this
walled garden she knows well
and which her body is.

Her eyes alone shall make
me blossom for her sake;
contained within her, all
my days shall flower or die,
birthday or funeral
concealed where no man's eye
finds me unless she says:
He is my flesh and I
am what he was.

### VALEDICTION TO MY CONTEMPORARIES

*The return after*
*ten years: New*
*York, Chicago,*
*Madison*

Entrain airport   New York   Chicago west
piercing the sunset's terminal where day
breaks midnight into stars before the dawn
Superior   Lake Erie   Michigan:
seawind but no saltsea in this lake spray
clear eyes and nostrils: drink our health: the sand
our shores.
            Stop signals   home again!

Awake at morning, spring coiled in the body
and at the narrow window slit in stone,
skylight and sun.
            Tilt the horizon down,
ride windward through Wisconsin miles of corn,
grazing the shallow valley and long plains.

        O Alma Mater on the hill! What green hills, Cicero,
        vanish, return. What stone embankments of hope, desire,
        what little almost islands Sirmio
        anchored within us rest, flower in sleep, Catullus,
        welcomed home.

### II

*The University*
*of Wisconsin:*
*1919*

Here was the campus of our hearts, my friends,
Plato's green-treed republic of the air:
see what miraculous fruit its branches bear,
oceans of maple spray, green harbored, flowing
against the sky: and from these shores Greek towers . . .

See how the white dome trembles in the sun,
dissolves at noon three thousand years away
where the antique nightingale engraved in bronze
still sways unheard forever, now entwined
within the steel crescendos of the mind.

### III

*The indecisive
peace after war
which lasted
until 1929*

Those who return, return to empty halls,
the crystal image in the sky, pellucid
limbs that fade in shadows on these walls:

This peace was ours: the slow guns still resounding
peace: *drive homeward angels from Versailles*
in limousines sunk under no man's land.
Run the machine guns through the arras—dead?
Not dead but much alive.

How shall we find
the bodies of those unslain, exiled from war
but now returned, furloughs of exile signed
from all green ports on earth?

The birth certificate of love
declared obscene: Faith of no faith, Our Father,
do not destroy this faithlessness to friend
or enemy, lest we perish to no end.

### IV

*Alternate
speeches: indi-
vidual lovers
walking in the
shadow of
Lucretius*

Measure the atoms of our souls, O Roman
death's astronomer Lucretius.

Spires of light ascend
discarnate memories: the four years spanned
by the quick, sinewy shadow of his hand:

(And in this shadow where she stood,
flight in her hair!
the limbs reveal undress that virgins wear
to meet the bridegroom on the wedding stair,
do not unsay her testament, O love:

"Live for this hour and we who die today
kiss lips that bloom forever underground."
And did you call me by his name who died
naked, Parian attitudes of death
entwined your limbs and his: kiss and restore
his body's heat in mine, this earth his grave:
sleepless, his blood drives home
niagaras in our veins)

—O Mors Aeterna,
lean from the fiery ramparts of world's end,
time's end and love's last image scrolled
in quicksilver across the mind—descend
voice of a million tongues, your elegies
(some say that suicide usurped his blood)
resound no more. . . .

Mount stairways to the sun!
We have survived your heritage, these years
consuming time toward death too swift for tears.

V

*The valediction*      The course of empire westward to Cathay
rides in the east: the circle breaks in fire:
these charred remains of what we were expire,
(O incandescent speed!) the hands, lips, eyes
anonymous. Rise atque vale, rise:
another generation shall disown
these years in darkness each to four winds blown
(the deeds are obsolete as Helen's war) . . .

Good-by, Il Penseroso of our spring,
forgive our ashes and destroy the urn:
unwind the clock, empty the seasons down
rivers of memory—do not return!

### ASK NO RETURN

Ask no return for love that's given
embracing mistress, wife or friend,
                    ask no return:
on this deep earth or in pale heaven,
awake and spend
hands, lips and eyes in love,
in darkness burn,
              the limbs entwined until the soul ascend.

Ask no return of seasons gone:
the fire of autumn and the first hour of spring,
the short bough blossoming
through city windows when night's done,
when fears adjourn
              backward in memory where all loves end
in self again, again the inward tree
growing against the heart
and no heart free.
From love that sleeps behind each eye
in double symmetry
             ask no return,
even in enmity, look! I shall take your hand;
nor can our limbs disjoin in separate ways again,
walking, even at night on foreign land
through houses open to the wind, through cold and rain,
waking alive, meet, kiss and understand.

### FOR YOU, MY SON

For you, my son,
I write of what we were:

Under cool skies, Wisconsin's April weather:
The lilac fragrance on our lips and hair,

Field and the lake where memories restore
Westward the wave to India, the passage
Chartered through night
                              and the returning dawn
Over the mast-head, spars:
                              New York,
Green Castle Gardens at thy side:
Brooklyn, the Battery, wide-breasted Whitman there,
Hand to the shoulder of the pioneer:
O many-footed echoing Manhattan,
Thy ships at harbor swaying with the tide.
Break here the lilac bough in April's weather,
Gather, foregather
                              in the pale mist of Juneau's city,
And in the valley, dry Menomenee
(Where forests were, clay-banked the silver river:
The trail in memory across the plain)

Turn where the earth's plowed under,
There at the root, the lilac flowering
In tombs that open when remembered spring
Comes home again beneath the pine roof-tree.

And did you hear the voices
Out of sand beach, lake waves?
                              The sound of water
Leaping in the dark:
                              remember shadowy limbs in darkness joined,
Pacing the forest to the inland sea.

Know what we were:
Our father's father
Ex-Dubliner, the tired eyes, bright laughter
Where the cold heart concealed disaster:

    "How many times before we fall,
    We fail:
    I am a tall man, handsome for my years,

    Erect three score, the six foot two and three hands taller
    Mounting to steer the horses beggars ride.
    And over Michigan the space too small
    For any man my size:
    Ex-patriarch, astronomer, engineer
    From the black-green growing turf where I was born
    The black-bird army wheeling close through cloud

    (breaking the sky through sunlight, rain
    until the violet, long archaic twilight
    empties its shadow over hills again)

Building my bridges to oblivion,
Even here, across the lake, across the sea.
See the cold island where I was born,
Peace where there is no peace,
                    always the blind
Violent war behind each blinded eye,
And darling Emmett dead, the cause in blood
Against gray walls.
                Priest over priest,
Walking in prayer to soothe the dead,
Over each friend betraying friend,
The dark stain spreading is a blood-clot in the mind.
Wherever I go now and even here
(Seeing sky break in spring new hemisphere)
There is no rest for me in the new land."

Know what we were; this is the hour.
White-haired millionaire
Starts from the dream:
    "The banks are broken, Gas has fallen;
    Consolidated Ice and Frigidaire
    Dropped down Chicago River;
    River swimming with rats, the poor:
    No virgin safe tonight, pack up your girls,
    Call the militia, ride
    Down blackened streets in hell
    Machine-gun fire until the pickets fall.
    Pity the poor, but not the undeserving poor,
    The right arm raised in blood,
    Whose hand is bleeding at my door,
    The million strong
    Army at my door and the lock sprung."

Turn here, my son
(No longer turn to what we were)
Build in the sunlight with strong men,
Beyond our barricade:
For even I remember the old war
And death in peace:
The neon sign 'Success' across our foreheads.

(Under the earth, shaken, as I am trembling now:
The small room where the body moves alone:
    sleepless I saw the dream;
    I saw my head upon the pillow
    and the blood)

                  *the naked bed, the folding chair*
*Voiceless we smile; we are not violent.*

And this is fear, fear,
The empty heart and the closed lung,

The broken song:
My classmates a republic of old men,

Yet even here, my hand to you, my son.

We shall be envious: O bitter eyes
Inward to see the dead,
                    those dead, our dead,
The bitter dying where the old world is dead.

I tell you love returns
Changing the hour:
                    break here the lilac bough,
Scatter the ashes in the tomb before the slow
Wind gathers into storm.
Over the cities and the yellowing plain
In bitter drought:
                    wait for new rain, welcome the men
Who shall survive, outface despair,
Terror and hate
                    to build new fire
At an empty hearth,
Burn doubt and fear.

As the map changes, through the cold sky,
Lean from the cockpit, read
The flower of prairie grass in seed
(Though here is war
                    my hand points where the body
Leaps its dead, the million poor,
Steel-staved and broken
                    and no grave shall hold them
Either in stone or sea; nor urn nor sand,
Skyline of city walls, their monument,
And on this field, lockstep in millions joined,
New world in fire opens where they stand.)

Wake to the song,
Only the young
                    shall outlive this dark hour
And night down streets the body walks alone;
Then up the stair; your portrait is my mirror;
Your features mine, and yours the quick, bright hair,
Read here my testament
                    when I am done,
This book is yours, the page uncut
                    Farewell, my brother
Comrade, son.

# Malcolm Cowley

MALCOLM COWLEY was born August 24, 1898, at Belsano in the valley between Laurel Hill and Chestnut Ridge, Pennsylvania. He was educated in the Pittsburgh public schools, at Harvard University, and the University of Montpellier. After going abroad he became identified for a while with the "left wing" group, helped edit "Secession," and contributed sporadically to the less popular magazines. Later he became one of the editors of *The New Republic*. Unrecognized as a creator, he became known for his translations from the French, and received especial praise for his version of Paul Valéry's *Variety* and Maurice Barrés' *The Sacred Hill*. It was not until his thirty-first year that he received serious appraisal as a critic and as an author of original gifts.

*Blue Juniata* (1929) traces, more or less chronologically, the genesis and growth of a poet. It begins in Cowley's west-central Pennsylvania and accompanies him on a fancied escape to Greenwich Village, through a further retreat (this time to Europe during the *Valuta* years of 1920-1924), a revulsion from self-imposed exile, to the final return. It has, therefore, the round development characteristic of the novel, a continuity and expansion one seldom finds in a book of poems. The first and, in many ways, the best section is sensitive and even lyrical; the second records that sentimental attachment to the sordid which, appropriate to youth, is a feverish and inverted nostalgia; the third registers a natural though somewhat elegant scorn for the *Valutaschweine* and the unrealities of a life which "ceased to have any values, only prices"; the fourth is a mixed paean and protest, a reaction to the speeded-up, machine-jazz-driven, overstimulated metropolis of "lasting impermanences"; the fifth and concluding section is the coda, self-described by its subtitle "Old Melodies: Love and Death."

Here is the material for a searching work and, even in the most experimental pages, there is nothing superficial about Cowley. But, except in the first section and parts of the last, Cowley penetrates fewer surfaces than he leaves undisturbed. This is chiefly due to a method which is disruptive and to an idiom which is staccato and often feverish. Cowley himself is quick to forestall his critics, saying in one instance, "I have ceased to value many of these poems; their emotions and their technique are too impermanent," and in another, "Our writings . . . had other qualities that were more questionable—a sort of crooked sentiment, a self-protective smirk." Much of this is the poetry of adolescence, but the adolescent who was responsible for "Kelly's Barroom," "Nocturne," and "Free Clinic" could turn, a few years later, to expression as ripe as "Three Hills" and as simple-startling as "Two Swans."

The title-poem, "Mine No. 6" and "The Farm Died," are further advances. They mark, with increasing confidence, the poet's attempt to record the conflict between time and timelessness, an accomplishment emphasized by the double sonnet "Winter."

### BLUE JUNIATA

Farmhouses curl like horns of plenty, hide
lean paintless shanks against a barn, or crouch

empty in the shadow of a mountain. Here
there is no house at all—

Only the bones of a house,
lilacs growing beside them,
roses in clumps between them,
honeysuckle over;
a door, a crooked chimney,
mud-chinked, a yawning fireplace,
the skeleton of a pine;

a railroad thirty yards from the empty door.

I heard a railroad section-man playing on a jew's-harp,
*Where is now that merry party I remember long ago?*
*Nelly was a lady* . . . twice . . . *Old Black Joe,*
as if he laid a hand upon my shoulder,
saying:
　　　　"Your father lived here long ago;
your father's father built the house, lies buried
under the pine—"
　　　　　　　Sing *Nelly was a lady*
. . . *Blue Juniata* . . . *Old Black Joe.*

For sometimes a familiar music hammers
like blood against the eardrums, paints a mist
across the eyes, as if the smell of lilac,
moss-roses and the past became a music
made visible, a monument of air.


### THE FARM DIED

I watched the agony of a mountain farm,
a gangrenous decay:
the farm died with the pines that sheltered it;
the farm died when the woodshed rotted away.

It died to the beat of a loose board on the barn
that flapped in the wind all night;
nobody came to drive a nail in it.
The farm died in a broken window-light,

a broken pane upstairs in the guest bedroom,
through which the autumn rain
beat down all night upon the Turkey carpet;
nobody thought to putty in a pane.

Nobody nailed another slat on the corncrib;
nobody mowed the hay;
nobody came to mend the rusty fences.
The farm died when the two boys went away,

or maybe lived till the old man was buried,
but after it was dead I loved it more,
though poison sumac grew in the empty pastures,
though ridgepoles fell, and though November winds
came all night whistling through an open door.

### MINE NO. 6

They scoured the hill with steel and living brooms
of fire, that nothing living might persist;
here crouch their cabins; here the tipple looms
uncompromising, black against the mist.

All day the wagons lumber past, the wide
squat wheels hub deep, the horses strained and still;
the headlong rain pours down all day to hide
the blackened stumps, the ulcerated hill.

Beauty, perfection, I have loved you fiercely
—even in this windy slum, where fear
drips from the eaves like August rain, and scarcely
a leaf sprouts, and a universe of pain
labors to bear its stillborn fruit—even here
. . . your long white cruel fingers at my brain.

### WINTER: TWO SONNETS

#### I

The year swings over slowly, like a pilot
southward now driving from the cold and dark
toward vertical suns and days of briefer twilight
and lights less promptly lighted in the park,

more definite nights, and days more sharply ending.
. . . How shrouded, empty of voice, the streets appear
in these December dusks, their skies distending
till Snow falls at the turning of the year.

Only in a dead city one man waking,
who tried to read the city by the glow
of towers feebly luminous and seeking
God in the skies grown suddenly bright with snow,
who listened, till he heard the city speaking
in mortuary whispers to the snow.

#### II

When little daily winds have died away,
and turkeys climb to roost in the apple tree,
across the snow night creeps so gradually
no eye can mark the cornerstone of day.

Now tightly draw the blinds against the dark
and see in lamplight how the room awakes,
Listen . . . through the tangible silence breaks,
out of the woodlot, a dog-fox's bark.

A creak of rusty hinges in the wind:
his voice was like the rasping of a door,
and when it ceased the darkness instantly
became so hugely silent that behind
a final range of hills we heard the sea
growling with all his voices at the shore.

# Hart Crane

HART CRANE was born in Garrettsville, Ohio, in 1899 and educated in the public schools of his state. Avoiding college, he worked in the ranks of advertising copywriters, chiefly in Cleveland and New York. In his early twenties his poetry—incomprehensible to some, extraordinary to others—began to appear in the more radical magazines. Crane traveled much, to England and the Continent, later to Mexico. After a chaotic life he committed suicide by jumping from a northbound steamer in the Gulf of Mexico, April 28, 1932.

*White Buildings* (1926) is obviously founded on rhetoric, but rhetoric of a new order. Influenced by Rimbaud, Poe, and Wallace Stevens—poets devoted to tonal gradations and color-values of words—Hart Crane's verbal ingenuity is often as accomplished as theirs.

Sometimes he transcends ingenuity, striking out phrases as felicitous as "Where the cedar leaf divides the sky" and "In sapphire arenas of the hills." But *White Buildings* is the record of esthetic as well as emotional conflict. Alternating between actual delineation and complete departure from representation, the verse approximates without quite achieving an "absolute" poetry. Romantic in inception, its gestures are larger than itself; as Allen Tate hints in his introduction, Crane has not yet discovered a theme to embody his uncoördinated visions.

In *The Bridge* (1930) the theme has been found. A set of disparate poems has been united by vital figures and national myths. The sense of time flows like a leading theme through variations in which Pocahontas, Rip Van Winkle, and the Subway are not isolated legends but significantly related phenomena. Crane's style has undergone only a slight change, but that change, necessitated by the larger work, is important. Surprise and a romantic strangeness are still principles of his work, but discipline controls singularity; the mystical rhetoric now plays about a central organization.

Crane's influences have not been wholly discarded; one does not have to look far to recognize the color-suggestions of Stevens and the contrast-methods of Pound and Eliot. Yet it is equally evident that Crane is not spiritually persuaded by any of these, but rather by poets who might be thought their opposites. His visions—his very mottoes—are those of Blake, the Book of Job, Emily Dickinson, Walt Whitman.

It is the spirit of Whitman, the spirit of "competent loam, the probable grass," which is apotheosized on a rising cadence and lifts a broken but finally sustained passion to prophetic rhapsody. *The Bridge* lacks the final integration, but its individual sections are eloquent. Such a passage as the one quoted from "Cape Hatteras" comes close to realizing Crane's dream of using images from contemporary life and science, of "acclimatizing" the machine with its "nasal whine of power." The phrasing here accomplishes the paradox of being both suggestive and brilliantly exact.

There will be those who will find Crane's poetry not merely tangential but cryptic. The difficulty is caused by his combination of allusiveness and allegory, especially since the allusions are often remote and the allegorical symbols personal to the point of privacy. But what Crane loses in directness he gains in implication; he has perfected a rounded locution from which the meaning is always sliding off and yet maintaining something more than the surface meaning. It is a triumph of suggestiveness, an exact inexactitude. *The Bridge,* in its lofty reach and inclusive intention, carries the rhetorician beyond himself and approximates a highly sophisticated, highly syncopated local epic.

Several critics consider Crane's early short pieces, such as "Voyages" and "Praise for an Urn" among his best. Speaking of the latter, Allen Tate wrote in his memoir, "although his later development gave us a poetry that the period would be much the less rich for not having, he never again had such perfect mastery of his subject. And I think this was because he never afterwards knew precisely what his subject was. . . . Crane was the archetype of the modern American poet whose fundamental mistake lay in thinking that an irrational surrender of the intellect to the will would be the basis of a new mentality."

The substitution of sensation for thought, of will for intellect, is completely revealed in *Collected Poems of Hart Crane* (1933). This posthumous volume includes, besides a sensitive if too rapturous preface by Waldo Frank, several new poems, particularly brilliant being the more "representational" West Indian verses of which Crane was fond and which appear in the following group.

VAN WINKLE

*(from "The Bridge")*

Macadam, gun-gray as the tunny's belt,
Leaps from Far Rockaway to Golden Gate:
Listen! the miles a hurdy-gurdy grinds—
Down gold arpeggios mile on mile unwinds.

Times earlier, when you hurried off to school,
—It is the same hour though a later day—
You walked with Pizarro in a copybook,
And Cortes rode up, reining tautly in—
Firmly as coffee grips the taste,—and away!

There was Priscilla's cheek close in the wind,
And Captain Smith, all beard and certainty,
And Rip Van Winkle, bowing by the way,—
"Is this Sleepy Hollow, friend—?" And he—

*And Rip forgot the office hours,*
              *and he forgot the pay;*
*Van Winkle sweeps a tenement*
              *down town on Avenue A,—*

The grind-organ says . . . Remember, remember
The cinder pile at the end of the backyard
Where we stoned the family of young
Garter snakes under . . . And the monoplanes
We launched—with paper wings and twisted
Rubber bands. . . . Recall—
                              the rapid tongues
That flittered from under the ash heap day
After day whenever your stick discovered
Some sunning inch of unsuspecting fiber—
It flashed back at your thrust, as clean as fire.

*And Rip was slowly made aware*
              *that he, Van Winkle, was not here*
*Nor there. He woke and swore he'd seen Broadway*
              *a Catskill daisy chain in May—*

So memory, that strikes a rhyme out of a box,
Or splits a random smell of flowers through glass—
Is it the whip stripped from the lilac tree
One day in spring my father took to me,
Or is it the Sabbatical, unconscious smile
My mother almost brought me once from church
And once only, as I recall—?

It flickered through the snow screen, blindly
It forsook her at the doorway; it was gone
Before I had left the window. It
Did not return with the kiss in the hall.

Macadam, gun-gray as the tunny's belt,
Leaps from Far Rockaway to Golden Gate . . .
Keep hold of that nickel for car-change, Rip,—
Have you got your paper—?
And hurry along, Van Winkle—it's getting late!

### ROYAL PALM

Green rustlings, more-than-regal charities
Drift coolly from that tower of whispered light.
Amid the noontide's blazed asperities
I watched the sun's most gracious anchorite

Climb up as my communings, year on year
Uneaten of the earth or aught earth holds,

And the gray trunk, that's elephantine, rear
Its frondings sighing in aetherial folds.

Forever fruitless, and beyond that yield
Of sweat the jungle presses with hot love
And tendril till our deathward breath is sealed—
It grazes the horizons, launched above

Mortality—ascending emerald-bright,
A fountain at salute, a crown in view—
Unshackled, casual of its azured height
As though it soared suchwise through heaven too.

### THE TUNNEL

*(from "The Bridge")*

*To find the Western path*
*Right thro' the Gates of Wrath*
                    —BLAKE.

Performances, assortments, résumés—
Up Times Square to Columbus Circle lights
Channel the congresses, nightly sessions,
Refractions of the thousand theaters, faces—
Mysterious kitchens . . . You shall search them all.
Some day by heart you'll learn each famous sight
And watch the curtain lift in hell's despite;
You'll find the garden in the third act dead,
Finger your knees—and wish yourself in bed
With tabloid crime-sheets perched in easy sight.

> Then let you reach your hat
> and go.
> As usual, let you—also
> walking down—exclaim
> to twelve upward leaving
> a subscription praise
> for what time slays . . .

Or can't you quite make up your mind to ride;
A walk is better underneath the L for a brisk
Ten blocks or so before? But you find yourself
Preparing penguin flexions of the arms—
As usual you will meet the scuttle yawn:
The subway yawns the quickest promise home.

Be minimum then, to swim the hiving swarms
Out of the Square, the Circle burning bright—
Avoid the glass doors gyring at your right,
Where boxed alone a second, eyes take fright
—Quite unprepared rush naked back to light:

And down beside the turnstile press the coin
Into the slot. The gongs already rattle.

> And so
> of cities you bespeak
> subways, rivered under streets
> and rivers . . . In the car
> the overtone of motion
> underground, the monotone
> of motion is the sound
> of other faces, also underground—

"Let's have a pencil Jimmy—living now
at Floral Park
Flatbush—on the fourth of July—
like a pigeon's muddy dream—potatoes
to dig in the field—travlin' the town too—
night after night—the Culver line—the
girls all shaping up—it used to be—"

Our tongues recant like beaten weather vanes.
This answer lives like verdigris, like hair
Beyond extinction, surcease of the bone;
And repetition freezes—"What
what do you want? getting weak on the links?
fandaddle daddy don't ask for change—IS THIS
FOURTEENTH? it's half-past six she said—if
you don't like my gate why did you
swing on it, why *didja*
swing on it
anyhow—"

> And somehow anyhow swing—

The phonographs of hades in the brain
Are tunnels that re-wind themselves, and love—
A burnt match skating in a urinal
Somewhere above Fourteenth TAKE THE EXPRESS
To brush some new presentiment of pain—

"But I want service in this office SERVICE
I said—after
the show she cried a little afterwards but—"

Whose head is swinging from the swollen strap?
Whose body smokes along the bitten rails,
Bursts from a smoldering bundle far behind
In back forks of the chasms of the brain—
Puffs from a riven stump far out behind
In interborough fissures of the mind . . . ?

And why do I often meet your visage here,
Your eyes like agate lanterns—on and on
Below the toothpaste and the dandruff ads?
—And did their riding eyes right through your side,
And did their eyes like unwashed platters ride?
And Death, aloft—gigantically down
Probing through you toward me, O Evermore!
And when they dragged your retching flesh,
Your trembling hands that night through Baltimore—
That last night on the ballot rounds, did you,
Shaking—did you deny the ticket, Poe?

For Gravesend Manor change at Chambers Street.
The platform hurries along to a dead stop.
The intent escalator lifts a serenade
Stilly
Of shoes, umbrellas, each eye attending its shoe, then
Bolting outright somewhere above where streets
Burst suddenly in rain . . . The gongs recur:
Elbows and levers, guard and hissing door.
Thunder is galvothermic here below . . . The car
Wheels off. The train rounds, bending to a scream,
Taking the final level for the dive
Under the river—

And somewhat emptier than before,
Demented, for a hitching second, humps; then
Lets go . . . Toward corners of the floor
Newspapers wing, revolve and wing.
Blank windows gargle signals through the roar.

And does the Daemon take you home, also,
Wop washerwoman, with the bandaged hair?
After the corridors are swept, the cuspidors—
The gaunt sky-barracks cleanly now, and bare,
O Genoese, do you bring mother-eyes and hands
Back home to children and to golden hair?

Daemon, demurring and eventful yawn!
Whose hideous laughter is the bellows mirth
—Or the muffled slaughter of a day in birth—
O cruelly to inoculate the brinking dawn
With antennae toward worlds that spark and sink—
To spoon us out more liquid than the dim
Locution of the eldest star, and pack
The conscience naveled in the plunging wind,
Umbilical to call—and straightway die!
O caught like pennies beneath soot and steam,
Kiss of our agony thou gatherest;
Condensed, thou takest all—shrill ganglia
Impassioned with some song we fail to keep.

And yet, like Lazarus, to feel the slope,
The sod and billow breaking—lifting ground,
—A sound of waters bending astride the sky
Unceasing with some word that will not die!

✦

A tugboat, wheezing wreaths of steam,
Lunged past, with one galvanic blare stove up the river.
I counted the echoes assembling, one after one,
Searching, thumbing the midnight on the piers.
Lights, coasting left the oily tympanum of waters;
The blackness somewhere gouged glass on a sky.

And this thy harbor, O my City, I have driven under,
Tossed from the coil of ticking towers . . . Tomorrow,
And to be . . . Here by the River that is East—
Here at the waters' edge the hands drop memory;
Shadowless in that abyss they unaccounting lie.
How far away the star has pooled the sea—
Or shall the hands be drawn away, to die?

Kiss of our agony Thou gatherest,
                    O Hand of Fire
                              gatherest—


VOYAGES: II

—And yet this great wink of eternity,
Of rimless floods, unfettered leewardings,
Samite sheeted and processioned where
Her undinal vast belly moonward bends,
Laughing the wrapt inflections of our love;

Take this Sea, whose diapason knells
On scrolls of silver snowy sentences,
The sceptered terror of whose sessions rends
As her demeanors motion well or ill,
All but the pieties of lovers' hands.

And onward, as bells off San Salvador
Salute the crocus lusters of the stars,
In these poinsettia meadows of her tides,—
Adagios of islands, O my Prodigal,
Complete the dark confessions her veins spell.

Mark how her turning shoulders wind the hours,
And hasten while her penniless rich palms
Pass superscription of bent foam and wave,—
Hasten, while they are true,—sleep, death, desire,
Close round one instant in one floating flower.

Bind us in time, O seasons clear, and awe.
O minstrel galleons of Carib fire,
Bequeath us to no earthly shore until
Is answered in the vortex of our grave
The seal's wide spindrift gaze toward paradise.

## VOYAGES: VI

Where icy and bright dungeons lift
Of swimmers their lost morning eyes,
And ocean rivers, churning, shift
Green borders under stranger skies,

Steadily as a shell secretes
Its beating leagues of monotone,
Or as many waters trough the sun's
Red kelson past the cape's wet stone;

O rivers mingling toward the sky
And harbor of the phoenix' breast—
My eyes pressed black against the prow,
—Thy derelict and blinded guest

Waiting, afire, what name, unspoke,
I cannot claim: let thy waves rear
More savage than the death of kings,
Some splintered garland for the seer.

Beyond siroccos harvesting
The solstice thunders, crept away,
Like a cliff swinging or a sail
Flung into April's inmost day—

Creation's blithe and petaled word
To the lounged goddess when she rose
Conceding dialogue with eyes
That smile unsearchable repose—

Still fervid covenant, Belle Isle,
—Unfolded floating dais before
Which rainbows twine continual hair—
Belle Isle, white echo of the oar!

The imaged word, it is, that holds
Hushed willows anchored in its glow.
It is the unbetrayable reply
Whose accent no farewell can know.

## PRAISE FOR AN URN

It was a kind and northern face
That mingled in such exile guise
The everlasting eyes of Pierrot
And, of Gargantua, the laughter.

His thoughts, delivered to me
From the white coverlet and pillow,
I see now, were inheritances—
Delicate riders of the storm.

The slant moon on the slanting hill
Once moved us toward presentiments
Of what the dead keep, living still,
And such assessments of the soul

As, perched in the crematory lobby,
The insistent clock commented on,
Touching as well upon our praise
Of glories proper to the time.

Still, having in mind gold hair,
I cannot see that broken brow
And miss the dry sound of bees
Stretching across a lucid space.

Scatter these well-meant idioms
Into the smoky spring that fills
The suburbs, where they will be lost.
They are no trophies of the sun.

## THE AIR PLANT

### (*Grand Cayman, W. I.*)

This tuft that thrives on saline nothingness,
Inverted octopus with heavenward arms
Thrust parching from a palm-bole hard by the cove—
A bird almost—of almost bird alarms,

Is pulmonary to the wind that jars
Its tentacles, horrific in their lurch.
The lizard's throat, held bloated for a fly,
Balloons but warily from this throbbing perch.

The needles and hacksaws of cactus bleed
A milk of earth when stricken off the stalk;
But this—defenseless, thornless, sheds no blood,
Scarce shadow even—but the air's thin talk.

Angelic Dynamo! Ventriloquist of the Blue!
While beachward creeps the shark-swept Spanish Main.
By what conjunctions do the winds appoint
Its apotheosis, at last—the hurricane!

### POWER

#### (from "Cape Hatteras")

The nasal whine of power whips a new universe . . .
Where spouting pillars spoor the evening sky,
Under the looming stacks of the gigantic power house
Stars prick the eyes with sharp ammoniac proverbs,
New verities, new inklings in the velvet hummed
Of dynamos where hearing's leash is strummed . . .
Power's script,—wound, bobbin-bound, refined—
Is stropped to the slap of belts on booming spools, spurred
Into the bulging bouillon, harnessed jelly of the stars.
Towards what? The forked crash of split thunder parts
Our hearing momentwise; but fast in whirling armatures,
As bright as frogs' eyes, giggling in the girth
Of steely gizzards—axle-bound, confined
In coiled precision, bunched in mutual glee
The bearings glint—O murmurless and shined
In oilrinsed circles of blind ecstasy!

Stars scribble on our eyes the frosty sagas,
The gleaming cantos of unvanquished space. . . .
O sinewy silver biplane, nudging the wind's withers!
There, from Kill Devils Hill at Kitty Hawk
Two brothers in their twinship left the dune;
Warping the gale, the Wright windwrestles veered
Capeward, then blading the wind's flank, banked and spun
What ciphers risen from prophetic script,
What marathons new-set between the stars!
The soul, by naphtha fledged into new reaches
Already knows the closer clasp of Mars,—
New latitudes, unknotting, soon give place
To what fierce schedules, rife of doom apace!

Behold the dragon's covey—amphibian, ubiquitous
To hedge the seaboard, wrap the headland, ride

The blue's unfeathered districts unto aether. . . .
While Iliads glimmer through eyes raised in pride
Hell's belt springs wider—into heaven's plumed side.
O bright circumferences, heights employed to fly
War's fiery kennel masked in downy offings,—
This tournament of space, the threshed and chiseled height,
Is baited by marauding circles, bludgeon flail
Of rancorous grenades whose screaming petals carve us
The wounds we wrap with theorems sharp as hail!

Wheeled swiftly, wings emerge from larval-silver hangars.
Taut motors surge, space-gnawing, into flight;
Through sparkling visibility, outspread, unsleeping
Wings clip the last peripheries of light. . . .
Tellurian wind-sleuths on dawn patrol,
Each plane a hurtling javelin of winged ordnance,
Bristle the heights above a screeching gale to hover;
Surely no eye that Sunward Escadrille can cover!
There, meaningful, fledged as the Pleiades
With razor sheen they zoom each rapid helix!
Up-chartered choristers of their own speeding
They, cavalcade on escapade, shear Cumulus—
Lay siege and hurdle Cirrus down the skies!
While Cetus-like, O thou Dirigible, enormous Lounger
Of pendulous auroral beaches,—satellited wide
By convoy planes, moonferrets that rejoin thee
On fleeing balconies as thou dost glide,
—Hast splintered space!

# Allen Tate

ALLEN TATE (whose full name, not often admitted, is John Orley Allen Tate) was born November 19, 1899, in Winchester, Clark County, Kentucky, and was educated in public and private schools in Louisville, Nashville, and Washington, D. C., and after some tergiversation was graduated from Vanderbilt University in 1922. Immediately thereafter, he engaged in free-lance literary criticism for which he is as well known as for his poetry. He was one of the founders, in 1922, of *The Fugitive,* sharing that distinction with John Crowe Ransom, Donald Davidson, and a few others. An avowed believer in sectionalism, his critical acumen runs parallel to his predilections in *Stonewall Jackson: The Good Soldier* (1928) and *Jefferson Davis: His Rise and Fall* (1929). Both biographies are skillfully constructed mosaics of fact and interpretation. His reviews and essays are among the most brilliant and provocative of his generation.

*Mr. Pope and Other Poems* (1928) reveals a mind that is critical and complex. His Ignis Fatuus, as acknowledged in Tate's Epilogue, has a "fierce latinity," and the adjective gives us an inkling of the paradox at the heart of his verse. Here Donne wrestles with Vergil; an essentially Gothic foundation shoots up into baroque efflorescences; the cultural tradition battles with vulgar aggressiveness. This clash between classicism and modernity—sublimated by Tate's transposition of romantic South and realistic North—strains to achieve a kind of harassed unity in *Mr. Pope and Other Poems*. A finesse of satire and a dissection of emotion combine to place most of the volume in the literature of wit, but poems like "Death of Little Boys" and "Ode to the Confederate Dead" are compact with feeling and so escape the category.

The more mature *Poems: 1928-1931* (1932) owes less to the intellectualist's conflict. Structure is still preëminent, but the poet emphasizes form without being a slave to it. Tate himself has said his method consists in playing the rôle of a hawk, "gradually circling round the subject, threatening it, filling it with suspense, and finally accomplishing its demise without ever quite using the ultimate violence upon it." The method has the disadvantages inherent in its aim. The reader waiting for forthright ideas expressed in the key of conversation, however heightened and intensified, will wait in vain. Tate is not concerned with the impulse that extends from Wordsworth to Frost, supplying "the charm of novelty to things of everyday"; he cannot flourish a finality or bring an emotion simply to the surface. In his circumlocutory, or circumambient, manner he is likely to leave the climax unsolved; the reader is not always certain that, in Tate's hawk-like swoop, the final capture is accomplished—not even in such poems as "Mother and Son" and "The Mediterranean," eloquent though they are.

Circulating "about" his subject, the poet gains a perspective, but loses a definiteness, even, at times, a direction which the reader is likely to require. The lines frequently suffer from excessive subjectivity, from a critical introspection at war with the lyric impulse. Thus Tate rewrites his poems so often that the original edge is sometimes lost. "His art," writes John Gould Fletcher, "is that of the lapidary, polishing and repolishing his work till it, literally, in many cases, has no life left." Although this is an exaggeration, it is true that such a fine poem as "Ode to the Confederate Dead" has been so much revised that where the new version gains in allusiveness, it loses in speed and directness. The new conclusion, however, is clearly superior, and it is the latest version which is given here.

In 1930, after two years abroad on a Guggenheim Foundation award, Tate returned to Tennessee, to an old estate a few miles from Clarksville on the Cumberland River. In 1934 he began lecturing in English literature at Southwestern College in Memphis, Tennessee. He was Southern editor of *Hound and Horn* from 1932 until the demise of that magazine in 1934, and a collection of his critical essays appeared in 1936. His later verse distinguishes *The Mediterranean and Other Poems* (1936).

### ODE TO THE CONFEDERATE DEAD

Row after row with strict impunity
The headstones yield their names to the element,
The wind whirrs without recollection;
In the riven troughs the splayed leaves
Pile up, of nature the casual sacrament
To the seasonal eternity of death,
Then driven by the fierce scrutiny
Of heaven to their business in the vast breath,
They sough the rumor of mortality.

Autumn is desolation in the plot
Of a thousand acres, where these memories grow
From the inexhaustible bodies that are not
Dead, but feed the grass row after rich row:
Remember now the autumns that have gone—
Ambitious November with the humors of the year,
With a particular zeal for every slab,
Staining the uncomfortable angels that rot
On the slabs, a wing chipped here, an arm there:
The brute curiosity of an angel's stare
Turns you like them to stone,
Transforms the heaving air,
Till plunged to a heavier world below
You shift your sea-space blindly,
Heaving, turning like the blind crab.

Dazed by the wind, only the wind
The leaves flying, plunge

You know who have waited by the wall
The twilit certainty of an animal;
Those midnight restitutions of the blood
You know—the immitigable pines, the smoky frieze
Of the sky, the sudden call; you know the rage—
The cold pool left by the mounting flood—
The rage of Zeno and Parmenides.
You who have waited for the angry resolution
Of those desires that should be yours tomorrow,
You know the unimportant shrift of death
And praise the vision
And praise the arrogant circumstance
Of those who fall
Rank upon rank, hurried beyond decision—
Here by the sagging gate, stopped by the wall.

Seeing, seeing only the leaves
Flying, plunge and expire

Turn your eyes to the immoderate past
Turn to the inscrutable infantry rising
Demons out of the earth—they will not last.
Stonewall, Stonewall—and the sunken fields of hemp,
Shiloh, Antietam, Malvern Hill, Bull Run.
Lost in that orient of the thick and fast
You will curse the setting sun.

Cursing only the leaves crying
Like an old man in a storm

You hear the shout—the crazy hemlocks point
With troubled fingers to the silence which
Smothers you, a mummy, in time. The hound bitch

Toothless and dying, in a musty cellar
Hears the wind only.
                         Now that the salt of their blood
Stiffens the saltier oblivion of the sea,
Seals the malignant purity of the flood,
What shall we, who count our days and bow
Our heads with a commemorial woe,
In the ribboned coats of grim felicity,
What shall we say of the bones, unclean—
Their verdurous anonymity will grow—
The ragged arms, the ragged heads and eyes
Lost in these acres of the insane green?
The gray lean spiders come; they come and go;
In a tangle of willows without light
The singular screech-owl's bright
Invisible lyric seeds the mind
With the furious murmur of their chivalry.

We shall say only, the leaves
Flying, plunge and expire

We shall say only, the leaves whispering
In the improbable mist of nightfall
That flies on multiple wing:
Night is the beginning and the end,
And in between the ends of distraction
Waits mute speculation, the patient curse
That stones the eyes, or like the jaguar leaps
For his own image in a jungle pool, his victim.

What shall we say who have knowledge
Carried to the heart? Shall we take the act
To the grave? Shall we, more hopeful, set up the grave
In the house? The ravenous grave?

                         Leave now
The turnstile and the old stone wall:
The gentle serpent, green in the mulberry bush,
Riots with his tongue through the hush—
Sentinel of the grave who counts us all!

### MR. POPE

When Alexander Pope strolled in the city
Strict was the glint of pearl and gold sedans.
Ladies leaned out, more out of fear than pity;
For Pope's tight back was rather a goat's than man's.

One often thinks the urn should have more bones
Than skeletons provide for speedy dust;
The urn gets hollow, cobwebs brittle as stones
Weave to the funeral shell a frivolous rust.

And he who dribbled couplets like the snake
Coiled to a lithe precision in the sun,
Is missing. The jar is empty; you may break
It only to find that Mr. Pope is gone.

What requisitions of a verity
Prompted the wit and rage between his teeth
One cannot say: around a crooked tree
A mortal climbs whose name should be a wreath.


### DEATH OF LITTLE BOYS

When little boys grow patient at last, weary,
Surrender their eyes immeasurably to the night,
The event will rage terrific as the sea;
Their bodies fill a crumbling room with light.

Then you will touch at the bedside, torn in two,
Gold curls now deftly intricate with gray
As the windowpane extends a fear to you
From one peeled aster drenched with the wind all day.

And over his chest the covers, in an ultimate dream,
Will mount to the teeth, ascend the eyes, press back
The locks—while round his sturdy belly gleam
The suspended breaths, white spars above the wreck:

Till all the guests, come in to look, turn down
Their palms; and delirium assails the cliff
Of Norway where you ponder, and your little town
Reels like a sailor drunk in his rotten skiff. . . .

The bleak sunshine shrieks its chipped music then
Out to the milkweed amid the fields of wheat.
There is a calm for you where men and women
Unroll the chill precision of moving feet.


### MOTHER AND SON

Now all day long the man who is not dead
Hastens the dark with inattentive eyes,
The lady of the white hand, of the erect head
Stares at the cover, leans for the son's replies
At last to her importunate womanhood—
That hand of death laid on the living bed;
Such is the fierce compositor of blood.

She waits; he lies upon the bed of sin
Where greed, avarice, anger writhed and slept
Till to their silence they were gathered in;
There, fallen with time, his tall and wicked kin

Once fired the passions that were never kept
In the permanent heart, and there his mother lay
To bear him on the impenetrable day.

Because of this she cannot will her hand
Up to the bed nor break the manacle
Her exile sets upon her harsh command
That he should say the time is beautiful,
Transfigured with her own devouring light:
The sick man craves the impalpable night.

Loosed betwixt eye and lid, the swimming beams
Of memory, that school of cuttlefish
Rise to the air, plunge to the cold streams,
Rising and plunging the half-forgotten wish
To tear his heart out in some slow disgrace
And freeze the hue of terror to her face.

Hate, misery and fear beat off his heart
To the dry fury of the woman's mind;
The son prone in his autumn, moves apart
A seed blown upon a returning wind:
O child, be vigilant till towards the South
On the flowered wall all the sweet afternoon
That reach of sun, swift as the cottonmouth
Strikes at the black crucifix on her breast
Where the cold dusk comes suddenly to rest—
Mortality will speak the victor soon!

The dreary flies lazy and casual
Stick to the ceiling, buzz along the wall—
O heart, the spider shuffles from the mold
Weaving between the pinks and grapes his pall.
The bright wallpaper imperishably old
Uncurls and flutters; it will never fall.

## THE CROSS

There is a place that some men know,
I cannot see the whole of it,
Nor how men come there. Long ago
Flame burst out of a secret pit
Crushing the world with such a light
The day sky fell to moonless black,
The kingly sun to hateful night
For those, once seeing, turning back:
For love so hates mortality,
Which is the providence of life,
She will not let it blessèd be
But curses it with mortal strife,
Until beside the blinding rood
Within that world-destroying pit
—Like young wolves that have tasted blood,
Of death, men taste no more of it:
So blind in so severe a place
(All life before in the black grave)
The last alternatives they face
Of life, without the life to save,
Being from all salvation weaned—
A stag charged both at heel and head:
Who would come back is turned a fiend
Instructed by the fiery dead.

## THE MEDITERRANEAN

*Quem das finem, rex magne, dolorum?*

Where we went in the boat was a long bay
A sling-shot wide walled in by towering
    stone—
Peaked margin of antiquity's delay,
And we went there out of time's monotone:

Where we went in the black hull no light
    moved
But a gull white-winged along the feckless
    wave;
The breeze unseen but fierce as a body loved,
That boat drove onward like a willing slave.

Where we went in the small ship the seaweed
Parted and gave to us the murmuring shore
And we made feast and in our secret need
Devoured the very plates Aeneas bore:

Where derelict you see through the low twi-
    light
The green coast that you thunder-tossed
    would win,
Drop sail, and hastening to drink all night
Eat dish and bowl—to take that sweet land
    in!

Where we feasted and caroused on the sand
    less
Pebbles, affecting our day of piracy,
What prophecy of eaten plates could landless
Wanderers fulfill by the ancient sea?

We for that time might taste the famous age
Eternal here yet hidden from our eyes
When lust of power undid its stuffless rage
They, in a wineskin, bore earth's paradise

—Let us lie down once more by the breath-
    ing side
Of ocean, where our live forefathers sleep
As if the Known Sea still were a month
    wide—
Atlantis howls but is no longer steep!

What country shall we conquer, what fair
    land
Unman our conquest and locate our blood?
We've cracked the hemispheres with careless
    hand!
Now, from the Gates of Hercules we flood

Westward, westward till the barbarous brine
Whelms us to the tired world where tasseling
    corn,
Fat beans, grapes sweeter than muscadine
Rot on the vine: in that land were we born.

# Léonie Adams

Léonie adams was born in Brooklyn, New York, December 9, 1899. After a public
school preparation she became a member of the class of 1922 at Barnard College, supported herself in New York in various capacities for five years, was awarded
a "traveling fellowship" by the Guggenheim Foundation, and went abroad for two
years in 1928. After her return she taught for a while at New York University.

At Barnard she wrote her first published poems "in secret." While still an undergraduate, her remarkable "April Mortality" was printed in *The New Republic,* but,
although this would have been sufficient stimulus for most young authors to rush
into print, Miss Adams remained more reticent than ever and rarely submitted any
of her verse for publication.

It was only through the persuasion of two or three friends that her volume, *Those
Not Elect* (1925), was made ready for the press. The author's evasion of "realism"
is apparent in all of her poetry. The poems themselves are of two sorts: the younger
and simpler verses, full of a shy ecstasy, and the later, more metaphysical expres-

sions of a rare and not lightly communicated wonder. Without imitating the Elizabethans, Miss Adams has caught something of the quality of Webster and Vaughan. But whatever her style, whether she is direct as in "Home-Coming" or more difficult as in "The Horn," her sensitivity makes even the obscure passages a succession of inevitable images. Few poets have fixed the changing aspects of earth and sky, the fluid seasons, the constant variability of light with such natural certainty. Her most candid descriptions take on an unearthly and intensified air; even her statement of a landscape, or the performance of a tragedy, or "the pointed grass" drinking the light "till light brimmed even," or the old cheating of the sun is translated in lines both pure and suggestive. One may sometimes mistake her meaning; there is no mistaking the beauty of her imagination which lifts emotion, holding it, as it were, in suspense. There is not a line in her first book which is without distinction.

The same is true of *High Falcon* (1929). This is abstract poetry in the highest sense; the word is more than a word; the letter is uplifted by pure spirit. The lyrical line, carried on wave after wave of music, transcends personality. The ecstasy, however, is no less ecstatic for being disembodied; every phrase carries its import of intensities, of vistas larger than the scene, of meaning beyond meaning. It is a rarefied atmosphere which Miss Adams breathes and only a height-loving reader can venture with her into that fine air. "Twilit Revelation," "Bell Tower," "Sundown," "Country Summer" are a few of the poems in which the heart "extracts the spirit of the temporal." Neither sense nor the senses can wholly interpret this poetry, but every figure and accent compel us with authority. What, at first glance, seems obscurely metaphysical is resolved into a spiritual clarity that approaches clairvoyance. Here, we are in the presence of greatness; here matter is sanctified, "dipped in a gold stain."

"The Mount" synthesizes Miss Adams' qualities. One of her finest poems, it creates a new symbol of time; the sense of continuity is expressed through an image which is a little remote but quickly recognizable, holding a nice balance between the strange and the familiar. As Miss Adams wrote, "It seems to me to bear a special relation to most of the other verses in *High Falcon;* with respect to some it repeats what they have essentially to say with greater decision; and, with respect to others, expresses a resolution of much that is in them at loose ends."

Her utterance is unique, but it is no posture of "difference," no straining singularity. On the contrary, this is verse of the most reticent dignity, in which nothing, not even the mystical note, is overstressed. Herein lies Miss Adams' danger—or rather the danger to her imitators, for, since she is obviously "a poet's poet," imitated she will be. The surface pattern is easy enough to master: the withdrawn loveliness, the muted music, the faint Elizabethanism; but, lacking her rapt and actually reverent touch, the result would be only an echo of delicate diction. Miss Adams would undoubtedly gain a wider audience were she to mix a little more flesh with her spirit, but she would lose that virginal radiance which rises from springs more profound than those of the too nimbly gushing heart.

### APRIL MORTALITY

Rebellion shook an ancient dust,
   And bones bleached dry of rottenness
Said: Heart, be bitter still, nor trust
   The earth, the sky, in their bright dress.

Heart, heart, dost thou not break to know
 This anguish thou wilt bear alone?
We sang of it an age ago,
 And traced it dimly upon stone.

With all the drifting race of men
 Thou also art begot to mourn
That she is crucified again,
 The lonely Beauty yet unborn.

And if thou dreamest to have won
 Some touch of her in permanence,
'Tis the old cheating of the sun,
 The intricate lovely play of sense.

Be bitter still, remember how
 Four petals, when a little breath
Of wind made stir the pear-tree bough,
 Blew delicately down to death.

## HOME-COMING

When I stepped homeward to my hill
 Dusk went before with quiet tread;
The bare laced branches of the trees
 Were as a mist about its head.

Upon its leaf-brown breast, the rocks
 Like great gray sheep lay silent-wise;
Between the birch trees' gleaming arms
 The faint stars trembled in the skies.

The white brook met me half-way up
 And laughed as one that knew me well,
To whose more clear than crystal voice
 The frost had joined a crystal spell.

The skies lay like pale-watered deep.
 Dusk ran before me to its strand
And cloudily leaned forth to touch
 The moon's slow wonder with her hand.

## THOUGHT'S END

I watched the hills drink the last color of light,
All shapes grow bright and wane on the pale air.
Till down the traitorous east there came the night,
And swept the circle of my seeing bare.
Its intimate beauty like a wanton's veil
Tore from the void as from an empty face.
I felt at being's rim all being fail,
And my one body pitted against space.

O heart more frightened than a wild bird's wings,
Beating at green, now is no fiery mark
Left on the quiet nothingness of things.
Be self no more against the flooding dark:
There thousandwise sown in that cloudy blot
Stars that are worlds look out and see you not.

### DEATH AND THE LADY

*Their bargain told again*

Death to the Lady said
While she to dancing-measures still
Would move, while beauties on her lay,
Simply as dews the buds do fill,
Death said: "Stay!
Tell me, Lady,
If in your breast the lively breath
May flicker for a little space,
What ransom will you give to death,
Lady?" he said.
"O not one joy, O not one grace,
And what is your will to my will?
I can outwit parched fancies still."
To Death said the Lady.

Death to that Lady said,
When blood went numb and wearily,
"In innocency dear breath you drew,
And marrow and bloom you rendered me,"
She said: "True."
"How now, Lady?"
"My heart sucked up its sweet at will,
Whose scent when substance' sweet is past,
Is lovely still, is lovely still,
Death," she said.
"For bones' reprieve the dreams go last:
Soon, soon your flowery show did part,
But preciously I cull the heart,"
Death said to the Lady.

Death to that Lady said:
"Is then not all our bargain done?
Or why do you beckon me so fast
To chaffer for a skeleton
Flesh must cast,
Ghostly Lady?"
"For, Death, that I would have you drain
From my dead heart the blood that stands
So chilly in the withered vein.
And, Death," she said,

"Give my due bones into your hands."
"Beauties I claim at morning-prime,
But the lack-luster in good time,"
Death said to the Lady.

### TWILIT REVELATION

This hour was set the time for heaven's descent
Come drooping toward us on the heavy air,
The sky, that's heaven's seat above us bent,
Blue faint as violet-ash, you near me there
In nether space so drenched in goblin blue,
I could touch Hesperus as soon as you.

Now I perceive you lapt in singling light,
Washed by that blue which sucks whole planets in,
And hung like those top jewels of the night,
A mournful gold too high for love to win.
And you, poor brief, poor melting star, you seem
Half sunk, and half to brighten in that stream.

And these rich-bodied hours of our delight
Show like a moth-wing's substance when the fall
Of confine-loosing, blue unending night
Extracts the spirit of this temporal.
So space can pierce the crevice wide between
Fast hearts, skies deep-descended intervene.

### GHOSTLY TREE

O beech, unbind your yellow leaf, for deep
The honeyed time lies sleeping, and lead shade
Seals up the eyelids of its golden sleep.
Long are your flutes, chimes, little bells at rest,
And here is only the cold scream of the fox,
Only the hunter following on the hound,
And your quaint-plumagèd,
The bird that your green happy boughs lapped round,
Bends south its soft bright breast.

Before the winter and the terror break,
Scatter the leaf that broadened with the rose,
Not for a tempest, but a sigh to take.
Four nights to exorcise the thing that stood,
Bound by these frail which dangle at your branch,
They ran a frosty dagger to its heart,
And it, wan substance,
No more remembered it might cry, or start,
Or stain a point with blood.

## THE HORN

In coming to the feast I found
A venerable silver-throated horn,
Which were I brave enough to sound,
Then all as from that moment born
Would breathe the honey of this clime,
And three times merry in their time,
Would praise the virtue of that horn.

The mist is risen like thin breath,
The young leaves of the ground smell chill,
So faintly are they strewn on death,
The road I came down a west hill.
But none can name as I can name
A little golden-bright thing flame,
Since bones have caught their marrow chill.

And in a thicket passed me by,
In the black brush a running hare,
Having a specter in his eye,
That sped in darkness to the snare;
And who but I can know in pride,
The heart set beating in the side
Has but the wisdom of a hare?

## THE RIVER IN THE MEADOWS

rystal parting the meads,
  boat drifted up it like a swan,
ranquil, lovely, its bright front to the
  waters,
  slow swan is gone.

ll waters, O flowing silver,
ure, level with the clover,
  will stain drowning a star,
ith the moon it will brim over.

unning through lands dewy and shorn,
attle stoop at its brink,
nd every fawny-colored throat
ill sway its bells and drink.

saw a boat sailing the river
ith a tranced gait; it seemed
oosed by a spell from its moorings,
r a thing the helmsman dreamed.

hey said it would carry no traveler,
ut the vessel would go down,

If a heart were heavy-winged,
Or the bosom it dwelt in, stone.

## COUNTRY SUMMER

Now the rich cherry whose sleek wood
And top with silver petals traced,
Like a strict box its gems encased,
Has spilt from out that cunning lid,
All in an innocent green round,
Those melting rubies which it hid;
With moss ripe-strawberry-encrusted,
So birds get half, and minds lapse merry
To taste that deep-red lark's-bite berry,
And blackcap-bloom is yellow-dusted.

The wren that thieved it in the eaves
A trailer of the rose could catch
To her poor droopy sloven thatch,
And side by side with the wren's brood,—
O lovely time of beggars' luck—
Opens the quaint and hairy bud.
And full and golden is the yield
Of cows that never have to house,

But all night nibble under boughs,
Or cool their sides in the moist field.

Into the rooms flow meadow airs,
The warm farm-baking smell blows round;
Inside and out and sky and ground
Are much the same; the wishing star,
Hesperus, kind and early-born,
Is risen only finger-far.
All stars stand close in summer air,
And tremble, and look mild as amber;
When wicks are lighted in the chamber
You might say stars were settling there.

Now straightening from the flowery hay,
Down the still light the mowers look;
Or turn, because their dreaming shook,
And they waked half to other days,
When left alone in yellow-stubble,
The rusty-coated mare would graze.
Yet thick the lazy dreams are born;
Another thought can come to mind,
But like the shivering of the wind,
Morning and evening in the corn.

## THE MOUNT

"No, I have tempered haste,"
The joyous traveler said,
"The steed has passed me now
Whose hurrying hooves I fled.
My specter rides thereon,
I learned what mount he has,
Upon what summers fed;
And wept to know again,
Beneath the saddle swung,
Treasure for whose great theft
This breast was wrung.
His bridle bells sang out,
I could not tell their chime,
So brilliantly he rings,
But called his name as Time.
His bin was morning light,
Those straws which gild his bed
Are of the fallen West.
Although green lands consume
Beneath their burning tread,
In everlasting bright
His hooves have rest."

## THIS MEASURE

This measure was a measure to my mind,
Still musical through the unlikely hush.
The cold goes wide as doors, and in will come
Those notes of May set ringing through the brush,
Where every voice by natural law is dumb.

How many seasons I have watched the boughs,
That first are happy-tongued and happy-leaved,
Then bleed, as though an autumn were the last,
While that great life was with them undeceived,
Which all a wintering world seals home more fast.

Now visibly indeed I am assailed,
Yet I seem come clap on my very thing;
And now I learn I only asked as much:
It was in blooming weeks I lacked a spring
Rooted and blowing beyond sense or touch.

## BELL TOWER

I have seen, O desolate one, the voice has its tower,
The voice also, builded at secret cost,
Its temple of precious tissue; not silent then,
Forever. Casting silence in your hour.

There marble boys are leant from the light throat,
Thick locks that hang with dew, and eyes dew-lashed,
Dazzled with morning,—angels of the wind,
With ear a-point for the enchanted note.

And these at length shall tip the hanging bell,
And first the sound must gather in deep bronze,
Till, rarer than ice, purer than a bubble of gold,
It fill the sky to beat on an airy shell.

## KINGDOM OF HEAVEN

Bleak the February light
On the dark threshold spread,
The frost stood thick against the lock,
The clock for the great cold stopped dead,
When old wits idle with their luck
Lay singing in the bed,
That heard, while white frost span by night,
A pigeon happy with its bread.

And sang: I wakened to a sound
Which the streams make at thaw,
And pity on the shape I found
Inside a looking-glass with light.
For looking on my heart I saw,
A time before the break of day,
And looking won to second-sight,
And cast my character away.

The fields lie bound beneath the sky,
The hedge-top and the furrow freeze,
And still old plow-wheels sigh,
As sweet as bones which stretch from sleep,
And sooner than their sound is by,
Will come a noise of yellow bees
When the hay is nodding deep,
And some wise throat that laughs for ease.

Till there was a soft voice which spoke:
Hush, for every sound you tell
Is out of an old horn I blew.
I have come down to see who woke
On earth's cold brink when night was
   through.
No wilder chance befell,
Than the starry breath I drew.
I am Gabriel.

## SUNDOWN

This is the time lean woods shall spend
A steeped-up twilight, and the pale evening drink,
And the perilous roe, the leaper to the west brink,
Trembling and bright, to the caverned cloud descend.

Now shall you see pent oak gone gusty and frantic,
Stooped with dry weeping, ruinously unloosing
The sparse disheveled leaf, or reared and tossing
A dreary scarecrow bough in funeral antic.

Aye, tatter you and rend,
Oak heart, to your profession mourning, not obscure
The outcome, not crepuscular, on the deep floor,
Sable and gold match lusters and contend.

And rags of shrouding will not muffle the slain.
This is the immortal extinction, the priceless wound
Not to be staunched; the live gold leaks beyond,
And matter's sanctified, dipped in a gold stain.

### NIGHT-PIECE

The moon above the milky field
Gleaning moves her one slant light,
The wind weeps from the cloud:
Then, weeping wind, unshroud
Pale Cassiopeia, blow
The true-swung pole-lamp bright.
To this room a midnight's come
Which speaks but with the beating clock,
While on glistening paws the mouse
Creeps night-master of the house.
Rust shall eat away the lock,
The door sag from the garner hoard,
And the sleeper lie unsphered.
Time's wheel frets on his finger still,
He bends no more his weight with time's.
He wept as long as wind,
And sleeps with an indifferent will.
Not airs, not climes unclose, behind
The lashes' scarcely faltering jet,
Which star he sees since Hesper set.

### LULLABY

Hush, lullay,
Your treasures all
        Encrust with rust.
Your trinket pleasures
        Fall
To dust.
Beneath the sapphire arch
Upon the grassy floor
Is nothing more
        To hold,
And play is over old.
Your eyes
        In sleepy fever gleam,
Your lids droop
        To their dream.
You wander late alone,
The flesh frets on the bone,
Your love fails
        In your breast.
Here is the pillow.
        Rest.

# Langston Hughes

LANGSTON HUGHES was born February 1, 1902, in Joplin, Missouri. He was brought up in cities in the Middle West, graduated from Central High School in Cleveland, and at eighteen became a teacher of English in Mexico, where he lived for a year and a half. He spent a year at Columbia University and some time as a worker on the high seas. Hughes' next move was a foreign hegira to Paris in midwinter with seven dollars in his pocket. He stayed in France ten months, worked his way through Italy and Spain, and returned to New York with twenty-five cents. Working as a busboy in Washington, he was discovered by Vachel Lindsay, who read several of his poems to a fashionable audience in the very hotel in which Hughes carried trays of dishes.

The Weary Blues, Hughes' first volume, appeared in January, 1926. One of the poems had already won first prize in a contest conducted by Opportunity, a magazine which did great service in fostering creative work by Negroes. Hughes' poetry appearing at the same time as Countee Cullen's justified those who claimed we were witnessing a revival of Negro art. The Negroes themselves began to prove the quality of their inheritance. Johnson's The Book of American Negro Poetry appeared, three collections of American Negro spirituals disclosed the melodic fertility of the black singers, and various collections of "blues" revealed how greatly contemporary American composers were indebted to the complicated rhythms of the dark musicians. Hughes was the first to express the spirit of these blues in words. In his note to his second volume, *Fine Clothes to the Jew* (1927), he writes, "The *Blues,* unlike the *Spirituals,* have a strict poetic pattern: one long line repeated and a third line to rhyme with the first two. Sometimes the second line in repetition is slightly changed and sometimes, but very seldom, it is omitted. The mood of the *Blues* is almost always despondency, but when they are sung people laugh."

Although at least half of Hughes' work centers about the blues, much of his poetry is grim in an essentially urban manner. His portraits of Negro workmen (as evidenced in the remarkable "Brass Spittoons" with its similarity in symbols to Anna Hempstead Branch's "The Monk in the Kitchen") are more memorable than those produced by any of his compatriots. Beneath the physical struggle one senses the more suffering spirit. *Dear Lovely Death* (1931), privately printed, is a proof that Hughes can turn from the "popular" to the proletarian and still remain on the level of poetry. His play *Mulatto* was produced early in 1936.

### HOMESICK BLUES

De railroad bridge's
A sad song in de air.
De railroad bridge's
A sad song in de air.
Ever' time de trains pass
I wants to go somewhere.

I went down to de station;
Ma heart was in ma mouth.
Went down to de station;
Heart was in ma mouth.
Lookin' for a box car
To roll me to de South.

Homesick blues, Lawd,
'S a terrible thing to have.
Homesick blues is
A terrible thing to have.
To keep from cryin'
I opens ma mouth an' laughs.

### BRASS SPITTOONS

Clean the spittoons, boy.
  Detroit,
  Chicago,
  Atlantic City,
  Palm Beach.
Clean the spittoons.
The steam in hotel kitchens,
And the smoke in hotel lobbies,
And the slime in hotel spittoons:

Part of my life.
  Hey, boy!
  A nickel,
  A dime, ·
  A dollar,
Two dollars a day.
  Hey, boy!
  A nickel,
  A dime,
  A dollar,
  Two dollars
Buys shoes for the baby.
House rent to pay.
Church on Sunday.
  My God!

Babies and church
and women and Sunday
all mixed up with dimes and
dollars and clean spittoons
and house rent to pay.
  Hey, boy!

A bright bowl of brass is beautiful to the
    Lord.
Bright polished brass like the cymbals
Of King David's dancers,
Like the wine cups of Solomon.
  Hey, boy!
A clean spittoon on the altar of the Lord.
A clean bright spittoon all newly polished,—
At least I can offer that.
  Com'mere, boy!

## SATURDAY NIGHT

Play it once.
O, play it some more.
Charlie is a gambler
An' Sadie is a whore.
    A glass o' whiskey
    An' a glass o' gin:
    Strut, Mr. Charlie,
    Till de dawn comes in.
Pawn yo' gold watch
An' diamond ring.
Git a quart o' licker.
Let's shake dat thing!
    Skee-de-dad! De-dad!
    Doo-doo-doo!
    Won't be nothin' left
    When de worms git through.
    An' you's a long time
    Dead
    When you is
    Dead, too.
So beat dat drum, boy!
Shout dat song:
Shake 'em up an' shake 'em up
All night long.
    Hey! Hey!
    Ho . . . Hum!
    Do it, Mr. Charlie,
    Till de red dawn come.

## JAZZ BAND IN A PARISIAN CABARET

Play that thing,
Jazz band!
Play it for the lords and ladies,
For the dukes and counts,
For the whores and gigolos,
For the American millionaires,
And the schoolteachers
Out for a spree.
Play it,
Jazz band!
You know that tune
That laughs and cries at the same time.
You know it.
    May I?
    Mais oui.
    Mein Gott!
    Parece una rumba.

Play it, jazz band!
You've got seven languages to speak in
And then some,
Even if you do come from Georgia.
    Can I go home wid yuh, sweetie?
    Sure.

## DRUM

Bear in mind
That death is a drum
Beating for ever
Till the last worms come
To answer its call,
Till the last stars fall,
Until the last atom
Is no atom at all,
Until time is lost
And there is no air
And space itself
Is nothing nowhere.
Death is a drum,
A signal drum,
Calling all life
To Come! Come!
Come!

## FLORIDA ROAD WORKERS

I'm makin' a road
For the cars
To fly by on.
Makin' a road
Through the palmetto thicket
For light and civilization
To travel on.

Makin' a road
For the rich old white men
To sweep over in their big cars
And leave me standin' here.

Sure,
A road helps all of us!
White folks ride—
And I get to see 'em ride.
I ain't never seen nobody
Ride so fine before.
Hey buddy!
Look at me.
I'm making a road!

# Countee Cullen

COUNTEE CULLEN was born in New York City, May 30, 1903. He was educated in the New York schools and at New York University, being graduated with the class of 1925. A year later he received his M.A. at Harvard (1926).

When *The Book of American Negro Poetry* was published in 1922, Cullen was still in his 'teens and his few verses were no more unusual than most youthful flights. Had the anthology been collected three years later, Cullen's work would have been one of its outstanding features. Beginning in 1924, poems by this hitherto unknown Negro began appearing in the magazines; within a year his name had reached the smallest of literary circles.

*Color* (1925) and *Copper Sun* (1927) suffer not only from the poet's influences but from his own juvenilia. There is, however, no gainsaying his gift of epigram and the neatness of his execution. Lacking the deep racial quality of Langston Hughes, his is a more literary accomplishment. If his verse is not as black as it might be painted, it is bold in concept and metaphor. "Heritage," which, in spite of reminiscences of Ralph Hodgson and Edna Millay, marks the peak of his first volume, still stands as one of the finest poems produced by an American Negro.

*The Ballad of the Brown Girl* (1927) appeared in the same year as his comprehensive anthology of Negro verse, *Caroling Dusk,* in which Cullen showed unexpected editorial acumen. *The Black Christ* (1930) suffers from the double handicap of formula in style and formula in feeling. Its program is ambitious and promises force; but here is no fire, only fluency. The poet seems to be victimized by his own epithets, and these lack surprise or conviction. As Harry Alan Potamkin wrote, reviewing the preceding volume, "Mr. Cullen has capitalized the fact of race without paying for such capitalization by the exploitation of the material and the essence of race. Once race becomes to him more than capital and its poetic form more than the statement of its fact, he will create, upon what are undoubtedly unusual gifts, poems of import."

*The Medea and Some Poems* (1935) contains an adequate but not inspired version of the poetic drama with several other verses.

## SIMON THE CYRENIAN SPEAKS

He never spoke a word to me,
And yet He called my name.
He never gave a sign to see,
And yet I knew and came.

At first I said, "I will not bear
His cross upon my back—
He only seeks to place it there
Because my skin is black."

But He was dying for a dream,
And He was very meek;

And in His eyes there shone a gleam
Men journey far to seek.

It was Himself my pity bought;
I did for Christ alone
What all of Rome could not have wrought
With bruise of lash or stone.

## THREE EPITAPHS

*For My Grandmother*
This lovely flower fell to seed.
Work gently, sun and rain—

She held it as her dying creed
That she would grow again.

*For a Virgin Lady*
For forty years I shunned the lust
Inherent in my clay:
Death only was so amorous
I let him have his way.

*A Lady I Know*
She thinks that even up in heaven
Her class lies late and snores,
While poor black cherubs rise at seven
To do celestial chores.

## HERITAGE

What is Africa to me:
Copper sun or scarlet sea,
Jungle star or jungle track,
Strong bronzed men, or regal black
Women from whose loins I sprang
When the birds of Eden sang?
*One three centuries removed*
*From the scenes his fathers loved,*
*Spicy grove, cinnamon tree,*
*What is Africa to me?*

So I lie, who all day long
Want no sound except the song
Sung by wild barbaric birds
Goading massive jungle herds,
Juggernauts of flesh that pass
Trampling tall defiant grass
Where young forest lovers lie,
Plighting troth beneath the sky.
So I lie, who always hear,
Though I cram against my ear
Both my thumbs and keep them there,
Great drums throbbing through the air.
So I lie, whose fount of pride,
Dear distress, and joy allied,
Is my somber flesh and skin,
With the dark blood dammed within
Like great pulsing tides of wine
That, I fear, must burst the fine
Channels of the chafing net
Where they surge and foam and fret.

Africa? A book one thumbs
Listlessly, till slumber comes.

Unremembered are her bats
Circling through the night, her cats
Crouching in the river reeds,
Stalking gentle flesh that feeds
By the river brink; no more
Does the bugle-throated roar
Cry that monarch claws have leapt
From the scabbards where they slept.
Silver snakes that once a year
Doff the lovely coats you wear,
Seek no covert in your fear
Lest a mortal eye should see;
What's your nakedness to me?
Here no leprous flowers rear
Fierce corollas in the air;
Here no bodies sleek and wet,
Dripping mingled rain and sweat,
Tread the savage measures of
Jungle boys and girls in love.

What is last year's snow to me,
Last year's anything? The tree
Budding yearly must forget
How its past arose or set—
Bough and blossom, flower, fruit,
Even what shy bird with mute
Wonder at her travail there,
Meekly labored in its hair.
*One three centuries removed*
*From the scenes his fathers loved,*
*Spicy grove, cinnamon tree,*
*What is Africa to me?*

So I lie, who find no peace
Night or day, no slight release
From the unremittent beat
Made by cruel padded feet
Walking through my body's street.
Up and down they go, and back,
Treading out a jungle track.
So I lie, who never quite
Safely sleep from rain at night—
I can never rest at all
When the rain begins to fall;
Like a soul gone mad with pain
I must match its weird refrain;
Ever must I twist and squirm,
Writhing like a baited worm,
While its primal measures drip
Through my body, crying, "Strip!

Doff this new exuberance.
Come and dance the Lover's Dance!"
In an old remembered way
Rain works on me night and day.

Quaint, outlandish heathen gods
Black men fashion out of rods,
Clay and brittle bits of stone,
In a likeness of their own,
My conversion came high-priced;
I belong to Jesus Christ,
Preacher of humility;
Heathen gods are naught to me.
Father, Son and Holy Ghost,
So I make an idle boast;
Jesus of the twice-turned cheek,
Lamb of God, although I speak
With my mouth thus, in my heart
Do I play a double part.
Even at Thy glowing altar
Must my heart grow sick and falter,
Wishing He I served were black,
Thinking then it would not lack
Precedent of pain to guide it,
Let who would or might deride it;

Surely then this flesh would know
Yours had borne a kindred woe.
Lord, I fashion dark gods, too,
Daring even to give You
Dark despairing features where,
Crowned with dark rebellious hair,
Patience wavers just so much as
Mortal grief compels, while touches
Quick and hot, of anger, rise
To smitten cheek and weary eyes.
Lord, forgive me if my need
Sometimes shapes a human creed.

*All day long and all night through,*
*One thing only must I do:*
*Quench my pride and cool my blood,*
*Lest I perish in the flood.*
*Lest a hidden ember set*
*Timber that I thought was wet*
*Burning like the dryest flax,*
*Melting like the merest wax,*
*Lest the grave restore its dead.*
*Not yet has my heart or head*
*In the least way realized*
*They and I are civilized.*

## Merrill Moore

MERRILL MOORE was born in Columbia, Tennessee, September 11, 1903. Although he served an internship in Boston and practiced there, his backgrounds are entirely Southern: his father, John Trotwood Moore, the historian, was from Alabama; his mother from Missouri. He was educated in Nashville, received his B.A. at Vanderbilt University in 1924, his M.D. in 1928, and he was one of the group which made *The Fugitive* so provocative a periodical.

His work is vividly modern and it seems, at first glance, a paradox that this experimental poet has chosen the most classic form as his medium. Typography and tradition notwithstanding, *The Noise That Time Makes* (1929) is composed entirely of sonnets—and it is an open secret that Merrill Moore at the age of twenty-five had composed no less than four thousand such sonnets. Nor is it a fiction that Moore learned shorthand in order to get more of his fourteen-liners done between classroom and laboratory. It should be said that neither Wyatt nor Philip Sidney would have sponsored had they even recognized Moore's employment of the key with which Shakespeare is supposed to have unlocked his heart. *The Noise That Time Makes* bears the first fruits of what might be considered a new hybrid: the American sonnet.

The characterization is not far-fetched, for Moore's cis-Atlantic accent, the native syncopated speed—so different from English and Italian tempi—the abrupt approach and swift abandonment are not only occasioned by local backgrounds but are the very essence of these poems. As a sonneteer in the strict sense, Moore commits every known heresy and invents several new ones. His rhyme-schemes seem as haphazard as they are numerous—the rhymes themselves are suspiciously unorthodox. His lines, instead of conforming to a precise meter, stretch themselves flexibly as their author throws in four or five extra syllables with prodigal nonchalance. His stanzas, instead of splitting neatly into customary octave and sestet, divide themselves anywhere with what seems sheer perversity. But there is nothing arbitrary about these "American sonnets." The innovations are essentially reasonable, and the reasons for them are quite simple. Merrill Moore's sonnets are, in some ways, the most spontaneous ever written in America, and their "naturalness" is reflected in their structure. The rhythms are based on the rise and fall of the breath rather than on the beat of the metronome. It is not scansion but stress which determines the line-length. Sometimes the author adds a title which, included in the rhyme-scheme, is actually a part of the poem (*vide* "Old Men and Old Women Going Home on the Street Car" or "Helen Told Me What Was in Her Head"), and so calmly manufactures a fifteen-line sonnet.

The charm of such poetry is the continual freshness, which gives it the quality of improvisation. This is, likewise, a danger; for when Moore, seated before his instrument, lets his fingers wander as they list, his spontaneous playing extends itself into a fluency which is neither a virtue nor virtuosity. But the best of his lines reveal the serious eye and sensitive touch. "What if small birds are peppering the sky," "allowing fish-like thoughts to escape in thin streams trickling through the mind," "birds' indeclinable twitter"—the sonnets are full of such swift exactitudes. Suiting their pace to subjects limited only by a seemingly unlimited imagination, scarcely two of these poems are alike in shape or theme. "Shot Who? Jim Lane!" is as realistic as it is sectional; "Warning to One" is a tribute etched with acid; "How She Resolved to Act" is intuitive as it is whimsical; "The Book of How" quietly mingles the casual and the colossal.

*Six Sides to a Man* (1935), like its predecessor, presents no sequence but, with kaleidoscopic changes, a set of unrelated patterns. It is as if a flood of quickly igniting thoughts were impelled by recollections, sights, sounds, smells, the look and feel of words, with all their complex associations. These associations, intuitions, and memories both help and hinder each other, and in the clash the poem appears. This paradox of creation and conflict, this order out of chaos, is common to every poet; in Moore's case the process is somewhat more self-revealing. The factor that frequently deranges his aim is probably that his intuitions and unconscious associations are not in league with and often even opposed to his conscious intention.

But if the consequence is a multiplicity of effects rather than a single finality, the result is a phenomenon of unusual interest. Everything is here in rich disorganization—a genre picture, a case history, a dream landscape, a seasoned philosophy, a story in journalese, a miniature drama, or the play of free associations—integrated only by the vision of the poet.

This, obviously, is not a poetry of perfection but of casual disassociation. It contains errors in taste and proportion, but has its own positive quality. Merrill Moore derives from no one; his mind is expansive, almost explosive; his energy incalculable

—at thirty he had written approximately twenty thousand sonnets—and he has that individualized tone which is the unmistakable property of the poet.

### OLD MEN AND OLD WOMEN GOING HOME
### ON THE STREET CAR

Carrying their packages of groceries in particular
With books under their arms that maybe they will read
And possibly understand, old women lead
Their weaker selves up to the front of the car.

And old men who for thirty years have sat at desks
Survey them harmlessly.
                    They regard each other
As forgotten sister looks at forgotten brother
On their way between two easily remembered tasks
And that is positively all there is to it.

But it was not that way thirty years ago!
Before desks and counters had tired their backs and feet,

When life for them was a bowl of odorous fruit
That they might take their pick of, then turn and go,
Saying, "This tastes so good!" or, "This smells so sweet!"

### IT IS WINTER, I KNOW

What if small birds are peppering the sky,
Scudding south with the clouds to an ultimate tip on lands
Where they may peck worms and slugs from moist sands
Rather muddily mixed with salt?
                    Or if wind dashes by
Insufferably filled with birds' indeclinable twitter
Not deigning to toy with the oak-twigs that it passes
And treading but lightly on all the delicate grasses
Under trees where crickets are silent, where mad leaves flutter?

It is winter, I know, there are too many Nays now confronting
The obdurate soul that would trick itself into believing
That buds are still ripe, that cells are all ready for cleaving;
It can only be winter, winter alone, when blunting
Winds rush over the ice, scattering leaves from their weeds
To rattle the sycamore tree's dry-shriveled seeds.

### SHOT WHO? JIM LANE!

When he was shot he toppled to the ground
As if the toughened posts that were his thighs
Had felt that all that held them up were lies,
Weak lies, that suddenly someone had found

Out all that was true about them.
                              It did not seem
Like the crashing of a stalwart forest oak
But like a frail staff that a sharp wind broke
Or something insubstantial in a dream.

I never thought Jim Lane would fall like that.

He'd sworn that bullets must be gold to find him;
That when they came toward him he made them mind him
By means he knew,
                  just as a barn-yard cat
Can keep a pack of leaping dogs at bay
By concentrating and looking a certain way.

### WARNING TO ONE

Death is the strongest of all living things
And when it happens do not look in the eyes
For a dead fire or a lack-luster there,
But listen for the words that fall from lips
Or do not fall. Silence is not death;
It merely means that the one who is conserving breath
Is not concerned with tattle and small quips.

Watch the quick fingers and the way they move
During unguarded moments—words of love
And love's caresses may be cold as ice
And cold the glitter of engagement rings;
Death is the sword that hangs on a single hair,
And that thin tenuous hair is no more than love
And yours is the silly head it hangs above.

### HOW SHE RESOLVED TO ACT

"I shall be careful to say nothing at all
About myself or what I know of him
Or the vaguest thought I have—no matter how dim,
Tonight if it so happen that he call."

And not ten minutes later the door-bell rang
And into the hall he stepped as he always did
With a face and a bearing that quite poorly hid
His brain that burned and his heart that fairly sang
And his tongue that wanted to be rid of the truth.

As well as she could, for she was very loath
To signify how she felt, she kept very still,
But soon her heart cracked loud as a coffee mill
And her brain swung like a comet in the dark
And her tongue raced like a squirrel in the park.

### PANDORA AND THE MOON

Minds awake in bodies that were asleep
Caused the winged troubles to be born
That made Pandora one time feel forlorn,

Because, in spite of the box, she could not keep
Her troubles there, the worrisome animalcules
Fluttered out never to be regained,
For every method of evil especially trained
And subject neither to God's nor the devil's rules.

What shall she do? Nothing; sit and ponder,
Watch the dying leaves drop from the tree
Until they all are gone and she may see
The same moon then that used to make her wonder
At the unbelievable stories she sits and reads.

And if she succeeds in that then she succeeds.

### VILLAGE NOON: MID-DAY BELLS

When both hands of the town clock stood at twelve
Eve ceased spinning, Adam ceased to delve.

A lusty cockerel crowed that noon had come,
The shadows stood beneath the trees and some
Were motionless a moment—then the people
Busied themselves for food, and in the steeple
Ubiquitous pigeons roucoulayed and slept
Above the watch the dogs below them kept
For nothing—or a dust cloud down the road
That might mean feet or might mean wheels or not.

Then as the noon sun with its ardor glowed
On man and beast and field and dwelling place
The hands moved past noon to another spot
And Time moved on a little way in Space.

### UNKNOWN MAN IN THE MORGUE

Tortured body, lie at rest alone
Finally on the long and merciless
Slab of now cool lava-molten stone,
And wait our mutual and final guess
At your identity, nameless, homeless one.

No suburb avenue, no numbered house
We know for you; no date of birth nor death
Are yours, though somewhere visitors may carouse
In a forgotten room where once you lived,
Fathered, soned and brothered, lovered, wived.

But here you come unfollowed to this place,
With an anonymous grimace on your face
In death, whose last name and whose last address
Will now be yours in your last loneliness.


### THE BOOK OF HOW

After the stars were all hung separately out
For mortal eyes to see that care to look
The one who did it sat down and wrote a book
On how he did it.
                          It took him about
As long to write the book as to do the deed
But he said, "It's things like this we mostly need."
And the angels approved but the devils screamed with laughter
For they knew exactly what would follow after.

For somehow he managed entirely to omit
The most important facts in accomplishing it,

Where he got the ladder to reach the stars
And how he lighted them, especially Mars,

And what he hung them on when he got them there
Eternally distant and luminous in the air.


### AND TO THE YOUNG MEN

And to the young men awaiting their sacrifice
You brought water in an invisible pail
And promised them the plans would surely fail
That were written against them, recorded in the stars.
And you brought straw and padded the cold bars
Of the prison beds whereon the young men lay,
And sung to some at night and fanned by day
Those who were fevering into paradise.

But even then you did not do enough.
For you remember a boy, the silent one?
With a silent eye, who scarcely loved the sun,
And felt too keenly the winter wind's dry sough?
Well, you should have brought him cresses from a far stream
Over which nymphs and under which naiads dream.


### AND THEN HER BURIAL

Motionless, gentle as it always was,
The earth is opened all upon the cause
Of her mere dying, and it is prepared
To cushion her as soon as it is bared.

Now, musicians, if you ever played,
Deafen us to grief, who are afraid
Of weeping at her parting, for we stand
Wringing useless hand with useless hand.

We fan our face that parches in the sight
Of all her beauty billowing too bright
In radiant waves against the saddest eye
Our face has ever matched our feeling by.

Gone, gone her smile, unless we can recall
Her friendly face beneath the lily-pall.

## "FINAL STATUS NEVER ASCERTAINED" *LLOYDS REGISTRY*

Where the drift went the waters answered it,
Where the drift went the lonely waters called
To cliffs along the shore grown gray and bald

As loudly crying seabirds used to flit
Over the headlands of that noisy coast
Where the *Aphis* and her crew were lost.

Humble, patient carpenters had made
Her hull, and simple sailors made her sails.

But what hands made the rocky reefs and gales
That tore the ship apart and picked the meat
Completely from her bones and far too neat
Swept the crew and carried them away
Into green chambers where they had to stay
And had no choice, nor ever a word to say?

# Robert Penn Warren

ROBERT PENN WARREN was born in Kentucky in 1905. His education was widely scattered: he received his B.A. at Vanderbilt University and his M.A. at the University of California. He attended Yale Graduate School for a time and, in 1929, New College, Oxford. He was the youngest of *The Fugitive* group, sharing their sectional differences, though less pronouncedly local than most. Upon his return to America he began teaching, first at Vanderbilt, later in Louisiana State University at Baton Rouge, besides conducting conferences in writing at the universities of Montana and Colorado. With Cleanth Brooks, Jr., he became one of the managing editors of *The Southern Review*.

*John Brown* (1929) is a biography in prose, differing radically in tone and treatment from Benét's *John Brown's Body*. Warren's poetry is more certain; it has iron beneath its grace. Intellectual in its origins, Warren's verse remains closer to the earth than the work of his confrères; fertile in strong images, its strength no less than its fecundity rises from Kentucky soil. The critical mind is always at work here, but not so insistently as to inhibit the creative imagination. In his early twenties, Warren has already accomplished a fusion: in his lime-tinctured phrases, form and feeling are one.

A volume, *Pondy Woods and Other Poems,* was announced as early as 1929, but never published. His best work appeared in *Thirty-Six Poems* (1935). Such poems as "Letter to a Friend," "Aubade for Hope," "The Owl," and others may not be as sharply delineated as the early "Pondy Woods" and "History Among the Rocks," but their more rounded contours reveal Warren's development, and his growing power. "The Return—An Elegy" confirms the vigor of "Pro Sua Vita" and reveals a poet who can combine the latest devices with an almost Saxon strength. This verse, intense in its visual perceptions as well as its inner keenness, is knotted even in its emotions, "strung with the bitter tendons of the stone."

### PONDY WOODS

The buzzards over Pondy Woods
Achieve the blue tense altitudes,
Black figments that the woods release,
Obscenity in form and grace,
Drifting high through the pure sunshine
Till the sun in gold decline.

Big Jim Todd was a slick black buck
Laying low in the mud and muck
Of Pondy Woods when the sun went down
In gold, and the buzzards tilted down
A windless vortex to the black-gum trees
To sit along the quiet boughs,
Devout and swollen, at their ease.

By the buzzard roost Big Jim Todd
Listened for hoofs on the corduroy road
Or for the foul and sucking sound
A man's foot makes on the marshy ground.
Past midnight, when the moccasin
Slipped from the log and, trailing in
Its obscured waters, broke
The dark algae, one lean bird spoke.

"Nigger, you went this afternoon
For your Saturday spree at the Blue Goose saloon,
So you've got on your Sunday clothes,
On your big splay feet got patent-leather shoes.
But a buzzard can smell the thing you've done;
The posse will get you—run, nigger, run—
There's a fellow behind you with a big shot-gun.

Nigger, nigger, you'll sweat cold sweat
In your patent-leather shoes and Sunday clothes
When down your track the steeljacket goes
Mean and whimpering over the wheat.

"Nigger, your breed ain't metaphysical."
The buzzard coughed. His words fell
In the darkness, mystic and ambrosial.
"But we maintain our ancient rite,
Eat gods by day and prophesy by night.
We swing against the sky and wait;
You seize the hour, more passionate
Than strong, and strive with time to die—
With Time, the beaked tribe's astute ally.

"The Jew-boy died. The Syrian vulture swung
Remotely above the cross whereon he hung
From dinner-time to supper-time, and all
The people gathered there watched him until
The lean brown chest no longer stirred,
Then idly watched the slow majestic bird
That in the last sun above the twilit hill
Gleamed for a moment at the height and slid
Down the hot wind and in the darkness hid.
Nigger, regard the circumstance of breath:
'Non omnis moriar,' the poet saith."

Pedantic, the bird clacked its gray beak,
With a Tennessee accent to the classic phrase;
Jim understood, and was about to speak,
But the buzzard drooped one wing and filmed the eyes.

At dawn unto the Sabbath wheat he came,
That gave to the dew its faithless yellow flame
From kindly loam in recollection of
The fires that in the brutal rock once strove.
To the ripe wheat fields he came at dawn.
Northward the printed smoke stood quiet above
The distant cabins of Squiggtown.
A train's far whistle blew and drifted away
Coldly; lucid and thin the morning lay
Along the farms, and here no sound
Touched the sweet earth miraculously stilled.
Then down the damp and sudden wood there belled
The musical white-throated hound.

In Pondy Woods in the August drouth
Lurks fever and the cottonmouth.
And buzzards over Pondy Woods
Achieve the blue tense altitudes,

Drifting high in the pure sunshine
Till the sun in gold decline;
Then golden and hieratic through
The night their eyes burn two by two.


### PRO SUA VITA

Nine months I waited in the dark beneath
Her tired heart for this precious breath,

And month by month since I left her breast
Her breath and blood I have given in waste,

Till now at length some peace she has got
That her breath and blood in me have not.

In the strictured nights of glimmering snow
The blood drives quick though breath is slow,

And through the August afternoon
Flees the breath faintly but too soon.

So blood is lost to the brutal gardens
Where the iron petal of dark frost hardens,

And breath, when the storm-black trees bowed under,
Waited the fanged astounding thunder.

Shall I say to my father then
Among the belted best of men:

"Fellow, you tupped her years ago
That tonight my boots might crunch the snow.

"And, woman, you show your son to wait
Till the breath and distraught blood abate;

"As my father began the tale of waste
When the sullen head slept on your breast,

"So the rigid hills had been forgot
In darkness, if God had wasted not."


### LETTER OF A MOTHER

Under the green lamp-light her letter there
Lies among cluttered papers, rusted pens,
Books and handkerchiefs, tobacco tins.
Shuffle of feet ascends the darkened stair.

The son, defined upon the superscription,
Inherits now his cubicled domain,
And reads. Indeed, should he possess again
The loneliness of time's slow mitigation?

Or spell the name, which is himself, and say:
"By now this woman's milk is out of me.
I have a debt of flesh, assuredly,
Which score the mintage of the breath might pay. . . .

"A certain weight of cunning flesh devised
So hunger is bred in the bitter bone
To cleave about his precious skeleton
Held mortmain of her womb and merchandised

"Unto the dark: a subtile engine, propped
In the sutured head beneath the coronal seam,
Whose illegal prodigality of dream
In shaking the escheat heart is quick estopped.

"Such is the substance of this legacy:
A fragile vision fed of acrid blood,
Whose sweet process may bloom in gratitude
For the worthier gift of her mortality."

But still the flesh cries out unto the black
Void, across the plains insistently
Where rivers wash their wastage to the sea. . . .
The mother flesh that cannot summon back

The tired child it would again possess
As shall a womb more tender than her own
That builds not tissue or the little bone,
But dissolves them to itself in weariness.

### HISTORY AMONG THE ROCKS

*(from "Kentucky Mountain Farm")*

There are many ways to die
Here among the rocks in any weather:
Wind, down the eastern gap, will lie
Level along the snow, beating the cedar,
And lull the drowsy head that it blows over
To startle a crystalline, cold dream forever.

The hound's black paw will print the grass in May,
And sycamores rise down a dark ravine,
Where a creek in flood, sucking the rock and clay,
Will tumble the sycamore, the laurel, away.
Think how a body, naked and lean

And white as the splintered sycamore, would go
Tumbling and turning, hushed in the end,
With hair afloat in waters that gently bend
To ocean where the blind tides flow.

Under the shadow of ripe wheat,
By flat limestone, will coil the copperhead,
Fanged as the sunlight, hearing the reaper's feet.
But there are other ways, the lean men said:
In these autumn orchards once young men lay dead—
Gray coats, blue coats. Young men on the mountainside
Clambered, fought. Heels muddied the rocky spring.
Their reason is hard to guess, remembering
Blood on their black mustaches in moonlight,
Cold musket-barrels glittering with frost.
Their reason is hard to guess and a long time past;
The apple falls, falling in the quiet night.


### LETTER FROM A COWARD TO A HERO

What did the day bring?
The sharp fragment,
The shard,
The promise half-meant,
The impaired thing,
At dusk the hard word,
Good action by good will marred . . .
All
In the trampled stall:

> *I think you deserved better;*
> *Therefore I am writing you this letter.*

The scenes of childhood were splendid,
And the light that there attended,
But is rescinded:
The cedar,
The lichened rocks,
The thicket where I saw the fox,
And where I swam, the river.
These things are hard
To reconstruct:
The word
Is memory's gelded usufruct.
But piety is simple,
And should be ample.

> *Though late at night we have talked,*
> *I cannot see what ways your feet in childhood walked.*
> *In what purlieus was courage early caulked?*

Guns blaze in autumn and
The quail falls and

Empires collide with a bang
That shakes the pictures where they hang
And democracy shows signs of dry rot
And Dives has and Lazarus not
And the time is out of joint:
But a good pointer holds the point
And is not gun-shy;
But I
Am gun-shy.

Though young, I do not like loud noise:
The sudden backfire,
The catcall of boys,
Drums beating for
The big war,
Or clocks that tick at night, and will not stop.
If you ever lose your compass and map
Or a mouse gets in the wall,
For sleep try love or veronal,
Though some prefer, I know, philology.
Does the airman scream in the flaming trajectory?

You have been strong in love and hate.
Disaster owns less speed than you have got,
But he will cut across the back lot
To lurk and lie in wait.
Admired of children, gathered for their games,
Disaster, like the dandelion, blooms,
And the delicate film is fanned
To seed the shaven lawn.
Rarely, you've been unmanned;
I have not seen your courage put to pawn.

At the blind hour of unaided grief,
Of addition and subtraction,
Of compromise,
Of the smoky lecher, the thief,
Of regretted action,
At the hour to close the eyes,
At the hour when lights go out in the houses . . .
Then wind rouses
The kildees from their sodden ground:
Their commentary is part of the wind's sound.
What is that other sound,
Surf or distant cannonade?
You are what you are without our aid.
No doubt, when corridors are dumb
And the bed is made,
It is your custom to recline,
Clutching between the forefinger and thumb
Honor, for death shy valentine.

THE OWL

Here was the sound of water falling only,
Which is not sound but silence musical
Tumbling forever down the gorge's wall.
Like late milkweed that blooms beside the lonely
And sunlit stone, peace bloomed all afternoon.
Where time is not is peace; and here the shadow,
That crept to him across the Western meadow
And climbed the hill to mark the dropping sun,
Seemed held a space, washed downward by the water
Whose music flowed against the flow of time.
It could not be. Dark fell along the stream,
And like a child grown suddenly afraid,
With shaking knees, hands bloody on the stone,
Toward the upland gleaming fields he fled.
Light burned against their rim, was quickly gone.

Later he would remember this, and start.
And once or twice again his tough old heart
Knew sickness that the rabbit's heart must know,
When star by star the great wings float,
And down the moonlit track below
Their mortal silken shadow sweeps the snow.
O scaled bent claw, infatuate deep throat!

LETTER TO A FRIEND

Our eyes have viewed the burnished vineyards where
No leaf falls, and the grape, unripening, ripes.
It was a dream without fruition as
Without our terror. We have seen it;

And seen the ever-rounding vaulty-structured
Ocean moveless, and the mortised keel
Unmoving o'er the sunlit lichened wave.
That voyage, then each to each we said, had rendered

Courage superfluous, hope a burden.
But living still, we live by them, and only
Thus, or thus, stuttering, eke them out,
Our huddled alms to crammed Necessity.

Fears rise, old wranglers out of sleep, and go:
The caterpillar knows its leaf, the mole
Its hummock, who has known his heart, or knows
The trigger of this action, set and sprung?

In this, the time of toads' engendering,
I write to you, to you unfrighted yet
Before the blunt experiment of Time.
Your triumph is not commensurate with stone.

AUBADE FOR HOPE

Dawn: and foot on the cold stair treading or
Thump of wood on the unswept hearth-stone is
Comment on the margin of consciousness,
A dirty thumb-smear by the printed page.

Thumb-smear: nay other, for the blessed light
Acclaimèd thus, as a ducal progress by
The scared cur, wakes them who wallowed in
The unaimed faceless appetite of dream.

All night the ice sought out the rotten bough:
In sleep they heard. And now they stir, as east
Beyond the formal gleam of landscape sun
Has struck the senatorial hooded hill.

Light; the groaning stair; the match aflame;
The negro woman's hand, horned gray with cold,
That lit the wood; a child's eyes sullen
In the August street . . . I name some things that shall,

As voices speaking from a farther room,
Muffled, bespeak us yet for time and hope:
For Hope that like a blockhead grandam ever
Above the ash and spittle croaks and leans.

# George Dillon

GEORGE DILLON was born November 12, 1906, in Jacksonville, Florida, and spent most of his childhood in Kentucky, his mother's region. He went to school in the Middle West and was graduated from the University of Chicago in 1927.

While still an undergraduate, his verses began to attract attention beyond the borders of Illinois; he was made president of the Poetry Club of his University, and in 1925 was given the John Billings Fiske Prize as well as the Young Poet's Prize awarded by *Poetry: A Magazine of Verse*. In the same year he joined the *Poetry* staff as Associate Editor.

*Boy in the Wind* (1927) is distinguished by much more than precocity; always musical, there is an edge to these water-color contours. Dillon is essentially a lyricist of half-tones, but he puts suavity to measures firm in outline.

*The Flowering Stone* (1931) was awarded the Pulitzer Prize in 1932. Here the poetry is less insistently dulcet. Maturity begins to underline his soft lights with shadows. But Dillon does not fall into a "daybreak of anguish"; he still declares for "the noble wave, the affluent wind." His defect is his fluency; he is sure of his craftsmanship, a little too sure. The subject-matter is conventional to the point of being stereotyped and the tone in the sonnets is a shade too pompous. Yet the verse is unusually flexible and few will question his gift of song.

### IN TWO MONTHS NOW

In two months now or maybe one
The sun will be a different sun
And earth that stretches white as straw
With stony ice will crack and thaw
And run in whistling streams and curve
In still blue-shadowed pools. The nerve
Of each pink root will quiver bare
And orchards in the April air
Will show black branches breaking white.
Red roses in the green twilight
Will glimmer ghostly blue and swell
Upon their vines with such a smell
As only floats when the breeze is loud
At dusk from roses in a crowd.
I know that there will be these things,
Remembering them from other springs.
All these and more shall soon be seen,
As beautiful as they have been;
But not so beautiful as they
Seem now to be, a month away.

### BOY IN THE WIND

How came this troubled one to stray
With fire and song in the wind's way?

Indifferent and dumb and sweet,
The seasons fall about his feet.

Frail flames are set behind his eyes,
And under his ribs his heart makes moan
Like a pent bird who throbs and dies.

He walks in the windy night alone.

And who would know if he should sing
Whose song is less than the murmuring
Of the wind full of the ruin of spring?

And who could say if he had flown
Like a flame blown out or a bird up-blown?

Or if his heart cries out in pain
Who hears the cry through wind and rain?

He wanders east. He wanders west.

Where will he ever come to rest,
With that fire blowing in his brain,
And that bird grieving in his breast?

### APRIL'S AMAZING MEANING

April's amazing meaning doubtless lies
    In tall hoarse boys and slips
Of slender girls with suddenly wider eyes
    And parted lips;

For girls will wander pensive in the spring
    When the green rain is over,
Doing some slow, inconsequential thing,
    Plucking clover;

And any boy alone upon a bench
    When his work's done will sit
And stare at the black ground and break a
    branch
    And whittle it

Slowly; and boys and girls, irresolute,
    Will curse the dreamy weather
Until they meet past the pale hedge and put
    Their lips together.

### MEMORY OF LAKE SUPERIOR

I know a country of bright anonymous beaches
Where the sand may sleep unprinted till it is stone.
Granite grows loud among the hills and ditches
Of the blown water when the water is blown.

Up on the mountain the sky is everywhere,
The lake fallen hugely underfoot as if
Into the bottom of a well of air,
The island upon it little as a leaf.

The woods are dark with the rank lace of hemlock and pine,
Beech, birch, and balsam, and the shadow of these.
There are mushrooms, and thimbleberries sweeter than wine,
And a far noise of wind in the tops of the trees.

That country was all the knowledge I shall ever learn;
It was all the wisdom I shall ever have.
It was there I looked for the driftwood boughs that burn
In colors like the memory of a wave.

It was there I looked along the forest floor
For the gray feather of the grouse's wing.
It was there I learned to look for nothing more,
Looking into the sea-blue eyes of spring.

## ONE BEAUTY STILL

One beauty still is faultless, not
Deflowered in the bed of thought:
It is a sound of sunken seas.
It is an avid wish for ease.
It is the earth, it is the sky
When passion is a lute put by,
And life a dancer out of breath.
It is the lovely face of death,
Adored and guessed at—never once
Beheld in chrysoprase or bronze;
Not in the temple or the grove,
Not in a hundred nights of love.

This was the morning sun, the wild
Daybreak of anguish in the child.
This is the sun at noon no less,
Deep in the dome of nothingness.
Wherefore, impoverished heart, be proud
To wear the purple of the shroud:
If you are friendless, take for friend
The noble wave, the affluent wind.
If you are homeless, do not care:
Inhabit the bright house of air.
If you are worn with wayfaring,
Lie down within the arms of spring.

# *James Agee*

JAMES AGEE was born in Knoxville, Tennessee, November 27, 1909. Although his early schooling was in Franklin County, Tennessee, the center of "The Fugitives," Agee did not enter Vanderbilt and never came under the influence of the Nashville group. Instead he came north, attended Exeter for three years and spent four years at Harvard. Subsequently he came to New York, where he worked on *Fortune*, where his chief "namable" interests were "music, words, the present, the future, and 'documentary' movies."

His first book, *Permit Me Voyage* (1934), with a foreword by Archibald Mac-Leish, was published in Agee's twenty-fifth year. It is an unusual book, remarkable in its vigor and its unevenness. The defects are obvious. The long "Dedication" is interesting as an exposé of the young poet's admirations, naïve in tone and almost comic in its incongruities. "Epithalamium" is an undergraduate's solemn exercise in the grand manner; the long and turgid "Ann Garner," written while Agee was still at school, is an unfortunate attempt to combine the subject matter of Robinson Jeffers with the tone and background of Robert Frost. But these failures, once dismissed, cannot obscure the originality of Agee's poetry. The title-poem alone proves the firmness and sentiency of his work; the title, taken from a poem by Hart Crane, suggests an indebtedness as well as sensitivity, but Agee makes the lines authentically his own.

The title-poem, the opening group of lyrics, and the twenty-five sonnets are the book's real reason for being. All of them are interesting and many are admirable; they show a dexterous balance of passion and restraint, of novelty and authority. Most of them are classical in tone, Elizabethan rather than experimental, declaring the influence of Donne and Shakespeare with an infusion of Hopkins. The lyrics suffer from occasional constriction; the images are almost too spare, the phrasing too tight. But they are rarely without charm, a charm that does not hesitate to employ humor and a purposeful awkwardness. The poems written after publication of *Permit Me Voyage* (three examples of the more recent work are here reprinted) emphasize the emotional tensity half hidden by the tart grace. Although the work does not, as yet, achieve an indisputable importance, it reveals a clear control, a personal vocabulary and, as Archibald MacLeish concludes, "the one poetic gift which no amount of application can purchase and which no amount of ingenuity can fake—a delicate and perceptive ear."

### LYRICS

No doubt left. Enough deceiving.
Now I know you do not love.
Now you know I do not love.
Now we know we do not love.
No more doubt. No more deceiving.

Yet there is pity in us for each other
And better times are almost fresh as true.
The dog returns. And the man to his mother.
And tides. And you to me. And I to you.
And we are cowardly kind the cruelest way,
Feeling the cliff unmorsel from our heels
And knowing balance gone, we smile, and stay
A little, whirling our arms like desperate wheels.

✦

Not met and marred with the year's whole turn of grief,
But easily on the mercy of the morning
Fell this still folded leaf:

Small that never Summer spread
Demented on the dusty heat;
And sweet that never Fall
Wrung sere and tarnished red;
Safe now that never knew
Stunning Winter's bitter blue
It fell fair in the fair season:

Therefore with reason
Dress all in cheer and lightly put away
   With music and glad will
This little child that cheated the long day
   Of the long day's ill:
Who knows this breathing joy, heavy on us all,
   Never, never, never.

✦

I loitered weeping with my bride for gladness
Her walking side against and both embracing
Through the brash brightening rain that now the season changes
White on the fallen air that now my fallen
                              the fallen girl her grave effaces.

### SONNETS

#### I

So it begins. Adam is in his earth
Tempted, and fallen, and his doom made sure,
O, in the very instant of his birth:
Whose deathly nature must all things endure.
The hungers of his flesh, and mind, and heart,
That governed him when he was in the womb,
These ravenings multiply in every part:
And shall release him only to the tomb.
Meantime he works the earth, and builds up nations,
And trades, and wars, and learns, and worships chance,
And looks to God, and weaves the generations
Which shall his many hungerings advance
When he is sunken dead among his sins.
Adam is in this earth. So it begins.

#### II

Our doom is in our being. We began
In hunger eager more than ache of hell:
And in that hunger became each a man
Ravened with hunger death alone may spell:
And in that hunger live, as lived the dead,
Who sought, as now we seek, in the same ways,
Nobly, and hatefully, what angel's-bread
Might ever stand us out these short few days.

So is this race in this wild hour confounded:
And though you rectify the big distress,
And kill all outward wrong where wrong abounded,
Your hunger cannot make this hunger less
Which breeds all wrath and right, and shall not die
In earth, and finds some hope upon the sky.

### XIX

Those former loves wherein our lives have run
Seeing them shining, following them far,
Were but a hot deflection of the sun,
The operation of a migrant star.
In that wrong time when still a shape of earth
Severed us far and stood our sight between,
Those loves were effigies of love whose worth
Was all our wandering nothing to have seen:
So toward those steep projections on our sky
We toiled though partners to their falsity
Who faintly in that falseness could descry
What now stands forth too marvelous to see:
Who one time loved in them the truth concealed:
And now must leave them in the truth revealed.

### XX

Now stands our love on that still verge of day
Where darkness loiters leaf to leaf releasing
Lone tree to silvering tree: then slopes away
Before the morning's deep-drawn strength increasing
Till the sweet land lies burnished in the dawn:
But sleeping still: nor stirs a thread of grass:
Large on the low hill and the spangled lawn
The pureleaved air dwells passionless as glass:
So stands our love new found and unaroused,
Appareled in all peace and innocence,
In all lost shadows of love past still drowsed
Against foreknowledge of such immanence
As now, with earth outshone and earth's wide air,
Shows each to other as this morning fair.

### PERMIT ME VOYAGE

Take these who will as may be: I
Am careless now of what they fail:
My heart and mind discharted lie
And surely as the nervèd nail

Appoints all quarters on the north
So now it designates him forth
My sovereign God my princely soul
Whereon my flesh is priestly stole:

Whenceforth shall my heart and mind
To God through soul entirely bow,

Therein such strong increase to find
In truth as is my fate to know:

Small though that be great God I know
I know in this gigantic day
What God is ruined and I know
How labors with Godhead this day:

How from the porches of our sky
The crested glory is declined:
And hear with that translated cry
The stridden soul is overshined:

And how this world of wildness through
True poets shall walk who herald you:
Of whom God grant me of your grace
To be, that shall preserve this race.

Permit me voyage, Love, into your hands.

### SONG WITH WORDS

When Eve first saw the glistering day
  Watch by the wan world side
She learned her worst and down she lay
  In the streaming land and cried.

When Adam saw the mastering night
  First board the wan world's lifted breast
He climbed his bride with all his might
  And sank to tenderest rest.

And night took both and day brought high
The children that must likewise die:

And all our grief and every joy
To time's deep end shall time destroy:

And weave us one and wave us under
Where is neither faith nor wonder.

### TWO SONGS ON THE ECONOMY OF ABUNDANCE

*Temperance Note: and Weather Prophecy*
  Watch well The Poor in this late hour
  Before the wretched wonder stop:
  Who march among a thundershower
  And never touch a drop.

*Red Sea*
  How long this way: that everywhere
  We make our march the water stands
  Apart and all our wine is air
  And all our ease the emptied sands?

### IN HEAVY MIND

In heavy mind I strayed the field
The chilly damp and devious air
The restiveness   the rags of snow
The mulled and matted blackness where

The summer overthroned with leaves
Had shown its cloudy loveliest
And I had lain along the shade
In tears that fully undistressed

Me among men upon the earth
In flowering sky of every doubt
But only so much natural joy
Might flare the flesh,   thaw the wick out:

But now was logy with the weight of brain,
Flat in the eyes and of my love most low,
Hate toward, and clambering thought, and
    failure sure,
And life a lean long while,   the starving slow:

When, not to see, some previous bird
Made whistling from a bramble tree:
And all my will was not enough
To hold the heavens out of me.

## *Margaret Marks*

M ARGARET MARKS was born in New York City, in 1909, educated at the Ethical Culture School and at Barnard College. A particular liking for the medieval impelled her to spend two years at the School of Art and Archaeology in Paris. She regards the metaphysical accent in her work with detachment and a little suspicion. "I have read," she says, "my Donne, his ancestors, and his descendants, as who has not; but I do not think I am one of his children."

  She has written little, but that little is marked by a scrupulous choice of idea, image, and epithet. The content of her poetry is original without straining for originality; her patterns present interesting departures but they are never freakish, being disciplined in their very differences. "Lady with Arrows," for example, pictures a woman conscious of her cruelty and destructiveness, yet unable to control either. But the poem is more than a portrait; it is a sensitive record done entirely in shades of suggestion. The art of nuance characterizes all this work.

This poet's stanzas have a certain kinship with Elinor Wylie's later metaphysical verse, but it is a remote relationship. Miss Marks's line is rounded where Elinor Wylie's is pointed; her perceptions are registered with a delicate and softened exactness instead of Mrs. Wylie's angular precision. Like Mrs. Wylie she never succumbs to mediocrity of thought or phrase. But even such a comparison is an injustice to Miss Marks. She owes little to any of her contemporaries, and her accent is quite her own.

### LADY WITH ARROWS

She is not mistress here, the arrows shake themselves
Free of her bow; they ride the carrying air
Straight to the mark that is forever there,
Contrive just not to lay it low, to leave it where
It sways a challenge to that practiced art
She most denies, in which she has no part.

Denies, mourns, even says: Is it indeed my hand,
This delicate blue-veined, is it indeed my arm
That so directs, that points the sinewy dart
On that poor flesh to which I wish no harm?
Believe me when I say it is not so.
I am for nothing here; I am possessed;
I am the house of ghostly skill, the host
Of power. It is this commanding guest
(Believe it!)
And not I, not I,
That bends the bow,
That bids the arrow fly.

### CHORUS FOR REFUSAL

In the dark room of her disinclination
She does rehearse how best she may say no,
Sharply or sweet to mouth it, high or low,
And stressed by the hand's lifting, or the head
Most levelly and in all kindness shaken;
Tries over the quick syllable and the slow,
And finds some methods good and some mistaken.

And as she walks in practice to and fro,
Behind her walk the disinclining dead,
Mimicking, lipless, her mouth shaped to no,
Mimicking, too, her delicate gestured no
With the hand's skeleton and the bony head.

### TACTIC

A little is he victor here;
A little is she vanquishèd;
As she bemusèd were, she stands
Her ground,
Receives into her flesh
The vulgar and unshapely wound,
Hoarding, for reasons she knows best,
Against what hour she also knows,
Weapons whereof she is possessed.

Her innocence, that steely thing,
She keeps well sheathed
(Oh, not so soon
Submit that singular blade to stain);
Neither takes flight
But keeps for flight
Pride's lovely and undirtied wing.

## *Nathalia Crane*

NATHALIA CLARA RUTH CRANE, the most remarkable phenomenon since the days of Marjorie Fleming, was born in New York City August 11, 1913. Through her father she is descended from John and Priscilla Alden, Stephen Crane being a not distant kinsman; on her mother's side she inherits the varied gifts of the Abarbanels, that famous family of Spanish Jews which counts among its members poets, musicians, and ministers of state.

Nathalia began to write when she was little more than eight years old. At nine she sent some of her verses to *The New York Sun* and they were accepted wholly on their merit, the editor having no idea that the lines were written by a child. For six years her volumes appeared in rapid succession. During her attendance at New Jersey College for Women and at Barnard she was kept from publishing, but at twenty-two she assembled another collection of her half-childish, half-pedantic verses, *Swear by the Night* (1936), with a foreword by the editor.

Nathalia's first volume, *The Janitor's Boy*, appeared when its author was ten and a half, in 1924. It went rapidly through six editions, and became one of the most discussed publications of the year. Some of the critics explained the work by insisting that the child was some sort of medium, an instrument unaware of what was played upon it; others, considering the book a hoax, scorned the fact that any child could have written verses so smooth in execution and so remarkable in spiritual overtones. Whatever the source may be, whether the inspiration derives from Nathalia's yarn-spinning father or some atavistic spark, the poetry speaks for itself, a firm and definite accomplishment.

The verse is sharply divided into two kinds: the light and childish jingle—the sort of thinking native to most children but which most of them are unable to compress into such facile rhyme—and the grave and cryptic poetry. Even in the first division there is a quality unusual to child verse; in such merry stanzas as "The Flathouse Roof," "Love," "Oh, Roger Jones" there is a sophistication which lifts them above many of Eugene Field's rhymes on similar themes. The turn of epigram is never lacking; even in her pattering syllables she speaks of "the tenseness of humiliating pain"; a visit to an ice-cream store leads her to conclude that she "could not stain romance with monetary fee"; an emotion suspiciously like humor leads her to write "The First Reformer" and to begin another poem:

> I linger on the flathouse roof, the moonlight is divine,
> But my heart is all a-flutter like the washing on the line.

The other division of Nathalia's work, which is no longer verse but indubitable poetry, reveals that Nathalia has read much not only in books of legends but in the dictionary. This juvenile mystic is as fond of archaic terms as Francis Thompson (she collects unusual words as other children postage stamps), and she enjoys using a string of glistening alliterations to express an intuition or a mere mathematical fact. But the fact rises from its foundations on an imaginative sweep which any poet might envy. The thought of heavenly spirits hankering for the world they have left assumes this form:

> A precious place is Paradise and none may know its worth,
> But Eden ever longeth for the knicknacks of the earth.
>
> The angels grow quite wistful over worldly things below;
> They hear the hurdy-gurdies in the Candle Maker's Row.
>
> They listen for the laughter from the attics of the earth;
> They lower pails from heaven's wall to catch the milkmaid's mirth.

She summons "birth-marked butterflies cruising across the mirrors of the skies"; she sends the humming-bird "pivoting on emptiness"; her *alter ego* in Gobi sees "the tombs Time left unlatched" and "wind-blown shrouds of sand"; she imagines Oriental bees sailing "in golden convoys to the mountains of the moon." She writes a poem to console a blind playmate to whom she has tried to picture the wonder of a Christmas tree. But the lines which result have little to do with the child and nothing with the actual event; what follows is a piece of musical philosophy in which the insight is nothing less than uncanny.

Other volumes followed swiftly. *Lava Lane* (1925), *The Singing Crow* (1926), *Venus Invisible* (1928), three volumes of poetry more sedate than her first book. Prose paralleled her verse: *The Sunken Garden* (1926) showed her curiously pompous style in a long alliterative account of the Children's Crusade; *An Alien from Heaven* (1929) is a novel on a more unusual theme in which the symbolism is seemingly autobiographical if suspiciously mature and dry in tone.

*Venus Invisible* and *Swear by the Night* are the most rewarding of these volumes. They continue her eccentric vocabulary and a journalistic tendency that causes her to fashion lyrics out of a current fad in psychology or an item in a newspaper. Thus the achievement of Lindbergh—celebrated in "The Wings of Lead," which won first prize in a contest for versifying the flight across the Atlantic—brings in Homer, David, Richard, Joan, Ephesian Diana, Indra, "the stony wings of Egypt," "the tambourine of Miriam." To her defects one might add Nathalia's dependence on roses were it not that some of her finest verse uplifts the flower-cliché. Such a metaphysical poem as the "Song" beginning "Great is the rose" has long overtones. The mingling of pathos and humor in "The Dead Bee" recalls Emily Dickinson. As a rule, there is little evidence of derivations, and finally one ceases to question whether the author is a conscious child or an influenced medium; one forgets who may have written the phrases and listens only to the long implication which "challenges the crypt, and quotes millenniums against the grave." "The Dust" reiterates the theme; condensations like "The Colors," and "Desire," with its recognition of the province of poetry, are distilled communications. They reach beyond cavil or controversy. The appeal of such lines is not that they have been written by a child but by a poet.

### THE BLIND GIRL

In the darkness, who would answer for the color of a rose,
Or the vestments of the May moth and the pilgrimage it goes.

In the darkness who would answer, in the darkness who would care,
If the odor of the roses and the wingèd things were there.

In the darkness who would cavil o'er the question of a line,
Since the darkness holds all loveliness beyond the mere design.

Oh, night, thy soothing prophecies companion all our ways,
Until releasing hands let fall the catalogue of days.

In the darkness, who would answer for the color of a rose,
Or the vestments of the May moth and the pilgrimage it goes?

In the darkness who would answer, in the darkness who would care,
If the odor of the roses and the wingèd things were there.

### THE VESTAL

Once a pallid vestal
  Doubted truth in blue;
Listed red as ruin,
  Harried every hue;

Barricaded vision,
  Garbed herself in sighs;
Ridiculed the birth marks
  Of the butterflies.

Dormant and disdainful,
  Never could she see
Why the golden powder
  Decorates the bee;

Why a summer pasture
  Lends itself to paint;

Why love unappareled
  Still remains the saint.

Finally she faltered;
  Saw at last, forsooth,
Every gaudy color
  Is a bit of truth.

Then the gates were opened;
  Miracles were seen;
That instructed damsel
  Donned a gown of green;

Wore it in a churchyard,
  All arrayed with care;
And a painted rainbow
  Shone above her there.

## THE GOSSIPS

The rosebud that grew by the settle
  Bowed low to the gossiping thrusts;
The poet was praising the nettle,
  The nettle that nobody trusts.

The pansies were painted in postures,
  The poppies have stood on their toes;
But long before mention of Moses
  Her rivals have flouted the rose.

Oh! Sweetness a-sway by the settle,
  Be still on thy beautiful stem;
For love never clung to the nettle—
  The nettle that burns to condemn.

Grieve not for a moment's defection,
  Though pansies and poppies may pose,
For after a bit of reflection
  The rover returns to the rose.

## DESTINY

The wind doth wander up and down,
  Forever seeking for a crown;
The rose, in stillness on a stem,
  Inherits love's own diadem.

## THE DUST

Crumpling a pyramid, humbling a rose,
The dust has its reasons wherever it goes.

Treating the sword blade the same as the staff,
Turning the chariot wheel into chaff.

Toppling a pillar and nudging a wall,
Building a sand pile to counter each fall.

Yielding to nothing, not even the rose,
The dust has its reasons wherever it goes.

## THE COLORS

You cannot choose your battlefield,
  The gods do that for you,
But you can plant a standard
  Where a standard never flew.

## ALLIANCES

The little *and,* the tiny *if,*
  The ardent *ahs* and *ohs,*
They haunt the lanes of poesy,
  The boulevards of prose.

Small primpers of the passages
  With very slender limbs—
And yet they make alliances
  With lordly paradigms.

## DESIRE

Oh, I would like to be a ghoul
  And ruffle the poet's mound,
To dig up the rhymes he laid aside
  For the sake of another sound.

And otherwise, if that were vain,
  A diver I would be,
To pick up the rings the doges dropped
  Whenever they married the sea.

## THE DEAD BEE

Beside me there is resting
  A great biography,
That crumpled panorama—
  The history of the bee.
A husk of ebon velvet,
  A powdering of gold,
Lies, at the end, a bankrupt
  With honey still unsold.
What an extensive failure—
  (Sheriffs are in the air)
Barrels of good wild honey—
  Nobody knows just where;
Only a little bankrupt,
  Truly too tired to care.

## SONG

(*from "Tadmor"*)

Great is the rose
Infected by the tomb,
Yet burgeoning
Indifferent to death.

Where dawn on dawn
Did stumble to fulfill,
The rose has told
In one simplicity

That never life
Relinquishes a bloom

But to bestow
An ancient confidence.

Great is the rose
That challenges the crypt,
And quotes millenniums
Against the grave.

## Muriel Rukeyser

MURIEL RUKEYSER was born in New York City, December 15, 1913. She began her education in Ethical Culture and Fieldston School, entered Vassar with the class of 1934, left college after two years, and attended summer sessions at Columbia for two years more. In 1932 she became literary editor of *The Student Review* and a member of committees investigating Negro and labor problems; she was arrested during the second Scottsboro trial in Alabama. She worked her way through the ground-course at Roosevelt Aviation School, but was not allowed to pilot a plane as her parents refused to sign a contract permitting a minor to fly. It was at this time that she wrote her first important long poem, "Theory of Flight," which became the title-poem of her first volume. Work in statistics took her in 1936 to England, from where a London magazine sent her to report the People's Olympics in Barcelona, which were to open on the day the Spanish Civil War began.

Unlike many of her generation Muriel Rukeyser did not begin writing by copying the literary fashions of the day; instead of imitating the popular experimenters, she schooled herself in the traditional measures, even in the rigid French forms. Although her original work follows no tradition, the early discipline helped her to direct the fluent course, the very contradictions, of consciousness, and give the loosest of her monologues a dignity and shapeliness.

*Theory of Flight* (1935) is startling without being theatrical, intense yet governed, alternating between vivid autobiography and deep impersonality, undeviatingly honest and uncannily mature. This poet not only uses the material of modern life, she uses it without self-consciousness or the impulse to challenge attention. For her the trucks rumbling along the city streets are a more native, a more natural, prelude to day than the lark at heaven's gate; the airplane is a more legitimate, and more poetic, symbol of man's longing for freedom than fluttering Psyches, butterflies, and picturesquely released doves. Her images, dramatic and often militant, are appropriate to one born in a period of national struggles and economic warfare. The very poignance of her dialogues—"Effort at Speech Between Two People" was written when she was a sophomore—reveals the tension and terror of the contemporary world.

*Theory of Flight,* the most important volume in the Yale Series of Younger Poets, won the admiration of writers at both extremes; it was equally praised by those on the unyielding right and those on the determined left, by Kenneth Burke in *New Masses,* by Horace Gregory in *The New Republic,* and by Stephen Vincent Benét, who wrote an introduction to the book, and who concluded, "She can write powerfully . . . her technique is sure, and developing in original directions." The poems written since the publication of her first volume show an even greater strength and distinction. They are firmer, clear of the occasional abstractions which weakened certain passages in the book, and, though the direction is leftish, free of both political and poetic shibboleths.

### CEILING UNLIMITED

The cattle-trains edge along the river, bringing morning on a white vibration
breaking the darkness split with beast-cries:      a milk-wagon proceeds
down the street leaving the cold bottles:      the Mack truck pushes
around the corner, tires hissing on the washed asphalt.      A clear sky
growing candid and later bright.
                          Ceiling unlimited.      Visibility unlimited.

They stir on the pillows, her leg moving, her face swung windowward
vacant with sleep still, modeled with light's coming; his dark head
among the softness of her arm and breast, nuzzled in dreams,
mumbling the old words, hardly roused.      They return to silence.
                         At the airport, the floodlights are snapped off.

Turning, he says, "Tell me how's the sky this morning?" "Fair," she answers,
"no clouds from where I lie; bluer and bluer."      "And later and later—
god, for some sleep into some noon, instead of all these mornings
with my mouth going stiff behind the cowling and wind brushing
away from me and my teeth freezing against the wind."
                     Light gales from the northwest:      tomorrow, rain.

The street is long, with a sprinkling of ashcans; panhandlers
begin to forage among banana-peels and cardboard boxes.
She moves to the window, tall and dark before a brightening sky,
full with her six months' pregnancy molded in ripeness.
                    Stands, watching the sky's blankness.

Very soon:      "How I love to see you when I wake," he says.
"How the child's meaning in you is my life's growing."
She faces him, hands brought to her belly's level, offering,
wordless, looking upon him.      She carries his desire well.
                Sun rises:      6:38 A.M.      Sun sets. . . .

"Flying is what makes you strange to me, dark as Asia,
almost removed from my world even in your closenesses:
that you should be familiar with those intricacies
and a hero in mysteries which all the world has wanted."
                Wind velocity changing from 19 to 30.

"No, that's wrong," and he laughs, "no personal hero's left
to make a legend.      Those centuries have gone.      If I fly,
why, I know that countries are not map-colored, that seas
belong to no one, that war's a pock-marking on Europe:"
            The Weather Bureau's forecast, effective until noon.

"Your friends sleep with strange women desperately,
drink liquor and sleep heavily to forget those skies.
You fly all day and come home truly returning
to me who know only land.     And we will have this child."
                              New York to Boston:     Scattered to broken clouds.


"The child will have a hard time to be an American,"
he says slowly, "fathered by a man whose country is air,
who believes there are no heroes to withstand
wind, or a loose bolt, or a tank empty of gas."
                              To Washington:     Broken clouds becoming overcast.


"It will be a brave child," she answers, smiling.
"We will show planes to it, and the bums in the street.
You will teach it to fly, and I will love it
very much."     He thinks of his job, dressing.
                              Strong west northwest winds above 1000 feet.


He thinks how many men have wanted flight.
He ties his tie, looking into his face.
Finishes breakfast, hurrying to be gone,
crossing the river to the airport and his place.
                              To Cleveland:     Broken clouds to overcast.


She does not imagine how the propeller turns
in a blinding speed, swinging the plane through space;
she never sees the cowling rattle and slip
forward and forward against the grim blades' grinding.
                              Cruising speed 1700 R.P.M.


Slipping, a failing desire; slipping like death
insidious against the propeller, until the blades shake,
bitten by steel, jagged against steel, broken,
and his face angry and raked by death, staring.
                              Strong west northwest or west winds above 2000 feet.


She watches the clock as his return time hurries,
the schedule ticking off, eating the short minutes.
She watches evening advance; she knows the child's stirring.
She knows night.     She knows he will not come.
                              Ceiling unlimited.     Visibility unlimited.


### EFFORT AT SPEECH BETWEEN TWO PEOPLE

Speak to me.     Take my hand.     What are you now?
I will tell you all.     I will conceal nothing.
When I was three, a little child read a story about a rabbit
who died, in the story, and I crawled under a chair:
a pink rabbit:     it was my birthday, and a candle
burnt a sore spot on my finger, and I was told to be happy.

Oh, grow to know me.      I am not happy.      I will be open:
Now I am thinking of white sails against a sky like music,
like glad horns blowing, and birds tilting, and an arm about me.
There was one I loved, who wanted to live, sailing.

Speak to me.      Take my hand.      What are you now?
When I was nine, I was fruitily sentimental,
fluid: and my widowed aunt played Chopin,
and I bent my head on the painted woodwork, and wept.
I want now to be close to you.      I would
link the minutes of my days close, somehow, to your days.

I am not happy.      I will be open.
I have liked lamps in evening corners, and quiet poems.
There has been fear in my life.      Sometimes I speculate
On what a tragedy his life was, really.

Take my hand.      Fist my mind in your hand.      What are you now?
When I was fourteen, I had dreams of suicide,
and I stood at a steep window, at sunset, hoping toward death:
if the light had not melted clouds and plains to beauty,
if light had not transformed that day, I would have leapt.
I am unhappy.      I am lonely.      Speak to me.

I will be open.      I think he never loved me:
he loved the bright beaches, the little lips of foam
that ride small waves, he loved the veer of gulls:
he said with a gay mouth: I love you.      Grow to know me.

What are you now?      If we could touch one another,
if these our separate entities could come to grips,
clenched like a Chinese puzzle . . . yesterday
I stood in a crowded street that was live with people,
and no one spoke a word, and the morning shone.
Everyone silent, moving. . . . Take my hand.      Speak to me.

# INDEX OF AUTHORS

*References in parentheses are to editorial mentions.*

# INDEX OF TITLES

*MODERN BRITISH POETRY*

*Fourth Revised Edition*

*A FOREWORD*

*To the Fourth Revised Edition*

THIS collection is a companion volume to the fifth edition of *Modern American Poetry*. As with the American anthology, the groups of poems by the more important authors have been considerably enlarged. The contributions by the outstanding older writers have been emphasized and increased in number, and considerable space has been directed to the more experimental younger men, particularly to W. H. Auden, C. Day Lewis, Louis MacNeice, and Stephen Spender. The Preface has been revised; the conclusions reappraised; the introductory notes—many of them completely rewritten—are fuller and more critical.

To permit these additions, to make room for longer poems, and to keep an already large book from becoming unwieldy, thirty-eight poets represented in earlier editions of this anthology have been omitted.

It should be repeated, as it was implied in the 1930 edition, that this compilation, in spite of its air of inclusiveness, is anything but a complete summary. The work of the poets in England and Ireland since the end of the Victorian era has been so varied, the recent revival is so energetic and full of promise, that not even the most enthusiastic editor can claim finality for his labors. It may be pleaded in extenuation that no anthology, no matter how liberal or spacious, can hope to be final. Nor should it be. The duty of the anthologist (as far as one editor sees it) is to whet the reader's appetite, not to satisfy it. Such a collection as this, if its purpose be successful, should stimulate the reader's interest and excite him to a closer inspection of the poet's own volumes. Thus the following pages pretend to be little more than a critical introduction, attempting to chart various movements and tendencies with certain outstanding personalities.

For the greatest help in the preparation of this volume, thanks must be given to most of the living poets represented here. In the majority of instances, they themselves have furnished not only invaluable data but have assisted the editor in the choice of selections, so that this gathering is, to a great extent, a record of their own taste as well as his.

A further acknowledgment must be made to the various publishers whose coöperation has been of such assistance. For permission to reprint the copyright material in this volume, the editor wishes to thank the following firms—his indebtedness being alphabetically acknowledged to:

ERNEST BENN, LTD.—for the selections from *Kensington Gardens* by Humbert Wolfe.

BASIL BLACKWOOD—for the selections from *Philip* by Richard Church, *The Happy Tree* by Gerald Gould, *Poems* by Camilla Doyle, *The Wooden Pegasus* by Edith

v

Sitwell, and the various volumes of *Wheels: an Anthology* edited by Edith Sitwell.

Brentano's—for the selections from Francis Ledwidge.

The Clarendon Press—for the selections from *The Shorter Poems of Robert Bridges* and the sonnet from *The Growth of Love* by Robert Bridges.

J. M. Dent & Sons, Ltd.—for the selection from *The Cherry Minder* by Frank Kendon.

The Dial Press: Lincoln Macveagh—for the selections from *The Espalier* by Sylvia Townsend Warner.

Doubleday, Doran and Company, Inc.—for the selections from *Leda* by Aldous Huxley, *The Cyder Feast* by Sacheverell Sitwell, *Beauty and the Pilgrim* by Gerald Gould, *The Land* by V. Sackville-West, and *Requiem* by Humbert Wolfe.

Doubleday, Doran and Company, Inc., and A. P. Watt and Sons—for the selections from *Collected Poems: Inclusive Edition* by Rudyard Kipling; for "Boots" and "The Return" from *The Five Nations* by Rudyard Kipling, copyright 1917; "An Astrologer's Song" from *Actions and Reactions,* by Rudyard Kipling, copyright 1909; "Sestina of the Tramp-Royal" "The Ladies," "The Last Chantey," and "For to Admire" from *The Seven Seas* by Rudyard Kipling, copyright 1893, 1905; and "The Land" from *A Diversity of Creatures,* by Rudyard Kipling, copyright 1917, all of which are reprinted by special permission of Rudyard Kipling and Doubleday, Doran and Company, Inc.

Doubleday, Doran and Company and Martin Secker—for the selections from *Collected Poems* by James Elroy Flecker.

Duckworth & Co.—for poems from *Bucolic Comedies* by Edith Sitwell.

E. P. Dutton and Company—for selections from *The Old Huntsman, Counter-Attack* and *Picture Show* by Siegfried Sassoon, *Prophet and Fool* by Louis Golding and *Fifty Poems* by Lord Dunsany.

Faber & Faber, Ltd.—for the selections from *Collected Poems* by Herbert Read.

Four Seas Company—for the selections from *War and Love* by Richard Aldington and *The Mountainy Singer* by Seosamh MacCathmhaoil (Joseph Campbell).

Golden Cockerel Press—for the selections from *Hips and Haws* and *Pelagea* by A. E. Coppard.

Laurence J. Gomme—for the selections from *Verses* by Hilaire Belloc.

Harcourt, Brace and Company—for the selections from *Poems New and Old* by John Freeman, *Secrets* and *Selected Poems* by W. H. Davies, *Poems 1914-1934* by Herbert Read, and *The Contemplative Quarry* by Anna Wickham, *The Unknown Goddess* by Humbert Wolfe.

Harper and Brothers—for the selections from *Hawthorn and Lavender* by W. E. Henley and *The Heart's Journey* by Siegfried Sassoon.

The Hogarth Press—for the poems from *New Signatures* by John Lehmann and W. H. Auden, and *A Time to Dance* by C. Day Lewis.

Henry Holt and Company—for the selections from *Wild Earth* by Padraic Colum, *Peacock Pie, The Listeners, The Veil* and *Collected Poems* by Walter De la Mare, *A Shropshire Lad* and *Last Poems* by A. E. Housman, and *Poems* by Edward Thomas.

Mitchell Kennerley—for the selections from *Love Poems and Others* by D. H. Lawrence.

ALFRED A. KNOPF—for the selections from *The Collected Poems of William H. Davies: First Series, The Waggoner* by Edmund Blunden, *Fairies and Fusiliers* by Robert Graves, *Argonaut and Juggernaut* by Osbert Sitwell, *Bucolic Comedies, Troy Park* and *The Sleeping Beauty* by Edith Sitwell, *Poems: First Series* by J. C. Squire.

JOHN LANE: THE BODLEY HEAD, LTD.—for the selections from *Poems and Sonnets* by Frank Kendon.

HORACE LIVERIGHT, INC.—for the selections from *Dublin Days* by L. A. G. Strong.

THE MACMILLAN COMPANY—for the selections from *Twenty* by Stella Benson, *Creatures* by Padraic Colum, *Fires,* Copyright 1912, and *Borderlands and Thoroughfares,* Copyright 1915, by Wilfrid Wilson Gibson, *Collected Poems* by Thomas Hardy, *Poems* by Ralph Hodgson, *Good Friday and Other Poems,* Copyright 1916, and *Salt-Water Ballads* by John Masefield, the passage (in this volume entitled "Rounding the Horn") from "Dauber" and two poems from *The Story of a Round-House,* Copyright 1913, and *Collected Poems* by John Masefield, *Saturday Market* by Charlotte Mew, *Collected Poems* by James Stephens, *Poems, Later Poems,* Copyright 1924, *The Tower,* Copyright 1928, and *Collected Poems,* Copyright 1932, by William Butler Yeats.

MACMILLAN AND CO., LIMITED—for the selections from *Collected Poems* and *Late Lyrics and Earlier* by Thomas Hardy.

ELKIN MATTHEWS—for the poem from *Chambers of Imagery* by Gordon Bottomley.

JOHN MURRAY—for the selections from *Poetical Works* by Robert Bridges.

THE OXFORD UNIVERSITY PRESS—for the selections from *The Poems of Gerard Manley Hopkins.*

JAMES B. PINKER—for the selections from *Whipperginny* and the recent work of Robert Graves.

THE POETRY BOOKSHOP (London)—for the selections from *Spring Morning* and *Autumn Midnight* by Frances Cornford, *The Farmer's Bride* and *The Rambling Sailor* by Charlotte Mew, *Strange Meetings, Children of Love* and *Real Property* by Harold Monro. Also for the poems reprinted, with the authors' permissions, from the volumes of *Georgian Poetry.*

RANDOM HOUSE—for the selections from *Poems* by W. H. Auden, *Collected Poems* by C. Day Lewis, *Poems* by Stephen Spender, and *The Complete Works of J. M. Synge,* all of which are reprinted by permission of Random House, Inc.

GRANT RICHARDS—for the selections from *The Hundred and One Harlequins* by Sacheverell Sitwell.

SIEGFRIED SASSOON—for the selections from his *Selected Poems, Recreations* and *Vigils.*

CHARLES SCRIBNER'S SONS—for the selections from the *Collected Poems* of Alice Meynell, *Poems* by William Ernest Henley and the works of Robert Louis Stevenson.

MARTIN SECKER—for the selections from *Collected Poems* by James Elroy Flecker, *Verses* by Viola Meynell and *Days and Nights* by Arthur Symons.

SIDGWICK AND JACKSON, LTD.—for the selections from *The Waggoner* by Edmund Blunden and *The Dark Fire* by W. J. Turner.

FREDERICK A. STOKES COMPANY—for the selections from *Ardours and Endurances* by Robert Nichols and *The World's Miser* by Theodore Maynard.

THE VIKING PRESS—for the selections from *Chamber Music* by James Joyce, *Amores, Look! We Have Come Through!,* and *New Poems* by D. H. Lawrence, *Poems* by Wilfred Owen, and *The Espalier* and *Time Importuned* by Sylvia Townsend Warner.

For permission to reprint certain poems from magazines and other periodicals, the editor thanks:

THE ENGLISH REVIEW—for a poem by Humbert Wolfe.
THE LONDON MERCURY—for a poem by Stephen Spender.
THE OBSERVER—for poems by Edmund Blunden and W. H. Davies.
THE NEW REPUBLIC—for poems by Sylvia Townsend Warner and Anna Wickham.
THE NEW STATESMAN—for a poem by Roy Campbell.
NEW VERSE—for a poem by W. H. Auden.
THE SATURDAY REVIEW OF LITERATURE—for poems by Siegfried Sassoon, Richard Hughes, Frances Cornford, and Sylvia Townsend Warner.
POETRY: A MAGAZINE OF VERSE—for a selection from Ford Madox Ford.

For permission to print certain poems in manuscript and other poems which have not yet appeared in their authors' volumes, the editor especially thanks Siegfried Sassoon, Sylvia Townsend Warner, Lascelles Abercrombie, Francis Meynell, John Lehmann, Anna Wickham, Richard Church, Frank Kendon, Roy Campbell, C. Day Lewis, Louis MacNeice, and Stephen Spender.

The poems of James Elroy Flecker are reprinted by permission of his executors. The poems of Alice Meynell are reprinted with the consent of her husband, Wilfred Meynell.

Two of the posthumous poems of Thomas Hardy are reprinted by permission of Mrs. Hardy and Mr. Sidney Cockerell, his executors.

Finally I must record my indebtedness to Robert Hillyer for several suggestions and especially for his paragraphs on Robert Bridges, and to my wife, Esther Antin, for her accurate and patient help in the preparation of the manuscript.

# CONTENTS

# CONTENTS

# CONTENTS

# PREFACE

## THE "MODERN" BOUNDARY

To say this is a collection of modern poetry calls at once for a definition of the term, and it is doubtful whether there is a less exact and more overused adjective in the language than "modern." In the case of this compilation the limits of the term are determined if not defined by the dates 1830-1935, or from the birth of Christina Rossetti in the midst of Victorianism to the emergence of the "post-war" poets in the midst of revolt and reappraisal.

One line of the arbitrary boundary—a deadline by which any poet born before 1830 is excluded—has been chosen for three reasons. First, it permits the other end to round out something more than a full century of poetic accomplishment, so that the book acts as a comparison as well as a companion to *Modern American Poetry*. Second, it begins with Christina Rossetti and T. E. Brown—the former, like Emily Dickinson on the other side of the Atlantic, anticipating the semi-autobiographical lyric verse by women, the latter foreshadowing the direct speech and colloquial rhythms adopted by succeeding generations. Third, it marks the end of four-square, Victorian conservatism and the beginning of the energetic experimentalism which still engages us.

Most of the great Victorian figures are thus eliminated; reaction takes the place of reflection. Nothing, it has been said, is more permanent than the spirit of change, and we have come a long way since the time when a poet was seriously praised (in 1870) because he held "the proud honor of never uttering one single line which an English mother once would wish unwritten or an English girl would wish unread." The poet was Tennyson who (in *Idylls of the King*) reduced Malory's Round Table to the board of a royal family in the best suburban manner, proving that no laureate could have been more appropriate to the era. But if Tennyson, as G. K. Chesterton dryly remarked, "did hold a great many of the same views as Queen Victoria, though he was gifted with a more fortunate literary style," it was his style even more than his views from which his successors revolted. He presented a conventionalized tightness of sentiment; Swinburne offered an equally conventionalized looseness of rhetoric. Taste tired of both. They suggested the extremes which Yeats defined in another connection, "Sentimentality is deceiving one's self; rhetoric is deceiving other people." Artificial emotions were waning. The inversions, the elaborate diction, the strained periods were doomed.

But I am proceeding too rapidly. Within the larger curve traced in this volume, there are the records of conflicting tendencies. In general—if I may be permitted an arbitrary grouping—these smaller movements may be classified as (1) The end of Victorianism and the growth of a purely decorative art, (2)

3

The Pre-Raphaelites and Swinburne, (3) The rise and decline of the esthetic philosophy, (4) The muscular influence of Henley, (5) William Butler Yeats and the Celtic revival in Ireland, (6) Rudyard Kipling and the ascendancy of mechanism in art, (7) John Masefield and the return of the rhymed narrative, (8) The war and its effects upon the Georgians, (9) The aftermath and the new bucolic poetry, (10) The "literature of nerves," and (11) The "post-war" group. It may be interesting to follow these developments in somewhat closer detail.

### THE END OF VICTORIANISM

The age commonly called Victorian came to an end in England about 1880. It was an age distinguished by many true idealists and many false ideals. It was, in spite of its notable artists, on an entirely different level from the epoch preceding. Its poetry was, in the main, not universal but parochial; its romanticism was gilt and tinsel; its realism was kin to its showy glass pendants, red plush, parlor chromos and antimacassars. The period was full of a pessimistic resignation (the note popularized by Fitzgerald's Omar Khayyám) and a kind of negation which, refusing to see any glamor in the present world, turned to the Middle Ages, to King Arthur, to the legend of Troy—to the suave surroundings of a dream-world instead of the hard contours of actual experience.

At its worst, it was a period of smugness, of placid and pious sentimentality, epitomized by the rhymed sermons of Martin Farquhar Tupper, whose *Proverbial Philosophy* was devoured, with all its cloying and indigestible sweetmeats, by tens of thousands. The same tendency is apparent, though a little less objectionably, in the moralizing lays of Lord Thomas Macaulay, in the theatrically emotionalized verses of Robert Buchanan, Edwin Arnold and Sir Lewis Morris, even in the lesser work of Alfred Lord Tennyson.

The poets of a generation before this time were fired with such ideas as freedom, an adoration of nature, an insatiable hunger for truth in all its forms and manifestations. The characteristic poets of the Victorian Era, says Max Plowman, "wrote under the dominance of churchliness, of 'sweetness and light,' and a thousand lesser theories that have not truth but comfort for their end."

The revolt against the tawdriness of the period had already begun; the best of Victorianism can be found not in men who were typically Victorian, but in pioneers like Browning and insurrectionary spirits like Swinburne, Rossetti, William Morris, who were completely out of sympathy with their time.

### THE PRE-RAPHAELITES AND SWINBURNE

That band of painters and poets who called themselves quaintly The Pre-Raphaelite Brotherhood hurried the demise of Victorianism. Their work was a continual denial of its forms; their poems aspired to be paintings, their paintings poems. Under the leadership of William Morris The Pre-Raphaelites enlisted the coöperation of Burne-Jones, the Rossettis, and the insecure loyalty of Swinburne. Morris, the most practical member of the group, sought to make over an entire culture; he designed everything from chintzes to stained-glass windows, created furniture, wrought iron, printed books, manufactured glass, needlework, tapestries, tools—all as a protest against the rapid commercialism of a period whose prosperity was essentially shoddy. Morris was a consistent protestant in his poetry and his politics. In the rôle of poet he rebuked the smallness of his times with epics like *The Earthly Paradise;* in the rôle of propagandist he answered narrow individualism with *News from Nowhere,* picturing an ideal England in which the principles of communism had triumphed. Here Morris, dreaming of a medieval Utopia, confused the future with the past. With a simplicity surpassed only by his energy, he turned back to passion in suits of antique armor and to gallants whose heroism was suspiciously like heroics.

Morris failed, partly because the trend toward standardized production was too sweeping to take account of his theories, partly because he himself was not so much concerned with humanity as with things. He advocated a knightly Socialism not because it would make a more beautiful race but more decorative objects. His sagas show that his preoccupation was with literature instead of life; and, by an ungrateful paradox, a literature that is preferred to life has a swift mortality.

Swinburne suffered from a similar defect. Flying from the prim domesticity sanctified by Tennyson, Swinburne rushed to the unholy (and purely literary) arms of Dolores, Faustine, Félise, Fragoletta, to the neo-paganism of *Atalanta in Calydon,* to the lush intransigence of *Songs Before Sunrise,* to Gautier and Hugo and Baudelaire, to a quick succession of enthusiasms and influences. But it was neither Swinburne's political convictions nor his vaguely revolutionary tendencies which made the young men of his day go about "chanting to one another these new, astonishing melodies." It was his mastery of the lightning phrase, cutting through murky philosophizing and wave-like rhythms rising and crashing on startled shores; it was his headlong fervor coming immediately after a decade of cautious hesitancy. Most of all, from a literary-historical point of view, it was his technique which affected the entire conception of English metrics. English poetry had been slavishly devoted to its norm, the *iamb;* Swinburne, by a lavish use of the dactyl, the choriambus and the anapest, gave poetry a new motion, a polyphonic freedom, an orchestral sweep and sonority. He enlarged the potentialities of English prosody. "Nor," writes Edmund Gosse, "was his singular vogue due only to this extraordinary metrical ingenuity; the effect of his artistic personality was itself intoxicating, even delirious. He was the poet of youth insurgent against all the restraints of conventionality and custom."

The "purest" poet of the group was one only loosely affiliated with it, the quiet sister of Dante Gabriel, Christina Rossetti. Her delicate reticences have been often portrayed, but it remained for Frances Winwar, in *Poor Splendid Wings: The Rossettis and Their Circle,* to depict the outer softness and the inner sharpness, "protecting, like a coat of armor, something she held above the treasures of the world." Struggling between the desires of her womanhood and a congenital refusal to face life, her philosophy grew more and more ascetic. Denial and loss became her favorite themes, she grew increasingly preoccupied with the thought of death as the undemanding lover, the final appeasement. But the thought of sundering to which she always returned, the tremulous abnegation, stirred the depths of her music and inspired her most memorable poetry.

### RISE AND DECLINE OF THE ESTHETIC PHILOSOPHY

A further, if more limited, revolt ensued. Oscar Wilde, dilettante *de luxe,* attempted to make the 'Nineties draw up an esthetic declaration of independence; the beauty they championed, taking a leaf from the French symbolists, was to be "its own excuse for being." Wilde's was, in the most outspoken manner, the first use of estheticism as a slogan; the battle-cry of the group was actually the now outworn but then revolutionary "Art for Art's sake"! And, so sick were people of the pinchbeck ornaments of the immediate past, that the slogan won. At least, temporarily.

*The Yellow Book,* the organ of the révoltés, appeared (1894-1897), representing a reasoned if limited reaction. The Rhymers' Club was the nucleus, and its members—among them Ernest Dowson, Lionel Johnson, Victor Plarr, John Davidson, Arthur Symons, William Butler Yeats—met at the Cheshire Cheese where, over their cakes and ale, they fondly hoped to restore the spirit of the Elizabethan age. Unfortunately they lacked both the gusto and the initiative of their Mermaid Tavern models. Where the Elizabethans were all for size, the sad young men were all for subtlety; instead of being large and careless, they were cramped and self-conscious, writing with one eye on the British public which they hoped to startle, and the other on the French poets whom they hoped to impress. But, underneath the desire to shock the middle-classes their standards were as prescribed as those they derided. To be mildly heretical was their unwritten orthodoxy; instead of being sentimental about virgins they were sentimental about street-walkers. Prostitutes were "soiled doves" and the street-lamps under which they plied their trade were "the iron lilies of the Strand."

Until its collapse after the trial of Wilde, the Esthetic Movement gathered a show of strength which was, however, weakened by its central fallacy. It tried to drag life down to literature instead of bringing literature up to life. The young men's prophet was Walter Pater; their stronghold the ivory tower; their program a mixture of Anglican intellectuality and Parnassian impressionism. "But," as C. E. Andrews and M. O. Percival point out in *Poetry of the Nineties,* "they left behind the intellectual side of Pater, and the 'gem-like flame' was fed purely by emotions. The esthetes' search for beauty became a search for sensations. They did not face the whole of life . . . but they selected from life its strange colors and its strange experiences. They loved to see in the real world glimpses that *seemed* exotic and remote."

Almost the first act of the "new" men was to rouse and outrage their immediate predecessors. This end-of-the-century desire to shock, which was so strong and natural an impulse, still has a place of its own as an antidote. Mid-Victorian propriety and self-satisfaction crumbled under the swift audacities of rebellious spirits. The old walls fell; the public, once so apathetic to *belles-lettres,* was more than attentive to every phase of literary experimentation. The last decade of the nineteenth century was so tolerant of novelty in art and ideas, that it would seem, says Holbrook Jackson in his penetrative summary, *The Eighteen-Nineties,* "as though the declining century wished to make amends for several decades of artistic monotony. It may indeed be something more than a coincidence that placed this decade at the close of a century, and *fin de siècle* may have been at once a swan song and a death-bed repentance."

Thereafter, the movement (if such it may be called) surfeited with its own excesses fell into the mere poses of revolt; it degenerated into a half-hearted defense of artificialities.

It scarcely needed W. S. Gilbert (in *Patience*) or Robert Hichens (in *The Green Carnation*) to satirize its distorted attitudinizing. It strained itself to death; it became its own burlesque of the bizarre, an extravaganza of extravagance. "The period" (I am again quoting Holbrook Jackson) "was as certainly a period of decadence as it was a period of renaissance. The decadence was to be seen in a perverse and finicking glorification of the fine arts and mere artistic virtuosity on the one hand, and a militant commercial movement on the other. . . . The eroticism which became so prevalent in the verse of many of the younger poets was minor because it was little more than a pose—not because it was erotic. . . . It was a passing mood which gave the poetry of the hour a hothouse fragrance; a perfume faint, yet unmistakable and strange."

But most of the elegant and disillusioned young men overshot their mark. Vulgar health reasserted itself; an inherent though long-repressed vitality sought new channels. Arthur Symons deserted his hectic Muse, Richard Le Gallienne abandoned his preciosity, and the group began to disintegrate. The esthetic philosophy was wearing thin; it had already begun to fray and reveal its essential shabbiness. Wilde, himself, possessed the three things which he said the English would never forgive—youth, power, and enthusiasm. But in trying to make an exclusive cult of beauty, Wilde had also tried to make it evade actuality; he urged that art should not, in any sense, be a part of life but an escape from it. "The proper school to learn art in is not Life—but Art." And in the same essay ("The Decay of Lying") he wrote, "All bad Art comes from returning to Life and Nature, and elevating them into ideals." Elsewhere he declared his motto: "The first duty in life is to be as artificial as possible. What the second duty is no one has discovered."

Such a cynical and, in essence, silly philosophy could not go unchallenged. Its snobbish fastidiousness, its very pretense, was bound to arouse the blood of common reality. This negative attitude received its answer in the work of that determined yea-sayer, W. E. Henley.

### WILLIAM ERNEST HENLEY

Henley repudiated languid estheticism; he scorned a mincing art which was out of touch with the world. His was a large and sweeping affirmation. He felt that mere existence was glorious: life was coarse, difficult, often dangerous and dirty, but splendid at the heart. Art, he knew, could not be separated from the dreams and hungers of man; it could not flourish only on its own essences or technical accomplishments. To live, poetry would have to share the fears, angers, hopes and struggles of the prosaic world. So Henley came like a salt breeze blowing through a perfumed, heavily screened studio. He sang loudly (often, indeed, too loudly) of the joy of living and the courage of the "unconquerable soul." He was a powerful influence not only as a poet but as a critic and editor. In the latter capacity he gathered about him such men as Robert Louis Stevenson, Rudyard Kipling, Thomas Hardy, H. G. Wells, William Butler Yeats, T. E. Brown, J. M. Barrie. None of these men were his disciples, some were much older, but none came into contact with him without being influenced in some way by his sharp and positive personality. A pioneer and something of a prophet, he was one of the first to champion the paintings of Whistler and to proclaim the genius of Rodin.

Historically considered, Henley represents another transition; his is the bridge between the loose optimism of Browning and the applied imperialism of Kipling. Both extremes find a voice—and a prolonged one—in his work. "Life! More life!" he shouted with the over-eagerness of one afflicted by physical infirmities. "More life!"—particularly English life which, with the authority of sword and gospel, must be broadcast over both hemispheres—but life, no matter how undisciplined, at any cost. And the more boisterous the better.

> Life—give me life until the end,
> That at the very top of being,
> The battle-spirit shouting in my blood,
> Out of the reddest hell of the fight
> I may be snatched and flung
> Into the everlasting lull,
> The immortal, incommunicable dream.

But Henley's verse was not always shrill. When he forgot to be muscular, he fashioned ballades and rondeaus with a dexterity scarcely surpassed by Swinburne, lyrics of surprisingly delicate texture, free verse that anticipated a movement two generations later, and "voluntaries" of the city on the Thames with Whistlerian glamor. Further than that, Henley's noisy periods are redeemed by his passionate enthusiasm for nobility in whatever cause it was joined. He loved the world in all its moods. Bus-drivers, hospital interiors, scrubwomen, a panting train, the mystery and squalor of London's alleys, all found a voice in his lines; his later work contains more than a hint of the delight in science and machinery which was later to be sounded more fully in the work of Rudyard Kipling.

### THE CELTIC REVIVAL AND J. M. SYNGE

In 1889, William Butler Yeats published his *Wanderings of Oisin;* in the same year Douglas Hyde, scholar and folk-lorist, brought out his *Book of Gaelic Stories.*

The revival of Gaelic and the renascence of Irish literature may be said to date from the publication of those two books. The fundamental idea of both men and their followers was the same. It was to create a literature which would express the national consciousness of Ireland through a purely national art. They began to reflect the strange background of dreams, politics, hopelessness, and heroism which is proverbially Irish. This community of fellowship and aims is to be found in the varied but allied work of William Butler Yeats, "Æ" (George W. Russell), Moira O'Neill, Lionel Johnson, Katharine Tynan, Padraic Colum, and others. The first fervor gone, a period of dullness set in. After reanimating the old myths, surcharging the legendary heroes with a new significance, it seemed that the movement was losing itself in a literary mysticism. But there followed an increasing concern with the peasant, the migratory laborer, the tramp; an interest that was a reaction against the influence of Yeats and his then arbitrary, over-symbolized otherworldliness. In 1904, the Celtic Revival reached its height with John Millington Synge, who was not only the greatest dramatist of the Irish Theater, but (to quote such contrary critics as George Moore and Harold Williams) "one of the greatest dramatists who has written in English." Synge's poetry, brusque and all too small in quantity, was a minor occupation with him, yet the quality and power of it is unmistakable. Its content was not great, but the raw vigor in it served as a bold banner—a sort of a brilliant Jolly Roger—for the younger men of a subsequent period.

In the introduction to *The Playboy of the Western World,* Synge declared, "When I was writing *The Shadow of the Glen* some years ago, I got more aid than any learning could have given me from a chink in the floor of the old Wicklow house where I was staying that let me hear what was being said by the servant girls in the kitchen. This matter is, I think, of some importance; for in countries where the imagination of the people and the language they use, is rich and living, it is possible for a writer to be rich and copious in his words —and at the same time to give the reality which is at the root of all poetry, in a natural and comprehensive form." This not only explains Synge's impulse but his idiom, possibly the raciest in modern literature.

Synge's poetic power is unquestionably greatest in his plays. In *The Well of the Saints, The Playboy of the Western World,* and *Riders to the Sea* there is more beauty of form, more richness of language than in any piece of dramatic writing since the Elizabethans. Yeats, when he first heard Synge's early one-act play, *The Shadow of the Glen,* is said to have exclaimed "Euripides." A half year later when Synge read him *Riders to the Sea,* Yeats again confined his enthusiasm to a single word:—"Aeschylus!" Time has shown that Yeats's exaggeration was not wholly a compatriot's *beau geste.*

Although Synge's poetry was not his major concern, numbering only twenty-four original pieces and eighteen translations, it had a surprising effect. It marked a point of departure, a reaction against the too-polished verse of his immediate predecessors as well as the dehumanized mysticism of many of his associates. In that memorable preface to his *Poems* he wrote what was a manifesto and at the same time a classic *credo* for all that called itself the "new" poetry. "I have often thought," it begins, "that at the side of poetic diction, which everyone condemns, modern verse contains a great deal of poetic material, using 'poetic' in the same special sense. The poetry of exaltation will be always the highest, but when men lose their poetic feeling for ordinary life and cannot write poetry of ordinary things, their exalted poetry is likely to lose its strength of exaltation in the way that men cease to build beautiful churches when they have lost happiness in building shops. . . . Even if we grant that exalted poetry can be kept successfully by itself, the strong things of life are needed in poetry also, to show that what is exalted or tender is not made by feeble blood."

### WILLIAM BUTLER YEATS

William Butler Yeats began by being part of the Celtic movement; before he was sixty he had inspired a movement of his own. With the publication of his *Collected Poems* in 1933 he was acclaimed Ireland's uncrowned laureate and was considered by many the finest poet of his day. Yeats's early poetry was in the style popularized by the Celtic twilight with all its musing and mistiness. Several volumes, such as *Crossways* (1889), *The Rose* (1893), *The Wind Among the Reeds* (1899), illustrate his gift for pure song. With *The Green Helmet* (1910) a more colloquial tone entered his verse and in *Responsibilities* (1914) a new articulation manifested itself. Yeats had met Ezra Pound and was greatly impressed with the young American's poetic idiom. His later work grew clearer in thought, more complex in harmony. He employed common speech with increasingly greater richness, mingling wit and wisdom in a way scarcely suggested by his early poetry. In "The Lake Isle of Innisfree" and other lyrics of that period Yeats was approximating the indefiniteness of music which was the chief aim of the Symbolists; in the later meditative poetry he traced the intricate patterns of the conscious mind.

The publication of the *Collected Poems* when Yeats was in his sixty-eighth year, was the signal for an international salute; poets of every school and tendency united to acclaim Yeats's increased power. Expressing it for all, Charles Powell wrote in the *Manchester Guardian,* "In Mr. Yeats there is, perhaps, the clearest link between the modern and the more traditional. There is no poet writing today, old or new, who gets so surely through to reality or who has so vitally the contemporary consciousness. But he gives the artist's allegiance to beauty; and, now that he has established something like an equipoise between the intellect and the imagination, his poetry has the energy of life that is at once passionate and serene."

### RUDYARD KIPLING

New tendencies are contagious. But they also disclose themselves simultaneously in places and people where there has been no point of contact. Even before Synge proclaimed the wild beauty in rude life, Kipling was illuminating, in a totally different manner, the wealth of poetic material in things hitherto regarded as too commonplace for poetry. Before literary England had quite recovered from a surfeit of Victorian priggishness and Pre-Raphaelite preciosity, the young Kipling came out of India with high spirits and a great tide of life, sweeping all before him. An obscure Anglo-Indian journalist, the publication of his *Barrack-room Ballads* in 1892 brought him sudden notice. By 1895, he was internationally famous. Plunging through the past as through a withered underbrush, he sprang into the open field of the present. Its mechanical obstacles did not deter him. Kipling gloried in the material world; he did more— he glorified it. He pierced the tough exteriors of seemingly prosaic things—

things like machinery, bridge-building, cockney soldiers, slang, steam, the dirty by-products of science (witness "M'Andrews Hymn" and "The Bell Buoy")—and uncovered their hidden glamor. "Romance is gone," sighed most of his contemporaries,

> . . . and all unseen
> Romance brought up the nine-fifteen.

That sentence (from his poem "The King") furnishes the key to his idiom; it explains how, without theories or technical innovations, the author of *Barrack-room Ballads* and *The Five Nations* helped rejuvenate English verse.

Reality is Kipling's romanticism; he rolls drums and sounds clarions for another "crowded hour of glorious life." But it is not Henley's abstraction for which Kipling fills his fife; he composes marches for soldiers, explorers, mechanics, foot-sloggers—for life which is no emotional generality, but life in action. Motion itself is apostrophized in his verse. Where the world is going is of no particular concern to Kipling; that it moves as a beneficent Britannia directs is gratifying, but that it moves is sufficient.

Kipling, with his perception of ordinary people in terms of ordinary life, is one of the strongest links between the Wordsworth-Browning era and the apostles of vigor, beginning with Masefield. There are serious defects in Kipling's work, particularly in his more facile poetry. He falls into a journalistic ease with a tendency to jingle; he is fond of a militaristic drum-banging as blatant as the insularity he condemns. But a burning if bland faith shines through his dogmas. His best work vibrates with an intensity that transforms the once tawdry, that lifts the vulgar and incidental to the universal—the universal, that is, in terms of the British Empire.

### JOHN MASEFIELD

All art is a twofold reviving—a reappraisal of subject and a reanimating of form. Poetry becomes perennially "new" by returning to the old with a different consciousness, a greater awareness. In 1911, when art was again searching for novelty, John Masefield created something startling and new by going back to 1385 and *The Canterbury Pilgrims*. Employing both the Chaucerian model and a form similar to the practically forgotten Byronic stanza, Masefield wrote in rapid succession, *The Everlasting Mercy* (1911), *The Widow in the Bye Street* (1912), *Dauber* (1912), *The Daffodil Fields* (1913)—four astonishing rhymed narratives and four of the most remarkable poems of his generation. Expressive of every rugged phase of life, these poems, uniting old and new manners, responded to Synge's proclamation that "the strong things of life are needed in poetry also . . . and it may almost be said that before verse can be human again it must be brutal."

Masefield brought back to poetry that mixture of beauty and brutality which is its most human and enduring quality. He brought back that rich and vulgar vividness which is the life-blood of Chaucer, of Shakespeare, of Burns, of Villon, of Heine—and of all those who were not only great artists but great humanists. As a purely descriptive poet, he won a place with the masters of seascape and landscape. As an imaginative realist, he showed those who were stumbling from one wild eccentricity to another that humanity itself was wilder, stranger, far more thrilling than anything in the world—or out of it. Few things in contemporary poetry are as powerful as the regeneration of Saul Kane (in *The Everlasting Mercy*) or the story of *Dauber,* the tale of a tragic sea-voyage and a dreamer who wanted to be a painter. The vigorous description of rounding Cape Horn in the latter poem is a masterpiece in itself. Masefield's later volumes are quieter in tone, more measured in technique; there is a genuinely religious ring to many of his Shakespearean sonnets. But the swinging surge is in all his work from *Salt Water Ballads* (1902) to *Reynard the Fox* (1919).

### THE WAR AND THE GEORGIANS

In 1914, the line of demarcation between Masefield and the younger men was not sharp. Realism was again in the ascendancy. So definite a style as Masefield's was bound to be imitated. It even attracted W. W. Gibson, who deserted bowery arcades to follow the rude trail Masefield had blazed. Gibson reënforced the interest in actuality by turning from a preoccupation with shining knights, faultless queens, ladies in distress, and all the paraphernalia of hackneyed medieval romances, to write about ferrymen, berry-pickers, stone-cutters, farmers, printers, circus-men, carpenters—dramatizing (and often theatricalizing) the primitive emotions of ordinary people in *Livelihood, Daily Bread,* and *Fires.* Candor had been asking new questions. It found unexpected answers in the war; repressed emotionalism discovered a new and terrible outlet.

The first volume of the biennial *Georgian Poetry* had just appeared when the war caught up the youth of England in a gust of national fervor. Not only the young men but their seniors joined what seemed then to be "the Great Adventure," only to find that it was, as one of them has since called it, "the Late Great Nightmare." After the early flush of romanticism had passed, the voices of bitter disillusion were heard. Not at first, for censorship was omnipresent. But Siegfried Sassoon's fierce satires and burning denunciations could not be stilled, the mocking lines of Robert Graves began to be quoted, Wilfred Owen's posthumous poems painted a picture the very opposite of the journalistic jingo verses which attempted to paint civilization's greatest horror in bright and cheerful colors.

Recently, in an article on a similar theme, Graves wrote: "The poetry written by actual soldiers is perhaps too familiar for discussion, but we may remind ourselves of one or two outstanding facts usually overlooked: that Rupert Brooke saw many warlike scenes but no actual fighting, that Robert Nichols, with the best of intentions, only saw three weeks' service in France and this on a quiet sector with the artillery: that of the other poets with reputations as War-poets not more than four or five (including Siegfried Sassoon, Wilfred Owen, who was killed just before the Armistice, Isaac Rosenberg, Edmund Blunden, and Herbert Read) bore the heat and burden of the War; and that these unanimously vilified rather than celebrated the War: and that of these only Siegfried Sassoon published his verse while the War was still on."

Rupert Brooke, the most popular of his group, remains, in most minds, as the type of romantic warrior, a symbolic figure not uncommon at the beginning of the War. But his poetry, as well as his correspondence, contains evidence that, had he survived the first few years of warfare, his verse—had he written at all—would have been akin to the unromanticized passion of those who, like Sassoon and Owen, saw the horror at close range and at length. Even his comrade, Charles Hamilton Sorley, that marvelous boy killed at twenty, hearing the news of Brooke's enlistment, wrote: "Rupert Brooke is far too obsessed with his own sacrifice, regarding the going to war of himself (and others) as a highly intense, remarkable and sacrificial exploit, whereas it is merely the conduct demanded of him (and others) by the turn of circumstances, where non-compliance with this demand would have made life intolerable. He has clothed his attitude in fine words: but his is, nevertheless, the sentimental attitude."

The effect of the War on the older and more established poets was definite if less direct. The Georgian group issued two more volumes (there were five in all, the last being *Georgian Poetry 1920-1922*), but the spirit had gone out of it. Rupert Brooke and Edward Thomas had been silenced by death. The work of Walter de la Mare grew increasingly somber; John Masefield no longer contributed; D. H. Lawrence—never a Georgian at heart and admitted to the volumes with a few circumspect poems—turned to prose and bitter *pensées;* Lascelles Abercrombie wrote little after 1919; Ralph Hodgson ceased to write at all. Only W. H. Davies, living in a world which, seemingly common-pastoral, was really a world of his own, continued to warble his delighted, thought-free bird-notes. The loss to the group of these men—or the loss of their power—was not compensated by the addition of Martin Armstrong, William Kerr, J. D. C. Pellow, Edward Shanks, Thomas Moult, and other fashioners of what Sassoon called "crocus-crowded lyrics."

## AFTERMATH

Peace brought back but few of the younger poets. The most brilliant of them, Charles Hamilton Sorley, was killed on the threshold of an indubitably great future. The career of Isaac Rosenberg, author of an amazing poetic drama, was ended almost before it had begun. Rupert Brooke died in the midst of his singing; so did Edward Thomas, Francis Ledwidge, Cameron Wilson. Wilfred Owen was struck down just as he had found his own full-throated utterance. It is impossible to calculate how much was lost to English poetry by the death of these singers.

One after-effect was particularly noticeable. English literature suffered not only from individual losses but from general shock. This shock affected the writers of every school and diverted where it did not arrest the current of contemporary verse. It threw Masefield back to the classic drama of half a century ago; it silenced such of its War-poets as refused to continue to write about "the collective madness" and yet could think of little else. It created the sharp division between the new group of English pastoral poets and the still younger intellectuals. The reactions of the two contradictory movements are easy to understand. Wishing to escape the mechanistic urban civilization which had scarred Europe with ruins, many of the poets turned hopefully to the traditional curlew-calling, plover-haunted English countryside. The machine is a dead thing spreading death, they cried; only the soil brings forth. "We have had enough of destructive ingenuities; let us go back to creative simplicities." Following, more or less consciously, the example of that genuinely naïf poet, W. H. Davies, a small cohort of writers began to sing exclusively about the charms of childhood, sunsets, and rural delights. But where Davies' innocence is natural and deep, the simplicity of most of the pastoral Georgians is predetermined and superficial. Much of the resulting poetry is inspired by the wish to avoid past memories rather than by a spontaneous affection for the present scene; much of it, indeed, seems a sort of spiritual convalescence.

The Georgian group developed a vocabulary built on the colloquial, but it failed to emphasize any conviction behind it. Although it was devoted to real objects, it favored a gentlemanly realism. It was, as L. A. G. Strong has written, "soothing, reassuring. Its outbursts of indignation were directed against precisely the right objects, and were timed for precisely the right moment." The technique was always enviably neat—a finical contrast to the vivid bucolic records of Edward Thomas—and the conceits were properly restrained. Sometimes they reached extremes of insipidity; one of the collections enshrines this *reductio ad absurdum,* in which one of the literary shepherds composes such unconsciously comic strophes as:

> I lingered at a gate and talked
> A little with a lonely lamb.
> He told me of the great still night,
> Of calm starlight,
> And of the lady moon, who'd stoop
> For a kiss sometimes. . . .
> Of how, when sheep grew old,
> As their faith told
> They went without a pang
> To far green fields, where fall
> Perpetual streams that call
> To deathless nightingales.

The true pastoral note was not without its singers. The bucolics of Edmund Blunden, W. J. Turner, Frank Prewett and others contain a quality which makes the verses significant, especially in view of the conditions which caused them.

### THE "LITERATURE OF NERVES"

Opposed to the rustic tendency, a group emerged headed by the three Sitwells. Revolting from the false naïveté of the Georgians—particularly that part of it dominated by J. C. Squire of *The London Mercury* and derisively nicknamed the Squirearchy—the expression at first took the form of satire. Sometimes the burlesque was broad, sometimes the allusions were so erudite and private that only the initiate found them intelligible. The Sitwells advertised themselves liberally, even caricatured their offerings as the "queer" products of a disordered age, bellowed their verses through megaphones, and capitalized their well-organized unpopularity. Their poetry was not always

compounded of wildness prepense; it was mad only north-north-west, and
soon it became evident that what they had to say was of some significance to
their times. Their patently artificial figures began to breathe; their pastiche was
humanized. Nostalgia welled up beneath the elegances, reminiscent of the
'Nineties, and (again reminding us of the *fin de siècle* esthetes) this yearning
back to a happier world clothed itself in foreign symbolism. Differing from the
Parnassian poets, they did not depict their objects—or objectives—by direct
statement; like the Symbolists, they relied on the power of elision and suggestion, compelling readers to participate in the process of creation, making
them fill the gaps between thought and figure, between meaning and mystery.
They would have agreed with Jules Huret who insisted,

It is the perfect use of this mystery that constitutes the symbol: little by little to
evoke an object in order to show a condition of the mind; or inversely to choose an
object, and from it to disengage a state of the mind by a series of decipherings. . . .
There should always be an enigma in poetry, and the aim of literature—it has no
other—is to evoke objects.

The movement, as may be deduced, was primarily intellectual; though it
developed an emotionalism, or at least a state of feeling of its own, it was
bound to arbitrary tenets. But Edith Sitwell, the creator, triumphed over the
tenets of Edith Sitwell, the theorist. The poet Herbert Read was not always in
agreement with the critic Herbert Read, who attempted to resolve the old
dispute by saying, "Poetry is creative expression: Prose is constructive expression," maintaining "we now see that poetry may inhere in a single word, in a
single syllable, and may therefore in an extreme case be without rhythm."
For several years the "anti-Georgians" sent up rockets of savage and esoteric
brilliance. Nor did all of these explosions end in a shower of burnt sticks.
Whatever their defects, they were faults of excess—more acceptable than the
extravagances of dearth—and their idiom (particularly Edith Sitwell's and
Peter Quennell's) was like no other's. Much of it, high-pitched and exacerbated, belongs to the literature of nerves. But its implicit challenge is always
provocative, sometimes thrilling, and never dull.

### THE POST-WAR POETS

In the early 1930s several poets emerged who had more than mere con-
temporaneousness in common. Their vocabulary, their taste, their technique,
most of all their social and political convictions, were in the greatest possible
contrast to those of the Georgians and the Sitwellians. They owed much to
two experimental predecessors: Gerard Manley Hopkins, that richly associative
and most original poet neglected during his lifetime, and the American T. S.
Eliot, who so strongly influenced English poetry at the beginning of the twentieth century. Eliot prepared the way for them, celebrating and satirizing the
end of a cycle, the cultural decay of a period and a system. But Eliot, retreating into Anglo-Catholicism and increasingly obscure allegories, declined to
face the outcome. Here the younger Englishmen broke with him; they refused
to follow his desperate evasions and final defeatism. They were revolutionaries;

to them, as to Hopkins, communism offered a better way of life. They borrowed from Eliot his style rather than his thought; they benefited from his manner, particularly his method of communication by symbol and atmosphere.

The members of this group—called "post-war" to characterize those who began to write only after the war—published their work in a collection *New Signatures* and in the periodical *New Verse*. The most important contributors were W. H. Auden, Stephen Spender, Cecil Day Lewis, John Lehmann, and Louis MacNeice. Their volumes appeared almost simultaneously in the early 1930s—they shared the same point of view toward art and nature, politics and poetry. Considering their contribution Alastair Miller, in *The Saturday Review of Literature,* summarized it, "Nature is no longer considered anthropomorphically, nor love religiously. The poet no longer looks out of his window in the country and, blinding himself to the railway track, sees a beneficent Providence creating the pleasures and necessities of men: he sees electric pylons conveying imprisoned power, telegraph wires defying distance, motor ploughs forcing fertility into the soil. There is no disrespect, as is sometimes maintained, for primroses and budding trees; but they are not accepted as a solution of, or consolation for, human misery." Stephen Spender makes this particularly explicit in his "Landscape near an Aerodrome" which begins:

> More beautiful and soft than any moth
> With burring furred antennae feeling its huge path
> Through dusk, the air-liner with shut-off engines
> Glides over suburbs and the sleeves set trailing tall
> To point the wind.

In "The Express" Spender pictures "the first powerful plain manifesto, the black statement of pistons," and at the end of one of his sonnets he emphasizes the post-war poet's attitude:

> Real were iron lines, and, smashing the grass
> The cars in which we ride, and real our compelled time:
> Painted on enamel beneath moving glass
> Unreal were cows, the wave-winged storks, the lime:
> These burned in a clear world from which we pass
> Like *rose* and *love* in a forgotten rhyme.

This is, obviously, an attitude that tempts controversy. Even so liberal a commentator as L. A. G. Strong considers it highly questionable. "First of all," he says, "it begs the question whether in contemplating nature a man is not living as intensely as when he is contesting an election on the Communistic ticket." But Mr. Strong is quick to perceive that it is an error to make the theory a basis for attack and he adds that what a poet believes is of no importance except for the results it may have on his poetry. "The theory from which a new movement in English poetry is rising may be sound or unsound, but it is in itself no grounds for attacking or defending that poetry, and its final importance must lie in the work which it inspires."

Much of that importance will be due to the diction of the post-war poets, a diction utterly unlike anything in English verse. Echoing the Symbolists, they maintained that the poet's chief aim was to communicate, not the exact details of an experience, but its quality, its tone and rhythm. Eliot was credited with having shown them the way to a new rhythmical freedom, Hopkins for the fresh arrangements and cadences of words. The constant shifting of tone and emphasis, the alternations of ecstasy and banality, were devices which Eliot had taken from the French; the post-war poets adopted and varied them. C. Day Lewis, in his revealing essay, "A Hope for Poetry," makes plain the salient characteristic of post-war verse technique. "The deliberate insertion into a lyrical context of pieces of slang and 'prosaic' words; the juxtaposition of highly charged 'poetical' images and dull, commonplace images; the use of bathos—all these have been taken over from the Symbolists, largely through the instrumentality of Eliot; and the verse that results offers an uneven, conversational surface shot through with gleams of lyricism, rather than a uniformly lyrical texture. . . . The desire for intensity and for freshness of language which leads these poets to syntactical ellipses, produces also that preoccupation with internal rhyme and assonance which may succeed in restablishing poetry as a delight to the ear."

As Lewis himself concludes, no amount of technical experiment can of itself produce poetry, but the intensive experimentation was conducted with an energy and optimism that was startling. The poetic art in England received a sudden increase in vitality impelled by a revolutionary fervor. It came with such exuberance that even those who challenged its philosophy could not dispute its stimulative effect. Quoting some lines of W. H. Auden, Hugh Walpole wrote, "It is the first time for years that the new poetry in England has had the energy to entrain or cut peat or light a fire. The Waste Land is, at last, to be cultivated. . . . The real importance comes from the undoubted fact that these poets accept life rather than curse or despise it." Auden, the most forceful if also the least simple, not only inspired Day Lewis and Spender, but seems to have engendered a poetry revival almost by himself.

If such active post-war poetry did not mark a complete return to health after a decade of "nerves," at least it indicated a lively convalescence.

## SUMMARY

Most of the representative poets of the end of the nineteenth and the first third of the twentieth century cannot be placed in any school or group. The work of such men as Thomas Hardy, Gerard Manley Hopkins, William Butler Yeats, and Wilfred Owen resists category. It is equally difficult to classify the poetry of Walter de la Mare—half moon-soaked fantasy and half morose reality—the fluent and unperturbed lyrics of Ralph Hodgson—lyrics in which the simplicity masks a powerful imagination, matched only by the genius of A. E. Housman—the brooding gravity of Charlotte Mew, the fretted energy of Anna Wickham, the whimsical mind of James Stephens, the wise innocence of Padraic Colum, the versatility of Humbert Wolfe, the fierce and self-flagellating introspection of D. H. Lawrence. Without imposing their theories upon the period they helped make the period what it is.

✦

This collection is a companion volume to *Modern American Poetry,* the period covered by both volumes being about the same. The two books aim to give a fairly representative picture of the two branches of our literature, revealing many contrasts and a few general differences. Broadly speaking, modern British poetry is smoother, more matured, and, molded by centuries of literature, richer in associations. American poetry, no longer colonially imitative, is sharper, more vigorously experimental; it is full of youth, with youth's occasional (and natural) crudities. Where the English product is formulated, precise, and (in spite of certain fluctuations) true to its past, the American expression is more varied and—being the reflection of partly indigenous, partly naturalized, and largely unassimilated ideas and temperaments—characteristically uncoördinated. American poetry might be described as a rush of unconnected mountain torrents and valley streams; instead of one placidly moving body there are a dozen turbulent currents. English poetry, on the other hand, may be compared to a broad and luxuriating river with a series of tributaries contributing to the now thinning, now widening channel.

Not that recent English poetry has been without its departures, even its extremes of experimentation. As in America, many of the younger men, and a few of the older ones, were accused of irreverence, infidelity to tradition, scorn of ideals, lack of standards, obscurity of aim, and general unintelligibility. In defense of the poets vaguely classed as members of the Left Wing, Alida Monro, in *Recent Poetry: 1923-1933,* agreed that the poet who is the product of the twentieth century is probably devoid of most of the qualities enumerated above as they are understood by persons born during the sixties, seventies, and eighties of the last century, but she added: "At no time in the history of man has there been so sudden and violent a change in his environment and circumstance as has taken place in the past twenty-five years. It is far easier, in some ways, to understand the past, even the past of two hundred years ago, than it is to understand our own time, or to try to imagine what life may be like twenty years hence. It is, then, not remarkable that, oppressed by every fresh scientific discovery, with the Great War behind, with the Greater and more horrible War before him, the poet today should be preoccupied with subjects and forms that do not seem to fit into the preconceived notions of what constitutes poetry according to the canons of an age in literature that is now as dead as is the Augustan age."

It is salutary to observe how the course of poetry in Great Britain has been deflected temporarily in the last fifty years, how it has swung from one tendency toward another, and how, for all its bends and twists, it has lost neither its strength nor its direction.

L. U.

# Christina Rossetti

CHRISTINA GEORGINA ROSSETTI was born in London, December 5, 1830. She was the youngest of the four children of Frances Mary Lavinia (Polidori) and Gabriele Rossetti, an Italian poet, exile and professor at King's College. The entire family was unusually creative as well as scholarly. Her father, an authority on Italian literature, had published a volume of religious verse in 1852; Dante Gabriel Rossetti, her oldest brother, established his reputation in painting as well as literature; her second brother, William Michael, was an essayist and man of letters; her older sister Maria Francesca, who later became an Anglican nun, was known for a searching commentary, *Shadow of Dante*.

Christina grew up in London, "enjoying," says Edmund Gosse, "the advantages and disadvantages of the strange society of Italian exiles and English eccentrics which her father gathered about him." The first mention of her name in the letters of her family shows her a poet at the age of twelve, Christina having contributed two poems to a magazine edited by her brothers. At eighteen (after having followed the Rossetti tradition of verse-and-picture-making) she posed for the Virgin in Dante Gabriel's first important picture. Infected from the cradle with over-seriousness, the child was preoccupied to the point of morbidity, delicate in health, detached in manner. "I was," she wrote many years later, "a very melancholy girl," and this early gravity gave her features that typical Pre-Raphaelite sadness which made her a fitting model for her brother as well as his confrères, Millais, Madox-Brown, and Holman Hunt.

Although she admired her father, it was her mother—and her mother's image reflected in her sister—that she worshiped. She actually applauded Maria Francesca's refusal to look at the mummies in the British Museum "because she realized how the general Resurrection might happen even as she looked at those solemn corpses turned into a sight for sight-seers."

When she was seventeen her grandfather, Gaetano Polidori, privately printed her first volume, *Verses*. A year later she met James Collinson, a minor painter of the Pre-Raphaelite Brotherhood whom Dante Gabriel considered "a stunner," and became engaged to him. Biographers have been unable to agree as to which of Christina's two attachments affected her most. Edmund Gosse says distinctly, "She was twice sought in marriage, but each time, from religious scruples, she refused her suitor; on the *former* of these occasions she sorrowed greatly and her suffering is reflected in much of her song." Her brother, William Michael, corroborates this, in his Memoir: "He (Collinson) had struck a staggering blow at Christina Rossetti's peace of mind on the very threshold of womanly life." But Elizabeth Luther Cary is of another opinion. With a reticence abnormal in a biographer, Mrs. Cary, refusing to give the name of either man, contents herself with: "In 1866 at the age of thirty-six,[1] she again suffered from her deep interest in a suitor, whom she could not marry owing to her religious scruples. This incident, which involved a genuine and strong attachment, is probably responsible for what is most moving and most exquisite in her poetry."

Twice, then, Christina refused to marry because of "religious scruples." Collinson, originally a member of the Church of England, had been converted to Catholicism, reverted to the English Church at Christina's request, and (possibly because he had religious scruples of his own) 'verted once more to Catholicism. And though Christina was a member of the Tractarian or Anglo-Catholic party, she would have none of him. But the case of Cayley, whom she loved, says her brother, "to the last days of his life, December 5, 1883," is more inexplicable. Cayley was of the same denomination as Christina and was "a singularly unworldly person." Yet their love was not consummated. Although Cayley was religious he was evidently not religious enough. "She loved him deeply and permanently, but," W. M. Rossetti remarks vaguely, "she must no doubt have probed his faith and found it either wrong or woefully defective." It needs no analyst to furnish the obvious clew not only to Christina's withdrawal from marriage, but, as evidenced in poem after poem, from the normal give-and-take of life. She could not surrender to any earthly lover, for she was committed—at first half-consciously, later candidly—to the Heavenly Bridegroom. She turned from the hands of Collinson and Cayley to the arms of Christ the more easily since, to her fixed faith, abnegation and affirmation were one. Her religion was "far more a thing of the heart than of the mind: she clung to and loved the Christian creed because she loved Jesus Christ." But even here her love was shame-faced, saintly but not serene. Unlike her sister Maria, whom she followed to the very threshold of the convent, she was confident neither of self nor salvation; she remained uncertain, unworthy. As she grew older, she retreated further and further into self-abasement. Her days were a succession of perpetual church-goings and communions, prayers and fasts, submission to clerical direction, oblations, confessions. She wrote literally hundreds of hymns, "Songs for Strangers and Pilgrims," and devotional verses whose sincerity cannot conceal their mawkish reiterations.

Meanwhile, without the slightest ambition for literary prominence, she had become established as one of the period's undoubted poets. At thirty-two she published *Goblin Market* (1862); four years later, *The Prince's Progress and Other Poems* (1866) appeared. Both volumes were widely circulated and applauded. At that time her poetry (now seen to be made of far finer substance than her brother's) was considered inferior to Dante Gabriel's—an opinion in which she concurred. It was natural that she should carry spiritual humility into her literary life, and she depreciated herself at every opportunity. In her introductory paragraph to the "Monna Innominata" sequence, she refers to Mrs. Browning as "the Great Poetess of our own day and nation," preferring the limp ardor of the "Portuguese" sonnets to her own impassioned fourteen-liners. But uncritical self-depreciation (not "over-scrupulosity" as her brother averred) was her weakness. Invited to contribute to a volume

[1] This is not in accord with W. M. Rossetti's dates. "I must next deal," he writes, "with a personage of higher type, Charles Bagot Cayley, a man of letters and an author, but less author than scholar. Christina may have first known him as far back as 1847 or so, and again in 1854; but the two did not meet much until some such date as 1860." Christina was, at the latest, not quite thirty when she became intimate with Cayley.

of *Representative Poems of Living Poets* in 1886, she chose only three: "A Christmas Carol," "An Apple Gathering" and "No, Thank You, John," the last two being as unrepresentative, and as unlovely, as anything she ever wrote.

It is impossible to say how many poems she wrote; a scant thousand are published in her *Collected Poems*. But, though numerous volumes appeared, her first two books contain most of her best. "Goblin Market" is her fairy-child, unlike anything she ever conceived. It has something of "The Pied Piper of Hamelin" combined with an unearthly color which is less light than translucence; it is Hans Christian Andersen played on an elfin flute. "The narrative," concluded the *London Quarterly Review,* "has so matter-of-fact and at the same time so bewildering an air, that we are fairly puzzled into acceptance of everything." Too long to reprint in these pages, attention must be called to its appropriately goblin-hopping rhythm; its childish legend and most unchildish moral; its catalogue of fruits, so tropical in imagery and so exact in epithet as to summon particularities of taste; and to its very Pre-Raphaelite picture of the two sisters, as lingering as the drawing of the younger:

> White and golden Lizzie stood,
> Like a lily in a flood,
> Like a rock of blue-veined stone
> Lashed by tides obstreperously,—
> Like a beacon left alone
> In a hoary roaring sea,
> Sending up a golden fire.
> Like a fruit-crowned orange-tree
> White with blossoms honey-sweet
> Sore beset by wasp and bee,—
> Like a royal virgin town
> Topped with gilded dome and spire
> Close beleaguered by a fleet
> Mad to tug her standard down.

The contrast between "Goblin Market" and all her other poems is startling. With one or two exceptions ("A Birthday" is one of them) the light spirit is gone; the nimble pace slows down to a measured solemnity. The prevailing note is melancholy, a sadness that searches the soul but never probes the intellect. She had the habit of automatic inquiry, of questioning, one might say, without curiosity. "Faith with her," says W. M. Rossetti, "was faith pure and absolute: an entire acceptance of a thing revealed, not a quest for confirmation or demonstrative proof. . . . Her attitude of mind was 'I believe because I am told to believe, and I know that the authority which tells me to believe is the only real authority, God.'"

This unreserved acceptance of dogma sharply differentiates Christina Rossetti from her transatlantic contemporary, Emily Dickinson, with whom she has been compared. Apart from the American's imagery and idiom, difficult enough to the Englishwoman, Christina would have been outraged at the attitude of the protesting Puritan; the style would have been incomprehensible, the spirit incredible. Here was a woman—presumably a Christian—who not only challenged her God, but dared interrogate, tease, berate, rally, and fling herself upon Him. Emily's flippant intimacy would have seemed no less than purposeful blasphemy. Yet it was Emily Dickinson not Christina Rossetti, who was the true mystic. Christina absorbed her faith, Emily translated it. Christina was devout, uplifted, sometimes *exalté;* Emily was impertinent, indirect, and always the metaphysician. Christina, continually submerging her personality, wrote only what might please her Creator; Emily, individual to the point of refusing a public, wrote only to please herself. One returned to God, with passionate meekness, all she had learned from Him; the other, less submissive, gave Him back a conception of Himself that was a separate creation. That Emily Dickinson's was the more original and entertaining genius—that, as a poet, she exercises a more impelling influence is, I think, indubitable. But it is equally plain that in her rare moments Christina Rossetti attained purer vision and serener heights. There is nobility surpassing charm of epithet, power beyond surprise or eloquence in the ecstatic "From House to Home"—which in concept and dimension is in the line of major poetry—in "Marvel of Marvels," in "Passing Away," of which Swinburne wrote, "It is so much the noblest sacred poem in our language that there is none which comes near enough to stand second."

"Passing Away" is one of the poems which display Christina Rossetti's technical as well as spiritual excellencies. Here, as in "Marvel of Marvels" and others, she delights to ring the changes on an organ-point of rhyme, playing upon a set of strong open vowels as dexterously as the early Italian composers. Her style is traditionally *bel canto,* although she does not disdain effects that are supposedly the product of our own generation. She employs balance with skill and uses repetition, that dangerous device, with complete security. Many of her lyrics are rich with adroit echoing, even a mocking, of similar sounds. Some of her finest sonnets (notably the one beginning "The irresponsive silence of the land") are achieved by the pairing of figures and the building up of tone on tone, the repeated word insinuating itself like a muffled but dramatic drum. Melodic grace lifts her preoccupations, whether they inform grave soliloquies or the inconsequential jingles of "Sing-Song," that mixture of delight and dogmatism in which an angel sings with the voice of Dr. Watts. Save at her best, she was not without mannerisms as irritating as Mrs. Browning's or Emily Dickinson's. She dwelt on her heartbreak, relied (poetically) on the broken reed. She was prone to pile up comparisons; some of her most admirable poems—such as "Goblin Market," an illustrative segment of which has been quoted, and "A Birthday"—are little more than a chain of threaded similes. She coddled her clichés; she never tired of writing about roses and lilies, always with the connotations of a minor poet, and of winter, which she saw only as something dismal and bitter.

But if this is true of her best, what is one to say of her worst? Here again, the paradox persists; first and fifth-rate mingle uncritically, inextricably. It is true that most of the "Songs for Strangers and Pilgrims," "Some Feasts and Fasts," "Gifts and Graces," "New Jerusalem and Its Citizens," are endlessly lugubrious. Her hatred—or fear—of the world found expression in these dull but undoubtedly autobiographical confessions.

> She gave up beauty in her tender youth,
> Gave all her hope and joy and pleasant ways;
> She covered up her eyes lest they should gaze
> On vanity, and chose the bitter truth.
> Harsh towards herself, towards other full of ruth,
> Servant of servants, little known to praise,

> Long prayers and fasts trenched on her nights and days:
> She schooled herself to sights and sounds uncouth
> That with the poor and stricken she might make
> A home, until the least of all sufficed
> Her wants; her own self learned she to forsake,
> Counting all earthly gain but hurt and loss.
> So with calm will she chose and bore the cross
> And hated all for love of Jesus Christ.

This is the heart of her secret, if secret it may be called. The world—she says it over and over—is evil, being the abode of the flesh which is the devil. All which is terrestrial and impermanent is Vanity; worse, it is dalliance with sin. Sin (and let the Freudians make what they will of it) fascinated her; her poetry, intent though she was on the soul's salvation, "covered up her eyes" to its multiple manifestations. In prose she declared explicitly, "Strip sin bare from the voluptuousness of music, fascination of gesture, entrancement of the stage, rapture of poetry. . . . Let it stand out bald as the Ten Commandments. Lavish sympathy on the sinner, never on the sin." She, herself, baptized her infant nephew just before his death and "I doubt," her brother assures us, "whether any act of her life yielded her more heart-felt satisfaction."

But if her disposition grew fixedly Calvinistic and her character became "a fountain sealed," the impulse checked in action was spontaneous as ever in composition. Buried among the four hundred and fifty devotional pieces given to the Society for Promoting Christian Knowledge, are some of the bitterest but most authentic verse she ever wrote. True, she reiterates with unvarying insistence, that life is not sweet, that the world is loathsome and foul, that death is merely sleeping from "risk," that earthly mornings are cold and all its twilights gray. But just when we would turn disheartened from these wailings in sackcloth, a voice, clear and compelling, makes us pause, and we know we are once more listening to the accents of authoritative poetry.

Christina Rossetti had suffered much of her life from a chronic weakness of heart. In 1892 she was operated for cancer, bearing the operation well. A year later it became evident that the disease had not been eradicated. It returned, complicated by dropsy. A further operation was impossible; palliatives were given; the end was foreseen. "At the close of a week of collapse and semiconsciousness, she died without a struggle, in the act of inarticulate prayer." This was on December 29, 1894, just as she had turned sixty-four.

Her spirit persists, though scarcely in the way Christina might have foreseen. Saintliness by withdrawal is not a program which wins general response. Though the world turn from physics to metaphysics, Christina Rossetti can never be one of its prophets. She was an ascetic, not a mystic—a feminine ascetic, lachrymose in preoccupation with death. Some of her noble verse is sullied with self-pity. But though she was not one of the world's prophets, she remains one of its undoubted poets—one of the three great women lyricists who wrote in English. She was the forerunner of a generation of women who learned from her the art of keeping expression simple and intense. Though not primarily a technician, and often too ready to rely on decorative generalities, her best work is so felicitous in music, so flexible a medium for emotion, that it has become a model of its kind. Lizette Woodworth

Reese, Sara Teasdale and a score of others have gone to school to her; the inflection of Edna St. Vincent Millay is already anticipated in sonnets like "Because you never yet have loved me, dear." In Christina Rossetti the singer and the saint combined. But it was the singer who had the clearer, actually the more spiritual, vision. The poetry opened vistas that could not be summoned by the repetition of a creed. The rapt ascetic bowed under a "strangling load"; the poet, winged in her rapture, escaped the yoke and set herself free.

### A BIRTHDAY

My heart is like a singing bird
  Whose nest is in a watered shoot;
My heart is like an apple-tree
  Whose boughs are bent with thickset fruit;
My heart is like a rainbow shell
  That paddles in a halcyon sea;
My heart is gladder than all these
  Because my love is come to me.

Raise me a dais of silk and down;
  Hang it with vair and purple dyes;
Carve it in doves and pomegranates,
  And peacocks with a hundred eyes;
Work it in gold and silver grapes,
  In leaves and silver fleurs-de-lys;
Because the birthday of my life
  Is come, my love is come to me.

### THE IRRESPONSIVE SILENCE OF THE LAND

The irresponsive silence of the land,
The irresponsive sounding of the sea,
Speak both one message of one sense to
  me:—
"Aloof, aloof, we stand aloof; so stand
Thou too aloof bound with the flawless band
In inner solitude; we bind not thee.
But who from thy self-chain shall set thee
  free?
What heart shall touch thy heart? what hand
  thy hand?"—

And I am sometimes proud and sometimes
  meek,
And sometimes I remember days of old
When fellowship seemed not so far to seek
And all the world and I seemed much less
  cold,
And at the rainbow's foot lay surely gold,
And hope felt strong and life itself not weak.

### THE BOURNE

Underneath the growing grass,
  Underneath the living flowers,
  Deeper than the sound of showers:
  There we shall not count the hours
By the shadows as they pass.

Youth and health will be but vain,
  Beauty reckoned of no worth:
  There a very little girth
  Can hold round what once the earth
Seemed too narrow to contain.

### COME BACK TO ME

Come back to me who wait and watch for
  you:—
Or come not yet, for it is over then,
And long it is before you come again,
So far between my pleasures are and few.
While, when you come not, what I do I do,
Thinking, "Now when he comes," my sweet-
  est "when":
For one man is my world of all the men
This wide world holds; O love, my world is
  you.
Howbeit, to meet you grows almost a pang
Because the pang of parting comes so soon;
My hope hangs waning, waxing, like a moon
Between the heavenly days on which we
  meet:
Ah me, but where are now the songs I sang
When life was sweet because you called them
  sweet?

### MIRAGE

The hope I dreamed of was a dream,
  Was but a dream; and now I wake
Exceeding comfortless, and worn, and old,
  For a dream's sake.

Lie still, lie still, my breaking heart;
  My silent heart, lie still and break;
Life, and the world, and mine own self, are
    changed
  For a dream's sake.

### DREAM LAND

Where sunless rivers weep
Their waves into the deep,
She sleeps a charmèd sleep:
  Awake her not.
Led by a single star,
She came from very far
To seek where shadows are
  Her pleasant lot.

She left the rosy morn,
She left the fields of corn,
For twilight cold and lorn
  And water springs.

Through sleep, as through a veil,
She sees the sky look pale,
And hears the nightingale
  That sadly sings.

Rest, rest, a perfect rest
Shed over brow and breast;
Her face is toward the west,
  The purple land.
She cannot see the grain
Ripening on hill and plain;
She cannot feel the rain
  Upon her hand.

Rest, rest, for evermore
Upon a mossy shore;
Rest, rest at the heart's core
  Till time shall cease:
Sleep that no pain shall wake,
Night that no morn shall break,
Till joy shall overtake
  Her perfect peace.

### IF THERE BE ANYONE

If there be anyone can take my place
And make you happy whom I grieve to grieve,
Think not that I can grudge it, but believe
I do commend you to that nobler grace,
That readier wit than mine, that sweeter face;
Yea, since your riches make me rich, conceive
I too am crowned, while bridal crowns I weave,
And thread the bridal dance with jocund pace.
For if I did not love you, it might be
That I should grudge you some one dear delight;
But since the heart is yours that was mine own,
Your pleasure is my pleasure, right my right,
Your honorable freedom makes me free,
And you companioned I am not alone.

### WHEN I AM DEAD, MY DEAREST

When I am dead, my dearest,
Sing no sad songs for me;
Plant thou no roses at my head,
Nor shady cypress tree:
Be the green grass above me
With showers and dewdrops wet:
And if thou wilt, remember,
And if thou wilt, forget.

I shall not see the shadows,
I shall not see the rain;
I shall not hear the nightingale
Sing on as if in pain:
And dreaming through the twilight
That doth not rise nor set,
Haply I may remember,
And haply may forget.

## REMEMBER ME WHEN I AM GONE AWAY

Remember me when I am gone away,
Gone far away into the silent land;
When you can no more hold me by the hand
Nor I half turn to go yet turning stay.
Remember me when no more day by day
You tell me of our future that you planned.
Only remember me; you understand
It will be late to counsel then or pray.
Yet if you should forget me for a while
And afterwards remember, do not grieve:
For if the darkness and corruption leave
A vestige of the thoughts that once I had,
Better by far you should forget and smile
Than that you should remember and be sad.

## O EARTH, LIE HEAVILY UPON HER EYES

O Earth, lie heavily upon her eyes;
Seal her sweet eyes weary of watching, Earth;
Lie close around her; leave no room for mirth
With its harsh laughter, nor for sound of sighs.
She hath no questions, she hath no replies,
Hushed in and curtained with a blessed dearth
Of all that irked her from the hour of birth;
With stillness that is almost Paradise.
Darkness more clear than noonday holdeth her,
Silence more musical than any song;
Even her very heart has ceased to stir:
Until the morning of Eternity
Her rest shall not begin nor end, but be;
And when she wakes she will not think it long.

## DREAM-LOVE

Young Love lies sleeping
  In May-time of the year,
Among the lilies,
  Lapped in tender light:
White lambs come grazing,
  White doves come building here;

And round about him
  The May-bushes are white.

Soft moss the pillow
  For O, a softer cheek;
Broad leaves cast shadow
  Upon the heavy eyes:

There winds and waters
   Grow lulled and scarcely speak;
There twilight lingers
   The longest in the skies.

Young Love lies dreaming;
   But who shall tell the dream?
A perfect sunlight
   On rustling forest tips;
A perfect moonlight
   Upon a rippling stream;
Or perfect silence,
   Or song of cherished lips.

Burn odors round him
   To fill the drowsy air;
Weave silent dances
   Around him to and fro;
For O, in waking,
   The sights are not so fair,
And song and silence
   Are not like these below.

Young Love lies drowsing
   Away to poppied death;
Cool shadows deepen
   Across the sleeping face:
So fails the summer
   With warm, delicious breath;
And what hath autumn
   To give us in its place?

Draw close the curtains
   Of branched evergreen;
Change cannot touch them
   With fading fingers sere:
Here the first violets
   Perhaps will bud unseen,
And a dove, maybe,
   Return to nestle here.

### SING-SONG

#### (Selections)

Dead in the cold, a song-singing thrush,
Dead at the foot of a snowberry bush,—
Weave him a coffin of rush,
Dig him a grave where the soft mosses grow,
Raise him a tombstone of snow.

✦

Hope is like a harebell trembling from its
   birth,
Love is like a rose the joy of all the earth;
Faith is like a lily lifted high and white,
Love is like a lovely rose the world's delight;
Harebells and sweet lilies show a thornless
   growth,
But the rose with all its thorns excels them
   both.

✦

Twist me a crown of wind-flowers;
   That I may fly away
To hear the singers at their song,
   And players at their play.

Put on your crown of wind-flowers:
   But whither would you go?
Beyond the surging of the sea
   And the storms that blow.

Alas! your crown of wind-flowers
   Can never make you fly:
I twist them in a crown today,
   And tonight they die.

✦

Where innocent bright-eyed daisies are,
   With blades of grass between,
Each daisy stands up like a star
   Out of a sky of green.

✦

If hope grew on a bush,
   And joy grew on a tree,
What a nosegay for the plucking
   There would be!

But, oh, in windy autumn,
   When frail flowers wither,
What should we do for hope and joy,
   Fading together?

✦

The wind has such a rainy sound
   Moaning through the town,
The sea has such a windy sound,—
   Will the ships go down?

The apples in the orchard
   Tumble from their tree—

Oh, will the ships go down, go down,
  In the windy sea?

✦

I planted a hand
  And there came up a palm.
I planted a heart
  And there came up balm.

Then I planted a wish,
  And there sprang a thorn,
While heaven frowned with thunder
  And earth sighed forlorn.

✦

Who has seen the wind?
  Neither I nor you:
But when the leaves hang trembling
  The wind is passing through.

Who has seen the wind?
  Neither you nor I:
But when the trees bow down their heads
  The wind is passing by.

✦

The lily has a smooth stalk,
  Will never hurt your hand;
But the rose upon her briar
  Is lady of the land.

There's sweetness in an apple tree,
  And profit in the corn;
But lady of all beauty
  Is a rose upon a thorn.

When with moss and honey
  She tips her bending briar,
And half unfolds her glowing heart,
  She sets the world on fire.

✦

When a mounting skylark sings
  In the sunlit summer morn,
I know that heaven is up on high,
  And on earth are fields of corn.

But when a nightingale sings
  In the moonlit summer even,
I know not if earth is merely earth,
  Only that heaven is heaven.

### ECHO

Come to me in the silence of the night;
  Come in the speaking silence of a dream;
Come with soft rounded cheeks and eyes as bright
    As sunlight on a stream;
      Come back in tears,
O memory, hope and love of finished years.

O dream how sweet, too sweet, too bitter-sweet,
  Whose wakening should have been in Paradise,
Where souls brim-full of love abide and meet;
    Where thirsting longing eyes
      Watch the slow door
That opening, letting in, lets out no more.

Yet come to me in dreams, that I may live
  My very life again though cold in death;
Come back to me in dreams, that I may give
    Pulse for pulse, breath for breath:
      Speak low, lean low,
As long ago my love, how long ago.

### PASSING AWAY

Passing away, saith the World, passing away:
Chances, beauty and youth sapped day by day:
Thy life never continueth in one stay.
Is the eye waxen dim, is the dark hair changing to gray
That hath won neither laurel nor bay?
I shall clothe myself in Spring and bud in May:
Thou, root-stricken, shalt not rebuild thy decay
On my bosom for aye.
Then I answered: Yea.

Passing away, saith my Soul, passing away:
With its burden of fear and hope, of labor and play;
Hearken what the past doth witness and say:
Rust in thy gold, a moth is in thine array,
A canker is in thy bud, thy leaf must decay.
At midnight, at cockcrow, at morning, one certain day
Lo, the Bridegroom shall come and shall not delay:
Watch thou and pray.
Then I answered: Yea.

Passing away, saith my God, passing away:
Winter passeth after the long delay:
New grapes on the vine, new figs on the tender spray,
Turtle calleth turtle in Heaven's May.
Though I tarry wait for Me, trust Me, watch and pray.
Arise, come away, night is past, and lo it is day,
My love, My sister, My spouse, thou shalt hear Me say.
Then I answered: Yea.

### MARVEL OF MARVELS

Marvel of marvels, if I myself shall behold
With mine own eyes my King in His city of gold;
Where the least of lambs is spotless white in the fold,
Where the least and last of saints in spotless white is stoled,
Where the dimmest head beyond a moon is aureoled.
O saints, my beloved, now moldering to mold in the mold,
Shall I see you lift your heads, see your cerements unrolled,
See with these very eyes? who now in darkness and cold
Tremble for the midnight cry, the rapture, the tale untold,—
*The Bridegroom cometh, cometh, His Bride to enfold!*

Cold it is, my beloved, since your funeral bell was tolled:
Cold it is, O my King, how cold alone on the wold!

A CHRISTMAS CAROL

In the bleak mid-winter
  Frosty wind made moan,
Earth stood hard as iron,
  Water like stone;
Snow had fallen, snow on snow,
  Snow on snow,
In the bleak mid-winter
  Long ago.

Our God, Heaven cannot hold Him
  Nor earth sustain;
Heaven and earth shall flee away
  When He comes to reign:
In the bleak mid-winter
  A stable-place sufficed
The Lord God Almighty
  Jesus Christ.

Enough for Him whom cherubim
  Worship night and day,
A breastful of milk
  And a manger full of hay;

Enough for Him whom angels
  Fall down before,
The ox and ass and camel
  Which adore.

Angels and archangels
  May have gathered there,
Cherubim and seraphim
  Throng'd the air
But only His mother
  In her maiden bliss
Worshiped her Beloved
  With a kiss.

What can I give Him,
  Poor as I am?
If I were a shepherd
  I would bring a lamb,
If I were a wise man
  I would do my part,—
Yet what I can I give Him,
  Give my heart.

FROM HOUSE TO HOME

(*Selection*)

I have no words to tell what way we walked,
  What unforgotten path now closed and sealed;
I have no words to tell all things we talked,
  All things that he revealed:

This only can I tell: that hour by hour
  I waxed more feastful, lifted up and glad;
I felt no thorn-prick when I plucked a flower,
  Felt not my friend was sad.

"Tomorrow," once I said to him with smiles:
  "Tonight," he answered gravely and was dumb.
But pointed out the stones that numbered miles
  And miles and miles to come.

"Not so," I said: "Tomorrow shall be sweet;
  Tonight is not so sweet as coming days."
Then first I saw that he had turned his feet,
  Had turned from me his face:

Running and flying miles and miles he went,
  But once looked back to beckon with his hand
And cry: "Come home, O love, from banishment:
  Come to the distant land."

That night destroyed me like an avalanche;
  One night turned all my summer back to snow:
Next morning not a bird upon my branch,
  Not a lamb woke below,—

No bird, no lamb, no living breathing thing;
  No squirrel scampered on my breezy lawn,
No mouse lodged by his hoard: all joys took wing
  And fled before that dawn.

Azure and sun were starved from heaven above,
  No dew had fallen, biting frost lay hoar:
O love, I knew that I should meet my love,
  Should find my love no more.

"My love no more," I muttered, stunned with pain:
  I shed no tear, I wrung no passionate hand,
Till something whispered: "You shall meet again,
  Meet in a distant land."

Then with a cry like famine I arose,
  I lit my candle, searched from room to room,
Searched up and down; a war of winds that froze
  Swept through the blank of gloom.

I searched day after day, night after night;
  Scant change there came to me of night or day:
"No more," I wailed, "no more": and trimmed my light,
  And gnashed but did not pray,

Until my heart broke and my spirit broke:
  Upon the frost-bound floor I stumbled, fell,
And moaned: "It is enough: withhold the stroke.
  Farewell, O love, farewell."

Then life swooned from me. And I heard the song
  Of spheres and spirits rejoicing over me:
One cried: "Our sister, she hath suffered long."—
  One answered: "Make her see."—

One cried: "Oh, blessed she who no more pain,
  Who no more disappointment shall receive."—
One answered: "Not so: she must live again;
  Strengthen thou her to live."

So while I lay entranced a curtain seemed
  To shrivel with crackling from before my face;
Across mine eyes a waxing radiance beamed
  And showed a certain place.

I saw a vision of a woman, where
  Night and new morning strive for domination;
Incomparably pale, and almost fair,
  And sad beyond expression.

Her eyes were like some fire-enshrining gem,
  Were stately like the stars, and yet were tender;
Her figure charmed me like a windy stem
  Quivering and drooped and slender.

I stood upon the outer barren ground,
  She stood on inner ground that budded flowers;
While circling in their never-slackening round
  Danced by the mystic hours.

But every flower was lifted on a thorn,
  And every thorn shot upright from its sands
To gall her feet; hoarse laughter pealed in scorn
  With cruel clapping hands.

She bled and wept, yet did not shrink; her strength
  Was strung up until daybreak of delight:
She measured measureless sorrow toward its length,
  And breadth, and depth, and height.

Then marked I how a chain sustained her form,
  A chain of living links not made nor riven:
It stretched sheer up through lightning, wind, and storm,
  And anchored fast in heaven.

One cried: "How long? yet founded on the Rock
  She shall do battle, suffer, and attain."—
One answered: "Faith quakes in the tempest shock:
  Strengthen her soul again."

I saw a cup sent down and come to her
  Brimfull of loathing and of bitterness:
She drank with livid lips that seemed to stir
  The depth, not make it less.

But as she drank I spied a hand distill
  New wine and virgin honey; making it
First bitter-sweet, then sweet indeed, until
  She tasted only sweet.

Her lips and cheeks waxed rosy-fresh and young;
  Drinking she sang: "My soul shall nothing want";
And drank anew: while soft a song was sung,
  A mystical slow chànt.

One cried: "The wounds are faithful of a friend:
  The wilderness shall blossom as a rose."
One answered: "Rend the veil, declare the end,
  Strengthen her ere she goes."

Then earth and heaven were rolled up like a scroll;
  Time, space, and change and death, had passed away;
Weight, number, measure, each had reached its whole;
  The day had come, that day.

Multitudes—multitudes—stood up in bliss,
 Made equal to the angels, glorious, fair;
With harps, palms, wedding-garments, kiss of peace·
 And crowned and haloed hair.

They sang a song, a new song in the height,
 Harping with harps to Him Who is Strong and True:
They drank new wine, their eyes saw with new light,
 Lo, all things were made new.

Tier beyond tier they rose and rose and rose
 So high that it was dreadful, flames with flames:
No man could number them, no tongue disclose
 Their secret sacred names.

As though one pulse stirred all, one rush of blood
 Fed all, one breath swept through them myriad-voiced,
They struck their harps, cast down their crowns, they stood
 And worshiped and rejoiced.

Each face looked one way like a moon new-lit,
 Each face looked one way towards its Sun of Love;
Drank love and bathed in love and mirrored it
 And knew no end thereof.

Glory touched glory on each blessèd head,
 Hands locked dear hands never to sunder more:
These were the new-begotten from the dead
 Whom the great birthday bore.

Heart answered heart, soul answered soul at rest,
 Double against each other, filled, sufficed:
All loving, loved of all; but loving best
 And best beloved of Christ.

I saw that one who lost her love in pain,
 Who trod on thorns, who drank the loathsome cup,
The lost in night, in day was found again;
 The fallen was lifted up.

They stood together in the blessèd noon,
 They sang together through the length of days;
Each loving face bent sunwards like a moon
 New-lit with love and praise.

Therefore, O friend, I would not if I might
 Rebuild my house of lies, wherein I joyed
One time to dwell: my soul shall walk in white,
 Cast down but not destroyed.

Therefore in patience I possess my soul;
 Yea, therefore as a flint I set my face,
To pluck down, to build up again the whole—
 But in a distant place.

These thorns are sharp, yet I can tread on them;
   This cup is loathsome, yet He makes it sweet:
My face is steadfast toward Jerusalem,
   My heart remembers it.

I lift the hanging hands, the feeble knees—
   I, precious more than seven times molten gold—
Until the day when from His storehouses
   God shall bring new and old;

Beauty for ashes, oil of joy for grief,
   Garment of praise for spirit of heaviness:
Although today I fade as doth a leaf,
   I languish and grow less.

Although today He prunes my twigs with pain,
   Yet doth His blood nourish and warm my root:
Tomorrow I shall put forth buds again
   And clothe myself with fruit.

Although today I walk in tedious ways,
   Today His staff is turned into a rod,
Yet will I wait for Him the appointed days
   And stay upon my God.

# T. E. Brown

THOMAS EDWARD BROWN was born May 5, 1830, at Douglas, in the Isle of Man, where his father was vicar at St. Matthew's Church. The family was poor and when the boy went to Christchurch, Oxford, he had to earn his way as a servitor. Here, at twenty-three, he took the coveted "Double First," but his servitorship was considered a bar to his election as Senior Student, the time being "one of the most intensely miserable I was ever called to endure." The year following, however, he attained "the summit of an Oxford man's ambition" and was elected Fellow of Oriel. Shortly after he was ordained deacon but "never took kindly to the life." Instead he became a schoolmaster at his old school on the Isle of Man, at Gloucester where, though unhappy, he taught and influenced the young W. E. Henley, and at Clifton College where he spent twenty-eight years, raising the inconspicuous private institution to one of the most important schools in England.

During his career as schoolmaster Brown had been writing quietly—*ohne Hast, ohne Rast*—verse of a singularly salty character. His labors as educator dissipated much of his creative energy and when he was offered the Archdeaconry of the Isle of Man, he refused, saying, "I need absolute freedom, freedom to go to church or not to go to church, freedom to commune with local preachers and occasionally to attend Methodist chapels, freedom to smoke a pipe in a Manx public-house, freedom to absent myself from church conferences and ruridecanal potterings—in short, absolute freedom." High-spirited, running the scale from burlesque to pathos ("I was a born sobber"), equally rich in love and humor, he could find no fuller outlet than his verse.

Although he had written much and printed a little, it was not until 1873 (in his forty-third year) that his first book was published. *Betty Lee, a Fo'c's'le Yarn* was republished with several other narratives as *Fo'c's'le Yarns* (1881), which latter work went through several editions. This was followed by three other volumes, all assembled a few years after his death—which occurred October 29, 1897—in *The Collected Poems of T. E. Brown* (1900), to which Henley supplied an Introduction to the edition of 1901. A popular *Poems of T. E. Brown* with a valuable biographical preface first appeared in 1908 and has often been reprinted.

The bulk of Brown's poetry is not large nor is all of it important. His tales are diffuse, although some (particularly "Mary Quayle") anticipate the rude strength of Masefield; his finest narratives are in the Manx dialect which, though lovingly used, is too local to win large audiences. The most interesting features of his *Fo'c's'le Yarns* are their technical irregularities and the identification of the character Tom Baynes with (Tom) Brown—"when I am alone I think and speak to myself always as Tom Baynes."

Brown is most characteristic and most himself in his lyrics. Here in that rhythmically "heightened prose" which is presumably a discovery of the twentieth century, he transmits a talk-tinctured verse, which is free in idiom, fresh in accent. His editor H. F. B. notes the vein of "quaintness" which permeates his work, and calls attention to a likeness with George Herbert, a comparison justified by stanzas like:

> Poor souls whose God is Mammon—
> Meanwhile, from Ocean's gate,
> Keen for the foaming spate,
> The true God rushes in the salmon.

"The emotion," says A. T. Quiller-Couch, "while almost equally explosive in mirth and in tears, remains an educated emotion, disciplined by a scholar's sense of language." While this conclusion is apt enough, it is only partially true. Brown's language was not always scholarly; his best passages have a tone not to be found in libraries but in the homely fields that Brown loved to frequent. The charm of his verse lies not so much in his intuitive philosophy nor even in the audacity of his fancy but in the unexpectedness of his speech.

### I BENDED UNTO ME

I bended unto me a bough of May,
That I might see and smell:
It bore it in a sort of way,
It bore it very well.
But when I let it backward sway,
Then it were hard to tell.
With what a toss, with what a swing,
The dainty thing

Resumed its proper level,
And sent me to the devil.
I know it did—you doubt it?
I turned, and saw them whispering about it.

### VESPERS

O blackbird, what a boy you are!
How you do go it!
Blowing your bugle to that one sweet star—

How you do blow it!
And does she hear you, blackbird boy, so far?
Or is it wasted breath?
"Good Lord! she is so bright
Tonight!"
The blackbird saith.

### PER OMNIA DEUS

What moves at Cardiff, how a man
At Newport ends the day as he began,
At Weston what adventures may befall,
What Bristol dreams, or if she dream at all,
Upon the pier, with step sedate,
I meditate—
Poor souls! whose God is Mammon—
Meanwhile, from Ocean's gate,
Keen for the foaming spate,
The true God rushes in the salmon.

### DISGUISES

High stretched upon the swinging yard,
I gather in the sheet;
But it is hard
And stiff, and one cries haste.
Then He that is most dear in my regard
Of all the crew gives aidance meet;
But from His hands, and from His feet,
A glory spreads wherewith the night is
    starred:
Moreover of a cup most bitter-sweet
With fragrance as of nard,
And myrrh, and cassia spiced,
He proffers me to taste.
Then I to Him:—"Art Thou the Christ?"
He saith—"Thou say'st."

Like to an ox
That staggers 'neath the mortal blow,
She grinds upon the rocks;—
Then straight and low
Leaps forth the leveled line, and in our
    quarter locks.
The cradle's rigged; with swerving of the
    blast
We go,
Our Captain last—
Demands
"Who fired that shot?" Each silent stands—

Ah, sweet perplexity!
This too was He.

I have an arbor wherein came a toad
Most hideous to see—
Immediate, seizing staff or goad,
I smote it cruelly.
Then all the place with subtle radiance
    glowed—
I looked, and it was He!

### DORA

She knelt upon her brother's grave,
    My little girl of six years old—
He used to be so good and brave,
    The sweetest lamb of all our fold;
He used to shout, he used to sing,
Of all our tribe the little king—
And so unto the turf her ear she laid,
To hark if still in that dark place he play'd.
    No sound! no sound!
    Death's silence was profound;
    And horror crept
Into her aching heart, and Dora wept.
    If this is as it ought to be,
    My God, I leave it unto Thee.

### JUVENTA PERENNIS

    If youth be thine,
    Spare not to drink its wine;
    If youth be fled,
        Hold up
        The golden cup—
    God's grapes are always red.

### MY GARDEN

A garden is a lovesome thing, God wot!
Rose plot,
Fringed pool,
Ferned grot—
The veriest school
Of peace; and yet the fool
Contends that God is not—
Not God! In gardens! When the eve is cool?
Nay, but I have a sign;
'Tis very sure God walks in mine.

### THE SCHOONER

Just mark that schooner westward far at sea—
  'Tis but an hour ago
When she was lying boggish at the quay,
  And men ran to and fro,
And tugged, and stamped, and shoved, and pushed, and swore,
And ever and anon, with crapulous glee,
Grinned homage to viragoes on the shore.

So to the jetty gradual she was hauled:
  Then one the tiller took,
And chewed, and spat upon his hand, and bawled;
  And one the canvas shook
Forth like a moldy bat; and one, with nods
And smiles, lay on the bowsprit-end, and called
And cursed the Harbor-master by his gods.

And, rotten from the gunwale to the keel,
  Rat-riddled, bilge-bestank,
Slime-slobbered, horrible, I saw her reel,
  And drag her oozy flank,
And sprawl among the deft young waves, that laughed,
And leapt, and turned in many a sportive wheel,
As she thumped onward with her lumbering draught.

And now, behold! a shadow of repose
  Upon a line of gray,
She sleeps, that transverse cuts the evening rose—
  She sleeps, and dreams away,
Soft-blended in a unity of rest
All jars, and strifes obscene, and turbulent throes
'Neath the broad benediction of the West—

Sleeps; and methinks she changes as she sleeps,
  And dies, and is a spirit pure.
Lo! on her deck an angel pilot keeps
  His lonely watch secure;
And at the entrance of Heaven's dockyard waits,
Till from Night's leash the fine-breath'd morning leaps,
And that strong hand within unbars the gates.

# Lewis Carroll

CHARLES LUTWIDGE DODGSON was born in Daresbury, Cheshire, January 27, 1832.
He entered Christchurch College at nineteen, was made Master of the House
at twenty-four, became a Deacon in Holy Orders at thirty. His first books published
under his own name were not only serious but mathematical: *A Syllabus of Plane*

*Algebraical Geometry* (1860) and *The Formulae of Plane Trigonometry* (1861). As the author of such grave works Dodgson did not wish his name familiarized as an entertainer of children; so when *Alice's Adventures in Wonderland* was published in 1865, it appeared under the *nom-de-plume* of "Lewis Carroll."

*Alice in Wonderland* (originally entitled *Alice's Adventures Underground*) and *Through the Looking Glass* (1871) are immortal, though relished far more by sophisticated maturity than by the children to whom the works are presented as "appropriate" gift-books. So with *Rhyme? and Reason?* (1883), which contains that triumph of the absurd, "The Hunting of the Snark" and the madcap *Sylvie and Bruno* (1889-1893). Here the Comic Spirit is a carefully adult one, not the inconsequential Punch-and-Judy dear to childhood. Dodgson's passions were divided between occasional preaching, the continual making of puzzles, and propounding mathematical problems. Parallel with the "Lewis Carroll" series he preoccupied himself by writing a succession of mathematical books until his death at Guildsford, January 14, 1898. To the last he refused to be identified with his pseudonym. Though it was generally known that he wrote the "Alice" books, he continually evaded the responsibility of authorship, saying, "Mr. Dodgson neither claimed nor acknowledged any connection with the books not published under his name."

"Dodgson's life," writes Eleanor Farjeon, "was in his work, and he produced indefatigably a quantity of books in which nonsensical and logical minds were so balanced that those on logic could not help being nonsensical, while his nonsense was irrepressibly logical. . . . He leaves the impression of a man who inhabited a slightly unreal world—and oddly enough, a world not of imagination, but of ingenuity. Even in his happiest work his genius was inventive rather than creative; and in all he did and thought there is a sense of arrangement, as though most of the affairs of life could be conducted delightfully through a series of games and tricks. The figure he cuts in Victorian annals is something that of a whimsical monk of the Middle Ages."

But while this résumé may be true of the man and his style, it is far from true of his characters. Alice has become a national heroine; The Mad Hatter is a recognizable neighbor; the Duchess, the Walrus and the Carpenter, even the Jabberwocky have lives—and evidently deathless ones—vividly their own. Even the absurdly logical words—"chortle" and "burble" for example—have ceased to be nonsense and have become part of our vocabulary. As for such poems as "Jabberwocky," "Father William" and "The Walrus and the Carpenter," they are gems in the treasury of English verse.

### JABBERWOCKY

'Twas brillig, and the slithy toves
  Did gyre and gimble in the wabe:
All mimsy were the borogoves,
  And the mome raths outgrabe.

"Beware the Jabberwock, my son!
  The jaws that bite, the claws that catch!
Beware the Jubjub bird, and shun
  The frumious Bandersnatch!"

He took his vorpal sword in hand;
  Long time the manxome foe he sought—
So rested he by the Tumtum tree,
  And stood awhile in thought.

And, as in uffish thought he stood,
  The Jabberwock, with eyes of flame,
Came whiffling through the tulgey wood,
  And burbled as it came!

ne, two! One, two! And through and
  through
The vorpal blade went snicker-snack!
[ e left it dead, and with its head
  He went galumphing back.

And hast thou slain the Jabberwock?
  Come to my arms, my beamish boy!
> frabjous day! Callooh! Callay!"
  He chortled in his joy.

[ was brillig, and the slithy toves
  Did gyre and gimble in the wabe:
ll mimsy were the borogoves,
  And the mome raths outgrabe.

### THE WALRUS AND THE CARPENTER

[ he sun was shining on the sea,
  Shining with all his might:
[ e did his very best to make
  The billows smooth and bright—
nd this was odd, because it was
  The middle of the night.

[ he moon was shining sulkily,
  Because she thought the sun
[ ad got no business to be there
  After the day was done—
[ t's very rude of him," she said,
  "To come and spoil the fun!"

[ he sea was wet as wet could be,
  The sands were dry as dry.
[ ou could not see a cloud because
  No cloud was in the sky:
[ o birds were flying overhead—
  There were no birds to fly.

[ he Walrus and the Carpenter
  Were walking close at hand:
[ hey wept like anything to see
  Such quantities of sand:
[ f this were only cleared away,"
  They said, "it *would* be grand!"

[ f seven maids with seven mops
  Swept it for half a year,
[ o you suppose," the Walrus said,
  "That they could get it clear?"

"I doubt it," said the Carpenter,
  And shed a bitter tear.

"O Oysters, come and walk with us!"
  The Walrus did beseech.
"A pleasant walk, a pleasant talk,
  Along the briny beach:
We cannot do with more than four,
  To give a hand to each."

The eldest Oyster looked at him,
  But never a word he said;
The eldest Oyster winked his eye,
  And shook his heavy head—
Meaning to say he did not choose
  To leave the oyster-bed.

But four young Oysters hurried up,
  All eager for the treat:
Their coats were brushed, their faces washed,
  Their shoes were clean and neat.
And this was odd, because, you know,
  They hadn't any feet.

Four other Oysters followed them,
  And yet another four;
And thick and fast they came at last,
  And more and more and more—
All hopping through the frothy waves,
  And scrambling to the shore.

The Walrus and the Carpenter
  Walked on a mile or so,
And then they rested on a rock
  Conveniently low:
And all the little Oysters stood
  And waited in a row.

"The time has come," the Walrus said,
  "To talk of many things:
Of shoes—and ships—and sealing-wax—
  Of cabbages—and kings—
And why the sea is boiling hot—
  And whether pigs have wings."

"But wait a bit," the Oysters cried,
  "Before we have our chat;
For some of us are out of breath,
  And all of us are fat!"
"No hurry!" said the Carpenter.
  They thanked him much for that.

"A loaf of bread," the Walrus said,
  "Is what we chiefly need:
Pepper and vinegar besides
  Are very good indeed—
Now, if you're ready, Oysters dear,
  We can begin to feed."

"But not on us!" the Oysters cried,
  Turning a little blue.
"After such kindness, that would be
  A dismal thing to do!"
"The night is fine," the Walrus said,
  "Do you admire the view?

"It was so kind of you to come!
  And you are very nice!"
The Carpenter said nothing but
  "Cut us another slice.
I wish you were not quite so deaf—
  I've had to ask you twice!"

"It seems a shame," the Walrus said,
  "To play them such a trick.
After we've brought them out so far,
  And made them trot so quick!"
The Carpenter said nothing but
  "The butter's spread too thick!"

"I weep for you," the Walrus said:
  "I deeply sympathize."
With sobs and tears he sorted out
  Those of the largest size,
Holding his pocket-handkerchief
  Before his streaming eyes.

"O Oysters," said the Carpenter,
  "You've had a pleasant run!
Shall we be trotting home again?"
  But answer came there none—
And this was scarcely odd, because
  They'd eaten every one.

### THE CROCODILE

How doth the little crocodile
  Improve his shining tail,
And pour the waters of the Nile
  On every golden scale!

How cheerfully he seems to grin,
  How neatly spreads his claws,
And welcomes little fishes in,
  With gently smiling jaws!

### FATHER WILLIAM

"You are old, Father William," the young man said,
  "And your hair has become very white;
And yet you incessantly stand on your head—
  Do you think, at your age, it is right?"

"In my youth," Father William replied to his son,
  "I feared it might injure the brain;
But, now that I'm perfectly sure I have none,
  Why, I do it again and again."

"You are old," said the youth, "as I mentioned before,
  And have grown most uncommonly fat;
Yet you turned a back-somersault in at the door—
  Pray, what is the reason of that?"

"In my youth," said the sage, as he shook his gray locks,
  "I kept all my limbs very supple
By the use of this ointment—one shilling the box—
  Allow me to sell you a couple?"

"You are old," said the youth, "and your jaws are too weak
  For anything tougher than suet;

Yet you finished the goose, with the bones and the beak—
Pray, how did you manage to do it?"

"In my youth," said his father, "I took to the law,
And argued each case with my wife;
And the muscular strength which it gave to my jaw
Has lasted the rest of my life."

"You are old," said the youth, "one would hardly suppose
That your eye was as steady as ever;
Yet you balanced an eel on the end of your nose—
What made you so awfully clever?"

"I have answered three questions, and that is enough,"
Said his father. "Don't give yourself airs!
Do you think I can listen all day to such stuff?
Be off, or I'll kick you down-stairs!"

## METAMORPHOSES

(from "Sylvie and Bruno")

He thought he saw an Elephant,
That practiced on a fife:
He looked again and found it was
A letter from his wife.
"At length I realize," he said,
"The bitterness of life!"

He thought he saw a Buffalo
Upon the chimney-piece:
He looked again, and found it was
His Sister's Husband's Niece.
"Unless you leave this house," he said,
"I'll send for the Police!"

He thought he saw a Rattlesnake
That questioned him in Greek:
He looked again, and found it was
The Middle of Next Week.
"The one thing I regret," he said,
"Is that it cannot speak!"

He thought he saw a Banker's Clerk
Descending from the 'Bus:

He looked again, and found it was
A Hippopotamus.
"If this should stay to dine," he said,
"There won't be much for us!"

He thought he saw a Coach-and-Four
That stood beside his bed:
He looked again, and found it was
A Bear without a Head.
"Poor thing," he said, "poor silly thing!
It's waiting to be fed!"

He thought he saw an Albatross
That fluttered round the lamp:
He looked again and found it was
A Penny-Postage-Stamp.
"You'd best be getting home," he said:
"The nights are very damp!"

He thought he saw a Garden Door
That opened with a key:
He looked again, and found it was
A Double-Rule-of-Three:
"And all its mystery," he said,
"Is clear as day to me!"

## THE BAKER'S TALE

(from "The Hunting of the Snark")

They roused him with muffins—they roused him with ice—
They roused him with mustard and cress—

They roused him with jam and judicious advice—
  They set him conundrums to guess.

When at length he sat up and was able to speak,
  His sad story he offered to tell;
And the Bellman cried, "Silence! Not even a shriek!"
  And excitedly tingled his bell.

There was silence supreme! Not a shriek, not a scream,
  Scarcely even a howl or a groan,
As the man they called "Ho!" told his story of woe
  In an antediluvian tone.

"My father and mother were honest, though poor—"
  "Skip all that!" cried the Bellman in haste.
"If it once becomes dark, there's no chance of a Snark—
  We have hardly a minute to waste!"

"I skip forty years," said the Baker, in tears,
  "And proceed without further remark
To the day when you took me aboard of your ship
  To help you in hunting the Snark.

"A dear uncle of mine (after whom I was named)
  Remarked when I bade him farewell—"
"Oh, skip your dear uncle!" the Bellman exclaimed,
  As he angrily tingled his bell.

"He remarked to me then," said the mildest of men,
  "If your Snark be a Snark, that is right:
"Fetch it home by all means—you may serve it with greens
  And it's handy for striking a light.

"You may seek it with thimbles, and seek it with care;
  You may hunt it with forks and hope;
You may threaten its life with a railway-share;
  You may charm it with smiles and soap—"

("That's exactly the method," the Bellman bold
  In a hasty parenthesis cried,
"That's exactly the way I have always been told
  That the capture of Snarks should be tried!")

"But oh, beamish nephew, beware of the day,
  If your Snark be a Boojum! For then
You will softly and suddenly vanish away
  And never be met with again!

"It is this, it is this that oppresses my soul,
  When I think of my uncle's last words:
And my heart is like nothing so much as a bowl
  Brimming over with quivering curds!

"It is this, it is this—" "We have had that before!"
  The Bellman indignantly said.
And the Baker replied, "Let me say it once more.
  It is this, it is this that I dread!

"I engage with the Snark—every night after dark—
  In a dreamy delirious fight;
I serve it with greens in those shadowy scenes,
  And I use it for striking a light:

"But if ever I meet with a Boojum, that day,
  In a moment (of this I am sure),
I shall softly and suddenly vanish away—
  And the notion I cannot endure!"

# William Morris

WILLIAM MORRIS, poet and artisan, was born at Walthamstow, March 24, 1834. The mercantile strain inherited from his grandfather, a prosperous tradesman in Worcester, stood him in good stead when he turned craftsman and set up his own shop. In youth, however, he was concerned only with literature; a precocious reader, it is said that he had read most of the Waverley novels at the age of four. Through such romances he steeped himself in a literary *moyen âge* which was to dominate him in maturity. A significant diversion of his childhood was his riding about Epping Forest at the age of six—when the chimney-factories were invading the countryside—in a toy suit of armor. He was educated in neighboring schools, matriculated at Exeter College, Oxford, in 1852 and, while at college, formed a friendship with Edward Burne-Jones that was to last all his life. Their mutual passions were medieval literature, ecclesiastical art, and theological history. For a while they considered taking holy orders, but, with a large if vague social reform in mind, Morris turned to architecture and Burne-Jones to painting.

Four years later Morris, not content with work in an architect's office, founded *The Oxford and Cambridge Magazine,* which, though it died within a year, brought him into close contact with Dante Gabriel Rossetti who convinced him that painting was the only occupation for a man of his talents. So, forsaking letters and blue prints for the nonce, Morris planted himself in front of canvases intent on realizing his dream of an up-to-date medievalism. But the poet was not to be so lightly extinguished. In 1858 he published *The Defense of Guenevere,* a long poem as different from Malory's treatment of the theme as it was from Tennyson's. It attracted little attention, and four years later, after furnishing his own home entirely with his own hands, Morris formed a company to supply interior decorations and household utensils of every kind, embodying guild principles and "guild conscience." This opposition to a machine-mad age expressed itself directly in his hand-made products and his social protests, indirectly in his poetry which turned back to what—to Morris at least—were larger issues and more spacious times. *The Life and Death of Jason*

(1867), *The Earthly Paradise* (1868-1870), *Love is Enough* (1872) announce and elaborate a theme of epic grandeur, the triumph of the imagination over stubborn material.

Having found his métier, Morris's energies, never long repressed, found new and varied outlets. Incited by a trip to Iceland, he began work on the Icelandic sagas— *Sigurd the Volsung* appeared in 1876. He finished a characteristic if inexact translation of the *Aeneid*. Becoming more concerned with economic determinism, he wrote the idealistic *News from Nowhere* (1891), *A Dream of John Ball* and the still-popular *Chants for Socialists*. When his pronouncements were considered not sufficiently "advanced," he drifted away from the movement and back to more subtle ways of educating the public.

Before 1890 Morris had established his reputation as a designer and manufacturer of tapestries in the old spirit, as an illuminator of manuscripts, and as the best of contemporary typographers. The Kelmscott Press was his creation and the darling of his later years, his last labor being the almost priceless Kelmscott Chaucer. He refused the laureateship offered him after the death of Tennyson, pleading that he was "too remote from the requirements of a court," but really fearing that his taste and the public's were too wide apart. He died October 3, 1896.

The importance of Morris has dwindled perceptibly; his influence remains. It is indisputable that his medievalism was a sentimental one, that as "the idle singer of an empty day" he enjoyed championing a lost cause. It is also true that his verse is muffled with too much tapestry and confused with the clash of too many arms. But one must remember the decorous dullness from which Morris reacted. He brought color into a gray and prosy world, reviving a feeling for handicraft which extends to our own time. Most of all he put vigor and a sharpened if spasmodic urgency into the thinning blood of English estheticism. His poetry lacks final authority because Morris himself could not adjust to any prolonged reality; it can never appeal profoundly to a large portion of mankind, since, for all his propaganda, Morris was more interested in the things he handled than the men he wanted to uplift. He loved humanity in the abstract; the individual—his poetry betrays it—was strange and somewhat repellent. Life to him was something to be found in a tapestry-hung library furnished with exquisitely printed books, or riding through a blossom-shedding wood, following the Gleam in a suit of toy armor. But underneath the outworn trappings the soul was knightly and real.

### LOVE IS ENOUGH

Love is enough: though the World be a-waning,
And the woods have no voice but the voice of complaining,
  Though the skies be too dark for dim eyes to discover
The gold-cups and daisies fair blooming thereunder,
Though the hills be held shadows, and the sea a dark wonder,
  And this day draw a veil over all deeds pass'd over,
Yet their hands shall not tremble, their feet shall not falter:
The void shall not weary, the fear shall not alter
  These lips and these eyes of the loved and the lover.

### THE GILLIFLOWER OF GOLD

A golden gilliflower today
I wore upon my helm alway
And won the prize of this tourney
 *Hah! hah! la belle jaune giroflée.*

However well Sir Giles might sit,
His sun was weak to wither it,
Lord Miles's blood was dew on it:
 *Hah! hah! la belle jaune giroflée.*

Although my spear in splinters flew
From John's steel-coat my eye was true;
I wheel'd about and cried for you,
 *Hah! hah! la belle jaune giroflée.*

Yea, do not doubt my heart was good,
Though my sword flew like rotten wood,
To shout, although I scarcely stood,
 *Hah! hah! la belle jaune giroflée.*

My hand was steady too, to take
My ax from round my neck, and break
John's steel-coat up for my love's sake.
 *Hah! hah! la belle jaune giroflée.*

When I stood in my tent again
Arming afresh I felt a pain
Take hold of me, I was so fain—
 *Hah! hah! la belle jaune giroflée.*

To hear: *"Honneur aux fils des preux!"*
Right in my ears again, and shew
The gilliflower blossom'd anew.
 *Hah! hah! la belle jaune giroflée.*

The Sieur Guillaume against me came,
His tabard bore three points of flame
From a red heart: with little blame—
 *Hah! hah! la belle jaune giroflée.*

Our tough spears crackled up like straw;
He was the first to turn and draw
His sword that had nor speck nor flaw,—
 *Hah! hah! la belle jaune giroflée.*

But I felt weaker than a maid,
And my brain, dizzied and afraid,
Within my helm a fierce tune play'd,—
 *Hah! hah! la belle jaune giroflée.*

Until I thought of your dear head,
Bow'd to the gilliflower bed,
The yellow flowers stain'd with red;—
 *Hah! hah! la belle jaune giroflée.*

Crash! how the swords met, *"giroflée!"*
The fierce tune in my helm would play,
*"La belle! la belle! jaune giroflée!"*
 *Hah! hah! la belle jaune giroflée.*

Once more the great swords met again,
*"La belle! la belle!"* but who fell then?
Le Sieur Guillaume, who struck down ten;—
 *Hah! hah! la belle jaune giroflée.*

And as with mazed and unarm'd face
Toward my own crown and the Queen's
  place,
They led me at a gentle pace—
 *Hah! hah! la belle jaune giroflée.*

I almost saw your quiet head
Bow'd o'er the gilliflower bed,
The yellow flowers stain'd with red—
 *Hah! hah! la belle jaune giroflée.*

### SHAMEFUL DEATH

There were four of us about that bed;
 The mass-priest knelt at the side,
I and his mother stood at the head,
 Over his feet lay the bride;
We were quite sure that he was dead,
 Though his eyes were open wide.

He did not die in the night,
 He did not die in the day,
But in the morning twilight
 His spirit pass'd away,
When neither sun nor moon was bright,
 And the trees were merely gray.

He was not slain with the sword,
 Knight's ax, or the knightly spear,
Yet spoke he never a word
 After he came in here;
I cut away the cord
 From the neck of my brother dear.

He did not strike one blow,
 For the recreants came behind,

In a place where the hornbeams grow,
　A path right hard to find,
For the hornbeam boughs swing so
　That the twilight makes it blind.

They lighted a great torch then,
　When his arms were pinioned fast
Sir John the knight of the Fen,
　Sir Guy of the Dolorous Blast,
With knights threescore and ten,
　Hung brave Lord Hugh at last.

I am threescore and ten,
　And my hair is all turn'd gray,
But I met Sir John of the Fen
　Long ago on a summer day,
And am glad to think of the moment when
　I took his life away.

I am threescore and ten
　And my strength is mostly pass'd,
But long ago I and my men
　When the sky was overcast,
And the smoke roll'd over the reeds of the
　　fen,
　Slew Guy of the Dolorous Blast.

And now, all knights of you,
I pray you pray for Sir Hugh,
　A good knight and a true,
And for Alice, his wife, pray too.

### THE HAYSTACK IN THE FLOODS

Had she come all the way for this,
To part at last without a kiss?
Yea, had she borne the dirt and rain
That her own eyes might see him slain
Beside the haystack in the floods?

Along the dripping leafless woods,
The stirrup touching either shoe,
She rode astride as troopers do;
With kirtle kilted to her knee,
To which the mud splash'd wretchedly;
And the wet dripped from every tree
Upon her head and heavy hair,
And on her eyelids broad and fair;
The tears and rain ran down her face.
By fits and starts they rode apace,
And very often was his place

Far off from her; he had to ride
Ahead to see what might betide
When the roads cross'd; and sometimes whe.
There rose a murmuring from his men,
Had to turn back with promises;
Ah me! she had but little ease;
And often for pure doubt and dread
She sobb'd, made giddy in the head
By the swift riding; while, for cold,
Her slender fingers scarce could hold
The wet reins; yea, and scarcely, too,
She felt the foot within her shoe
Against the stirrup: all for this
To part at last without a kiss
Beside the haystack in the floods.

For when they near'd that old soak'd hay,
They saw across the only way
That Judas, Godmar, and the three
Red running lions dismally
Grinn'd from his pennon, under which,
In one straight line along the ditch,
They counted thirty heads.
　　　　　　　　　　　So then,
While Robert turn'd round to his men,
She saw at once the wretched end,
And, stooping down, tried hard to rend
Her coif the wrong way from her head,
And hid her eyes; while Robert said:
"Nay, love, 'tis scarcely two to one,
At Poictiers where we made them run
So fast—why, sweet my love, good cheer.
Nought after this."
　　　　　　　　But, "O," she said,
"My God! my God! I have to tread
The long way back without you; then
The court at Paris; those six men;
The gratings of the Chatelet;
The swift Seine on some rainy day
Like this, and people standing by,
And laughing, while my weak hands try
To recollect how strong men swim.
All this, or else a life with him,
For which I should be damned at last,
Would God that this next hour were past!"

He answer'd not but cried his cry,
"St. George for Marny!" cheerily;
And laid his hand upon her rein.
Alas! no man of all his train
Gave back that cheery cry again;

And, while for rage his thumb beat fast
Upon his sword-hilts, someone cast
About his neck a kerchief long,
And bound him.
             Then they went along
To Godmar; who said: "Now, Jehane,
Your lover's life is on the wane
So fast, that, if this very hour
You yield not as my paramour,
He will not see the rain leave off—
Nay, keep thy tongue from gibe and scoff,
Sir Robert, or I slay you now."

She laid her hand upon her brow,
Then gazed upon her palm, as though
She thought her forehead bled, and—"No."
She said, and turn'd her head away,
As there were nothing else to say,
And everything were settled: red
Grew Godmar's face from chin to head:
"Jehane, on yonder hill there stands
My castle, guarding well my lands:
What hinders me from taking you,
And doing what I list to do
To your fair willful body, while
Your knight lies dead?"
             A wicked smile
Wrinkled her face, her lips grew thin,
A long way out she thrust her chin:
"You know that I would strangle you
While you were sleeping; or bite through
Your throat, by God's help—ah!" she said,
"Lord Jesus, pity your poor maid!
For in such wise they hem me in,
 cannot choose but sin and sin,
Whatever happens: yet I think
They could not make me eat or drink,
And so should I just reach my rest."
"Nay, if you do not my behest,
O Jehane! though I love you well,"
Said Godmar, "would I fail to tell
All that I know?" "Foul lies," she said.
"Eh? lies, my Jehane? by God's head,
At Paris folks would deem them true!
Do you know, Jehane, they cry for you,
Jehane the brown! Jehane the brown!
Give us Jehane to burn or drown!'—
Eh—gag me, Robert!—sweet my friend,
This were indeed a piteous end
For those long fingers and long feet,
And long neck and smooth shoulders sweet;

An end that few men would forget
That saw it— So, an hour yet:
Consider, Jehane, which to take
Of life or death!"
             So, scarce awake,
Dismounting, did she leave that place,
And totter some yards: with her face
Turn'd upward to the sky she lay,
Her head on a wet heap of hay,
And fell asleep: and while she slept,
And did not dream, the minutes crept
Round to the twelve again; but she
Being waked at last, sigh'd quietly,
And strangely childlike came, and said:
"I will not." Straightway Godmar's head,
As though it hung on strong wires turn'd
Most sharply round and his face burn'd.
For Robert—both his eyes were dry,
He could not weep, but gloomily
He seemed to watch the rain; yea, too,
His lips were firm; he tried once more
To touch her lips; she reach'd out, sore
And vain desire so tortured them,
The poor gray lips, and now the hem
Of his sleeve brush'd them.
             With a start
Up Godmar rose, thrust them apart;
From Robert's throat he loosed the bands
Of silk and mail; with empty hands
Held out, she stood and gazed, and saw,
The long bright blade without a flaw
Glide out from Godmar's sheath, his hand
In Robert's hair; she saw him bend
Back Robert's head; she saw him send
The thin steel down; the blow told well,
Right backward the knight Robert fell,
And moan'd as dogs do, being half dead,
Unwitting, as I deem: so then
Godmar turned grinning to his men,
Who ran some five or six, and beat
His head to pieces at their feet.

Then Godmar turn'd again and said:
"So, Jehane, the first fitte is read!
Take note, my lady, that your way
Lies backward to the Chatelet!"
She shook her head and gazed awhile
At her cold hands with a rueful smile,
As though this thing had made her mad.

This was the parting that they had
Beside the haystack in the floods.

# James Thomson

JAMES THOMSON, who signed his work "B. V." to distinguish himself from the eighteenth century author of "The Seasons," was born at Port-Glasgow, in Renfrewshire, November 23, 1834. His life was unhappy from the beginning. His boyhood was spent in Orphan and Military asylums; his youth was passed as an Army schoolmaster among surroundings oppressive to his solitary nature. The sun broke through for a short period while he was stationed at a garrison near Cork, when he fell violently in love and was loved by the sergeant's daughter. Her death two years later plunged Thomson into a profound gloom from which he never emerged. It is significant that his first work (in 1858) was published under the pseudonym "Crepusculus." In 1862 he was dismissed from the Army. From 1866 to the time of his death—except for two brief intervals—he lived in a single room in the purlieus of London, suffering from insomnia and intemperance, increasing pessimism and dipsomania interacting upon each other. In 1872 he went to America as agent for a silver mine, and discovered it to be fraudulent; in 1873 he went to Spain as warcorrespondent for *The New York World,* and was prostrated by sun-stroke. Meanwhile he had produced several books, the most famous of which was that somber masterpiece, *The City of Dreadful Night,* which was published in 1880. *Vane's Story and Other Poems,* published in the same year, and *Essays and Phantasies* (1881) did little to enhance his reputation. He sank back into the morbidity from which he had scarcely risen, died June 3, 1882, and was buried in unconsecrated ground.

Writing of Thomson, John Davidson (probably with self-identification) exceeded the excessive tributes of George Meredith and George Eliot, saying: "I think he was by Nature endowed beyond any English poet of his time. There are no half-measures with Nature. . . . Nature is the great spendthrift. She will burn up the world some day to attain what will probably seem to us a very inadequate end; and in order to have things stated at their worst, once for all, in English, she took a splendid genius and made him—an Army schoolmaster, starved his intellect, starved his heart, starved his body." Davidson's tribute is uncritically generous, but though Thomson's main work, *The City of Dreadful Night,* suffers from unrelieved darkness and a very concentration of pessimism, no one can question its sincerity or imaginative strength. He wrote as one who had never experienced a noon, whose only season was a protracted and relentless winter, whose only hour was midnight, whose only food was want. Considering his life and the effects upon his temperament, it can be seen that this was no mere attitude, and the resulting poetry sounded a depth, a very abyss of self-confession. In this abyss where no light penetrated, he attempted to paint black on black, and almost succeeded in conveying a sense of cosmic hopelessness.

This is the keynote and cadence of his philosophy, which, though bitter, never becomes perverse. For him, the city was a projection of that Nothingness in which night and death held supreme court. Sun never visits this city and dawn glooms "in her tenebrous regard" because:

The sense that every struggle brings defeat
   Because Fate holds no prize to crown success;
That all the oracles are dumb or cheat
   Because they have no secret to express;'
That none can pierce the vast black veil uncertain
Because there is no light beyond the curtain;
   That all is vanity and nothingness.

  A few of Thomson's smaller verses have found their way into a few anthologies, but his lyrics are occasional and uncharacteristic. His sonorities require amplitude and reverberate in a kind of haunted space. His heavily weighted stresses communicate nightmare depression, nowhere more effectively than in the description of the "Melancholia" which epitomized Thomson far more than Dürer.

### AS I CAME THROUGH THE DESERT

#### (*from "The City of Dreadful Night"*)

As I came through the desert thus it was,
As I came through the desert: All was black,
In heaven no single star, on earth no track;
A brooding hush without a stir or note,
The air so thick it clotted in my throat;
And thus for hours; then some enormous things
Swooped past with savage cries and clanking wings:
       But I strode on austere;
       No hope could have no fear.

As I came through the desert, thus it was,
As I came through the desert: Eyes of fire
Glared at me throbbing with a starved desire;
The hoarse and heavy and carnivorous breath
Was hot upon me from deep jaws of death;
Sharp claws, swift talons, fleshless fingers cold
Plucked at me from the bushes, tried to hold:
       But I strode on austere;
       No hope could have no fear.

As I came through the desert thus it was,
As I came through the desert: Lo you, there,
That hillock burning with a brazen glare;
Those myriad dusky flames with points a-glow
Which writhed and hissed and darted to and fro;
A Sabbath of the Serpents, heaped pell-mell
For Devil's roll-call and some fête of Hell:
       Yet I strode on austere;
       No hope could have no fear.

As I came through the desert thus it was,
As I came through the desert: Meteors ran
And crossed their javelins on the black sky-span;

The zenith opened to a gulf of flame,
The dreadful thunderbolts jarred earth's fixed frame:
The ground all heaved in waves of fire that surged
And weltered round me sole there unsubmerged:
   Yet I strode on austere;
   No hope could have no fear.

As I came through the desert thus it was,
As I came through the desert: Air once more,
And I was close upon a wild sea-shore;
Enormous cliffs arose on either hand,
The deep tide thundered up a league-broad strand;
White foam-belts seethed there, wan spray swept and flew;
The sky broke, moon and stars and clouds and blue:
   And I strode on austere;
   No hope could have no fear.

As I came through the desert thus it was,
As I came through the desert: On the left
The sun arose and crowned a broad crag-cleft;
There stopped and burned out black, except a rim,
A bleeding eyeless socket, red and dim;
Whereon the moon fell suddenly south-west,
And stood above the right-hand cliffs at rest:
   Still I stood on austere;
   No hope could have no fear.

As I came through the desert thus it was,
As I came through the desert: From the right
A shape came slowly with a ruddy light;
A woman with a red lamp in her hand,
Bareheaded and barefooted on that strand;
O desolation moving with such grace!
O anguish with such beauty in thy face.
   I fell as on my bier,
   Hope travailed with such fear.

As I came through the desert thus it was,
As I came through the desert: I was twain,
Two selves distinct that cannot join again;
One stood apart and knew but could not stir,
And watched the other stark in swoon and her;
And she came on, and never turned aside,
Between such sun and moon and roaring tide:
   And as she came more near
   My soul grew mad with fear.

     ✦

As I came through the desert thus it was,
As I came through the desert: When the tide
Swept up to her there kneeling by my side,

She clasped that corpse-like me, and they were borne
Away, and this vile me was left forlorn;
I know the whole sea cannot quench that heart,
Or cleanse that brow, or wash those two apart:
> They love; their doom is drear,
> Yet they nor hope nor fear;
> But I, what do I here?

## MELANCHOLIA

*(from "The City of Dreadful Night")*

Anear the center of that northern crest
  Stands out a level upland bleak and bare,
From which the city east and south and west
  Sinks gentle in long waves; and thrònèd there
An Image sits, stupendous, superhuman,
The bronze colossus of a wingèd woman,
  Upon a graded granite base foursquare.

Low-seated she leans forward massively,
  With cheek on clenched left hand, the forearm's might
Erect, its elbow on her rounded knee;
  Across a clasped book in her lap the right
Upholds a pair of compasses; she gazes
With full set eyes but wandering in thick mazes
  Of somber thought beholds no outward sight.

Words cannot picture her; but all men know
  That solemn sketch the pure sad artist wrought
Three centuries and threescore years ago,
  With phantasies of his peculiar thought:
The instruments of carpentry and science
Scattered about her feet, in strange alliance
  With the keen wolf-hound sleeping undistraught;

Scales, hour-glass, bell, and magic-square above;
  The grave and solid infant perched beside,
With open winglets that might bear a dove,
  Intent upon its tablets, heavy-eyed;
Her folded wings as of a mighty-eagle,
But all too impotent to lift the regal
  Robustness of her earth-born strength and pride;

And with those wings, and that light wreath which seems
  To mock her grand head and the knotted frown
Of forehead charged with baleful thoughts and dreams,
  The household bunch of keys, the housewife's gown
Voluminous, indented, and yet rigid
As if a shell of burnished metal frigid,
  The feet thick shod to tread all weakness down;

The comet hanging o'er the waste dark seas,
    The massy rainbow curved in front of it,
Beyond the village with the masts and trees;
    The snaky-imp, dog-headed, from the Pit,
Bearing upon its batlike leathern pinions
Her name unfolded in the sun's dominions,
    The "Melancholia" that transcends all wit.

Thus has the artist copied her, and thus
    Surrounded to expound her form sublime,
Her fate heroic and calamitous;
    Fronting the dreadful mysteries of Time,
Unvanquished in defeat and desolation,
Undaunted in the hopeless conflagration
    Of the day setting on her baffled prime.


THE VINE

The wine of Love is music,
    And the feast of Love is song:
When Love sits down to banquet,
    Love sits long:

Sits long and rises drunken,
    But not with the feast and the wine;
He reeleth with his own heart,
    That great, rich Vine.


# *W. S. Gilbert*

WILLIAM SCHWENK GILBERT was born in London, November 18, 1836. He was educated at Boulogne and at King's College, received his B.A. from the University of London in 1856. He entered the Civil Service in 1857, left it in 1861, was called to the bar in 1864, became a magistrate in 1891.

Thus his "official" career. But Gilbert's was too exuberant a nature to be satisfied with civic duties alone. His avocation, and later his profession, was art and letters, a penchant manifested early in youth when he illustrated his father's novels with that whimsical line which was to be his hallmark. In 1861 he began contributing verses to *Fun,* a short-lived rival of *Punch,* which had refused his contributions, returning the famous "Yarn of the Nancy Bell" on the ground that it was "too cannibalistic for its readers' tastes." These rhymes, ranging from the deftly ironic to the wildly absurd, were published under the title *The Bab Ballads* (1869) and were followed a few years later by *More Bab Ballads,* both volumes characteristically illustrated by Gilbert himself.

Gilbert turned to the stage in 1866, writing burlesque, pantomimes, melodramas, and sentimental pieces full of hearts and flowers. It was not until *Trial by Jury*

(1875) that he found his collaborator and, at the same time, his métier. In Arthur Sullivan, Gilbert met the ideal partner. Sullivan's music combined the mock-gravity and the serious humor which we know as "Gilbertian," and which in turn and rhythm was characteristically English. The alliance was phenomenal, artistically and financially. Success followed success: *The Sorcerer* (1877), *H.M.S. Pinafore* (1878), *The Pirates of Penzance* (1880), *Patience or Bunthorne's Bride* (1881), *Iolanthe* (1882), *Princess Ida,* "a respectful perversion of Mr. Tennyson's exquisite poem" (1884), *The Mikado* (1885), *Ruddigore* (1887), *The Yeomen of the Guard* (1888), *The Gondoliers* (1889).

Most of these were brilliant extensions of various Bab Ballads, aimed at the outstanding foibles of his time. Masquerading as nonsense, his librettos were never without purpose; his pattering syllables, jingling to heel-and-toe measures, carried literary as well as social criticism. In the staid shadow of the Victorian court, Gilbert bore the self-elected office of the Court Fool, satirizing the complacent insularity of that era. *Pinafore* is a sardonic commentary on parochial office-holders and the British Navy; *Iolanthe* mocks the Peerage in general and the House of Lords in particular; *The Pirates of Penzance* and *Ruddigore* are slyer in their ridicule of "blue blood." But none offers so much literary refreshment as *Patience,* founded on the Bab Ballad called "The Rival Curates." Here Gilbert, changing his clergymen to a couple of yearning esthetes, delightfully victimized a movement and an outstanding personality. Although Gilbert never specifically acknowledged it, there is little doubt that the figure of Bunthorne "uttering platitudes in stained-glass attitudes" was suggested by, if not actually derived from, Oscar Wilde. The "esthetic craze" died at the beginning of the century, but Gilbert's unvenomed irony is so universal that it persists beyond the movement that incited it, and applies to similar exaggerations in any time.

Most of the Gilbert and Sullivan operas were produced at The Savoy, a theater especially built for them, and so, when Gilbert selected the best lyrics from his librettos, he published them under the title, *Songs of a Savoyard* (1890). In these, even more than in *The Bab Ballads,* he showed himself a master of not only wit and intricate rhyme, but of meter, fitting his sly parables to gay paradoxes in new and extraordinary supple rhythms. Scores of emulators have attempted his manner, but none has captured his dexterity.

In 1908 Gilbert was knighted. He died three years later after attempting to rescue a young woman from drowning at Harrow Weald, May, 1911.

### RECITATION AND SONG

*(from "Patience")*

Bunthorne:

> Am I alone,
>> And unobserved? I am!
> Then let me own
>> I'm an esthetic sham!
> This air severe
>> Is but a mere
>> Veneer!

This cynic smile
Is but a wile
Of guile!
This costume chaste
Is but good taste
Misplaced!
Let me confess
A languid love for lilies does *not* blight me!
Lank limbs and haggard cheeks do *not* delight me!
I do *not* care for dirty greens
By any means.
I do *not* long for all one sees
That's Japanese.
I am *not* fond of uttering platitudes
In stained-glass attitudes.
In short, my medievalism's affectation,
Born of a morbid love of admiration!

### Song

If you're anxious for to shine in the high esthetic line as a man of culture rare,
You must get up all the germs of the transcendental terms, and plant them every-
where.
You must lie upon the daisies and discourse in novel phrases of your complicated
state of mind,
The meaning doesn't matter if it's only idle chatter of a transcendental kind.
And everyone will say
As you walk your mystic way,
"If this young man expresses himself in terms too deep for *me,*
Why, what a very singularly deep young man this deep young man must be!"

Be eloquent in praise of the very dull old days which have long since passed away,
And convince 'em, if you can, that the reign of good Queen Anne was Culture's
palmiest day.
Of course you will pooh-pooh whatever's fresh and new, and declare it's crude and
mean;
For art stopped short in the cultivated court of the Empress Josephine.
And everyone will say
As you walk your mystic way,
"If that's not good enough for him which is good enough for *me,*
Why, what a very cultivated kind of youth this kind of youth must be!"

Then a sentimental passion of a vegetable fashion must excite your languid spleen,
An attachment *à la* Plato for a bashful young potato, or a not-too-French French
bean!
Though the Philistines may jostle, you will rank as an apostle in the high esthetic
band,
If you walk down Piccadilly, with a poppy or a lily in your medieval hand.
And everyone will say,
As you walk your flowery way,
"If he's content with a vegetable love which would certainly not suit *me,*
Why, what a particularly pure young man this pure young man must be!"

## THE HOUSE OF PEERS

*(from "Iolanthe")*

When Britain *really* ruled the waves
  (In good Queen Bess's time)
The House of Peers made no pretense
To intellectual eminence
  Or scholarship sublime;
Yet Britain won her proudest bays
In good Queen Bess's glorious days.

When Wellington thrashed Bonaparte,
  As every child can tell,
The House of Peers throughout the war
Did nothing in particular,
  And did it very well;
Yet Britain set the world ablaze
In good King George's glorious days.

And while the House of Peers withholds
  Its legislative hand,
And noble statesmen do not itch
To interfere with matters which
  They do not understand,
As bright will shine Great Britain's rays
As in King George's glorious days.

## TO THE TERRESTRIAL GLOBE

*(By a Miserable Wretch)*

Roll on, thou ball, roll on!
Through pathless realms of Space
  Roll on!
What though I'm in a sorry case?
What though I cannot meet my bills?
What though I suffer toothache's ills?
What though I swallow countless pills?
  Never *you* mind!
  Roll on!

Roll on, thou ball, roll on!
Through seas of inky air
  Roll on!
It's true I've got no shirts to wear;
It's true my butcher's bill is due;
It's true my prospects all look blue—
But don't let that unsettle you!
  Never *you* mind!
  Roll on!
         *(It rolls on.)*

## THE RIVAL CURATES

List while the poet trolls
  Of Mr. Clayton Hooper,
Who had a cure of souls
  At Spiffton-extra-Sooper.

He lived on curds and whey,
  And daily sang their praises,
And then he'd go and play
  With buttercups and daisies.

Wild croquet Hooper banned,
  And all the sports of Mammon,
He warred with cribbage, and
  He exorcised backgammon.

His helmet was a glance
  That spoke of holy gladness;
A saintly smile his lance;
  His shield a tear of sadness.

His Vicar smiled to see
  This armor on him buckled:
With pardonable glee
  He blessed himself and chuckled:

"In mildness to abound
  My curate's sole design is;
In all the country round
  There's none so mild as mine is!"

And Hooper, disinclined
  His trumpet to be blowing,
Yet didn't think you'd find
  A milder curate going.

A friend arrived one day
  At Spiffton-extra-Sooper,
And in this shameful way
  He spoke to Mr. Hooper.

"You think your famous name
  For mildness can't be shaken,
That none can blot your fame—
  But, Hooper, you're mistaken!

"Your mind is not as blank
  As that of Hopley Porter,
Who holds a curate's rank
  At Assesmilk-cum-Worter.

"*He* plays the airy flute,
  And looks depressed and blighted,
Doves round about him 'toot,'
  And lambkins dance delighted.

"He labors more than you
  At worsted work, and frames it;
In old maids' albums too,
  Sticks seaweed—yes, and names it!"

The tempter said his say,
  Which pierced him like a needle—
He summoned straight away
  His sexton and his beadle.

(These men were men who could
  Hold liberal opinions:
On Sundays they were good—
  On week-days they were minions.)

"To Hopley Porter go,
  Your fare I will afford you—
Deal him a deadly blow,
  And blessings shall reward you.

"But stay—I do not like
  Undue assassination,
And so before you strike,
  Make this communication:

"I'll give him this one chance—
  If he'll more gayly bear him,

Play croquet, smoke and dance,
  I willingly will spare him."

They went, those minions true,
  To Assesmilk-cum-Worter,
And told their errand to
  The Reverend Hopley Porter.

"What?" said that reverend gent,
  "Dance through my hours of leisure?
Smoke?—bathe myself with scent?—
  Play croquet? Oh, with pleasure!

"Wear all my hair in curl?
  Stand at my door and wink—so—
At every passing girl?
  My brothers, I should think so!

"For years I've longed for some
  Excuse for this revulsion:
Now that excuse has come—
  I do it on compulsion!"

He smoked and winked away—
  This Reverend Hopley Porter—
The deuce there was to pay
  At Assesmilk-cum-Worter.

And Hooper holds his ground,
  In mildness daily growing—
They think him, all around,
  The mildest curate going.

### GENTLE ALICE BROWN

It was a robber's daughter, and her name was Alice Brown,
Her father was the terror of a small Italian town;
Her mother was a foolish, weak, but amiable old thing;
But it isn't of her parents that I'm going for to sing.

As Alice was a-sitting at her window-sill one day,
A beautiful young gentleman he chanced to pass that way;
She cast her eyes upon him, and he looked so good and true,
That she thought, "I could be happy with a gentleman like you!"

And every morning passed her house that cream of gentlemen,
She knew she might expect him at a quarter unto ten;
A sorter in the Custom-house, it was his daily road
(The Custom-house was fifteen minutes' walk from her abode).

But Alice was a pious girl, who knew it wasn't wise
To look at strange young sorters with expressive purple eyes;

So she sought the village priest to whom her family confessed,
The priest by whom their little sins were carefully assessed.

"Oh, holy father," Alice said, " 'twould grieve you, would it not,
To discover that I was a most disreputable lot?
Of all unhappy sinners, I'm the most unhappy one!"
The padre said, "Whatever have you been and gone and done?"

"I have helped mamma to steal a little kiddy from its dad,
I've assisted dear papa in cutting up a little lad,
I've planned a little burglary and forged a little check,
And slain a little baby for the coral on its neck!"

The worthy pastor heaved a sigh, and dropped a silent tear,
And said, "You mustn't judge yourself too heavily, my dear:
It's wrong to murder babies, little corals for to fleece;
But sins like these one expiates at half-a-crown apiece.

"Girls will be girls—you're very young, and flighty in your mind;
Old heads upon young shoulders we must not expect to find:
We mustn't be too hard upon these little girlish tricks.
Let's see—five crimes at half-a-crown—exactly twelve-and-six."

"Oh, father," little Alice cried, "your kindness makes me weep,
You do these little things for me so singularly cheap—
Your thoughtful liberality I never can forget;
But, oh! there is another crime I haven't mentioned yet!

"A pleasant-looking gentleman, with pretty purple eyes,
I've noticed at my window, as I've sat a-catching flies;
He passes by it every day as certain as can be—
I blush to say I've winked at him, and he has winked at me!"

"For shame!" said Father Paul, "my erring daughter! On my word
This is the most distressing news that I have ever heard.
Why, naughty girl, your excellent papa has pledged your hand
To a promising young robber, the lieutenant of his band!

"This dreadful piece of news will pain your worthy parents so!
They are the most remunerative customers I know;
For many many years they've kept starvation from my doors:
I never knew so criminal a family as yours!

"The common country folk in this insipid neighborhood
Have nothing to confess, they're so ridiculously good;
And if you marry anyone respectable at all,
Why, you'll reform, and what then will become of Father Paul?"

The worthy priest, he up and drew his cowl upon his crown,
And started off in haste to tell the news to Robber Brown—
To tell him how his daughter, who was now for marriage fit,
Had winked upon a sorter, who reciprocated it.

Good Robber Brown he muffled up his anger pretty well:
He said, "I have a notion, and that notion I will tell;
I will nab this gay young sorter, terrify him into fits,
And get my gentle wife to chop him into little bits.

"I've studied human nature, and I know a thing or two;
Though a girl may fondly love a living gent, as many do,
A feeling of disgust upon her senses there will fall
When she looks upon his body chopped particularly small."

He traced that gallant sorter to a still suburban square;
He watched his opportunity, and seized him unaware;
He took a life-preserver and he hit him on the head,
And Mrs. Brown dissected him before she went to bed.

And pretty little Alice grew more settled in her mind,
She never more was guilty of a weakness of the kind,
Until at length good Robber Brown bestowed her pretty hand
On the promising young robber, the lieutenant of his band.

## THE PERIWINKLE GIRL

I've often thought that headstrong youths
  Of decent education,
Determine all-important truths
  With strange precipitation.

The over-ready victims they
  Of logical illusions,
And in a self-assertive way
  They jump at strange conclusions.

Now take my case: Ere sorrow could
  My ample forehead wrinkle,
I had determined that I would
  Not like to be a winkle.

"A winkle," I would oft advance
  With readiness provoking,
"Can seldom flirt, and never dance,
  Or soothe his mind by smoking."

In short, I spurned the shelly joy,
  And spoke with strange decision:
Men pointed to me as a boy
  Who held them in derision.

But I was young—too young by far—
  Or I had been more wary:
I knew not then that winkles are
  The stock-in-trade of Mary.

I had not seen her sunlight blithe
  As o'er their shells it dances;
I've seen those winkles almost writhe
  Beneath her beaming glances.

Both high and low and great and small
  Fell prostrate at her tootsies;
They all were noblemen, and all
  Had balances at Coutts's.

Dukes with the lovely maiden dealt,
  Duke Bailey and Duke Humphy,
Who ate her winkles till they felt
  Exceedingly uncomfy.

Duke Bailey greatest wealth computes,
  And sticks, they say, at no-thing;
He wears a pair of golden boots,
  And silver underclothing.

Duke Humphy, as I understand,
  Though mentally acuter,
His boots are only silver, and
  His underclothing pewter.

A third adorer had the girl,
  A man of lowly station—
A miserable grov'ling Earl
  Besought her approbation.

This humble cad she did refuse
  With much contempt and loathing:
He wore a pair of leather shoes,
  And cambric underclothing!

"Ha! ha!" she cried. "Upon my word!
  Well, really—come, I never!
Oh, go along, it's too absurd!
  My goodness! Did you ever?

"Two Dukes would make their Bowles a
    bride,
  And from her foes defend her."
"Well, not exactly that," they cried,
  "We offer guilty splendor.

"We do not offer marriage rite,
  So please dismiss the notion!"
"Oh, dear!" said she: "that alters quite
  The state of my emotion."

The Earl he up, and says, says he,
  "Dismiss them to their orgies,
For I am game to marry thee
  Quite reg'lar at St. George's."

He'd had, it happily befell,
  A decent education,
His views would have befitted well
  A far superior station.

His sterling worth had worked a cure,
  She never heard him grumble;
She saw his soul was good and pure,
  Although his rank was humble.

Her views of earldoms and their lot
  All underwent expansion:
Come, Virtue in an earldom's cot!
  Go, Vice in ducal mansion!

## Algernon Charles Swinburne

ALGERNON CHARLES SWINBURNE was born in London, April 5, 1837. His father was
Admiral Charles Henry Swinburne, descendant of an old Northumbrian family,
and though the son was born in the capital, his boyhood was spent in the country,
half the year at his grandfather's estate in Northumberland, the other half at his
father's home on the Isle of Wight. Thus he was exposed to two contrary influences,
although his poetry, full of southern luxuriance, reflects little of the rigorous north.
After some private tuition, young Swinburne attended Eton for five years, Balliol
College (Oxford) for three, and though he won a prize in Italian and French, left
the University without taking a degree.

Immediately upon leaving Oxford, Swinburne published his first work, *The
Queen Mother* and *Rosamond* (1860), two poetic dramas, eloquent enough in their
own right and remarkable for a youth of twenty-three. Although the volume has an
energetic sweep and freshness lacking in the later plays—being to his Mary Stuart
trilogy what Wagner's "Tannhäuser" is to the "Ring"—the work passed unnoticed
and Swinburne departed for Italy. His sojourn there, during which he became acquainted with Walter Savage Landor, was of short duration, but the richness of
color and climate must have acted like a forcing-ground and quickened a seed ready
for ripening. A few years later, *Atalanta in Calydon* (1865) attracted the attention
of the *literati*. *Chastelard* (the first of the three tragedies dealing with Mary, Queen
of Scots) followed and was respectfully considered. But Swinburne was not a name
which held glamor until the publication of *Poems and Ballads* in 1866. Critics and
the lay public were taken by storm. "There had been," says William Morton Payne
in his introduction to Swinburne's *Selected Poems,* "no such sensation in English

poetry since the appearance of the first two cantos of *Childe Harold.*" But whereas Byron's work was followed equally by the literary and unliterary, Swinburne's appealed—and still appeals—only to the poetic. By the end of his thirtieth year, his reputation was second to none in his time and country and Swinburne became a name for conjuration and controversy.

Influences were already noticeable, influences that, at first disguised by the rush and roar of Swinburne's syllables, have become increasingly more apparent. *Atalanta in Calydon,* in spite of its attempt to mingle lyric abandon and tragic portentousness, is an exotic which, with its Greek mode and Attic idioms, has the taint of translation. Its ringing choruses are all that have survived, enlarging English poetry with new figures and rhythms. *Song of Italy* (1867) and *Songs Before Sunrise* (1871) reveal another side of the poet, the political insurgent—and another derivation. "His first book," Edmund Gosse admits in his comprehensive article in the *Encyclopaedia Britannica,* "is deliberately Shakespearian in design and expression; the *Atalanta,* of course, is equally deliberate in its pursuit of the Hellenic spirit." *Poems and Ballads* is a hybrid in which the lank lilies of Pre-Raphaelitism are grafted on the evil flowers of Baudelaire—a lesser and lighter Baudelaire for, as Edward Thomas pointed out, his hymn to the roses and raptures of vice is "from the lips outward. In a spirit of gay and amateur perversity he flatters sin with appellations of virtue, as George Herbert gave his religious poetry the unction of love."

*Song of Italy* and *Songs Before Sunrise* present if not a *volte face* a new turn. Here Swinburne revolted against political and churchly conventions rather than against moral restraint. In *Poems and Ballads—Second Series* (1878) the forty-year-old Swinburne, discarding Baudelaire and Mazzini, devoted himself to Victor Hugo. He was now at the peak of his creative—and adaptive—powers; volume after volume flew from under his facile hand. His *Study of Shakespeare* (1879) is a mixture of eloquence and exaggeration, a hearty instance of "the noble pleasure of praising" as opposed to pedantic dusting of dry bones. In 1880 he published three wholly different kinds of books: *Songs of the Springtides, Studies in Song,* and *The Modern Heptalogia* (published anonymously), a set of devastating parodies subtitled "The Seven Against Sense," burlesques of Tennyson's pantheism, Browning's cacophony, Mrs. Browning's lax sentimentality, and Swinburne's own alliterative wordiness. The flow of verse grew still more voluminous after Swinburne met Theodore Watts-Dunton, poet and essayist, who guarded the erratic poet with the love of a brother and the scrutiny of a father and with whom he lived until his death. *Mary Stuart,* concluding the trilogy, appeared in 1881. Less than a year later, he had completed *Tristram of Lyonnesse,* a shower of wild rockets compared to the domestic oil-lamps of *Idylls of the King,* restoring to Malory some of the grossness and strength which Tennyson had emasculated. Swinburne's versatility was emphasized by *A Century of Roundels* (1883) which, as the title suggests, contains a hundred variations of the French rondeau in a form which he himself devised, by *A Midsummer Holiday* (1884), which extended his mannerisms, by *Marino Faliero* (1885), a far richer narrative than Byron's story on the same theme, by *Miscellanies* (1886), by the adroit *Astrophel* (1894), and by *The Tale of Balen* (1896), a faithfully versified section of the *Morte d'Arthur* in more than two thousand lines. And so on, without breath-taking, until *A Channel Passage and Other Poems* in 1904, in which year the eleven volume edition of his *Poems and Dramas* was begun. A short pause fol-

lowed. Then a novel (*Love's Cross Currents*) rescued and revised from an old periodical, then the *Duke of Gardia* (1908). Then the richly accoutered *Age of Shakespeare*. Then death, after a sudden attack of pneumonia, at the home of Watts-
Dunton, April 10, 1909.

What remains of the huge mass of epics, Latin imitations, experiments, sestinas,
ballades and double-ballades, excoriations, enthusiasms, *tours de force* in every con-
ceivable meter? There remain, chiefly, the meters themselves and their resonance.
Swinburne's phrasing and philosophy seem to matter little; we are no longer exercised by their morality or immorality. The fury is gone, only the sound is left. And
even this, to be relished, has to be sampled sparingly. As Edmund Gosse was forced
to concede, "The young lover of poetry, when first he encounters Swinburne's influence, is almost bound to be swept away by it; the wild, extravagant license, the
apparent sincerity, the vigor and the verve, cry directly to the aspirations of youth
like a clarion in the wilderness. But while this is inevitable, it is also true that the
critical lover of poetry outgrows an unquestioning allegiance to the Swinburnian
mood more quickly than any other of the diverse emotions aroused by the study of
the great poets." Edward Thomas, whose *Algernon Charles Swinburne: A Critical
Study* (1912) is a most penetrating synthesis, summarizes the lack of finality in
Swinburne's smooth flowing phrases: "He can astonish and melt, but seldom thrill;
and when he does it is not by any felicity of, as it were, God-given inevitable words.
He has to depend on sound and an atmosphere of words which is now and then
concentrated and crystallized into an intensity of effect which is almost magical,
perhaps never quite magical. This atmosphere comes from a vocabulary very rich in
words connected with objects, sensations, emotions of pleasure and beauty, but used
somewhat lightly and even in appearance indiscriminately."

His philosophical verses, praised as much as the early "libidinous" lyrics were
condemned, have suffered by reappraisal. To his generation Swinburne seemed both
a dark, lawless satyr and a bright herald of new laws. He was, we see, neither. He
was a rhyme-intoxicated genius whose vision of another heaven was violent but
vague, whose loose ideas were held in a set of fixed symbols, whose concept of liberty was little more than a large summoning of winds, seas, and lightnings.

Swinburne's reliance on alliteration—the hallmark of familiar parodies—degenerated into a trick that is first titillating, then amusing, and finally wearisome. Nevertheless the weakness of his verse is not that it is too alliterative but too literary.
His preoccupation is with life at second-hand, with its recording or rebellious spirits,
rather than with life itself. Thus his volumes are crammed with tributes to poets,
to Shelley, Sappho, Chaucer, Catullus, Sidney, Browning, Baudelaire, Gautier,
Landor, with apostrophes to Carlyle, Hugo, Mazzini, Wagner, with sonnets to
Massinger, Jonson, Webster, and seventeen other Elizabethan dramatists. Here, as
elsewhere, his rhythms so easily liberated dictate the course of his thought.

If much of this poetry is a sea of syllables which first entice then engulf the
reader, if, as Saintsbury says in what is meant to be a paragraph of praise, Swinburne planned "sea serpents in verse in order to show how easily and gracefully
he can make them coil and uncoil," the metaphors remind us that no English
poet has written more rapturously about the sea or with more passion for the
renewal of spirit which that element symbolizes. Where Keats identifies himself
with the nightingale, Shelley with the skylark, Poe with the raven, Swinburne's

bird is, appropriately, the seamew. Yet after prolixity is forgotten, there persists the pantheistic pean of "Hertha," the Pre-Raphaelite picture of "Madonna Mia," the giddy music of "Itylus," "When the Hounds of Spring," "Hymn to Proserpine," "The Triumph of Time," "A Forsaken Garden," and a dozen others. The worst of Swinburne has been caricatured by himself in "Nephelidia" which begins:

From the depths of the dreamy decline of the dawn through a notable nimbus of
  nebulous noonshine,
Pallid and pink as the palm of the flag-flower that flickers with fear of the flies
  as they float
Are the looks of our lovers that lustrously lean from a marvel of mystic miraculous
  moonshine,
These that we feel in the blood of our blushes that thicken and threaten with
  throbs through the throat.

What is best lives in his lyrics, in the generous spirit and the impetuous movement of his syllables. Here is richness of sound and spirit, a zest which, even in the later work, never outgrew headlong, eloquent, and often grandiloquent youth.

### THE GARDEN OF PROSERPINE

Here, where the world is quiet,
  Here, where all trouble seems
Dead winds' and spent waves' riot
  In doubtful dreams of dreams;
I watch the green field growing
For reaping folk and sowing,
For harvest time and mowing,
  A sleepy world of streams.

I am tired of tears and laughter,
  And men that laugh and weep,
Of what may come hereafter
  For men that sow to reap:
I am weary of days and hours,
Blown buds of barren flowers,
Desires and dreams and powers
  And everything but sleep.

Here life has death for neighbor,
  And far from eye or ear
Wan waves and wet winds labor,
  Weak ships and spirits steer;
They drive adrift, and whither
They wot not who make thither;
But no such winds blow hither,
  And no such things grow here.

No growth of moor or coppice,
  No heather-flower or vine,
But bloomless buds of poppies,
  Green grapes of Proserpine,

Pale beds of blowing rushes
Where no leaf blooms or blushes,
Save this whereout she crushes
  For dead men deadly wine.

Pale, without name or number,
  In fruitless fields of corn,
They bow themselves and slumber
  All night till light is born;
And like a soul belated,
In hell and heaven unmated,
By cloud and mist abated
  Comes out of darkness morn.

Though one were strong as seven,
  He too with death shall dwell,
Nor wake with wings in heaven,
  Nor weep for pains in hell;
Though one were fair as roses,
His beauty clouds and closes;
And well though love reposes,
  In the end it is not well.

Pale, beyond porch and portal,
  Crowned with calm leaves, she stands
Who gathers all things mortal
  With cold immortal hands;
Her languid lips are sweeter
Than love's who fears to greet her
To men that mix and meet her
  From many times and lands.

She waits for each and other,
　She waits for all men born;
Forgets the earth her mother,
　The life of fruits and corn;
And spring and seed and swallow
Take wing for her and follow
Where summer song rings hollow
　And flowers are put to scorn.

There go the loves that wither,
　The old loves with wearier wings;
And all dead years draw thither,
　And all disastrous things;
Dead dreams of days forsaken
Blind buds that snows have shaken,
Wild leaves that winds have taken,
　Red strays of ruined springs.

We are not sure of sorrow,
　And joy was never sure;
Today will die tomorrow;
　Time stoops to no man's lure;

And love, grown faint and fretful,
With lips but half regretful
Sighs, and with eyes forgetful
　Weeps that no loves endure.

From too much love of living,
　From hope and fear set free,
We thank with brief thanksgiving
　Whatever gods may be
That no life lives for ever;
That dead men rise up never;
That even the weariest river
　Winds somewhere safe to sea.

Then star nor sun shall waken,
　Nor any change of light:
Nor sound of waters shaken
　Nor any sound or sight:
Nor wintry leaves nor vernal,
Nor days nor things diurnal;
Only the sleep eternal
　In an eternal night.

## ITYLUS

Swallow, my sister, O sister swallow,
　How can thine heart be full of the spring?
　A thousand summers are over and dead.
What hast thou found in the spring to follow?
　What hast thou found in thine heart to sing?
　What wilt thou do when the summer is shed?

O swallow, sister, O fair swift swallow,
　Why wilt thou fly after spring to the south,
　The soft south whither thine heart is set?
Shall not the grief of the old time follow?
　Shall not the song thereof cleave to thy mouth?
　Hast thou forgotten ere I forget?

Sister, my sister, O fleet sweet swallow,
　Thy way is long to the sun and the south;
　But I, fulfilled of my heart's desire,
Shedding my song upon height, upon hollow,
　From tawny body and sweet small mouth
　Feed the heart of the night with fire.

I the nightingale all spring through,
　O swallow, sister, O fair swift swallow,
　All spring through till the spring be done,
Clothed with the light of the night on the dew,
　Sing, while the hours and the wild birds follow,
　Take flight and follow and find the sun.

Sister, my sister, O soft light swallow,
  Though all things feast in the spring's guest-chamber,
    How hast thou heart to be glad there of yet?
For where thou fliest I shall not follow,
  Till life forget and death remember,
    Till thou remember and I forget.

Swallow, my sister, O singing swallow,
  I know not how thou hast heart to sing.
    Hast thou the heart? is it all past over?
Thy lord the summer is good to follow,
  And fair the feet of thy lover the spring:
    But what wilt thou say to the spring thy lover?

O swallow, sister, O fleeting swallow,
  My heart in me is a molten ember
    And over my head the waves have met.
But thou wouldst tarry or I would follow,
  Could I forget or thou remember,
    Couldst thou remember and I forget.

O sweet stray sister, O shifting swallow,
  The heart's division divideth us.
    Thy heart is light as a leaf of a tree;
But mine goes forth among sea-gulfs hollow
  To the place of the slaying of Itylus,
    The feast of Daulis, the Thracian sea.

O swallow, sister, O rapid swallow,
  I pray thee sing not a little space.
    Are not the roofs and the lintels wet?
The woven web that was plain to follow,
  The small slain body, the flower-like face,
    Can I remember if thou forget?

O sister, sister, thy first-begotten!
  The hands that cling and the feet that follow,
    The voice of the child's blood crying yet
*Who hath remembered me? who hath forgotten?*
  Thou hast forgotten, O summer swallow,
    But the world shall end when I forget.

### A LEAVE-TAKING

Let us go hence, my songs; she will not hear.
Let us go hence together without fear;
Keep silence now, for singing-time is over
And over all old things and all things dear.
She loves not you nor me as all we love her.
Yea, though we sang as angels in her ear,
    She would not hear.

Let us rise up and part; she will not know.
Let us go seaward as the great winds go,
Full of blown sand and foam; what help is there?
There is no help, for all these things are so,
And all the world is bitter as a tear.
And how these things are, though ye strove to show,
She would not know.

Let us go home and hence; she will not weep,
We gave love many dreams and days to keep,
Flowers without scent, and fruits that would not grow,
Saying, "If thou wilt, thrust in thy sickle and reap."
All is reaped now; no grass is left to mow;
And we that sowed, though all we fell on sleep,
She would not weep.

Let us go hence and rest; she will not love.
She shall not hear us if we sing hereof,
Nor see love's ways, how sore they are and steep.
Come hence, let be, lie still; it is enough.
Love is a barren sea, bitter and deep;
And though she saw all heaven in flower above,
She would not love.

Let us give up, go down; she will not care.
Though all the stars made gold of all the air,
And the sea moving saw before it move
One moon-flower making all the foam-flowers fair;
Though all those waves went over us, and drove
Deep down the stifling lips and drowning hair
She would not care.

Let us go hence, go hence; she will not see.
Sing all once more together: surely she,
She too, remembering days and words that were,
Will turn a little toward us, sighing; but we,
We are hence, we are gone, as though we had not been there.
Nay, and though all men seeing had pity on me,
She would not see.

### FROM "THE TRIUMPH OF TIME"

I will go back to the great sweet mother,
    Mother and lover of men, the sea.
I will go down to her, I and none other,
    Close with her, kiss her and mix her with me;
Cling to her, strive with her, hold her fast;
O fair white mother, in days long past
Born without sister, born without brother,
    Set free my soul as thy soul is free.

O fair green-girdled mother of mine,
    Sea, that art clothed with the sun and the rain,
Thy sweet hard kisses are strong like wine,
    Thy large embraces are keen like pain.
Save me and hide me with all thy waves,
Find me one grave of thy thousand graves,
Those pure cold populous graves of thine,
    Wrought without hand in a world without stain.

I shall sleep, and move with the moving ships,
    Change as the winds change, veer in the tide;
My lips will feast on the foam of thy lips,
    I shall rise with thy rising, with thee subside;
Sleep, and not know if she be, if she were,
Filled full with life to the eyes and hair,
As a rose is fulfilled to the roseleaf tips
    With splendid summer and perfume and pride.

This woven raiment of nights and days,
    Were it once cast off and unwound from me,
Naked and glad would I walk in thy ways,
    Alive and aware of thy ways and thee;
Clear of the whole world, hidden at home,
Clothed with the green and crowned with the foam,
A pulse of the life of thy straits and bays,
    A vein in the heart of the streams of the sea.

Fair mother, fed with the lives of men,
    Thou art subtle and cruel of heart, men say
Thou hast taken, and shalt not render again;
    Thou art full of thy dead, and cold as they.
But death is the worst that comes of thee;
Thou art fed with our dead, O mother, O sea,
But when hast thou fed on our hearts? or when,
    Having given us love, hast thou taken away?

O tender-hearted, O perfect lover,
    Thy lips are bitter, and sweet thine heart.
The hopes that hurt and the dreams that hover,
    Shall they not vanish away and apart?
But thou, thou art sure, thou art older than earth;
Thou art strong for death and fruitful of birth;
Thy depths conceal and thy gulfs discover;
    From the first thou wert; in the end thou art.


FROM "HYMN TO PROSERPINE"

(*After the Proclamation in Rome of the Christian Faith*)

*Vicisti, Galilaee*

Thou hast conquered, O pale Galilean; the world has grown gray from thy breath;
We have drunken of things Lethean, and fed on the fullness of death.

Laurel is green for a season, and love is sweet for a day;
But love grows bitter with treason, and laurel outlives not May.
Sleep, shall we sleep after all? for the world is not sweet in the end;
For the old faiths loosen and fall, the new years ruin and rend.
Fate is a sea without shore, and the soul is a rock that abides;
But her ears are vexed with the roar and her face with the foam of the tides.
O lips that the live blood faints in, the leavings of racks and rods!
O ghastly glories of saints, dead limbs of gibbeted Gods!
Though all men abase them before you in spirit, and all knees bend,
I kneel not, neither adore you, but standing, look to the end.
All delicate days and pleasant, all spirits and sorrows are cast
Far out with the foam of the present that sweeps to the surf of the past;
Where beyond the extreme sea-wall, and between the remote sea-gates,
Waste water washes, and tall ships founder, and deep death waits:
Where, mighty with deepening sides, clad about with the seas as with wings,
And impelled of invisible tides, and fulfilled of unspeakable things,
White-eyed and poisonous finned, shark-toothed and serpentine-curled,
Rolls, under the whitening wind of the future, the wave of the world.
The depths stand naked in sunder behind it, the storms flee away;
In the hollow before it the thunder is taken and snared as a prey;
In its sides is the north-wind bound; and its salt is of all men's tears;
With light of ruin, and sound of changes, and pulse of years:
With travail of day after day, and with trouble of hour upon hour;
And bitter as blood is the spray; and the crests are as fangs that devour:
And its vapor and storm of its steam as the sighing of spirits to be;
And its noise as the noise in a dream; and its depth as the roots of the sea:
And the height of its heads as the height of the utmost stars of the air:
And the ends of the earth at the might thereof tremble, and time is made bare.
Will ye bridle the deep sea with reins, will ye chasten the high sea with rods?
Will ye take her to chain her with chains, who is older than all ye Gods?
All ye as a wind shall go by, as a fire shall ye pass and be past;
Ye are Gods, and behold ye shall die, and the waves be upon you at last.
In the darkness of time, in the deeps of the years, in the changes of things,
Ye shall sleep as a slain man sleeps, and the world shall forget you for kings.
Though the feet of thine high priests tread where thy lords and our forefathers trod,
Though these that were Gods are dead and thou being dead art a God.
Though before thee the throned Cytherian be fallen, and hidden her head,
Yet thy kingdom shall pass, Galilean, thy dead shall go down to thee dead.
Of the maiden thy mother, men sing as a goddess with grace clad around;
Thou art throned where another was king; where another was queen she is
    crowned.
Yea, once we had sight of another: but now she is queen, say these.
Not as thine, not as thine was our mother, a blossom of flowering seas,
Clothed round with the world's desire as with raiment, and fair as the foam,
And fleeter than kindled fire, and a goddess, and mother of Rome.
For thine came pale and a maiden, and sister to sorrow; but ours,
Her deep hair heavily laden with odor and color of flowers,
White rose of the rose-white water, a silver splendor, a flame,
Bent down unto us that besought her, and earth grew sweet with her name.
For thine came weeping, a slave among slaves, and rejected; but she
Came flushed from the full-flushed wave, and imperial, her foot on the sea,

And the wonderful waters knew her, the winds and the viewless ways,
And the roses grew rosier, and bluer the sea-blue stream of the bays.
Ye are fallen, our lords, by what token? we wist that ye should not fall.
Ye were all so fair that are broken; and one more fair than ye all.
But I turn to her still, having seen she shall surely abide in the end;
Goddess and maiden and queen, be near me now and befriend.
O daughter of earth, of my mother, her crown and blossom of birth,
I am also, I also, thy brother; I go as I came unto earth.
In the night where thine eyes are as moons are in heaven, the night where thou art,
Where the silence is more than all tunes, where sleep overflows from the heart,
Where the poppies are sweet as the rose in our world, and the red rose is white,
And the wind falls faint as it blows with the fume of the flowers of the night.
And the murmur of spirits that sleep in the shadow of Gods from afar
Grows dim in thine ears and deep as the deep dim soul of a star,
In the sweet low light of thy face, under heavens untrod by the sun,
Let my soul with their souls find place, and forget what is done and undone.
Thou art more than the Gods who number the days of our temporal breath;
For these give labor and slumber; but thou, Proserpina, death.
Therefore now at thy feet I abide for a season in silence. I know
I shall die as my fathers died, and sleep as they sleep; even so.
For the glass of the years is brittle wherein we gaze for a span;
A little soul for a little bears up this corpse which is man.
So long I endure, no longer; and laugh not again, neither weep.
For there is no God found stronger than death; and death is a sleep.

### RONDEL

> Kissing her hair I sat against her feet,
> Wove and unwove it, wound and found it sweet,
> Made fast therewith her hands, drew down her eyes,
> Deep as deep flowers and dreamy like dim skies;
> With her own tresses bound and found her fair,
>   Kissing her hair.
>
> Sleep were no sweeter than her face to me,
> Sleep of cold sea-bloom under the cold sea;
> What pain could get between my face and hers?
> What new sweet thing would love not relish worse?
> Unless, perhaps, white death had kissed me there,
>   Kissing her hair?

### A BALLADE OF DREAMLAND

> I hid my heart in a nest of roses,
>   Out of the sun's way, hidden apart;
> In a softer bed than the soft white snow's is,
>   Under the roses I hid my heart.
>   Why would it sleep not? why should it start,
> When never a leaf of the rose-trees stirred?
>   What made sleep flutter his wings and part?
> Only the song of a secret bird.

Lie still, I said, for the wind's wing closes,
  And mild leaves muffle the keen sun's dart;
Lie still, for the wind on the warm sea dozes,
  And the wind is unquieter yet than thou art.
    Does a thought in thee still as a thorn's wound smart?
Does the fang still fret thee of hope deferred?
  What bids the lids of thy sleep dispart?
Only the song of a secret bird.

The green land's name that a charm encloses,
  It never was writ in the traveler's chart,
And sweet on its trees as the fruit that grows is,
  It never was sold in the merchant's mart.
    The swallows of dreams through its dim fields dart,
And sleep's are the tunes in its tree-tops heard;
  No hound's note wakens the wildwood hart,
Only the song of a secret bird.

### Envoi

In the world of dreams I have chosen my part.
  To sleep for a season and hear no word
Of true love's truth or of light love's art,
  Only the song of a secret bird.

#### A FORSAKEN GARDEN

In a coign of the cliff between lowland and highland,
  At the sea-down's edge between windward and lee,
Walled round with rocks as an inland island,
  The ghost of a garden fronts the sea.
A girdle of brushwood and thorn encloses
  The steep square slope of the blossomless bed
Where the weeds that grew green from the graves of its roses
          Now lie dead.

The fields fall southward, abrupt and broken,
  To the low last edge of the long lone land.
If a step should sound or a word be spoken,
  Would a ghost not rise at the strange guest's hand?
So long have the gray bare walks lain guestless,
  Through branches and briars if a man make way,
He shall find no life but the sea-wind's, restless
          Night and day.

The dense hard passage is blind and stifled
  That crawls by a track none turn to climb
To the strait waste place that the years have rifled
  Of all but the thorns that are touched not of time.
The thorns he spares when the rose is taken;
  The rocks are left when he wastes the plain.
The wind that wanders, the weeds wind-shaken,
          These remain.

Not a flower to be prest of the foot that falls not;
  As the heart of a dead man the seed-plots are dry;
From the thicket of thorns whence the nightingale calls not,
  Could she call, there were never a rose to reply.
Over the meadows that blossom and wither
  Rings but the note of a sea-bird's song;
Only the sun and the rain come hither
      All year long.

The sun burns sere and the rain dishevels
  One gaunt bleak blossom of scentless breath.
Only the wind here hovers and revels
  In a round where life seems barren as death.
Here there was laughing of old, there was weeping,
  Haply, of lovers none ever will know,
Whose eyes went seaward a hundred sleeping
      Years ago.

Heart handfast in heart as they stood, "Look thither,"
  Did he whisper? "Look forth from the flowers to the sea;
For the foam-flowers endure when the rose-blossoms wither
  And men that love lightly may die—but we?"
And the same wind sang and the same waves whitened,
  And or ever the garden's last petals were shed,
In the lips that had whispered, the eyes that had lightened,
      Love was dead.

Or they loved their life through, and then went whither?
  And were one to the end—but what end who knows?
Love deep as the sea as a rose must wither,
  As the rose-red seaweed that mocks the rose.
Shall the dead take thought for the dead to love them?
  What love was ever as deep as a grave?
They are loveless now as the grass above them
      Or the wave.

All are at one now, roses and lovers,
  Not known of the cliffs and the fields and the sea.
Not a breath of the time that has been hovers
  In the air now soft with a summer to be.
Not a breath shall there sweeten the seasons hereafter
  Of the flowers or the lovers that laugh now or weep,
When as they that are free now of weeping and laughter
      We shall sleep.

Here death may deal not again forever;
  Here change may come not till all change end.
From the graves they have made they shall rise up never,
  Who have left nought living to ravage and rend.
Earth, stones, and thorns of the wild ground growing,
  While the sun and the rain live, these shall be;
Till a last wind's breath upon all these blowing
      Roll the sea.

Till the slow sea rise and the sheer cliff crumble,
  Till terrace and meadow the deep gulfs drink,
Till the strength of the waves of the high tides humble
  The fields that lessen, the rocks that shrink,
Here now in his triumph where all things falter,
  Stretched out on the spoils that his own hand spread,
As a god self-slain on his own strange altar,
  Death lies dead.

### MADONNA MIA

Under green apple-boughs
That never a storm will rouse,
My lady hath her house
  Between two bowers;
In either of the twain
Red roses full of rain;
She hath for bondwomen
  All kind of flowers.

She hath no handmaid fair
To draw her curled gold hair
Through rings of gold that bear
  Her whole hair's weight;
She hath no maids to stand
Gold-clothed on either hand;
In all the great green land
  None is so great.

She hath no more to wear
But one white hood of vair
Drawn over eyes and hair,
  Wrought with strange gold,
Made for some great queen's head,
Some fair great queen since dead;
And one strait gown of red
  Against the cold.

Beneath her eyelids deep
Love lying seems asleep,
Love, swift to wake, to weep,
  To laugh, to gaze;
Her breasts are like white birds,
And all her gracious words
As water-grass to herds
  In the June-days.

To her all dews that fall
And rains are musical;
Her flowers are fed from all,
  Her joys from these;

In the deep-feather firs
Their gift of joy is hers,
In the least breath that stirs
  Across the trees.

She grows with greenest leaves,
Ripens with reddest sheaves,
Forgets, remembers, grieves,
  And is not sad;
The quiet lands and skies
Leave light upon her eyes;
None knows her, weak or wise,
  Or tired or glad.

None knows, none understands,
What flowers are like her hands;
Though you should search all lands.
  Wherein time grows,
What snows are like her feet,
Though his eyes burn with heat
Through gazing on my sweet,
  Yet no man knows.

Only this thing is said;
That white and gold and red,
God's three chief words, man's bread
  And oil and wine,
Were given her for dowers,
And kingdom of all hours,
And grace of goodly flowers
  And various wine.

This is my lady's praise:
God after many days
Wrought her in unknown ways,
  In sunset lands;
This was my lady's birth;
God gave her might and mirth
And laid his whole sweet earth
  Between her hands.

Under deep apple-boughs
My lady hath her house;
She wears upon her brows
  The flower thereof;
All saying but what God saith
To her is as vain breath;
She is more strong than death,
  Being strong as love.

## CHORUS

### (from "Atalanta in Calydon")

Before the beginning of years,
  There came to the making of man
Time, with a gift of tears;
  Grief, with a glass that ran;
Pleasure, with pain for leaven;
  Summer, with flowers that fell;
Remembrance fallen from heaven,
  And madness risen from hell;
Strength without hands to smite;
  Love that endures for a breath;
Night, the shadow of light,
  And life, the shadow of death.
And the high gods took in hand
  Fire, and the falling of tears,
And a measure of sliding sand
  From under the feet of the years;
And froth and drift of the sea;
  And dust of the laboring earth;

And bodies of things to be
  In the houses of death and of birth;
And wrought with weeping and laughter,
  And fashioned with loathing and love,
With life before and after
  And death beneath and above,
For a day and a night and a morrow,
  That his strength might endure for a span
With travail and heavy sorrow,
  The holy spirit of man.

From the winds of the north and the south
  They gathered as unto strife;
They breathed upon his mouth,
  They filled his body with life;
Eyesight and speech they wrought
  For the veils of the soul therein,
A time for labor and thought,
  A time to serve and to sin;
They gave him light in his ways,
  And love, and a space for delight,
And beauty and length of days,
  And night, and sleep in the night.
His speech is a burning fire;
  With his lips he travaileth;
In his heart is a blind desire,
  In his eyes foreknowledge of death;
He weaves, and is clothed with derision;
  Sows, and he shall not reap;
His life is a watch or a vision
  Between a sleep and a sleep.

## WHEN THE HOUNDS OF SPRING

### (from "Atalanta in Calydon")

When the hounds of spring are on winter's traces,
  The mother of months in meadow or plain
Fills the shadows and windy places
  With lisp of leaves and ripple of rain;
And the brown bright nightingale amorous
Is half assuaged for Itylus,
For the Thracian ships and the foreign faces,
  The tongueless vigil, and all the pain.

Come with bows bent and with emptying of quivers,
  Maiden most perfect, lady of light,
With a noise of winds and many rivers,
  With a clamor of waters, and with might;
Bind on thy sandals, O thou most fleet,
Over the splendor and speed of thy feet;
For the faint east quickens, the wan west shivers,
  Round the feet of the day and the feet of the night.

Where shall we find her, how shall we sing to her,
    Fold our hands round her knees, and cling?
O that man's heart were as fire and could spring to her,
    Fire, or the strength of the streams that spring!
For the stars and the winds are unto her
As raiment, as songs of the harp-player;
For the risen stars and the fallen cling to her,
    And the southwest-wind and the west-wind sing.

For winter's rains and ruins are over,
    And all the season of snows and sins;
The days dividing lover and lover,
    The light that loses, the night that wins;
And time remembered is grief forgotten,
And frosts are slain and flowers begotten,
And in green underwood and cover
    Blossom by blossom the spring begins.

The full streams feed on flower of rushes,
    Ripe grasses trammel a traveling foot,
The faint fresh flame of the young year flushes
    From leaf to flower and flower to fruit;
And fruit and leaf are as gold and fire,
And the oat is heard above the lyre,
And the hoofèd heel of a satyr crushes
    The chestnut-husk at the chestnut-root.

And Pan by noon and Bacchus by night,
    Fleeter of foot than the fleet-foot kid,
Follows with dancing and fills with delight
    The Maenad and the Bassarid;
And soft as lips that laugh and hide
The laughing leaves of the trees divide,
And screen from seeing and leave in sight
    The god pursuing, the maiden hid.

The ivy falls with the Bacchanal's hair
    Over her eyebrows hiding her eyes;
The wild vine slipping down leaves bare
    Her bright breast shortening into sighs;
The wild vine slips with the weight of its leaves,
But the berried ivy catches and cleaves
To the limbs that glitter, the feet that scare
    The wolf that follows, the fawn that flies.

### HERTHA

I am that which began;
    Out of me the years roll;
Out of me God and man;
    I am equal and Whole;
God changes, and man, and the form of them bodily; I am the soul.

Before ever land was,
    Before ever the sea,
Or soft hair of the grass,
    Or fair limbs of the tree,
Or the flesh-colored fruit of my branches, I was, and thy soul was in me.

    First life on my sources
        First drifted and swam;
    Out of me are the forces
        That save it or damn;
Out of me man and woman, and wild-beast and bird; before God was, I am.

    Beside or above me
        Nought is there to go;
Love or unlove me,
        Unknow me or know,
I am that which unloves me and loves; I am stricken, and I am the blow.

    I the mark that is missed
        And the arrows that miss,
    I the mouth that is kissed
        And the breath in the kiss,
The search, and the sought, and the seeker, the soul and the body that is.

    I am the thing which blesses
        My spirit elate;
    That which caresses
        With hands uncreate
My limbs unbegotten that measure the length of the measure of fate.

    But what thing dost thou now,
        Looking Godward, to cry,
    "I am I, thou art thou,
        I am low, thou art high"?
I am thou, whom thou seekest to find him; find thou but myself, thou art I.

    I the grain and the furrow,
        The plow-cloven clod
And the plowshare drawn thorough,
        The germ and the sod,
The deed and the doer, the seed and the sower, the dust which is God.

    Hast thou known how I fashioned thee,
        Child, underground?
Fire that impassioned thee,
        Iron that bound,
Dim changes of water, what thing of all these hast thou known of or found?

    Canst thou say in thine heart
        Thou hast seen with thine eyes
With what cunning of art
        Thou wast wrought in what wise,
By what force of what stuff thou wast shapen, and shown on my breast to the skies?

✦

A creed is a rod,
    And a crown is of night;
But this thing is God,
    To be man with thy might,
To grow straight in the strength of thy spirit, and live out thy life as the light.

I am in thee to save thee,
    As my soul in thee saith,
Give thou as I gave thee,
    Thy life-blood and breath,
Green leaves of thy labor, white flowers of thy thought, and red fruit of thy death.

Be the ways of thy giving
    As mine were to thee;
The free life of thy living,
    Be the gift of it free;
Not as servant to lord, nor as master to slave, shalt thou give thee to me.

✦

I bid you but be;
    I have need not of prayer;
I have need of you free
    As your mouths of mine air;
That my heart may be greater within me, beholding the fruits of me fair.

Lo, winged with world's wonders,
    With miracles shod,
With the fires of his thunders
    For raiment and rod,
God trembles in heaven, and his angels are white with the terror of God.

For his twilight is come on him,
    His anguish is here;
And his spirits gaze dumb on him,
    Grown gray from his fear;
And his hour taketh hold on him stricken, the last of his infinite year.

Thought made him and breaks him,
    Truth slays and forgives;
But to you, as time takes him,
    This new thing it gives,
Even love, the beloved Republic, that feeds upon freedom and lives.

For truth only is living,
    Truth only is whole,
And the love of his giving
    Man's polestar and pole;
Man, pulse of my center, and fruit of my body, and seed of my soul.

One birth of my bosom;
    One beam of mine eye:
One topmost blossom
    That scales the sky;
Man, equal and one with me, man that is made of me, man that is I.

# Thomas Hardy

THOMAS HARDY was born at Upper Bockhampton, near Dorchester, June 2, 1840, of parents in humble circumstances, his father being a stone-mason. His schooling was fitful. When sixteen, he was apprenticed to an ecclesiastical architect. Later, he left his native village and worked in London, where he won the prize offered by the Royal Institute of British Architects. This was in 1863. A few years after, he abandoned architecture and, in 1871, his first novel, *Desperate Remedies,* was published anonymously. It was a failure, little attention being paid to the author until the publication of *Under the Greenwood Tree.* From that time on his success as a writer was assured.

It was not until he was almost sixty—in 1898, to be precise—that Hardy abandoned prose and challenged attention as a poet, verse having been the form of expression with which he began and, as many (including the editor and Hardy himself) believe, the form by which he will be remembered longest. Technically considered, the rhythms of his verse are, at first reading, irritatingly rude; his syntax is often clumsy; his language involved. But, beneath the surface crudities— and many of them are efforts to achieve particular effects—Hardy's poetry is as disciplined as it is original. If its idiom is sometimes overweighted, it corresponds to the large design and complexities of his thought. "It has," says Dorothy Martin, in an essay on Hardy's lyrics, "an elemental power which, in its wide range of emotion, its sense of inner conflict between mind and heart, affords something like a counterpart in poetry to the art of Rodin in sculpture. To the horror of the orthodox, it has outwardly the same challenging roughnesses and acerbities; it has also the same profundity and stimulating power for those who, refusing to be put off by a difficult exterior, push on to the inner spirit of which this exterior is the vigorous, provocative but fitting expression."

As has been said, by Hardy himself, he "was *compelled* to give up verse for prose," but at no time did he prefer the many works of fiction which won him an international reputation. On the contrary, he was bitter that necessity had forced him to discontinue the creation of poetry for the writing of novels, and in private life would refer to the latter as "pot-boilers" and "wretched stuff." Nevertheless, between the ages of thirty-four and fifty-seven, Hardy published eleven novels and three collections of stories, of which *The Return of the Native* and *The Mayor of Casterbridge* are the sharpest in characterization although *Tess of the D'Urbervilles* (1891) and *Jude the Obscure* (1896) caused more comment. The former started a controversy which grew into an attack, chiefly because of the social criticism which had been implicit in his previous work but which was now openly expressed. With greater violence, almost with vituperation, Hardy was called to account for *Jude the Obscure.* This further example of critical stupidity hurt Hardy so deeply that he said it "cured him of all interest in novel-writing."

Two years later he turned definitely and exclusively to poetry, publishing *Wessex Poems* (1898) with his own drawings, and *Poems of the Past and Present* (1902). Both volumes were respectfully but unenthusiastically received. Then, when Hardy was sixty-four years old and critics had decided that his power had waned, he published the first part of *The Dynasts* (1904), that epic which was to spread itself on the largest canvas of his time. By 1908 the work was complete, a huge drama of the Napoleonic Wars in three books, nineteen acts, and one hundred and thirty scenes. This triumph is the apotheosis of the poet. Of it, the *London Times* wrote: "A work which combines as only a work of genius could combine, a poetic philosophy with minute historical knowledge and a shrewd eye for the tragical and comical ways of men and women." Lascelles Abercrombie, a most conservative appraiser, unhesitatingly called it "the biggest and most consistent exhibition of fatalism in literature." Hardy himself liked, so he informed the editor, two or three of the lyrics in *The Dynasts* (particularly "Trafalgár") as well as anything in his *Collected Poems*.

As Hardy grew older, his poems increased, and his powers with them. Explaining the large number of verses written after his sixtieth year, he said that he would merely "go to a drawer and take something out." But, although it is true that he resuscitated and refurbished many lyrics of an earlier period, Hardy continued to create new ones no less knotted, no less characteristically acrid, delicately nostalgic, pungently bitter-sweet, until he was almost ninety. When he was seventy-nine his *Collected Poems* (1919) displayed the range and fecundity but not the end of his gifts. As an octogenarian, he published *Late Lyrics and Earlier* (1922), *Human Shows: Far Phantasies, Songs and Trifles* (1925), and *Winter Words in Various Moods and Metres,* which, though appearing posthumously, had been arranged and selected by Hardy before his death.

Hardy's death in his eighty-eighth year on January 11, 1928, deprived contemporary England of its most honored author. Although his ashes were placed in Westminster Abbey, his heart (as requested in his Will) was buried in the churchyard of his own village, in the soil he loved so faithfully.

His work resists a pat synthesis. Hardy wrote in almost every manner, good and bad, in every meter, old and new, mixing novelty and banality, dropping heavy cacophonies into the lightest melodies, balancing the profound with the trivial, the cosmic with the comic. Most readers prefer him in that curiously lyric-narrative style which he perfected, but his intensities escape category. Each of his collections runs the gamut of life and its reflection in literature, and his style follows the scale. Modern and ancient, his technique is as advanced as the youngest contemporary's, as formal as a poetic ballet-master's. "In the Servants' Quarters" is a splendid instance of Hardy's talk-flavored verse, which ascends from casual speech on a *crescendo* of dramatic effect, to a half-expected yet startling climax. In quite another manner, his *Satires of Circumstance* (reminding an American reader of Masters' *Spoon River Anthology,* which it anticipated by a generation) are epigrammatic vignettes in which he condensed whole domestic dramas. "The Dark-Eyed Gentleman," on the other hand, is as simple-spontaneous as a folk-tune and quite unlike Hardy's other verse.

Hardy's resources are seemingly endless. At one moment he plays the pathetic fanciful as in "The Tree and the Lady," the next moment he strikes the ironically bizarre in "Ah, Are You Digging on My Grave?" "In Time of 'The Breaking of Nations'" packs an epic into twelve quiet-colored lines; "Snow in the Suburbs" is a purely objective delineation in black and white; "When I Set Out for Lyonnesse" (one of Hardy's favorites among his own poems) is pure song; "The Oxen" turns a superstition to tender humor. And, though each of these is a lyric and all are straightforward in rhythm, each has its own dexterous difference in meter. It has passed unnoted, but Hardy even ventured into the French forms for occasional effects; "The Roman Road" is as neat a rondeau as Austin Dobson ever fashioned; "Winter in Durnover Field" and "Birds at Winter Nightfall" are thoroughly Hardyesque and yet precise if unusual triolets.

Hardy's questioning the beneficence of Nature led to accusations of pessimism, a charge that he continually but ineffectually denied. Actually the poet was an unorthodox moralist whose heart went out to the things, people, and elements he loved. These elements—as he says ironically in "New Year's Eve," affirmatively in "The Subalterns"—are not actuated either by blind hate or blinder chance, but are subject to laws beyond the rules of logic. Hardy denied no God, but sensed design in chaos. Even when he could not rationalize a universe struggling to establish order in imperfection, he praised it, "hoping it might be so."

In the brief note preceding Hardy's contribution in *Great Names* (1926) Siegfried Sassoon wrote, "Without laboring the analogy between poetry and religion, it may be said that sham poetry is as pernicious as sham religion; and that for poets a merely poetical state of mind is as dangerous as a religious belief based on superficial religious emotion. That is why Hardy's poetry of experience is so significant. He records with microscopic exactitude, preserving a flawless artistic integrity. In his short poems he fuses all that he has learned from the past and endured in the present, in a supreme imaginative vision with masterly and original craft in words and subtle ironic sense. He realizes that the true satisfaction of life lies in imaginative conflict. Whatever their ultimate purpose, men are alive only while they struggle. When they grow aware of the futility of their effort, and yet strive to fashion something from it, they become noble and tragic. Such is Hardy; but his despair is mitigated by tenderness and pity for his fellows. . . . With a wistful understanding he surveys the human scene."

No consideration of Hardy could end on a finer coda. Throughout Hardy's work there shines a greater triumph than the technician's: a triumphant personality.

Three excellent studies of Hardy, presenting the novelist and poet from three distinctly different points of view, are those by Lionel Johnson (1894), Lascelles Abercrombie (1912), and Ernst Brennecke (1925).

### IN TIME OF "THE BREAKING OF NATIONS"

Only a man harrowing clods
    In a slow silent walk,
With an old horse that stumbles and nods
    Half asleep as they stalk.

Only thin smoke without flame
    From the heaps of couch grass:
Yet this will go onward the same
    Though Dynasties pass.

Yonder a maid and her wight
    Come whispering by;
War's annals will fade into night
    Ere their story die.

### THE DARKLING THRUSH

I leaned upon a coppice gate
    When Frost was specter-gray,
And Winter's dregs made desolate
    The weakening eye of day.

The tangled bine-stems scored the sky
  Like strings from broken lyres,
And all mankind that haunted nigh
  Had sought their household fires.

The land's sharp features seemed to be
  The Century's corpse outleant;
His crypt the cloudy canopy,
  The wind his death-lament.
The ancient pulse of germ and birth
  Was shrunken hard and dry,
And every spirit upon earth
  Seemed fervorless as I.

At once a voice burst forth among
  The bleak twigs overhead
In a full-hearted evensong
  Of joy illimited;
An aged thrush, frail, gaunt and small,
  In blast-beruffled plume,
Had chosen thus to fling his soul
  Upon the growing gloom.

So little cause for carolings
  Of such ecstatic sound
Was written on terrestrial things
  Afar or nigh around,
That I could think there trembled through
  His happy good-night air

Some blessed hope, whereof he knew
And I was unaware.

## THE MAN HE KILLED

"Had he and I but met
    By some old ancient inn,
We should have sat us down to wet
    Right many a nipperkin!

"But ranged as infantry,
    And staring face to face,
I shot at him as he at me,
    And killed him in his place.

"I shot him dead because—
    Because he was my foe,
Just so: my foe of course he was;
    That's clear enough; although

"He thought he'd 'list, perhaps,
    Off-hand-like—just as I—
Was out of work—had sold his traps—
    No other reason why.

"Yes; quaint and curious war is!
    You shoot a fellow down
You'd treat, if met where any bar is,
    Or help to half-a-crown."

## IN THE SERVANTS' QUARTERS

"Man, you too, aren't you, one of these rough followers of the criminal?
All hanging hereabout to gather how he's going to bear
Examination in the hall." She flung disdainful glances on
The shabby figure standing at the fire with others there,
      Who warmed them by its flare.

"No, indeed, my skipping maiden: I know nothing of the trial here,
Or criminal, if so he be.—I chanced to come this way,
And the fire shone out into the dawn, and morning airs are cold now;
I, too, was drawn in part by charms I see before me play,
      That I see not every day."

"Ha, ha!" then laughed the constables who also stood to warm themselves,
The while another maiden scrutinized his features hard,
As the blaze threw into contrast every knot and line that wrinkled them,
Exclaiming, "Why, last night when he was brought in by the guard,
      You were with him in the yard!"

"Nay, nay, you teasing wench, I say! You know you speak mistakenly.
Cannot a tired pedestrian who has legged it long and far
Here on his way from northern parts, engrossed in humble marketings,
Come in and rest awhile, although judicial doings are
      Afoot by morning star?"

"O come, come!" laughed the constables. "Why, man, you speak the dialect
He uses in his answers; you can hear him up the stairs.
So own it. We sha'n't hurt ye. There, he's speaking now! His syllables
Are those you sound yourself when you are talking unawares,
      As this pretty girl declares."

"And you shudder when his chain clinks!" she rejoined. "O yes, I noticed it.
And you winced, too, when those cuffs they gave him echoed to us here.
They'll soon be coming down, and you may then have to defend yourself
Unless you hold your tongue, or go away and keep you clear
      When he's led to judgment near!"

"No! I'll be damned in hell if I know anything about the man!
No single thing about him more than everybody knows!
Must not I even warm my hands but I am charged with blasphemies?" . . .
—His face convulses as the morning cock that moment crows,
      And he droops, and turns, and goes.

## NEUTRAL TONES

We stood by a pond that winter day,
And the sun was white, as though chidden
   of God,
And a few leaves lay on the starving sod;
  They had fallen from an ash, and were
   gray.

Your eyes on me were as eyes that rove
Over tedious riddles solved years ago;
And some words played between us to and
   fro
  On which lost the more by our love.

The smile on your mouth was the deadest
   thing
Alive enough to have strength to die;
And a grin of bitterness swept thereby
  Like an ominous bird a-wing. . . .

Since then, keen lessons that love deceives,
And wrings with wrong, have shaped to me
Your face, and the God-curst sun, and a tree,
  And a pond edged with grayish leaves.

## NEW YEAR'S EVE

"I have finished another year," said God,
  "In gray, green, white and brown;
I have strewn the leaf upon the sod,
Sealed up the worm within the clod,
   And let the last sun down."

"And what's the good of it?" I said,
  "What reasons made you call
From formless void this earth we tread,
When nine-and-ninety can be read
   Why nought should be at all?

"Yea, Sire; why shaped you us, 'who in
  This tabernacle groan'—
If ever a joy be found herein,
Such joy no man had wished to win
   If he had never known!"

Then he: "My labors—logicless—
  You may explain; not I:
Sense-sealed I have wrought, without a guess
That I evolved a Consciousness
   To ask for reasons why.

"Strange that ephemeral creatures who
  By my own ordering are,
Should see the shortness of my view,
Use ethic tests I never knew,
  Or made provision for!"

He sank to raptness as of yore,
  And opening New Year's Day
Wove it by rote as theretofore,
And went on working evermore
  In his unweeting way.

### THE NIGHT OF TRAFALGÁR

#### (from "The Dynasts")

In the wild October night-time, when the wind raved round the land,
And the Back-sea met the Front-sea, and our doors were blocked with sand,
And we heard the drub of Dead-man's Bay, where bones of thousands are,
We knew not what the day had done for us at Trafalgár.
          Had done,
          Had done,
      For us at Trafalgár!

"Pull hard, and make the Nothe, or down we go!" one says, says he.
We pulled; and bedtime brought the storm; but snug at home slept we.
Yet all the while our gallants after fighting through the day,
Were beating up and down the dark, sou'-west of Cadiz Bay.
          The dark,
          The dark,
      Sou'-west of Cadiz Bay!

The victors and the vanquished then the storm it tossed and tore,
As hard they strove, those worn-out men, upon that surly shore;
Dead Nelson and his half-dead crew, his foes from near and far,
Were rolled together on the deep that night at Trafalgár!
          The deep,
          The deep,
      That night at Trafalgár!

### WEATHERS

This is the weather the cuckoo likes,
      And so do I;
When showers betumble the chestnut spikes,
      And nestlings fly;
And the little brown nightingale bills his
      best,
And they sit outside the "Traveler's Rest,"
And maids come forth sprig-muslin drest,
And citizens dream of the South and West,
      And so do I.

This is the weather the shepherd shuns,
      And so do I;
When beeches drip in browns and duns,
      And thresh, and ply;

And hill-hid tides throb, throe on throe,
And meadow rivulets overflow,
And drops on gate-bars hang in a row,
And rooks in families homeward go,
      And so do I.

### "AH, ARE YOU DIGGING ON MY GRAVE?"

"Ah, are you digging on my grave
      My beloved one?—planting rue?"
—"No: yesterday he went to wed
One of the brightest wealth has bred,
'It cannot hurt her now,' he said,
      'That I should not be true.'"

"Then who is digging on my grave?
  My nearest, dearest kin?"
—"Ah, no: they sit and think, 'What use!
What good will planting flowers produce?
No tendance of her mound can loose
  Her spirit from Death's gin.' "

"But someone digs upon my grave?
  My enemy?—prodding sly?"
—"Nay: when she heard you had passed the
  Gate
That shuts on all flesh soon or late,
She thought you no more worth her hate,
  And cares not where you lie."

"Then, who is digging on my grave?
  Say—since I have not guessed!"

—"O it is I, my mistress dear,
Your little dog, who still lives near,
And much I hope my movements here
  Have not disturbed your rest?"

"Ah, yes! *You* dig upon my grave. . . .
  Why flashed it not on me
That one true heart was left behind!
What feeling do we ever find
To equal among human kind
  A dog's fidelity!"

"Mistress, I dug upon your grave
  To bury a bone, in case
I should be hungry near this spot
When passing on my daily trot.
I am sorry, but I quite forgot
  It was your resting-place."

FIVE "SATIRES OF CIRCUMSTANCE"

### In Church

"And now to God the Father," he ends,
And his voice thrills up to the topmost tiles:
Each listener chokes as he bows and bends,
And emotion pervades the crowded aisles.
Then the preacher glides to the vestry-door,
And shuts it, and thinks he is seen no more.

The door swings softly ajar meanwhile,
And a pupil of his in the Bible class,
Who adores him as one without gloss or guile,
Sees her idol stand with a satisfied smile
And reënact at the vestry-glass
Each pulpit gesture in deft dumb-show
That had moved the congregation so.

### By Her Aunt's Grave

"Sixpence a week," says the girl to her lover,
"Aunt used to bring me, for she could confide
In me alone, she vowed. It was to cover
The cost of her headstone when she died.
And that was a year ago last June;
I've not yet fixed it. But I must soon."

"And where is the money now, my dear?"
"O, snug in my purse. . . . Aunt was *so* slow
In saving it—eighty weeks, or near." . . .
"Let's spend it," he hints. "For she won't know.
There's a dance tonight at the *Load of Hay*."
She passively nods. And they go that way.

### At the Altar-rail

"My bride is not coming, alas!" says the groom,
And the telegram shakes in his hand. "I own
It was hurried! We met at a dancing-room
When I went to the Cattle-Show alone,
And then, next night, where the Fountain leaps,
And the Street of the Quarter-Circle sweeps.

"Aye, she won me to ask her to be my wife—
'Twas foolish perhaps!—to forsake the ways
Of the flaring town for a farmer's life.
She agreed. And we fixed it. Now she says:
*'It's sweet of you, dear, to prepare me a nest,*
*But a swift, short, gay life suits me best.*
*What I really am you have never gleaned;*
*I had eaten the apple ere you were weaned.'* "

### In the Restaurant

"But hear. If you stay, and the child be born,
It will pass as your husband's with the rest,
While, if we fly, the teeth of scorn
Will be gleaming at us from east to west;
And the child will come as a life despised.
I feel an elopement is ill-advised!"

"O you realize not what it is, my dear,
To a woman! Daily and hourly alarms
Lest the truth should out. How can I stay here
And nightly take him into my arms!
Come to the child no name or fame,
Let us go, and face it, and bear the shame."

### At the Draper's

"I stood at the back of the shop, my dear,
    But you did not perceive me.
Well, when they deliver what you were shown
    I shall know nothing of it, believe me!"

And he coughed and coughed as she paled and said,
    "O, I didn't see you come in there—
Why couldn't you speak?"—"Well, I didn't. I left
    That you should not notice I'd been there.

"You were viewing some lovely things. *'Soon required*
    *For a widow, of latest fashion';*
And I knew 'twould upset you to meet the man
    Who had to be cold and ashen

"And screwed in a box before they could dress you
    *'In the last new note in mourning,'*
As they defined it. So, not to distress you,
    I left you to your adorning."

### AFTERWARDS

When the Present has latched its postern behind my tremulous stay,
    And the May month flaps its glad green leaves like wings,
Delicate-filmed as new-spun silk, will the neighbors say,
    "He was a man who used to notice such things"?

If it be in the dusk when, like an eyelid's soundless blink,
    The dewfall-hawk comes crossing the shades to alight
Upon the wind-warped upland thorn, a gazer may think,
    "To him this must have been a familiar sight."

If I pass during some nocturnal blackness, mothy and warm,
    When the hedgehog travels furtively over the lawn,
One may say, "He strove that such innocent creatures should come to no harm,
    But he could do little for them; and now he is gone."

If, when hearing that I have been stilled at last, they stand at the door,
    Watching the full-starred heavens that winter sees,
Will this thought rise on those who will meet my face no more,
    "He was one who had an eye for such mysteries"?

And will any say when my bell of quittance is heard in the gloom,
    And a crossing breeze cuts a pause in its outrollings,
Till they rise again, as they were a new bell's boom,
    "He hears it not now, but used to notice such things"?

### BIRDS AT WINTER NIGHTFALL

Around the house the flakes fly faster,
And all the berries now are gone
From holly and cotoneaster
Around the house. The flakes fly!—faster
Shutting indoors that crumb-outcaster
We used to see upon the lawn
Around the house. The flakes fly faster,
And all the berries now are gone!

### WINTER IN DURNOVER FIELD

Scene.—*A wide stretch of fallow ground recently sown with wheat, and frozen to
iron hardness. Three large birds walking about thereon, and wistfully eyeing
the surface. Wind keen from north-east: sky a dull gray.*

Rook:      Throughout the field I find no grain;
           The cruel frost encrusts the cornland!
Starling:  Aye: patient pecking now is vain
           Throughout the field, I find . . .
Rook:                                      No grain!
Pigeon:    Nor will be, comrade, till it rain,
           Or genial thawings loose the lorn land
           Throughout the field.
Rook:                            I find no grain:
           The cruel frost encrusts the cornland!

### THE ROMAN ROAD

The Roman Road runs straight and bare
As the pale parting-line in hair
Across the heath. And thoughtful men
Contrast its days of Now and Then,
And delve, and measure, and compare;

Visioning on the vacant air
Helmed legionnaires, who proudly rear
The Eagle, as they pace again
    The Roman Road.

But no tall brass-helmed legionnaire
Haunts it for me. Uprises there
A mother's form upon my ken,
Guiding my infant steps, as when
We walked that ancient thoroughfare,
    The Roman Road.

### MY SPIRIT WILL NOT HAUNT THE MOUND

My spirit will not haunt the mound
    Above my breast,
But travel, memory-possessed,
To where my tremulous being found
    Life largest, best.

My phantom-footed shape will go
    When nightfall grays
Hither and thither along the ways
I and another used to know
    In backward days.

And there you'll find me, if a jot
    You still should care
For me, and for my curious air;
If otherwise, then I shall not,
    For you, be there.

### WHEN I SET OUT FOR LYONNESSE

When I set out for Lyonnesse,
    A hundred miles away,
    The rime was on the spray,
And starlight lit my lonesomeness
When I set out for Lyonnesse
    A hundred miles away.

What could bechance at Lyonnesse
    While I should sojourn there
    No prophet durst declare,
Nor did the wisest wizard guess
What would bechance at Lyonnesse
    While I should sojourn there.

When I came back from Lyonnesse
    With magic in my eyes,
    All marked with mute surmise
My radiance rare and fathomless,
When I came back from Lyonnesse
    With magic in my eyes.

### THE DARK-EYED GENTLEMAN

I pitched my day's leazings [1] in Crimmercrock Lane,
To tie up my garter and jog on again,
When a dear dark-eyed gentleman passed there and said,
In a way that made all o' me color rose-red,
    "What do I see—
    O pretty knee!"
And he came and he tied up my garter for me.

'Twixt sunset and moonrise it was, I can mind:
Ah, 'tis easy to lose what we nevermore find!—
Of the dear stranger's home, of his name, I knew nought,
But I soon knew his nature and all that it brought.
    Then bitterly
    Sobbed I that he
Should ever have tied up my garter for me!

[1] "Leazings"; bundles of gleaned corn.

Yet now I've beside me a fine lissom lad,
And my slip's nigh forgot, and my days are not sad;
My own dearest joy is he, comrade, and friend,
He it is who safe-guards me, on him I depend;
No sorrow brings he,
And thankful I be
That his daddy once tied up my garter for me!

### THE SUBALTERNS

"Poor wanderer," said the leaden sky,
"I fain would lighten thee,
But there be laws in force on high
Which say it must not be."

"I would not freeze thee, shorn one," cried
The North, "knew I but how
To warm my breath, to slack my stride;
But I am ruled as thou."

"Tomorrow I attack thee, wight,"
Said Sickness. "Yet I swear
I bear thy little ark no spite,
But am bid enter there."

"Come hither, Son," I heard Death say;
"I did not will a grave
Should end thy pilgrimage today,
But I, too, am a slave!"

We smiled upon each other then,
And life to me wore less

Of that fell guise it wore ere when
They owned their passiveness.

### THE OXEN

Christmas Eve, and twelve of the clock,
"Now they are all on their knees,"
An elder said as we sat in a flock
By the embers in hearthside ease.

We pictured the meek mild creatures where
They dwelt in their strawy pen,
Nor did it occur to one of us there
To doubt they were kneeling then.

So fair a fancy few would weave
In these years! Yet, I feel,
If someone said on Christmas Eve,
"Come; see the oxen kneel

"In the lonely barton [1] by yonder coomb [2]
Our childhood used to know,"
I should go with him in the gloom,
Hoping it might be so.

### THE TREE AND THE LADY

I have done all I could
For that lady I knew! Through the heats I have shaded her,
Drawn to her songsters when summer has jaded her,
Home from the heath or the wood.

At the mirth-time of May,
When my shadow first lured her, I'd donned my new bravery
Of greenth: 'twas my all. Now I shiver in slavery,
Icicles grieving me gray.

Plumed to every twig's end
I could tempt her chair under me. Much did I treasure her
During those days she had nothing to pleasure her;
Mutely she used me as friend.

[1] Barton: farmyard.          [2] Coomb: valley, hollow.

I'm a skeleton now,
And she's gone, craving warmth. The rime sticks like skin to me;
Through me Arcturus peers; Nor'lights shoot into me;
Gone is she, scorning my bough!

## SNOW IN THE SUBURBS

Every branch big with it,
Bent every twig with it;
Every fork like a white web-foot;
Every street and pavement mute:
Some flakes have lost their way, and grope back upward, when
Meeting those meandering down they turn and descend again.
The palings are glued together like a wall,
And there is no waft of wind with the fleecy fall.

A sparrow enters the tree
Whereon immediately
A snow-lump thrice his own slight size
Descends on him and showers his head and eyes.
And overturns him,
And near inurns him,
And lights on a nether twig, when its brush
Starts off a volley of other lodging lumps with a rush.

The steps are a blanched slope,
Up which, with feeble hope,
A black cat comes, wide-eyed and thin;
And we take him in.

## A PLACID MAN'S EPITAPH

As for my life, I've led it
With fair content and credit:
It said: "Take this." I took it:
Said: "Leave." And I forsook it.
If I had done without it
None would have cared about it,
Or said: "One has refused it
Who might have meetly used it."

## WAITING BOTH

A star looks down at me,
And says: "Here I and you
Stand, each in our degree:
What do you mean to do—
    Mean to do?"

I say: "For all I know,
Wait, and let Time go by,
Till my change come."—"Just so,"
The star says: "So mean I—
    So mean I."

# Wilfrid Scawen Blunt

WILFRID SCAWEN BLUNT was born at Petworth House, Crawley, Sussex, in 1840. He was educated at St. Mary's College, Oscott, and was a member of the diplomatic service from 1858 to 1870. He spent many years in the East, his observations making him strongly sympathetic to lesser nationalities and all the downtrodden. Traveling in North Africa, Asia Minor, and Arabia in the late seventies, all he saw caused him to support the Islamic movement (anticipating T. E. Lawrence) and to oppose the British government's control until his death. He favored the cause of the Egyptians; his voice was lifted for justice to Ireland; he joined Lloyd George in condemning the Boer War.

As a poet, he is best known by his *The Love Sonnets of Proteus* (1881) and *The New Pilgrimage* (1889). Both volumes reveal a deep, philosophical nature expressing itself in terms of high seriousness. A collected edition of his works was published in 1914, and *Selected Poems,* edited by Floyd Dell, was brought out in America in 1923.

His remarkable *My Diaries* [*1888-1914*] appeared when Blunt was an octogenarian, in 1921, a work which its British publisher quickly withdrew from the market because of its blunt revelations of British secret diplomacy. Shortly before his death, he wrote, "I have lived my life in full. No life is perfect that has not been lived youth in feeling, manhood in battle, old age in meditation." Blunt died in London, September 11, 1922.

Although Blunt produced a considerable body of verse, little of it survives. His experiments in assonance and echoing vowels are interesting mainly to the technician; his sonnet sequences, for all their attempts at dramatic narration, are sadly "dated." Five or six of his sonnets have the ring of true metal, and "The Desolate City" moves like an ebbing melody. However, says T. Earle Welby in *A Popular History of English Poetry,* "to have married Byron's granddaughter, bred Arab horses, and been admired by Henley and George Wyndham is to have made a great deal of life."

## ON THE SHORTNESS OF TIME

If I could live without the thought of death,
Forgetful of time's waste, the soul's decay,
I would not ask for other joy than breath
With light and sound of birds and the sun's
    ray.
I could sit on untroubled day by day
Watching the grass grow, and the wild flow-
    ers range
From blue to yellow and from red to gray
In natural sequence as the seasons change.
I could afford to wait, but for the hurt
Of this dull tick of time which chides my
    ear.
But now I dare not sit with loins ungirt
And staff unlifted, for death stands too near
I must be up and going—aye, each minute
The grave gives time for rest when we are
    in it.

## THE TWO HIGHWAYMEN

I long have had a quarrel set with Time
Because he robb'd me. Every day of life
Was wrested from me after bitter strife;
I never yet could see the sun go down
But I was angry in my heart, nor hear
The leaves fall in the wind without a tear
Over the dying summer. I have known

No truce with Time nor Time's accomplice,
　Death.
The fair world is the witness of a crime
Repeated every hour. For life and breath
Are sweet to all who live; and bitterly
The voices of these robbers of the heath
Sound in each ear and chill the passer-by.
—What have we done to thee, thou monstrous Time?
What have we done to Death that we must die?

## THE DESOLATE CITY

Dark to me is the earth. Dark to me are the heavens.
　Where is she that I loved, the woman with eyes like stars?
Desolate are the streets. Desolate is the city.
　A city taken by storm, where none are left but the slain.

Sadly I rose at dawn, undid the latch of my shutters,
　Thinking to let in light, but I only let in love.
Birds in the boughs were awake; I listened to their chaunting;
　Each one sang to his love; only I was alone.

This, I said in my heart, is the hour of life and of pleasure.
　Now each creature on earth has his joy, and lives in the sun,
Each in another's eyes finds light, the light of compassion,
　This is the moment of pity, this is the moment of love.

Speak, O desolate city! Speak, O silence in sadness!
　Where is she that I loved in my strength, that spoke to my soul?
Where are those passionate eyes that appeal'd to my eyes in passion?
　Where is the mouth that kiss'd me, the breast I laid to my own?

Groping I went, as blind. I sought her house, my belovèd's.
　There I stopp'd at the silent door, and listen'd and tried the latch.
Love, I cried, dost thou slumber? This is no hour for slumber,
　This is the hour of love, and love I bring in my hand.

I knew the house, with its windows barr'd, and its leafless fig-tree,
　Climbing round by the doorstep, the only one in the street;
I knew where my hope had climb'd to its goal and there encircled
　All that those desolate walls once held, my belovèd's heart.

There in my grief she consoled me. She loved me when I loved not.
　She put her hand in my hand, and set her lips to my lips.
She told me all her pain and show'd me all her trouble.
　I, like a fool, scarce heard, hardly return'd her kiss.

Weeping strangled my voice. I call'd out, but none answer'd;
　Blindly the windows gazed back at me, dumbly the door;
She whom I love, who loved me, look'd not on my yearning,
　Gave me no more her hands to kiss, show'd me no more her soul.

Therefore the earth is dark to me, the sunlight blackness,
　Therefore I go in tears and alone, by night and day;
Therefore I find no love in heaven, no light, no beauty,
　A heaven taken by storm, where none are left but the slain!

### FAREWELL

Farewell, then. It is finished. I forgo
With this all right in you, even that of tears.
If I have spoken hardly, it will show
How much I loved you. With you disappears
A glory, a romance of many years.
What you may be henceforth I will not know.
The phantom of your presence on my fears
Is impotent at length for weal or woe.
Your past, your present, all alike must fade
In a new land of dreams where love is not.
Then kiss me and farewell. The choice is made
And we shall live to see the past forgot,
If not forgiven. See, I came to curse,
Yet stay to bless. I know not which is worse.

### FROM "ESTHER"

When I hear laughter from a tavern door,
   When I see crowds agape and in the rain
Watching on tiptoe and with stifled roar
   To see a rocket fired or a bull slain,
When misers handle gold, when orators
   Touch strong men's hearts with glory till they weep,
When cities deck their streets for barren wars
   Which have laid waste their youth, and when I keep
Calmly the count of my own life and see
   On what poor stuff my manhood's dreams were fed
Till I too learned what dole of vanity
   Will serve a human soul for daily bread,
—Then I remember that I once was young
And lived with Esther the world's gods among.

### LAUGHTER AND DEATH

There is no laughter in the natural world
Of beast or fish or bird, though no sad doubt
Of their futurity to them unfurled
Has dared to check the mirth-compelling shout.
The lion roars his solemn thunder out
To sleeping woods. The eagle screams her cry.
Even the lark must strain a serious throat
To hurl his blest defiance at the sky.

Fear, anger, jealousy, have found a voice.
Love's pain or rapture the brute bosoms swell.
Nature has symbols for her nobler joys,
Her nobler sorrows. Who has dared foretell
That only man, by some sad mockery,
Should learn to laugh who learns that he must die?

# Austin Dobson

(Henry) Austin Dobson was born at Plymouth, in 1840, and was educated in Wales and on the Continent. In 1856, he received a clerkship in The Board of Trade and remained in official life a great part of his life.

His first collection, *Vignettes in Rhyme* (1873), attracted attention by the ease with which the author managed his dexterous and sometimes difficult effects. With *Proverbs in Porcelain* (1877), *Old World Idylls* (1883), and *At the Sign of the Lyre* (1885), it was evident that a new master of *vers de société* had arisen. The crispness and clean delicacy of his verse made Dobson the peer of Prior, Praed, and sometimes of Thomas Hood.

During the latter part of his life, he devoted himself to a type of semi-biographical essay, intended to preserve the spirit of some nearly or wholly forgotten celebrity. In this form, his prose is scarcely less distinctive than his verse; his detailed and charmingly dispensed knowledge of the time of Queen Anne gives to his writings its own special flavor of "archaic gentility."

His *Complete Poetical Works,* contained in a volume of over five hundred closely printed pages, display his resourcefulness in all modes, especially the French forms. Although most of his rhymes are charming rather than profound, certain pages, like the famous rondeaux "In After Days" and "Before Sedan," are memorable for their serious clarity. "Ars Victrix" is something more than an admonition; it is a craftsman's confession of faith which any artist might heed.

Once in a while, as in "The Prayer of the Swine to Circe" and "The Sick Man and the Birds," Dobson attempted a note wholly solemn, but in spite of the occasional pathos masked in graceful dominos, he is enjoyed most—and deservedly so— for the frivolous triolets made of rose-leaves, the lacy rondels, and the ballades compounded of nothing graver than "the ripple of laughing rhyme."

Dobson died just after having passed the height of popularity, September 3, 1921.

## FAREWELL, RENOWN!

Farewell, Renown! Too fleeting flower,
That grows a year to last an hour;
  Prize of the race's dust and heat,
  Too often trodden under feet,—
Why should I court your "barren dower"?

Nay; had I Dryden's angry power,
The thews of Ben, the wind of Gower,
  Not less my voice should still repeat
    "Farewell, Renown!"

Farewell! Because the Muses' bower
Is filled with rival brows that lower;
  Because, howe'er his pipe be sweet,
  The Bard, that "pays," must please the
    street;

But most . . . because the grapes are sour—
    "Farewell, Renown!"

## BEFORE SEDAN

*"The dead hand clasped a letter."*
    —SPECIAL CORRESPONDENCE.

Here in this leafy place
  Quiet he lies,
Cold with his sightless face
  Turned to the skies;
'Tis but another dead;
All you can say is said.

Carry his body hence,—
  Kings must have slaves;

Kings climb to eminence
  Over men's graves:
So this man's eye is dim;—
  Throw the earth over him.

What was the white you touched,
  There, at his side?
Paper his hand had clutched
  Tight ere he died;—
Message or wish, may be;
Smooth the folds out and see.

Hardly the worst of us
  Here could have smiled!
Only the tremulous
  Words of a child;
Prattle, that has for stops
Just a few ruddy drops.

Look. She is sad to miss,
  Morning and night,
His—her dead father's—kiss;
  Tries to be bright,
Good to mamma, and sweet.
That is all. "Marguerite."

Ah, if beside the dead
  Slumbered the pain!
Ah, if the hearts that bled
  Slept with the slain!
If the grief died;—but no.
Death will not have it so.

### ROSE-LEAVES

#### A Kiss

Rose kissed me today.
Will she kiss me tomorrow?
Let it be as it may,
Rose kissed me today

But the pleasure gives way
  To a savor of sorrow.
Rose kissed me today,—
  *Will* she kiss me tomorrow?

#### A Greek Gift

Here's a present for Rose,
  How pleased she is looking!
Is it verse? Is it prose?
  Here's a present for Rose!
"*Plats,*" "*Entrées,*" and "*Rôts,*"—
  Why, it's "Gouffé on Cooking"!
*Here's* a present for Rose,
  How *pleased* she is looking.

#### "Urceus Exit"

I intended an Ode,
  And it turned to a Sonnet.
It began à la mode,
I intended an Ode;
But Rose crossed the road
  In her latest new bonnet;
I intended an Ode;
  And it turned to a Sonnet.

### IN VAIN TODAY

In vain today I scrape and blot:
  The nimble words, the phrases neat,
  Decline to mingle or to meet;
My skill is all foregone—forgot.

He will not canter, walk nor trot,
  My Pegasus. I spur, I beat,
    In vain today!

And yet 'twere sure the saddest lot
  That I should fail to leave complete
  One poor . . . the rhyme suggests "con-
    ceit!"
Alas! 'Tis all too clear I'm not
    In *vein* today.

### THE BALLADE OF PROSE AND RHYME

When the ways are heavy with mire and rut,
  In November fogs, in December snows,
When the North Wind howls, and the doors are shut,—
  There is place and enough for the pains of prose;

But whenever a scent from the whitethorn blows,
  And the jasmine-stars at the casement climb,
  And a Rosalind-face at the lattice shows,
Then hey!—for the ripple of laughing rhyme!

When the brain gets dry as an empty nut,
  When the reason stands on its squarest toes,
When the mind (like a beard) has a "formal cut,"—
    There is place and enough for the pains of prose;
  But whenever the May-blood stirs and glows,
And the young year draws to the "golden prime,"
  And Sir Romeo sticks in his ear a rose,
Then hey!—for the ripple of laughing rhyme!

In a theme where the thoughts have a pedant-strut,
  In a changing quarrel of "Ayes" and "Noes,"
In a starched procession of "If" and "But,"—
    There is place and enough for the pains of prose;
  But wherever a soft glance softer grows,
And the light hours dance to the trysting-time,
  And the secret is told "that no one knows,"
Then hey!—for the ripple of laughing rhyme!

*Envoy*

In the work-a-day world, for its needs and woes,
  There is place and enough for the pains of prose;
  But whenever the May-bells clash and chime,
Then hey!—for the ripple of laughing rhyme!

### RONDEL: THE WANDERER

Love comes back to his vacant dwelling,—
  The old, old Love that we knew of yore!
  We see him stand by the open door,
With his great eyes sad, and his bosom swell-
    ing.

He makes as though in our arms repelling,
  He fain would lie as he lay before;—
Love comes back to his vacant dwelling,—
  The old, old Love that we knew of yore!

Ah, who shall help us from over-spelling
  That sweet, forgotten, forbidden lore!
  E'en as we doubt in our heart once more,
With a rush of tears to our eyelids welling,
Love comes back to his vacant dwelling.

### IN AFTER DAYS

In after days when grasses high
O'ertop the stone where I shall lie,
  Though ill or well the world adjust
  My slender claim to honored dust,
I shall not question or reply.

I shall not see the morning sky;
I shall not hear the night-wind's sigh;
  I shall be mute, as all men must
    In after days!

But yet, now living, fain were I
That someone then should testify,
  Saying—"He held his pen in trust
  To Art, not serving shame or lust."
Will none?—Then let my memory die
    In after days!

ARS VICTRIX

(*Imitated from Théophile Gautier*)

Yes; when the ways oppose—
    When the hard means rebel,
Fairer the work out-grows,—
    More potent far the spell.

O Poet, then, forbear
    The loosely sandaled verse,
Choose rather thou to wear
    The buskin—strait and terse;

Leave to the tyro's hand
    The limp and shapeless style,
See that thy form demand
    The labor of the file.

Sculptor, do thou discard
    The yielding clay, consign
To Paros marble hard
    The beauty of thy line;

Model thy Satyr's face
    For bronze of Syracuse;
In the veined agate trace
    The profile of thy Muse.

Painter, that still must mix
    But transient tints anew,
Thou in the furnace fix
    The firm enamel's hue.

All passes. Art alone
    Enduring stays to us;
The Bust outlasts the throne,
    The Coin, Tiberius:

Even the gods must go;
    Only the lofty Rhyme
Not countless years o'erthrow,
    Not long array of time.

Paint, chisel, then, or write;
    But, that the work surpass,
With the hard fashion fight,
    With the resisting mass.

FAME

Fame is a food that dead men eat,—
I have no stomach for such meat.
In little light and narrow room,
They eat it in the silent tomb,
With no kind voice of comrade near
To bid the feaster be of cheer.

But friendship is a nobler thing,—
Of friendship it is good to sing.
For truly, when a man shall end,
He lives in memory of his friend,
Who doth his better part recall
And of his fault make funeral.

# Charles Doughty

CHARLES (MONTAGU) DOUGHTY was born in 1843 at Suffolk, and his eighty-three years were filled with a variety and strangeness rare in the strangest and most varied of lives. He studied for the law; then decided to enter the navy; turned from the sea to science; pursued his studies in geology through four universities. His educational career was equally mixed. He attended Cambridge and Oxford; went abroad to the universities of Leyden and Louvain. His travels brought him to Norway, where he lived twelve months, to Italy where he remained for several years, to France, Spain, Greece, Tunis, and Algeria. It was in Damascus he discovered a passion that was to last him the rest of his life: the passion for Arabia. After learning different Arabic dialects, he joined a caravan to make researches in old stone inscriptions. He became separated from his companions, wandered in the desert for two years, was taken prisoner, was released and, after almost fatal escapades, kept himself alive by treating sick Arabs with a small supply of drugs he still had.

In Doughty's late thirties, he began compiling, from notebooks kept during travel, his large prose work. In 1888 *Travels in Arabia Deserta* was first published. Though formidable in proportion and difficult in style, the book was recognized as a masterpiece. Its idiom proved the chief barrier to popularity—the language being a mixture of heavy Orientalism and early English archaism—and twenty years later Edward Garnett undertook an abridgement of the *magnum opus,* issuing it under the title of *Wanderings in Arabia* (1908). No book before or since—including T. E. Lawrence's *Revolt in the Desert* (1927)—has interpreted Arabia with such vivid power and indubitable authority.

Doughty's poetry—of which seven volumes appeared before his death—presents to the casual reader the same obstacles as his prose. *Dawn in Britain* (1906), the most imposing of his verse, *Adam Cast Forth* (1908), *The Titans* (1916), *Mansoul, or The Riddle of the World* (1920) are so rankly overgrown with archaic eccentricities as to seem, at first glance, impenetrable. But once Doughty's code is deciphered the reader is rewarded with a message whose whole import may still elude him, but whose impact is unquestionable. This is a poetry of accretion and accumulation, not a poetry of telling details. It is so knit in a kind of gnarled unity, so intricately epic, that brief quotation is impossible; one must go to any of his volumes—preferably to *Dawn in Britain*—to get the first full flavor of his quality.

Doughty died in his eighty-fourth year, in 1926.

# *Arthur O'Shaughnessy*

THE IRISH-ENGLISH singer, Arthur (William Edgar) O'Shaughnessy, was born in London in 1844. He was connected, for a while, with the British Museum, and was transferred later to the Department of Natural History. His first literary success, *Epic of Women* (1870), promised a splendid future for the young poet, a promise strengthened by *Music and Moonlight* (1874). Always delicate in health, his hopes were dashed by periods of illness and an early death in London in 1881.

The poems here reprinted, like all of O'Shaughnessy's, owe much to their editors. The "Ode," which is one of the classics of his age, originally had seven verses, the last four being mediocre versifying. When Palgrave compiled his *Golden Treasury,* he recognized the difference between the first three inspired stanzas and the others—and calmly and courageously dropped the final four.

William Alexander Percy performed a similar service for this singer who, nine-tenths of the time, was an undistinguished minor poet. It is a series of liberties taken in his *Poems of Arthur O'Shaughnessy* (1922), but the editorial omissions are justifiable. As Percy says, "In O'Shaughnessy's case, it is the only way to save him from himself and for posterity." One hesitates to approve such cavalier disposals; one would like to believe that a poet should be protected against editorial excisions. But no one ever called for the blue pencil more imperatively than O'Shaughnessy. He allowed his melodic stream, thin at the best, to trickle out into the merest flow of sound and all but disappear in rivulets of rhyme.

## ODE

We are the music-makers,
  And we are the dreamers of dreams,
Wandering by lone sea-breakers,
  And sitting by desolate streams;
World-losers and world-forsakers,
  On whom the pale moon gleams:
Yet we are the movers and shakers
  Of the world for ever, it seems.

With wonderful deathless ditties
We build up the world's great cities,
  And out of a fabulous story
  We fashion an empire's glory:
One man with a dream, at pleasure,
  Shall go forth and conquer a crown;
And three with a new song's measure
  Can trample an empire down.

We, in the ages lying
  In the buried past of the earth,
Built Nineveh with our sighing,
  And Babel itself with our mirth;
And o'erthrew them with prophesying
  To the old of the new world's worth;
For each age is a dream that is dying,
  Or one that is coming to birth.

## THE NEW LOVE AND THE OLD

I made another garden, yea,
  For my new Love:
I left the dead rose where it lay
  And set the new above.

Why did my Summer not begin?
  Why did my heart not haste?
My old Love came and walk'd therein,
  And laid the garden waste.

She enter'd with her weary smile,
  Just as of old;
She look'd around a little while
  And shiver'd with the cold:
Her passing touch was death to all,
  Her passing look a blight;
She made the white rose-petals fall,
  And turn'd the red rose white.

Her pale robe clinging to the grass
  Seem'd like a snake
That bit the grass and ground, alas!
  And a sad trail did make.
She went up slowly to the gate,
  And then, just as of yore,
She turn'd back at the last to wait
  And say farewell once more.

## DOOM

In either mood, to bless or curse
  God bringeth forth the breath of man;
No angel sire, no woman nurse
  Shall change the work that God began

One spirit shall be like a star,
  He shall delight to honor one:
Another spirit he shall mar:
  None shall undo what God hath done.

# Gerard Manley Hopkins

GERARD MANLEY HOPKINS was born in 1844, became a Jesuit, and was an instructor in Greek and Greek meters at University College in Dublin. He was, in addition, a painter and a musician of no little ability, and his various gifts equipped him to be an innovator in poetic structure. Although he wrote much during an intensely spiritual life, none of his poetry appeared during his lifetime, and it was not until thirty years after his death that his extraordinary verse was collected. Hopkins died in 1889 and the world was not given the *Poems of Gerard Hopkins, Now First Published, with Notes by Robert Bridges* until 1919. Many of the verses in this posthumous volume were deciphered from manuscript by the

Poet-Laureate and it is to him that one must be grateful for rescuing the work of a most original though complicated mind from oblivion.

A casual reader of Hopkins should expect obstacles; he must be prepared for difficulties that, at first, seem insuperable. He must be willing to accept a series of musical dissonances, compared to which the most cacophonous passages in Browning are limpid and bird-like. He must penetrate obscurities which are cloudy to the point of confusion. But he will be rewarded. Behind the tortured constructions and heaped-up epithets there is magnificence. In spite of the verbal excesses and idiomatic oddities there is an originality of vision which is nothing less than startling. In its intimate fancifulness, the imagery is sometimes reminiscent of the more controlled extravagances of Emily Dickinson. Like the New England poetess, Hopkins' poetry is sometimes eccentric, but it is always logical, never arbitrary or perverse.

Hopkins himself worked out a curious scheme of prosody (he even invented a system of signs to make plain the effects he wished to achieve) and his lines (as his own preface tells us) are "written in Running Rhythm, the common rhythm in English use, some in Sprung Rhythm (a free beat strongly suggestive of later *vers libre*) and some in a mixture of both." The peculiar beauty in his poems makes it lamentable that Hopkins (to quote his editor) "died when, to judge by his latest work, he was beginning to concentrate the force of all his luxuriant experiments in rhythm and diction, and castigate his art into a more reserved style." Even in the cloudiest of his effects there is a splendor, a rush of rhyme, a cataract of color, attained by scarcely any of his plainer-speaking contemporaries.

The most outspoken admirer of this highly imaginative and highly elliptical poetry must admit its structural awkwardness. Hopkins himself wrote, "No doubt my poetry errs on the side of oddness. I hope in time to have a more balanced and Miltonic style. But as air, melody, is what strikes me most of all in music, and design in painting, so design, pattern, or what I am in the habit of calling *inscape* is what above all I aim at in poetry. Now it is the virtue of design, pattern, or 'inscape' to be distinctive, and it is the vice of distinctiveness to become queer. This vice I cannot have escaped." Yet Dr. Robert Bridges has made too much of Hopkins' mannerisms. If these poems, Bridges comments, "were to be arraigned for errors of what might be called taste, they might be convicted of occasional affectation in metaphor, as where the hills are 'as a stallion stalwart, very-violet-sweet'" . . . As Robert Graves and Laura Riding inquire in *A Survey of Modernist Poetry,* "Why cannot what Dr. Bridges calls a fault of taste, an affectation, in the description of hills as 'a stallion stalwart, very-violet-sweet' be, with the proper sympathy for Hopkins' enthusiasm, appreciated as a phrase reconciling the two seemingly opposed qualities of mountains, their male, animal-like roughness and strength and, at the same time, their ethereal quality under soft light for which the violet in the gentle eye of the horse makes exactly the proper association?" That Bridges never understood Hopkins is proved by Bridges' other comments in the introduction, and emphasized by Hopkins' letters—Bridges having (significantly, it seems) destroyed his side of the correspondence.

Continually daring, Hopkins' work has never the note of ostentatious bravado. His boldness is instinctive; even such extraordinary departures as "Hurrahing in

Harvest" and "Felix Randal" are extensions of the sonnet form but not violations of its spirit.

One of the more enthusiastic disciples (C. Day Lewis) has compared Hopkins to Shakespeare, not only because of Hopkins' continual "re-creation of word and image," but because of the exuberant quality of his images.

> I caught this morning morning's minion, king-
> dom of daylight's Dauphin, dapple-dawn-drawn Falcon, in his riding
> Of the rolling level underneath him steady air.

In such lines Hopkins explores the limbo which divides the ridiculous from the sublime. Here is a riotous alliteration which even the prodigal Swinburne might have hesitated to use, and yet Hopkins lifts the device into grandeur. Here, and almost everywhere in his poetry, is the concealed music, the subtle modulation, which breaks down the current poetic speech and forms it into a new language. "The poetic language of an age," Hopkins wrote, improving on Wordsworth, "should be the current language heightened, to any degree heightened and unlike itself, but not an obsolete one." Such heightening sometimes causes the reader to confess his inability to follow the poet's vision, but, as Day Lewis remarked in *A Hope for Poetry,* "what obscurity we may find is due, not to a clouded imagination or an unsettled intellect, but to his lightning dashes from image to image, so quick that we are unable at first to perceive the points of contact."

Hopkins' epithets may seem erratic but they are actually if oddly precise. As with his punctuation, he could give a rule for everything, even for the frequent and deliberate omission of the relative pronoun which he dropped not only "to crowd out every merely grammatical or toneless element" but to stress the heavy accents of his verse. "The Habit of Perfection," "The Starlight Night," "The Golden Echo," its companion piece, "The Leaden Echo," and "God's Grandeur" will not be shaken out of the mind. If "emphasis seems to oust euphony" in a struggle of intense contractions, his style, pushed by the extremities of his theories, is a triumph of elisions. Far from being a "fascinating failure" (T. Earle Welby's summary), his poetry lifts exact if unfamiliar verity of phrase to a burning beauty.

Hopkins having found an audience thirty-five years after his death, his least fragments were collated and an enlarged edition of his *Poems* was issued in 1934. A year later there appeared *The Letters of Gerard Manley Hopkins to Robert Bridges* (1935) and *The Correspondence of Gerard Manley Hopkins and Richard Watson Dixon* (1935), two volumes rich in delicate humor, insight, and discrimination, possibly the finest criticism written in English. Memorable are his disposals of Dickens, Wordsworth, Tennyson—he called the Idylls "Charades of the Middle Ages"—and Swinburne of the "delirium-tremendous imagination." And who, after once reading his estimate of Browning, can forget that Browning has "a way of talking and making his people talk with the air and spirit of a man bouncing up from table with his mouth full of bread and cheese and saying that he meant to stand no blasted nonsense."

*Gerard Manley Hopkins: A Biography* (1934) by G. F. Lahey, and *Three Friends,* by Robert Bridges, memoirs of Digby Mackworth Dolben, Richard Watson Dixon and Henry Bradley, shed further light on this rich personality.

One of the most erudite critics and certainly the most inventive poet of his day—

such was the man who refused to fight for fame because, as a Jesuit, he had vowed to serve God. Like the things he loved most, he, too, was "counter, original, spare, strange," possibly the most original genius of his generation.

### PIED BEAUTY

Glory be to God for dappled things—
   For skies as couple-colored as a brinded cow;
     For rose-moles all in stipple upon trout that swim;
Fresh-firecoal chestnut-falls; finches' wings;
   Landscapes plotted and pieced—fold, fallow, and plow;
     And all trades, their gear and tackle and trim.
All things counter, original, spare, strange;
   Whatever is fickle, freckled (who knows how?)
     With swift, slow; sweet, sour; adazzle, dim;
He fathers-forth whose beauty is past change:
     Praise Him.

### THE HABIT OF PERFECTION

Elected Silence, sing to me
And beat upon my whorlèd ear,
Pipe me to pastures still, and be
The music that I care to hear.

Shape nothing, lips; be lovely-dumb;
It is the shut, the curfew sent
From there where all surrenders come
Which only makes you eloquent.

Be shellèd, eyes, with double dark
And find the uncreated light:
This ruck and reel which you remark
Coils, keeps, and teases simple sight.

Palate, the hatch of tasty lust,
Desire not to be rinsed with wine:

The can must be so sweet, the crust
So fresh that come in fasts divine!

Nostrils, your careless breath that spend
Upon the stir and keep of pride,
What relish shall the censers send
Along the sanctuary side!

O feel-of-primrose hands, O feet
That want the yield of plushy sward,
But you shall walk the golden street
And you unhouse and house the Lord.

And, Poverty, be thou the bride
And now the marriage feast begun,
And lily-colored clothes provide
Your spouse not labored-at nor spun.

### THE LEADEN ECHO

How to keep—is there any, any, is there none such, nowhere known, some bow or
    brooch or braid or brace, lace, latch or catch or key to keep
Back beauty, keep it, beauty, beauty, beauty, . . . from vanishing away?
Oh, is there no frowning of these wrinkles, ranked wrinkles deep,
Down? no waving-off of these most mournful messengers, still messengers, sad and
    stealing messengers of gray?
No, there's none, there's none—oh, no, there's none!
Nor can you long be, what you now are, called fair—
Do what you may do, do what you may,
And wisdom is early to despair:

Be beginning; since, no, nothing can be done
To keep at bay
Age and age's evils—hoar hair,
Ruck and wrinkle, drooping, dying, death's worst, winding sheets, tombs and
    worms, and tumbling to decay;
So be beginning, be beginning to despair.
Oh, there's none—no, no, no, there's none:
      Be beginning to despair, to despair,
      Despair, despair, despair, despair.


### THE GOLDEN ECHO

    Spare!
There is one, yes, I have one (Hush there!);
Only not within seeing of the sun,
Not within the singeing of the strong sun,
Tall sun's tingeing, or treacherous the tainting of the earth's air,
Somewhere elsewhere there is ah, well, where! one,
One. Yes, I can tell such a key, I do know such a place,
Where whatever's prized and passed of us, everything that's fresh and fast-flying
    of us, seems to us sweet of us and swiftly away with, done away with, undone,
Undone, done with, soon done with, and yet dearly and dangerously sweet
Of us, the wimpled-water-dimpled, not-by-morning-matchèd face,
The flower of beauty, fleece of beauty, too too apt to, ah! to fleet,
Never fleets more, fastened with the tenderest truth
To its own best being and its loveliness of youth: it is an everlastingness of, O it is
    an all youth!
Come then, your ways and airs and looks, locks, maiden gear, gallantry and gayety
    and grace,
Winning ways, airs innocent, maiden manners, sweet looks, loose locks, long locks,
    lovelocks, gaygear, going gallant, girlgrace—
Resign them, sign them, seal them, send them, motion them with breath,
And with sighs soaring, soaring sighs deliver
Then; beauty-in-the-ghost, deliver it, early now, long before death
Give beauty back, beauty, beauty, beauty, back to God, beauty's self and beauty's
    giver.
See; not a hair is, not an eyelash, not the least lash lost; every hair
Is, hair of the head, numbered.
Nay, what we had lighthanded left in surely the mere mold
Will have waked and have waxed and have walked with the wind whatwhile we
    slept,
This side, that side hurling a heavyheaded hundredfold
What while we, while we slumbered.
O then, weary then why should we tread? O why are we so haggard at the heart,
    so care-coiled, care-killed, so fagged, so fashed, so cogged, so cumbered,
When the thing we freely forfeit is kept with fonder a care,
Fonder a care kept than we could have kept it, kept
Far with fonder a care (and we, we should have lost it) finer, fonder
A care kept.—Where kept? Do but tell us where kept, where.—
Yonder.—What high as that! We follow, now we follow.—Yonder, yes, yonder,
    yonder,
Yonder.

### GOD'S GRANDEUR

The world is charged with the grandeur of God.
　It will flame out, like shining from shook foil;
　It gathers to a greatness, like the ooze of oil
Crushed. Why do men then now not reck his rod?
Generations have trod, have trod, have trod;
　And all is seared with trade; bleared, smeared with toil;
　And, wears man's smudge and shares man's smell: the soil
Is bare now, nor can foot feel, being shod.

And for all this, nature is never spent;
　There lives the dearest freshness deep down things;
And though the last lights off the black West went
　Oh, morning, at the brown brink eastward, springs—
Because the Holy Ghost over the bent
　World broods with warm breast and with ah! bright wings.

### THE STARLIGHT NIGHT

Look at the stars! look, look up at the skies!
　O look at all the fire-folk sitting in the air!
　The bright boroughs, the circle-citadels there!
Down in dim woods the diamond delves! the elves'-eyes!
The gray lawns cold where gold, where quickgold lies!
　Wind-beat whitebeam! airy abeles set on a flare!
　Flake-doves sent floating forth at a farmyard scare!
Ah, well! it is all a purchase, all is a prize.
Buy then! bid then!—What?—Prayer, patience, alms, vows.
Look, look: a May-mess, like on orchard boughs!
　Look! March-bloom, like on mealed-with-yellow sallows!
These are indeed the barn; withindoors house
The shocks. This piece-bright paling shuts the spouse
　Christ home, Christ and his mother and all his hallows.

### SPRING

Nothing is so beautiful as spring—
　When weeds, in wheels, shoot long and lovely and lush;
　Thrush's eggs look little low heavens, and thrush
Through the echoing timber does so rinse and wring
The ear, it strikes like lightning to hear him sing;
　The glassy peartree leaves and blooms, they brush
　The descending blue; that blue is all in a rush
With richness; the racing lambs too have fair their fling.

What is all this juice and all this joy?
　A strain of the earth's sweet being in the beginning
In Eden garden.—Have, get, before it cloy,
　Before it cloud, Christ, lord, and sour with sinning,
Innocent mind and Mayday in girl and boy,
　Most, O maid's child, thy choice and worthy the winning.

### HURRAHING IN HARVEST

Summer ends now; now, barbarous in beauty, the stooks rise
   Around; up above, what wind-walks! what lovely behavior
   Of silk-sack clouds! has wilder, willful-wavier
Meal-drift molded ever and melted across skies?

I walk, I lift up, I lift up heart, eyes,
   Down all that glory in the heavens to glean our Saviour;
   And, eyes, heart, what looks, what lips yet gave you a
Rapturous love's greeting of realer, of rounder replies?

And the azurous hung hills are his world-wielding shoulder
   Majestic—as a stallion stalwart, very-violet-sweet!—
These things, these things were here and but the beholder
   Wanting; which two when they once meet,
The heart rears wings bold and bolder
   And hurls for him, O half hurls earth for him off under his feet.

### THE CAGED SKYLARK

As a dare-gale skylark scanted in a dull cage
   Man's mounting spirit in his bone-house, mean house, dwells—
   That bird beyond the remembering his free fells;
This in drudgery, day-laboring-out life's age.

Though aloft on turf or perch or poor low stage,
   Both sing sometimes the sweetest, sweetest spells,
   Yet both droop deadly sometimes in their cells
Or wring their barriers in bursts of fear or rage.

Not that the sweet-fowl, song-fowl, needs no rest—
   Why, hear him, hear him babble and drop down to his nest,
   But his own nest, wild nest, no prison.

Man's spirit will be flesh-bound when found at best,
   But uncumbered: meadow-down is not distressed
   For a rainbow footing it nor he for his bones risen.

### MOONRISE

I awoke in the Midsummer not to call night, in the white and the walk of the
   morning:
The moon, dwindled and thinned to the fringe of a finger-nail held to the candle,
Or paring of paradisaïcal fruit, lovely in waning but lusterless,
Stepped from the stool, drew back from the barrow, of dark Maenefa the mountain;
A cusp still clasped him, a fluke yet fanged him, entangled him, not quit utterly.
This was the prized, the desirable sight, unsought, presented so easily,
Parted me leaf and leaf, divided me, eyelid and eyelid of slumber.

## FELIX RANDAL

Felix Randal the farrier, O he is dead then? my duty all ended,
Who have watched his mold of man, big-boned and hardy-handsome
Pining, pining, till time when reason rambled in it and some
Fatal four disorders, fleshed there, all contended?

Sickness broke him. Impatient he cursed at first, but mended
Being anointed and all; though a heavenlier heart began some
Months earlier, since I had our sweet reprieve and ransom
Tendered to him. Ah, well, God rest him all road ever he offended!

This seeing the sick endears them to us, us too it endears.
My tongue had taught thee comfort, touch had quenched thy tears,
Thy tears that touched my heart, child, Felix, poor Felix Randal;

How far from then forethought of, all thy more boisterous years,
When thou at the random grim forge, powerful amidst peers,
Didst fettle for the great gray drayhorse his bright and battering sandal!

## TO HIS WATCH

### (*unfinished*)

Mortal my mate, bearing my rock-a-heart
Warm beat with cold beat company, shall I
Earlier or you fail at our force, and lie
The ruins of, rifled, once a world of art?
The telling time our task is; time's some part,
Not all, but we were framed to fail and die—
One spell and well that one. There, ah, thereby
Is comfort's carol of all or woe's worst smart.

Field-flown the departed day no morning brings
Saying "This was yours" with her, but new one, worse,
And then that last and shortest . . .

## THE CUCKOO

Repeat that, repeat,
Cuckoo, bird, and open ear wells, heart-springs, delightfully sweet,
With a ballad, with a ballad, a rebound
Off trundled timber and scoops of the hillside ground, hollow hollow hollow ground:
The whole landscape flushes on a sudden at a sound.

## HEAVEN-HAVEN

### A Nun Takes the Veil

I have desired to go
   Where springs not fail,
To fields where flies no sharp and sided hail,
   And a few lilies blow.

And I have asked to be
Where no storms come,
Where the green swell is in the havens dumb
And out of the swing of the sea.

# Robert Bridges

ROBERT (SEYMOUR) BRIDGES was born October 23, 1844. He was educated at Eton and Corpus Christi, Oxford, and, after having traveled, studied medicine, taking the post of Casualty Surgeon at St. Bartholomew's Hospital, London. He retired from the medical profession in 1882 to devote himself entirely to literature. Although many more prominent poets were suggested for the office, the classic restraint of his verse won him the highest official honor: he became Poet Laureate in 1913. So often has the Laureateship been nothing more than a political prize that it is gratifying to observe that the award went to one distinguished for nothing more zealous than his art. As essayist, he wrote considerably for the Society of Pure English which, largely through his efforts, was founded in 1913. He was among the first to advocate a resumption of friendly relations between the English and German universities after the war—and was scolded in Parliament for doing so. His interests were unusually varied and included cricket, hymnology (he collaborated in the editing of a hymnal), spoken English, reformed spelling, the encouragement of fellow poets (Hopkins, for example), and music, especially music for the harpsichord. He died, after a short illness, in his seventy-sixth year, on April 21, 1930.

The subjects of his many volumes are indicative of his expression; a few of the titles are: *Prometheus the Firegiver; Eros and Psyche; Achilles in Scyros; The Feast of Bacchus. Poems* appeared as early as 1873. His more recent work, although not strictly modern, is closer in spirit to our own time. The distinguishing features of his *Shorter Poems* (1894) are a subtlety of rhythm, a precise command of metrical delicacies. It is, in fact, as a metrician that his work is most interesting; even his most academic lines bear a beauty of pattern. Apart from the skill of versification, there are many delights for the most casual reader in his collected *Poetical Works* (excluding the dramas) which appeared in 1913.

Robert Hillyer, the American poet and teacher, has made a study of Bridges' poems and a particularly delicate analysis of his major work. The following paragraphs are a summary of Mr. Hillyer's findings and have been prepared by him for this volume.

"Until the publication of *The Testament of Beauty* (1929)," writes Mr. Hillyer, "the genius of Robert Bridges was known to comparatively few. At the time of his appointment as Poet Laureate, *The New York Times* published a querulous editorial to the effect that Bridges was a nonentity. The same newspaper in recent editorials has more than once admiringly quoted the late laureate. In spite of the prolonged neglect of his earlier works on the part of the large public, most of the poets of England and a few in America recognized him as a master. W. B. Yeats devoted enthusiastic essays to the poetic dramas of Bridges, and the future laureate's *Shorter Poems* were accounted the height of lyric artistry. Some of these, such as 'A Passer-by,' 'London Snow,' and 'Awake, My Heart, to Be Loved,' found a more general audience; but, for the most part, Bridges remained a poet's poet until the publication of *The Testament of Beauty.*

"The reasons for this are simple. In the first place, Bridges, like Spenser before him, did not hesitate to employ archaic diction and syntax where he desired to gain a particular effect. In England the practice is frowned on (we are reminded of Ben Jonson's outburst against Spenser's 'Chaucerisms'), and in America it is taboo. Secondly, his diction is so simple and lucid that a casual reader might easily glance through one of his poems convinced that the work was merely conventional phrasing. Thirdly, in Bridges we find no violence—the mood most congenial to many today. To quote Mr. Charles Williams, whose essay on Bridges in *Poetry at Present* is well worth study: 'Love, diligence, wit, justice, courage, temperance, reason: these are the qualities Mr. Bridges praises and recommends to the young adventurer. They are, transmuted into poetry, the qualities of his verse; they are the analyzed elements of its beauty as it praises Beauty. Besides great art, a few things are preëminent in his poetic knowledge—the English landscape, man in society, Hellenism, solitude, piety. These things cause a profound and still delight. But it is a delight which may require a certain similarity of temperament or a certain prolonged discipline before it can be accepted, especially from a reader used to more violent effects.' Another obstacle between the careless or tone-deaf reader is yet one of the greatest virtues in the poetry of Bridges,—a muted, delicate music which yields its full loveliness only to one who is willing to study this verse as a virtuoso might study an intricate fugue.

"Both those who admire and those who dislike the poetry of Bridges agree on one point: that technically he was one of the masters of English verse. His experiments within the tradition are bolder and more informed than most of those outside it. His skill has often been cited against him by the school of modern critics who prefer verse to be slip-shod or, as they would express it, 'unacademic.' Starting early with Gerard Manley Hopkins and other friends a systematic study of what could be done in English meters without breaking down the instrument, he explored possibilities which, though not so obviously startling as Hopkins's 'sprung rhythm,' were subtly quite as adventurous. His main impulse came from Classical prosody, and his early adaptations of quantity to English metrics have never been equaled. In his later work, notably in the 'loose Alexandrines' of *The Testament of Beauty,* he combined with this strong quantitative influence an element wholly derived from our own ancient verse; that is, great liberty in the number of syllables within the single line. Professor Garrod, in his otherwise excellent essay on Bridges, makes one curious slip: he asserts that the versification of *The Testament of Beauty* was quite unprepared for in the earlier works. On the contrary, the volume just preceding, *New Verse* (a title to be taken quite literally as indicating a new technique), anticipates the loose rhythms of the *Testament,* though generally in a five-foot rather than a six-foot line. One superficial flaw mars Bridges's masterpiece. Like the sixteenth century poet Stanyhurst, Bridges had a notion that the length of syllables could be indicated by different spellings. The system is pedantic and sets up a typographical obstacle between the reader and the poem. (Quotation from the work is impossible, partly because of its character, partly because Bridges left instructions prohibiting the use of extracts.)

"Space forbids any detailed analysis of this great work. It has been compared to Wordsworth's *Prelude* and to Lucretius's *De Rerum Natura*. The main theme, based on Christian teleology, is the evolution of the human soul toward perfection, the reunion of all things in God through the growth of spiritual love. The poet shows how in Man the blind instincts of Nature become transformed, through influences such as that of beauty, into spiritual forces. Thus, the indiscriminate mating of lower forms of life rises to love inspired by the beauty of the beloved, and in higher natures becomes completely transmuted, as in Dante's love for Beatrice. The theme is developed by the high logic of poetry, which combines with the philosopher's learning and reasoning, the persuasion of beauty itself."

### A PASSER-BY

Whither, O splendid ship, thy white sails crowding,
    Leaning across the bosom of the urgent West,
That fearest nor sea rising nor sky clouding,
    Whither away, fair rover, and what thy quest?
    Ah! soon, when Winter has all our vales opprest,
When skies are cold and misty, and hail is hurling,
    Wilt thou glide on the blue Pacific, or rest
In a summer haven asleep, thy white sails furling.

I there before thee, in the country that well thou knowest,
    Already arrived am inhaling the odorous air:
I watch thee enter unerringly where thou goest,
    And anchor queen of the strange shipping there,
    Thy sails for awnings spread, thy masts bare;
Nor is aught from the foaming reef to the snow-capp'd, grandest
    Peak, that is over the feathery palms, more fair
Than thou, so upright, so stately, and still thou standest.

And yet, O splendid ship, unhail'd and nameless,
    I know not if, aiming a fancy, I rightly divine
That thou hast a purpose joyful, a courage blameless,
    Thy port assured in a happier land than mine.
    But for all I have given thee, beauty enough is thine,
As thou, aslant with trim tackle and shrouding,
    From the proud nostril curve of a prow's line
In the offing scatterest foam, thy white sails crowding.

### AWAKE, MY HEART, TO BE LOVED

Awake, my heart, to be loved, awake, awake!
The darkness silvers away, the morn doth break,
It leaps in the sky: unrisen lusters slake
The o'ertaken moon. Awake, O heart, awake!

She too that loveth awaketh and hopes for thee;
Her eyes already have sped the shades that flee,
Already they watch the path thy feet shall take:
Awake, O heart, to be loved, awake, awake!

And if thou tarry from her,—if this could be,—
She cometh herself, O heart, to be loved, to thee;
For thee would unashamèd herself forsake:
Awake to be loved, my heart, awake, awake!

Awake! the land is scattered with light, and see,
Uncanopied sleep is flying from field and tree:
And blossoming boughs of April in laughter shake;
Awake, O heart, to be loved, awake, awake!

Lo all things wake and tarry and look for thee:
She looketh and saith, "O sun, now bring him to me.
Come more adored, O adored, for his coming's sake,
And awake, my heart, to be loved: awake, awake!"

## O WEARY PILGRIMS

### (from "The Growth of Love")

O weary pilgrims, chanting of your woe,
That turn your eyes to all the peaks that shine,
Hailing in each the citadel divine
The which ye thought to have entered long ago;
Until at length your feeble steps and slow
Falter upon the threshold of the shrine,
And your hearts overburdened doubt in fine
Whether it be Jerusalem or no:
Disheartened pilgrims, I am one of you;
For, having worshiped many a barren face,
I scarce now greet the goal I journeyed to:
I stand a pagan in the holy place;
Beneath the lamp of truth I am found untrue,
And question with the God that I embrace.

## THOU DIDST DELIGHT MY EYES

Thou didst delight my eyes:
Yet who am I? nor first
Nor last nor best, that durst
Once dream of thee for prize;
Nor this the only time
Thou shalt set love to rhyme.

Thou didst delight my ear:
Ah! little praise; thy voice
Makes other hearts rejoice,
Makes all ears glad that hear;
And short my joy: but yet,
O song, do not forget.

For what wert thou to me?
How shall I say? The moon,
That poured her midnight noon
Upon his wrecking sea;—
A sail, that for a day
Has cheered the castaway.

WINTER NIGHTFALL

The day begins to droop,—
  Its course is done:
But nothing tells the place
  Of the setting sun.

The hazy darkness deepens,
  And up the lane
You may hear, but cannot see,
  The homing wain.

An engine pants and hums
  In the farm hard by:
Its lowering smoke is lost
  In the lowering sky.

The soaking branches drip,
  And all night through

The dropping will not cease
  In the avenue.

A tall man there in the house
  Must keep his chair:
He knows he will never again
  Breathe the spring air:

His heart is worn with work;
  He is giddy and sick
If he rise to go as far
  As the nearest rick:

He thinks of his morn of life,
  His hale, strong years;
And braves as he may the night
  Of darkness and tears.

LONDON SNOW

When men were all asleep the snow came flying,
In large white flakes falling on the city brown,
Stealthily and perpetually settling and loosely lying,
  Hushing the latest traffic of the drowsy town;
Deadening, muffling, stifling its murmurs failing;
Lazily and incessantly floating down and down;
  Silently sifting and veiling road, roof and railing;
Hiding difference, making unevenness even,
Into angles and crevices softly drifting and sailing.
  All night it fell, and when full inches seven
It lay in the depth of its uncompacted lightness,
The clouds blew off from a high and frosty heaven;
  And all woke earlier for the unaccustomed brightness
Of the winter dawning, the strange unheavenly glare:
The eye marveled—marveled at the dazzling whiteness;
  The ear hearkened to the stillness of the solemn air;
No sound of wheel rumbling nor of foot falling,
And the busy morning cries came thin and spare.
  Then boys I heard, as they went to school, calling;
They gathered up the crystal manna to freeze
Their tongues with tasting, their hands with snow-balling;
  Or rioted in a drift, plunging up to the knees;
Or peering up from under the white-mossed wonder,
"O look at the trees!" they cried. "O look at the trees!"
  With lessened load, a few carts creak and blunder,
Following along the white deserted way,
A country company long dispersed asunder:
  When now already the sun, in pale display
Standing by Paul's high dome, spread forth below

His sparkling beams, and awoke the stir of the day.
   For now doors open, and war is waged with the snow;
And trains of somber men, past tale of number,
Tread long brown paths, as toward their toil they go:
   But even for them awhile no cares encumber
Their minds diverted; the daily word is unspoken,
The daily thoughts of labor and sorrow slumber
   At the sight of the beauty that greets them, for the charm they
      have broken.

## NIGHTINGALES

Beautiful must be the mountains whence ye come,
And bright in the fruitful valleys the streams wherefrom
    Ye learn your song:
Where are those starry woods? O might I wander there,
  Among the flowers, which in that heavenly air
    Bloom the year long!

Nay, barren are those mountains and spent the streams:
Our song is the voice of desire, that haunts our dreams,
    A throe of the heart,
Whose pining visions dim, forbidden hopes profound,
  No dying cadence nor long sigh can sound,
    For all our art.

Alone, aloud in the raptured ear of men
We pour our dark nocturnal secret; and then,
    As night is withdrawn
From these sweet-springing meads and bursting boughs of May,
  Dream, while the innumerable choir of day
    Welcome the dawn.

### I HAVE LOVED FLOWERS

I have loved flowers that fade,
Within whose magic tents
Rich hues have marriage made
With sweet unmemoried scents:
A honeymoon delight,—
A joy of love at sight,
That ages in an hour:—
My song be like a flower!

I have loved airs that die
Before their charm is writ
Along a liquid sky
Trembling to welcome it.
Notes that with pulse of fire
Proclaim the spirit's desire,
Then die, and are nowhere:—
My song be like an air!

Die, song, die like a breath,
And wither as a bloom:
Fear not a flowery death,
Dread not an airy tomb!
Fly with delight, fly hence!
'Twas thine love's tender sense
To feast; now on thy bier
Beauty shall shed a tear.

### NIMIUM FORTUNATUS

I have lain in the sun,
I have toil'd as I might,
I have thought as I would,
And now it is night.

My bed full of sleep,
My heart of content
For friends that I met
The way that I went.

I welcome fatigue
While frenzy and care
Like thin summer clouds
Go melting in air.

To dream as I may
And awake when I will
With the song of the birds
And the sun on the hill.

Or death—were it death—
To what should I wake
Who loved in my home
All life for its sake?

What good have I wrought?
I laugh to have learned
That joy cannot come
Unless it be earned;

For a happier lot
Than God giveth me
It never hath been
Nor ever shall be.

# Michael Field

MICHAEL FIELD was the pen-name adopted by two women: an aunt, Katherine Harris Bradley, born in 1846, and her niece, Edith Emma Cooper, born in 1862. The affection between the two was unusually deep; it is evident that many of their poems were written to each other. But, during their lifetime, few discovered the secret of their disguise. Robert Browning was the first to hail Michael Field with enthusiasm, and the early work had a great vogue in the 'eighties. Reviewers hailed Field's *Callirhoë* as a work of genius; Swinburne and Meredith were lavish in praise of subsequent volumes. But—possibly due to the waning interest in classicism, possibly because of their overproductiveness—the twinned poets lost the public's interest; "the literary world," to quote Sturge Moore, "having been plunged into a disproprotionate eagerness, next plunged into an equally unintelligent neglect."

Between 1887 and 1912, the two authors published more than twenty-five plays and eight volumes of poems; two other books were issued posthumously. In 1913, Edith Cooper died of cancer, a disease which she had concealed from her aunt and fellow-worker; a few months later, in 1914, the older, Katherine Bradley, died of the same illness.

The best known of Michael Field's volumes is the set of adaptations from Sappho entitled *Long Ago*. But, though the collections of their original verse suffer from unevenness and lack of condensation, a few lyrics, such as the one beginning "I could wish to be dead," are poignantly direct and such an outcry as "Descent from the Cross" burns with an ecstatic fire. *The Accuser and Other Plays* (1911) contains the most vivid of the dramas; *Dedicated* (1914) and *In the Name of Time* (1919) were issued after the death of the two collaborators.

Though Michael Field's work can never be popular, it should not be neglected. Even the greater figures of the period cannot dwarf what is large and essentially noble in the best of the monologues and dramas. What militates against them is a mood prevailingly overcast. This work is somber, for Michael Field was a tragic rather than a lyric poet, obsessed with the struggle of man against the apathy of nature. A carefully selected edition in one volume is needed in this country. It is lamentable that a body of work so high in purpose, so rare in attainment remains practically unknown.

*A Selection from the Poems of Michael Field* with a Preface by T. Sturge Moore was published by The Poetry Bookshop in 1923. An invaluable study, *Michael Field,* the result of years of patient labor by Mary Sturgeon, appeared in 1922.

### THE TRAGIC MARY QUEEN
### OF SCOTS

I could wish to be dead!
Too quick with life were the tears I shed,
Too sweet for tears is the life I led;
And, ah, too lonesome my marriage-bed!
I could wish to be dead.

I could wish to be dead,
For just a word that rings in my head;
Too dear, too dear are the words he said,
They must never be rememberèd.
I could wish to be dead.

I could wish to be dead:
The wish to be loved is all mis-read,
And to love, one learns when one is wed,

Is to suffer bitter shame; instead
I could wish to be dead.

### AFTER SOUFRIÈRE[1]

It is not grief or pain;
But like the even dropping of the rain,
That thou art gone.
It is not like a grave
To weep upon;
But like the rise and falling of a wave
When the vessel's gone.
It is like the sudden void
When the city is destroyed,
Where the sun shone:
There is neither grief nor pain,
But the wide waste come again.

### TOO LATE

"O Virgins, very lovely in your troop,
O Virgins, very lovely, very white,
How is it that your lilies droop?
How is it that the lamps you bear are not alight?

"Why are you bending downward from the hill?
Bright is it on the hill as for a feast."
Trembling they sped as to fulfill
Some grievous prophecy; nor heeded me the least.

Downward they passed. . . . Oh, they were very fair,
But stricken as the frosted leaves to doom!
Their eyes I saw. . . . Bright with despair
Their eyes, and very lamps to light them to their doom.

Full were their looks of love and sorrowing
As they passed by me, shaking out a spell
Of sighs, of balms. And is it such a thing
Can be, that they were hurrying to Hell?

[1] T. Sturge Moore says: "I believe this title to refer to a volcanic cataclysm in which the town of Soufrière in Guadeloupe was destroyed, and which had occurred just before the poem was written."

### METE ME OUT MY LONELINESS

Come, mete me out my loneliness, O wind,
For I would know
How far the living who must stay behind
Are from the dead who go.

Eternal Passer-by, I feel there is
In thee a stir,
A strength to span the yawning distances
From her gravestone to her.

### MORE GOLD THAN GOLD

#### (*After Sappho*)

Yea, gold is son of Zeus: no rust
  Its timeless light can stain;
The worm that brings man's flesh to dust
  Assaults its strength in vain:
More gold than gold the love I sing,
A hard, inviolable thing.

Men say the passions should grow old
  With waning years; my heart
Is incorruptible as gold,
  'Tis my immortal part;
Nor is there any god can lay
On love the finger of decay.

### DESCENT FROM THE CROSS[1]

Come down from the Cross, my soul, and save thyself—come down!
Thou wilt be free as wind. None meeting thee will know
How thou wert hanging stark, my soul, outside the town,
Thou wilt fare to and fro;
Thy feet in grass will smell of faithful thyme; thy head. . . .
Think of the thorns, my soul—how thou wilt cast them off,
With shudder at the bleeding clench they hold!
But on their wounds thou wilt a balsam spread,
And over that a verdurous circle rolled
With gathered violets, sweet bright violets, sweet
As incense of the thyme on thy free feet;
A wreath thou wilt not give away, nor wilt thou doff.

Come down from the Cross, my soul, and save thyself; yea, move
As scudding swans pass lithely on a seaward stream!
Thou wilt have everything; thou wert made great to love;
Thou wilt have ease for every dream;
No nails with fang will hold thy purpose to one aim;

[1] This poem is from *Poems of Adoration* (1912), which was entirely written (with the exception of a few pages) by Edith Cooper after her conversion.

There will be arbors round about thee, not one trunk
Against thy shoulders pressed and burning them with hate,
Yea, burning with intolerable flame.
O lips, such noxious vinegar have drunk,
There are, through valley-woods and mountain glades,
Rivers where thirst in naked prowess wades;
And there are wells in solitude whose chill no hour abates!

Come down from the Cross, my soul, and save thyself! A sign
Thou wilt become to many as a shooting star.
They will believe thou art ethereal, divine,
When thou art where they are;
They will believe in thee and give thee feasts and praise.
They will believe thy power when thou hast loosed thy nails;
For power to them is fetterless and grand:
For destiny to them, along their ways,
Is one whose earthly Kingdom never fails.
Thou wilt be as a prophet or a king
In thy tremendous term of flourishing—
And thy hot royalty with acclamations fanned.

Come down from the Cross, my soul, and save thyself! . . . Beware!
Art thou not crucified with God, who is thy breath?
Wilt thou not hang as He while mockers laugh and stare?
Wilt thou not die His death?
Wilt thou not stay as He with nails and thorns and thirst?
Wilt thou not choose to conquer faith in His lone style?
Wilt thou not be with Him and hold thee still?
Voices have cried to him, *Come Down!* Accursed
And vain those voices, striving to beguile!
How heedless, solemn-gray in powerful mass,
Christ droops among the echoes as they pass!
O soul, remain with Him, with Him thy doom fulfill!

# William Ernest Henley

WILLIAM ERNEST HENLEY was born August 23, 1849, at Gloucester, and was
educated at the Grammar School of Gloucester. From childhood he was afflicted with a tuberculous disease which finally necessitated the amputation of a
foot. His *Hospital Sketches,* those vivid precursors of free verse, were a record of the
time when he was at the infirmary at Edinburgh; they are sharp with the sights,
sensations, even the smells, of the sick-room. In spite (or, more probably, because)
of his continued poor health, Henley never ceased to worship strength and energy;
courage and a triumphant belief shine out of the athletic *London Voluntaries* (1892)
and the light lyrics in *Hawthorn and Lavender* (1901).

The buoyancy, rousing at first, becomes wearing; it is too insistent, a little shrill.

When Henley ceased to overrate animal energy he was no less himself and a better poet. When not banging drums and flashing swords, he could distill the essence of a lyric, turn a triolet or ballade with the most expert practitioner of the French forms, paint impressionistic side-lights of intimate London, and, in such pieces as "Madame Life," combine grimness and gay *bizarrerie.*

The mixture of lightness and lustiness dates from his early youth. An infectious idiom, it flowered under his first influence which was that of his schoolmaster, T. E. Brown (see page 34) and remained to the end.

The bulk of Henley's poetry is not great in volume. He has himself explained the small quantity of his work in a Preface to his *Poems,* first published in 1888. "A principal reason," he says, "is that, after spending the better part of my life in the pursuit of poetry, I found myself (about 1877) so utterly unmarketable that I had to own myself beaten in art, and to indict myself to journalism for the next ten years." Later on, he began to write again—"old dusty sheaves were dragged to light; the work of selection and correction was begun; I burned much; I found that, after all, the lyrical instinct had slept—not died."

As editor he was fearless, prejudiced, violent in preferences and antipathies, and always sincere. His unflinching candor won over even those who completely disagreed with him. His friendships were many; one of the closest was with Robert Louis Stevenson, with whom he wrote three plays published in 1892. Though continually in conflict, he remained belligerent until 1894; in that year the death of his six-year-old daughter broke the heart of one whose head had been "bloody but unbowed."

In 1901 he published *Hawthorn and Lavender,* releasing a far finer though smaller music than he had ever uttered. His unrhymed rhythms, reminiscent of Heine's *North Sea* cycles, anticipated in color and accent the subsequent vogue of *vers libre.* Although he was not one of the great poets of his period, his period, as well as ours, would be incomplete without him. After a brilliant and varied career devoted mostly to journalism, Henley died in 1903.

### INVICTUS

Out of the night that covers me,
  Black as the Pit from pole to pole,
I thank whatever gods may be
  For my unconquerable soul.

In the fell clutch of circumstance
  I have not winced nor cried aloud.
Under the bludgeonings of chance
  My head is bloody, but unbowed.

Beyond this place of wrath and tears
  Looms but the horror of the shade,
And yet the menace of the years
  Finds, and shall find me, unafraid.

It matters not how strait the gate,
  How charged with punishments the scroll,
I am the master of my fate:
  I am the captain of my soul.

### THE BLACKBIRD

The nightingale has a lyre of gold,
  The lark's is a clarion call,
And the blackbird plays but a boxwood flute,
  But I love him best of all.

For his song is all of the joy of life,
  And we in the mad, spring weather,
We two have listened till he sang
  Our hearts and lips together.

### A BOWL OF ROSES

It was a bowl of roses:
  There in the light they lay,
Languishing, glorying, glowing
  Their life away.

And the soul of them rose like a presence,
  Into me crept and grew,
And filled me with something—someone—
  O, was it you?

### BEFORE

Behold me waiting—waiting for the knife.
A little while, and at a leap I storm
The thick sweet mystery of chloroform,
The drunken dark, the little death-in-life.
The gods are good to me: I have no wife,
No innocent child, to think of as I near
The fateful minute; nothing all-too dear
Unmans me for my bout of passive strife.
Yet I am tremulous and a trifle sick,
And, face to face with chance, I shrink a
  little:
My hopes are strong, my will is something
  weak.
Here comes the basket? Thank you. I am
  ready.
But, gentlemen my porters, life is brittle:
You carry Caesar and his fortunes—Steady!

### BALLADE

#### Made in the Hot Weather

Fountains that frisk and sprinkle
  The moss they overspill;
Pools that the breezes crinkle;

The wheel beside the mill,
With its wet, weedy frill;
Wind-shadows in the wheat;
A water-cart in the street;
The fringe of foam that girds
An islet's ferneries;
A green sky's minor thirds—
To live, I think of these!

Of ice and glass the tinkle,
Pellucid, silver-shrill;
Peaches without a wrinkle;
Cherries and snow at will,
From china bowls that fill
The senses with a sweet
Incuriousness of heat;
A melon's dripping sherds;
Cream-clotted strawberries;
Dusk dairies set with curds—
To live, I think of these!

Vale-lily and periwinkle;
Wet stone-crop on the sill;
The look of leaves a-twinkle
With windlets clear and still;
The feel of a forest rill
That wimples fresh and fleet
About one's naked feet;
The muzzles of drinking herds;
Lush flags and bulrushes;
The chirp of rain-bound birds—
To live, I think of these!

#### Envoy

Dark aisles, new packs of cards,
Mermaidens' tails, cool swards,
Dawn dews and starlit seas,
White marbles, whiter words—
To live, I think of these!

### WE'LL GO NO MORE A-ROVING

We'll go no more a-roving by the light of the moon.
November glooms are barren beside the dusk of June.
The summer flowers are faded, the summer thoughts are sere.
We'll go no more a-roving, lest worse befall, my dear.

We'll go no more a-roving by the light of the moon.
The song we sang rings hollow, and heavy runs the tune.
Glad ways and words remembered would shame the wretched year.
We'll go no more a-roving, nor dream we did, my dear.

We'll go no more a-roving by the light of the moon.
If yet we walk together, we need not shun the noon.
No sweet thing left to savor, no sad thing left to fear,
We'll go no more a-roving, but weep at home, my dear.

## MADAM LIFE

Madam Life's a piece in bloom
   Death goes dogging everywhere:
She's the tenant of the room,
   He's the ruffian on the stair.

You shall see her as a friend,
   You shall bilk him once and twice;
But he'll trap you in the end,
   And he'll stick you for her price.

With his kneebones at your chest,
   And his knuckles in your throat,
You would reason—plead—protest!
   Clutching at her petticoat;

But she's heard it all before,
   Well she knows you've had your fun,
Gingerly she gains the door,
   And your little job is done.

## OUT OF TUNE

The spring, my dear,
Is no longer spring.
Does the blackbird sing
What he sang last year?
Are the skies the old
Immemorial blue?
Or am I, or are you,
Grown cold?

Though life be change,
It is hard to bear
When the old sweet air
Sounds forced and strange.
To be out of tune,
Plain You and I . . .
It were better to die,
And soon!

## FALMOUTH[1]

O, Falmouth is a fine town with ships in the bay,
And I wish from my heart it's there I was today;
I wish from my heart I was far away from here,
Sitting in my parlor and talking to my dear.
   For it's home, dearie, home—it's home I want to be.
   Our topsails are hoisted, and we'll away to sea.
   O, the oak and the ash and the bonnie birken tree
   They're all growing green in the old countrie.

In Baltimore a-walking a lady I did meet
With her babe on her arm, as she came down the street;
And I thought how I sailed, and the cradle standing ready
For the pretty little babe that has never seen its daddie.
   And it's home, dearie, home . . .

O, if it be a lass, she shall wear a golden ring;
And if it be a lad, he shall fight for his king:
With his dirk and his hat and his little jacket blue
He shall walk the quarter-deck as his daddie used to do.
   And it's home, dearie, home . . .

[1] The burden and the third stanza are adapted from an old song.

O, there's a wind a-blowing, a-blowing from the west,
And that of all the winds is the one I like the best,
For it blows at our backs, and it shakes our pennon free,
And it soon will blow us home to the old countrie.
  For it's home, dearie, home—it's home I want to be.
  Our topsails are hoisted, and we'll away to sea.
  O, the oak and the ash and the bonnie birken tree
  They're all growing green in the old countrie.

## ENGLAND, MY ENGLAND

What have I done for you,
  England, my England?
What is there that I would not do,
  England, my own?
With your glorious eyes austere,
As the Lord were walking near,
Whispering terrible things and dear
  As the Song on your bugles blown,
    England—
  Round the world on your bugles blown!

Where shall the watchful Sun,
  England, my England,
Match the master-work you've done,
  England, my own?
When shall he rejoice again
Such a breed of mighty men
As come forward, one to ten,
  To the Song on your bugles blown,
    England—
  Down the years on your bugles blown?

Ever the faith endures,
  England, my England:—
"Take and break us: we are yours,
  "England, my own!
"Life is good, and joy runs high
"Between English earth and sky:
"Death is death; but we shall die
  "To the Song on your bugles blown,
    "England—
  "To the stars on your bugles blown!"

They call you proud and hard,
  England, my England:
You with worlds to watch and ward,
  England, my own!
You whose mailed hand keeps the keys
Of such teeming destinies
You could know nor dread nor ease

Were the Song on your bugles blown,
  England,
Round the Pit on your bugles blown!

Mother of Ships whose might,
  England, my England,
Is the fierce old Sea's delight,
  England, my own,
Chosen daughter of the Lord,
Spouse-in-Chief of the ancient sword,
There's the menace of the Word
  In the Song on your bugles blown,
    England—
  Out of heaven on your bugles blown!

## O GATHER ME THE ROSE

O gather me the rose, the rose,
  While yet in flower we find it,
For summer smiles, but summer goes,
  And winter waits behind it.

For with the dream foregone, foregone,
  The deed forborne for ever,
The worm Regret will canker on,
  And time will turn him never.

So were it well to love, my love,
  And cheat of any laughter
The fate beneath us and above,
  The dark before and after.

The myrtle and the rose, the rose,
  The sunshine and the swallow,
The dream that comes, the wish that goes,
  The memories that follow!

## TO ROBERT LOUIS STEVENSON

A child,
Curious and innocent,
Slips from his Nurse, and rejoicing
Loses himself in the Fair.

Thro' the jostle and din
Wandering, he revels,
Dreaming, desiring, possessing;
Till, of a sudden
Tired and afraid, he beholds
The sordid assemblage
Just as it is; and he runs
With a sob to his Nurse
(Lighting at last on him),
And in her motherly bosom
Cries him to sleep.

Thus thro' the World,
Seeing and feeling and knowing,
Goes Man: till at last,
Tired of experience, he turns
To the friendly and comforting breast
Of the old nurse, Death.

### MARGARITAE SORORI

A late lark twitters from the quiet skies;
And from the west,

Where the sun, his day's work ended,
Lingers as in content,
There falls on the old, gray city
An influence luminous and serene,
A shining peace.

The smoke ascends
In a rosy-and-golden haze. The spires
Shine, and are changed. In the valley
Shadows rise. The lark sings on. The sun,
Closing his benediction,
Sinks, and the darkening air
Thrills with a sense of the triumphing
  night—
Night with her train of stars
And her great gift of sleep.

So be my passing!
My task accomplished and the long day done,
My wages taken, and in my heart
Some late lark singing,
Let me be gathered to the quiet west,
The sundown splendid and serene,
Death.

# Robert Louis Stevenson

R OBERT LOUIS STEVENSON was born at Edinburgh in 1850 and attended the university there. From infancy he was afflicted with illness, nearly dying of gastric fever at the age of eight, a sickness which left him constitutionally weak. The rest of his life was a struggle between his work and a search for health in Switzerland, America, and the South Seas. He was at first trained to be a lighthouse engineer, following the profession of his family. However, he studied law instead, was admitted to the bar in 1875, and abandoned law for literature a few years later. After wandering several years about Europe, he recorded his peregrinations in *An Inland Voyage* (1878) and *Travels with a Donkey* (1879). Although he had written much before his thirtieth year, it was not until the publication of *Treasure Island* (1883) that he became popular. In 1885 he published, with misgivings, *A Child's Garden of Verses;* and again won public favor a year later with that *tour de force, The Strange Case of Dr. Jekyll and Mr. Hyde.*

In 1887, after a prolonged breakdown, he left England never to return. In rapid succession he tried the Adirondacks, New Jersey, California, and, in 1888 sailed, as Sidney Colvin said, "on what was only intended to be an excursion, but turned into a voluntary exile, prolonged until the hour of his death." He lived in Honolulu, Australia, and finally Samoa, where, after a long fight, he succumbed to tuberculosis in 1894.

Though primarily a novelist, Stevenson has left one book which is equally at home in the nursery and the library: *A Child's Garden of Verses* is second only to Mother Goose's own collection in simplicity and universal appeal. With the exception of these favorite verses and a posthumous *New Poems* (1918), *Underwoods* (1887) and *Ballads* (1890) comprise his entire poetic output. As a genial essayist, he is usually ranked with Charles Lamb. As a romancer, his fame rests on *Kidnapped,* the unfinished masterpiece, *Weir of Hermiston,* and that classic of youth, *Treasure Island.*

Stevenson's writing is inseparable from his charm and the personal appeal of his life-story. He is persuasive, not profound, too concerned with his craft, but never dull, and finally winning.

### SUMMER SUN

Great is the sun, and wide he goes
Through empty heaven without repose;
And in the blue and glowing days
More thick than rain he showers his rays.

Though closer still the blinds we pull
To keep the shady parlor cool,
Yet he will find a chink or two
To slip his golden fingers through.

The dusty attic, spider-clad,
He, through the keyhole, maketh glad;
And through the broken edge of tiles
Into the laddered hay-loft smiles.

Meantime his golden face around
He bares to all the garden ground,
And sheds a warm and glittering look
Among the ivy's inmost nook.

Above the hills, along the blue,
Round the bright air with footing true,
To please the child, to paint the rose,
The gardener of the World, he goes.

### WINTER TIME

Late lies the wintry sun a-bed,
A frosty, fiery sleepy-head;
Blinks but an hour or two; and then,
A blood-red orange, sets again.

Before the stars have left the skies
At morning in the dark I rise;

And, shivering in my nakedness,
By the cold candle, bathe and dress.

Close by the jolly fire I sit
To warm my frozen bones a bit;
Or, with a reindeer-sled, explore
The colder countries round the door.

When to go out, my nurse doth wrap
Me in my comforter and cap;
The cold wind burns my face, and blows
Its frosty pepper up my nose.

Black are my steps on silver sod;
Thick blows my frosty breath abroad;
And tree and house, and hill and lake,
Are frosted like a wedding-cake.

### THE CELESTIAL SURGEON

If I have faltered more or less
In my great task of happiness;
If I have moved among my race
And shown no glorious morning face;
If beams from happy human eyes
Have moved me not; if morning skies,
Books, and my food, and summer rain
Knocked on my sullen heart in vain:—
Lord, thy most pointed pleasure take
And stab my spirit broad awake;
Or, Lord, if still too obdurate I,
Choose thou, before that spirit die,
A piercing pain, a killing sin,
And to my dead heart run them in!

### ROMANCE

I will make you brooches and toys for your delight
Of bird-song at morning and star-shine at night.
I will make a palace fit for you and me,
Of green days in forests and blue days at sea.

I will make my kitchen, and you shall keep your room,
Where white flows the river and bright blows the broom
And you shall wash your linen and keep your body white
In rainfall at morning and dewfall at night.

And this shall be for music when no one else is near,
The fine song for singing, the rare song to hear!
That only I remember, that only you admire,
Of the broad road that stretches and the roadside fire.

### REQUIEM

Under the wide and starry sky
  Dig the grave and let me lie:
Glad did I live and gladly die,
  And I laid me down with a will.

This be the verse you 'grave for me:
  *Here he lies where he long'd to be;*
*Home is the sailor, home from sea,*
  *And the hunter home from the hill.*

### GO, LITTLE BOOK

Go, little book, and wish to all
Flowers in the garden, meat in the hall,
A bin of wine, a spice of wit,
A house with lawns enclosing it,
A living river by the door,
A nightingale in the sycamore.

## Alice Meynell

ALICE (CHRISTIANA THOMPSON) MEYNELL was born in 1850, educated at home and spent a great part of her early life in Italy. Later, she married Wilfred Meynell, friend, editor, and literary executor of Francis Thompson. For eighteen years she contributed to the *Weekly Register* of which her husband was editor; for twelve years was co-editor with him on *Merrie England;* wrote countless essays, columns for other periodicals, issued several volumes of poetry, made innumerable contacts—

not the least of which was the sponsorship of Francis Thompson which saved him from ruin—all with a huge family growing up about her. There were seven Meynell children, among them being Francis, typographer and poet (see page 431), Viola, the novelist (see page 428), Monica, the critical, and Everard, author of *The Life of Francis Thompson*. As described in the authorized Memoir *Alice Meynell* (1929) by her daughter, Viola, the children, aping their elders, conceived editing as a species of indoor sport and made up papers of their own. In one of these, the youngsters, attempting to answer Mrs. Meynell's critics, unconsciously appraised her:

"Her thought is a thought which very few writers got. It is mystical but excucite. She is a little obscure to readers who are not up in literature sufficiently to understand mystical touches. . . . Hers is a very docile temperament and thoroughly sympathetic. When she is singing a sympathetic song you can tell that she must have some excellent powers in her head."

The child Monica, touched with the family passion for salvation and trying to save her mother from literature, put the case against "ecstasy" in these delightful sentences:

"Dear Mother,—I hope you will in time give up your absurd thoughts about litreture. It makes my mind quite feverish when I think of the exhaltation your undergoing. I'm getting quite frightened about calling you 'dear Mother' because you will begin to take it quite seriously. Just because Mr. Henley and those sort of unsencere men say you write well simply because they know if they don't flatter you they'll never get anything for their paper. Now mother take my advise and don't be quite so estatic, you'll get on just as well in the world and much better because you'll be respected. Now just see. MONNIE."

Whatever form Alice Meynell chose, her work was always a reflection of her spirit. She scorned sentimentality, "the facile literary opportunity," despised slovenliness, "the fashion of an animated strut of style," and kept herself aloof from them. Her later years were spent collecting her poems, revising her early prose and publishing the best of it in *Essays*. She died in 1923.

*Preludes* was published in 1876. Since then, various collections of her poems and essays have appeared at irregular intervals, and, in 1923, Charles Scribner's Sons published *The Poems of Alice Meynell*. From the earliest restrained verses to the later more ornate conceits, one strain is dominant: the music of religious emotion. It is, obviously, emotion controlled, almost intellectualized. Yet the poetry is never dull. The reader is always aware of a nature disciplined, but which, for all its self-imposed strictures, is rich in feeling, exquisite in communication.

*Selected Poems of Alice Meynell* (1931), with a valuable introductory note by Wilfred Meynell, is a careful winnowing of her best, although one of her finest short lyrics ("Chimes") is omitted. The book begins appropriately with the quietly original and wholly beautiful "A Letter from a Girl to Her Own Old Age" and ends with tributes from Ruskin, Meredith, Coventry Patmore, Chesterton and others.

Dante Gabriel Rossetti considered her "Renouncement" one of the three finest sonnets ever written by women. "Christ in the Universe," "To a Daisy," and "A Thrush Before Dawn," show a literary as well as spiritual kinship with Francis

Thompson; but where Thompson is lavish to the point of gaudiness, Mrs. Meynell's fastidiousness dictates a fine economy. .

### TO A DAISY

Slight as thou art, thou art enough to hide,
  Like all created things, secrets from me,
  And stand a barrier to eternity.
And I, how can I praise thee well and wide
From where I dwell—upon the hither side?
  Thou little veil for so great mystery,
  When shall I penetrate all things and thee,
And then look back? For this I must abide,
Till thou shalt grow and fold and be unfurled
Literally between me and the world.
  Then I shall drink from in beneath a spring,
  And from a poet's side shall read his book.
O daisy mine, what will it be to look
  From God's side even on such a simple thing?

### THE SHEPHERDESS

She walks—the lady of my delight—
  A shepherdess of sheep.
Her flocks are thoughts. She keeps them
    white;
  She guards them from the steep;
She feeds them on the fragrant height,
  And folds them in for sleep.

She roams maternal hills and bright
  Dark valleys safe and deep.
Into that tender breast at night,
  The chastest stars may peep.
She walks—the lady of my delight—
  A shepherdess of sheep.

She holds her little thoughts in sight,
  Though gay they run and leap.
She is so circumspect and right;
  She has her soul to keep.
She walks—the lady of my delight—
  A shepherdess of sheep.

### THE WIND IS BLIND

*"Eyeless, in Gaza, at the mill, with slaves."*
  —MILTON'S SAMSON.

The wind is blind.
The earth sees sun and moon; the height
Is watch-tower to the dawn; the plain

Shines to the summer; visible light
Is scattered in the drops of rain.

  The wind is blind.
The flashing billows are aware;
With open eyes the cities see;
Light leaves the ether, everywhere
Known to the homing bird and bee.

  The wind is blind,
Is blind alone. How has he hurled
His ignorant lash, his sinless dart,
His eyeless rush upon the world,
Unseeing, to break his unknown heart!

  The wind is blind.
And the sail traps him, and the mill
Captures him; and he cannot save
His swiftness and his desperate will
From those blind uses of the slave.

### NOVEMBER BLUE

*The golden tint of the electric lights seems to giv*
*a complementary color to the air in the early evenin,*
  —ESSAY ON LONDO

O heavenly color, London town
  Has blurred it from her skies;

And, hooded in an earthly brown,
  Unheaven'd the city lies.
No longer, standard-like, this hue
  Above the broad road flies;
Nor does the narrow street the blue
  Wear, slender pennon-wise.

But when the gold and silver lamps
  Color the London dew,
And, misted by the winter damps,
  The shops shine bright, anew—
Blue comes to earth, it walks the street,
  It dyes the wide air through;
A mimic sky about their feet
  The throng go crowned with blue.

CHIMES

Brief, on a flying night
  From the shaken tower,
A flock of bells take flight,
  And go with the hour.

Like birds from the cote to the gales,
  Abrupt—O hark!
A fleet of bells set sails,
  And go to the dark.

Sudden the cold airs swing,
  Alone, aloud,
A verse of bells takes wing
  And flies with the cloud.

A LETTER FROM A GIRL TO HER OWN OLD AGE

Listen, and when thy hand this paper presses,
O time-worn woman, think of her who blesses
What thy thin fingers touch, with her caresses.

O mother, for the weight of years that break thee!
O daughter, for slow time must yet awake thee,
And from the changes of my heart must make thee!

O fainting traveler, morn is gray in heaven.
Dost thou remember how the clouds were driven?
And are they calm about the fall of even?

Pause near the ending of thy long migration;
For this one sudden hour of desolation
Appeals to one hour of thy meditation.

Suffer, O silent one, that I remind thee
Of the great hills that stormed the sky behind thee,
Of the wild winds of power that have resigned thee.

Know that the mournful plain where thou must wander
Is but a gray and silent world; but ponder
The misty mountains of the morning yonder.

Listen:—the mountain winds with rain were fretting,
And sudden gleams the mountain-tops besetting.
I cannot let thee fade to death, forgetting.

What part of this wild heart of mine I know not
Will follow with thee where the great winds blow not,
And where the young flowers of the mountain grow not.

Yet let my letter with thy lost thoughts in it
Tell what the way was when thou didst begin it,
And win with thee the goal when thou shalt win it.

I have not writ this letter of divining
To make a glory of thy silent pining,
A triumph of thy mute and strange declining.

Only one youth, and the bright life was shrouded;
Only one morning, and the day was clouded;
And one old age with all regrets is crowded.

O hush, O hush! Thy tears my words are steeping.
O hush, hush, hush! So full, the fount of weeping?
Poor eyes, so quickly moved, so near to sleeping?

Pardon the girl; such strange desires beset her.
Poor woman, lay aside the mournful letter
That breaks thy heart; the one who wrote, forget her:

The one who now thy faded features guesses,
With filial fingers thy gray hair caresses,
With morning tears thy mournful twilight blesses.

### THE OCTOBER REDBREAST

Autumn is weary, halt, and old;
  Ah, but she owns the song of joy!
Her colors fade, her woods are cold.
  Her singing-bird's a boy, a boy.

In lovely Spring the birds were bent
  On nests, on use, on love, forsooth!
Grown-up were they. This boy's content,
  For his is liberty, his is youth.

The musical stripling sings for play
  Taking no thought, and virgin-glad.
For duty sang those mates in May.
  This singing-bird's a lad, a lad.

### A THRUSH BEFORE DAWN

A voice peals in this end of night
  A phrase of notes resembling stars,
Single and spiritual notes of light.
  What call they at my window-bars?
    The South, the past, the day to be,
    An ancient infelicity.

Darkling, deliberate, what sings
  This wonderful one, alone, at peace?
What wilder things than song, what things
  Sweeter than youth, clearer than Greece,
    Dearer than Italy, untold
    Delight, and freshness centuries old?

And first first-loves, a multitude,
  The exaltation of their pain;
Ancestral childhood long renewed;
  And midnights of invisible rain;
    And gardens, gardens, night and day,
    Gardens and childhood all the way.

What Middle Ages passionate,
  O passionless voice! What distant bells
Lodged in the hills, what palace state
  Illyrian! For it speaks, it tells,
    Without desire, without dismay
    Some morrow and some yesterday.

All-natural things! But more— Whence came
  This yet remoter mystery?
How do these starry notes proclaim
  A graver still divinity?
    This hope, this sanctity of fear?
    *O innocent throat! O human ear!*

### RENOUNCEMENT

I must not think of thee; and, tired yet strong,
  I shun the thought that lurks in all delight—
  The thought of thee—and in the blue Heaven's height,
And in the sweetest passage of a song.

O just beyond the fairest thoughts that throng
  This breast, the thought of thee waits hidden yet bright;
  But it must never, never come in sight;
I must stop short of thee the whole day long.

But when sleep comes to close each difficult day,
  When night gives pause to the long watch I keep,
  And all my bonds I needs must loose apart,

Must doff my will as raiment laid away,
  With the first dream that comes with the first sleep
  I run, I run, I am gathered to thy heart.

### CHRIST IN THE UNIVERSE

With this ambiguous earth
His dealings have been told us. These abide:
The signal to a maid, the human birth,
The lesson, and the young Man crucified.

But not a star of all
The innumerable hosts of stars has heard
How He administered this terrestrial ball.
Our race have kept their Lord's entrusted Word.

Of His earth-visiting feet
None knows the secret, cherished, perilous,
The terrible, shamefast, frightened, whispered, sweet,
Heart-shattering secret of His way with us.

No planet knows of this.
Our wayside planet, carrying land and wave,
Love and life multiplied, and pain and bliss,
Bears, as chief treasure, one forsaken grave.

Nor, in our little day,
May His devices with the heavens be guessed;
His pilgrimage to thread the Milky Way,
Or His bestowals there, be manifest.

But, in the eternities,
Doubtless we shall compare together, hear
A million alien Gospels, in what guise
He trod the Pleiades, the Lyre, the Bear.

O be prepared, my soul!
To read the inconceivable, to scan
The million forms of God those stars unroll
When, in our turn, we show to them a Man.

# Oscar Wilde

OSCAR (FINGALL O'FLAHERTIE) WILDE was born at Dublin, Ireland, October 16, 1856, and even as an undergraduate at Oxford was marked for a brilliant career. When he was scarcely twenty-one years of age, he won the Newdigate Prize with his poem "Ravenna." Devoting himself almost entirely to prose, he speedily became known as a writer of brilliant epigrammatic essays and even more brilliant paradoxical plays, such as *An Ideal Husband* and *The Importance of Being Earnest.* Wilde's aphorisms and flippancies were quoted everywhere; his fame as a wit was only surpassed by his notoriety as an esthete, the scandal of his trial, and the final prison sentence.

Most of his poems in prose (such as "The Happy Prince," "The Birthday of the Infanta," and "The Fisherman and His Soul") are more imaginative and richly colored than his rococo verse which suffers from deliberate decadence. But in one long poem, "The Ballad of Reading Gaol" (1898), he sounded his simplest and most enduring note. Prison was, in some ways, a regeneration for Wilde. It not only produced "The Ballad of Reading Gaol," but made possible his finest piece of writing, "De Profundis," only a small part of which has been published. "Salomé," which has made the author's name a household word, was originally written in French in 1892 and later translated into English by Lord Alfred Douglas, accompanied by the famous illustrations by Aubrey Beardsley. More recently, this heated drama, based on the story of Herod and Herodias, was made into an opera by Richard Strauss and performed in a dozen countries and several languages.

Wilde's society plays, flashing and cynical, were the forerunners of Bernard Shaw's audacious and far more searching ironies. One sees the origin of a whole school of drama in such epigrams as "The history of woman is the history of the worst form of tyranny the world has ever known: the tyranny of the weak over the strong. It is the only tyranny that lasts." Or "There is only one thing in the world worse than being talked about, and that is not being talked about."

Wilde's flair for publicity, avowed in the last quotation, was gratified to the full. No man of his time was more talked about. The end of the Esthetic Movement came coincidentally—and ironically—with the trial of Oscar Wilde and his indictment for a social crime. His predilection for extremes caused his artistic ruin: in youth he was ultra-Keatsian; in early manhood, ultra-Rossettian; in maturity, ultra-Wilde—and he pushed preciosity to the limits of the absurd. He believed in nothing, not even himself, except for the passing effect; he was essentially the "Pierrot of the minute"—a Pierrot whose shifting passions and impertinences convinced no one. Even his Pierroticism was a pose.

"Impression du Matin" and "Symphony in Yellow" are among the poems which suggest a verbal Whistler, with whom Wilde waged many an epigrammatic battle, and "Hélas" is an unusually honest fragment of self-analysis.

Wilde borrowed from Swinburne no little of his spirit and as much of his technique as he could master. But Swinburne's rebelliousness, though vague and general, was sincere; Wilde, the antithesis of a rebel by instinct, was a social snob who clung to his insurgence for the entrée it won him in properly breathless gatherings. His success was without dignity, his failure without pathos.

Wilde died at Paris, November 30, 1900, his body being buried in the Cemetery of Bagneux. On July 20, 1909, it was transferred to the great Cemetery of Père Lachaise, where later a striking monument by Epstein was erected to his memory.

### REQUIESCAT

Tread lightly, she is near
　Under the snow,
Speak gently, she can hear
　The daisies grow.

All her bright golden hair
　Tarnished with rust,
She that was young and fair
　Fallen to dust.

Lily-like, white as snow,
　She hardly knew
She was a woman, so
　Sweetly she grew.

Coffin-board, heavy stone,
　Lie on her breast;
I vex my heart alone,
　She is at rest.

Peace, peace; she cannot hear
　Lyre or sonnet;
All my life's buried here.
　Heap earth upon it.

### IMPRESSION DU MATIN

The Thames nocturne of blue and gold
　Changed to a harmony in gray;
　A barge with ocher-colored hay
Dropt from the wharf: and chill and cold

The yellow fog came creeping down
　The bridges, till the houses' walls
　Seemed changed to shadows, and St. Paul's
Loomed like a bubble o'er the town.

Then suddenly arose the clang
　Of waking life; the streets were stirred
　With country wagons; and a bird
Flew to the glistening roofs and sang.

But one pale woman all alone,
　The daylight kissing her wan hair,
　Loitered beneath the gas lamps' flare,
With lips of flame and heart of stone.

### HÉLAS

To drift with every passion till my soul
Is a stringed lute on which all winds can play,
Is it for this that I have given away
Mine ancient wisdom, and austere control?
Methinks my life is a twice-written scroll
Scrawled over on some boyish holiday
With idle songs for pipe and virelay,
Which do but mar the secret of the whole.
Surely there was a time I might have trod
The sunlit heights, and from life's dissonance
Struck one clear chord to reach the ears of
　God:
Is that time dead? lo! with a little rod
I did but touch the honey of romance—
And must I lose a soul's inheritance?

### MAGDALEN WALKS

The little white clouds are racing over the sky,
　And the fields are strewn with the gold of the flower of March,
　The daffodil breaks under foot, and the tasseled larch
Sways and swings as the thrush goes hurrying by.

A delicate odor is borne on the wings of the morning breeze,
   The odor of deep wet grass, and of brown new-furrowed earth,
   The birds are singing for joy of the Spring's glad birth,
Hopping from branch to branch on the rocking trees.

And all the woods are alive with the murmur and sound of Spring,
   And the rose-bud breaks into pink on the climbing briar,
   And the crocus-bed is a quivering moon of fire
Girdled round with the belt of an amethyst ring.

And the plane of the pine-tree is whispering some tale of love
   Till it rustles with laughter and tosses its mantle of green,
   And the gloom of the wych-elm's hollow is lit with the iris sheen
Of the burnished rainbow throat and the silver breast of a dove.

See! the lark starts up from his bed in the meadow there,
   Breaking the gossamer threads and the nets of dew,
   And flashing adown the river, a flame of blue!
The kingfisher flies like an arrow, and wounds the air.

And the sense of my life is sweet! though I know that the end is nigh:
   For the ruin and rain of winter will shortly come,
   The lily will lose its gold, and the chestnut-bloom
In billows of red and white on the grass will lie.

And even the light of the sun will fade at the last,
   And the leaves will fall, and the birds will hasten away,
   And I will be left in the snow of a flowerless day
To think on the glories of Spring, and the joys of a youth long past.

Yet be silent, my heart! do not count it a profitless thing
   To have seen the splendor of the sun, and of grass, and of flower!
   To have lived and loved! for I hold that to love for an hour
Is better for man and woman than cycles of blossoming Spring.

### E TENEBRIS

Come down, O Christ, and help me! reach thy hand,
   For I am drowning in a stormier sea
   Than Simon on thy lake of Galilee:
The wine of life is spilt upon the sand,
My heart is as some famine-murdered land
   Whence all good things have perished utterly,
   And well I know my soul in Hell must lie
If I this night before God's throne should stand.
"He sleeps perchance, or rideth to the chase,
   Like Baal, when his prophets howled that name
   From morn to noon on Carmel's smitten height."
Nay, peace, I shall behold, before the night,
   The feet of brass, the robe more white than flame,
The wounded hands, the weary human face.

## SYMPHONY IN YELLOW

An omnibus across the bridge
  Crawls like a yellow butterfly,
  And, here and there, a passer-by
Shows like a little restless midge.

Big barges full of yellow hay
  Are moved against the shadowy wharf,
  And, like a yellow silken scarf,
The thick fog hangs along the quay.

The yellow leaves begin to fade
  And flutter from the Temple elms,
  And at my feet the pale green Thames
Lies like a rod of rippled jade.

## THE HARLOT'S HOUSE

We caught the tread of dancing feet,
We loitered down the moonlit street,
And stopped beneath the harlot's house.

Inside, above the din and fray,
We heard the loud musicians play
The "Treues Liebes Herz" of Strauss.

Like strange mechanical grotesques,
Making fantastic arabesques,
The shadows raced across the blind.

We watched the ghostly dancers spin
To sound of horn and violin,
Like black leaves wheeling in the wind.

Like wire-pulled automatons,
Slim silhouetted skeletons
Went sidling through the slow quadrille.

They took each other by the hand,
And danced a stately saraband;
Their laughter echoed thin and shrill.

Sometimes a clockwork puppet pressed
A phantom lover to her breast,
Sometimes they seemed to try to sing.

Sometimes a horrible marionette
Came out, and smoked its cigarette
Upon the steps like a live thing.

Then, turning to my love, I said,
"The dead are dancing with the dead,
The dust is whirling with the dust."

But she—she heard the violin,
And left my side and entered in:
Love passed into the house of lust.

Then suddenly the tune went false,
The dancers wearied of the waltz,
The shadows ceased to wheel and whirl.

And down the long and silent street,
The dawn, with silver-sandaled feet,
Crept like a frightened girl.

## FROM "THE SPHINX"

How subtle-secret is your smile! Did you love none then? Nay, I know
Great Ammon was your bedfellow! He lay with you beside the Nile!

The river-horses in the slime trumpeted when they saw him come
Odorous with Syrian galbanum and smeared with spikenard and with thyme.

He came along the river bank like some tall galley argent-sailed,
He strode across the waters, mailed in beauty, and the waters sank.

He strode across the desert sand: he reached the valley where you lay:
He waited till the dawn of day: then touched your black breasts with his hand.

You kissed his mouth with mouth of flame: you made the hornèd god your own:
You stood behind him on his throne: you called him by his secret name.

You whispered monstrous oracles into the caverns of his ears:
With blood of goats and blood of steers you taught him monstrous miracles.

White Ammon was your bedfellow! Your chamber was the steaming Nile!
And with your curved archaic smile you watched his passion come and go.

### FROM "THE BALLAD OF READING GAOL"

He did not wear his scarlet coat,
  For blood and wine are red,
And blood and wine were on his hands
  When they found him with the dead,
The poor dead woman whom he loved,
  And murdered in her bed.

He walked amongst the Trial Men
  In a suit of shabby gray;
A cricket cap was on his head,
  And his step seemed light and gay;
But I never saw a man who looked
  So wistfully at the day.

I never saw a man who looked
  With such a wistful eye
Upon that little tent of blue
  Which prisoners call the sky,
And at every drifting cloud that went
  With sails of silver by.

I walked, with other souls in pain,
  Within another ring,
And was wondering if the man had done
  A great or little thing,
When a voice behind me whispered low,
  *"That fellow's got to swing."*

Dear Christ! the very prison walls
  Suddenly seemed to reel,
And the sky above my head became
  Like a casque of scorching steel;
And, though I was a soul in pain,
  My pain I could not feel.

I only knew what hunted thought
  Quickened his step, and why
He looked upon the garish day
  With such a wistful eye:
The man had killed the thing he loved,
  And so he had to die.

✦

Yet each man kills the thing he loves,
  By each let this be heard,
Some do it with a bitter look,
  Some with a flattering word,
The coward does it with a kiss,
  The brave man with a sword!

Some kill their love when they are young
  And some when they are old;
Some strangle with the hands of Lust,
  Some with the hands of Gold:
The kindest use a knife, because
  The dead so soon grow cold.

Some love too little, some too long,
  Some sell, and others buy;
Some do the deed with many tears,
  And some without a sigh:
For each man kills the thing he loves,
  Yet each man does not die.

He does not die a death of shame
  On a day of dark disgrace,
Nor have a noose about his neck,
  Nor a cloth upon his face,
Nor drop feet foremost through the floor
  Into an empty space.

He did not wring his hands nor weep,
  Nor did he peak or pine,
But he drank the air as though it held
  Some healthful anodyne;
With open mouth he drank the sun
  As though it had been wine!

And I and all the souls in pain,
  Who tramped the other ring,
Forgot if we ourselves had done
  A great or little thing,
And watched with gaze of dull amaze
  The man who had to swing.

And strange it was to see him pass
  With a step so light and gay,

And strange it was to see him look
 So wistfully at the day,
And strange it was to think that he
 Had such a debt to pay.

✦

For oak and elm have pleasant leaves
 That in the spring-time shoot:
But grim to see is the gallows-tree,
 With its adder-bitten root,
And, green or dry, a man must die
 Before it bears its fruit!

The loftiest place is that seat of grace
 For which all worldlings try:
But who would stand in hempen band
 Upon a scaffold high,
And through a murderer's collar take
 His last look at the sky?

It is sweet to dance to violins
 When Love and Life are fair:
To dance to flutes, to dance to lutes
 Is delicate and rare:
But it is not sweet with nimble feet
 To dance upon the air!

So with curious eyes and sick surmise
 We watched him day by day,
And wondered if each one of us
 Would end the self-same way,
For none can tell to what red Hell
 His sightless soul may stray.

At last the dead man walked no more
 Amongst the Trial Men,
And I knew that he was standing up
 In the black dock's dreadful pen,
And that never would I see his face
 In God's sweet world again.

Like two doomed ships that pass in storm
 We had crossed each other's way:
But we made no sign, we said no word,
 We had no word to say;
For we did not meet in the holy night,
 But in the shameful day.

A prison wall was round us both,
 Two outcast men we were:
The world had thrust us from its heart,
 And God from out His care:
And the iron gin that waits for Sin
 Had caught us in its snare.

# John Davidson

JOHN DAVIDSON was born at Barrhead, Renfrewshire, in 1857. His *Ballads and Songs* (1895) and *New Ballads* (1897) attained a sudden but too short-lived popularity; his great promise was quenched by an apathetic public and by his own growing disillusion and despair. Neither the later *Holiday and Other Poems* (1906) nor the ambitious trilogy, *God and Mammon* (the first volume of which appeared in 1907) received anything more than frozen respect. His somber poetry never tired of repeating his favorite theme: "Man is but the Universe grown conscious." Author of some four "testaments," six plays, three novels, and various collections of poems and essays, Davidson died by his own hand at Penzance in 1909.

The theme of "A Ballad of a Nun" is one which has attracted many writers since the Middle Ages, but Davidson has given it a turn which makes the tale sound far fresher than Vollmoeller's employment of it in *The Miracle*. "A Ballad of Hell," Davidson's only "popular" poem, is wholly his own material.

Davidson's work may be divided into three stages. His first phase, announced in *The North Wall* (1885), was conscious cleverness. In the second stage he tried to reach sophisticated audiences, attempting the metropolitan note with sketches, plays, and novels in the manner of the febrile Nineties. It was not until *Ballads and Songs* and *The Last Ballad* (1899) that he struck what for him and his readers was the true note. "A Ballad of Hell" and "A Ballad of a Nun," among others, are infused with the old ballad spirit; they have the traditional reach and vigor, modernized without becoming topical, pointed but not over-personalized.

After 1900 Davidson's work suffered. As his biographer R. M. Wenley puts it, "cosmogonic passion overwhelming him, the artist pales before the prophet in travail." Somberness developed into pessimism, pessimism into self-persecution. He identified himself with James Thomson (see page 48), another maladjusted soul; he became paranoiac, losing himself in "strange passions, outlandish affaires, overstrung rhetoric." Over-emphasizing extremes, his later work was not only neurotic but melodramatic. Hysteria tainted a half-Nietzschean, half-Calvinistic philosophy; his twisted apprehension of the "hero" concept of history (in which he seemed to himself one of the defeated martyrs) was, as Wenley remarks, "like other Neo-Romantics'—from Nietzsche *in excelsis* to D'Annunzio *in inferis.*"

But it is only in his last phase that Davidson turned from singing to shrieking. His huge and misshapen trilogies are forgotten; his exaggerated colors have faded; the ballads and a few of the lyrics remain. They have persistent if not permanent stuff.

### A BALLAD OF HELL

"A letter from my love today!
  Oh, unexpected, dear appeal!"
She struck a happy tear away,
  And broke the crimson seal.

"My love, there is no help on earth,
  No help in heaven; the dead-man's bell
Must toll our wedding; our first hearth
  Must be the well-paved floor of hell."

The color died from out her face,
  Her eyes like ghostly candles shone;
She cast dread looks about the place,
  Then clenched her teeth and read right on.

"I may not pass the prison door;
  Here must I rot from day to day,
Unless I wed whom I abhor,
  My cousin, Blanche of Valencay.

"At midnight with my dagger keen,
  I'll take my life; it must be so.
Meet me in hell tonight, my queen,
  For weal and woe."

She laughed, although her face was wan,
  She girded on her golden belt,
She took her jeweled ivory fan,
  And at her glowing missal knelt.

Then rose, "And am I mad?" she said:
  She broke her fan, her belt untied;
With leather girt herself instead,
  And stuck a dagger at her side.

She waited, shuddering in her room,
  Till sleep had fallen on all the house.
She never flinched; she faced her doom:
  They two must sin to keep their vows.

Then out into the night she went,
  And, stooping, crept by hedge and tree;
Her rose-bush flung a snare of scent,
  And caught a happy memory.

She fell, and lay a minute's space;
  She tore the sward in her distress;
The dewy grass refreshed her face;
  She rose and ran with lifted dress.

She started like a morn-caught ghost
  Once when the moon came out and stood
To watch; the naked road she crossed,
  And dived into the murmuring wood.

The branches snatched her streaming cloak
  A live thing shrieked; she made no stay
She hurried to the trysting-oak—
  Right well she knew the way.

Without a pause she bared her breast,
  And drove her dagger home and fell,
And lay like one that takes her rest,
  And died and wakened up in hell.

She bathed her spirit in the flame,
  And near the center took her post;
From all sides to her ears there came
  The dreary anguish of the lost.

The devil started at her side,
  Comely, and tall, and black as jet.
"I am young Malespina's bride;
  Has he come hither yet?"

"My poppet, welcome to your bed."
  "Is Malespina here?"
"Not he! Tomorrow he must wed
  His cousin Blanche, my dear!"

"You lie, he died with me tonight."
  "Not he! it was a plot" . . . "You lie."
"My dear, I never lie outright."
  "We died at midnight, he and I."

The devil went. Without a groan
  She, gathered up in one fierce prayer,
Took root in hell's midst all alone,
  And waited for him there.

She dared to make herself at home
  Amidst the wail, the uneasy stir.
The blood-stained flame that filled the dome,
  Scentless and silent, shrouded her.

How long she stayed I cannot tell;
  But when she felt his perfidy,
She marched across the floor of hell;
  And all the damned stood up to see.

The devil stopped her at the brink:
  She shook him off; she cried, "Away!"
"My dear, you have gone mad, I think."
  "I was betrayed: I will not stay."

Across the weltering deep she ran;
  A stranger thing was never seen:
The damned stood silent to a man;
  They saw the great gulf set between.

To her it seemed a meadow fair;
  And flowers sprang up about her feet.
She entered heaven; she climbed the stair
  And knelt down at the mercy-seat.

Seraphs and saints with one great voice
  Welcomed that soul that knew not fear.
Amazed to find it could rejoice,
  Hell raised a hoarse, half-human cheer.

## IMAGINATION

### (*from "New Year's Eve"*)

There is a dish to hold the sea,
  A brazier to contain the sun,
A compass for the galaxy,
  A voice to wake the dead and done!

That minister of ministers,
  Imagination, gathers up
The undiscovered Universe,
  Like jewels in a jasper cup.

Its flame can mingle north and south;
  Its accent with the thunder strive;
The ruddy sentence of its mouth
  Can make the ancient dead alive.

The mart of power, the fount of will,
  The form and mold of every star,
The source and bound of good and ill,
  The key of all the things that are,

Imagination, new and strange
  In every age, can turn the year;
Can shift the poles and lightly change
  The mood of men, the world's career.

## THE OUTCAST

Soul, be your own
  Pleasance and mart,
A land unknown,
  A state apart.

Scowl and be rude
  Should love entice;
Call gratitude
  The costliest vice.

Deride the ill
  By fortune sent;
Be scornful still
  If foes repent.

When curse and stone
  Are hissed and hurled,
Aloof, alone
  Disdain the world.

Soul, disregard
  The bad, the good;
Be haughty, hard,
  Misunderstood.

Be neutral; spare
  No humblest lie,
And overbear
  Authority.

Laugh wisdom down;
  Abandon fate;
Shame the renown
  Of all the great.

Dethrone the past;
  Deed, vision—naught
Avails at last
  Save your own thought.

Though on all hands
  The powers unsheathe
Their lightning-brands
  And from beneath,

And from above
  One curse be hurled
With scorn, with love
  Affront the world.

### THE UNKNOWN

### (*Vilanelle*)

To brave and to know the unknown
  Is the high world's motive and mark,
Though the way with snares be strewn.

The earth itself alone
  Wheels through the light and the dark
Onward to meet the unknown.

Each soul, upright or prone,
  While the owl sings or the lark,
Must pass where the bones are strewn.

Power on the loftiest throne
  Can fashion no certain ark
That shall stem and outride the unknown.

Beauty must doff her zone,
  Strength trudge unarmed and stark
Though the way with eyes be strewn.

This only can atone,
  The high world's motive and mark,
To brave and to know the unknown
Though the way with fire be strewn.

### A BALLAD OF A NUN

From Eastertide to Eastertide
  For ten long years her patient knees
Engraved the stones—the fittest bride
  Of Christ in all the diocese.

She conquered every earthly lust;
  The abbess loved her more and more;
And, as a mark of perfect trust,
  Made her the keeper of the door.

High on a hill the convent hung,
  Across a duchy looking down,
Where everlasting mountains flung
  Their shadows over tower and town.

The jewels of their lofty snows
  In constellations flashed at night;
Above their crests the moon arose;
  The deep earth shuddered with delight.

Long ere she left her cloudy bed,
  Still dreaming in the orient land,
On many a mountain's happy head
  Dawn lightly laid her rosy hand.

The adventurous sun took heaven by storm;
  Clouds scattered largesses of rain;
The sounding cities, rich and warm,
  Smoldered and glittered in the plain.

Sometimes it was a wandering wind,
  Sometimes the fragrance of the pine,
Sometimes the thought how others sinned,
  That turned her sweet blood into wine.

Sometimes she heard a serenade
  Complaining sweetly far away:
She said, "A young man woos a maid";
  And dreamt of love till break of day.

Then she would ply her knotted scourge
  Until she swooned; but evermore
She had the same red sin to purge,
  Poor, passionate keeper of the door!

For still night's starry scroll unfurled,
  And still the day came like a flood:
It was the greatness of the world
  That made her long to use her blood.

In winter-time when Lent drew nigh,
  And hill and plain were wrapped in snow,
She watched beneath the frosty sky
  The nearest city nightly glow.

Like peals of airy bells outworn
  Faint laughter died above her head
In gusts of broken music borne:
  "They keep the Carnival," she said.

Her hungry heart devoured the town:
  "Heaven save me by a miracle!
Unless God sends an angel down,
  Thither I go though it were Hell."

Fillet and veil in strips she tore;
  Her golden tresses floated wide;
The ring and bracelet that she wore
  As Christ's betrothed, she cast aside.

"Life's dearest meaning I shall probe;
  Lo! I shall taste of love at last!
Away!" She doffed her outer robe,
  And sent it sailing down the blast.

Her body seemed to warm the wind;
  With bleeding feet o'er ice she ran:
"I leave the righteous God behind;
  I go to worship sinful man."

She reached the sounding city's gate;
  No question did the warder ask:
He passed her in: "Welcome, wild mate!"
  He thought her some fantastic mask.

Half-naked through the town she went;
  Each footstep left a bloody mark;
Crowds followed her with looks intent;
  Her bright eyes made the torches dark.

Alone and watching in the street
  There stood a grave youth nobly dressed;
To him she knelt and kissed his feet;
  Her face her great desire confessed.

Straight to his house the nun he led:
  "Strange lady, what would you with me?"
"Your love, your love, sweet lord," she said;
  "I bring you my virginity."

He healed her bosom with a kiss;
  She gave him all her passion's hoard;
And sobbed and murmured ever, "This
  Is life's great meaning, dear, my lord.

"I care not for my broken vows;
  Though God should come in thunder soon,
I am sister to the mountains now,
  And sister to the sun and moon."

Through all the towns of Belmarie
  She made a progress like a queen.
"She is," they said, "whate'er she be,
  The strangest woman ever seen.

"From fairyland she must have come,
  Or else she is a mermaiden."
Some said she was a ghoul, and some
  A heathen goddess born again.

But soon her fire to ashes burned;
  Her beauty changed to haggardness;
Her golden hair to silver turned;
  The hour came of her last caress.

At midnight from her lonely bed
  She rose, and said, "I have had my will."
The old ragged robe she donned, and fled
  Back to the convent on the hill.

Half-naked as she went before,
  She hurried to the city wall,
Unnoticed in the rush and roar
  And splendor of the Carnival.

She ran across the icy plain;
  Her worn blood curdled in the blast;
Each footstep left a crimson stain;
  The white-faced moon looked on aghast.

She said between her chattering jaws,
  "Deep peace is mine, I cease to strive;
Oh, comfortable convent laws,
  That bury foolish nuns alive!

"A trowel for my passing-bell,
  A little bed within the wall,
A coverlet of stones; how well
  I there shall keep the Carnival!"

Like tired bells chiming in their sleep,
  The wind faint peals of laughter bore;
She stopped her ears and climbed the steep
  And thundered at the convent door.

It opened straight: she entered in,
  And at the wardress' feet fell prone:
"I come to purge away my sin;
  Bury me, close me up in stone."

The wardress raised her tenderly;
  She touched her wet and fast-shut eyes:
"Look, sister; sister, look at me;
  Look; can you see through my disguise?"

She looked and saw her own sad face,
  And trembled, wondering, "Who art
    thou?"
"God sent me down to fill your place:
  I am the Virgin Mary now."

And with the word, God's mother shone:
  The wanderer whispered, "Mary, hail!"
The vision helped her to put on
  Bracelet and fillet, ring and veil.

"You are sister to the mountains now,
  And sister to the day and night;
Sister to God." And on the brow
  She kissed her thrice, and left her sight,

While dreaming in her cloudy bed,
  Far in the crimson orient land,
On many a mountain's happy head
  Dawn lightly laid her rosy hand.

# William Watson

WILLIAM WATSON was born at Burley-in-Wharfedale, Yorkshire, August 2, 1858. He achieved his first success through his long poems on Wordsworth, Shelley, and Tennyson—poems that attempted, almost successfully, to combine the manners of these masters. Upon the death of Tennyson, Watson was inspired to write his most famous elegy. Without stopping for food or rest he wrote "Lacrymae Musarum" in fifty hours. The poem caused a deep impression; Queen Victoria admired it, Gladstone suggested that the author be made Poet Laureate. The conservatives, however, felt that Watson, just turned thirty-four, was too young; moreover, he was suspiciously "liberal," so the honor went to the dull but politically dependable Alfred Austin. This was the peak of Watson's career. A few years later he was snubbed by a Prime Minister for some tactless verses; the younger men were contemptuous of him; at sixty he was, worse than condemned, forgotten. In 1930 his circumstances were so reduced that a committee of well-wishers had to exert themselves to raise a fund for his sustenance.

    Yet his early work—the best of which is in *Selected Poems* (1902)—has a dignity and a molded imagination. A rare reflective temper illumines *Odes and Other Poems* (1894) and *The Hope of the World* (1896). Less interesting is *The Man Who Saw* (1917), and *The Superhuman Antagonists* is high-pitched but feeble. Like his later work, the poet himself lost favor rapidly. At the beginning of his seventy-eighth year he died, obscurely, almost in poverty, at his old Sussex home, August 13, 1935.

A somewhat too-inclusive *Selected Poems of Sir William Watson,* chosen by the poet himself, was published in 1927. This volume shows, rather pathetically, the rise and decline of a poet miscast in the rôle of prophet. The vatic note seems to have dwindled to irritation, an irritation caused mainly by a younger order of writers. Too much of Watson's time was devoted to extolling the tradition he worshiped and attacking a kind of poetry he disliked and which, one suspects, he did not understand. His exasperations aside, Watson produced a few effects both large and fine. "Ode in May" is a flawless expression of its kind; the song, "April, April" is deservedly famous; the "Epigrams" have certainty and wit. It is in the longer poems that Watson is paradoxically most and least himself. Summoning the wraiths of Wordsworth, Milton, Tennyson, he achieved the state of the devotee who merges his own identity in that which he worships. But Watson, alas, was not an illumined disciple, only a bemused priest repeating an old ritual. Since his idol was not a single or defined figure, he lost his own identity without reflecting a better one, becoming almost a composite parody of the Royal Purple trend in English letters. The shorter poems escape this stricture.

### ODE IN MAY

Let me go forth, and share
The overflowing Sun
With one wise friend, or one
Better than wise, being fair,
Where the pewit wheels and dips
On heights of bracken and ling,
And Earth, unto her leaflet tips,
Tingles with the Spring.

What is so sweet and dear
As a prosperous morn in May,
The confident prime of the day,
And the dauntless youth of the year,
When nothing that asks for bliss,
Asking aright, is denied,
And half of the world a bridegroom is,
And half of the world a bride?

The Song of Mingling flows,
Grave, ceremonial, pure,
As once, from lips that endure,
The cosmic descant rose,
When the temporal lord of life,
Going his golden way,
Had taken a wondrous maid to wife
That long had said him nay.

For of old the Sun, our sire,
Came wooing the mother of men,
Earth, that was virginal then,
Vestal fire to his fire.

Silent her bosom and coy,
But the strong god sued and pressed;
And born of their starry nuptial joy
Are all that drink of her breast.

And the triumph of him that begot,
And the travail of her that bore,
Behold, they are evermore
As warp and weft in our lot.
We are children of splendor and flame,
Of shuddering, also, and tears.
Magnificent out of the dust we came,
And abject from the Spheres.

O bright irresistible lord,
We are fruit of Earth's womb, each one,
And fruit of thy loins, O Sun,
Whence first was the seed outpoured.
To thee as our Father we bow,
Forbidden thy Father to see,
Who is older and greater than thou, as thou
Art greater and older than we.

Thou art but as a word of his speech,
Thou art but as a wave of his hand;
Thou art brief as a glitter of sand
'Twixt tide and tide on his beach;
Thou art less than a spark of his fire,
Or a moment's mood of his soul:
Thou art lost in the notes on the lips of his
    choir
That chant the chant of the Whole.

### ESTRANGEMENT

So, without overt breach, we fall apart,
Tacitly sunder—neither you nor I
Conscious of one intelligible Why,
And both, from severance, winning equal
    smart.
So, with resigned and acquiescent heart,
Whene'er your name on some chance lip
    may lie,
I seem to see an alien shade pass by,
A spirit wherein I have no lot or part.

Thus may a captive, in some fortress grim,
From casual speech betwixt his warders, learn
That June on her triumphal progress goes
Through arched and bannered woodlands;
    while for him
She is a legend emptied of concern,
And idle is the rumor of the rose.

### SONG

April, April,
Laugh thy girlish laughter;
Then, the moment after,
Weep thy girlish tears,
April, that mine ears
Like a lover greetest,
If I tell thee, sweetest,
All my hopes and fear.
April, April,
Laugh thy golden laughter,
But, the moment after,
Weep thy golden tears!

### WORLD-STRANGENESS

Strange the world about me lies,
    Never yet familiar grown—
Still disturbs me with surprise,
    Haunts me like a face half-known.

In this house with starry dome,
    Floored with gemlike plains and seas,
Shall I never feel at home,
    Never wholly be at ease?

On from room to room I stray,
    Yet my Host can ne'er espy,
And I know not to this day
    Whether guest or captive I.

So, between the starry dome
    And the floor of plains and seas,
I have never felt at home,
    Never wholly been at ease.

### FOUR EPIGRAMS

The statue—Buonarroti said—doth wait,
Thralled in the block for me to liberate.
The poem—saith the poet—wanders free
Till I betray it to captivity.

✦

The Poet gathers fruit from every tree,
Yea, grapes from thorns and figs from
    thistles he.
Pluck'd by his hand, the basest weed that
    grows
Towers to a lily, reddens to a rose.

✦

Love, like a bird, hath perch'd upon a spray
    For thee and me to hearken what he sings.
Contented, he forgets to fly away;
    But hush! . . . remind not Eros of his
    wings.

✦

The children romp within the graveyard's
    pale;
The lark sings o'er a madhouse or a jail;
Such nice antitheses of perfect poise
Chance in her curious rhetoric employs.

# Francis Thompson

FRANCIS THOMPSON was born at Ashton in Lancashire in 1859. The son of a doctor, he was intended for the profession and took the medical course at Owens College, Manchester. He had, however, no interest in medicine, but from youth evinced a passion for religion, particularly for the ritual of Catholicism.

His attempts to earn a living were a succession of failures. He was employed as a book-agent, and sold no books; he was apprenticed to the boot trade, and spent many hours of his apprenticeship in public libraries; he enlisted as a soldier, and was discharged as incompetent. He went to London, as Francis Meynell says, "not so much to seek his fortune as to escape his bad fortune. He lost in the gamble, but literature gained. He lived for four years as errand man, seller of matches, holder of horses' heads. Soon he became too shabby to gain admittance into the public libraries, so that when one says that desire of reading was with him a passion, one restores to its literal meaning that abused word. He slept on the Embankment, and 'saw the traffic of Jacob's ladder Pitched betwixt Heaven and Charing Cross.' A woman of the streets took pity on him and kept him alive by her charity—the spirit and the deed. He began to write—now for the first time. His poem, 'Dream Tryst,' written on blue sugar wrapping, found after many months an editorial welcome. Thereafter he was persuaded, though with difficulty, to come off the streets; and even to give up for many years the laudanum he had been taking. For the remaining nineteen years of his life he had an existence at any rate three-quarters protected from the physical tragedies of his starved and homeless young manhood."

Francis Meynell does not name the persons who gave Thompson "an editorial welcome" and who provided him with the shelter which made it possible for him to continue writing and, for that matter, living. These persons were Wilfred Meynell (later to become Thompson's editor and executor) and the poet Alice Meynell (see page 120), who named their son Francis after the genius who became his godfather.

Thompson's first volume, *Poems,* appeared in 1893, disclosing beneath a surface of wild metaphors and violent neologisms an affinity with the august. This volume was followed by *Sister Songs* (1895) and *New Poems* (1897). In these, as well as in the essays on De Quincey and Shelley, there was tropical strangeness. Plenitude is here not only in the large concept but in the small detail. Here are metaphors as bold as

> . . . laden with its lampèd clusters bright
> The fiery-fruited vineyard of this night.

and

> I broke through the doors of sunset,
> Ran before the hooves of sunrise.

The "Anthem of Earth," from which the last quotation is taken, is second only to Thompson's highest achievement. "The Hound of Heaven," which Coventry Patmore declared "one of the very few 'great' odes the language can boast," has captured more readers than any religious poem of this century. In a mystic circle, in which the God-pursuing is the God-pursued, the poem moves with the unhurried majesty of a Bach Chorale, building verse upon fugual verse into an unterrestrial architecture. Recognition of a divine order is celebrated with an almost divine excess. Everything, like Thompson's bright laburnum, spills its "honey of wild flame."

Thompson's poetry was embedded in his philosophy to an unusual degree; he saw all things related and linked by immortal power. It was a super-Berkeley who wrote:

> . . . thou canst not stir a flower
> Without troubling of a star.

Thompson's philosophy, however, exalted though it was, could not maintain him on the heights. Rapture and despair fought within him. "Down the arcane where Night would perish in night," he wandered, lost in "incredible excess"; the heart's cry in "The Dread of Height" sounds the ecstatic reaches and profound depths which his spirit touched. His suspensions were unresolved. But if neither man nor nature granted him final solution, the Church offered him serenity, and no singer has ever put the Catholic creed to more inspired measures.

Influenced at first by the dazzling Crashaw and the conceits of the seventeenth century metaphysicians, Thompson allowed himself the fullest play of purple-pompous tropes. He was as prodigal with strange colors and curious words as a child; the words he applied to characterize Shelley might be used with even greater justice to describe Thompson himself: "To the last, in a degree uncommon even among poets, he retained the idiosyncrasy of childhood, expanded and matured without differentiation. To the last, he was the enchanted child."

Riotous images and extravagant archaisms were Thompson's delight and his defect; he toyed with a style that loved to toss the stars and swing constellations by the hair. His was, not infrequently, a baroque magnificence. He often confused glitter with gold, painting the sublime in terms of the theatrical, falling from the grand manner into the grand-opera manner. At worst, Thompson overdressed his lines with a showy vocabulary; at his best, he attained sublimity. Such poems as "A Fallen Yew," "Ode to the Setting Sun," "Any Saint," "In No Strange Land," and, first and last, "The Hound of Heaven," provide a noble shrine for a noble vision. Here he captured, if only for glowing moments, a glory of which most of his contemporaries were not even aware.

Thompson died, after a fragile and spasmodic life, in St. John's Wood, London, in November, 1907. Since that time, several *Selected Poems* have revealed Thompson's pomp and prodigality to a new generation; an inexpensive *Complete Poetical Works* may be found in The Modern Library.

### DAISY

Where the thistle lifts a purple crown
 Six foot out of the turf,
And the harebell shakes on the windy hill—
 O breath of the distant surf!—

The hills look over on the South,
 And southward dreams the sea;

And with the sea-breeze hand in hand
 Came innocence and she.

Where 'mid the gorse the raspberry
 Red for the gatherer springs;
Two children did we stray and talk
 Wise, idle, childish things.

She listened with big-lipped surprise,
 Breast-deep 'mid flower and spine:

Her skin was like a grape whose veins
  Run snow instead of wine.

She knew not those sweet words she spake,
  Nor knew her own sweet way;
But there's never a bird, so sweet a song
  Thronged in whose throat all day.

Oh, there were flowers in Storrington
  On the turf and on the spray;
But the sweetest flower on Sussex hills
  Was the Daisy-flower that day!

Her beauty smoothed earth's furrowed face.
  She gave me tokens three:—
A look, a word of her winsome mouth,
  And a wild raspberry.

A berry red, a guileless look,
  A still word,—strings of sand!
And yet they made my wild, wild heart
  Fly down to her little hand.

For standing artless as the air
  And candid as the skies,
She took the berries with her hand
  And the love with her sweet eyes.

The fairest things have fleetest end,
  Their scent survives their close:
But the rose's scent is bitterness
  To him that loved the rose.

She looked a little wistfully,
  Then went her sunshine way:—
The sea's eye had a mist on it,
  And the leaves fell from the day.

She went her unremembering way,
  She went and left in me
The pang of all the partings gone,
  And partings yet to be.

She left me marveling why my soul
  Was sad that she was glad;
At all the sadness in the sweet,
  The sweetness in the sad.

Still, still I seemed to see her, still
  Look up with soft replies,
And take the berries with her hand,
  And the love with her lovely eyes.

Nothing begins, and nothing ends,
  That is not paid with moan,
For we are born in other's pain,
  And perish in our own.

## TO A SNOWFLAKE

What heart could have thought you?—
Past our devisal
(O filigree petal!)
Fashioned so purely,
Fragilely, surely,
From what Paradisal
Imagineless metal,
Too costly for cost?
Who hammered you, wrought you,
From argentine vapor?—

"God was my shaper.
Passing surmisal,
He hammered, He wrought me,
From curled silver vapor,
To lust of his mind:—
Thou couldst not have thought me!
So purely, so palely,
Tinily, surely,
Mightily, frailly,
Insculped and embossed,
With His hammer of wind,
And His graver of frost."

## AN ARAB LOVE-SONG

The hunchèd camels of the night [1]
Trouble the bright
And silver waters of the moon.
The Maiden of the Morn will soon
Through Heaven stray and sing,
Star gathering.

[1] Cloud-shapes observed by travelers in the East.

Now while the dark about our loves is strewn,
Light of my dark, blood of my heart, O come!
And night will catch her breath up, and be dumb.

Leave thy father, leave thy mother
And thy brother;
Leave the black tents of thy tribe apart!
Am I not thy father and thy brother,
And thy mother?
And thou—what needest with thy tribe's black tents
Who hast the red pavilion of my heart?

### ALL'S VAST

O nothing, in this corporal earth of man,
    That to the imminent heaven of his high soul
Responds with color and with shadow, can
    Lack correlated greatness. If the scroll
Where thoughts lie fast in spell of hieroglyph
    Be mighty through its mighty inhabitants;
If God be in His Name; grave potence if
    The sounds unbind of hieratic chants;
All's vast that vastness means. Nay, I affirm
    Nature is whole in her least things exprest,
Nor know we with what scope God builds the worm.
    Our towns are copied fragments from our breast;
        And all man's Babylons strive but to impart
        The grandeurs of his Babylonian heart.

### EPILOGUE

*(from "A Judgment in Heaven")*

Heaven, which man's generations draws,
Nor deviates into replicas,
Must of as deep diversity
In judgment as creation be.
There is no expeditious road
To pack and label men for God,
And save them by the barrel-load.
Some may perchance, with strange surprise,
Have blundered into Paradise.
In vasty dusk of life abroad,
They fondly thought to err from God,
Nor knew the circle that they trod;
And, wandering all the night about,
Found them at morn where they set out.
Death dawned; Heaven lay in prospect wide:—
Lo! they were standing by His side!

THE POPPY

(*To Monica*)

Summer set lip to earth's bosom bare,
And left the flushed print in a poppy there:
Like a yawn of fire from the grass it came,
And the fanning wind puffed it to flapping flame.

With burnt mouth, red like a lion's, it drank
The blood of the sun as he slaughtered sank,
And dipped its cup in the purpurate shine
When the Eastern conduits ran with wine.

Till it grew lethargied with fierce bliss,
And hot as a swinked gypsy is,
And drowsed in sleepy savageries,
With mouth wide a-pout for a sultry kiss.

A child and man paced side by side,
Treading the skirts of eventide;
But between the clasp of his hand and hers
Lay, felt not, twenty withered years.

She turned, with the rout of her dusk South hair,
And saw the sleeping gypsy there:
And snatched and snapped it in swift child's whim,
With—"Keep it, long as you live!"—to him.

And his smile, as nymphs from their laving meres,
Trembled up from a bath of tears;
And joy, like a mew sea-rocked apart,
Tossed on the waves of his troubled heart.

For *he* saw what she did not see,
That—as kindled by its own fervency—
The verge shriveled inward smolderingly:
And suddenly 'twixt his hand and hers
He knew the twenty withered years—
No flower, but twenty shriveled years.

"Was never such thing until this hour,"
Low to his heart he said; "the flower
Of sleep brings wakening to me,
And of oblivion, memory.

"Was never this thing to me," he said,
"Though with bruisèd poppies my feet are red!"
And again to his own heart very low:
"O child! I love, for I love and know;

"But you, who love nor know at all
The diverse chambers in Love's guest-hall,
Where some rise early, few sit long:
In how differing accents hear the throng
His great Pentecostal tongue;

"Who know not love from amity,
Nor my reported self from me;
A fair fit gift is this, meseems,
You give—this withering flower of dreams.

"O frankly fickle, and fickly true,
Do you know what the days will do to you?
To your love and you what the days will do,
O frankly fickle, and fickly true?

"You have loved me, Fair, three lives—or days:
'Twill pass with the passing of my face.
But where *I* go, your face goes too,
To watch lest I play false to you.

"I am but, my sweet, your foster-lover,
Knowing well when certain years are over
You vanish from me to another;
Yet I know, and love, like the foster-mother.

"So, frankly fickle, and fickly true!
For my brief life-while I take from you
This token, fair and fit, meseems,
For me—this withering flower of dreams."

The sleep-flower sways in the wheat its head,
Heavy with dreams, as that with bread:
The goodly grain and the sun-flushed sleeper
The reaper reaps, and Time the reaper.

I hang 'mid men my needless head,
And my fruit is dreams, as theirs is bread:
The goodly men and the sun-hazed sleeper
Time shall reap, but after the reaper
The world shall glean of me, me the sleeper.

Love, love! your flower of withered dream
In leavèd rhyme lies safe, I deem,
Sheltered and shut in a nook of rhyme,
From the reaper man, and his reaper Time.

Love! *I* fall into the claws of Time:
But lasts within a leavèd rhyme
All that the world of me esteems—
My withered dreams, my withered dreams.

### THE SUN

*(from "Ode to the Setting Sun")*

Who lit the furnace of the mammoth's heart?
  Who shagged him like Pilatus' ribbèd flanks?
    Who raised the columned ranks
Of that old pre-diluvian forestry,
Which like a continent torn oppressed the sea,
  When the ancient heavens did in rains depart,
    While the high-dancèd whirls
Of the tossed scud made hiss thy drenchèd curls?
    Thou rear'dst the enormous brood;
    Who hast with life imbued
The lion maned in tawny majesty,
    The tiger velvet-barred,
    The stealthy-stepping pard,
And the lithe panther's flexous symmetry?

How came the entombèd tree a light-bearer,
    Though sunk in lightless lair?
    Friend of the forgers of earth,
    Mate of the earthquake and thunders volcanic,
  Clasped in the arms of the forces Titanic
    Which rock like a cradle the girth
      Of the ether-hung world;
    Swart son of the swarthy mine,
  When flame on the breath of his nostrils feeds
    How is his countenance half-divine,
    Like thee in thy sanguine weeds?
    Thou gavest him his light,
    Though sepultured in night
Beneath the dead bones of a perished world;
    Over his prostrate form
    Though cold, and heat, and storm,
The mountainous wrack of a creation hurled.

    Who made the splendid rose
    Saturate with purple glows;
Cupped to the marge with beauty; a perfume-press
    Whence the wind vintages
Gushes of warmèd fragrance richer far
  Than all the flavorous ooze of Cyprus' vats?
Lo, in yon gale which waves her green cymar,
    With dusky cheeks burnt red
    She sways her heavy head,
Drunk with the must of her own odorousness;
  While in a moted trouble the vexed gnats
Maze, and vibrate, and tease the noontide hush.
  Who girt dissolvèd lightnings in the grape?
Summered the opal with an Irised flush?
  Is it not thou that dost the tulip drape,

And huest the daffodilly,
Yet who hast snowed the lily,
And her frail sister, whom the waters name,
Dost vestal-vesture 'mid the blaze of June,
Cold as the new-sprung girlhood of the moon
Ere Autumn's kiss sultry her cheek with flame?
Thou sway'st thy sceptered beam
O'er all delight and dream,
Beauty is beautiful but in thy glance:
And like a jocund maid
In garland-flowers arrayed,
Before thy ark Earth keeps her sacred dance.


### A FALLEN YEW

It seemed corrival of the world's great prime,
Made to un-edge the scythe of Time,
And last with stateliest rhyme.

No tender Dryad ever did indue
That rigid chiton of rough yew,
To fret her white flesh through:

But some god like to those grim Asgard lords,
Who walk the fables of the hordes
From Scandinavian fjords,

Upheaved its stubborn girth, and raised unriven,
Against the whirl-blast and the levin,
Defiant arms to Heaven.

When doom puffed out the stars, we might have said,
It would decline its heavy head,
And see the world to bed.

For this firm yew did from the vassal leas,
And rain and air, its tributaries,
Its revenues increase,

And levy impost on the golden sun,
Take the blind years as they might run,
And no fate seek or shun.

But now our yew is strook, is fallen—yea,
Hacked like dull wood of every day
To this and that, men say.

Never!—To Hades' shadowy shipyards gone,
Dim barge of Dis, down Acheron
It drops, or Lethe wan.

Stirred by its fall—poor destined bark of Dis!—
Along my soul a bruit there is
Of echoing images,

Reverberations of mortality:
　Spelt backward from its death, to me
　　Its life reads saddenedly.

Its breast was hollowed as the tooth of eld;
　And boys, there creeping unbeheld,
　　A laughing moment dwelled.

Yet they, within its very heart so crept,
　Reached not the heart that courage kept
　　With winds and years beswept.

And in its boughs did close and kindly nest
　The birds, as they within its breast,
　　By all its leaves caressed.

But bird nor child might touch by any art
　Each other's or the tree's hid heart,
　　A whole God's breadth apart;

The breadth of God, the breadth of death and life!
　Even so, even so, in undreamed strife
　　With pulseless Law, the wife,—

The sweetest wife on sweetest marriage-day,—
　Their souls at grapple in mid-way,
　　Sweet to her sweet may say:

"I take you to my inmost heart, my true!"
　Ah, fool! but there is one heart you
　　Shall never take him to!

The hold that falls not when the town is got,
　The heart's heart, whose immurèd plot
　　Hath keys yourself keep not!

Its ports you cannot burst—you are withstood—
　For him that to your listening blood
　　Sends precepts as he would.

Its gates are deaf to Love, high summoner;
　Yea, love's great warrant runs not there:
　　You are your prisoner.

Yourself are with yourself the sole consortress
　In that unleaguerable fortress;
　　It knows you not for portress.

Its keys are at the cincture hung of God;
　Its gates are trepidant to His nod;
　　By Him its floors are trod.

And if His feet shall rock those floors in wrath,
　Or blest aspersion sleek His path,
　　Is only choice it hath.

Yea, in that ultimate heart's occult abode
To lie as in an oubliette of God,
    Or in a bower untrod,

Built by a secret Lover for His Spouse;—
Sole choice is this your life allows,
    Sad tree, whose perishing boughs
        So few birds house!


### A COUNSEL OF MODERATION

On him the unpetitioned heavens descend,
Who heaven on earth proposes not for end;
The perilous and celestial excess
Taking with peace, lacking with thankfulness.
Bliss in extreme befits thee not until
Thou'rt not extreme in bliss; be equal still:
Sweets to be granted think thyself unmeet
Till thou have learned to hold sweet not too sweet.

This thing not far is he from wise in art
Who teacheth; nor who doth, from wise in heart.


### ANY SAINT

(*Condensed*)

His shoulder did I hold
Too high that I, o'erbold
        Weak one,
    Should lean thereon.

But He a little hath
Declined His stately path
        And my
    Feet set more high;

That the slack arm may reach
His shoulder, and faint speech
        Stir
    His unwithering hair.

And bolder now and bolder
I lean upon that shoulder,
        So dear
    He is and near:

And with His aureole
The tresses of my soul
        Are blent
    In wished content.

Yea, this too gentle Lover
Hath flattering words to move her
        To pride
    By His sweet side.

Ah, Love! somewhat let be—
Lest my humility
        Grow weak
    When Thou dost speak.

Rebate Thy tender suit,
Lest to herself impute
        Some worth
    Thy bride of earth!

A maid too easily
Conceits herself to be
        Those things
    Her lover sings;

And being straitly wooed,
Believes herself the Good
        And Fair
    He seeks in her.

Turn something of Thy look,
And fear me with rebuke,
That I
May timorously

Take tremors in Thy arms,
And with contrivèd charms
Allure
A love unsure.

Not to me, not to me,
Builded so flawfully,
O God,
Thy humbling laud!

Not to this man, but Man,—
Universe in a span;
Point
Of the spheres conjoint;

In whom eternally
Thou, Light, dost focus Thee!—
Didst pave
The way o' the wave.

✦

Thou meaning, couldst thou see,
Of all which dafteth thee;
So plain,
It mocks thy pain.

Stone of the Law indeed,
Thine own self couldst thou read;
Thy bliss
Within thee is.

Compost of Heaven and mire,
Slow foot and swift desire!
Lo,
To have Yes, choose No;

✦

To feel thyself and be
His dear nonentity—
Caught
Beyond human thought

In the thunder-spout of Him,
Until thy being dim,
And be
Dead deathlessly.

Stoop, stoop; for thou dost fear
The nettle's wrathful spear,
So slight
Art thou of might!

Rise; for Heaven hath no frown
When thou to thee pluck'st down,
Strong clod!
The neck of God.

## THE HOUND OF HEAVEN

I fled Him, down the nights and down the days;
  I fled Him, down the arches of the years;
I fled Him, down the labyrinthine ways
  Of my own mind; and in the mist of tears
I hid from Him, and under running laughter.
    Up vistaed hopes I sped;
    And shot, precipitated,
Adown Titanic glooms of chasmèd fears,
  From those strong Feet that followed, followed after.
    But with unhurrying chase,
    And unperturbèd pace,
Deliberate speed, majestic instancy,
    They beat—and a Voice beat
    More instant than the Feet—
"All things betray thee, who betrayest Me."

    I pleaded, outlaw-wise,
By many a hearted casement, curtained red,
  Trellised with intertwining charities
(For, though I knew His love Who followèd,

Yet was I sore adread
Lest, having Him, I must have naught beside);
But, if one little casement parted wide,
   The gust of His approach would clash it to:
Fear wist not to evade, as Love wist to pursue.
Across the margent of the world I fled,
   And troubled the gold gateways of the stars,
   Smiting for shelter on their clangèd bars;
      Fretted to dulcet jars
And silvern chatter the pale ports o' the moon.
I said to Dawn: Be sudden—to Eve: Be soon;
   With thy young skiey blossoms heap me over
     From this tremendous Lover—
Float thy vague veil about me, lest He see!
   I tempted all His servitors, but to find
My own betrayal in their constancy,
In faith to Him their fickleness to me,
   Their traitorous trueness, and their loyal deceit.
To all swift things for swiftness did I sue;
  Clung to the whistling mane of every wind.
     But whether they swept, smoothly fleet,
    The long savannahs of the blue;
     Or whether, Thunder-driven,
     They clanged his chariot 'thwart a heaven,
Plashy with flying lightnings round the spurn o' their feet:—
Fear wist not to evade as Love wist to pursue.
     Still with unhurrying chase,
     And unperturbèd pace,
    Deliberate speed, majestic instancy,
     Came on the following Feet,
     And a Voice above their beat—
  "Naught shelters thee, who wilt not shelter Me."

I sought no more that after which I strayed
     In face of man or maid;
But still within the little children's eyes
    Seems something, something that replies,
*They* at least are for me, surely for me!
I turned me to them very wistfully;
But just as their young eyes grew sudden fair
    With dawning answers there,
Their angel plucked them from me by the hair.
"Come then, ye other children, Nature's—share
With me" (said I) "your delicate fellowship;
    Let me greet you lip to lip,
    Let me twine with you caresses,
     Wantoning
     With our Lady-Mother's vagrant tresses,
     Banqueting

With her in her wind-walled palace,
Underneath her azured daïs,
Quaffing, as your taintless way is,
    From a chalice
Lucent-weeping out of the dayspring."
        So it was done:
*I* in their delicate fellowship was one—
Drew the bolt of Nature's secrecies.
    *I* knew all the swift importings
    On the willful face of skies;
    I knew how the clouds arise
    Spumèd of the wild sea-snortings;
        All that's born or dies
    Rose and drooped with; made them shapers
Of mine own moods, or wailful or divine;
    With them joyed and was bereaven.
    I was heavy with the even,
    When she lit her glimmering tapers
    Round the day's dead sanctities.
    I laughed in the morning's eyes.
I triumphed and I saddened with all weather,
    Heaven and I wept together,
And its sweet tears were salt with mortal mine;

Against the red throb of its sunset-heart
    I laid my own to beat,
    And share commingling heat;
But not by that, by that, was eased my human smart.
In vain my tears were wet on Heaven's gray cheek.
For ah! we know not what each other says,
    These things and I; in sound *I* speak—
*Their* sound is but their stir, they speak by silences.
Nature, poor stepdame, cannot slake my drouth;
    Let her, if she would owe me,
Drop yon blue bosom-veil of sky, and show me
    The breasts o' her tenderness:
Never did any milk of hers once bless
        My thirsting mouth.
        Nigh and nigh draws the chase,
        With unperturbèd pace,
    Deliberate speed, majestic instancy;
        And past those noisèd Feet
        A Voice comes yet more fleet—
    "Lo! naught contents thee, who content'st not Me."

Naked I wait Thy love's uplifted stroke!
My harness piece by piece Thou hast hewn from me,
    And smitten me to my knee;
    I am defenseless utterly.
    I slept, methinks, and woke,

And, slowly gazing, find me stripped in sleep.
In the rash lustihead of my young powers,
   I shook the pillaring hours
And pulled my life upon me; grimed with smears,
I stand amid the dust o' the mounded years—
My mangled youth lies dead beneath the heap.
My days have crackled and gone up in smoke,
Have puffed and burst as sun-starts on a stream.
     Yea, faileth now even dream
The dreamer, and the lute the lutanist;
Even the linked fantasies, in whose blossomy twist
I swung the earth a trinket at my wrist,
Are yielding; cords of all too weak account
For earth with heavy griefs so overplused.
    Ah! is Thy love indeed
A weed, albeit an amaranthine weed,
Suffering no flowers except its own to mount?
    Ah! must—
    Designer infinite!—
Ah! must Thou char the wood ere Thou canst limn with it?
My freshness spent its wavering shower i' the dust;
And now my heart is as a broken fount,
Wherein tear-dripping stagnate, spilt down ever
    From the dank thoughts that shiver
Upon the sighful branches of my mind.
    Such is; what is to be?
The pulp so bitter, how shall taste the rind?
I dimly guess what Time in mists confounds;
Yet ever and anon a trumpet sounds
From the hid battlements of Eternity;
Those shaken mists a space unsettle, then
Round the half-glimpsèd turrets slowly wash again.
    But not ere him who summoneth
    I first have seen, enwound
With glooming robes purpureal, cypress-crowned;
His name I know, and what his trumpet saith.
Whether man's heart or life it be which yields
    Thee harvest, must Thy harvest-fields
    Be dunged with rotten death?

    Now of that long pursuit
    Comes on at hand the bruit;
   That Voice is round me like a bursting sea:
    "And is thy earth so marred,
    Shattered in shard on shard?
  Lo, all things fly thee, for thou fliest Me!
    Strange, piteous, futile thing!
Wherefore should any set thee love apart?
Seeing none but I makes much of naught" (He said),
"And human love needs human meriting:
    How hast thou merited—

Of all man's clotted clay the dingiest clot?
　　　Alack, thou knowest not
How little worthy of any love thou art!
Whom wilt thou find to love ignoble thee
　　　Save Me, save only Me?
All which I took from thee I did but take,
　　　Not for thy harms,
But just that thou might'st seek it in My arms.
　　　All which thy child's mistake
Fancies as lost, I have stored for thee at home:
　　　Rise, clasp My hand, and come!"


　　　Halts by me that footfall:
　　　Is my gloom, after all,
Shade of His hand, outstretched caressingly?
　　　"Ah, fondest, blindest, weakest,
　　　I am He Whom thou seekest!
Thou dravest love from thee, who dravest Me."


FROM "GRACE OF THE WAY"

Now of that vision I, bereaven,
　This knowledge keep, that may not dim:
Short arm needs man to reach to Heaven,
　So ready is Heaven to stoop to him.


TO OLIVIA

I fear to love thee, Sweet, because
Love's the ambassador of loss;
White flake of childhood, clinging so
To my soiled raiment, thy shy snow
At tenderest touch will shrink and go.
Love me not, delightful child.
My heart, by many snares beguiled,
Has grown timorous and wild.
It would fear thee not at all,
Wert thou not so harmless-small.
Because thy arrows, not yet dire,
Are still unbarbed with destined fire,
I fear thee more than hadst thou stood
Full-panoplied in womanhood.


"IN NO STRANGE LAND"[1]

O world invisible, we view thee,
O world intangible, we touch thee,
O world unknowable, we know thee,
Inapprehensible, we clutch thee!

Does the fish soar to find the ocean,
The eagle plunge to find the air—
That we ask of the stars in motion
If they have rumor of thee there?

Not where the wheeling systems darken,
And our benumbed conceiving soars!—
The drift of pinions, would we hearken,
Beats at our own clay-shuttered doors.

The angels keep their ancient places;
Turn but a stone, and start a wing!
'Tis ye, 'tis your estrangèd faces,
That miss the many-splendored thing.

But, when so sad thou canst not sadder,
Cry;—and upon thy so sore loss
Shall shine the traffic of Jacob's ladder
Pitched betwixt Heaven and Charing Cross.

Yea, in the night, my Soul, my daughter,
Cry,—clinging Heaven by the hems;
And lo, Christ walking on the water
Not of Gennesareth, but Thames!

[1] These verses, unpublished during his lifetime, were found among Francis Thompson's papers after his death.

ENVOY

Go, songs, for ended is our brief, sweet play;
  Go, children of swift joy and tardy sorrow:
And some are sung, and that was yesterday,
  And some unsung, and that may be tomorrow.

Go forth; and if it be o'er stony way,
  Old joy can lend what newer grief must borrow:
And it was sweet, and that was yesterday,
  And sweet is sweet, though purchasèd with sorrow.

Go, songs, and come not back from your far way:
  And if men ask you why ye smile and sorrow,
Tell them ye grieve, for your hearts know Today,
  Tell them ye smile, for your eyes know Tomorrow.

# A. E. Housman

A(LFRED) E(DWARD) HOUSMAN was born March 26, 1859, and educated at Oxford
where he received his M.A. He was a Higher Division Clerk in the British
Patent Office for ten years (1882-1892), leaving the office to become a teacher.
Professor of Latin at University College, London, from 1892 to 1911, at Cambridge
after 1911, he is one of the finest classical scholars of his time.

He is known to the world at large as the author of *A Shropshire Lad;* his entire
non-classical output consisting of only two small volumes of poems, published nearly
thirty years apart. The popularity of the first of these was exceeded only by Fitzgerald's *Rubáiyát of Omar Khayyám.* The extraordinary success of both Fitzgerald and Housman is the more curious since both voice a philosophy compounded
of pessimism and defeat. Though obviously not Oriental, Housman's fatalism is
the darker of the two. Fitzgerald escapes from a world of frustration to a world
of sensation; Housman does not even make the gesture of escape. Khayyám's
remedy is drink; Housman's is suicide. Such concepts, dismal at the core, could
never have found favor had they not been expressed in peculiarly glamorous
music. Both Fitzgerald and Housman wrote with such compelling grace that, for
the moment, they make darkness seem desirable. It is, however, doubtful whether
readers pay much heed to the central philosophy, but rather are carried on if not
convinced by the brisk and brilliant measures.

*A Shropshire Lad* is limited in range and idea. Nature is not kind; lovers are
untrue; men cheat and girls betray; lads, though lightfoot, drink and die; an occasional drum calls to a conflict without reason, a struggle without hope. Nevertheless,
courage is dominant, declared over and over in such poems as "Reveillé," "When
Smoke Stood Up from Ludlow," "The Chestnut Casts His Flambeaux," and
Housman's bitter but fearless philosophy reaches the heights in his "Epilogue."

Purely as writing, however, *A Shropshire Lad* is incomparable. Owing nothing to any poet of his own generation and showing few influences other than Heine's, Housman's verse is condensed to the uttermost, stripped of every superfluous ornament, pared and precise. Not the least of his triumph is the mingling of pungent humor and poignance. Possibly the outstanding virtue is the seemingly artless but extraordinarily skillful simplicity of tone. This is song sharpened, acid-flavored, yet always song.

*A Shropshire Lad* was first published in 1896 when Housman was thirty-seven, although several of the lyrics were written when the poet was younger. After a silence of twenty-six years, there appeared his *Last Poems* (1922). The title is significant, Housman saying, "I publish these poems, few though they are, because it is not likely that I shall ever be impelled to write much more. I can no longer expect to be revisited by the continuous excitement under which in the early months of 1895 I wrote the greater part of my other book, nor indeed could I well sustain it if it came." Most of the second volume belongs to an earlier period, to the years between 1895 and 1910. Here in *Last Poems* the Shropshire lad lives again to pipe his mournful-merry tunes; here again the rose-lipt maiden kisses carelessly as ever, and the heart out of the bosom is given in vain. Here Wenlock Edge is still in trouble, young men shoulder the sky and face the hills whose comfort cannot delay "the beautiful and deathstruck year." The pessimism assumes a half-careless, half-heroic note.

*A Shropshire Lad* sounded the note of a wry surrender:

> Be still, be still, my soul; it is but for a season:
> Let us endure an hour and see injustice done.
>
> Aye, look, high heaven and earth ail from the prime foundation;
> All thoughts to rive the heart are here, and all in vain:
> Horror and scorn and hate and fear and indignation—
> Oh, why did I awake? When shall I sleep again?

And in *Last Poems* the no less disillusioned spirit cries:

> We of a certainty are not the first
> Have sat in taverns while the tempest hurled
> Their hopeful plans to emptiness, and cursed
> Whatever brute or blackguard made the world.

The rhythms of *Last Poems* are a trifle slower, the cadences somewhat more acrid, but Housman's command of his instrument is still unfaltering. Some critics have pointed out Housman's "echoes" and John Sparrow, in *The Nineteenth Century,* has traced certain general resemblances and a few specific phrases to earlier writers, especially Shakespeare, Heine, and the Greek lyrists. But Housman's touch is so definitely his own, his accent so individualized that the occasional (and usually intentional) allusions are absorbed in the English poet's idiom. Who else could modernize the story of Jesus as concisely as Housman has done in "The Carpenter's Son"; who but he could have turned such simple material as "Loveliest of Trees" to the words and music of possibly the finest lyric in the English language? Each reader will have his favorites, and those admirers who know the two volumes almost by heart will even resent learning that Thomas Hardy considered "Is my team ploughing" one of the most dramatic short poems in the language.

Besides his poetry Housman has written a little provocative verse. He edited Juvenal and the works of Manilius, supplying the latter with a trenchant preface which reveals a caustic, though not wholly unsuspected, side of the scholar. A similar tone—informed, intuitive, and teasing—was heard in *The Name and Nature of Poetry* (1933), a lecture (delivered at Cambridge in May, 1933) which concealed as much about the process of creation as it revealed.

But it is as a poet that Housman will live for his two small books seem marked for permanence. Containing poems which are often extended epigrams they are part of the world's treasures, a set of almost flawless songs, probably as near lyric perfection as can be attained by the written word.

### REVEILLÉ

Wake: the silver dusk returning
  Up the beach of darkness brims,
And the ship of sunrise burning
  Strands upon the eastern rims.

Wake: the vaulted shadow shatters,
  Trampled to the floor it spanned,
And the tent of night in tatters
  Straws the sky-pavilioned land.

Up, lad, up, 'tis late for lying:
  Hear the drums of morning play;
Hark, the empty highways crying
  "Who'll beyond the hills away?"

Towns and countries woo together,
  Forelands beacon, belfries call;
Never lad that trod on leather
  Lived to feast his heart with all.

Up, lad: thews that lie and cumber
  Sunlit pallets never thrive;
Morns abed and daylight slumber
  Were not meant for man alive.

Clay lies still, but blood's a rover;
  Breath's a ware that will not keep.
Up, lad: when the journey's over
  There'll be time enough to sleep.

### WHEN I WAS ONE-AND-TWENTY

When I was one-and-twenty
  I heard a wise man say,
"Give crowns and pounds and guineas
  But not your heart away;

Give pearls away and rubies
  But keep your fancy free."
But I was one-and-twenty,
  No use to talk to me.

When I was one-and-twenty
  I heard him say again,
"The heart out of the bosom
  Was never given in vain;
'Tis paid with sighs a-plenty
  And sold for endless rue."
And I am two-and-twenty,
  And oh, 'tis true, 'tis true.

### WITH RUE MY HEART IS LADEN

With rue my heart is laden
  For golden friends I had,
For many a rose-lipt maiden
  And many a lightfoot lad.

By brooks too broad for leaping
  The lightfoot boys are laid;
The rose-lipt girls are sleeping
  In fields where roses fade.

### TO AN ATHLETE DYING YOUNG

The time you won your town the race
We chaired you through the market-place
Man and boy stood cheering by,
And home we brought you shoulder-high.

Today, the road all runners come,
Shoulder-high we bring you home,
And set you at your threshold down,
Townsman of a stiller town.

Smart lad, to slip betimes away
From fields where glory does not stay,
And early though the laurel grows
It withers quicker than the rose.

Eyes the shady night has shut
Cannot see the record cut,
And silence sounds no worse than cheers
After earth has stopped the ears:

Now you will not swell the rout
Of lads that wore their honors out,
Runners whom renown outran
And the name died before the man.

So set, before its echoes fade,
The fleet foot on the sill of shade,
And hold to the low lintel up
The still-defended challenge-cup.

And round that early-laureled head
Will flock to gaze the strengthless dead,
And find unwithered on its curls
The garland briefer than a girl's.

### LOVELIEST OF TREES

Loveliest of trees, the cherry now
Is hung with bloom along the bough,
And stands about the woodland ride
Wearing white for Eastertide.

Now, of my threescore years and ten,
Twenty will not come again,
And take from seventy springs a score,
It only leaves me fifty more.

And since to look at things in bloom
Fifty springs are little room,
About the woodlands I will go
To see the cherry hung with snow.

### IS MY TEAM PLOUGHING

"Is my team ploughing,
   That I used to drive
And hear the harness jingle
   When I was man alive?"

Aye, the horses trample,
   The harness jingles now;
No change though you lie under
   The land you used to plough.

"Is football playing
   Along the river shore,
With lads to chase the leather,
   Now I stand up no more?"

Aye, the ball is flying,
   The lads play heart and soul;
The goal stands up, the keeper
   Stands up to keep the goal.

"Is my girl happy,
   That I thought hard to leave,
And has she tired of weeping
   As she lies down at eve?"

Aye, she lies down lightly,
   She lies not down to weep:
Your girl is well contented.
   Be still, my lad, and sleep.

"Is my friend hearty,
   Now I am thin and pine;
And has he found to sleep in
   A better bed than mine?"

Aye, lad, I lie easy,
   I lie as lads would choose;
I cheer a dead man's sweetheart.
   Never ask me whose.

### WHEN SMOKE STOOD UP
### FROM LUDLOW

When smoke stood up from Ludlow,
   And mist blew off from Teme,
And blithe afield to ploughing
   Against the morning beam
   I strode beside my team,

The blackbird in the coppice
   Looked out to see me stride,
And hearkened as I whistled
   The trampling team beside,
   And fluted and replied:

"Lie down, lie down, young yeoman;
   What use to rise and rise?
Rise man a thousand mornings
   Yet down at last he lies,
   And then the man is wise."

I heard the tune he sang me,
   And spied his yellow bill;

I picked a stone and aimed it
  And threw it with a will:
And then the bird was still.

Then my soul within me
  Took up the blackbird's strain,
And still beside the horses
  Along the dewy lane
  It sang the song again:

"Lie down, lie down, young yeoman;
  The sun moves always west;
The road one treads to labor
  Will lead one home to rest,
  And that will be the best."

### WHEN I WATCH THE LIVING MEET

When I watch the living meet,
  And the moving pageant file
Warm and breathing through the street
  Where I lodge a little while,

If the heats of hate and lust
  In the house of flesh are strong,
Let me mind the house of dust
  Where my sojourn shall be long.

In the nation that is not
  Nothing stands that stood before;
There revenges are forgot,
  And the hater hates no more;

Lovers lying two and two
  Ask not whom they sleep beside,
And the bridegroom all night through
  Never turns him to the bride.

### OH, SEE HOW THICK THE GOLDCUP FLOWERS

Oh, see how thick the goldcup flowers
  Are lying in field and lane,
With dandelions to tell the hours
  That never are told again,
Oh, may I squire you round the meads
  And pick you posies gay?
—'Twill do no harm to take my arm.
  "You may, young man, you may."

Ah, spring was sent for lass and lad,
  'Tis now the blood runs gold,
And man and maid had best be glad
  Before the world is old.
What flowers today may flower tomorrow,
  But never as good as new.
—Suppose I wound my arm right round.
  " 'Tis true, young man, 'tis true."

Some lads there are, 'tis shame to say,
  That only court to thieve,
And once they bear the bloom away
  'Tis little enough they leave.
Then keep your heart for men like me
  And safe from trustless chaps.
My love is true and all for you.
  "Perhaps, young man, perhaps."

Oh, look in my eyes then, can you doubt.
  —Why, 'tis a mile from town.
How green the grass is all about!
  We might as well sit down.
—Ah, life, what is it but a flower?
  Why must true lovers sigh?
Be kind, have pity, my own, my pretty,—
  "Good-by, young man, good-by."

### THE LADS IN THEIR HUNDREDS

The lads in their hundreds to Ludlow come in for the fair,
  There's men from the barn and the forge and the mill and the fold,
The lads for the girls and the lads for the liquor are there,
  And there with the rest are the lads that will never be old.

There's chaps from the town and the field and the till and the cart,
  And many to count are the stalwart, and many the brave,
And many the handsome of face and the handsome of heart,
  And few that will carry their looks or their truth to the grave.

I wish one could know them, I wish there were tokens to tell
    The fortunate fellows that now you can never discern;
And then one could talk with them friendly and wish them farewell
    And watch them depart on the way that they will not return.

But now you may stare as you like and there's nothing to scan;
    And brushing your elbow unguessed-at and not to be told
They carry back bright to the coiner the mintage of man,
    The lads that will die in their glory and never be old.

### WHEN THE LAD FOR LONGING SIGHS

When the lad for longing sighs,
    Mute and dull of cheer and pale,
If at death's own door he lies,
    Maiden, you can heal his ail.

Lovers' ills are all to buy:
    The wan look, the hollow tone,
The hung head, the sunken eye,
    You can have them for your own.

Buy them, buy them: eve and morn
    Lovers' ills are all to sell.
Then you can lie down forlorn;
    But the lover will be well.

### THE IMMORTAL PART

When I meet the morning beam,
Or lay me down at night to dream,
  I hear my bones within me say,
"Another night, another day.

"When shall this slough of sense be cast,
This dust of thoughts be laid at last,
The man of flesh and soul be slain
And the man of bone remain?

"This tongue that talks, these lungs that
    shout,
These thews that hustle us about,
This brain that fills the skull with schemes,
And its humming hive of dreams,—

"These today are proud in power
And lord it in their little hour:
The immortal bones obey control
Of dying flesh and dying soul.

" 'Tis long till eve and morn are gone:
Slow the endless night comes on,
And late to fullness grows the birth
That shall last as long as earth.

"Wanderers eastward, wanderers west,
Know you why you cannot rest?
'Tis that every mother's son
Travails with a skeleton.

"Lie down in the bed of dust;
Bear the fruit that bear you must;
Bring the eternal seed to light,
And morn is all the same as night.

"Rest you so from trouble sore,
Fear the heat o' the sun no more,
Nor the snowing winter wild,
Now you labor not with child.

"Empty vessel, garment cast,
We that wore you long shall last.
—Another night, another day."
    So my bones within me say.

Therefore they shall do my will
Today while I am master still,
And flesh and soul, now both are strong,
Shall hale the sullen slaves along,

Before this fire of sense decay,
This smoke of thought blow clean away,
And leave with ancient night alone
The steadfast and enduring bone.

### ON WENLOCK EDGE

On Wenlock Edge the wood's in trouble;
His forest fleece the Wrekin heaves;
The gale, it plies the saplings double,
And thick on Severn snow the leaves.

'Twould blow like this through hold and
  hangar
When Uricon the city stood:
'Tis the old wind in the old anger,
But then it threshed another wood.

Then, 'twas before my time, the Roman
At yonder heaving hill would stare:
The blood that warms an English yeoman,
The thoughts that hurt him, they were there.

There, like the wind through woods in riot,
Through him the gale of life blew high;
The tree of man was never quiet:
Then 'twas the Roman, now 'tis I.

The gale, it plies the saplings double,
It blows so hard, 'twill soon be gone:
Today the Roman and his trouble
Are ashes under Uricon.

### OH, WHEN I WAS IN LOVE WITH YOU

Oh, when I was in love with you,
  Then I was clean and brave,
And miles around the wonder grew
  How well did I behave.

And now the fancy passes by,
  And nothing will remain,
And miles around they'll say that I
  Am quite myself again.

### ALONG THE FIELD AS WE CAME BY

Along the field as we came by
A year ago, my love and I,
The aspen over stile and stone
Was talking to itself alone.
"Oh, who are these that kiss and pass?
A country lover and his lass;
Two lovers looking to be wed;
And time shall put them both to bed,
But she shall lie with earth above,
And he beside another love."

And sure enough beneath the tree
There walks another love with me,
And overhead the aspen heaves
Its rainy-sounding silver leaves;

And I spell nothing in their stir,
But now perhaps they speak to her,
And plain for her to understand
They talk about a time at hand
When I shall sleep with clover clad,
And she beside another lad.

### ON THE IDLE HILL OF SUMMER

On the idle hill of summer,
  Sleepy with the flow of streams,
Far I hear the steady drummer
  Drumming like a noise in dreams.

Far and near and low and louder
  On the roads of earth go by,
Dear to friends and food for powder,
  Soldiers marching, all to die.

East and west on fields forgotten
  Bleach the bones of comrades slain,
Lovely lads and dead and rotten;
  None that go return again.

Far the calling bugles hollo,
  High the screaming fife replies,
Gay the files of scarlet follow:
  Woman bore me, I will rise.

### BREDON HILL

In summertime on Bredon
  The bells they sound so clear;
Round both the shires they ring them
  In steeples far and near,
  A happy noise to hear.

Here of a Sunday morning
  My love and I would lie,
And see the colored counties,
  And hear the larks so high
  About us in the sky.

The bells would ring to call her
  In valleys miles away:
"Come all to church, good people;
  Good people, come and pray."
  But here my love would stay.

And I would turn and answer
  Among the springing thyme,
"Oh, peal upon our wedding,

And we will hear the chime,
  And come to church in time."

But when the snows at Christmas
  On Bredon top were strown,
My love rose up so early
  And stole out unbeknown
  And went to church alone.

They tolled the one bell only,
  Groom there was none to see,
The mourners followed after,
  And so to church went she,
  And would not wait for me.

The bells they sound on Bredon,
  And still the steeples hum.
"Come all to church, good people,—"
  Oh, noisy bells, be dumb;
  I hear you, I will come.

### LANCER

I 'listed at home for a lancer,
  *Oh who would not sleep with the brave?*
I 'listed at home for a lancer
  To ride on a horse to my grave.

And over the seas we were bidden
  A country to take and to keep;
And far with the brave I have ridden,
  And now with the brave I shall sleep.

For round me the men will be lying
  That learned me the way to behave,
And showed me my business of dying:
  *Oh who would not sleep with the brave?*

They ask and there is not an answer;
Says I, I will 'list for a lancer,
  *Oh who would not sleep with the brave?*

And I with the brave shall be sleeping
  At ease on my mattress of loam,
When back from their taking and keeping
  The squadron is riding at home.

The wind with the plumes will be playing,
  The girls will stand watching them wave,
And eyeing my comrades and saying
  *Oh who would not sleep with the brave?*

They ask and there is not an answer;
Says you, I will 'list for a lancer,
  *Oh who would not sleep with the brave?*

## THE CHESTNUT CASTS HIS FLAMBEAUX, AND THE FLOWERS

The chestnut casts his flambeaux, and the flowers
  Stream from the hawthorn on the wind away,
The doors clap to, the pane is blind with showers.
  Pass me the can, lad; there's an end of May.

There's one spoilt spring to scant our mortal lot,
  One season ruined of our little store.
May will be fine next year as like as not:
  Oh, aye, but then we shall be twenty-four.

We for a certainty are not the first
  Have sat in taverns while the tempest hurled
Their hopeful plans to emptiness, and cursed
  Whatever brute and blackguard made the world.

It is in truth iniquity on high
  To cheat our sentenced souls of aught they crave,
And mar the merriment as you and I
  Fare on our long fool's errand to the grave.

Iniquity it is; but pass the can.
  My lad, no pair of kings our mothers bore;
Our only portion is the estate of man:
  We want the moon, but we shall get no more.

If here today the cloud of thunder lours
   Tomorrow it will hie on far behests;
The flesh will grieve on other bones than ours
   Soon, and the soul will mourn in other breasts.

The troubles of our proud and angry dust
   Are from eternity, and shall not fail.
Bear them we can, and if we can we must.
   Shoulder the sky, my lad, and drink your ale.

### EIGHT O'CLOCK

He stood, and heard the steeple
   Sprinkle the quarters on the morning town.
One, two, three, four, to market-place and people
   It tossed them down.

Strapped, noosed, nighing his hour,
   He stood and counted them and cursed his luck;
And then the clock collected in the tower
   Its strength, and struck.

### EPILOGUE

"Terence, this is stupid stuff;
You eat your victuals fast enough;
There can't be much amiss, 'tis clear,
To see the rate you drink your beer.
But oh, good Lord, the verse you make,
It gives a chap the belly-ache.
The cow, the old cow, she is dead;
It sleeps well, the horned head:
We poor lads, 'tis our turn now
To hear such tunes as killed the cow.
Pretty friendship 'tis to rhyme
Your friends to death before their time
Moping melancholy mad:
Come, pipe a tune to dance to, lad."

Why, if 'tis dancing you would be,
There's brisker pipes than poetry.
Say, for what were hop-yards meant,
Or why was Burton built on Trent?
Oh, many a peer of England brews
Livelier liquor than the Muse,
And malt does more than Milton can
To justify God's ways to man.
Ale, man, ale's the stuff to drink
For fellows whom it hurts to think:
Look into the pewter pot
To see the world as the world's not.

And faith, 'tis pleasant till 'tis past:
The mischief is that 'twill not last.
Oh, I have been to Ludlow fair
And left my necktie God knows where,
And carried half way home, or near,
Pints and quarts of Ludlow beer:
Then the world seemed none so bad,
And I myself a sterling lad;
And down in lovely muck I've lain,
Happy till I woke again.
Then I saw the morning sky:
Heigho, the tale was all a lie;
The world, it was the old world yet,
I was I, my things were wet,
And nothing now remained to do
But begin the game anew.

Therefore, since the world has still
Much good, but much less good than ill,
And while the sun and moon endure
Luck's a chance, but trouble's sure,
I'd face it as a wise man would,
And train for ill and not for good.
'Tis true, the stuff I bring for sale
Is not so brisk a brew as ale:
Out of a stem that scored the hand
I wrung it in a weary land.
But take it: if the smack is sour,
The better for the embittered hour;

t should do good to heart and head
When your soul is in my soul's stead;
And I will friend you, if I may,
n the dark and cloudy day.

There was a king reigned in the East:
There, when kings will sit to feast,
They get their fill before they think
With poisoned meat and poisoned drink.
He gathered all that springs to birth
From the many-venomed earth;
First a little, thence to more,

He sampled all her killing store;
And easy, smiling, seasoned sound,
Sate the king when healths went round.
They put arsenic in his meat
And stared aghast to watch him eat;
They poured strychnine in his cup
And shook to see him drink it up:
They shook, they stared as white's their
     shirt:
Them it was their poison hurt.
—I tell the tale that I heard told.
Mithridates, he died old.

## Douglas Hyde

DOCTOR DOUGLAS HYDE was born in Roscommon County, Ireland, in, as nearly as can be ascertained, 1860. One of the most brilliant Irish scholars of his day, he worked indefatigably for the cause of his native letters. He wrote a comprehensive history of Irish literature; compiled, edited, and translated into English the *Love Songs of Connaught;* was President of The Irish National Literary Society; and is the author of innumerable poems in Gaelic—far more than he ever wrote in English. His collections of Irish folk-lore are among the most notable contributions to the Celtic revival; they were to a large extent responsible for it. Since 1909 he has been Professor of Modern Irish in University College, Dublin.

The poems here quoted are two of his sensitive and reanimating translations. In the peculiar rhyme-scheme of the first, the paraphraser reproduces the music as well as the color of the West Irish original.

### I SHALL NOT DIE FOR THEE

#### (from the Irish)

For thee, I shall not die,
   Woman of high fame and name;
Foolish men thou mayest slay.
   I and they are not the same.

Why should I expire
   For the fire of an eye,
Slender waist or swan-like limb,
   Is't for them that I should die?

The round breasts, the fresh skin,
   Cheeks crimson, hair so long and rich;

Indeed, indeed, I shall not die,
   Please God, not I, for any such.

The golden hair, the forehead thin,
   The chaste mien, the gracious ease,
The rounded heel, the languid tone,—
   Fools alone find death from these.

Thy sharp wit, thy perfect calm,
   Thy thin palm like foam o' the sea;
Thy white neck, thy blue eye,
   I shall not die for thee.

Woman, graceful as the swan,
   A wise man did nurture me.
Little palm, white neck, bright eye,
   I shall not die for ye.

MY GRIEF ON THE SEA

(*from the Irish*)

My grief on the sea,
  How the waves of it roll!
For they heave between me
  And the love of my soul!

Abandon'd, forsaken,
  To grief and to care,
Will the sea ever waken
  Relief from despair?

My grief and my trouble!
  Would he and I were

In the province of Leinster,
  Or County of Clare!

Would I and my darling—
  O heart-bitter wound!—
On board of the ship
  For America bound.

On a green bed of rushes
  All last night I lay,
And I flung it abroad
  With the heat of the day.

And my Love came behind me,
  He came from the South;
His breast to my bosom,
  His mouth to my mouth.

## Katharine Tynan Hinkson

K ATHARINE TYNAN was born at Dublin in 1861, and educated at the Convent of
  St. Catherine at Drogheda. She married Henry Hinkson in 1893. Her poetry
is largely actuated by religious themes, devotional yet distinctive. She was one of
the members though not one of the leaders of the Irish Renaissance.

Although she wrote many novels, miracle plays, memoirs and books of verse, she
is at her best in *New Poems* (1911). The lines are graceful and meditative, with
occasional notes of deep pathos. Of the later volumes, the most interesting are
*Flower of Youth* (1914), *Late Songs* (1917) and *Evensong* (1922).

Her autobiographical account of the Irish Renaissance is set forth in *Twenty-Five
Years* (1913) and *Memories* (1924). She died, after a brief illness, April 2, 1931.

SHEEP AND LAMBS

All in the April morning,
  April airs were abroad;
The sheep with their little lambs
  Pass'd me by on the road.

The sheep with their little lambs
  Pass'd me by on the road;
All in an April evening
  I thought on the Lamb of God.

The lambs were weary, and crying
  With a weak human cry;
I thought on the Lamb of God
  Going meekly to die.

Up in the blue, blue mountains
  Dewy pastures are sweet:
Rest for the little bodies,
  Rest for the little feet.

Rest for the Lamb of God
  Up on the hill-top green;
Only a cross of shame
  Two stark crosses between.

All in the April evening,
  April airs were abroad;
I saw the sheep with their lambs,
  And thought on the Lamb of God.

### ALL SOULS

The door of Heaven is on the latch
  Tonight, and many a one is fain
To go home for one's night's watch
  With his love again.

Oh, where the father and mother sit
  There's a drift of dead leaves at the door
Like pitter-patter of little feet
  That come no more.

Their thoughts are in the night and cold,
  Their tears are heavier than the clay,
But who is this at the threshold
  So young and gay?

They are come from the land o' the young,
  They have forgotten how to weep;
Words of comfort on the tongue,
  And a kiss to keep.

They sit down and they stay awhile,
  Kisses and comfort none shall lack;
At morn they steal forth with a smile
  And a long look back.

### SLOW SPRING

O year, grow slowly. Exquisite, holy,
  The days go on
With almonds showing the pink stars blow-
    ing,
  And birds in the dawn.

Grow slowly, year, like a child that is dear,
  Or a lamb that is mild,
By little steps, and by little skips,
  Like a lamb or a child.

## Mary E. Coleridge

MARY ELIZABETH COLERIDGE, great-niece of Samuel T. Coleridge, was born in September, 1861. Her childhood was, she wrote, "vague and twilit, and I can recall scarcely anything except sharp sensations of fear that broke the dull dream of my days." She dwelt in books, reading Shakespeare before she entered her teens. At thirteen, she became acquainted with her father's friend, William Johnson (the William Cory of *Ionica*) and the influence of this poet and scholar remained throughout her life. Her taste in literature was catholic; she was a passionate ad-mirer of Browning, and Tolstoy so affected her that it was only after a great struggle and with the realization of her own physical incapacity, that she abandoned the idea of devoting her life to the poor. As it was, she helped needy girls desiring educa-tion, and during the last twelve years of her life taught at The Working Women's College. She died in August 1907.

Her first novel, *The Seven Sleepers of Ephesus* (1893), was a fantasia ignored by the public though praised by Stevenson. Two years later Robert Bridges saw a manuscript of her verse and urged its publication. It appeared as *Fancy's Following* (1896), over the pseudonym of "Anodos." Tales, essays, novels followed, one of which—*The King with Two Faces* (1897)—was a success. Two posthumous vol-umes furnish a summary of her qualities: *Gathered Leaves from the Prose of Mary E. Coleridge,* with a Memoir by Edith Sichel (1911) and *Collected Poems,* in which the original forty-five have grown to two hundred and twenty-seven.

Her novels were never wholly satisfactory; they were, says Edith Sichel, "the novels of a poet, and this was her weakness, and her strength." It is as a poet that she survives. Robert Bridges, in an essay in *The Cornhill Magazine* for November,

1907, compares her to Blake, Heine, and Canon Dixon. There is some justification
for summoning this queerly combined trio, since Mary Coleridge mingled, in a
muted way, the clarity of the first, the *Minnesinger* simplicity of the second, and the
religious convictions (not mere religiosity) of the third. Hers is throughout a noble
if diminishing verse, a quiet verse, not so much disciplined as inherently low-
spoken. Poems like "Our Lady" and such brief lyrics as "I Saw a Stable" attest to
the spontaneity which made this poet see the heavenly in the humble and the
miraculous within the casual.

## OUR LADY

Mother of God—no lady thou:
　Common woman of common earth.
"Our Lady" ladies call thee now,
　But Christ was never of gentle birth;
　A common man of common earth.

For God's ways are not our ways.
　The noblest lady in the land
Would have given up half her days,
　Would have cut off her right hand
　To bear the child that was God of the
　　land.

Never a lady did He choose,
　Only a maid of low degree,
So humble she might not refuse
　The carpenter of Galilee:
　A daughter of the people, she.

Out she sang the song of her heart.
　Never a lady so had sung.
She knew no letters, had no art;
　To all mankind, in woman's tongue,
　Hath Israelitish Mary sung.

And still for men to come she sings,
　Nor shall her singing pass away.
*"He hath fillèd the hungry with good
　things"*—
Oh, listen, lords and ladies gay—
*"And the rich He hath sent empty away."*

## I SAW A STABLE

I saw a stable, low and very bare,
　A little child in a manger.
The oxen knew Him, had Him in care,
　To men he was a stranger.
The safety of the world was lying there—
　And the world's danger.

## MORTAL COMBAT

It is because you were my friend,
　I fought you as the devil fights.
Whatever fortune God may send,
　For once I set the world to rights.

And that was when I thrust you down,
　And stabbed you twice and twice again
Because you dared take off your crown
　And be a man like other men.

## GONE

About the chambers of my heart
Friends have been coming—going—many
　　year.
　The doors stand open here.
Some, lightly stepping, enter; some depart.

Freely they come and freely go, at will,
The walls give back their laughter; all da
　long
　They fill the house with song.
One door alone is shut, one chamber still.

# Henry Newbolt

HENRY (JOHN) NEWBOLT was born at Bilston in 1862 and educated at Corpus Christi College, Oxford. He was called to the Bar in 1887 but retired from practice in 1899.

After editing *The Monthly Review* (1900-1904), he gave himself wholly to creative labor. His early work was frankly imitative of Tennyson; he even attempted to add to the Arthurian legends with a drama in blank verse entitled *Mordred* (1895). It was not until he wrote his sea-ballads that he struck his own note. With the publication of *Admirals All* (1897) and *The Island Race* (1898) his fame was widespread. The popularity of his lines was due not so much to the subject-matter of Newbolt's verse as to the breeziness of his music, the solid beat of rhythm, the vigorous swing of his stanzas. William Rose Benét wrote that "The Guides at Cabul" was "not only a trumpet-note, but a triumphant achievement in meter." *Songs of the Fleet* (1910) repeats a sometimes too "salty" strain, but *The Linnet's Nest* (1927) discloses a quieter—and better—poet.

Besides being a personality of unusual persuasiveness as well as a poet, Newbolt has written many essays; his critical volume, *A New Study of English Poetry* (1917), is a collection of articles that are both analytical and alive. *New Paths on Helicon* (1927) is a balanced, non-partisan anthology of contemporary verse.

### DRAKE'S DRUM

Drake he's in his hammock an' a thousand mile away,
  (Capten, art tha sleepin' there below?)
Slung atween the round shot in Nombre Dios Bay,
  An' dreamin' arl the time o' Plymouth Hoe.
Yarnder lumes the island, yarnder lie the ships,
  Wi' sailor lads a-dancin' heel-an'-toe,
An' the shore-lights flashin', an' the night-tide dashin'
  He sees et arl so plainly as he saw et long ago.

Drake he was a Devon man, an' ruled the Devon seas,
  (Capten, art tha sleepin' there below?)
Rovin' tho' his death fell, he went wi' heart at ease,
  An' dreamin' arl the time o' Plymouth Hoe,
"Take my drum to England, hang et by the shore,
  Strike et when your powder's runnin' low;
If the Dons sight Devon, I'll quit the port o' Heaven,
  An' drum them up the Channel as we drummed them long ago."

Drake he's in his hammock till the great Armadas come.
  (Capten, art tha sleepin' there below?)
Slung atween the round shot, listenin' for the drum,
  An' dreamin' arl the time o' Plymouth Hoe.

Call him on the deep sea, call him up the Sound,
   Call him when ye sail to meet the foe;
Where the old trade's plyin' an' the old flag flyin',
   They shall find him, ware an' wakin', as they found him long ago.

### THE NIGHTJAR

We loved our Nightjar, but she would not stay with us.
We had found her lying as dead, but soft and warm,
Under the apple tree beside the old thatched wall.
Two days we kept her in a basket by the fire,
Fed her, and thought she well might live—till suddenly
In the very moment of most confiding hope
She raised herself all tense, quivered, and drooped, and died.
Tears sprang into my eyes—why not? the heart of man
Soon sets itself to love a living companion
And more so if by chance it asks some care of him.
And this one had the kind of loveliness that goes
Far deeper than the optic nerve—full fathom five
To the soul's ocean cave, where Wonder and Reason
Tell their alternate dreams of how the world was made.
So wonderful she was—her wings the wings of night
But powdered here and there with tiny golden clouds
And wave-line markings like sea-ripples on the sand.
O how I wish I might never forget that bird—
Never!—but even now, like all beauty of earth,
She is fading from me into the dusk of Time.

### THE GUIDES AT CABUL, 1879

Sons of the Island race, wherever ye dwell,
   Who speak of your fathers' battles with lips that burn,
The deeds of an alien legion hear me tell,
   And think not shame from the hearts ye tamed to learn,
   When succor shall fail and the tide for a season turn,
To fight with a joyful courage, a passionate pride,
To die at the last as the Guides at Cabul died.

For a handful of seventy men in a barrack of mud,
   Foodless, waterless, dwindling one by one,
Answered a thousand yelling for English blood
   With stormy volleys that swept them gunner from gun,
   And charge on charge in the glare of the Afghan sun,
Till the walls were shattered wherein they couched at bay,
And dead or dying half of the seventy lay.

Twice they had taken the cannon that wrecked their hold,
   Twice toiled in vain to drag it back,
Thrice they toiled, and alone, wary and bold,

Whirling a hurricane sword to scatter the rack,
Hamilton, last of the English, covered their track.
"Never give in!" he cried, and he heard them shout,
And grappled with death as a man that knows no doubt.

And the Guides looked down from their smoldering barrack again,
And behold, a banner of truce, and a voice that spoke:
"Come, for we know that the English all are slain,
We keep no feud with men of a kindred folk;
Rejoice with us to be free of the conqueror's yoke."
Silence fell for a moment, then was heard
A sound of laughter and scorn, and an answering word.

"Is it we or the lords we serve who have earned this wrong,
That ye call us to flinch from the battle they bade us fight?
We that live—do ye doubt that our hands are strong?
They that are fallen—ye know that their blood was bright!
Think ye the Guides will barter for lust of the light
The pride of an ancient people in warfare bred,
Honor of comrades living, and faith to the dead?"

Then the joy that spurs the warrior's heart
To the last thundering gallop and sheer leap
Came on the men of the Guides: they flung apart
The doors not all their valor could longer keep;
They dressed their slender line; they breathed deep,
And with never a foot lagging or head bent
To the clash and clamor and dust of death they went.

# Eden Phillpotts

EDEN PHILLPOTTS was born November 4, 1862, at Mount Abu, India, son of an English army officer. He was educated at Plymouth, England, and at seventeen entered the fire insurance business, and remained in it for more than ten years. It was during this time that Phillpotts began his stories, writing steadily at night. Finding literature a dubious profession at first, he tried acting and, though he was not a spectacularly successful player, his stage experience undoubtedly gave him a technique which he employed later in the construction of successful dramas.

Phillpotts is best known for his Devonshire tales—an enthusiastic critic has said that Phillpotts did for Dartmoor what Hardy accomplished for Wessex—but his later work concerned itself more with medieval and classical backgrounds. He even wrote detective stories and tales of horror. An extraordinarily fecund author, a check-list as of 1935 shows four dozen publications since *Children of the Mist* in 1898. This list includes ten Devonshire novels, eight historical narratives, four collections of short stories, four volumes of studies, four mystery tales, four plays (of which *The Farmer's Wife,* 1916, ran for years) and four books of poetry.

*A Dish of Apples* (1921), *A Harvesting* (1924) and *Brother Man* (1926) are frequently derivative and undistinguished. But they are not without character. In the midst of much versifying, there is no little of the acrid, earthy flavor which abounds in the best of his stories of the soil.

### LITANY TO PAN

By the abortions of the teeming Spring,
By Summer's starved and withered offering,
By Autumn's stricken hope and Winter's
    sting,
Oh, hear!

By the ichneumon on the writhing worm,
By the swift far-flung poison of the germ,
By soft and foul brought out of hard and
    firm,
Oh, hear!

By the fierce battle under every blade,
By the etiolation of the shade,
By drought and thirst and things undone half
    made,
Oh, hear!

By all the horrors of re-quickened dust,
By the eternal waste of baffled lust,
By mildews and by cankers and by rust,
Oh, hear!

By the fierce scythe of Spring upon the wold,
By the dead weaning mother in the fold,
By stillborn, stricken young and tortured old,
Oh, hear!

By fading eyes pecked from a dying head,
By the hot mouthful of a thing not dead,
By all thy bleeding, struggling, shrieking red,
Oh, hear!

By all the agonies of all the past,
By earth's cold dust and ashes at the last,
By her return to the unconscious vast,
Oh, hear!

### THE HUNTING

When red sun fox steals down the sky,
And darkness dims the heavens high,
There leap again upon his tracks
The eager, starry, hunting packs.

They glitter, glitter, gold and green,
With sparks of frosty fire between,
And Dian bright as day;
While in the gloaming, far below,
Brown owl doth shout, "Hi! Tally Ho!
Sun fox hath gone away!"

To music of the spheres they sweep
Over the western world asleep;
Then in the east, with sudden rush,
Sun fox shall whisk his white-tipped brush.
    The field is fading, gold and green,
    With sparks of frosty fire between,
    And Dian growing gray;
    While morning leaps the hither hill
    And herald lark shouts with a will,
    "Sun fox hath gone away!"

Oh, Huntress fond and silly stars—
White Venus, fiery, futile Mars,
In vain your pack ye whirl and cast
Upon the marches of the vast;
    Vainly ye glitter, gold and green,
    With sparks of frosty fire between,
    And Dian's arrows fly
    In shattered shafts of ebbing light;
    For ne'er shall day be caught by night,
    And sun fox cannot die.

### THE GAFFER'S SONG

A sudden wakin', a sudden weepin';
A li'l suckin', a li'l sleepin';
A cheel's full joys an' a cheel's short sorrows,
Wi' a power o' faith in gert tomorrows.

Young blood red-hot an' the love of a maid;
Wan glorious hour as'll never fade;
Then shadows an' sunshine an' triumphs an'
    tears
Pile the gatherin' weight o' the flyin' years.

Now auld man's talk o' the days behind me;
My darter's youngest darter to mind me;
A li'l dreamin', a li'l dyin',
A li'l, lew corner o' airth to lie in.

# Victor Plarr

VICTOR (GUSTAVE) PLARR was born June 21, 1863, near Strasbourg and came to
Scotland at the age of seven, his father's house having been burnt in the Franco-
German war of 1870. He was educated at St. Andrew's, studied medicine and, in
1897, became the librarian of the Royal College of Surgeons of England.

Plarr was one of the less conspicuous members of the group which made the
Nineties famous. One of the founders of the Rhymers' Club, he appeared in both
volumes of its selected poems. His own collection, *In the Dorian Mood,* was acclaimed upon its publication in 1896.

Although most of his lines scarcely rise above the level of competent verse-making,
the tiny epitaph here reprinted bids fair to survive Plarr's more ambitious but less
successful poetry. Plarr seems fated to be known as the author of "Epitaphium
Citharistriae," yet "Ad Cinerarium," far from being a less worthy example of his
work, may be said to equal if not surpass the better-known poem.

Plarr died in London, January 28, 1929.

## EPITAPHIUM CITHARISTRIAE

Stand not uttering sedately
    Trite oblivious praise above her!
Rather say you saw her lately
    Lightly kissing her last lover.

Whisper not, "There is a reason
    Why we bring her no white blossom":
Since the snowy bloom's in season
    Strow it on her sleeping bosom:

Oh, for it would be a pity
    To o'erpraise her or to flout her:
She was wild, and sweet, and witty—
    Let's not say dull things about her.


## AD CINERARIUM

Who in this small urn reposes,
    Celt or Roman, man or woman,
Steel of steel, or rose of roses?

Whose the dust set rustling slightly,
    In its hiding-place abiding,
When this urn is lifted lightly?

Sure some mourner deemed immortal
    What thou holdest and enfoldest,
Little house without a portal!

When the artificers had slowly
    Formed thee, turned thee, sealed thee,
        burned thee,
Freighted with thy freightage holy,

Sure he thought there's no forgetting
    All the sweetness and completeness
Of his rising, of her setting,

And so bade them grave no token,
    Generation, age, or nation,
On thy round side still unbroken;—

Let them score no cypress verses,
    Funeral glories, prayers, or stories,
Mourners' tears, or mourners' curses,

Round thy brown rim time has polished,—
    Left thee dumbly cold and comely
As some shrine of gods abolished.

Ah, 'tis well! It scarcely matters
    What is sleeping in the keeping
Of this house of human tatters,

Steel of steel, or rose of roses,
    Man or woman, Celt or Roman,
If but soundly he reposes!

## *Arthur Symons*

Born in 1865 in Wales, of Cornish parents, Arthur Symons was educated at private schools. Attracted at an early age to the Symbolist movement, he became one of its leaders in England. His first few publications reveal an intellectual rather than an emotional passion. Those volumes—*Days and Nights* (1889), *Silhouettes* (1892), *London Nights* (1895)—are full of the artifice of the period, but Symons' technical skill often saves the poems from complete decadence. His later books are less imitative; the influence of Verlaine and Baudelaire is not so apparent. The scent of patchouli, the breath of heavy, narcotic blossoms still cling to many of the pages, but there is no longer the obsession with strange sensations, with what might be called the Deadly Nightshade school of poetry.

The best of Symons' poems have a firm delicacy of touch; they breathe an intimacy in which sophistication is not cynical and sensuousness is restrained. His various collections of essays and stories before 1900 reflect the same blend of intellectuality and perfumed romanticism one finds in his poems.

After a silence of some years, Symons began to write in a less nostalgic and more critical vein. *Dramatis Personae* appeared in 1923; a limited edition of his *Collected Works* a year later. *The Symbolist Movement in Literature,* originally published in 1899, remains one of the best studies of the period.

Of his many volumes in prose, *Spiritual Adventures* (1905), while obviously influenced by Walter Pater, is by far the most original, an undeservedly neglected volume of psychological short stories. His poetry up to 1902 was collected in two volumes, *Poems. The Fool of the World* appeared in 1907; *Tragedies* in 1916.

Appraisals of Symons' work have touched the extremes of adulation and denunciation. A final estimate of his work has not yet been reached. It is obvious that his early poetry, generated from weariness and literary wantonness, belongs to the literature of decadence. His later work is no longer preoccupied with orchids, scented handkerchiefs, and the nuances of sensation. His mind, essentially healthy, threw off its infection and produced work of a clean and admirable precision.

"In the Wood of Finvara," "Modern Beauty," "The Turning Dervish," "The Crying of Water" and a dozen other lyrics are as simple as they are sensuous.

### IN THE WOOD OF FINVARA

I have grown tired of sorrow and human tears;
Life is a dream in the night, a fear among fears,
A naked runner lost in a storm of spears.

I have grown tired of rapture and love's desire;
Love is a flaming heart, and its flames aspire
Till they cloud the soul in the smoke of a windy fire.

I would wash the dust of the world in a soft green flood;
Here between sea and sea, in the fairy wood,
I have found a delicate, wave-green solitude.

Here, in the fairy wood, between sea and sea,
I have heard the song of a fairy bird in a tree,
And the peace that is not in the world has flown to me.

## MODERN BEAUTY

I am the torch, she saith, and what to me
If the moth die of me? I am the flame
Of beauty, and I burn that all may see
Beauty, and I have neither joy nor shame,
But live with that clear light of perfect fire
Which is to men the death of their desire.

I am Yseult and Helen. I have seen
Troy burn, and the most loving knight lie dead.
The world has been my mirror, time has been
My breath upon the glass; and men have said,
Age after age, in rapture and despair,
Love's poor few words before my image there.

I live, and am immortal; in my eyes
The sorrow of the world, and on my lips
The joy of life, mingle to make me wise;
Yet now the day is darkened with eclipse:
Who is there still lives for beauty? Still am I
The torch, but where's the moth that still dares die?

## THE CRYING OF WATER

O water, voice of my heart, crying in the sand,
All night long crying with a mournful cry,
As I lie and listen, and cannot understand
The voice of my heart in my side or the voice of the sea,
O water crying for rest, is it I, is it I?
All night long the water is crying to me.

Unresting water, there shall never be rest
Till the last moon drop and the last tide fail,
And the fire of the end begin to burn in the west;
And the heart shall be weary and wonder and cry like the sea,
All life long crying without avail,
As the water all night long is crying to me.

## THE TURNING DERVISH

Stars in the heaven turn,
I worship like a star,
And in its footsteps learn
Where peace and wisdom are.

Man crawls as a worm crawls;
Till dust with dust he lies,

A crooked line he scrawls
Between the earth and skies.

Yet God, having ordained
The course of star and sun,
No creature hath constrained
A meaner course to run.

I, by his lesson taught,
Imaging his design,
Have diligently wrought
Motion to be divine.

I turn until my sense,
Dizzied with waves of air,
Spins to a point intense,
And spires and centers there.

There, motionless in speed,
I drink that flaming peace,
Which in the heavens doth feed
The stars with bright increase.

Some spirit in me doth move
Through ways of light untrod,

Till, with excessive love,
I drown, and am in God.

## NIGHT

The night's held breath,
And the stars' steady eyes:
Is it sleep, is it death,
In the earth, in the skies?

In my heart of hope,
In my restless will,
There is that should not stop
Though the earth stood still,

Though the heavens shook aghast,
As the frost shakes a tree,
And a strong wind cast
The stars in the sea.

## WANDERER'S SONG

I have had enough of women, and enough of love,
But the land waits, and the sea waits, and day and night is enough;
Give me a long white road, and the gray wide path of the sea,
And the wind's will and the bird's will, and the heart-ache still in me.

Why should I seek out sorrow, and give gold for strife?
I have loved much and wept much, but tears and love are not life;
The grass calls to my heart, and the foam to my blood cries up,
And the sun shines and the road shines, and the wine's in the cup.

I have had enough of wisdom, and enough of mirth,
For the way's one and the end's one, and it's soon to the ends of the earth;
And it's then good-night and to bed, and if heels or heart ache,
Well, it's sound sleep and long sleep, and sleep too deep to wake.

## DURING MUSIC

The music had the heat of blood,
A passion no words can reach;
We sat together, and understood
Our own heart's speech.

We had no need of word or sign,
The music spoke for us, and said
All that her eyes could read in mine
Or mine in hers had read.

## NERVES

The modern malady of love is nerves.
Love, once a simple madness, now observes
The stages of his passionate disease,
And is twice sorrowful because he sees,
Inch by inch entering, the fatal knife.
O health of simple minds, give me your life,
And let me for one midnight cease to hear
The clock forever ticking in my ear,
The clock that tells the minutes in my
  brain
It is not love, nor love's despair, this pain
That shoots a witness, keener pang across
The simple agony of love and loss.
Nerves, nerves! O folly of a child who
  dreams
Of heaven and, waking in the darkness,
  screams.

# William Butler Yeats

WILLIAM BUTLER YEATS, son of John B. Yeats, the Irish artist, was born at Sandy-mount, Ireland, June 13, 1865. He studied art for a short time at the Royal Dublin Society, but his childhood was spent in the wild district of Sligo. He was educated at Godolphin School, Hammersmith, and Erasmus Smith School, Dublin. In 1888 he came to London where he lived many years. Later in life he spent much time abroad, in Paris, on the Italian Riviera, always returning to his Ireland as the source of his inspiration and from which he absorbed that mixture of straightfor-wardness and symbolism which pronounced his individual accent.

It is not easy to summarize Yeats' contribution, for his activities have been so varied and his work does not divide in fixed periods nor fit into convenient cate-gories. He was folk-lorist, playwright, pamphleteer, editor, experimenter in Spirit-ualism—and above these rôles, prompting them all, he was a poet.

In the capacity of folk-lorist he prepared the collections of old wives' tales and mythical legends: *Fairy and Folk Tales* (1890) and *Irish Representative Tales* (1904). As essayist he wrote *The Celtic Twilight* (1893); as editor he collaborated with Edwin T. Ellis on an invaluable edition of *The Works of William Blake* (1893); as playwright, he helped organize a native Theater and impel the move-ment known as the Celtic revival.

It was through the "Young Ireland" society that Yeats became identified with an Irish literary theater. He dreamed of a national poetry which would be traditional yet dramatic, written in simple English but spiritually Irish. He founded and edited a paper, the first number appearing in May, 1899, to expound his views. He col-laborated with George Moore, with whom he had become associated, wrote his first original play in prose, *Kathleen ni Houlihan* (1902), and became one of the leaders of the movement, his chief associates being J. M. Synge, Douglas Hyde, Moore, and Lady Gregory. He worked incessantly for the cause both as propagandist and play-wright; his *Plays for an Irish Theatre* (1913) containing *Where There Is Nothing, The Hour-Glass, Kathleen ni Houlihan, The Pot of Broth, The King's Threshold,* and *On Baile's Strand.*

Others who followed Yeats intensified the Irish drama; they established a closer contact between the peasant and poet. No one, however, had so great a part as Yeats in the actual shaping of modern drama in Ireland. His *Deirdre* (1907), a beautiful retelling of the great Gaelic legend, is far more dramatic than the earlier plays; it is particularly interesting to read as a complement to Synge's more idiomatic play on the same theme, *Deirdre of the Sorrows.*

The poet was already at work—*Mosada: A Poem* was published in 1886, in Yeats' twenty-first year—but he was not yet ready to declare himself definitely. Be-fore his verse marked the rise of a new Irish school he was one of the group con-tributing to the *fin de siècle* publication *The Yellow Book;* he became the friend of Lionel Johnson and Oscar Wilde, and with them founded the Rhymer's Club; he was represented in both its anthologies. But, as he has told in his autobiographical volumes, *Reveries over Childhood and Youth* (1915) and *The Trembling of the*

*Veil* (1922), he was forced to walk about London because he could not afford the bus fare, and tea with hospitable friends was not only a social function but a meal that kept him from days of hunger. Accepting his enforced asceticism he turned it into a discipline, and those critics who consider his mysticism a later affectation might well study this period of Yeats' life and trace its essential reality.

It was in London, at the age of twenty-four, that he decided to devote himself to poetry, and it was there that his first representative volume was published in 1889, *The Wanderings of Oisin*. There appeared in rapid succession *The Countess Kathleen and Various Lyrics* (1892), a drama with appended verses; *A Book of Irish Verse* (1895); *The Wind Among the Reeds* (1899), which contains some of Yeats' finest early lyrics; and *The Shadowy Waters* (1900), another poetic play.

By this time Yeats had established himself as a poet of delicate effects and inconclusive loveliness. His was both a vague and personal music—the translation of faery charms and elfin songs into traditionally romantic yet highly individualized lyrics. The very music of the early lyrics—favored by those who prefer sensuousness to depth of feeling—is a limitation. They are almost too musical; they sacrifice strength of thought and utterance to limpidity. In this period Yeats presumably depended on a small set of colorful symbols, symbols which were both arbitrary and facile. It seemed that Yeats had found his métier and that he would continue to sound the charming if restricted gamut of fancy. But the poet revolted against fancifulness; he turned away from the comfort of sheer sentiment and the reliance on rhetoric. "Sentimentality," he said, "is deceiving one's self; rhetoric is deceiving other people."

With *Responsibilities* (1914) and *The Wild Swans at Coole* (1919) a change in tone is immediately apparent. The idiom is sharper, the imagery sparser. The language, no longer richly colored, is almost bare of ornament, the tone pitched on a conversational plane. This contrast to the earlier poetry was emphasized in *Later Poems* (1922), *Michael Robartes and the Dancer* (1923), *The Tower* (1928), and *The Winding Stair* (1932). One likes to believe that it was the later work which won Yeats the Nobel Prize for literature in 1924. In the comprehensive *Collected Poems* of 1933 the complete change is fully revealed not only in the quality of the later work but in the alterations Yeats had made in the earlier poems, often substituting the exact and sometimes harsh word for the smooth and dreamlike one.

In changing the wavering outlines of his poetry to a more rigorous line Yeats did not sacrifice music. On the contrary, the revisions disclose a music which is, at the same time, subtler and more precise. The poet has freed himself from his preoccupations with shadowy waters, Gaelic gods, and the mystic Rose's multiple meanings; he has emerged from his "labyrinth of images." Not that he has discarded symbolism, but his symbols now have a greater value; they are intellectually finer and firmer. Originally influenced by Blake and the French Symbolists, he finally accomplished a "more subtle rhythm, a more organic form."

> I made my song a coat
> Covered with embroideries
> Out of old mythologies
> From heel to throat;
> But the fools caught it,

> Wore it in the world's eyes
> As though they'd wrought it.
> Song, let them take it,
> For there's more enterprise
> In walking naked.

Here Yeats says explicitly what so many of the later poems imply. He repudiates his imitators and mocks his own early mythological manner. Instead of the purple patches and the multicolored "cloths of Heaven" Yeats seems less interested in talking to poets and more concerned with the simple people he used to live among. Desire for direct communication must have prompted such a poem as the one which begins

> Although I see him still
> The freckled man who goes
> To a gray place on the hill

and ends

> I shall have written him one
> Poem maybe as cold
> And passionate as the dawn.

"Leda" (a modern poem in spite of its classical subject), "The Wild Swans at Coole," some of the political poems, "Among School Children," and "Sailing to Byzantium" are among the many verses illustrating the deeper contemplative manner with which "the last of the romantics," as Yeats called himself, rose from remote fantasies into immediate experience. More intensely self-searching the poet turns, regretfully but resolutely, to a new set of symbols expressing his adjustment with the actual world. "Sailing to Byzantium" shows the conflict and its solution with particular clarity. Cleanth Brooks, in "A Note on Symbol and Conceit" (in *The American Review* for May, 1934), summarizes it thus: "The poet's own country is a land of natural beauty, beauty of the body. But his own body is old. The soul must, therefore, sing the louder to compensate for the old and dying flesh.

> An aged man is but a paltry thing,
> A tattered coat upon a stick, unless
> Soul clap its hands and sing, and louder sing
> For every tatter in its mortal dress.

But there is no singing school for the soul except in studying the works of the soul. 'And therefore' he has sailed to Byzantium, for the artists of Byzantium do not follow the forms of nature but intellectual forms, ideal patterns. He appears to them to

> Consume my heart away; sick with desire
> And fastened to a dying animal

and by severing him from the dying world of the body, to gather him into what is at least 'the artifice of eternity.'

"A comparison of this clumsy paraphrase with the poem in its entirety illustrates better than anything else why the poet must write as he does—how much we lose by substituting concepts for his richer 'symbols.' Byzantium is, for instance, a very rich symbol. It may be thought a very indefinite one. But richness and complexity are not vagueness, and it will be easy to show that the symbol has its precision. It means many things, but if one misses the connection with intellectual art, one has missed the poem. The whole poem demands, as do the poems of Donne and Marvell, mental agility on the part of the reader."

Such verse reveals how Yeats has grown from a maker of pure melodies into a poet of intellectual power. Nor has intellect destroyed intuition. *The King of the Great Clock Tower* (1935), published in Yeats' seventieth year, includes several supernatural songs, some keen political poems, and much shrewd commentary. The imagination is still alert although it is linked with wit and a disillusioned mind; the music is still potent, but it is more flexible, less "tuneful," perhaps, being full of increased sensibility and conviction. It is in the graver cadences, the greater and more thoughtful poetry, that Yeats finally freed himself from the spell of verbal magic, which, lovely though it was, threatened to constrict him. Outgrowing the pattern imposed upon himself he developed a restrained and noble music unsurpassed by any poet of his times.

### THE LAKE ISLE OF INNISFREE

I will arise and go now, and go to Innisfree,
And a small cabin build there, of clay and wattles made;
Nine bean rows will I have there, a hive for the honey bee,
  And live alone in the bee-loud glade.

And I shall have some peace there, for peace comes dropping slow,
Dropping from the veils of the morning to where the cricket sings;
There midnight's all a glimmer, and noon a purple glow,
  And evening full of the linnet's wings.

I will arise and go now, for always night and day
I hear lake water lapping with low sounds by the shore;
While I stand on the roadway, or on the pavements gray,
  I hear it in the deep heart's core.

### AEDH WISHES FOR THE CLOTHS OF HEAVEN

Had I the heavens' embroidered cloths,
Enwrought with golden and silver light,
The blue and the dim and the dark cloths
Of night and light and the half-light,
I would spread the cloths under your feet:
But I, being poor, have only my dreams;
I have spread my dreams under your feet;
Tread softly because you tread on my dreams.

### THE SONG OF WANDERING AENGUS

I went out to the hazel wood,
Because a fire was in my head,
And cut and peeled a hazel wand,
And hooked a berry to a thread,
And when white moths were on the wing,
And moth-like stars were flickering out,
I dropped the berry in a stream
And caught a little silver trout.

When I had laid it on the floor
I went to blow the fire a-flame,
But something rustled on the floor,
And someone called me by my name:
It had become a glimmering girl
With apple blossoms in her hair
Who called me by my name and ran
And faded through the brightening air.

Though I am old with wandering
Through hollow lands and hilly lands,
I will find out where she has gone,
And kiss her lips and take her hands;

And walk among long dappled grass,
And pluck till time and times are done,
The silver apples of the moon,
The golden apples of the sun.

### AEDH TELLS OF THE ROSE IN HIS HEART

All things uncomely and broken, all things worn out and old,
The cry of a child by the roadway, the creak of a lumbering cart,
The heavy steps of the plowman, splashing the wintry mold,
Are wronging your image that blossoms a rose in the deeps of my heart.

The wrong of unshapely things is a wrong too great to be told;
I hunger to build them anew and sit on a green knoll apart,
With the earth and the sky and the water, remade, like a casket of gold
For my dreams of your image that blossoms a rose in the deeps of my heart.

### FAIRY SONG

#### (from "The Land of Heart's Desire")

The wind blows out of the gates of day,
The wind blows over the lonely heart,
And the lonely of heart is withered away,
While the faëries dance in a place apart,
Shaking their milk-white feet in a ring,
Tossing their milk-white arms in the air:
For they hear the wind laugh, and murmur and sing
Of a land where even the old are fair,
And even the wise are merry of tongue;
But I heard a reed of Coolaney say,
"When the wind has laughed and murmured and sung,
The lonely of heart is withered away!"

### WHEN YOU ARE OLD

When you are old and gray and full of sleep,
And nodding by the fire, take down this book,
And slowly read, and dream of the soft look
Your eyes had once, and of their shadows deep;

How many loved your moments of glad grace,
And loved your beauty with love false or true;
But one man loved the pilgrim soul in you,
And loved the sorrows of your changing face.

And bending down beside the glowing bars
Murmur, a little sadly, how love fled
And paced upon the mountains overhead
And hid his face amid a crowd of stars.

### THE CAP AND BELLS

A Queen was beloved by a jester,
  And once when the owls grew still
He made his soul go upward
  And stand on her window sill.

In a long and straight blue garment,
  It talked before morn was white,
And it had grown wise by thinking
  Of a footfall hushed and light.

But the young queen would not listen;
  She rose in her pale nightgown,
She drew in the brightening casement
  And pushed the brass bolt down.

He bade his heart go to her,
  When the bats cried out no more,
In a red and quivering garment
  It sang to her through the door.

The tongue of it sweet with dreaming
  Of a flutter of flower-like hair,

But she took up her fan from the table
  And waved it off on the air.

"I've cap and bells," he pondered,
  "I will send them to her and die."
And as soon as the morn had whitened
  He left them where she went by.

She laid them upon her bosom,
  Under a cloud of her hair,
And her red lips sang them a love song.
  The stars grew out of the air.

She opened her door and her window,
  And the heart and the soul came through,
To her right hand came the red one,
  To her left hand came the blue.

They set up a noise like crickets,
  A chattering wise and sweet,
And her hair was a folded flower,
  And the quiet of love her feet.

### THE INDIAN UPON GOD

I passed along the water's edge below the humid trees,
My spirit rocked in evening light, the rushes round my knees,
My spirit rocked in sleep and sighs; and saw the moorfowl pace
All dripping on a grassy slope, and saw them cease to chase
Each other round in circles, and heard the eldest speak:
*Who holds the world between His bill and made us strong or weak*
*Is an undying moorfowl, and He lives beyond the sky.*
*The rains are from His dripping wing, the moonbeams from His eye.*
I passed a little further on and heard a lotus talk:
*Who made the world and ruleth it, He hangeth on a stalk,*
*For I am in His image made, and all this tinkling tide*
*Is but a sliding drop of rain between His petals wide.*
A little way within the gloom a roebuck raised his eyes
Brimful of starlight, and he said: *The Stamper of the Skies,*
*He is a gentle roebuck; for how else, I pray, could He*
*Conceive a thing so sad and soft, a gentle thing like me?*
I passed a little further on and heard a peacock say:
*Who made the grass and made the worms and made my feathers gay,*
*He is a monstrous peacock, and He waveth all the night*
*His languid tail above us, lit with myriad spots of light.*

## AN OLD SONG RESUNG[1]

Down by the salley gardens my love and I did meet;
She passed the salley gardens with little snow-white feet.
She bid me take love easy, as the leaves grow on the tree;
But I, being young and foolish, with her would not agree.

In a field by the river my love and I did stand,
And on my leaning shoulder she laid her snow-white hand.
She bid me take life easy, as the grass grows on the weirs;
But I was young and foolish, and now am full of tears.

## THE ROSE OF THE WORLD

Who dreamed that beauty passes like a dream?
  For these red lips, with all their mournful pride,
  Mournful that no new wonder may betide,
Troy passed away in one high funeral gleam,
  And Usna's children died.

We and the laboring world are passing by:
  Amid men's souls, that waver and give place,
  Like the pale waters in their wintry race,
Under the passing stars, frame of the sky,
  Lives on this lonely face.

Bow down, archangels, in your dim abode:
  Before you were, or any hearts to beat,
  Weary and kind, one lingered by His seat;
He made the world to be a grassy road
  Before her wandering feet.

## THE SORROW OF LOVE

The quarrel of the sparrows in the eaves,
The full round moon and the star-laden sky,
And the loud song of the ever-singing leaves,
Has hid away earth's old and weary cry.

And then you came with those red mournful lips,
And with you came the whole of the world's tears,
And all the trouble of her laboring ships,
And all the trouble of her myriad years.

And now the sparrows warring in the eaves,
The curd-pale moon, the white stars in the sky,
And the loud chaunting of the unquiet leaves,
Are shaken with earth's old and weary cry.

[1] "This," Yeats wrote in a footnote in one of the early editions, "is an extension of three lines
sung to me by an old woman of Ballisodare."

## THE SONG OF THE OLD MOTHER

I rise in the dawn, and I kneel and blow
Till the seed of the fire flicker and glow.
And then I must scrub, and bake, and sweep,
Till stars are beginning to blink and peep;
But the young lie long and dream in their bed
Of the matching of ribbons, the blue and the red,
And their day goes over in idleness,
And they sigh if the wind but lift up a tress.
While I must work, because I am old
And the seed of the fire gets feeble and cold.

## THE BALLAD OF FATHER GILLIGAN

The old priest Peter Gilligan
Was weary night and day;
For half his flock were in their beds,
Or under green sods lay.

Once, while he nodded on a chair,
At the moth-hour of eve,
Another poor man sent for him,
And he began to grieve.

"I have no rest, nor joy, nor peace,
"For people die and die";
And after cried he, "God forgive!
"My body spake, not I."

He knelt, and leaning on the chair
He prayed and fell asleep;
And the moth-hour went from the fields,
And stars began to peep.

They slowly into millions grew,
And leaves shook in the wind;
And God covered the world with shade,
And whispered to mankind.

Upon the time of sparrow chirp
When the moths came once more,

The old priest Peter Gilligan
Stood upright on the floor.

"Mavrone, mavrone! the man has died,
"While I slept on the chair";
He roused his horse out of its sleep
And rode with little care.

He rode now as he never rode,
By rocky lane and fen;
The sick man's wife opened the door;
"Father! You come again!"

"And is the poor man dead?" he cried.
"He died an hour ago."
The old priest Peter Gilligan
In grief swayed to and fro.

"When you were gone, he turned and died
"As merry as a bird."
The old priest Peter Gilligan
He knelt him at that word.

"He who hath made the night of stars
"For souls, who tire and bleed,
"Sent one of His great angels down
"To help me in my need.

"He who is wrapped in purple robes,
"With planets in His care,
"Had pity on the least of things
"Asleep upon a chair."

## THE WILD SWANS AT COOLE

The trees are in their autumn beauty,
The woodland paths are dry,
Under the October twilight the water
Mirrors a still sky;

Upon the brimming water among the stones
Are nine and fifty swans.

The nineteenth Autumn has come upon me
Since I first made my count;
I saw, before I had well finished,
All suddenly mount
And scatter, wheeling, in great broken rings
Upon their clamorous wings.

I have looked upon those brilliant creatures,
And now my heart is sore.
All's changed since I, hearing at twilight,
The first time on this shore,
The bell-beat of their wings above my head,
Trod with a lighter tread.

Unwearied still, lover by lover,
They paddle in the cold,
Companionable streams or climb the air;
Their hearts have not grown old;
Passion or conquest, wander where they will,
Attend upon them still.

But now they drift on the still water
Mysterious, beautiful;
Among what rushes will they build,
By what lake's edge or pool
Delight men's eyes, when I awake some day
To find they have flown away?

### LEDA AND THE SWAN

A sudden blow: the great wings beating still
Above the staggering girl, her thighs caressed
By the dark webs, her nape caught in his bill,
He holds her helpless breast upon his breast.

How can those terrified vague fingers push
The feathered glory from her loosening thighs?
And how can body, laid in that white rush,
But feel the strange heart beating where it lies?

A shudder in the loins engenders there
The broken wall, the burning roof and tower
And Agamemnon dead.
              Being so caught up,
So mastered by the brute blood of the air,
Did she put on his knowledge with his power
Before the indifferent beak could let her drop?

### SAILING TO BYZANTIUM

#### I

That is no country for old men. The young
In one another's arms, birds in the trees,
—Those dying generations—at their song,
The salmon-falls, the mackerel-crowded seas,
Fish, flesh, or fowl, commend all summer long
Whatever is begotten, born, and dies.
Caught in that sensual music all neglect
Monuments of unaging intellect.

#### II

An aged man is but a paltry thing,
A tattered coat upon a stick, unless
Soul clap its hands and sing, and louder sing
For every tatter in its mortal dress,
Nor is there singing school but studying
Monuments of its own magnificence;
And therefore I have sailed the seas and come
To the holy city of Byzantium.

#### III

O sages standing in God's holy fire
As in the gold mosaic of a wall,
Come from the holy fire, perne [1] in a gyre,
And be the singing-masters of my soul.
Consume my heart away; sick with desire
And fastened to a dying animal
It knows not what it is; and gather me
Into the artifice of eternity.

#### IV

Once out of nature I shall never take
My bodily form from any natural thing,
But such a form as Grecian goldsmiths make
Of hammered gold and gold enameling
To keep a drowsy Emperor awake;
Or set upon a golden bough to sing
To lords and ladies of Byzantium
Of what is past, or passing, or to come.

### AMONG SCHOOL CHILDREN

#### I

I walk through the long schoolroom questioning;
A kind old nun in a white hood replies;
The children learn to cipher and to sing,
To study reading-books and history,

[1] Perne: Change attitude.

To cut and sew, be neat in everything
In the best modern way—the children's eyes
In momentary wonder stare upon
A sixty-year-old smiling public man.

### II

I dream of a Ledaean body, bent
Above a sinking fire, a tale that she
Told of a harsh reproof, or trivial event
That changed some childish day to tragedy—
Told, and it seemed that our two natures blent
Into a sphere from youthful sympathy,
Or else, to alter Plato's parable,
Into the yolk and the white of one shell.

### III

And thinking of that fit of grief or rage
I look upon one child or t'other there
And wonder if she stood so at that age—
For even daughters of the swan can share
Something of every paddler's heritage—
And had that color upon cheek or hair,
And thereupon my heart is driven wild:
She stands before me as a living child.

### IV

Her present image floats into the mind—
Did Quattrocento finger fashion it
Hollow of cheek as though it drank the wind
And took a mess of shadows for its meat?
And I though never of Ledaean kind
Had pretty plumage once—enough of that,
Better to smile on all that smile, and show
There is a comfortable kind of scarecrow.

### V

What youthful mother, a shape upon her lap
Honey of generation had betrayed,
And that must sleep, shriek, struggle to escape
As recollection or the drug decide,
Would think her son, did she but see that shape
With sixty or more winters on its head,
A compensation for the pang of his birth,
Or the uncertainty of his setting forth?

### VI

Plato thought nature but a spume that plays
Upon a ghostly paradigm of things;
Solider Aristotle played the taws
Upon the bottom of a king of kings;

World-famous golden-thighed Pythagoras
Fingered upon a fiddle-stick or strings
What a star sang and careless Muses heard:
Old clothes upon old sticks to scare a bird.

### VII

Both nuns and mothers worship images,
But those the candles light are not as those
That animate a mother's reveries,
But keep a marble or a bronze repose.
And yet they too break hearts—O Presences
That passion, piety or affection knows,
And that all heavenly glory symbolize—
O self-born mockers of man's enterprise;

### VIII

Labor is blossoming or dancing where
The body is not bruised to pleasure soul,
Nor beauty born out of its own despair,
Nor blear-eyed wisdom out of midnight oil.
O chestnut tree, great rooted blossomer,
Are you the leaf, the blossom or the bole?
O body swayed to music, O brightening glance,
How can we know the dancer from the dance?

### THE LEADERS OF THE CROWD

They must to keep their certainty accuse
All that are different of a base intent;
Pull down established honor; hawk for news
Whatever their loose phantasy invent
And murmur it with bated breath, as though
The abounding gutter had been Helicon
Or calumny a song. How can they know
Truth flourishes where the student's lamp has shone,
And there alone, that have no solitude?
So the crowd come they care not what may come.
They have loud music, hope every day renewed
And heartier loves; that lamp is from the tomb.

# Herbert Trench

(Frederic) Herbert Trench was born in November, 1865, at Avoncore, County
Cork, Ireland. He was educated at Haileybury and Oxford, became a Fellow of
the Royal Society of Literature, and was Director of Special Enquiries at the Board
of Education, from which he retired in 1908. After his extensive travels, he decided

"to risk everything on literature," although he was at one time Director of the Haymarket Theatre. He died in July, 1923.

Although the greater part of his work is an attempt to scale profound heights, his poetry in "the grand manner" is rarely impressive; it is noble in intention but ineffectual as communication. Trench's all too frequent excursions into the realm of the metaphysical achieved far less than a few of his unambitious lyrics. Rid of his nebular philosophy, the shorter verses shine with a natural clarity. "I Heard a Soldier," "Song," and three or four others deserve more than passing patronization.

The best of Trench may be found in *Deirdre Wedded* (1900) and *Lyrics and Narrative Poems* (1911). *Selected Poems* as well as *The Complete Works of Herbert Trench*, edited by Harold Williams, were published in 1924.

### I HEARD A SOLDIER

I heard a soldier sing some trifle
   Out in the sun-dried veldt alone.
He lay and cleaned his grimy rifle
   Idly, behind a stone.

"If after death, love, comes a waking,
   And in their camp so dark and still
The men of dust hear bugles, breaking
   Their halt upon the hill,

"To me the slow and silver pealing
   That then the last high trumpet pours,
Shall softer than the dawn come stealing,
   For, with its call, comes yours!"

What grief of love had he to stifle,
   Basking so idly by his stone,
That grimy soldier with his rifle
   Out in the veldt, alone?

### SONG

She comes not when Noon is on the roses—
   Too bright is Day.
She comes not to the soul till it reposes
   From work and play.

But when Night is on the hills, and the great voices
   Roll in from sea,
By starlight and by candlelight and dreamlight
   She comes to me.

COME, LET US MAKE LOVE DEATHLESS

Come, let us make love deathless, thou and I,
  ' Seeing that our footing on earth is brief—
Seeing that her multitudes sweep out to die
  Mocking at all that passes their belief.
For standard of our love not theirs we take:
  If we go hence today
Fill the high cup that is so soon to break
  With richer wine than they!

Aye, since beyond these walls no heavens there be
  Joy to revive or wasted youth repair,
I'll not bedim the lovely flame in thee
  Nor sully the sad splendor that we wear.
Great be the love, if with the lover dies
  Our greatness past recall,
And nobler for the fading of those eyes
  The world seen once for all.

# *Rudyard Kipling*

BORN at Bombay, India, December 30, 1865 (Joseph) Rudyard Kipling was educated at the United Services College in England. He returned, however, to India
and took a position on the staff of *The Lahore Civil and Military Gazette,* writing
for the Indian press until about 1890, when he went to England, where, with the
exception of a short sojourn in America, he lived until his death January 17, 1936.
Even while he was still in India, he achieved a popular as well as a literary success
with his dramatic tales and high-spirited ballads of Anglo-Indian life.

*Soldiers Three* (1888) was the first of six collections of short stories brought out
in "Wheeler's Railway Library." They were followed by the more sensitive *Plain
Tales from the Hills, Under the Deodars* and *The Phantom 'Rikshaw,* which contains two of the best and most convincing ghost-stories in recent literature.

These tales, however, display only one side of Kipling's extraordinary talents.
As a writer of children's stories, he has few living equals. *Wee Willie Winkie,*
which contains that stirring, heroic fragment "Drums of the Fore and Aft," is only
a trifle less delightful than his more obviously juvenile collections. *Just-So Stories*
and the two *Jungle Books* (prose interspersed with lively rhymes) are for young
people of all ages. *Kim,* the novel of a super-Mowgli grown up, is a more
mature canvas painted against the background of the great Indian roads.

Considered solely as a poet, Kipling is one of the most vigorous figures of his
time. The spirit of romance surges under his realities. His brisk lines conjure up
a countryside in autumn, the tingle of salt spray, the rude sentiment of ruder
natures, the snapping of a banner, the lurch and rumble of the sea. His poetry is

woven of the stuff of myths, but it never loses its hold on actualities. Kipling himself in his poem "The Benefactors" (from *The Years Between* [1919]) writes:

> Ah! What avails the classic bent
> And what the cultured word,
> Against the undoctored incident
> That actually occurred?

What attracted the average reader to Kipling was this attitude to the world's work. Where others sang of lilies and leisure, Kipling celebrated difficulties, duty, hard labor; where others evoked Greek nymphs, he hailed bridge-builders, engineers, sweating stokers—all those who exulted in the job. If he sometimes lost his head in a general hurrahing, his high spirits carried off specious prophesying and brought sing-song meters to a pitch of excitement. Gusto was not the least of his gods.

Kipling won the Nobel Prize for Literature in 1907. His varied poems, ranging from the lusty *Barrack-Room Ballads* to the quieter verse in *The Five Nations, The Seven Seas* and the later work, were collected in a remarkable one-volume *Inclusive Edition* (1885-1918), an indispensable part of any student's library. Subsequent to this collection, a new volume, *The Years Between,* was published in 1919.

The best and worst of Kipling are obvious to the least critical reader. His worst is inherent in a heartiness which is too loud and too prolonged, a vehemence which changes robustiousness into rowdiness. Max Beerbohm excoriated this Kipling in the cartoon showing an irate little man, helmeted and spectacled, blowing a tin trumpet, waving a Union Jack, and dancing himself into a paroxysm of patriotic fury. This Kipling, overcome by the conquering chauvinism of the Colonist, loses his sense of values, belittling the weak to the tune of British imperialism. The tune, one must admit, is an attractive one, and even those who object to its burden of bombast have learned to whistle it by heart. The rhythms are often the beat of journalistic verse, but they communicate to the "average man" something he seeks and which he would not recognize in finer measures. It is indisputable that Kipling too often tries to force beauty in a rape of violence. But there are also those poems in which, as T. Earle Welby says in *A Popular History of English Poetry,* "he has been humbler and more passive, and in which beauty is a voluntary captive. One emotion has never failed to inspire him, the inverted nostalgia of the man returned home and yearning for far and once familiar scenes of exile. It arouses all the poet in him, puts wistfulness into his generally brazen music, clears his style of semi-Biblical claptrap, and sets his extraordinary descriptive talent to work more legitimately than usual." Such a descriptive talent is illustrated by "Mandalay," "Fuzzy Wuzzy," "Chant-Pagan," "The Return," even by such a stanza as:

> Rivers at night that cluck an' jeer,
>   Plains which the moonshine turns to sea,
> Mountains which never let you near,
>   An' stars to all eternity;
> An' the quick-breathin' dark that fills
>   The 'ollows of the wilderness,
> When the wind worries through the 'ills—
>   These may 'ave taught me more or less.

Such work shows that Kipling, though a poet, is something besides a poet. He is not so much a writer for those who enjoy writing—although his craftsmanship will repay study—as he is the singer of those who have never risen to an understanding of song. Yet after the War it became the fashion to disparage Kipling's work as well as his philosophy. When his name was mentioned it was accompanied by a deprecatory shrug or a remark about the decline of his fame; in 1935 a New York newspaper referred to him as "the forgotten man of English letters."

Reaction follows reaction, and if Kipling is underpraised today for the very qualities which were overpraised thirty years ago his hour will strike again. Few poems have revealed a richer and more resigned understanding of the soil and those who live close to it than "The Land"; the wanderlust has never been so poignantly expressed as in "For to Admire." His ballads have not only the swing but the vitality of the ancient Border Ballads, and it is altogether possible that he will outlast most of his contemporaries, and go down to posterity as a people's poet, a balladist whose songs were the popular tunes of one age and the folk-classics of another.

GUNGA DIN

You may talk o' gin an' beer
When you're quartered safe out 'ere,
An' you're sent to penny-fights an' Aldershot it;
But when it comes to slaughter
You will do your work on water,
An' you'll lick the bloomin' boots of 'im that's got it.
Now in Injia's sunny clime,
Where I used to spend my time
A-servin' of 'Er Majesty the Queen,
Of all them black-faced crew
The finest man I knew
Was our regimental *bhisti*,[1] Gunga Din.

It was "Din! Din! Din!
You limping lump o' brick-dust, Gunga Din!
Hi! *slippy hitherao!*
Water, get it! *Panee lao!*[2]
You squidgy-nosed old idol, Gunga Din!"

The uniform 'e wore
Was nothin' much before,
An' rather less than 'arf o' that be'ind,
For a twisty piece o' rag
An' a goatskin water-bag
Was all the field-equipment 'e could find.
When the sweatin' troop-train lay
In a sidin' through the day,
Where the 'eat would make your bloomin' eyebrows crawl,
We shouted *"Harry By!"*[3]

---

[1] The *bhisti*, or water-carrier, attached to regiments in India, is often one of the most devoted of the Queen's servants. He is also appreciated by the men.

[2] Bring water swiftly.                    [3] Tommy Atkins' equivalent for "O Brother!"

Till our throats were bricky-dry,
Then we wopped 'im 'cause 'e couldn't serve us all.

    It was "Din! Din! Din!
    You 'eathen, where the mischief 'ave you been?
    You put some *juldee* [1] in it,
    Or I'll *marrow* [2] you this minute,
    If you don't fill up my helmet, Gunga Din!"

'E would dot an' carry one
Till the longest day was done,
An' 'e didn't seem to know the use o' fear.
If we charged or broke or cut,
You could bet your bloomin' nut,
'E'd be waitin' fifty paces right flank rear.
With 'is *mussick* [3] on 'is back,
'E would skip with our attack,
An' watch us till the bugles made "Retire."
An' for all 'is dirty 'ide,
'E was white, clear white, inside
When 'e went to tend the wounded under fire!

    It was "Din! Din! Din!"
    With the bullets kickin' dust-spots on the green.
    When the cartridges ran out,
    You could 'ear the front-files shout:
    "Hi! ammunition-mules an' Gunga Din!"

I sha'n't forgit the night
When I dropped be'ind the fight
With a bullet where my belt-plate should 'a' been.
I was chokin' mad with thirst,
An' the man that spied me first
Was our good old grinnin', gruntin' Gunga Din.
'E lifted up my 'ead,
An' 'e plugged me where I bled,
An' 'e guv me 'arf-a-pint o' water—green;
It was crawlin' an' it stunk,
But of all the drinks I've drunk,
I'm gratefulest to one from Gunga Din.

    It was "Din! Din! Din!
    'Ere's a beggar with a bullet through 'is spleen;
    'E's chawin' up the ground an' 'e's kickin' all around:
    For Gawd's sake, git the water, Gunga Din!"

'E carried me away
To where a *dooli* lay,
An' a bullet come an' drilled the beggar clean.
'E put me safe inside,
An' just before 'e died:
"I 'ope you liked your drink," sez Gunga Din.

---

[1] Speed.        [2] Hit you.        [3] Water-skin.

So I'll meet 'im later on
In the place where 'e is gone—
Where it's always double drill and no canteen;
'E'll be squattin' on the coals
Givin' drink to pore damned souls,
An' I'll get a swig in Hell from Gunga Din!

Din! Din! Din!
You Lazarushian-leather Gunga Din!
Tho' I've belted you an' flayed you,
By the livin' Gawd that made you,
You're a better man than I am, Gunga Din!

### DANNY DEEVER

"What are the bugles blowin' for?" said Files-on-Parade.
"To turn you out, to turn you out," the Color-Sergeant said.
"What makes you look so white, so white?" said Files-on-Parade.
"I'm dreadin' what I've got to watch," the Color-Sergeant said.
    For they're hangin' Danny Deever, you can 'ear the Dead March play,
    The regiment's in 'ollow square—they're hangin' him today;
    They've taken of his buttons off an' cut his stripes away,
    An' they're hangin' Danny Deever in the mornin'.

"What makes the rear-rank breathe so 'ard?" said Files-on-Parade.
"It's bitter cold, it's bitter cold," the Color-Sergeant said.
"What makes that front-rank man fall down?" says Files-on-Parade.
"A touch of sun, a touch of sun," the Color-Sergeant said.
    They are hangin' Danny Deever, they are marchin' of 'im round.
    They 'ave 'alted Danny Deever by 'is coffin on the ground;
    An 'e'll swing in 'arf a minute for a sneakin' shootin' hound—
    O they're hangin' Danny Deever in the mornin'!

" 'Is cot was right-'and cot to mine," said Files-on-Parade.
" 'E's sleepin' out an' far tonight," the Color-Sergeant said.
"I've drunk 'is beer a score o' times," said Files-on-Parade.
" 'E's drinkin' bitter beer alone," the Color-Sergeant said.
    They are hangin' Danny Deever, you must mark 'im to 'is place,
    For 'e shot a comrade sleepin'—you must look 'im in the face;
    Nine 'undred of 'is county an' the regiment's disgrace,
    While they're hangin' Danny Deever in the mornin'.

"What's that so black agin the sun?" said Files-on-Parade.
"It's Danny fightin' 'ard for life," the Color-Sergeant said.
"What's that that whimpers over'ead?" said Files-on-Parade.
"It's Danny's soul that's passin' now," the Color-Sergeant said.
    For they're done with Danny Deever, you can 'ear the quickstep play,
    The regiment's in column, an' they're marchin' us away;
    Ho! the young recruits are shakin', an' they'll want their beer today,
    After hangin' Danny Deever in the mornin'.

### MANDALAY

By the old Moulmein Pagoda, lookin' eastward to the sea,
There's a Burma girl a-settin', an' I know she thinks o' me;
For the wind is in the palm-trees, an' the temple-bells they say:
"Come you back, you British soldier; come you back to Mandalay!"
    Come you back to Mandalay,
    Where the old Flotilla lay:
    Can't you 'ear their paddles chunkin' from Rangoon to Mandalay?
    On the road to Mandalay,
    Where the flyin'-fishes play,
    An' the dawn comes up like thunder outer China 'crost the Bay!

'Er petticut was yaller an' 'er little cap was green,
An' 'er name was Supi-yaw-let—jes' the same as Theebaw's Queen,
An' I seed her fust a-smokin' of a whackin' white cheroot,
An' a-wastin' Christian kisses on an 'eathen idol's foot:
    Bloomin' idol made o' mud—
    What they called the Great Gawd Budd—
    Plucky lot she cared for idols when I kissed 'er where she stud!
    On the road to Mandalay—

When the mist was on the rice-fields an' the sun was droppin' slow,
She'd git 'er little banjo an' she'd sing *"Kulla-lo-lo!"*
With 'er arm upon my shoulder an' her cheek agin my cheek
We useter watch the steamers an' the *hathis* pilin' teak.
    Elephints a-pilin' teak
    In the sludgy, squdgy creek,
    Where the silence 'ung that 'eavy you was 'arf afraid to speak!
    On the road to Mandalay—

But that's all shove be'ind me—long ago an' fur away,
An' there ain't no 'busses runnin' from the Benk to Mandalay;
An' I'm learnin' 'ere in London what the ten-year sodger tells:
"If you've 'eard the East a-callin', why, you won't 'eed nothin' else."
    No! you won't 'eed nothin' else
    But them spicy garlic smells
    An' the sunshine an' the palm-trees an' the tinkly temple bells!
    On the road to Mandalay—

I am sick o' wastin' leather on these gritty pavin'-stones,
An' the blasted Henglish drizzle wakes the fever in my bones;
Tho' I walks with fifty 'ousemaids outer Chelsea to the Strand,
An' they talks a lot o' lovin', but wot do they understand?
    Beefy face an' grubby 'and—
    Law! wot *do* they understand?
    I've a neater, sweeter maiden in a cleaner, greener land!
    On the road to Mandalay—

Ship me somewheres east of Suez where the best is like the worst,
Where there aren't no Ten Commandments, an' a man can raise a thirst;

For the temple-bells are callin', an' it's there that I would be—
By the old Moulmein Pagoda, lookin' lazy at the sea—
    On the road to Mandalay,
    Where the old Flotilla lay,
    With our sick beneath the awnings when we went to Mandalay!
    Oh, the road to Mandalay,
    Where the flyin'-fishes play,
    An' the dawn comes up like thunder outer China 'crost the Bay!

## "FUZZY-WUZZY"

### (*Soudan Expeditionary Force*)

We've fought with many men acrost the seas,
    An' some of 'em was brave an' some was not:
The Paythan an' the Zulu an' Burmese;
    But the Fuzzy was the finest o' the lot.
We never got a ha'porth's change of 'im:
    'E squatted in the scrub an' 'ocked our 'orses,
'E cut our sentries up at Sua*kim,*
    An' 'e played the cat an' banjo with our forces.
        So 'ere's *to* you, Fuzzy-Wuzzy, at your 'ome in the Sowdan;
        You're a pore benighted 'eathen but a first-class fightin' man;
        We gives you your certifikit, an' if you want it signed
        We'll come an' 'ave a romp with you whenever you're inclined.

We took our chanst among the Kyber 'ills,
    The Boers knocked us silly at a mile,
The Burman guv us Irriwaddy chills,
    An' a Zulu *impi* dished us up in style:
But all we ever got from such as they
    Was pop to what the Fuzzy made us swaller;
We 'eld our bloomin' own, the papers say,
    But man for man the Fuzzy knocked us 'oller.
        Then 'ere's *to* you, Fuzzy-Wuzzy, an' the missis and the kid;
        Our orders was to break you, an' of course we went an' did.
        We sloshed you with Martinis, an' it wasn't 'ardly fair;
        But for all the odds agin you, Fuzzy-Wuz, you bruk the square.

'E 'asn't got no papers of 'is own,
    'E 'asn't got no medals nor rewards,
So we must certify the skill 'e's shown
    In usin' of 'is long two-'anded swords;
When 'e's 'oppin' in an' out among the bush
    With 'is coffin-'eaded shield an' shovel-spear,
A 'appy day with Fuzzy on the rush
    Will last a 'ealthy Tommy for a year.
        So 'ere's *to* you, Fuzzy-Wuzzy, an' your friends which is no more,
        If we 'adn't lost some messmates we would 'elp you to deplore;
        But give an' take's the gospel, an' we'll call the bargain fair,
        For if you 'ave lost more than us, you crumpled up the square!

'E rushes at the smoke when we let drive,
  An', before we know, 'e's 'ackin' at our 'ead;
'E's all 'ot sand an' ginger when alive,
  An' 'e's generally shammin' when 'e's dead.
'E's a daisy, 'e's a ducky, 'e's a lamb!
  'E's a injia-rubber idiot on the spree,
'E's the on'y thing that doesn't care a damn
  For the Regiment o' British Infantree.
    So 'ere's *to* you, Fuzzy-Wuzzy, at your 'ome in the Sowdan;
    You're a pore benighted 'eathen but a first-class fightin' man;
    An 'ere's *to* you, Fuzzy-Wuzzy, with your 'ayrick 'ead of 'air—
    You big black boundin' beggar—for you bruk a British square.

## TOMMY

I went into a public-'ouse to get a pint o' beer,
The publican 'e up an' sez, "We serve no red-coats here."
The girls be'ind the bar they laughed an' giggled fit to die,
I outs into the street again, an' to myself sez I:
    O it's Tommy this, an' Tommy that, an' "Tommy go away";
    But it's "Thank you, Mister Atkins," when the band begins to play,
    The band begins to play, my boys, the band begins to play,
    O it's "Thank you, Mister Atkins," when the band begins to play.

I went into a theater as sober as could be,
They give a drunk civilian room, but 'adn't none for me;
They sent me to the gallery or round the music-'alls,
But when it comes to fightin', Lord! they'll shove me in the stalls.
    For it's Tommy this, an' Tommy that, an' "Tommy wait outside";
    But it's "Special train for Atkins," when the trooper's on the tide,
    The troopship's on the tide, my boys, etc.

O makin' mock o' uniforms that guard you while you sleep
Is cheaper than them uniforms, an' they're starvation cheap;
An' hustlin' drunken sodgers when they're goin' large a bit
Is five times better business than paradin' in full kit.
    Then it's Tommy this, an' Tommy that, an' "Tommy 'ow's yer soul?"
    But it's "Thin red line of 'eroes" when the drums begin to roll,
    The drums begin to roll, my boys, etc.

We aren't no thin red 'eroes, nor we aren't no blackguards too,
But single men in barricks, most remarkable like you;
An' if sometimes our conduck isn't all your fancy paints,
Why, single men in barricks don't grow into plaster saints.
    While it's Tommy this, an' Tommy that, an' "Tommy fall be'ind";
    But it's "Please to walk in front, sir," when there's trouble in the wind,
    There's trouble in the wind, my boys, etc.

You talk o' better food for us, an' schools, an' fires, an' all:
We'll wait for extry rations if you treat us rational.
Don't mess about the cook-room slops, but prove it to our face
The Widow's uniform is not the soldier-man's disgrace.

But it's Tommy this, an' Tommy that, an' "Chuck him out, the brute!"
But it's "Savior of 'is country" when the guns begin to shoot;
An' it's Tommy this, an' Tommy that, an' anything you please;
An' Tommy ain't a bloomin' fool—you bet that Tommy sees!

## THE LADIES

I've taken my fun where I've found it;
   I've rogued an' I've ranged in my time;
I've 'ad my pickin' o' sweet'earts,
   An' four o' the lot was prime.
One was an 'arf-caste widow,
   One was a woman at Prome,
One was the wife of a *jemadar-sais,*
   An' one is a girl at 'ome.

*Now I aren't no 'and with the ladies,*
   *For, takin' 'em all along,*
*You never can say till you've tried 'em,*
   *An' then you are like to be wrong.*
*There's times when you'll think that you mightn't,*
   *There's times when you'll know that you might;*
*But the things you will learn from the Yellow an' Brown,*
   *They'll 'elp you a lot with the White!*

I was a young un at 'Oogli,
   Shy as a girl to begin;
Aggie de Castrer she made me,
   An' Aggie was clever as sin;
Older than me, but my first un—
   More like a mother she were—
Showed me the way to promotion an' pay,
   An' I learned about women from 'er!

Then I was ordered to Burma,
   Actin' in charge o' Bazar,
An' I got me a tiddy live 'eathen
   Through buyin' supplies off 'er pa.
Funny an' yellow an' faithful—
   Doll in a teacup she were,
But we lived on the square, like a true-married pair,
   An' I learned about women from 'er!

Then we was shifted to Neemuch
   (Or I might ha' been keepin' 'er now),
An' I took with a shiny she-devil,
   The wife of a nigger at Mhow;
Taught me the gypsy-folks' *bolee;*
   Kind o' volcano she were,
For she knifed me one night 'cause I wished she was white,
   An' I learned about women from 'er!

Then I come 'ome in the trooper,
  'Long of a kid o' sixteen—
Girl from a convent at Meerut,
  The straightest I ever 'ave seen.
Love at first sight was 'er trouble,
  *She* didn't know what it were;
An' I wouldn't do such, 'cause I liked 'er too much,
  But—I learned about women from 'er!

I've taken my fun where I've found it,
  An' now I must pay for my fun,
For the more you 'ave known o' the others
  The less you will settle to one;
An' the end of it's sittin' and thinkin',
  An' dreamin' Hell-fires to see;
So be warned by my lot (which I know you will not),
  An' learn about women from me!

     *What did the Colonel's Lady think?*
      *Nobody never knew.*
     *Somebody asked the Sergeant's wife,*
      *An' she told 'em true!*
     *When you get to a man in the case,*
      *They're like as a row of pins—*
     *For the Colonel's Lady an' Judy O'Grady*
     *Are sisters under their skins!*

### BOOTS

#### (*Infantry Columns of the Earlier War*)

We're foot—slog—slog—slog—sloggin' over Africa!
Foot—foot—foot—foot—sloggin' over Africa—
(Boots—boots—boots—boots, movin' up an' down again!)
    There's no discharge in the war!

Seven—six—eleven—five—nine-an'-twenty mile today—
Four—eleven—seventeen—thirty-two the day before—
(Boots—boots—boots—boots, movin' up an' down again!)
    There's no discharge in the war!

Don't—don't—don't—don't—look at what's in front of you
(Boots—boots—boots—boots, movin' up an' down again);
Men—men—men—men—men go mad with watchin' 'em,
    An' there's no discharge in the war!

Try—try—try—try—to think o' something different—
Oh—my—God—keep—me from goin' lunatic!
(Boots—boots—boots—boots, movin' up an' down again!)
    There's no discharge in the war!

Count—count—count—count—the bullets in the bandoliers;
If—your—eyes—drop—they will get atop o' you
(Boots—boots—boots—boots, movin' up an' down again)—
    There's no discharge in the war!

We—can—stick—out—'unger, thirst, an' weariness,
But—not—not—not—not the chronic sight of 'em—
Boots—boots—boots—boots, movin' up an' down again,
    An' there's no discharge in the war!

'Tain't—so—bad—by—day because o' company,
But night—brings—long—strings o' forty thousand million
Boots—boots—boots—boots, movin' up an' down again.
    There's no discharge in the war!

I—'ave—marched—six—weeks in 'Ell an' certify
It—is—not—fire—devils, dark or anything
But boots—boots—boots, movin' up an' down again,
    An' there's no discharge in the war!

### THE RETURN

Peace is declared, and I return
  To 'Ackneystadt, but not the same;
Things 'ave transpired which made me learn
  The size and meanin' of the game.
I did no more than others did,
  I don't know where the change began;
I started as a average kid,
  I finished as a thinkin' man.

*If England was what England seems*
  *An' not the England of our dreams,*
*But only putty, brass, an' paint,*
  *'Ow quick we'd drop 'er! But she ain't!*

Before my gappin' mouth could speak
  I 'eard it in my comrade's tone;
I saw it on my neighbor's cheek
  Before I felt it flush my own.
An' last it come to me—not pride,
  Nor yet conceit, but on the 'ole
(If such a term may be applied)
  The makin's of a bloomin' soul.

Rivers at night that cluck an' jeer,
  Plains which the moonshine turns to sea,
Mountains that never let you near,
  An' stars to all eternity;

An' the quick-breathin' dark that fills
 The 'ollows of the wilderness,
When the wind worries through the 'ills—
 These may 'ave taught me more or less.

Towns without people, ten times took,
 An' ten times left an' burned at last;
An' starvin' dogs that come to look
 For owners when a column passed;
An' quiet, 'omesick talks between
 Men, met by night, you never knew
Until—'is face—by shellfire seen—
 Once—an' struck off. They taught me, too.

The day's lay-out—the mornin' sun
 Beneath your 'at-brim as you sight;
The dinner-'ush from noon till one,
 An' the full roar that lasts till night;
An' the pore dead that look so old
 An' was so young an hour ago,
An' legs tied down before they're cold—
 These are the things which make you know.

Also Time runnin' into years—
 A thousand Places left be'ind—
An' Men from both two 'emispheres
 Discussin' things of every kind;
So much more near than I 'ad known,
 So much more great than I 'ad guessed—
An' me, like all the rest, alone—
 But reachin' out to all the rest!

So 'ath it come to me—not pride,
 Nor yet conceit, but on the 'ole
(If such a term may be applied)
 The makin's of a bloomin' soul.
But now, discharged, I fall away
 To do with little things again. . . .
Gawd, 'oo knows all I cannot say,
 Look after me in Thamesfontein!

*If England was what England seems*
 *An' not the England of our dreams,*
*But only putty, brass, an' paint,*
 *'Ow quick we'd chuck 'er! But she ain't!*

## THE CONUNDRUM OF THE WORKSHOPS

When the flush of a newborn sun fell first on Eden's green and gold,
Our father Adam sat under the Tree and scratched with a stick in the mold;
And the first rude sketch that the world had seen was joy to his mighty heart,
Till the Devil whispered behind the leaves: "It's pretty, but is it Art?"

Wherefore he called to his wife and fled to fashion his work anew—
The first of his race who cared a fig for the first, most dread review;
And he left his lore to the use of his sons—and that was a glorious gain
When the Devil chuckled: "Is it Art?" in the ear of the branded Cain.

They builded a tower to shiver the sky and wrench the stars apart,
Till the Devil grunted behind the bricks: "It's striking, but is it Art?"
The stone was dropped by the quarry-side, and the idle derrick swung,
While each man talked of the aims of art, and each in an alien tongue.

They fought and they talked in the north and the south, they talked and they
        fought in the west,
Till the waters rose on the jabbering land, and the poor Red Clay had rest—
Had rest till the dank blank-canvas dawn when the dove was preened to start,
And the Devil bubbled below the keel: "It's human, but is it Art?"

The tale is old as the Eden Tree—as new as the new-cut tooth—
For each man knows ere his lip-thatch grows he is master of Art and Truth;
And each man hears as the twilight nears, to the beat of his dying heart,
The Devil drum on the darkened pane: "You did it, but was it Art?"

We have learned to whittle the Eden Tree to the shape of a surplice-peg,
We have learned to bottle our parents twain in the yolk of an addled egg,
We know that the tail must wag the dog, as the horse is drawn by the cart;
But the Devil whoops, as he whooped of old: "It's clever, but is it Art?"

When the flicker of London's sun falls faint on the club-room's green and gold,
The sons of Adam sit them down and scratch with their pens in the mold—
They scratch with their pens in the mold of their graves, and the ink and the
        anguish start
When the Devil mutters behind the leaves: "It's pretty, but is it Art?"

Now, if we could win to the Eden Tree where the four great rivers flow,
And the wreath of Eve is red on the turf as she left it long ago,
And if we could come when the sentry slept, and softly scurry through,
By the favor of God we might know as much—as our father Adam knew.


### EVARRA AND HIS GODS

*Read here,*
*This is the story of Evarra—man—*
*Maker of Gods in lands beyond the sea.*
    Because the city gave him of her gold,
    Because the caravans brought turquoises,
    Because his life was sheltered by the King,
    So that no man should maim him, none should steal,
    Or break his rest with babble in the streets
    When he was weary after toil, he made
    An image of his God in gold and pearl,
    With turquoise diadem and human eyes,
    A wonder in the sunshine, known afar
    And worshiped by the King; but, drunk with pride,

Because the city bowed to him for God,
He wrote above the shrine: *"Thus Gods are made,*
*And whoso makes them otherwise shall die."*
And all the city praised him. . . . Then he died.

*Read here the story of Evarra—man—*
*Maker of Gods in lands beyond the sea.*
Because his city had no wealth to give,
Because the caravans were spoiled afar,
Because his life was threatened by the King,
So that all men despised him in the streets,
He hacked the living rock, with sweat and tears,
And reared a God against the morning-gold,
A terror in the sunshine, seen afar,
And worshiped by the King; but, drunk with pride,
Because the city fawned to bring him back,
He carved upon the plinth: *"Thus Gods are made,*
*And whoso makes them otherwise shall die."*
And all the people praised him. . . . Then he died.

*Read here the story of Evarra—man—*
*Maker of Gods in lands beyond the sea.*
Because he lived among the simple folk,
Because his village was between the hills,
Because he smeared his cheeks with blood of ewes,
He cut an idol from a fallen pine,
Smeared blood upon its cheeks, and wedged a shell
Above its brow for eye, and gave it hair
Of trailing moss, and plaited straw for crown.
And all the village praised him for his craft,
And brought him butter, honey, milk, and curds.
Wherefore, because the shoutings drove him mad,
He scratched upon that log: *"Thus Gods are made,*
*And whoso makes them otherwise shall die."*
And all the people praised him. . . . Then he died.

*Read here the story of Evarra—man—*
*Maker of Gods in lands beyond the sea.*
Because his God decreed one clot of blood
Should swerve a hair's-breadth from the pulse's path,
And chafe his brain, Evarra mowed alone,
Rag-wrapped, among the cattle in the fields,
Counting his fingers, jesting with the trees,
And mocking at the mist, until his God
Drove him to labor. Out of dung and horns
Dropped in the mire he made a monstrous God,
Abhorrent, shapeless, crowned with plantain tufts.
And when the cattle lowed at twilight-time,
He dreamed it was the clamor of lost crowds,
And howled among the beasts: *"Thus Gods are made,*
*And whoso makes them otherwise shall die."*
Thereat the cattle bellowed. . . . Then he died.

Yet at the last he came to Paradise,
And found his own four Gods, and that he wrote;
And marveled, being very near to God,
What oaf on earth had made his toil God's law,
Till God said, mocking: "Mock not. These be thine."
Then cried Evarra: "I have sinned!"—"Not so.
If thou hadst written otherwise, thy Gods
Had rested in the mountain and the mine,
And I were poorer by four wondrous Gods,
And thy more wondrous law, Evarra. Thine,
Servant of shouting crowds and lowing kine."
Thereat with laughing mouth, but tear-wet eyes,
Evarra cast his Gods from Paradise.

*This is the story of Evarra—man—*
*Maker of Gods in lands beyond the sea.*

### LA NUIT BLANCHE

*A Much-Discerning Public hold*
*The Singer generally sings*
*Of personal and private things,*
*And prints and sells his past for gold.*

*Whatever I may here disclaim,*
*The very clever folk I sing to*
*Will most indubitably cling to*
*Their pet delusion, just the same.*

I had seen, as dawn was breaking
And I staggered to my rest,
Tari Devi softly shaking
From the Cart Road to the crest.
I had seen the spurs of Jakko
Heave and quiver, swell and sink.
Was it Earthquake or tobacco,
Day of Doom or Night of Drink?

In the full, fresh, fragrant morning
I observed a camel crawl,
Laws of gravitation scorning,
On the ceiling and the wall;
Then I watched a fender walking,
And I heard gray leeches sing,
And a red-hot monkey talking
Did not seem the proper thing.

Half the night I watch the Heavens
Fizz like '81 champagne—
Fly to sixes and to sevens,
Wheel and thunder back again;
And when all was peace and order
Save one planet nailed askew,
Much I wept because my warder
Would not let me set it true.

After frenzied hours of waiting,
When the Earth and Skies were dumb,
Pealed an awful voice dictating
An interminable sum,
Changing to a tangled story—
"What she said you said I said—"
Till the Moon arose in glory,
And I found her . . . in my head;

Then a Face came, blind and weeping,
And It couldn't wipe Its eyes,
And It muttered I was keeping
Back the moonlight from the skies;
So I patted it for pity,
But it whistled shrill with wrath,
And a huge black Devil City
Poured its peoples on my path.

So I fled with steps uncertain
On a thousand-year long race,
But the bellying of the curtain
Kept me always in one place;
While the tumult rose and maddened
To the roar of Earth on fire,
Ere it ebbed and sank and saddened
To a whisper tense as wire.

In intolerable stillness
Rose one little, little star,
And it chuckled at my illness,
And it mocked me from afar;
And its brethren came and eyed me,
Called the Universe to aid,
Till I lay, with naught to hide me,
'Neath the Scorn of All Things Made.

Dun and saffron, robed and splendid,
  Broke the solemn, pitying Day,
And I knew my pains were ended,
  And I turned and tried to pray;
But my speech was shattered wholly,
  And I wept as children weep,
Till the dawn-wind, softly, slowly,
  Brought to burning eyelids sleep.

## AN ASTROLOGER'S SONG

To the Heavens above us
  Oh, look and behold
The Planets that love us
  All harnessed in gold!
What chariots, what horses
  Against us shall bide
While the Stars in their courses
  Do fight on our side?

All thought, all desires,
  That are under the sun,
Are one with their fires,
  As we also are one:
All matter, all spirit,
  All fashion, all frame,
Receive and inherit
  Their strength from the same.

(Oh, man that deniest
  All power save thine own,
Their power in the highest
  Is mightily shown.
Not less in the lowest
  That power is made clear.
Oh, man, if thou knowest,
  What treasure is here!)

Earth quakes in her throes
  And we wonder for why!
But the blind planet knows
  When her ruler is nigh;
And, attuned since Creation
  To perfect accord,
She thrills in her station
  And yearns to her Lord.

The waters have risen,
  The springs are unbound—
The floods break their prison,
  And ravin around.

No rampart withstands 'em,
  Their fury will last,
Till the Sign that commands 'em
  Sinks low or swings past.

Through abysses unproven
  And gulfs beyond thought,
Our portion is woven,
  Our burden is brought.
Yet They that prepare it,
  Whose Nature we share,
Make us who must bear it
  Well able to bear.

Though terrors o'ertake us
  We'll not be afraid.
No power can unmake us
  Save that which has made.
Nor yet beyond reason
  Or hope shall we fall—
All things have their season,
  And Mercy crowns all!

Then doubt not, ye fearful—
  The Eternal is King—
Up, heart, and be cheerful,
  And lustily sing:—
*What chariots, what horses*
  *Against us shall bide*
*While the Stars in their courses*
  *Do fight on our side?*

## RECESSIONAL

God of our fathers, known of old,
  Lord of our far-flung battle-line,
Beneath whose awful hand we hold
  Dominion over palm and pine—
Lord God of Hosts, be with us yet,
Lest we forget—lest we forget!

The tumult and the shouting dies;
  The captains and the kings depart:
Still stands Thine ancient sacrifice,
  An humble and a contrite heart.
Lord God of Hosts, be with us yet,
Lest we forget—lest we forget!

Far-called, our navies melt away;
  On dune and headland sinks the fire:

Lo, all our pomp of yesterday
  Is one with Nineveh and Tyre!
Judge of the Nations, spare us yet,
Lest we forget—lest we forget!

If, drunk with sight of power, we loose
  Wild tongues that have not Thee in awe,
Such boastings as the Gentiles use,
  Or lesser breeds without the Law—

Lord God of Hosts, be with us yet,
  Lest we forget—lest we forget!

For heathen heart that puts her trust
  In reeking tube and iron shard,
All valiant dust that builds on dust,
  And, guarding, calls not Thee to guard,
For frantic boast and foolish word—
Thy Mercy on Thy People, Lord!

### THE LAST CHANTEY

*"And there was no more sea"*

Thus said the Lord in the Vault above the Cherubim,
  Calling to the Angels and the Souls in their degree:
    "Lo! Earth has passed away
    On the smoke of Judgment Day.
  That Our word may be established shall We gather up the sea?"

Loud sang the souls of the jolly, jolly mariners:
  "Plague upon the hurricane that made us furl and flee!
    But the war is done between us,
    In the deep the Lord hath seen us—
  Our bones we'll leave the barracout', and God may sink the sea!"

Then said the soul of Judas that betrayed Him:
  "Lord, hast Thou forgotten Thy covenant with me?
    How once a year I go
    To cool me on the floe?
  And Ye take my day of mercy if Ye take away the sea."

Then said the soul of the Angel of the Off-shore Wind:
  (He that bits the thunder when the bull-mouthed breakers flee):
    "I have watch and ward to keep
    O'er Thy wonders on the deep,
  And Ye take mine honor from me if Ye take away the sea!"

Loud sang the souls of the jolly, jolly mariners:
  "Nay, but we were angry, and a hasty folk are we.
    If we worked the ship together
    Till she foundered in foul weather,
  Are we babes that we should clamor for a vengeance on the sea?"

Then said the souls of the slaves that men threw overboard:
  "Kenneled in the picaroon a weary band were we;
    But Thy arm was strong to save,
    And it touched us on the wave,
  And we drowsed the long tides idle till Thy Trumpets tore the sea."

Then cried the soul of the stout Apostle Paul to God:
  "Once we frapped a ship, and she labored woundily.

> There were fourteen score of these,
>    And they blessed Thee on their knees,
> When they learned Thy Grace and Glory under Malta by the sea!"

Loud sang the souls of the jolly, jolly mariners,
   Plucking at their harps, and they plucked unhandily:
      "Our thumbs are rough and tarred,
      And the tune is something hard—
May we lift a Deepsea Chantey such as seamen use at sea?"

Then said the souls of the gentlemen-adventurers—
   Fettered wrist to bar all for red iniquity:
      "Ho, we revel in our chains
      O'er the sorrow that was Spain's;
Heave or sink it, leave or drink it, we were masters of the sea!"

Up spake the soul of a gray Gothavn 'speckshioner—
   (He that led the flenching in the fleets of fair Fundee):
      "Oh, the ice-blink white and near,
      And the bowhead breaching clear!
Will Ye whelm them all for wantonness that wallow in the sea?"

Loud sang the souls of the jolly, jolly mariners,
   Crying: "Under Heaven, here is neither lead nor lea!
      Must we sing for evermore
      On the windless, glassy floor?
Take back your golden fiddles and we'll beat to open sea!"

Then stooped the Lord, and He called the good sea up to Him,
   And 'stablished its borders unto all eternity,
      That such as have no pleasure
      For to praise the Lord by measure,
They may enter into galleons and serve Him on the sea.

*Sun, Wind, and Cloud shall fail not from the face of it,*
   *Stinging, ringing spindrift, nor the fulmar flying free;*
      *And the ships shall go abroad*
      *To the Glory of the Lord*
*Who heard the silly sailor-folk and gave them back their sea!*

## SESTINA OF THE TRAMP-ROYAL

Speakin' in general, I 'ave tried 'em all—
The 'appy roads that take you o'er the world.
Speakin' in general, I 'ave found them good
For such as cannot use one bed too long,
But must get 'ence, the same as I 'ave done,
An' go observin' matters till they die.

What do it matter where or 'ow we die,
So long as we've our 'ealth to watch it all—
The different ways that different things are done,

An' men an' women lovin' in this world;
Takin' our chances as they come along,
An' when they ain't, pretendin' they are good?

In cash or credit—no, it aren't no good;
You 'ave to 'ave the 'abit or you'd die,
Unless you lived your life but one day long,
Nor didn't prophesy nor fret at all,
But drew your tucker some'ow from the world,
An' never bothered what you might ha' done.

But, Gawd, what things are they I 'aven't done!
I've turned my 'and to most, an' turned it good,
In various situations round the world—
For 'im that doth not work must surely die;
But that's no reason man should labor all
'Is life on one same shift—life's none so long.

Therefore, from job to job I've moved along.
Pay couldn't 'old me when my time was done,
For something in my 'ead upset it all,
Till I 'ad dropped whatever 't was for good,
An' out at sea, be'eld the dock-lights die,
An' met my mate—the wind that tramps the world!

It's like a book, I think, this bloomin' world,
Which you can read and care for just so long,
But presently you feel that you will die
Unless you get the page you're readin' done,
An' turn another—likely not so good;
But what you're after is to turn 'em all.

Gawd bless this world! Whatever she 'ath done—
Excep' when awful long—I've found it good.
So write, before I die, " 'E liked it all!"

### THE LAND

When Julius Fabricius, Sub-Prefect of the Weald,
In the days of Diocletian owned our Lower River-field,
He called to him Hobdenius—a Briton of the Clay,
Saying, "What about that River-piece for layin' in to hay?"

And the aged Hobden answered: "I remember as a lad
My father told your father that she wanted dreenin' bad.
An' the more that you neeglect her the less you'll get her clean.
Have it jest *as* you've a mind to, but, if I was you, I'd dreen."

So they drained it long and crossways in the lavish Roman style.
Still we find among the river-drift their flakes of ancient tile,
And in drouthy middle August, when the bones of meadows show,
We can trace the lines they followed sixteen hundred years ago.

Then Julius Fabricius died as even Prefects do,
And after certain centuries, Imperial Rome died too.
Then did robbers enter Britain from across the Northern main
And our Lower River-field was won by Ogier the Dane.

Well could Ogier work his war-boat—well could Ogier wield his brand—
Much he knew of foaming waters—not so much of farming land.
So he called to him a Hobden of the old unaltered blood,
Saying: "What about that River-bit, she doesn't look so good."

And that aged Hobden answered: " 'Tain't for *me* to interfere,
But I've known that bit o' meadow now for five and fifty year.
Have it *jest* as you've a mind to, but I've proved it time on time,
If you want to change her nature you have *got* to give her lime!"

Ogier sent his wains to Lewes, twenty hours' solemn walk,
And drew back great abundance of the cool, gray, healing chalk.
And old Hobden spread it broadcast, never heeding what was in't;
Which is why in cleaning ditches, now and then we find a flint.

Ogier died. His sons grew English. Anglo-Saxon was their name,
Till out of blossomed Normandy another pirate came;
For Duke William conquered England and divided with his men,
And our Lower River-field he gave to William of Warenne.

But the Brook (you know her habit) rose one rainy Autumn night
And tore down sodden flitches of the bank to left and right.
So, said William to his Bailiff as they rode their dripping rounds:
"Hob, what about that River-bit—the Brook's got up no bounds?"

And that aged Hobden answered: " 'Tain't my business to advise,
But ye might ha' known 'twould happen from the way the valley lies.
When ye can't hold back the water you must try and save the sile.
Hev it jest as you've a *mind* to, but if I was you I'd spile!"

They spiled along the water-course with trunks of willow-trees
And planks of elms behind 'em and immortal oaken knees.
And when the spates of Autumn whirl the gravel-beds away
You can see their faithful fragments iron-hard in iron clay.

*Georgii Quinti, Anno Sexto,* I, who own the River-field,
Am fortified with title-deeds, attested, signed and sealed,
Guaranteeing me, my assigns, my executors and heirs
All sorts of powers and profits which—are neither mine nor theirs.

I have rights of chase and warren, as my dignity requires.
I can fish—but Hobden tickles. I can shoot—but Hobden wires.
I repair, but he reopens, certain gaps which, men allege,
Have been used by every Hobden since a Hobden swapped a hedge.

Shall I dog his morning progress o'er the track-betraying dew?
Demand his dinner-basket into which my pheasant flew?
Confiscate his evening faggot into which the conies ran,
And summons him to judgment? I would sooner summons Pan.

His dead are in the churchyard—thirty generations laid.
Their names went down in Domesday Book when Domesday Book was made.
And the passion and the piety and prowess of his line
Have seeded, rooted, fruited in some land the Law calls mine.

Not for any beast that burrows, nor for any bird that flies,
Would I lose his large sound council, miss his keen amending eyes.
He is bailiff, woodman, wheelwright, field-surveyor, engineer,
And if flagrantly a poacher—'tain't for me to interfere.

"Hob, what about that River-bit?" I turn to him again
With Fabricius and Ogier and William of Warenne.
"Hev it jest as you've a mind to, *but*"—and so he takes command.
For whoever pays the taxes, old Mus' Hobden owns the land.

## FOR TO ADMIRE

The Injian Ocean sets an' smiles
    So sof', so bright, so bloomin' blue;
There aren't a wave for miles an' miles
    Excep' the jiggle from the screw.
The ship is swep', the day is done,
    The bugle's gone for smoke and play;
An' black agin' the settin' sun
    The Lascar sings, *"Hum deckty hail"* [1]

    *For to admire an' for to see,*
      *For to be'old this world so wide—*
    *It never done no good to me,*
      *But I can't drop it if I tried!*

I see the sergeants pitchin' quoits,
    I 'ear the women laugh an' talk,
I spy upon the quarter-deck
    The orficers an' lydies walk.
I thinks about the things that was,
    An' leans an' looks acrost the sea,
Till spite of all the crowded ship
    There's no one lef' alive but me.

The things that was which I 'ave seen,
    In barrick, camp, an' action too,
I tells them over by myself,
    An' sometimes wonders if they're true;
For they was odd—most awful odd—
    But all the same now they are o'er,
There must be 'eaps o' plenty such,
    An' if I wait I'll see some more.

[1] "I'm looking out."

Oh, I 'ave come upon the books,
    An' frequent broke a barrick rule,
An' stood beside an' watched myself
    Be'avin' like a bloomin' fool.
I paid my price for findin' out,
    Nor never grutched the price I paid,
But sat in Clink without my boots,
    Admirin' 'ow the world was made.

Be'old a crowd upon the beam,
    An' 'umped above the sea appears
Old Aden, like a barrick-stove
    That no one's lit for years an' years!
I passed by that when I began,
    An' I go 'ome the road I came,
A time-expired soldier-man
    With six years' service to 'is name.

My girl she said, "Oh, stay with me!"
    My mother 'eld me to 'er breast.
They've never written none, an' so
    They must 'ave gone with all the rest—
With all the rest which I 'ave seen
    An' found an' known an' met along.
I cannot say the things I feel,
    And so I sing my evenin' song:

    *For to admire an' for to see,*
      *For to be'old this world so wide—*
    *It never done no good to me,*
      *But I can't drop it if I tried!*

# "ÆE"

G EORGE WILLIAM RUSSELL was born April 10, 1867, in the small town of Lurgan, County Armagh, Ireland. At sixteen he studied painting in the School of Art in Dublin, and became the close friend of W. B. Yeats and, later, James Stephens. While working as an accountant in a draper's establishment, he read much in Oriental mystical literature, becoming the leader of a small theosophical group. At that time he wrote an article for *The Irish Theosophist* under the pseudonym "Æon" but the compositor omitted the two last letters and the piece appeared under the diphthong "Æ," a pen-name which Russell adopted and used ever since.

In 1897 he became active in Irish politics. For several years he devoted himself to establishing coöperative societies, aiding rural communities, editing (in 1904) *The Irish Homestead* and (in 1923) *The Irish Statesman.* Upon his death, July 17, 1935, it was agreed that as an economist he had pulled his native Ireland out of its ruinously medieval farming methods.

With maturity he cultivated all his gifts, alternating and sometimes combining the rôles of sociologist, public speaker, poet, painter, and propagandist. His landscapes have the misty-mystical color of his poems, which, unconcerned with issues of agrarianism or, for that matter, any other problem, are serene if appropriately vague in their otherworldliness. "Continuity" and "The Secret" embody his faith *in petto.*

The best of his poetry is in *Homeward Songs by the Way* (1894) and *The Earth Breath and Other Poems* (1897). Yeats has spoken of these poems as "revealing in all things a kind of scented flame consuming them from within." *Collected Poems,* including later work, appeared in 1914. A more recent collection, *Mid-Summer Eve* (1928), contains only twelve poems. It is the clear expression of one who is not so much God-fearing as God-loving; not particularly original as poetry, but fine and mellow in spirit.

### THE GREAT BREATH

Its edges foamed with amethyst and rose,
Withers once more the old blue flower of day:
There where the ether like a diamond glows,
    Its petals fade away.

A shadowy tumult stirs the dusky air;
Sparkle the delicate dews, the distant snows;
The great deep thrills—for through it everywhere
    The breath of Beauty blows.

I saw how all the trembling ages past,
Molded to her by deep and deeper breath,
Near'd to the hour when Beauty breathes her last
    And knows herself in death.

## FROLIC

The children were shouting together
And racing along the sands,
A glimmer of dancing shadows,
A dovelike flutter of hands.

The stars were shouting in heaven,
The sun was chasing the moon:
The game was the same as the children's,
They danced to the self-same tune.

The whole of the world was merry,
One joy from the vale to the height,
Where the blue woods of twilight encircled
The love-lawns of the light.

## THE SECRET

One thing in all things have I seen:
One thought has haunted earth and air:
Clangor and silence both have been
Its palace chambers. Everywhere

I saw the mystic vision flow
And live in men and woods and streams,
Until I could no longer know
The dream of life from my own dreams.

Sometimes it rose like fire in me
Within the depths of my own mind,
And spreading to infinity,
It took the voices of the wind:

It scrawled the human mystery—
Dim heraldry—on light and air;
Wavering along the starry sea
I saw the flying vision there.

Each fire that in God's temple lit
Burns fierce before the inner shrine,
Dimmed as my fire grew near to it
And darkened at the light of mine.

At last, at last, the meaning caught—
The Spirit wears its diadem;
It shakes its wondrous plumes of thought
And trails the stars along with them.

## THE UNKNOWN GOD

Far up the dim twilight fluttered
    Moth-wings of vapor and flame:
The lights danced over the mountains,
    Star after star they came.

The lights grew thicker unheeded,
    For silent and still were we;
Our hearts were drunk with a beauty
    Our eyes could never see.

## CONTINUITY

No sign is made while empires pass,
The flowers and stars are still His care,
The constellations hid in grass,
The golden miracles in air.

Life in an instant will be rent,
Where death is glittering blind and wild—
The Heavenly Brooding is intent
To that last instant on Its child.

It breathes the glow in brain and heart,
Life is made magical. Until
Body and spirit are apart,
The Everlasting works Its will.

In that wild orchid that your feet
In their next falling shall destroy,
Minute and passionate and sweet
The Mighty Master holds His joy.

Though the crushed jewels droop and fade,
The Artist's labors will not cease,
And of the ruins shall be made
Some yet more lovely masterpiece.

# Richard Le Gallienne

RICHARD LE GALLIENNE, who, in spite of long residence in the United States, must be considered an English poet, was born at Liverpool in 1867. He entered on a business career soon after leaving Liverpool College, but, after five or six years, gave up commercial life to become a man of letters.

His early work was strongly influenced by the artificialities of the esthetic movement; the indebtedness to Oscar Wilde is especially evident. A little later, Keats was the dominant influence, and *English Poems* (1892) betray how deep and almost undermining were Le Gallienne's admirations. His poems in *The Lonely Dancer* (1913) show a keener individuality. His prose fancies are well known—particularly *The Book Bills of Narcissus* and the high-spirited fantasia, *The Quest of the Golden Girl*. *The Junkman and Other Poems* appeared in 1921.

Le Gallienne came to America about 1905 and, engaging in spasmodic journalism, lived in Rowayton, Conn., and New York City for about twenty years, after which he made his home in Paris.

## A BALLAD OF LONDON

Ah, London! London! our delight,
Great flower that opens but at night,
Great City of the midnight sun,
Whose day begins when day is done.

Lamp after lamp against the sky
Opens a sudden beaming eye,
Leaping alight on either hand,
The iron lilies of the Strand.

Like dragonflies, the hansoms hover,
With jeweled eyes, to catch the lover;
The streets are full of lights and loves,
Soft gowns, and flutter of soiled doves.

The human moths about the light
Dash and cling close in dazed delight,
And burn and laugh, the world and wife,
For this is London, this is life!

Upon thy petals butterflies,
But at thy root, some say, there lies
A world of weeping trodden things,
Poor worms that have not eyes or wings.

From out corruption of their woe
Springs this bright flower that charms us so,
Men die and rot deep out of sight
To keep this jungle-flower bright.

Paris and London, World-Flowers twain
Wherewith the World-Tree blooms again,
Since Time hath gathered Babylon,
And withered Rome still withers on.

Sidon and Tyre were such as ye,
How bright they shone upon the tree!
But Time hath gathered, both are gone,
And no man sails to Babylon.

## REGRET

One asked of regret,
  And I made reply:
To have held the bird,
  And let it fly;
To have seen the star
  For a moment nigh,
And lost it
  Through a slothful eye;
To have plucked the flower
  And cast it by;
To have one only hope—
  To die.

# Ernest Dowson

Eᴿɴᴇꜱᴛ ᴅᴏᴡꜱᴏɴ was born at Belmont Hill in Kent, August 2, 1867. His great-uncle was Alfred Domett (Browning's "Waring"), one time Prime Minister of New Zealand. Dowson, practically an invalid all his life, lived intermittently in London, Paris, Normandy, and on the Riviera. He was reckless with himself and, as disease weakened him more and more, hid in miserable surroundings; for almost two years he lived in sordid supper-houses known as "cabmen's shelters."

He formed only one passion but that one was final and devastating. He fell in love with a restaurant-keeper's daughter, paid court to her with the most delicate reserve, and she—impatient alike of his words and his reticences—married a waiter. The shock to Dowson was profound. He grew more and more withdrawn, even his contacts with fellow-members of the Rhymers' Club became slighter. He sank into despondency and dissipation; he literally drank himself to death.

Dowson's delicate and fantastic poetry was an attempt to escape from a reality too brutal for him. It is not only typically *fin de siécle;* it is, as any psychoanalytical critic will recognize, curiously autobiographical. He, himself, was his own pitiful "Pierrot of the Minute," throwing "roses, riotously with the throng"—even though the throng was ignorant of him. His passionate lyric, "I have been faithful to thee, Cynara! in my fashion," a triumph of despair and disillusion, is an outburst in which Dowson epitomized himself. "One of the greatest lyrical poems of our time," writes Arthur Symons; "in it he has for once said everything, and he has said it to an intoxicating and perhaps immortal music."

Yet, in spite of the fact that this familiar poem has been quoted in almost every contemporary collection, several of Dowson's less well-known poems strike a higher and far more resonant note. Among such poems are "Extreme Unction," possibly the finest expression of his Catholicism, and "A Last Word," which expresses his revulsion from the "perverse and aimless band."

Dowson's poems of decadence are no less typical than his religious poems; both, unlike the product of much of his period, are sincere. His mysticism, no less than his idealization of preciosity, is an esthetic one. Unable to find fulfillment in either, he wavered, as C. E. Andrews and M. O. Percival say in *Poetry of the Nineties,* "between heaping garlands upon the altars of Aphrodite and lighting candles to the Blessed Virgin."

Dowson died obscure in 1900, one of the least effectual but one of the most gifted of modern minor poets. His life was a tragedy of a weak nature buffeted by a strong and merciless environment. His poetry, highly special but never specious, survives.

### A LAST WORD

Let us go hence: the night is now at hand;
   The day is overworn, the birds all flown;
   And we have reaped the crops the gods have sown;
Despair and death; deep darkness o'er the land,

Broods like an owl; we cannot understand
   Laughter or tears, for we have only known
   Surpassing vanity: vain things alone
Have driven our perverse and aimless band.

Let us go hence, somewhither strange and cold,
   To Hollow Lands where just men and unjust
   Find end of labor, where's rest for the old,
Freedom to all from love and fear and lust.
Twine our torn hands! O pray the earth enfold
Our life-sick hearts and turn them into dust.


## NON SUM QUALIS ERAM BONAE SUB REGNO CYNARAE

Last night, ah, yesternight, betwixt her lips and mine
There fell thy shadow, Cynara! thy breath was shed
Upon my soul between the kisses and the wine;
And I was desolate and sick of an old passion,
   Yea, I was desolate and bowed my head:
I have been faithful to thee, Cynara! in my fashion.

All night upon mine heart I felt her warm heart beat,
Night-long within mine arms in love and sleep she lay;
Surely the kisses of her bought red mouth were sweet;
But I was desolate and sick of an old passion,
   When I awoke and found the dawn was gray:
I have been faithful to thee, Cynara! in my fashion.

I have forgot much, Cynara! gone with the wind,
Flung roses, roses riotously with the throng,
Dancing, to put thy pale, lost lilies out of mind;
But I was desolate and sick of an old passion,
   Yea, all the time, because the dance was long:
I have been faithful to thee, Cynara! in my fashion.

I cried for madder music and for stronger wine,
But when the feast is finished and the lamps expire,
Then falls thy shadow, Cynara! the night is thine;
And I am desolate and sick of an old passion,
   Yea, hungry for the lips of my desire:
I have been faithful to thee, Cynara! in my fashion.


## SPLEEN

I was not sorrowful, I could not weep,
And all my memories were put to sleep.

I watched the river grow more white and strange,
All day till evening I watched it change.

All day till evening I watched the rain
Beat wearily upon the window-pane.

I was not sorrowful, but only tired
Of everything that ever I desired.

Her lips, her eyes, all day became to me
The shadow of a shadow utterly.

All day mine hunger for her heart became
Oblivion, until the evening came.

And left me sorrowful, inclined to weep,
With all my memories that could not sleep.


## TO ONE IN BEDLAM

With delicate, mad hands, behind his sordid bars,
Surely he hath his posies, which they tear and twine;
Those scentless wisps of straw that, miserable, line
His strait, caged universe, whereat the dull world stares.

Pedant and pitiful. O, how his rapt gaze wars
With their stupidity! Know they what dreams divine
Lift his long, laughing reveries like enchanted wine,
And make his melancholy germane to the stars?

O lamentable brother! if those pity thee,
Am I not fain of all thy lone eyes promise me;
Half a fool's kingdom, far from men who sow and reap,
All their days, vanity? Better than mortal flowers,
Thy moon-kissed roses seem: better than love or sleep,
The star-crowned solitude of thine oblivious hours!


## EXTREME UNCTION

Upon the eyes, the lips, the feet,
  On all the passages of sense,
The atoning oil is spread with sweet
  Renewal of lost innocence.

The feet, that lately ran so fast
  To meet desire, are soothly sealed;
The eyes that were so often cast
  On vanity, are touched and healed.

From troublous sights and sounds set free;
  In such a twilight hour of breath

Shall one retrace his life, or see
  Through shadows the true face of death?

Vials of mercy! Sacring oils!
  I know not where nor when I come,
Nor through what wanderings and toils,
  To crave of you Viaticum.

Yet, when the walls of flesh grow weak,
  In such an hour, it well may be,
Through mist and darkness, light will break,
  And each anointed sense will see!


## YOU WOULD HAVE UNDERSTOOD ME

You would have understood me had you waited;
  I could have loved you, dear! as well as he:
Had we not been impatient, dear! and fated
  Always to disagree.

What is the use of speech? Silence were fitter:
　　Lest we should still be wishing things unsaid.
Though all the words we ever spake were bitter,
　　　　Shall I reproach you, dead?

Nay, let this earth, your portion, likewise cover
　　All the old anger, setting us apart:
Always, in all, in truth was I your lover;
　　　　Always, I held your heart.

I have met other women who were tender,
　　As you were cold, dear! with a grace as rare.
Think you, I turned to them, or made surrender,
　　　　I who had found you fair?

Had we been patient, dear! ah, had you waited,
　　I had fought death for you, better than he:
But from the very first, dear! we were fated
　　　　Always to disagree.

Late, late, I come to you, now death discloses
　　Love that in life was not to be our part:
On your low lying mound between the roses,
　　　　Sadly I cast my heart.

I would not waken you: nay! this is fitter;
　　Death and the darkness give you unto me;
Here we who loved so, were so cold and bitter,
　　　　Hardly can disagree.

## VILLANELLE OF MARGUERITES

*"A little, passionately, not at all?"*
　　She casts the snowy petals on the air;
And what care we how many petals fall?

　　Nay, wherefore seek the seasons to forestall?
　　It is but playing, and she will not care,
A little, passionately, not at all!

　　She would not answer us if we should call
　　Across the years; her visions are too fair;
And what care we how many petals fall!

　　She knows us not, nor recks if she enthrall
　　With voice and eyes and fashion of her hair,
A little, passionately, not at all!

　　Knee-deep she goes in meadow-grasses tall,
　　Kissed by the daisies that her fingers tear;
And what care we how many petals fall!

We pass and go; but she shall not recall
What men we were, nor all she made us bear;
*"A little, passionately, not at all!"*
And what care we how many petals fall!

ENVOY

*(Vitae summa brevis spem nos vetat incohare longam)*

They are not long, the weeping and the laughter,
   Love and desire and hate;
I think they have no portion in us after
   We pass the gate.

They are not long, the days of wine and roses:
   Out of a misty dream
Our path emerges for a while, then closes
   Within a dream.

# *Lionel Johnson*

B ORN in 1867, at Broadstairs in Kent, Lionel (Pigot) Johnson received a classical
education at Oxford; his poetry is a reflection of his studies in Greek and Latin
literatures. Though he allied himself with the modern Irish poets, his Celtic origin
is a literary myth; Johnson, having been converted to Catholicism in 1891, became
imbued with Catholic and Irish traditions. Yeats, who became his intimate friend,
says it was Johnson's habit to sleep all day and read and write all night, the ordinary world about him having no significance to the recluse. "In my library," Johnson said, "I have all the knowledge I need of the world."

Before any of his poetry was collected in a volume, he published a book on *The
Art of Thomas Hardy* (1894) which, though planned before the appearance of *Jude
the Obscure* or *The Dynasts,* remains one of the most sensitive studies of Hardy
yet written. His verse, published originally among the bizarre novelties of *The
Yellow Book,* was curiously cool and removed; he seemed, as one of his associates
had said, a young monk surrounded by dancing pagans. "Divine austerity" is the
goal to which his verse aspires. While sometimes over-decorated, it is chastely designed, and, like that of the Cavalier poets of the seventeenth century, fiercely devotional. Today, with such poems as "Mystic and Cavalier," "The Precept of
Silence," and "The Dark Angel," he seems the most important of his group; his
voice has found echoes in recent poetry, particularly in the poems of Yeats.

Johnson was one of the many poets to whom conversion to the Church supplied
not only a new color but a new impetus. It is a subject rich in speculation why this
period should have yielded so many artists who turned to the Catholic Church for
inspiration in their life and work; among the most eminent converts, besides Johnson, were Alice Meynell, Ernest Dowson, Oscar Wilde, and Aubrey Beardsley.

Poems (1895) and *Ireland* (1897) were published during his lifetime; a posthumous collection of essays, *Post Liminium,* appeared in 1911. A collected edition of his poems was brought out in 1915. Johnson died tragically in 1902.

### MYSTIC AND CAVALIER

Go from me: I am one of those who fall.
What! hath no cold wind swept your heart at all,
In my sad company? Before the end,
    Go from me, dear my friend!

Yours are the victories of light: your feet
Rest from good toil, where rest is brave and sweet:
But after warfare in a mourning gloom,
    I rest in clouds of doom.

Have you not read so, looking in these eyes?
Is it the common light of the pure skies
Lights up their shadowy depths? The end is set:
    Though the end be not yet.

When gracious music stirs, and all is bright,
And beauty triumphs through a courtly night;
When I too joy, a man like other men:
    Yet, am I like them, then?

And in the battle, when the horsemen sweep
Against a thousand deaths, and fall on sleep:
Who ever sought that sudden calm, if I
    Sought not? yet could not die!

Seek with thine eyes to pierce this crystal sphere:
Canst read a fate there, prosperous and clear?
Only the mists, only the weeping clouds,
    Dimness and airy shrouds.

Beneath, what angels are at work? What powers
Prepare the secret of the fatal hours?
See! the mists tremble, and the clouds are stirred:
    When comes the calling word?

The clouds are breaking from the crystal ball,
Breaking and clearing: and I look to fall.
When the cold winds and airs of portent sweep,
    My spirit may have sleep.

O rich and sounding voices of the air!
Interpreters and prophets of despair:
Priests of a fearful sacrament! I come
    To make with you mine home.

## TO MORFYDD

A voice on the winds,
A voice by the waters,
    Wanders and cries:
*Oh! what are the winds?*
*And what are the waters?*
    *Mine are your eyes!*

Western the winds are,
And western the waters,
    Where the light lies:
*Oh! what are the winds?*
*And what are the waters?*
    *Mine are your eyes!*

Cold, cold grow the winds,
And wild grow the waters,
    Where the sun dies:
*Oh! what are the winds?*
*And what are the waters?*
    *Mine are your eyes!*

And down the night winds,
And down the night waters,
    The music flies:
*Oh! what are the winds?*
*And what are the waters?*
*Cold be the winds,*
*And wild be the waters,*
    *So mine be your eyes!*

## BY THE STATUE OF KING CHARLES AT CHARING CROSS

Somber and rich, the skies,
Great glooms, and starry plains;
Gently the night wind sighs;
Else a vast silence reigns.

The splendid silence clings
Around me: and around
The saddest of all Kings,
Crown'd, and again discrown'd.

Comely and calm, he rides
Hard by his own Whitehall.
Only the night wind glides:
No crowds, no rebels, brawl.

Gone, too, his Court: and yet,
The stars his courtiers are:
Stars in their stations set;
And every wandering star.

Alone he rides, alone,
The fair and fatal King:
Dark night is all his own,
That strange and solemn thing.

Which are more full of fate:
The stars, or those sad eyes?
Which are more still and great:
Those brows, or the dark skies?

Although his whole heart yearn
In passionate tragedy,
Never was face so stern,
With sweet austerity.

Vanquish'd in life, his death
By beauty made amends:
The passing of his breath
Won his defeated ends.

Brief life and hapless? Nay:
Through death, life grew sublime.
*Speak after sentence?* Yea:
And to the end of time.

Armor'd he rides, his head
Bare to the stars of doom;
He triumphs now, the dead,
Beholding London's gloom.

Our wearier spirit faints,
Vex'd in the world's employ:
His soul was of the saints;
And art to him was joy.

King, tried in fires of woe!
Men hunger for thy grace:
And through the night I go,
Loving thy mournful face.

Yet, when the city sleeps,
When all the cries are still,
The stars and heavenly deeps
Work out a perfect will.

## TO A TRAVELER

The mountains, and the lonely death at last
Upon the lonely mountains: O strong friend!
The wandering over, and the labor passed,
    Thou art indeed at rest:
    Earth gave thee of her best,
    That labor and this end.

Earth was thy mother, and her true son thou:
Earth called thee to a knowledge of her ways,
Upon the great hills, up the great streams: now:
    Upon earth's kindly breast
    Thou art indeed at rest:
    Thou, and thine arduous days.

Fare thee well, O strong heart! The tranquil night
Looks calmly on thee: and the sun pours down
His glory over thee, O heart of might!
    Earth gives thee perfect rest:
    Earth, whom thy swift feet pressed:
    Earth, whom the vast stars crown.

## THE DARK ANGEL

Dark Angel, with thine aching lust
To rid the world of penitence:
Malicious Angel, who still dost
My soul such subtile violence!

Because of thee, no thought, no thing,
Abides for me undesecrate:
Dark Angel, ever on the wing,
Who never reachest me too late!

When music sounds, then changest thou
Its silvery to a sultry fire:
Nor will thine envious heart allow
Delight untortured by desire.

Through thee, the gracious Muses turn
To Furies, O mine Enemy!
And all the things of beauty burn
With flames of evil ecstasy.

Because of thee, the land of dreams
Becomes a gathering place of fears:
Until tormented slumber seems
One vehemence of useless tears.

When sunlight glows upon the flowers,
Or ripples down the dancing sea:
Thou, with thy troop of passionate powers,
Beleaguerest, bewilderest, me.

Within the breath of autumn woods,
Within the winter silences:
Thy venomous spirit stirs and broods,
O Master of impieties!

The ardor of red flames is thine,
And thine the steely soul of ice:
Thou poisonest the fair design
Of nature, with unfair device.

Apples of ashes, golden bright;
Waters of bitterness, how sweet!
O banquet of a foul delight,
Prepared by thee, dark Paraclete!

Thou art the whisper in the gloom,
The hinting tone, the haunting laugh:
Thou art the adorner of my tomb,
The minstrel of mine epitaph.

I fight thee, in the Holy Name!
Yet, what thou dost is what God saith:

Tempter! should I escape thy flame,
Thou wilt have helped my soul from Death:

The second Death, that never dies,
That cannot die, when time is dead:
Live Death, wherein the lost soul cries,
Eternally uncomforted.

Dark Angel, with thine aching lust!
Of two defeats, of two despairs;
Less dread, a change to drifting dust,
Than thine eternity of cares.

Do what thou wilt, thou shalt not so,
Dark Angel! triumph over me:
Lonely, unto the Lone I go;
Divine, to the Divinity.

THE PRECEPT OF SILENCE

I know you: solitary griefs,
Desolate passions, aching hours!
I know you: tremulous beliefs,
Agonized hopes, and ashen flowers!

The winds are sometimes sad to me;
The starry spaces, full of fear:
Mine is the sorrow on the sea,
And mine the sigh of places drear.

Some players upon plaintive strings
Publish their wistfulness abroad:
I have not spoken of these things,
Save to one man, and unto God.

# *Stephen Phillips*

Born in 1868, Stephen Phillips is best known as the author of *Herod* (1900), *Paola and Francesca* (1899), and *Ulysses* (1902); he was a poetic playwright who succeeded in reviving, for a brief interval, the blank verse drama on the modern stage. Hailed at first with extravagant praise, likened to Milton and Shakespeare, Phillips lived to see his once popular dramas discarded and his new ones unproduced and unnoticed.

Phillips failed to "restore" poetic drama because he was, first of all, a lyric rather than a dramatic poet. In spite of certain moments of rhetorical splendor, his scenes are spectacular instead of genuinely emotional; his inspiration is too often derived, and his highly colored passages bear the same relation to eloquence that paste coronets of the stage bear to crown jewels. As J. C. Squire remarked, reviewing a posthumous play, "Phillips tended to make all his characters minor poets, who were willing at any moment to hang up the play with unrevealing irrelevancies, faintly reminiscent of the great passages in great poets." In his prime, Squire concedes, "with his remarkable gift of serious and unconscious parody, and his instinct for crude effects of situation, he was as near being a good dramatic poet as a man could be without actually being one."

From the late 1890s until about 1905, Phillips was in his heyday. The reversal was sudden and severe. By 1913, Phillips had lost his readers and his fortune. His ambitiously patriotic *Harold* was not published until 1927, twelve years after his death. Even the purple patches had faded to foggy lavender. He died, almost neglected, in 1915.

As a lyrical poet, Phillips' reputation shrunk almost as much as his popularity as a dramatist. Yet, in spite of a too ornate, artificial diction, parts of *Marpessa* (1900) and *Lyrics and Dramas* (1913) achieve a ringing if mimetic eloquence.

### A DREAM

My dear love came to me, and said:
  "God gives me one hour's rest
To spend with thee on earth again:
  How shall we spend it best?"

"Why, as of old," I said; and so
  We quarreled, as of old:
But, when I turned to make my peace,
  That one short hour was told.

### BEAUTIFUL LIE THE DEAD

Beautiful lie the dead;
  Clear comes each feature;
Satisfied not to be,
  Strangely contented.

Like ships, the anchor dropped,
  Furled every sail is;
Mirrored with all their masts
  In a deep water.

### TO MILTON—BLIND

He who said suddenly, "Let there be light!"
To thee the dark deliberately gave;
That those full eyes might undistracted be
By this beguiling show of sky and field,
This brilliance, that so lures us from the Truth.
He gave thee back original night, His own
Tremendous canvas, large and blank and free,
Where at each thought a star flashed out and sang.
O blinded with a special lightning, thou
Hadst once again the virgin Dark! and when
The pleasant flowery sight, which had deterred
Thine eyes from seeing, when this recent world
Was quite withdrawn; then burst upon thy view
The elder glory; space again in pangs,
And Eden odorous in the early mist,
That heaving watery plain that *was* the world;
Then the burned earth, and Christ coming in clouds.
Or rather a special leave to thee was given
By the high power, and thou with bandaged eyes
Wast guided through the glimmering camp of God.
Thy hand was taken by angels, who patrol
The evening, or are sentries to the dawn,
Or pace the wide air everlastingly.
Thou wast admitted to the presence, and deep
Argument heardest, and the large design
That brings this world out of the woe to bliss.

## Laurence Binyon

(Robert) Laurence Binyon was born at Lancaster, August 10, 1869, a cousin
of Stephen Phillips, and was educated at Trinity College, Oxford. He won the
Newdigate Prize in 1890; and collaborated with Phillips, poems by both cousins appearing together the same year in *Primavera*. Binyon's subsequent volumes showed

little distinction until he published *London Visions,* which, in an enlarged edition in 1908, revealed a gift of characterization and a turn of speech in surprising contrast to his previous academic *Lyrical Poems* (1894). His *Odes* (1901) contains his ripest work; two poems in particular, "The Threshold" and "The Bacchanal of Alexander," are glowing and unusually spontaneous.

Binyon's talent continued to grow; age gave his verse a new sharpness. Sixty poems were published in *The Secret* (1920), some of which embody all Binyon's dignity with a definiteness which he never before attained. *Selected Poems* (1924) is an excellently arranged sequence which includes Binyon's finest work with the exception of *The Sirens* (1927), a long, elaborate ode in which the slow-paced rhythms have wide scope.

Binyon's *Collected Poems* (1931), in two volumes, reveal his progress from purely scholarly patterns to flexibility. The later verses are deepened with the power of thought and with a restrained music.

Since 1893 Binyon has been head of the Department of Printed Books and Deputy Keeper of Prints and Drawings in the British Museum. One volume of his Critical Studies—*English Poetry in its Relation to Painting and the Other Arts* (1919)—is especially rewarding to those interested in the kinship of the arts.

### THE LITTLE DANCERS

Lonely, save for a few faint stars, the sky
Dreams; and lonely, below, the little street
Into its gloom retires, secluded and shy.
Scarcely the dumb roar enters this soft retreat;
And all is dark, save where come flooding rays
From a tavern window; there, to the brisk measure
Of an organ that down in an alley merrily plays,
Two children, all alone and no one by,
Holding their tattered frocks, thro' an airy maze
Of motion lightly threaded with nimble feet
Dance sedately; face to face they gaze,
Their eyes shining, grave with a perfect pleasure.

### O WORLD, BE NOBLER

O world, be nobler, for her sake!
  If she but knew thee what thou art,
What wrongs are borne, what deeds are done
In thee, beneath thy daily sun,
  Know'st thou not that her tender heart
For pain and very shame would break?
  O World, be nobler, for her sake!

### NOTHING IS ENOUGH

Nothing is enough!
No, though our all be spent—

Heart's extremest love,
Spirit's whole intent,
All that nerve can feel,
All that brain invent,—
Still beyond appeal
Will Divine Desire
Yet more excellent
Precious cost require
Of this mortal stuff,—
Never be content
Till ourselves be fire.
Nothing is enough!

### BEAUTY

I think of a flower that no eye has ever seen,
    That springs in a solitary air.
Is it no one's joy? It is beautiful as a queen
    Without a kingdom's care.

We have built houses for Beauty, and costly shrines,
    And a throne in all men's view:
But she was far on a hill where the morning shines
    And her steps were lost in the dew.

### A SONG

For Mercy, Courage, Kindness, Mirth,
There is no measure upon earth.
Nay, they wither, root and stem,
If an end be set to them.

Overbrim and overflow,
If your own heart you would know;
For the spirit born to bless
Lives but in its own excess.

### THE HOUSE THAT WAS

Of the old house, only a few crumbled
    Courses of brick, smothered in nettle and dock,
Or a squared stone, lying mossy where it tumbled.
    Sprawling bramble and saucy thistle mock
What once was firelit floor and private charm
    Whence, seen in a windowed picture, were hills fading
At dusk, and all was memory-colored and warm,
    And voices talked, secure from the wind's invading.

Of the old garden, only a stray shining
    Of daffodil flames amid April's cuckoo-flowers,

Or a cluster of aconite mixt with weeds entwining!
  But, dark and lofty, a royal cedar towers
By homely thorns; and whether the white rain drifts
  Or sun scorches, he holds the downs in ken,
The western vales; his branchy tiers he lifts,
  Older than many a generation of men.

# Charlotte Mew

CHARLOTTE (MARY) MEW was born November 15, 1869, the daughter of an architect of distinction, who died when she was an infant. Little is generally known
of her life except that it was a long struggle not only with poverty but with ad-
versity and private sorrows that finally overcame her. In her late fifties, through the
joint efforts of Hardy, De la Mare, and Masefield, she was granted a Civil List
pension. Though she loved the country, she was forced to live almost continually
in London, in the very heart of Bloomsbury, becoming more and more of a recluse.
One of her few excursions was a week-end at Max Gate, where she was the guest
of Thomas Hardy, who considered her the best woman poet of her day. The death
of her mother was a blow from which she never recovered; the death of her sister
hastened her end. As Sidney C. Cockerell wrote, "Charlotte and Anne Mew had
more than a little in them of what made another Charlotte and Anne, and their
sister Emily, what they were. They were indeed like two Brontë sisters reincarnate."
  Charlotte Mew died by her own hand in a nursing home March 24, 1928.
  In the obituary note which Sidney Cockerell wrote for the *London Times* few
new facts came to light. It was learned that Charlotte Mew wrote much more than
was suspected, but "how much she destroyed at house-movings and during periods
of overwhelming depression, we shall never know. There can be no doubt that her
fastidious self-criticism proved fatal to much work that was really good, and that
the printed poems are far less than a tithe of what she composed. These first appeared in various periodicals. In 1916, seventeen of them were collected into a thin
volume which was issued by the Poetry Book Shop for a shilling. In 1921 this
volume, named *The Farmer's Bride,* after the opening poem, was re-issued with
the addition of 11 new poems, 28 in all. Perhaps not more than another 20 have
seen the light. But, although the visible output was so small, the quality was in each
case poignant and arresting. These poems are written as though with the life-blood
of a noble and passionate heart."
  One of Charlotte Mew's first discoverers was Alida Klemantaski (later Mrs.
Harold Monro), who was not only responsible for the publication of *The Farmer's
Bride,* but for the printing of the posthumous *The Rambling Sailor* (1929) to which
she furnished a Memoir. The first book was brought out in America under the title
of *Saturday Market* in 1921. Had Miss Mew printed nothing but the original
booklet, it would have been sufficient to rank her among the most distinctive and
intense of living poets. Hers is the distillation, the essence of emotion, rather than
the stirring up of passion. Her most remarkable work is in dramatic projections and

monologues (unfortunately too long to quote) like "The Changeling," with its fantastic pathos, and that powerful meditation, "Madeleine in Church." But lyrics as swift as "Sea Love," or as ageless as "Song," with its simple finality, or as hymnlike as "I Have Been Through the Gates" are equally sure of their place in English literature. They are, in common with all of Charlotte Mew's work, disturbing in their direct beauty; full of a speech that is noble and profound without ever becoming pompous. Apart from her other qualities (not the least of which is her control of an unusually long and extraordinarily flexible line) Miss Mew's work is a series of triumphs in condensation.

"To a Child in Death," a strangely premonitory poem, "In the Fields," and "Old Shepherd's Prayer" are among those given in manuscript by Charlotte Mew to the editor shortly before her death. These, with thirty other posthumous poems, appeared in *The Rambling Sailor*.

### IN THE FIELDS

Lord, when I look at lovely things which pass,
　　Under old trees the shadow of young leaves
Dancing to please the wind along the grass,
　　Or the gold stillness of the August sun on the August sheaves;
Can I believe there is a heavenlier world than this?
　　And if there is
Will the strange heart of any everlasting thing
　　Bring me these dreams that take my breath away?
They come at evening with the home-flying rooks and the scent of hay,
　　Over the fields. They come in Spring.

### SEA LOVE

Tide be runnin' the great world over:
　　'Twas only last June month I mind that we
Was thinkin' the toss and the call in the breast of the lover
　　So everlastin' as the sea.

Here's the same little fishes that sputter and swim,
　　Wi' the moon's old glim on the gray, wet sand;
An' him no more to me nor me to him
　　Than the wind goin' over my hand.

### I HAVE BEEN THROUGH THE GATES

His heart, to me, was a place of palaces and pinnacles and shining towers;
I saw it then as we see things in dreams,—I do not remember how long I slept;
I remember the trees, and the high, white walls, and how the sun was always on the towers;
The walls are standing today, and the gates: I have been through the gates, I have groped, I have crept
Back, back. There is dust in the streets, and blood; they are empty; darkness is over them;

His heart is a place with the lights gone out, forsaken by great winds and the
    heavenly rain, unclean and unswept,
Like the heart of the holy city, old, blind, beautiful Jerusalem,
Over which Christ wept.


### TO A CHILD IN DEATH

You would have scoffed if we had told you yesterday
Love made us feel—or so it was with me—like some great bird
    Trying to hold and shelter you in its strong wing;—
A gay little shadowy smile would have tossed us back such a solemn word,
    And it was not for that you were listening
    When so quietly you slipped away
With half the music of the world unheard.
What shall we do with this strange Summer, meant for you,—
    Dear, if we see the Winter through
    What shall be done with Spring—?
This, this is the victory of the grave; here is death's sting.
That it is not strong enough, our strongest wing.

But what of His who like a Father pitieth—?
His Son was also, once, a little thing,
The wistfulest child that ever drew breath,
Chased by a sword from Bethlehem and in the busy house at Nazareth
Playing with little rows of nails, watching the carpenter's hammer swing,
Long years before His hands and feet were tied
And by a hammer and the three great nails He died,
    Of youth, of Spring,
Of sorrow, of loneliness, of victory the king,
    Under the shadow of that wing.


### SONG

Love, Love today, my dear,
Love is not always here;
Wise maids know how soon grows sere
The greenest leaf of Spring;
But no man knoweth
Whither it goeth
When the wind bloweth
So frail a thing.

Love, Love, my dear, today,
If the ship's in the bay,
If the bird has come your way
That sings on summer trees;
When his song faileth
And the ship saileth
No voice availeth
To call back these.

THE FARMER'S BRIDE

Three Summers since I chose a maid,
Too young maybe—but more's to do
At harvest-time than bide and woo.
    When us was wed she turned afraid
Of love and me and all things human;
Like the shut of a winter's day.
Her smile went out, and 'twasn't a woman—
    More like a little frightened fay.
        One night, in the Fall, she runned away.

"Out 'mong the sheep, her be," they said,
'Should properly have been abed;
But sure enough she wasn't there
Lying awake with her wide brown stare.
So over seven-acre field and up-along across the down
We chased her, flying like a hare
Before our lanterns. To Church-Town
    All in a shiver and a scare
We caught her, fetched her home at last
And turned the key upon her, fast.

She does the work about the house
As well as most, but like a mouse:
    Happy enough to chat and play
    With birds and rabbits and such as they,
    So long as men-folk keep away.
"Not near, not near!" her eyes beseech
When one of us comes within reach.
    The women say that beasts in stall
    Look round like children at her call.
    *I've* hardly heard her speak at all.

Shy as a leveret, swift as he,
Straight and slight as a young larch tree,
Sweet as the first wild violets, she
To her wild self. But what to me?

The short days shorten and the oaks are brown,
    The blue smoke rises to the low gray sky,
One leaf in the still air falls slowly down,
    A magpie's spotted feathers lie
On the black earth spread white with rime,
The berries redden up to Christmas-time.
    What's Christmas-time without there be
    Some other in the house than we!

    She sleeps up in the attic there
    Alone, poor maid. 'Tis but a stair
Betwixt us. Oh! my God! the down,
The soft young down of her, the brown,
The brown of her—her eyes, her hair, her hair . . .

### BESIDE THE BED

Someone has shut the shining eyes, straightened and folded
　The wandering hands quietly covering the unquiet breast:
So, smoothed and silenced you lie, like a child, not again to be questioned or scolded:
　But, for you, not one of us believes that this is rest.

Not so to close the windows down can cloud and deaden
　The blue beyond: or to screen the wavering flame subdue its breath:
Why, if I lay my cheek to your cheek, your gray lips, like dawn, would quiver and
　　redden,
　Breaking into the old, odd smile at this fraud of death.

Because all night you have not turned to us or spoken
　It is time for you to wake; your dreams were never very deep:
I, for one, have seen the thin bright, twisted threads of them dimmed suddenly and
　　broken.
　This is only a most piteous pretense of sleep!

### FROM "MADELEINE IN CHURCH"

　How old was Mary out of whom you cast
　So many devils? Was she young or perhaps for years
She had sat staring, with dry eyes, at this and that man going past
　Till suddenly she saw You on the steps of Simon's house
　　And stood and looked at You through tears.
　　　I think she must have known by those
　　The thing, for what it was that had come to her.
　　For some of us there is a passion, I suppose,
　　So far from earthly cares and earthly fears
　　That in its stillness you can hardly stir
　　　Or in its nearness lift your hand,
　　So great that you have simply got to stand
　　Looking at it through tears, through tears.
　　Then straight from these there broke the kiss.
　　　I think You must have known by this
　　The thing, for what it was that had come to You:
　　　She did not love You like the rest,
　　It was in her own way, but at the worst, the best,
　　　She gave you something altogether new.
　　And through it all, from her, no word,
　　　She scarcely saw You, scarcely heard:
　　Surely You knew when she so touched You with her hair,
　　　Or by the wet cheek lying there,
And while her perfume clung to You from head to feet all through the day
　　That You can change the things for which we care,
　　But even You, unless You kill us, not the way.

　　This then was peace for her, but passion too.
　　I wonder was it like a kiss that once I knew,

The only one that I would care to take
Into the grave with me, to which if there were afterwards, to wake
Almost as happy as the carven dead
In some dim chancel lying head to head
We slept with it, but face to face, the whole night through—
One breath, one throbbing quietness, as if the thing behind our lips was endless life,
Lost, as I woke, to hear in the strange earthly dawn, his "Are you there?"
And lie still, listening to the wind outside, among the firs.

So Mary chose the dream of Him for what was left to her of night and day.
It is the only truth: it is the dream in us that neither life nor death nor any other
thing can take away:
But if she had not touched Him in the doorway of the dream could she
have cared so much?
She was a sinner, we are what we are: the spirit afterwards, but first, the
touch.

And He has never shared with me my haunted house beneath the trees
Of Eden and Calvary, with its ghosts that have not any eyes for tears,
And the happier guests, who would not see, or if they did, remember these,
Though they lived here a thousand years.
Outside, too gravely looking at me, He seems to stand,
And looking at Him if my forgotten spirit came
Unwillingly back, what could it claim
Of those calm eyes, that quiet speech,
Breaking like a slow tide upon the beach,
The scarred, not quite human hand?—
Unwillingly back to the burden of old imaginings
When it has learned so long not to think, not to be,
Again, again it would speak as it has spoken to me of things
That I shall not see!

### AGAIN

One day, not here, you will find a hand
Stretched out to you as you walk down some heavenly street;
You will see a stranger scarred from head to feet;
But when he speaks to you you will not understand,
Nor yet who wounded him nor why his wounds are sweet.
And saying nothing, letting go his hand,
You will leave him in the heavenly street—
So we shall meet!

### OLD SHEPHERD'S PRAYER

Up to the bed by the window, where I be lyin',
Comes bells and bleats of the flock wi' they two children's clack.
Over, from under the eaves there's the starlings flyin',
And down in yard, fit to burst his chain, yapping out at Sue I do hear young Mac.

Turning around like a falled-over sack
I can see team plowin' in Whithy-bush field and meal carts startin' up road to
    Church-Town;
Saturday arternoon then men goin' back
And the women from market, trapin' home over the down.

Heavenly Master, I wud like to wake to they same green places
Where I be know'd for breakin' dogs and follerin' sheep.
And if I may not walk in th' old ways and look on th' old faces
    wud sooner sleep.


THE TREES ARE DOWN

*—and he cried with a loud voice:*
*Hurt not the earth, neither the sea, nor the trees—*
                                *(Revelation.)*

They are cutting down the great plane-trees at the end of the gardens.
For days there has been the grate of the saw, the swish of the branches as they fall,
The crash of trunks, the rustle of trodden leaves,
With the "Whoops" and the "Whoas," the loud common talk, the loud common
    laughs of the men, above it all.

I remember one evening of a long past Spring
Turning in at a gate, getting out of a cart, and finding a large dead rat in the
    mud of the drive.
I remember thinking: alive or dead, a rat was a god-forsaken thing,
But at least, in May, that even a rat should be alive.

The week's work here is as good as done. There is just one bough
    On the roped bole, in the fine gray rain,
        Green and high
        And lonely against the sky.
            (Down now!—)
        And but for that,
        If an old dead rat
Did once, for a moment, unmake the Spring, I might never have thought of him
    again.

It is not for a moment the Spring is unmade today;
These were great trees, it was in them from root to stem:
When the men with the "Whoops" and the "Whoas" have carted the whole of the
    whispering loveliness away
Half the Spring, for me, will have gone with them.

It is going now, and my heart has been struck with the hearts of the planes;
Half my life it has beat with these, in the sun, in the rains,
    In the March wind, the May breeze,
In the great gales that came over to them across the roofs from the great seas.
    There was only a quiet rain when they were dying;
    They must have heard the sparrows flying,
And the small creeping creatures in the earth where they were lying—
    But I, all day, I heard an angel crying:
        "Hurt not the trees."

# Alfred Douglas

(Lord) Alfred Douglas was born in 1870 and educated at Magdalen College, Oxford. He was the editor of *The Academy* from 1907 to 1910 and was at one time the intimate friend of Oscar Wilde. One of the minor poets of "the eighteen-nineties," several of his poems rise above affectation and the end-of-the-century decadence. *The City of the Soul* (1899) and *Sonnets* (1900) contain something more than graceful writing, the latter volume disclosing Douglas's gift of phrase-making and fidelity to form.

The friendship with Oscar Wilde brought contumely upon him socially and depreciation poetically. In 1929 a convincing defense was published, and his *Selected Poems* (reissued in a popular edition in 1926) proved him, on the whole, a better poet than his more notorious friend, though nothing Douglas did can equal "The Ballad of Reading Gaol." Overshadowed at first, it is evident that Douglas freed himself from specious glamor. "Perkin Warbeck" is a remarkable combination of ballad and dramatic lyric; "Night-Coming Out of a Garden" is a memorable lyric; and several of the sonnets illustrate his individuality as well as his enviable command of the structure.

### THE GREEN RIVER

I know a green grass path that leaves the field
    And, like a running river, winds along
    Into a leafy wood, where is no throng
Of birds at noon-day; and no soft throats yield
Their music to the moon. The place is sealed,
    An unclaimed sovereignty of voiceless song,
    And all the unravished silences belong
To some sweet singer lost or unrevealed.

So is my soul become a silent place. . . .
    Oh, may I wake from this uneasy night
        To find some voice of music manifold.
Let it be shape of sorrow with wan face,
    Or love that swoons on sleep, or else delight
        That is as wide-eyed as a marigold.

### FROM "THE CITY OF THE SOUL"

Each new hour's passage is the acolyte
Of inarticulate song and syllable,
And every passing moment is a bell,
To mourn the death of undiscerned delight.
Where is the sun that made the noon-day bright,
And where the midnight moon? O let us tell,
In long carved line and painted parable,
How the white road curves down into the night.

Only to build one crystal barrier
Against this sea which beats upon our days;
To ransom one lost moment with a rhyme.
Or if fate cries and grudging gods demur,
To clutch Life's hair, and thrust one naked phrase.
Like a lean knife between the ribs of Time.


### NIGHT COMING OUT OF A GARDEN

Through the still air of night
    Suddenly comes, alone and shrill,
Like the far-off voice of the distant light,
    The single piping trill
Of a bird that has caught the scent of the dawn,
    And knows that the night is over;
(She has poured her dews on the velvet lawn
    And drenched the long grass and the clover),
And now with her naked white feet
    She is silently passing away,
Out of the garden and into the street,
Over the long yellow fields of the wheat,
    Till she melts in the arms of the day.
And from the great gates of the East,
    With a clang and a brazen blare,
Forth from the rosy wine and the feast
    Comes the god with flame-flaked hair;
The hoofs of his horses ring
    On the golden stones, and the wheels
Of his chariot burn and sing,
    And the earth beneath him reels;
And forth with a rush and a rout
    His myriad angels run,
And the world is awake with a shout,
    "He is coming! The sun! The sun!"


### THE DEAD POET

I dreamed of him last night, I saw his face
All radiant and unshadowed of distress,
And as of old, in music measureless,
I heard his golden voice and marked him trace
Under the common thing the hidden grace,
And conjure wonder out of emptiness,
Till mean things put on beauty like a dress
And all the world was an enchanted place.

And then methought outside a fast-locked gate
I mourned the loss of unrecorded words,
Forgotten tales and mysteries half said,

Wonders that might have been articulate,
And voiceless thoughts like murdered singing birds.
And so I woke and knew that he was dead.

### SONNET ON THE SONNET

To see the moment hold a madrigal,
To find some cloistered place, some hermitage
For free devices, some deliberate cage
Wherein to keep wild thoughts like birds in thrall,
To eat sweet honey and to taste black gall,
To fight with form, to wrestle and to rage,
Till at the last upon the conquered page
The shadows of created Beauty fall—

This is the sonnet, this is all delight
Of every flower that blows in every Spring,
And all desire of every desert place,
This is the joy that fills a cloudy night
When, bursting from her misty following,
A perfect moon wins to an empty space.

# T. Sturge Moore

T(HOMAS) STURGE MOORE was born at Hastings, March 4, 1870. He is well known not only as an author, but as a critic, wood-engraver, and designer of book-plates. As an artist, he has achieved no little distinction and has designed the covers for the poetry of W. B. Yeats and others. As a poet, the greater portion of his verse is severely classical in tone, academic in expression but, of its kind, distinctive and finely chiseled. Its precision has been praised, even envied, by several "advanced" poets on both sides of the Atlantic. Among his many volumes, the most outstanding are *The Vinedresser and Other Poems* (1899), *A Sicilian Idyll* (1911) and *The Sea Is Kind* (1914). *Danaë,* a volume of later poems, was published in 1920. After that date, Moore devoted himself to plays and dialogues: *The Tragic Mothers* (1921), *The Powers of the Air* (1921) and *Judas* (1923).

As critic, Sturge Moore has written works on Correggio, Dürer, Blake, and other artists, his prose being as delicately balanced as his verse.

### SILENCE SINGS

So faint, no ear is sure it hears,
So faint and far;
So vast that very near appears
My voice, both here and in each star
Unmeasured leagues do bridge between;
Like that which on a face is seen

Where secrets are;
Sweeping, like veils of lofty balm,
Tresses unbound
O'er desert sand, o'er ocean calm,
I am wherever is not sound;
And, goddess of the truthful face,
My beauty doth instill its grace
That joy abound.

## A DUET

"Flowers nodding gayly, scent in air,
Flowers poised, flowers for the hair,
Sleepy flowers, flowers bold to stare—"
　　"O pick me some!"

"Shells with lip, or tooth, or bleeding gum,
Tell-tale shells, and shells that whisper *Come,*
Shells that stammer, blush, and yet are dumb—"
　　"O let me hear."

"Eyes so black they draw one trembling near,
Brown eyes, caverns flooded with a tear,
Cloudless eyes, blue eyes so windy clear—"
　　"O look at me!"

"Kisses sadly blown across the sea,
Darkling kisses, kisses fair and free,
Bob-a-cherry kisses 'neath a tree—"
　　"O give me one!"

Thus sang a king and queen in Babylon.

## THE DYING SWAN

O silver-throated Swan,
Struck, struck! A golden dart
Clean through thy breast has gone
Home to thy heart.

Thrill, thrill, O silver throat!
O silver trumpet, pour
Love for defiance back
On him who smote!
And brim, brim o'er
With love; and ruby-dye thy track
Down thy last living reach
Of river, sail the golden light—
Enter the sun's heart—even teach,
O wondrous-gifted Pain, teach Thou
The God of love, let him learn how!

# Hilaire Belloc

(Joseph) Hilaire (Pierre) Belloc, who has been described as "a Frenchman, an Englishman, an Oxford man, a country gentleman, a soldier, a satirist, a democrat, a novelist, and a practical journalist," was born near Paris, July 27, 1870. After leaving school he served as a driver in the 8th Regiment of French Artillery at Toul, in the departement of Meurthe-et-Moselle, as at that time Belloc was a French citizen. He became a naturalized British subject somewhat later, finished his education at Balliol College, Oxford, and in 1906 entered the House of Commons as Liberal Member for South Salford. He was a member of Parliament from 1906 to 1910.

Besides his other multifarious activities, he was the author (by 1930) of some forty-five volumes. These books range the gamut of literature: from travel-sketches to essays significantly entitled *On Nothing and Kindred Subjects* (1908), *On Everything* (1909), *On Anything* (1910) and simply *On* (1923); from *A Book of Beasts* (1896) to a *History of England,* three volumes of which were published by 1927. He has written several books of satirical fiction, one of which, *Mr. Clutterbuck's Election* (1908), exposes British underground politics, and which, together with his other work, bristles with what might be termed affable Bellocosity.

Belloc's *Path to Rome* (1902) is a high-spirited travel book which has passed through many editions. His historical studies and biographies of *Robespierre* and *Marie Antoinette* (1909) are classics of their kind. His nonsense-rhymes (*Cautionary Tales, The Bad Child's Book of Beasts,* and *More Beasts for Worse Children*) are comparable to Edward Lear's. As a serious poet, he is engaging but somewhat less original. His *Verses* (1910) is a brief collection of poems on a variety of themes. Although his humorous and burlesque stanzas are refreshing, Belloc is most himself when he writes either of malt liquor or his beloved Sussex. His religious poems are full of a fine romanticism; "The South Country" and the "Lines to a Don" in defense of his friend Chesterton are the most persuasive of his earnest poems. His poetic as well as spiritual kinship with that other protagonist of a burly Catholicism, G. K. Chesterton, is obvious.

As an agile maker of epigrams, he has few equals, a fact proved by the inclusion of most of his rhymed *bons mots* in Belloc's *Collected Poems* in 1923.

## THE SOUTH COUNTRY

When I am living in the Midlands
    That are sodden and unkind,
I light my lamp in the evening:
    My work is left behind;
And the great hills of the South Country
    Come back into my mind.

The great hills of the South Country
    They stand along the sea;

And it's there walking in the high woods
  That I could wish to be,
And the men that were boys when I was a boy
  Walking along with me.

The men that live in North England
  I saw them for a day:
Their hearts are set upon the waste fells,
  Their skies are fast and gray;
From their castle-walls a man may see
  The mountains far away.

The men that live in West England
  They see the Severn strong,
A-rolling on rough water brown
  Light aspen leaves along.
They have the secret of the rocks,
  And the oldest kind of song.

But the men that live in the South Country
  Are the kindest and most wise,
They get their laughter from the loud surf,
  And the faith in their happy eyes
Comes surely from our Sister the Spring
  When over the sea she flies;
The violets suddenly bloom at her feet,
  She blesses us with surprise.

I never get between the pines
  But I smell the Sussex air;
Nor I never come on a belt of sand
  But my home is there.
And along the sky the line of the Downs
  So noble and so bare.

A lost thing could I never find,
  Nor a broken thing mend:
And I fear I shall be all alone
  When I get towards the end.
Who will there be to comfort me
  Or who will be my friend?

I will gather and carefully make my friends
  Of the men of the Sussex Weald;
They watch the stars from silent folds,
  They stiffly plow the field.
By them and the God of the South Country
  My poor soul shall be healed.

If I ever become a rich man,
  Or if ever I grow to be old,
I will build a house with deep thatch
  To shelter me from the cold,

And there shall the Sussex songs be sung
   And the story of Sussex told.

I will hold my house in the high wood
   Within a walk of the sea,
And the men that were boys when I was a boy
   Shall sit and drink with me.

### HA'NACKER MILL

Sally is gone that was so kindly,
   Sally is gone from Ha'nacker Hill.
And the Briar grows ever since then so blindly
   And ever since then the clapper is still,
   And the sweeps have fallen from Ha'nacker Mill.

Ha'nacker Hill is in Desolation:
   Ruin a-top and a field unplowed,
And Spirits that call on a fallen nation,
   Spirits that loved her calling aloud:
   Spirits abroad in a windy cloud.

Spirits that call and no one answers;
   Ha'nacker's down and England's done.
Wind and Thistle for pipe and dancers
   And never a plowman under the Sun.
   Never a plowman. Never a one.

### FOUR BEASTS

#### *The Big Baboon*

The Big Baboon is found upon
   The plains of Cariboo;
He goes about with nothing on
   (A shocking thing to do.)
But if he dressed respectably
   And let his whiskers grow
How like this Big Baboon would be
   To Mister So-and-So!

#### *The Yak*

As a friend to the children commend me the Yak;
   You will find it exactly the thing:
It will carry and fetch, you can ride on its back,
   Or lead it about with a string.

The Tartar who dwells on the plains of Thibet
   (A desolate region of snow)
Has for centuries made it a nursery pet,
   And surely the Tartar should know!

Then tell your papa where the Yak can be got,
And if he is awfully rich
He will buy you the creature—or else he will not.
(I cannot be positive which.)

### The Lion

The Lion, the Lion, he dwells in the waste,
He has a big head and a very small waist;
But his shoulders are stark, and his jaws they are grim,
And a good little child will not play with him.

### The Tiger

The Tiger, on the other hand, is kittenish and mild,
He makes a pretty playfellow for any little child;
And mothers of large families (who claim to common sense)
Will find a Tiger well repays the trouble and expense.

### LINES TO A DON

Remote and ineffectual Don
That dared attack my Chesterton,
With that poor weapon, half-impelled,
Unlearnt, unsteady, hardly held,
Unworthy for a tilt with men—
Your quavering and corroded pen;
Don poor at Bed and worse at Table,
Don pinched, Don starved, Don miserable;
Don stuttering, Don with roving eyes,
Don nervous, Don of crudities;
Don clerical, Don ordinary,
Don self-absorbed and solitary;
Don here-and-there, Don epileptic;
Don puffed and empty, Don dyspeptic;
Don middle-class, Don sycophantic,
Don dull, Don brutish, Don pedantic;
Don hypocritical, Don bad,
Don furtive, Don three-quarters mad;
Don (since a man must make an end),
Don that shall never be my friend.

✦

Don different from those regal Dons!
With hearts of gold and lungs of bronze,
Who shout and bang and roar and bawl
The Absolute across the hall,
Or sail in amply bellowing gown
Enormous through the Sacred Town,
Bearing from College to their homes
Deep cargoes of gigantic tomes;

Dons admirable! Dons of Might!
Uprising on my inward sight
Compact of ancient tales, and port
And sleep—and learning of a sort.
Dons English, worthy of the land;
Dons rooted; Dons that understand.
Good Dons perpetual that remain
A landmark, walling in the plain—
The horizon of my memories—
Like large and comfortable trees.

Don very much apart from these,
Thou scapegoat Don, thou Don devoted,
Don to thine own damnation quoted,
Perplexed to find thy trivial name
Reared in my verse to lasting shame.
Don dreadful, rasping Don and wearing,
Repulsive Don—Don past all bearing,
Don of the cold and doubtful breath,
Don despicable, Don of death;
Don nasty, skimpy, silent, level;
Don evil; Don that serves the devil.
Don ugly—that makes fifty lines.
There is a Canon which confines
A Rhymed Octosyllabic Curse
If written in Iambic Verse
To fifty lines. I never cut;
I far prefer to end it—but
Believe me I shall soon return.
My fires are banked, but still they burn
To write some more about the Don
That dared attack my Chesterton.

### SONNET

We will not whisper, we have found the place
Of silence and the endless halls of sleep.
Of that which breathes alone throughout the deep
The end and the beginning; and the face
Between the level brows of whose blind eyes
Lie plenary contentment, full surcease
Of violence, and the passionless long peace
Wherein we lose our human lullabies.

Look up and tell the immeasurable height
Between the vault of the world and your dear head;
That's death, my little sister, and the night
Which was our Mother beckons us to bed,
    Where large oblivion in her house is laid
    For us tired children, now our games are played.

### SIX EPIGRAMS

#### On Lady Poltagrue, a Public Peril

The Devil, having nothing else to do,
Went off to tempt My Lady Poltagrue.
My Lady, tempted by a private whim,
To his extreme annoyance, tempted him.

#### On a Dead Hostess

Of this bad world the loveliest and the best
Has smiled and said "Good Night," and gone to rest.

#### On Hygiene

Of old when folk lay sick and sorely tried,
The doctors gave them physic, and they died.
But here's a happier age: for now we know
Both how to make men sick and keep them so.

#### On His Books

When I am dead, I hope it may be said:
"His sins were scarlet, but his books were read."

#### Epitaph on the Politician

Here, richly, with ridiculous display,
The Politician's corpse was laid away.
While all of his acquaintance sneered and slanged,
I wept: for I had longed to see him hanged.

#### For False Heart

I said to Heart, "How goes it?" Heart replied:
"Right as a Ribstone Pippin!" But it lied.

# W. H. Davies

ACCORDING to his own biography, W(illiam) H(enry) Davies was born in a public-house called Church House at Newport, in the County of Monmouthshire, April 20, 1870, of Welsh parents. He was, until Bernard Shaw "discovered" him, a cattleman, a berry-picker, a panhandler—in short, a vagabond. In a preface to Davies' *The Autobiography of a Super-Tramp* (1906), Shaw describes how the manuscript came into his hands:

"In the year 1905 I received by post a volume of poems by one William H. Davies, whose address was The Farm House, Kennington, S.E. I was surprised to learn that there was still a farmhouse left in Kennington; for I did not then suspect that The Farm House, like the Shepherdess Walks and Nightingale Lane and Whetstone Parks of Bethnal Green and Holborn, is so called nowadays in irony, and is, in fact, a doss-house, or hostelry, where single men can have a night's lodging, for, at most, sixpence. . . . The author, as far as I could guess, had walked into a printer's or stationer's shop; handed in his manuscript; and ordered his book as he might have ordered a pair of boots. It was marked 'price, half a crown.' An accompanying letter asked me very civilly if I required a half-crown book of verses; and if so, would I please send the author the half-crown: if not, would I return the book. This was attractively simple and sensible. I opened the book, and was more puzzled than ever; for before I had read three lines I perceived that the author was a real poet. His work was not in the least strenuous or modern; there was indeed no sign of his ever having read anything otherwise than as a child reads. . . . Here, I saw, was a genuine innocent, writing odds and ends of verse about odds and ends of things; living quite out of the world in which such things are usually done, and knowing no better (or rather no worse) than to get his book made by the appropriate craftsman and hawk it round like any other ware."

It is more than likely that Davies' first notoriety as a tramp-poet who had ridden the rails in the United States and had had his right foot cut off by a train in Canada, obscured his merit as a singer. Even his early *The Soul's Destroyer* (1907) revealed that simplicity which is as *naïf* as it is unexpected.

Between 1906, when Davies published his first book, and 1935, the poet issued twenty-two volumes, five of autobiography, seventeen of verse. Besides these, there were four different *Collected Poems,* appearing in 1916, 1923, 1929, and 1935. The difficulty of keeping track of this verse is the greater since the Welsh-English poet is still in the very flush of fecundity and his continuous output shows no sign of diminishing. *Love Poems* (1935) is a queer mixture of Davies' plain-song sagacities and painful banalities. It needs all one's faith in a poet to forgive him such a stanza as:

> The sun has his spots, the moon has her shadows,
> The sea has his wrinkles, the land has her warts;
> Sweet faith has her doubts and lovers their quarrels,
> And nothing is perfect in all its parts.

But Davies merits our faith, for his best, like the best of the Caroline poets, moves us not only because of the innocence of vision but because of the adequacy of communicating it. If, in his later work, his thought is confused and tempts Davies out of his depth, his ear remains quick and sensitive as the thrush he celebrates:

> That speckled thrush, that stands so still,
>   Is listening for the worms to stir;
> He hears a worm—what marvelous ears
>   That he can live by ear alone,
> And save his eyes to guard his fears!

*Collected Poems* (1935) contains some five hundred poems in which good, indifferent, and bad mingle so inextricably that the reader must accept Davies *en masse* or reject him *in toto*. One can no more imagine Davies self-critical than one can imagine him in the labor of creation, his "labor" being about as arduous as a bird's and his song being no less recreational. The figure is not far-fetched, for no poetry has ever been more obviously bird-like. But, it may be asked with a proper regard for ornithology, what bird? Not the lark, for Davies is no Shelley hurling himself and his cry far above the comfortable altitudes of man. Not the nightingale, for his is not Keats' clear passion nor Swinburne's operatic coloratura. It is the English robin that Davies most resembles or the American goldfinch, whose song, limited in range, is cleanly, sharply pitched. Without the variability of greater singers, his notes are only three or four, but the tones are so cool, the delivery so fresh that we would not exchange the crisp spontaneity even for the versatile brilliance of the hermit-thrush. No less than thirty-three poems begin: "When I in praise of babies speak," "When on a summer morn I wake," "When I came forth this morn I saw," "When I am old," "When I complained," "When . . ."

It is easy enough to deride such naïveté, easy enough to confuse Davies with his compatriots who pipe their placid week-end pastorals. But, although a Georgian in point of time, Davies shakes himself free of "Georgianism," that false simplicity sicklied o'er with the pale cast of thoughtlessness. He does not study his subjects from the outside; it is doubtful if he studies them at all; he is always within his bucolics. Thus his sympathies are as genuine as they are ingenuous. His sense of wonder is as direct, as unmistakable as an untutored child's. He looks at clouds, cowslips, lovely ladies, glow-worms, sheep, dogs, dolls, and daisies, as though they had never existed prior to his observation; and he puts them to rhyme as unselfconsciously as though never before had they been employed in verse. Davies rediscovers the common objects which everyone takes for granted; he regards them with an air of surprise and what is more, communicates his astonished wonder.

Observe the poem entitled "A Great Time" and note what details prompt his adjective. Beauty to Davies is not in the elaboration but in the mere being; greatness is, therefore, implicit in the coming together of a rainbow and a cuckoo. These are his auguries of innocence; for him, also, "a dog starv'd at his master's gate Predicts the ruin of the State." His rapport with lamb and bat and game-cock may lead us to imply a kinship with Blake, but he is, at the best, a Blake in words of one syllable. Where Blake projects apocalypses and flaming images, Davies offers a panorama of quiet pictures; we drop from passionate vision into pleasant reverie.

And if the world is neither as simple nor spontaneous as his homely dream, Davies almost persuades us that it ought to be.

## THE HOUR OF MAGIC

This is the hour of magic, when the Moon
  With her bright wand has charmed the tallest tree
To stand stone-still with all his million leaves!
  I feel around me things I cannot see;
I hold my breath, as Nature holds her own.
  And do the mice and birds, the horse and cow,
Sleepless in this deep silence, so intense,
  Believe a miracle has happened now,
And wait to hear a sound they'll recognize,
To prove they still have life with earthly ties?

## A GREETING

Good morning, Life—and all
Things glad and beautiful.
My pockets nothing hold,
But he that owns the gold,
The Sun, is my great friend—
His spending has no end.

Hail to the morning sky,
Which bright clouds measure high;
Hail to you birds whose throats
Would number leaves by notes;
Hail to you shady bowers,
And you green fields of flowers.

Hail to you women fair,
That make a show so rare
In cloth as white as milk—
Be't calico or silk:
Good morning, Life—and all
Things glad and beautiful.

## DAYS TOO SHORT

When primroses are out in Spring,
  And small, blue violets come between;
  When merry birds sing on boughs green,
And rills, as soon as born, must sing;

When butterflies will make side-leaps,
  As though escaped from Nature's hand
  Ere perfect quite; and bees will stand
Upon their heads in fragrant deeps;

When small clouds are so silvery white
  Each seems a broken rimmèd moon—
  When such things are, this world too soon
For me, doth wear the veil of Night.

## THE MOON

Thy beauty haunts me heart and soul,
  O thou fair Moon, so close and bright;
Thy beauty makes me like the child
  That cries aloud to own thy light:
The little child that lifts each arm
To press thee to her bosom warm.

Though there are birds that sing this night
  With thy white beams across their throats
Let my deep silence speak for me
  More than for them their sweetest notes
Who worships thee till music fails
Is greater than thy nightingales.

## THE VILLAIN

While joy gave clouds the light of stars,
  That beamed where'er they looked;
And calves and lambs had tottering knees,
  Excited, while they sucked;
While every bird enjoyed his song,
  Without one thought of harm or wrong—
I turned my head and saw the wind,
  Not far from where I stood,
Dragging the corn by her golden hair,
  Into a dark and lonely wood.

## THE EXAMPLE

Here's an example from
   A Butterfly;
That on a rough, hard rock
   Happy can lie;
Friendless and all alone
On this unsweetened stone.

Now let my bed be hard,
   No care take I;
I'll make my joy like this
   Small Butterfly,
Whose happy heart has power
To make a stone a flower.

## THE TWO STARS

Day has her star, as well as Night,
One star is black, the other white.
I saw a white star burn and pant
   And swirl with such a wildness, once—
That I stood still, and almost stared
   Myself into a trance!

The star of Day, both seen and heard,
Is but a little, English bird:
The Lark, whose wings beat time to his
   Wild rapture, sings, high overhead;
When silence comes, we almost fear
   That Earth receives its dead.

## THE DOG

The dog was there, outside her door,
   She gave it food and drink,
She gave it shelter from the cold:
   It was the night young Molly robbed
An old fool of his gold.

"Molly," I said, "you'll go to hell—"
   And yet I half believed

That ugly, famished, tottering cur
   Would bark outside the gates of Heaven,
To open them for Her!

## JENNY WREN

Her sight is short, she comes quite near;
A foot to me's a mile to her;
And she is known as Jenny Wren,
The smallest bird in England. When
I heard that little bird at first,
Methought her frame would surely burst
With earnest song. Oft had I seen
Her running under leaves so green,
Or in the grass when fresh and wet,
As though her wings she would forget.
And, seeing this, I said to her—
"My pretty runner, you prefer
To be a thing to run unheard
Through leaves and grass, and not a bird!"
'Twas then she burst, to prove me wrong,
Into a sudden storm of song;
So very loud and earnest, I
Feared she would break her heart and die.
"Nay, nay," I laughed, "be you no thing
To run unheard, sweet scold, but sing!
O I could hear your voice near me,
Above the din in that oak tree,
When almost all the twigs on top
Had starlings chattering without stop."

## AMBITION

I had Ambition, by which sin
   The angels fell;
I climbed and, step by step, O Lord,
   Ascended into Hell.

Returning now to peace and quiet,
   And made more wise,
Let my descent and fall, O Lord,
   Be into Paradise.

## THE HERMIT

What moves that lonely man is not the boom
   Of waves that break against the cliff so strong;
Nor roar of thunder, when that traveling voice
   Is caught by rocks that carry far along.

'Tis not the groan of oak tree in its prime,
  When lightning strikes its solid heart to dust.
Nor frozen pond when, melted by the sun,
  It suddenly doth break its sparkling crust.

What moves that man is when the blind bat taps
  His window where he sits alone at night;
Or when the small bird sounds like some great beast
  Among the dead, dry leaves so frail and light;

Or when the moths on his night-pillow beat
  Such heavy blows he fears they'll break his bones;
Or when a mouse inside the papered walls,
  Comes like a tiger crunching through the stones.


## WHEN YON FULL MOON

When yon full moon's with her white fleet of stars,
  And but one bird makes music in the grove;
When you and I are breathing side by side,
  Where our two bodies make one shadow, love;

Not for her beauty will I praise the moon,
  But that she lights thy purer face and throat;
The only praise I'll give the nightingale
  Is that she draws from thee a richer note.

For, blinded with thy beauty, I am filled,
  Like Saul of Tarsus, with a greater light;
When he had heard that warning voice in Heaven,
  And lost his eyes to find a deeper sight.

Come, let us sit in that deep silence then,
  Launched on love's rapids, with our passions proud,
That makes all music hollow—though the lark
  Raves in his windy heights above a cloud.


## SHEEP

When I was once in Baltimore,
  A man came up to me and cried,
"Come, I have eighteen hundred sheep,
  And we will sail on Tuesday's tide.

"If you will sail with me, young man,
  I'll pay you fifty shillings down;
These eighteen hundred sheep I take
  From Baltimore to Glasgow town."

He paid me fifty shillings down,
  I sailed with eighteen hundred sheep;

We soon had cleared the harbor's mouth,
  We soon were in the salt sea deep.

The first night we were out at sea
  Those sheep were quiet in their mind;
The second night they cried with fear—
  They smelt no pastures in the wind.

They sniffed, poor things, for their green fields,
  They cried so loud I could not sleep;
For fifty thousand shillings down
  I would not sail again with sheep.

## THE MIND'S LIBERTY

The mind, with its own eyes and ears,
  May for these others have no care;
No matter where this body is,
  The mind is free to go elsewhere.
My mind can be a sailor, when
  This body's still confined to land;
And turn these mortals into trees,
  That walk in Fleet Street or the Strand.

So, when I'm passing Charing Cross,
  Where porters work both night and day,
I ofttimes hear sweet Malpas Brook,
  That flows thrice fifty miles away.
And when I'm passing near St. Paul's,
  I see, beyond the dome and crowd,
Twm Barlum, that green pap in Gwent,
  With its dark nipple in a cloud.

## A GREAT TIME

Sweet Chance, that led my steps abroad,
  Beyond the town, where wild flowers
    grow—
A rainbow and a cuckoo, Lord!
  How rich and great the times are now!
    Know, all ye sheep
    And cows that keep
On staring that I stand so long
In grass that's wet from heavy rain—
A rainbow and a cuckoo's song
  May never come together again;
    May never come
    This side the tomb.

## THE ELEMENTS

No house of stone
  Was built for me;
When the Sun shines—
  I am a bee.

No sooner comes
  The Rain so warm,
I come to light—
  I am a worm.

When the Winds blow,
  I do not strip,
But set my sails—
  I am a ship.

When Lightning comes,
  It plays with me
And I with it—
  I am a tree.

When drowned men rise
  At Thunder's word,
Sings Nightingale—
  I am a bird.

## LEAVES

Peace to these little broken leaves,
  That strew our common ground;
That chase their tails, like silly dogs,
  As they go round and round.

For though in winter boughs are bare,
  Let us not once forget
Their summer glory, when these leaves
  Caught the great Sun in their strong net;
And made him, in the lower air,
Tremble—no bigger than a star!

## SONGS OF JOY

Sing out, my Soul, thy songs of joy;
  Such as a happy bird will sing
Beneath a Rainbow's lovely arch
  In early spring.

Think not of Death in thy young days;
  Why shouldst thou that grim tyrant fear,
And fear him not when thou art old,
  And he is near.

Strive not for gold, for greedy fools
  Measure themselves by poor men never;
Their standards still being richer men,
  Makes them poor ever.

Train up thy mind to feel content,
  What matters then how low thy store!
What we enjoy, and not possess,
  Makes rich or poor.

Filled with sweet thought, then happy I
  Take not my state from others' eyes;
What's in my mind—not on my flesh
  Or theirs—I prize.

Sing, happy Soul, thy songs of joy;
  Such as a Brook sings in the wood,
That all night had been strengthened by
  Heaven's purer flood.


### TO A LADY FRIEND

Since you have turned unkind,
  Then let the truth be known:
We poets give our praise
  To any weed or stone,
Or sulking bird that in
  The cold, sharp wind is dumb;
To this, or that, or you—
  Whatever's first to come.

You came my way the first,
  When the life-force in my blood—
Coming from none knows where—
  Had reached its highest flood;
A time when anything,
  No matter old or new,
Could bring my song to birth—
  Sticks, bones, or rags, or you!


### LEISURE

What is this life if, full of care,
We have no time to stand and stare.

No time to stand beneath the boughs
And stare as long as sheep or cows.

No time to see, when woods we pass,
Where squirrels hide their nuts in grass.

No time to see, in broad daylight,
Streams full of stars, like skies at night.

No time to turn at Beauty's glance,
And watch her feet, how they can dance.

No time to wait till her mouth can
Enrich that smile her eyes began.

A poor life this if, full of care,
We have no time to stand and stare.


# *J. M. Synge*

JOHN M. SYNGE, the most brilliant star of the Celtic revival, was born at Rathfarn-
ham, near Dublin, in 1871, his maternal grandfather, Robert Traill, being famous
for a splendid translation of Josephus. As a child in Wicklow, Synge was already
fascinated by the strange idioms and rhythmic speech he heard there, a native utterance which was his delight and which was rare material for his greatest work. He
did not use this folk-language merely as he heard it; he was an artist first, and, as
an artist, he bent and shaped the rough matter, selecting with fastidiousness, so that
in his plays every speech is, as he himself declared all good speech should be, "as
fully flavored as a nut or apple." Even in *The Tinker's Wedding* (1907), the least
important of his plays, Synge's peculiarly inflected sentences vivify every scene; one
is arrested by snatches of illuminated prose like:

"That's a sweet tongue you have, Sarah Casey; but if sleep's a grand thing, it's a
grand thing to be waking up a day the like of this, when there's a warm sun in it,
and a kind of air, and you'll hear the cuckoos singing and crying out on the top of
the hill."

For some time, Synge's career was uncertain. He went to Germany half intending
to become a professional musician. There he studied the theory of music, perfecting
himself meanwhile in Gaelic and Hebrew, winning prizes in both of these languages.
He took up Heine with great interest, familiarized himself with the peasant-dramas

of Anzengruber, and was planning to translate the ballads of the old German min-nesingers into Anglo-Irish dialect. Then he went to Paris.

Yeats found him in France in 1898 and advised him to go to the Aran Islands, to live there as if he were one of the people. "Express a life," said Yeats, "that has never found expression." Synge went. He became part of the life of Aran, living upon salt fish and eggs, talking Irish for the most part, but listening also to that beautiful English which, to quote Yeats again, "has grown up in Irish-speaking dis-tricts and takes its vocabulary from the time of Malory and of the translators of the Bible, but its idiom and vivid metaphor from Irish." The result of this close contact was five of the greatest poetic-prose dramas not only of Synge's own generation, but of several generations preceding it.

In *Riders to the Sea* (1903), *The Well of the Saints* (1905), and *The Playboy of the Western World* (1907), there is a richness of imagery, a new language startling in its vigor; a wildness and passion that contrast strangely with the suave mysticism and delicate spirituality of the playwright's associates in the Irish Theatre.

Synge's *Poems and Translations* (1910), a volume which was not issued until after his death, contains not only his few hard and earthy verses, but also the famous preface embodying his theory of poetry. The translations, which have been rendered in a highly intensified prose, are as racy as anything in his plays; his versions of Villon and Petrarch are remarkable for their adherence to the original though they radiate the adapter's own personality.

Synge died of an old illness, just as his reputation had broken down borders, at a private hospital in Dublin, March 24, 1909.

### PRELUDE

Still south I went and west and south again,
Through Wicklow from the morning till the night,
And, far from cities and the sights of men,
Lived with the sunshine and the moon's delight.

I knew the stars, the flowers, and the birds,
The gray and wintry sides of many glens,
And did but half remember human words,
In converse with the mountains, moors and fens.

### BEG-INNISH

Bring Kateen-beug and Maurya Jude
To dance in Beg-Innish,[1]
And when the lads (they're in Dunquin)
Have sold their crabs and fish,
Wave fawny shawls and call them in,
And call the little girls who spin,
And seven weavers from Dunquin,
To dance in Beg-Innish.

[1] The accent is on the last syllable.

I'll play you jigs, and Maurice Kean,
Where nets are laid to dry,
I've silken strings would draw a dance
From girls are lame or shy;
Four strings I've brought from Spain and France
To make your long men skip and prance,
Till stars look out to see the dance
Where nets are laid to dry.

We'll have no priest or peeler in
To dance in Beg-Innish;
But we'll have drink from M'riarty Jim
Rowed round while gannets fish,
A keg with porter to the brim,
That every lad may have his whim,
Till we up sails with M'riarty Jim
And sail from Beg-Innish.

### IN KERRY

We heard the thrushes by the shore and sea,
And saw the golden stars' nativity,
Then round we went the lane by Thomas Flynn,
Across the church where bones lie out and in;
And there I asked beneath a lonely cloud
Of strange delight, with one bird singing loud,
What change you'd wrought in graveyard, rock and sea,
To wake this new wild paradise for me. . . .
Yet knew no more than knew those merry sins
Had built this stack of thigh-bones, jaws and shins.

### A QUESTION

I asked if I got sick and died, would you
With my black funeral go walking too,
If you'd stand close to hear them talk or pray
While I'm let down in that steep bank of clay.

And, No, you said, for if you saw a crew
Of living idiots pressing round that new
Oak coffin—they alive, I dead beneath
That board—you'd rave and rend them with your teeth.

### ON AN ISLAND

You've plucked a curlew, drawn a hen,
Washed the shirts of seven men,
You've stuffed my pillow, stretched the sheet,
And filled the pan to wash your feet,

You've cooped the pullets, wound the clock,
And rinsed the young men's drinking crock;
And now we'll dance to jigs and reels,
Nailed boots chasing girls' naked heels,
Until your father'll start to snore,
And Jude, now you're married, will stretch on the floor.

### DREAD

Beside a chapel I'd a room looked down,
Where all the women from the farms and town
On Holy-days and Sundays used to pass
To marriages, and christenings, and to Mass.

Then I sat lonely watching score and score,
Till I turned jealous of the Lord next door. . . .
Now by this window, where there's none can see,
The Lord God's jealous of yourself and me.

### IN MAY

In a nook
That opened south,
You and I
Lay mouth to mouth.

A snowy gull
And sooty daw
Came and looked
With many a caw;

"Such," I said,
"Are I and you,
When you've kissed me
Black and blue!"

### A TRANSLATION FROM PETRARCH

#### (*He is Jealous of the Heavens and the Earth*)

What a grudge I am bearing the earth that has its arms about her, and is holding
that face away from me, where I was finding peace from great sadness.

What a grudge I am bearing the Heavens that are after taking her, and shutting
her in with greediness, the Heavens that do push their bolt against so many.

What a grudge I am bearing the blessed saints that have got her sweet company,
that I am always seeking; and what a grudge I am bearing against Death, that is
standing in her two eyes, and will not call me with a word.

### TO THE OAKS OF GLENCREE

My arms are round you, and I lean
Against you, while the lark
Sings over us, and golden lights and green
Shadows are on your bark.

There'll come a season when you'll stretch
Black boards to cover me;
Then in Mount Jerome I will lie, poor wretch,
With worms eternally.


# *Eva Gore-Booth*

Eva gore-booth, the second daughter of Sir Henry Gore-Booth and the sister of Countess Marcievicz, was born in Sligo, Ireland, in 1871. She first appeared in "Æ" 's anthology, *New Songs,* in which so many of the modern Irish poets first came forward.

Her initial volume, *Poems* (1898), showed practically no distinction—not even the customary "promise." But *The One and the Many* (1904), *The Sorrowful Princess* (1907) and the later *The Sword of Justice* (1918) reveal the gift of the Celtic singer who is half mystic, half minstrel. Primarily philosophic, her verse often turns to lyrics as musical and generally quotable as the two examples here reprinted.


### THE WAVES OF BREFFNY

The grand road from the mountain goes shining to the sea,
    And there is traffic on it and many a horse and cart
But the little roads of Cloonagh are dearer far to me
    And the little roads of Cloonagh go rambling through my heart.

A great storm from the ocean goes shouting o'er the hill,
    And there is glory in it; and terror on the wind:
But the haunted air of twilight is very strange and still,
    And the little winds of twilight are dearer to my mind.

The great waves of the Atlantic sweep storming on their way,
    Shining green and silver with the hidden herring shoal;
But the little waves of Breffny have drenched my heart in spray,
    And the little waves of Breffny go stumbling through my soul.


### WALLS

Free to all souls the hidden beauty calls,
The sea thrift dwelling on her spray-swept height,
The lofty rose, the low-grown aconite,

The gliding river and the stream that brawls
Down the sharp cliffs with constant breaks and falls—
All these are equal in the equal light—
All waters mirror the one Infinite.

God made a garden; it was men built walls.
But the wide sea from men is wholly freed;
Freely the great waves rise and storm and break,
Nor softlier go for any landlord's need,
Where rhythmic tides flow for no miser's sake
And none hath profit of the brown sea-weed,
But all things give themselves, yet none may take.

## *Moira O'Neill*

MOIRA O'NEILL, a writer who has shunned public scrutiny, is known chiefly by a remarkable little collection of twenty-five lyrics, *Songs of the Glens of Antrim* (1900), simple tunes as unaffected as the peasants of whom she sings. A second volume, *More Songs of the Glens of Antrim,* was published in 1921. The best of her poetry is dramatic without being theatrical; melodious without falling into the tinkle of most "popular" sentimental verse.

### A BROKEN SONG

*"Where am I from?"* From the green hills of Erin.
*"Have I no song then?"* My songs are all sung.
*"What o' my love?"* 'Tis alone I am farin'.
Old grows my heart, an' my voice yet is young.

*"If she was tall?"* Like a king's own daughter.
*"If she was fair?"* Like a mornin' o' May.
When she'd come laughin' 'twas the running wather,
When she'd come blushin' 'twas the break o' day.

*"Where did she dwell?"* Where one'st I had my dwellin'.
*"Who loved her best?"* There's no one now will know.
*"Where is she gone?"* Och, why would I be tellin'!
Where she is gone there I can never go.

### BEAUTY'S A FLOWER

*Youth's for an hour,*
*Beauty's a flower,*
*But love is the jewel that wins the world.*

Youth's for an hour, an' the taste o' life is sweet,
Ailes was a girl that stepped on two bare feet;
In all my days I never seen the one as fair as she,
I'd have lost my life for Ailes, an' she never cared for me.

Beauty's a flower, an' the days o' life are long,
There's little knowin' who may live to sing another song;
For Ailes was the fairest, but another is my wife,
An' Mary—God be good to her!—is all I love in life.

> *Youth's for an hour,*
> *Beauty's a flower,*
> *But love is the jewel that wins the world.*

# Ralph Hodgson

RALPH HODGSON was born in Yorkshire, in 1872. Though he has been most reticent regarding the facts of his life, separating the poet from the casual man by the intimation that "the poet should live in his poetry," this much has been gathered: He lived for a while in America; he worked as a pressman in Fleet Street; he was a professional draughtsman, employed on the pictorial staff of an evening paper; he edited *Fry's Magazine;* he has bred bull terriers and, as a leading authority, has judged them; pugilism is one of his private enthusiasms. In 1924, Hodgson accepted an invitation to visit Japan as lecturer in English literature at Sendai University, about two hundred miles from Tokio. In 1928 the invitation was renewed and again accepted.

Although Hodgson has earned a livelihood in many capacities, he kept his writing severely apart; he refused to stain his pen with hack-work of any sort. He has given only his highest moments to his art, believing with Housman that lyric poetry—and Hodgson is one of the purest lyric poets of his age—is not a casual recreation. Writing little and publishing less, Hodgson was unknown until he was thirty-six; his first book, *The Last Blackbird and Other Lines,* appeared in 1907. In 1913, he went into partnership with Lovat Fraser and Holbrook Jackson to publish broadsides and chapbooks; many of his most famous poems appeared in the exquisite booklets issued by their press and illustrated by Fraser, "The Sign of Flying Fame." *Eve, The Bull, The Song of Honor, The Mystery and Other Poems* (1913-1914) found a wide circle of delighted readers in this format. A collected edition (entitled simply *Poems*) was published in 1917 and reissued in America some months later.

Hodgson's verses, full of the love of all natural things, a love that goes out to

> "an idle rainbow
> No less than laboring-seas,"

establish, like Davies' and De la Mare's, the wonder of essentially simple objects, or they (as in "Time, You Old Gypsy Man") personify abstractions.

One of the most graceful of word-magicians, Ralph Hodgson will retain his freshness as long as there are lovers of fresh and timeless songs. It is difficult to think of any showing of contemporary English poetry that could omit "Eve," "The Bull," "The Song of Honor," and that memorable snatch of music, "Time, You Old Gypsy Man." One succumbs to the charm of "Eve" at the first reading; here is the oldest of all legends told with a surprising simplicity and still more surprising difference. This Eve is neither the conscious sinner nor the symbolic Mother of men; she is, in Hodgson's candid lines, any young English country girl filling her basket, regarding the world and the serpent itself with a frank and childlike wonder.

Outstanding in Hodgson's work is his sympathy with animal life. This wide humanitarianism is implicit in poems like "The Bull," but it is explicit in his outrage against the slaughter of birds for fine feathers ("Stupidity Street") and the irony of "The Bells of Heaven."

Influences are far to seek in this work, although one scents rather than sees a trace of Christina Rossetti's "Goblin Market" in "Eve" and Christopher Smart's "Song to David" in "The Song of Honor." While Hodgson's poetry remains in the tradition, making no pretense to singularity or even originality, it has, because of an inherent candor, the spontaneity of a new genre.

### REASON

Reason has moons, but moons not hers
  Lie mirrored on her sea,
Confusing her astronomers,
  But O! delighting me.

### EVE

Eve, with her basket, was
Deep in the bells and grass,
Wading in bells and grass
Up to her knees.
Picking a dish of sweet
Berries and plums to eat,
Down in the bells and grass
Under the trees.

Mute as a mouse in a
Corner the cobra lay,
Curled round a bough of the
Cinnamon tall. . . .
Now to get even and
Humble proud heaven and
Now was the moment or
Never at all.

"Eva!" Each syllable
Light as a flower fell,
"Eva!" he whispered the
Wondering maid,

Soft as a bubble sung
Out of a linnet's lung,
Soft and most silverly
"Eva!" he said.

Picture that orchard sprite;
Eve, with her body white,
Supple and smooth to her
Slim finger tips;
Wondering, listening,
Listening, wondering,
Eve with a berry
Half-way to her lips.

Oh, had our simple Eve
Seen through the make-believe!
Had she but known the
Pretender he was!
Out of the boughs he came,
Whispering still her name,
Tumbling in twenty rings
Into the grass.

Here was the strangest pair
In the world anywhere,
Eve in the bells and grass
Kneeling, and he
Telling his story low. . . .
Singing birds saw them go
Down the dark path to
The Blasphemous Tree.

Oh, what a clatter when
Titmouse and Jenny Wren
Saw him successful and
Taking his leave!
How the birds rated him,
How they all hated him!
How they all pitied
Poor motherless Eve!

Picture her crying
Outside in the lane,
Eve, with no dish of sweet
Berries and plums to eat,
Haunting the gate of the
Orchard in vain. . . .
Picture the lewd delight
Under the hill tonight—
"Eva!" the toast goes round,
"Eva!" again.

## TIME, YOU OLD GYPSY MAN

Time, you old gypsy man,
  Will you not stay,
Put up your caravan
  Just for one day?

All things I'll give you
Will you be my guest,
Bells for your jennet
Of silver the best,
Goldsmiths shall beat you
A great golden ring,
Peacocks shall bow to you,
Little boys sing,
Oh, and sweet girls will
Festoon you with may.
Time, you old gypsy,
Why hasten away?

Last week in Babylon,
Last night in Rome,
Morning, and in the crush
Under Paul's dome;
Under Paul's dial
You tighten your rein—
Only a moment,
And off once again;
Off to some city
Now blind in the womb,
Off to another
Ere that's in the tomb.

Time, you old gypsy man,
  Will you not stay,
Put up your caravan
  Just for one day?

## THE BIRDCATCHER

When flighting time is on, I go
With clap-net and decoy,
A-fowling after goldfinches
And other birds of joy;

I lurk among the thickets of
The Heart where they are bred,
And catch the twittering beauties as
They fly into my Head.

## THE MOOR

The world's gone forward to its latest fair
And dropt an old man done with by the way,
To sit alone among the bats and stare
At miles and miles and miles of moorland
    bare
Lit only with last shreds of dying day.

Not all the world, not all the world's gone by:
Old man, you're like to meet one traveler
    still,
A journeyman well kenned for courtesy
To all that walk at odds with life and limb;
If this be he now riding up the hill
Maybe he'll stop and take you up with him. . . .

"But thou art Death?" "Of Heavenly Sera-
    phim
None else to seek thee out and bid thee
    come."
"I only care that thou art come from Him,
Unbody me—I'm tired—and get me home."

## AFTER

"How fared you when you mortal were?
  "What did you see on my peopled star?"
"Oh well enough," I answered her,
  "It went for me where mortals are!

"I saw blue flowers and the merlin's flight
  "And the rime on the wintry tree,
"Blue doves I saw and summer light
  "On the wings of the cinnamon bee."

THE SONG OF HONOR

climbed the hill as light fell short,
And rooks came home in scramble sort,
And filled the trees and flapped and fought
And sang themselves to sleep;
An owl from nowhere with no sound
Swung by and soon was nowhere found,
I heard him calling half-way round,
Holloing loud and deep;
A pair of stars, faint pins of light,
Then many a star, sailed into sight,
And all the stars, the flower of night,
Were round me at a leap;
To tell how still the valleys lay
I heard the watchdog miles away
And bells of distant sheep;
I heard no more of bird or bell,
The mastiff in a slumber fell,
I stared into the sky,
As wondering men have always done
Since beauty and the stars were one,
Though none so hard as I.

It seemed, so still the valleys were,
As if the whole world knelt at prayer,
Save me and me alone;
So pure and wide that silence was
I feared to bend a blade of grass,
And there I stood like stone.

There, sharp and sudden, there I heard—
*Ah! some wild lovesick singing bird*
*Woke singing in the trees?*
*The nightingale and babble-wren*
*Were in the English greenwood then,*
*And you heard one of these?*
The babble-wren and nightingale
Sang in the Abyssinian vale
That season of the year!
Yet, true enough, I heard them plain,
I heard them both again, again,
As sharp and sweet and clear
As if the Abyssinian tree
Had thrust a bough across the sea,
Had thrust a bough across to me
With music for my ear!

I heard them both, and, oh! I heard
The song of every singing bird
That sings beneath the sky,

And with the song of lark and wren
The song of mountains, moths and men
And seas and rainbows vie!

I heard the universal choir,
The Sons of Light exalt their Sire
With universal song,
Earth's lowliest and loudest notes,
Her million times ten million throats
Exalt Him loud and long,
And lips and lungs and tongues of Grace
From every part and every place
Within the shining of His face,
The universal throng.

I heard the hymn of being sound
From every well of honor found
In human sense and soul:
The song of poets when they write
The testament of Beautysprite
Upon a flying scroll,
The song of painters when they take
A burning brush for Beauty's sake
And limn her features whole—

The song of men divinely wise
Who look and see in starry skies
Not stars so much as robins' eyes,
And when these pale away
Hear flocks of shiny pleiades
Among the plums and apple trees
Sing in the summer day—

The song of all both high and low
To some blest vision true,
The song of beggars when they throw
The crust of pity all men owe
To hungry sparrows in the snow,
Old beggars hungry too—
The song of kings of kingdoms when
They rise above their fortune men,
And crown themselves anew—

The song of courage, heart and will
And gladness in a fight,
Of men who face a hopeless hill
With sparkling and delight,
The bells and bells of song that ring
Round banners of a cause or king
From armies bleeding white—

The song of sailors every one
When monstrous tide and tempest run
At ships like bulls at red,
When stately ships are twirled and spun
Like whipping tops and help there's none
And mighty ships ten thousand ton
Go down like lumps of lead—

And song of fighters stern as they
At odds with fortune night and day,
Crammed up in cities grim and gray
As thick as bees in hives,
Hosannas of a lowly throng
Who sing unconscious of their song,
Whose lips are in their lives—

And song of some at holy war
With spells and ghouls more dread by far
Than deadly seas and cities are,
Or hordes of quarreling kings—
The song of fighters great and small
The song of petty fighters all
And high heroic things—

The song of lovers—who knows how
Twitched up from place and time
Upon a sigh, a blush, a vow,
A curve or hue of cheek or brow,
Borne up and off from here and now
Into the void sublime!

And crying loves and passions still
In every key from soft to shrill
And numbers never done,
Dog-loyalties to faith and friend,
And loves like Ruth's of old no end,
And intermissions none—

And burst on burst for beauty and
For numbers not behind,
From men whose love of motherland
Is like a dog's for one dear hand,
Sole, selfless, boundless, blind—
And song of some with hearts beside
For men and sorrows far and wide,
Who watch the world with pity and pride
And warm to all mankind—

And endless joyous music rise
From children at their play,

And endless soaring lullabies
From happy, happy mothers' eyes,
And answering crows and baby cries,
How many who shall say!
And many a song as wondrous well
With pangs and sweets intolerable
From lonely hearths too gray to tell,
God knows how utter gray!
And song from many a house of care
When pain has forced a footing there
And there's a Darkness on the stair
Will not be turned away—

And song—that song whose singers come
With old kind tales of pity from
The Great Compassion's lips,
That make the bells of Heaven to peal
Round pillows frosty with the feel
Of Death's cold finger tips—

The song of men all sorts and kinds,
As many tempers, moods and minds
As leaves are on a tree,
As many faiths and castes and creeds,
As many human bloods and breeds
As in the world may be;

The song of each and all who gaze
On Beauty in her naked blaze,
Or see her dimly in a haze,
Or get her light in fitful rays
And tiniest needles even,
The song of all not wholly dark,
Not wholly sunk in stupor stark
Too deep for groping Heaven—

And alleluias sweet and clear
And wild with beauty men mishear,
From choirs of song as near and dear
To Paradise as they,
The everlasting pipe and flute
Of wind and sea and bird and brute,
And lips deaf men imagine mute
In wood and stone and clay,
The music of a lion strong
That shakes a hill a whole night long,
A hill as loud as he,
The twitter of a mouse among
Melodious greenery,
The ruby and the night-owl's song,
The nightingale's—all three,

The song of life that wells and flows
From every leopard, lark and rose
And everything that gleams or goes
Lack-luster in the sea.

I heard it all, each, every note
Of every lung and tongue and throat,
Aye, every rhythm and rhyme
Of everything that lives and loves
And upward ever upward moves
From lowly to sublime!
Earth's multitudinous Sons of Light,
I heard them lift their lyric might
With each and every chanting sprite
That lit the sky that wondrous night
As far as eye could climb!

I heard it all, I heard the whole
Harmonious hymn of being roll
Up through the chapel of my soul
And at the altar die,
And in the awful quiet then
Myself I heard, Amen, Amen,
Amen I heard me cry!
I heard it all and then although
I caught my flying senses, oh,
A dizzy man was I!
I stood and stared; the sky was lit,
The sky was stars all over it,
I stood, I knew not why,
Without a wish, without a will,
I stood upon that silent hill
And stared into the sky until
My eyes were blind with stars and still
I stared into the sky.

### THE LATE, LAST ROOK

The old gilt vane and spire receive
The last beam eastward striking;
The first shy bat to peep at eve
Has found her to his liking.
The western heaven is dull and gray,
The last red glow has followed day.

The late, last rook is housed and will
With cronies lie till morrow;
If there's a rook loquacious still
In dream he hunts a furrow,
And flaps behind a specter team,
Or ghostly scarecrows walk his dream.

### THE BULL

See an old unhappy bull,
Sick in soul and body both,
Slouching in the undergrowth
Of the forest beautiful,
Banished from the herd he led,
Bulls and cows a thousand head.

Cranes and gaudy parrots go
Up and down the burning sky;
Tree-top cats purr drowsily
In the dim-day green below;
And troops of monkeys, nutting some,
All disputing, go and come;
And things abominable sit
Picking offal buck or swine,
On the mess and over it
Burnished flies and beetles shine,
And spiders big as bladders lie
Under hemlocks ten foot high;

And a dotted serpent curled
Round and round and round a tree,
Yellowing its greenery,
Keeps a watch on all the world,
All the world and this old bull
In the forest beautiful.

Bravely by his fall he came:
One he led, a bull of blood
Newly come to lustihood,
Fought and put his prince to shame,
Snuffed and pawed the prostrate head
Tameless even while it bled.

There they left him, every one,
Left him there without a lick,
Left him for the birds to pick,
Left him for the carrion,
Vilely from their bosom cast
Wisdom, worth and love at last.
When the lion left his lair
And roared his beauty through the hills,
And the vultures pecked their quills
And flew into the middle air,
Then this prince no more to reign
Came to life and lived again.
He snuffed the herd in far retreat,
He saw the blood upon the ground,
And snuffed the burning airs around

Still with beevish odors sweet,
While the blood ran down his head
And his mouth ran slaver red.
Pity him, this fallen chief,
All his splendor, all his strength
All his beauty's breadth and length
Dwindled down with shame and grief,
Half the bull he was before,
Bones and leather, nothing more.

See him standing dewlap-deep
In the rushes at the lake,
Surly, stupid, half asleep,
Waiting for his heart to break
And the birds to join the flies
Feasting at his bloodshot eyes,—
Standing with his head hung down
In a stupor, dreaming things:
Green savannas, jungles brown,
Battlefields and bellowings,
Bulls undone and lions dead
And vultures flapping overhead.
Dreaming things: of days he spent
With his mother gaunt and lean
In the valley warm and green,
Full of baby wonderment,
Blinking out of silly eyes
At a hundred mysteries;
Dreaming over once again
How he wandered with a throng
Of bulls and cows a thousand strong,
Wandered on from plain to plain,
Up the hill and down the dale,
Always at his mother's tail;
How he lagged behind the herd,
Lagged and tottered, weak of limb,
And she turned and ran to him
Blaring at the loathly bird
Stationed always in the skies,
Waiting for the flesh that dies.

Dreaming maybe of a day,
When her drained and drying paps
Turned him to the sweets and saps,
Richer fountains by the way,
And she left the bull she bore
And he looked to her no more;
And his little frame grew stout,
And his little legs grew strong,
And the way was not so long;
And his little horns came out,

And he played at butting trees
And bowlder-stones and tortoises,
Joined a game of knobby skulls
With the youngsters of his year,
All the other little bulls,
Learning both to bruise and bear,
Learning how to stand a shock
Like a little bull of rock.

Dreaming of a day less dim,
Dreaming of a time less far,
When the faint but certain star
Of destiny burned clear for him,
And a fierce and wild unrest
Broke the quiet of his breast,
And the gristles of his youth
Hardened in his comely pow,
And he came to fighting growth,
Beat his bull and won his cow,
And flew his tail and trampled off
Past the tallest, vain enough.
And curved about in splendor full
And curved again and snuffed the airs
As who should say, Come out who dares!
And all beheld a bull, a Bull,
And knew that here was surely one
That backed for no bull, fearing none.
And the leader of the herd
Looked and saw, and beat the ground,
And shook the forest with his sound,
Bellowed at the loathly bird
Stationed always in the skies,
Waiting for the flesh that dies.

Dreaming, this old bull forlorn,
Surely dreaming of the hour
When he came to sultan power,
And they owned him master-horn,
Chiefest bull of all among
Bulls and cows a thousand strong,
And in all the trampling herd
Not a bull that barred his way,
Not a cow that said him nay,
Not a bull or cow that erred
In the furnace of his look
Dared a second, worse rebuke;
Not in all the forest wide,
Jungle, thicket, pasture, fen,
Not another dared him then,
Dared him and again defied;

Not a sovereign buck or boar
Came a second time for more.
Not a serpent that survived
Once the terrors of his hoof,
Risked a second time reproof,
Came a second time and lived,
Not a serpent in its skin
Came again for discipline;

Not a leopard bright as flame,
Flashing fingerhooks of steel,
That a wooden tree might feel,
Met his fury once and came
For a second reprimand,
Not a leopard in the land,
Not a lion of them all,
Not a lion of the hills,
Hero of a thousand kills,
Dared a second fight and fall,
Dared that ram terrific twice,
Paid a second time the price. . . .

Pity him, this dupe of dream,
Leader of the herd again
Only in his daft old brain,
Once again the bull supreme
And bull enough to bear the part
Only in his tameless heart.

Pity him that he must wake.
Even now the swarm of flies
Blackening his bloodshot eyes
Bursts and blusters round the lake,
Scattered from the feast half-fed,
By great shadows overhead,
And the dreamer turns away
From his visionary herds
And his splendid yesterday,
Turns to meet the loathly birds
Flocking round him from the skies,
Waiting for the flesh that dies.

### THE BELLS OF HEAVEN

'Twould ring the bells of Heaven
The wildest peal for years,
If Parson lost his senses
And people came to theirs,
And he and they together

Knelt down with angry prayers
For tamed and shabby tigers
And dancing dogs and bears,
And wretched, blind pit ponies,
And little hunted hares.

### THE HAMMERS

Noise of hammers once I heard
Many hammers, busy hammers,
Beating, shaping night and day,
Shaping, beating dust and clay
To a palace; saw it reared;
Saw the hammers laid away.

And I listened, and I heard
Hammers beating, night and day,
In the palace newly reared,
Beating it to dust and clay:
Other hammers, muffled hammers,
Silent hammers of decay.

### STUPIDITY STREET

I saw with open eyes
Singing birds sweet
Sold in the shops
For the people to eat,
Sold in the shops of
Stupidity Street.

I saw in a vision
The worm in the wheat,
And in the shops nothing
For people to eat:
Nothing for sale in
Stupidity Street.

### THE MYSTERY

He came and took me by the hand
Up to a red rose tree,
He kept His meaning to Himself
But gave a rose to me.

I did not pray Him to lay bare
The mystery to me,
Enough the rose was Heaven to smell,
And His own face to see.

## Ford Madox (Hueffer) Ford

FORD MADOX HUEFFER (who, later in life, became Ford Madox Ford) was born in 1873, the grandson of Ford Madox Brown, a cousin of the Rossettis. He was educated at University College, London, and abroad, but returned to edit *The English Review*. During his editorship he discovered many unknown writers who have since made reputations.

As an author, Ford first came into prominence as a collaborator of Joseph Conrad on *The Inheritors* (1901) and *Romance* (1901). As a novelist in his own right, his fame rests on the Tietjens series: *Some Do Not* (1924), *No More Parades* (1925), *A Man Could Stand Up* (1926) and *Last Post* (1928). Although utterly different from Galsworthy's cycle, the Tietjens novels prompt inevitable comparison with *The Forsyte Saga*. Ford's protagonist is a single man, not a family, and he deals with the impact of events in rapid succession on an individual, instead of social forces reacting through a period on a group. With the War as a living backdrop and in a style utterly his own, Ford has projected a figure, nervously intense, dully heroic, and wholly characteristic of his times.

Although known primarily as a novelist, Ford has been a poet at intervals most of his life. *Collected Poems* (1913), *On Heaven and Poems Written on Active Service* (1918) and *New Poems* (1927) show a style that never strives to be "poetic" and is as personal as Ford's prose. Allied to no "school" Ford displays, in such poems as "Gray Matter" and "A House," a definite but unspectacular modernity.

### GRAY MATTER

*She.* They leave us nothing.
*He.*                      Still, a little's left.
*She.* A crabbed, ancient, dried biologist,
Somewhere very far from the sea, closed up from the sky,
Shut in from the leaves, destroys our hopes and us.
*He.* Why no, our hopes and . . .
*She.*                      In his "Erster Heft"
Page something, I forget the line, he says
That, hidden as deep in the brain as he himself from hope,
There's this gray matter.
*He.*                      Why, 'tis there, dear heart.
*She.* That, if that hidden matter cools, decays,
Dies—what you will—our souls die out as well;
Since, hidden in the millionth of a cell,
Is all we have to give us consciousness.
*He.* Suppose it true.
*She.*                      Ah, never; better die,
Better have never lived than face this mist,
Better have never toiled to such distress.
*He.* It matters little.

*She.*                    Little!—Where shall I,
The woman, where shall you take part,
My poet? Where has either of us scope
In all this dead-dawning century that lacks all faith,
All hope, all aim, and all the mystery
That comforteth. Since he victorious
With his cold vapors chill out you and me,
The woman and the poet?
  *He.*                    Never, dear.
For you and I remain,
The woman and the poet. And soft rain
Still falls and still the crocus flames,
The blackbird calls.
  *She.*          But half the sweet is gone.
The voices of our children at their games
Lack half their ring.
  *He.*          Why, never, dear. Out there
The sea's a cord of silver, still to south
Beyond the marsh.
  *She.*          Aye, but beyond it all,
And all beneath and all above, half of the glory's done.
And I and you . . .
  *He.*          Why, no. The ancient sun
Shines as it ever shone, and still your mouth
Is sweet as of old it was.
  *She.*          But what remains?
  *He.* All the old pains,
And all the old sweet pleasures and the mystery
Of time, slow travel and unfathomed deep.
  *She.* And then this cold extinction? . . .
  *He.*          Dreamless sleep.
  *She.* And nothing matters?
  *He.*          All the old, old things.
    Whether to Church or College rings
     The clamorous bell of creeds,
    We, in the lush, far meads,
Poet and woman, past the city walls,
Hear turn by turn the burden of their calls,
Believe what we believe, feel what we feel,
Like what we list of what they cry within
    Cathedral or laborat'ry,
Since by the revolution of the wheel,
The one swings under, let us wait content.
  *She.* Yet it is hard.
  *He.*          Ah, no. A sure intent,
    For me and you.
The right, true, joyful word, the sweet, true phrase,
The calling of our children from the woods these garden days
Remain.—These drops of rain have laid the dust
And in our soft brown seed-beds formed the crust

We needed for our sowings. Bring your seed,
And you shall prick it in, I close the row.
Be sure the little grains your hands have pressed
Tenderly, lovingly, home, shall flourish best.
   *She.* Aye, you are still my poet.
   *He.*             Even so
Betwixt the rain and shine. Half true's still true
More truly than the thing that's proved and dead.
The sun lends flame to every crocus head
Once more, and we once more must sow and weed
Since in the earth the newly stirring seed
Begins the ancient mystery anew.

## "THERE SHALL BE MORE JOY . . ."

The little angels of Heaven
Each wear a long white dress,
And in the tall arcadings
Play ball and play at chess;

With never a soil on their garments,
Not a sigh the whole day long,
Not a bitter note in their pleasure,
Not a bitter note in their song.

But they shall know keener pleasure,
And they shall know joy more rare—
Keener, keener pleasure
When you, my dear, come there.

✦

The little angels of Heaven
Each wear a long white gown,
And they lean over the ramparts
Waiting and looking down.

## A HOUSE

### (*first part*)

*The House.* I am the House!
  I resemble
  The drawing of a child
  That draws "just a house." Two windows and two doors,
  Two chimney pots;
  Only two floors.
  Three windows on the upper one; a fourth
  Looks towards the north.
  I am very simple and mild;
  I am very gentle and sad and old.
  I have stood too long.
*The Tree.* I am the great Tree over above this House.
  I resemble
  The drawing of a child. Drawing "just a tree"
  The child draws Me!
  Heavy leaves, old branches, old knots:
  I am more old than the house is old.
  I have known nights so cold
  I used to tremble;
  For the sap was frozen in my branches,
  And the mouse,

That stored her nuts in my knot-holes, died. I am strong
Now . . . Let a storm come wild
Over the Sussex Wold,
I no longer fear it.
I have stood too long!
*The Nightingale.* I am the Nightingale. The summer through I sit
In the great tree, watching the house, and throw jewels over it!
There is no one watching but I; no other soul to waken
Echoes in this valley night.
*The Unborn Son of the House.* You are mistaken!
I am the Son of the House!—
That shall have silver limbs, and clean straight haunches,
Lean hips, clean lips and a tongue of gold;
That shall inherit
A golden voice, and waken
A whole world's wonder!
*The Nightingale.* Young blood! You are right,
So you and I only
Listen and watch and waken
Under
The stars of the night.
*The Dog of the House.* You are mistaken!
This house stands lonely.
Let but a sound sound in the seven acres that surround
Their sleeping house,
And I, seeming to sleep, shall awaken.
Let but a mouse
Creep in the bracken,
I seeming to drowse, I shall hearken.
Let but a shadow darken
Their threshold; let but a finger
Lie long or linger,
Holding their latch:
I am their Dog. And I watch.
I am just Dog. And being His hound
I lie
All night with my head on my paws,
Watchful and whist!
*The Nightingale.* So you and I and their Son and I
Watch alone under the stars of the sky.
*The Cat of the House.* I am the Cat. And you lie!
I am the Atheist!
All laws
I coldly despise.
I have yellow eyes;
I am the Cat on the Mat the child draws
When it first has a pencil to use.
*The Milch-goat.* I am the Goat. I give milk!
*The Cat of the House.* I muse
Over the hearth with my 'minishing eyes
Until after

The last coal dies.
Every tunnel of the mouse,
Every channel of the cricket,
I have smelt.
I have felt
The secret shifting of the moldered rafter,
And heard
Every bird in the thicket.
I see
You,
Nightingale up in your tree!

*The Nightingale.* The night takes a turn towards coldness; the stars
Waver and shake.
Truly more wake,
More thoughts are afloat;
More folk are afoot than I knew!

*The Milch-goat.* I, even I, am the Goat!

*Cat of the House.* Enough of your stuff of dust and of mud!
I, born of a race of strange things,
Of deserts, great temples, great kings,
In the hot sand where the nightingale never sings!
Old he-gods of ingle and hearth,
Young she-gods of fur and of silk—
Not the mud of the earth—
Are the things that I dream of!

*The Milch-goat.* Tibby-Tab, more than you deem of
I dream of when chewing the cud
For my milk:
Who was born
Of a Nan with one horn and a liking for gin
In the backyard of an inn.
A child of Original Sin,
With a fleece of spun-silk
And two horns in the bud—
I, made in the image of Pan,
With my corrugate, vicious-cocked horn,
Now make milk for a child yet unborn.
That's a come-down!
And you with your mouse-colored ruff,
Discoursing your stuff-of-a-dream,
Sell your birthright for cream,
And bolt from a cuff or a frown.
That's a come-down!
So let it be! That's enough.

*The House.* The top star of the Plow now mounts
Up to his highest place;
The dace
Hang silent in the pool.
The night is cool
Before the dawn. Behind the blind

Dies down the one thin candle.
Our harried man,
My lease-of-a-life-long Master,
Studies against disaster;
Gropes for some handle
Against too heavy Fate; pores over his accounts,
Studying into the morn
For the sake of his child unborn.
*The Unborn Son of the House.* The vibrant notes of the spheres,
   Thin, sifting sounds of the dew,
   I hear. The mist on the meres
   Rising I hear . . . So here's
   To a lad shall be lusty and bold,
   With a voice and a heart ringing true!
   To a house of a livelier hue!
*The House.* That is true!
   I have stood here too long and grown old.
*Himself.* What is the matter with the wicks?
   What on earth's the matter with the wax?
   The candle wastes in the draught;
   The blind's worn thin!
   . . . Thirty-four and four, ten . . .
   And ten . . . are forty-nine!
   And twenty pun' twelve and six was all
   I made by the clover.
   It's a month since I laughed:
   I have given up wine.
   And then . . .
   The Income Tax!
*The Dog of the House.* The mare's got out of the stable!
*The Cat of the House.* She's able, over and over,
   To push up the stable latch . . .
   Over and over again. You would say she's a witch,
   With a spite on our Man!
*The Milch-goat.* Heu! Did you see how she ran!
   She's after the clover; she's over the ditch,
   Doing more harm than a dozen of goats
   When there's no one to watch.
   Yet she is the sober old mare with her skin full of oats,
   Whereas we get dry bracken and heather;
   Snatching now and then a scrap of old leather,
   Or half an old tin,
   As the price of original sin!
*Himself.* I shall live to sell
   The clock from the hall;
   I shall have to pawn my old Dad's watch,
   Or fell
   The last old oak; or sell half the stock . . .
   Or all!

Or the oak chest out of the hall.
One or the other—or all.
God, it is hell to be poor
For ever and ever, keeping the Wolf from the door!

*The Cat of the House.* Wouldn't you say
  That Something, heavy and furry and gray,
  Was sniffing round the door?
  Wouldn't you say
  Skinny fingers, stretching from the thicket,
  Felt for the latch of the wicket?

*Himself.* You would almost say
  These blows were repercussions
  Of an avenging Fate!
  But how have we earned them . . .
  The sparks that fell on the cornricks and burned them
  Still in the ear;
  And all the set-backs of the year—
  Frost, drought and demurrage,
  The tiles blown half off the roof?
  What is it, what is it all for?
  Chastisement of pride? I swear we have no pride!
  We ride
  Behind an old mare with a flea-bitten hide!
  Or over-much love for a year-old bride?
  But it's your duty to love your bride! . . . But still,
  All the sows that died,
  And the cows all going off milk;
  The cream coming out under proof;
  The hens giving over laying;
  The bullocks straying,
  Getting pounded over the hill!
  It used to be something—cold feet going over
  The front of a trench after Stand-to at four!
  But these other things—God, how they make you blench!
  Aye, these are the pip-squeaks that call for
  Four-in-the-morning courage . . .
  May you never know, my wench,
  That's asleep up the stair!

*Herself (In her sleep).* I'll have a kitchen all white tiles;
  And a dairy, all marble the shelves and the floor;
  And a larder, cream-white and full of air.
  I'll have whitewood kegs for the flour,
  And blackwood kegs for the rice and barley,
  And silvery jugs for the milk and cream . . .
  O glorious Me!
  And hour by hour by hour by hour,
  On piles of cushions from hearth to door,
  I'll sit sewing my silken seams,
  I'll sit just dreaming my silver dreams;
  With a little, mettlesome, brown-legged Charley,

To leave his ploys [1] and come to my knee,
And question how God can be Three-in-One
And One-in-Three.
And all the day and all the day
Nothing but hoys [2] for my dearest one;
And no care at all but to kiss and twine;
And nought to contrive for but ploys and play
For my son, my son, my son, my son!
Only at nine,
With the dinner finished, the men at their wine;
And the girls in the parlor at forfeits for toffee,
I'll make such after-dinner coffee . . .
But it's all like a dream!

*Himself.* If Dixon could pay! . . . But he never will.
He promised to do it yesterday . . . But poor old Dicky's been through the mill.
And it's late—it's too late to sit railing at Fate!
He'd pay if he could: but he's got *his* fix on . . .
Yet . . . If he *could* pay—
God!—It would carry us over the day
Of Herself!

*The Clock in the Room.* I am the Clock on the Shelf!
Is . . . Was . . . Is . . . Was!
Too late . . . Because . . . Too late . . . Because . . .
One! . . . Two! . . . Three! . . . Four!

*Himself.* Just over The Day and a week or two more!
And we'd maybe get through.
Not with a hell of a lot
Of margin to spare . . . But just through!

*The Clock in the Hall.* One! . . . Two! . . . One! . . . Two!
As . . . your . . . hours . . . pass
I re . . . cord them
Though you . . . waste them
Or have . . . stored them
ALL . . .
  One!
  Two!
  Three!
  Four!
  Begun!
  Half through!
  Let be!
  No more at all!
  I am the Great Clock in the Hall!

---

[1] Ploys = games, sports.      [2] Hoys = enticements.

# *Walter De la Mare*

WALTER (JOHN) DE LA MARE was born at Charlton, in Kent, in 1873. He was educated at St. Paul's school in London and was employed for eighteen years in the English branch of The Standard Oil Company of America. Later he retired to the village of Taplow near London.

His first volume, *Songs of Childhood* (1902), was published under the pseudonym of "Walter Ramal," an anagram of part of his name. The first volume published under his own name was the novel *Henry Brocken* (1904), a form to which he returned with phenomenal success in *Memoirs of a Midget* (1921), a permanent edition to the world's small stock of philosophic fiction.

By 1929 De la Mare was the author of some twenty-three volumes which seem to fall into four categories: (1) The poetry of metaphysical phantasy. (2) The poems to and of children. (3) The mixture of prose and verse achieved in *Ding Dong Bell* (1924). (4) The introspective prose.

Although not the most important, his most popular verse is that which is centered in the child's sphere. As Harold Williams has written, "De la Mare is the singer of a young and romantic world, understanding and perceiving as a child." This poet paints simple scenes of miniature loveliness; he uses fragments of fairy-like delicacy and, with the least consequential matter, achieves a grace remarkable in its appeal. "In a few words, seemingly artless and unsought" (to quote Williams again) "he can express a pathos or a hope as wide as man's life."

De la Mare is an astonishing joiner of words; in *Peacock Pie* (1913) and *Down-a-Down Derry* (1922) he surprises us again and again by transforming what began as a child's nonsense-rhyme into a thrilling snatch of music. A score of times he takes events as casual as the feeding of chickens, or the swallowing of physic, berry-picking, eating, hair-cutting—and turns them into magic. These poems read like lyrics of William Shakespeare rendered by Mother Goose. The trick of revealing the ordinary in whimsical colors, of catching the commonplace off its guard, as in "Martha" and "The Sleeper," is the first of De la Mare's two chief gifts.

This poet's second gift is his sense of the supernatural, of the fantastic other-world that lies on the edges of our consciousness. Sometimes, as in "At the Key-hole" and "The Mocking Fairy," the sinister turns into the lightly *macabre;* often the unbelievable, as in "Sam" and "Berries," is more homely-natural than the real. *The Listeners* (1912) is a book that, like all the best of De la Mare, is full of half-heard whispers. Moonlight and mystery seem soaked in the lines, and a cool wind from Nowhere blows over them. That most suggestive of modern verses, "The Listeners," and the brief music of "An Epitaph" are two examples among many. In the first of these poems there is an uncanny splendor. What we have here is the effect, the thrill, the overtones, of a ghost story rather than the narrative itself—the less than half-told adventure of some new Childe Roland heroically challenging a heedless universe. Never have silence and black night been reproduced more creepily, nor has the symbolism of man's courage facing the cryptic riddle of life been more memorably expressed.

De la Mare's chief distinction, however, lies not so much in what he says as in how he says it; he can take outworn words like "thridding," "athwart," "amaranthine" and make them live again in a poetry that is of no time and of all time. He writes, it has been said, as much for antiquity as for posterity; he is a poet who is distinctively in the world and yet not wholly of it.

*Motley and Other Poems* (1918) was followed by *Collected Poems, 1901-1918*, published in 1920, and *The Veil and Other Poems* (1921). *Come Hither* (1923), a collection apparently designed for children, is actually for mature minds. In all of these—even in the anthology—De la Mare betrays a speculation which is kin to a preoccupation: the paradox of mortality and immortality. Henry Newbolt, in *New Paths on Helicon,* recognizes this pervading quality, but prefers to call it "an inveterate habit of questioning. . . . Even the descriptions in which he excels are of the nature of a search: he attempts, like the Pre-Raphaelite painters, to pierce by intensity of vision through to the reality behind the visible word."

*The Fleeting and Other Poems* (1934) displays less of De la Mare's technical virtuosity than its forerunners; the awareness of the dream world, so characteristic of De la Mare, is a little strained and the spirit seems tired. But the vocabulary is still supple, the harmonies delicate and often exquisite.

Technically, De la Mare's poetry is most interesting for the manner in which he achieves a new music merely by extending the line of an old one. His extra syllables, turns, and grace-notes give novelty to themes and measures in themselves traditional. His idiom, while not spectacular, is singular and unmistakable as a finger-print. His form, like that of every true poet, does not rise from cultivated ingenuity nor conscious difference, but is a reflection of his individuality.

### THE LISTENERS

"Is there anybody there?" said the Traveler,
  Knocking on the moonlit door;
And his horse in the silence champed the grasses
  Of the forest's ferny floor.
And a bird flew up out of the turret,
  Above the Traveler's head:
And he smote upon the door again a second time;
  "Is there anybody there?" he said.
But no one descended to the Traveler;
  No head from the leaf-fringed sill
Leaned over and looked into his gray eyes,
  Where he stood perplexed and still.
But only a host of phantom listeners
  That dwelt in the lone house then
Stood listening in the quiet of the moonlight
  To that voice from the world of men:
Stood thronging the faint moonbeams on the dark stair
  That goes down to the empty hall,
Hearkening in an air stirred and shaken
  By the lonely Traveler's call.
And he felt in his heart their strangeness,
  Their stillness answering his cry,

While his horse moved, cropping the dark turf,
  'Neath the starred and leafy sky;
For he suddenly smote on the door, even
  Louder, and lifted his head:—
"Tell them I came, and no one answered,
  That I kept my word," he said.
Never the least stir made the listeners,
  Though every word he spake
Fell echoing through the shadowiness of the still house
  From the one man left awake:
Aye, they heard his foot upon the stirrup,
  And the sound of iron on stone,
And how the silence surged softly backward,
  When the plunging hoofs were gone.

### AN EPITAPH

Here lies a most beautiful lady,
  Light of step and heart was she;
I think she was the most beautiful lady
  That ever was in the West Country.

But beauty vanishes; beauty passes;
  However rare—rare it be;
And when I crumble, who will remember
  This lady of the West Country?

### THE TRUANTS

Ere my heart beats too coldly and faintly
  To remember sad things, yet be gay,
I would sing a brief song of the world's little children
  Magic hath stolen away.

The primroses scattered by April,
  The stars of the wide Milky Way,
Cannot outnumber the hosts of the children
  Magic hath stolen away.

The buttercup green of the meadows,
  The snow of the blossoming may,
Lovelier are not than the legions of children
  Magic hath stolen away.

The waves tossing surf in the moonbeam,
  The albatross lone on the spray,
Alone knew the tears wept in vain for the children
  Magic hath stolen away.

In vain: for at hush of the evening,
  When the stars twinkle into the gray,
Seems to echo the far-away calling of children
  Magic hath stolen away.

## OLD SUSAN

When Susan's work was done, she'd sit
With one fat guttering candle lit,
And window opened wide to win
The sweet night air to enter in;
There, with a thumb to keep her place
She'd read, with stern and wrinkled face.
Her mild eyes gliding very slow
Across the letters to and fro,
While wagged the guttering candle flame
In the wind that through the window came.
And sometimes in the silence she
Would mumble a sentence audibly,
Or shake her head as if to say,
"You silly souls, to act this way!"
And never a sound from night I'd hear,
Unless some far-off cock crowed clear;
Or her old shuffling thumb should turn
Another page; and rapt and stern,
Through her great glasses bent on me,
She'd glance into reality;
And shake her round old silvery head,
With—"You!—I thought you was in bed!"—
Only to tilt her book again,
And rooted in Romance remain.

## MARTHA

"Once . . . once upon a time . . ."
  Over and over again,
Martha would tell us her stories,
  In the hazel glen.

Hers were those clear gray eyes
  You watch, and the story seems
Told by their beautifulness
  Tranquil as dreams.

She'd sit with her two slim hands
  Clasped round her bended knees;
While we on our elbows lolled,
  And stared at ease.

Her voice and her narrow chin,
  Her grave small lovely head,
Seemed half the meaning
  Of the words she said.

"Once . . . once upon a time . . ."
  Like a dream you dream in the night,

Fairies and gnomes stole out
  In the leaf-green light.

And her beauty far away
  Would fade, as her voice ran on,
Till hazel and summer sun
  And all were gone:—

All fordone and forgot;
  And like clouds in the height of the sky,
Our hearts stood still in the hush
  Of an age gone by.

## SOMEONE

Someone came knocking
  At my wee, small door;
Someone came knocking,
  I'm sure—sure—sure;
I listened, I opened,
  I looked to left and right,
But nought there was a-stirring
  In the still dark night;
Only the busy beetle
  Tap-tapping in the wall,
Only from the forest
  The screech-owl's call,
Only the cricket whistling
  While the dewdrops fall,
So I know not who came knocking,
  At all, at all, at all.

## THE SLEEPER

As Ann came in one summer's day,
  She felt that she must creep,
So silent was the clear cool house,
  It seemed a house of sleep.
And sure, when she pushed open the door,
  Rapt in the stillness there,
Her mother sat with stooping head,
  Asleep upon a chair;
Fast—fast asleep; her two hands laid
  Loose-folded on her knee,
So that her small unconscious face
  Looked half unreal to be:
So calmly lit with sleep's pale light
  Each feature was; so fair
Her forehead—every trouble was
  Smooth'd out beneath her hair.

But though her mind in dream now moved,
　　Still seemed her gaze to rest
From out beneath her fast-sealed lids,
　　Above her moving breast,
On Ann, as quite, quite still she stood;
　　Yet slumber lay so deep
Even her hands upon her lap
　　Seemed saturate with sleep.
And as Ann peeped, a cloudlike dread
　　Stole over her, and then,
On stealthy, mouselike feet she trod,
　　And tiptoed out again.

### THE OLD MEN

Old and alone sit we,
Caged, riddle-rid men;
Lost to earth's "Listen!" and "See!"
Thought's "Wherefore?" and "When?"
Only far memories stray
Of a past once lovely, but now
Wasted and faded away,
Like green leaves from the bough.
Vast broods the silence of night;
And the ruinous moon
Lifts on our faces her light,
Whence all dreaming is gone.
We speak not; trembles each head;
In their sockets our eyes are still;
Desire as cold as the dead,
Without wonder or will.

And one, with a lanthorn, draws near,
At clash with the moon in our eyes:
"Where art thou?" he asks: "I am here!"
One by one we arise.
And none lifts a hand to withhold
A friend from the touch of that foe:
Heart cries unto heart, "Thou art old!"
Yet reluctant we go.

### AT THE KEYHOLE

"Grill me some bones," said the Cobbler,
　　"Some bones, my pretty Sue;
I'm tired of my lonesome with heels and
　　soles,
Springsides and uppers too;
A mouse in the wainscot is nibbling;
A wind in the keyhole drones;
And a sheet webbed over my candle
　　Susie,
　　Grill me some bones!"

"Grill me some bones," said the Cobbler,
　　"I sat at my tic-tac-to;
And a footstep came to my door and stopped,
And a hand groped to and fro;
And I peered up over my boot and last;
And my feet went cold as stones:—
I saw an eye at the keyhole, Susie!—
　　Grill me some bones!"

### THE MOCKING FAIRY

"Won't you look out of your window, Mrs. Gill?"
　　Quoth the Fairy, nidding, nodding in the garden;
"*Can't* you look out of your window, Mrs. Gill?"
　　Quoth the Fairy, laughing softly in the garden;
But the air was still, the cherry boughs were still,
And the ivy-tod [1] 'neath the empty sill,
And never from her window looked out Mrs. Gill
　　On the Fairy shrilly mocking in the garden.

"What have they done with you, you poor Mrs. Gill?"
　　Quoth the Fairy brightly glancing in the garden;
"Where have they hidden you, you poor old Mrs. Gill?"
　　Quoth the Fairy dancing lightly in the garden;
But night's faint veil now wrapped the hill,
Stark 'neath the stars stood the dead-still Mill,
And out of her cold cottage never answered Mrs. Gill
　　The Fairy mimbling mambling in the garden.

[1] Tod = dense foliage.

### SAM

When Sam goes back in memory,
  It is to where the sea
Breaks on the shingle, emerald-green,
  In white foam, endlessly;
He says—with small brown eye on mine—
  "I used to keep awake,
And lean from my window in the moon,
  Watching those billows break.
And half a million tiny hands,
  And eyes, like sparks of frost,
Would dance and come tumbling into the moon,
  On every breaker tossed.
And all across from star to star,
  I've seen the watery sea,
With not a single ship in sight,
  Just ocean there, and me;
And heard my father snore. And once,
  As sure as I'm alive,
Out of those wallowing, moon-flecked waves
  I saw a mermaid dive;
Head and shoulders above the wave,
  Plain as I now see you,
Combing her hair, now back, now front,
  Her two eyes peeping through;
Calling me, 'Sam!'—quietlike—'Sam!' . . .
  But me . . . I never went,
Making believe I kind of thought
  'Twas someone else she meant . . .
Wonderful lovely there she sat,
  Singing the night away,
All in the solitudinous sea
  Of that there lonely bay.
P'raps," and he'd smooth his hairless mouth,
  "P'raps, if 'twere now, my son,
P'raps, if I heard a voice say, 'Sam!'
  Morning would find me gone."

### BERRIES

There was an old woman
  Went blackberry picking
Along the hedges
  From Weep to Wicking.
Half a pottle—
  No more she had got,
When out steps a Fairy
  From her green grot;
And says, "Well, Jill,
  Would 'ee pick 'ee mo?"

And Jill, she curtseys,
  And looks just so.
"Be off," says the Fairy,
  "As quick as you can,
Over the meadows
  To the little green lane,
That dips to the hayfields
  Of Farmer Grimes:
I've berried those hedges
  A score of times;
Bushel on bushel
  I'll promise 'ee, Jill,

This side of supper
  If 'ee pick with a will."
She glints very bright,
  And speaks her fair;
Then lo, and behold!
  She had faded in air.

Be sure Old Goodie
  She trots betimes
Over the meadows
  To Farmer Grimes.
And never was queen
  With jewelry rich
As those same hedges
  From twig to ditch;
Like Dutchmen's coffers,
  Fruit, thorn, and flower—
They shone like William
  And Mary's Bower.
And be sure Old Goodie
  Went back to Weep,
So tired with her basket
  She scarce could creep.

When she comes in the dusk
  To her cottage door,
There's Towser wagging
  As never before,
To see his Missus
  So glad to be
Come from her fruit-picking
  Back to he.
As soon as next morning
  Dawn was gray,
The pot on the hob
  Was simmering away;
And all in a stew
  And a hugger-mugger
Towser and Jill
  A-boiling of sugar,
And the dark clear fruit
  That from Faërie came
For syrup and jelly
  And blackberry jam.

Twelve jolly gallipots
  Jill put by;
And one little teeny one,
  One inch high;

And that she's hidden
  A good thumb deep,
Half way over
  From Wicking to Weep.

### ALL BUT BLIND

All but blind
  In his chambered hole
Gropes for worms
  The four-clawed Mole.

All but blind
  In the evening sky,
The hooded Bat
  Twirls softly by.

All but blind
  In the burning day
The Barn-Owl blunders
  On her way.

And blind as are
  These three to me,
So, blind to Someone
  I must be.

### SUMMER EVENING

The sandy cat by the Farmer's chair
Mews at his knee for dainty fare;
Old Rover in his moss-greened house
Mumbles a bone, and barks at a mouse.
In the dewy fields the cattle lie
Chewing the cud 'neath a fading sky.
Dobbin at manger pulls his hay:
Gone is another summer's day.

### THERE BLOOMS NO BUD IN MAY

There blooms no bud in May
Can for its white compare
With snow at break of day,
On fields forlorn and bare.

For shadow it hath rose,
Azure, and amethyst;
And every air that blows
Dies out in beauteous mist.

It hangs the frozen bough
With flowers on which the night
Wheeling her darkness through
Scatters a starry light.

Fearful of its pale glare
In flocks the starlings rise;
Slide through the frosty air,
And perch with plaintive cries.

Only the inky rook,
Hunched cold in ruffled wings,
Its snowy nest forsook,
Caws of unnumbered Springs.

### THE SCARECROW

All winter through I bow my head
  Beneath the driving rain;
The North wind powders me with snow
  And blows me black again;
At midnight 'neath a maze of stars
  I flame with glittering rime,
And stand, above the stubble, stiff
  As mail at morning-prime.
But when that child, called Spring, and all
  His host of children, come,
Scattering their buds and dew upon
  These acres of my home,
Some rapture in my rags awakes;
  I lift void eyes and scan
The skies for crows, those ravening foes
  Of my strange master, Man.
I watch him striding lank behind
  His clashing team, and know
Soon will the wheat swish body high
  Where once lay sterile snow;
Soon shall I gaze across a sea
  Of sun-begotten grain,
Which my unflinching watch hath sealed
  For harvest once again.

### THE GHOST

"Who knocks?" "I, who was beautiful,
Beyond all dreams to restore,
I, from the roots of the dark thorn am hither,
And knock on the door."

"Who speaks?" "I—once was my speech
Sweet as the bird's on the air.

When echo lurks by the waters to heed;
'Tis I speak thee fair."

"Dark is the hour!" "Aye, and cold."
"Lone is my house." "Ah, but mine?"
"Sight, touch, lips, eyes yearned in vain."
"Long dead these to thine. . . ."

Silence. Still faint on the porch
Brake the flames of the stars.
In gloom groped a hope-wearied hand
Over keys, bolts, and bars.

Dews were still betwixt us twain;
Stars a trembling beauty shed;
Yet—not a whisper comes again
Of the words he said.

### SILVER

Slowly, silently, now the moon
Walks the night in her silver shoon;
This way, and that, she peers, and sees
Silver fruit upon silver trees;
One by one the casements catch
Her beams beneath the silvery thatch;
Couched in his kennel, like a log,
With paws of silver sleeps the dog;
From their shadowy cote the white breasts
    peep
Of doves in a silver-feathered sleep;
A harvest mouse goes scampering by,
With silver claws and a silver eye;
And moveless fish in the water gleam,
By silver reeds in a silver stream.

### THE SONG OF SHADOWS

Sweep thy faint strings, Musician,
  With thy long lean hand;
Downward the starry tapers burn,
  Sinks soft the waning sand;
The old hound whimpers couched in sleep,
  The embers smolder low;
Across the walls the shadows
  Come, and go.

Sweep softly thy strings, Musician,
  The minutes mount to hours;
Frost on the windless casement weaves
  A labyrinth of flowers;

Ghosts linger in the darkening air,
  Hearken at the open door;
Music hath called them, dreaming,
  Home once more.


NOD

Softly along the road of evening,
  In a twilight dim with rose,
Wrinkled with age, and drenched with dew
  Old Nod, the shepherd, goes.

His drowsy flock streams on before him,
  Their fleeces charged with gold,
To where the sun's last beam leans low
  On Nod the shepherd's fold.

The hedge is quick and green with briar,
  From their sand the conies creep;
And all the birds that fly in heaven
  Flock singing home to sleep.


His lambs outnumber a noon's roses,
  Yet, when night's shadows fall,
His blind old sheep-dog, Slumber-soon,
  Misses not one of all.


His are the quiet steeps of dreamland,
  The waters of no-more-pain;
His ram's bell rings 'neath an arch of stars,
  "Rest, rest, and rest again."


# G. K. Chesterton

THAT brilliant journalist, novelist, essayist, publicist and lyricist, Gilbert Keith
Chesterton, was born at Campden Hill, Kensington, May 29, 1874, and began
his literary life by reviewing books on art for various magazines. He is best known
as a writer of paradoxical essays on anything and everything, such as *Tremendous
Trifles* (1909), *Varied Types* (1905), and *All Things Considered* (1910), but he is
also a stimulating critic; a keen appraiser, as shown in his volume *Heretics* (1905)
and his analytical studies of Robert Browning, Charles Dickens, and George Bernard
Shaw; a writer of strange and grotesque romances like *The Napoleon of Notting
Hill* (1906), *The Man Who Was Thursday* (1908), which Chesterton himself has
sub-titled "A Nightmare," and that mad extravaganza with songs for a sublimated
comic-opera, *The Flying Inn* (1914). This being insufficient to exhaust his creative
energy, he is also the author of several books of fantastic short stories, ranging from
the whimsical narratives in *The Club of Queer Trades* (1905) to that amazing
sequence begun with *The Innocence of Father Brown* (1911)—which is a series of
religious detective stories!

Besides being the creator of all these, Chesterton finds time to be a prolific if
sometimes too acrobatic newspaperman, a lay preacher in disguise (witness *Orthodoxy* [1908], *What's Wrong with the World* [1910], *The Ball and the Cross*
[1909]) and a pamphleteer. He is also—his admirers say, primarily—a poet. His
first volume of verse, *The Wild Knight and Other Poems* (1900), a collection
of quaintly flavored affirmative verses, was followed by *The Ballad of the White
Horse* (1911), one long poem which, in spite of Chesterton's ever-present sermoniz-
ing, is possibly the most stirring creation he has achieved. This poem has the vigor,
the spontaneity, if not quite the simplicity of the true ballad.

Scarcely less notable is the ringing "Lepanto" from his later, more epigrammatic
*Poems* (1915) which, anticipating the clanging verses of Vachel Lindsay's "The

Congo," is one of the finest of modern chants. It is interesting to see how the
syllables beat, as though on brass; it is thrilling to feel how, in one's pulses, the
armies sing, the feet tramp, the drums snarl, and all the tides of marching crusaders
roll out of lines like:

> Strong gongs groaning as the guns boom far,
> Don John of Austria is going to the war;
> Stiff flags straining in the night-blasts cold
> In the gloom black-purple, in the glint old-gold;
> Torchlight crimson on the copper kettle-drums,
> Then the tuckets, then the trumpets, then the cannon, and he comes. . . .

Subsequent volumes have established the poet's rollicking medievalism, his
mingled high spirits and high optimism. *Wine, Water and Song* (1915) and *The
Ballad of St. Barbara* (1922) have a humor—and a humanity—that is "at home
in the streets and familiar among the stars."

Chesterton seemed to grow more prolific with every year. Two plays were complete successes: *Magic* (1913) and *Johnson* (1928). *Tales of the Long Bow* (1925) is,
as the title implies, a set of incredible short stories. The Father Brown series grew
into six volumes; the best of the later ones is *The Incredulity of Father Brown*
(1926). His transatlantic visit was recorded in *What I Saw in America* (1922). In
an era devoted to quickly assimilated culture in the form of "outlines," he yielded
to the fashion—and satirized it—in *The Outline of Sanity* (1926). His colorful
*Collected Poems* appeared in 1927. The fantastic exploration of the limbo between
reason and insanity—a subject which has always compelled Chesterton—resulted
in fiction like *The Return of Don Quixote* (1927) and *The Poet and the Lunatics*
(1929).

Chesterton, the prose-paradoxer, is a furiously yea-saying antagonist of a skeptical
age. But it is Chesterton the poet who is more likely to outlive his period.

### LEPANTO

> White founts falling in the Courts of the sun,
> And the Soldan of Byzantium is smiling as they run;
> There is laughter like the fountains in that face of all men feared,
> It stirs the forest darkness, the darkness of his beard;
> It curls the blood-red crescent, the crescent of his lips;
> For the inmost sea of all the earth is shaken with his ships.
> They have dared the white republics up the capes of Italy,
> They have dashed the Adriatic round the Lion of the Sea,
> And the Pope has cast his arms abroad for agony and loss,
> And called the kings of Christendom for swords about the Cross.
> The cold queen of England is looking in the glass;
> The shadow of the Valois is yawning at the Mass;
> From evening isles fantastical rings faint the Spanish gun,
> And the Lord upon the Golden Horn is laughing in the sun.
>
> Dim drums throbbing, in the hills half heard,
> Where only on a nameless throne a crownless prince has stirred,

Where, risen from a doubtful seat and half-attainted stall,
The last knight of Europe takes weapons from the wall,
The last and lingering troubadour to whom the bird has sung,
That once went singing southward when all the world was young.
In that enormous silence, tiny and unafraid,
Comes up along a winding road the noise of the Crusade.
Strong gongs groaning as the guns boom far,
Don John of Austria is going to the war;
Stiff flags straining in the night-blasts cold
In the gloom black-purple, in the glint old-gold,
Torchlight crimson on the copper kettle-drums,
Then the tuckets, then the trumpets, then the cannon, and he comes.
Don John laughing in the brave beard curled,
Spurning of his stirrups like the thrones of all the world,
Holding his head up for a flag of all the free.
Love-light of Spain—hurrah!
Death-light of Africa!
Don John of Austria
Is riding to the sea.

Mahound is in his paradise above the evening star,
(*Don John of Austria is going to the war.*)
He moves a mighty turban on the timeless houri's knees,
His turban that is woven of the sunsets and the seas.
He shakes the peacock gardens as he rises from his ease,
And he strides among the tree-tops and is taller than the trees;
And his voice through all the garden is a thunder sent to bring
Black Azrael and Ariel and Ammon on the wing.
Giants and the Genii,
Multiplex of wing and eye,
Whose strong obedience broke the sky
When Solomon was king.

They rush in red and purple from the red clouds of the morn,
From the temples where the yellow gods shut up their eyes in scorn;
They rise in green robes roaring from the green hells of the sea
Where fallen skies and evil hues and eyeless creatures be,
On them the sea-valves cluster and the gray sea-forests curl,
Splashed with a splendid sickness, the sickness of the pearl;
They swell in sapphire smoke out of the blue cracks of the ground,—
They gather and they wonder and give worship to Mahound.
And he saith, "Break up the mountains where the hermit-folk can hide,
And sift the red and silver sands lest bone of saint abide,
And chase the Giaours flying night and day, not giving rest,
For that which was our trouble comes again out of the west.
We have set the seal of Solomon on all things under sun,
Of knowledge and of sorrow and endurance of things done.
But a noise is in the mountains, in the mountains; and I know
The voice that shook our palaces—four hundred years ago:
It is he that saith not 'Kismet'; it is he that knows not Fate;
It is Richard, it is Raymond, it is Godfrey at the gate!

It is he whose loss is laughter when he counts the wager worth,
Put down your feet upon him, that our peace be on the earth."
For he heard drums groaning and he heard guns jar,
(*Don John of Austria is going to the war.*)
Sudden and still—hurrah!
Bolt from Iberia!
Don John of Austria
Is gone by Alcalar.

St. Michael's on his Mountain in the sea-roads of the north
(*Don John of Austria is girt and going forth.*)
Where the gray seas glitter and the sharp tides shift
And the sea-folk labor and the red sails lift.
He shakes his lance of iron and he claps his wings of stone;
The noise is gone through Normandy; the noise is gone alone;
The North is full of tangled things and texts and aching eyes,
And dead is all the innocence of anger and surprise,
And Christian killeth Christian in a narrow dusty room,
And Christian dreadeth Christ that hath a newer face of doom,
And Christian hateth Mary that God kissed in Galilee,—
But Don John of Austria is riding to the sea.
Don John calling through the blast and the eclipse,
Crying with the trumpet, with the trumpet to his lips,
Trumpet that sayeth *ha!*
    *Domino Gloria!*
Don John of Austria
Is shouting to the ships.

King Philip's in his closet with the Fleece about his neck
(*Don John of Austria is armed upon the deck.*)
The walls are hung with velvet that is black and soft as sin,
And little dwarfs creep out of it and little dwarfs creep in.
He holds a crystal phial that has colors like the moon,
He touches, and it tingles, and he trembles very soon,
And his face is as a fungus of a leprous white and gray
Like plants in the high houses that are shuttered from the day,
And death is in the phial and the end of noble work,
But Don John of Austria has fired upon the Turk.
Don John's hunting, and his hounds have bayed—
Booms away past Italy the rumor of his raid.
Gun upon gun, ha! ha!
Gun upon gun, hurrah!
Don John of Austria
Has loosed the cannonade.

The Pope was in his chapel before day or battle broke,
(*Don John of Austria is hidden in the smoke.*)
The hidden room in man's house where God sits all the year,
The secret window whence the world looks small and very dear.
He sees as in a mirror on the monstrous twilight sea
The crescent of his cruel ships whose name is mystery;

They fling great shadows foe-wards, making Cross and Castle dark,
They veil the plumèd lions on the galleys of St. Mark;
And above the ships are palaces of brown, black-bearded chiefs,
And below the ships are prisons, where with multitudinous griefs,
Christian captives, sick and sunless, all a laboring race repines
Like a race in sunken cities, like a nation in the mines.
They are lost like slaves that swat, and in the skies of morning hung
The stair-ways of the tallest gods when tyranny was young.
They are countless, voiceless, hopeless as those, fallen or fleeing on
Before the high Kings' horses in the granite of Babylon.
And many a one grows witless in his quiet room in hell
Where a yellow face looks inward through the lattice of his cell,
And he finds his God forgotten, and he seeks no more a sign—
(*But Don John of Austria has burst the battle-line!*)
Don John pounding from the slaughter-painted poop,
Purpling all the ocean like a bloody pirate's sloop,
Scarlet running over on the silvers and the golds,
Breaking of the hatches up and bursting of the holds,
Thronging of the thousands up that labor under sea
White for bliss and blind for sun and stunned for liberty.
*Vivat Hispania!*
*Domino Gloria!*
Don John of Austria
Has set his people free!

Cervantes on his galley sets the sword back in the sheath
(*Don John of Austria rides homeward with a wreath.*)
And he sees across a weary land a straggling road in Spain,
Up which a lean and foolish knight for ever rides in vain,
And he smiles, but not as Sultans smile, and settles back the blade. . . .
(*But Don John of Austria rides home from the Crusade.*)


A PRAYER IN DARKNESS

This much, O heaven—if I should brood or rave,
    Pity me not; but let the world be fed,
    Yea, in my madness if I strike me dead,
Heed you the grass that grows upon my grave.

If I dare snarl between this sun and sod,
    Whimper and clamor, give me grace to own,
    In sun and rain and fruit in season shown,
The shining silence of the scorn of God.

Thank God the stars are set beyond my power,
    If I must travail in a night of wrath;
    Thank God my tears will never vex a moth,
Nor any curse of mine cut down a flower.

Men say the sun was darkened: yet I had
    Thought it beat brightly, even on—Calvary:
    And He that hung upon the Torturing Tree
Heard all the crickets singing, and was glad.

## ELEGY IN A COUNTRY CHURCHYARD

The men that worked for England
They have their graves at home;
And bees and birds of England
About the cross can roam.

But they that fought for England,
Following a falling star,
Alas, alas, for England
They have their graves afar.

And they that rule in England
In stately conclave met,
Alas, alas, for England
They have no graves as yet.

## THE DONKEY

When fishes flew and forests walked
  And figs grew upon thorn,
Some moment when the moon was blood,
  Then surely I was born;

With monstrous head and sickening cry
  And ears like errant wings,
The devil's walking parody
  On all four-footed things.

The tattered outlaw of the earth,
  Of ancient crooked will;
Starve, scourge, deride me: I am dumb,
  I keep my secret still.

Fools! For I also had my hour;
  One far fierce hour and sweet:
There was a shout about my ears,
  And palms before my feet!

## THE PRAISE OF DUST

"What of vile dust?" the preacher said.
  Methought the whole world woke,
The dead stone lived beneath my foot,
  And my whole body spoke.

"You, that play tyrant to the dust,
  And stamp its wrinkled face,
This patient star that flings you not
  Far into homeless space,

"Come down out of your dusty shrine
  The living dust to see,
The flowers that at your sermon's end
  Stand blazing silently.

"Rich white and blood-red blossom; stones,
  Lichens like fire encrust;
A gleam of blue, a glare of gold,
  The vision of the dust.

"Pass them all by: till, as you come
  Where, at a city's edge,
Under a tree—I know it well—
  Under a lattice ledge,

"The sunshine falls on one brown head.
  You, too, O cold of clay,
Eater of stones, may haply hear
  The trumpets of that day.

"When God to all his paladins
  By his own splendor swore
To make a fairer face than heaven,
  Of dust and nothing more."

## WINE AND WATER

Old Noah he had an ostrich farm and fowls on the largest scale,
He ate his egg with a ladle in an egg-cup big as a pail,
And the soup he took was Elephant Soup, and the fish he took was Whale,
But they all were small to the cellar he took when he set out to sail,
And Noah he often said to his wife when he sat down to dine,
"I don't care where the water goes if it doesn't get into the wine."

The cataract of the cliff of heaven fell blinding off the brink
As if it would wash the stars away as suds go down a sink,
The seven heavens came roaring down for the throats of hell to drink,
And Noah he cocked his eye and said, "It looks like rain, I think,

The water has drowned the Matterhorn as deep as a Mendip mine,
But I don't care where the water goes if it doesn't get into the wine."

But Noah he sinned, and we have sinned; on tipsy feet we trod,
Till a great big, black teetotaler was sent to us for a rod,
And you can't get wine at a P. S. A., or chapel, or Eisteddfod.
For the Curse of Water has come again because of the wrath of God,
And water is on the Bishop's board and the Higher Thinker's shrine,
But I don't care where the water goes if it doesn't get into the wine.

### THE SWORD OF SURPRISE

Sunder me from my bones, O sword of God,
Till they stand stark and strange as do the trees;
That I whose heart goes up with the soaring woods
May marvel as much at these.

Sunder me from my blood that in the dark
I hear that red ancestral river run,
Like branching buried floods that find the sea
But never find the sun.

Give me miraculous eyes to see my eyes,
Those rolling mirrors made alive in me,
Terrible crystal more incredible
Than all the things they see.

Sunder me from my soul, that I may see
The sins like streaming wounds, the life's brave beat
Till I shall save myself, as I would save
A stranger in the street.

### THE HOUSE OF CHRISTMAS

There fared a mother driven forth
    Out of an inn to roam;
In the place where she was homeless
    All men are at home.
The crazy stable close at hand,
With shaking timber and shifting sand,
Grew a stronger thing to abide and stand
    Than the square stones of Rome.

For men are homesick in their homes,
    And strangers under the sun,
And they lay their heads in a foreign land
    Whenever the day is done.
Here we have battle and blazing eyes,
And chance and honor and high surprise;
But our homes are under miraculous skies
    Where the yule tale was begun.

A child in a foul stable,
  Where the beasts feed and foam;
Only where He was homeless
  Are you and I at home;
We have hands that fashion and heads that know,
But our hearts we lost—how long ago!
In a place no chart nor ship can show
  Under the sky's dome.

This world is wild as an old wives' tale,
  And strange the plain things are,
The earth is enough and the air is enough
  For our wonder and our war;
But our rest is as far as the fire-drake swings,
And our peace is put in impossible things
Where clashed and thundered unthinkable wings
  Round an incredible star.

To an open house in the evening
  Home shall men come,
To an older place than Eden
  And a taller town than Rome;
To the end of the way of the wandering star,
To the things that cannot be and that are,
To the place where God was homeless
  And all men are at home.

## Gordon Bottomley

GORDON BOTTOMLEY was born at Keighley in 1874 and educated at the Grammar
School. He is best known as a dramatist, his volumes—and there are ten of
them dating from 1904—having elicited high praise upon publication. When the
dramas were collected in two volumes, *King Lear's Wife and Other Plays* (1920)
and *Gruach and Britain's Daughter* (1921), the tributes were still more enthusiastic.
Referring to *Gruach,* which is a portrait of the Lady Macbeth at the time of her
first meeting with the Thane, Lascelles Abercrombie wrote, "It was remarkable
enough that Mr. Bottomley should have proved himself capable of worthily invent-
ing a prelude to 'Lear'; it is astonishing that the success should be repeated in a
prelude to 'Macbeth.' But it has become clear now that at no time in the history
of English poetry since the seventeenth century has the requisite combination of
dramatic and poetic talents existed until now in the person of Mr. Bottomley."

His poetry, collected in *Chambers of Imagery, First Series* (1907), *Second Series*
(1912), displays the same command of vivid characterization and imaginative vigor
one finds in his poetic dramas. What lends technical, if contemporary, interest to
both volumes is that they anticipated the effects of the Imagists long before the
group created a movement. A comprehensive collection, *Poems of Thirty Years*
(1925), synthesizes the combination of force and delicacy which is Bottomley's own.

"The End of the World" (which should be read in connection with Abercrombie's play of the same title) is typical, simple in language, dramatic in effect, and extraordinarily supple in rhythm. Here, as in his dramas, the fine intricacies of phrase are paralleled by a knit power of thought.

### THE END OF THE WORLD

The snow had fallen many nights and days;
The sky was come upon the earth at last,
Sifting thinly down as endlessly
As though within the system of blind planets
Something had been forgot or overdriven.
The dawn now seemed neglected in the gray,
Where mountains were unbuilt and shadowless trees
Rootlessly paused or hung upon the air.
There was no wind, but now and then a sigh
Crossed that dry falling dust and rifted it
Through crevices of slate and door and casement.
Perhaps the new moon's time was even past.
Outside, the first white twilights were too void
Until a sheep called once, as to a lamb,
And tenderness crept everywhere from it;
But now the flock must have strayed far away.
The lights across the valley must be veiled,
The smoke lost in the grayness or the dusk.
For more than three days now the snow had thatched
That cow-house roof where it had ever melted
With yellow stains from the beasts' breath inside;
But yet a dog howled there, though not quite lately.
Someone passed down the valley swift and singing,
Yes, with locks spreaded like a son of morning;
But if he seemed too tall to be a man
It was that men had been so long unseen,
Or shapes loom larger through a moving snow.
And he was gone and food had not been given him.
When snow slid from an overweighted leaf
Shaking the tree, it might have been a bird
Slipping in sleep or shelter, whirring wings;
Yet never bird fell out, save once a dead one—
And in two days the snow had covered it.
The dog had howled again—or thus it seemed
Until a lean fox passed and cried no more.
All was so safe indoors where life went on
Glad of the close enfolding snow—O glad
To be so safe and secret at its heart,
Watching the strangeness of familiar things.
They knew not what dim hours went on, went by,
For while they slept the clock stopt newly wound
As the cold hardened. Once they watched the road,
Thinking to be remembered. Once they doubted
If they had kept the sequence of the days,

Because they heard not any sound of bells.
A butterfly, that hid until the Spring
Under a ceiling's shadow, dropt, was dead.
The coldness seemed more nigh, the coldness deepened
As a sound deepens into silences;
It was of earth and came not by the air;
The earth was cooling and drew down the sky.
The air was crumbling. There was no more sky.
Rails of a broken bed charred in the grate,
And when he touched the bars he thought the sting
Came from their heat—he could not feel such cold . . .
She said, "O do not sleep,
Heart, heart of mine, keep near me. No, no; sleep.
I will not lift his fallen, quiet eyelids,
Although I know he would awaken then—
He closed them thus but not of his own will.
He can stay with me while I do not lift them."

### DAWN

A thrush is tapping a stone
With a snail-shell in its beak;
A small bird hangs from a cherry
Until the stem shall break.
No waking song has begun,
And yet birds chatter and hurry
And throng in the elm's gloom
Because an owl goes home.

### EAGER SPRING

Whirl, snow, on the blackbird's chatter;
You will not hinder his song to come.
East wind, sleepless, you cannot scatter
Quince-bud, almond-bud,
Little grape-hyacinth's
Clustering brood.
Nor unfurl the tips of the plum.
No half-born stalk of a lily stops;
There is sap in the storm-torn bush;
And, ruffled by gusts in a snow-blurred copse,
"Pity to wait" sings a thrush.

Love, there are few Springs left for us;
They go, and the count of them as they go
Makes surer the count that is left for us.
More than the East wind, more than the
    snow,
I would put back these hours that bring
Buds and bees and are lost;
I would hold the night and the frost,
To save for us one more Spring.

### EAGLE SONG

*(from "Suilven and the Eagle")*

O deep, creating Light,
My energy, my desire,
Receive me into you in the height
And force me to aspire.

Alone I am made for you;
I alone rise and gaze
With lidless eyes, alone pursue
Like spiring flame your ways.

I am that part of life
Which will not live but to dare:
When I must rest from joyful strife
I climb the lonely air,

And climbing strive again.
On fellow life I prey,
Know that immaterial pain
Passes and things remain

In me or outside me,
Which deepen in that fierce way
Life, and by wisdom and cruelty
Continue it for a day.

Out of the fathomless height,
Come, show to me here
This thing I have held in my breast all night,
Desired, devoted, dear.
On strange, small limb and brow
Come, Light, now.

# A. E. Coppard

A. E. COPPARD was born January 4, 1878, at Folkestone, Kent, and has lived all his life in close contact with the soil of which he writes so faithfully. Unknown until 1921, his first volume, *Adam and Eve and Pinch Me,* immediately created an enthusiastic circle of readers on both sides of the Atlantic. *Clorinda Walks in Heaven* (1922) increased the number of his readers, and with *The Black Dog* (1923), *Fishmonger's Fiddle* (1925) and *The Field of Mustard* (1927) his following has grown greatly in size and admiration.

These volumes of short tales vibrate with a prose so pointed and colorful that it is seldom without the glow of poetry. But Coppard is no less a poet when he writes in rhyme. Two privately printed volumes—*Hips and Haws* (1922) and *Pelagea* (1927)—communicate his half-earthly, half-eerie quality. The latter volume is particularly rich in those concisions which point his prose; landscape and figure are fixed in a few lines. "Betty Perrin" is a common enough figure; Coppard gives her a new dimension. "Winter Field" is another example of the ordinary in terms of the illuminating.

*Collected Poems,* a volume awaited by Coppard's admirers, appeared in 1929 and was neglected by all but a few appreciators of his special quality.

### STAY, O STAY

Of love's designèd joys,
   Dream only, do not speak,
Lest every noting hour
   A separate vengeance take.

Holy is love, but frail
   With love's confined desires,
Against whose chosen urn
   Time like a thief conspires.

Keep silence; love will grow
   In its own darkened air,
A moon whose clouds do make
   Heaven and itself more fair.

### WINTER FIELD

Sorrow on the acres,
   Wind in the thorn,
And an old man plowing
   Through the frosty morn.

A flock of the dark birds,
   Rooks and their wives,

Follow the plow team
   The old man drives;

And troops of starlings,
   A-tittle-tat and prim,
Follow the rooks
   That follow him.

### BETTY PERRIN

Up the pound path
   Long o' Lag Lane,
Lives an old woman
   As never saw the rain,
Never saw the sea,
   Nor the sun upon the earth:
Poor Betty Perrin,
   Blind from her birth!

Chick nor child
   Never blessed her day,
Nor a loving man
   Ever came her way
With blessings in his heart
   And the blarney on his tongue;
Blind was Betty Perrin
   Since she was young.

She had sisters nine—
  O, such pretty maidies!—
Two went on the town,
  But most were decent ladies;
And Betty's pious pride
  Bethanked the Lord for that:
Poor Miss Perrin,
  Blind as a bat!

Both the saucy sisters
  Cherished her and fed,
Bought her beer and skittles
  Until they both were dead.
Dying thus so young,
  Be sure they died of sin:
Pray, lovely daughters,
  Never you begin!

Then the seven sisters
  Put her on the parish,
For they were truly wedded
  And she was hard to nourish.
Betty was a burden,
  A burden from her birth:
It would not hurt the living
  To give her to the earth.

Long o' Lag Lane,
  Up 'ayond the pound,
Still Betty Perrin
  Cumbereth the ground,
Sisterless as Eve
  With the Sword against the Door:
Poor Betty Perrin,
  Blind for evermore!

### THE SLUGGARD

On our last night together
My love rose early:
Come—said my dear—will you not come with me
To see the sun arise?

But I lay still,
Mum as a Christmas lark.
"Will you not come with me?
The clock has struck the hour,
Night wavers and the birds will soon begin."
But I lay a-mumbling:
"There'll be ten thousand dawns before we die;
One dawn is like another;
It is dark and freezing on the wold;
Do not go, I do not care to go;
Lie here and sleep again."

I heard the sharp latch fall as she went forth alone,
Alone to see day break—the last of days—
Beyond the wood, that well of moving shade
From whence all shadows rise;
I heard the latch fall and I could not sleep.

The gold rays slanted on the bedroom wall
When she came back again.
She had seen the couth hills flow into the sky
And the coloring sun glide out of them,
And as the sun soared up—
A blooded hawk from Abyssinia—
The moon came too:
His rose was in the river,
Her lily in the sky.
And O the cowslips nodding in the warren!

And the coney babe no bigger than a purse!
O the enriching beams athwart the wood,
Where the white windflowers hid their timid lips
Pondering, and buds of beech were locked in bronze!

When I arose she set the dishes out,
And cooked a haddock,
And we ate together,
And then she said Good-by;
For she was a stranger,
Wandering far from home:
Good-by, Good-by.
So long, my dear and tender love,
So long.

How often now I go to greet the dawns!
I do not care for them,
It is tiring to rise and go,
And one dawn is much like another,
But I do see them often, often now,
Seeking for what may bless me in her eyes.

I shall see ten thousand dawns before I die.


### THE PRODIGAL SON

When I forsook my homely town
    And bade my luck good-by,
The lord of freedom flung me down
    His sweet scourge from the sky;
But all the passionate winds ordained
    His purpose to fulfill
Blew to a burning goal ungained,
    Left me my idle will.

Sad are the harvests I amass,
    And empty of all grain;
Thickens the dust upon the grass
    No dews shall wash again;
Nought can unclog the unconfined
    From pride so falsely kept,
Nor from my void but living mind
    May its dead dreams be swept.

Ten thousand finer dreams of sleep,
    And old songs sweet to hear,
Mock at my anguish as I keep
    My journeying otherwhere;
I would not need one kingly frown,
    Or yet bequeath one sigh,
Had I not left my shining town,
    Nor bade my heart good-by.

# Thomas Macdonagh

THOMAS MACDONAGH was born in Ireland in 1878. Like his fellow-martyrs, he gave up the promise of a great career to devote himself to the liberation of his country. His poems are few in number, but they are filled with that affection and intensity which made him so striking as a leader of his political group.

In company with his compatriot-poets (see page 407), he was arrested and executed after the Easter Week Rising in Dublin in 1916. The poem "Of a Poet-Patriot," although written to commemorate a fellow-singer, might well serve as his own epitaph.

*The Collected Poems of Thomas Macdonagh* appeared posthumously in 1919. In the introduction, James Stephens wrote, "Here are the poems of a good man; and if, outside of rebellion and violence, you wish to know what his thoughts were like, you will find all his best here."

## OF A POET-PATRIOT

His songs were a little phrase
  Of eternal song.
Drowned in the harping of lays
  More loud and long.

His deed was a single word,
  Called out alone
In a night when no echo stirred
  To laughter or moan.

But his songs new souls shall thrill,
  The loud harps dumb,
And his deed the echoes fill
  When the dawn is come.

## WISHES FOR MY SON

*(Born on St. Cecilia's Day, 1912)*

Now, my son, is life for you,
And I wish you joy of it,—
Joy of power in all you do,
Deeper passion, better wit
Than I had who had enough,
Quicker life and length thereof,
More of every gift but love.

Love I have beyond all men,
Love that now you share with me—
What have I to wish you then

But that you be good and free,
And that God to you may give
Grace in stronger days to live?

For I wish you more than I
Ever knew of glorious deed,
Though no rapture passed me by
That an eager heart could heed,
Though I followed heights and sought
Things the sequel never brought:

Wild and perilous holy things
Flaming with a martyr's blood,
And the joy that laughs and sings
Where a foe must be withstood,
Joy of headlong happy chance
Leading on the battle dance.

But I found no enemy,
No man in a world of wrong.
That Christ's word of charity
Did not render clean and strong—
Who was I to judge my kind,
Blindest groper of the blind?

God to you may give the sight
And the clear undoubting strength,
Wars to knit for single right,
Freedom's war to knit at length,
And to win, through wrath and strife,
To the sequel of my life.

But for you, so small and young,
Born on St. Cecilia's Day,
I in more harmonious song
Now for nearer joys should pray—
Simple joys: the natural growth

Of your childhood and your youth,
Courage, innocence, and truth:

These for you, so small and young,
In your hand and heart and tongue.

## Seumas O'Sullivan

J AMES STARKEY was born in Dublin in 1878. Writing under the pseudonym of
Seumas O'Sullivan, he contributed a great variety of prose and verse to various
Irish papers. His reputation as a poet began with his appearance in *New Songs,*
edited by George Russell ("Æ"). Later, he published *The Twilight People* (1905),
*The Earth Lover* (1909), *Poems* (1912), and *Mud and Purple* (1918). His *Collected Poems* carry an Introduction by Padraic Colum, a selection in *The Bibelot*
having been prefaced by "Æ."

### PRAISE

Dear, they are praising your beauty,
The grass and the sky:
The sky in a silence of wonder,
The grass in a sigh.

I too would sing for your praising,
Dearest, had I
Speech as the whispering grass,
Or the silent sky.

These have an art for the praising
Beauty so high.
Sweet, you are praised in a silence,
Sung in a sigh.

### CREDO

I cannot pray, as Christians used to pray,
Before the holy Rood,
Nor on the sacred mysteries seven, as they,
Believing, brood.

Nor can I say with those whom pride makes sure,
Our hearts emancipate
Have scorn of ancient symbols that endure
Out-lasting late.

For I have seen Lord Angus in the trees,
And bowing heard
When Spring a lover whispered in their leaves
The living word.

Have known the sun, the wind's sweet agency
And the soft rains that bless
And lead the year through colored pageantry
To fruitfulness.

Yea, by the outstretched hands, the dimming sight,
The piercèd side,
Known when in every bough that shrinks from light
The Lord of life has died.

# Edward Thomas

(Philip) Edward Thomas was born in 1878 and educated at Lincoln College, Oxford. For many years before he turned to verse, Thomas had a large following as a critic and author of travel books, biographies, tired pot-boilers. Hating his hackwork, yet unable to get free of it, he had so repressed his creative ability that he had grown doubtful concerning his power. It needed something foreign to stir and animate what was native in him. So when Robert Frost, the New England poet, went abroad in 1912 for two years and became an intimate of Thomas's, the English critic began to write poetry.

His verse was first published under the pseudonym of "Edward Eastaway" and immediately attracted the attention of a small circle, but (as with his American preceptor) editors were slow to recognize the distinction of his rusticities. Loving, like Frost, the *minutiae* of existence, the quaint and casual turn of ordinary life, Thomas caught the magic of the English countryside in its unpoeticized quietude. Many of his poems are full of a slow, sad contemplation of life and a reflection of its brave futility. It is not exactly disillusion; it is rather an absence of illusion. *Poems* (1917), dedicated to Robert Frost, is full of Thomas's fidelity to little things, things as unglorified as the unfreezing of the "rock-like' mud," a child's path, a list of quaint-sounding villages, birds' nests uncovered by the autumn wind, dusty nettles. Whatever the subject, the lines glow with a deep and almost abject reverence for the soil.

Thomas was killed at Arras at an observatory outpost, ironically enough, on Easter Monday, 1917. *Last Poems* (published posthumously in 1919) has less of Frost's idiom (apparent in such poems as "Fifty Faggots," "Tall Nettles," "Haymaking") and more of Thomas's darkening concern. Faithful to a beauty unseen or scorned by others, his heart "floats through the window to a tree down in the misting, quiet vale":

Not like a peewit that returns to wail
For something it has lost, but like a dove
That slants unswerving to its home and love.
There I find my rest, and through the dark air
Flies what yet lives in me. Beauty is there.

This poetry is a constant search for neglected loveliness: the vortex in an eddy of dead leaves, the dying sun in a fading sunflower, the sedgewater's pipe, a music of songlessness:

> Song that lacks all words, all melody,
> All sweetness almost, was dearer to me then
> Than sweetest voice that sings in tune sweet words.

*Collected Poems,* a richly inclusive volume with an Introduction by Walter De la Mare, was published in 1929. Thomas must be reckoned among the most natural —and most English—of nature poets. As De la Mare wrote, "When Edward Thomas was killed in Flanders, a mirror of England was shattered of so pure a crystal that a clearer and tenderer reflection can be found no otherwhere than in these poems." Behind the accuracy of observation there is an emotional tensity, a vision of things seen "not with but through the eye."

### TALL NETTLES

> Tall nettles cover up, as they have done
> These many springs, the rusty harrow, the plow
> Long worn out, and the roller made of stone:
> Only the elm butt tops the nettles now.
>
> This corner of the farmyard I like most:
> As well as any bloom upon a flower
> I like the dust on the nettles, never lost
> Except to prove the sweetness of a shower.

### IF I SHOULD EVER BY CHANCE

> If I should ever by chance grow rich
> I'll buy Codham, Cockridden, and Childerditch,
> Roses, Pyrgo, and Lapwater,
> And let them all to my elder daughter.
> The rent I shall ask of her will be only
> Each year's first violets, white and lonely,
> The first primroses and orchises—
> She must find them before I do, that is.
> But if she finds a blossom on furze
> Without rent they shall all for ever be hers,
> Codham, Cockridden, and Childerditch,
> Roses, Pyrgo and Lapwater,—
> I shall give them all to my elder daughter.

### COCK-CROW

> Out of the wood of thoughts that grows by night
> To be cut down by the sharp ax of light,—
> Out of the night, two cocks together crow,
> Cleaving the darkness with a silver blow:

And bright before my eyes twin trumpeters stand,
Heralds of splendor, one at either hand,
Each facing each as in a coat of arms:—
The milkers lace their boots up at the farms.


### THE PENNY WHISTLE

The new moon hangs like an ivory bugle
  In the naked frosty blue;
And the ghylls of the forest, already blackened
  By Winter, are blackened anew.

The brooks that cut up and increase the forest,
  As if they had never known
The sun, are roaring with black hollow voices
  Betwixt rage and a moan.

But still the caravan-hut by the hollies
  Like a kingfisher gleams between;
Round the mossed old hearths of the charcoal-burners,
  First primroses ask to be seen.

The charcoal-burners are black, but their linen
  Blows white on the line;
And white the letter the girl is reading
  Under that crescent fine:

And her brother who hides apart in a thicket,
  Slowly and surely playing
On a whistle an olden nursery melody,
  Says far more than I am saying.


### THE TRUMPET

Rise up, rise up,
And, as the trumpet blowing
Chases the dreams of men,
As the dawn glowing
The stars that left unlit
The land and water,
Rise up and scatter
The dew that covers
The print of last night's lovers—
Scatter it, scatter it!

While you are listening
To the clear horn,
Forget, men, everything
On this earth newborn,
Except that it is lovelier
Than any mysteries.

Open your eyes to the air
That has washed the eyes of stars
Through all the dewy night:
Up with the light,
To the old wars;
Arise, arise!


### DIGGING

Today I think
Only with scents,—scents dead leaves yield,
And bracken and wild carrot's seed,
And the square mustard field;

Odors that rise
When the spade wounds the root of a tree,
Rose, currant, raspberry, or goutweed,
Rhubarb or celery;

The smoke's smell, too,
Flowing from where a bonfire burns
The dead, the waste, the dangerous,
And all to sweetness turns.

It is enough
To smell, to crumble the dark earth,
While the robin sings over again
Sad songs of Autumn mirth.

## THAW

Over the land freckled with snow half-thawed
The speculating rooks at their nests cawed,
And saw from elm-tops, delicate as flower of grass,
What we below could not see, Winter pass.

### GALLOWS

There was a weasel lived in the sun
With all his family,
Till a keeper shot him with his gun
And hung him up on a tree,
Where he swings in the wind and the rain,
In the sun and in the snow,
Without pleasure, without pain
On the dead oak tree bough.

There was a crow who was no sleeper,
But a thief and a murderer
Till a very late hour; and this keeper
Made him one of the things that were,
To hang and flap in the rain and wind,
In the sun and in the snow.
There are no more sins to be sinned
On the dead oak tree bough.

There was a magpie, too,
Had a long tongue and a long tail;
He could both talk and do—
But what did that avail?
He, too, flaps in the wind and rain
Alongside weasel and crow.
Without pleasure, without pain,
On the dead oak tree bough.

And many other beasts
And birds, skin, bone and feather,
Have been taken from their feasts
And hung up there together,
To swing and have endless leisure
In the sun and in the snow,
Without pain, without pleasure,
On the dead oak tree bough.

### FIFTY FAGGOTS

There they stand, on their ends, the fifty faggots
That once were underwood of hazel and ash
In Jenny Pink's copse. Now, by the hedge
Close packed they make a thicket fancy alone
Can creep through with the mouse and wren. Next Spring
A blackbird or a robin will nest there,
Accustomed to them, thinking they will remain
Whatever is forever to a bird:
This Spring it is too late; the swift has come.
'Twas a hot day for carrying them up:
Better they will never warm me, though they must
Light several Winters' fires. Before they are done
The war will have ended, many other things
Have ended, maybe, that I can no more
Foresee or more control than robin and wren.

## HAYMAKING

After night's slumber far away had rolled,
The fiery day had a sweet kernel of cold,
And in the perfect blue the clouds uncurled,
Like the first gods before they made the world
And misery, swimming the stormless sea
In beauty and in divine gayety.
The smooth white empty road was lightly strewn
With leaves—the holly's Autumn falls in June—
And fir cones standing stiff up in the heat.
The mill-foot water tumbled white and lit
With tossing crystals, happier than any crowd
Of children pouring out of school aloud.
And in the little thickets where a sleeper
For ever might lie lost, the nettle-creeper
And garden warbler sang unceasingly;
While over them shrill shrieked in his fierce glee
The swift with wings and tail as sharp and narrow
As if the bow had flown off with the arrow.
Only the scent of woodbine and hay new-mown
Traveled the road. In the field sloping down,
Park-like to where its willows showed the brook,
Haymakers rested. The tosser lay forsook
Out in the sun; and the long wagon stood
Without its team, it seemed it never would
Move from the shadow of that single yew.
The team, as still, until their task was due,
Beside the laborers enjoyed the shade
That three squat oaks mid-field together made
Upon a circle of grass and weed uncut,
And on the hollow, once a chalk-pit, but
Now brimmed with nut and elder-flower so clean.
The men leaned on their rakes, about to begin,
But still. And all were silent. All was old,
This morning time, with a great age untold,
Older than Clare and Cobbett, Morland and Crome,
Than, at the field's far edge, the farmer's home,
A white house crouched at the foot of a great tree.
Under the heavens that know not what years be
The men, the beasts, the trees, the implements
Uttered even what they will in times far hence—
All of us gone out of the reach of change—
Immortal in a picture of an old grange.

### OUT IN THE DARK

Out in the dark over the snow
The fallow fawns invisible go
With the fallow doe;

And the winds blow
Fast as the stars are slow.

Stealthily the dark haunts round
And, when a lamp goes, without sound
At a swifter bound
Than the swiftest hound,
Arrives, and all else is drowned;

And I and star and wind and deer,
Are in the dark together,—near,
Yet far,—and fear
Drums on my ear
In that sage company drear.

How weak and little is the light,
All the universe of sight,
Love and delight,
Before the might,
If you love it not, of night.

## John Masefield

JOHN MASEFIELD was born June 1, 1878, in Ledbury, Herefordshire. Although the son of a lawyer, he went to sea at an early age and became a wanderer for several years. At one time (in 1895, to be exact) he worked for a few months as a sort of third assistant barkeeper in Luke O'Connor's saloon, the Columbia Hotel, on the corner of Sixth and Greenwich Avenues, New York City. In 1897, he returned to England where he made friends with Synge in London, living, for a time, in Bloomsbury. The Royal Society of Literature awarded him the Edmond de Polignac prize for poetry in 1912. During the war, Masefield made a lecture tour in America in 1916. Since that time, he has had his home at Boar's Hill, near Oxford. After the death of Robert Bridges he was appointed Poet Laureate in 1930.

The results of his wanderings showed in his early works, *Salt-Water Ballads* (1902), *Ballads* (1903), frank, often crude but rightly measured poems of sailors written in their own dialect, and *A Mainsail Haul* (1905), a collection of short nautical stories. In these books Masefield occasionally overemphasized passion and brutality, yet, underneath the violence, he captured a highly colored realism. But all of Masefield is not fortissimo. He has sounded notes as lightly satiric as "Cargoes," as solemnly restrained as "The Choice," as quietly unaffected—and affecting —as "C. L. M."

It was not until he published *The Everlasting Mercy* (1911) that he became famous. Followed quickly by those remarkable long narrative poems, *The Widow in the Bye Street* (1912), *Dauber* (1912), and *The Daffodil Fields* (1913), these works vibrate with a blend of physical exulting and spiritual exaltation. It is striking and typical of Masefield that the very rudeness is lifted to a plane of religious intensity. Pictorially, Masefield is even more telling. The finest moment in *The Widow in the Bye Street* is the portrayal of the mother alone in her cottage; the public-house scene and the passage describing the birds following the plow are the most intense touches in *The Everlasting Mercy*. Nothing more vigorous or contagious than the description of the storm at sea in *Dauber* has appeared in current literature; "The Wanderer" is perhaps the most persuasive sea-poem in modern English.

The war, in which Masefield served with the Red Cross in France and on the Gallipoli peninsula (of which campaign he wrote a study for the government), softened his style; *Good Friday and Other Poems* (1916) is as restrained and dignified a collection as that of any of his contemporaries.

*Reynard the Fox* (1919) and *Right Royal* (1920) attempt a return to the early vigor. But the attempt is too evident; a sense of strain pervades the too-packed, too-rapidly propelled stanzas. Influenced by Chaucer (Masefield says he first took to writing after reading the *Parliament of Fowls*), they are marred by their excesses. "There is," says Middleton Murry, speaking of the former, "in Chaucer, a naturalness, a lack of emphasis, a confidence that the object will not fail to make its own impression, beside which Mr. Masefield's demonstration and underlining seem almost *malsain* . . . tainted by the desperate *bergerie* of the Georgian era. Chaucer is at home with his speech and at home with his world; by his side Mr. Masefield seems nervous and uncertain about both." But though the Chaucerian influence is obvious, it is not wholly a handicap to Masefield; it stimulates him to overcome a nostalgia, roused (if overanimated) by the English countryside. It is said that *Reynard the Fox* did more than any other single poem to earn him the Laureateship.

After 1930 Masefield grew less self-critical and his work suffered from prolixity. *Midsummer Night* (1928) still has the full narrative sweep of the earlier poems, but *Minnie Maylow's Story and Other Tales and Scenes* (1931) is a sort of British Night's Entertainment neither interesting in ideas nor technique. The thirteen "tales and scenes" ranging from the Chaucerian "Adamas and Eva" to the outworn theme of Tristan and Isolt, will not bear close scrutiny; though the *London Times* reported "there is no denying the zeal and cordiality with which he combines his invention with the traditional," the inventiveness is slight and the tradition overpowering. *A Tale of Troy* (1932) shows Masefield, for no discernible reason, retelling the drama of the Trojan war. *End and Beginning* (1933) is a poem-drama of the last days and execution of Mary, Queen of Scots, the title being from her prophetic remark when notified of her death sentence, "In the end is my beginning." A generous *Collected Poems* was issued in 1923 and enlarged in 1935. The former is the more commendable since it contains the best of his poetry from youth to maturity and does not include the later tedious work. The 1935 edition, however, is valuable since it contains, besides its seven hundred pages, a long preface in which Masefield tells of his first interest in verse and his indebtedness to Chaucer, Keats, Milton, Shelley, Swinburne, and Yeats.

Compared to the early exciting verse, Masefield's novels are conventional. The later novels gather speed, but even *Sard Harker* (1924), *Odtaa* (1926), *The Midnight Folk* (1927), and *The Wanderer of Liverpool* (1930), for all their surface differences, are little more than perfunctory. His books for boys are scarcely more enlivening. His plays come nearer the heart of the poet, although the influence of

Synge, Shakespeare, and Hardy can be traced. The early dramas, unlike the early novels, are his best: *The Tragedy of Nan* (1909), *The Tragedy of Pompey the Great* (1910) and *The Faithful* (1915) are far superior to his adaptations of Racine, his revamping of *Tristan and Isolt* (1927) or the dignified but dull *Coming of Christ* (1928).

Among his essays, *William Shakespeare* (1911) remains his most creative critique, although Masefield returned to the subject in *Shakespeare and Spiritual Life* (1924).

### A CONSECRATION

Not of the princes and prelates with periwigged charioteers
Riding triumphantly laureled to lap the fat of the years,—
Rather the scorned—the rejected—the men hemmed in with the spears;

The men of the tattered battalion which fights till it dies,
Dazed with the dust of the battle, the din and the cries.
The men with the broken heads and the blood running into their eyes.

Not the be-medaled Commander, beloved of the throne,
Riding cock-horse to parade when the bugles are blown,
But the lads who carried the koppie and cannot be known.

Not the ruler for me, but the ranker, the tramp of the road,
The slave with the sack on his shoulders pricked on with the goad,
The man with too weighty a burden, too weary a load.

The sailor, the stoker of steamers, the man with the clout,
The chantyman bent at the halliards putting a tune to the shout,
The drowsy man at the wheel and the tired look-out.

Others may sing of the wine and the wealth and the mirth,
The portly presence of potentates goodly in girth;—
Mine be the dirt and the dross, the dust and scum of the earth!

Theirs be the music, the color, the glory, the gold;
Mine be a handful of ashes, a mouthful of mold.
Of the maimed, of the halt and the blind in the rain and the cold—
Of these shall my songs be fashioned, my tales be told.

                                                   AMEN.

### SEA-FEVER

I must down to the seas again, to the lonely sea and the sky,
And all I ask is a tall ship and a star to steer her by,
And the wheel's kick and the wind's song and the white sail's shaking,
And a gray mist on the sea's face and a gray dawn breaking.

I must down to the seas again, for the call of the running tide
Is a wild call and a clear call that may not be denied;
And all I ask is a windy day with the white clouds flying,
And the flung spray and the blown spume, and the sea-gulls crying.

I must down to the seas again to the vagrant gypsy life.
To the gull's way and the whale's way where the wind's like a whetted knife;
And all I ask is a merry yarn from a laughing fellow-rover,
And quiet sleep and a sweet dream when the long trick's over.

### A WANDERER'S SONG

A wind's in the heart of me, a fire's in my heels,
I am tired of brick and stone and rumbling wagon-wheels;
I hunger for the sea's edge, the limits of the land,
Where the wild old Atlantic is shouting on the sand.

Oh I'll be going, leaving the noises of the street,
To where a lifting foresail-foot is yanking at the sheet;
To a windy, tossing anchorage where yawls and ketches ride,
Oh I'll be going, going, until I meet the tide.

And first I'll hear the sea-wind, the mewing of the gulls,
The clucking, sucking of the sea about the rusty hulls,
The songs at the capstan in the hooker warping out,
And then the heart of me'll know I'm there or thereabout.

Oh I am sick of brick and stone, the heart of me is sick,
For windy green, unquiet sea, the realm of Moby Dick;
And I'll be going, going, from the roaring of the wheels,
For a wind's in the heart of me, a fire's in my heels.

### SORROW OF MYDATH

Weary the cry of the wind is, weary the sea,
Weary the heart and the mind and the body of me.
Would I were out of it, done with it, would I could be
    A white gull crying along the desolate sands!

Outcast, derelict soul in a body accurst,
Standing drenched with the spindrift, standing athirst,
For the cool green waves of death to arise and burst
    In a tide of quiet for me on the desolate sands!

Would that the waves and the long white hair of the spray
Would gather in splendid terror and blot me away
To the sunless place of the wrecks where the waters sway
    Gently, dreamily, quietly over desolate sands!

### TOMORROW

Oh yesterday the cutting edge drank thirstily and deep,
The upland outlaws ringed us in and herded us as sheep,
They drove us from the stricken field and bayed us into keep;
    But tomorrow,
    By the living God, we'll try the game again!

Oh yesterday our little troop was ridden through and through,
Our swaying, tattered pennons fled, a broken, beaten few,
And all a summer afternoon they hunted us and slew;
      But tomorrow,
   By the living God, we'll try the game again!

And here upon the turret-top the bale-fire glowers red,
The wake-lights burn and drip about our hacked, disfigured dead,
And many a broken heart is here and many a broken head;
      But tomorrow,
   By the living God, we'll try the game again!

### THE WEST WIND

It's a warm wind, the west wind, full of birds' cries;
I never hear the west wind but tears are in my eyes.
For it comes from the west lands, the old brown hills,
And April's in the west wind, and daffodils.

It's a fine land, the west land, for hearts as tired as mine,
Apple orchards blossom there, and the air's like wine.
There is cool green grass there, where men may lie at rest,
And the thrushes are in song there, fluting from the nest.

"Will ye not come home, brother? ye have been long away,
It's April, and blossom time, and white is the may;
And bright is the sun, brother, and warm is the rain,—
Will ye not come home, brother, home to us again?

"The young corn is green, brother, where the rabbits run,
It's blue sky, and white clouds, and warm rain and sun.
It's song to a man's soul, brother, fire to a man's brain,
To hear the wild bees and see the merry spring again.

"Larks are singing in the west, brother, above the green wheat,
So will ye not come home, brother, and rest your tired feet?
I've a balm for bruised hearts, brother, sleep for aching eyes,"
Says the warm wind, the west wind, full of birds' cries.

It's the white road westwards is the road I must tread
To the green grass, the cool grass, and rest for heart and head,
To the violets and the warm hearts and the thrushes' song,
In the fine land, the west land, the land where I belong.

### ROUNDING THE HORN

#### (from "Dauber")

Then came the cry of "Call all hands on deck!"
The Dauber knew its meaning; it was come:
Cape Horn, that tramples beauty into wreck,
And crumples steel and smites the strong man dumb.

Down clattered flying kites and staysails; some
Sang out in quick, high calls: the fair-leads skirled,
And from the south-west came the end of the world . . .

"Lay out!" the Bosun yelled. The Dauber laid
Out on the yard, gripping the yard, and feeling
Sick at the mighty space of air displayed
Below his feet, where mewing birds were wheeling.
A giddy fear was on him; he was reeling.
He bit his lip half through, clutching the jack.
A cold sweat glued the shirt upon his back.

The yard was shaking, for a brace was loose.
He felt that he would fall; he clutched, he bent,
Clammy with natural terror to the shoes
While idiotic promptings came and went.
Snow fluttered on a wind-flaw and was spent;
He saw the water darken. Someone yelled,
"Frap it; don't stay to furl! Hold on!" He held.

Darkness came down—half darkness—in a whirl;
The sky went out, the waters disappeared.
He felt a shocking pressure of blowing hurl
The ship upon her side. The darkness speared
At her with wind; she staggered, she careered;
Then down she lay. The Dauber felt her go,
He saw her yard tilt downwards. Then the snow

Whirled all about—dense, multitudinous, çold—
Mixed with the wind's one devilish thrust and shriek,
Which whiffled out men's tears, defeated, took hold,
Flattening the flying drift against the cheek.
The yards buckled and bent, man could not speak.
The ship lay on her broadside; the wind's sound
Had devilish malice at having got her downed.

How long the gale had blown he could not tell,
Only the world had changed, his life had died.
A moment now was everlasting hell.
Nature an onslaught from the weather side,
A withering rush of death, a frost that cried,
Shrieked, till he withered at the heart; a hail
Plastered his oilskins with an icy mail. . . .

"Up!" yelled the Bosun; "up and clear the wreck!"
The Dauber followed where he led; below
He caught one giddy glimpsing of the deck
Filled with white water, as though heaped with snow.
He saw the streamers of the rigging blow
Straight out like pennons from the splintered mast,
Then, all sense dimmed, all was an icy blast.

Roaring from nether hell and filled with ice,
Roaring and crashing on the jerking stage,
An utter bridle given to utter vice,
Limitless power mad with endless rage
Withering the soul; a minute seemed an age.
He clutched and hacked at ropes, at rags of sail,
Thinking that comfort was a fairy tale,

Told long ago—long, long ago—long since
Heard of in other lives—imagined, dreamed—
There where the basest beggar was a prince.
To him in torment where the tempest screamed,
Comfort and warmth and ease no longer seemed
Things that a man could know; soul, body, brain,
Knew nothing but the wind, the cold, the pain.

## C. L. M.

In the dark womb where I began
My mother's life made me a man.
Through all the months of human birth
Her beauty fed my common earth.
I cannot see, nor breathe, nor stir,
But through the death of some of her.

Down in the darkness of the grave
She cannot see the life she gave.
For all her love, she cannot tell
Whether I use it ill or well,
Nor knock at dusty doors to find
Her beauty dusty in the mind.

If the grave's gates could be undone,
She would not know her little son,
I am so grown. If we should meet,
She would pass by me in the street,
Unless my soul's face let her see
My sense of what she did for me.

What have I done to keep in mind
My debt to her and womankind?
What woman's happier life repays
Her for those months of wretched days?
For all my mouthless body leech'd
Ere Birth's releasing hell was reach'd?

What have I done, or tried, or said
In thanks to that dear woman dead?
Men triumph over women still,
Men trample women's rights at will,
And man's lust roves the world untamed.

O grave, keep shut lest I be shamed.

## CARGOES

Quinquireme of Nineveh from distant Ophir
Rowing home to haven in sunny Palestine,
With a cargo of ivory,
And apes and peacocks,
Sandalwood, cedarwood, and sweet white wine.

Stately Spanish galleon coming from the Isthmus,
Dipping through the Tropics by the palm-green shores,
With a cargo of diamonds,
Emeralds, amethysts,
Topazes, and cinnamon, and gold moidores.

Dirty British coaster with a salt-caked smoke-stack
Butting through the Channel in the mad March days,
With a cargo of Tyne coal,
Road-rail, pig-lead,
Firewood, iron-ware, and cheap tin trays.

## CAPTAIN STRATTON'S FANCY

Oh some are fond of red wine, and some are fond of white,
And some are all for dancing in the pale moonlight;
But rum alone's the tipple and the heart's delight
    Of the old bold mate of Henry Morgan.

Oh some are fond of Spanish wine, and some are fond of French,
And some'll swallow tay and stuff fit only for a wench;
But I'm for right Jamaica till I roll beneath the bench,
    Says the old bold mate of Henry Morgan.

Oh some are for the lily, and some are for the rose,
But I am for the sugar-cane that in Jamaica grows;
For it's that makes the bonny drink to warm my copper nose,
    Says the old bold mate of Henry Morgan.

Oh some are fond of fiddles and a song well sung,
And some are all for music for to lilt upon the tongue;
But mouths were made for tankards, and for sucking at the bung,
    Says the old bold mate of Henry Morgan.

And some are fond of dancing, and some are fond of dice,
And some are all for red lips and pretty lasses' eyes;
But a right Jamaica puncheon is a finer prize
    To the old bold mate of Henry Morgan.

Oh some that's good and godly ones they hold that it's a sin
To troll the jolly bowl around and let the dollars spin;
But I'm for toleration and for drinking at an inn,
    Says the old bold mate of Henry Morgan.

Oh some are sad and wretched folk that go in silken suits,
And there's a mort of wicked rogues that live in good reputes;
So I'm for drinking honestly, and dying in my boots,
    Like an old bold mate of Henry Morgan.

## NIGHT ON THE DOWNLAND

Night is on the downland, on the lonely moorland,
On the hills where the wind goes over sheep-bitten turf,
Where the bent grass beats upon the unplowed poorland
And the pine-woods roar like the surf.

Here the Roman lived on the wind-barren lonely,
Dark now and haunted by the moorland fowl;
None comes here now but the peewit only,
And moth-like death in the owl.

Beauty was here on this beetle-droning downland;
The thought of a Caesar in the purple came
From the palace by the Tiber in the Roman townland
To this wind-swept hill with no name.

Lonely Beauty came here and was here in sadness,
Brave as a thought on the frontier of the mind,
In the camp of the wild upon the march of madness,
The bright-eyed Queen of the Blind.

Now where Beauty was are the wind-withered gorses,
Moaning like old men in the hill-wind's blast;
The flying sky is dark with running horses,
And the night is full of the past.


ON GROWING OLD

Be with me, Beauty, for the fire is dying;
My dog and I are old, too old for roving.
Man, whose young passion sets the spindrift flying,
Is soon too lame to march, too cold for loving.
I take the book and gather to the fire,
Turning old yellow leaves; minute by minute
The clock ticks to my heart. A withered wire,
Moves a thin ghost of music in the spinet.
I cannot sail your seas, I cannot wander
Your cornland, nor your hill-land, nor your valleys
Ever again, nor share the battle yonder
Where the young knight the broken squadron rallies.
Only stay quiet while my mind remembers
The beauty of fire from the beauty of embers.

Beauty, have pity! for the strong have power,
The rich their wealth, the beautiful their grace,
Summer of man its sunlight and its flower.
Spring-time of man all April in a face.
Only, as in the jostling in the Strand,
Where the mob thrusts or loiters or is loud,
The beggar with the saucer in his hand
Asks only a penny from the passing crowd,
So, from this glittering world with all its fashion,
Its fire, and play of men, its stir, its march,
Let me have wisdom, Beauty, wisdom and passion,
Bread to the soul, rain when the summers parch.
Give me but these, and though the darkness close
Even the night will blossom as the rose.

### SONNET

Flesh, I have knocked at many a dusty door,
Gone down full many a windy midnight lane,
Probed in old walls and felt along the floor,
Pressed in blind hope the lighted window-pane,
But useless all, though sometimes when the moon
Was full in heaven and the sea was full,
Along my body's alleys came a tune
Played in the tavern by the Beautiful.
Then for an instant I have felt at point
To find and seize her, whosoe'er she be,
Whether some saint whose glory doth anoint
Those whom she loves, or but a part of me,
Or something that the things not understood
Make for their uses out of flesh and blood.

### SONNET

Is there a great green commonwealth of Thought
Which ranks the yearly pageant, and decides
How Summer's royal progress shall be wrought,
By secret stir which in each plant abides?
Does rocking daffodil consent that she,
The snowdrop of wet winters, shall be first?
Does spotted cowslip with the grass agree
To hold her pride before the rattle burst?
And in the hedge what quick agreement goes,
When hawthorn blossoms redden to decay,
That Summer's pride shall come, the Summer's rose,
Before the flower be on the bramble spray?
Or is it, as with us, unresting strife,
And each consent a lucky gasp for life?

### LAUGH AND BE MERRY

Laugh and be merry, remember, better the world with a song,
Better the world with a blow in the teeth of a wrong.
Laugh, for the time is brief, a thread the length of a span.
Laugh, and be proud to belong to the old proud pageant of man.

Laugh and be merry: remember, in olden time,
God made Heaven and Earth for joy He took in a rhyme,
Made them, and filled them full with the strong red wine of His mirth,
The splendid joy of the stars: the joy of the earth.

So we must laugh and drink from the deep blue cup of the sky,
Join the jubilant song of the great stars sweeping by,
Laugh, and battle, and work, and drink of the wine outpoured
In the dear green earth, the sign of the joy of the Lord.

Laugh and be merry together, like brothers akin,
Guesting awhile in the rooms of a beautiful inn,
Glad till the dancing stops, and the lilt of the music ends.
Laugh till the game is played; and be you merry, my friends.

## THE CHOICE

The Kings go by with jeweled crowns;
Their horses gleam, their banners shake, their spears are many.
The sack of many-peopled towns
Is all their dream:
The way they take
Leaves but a ruin in the brake,
And, in the furrow that the plowmen make,
A stampless penny; a tale, a dream.

The Merchants reckon up their gold,
Their letters come, their ships arrive, their freights are glories;
The profits of their treasures sold
They tell and sum;
Their foremen drive
Their servants, starved to half-alive,
Whose labors do but make the earth a hive
Of stinking stories; a tale, a dream.

The Priests are singing in their stalls,
Their singing lifts, their incense burns, their praying clamors;
Yet God is as the sparrow falls,
The ivy drifts;
The votive urns
Are all left void when Fortune turns,
The god is but a marble for the kerns
To break with hammers; a tale, a dream.

O Beauty, let me know again
The green earth cold, the April rain, the quiet waters figuring sky,
The one star risen.
So shall I pass into the feast
Not touched by King, Merchant, or Priest;
Know the red spirit of the beast,
Be the green grain;
Escape from prison.

## THE PASSING STRANGE

Out of the earth to rest or range
Perpetual in perpetual change,
The unknown passing through the strange.

Water and saltness held together
To tread the dust and stand the weather,
And plow the field and stretch the tether,

To pass the wine-cup and be witty,
Water the sands and build the city,
Slaughter like devils and have pity,

Be red with rage and pale with lust,
Make beauty come, make peace, make
    trust,
Water and saltness mixed with dust;

Drive over earth, swim under sea,
Fly in the eagle's secrecy,
Guess where the hidden comets be;

Know all the deathy seeds that still
Queen Helen's beauty, Caesar's will,
And slay them even as they kill;

Fashion an altar for a rood,
Defile a continent with blood,
And watch a brother starve for food:

Love like a madman, shaking, blind,
Till self is burnt into a kind
Possession of another mind;

Brood upon beauty, till the grace
Of beauty with the holy face
Brings peace into the bitter place;

Prove in the lifeless granites, scan
The stars for hope, for guide, for plan;
Live as a woman or a man;

Fasten to lover or to friend,
Until the heart break at the end
The break of death that cannot mend:

Then to lie useless, helpless, still,
Down in the earth, in dark, to fill
The roots of grass or daffodil.

Down in the earth, in dark, alone,
A mockery of the ghost in bone,
The strangeness, passing the unknown.

Time will go by, that outlasts clocks,
Dawn in the thorps will rouse the cocks,
Sunset be glory on the rocks:

But it, the thing, will never heed
Even the rootling from the seed
Thrusting to suck it for its need.

✦

Since moons decay and suns decline,
How else should end this life of mine?
Water and saltness are not wine.

But in the darkest hour of night,
When even the foxes peer for sight,
The byre-cock crows; he feels the light.

So, in this water mixed with dust,
The byre-cock spirit crows from trust
That death will change because it must.

For all things change: the darkness changes,
The wandering spirits change their ranges,
The corn is gathered to the granges.

The corn is sown again, it grows;
The stars burn out, the darkness goes;
The rhythms change, they do not close.

They change, and we, who pass like foam,
Like dust blown through the streets of Rome,
Change ever, too; we have no home,

Only a beauty, only a power,
Sad in the fruit, bright in the flower,
Endlessly erring for its hour,

But gathering as we stray, a sense
Of Life, so lovely and intense,
It lingers when we wander hence,

That those who follow feel behind
Their backs, when all before is blind,
Our joy, a rampart to the mind.

## Lord Dunsany

Edward John Moreton Drax Plunkett, Lord Dunsany, the eighteenth Baron of his line, with estates in Meath, Ireland, and in Kent, was born July 24, 1878, and was educated at Eton and Sandhurst. He is best known as an author of fantastic fairy tales and still more fantastic plays. *The Gods of the Mountain* (1911) and *The Golden Doom* (1912) are highly dramatic and intensely poetic; *A Night at an Inn* (1916) is that peculiar novelty, an eerie and plausible melodrama.

Dunsany's prime quality is a highly colored imagination rich in symbolism. This symbolism, part modern, part Oriental, shows itself in situation, in the juxtaposition of the grotesque and the casual, even in the employment of curious fictitious names. *Five Plays* (1914) and *Plays of Gods and Men* (1917) include the best of Dunsany's one-acters.

After the World War, in which he served as captain in the Royal Inniskilling Fusiliers, Dunsany visited America and revised the reissue of his early tales and prose poems collected in his *The Book of Wonder,* originally published in 1912. Then followed *The Last Book of Wonder* (1916), *Unhappy Far-off Things* and *The King of Elfland's Daughter* (1924).

*Fifty Poems* (1930) is marred by too great an amount of occasional verse. Most of it seems the product of a mind whose edge is by no means dull but whose emotions are remembered in too tranquil a tranquillity. The Dunsany touch is not wholly lacking. "The Watchers," for all its resemblance to De la Mare's "The Listeners," is one of the best in the volume, and "Snow on the East Wind" is an apt and imagistic picturing of the dying down of the wind with the coming of snow.

### SNOW ON THE EAST WIND

A black horse came to visit us,
　His hooves on the hills drumming
All the way from the Caucasus,
　And was three days coming.

On his back was a lady light,
　And cruelly did she ride him.
He dropped dead at our doors by night
　As she softly stepped from astride him.

### SONGS FROM AN EVIL WOOD

#### I

There is no wrath in the stars,
　They do not rage in the sky;
I look from the evil wood
　And find myself wondering why.

Why do they not scream out
　And grapple star against star,
Seeking for blood in the wood
　As all things round me are?

They do not glare like the sky
　Or flash like the deeps of the wood;
But they shine softly on
　In their sacred solitude.

To their high, happy haunts
　Silence from us has flown,

She whom we loved of old
　And know it now she is gone.

When will she come again,
　Though for one second only?
She whom we loved is gone
　And the whole world is lonely.

#### II

Somewhere lost in the haze
　The sun goes down in the cold,
And birds in this evil wood
　Chirrup home as of old;

Chirrup, stir and are still,
　On the high twigs frozen and thin.
There is no more noise of them now,
　And the long night sets in.

Of all the wonderful things
　That I have seen in the wood
I marvel most at the birds
　And their wonderful quietude.

For a giant smites with his club
　All day the tops of the hill,
Sometimes he rests at night,
　Oftener he beats them still.

And a dwarf with a grim black mane
　Raps with repeated rage
All night in the valley below
　On the wooden walls of his cage.

And the elder giants come
  Sometimes, tramping from far
Through the weird and flickering light
  Made by an earthly star.

And the giant with his club,
  And the dwarf with rage in his breath,
And the elder giants from far,
  They are all the children of Death.

They are all abroad tonight
  And are breaking the hills with their
    brood,—
And the birds are all asleep
  Even in Plug Street Wood!

III

I met with Death in his country,
  With his scythe and his hollow eye
Walking the roads of Belgium.
  I looked and he passed me by.

Since he passed me by in Plug Street,
  In the wood of the evil name,
I shall not now lie with the heroes,
  I shall not share their fame;

I shall never be as they are,
  A name in the lands of the Free,
Since I looked on Death in Flanders
  And he did not look at me.

# Harold Monro

HAROLD MONRO was born in Brussels in 1879 and educated at Caius College, Cambridge. He described himself as "author, publisher, editor and book-seller." Monro founded The Poetry Bookshop in London in 1912, a unique establishment having as its object a practical relation between poetry and the public: it kept in stock nothing but poetry, the drama, and books connected with these subjects. His quarterly, *Poetry and Drama* (discontinued during the war and revived in 1919 as *The Chapbook*), was in a sense the organ of the younger men; and his shop, in which he lived for the last twenty years of his life except while he was in the army, became a literary center. In spite of changing fashions Monro remained an influence until his death. He died at Broadstairs, March 16, 1932.

Monro's poetry depicts the play between the world of reality and the limbo of fantasy. *Before Dawn* (1911) has little of his peculiar mysticism, but *Children of Love* (1914), *Trees* (1915) and *Strange Meetings* (1917) present, with indubitable originality, the relation of man, not only to the earth he rose from, but to the inanimate things among which he moves. Even the most whimsical poems disclose an emotional intensity beneath the skillful rhythms. Monro's kettles are as animated as his cats; his machines, domestic furniture, ordinary interiors are both surprising and natural—surprising in the revelation of what might well be their "inner selves," natural in the way their speech is communicated.

Monro has been criticized as being a poet by intention, but not a singer by intuition. Defending certain of the more determined "modernist" poets—and, by implication, himself—Monro has written, "It will be no use to say that their poetry 'does not sing.' It is not meant to. The word *Song* has been abandoned and swept out, with *Ode, Sonnet, Quatrain,* and other similar verbal lumber. The test of intellect is more important to them than tests of prosody, or tradition. The passing event and its effect on the mind is everything to them. . . . Thus they think in terms of the whole poem rather than of the single line, and thus they are often unquotable except in *extenso.*" While this is interesting (and only partially true) Monro's own poetry is at its best when intellect is subservient to imagination.

*Real Property* (1922) represents a further advance. Although Monro has not lost his whimsical appraisal of "still life," the note is graver, the implications larger. Some of the poems, as Monro states in a prefatory note, are "tainted with slight Georgian affectations." But such verses as the metaphysical "Earthliness" (too long for quotation) and the simpler poems of Part Two, four of which are reprinted in the group below, mark this poet as one of the most original though, undeservedly, one of the least popular creators of the period.

*The Earth for Sale* (1928) is a continuation and extension of the more somber speculations. Besides his poetry, Monro is the author of *Some Contemporary Poets* (1920), a set of sharply critical estimates.

### EVERY THING

Since man has been articulate,
Mechanical, improvidently wise
(Servant of Fate),
He has not understood the little cries
And foreign conversations of the small
Delightful creatures that have followed him
Not far behind;
Has failed to hear the sympathetic call
Of Crockery and Cutlery, those kind
Reposeful Teraphim
Of his domestic happiness; the Stool
He sat on, or the Door he entered through:
He has not thanked them, overbearing fool!
What is he coming to?

But you should listen to the talk of these.
Honest they are, and patient they have kept;
Served him without his Thank you or his Please . . .
I often heard
The gentle Bed, a sigh between each word,
Murmuring, before I slept.
The Candle, as I blew it, cried aloud,
Then bowed,
And in a smoky argument
Into the darkness went.
The Kettle puffed a tentacle of breath:—
"Pooh! I have boiled his water, I don't know
Why; and he always says I boil too slow.
He never calls me 'Sukie, dear,' and oh,
I wonder why I squander my desire
Sitting submissive on his kitchen fire."

Now the old Copper Basin suddenly
Rattled and tumbled from the shelf,
Bumping and crying: "I can fall by myself;

Without a woman's hand
To patronize and coax and flatter me,
I understand
The lean and poise of gravitable land."
It gave a raucous and tumultuous shout,
Twisted itself convulsively about,
Rested upon the floor, and, while I stare,
It stares and grins at me.

The old impetuous Gas above my head
Begins irascibly to flare and fret,
Wheezing into its epileptic jet,
Reminding me I ought to go to bed.

The rafters creak; an Empty-Cupboard door
Swings open; now a wild Plank of the floor
Breaks from its joist, and leaps behind my foot.
Down from the chimney, half a pound of Soot
Tumbles and lies, and shakes itself again.
The Putty cracks against the window-pane.
A piece of Paper in the basket shoves
Another piece, and toward the bottom moves.
My independent Pencil, while I write,
Breaks at the point: the ruminating Clock
Stirs all its body and begins to rock,
Warning the waiting presence of the Night,
Strikes the dead hour, and tumbles to the plain
Ticking of ordinary work again.

You do well to remind me, and I praise
Your strangely individual foreign ways.
You call me from myself to recognize
Companionship in your unselfish eyes.
I want your dear acquaintances, although
I pass you arrogantly over, throw
Your lovely sounds, and squander them along
My busy days. I'll do you no more wrong.

Purr for me, Sukie, like a faithful cat.
You, my well-trampled Boots, and you, my Hat,
Remain my friends: I feel, though I don't speak,
Your touch grow kindlier from week to week.
It well becomes our mutual happiness
To go toward the same end more or less.
There is not much dissimilarity,
Not much to choose, I know it well, in fine,
Between the purposes of you and me,
And your eventual Rubbish Heap, and mine.

## CHILDREN OF LOVE

The holy boy
Went from his mother out in the cool of day
Over the sun-parched fields
And in among the olives shining green and shining gray.

There was no sound,
No smallest voice of any shivering stream.
Poor sinless little boy,
He desired to play, and to sing; he could only sigh and dream.

Suddenly came
Running along to him naked, with curly hair,
That rogue of the lovely world,
That other beautiful child whom the virgin Venus bare.

The holy boy
Gazed with those sad blue eyes that all men know.
Impudent Cupid stood
Panting, holding an arrow and pointing his bow.

("Will you not play?
Jesus, run to him, run to him, swift for our joy.
Is he not holy, like you?
Are you afraid of his arrows, O beautiful dreaming boy?")

And now they stand
Watching one another with timid gaze;
Youth has met youth in the wood,
But holiness will not change its melancholy ways.

Cupid at last
Draws his bow and softly lets fly a dart.
Smile for a moment, sad world!—
It has grazed the white skin and drawn blood from the sorrowful heart.

Now for delight,
Cupid tosses his locks and goes wantonly near;
But the child that was born to the cross
Has let fall on his cheek, for the sadness of life a compassionate tear.

Marvelous dream!
Cupid has offered his arrows for Jesus to try;
He has offered his bow for the game,
But Jesus went weeping away, and left him there wondering why.

## STRANGE MEETINGS

### *If Suddenly a Clod of Earth*

If suddenly a clod of earth should rise,
And walk about, and breathe, and speak, and love,
How one would tremble, and in what surprise
Gasp: "Can *you* move"?

I see men walking and I always feel:
"Earth! How have you done this? What can you be?"
I can't learn how to know men, or conceal
How strange they are to me.

### A Flower Is Looking

A flower is looking through the ground,
Blinking at the April weather;
Now a child has seen the flower:
Now they go and play together.

Now it seems the flower will speak,
And will call the child its brother—
But, oh strange forgetfulness!—
They don't recognize each other.

### SOLITUDE

When you have tidied all things for the night,
And while your thoughts are fading to their sleep,
You'll pause a moment in the late firelight,
Too sorrowful to weep.

The large and gentle furniture has stood
In sympathetic silence all the day
With that old kindness of domestic wood;
Nevertheless the haunted room will say:
"Someone must be away."

The little dog rolls over half awake,
Stretches his paws, yawns, looking up at you,
Wags his tail very slightly for your sake,
That you may feel he is unhappy too.

A distant engine whistles, or the floor
Creaks, or the wandering night-wind bangs a door.

Silence is scattered like a broken glass.
The minutes prick their ears and run about,
Then one by one subside again and pass
Sedately in, monotonously out.

You bend your head and wipe away a tear.
Solitude walks one heavy step more near.

### MILK FOR THE CAT

When the tea is brought at five o'clock,
And all the neat curtains are drawn with care,
The little black cat with bright green eyes
Is suddenly purring there.

At first she pretends, having nothing to do,
She has come in merely to blink by the grate,
But, though tea may be late or the milk may be sour,
She is never late.

And presently her agate eyes
Take a soft large milky haze,
And her independent casual glance
Becomes a stiff hard gaze.

Then she stamps her claws or lifts her ears
Or twists her tail and begins to stir,
Till suddenly all her little body becomes
One breathing trembling purr.

The children eat and wriggle and laugh;
The two old ladies stroke their silk:
But the cat is grown small and thin with desire,
Transformed to a creeping lust for milk.

The white saucer like some full moon descends
At last from the clouds of the table above;
She sighs and dreams and thrills and glows,
Transfigured with love.

She nestles over the shining rim,
Buries her chin in the creamy sea;
Her tail hangs loose; each drowsy paw
Is doubled under each bending knee.

A long dim ecstasy holds her life;
Her world is an infinite shapeless white,
Till her tongue has curled the last holy drop,
Then she sinks back into the night,

Draws and dips her body to heap
Her sleepy nerves in the great arm-chair,
Lies defeated and buried deep
Three or four hours unconscious there.


DOG

O little friend, your nose is ready; you sniff,
Asking for that expected walk,
(Your nostrils full of the happy rabbit-whiff)
And almost talk.

And so the moment becomes a moving force;
Coats glide down from their pegs in the humble dark;
You scamper the stairs,
Your body informed with the scent and the track and the mark
Of stoats and weasels, moles and badgers and hares.

We are going *Out*. You know the pitch of the word,
Probing the tone of thought as it comes through fog
And reaches by devious means (half-smelt, half-heard)
The four-legged brain of a walk-ecstatic dog.

*Out* through the garden your head is already low.
You are going your walk, you know,
And your limbs will draw
Joy from the earth through the touch of your padded paw.

Now, sending a look to us behind,
Who follow slowly the track of your lovely play,
You fetch our bodies forward away from mind
Into the light and fun of your useless day.

Thus, for your walk, we took ourselves, and went
Out by the hedge, and tree, to the open ground.
You ran, in delightful strata of wafted scent,
Over the hill without seeing the view;
Beauty is hinted through primitive smells to you:
And that ultimate Beauty you track is but rarely found.

✦

Home . . . and further joy will be waiting there:
Supper full of the lovely taste of bone,
You lift up your nose again, and sniff, and stare
For the rapture known
Of the quick wild gorge of food, then the still lie-down;
While your people will talk above you in the light
Of candles, and your dreams will merge and drown
Into the bed-delicious hours of night.

### MAN CARRYING BALE

The tough hand closes gently on the load;
  Out of the mind a voice
Calls "Lift!" and the arms, remembering well their work,
  Lengthen and pause for help.
Then a slow ripple flows along the body,
While all the muscles call to one another:
  "Lift!" and the bulging bale
  Floats like a butterfly in June.

So moved the earliest carrier of bales,
  And the same watchful sun
Glowed through his body feeding it with light.
  So will the last one move,
And halt, and dip his head, and lay his load
Down, and the muscles will relax and tremble . . .
  Earth, you designed your man
Beautiful both in labor and repose.

### THE NIGHTINGALE NEAR THE HOUSE

Here is the soundless cypress on the lawn:
It listens, listens. Taller trees beyond
Listen. The moon at the unruffled pond
    Stares. And you sing, you sing.

That star-enchanted song falls through the air
From lawn to lawn down terraces of sound,
Darts in white arrows on the shadowed ground;
    And all the night you sing.

My dreams are flowers to which you are a bee
As all night long I listen, and my brain
Receives your song; then loses it again
    In moonlight on the lawn.

Now is your voice a marble high and white,
Then like a mist on fields of paradise,
Now is a raging fire, then is like ice,
    Then breaks, and it is dawn.

### CITY-STORM

The heavy sounds are over-sweet
That droop above the hooded street,
At any moment ripe to fall and lie,
And when the Wind will swagger up the town
They'll bend a moment, then will fly
All clattering down.

Troupes come and go of urchin breeze:
They flick your face or smack the trees,
Then round the corner spin and leap
With whistling cries,
Rake their rubbish in a heap
And throw it in your eyes.

(Much preparation of the earth and air
Is needed everywhere
Before that first large drop of rain can fall.)

Smells of the Sea, or inland Grass,
Come staring through the town and pass.
Brilliant old Memories drive in state
Along the way, but cannot wait;
And many a large unusual bird
Hovers across the sky, half-heard.

But listen. It is He;
At last he comes:
Gigantic tyrant panting through the street,
Slamming the windows of our little homes,

Banging the doors, knocking the chimneys down.
Oh, his loud tramp: how scornfully he can meet
Great citizens, and lash them with his sleet!
Everything will be altered in our town.
He'll wipe the film of habit clean away,
While he remains,
His cloak is over everything we do,
And the whole town complains:—

A somber scroll;
An inner room.
A crystal bowl:
Waters of gloom.
Oh, the darkened house—
Into silence creep!
The world is cold.
All people weep.

### THE HURRIER

O furrowed plaintive face,
No time for peace?
Your grim appointment will not wait?
No, our great earthly clock
Ticks through your spine, and locomotion wags
An angry tail.
Quick, do not miss the toiling trailing tram.
Hurry, or you are lost, for anywhere
Hunger may lurk and leer.
You may have been elected, mid so many,
To be his prey,
Even today.
On horned imagination drive your limbs.
It will need your whole life to be at peace:
Then all appointments cease.
But now you neither have the time for death,
Nor time conveniently to draw your breath.

# W. W. Gibson

W(ILFRID) W(ILSON) GIBSON was born in 1880 at Hexham, Northumberland, and, by his fiftieth year, was the author of some twenty-two books of poems and five volumes of poetic plays and dialogues. The first five or six of these were pseudo-Tennysonian, imitative in manner and sentimental in tone. Their titles give the key: *Urlyn the Harper* (1902), *The Queen's Vigil* (1902), *The Golden Helm* (1903), *The Nets of Love* (1905).

With *Daily Bread* (1910), *Fires* (1912), and *Borderlands* (1914) Gibson executed a complete right-about-face and, with dramatic brevity, wrote a series of poems mirroring the dreams, pursuits, and fears of common humanity. *Thorough-fares* (1914) marks an advance in technique and power. In *Livelihood* (1917) Gibson seems to be theatricalizing and merely exploiting his working-people, yet several of his later lyrics recapture the quality of such poems as "The Old Man," "The Stone" and "The Machine." *Hill-Tracks* (1918) attempts to hold (as Edward Thomas actually did hold) the beauty of village-names through the glamor of the English countryside. *Neighbors* (1920) again takes up the strain of a somewhat too conscious poeticizing of the casual.

Gibson's later work suffers from his facility; a thinning out of power, even of feeling, is evident in *Krindlesyke* (1922), *Kestrel Edge* (1924) and *I Heard a Sailor* (1925). The best of Gibson is in the first *Collected Poems* (1923), a further *Collected Poems, 1905-1925,* having been published in 1926.

### PRELUDE

As one, at midnight, wakened by the call
Of golden-plovers in their seaward flight,
Who lies and listens, as the clear notes fall
Through tingling silence of the frosty night—
Who lies and listens, till the last note fails,
And then, in fancy, faring with the flock
Far over slumbering hills and dreaming dales,
Soon hears the surges break on reef and rock;
And, hearkening, till all sense of self is drowned
Within the mightier music of the deep,
No more remembers the sweet piping sound
That startled him from dull, undreaming sleep;
So I, first waking from oblivion, heard,
With heart that kindled to the call of song,
The voice of young life, fluting like a bird,
And echoed that light lilting; till, ere long,
Lured onward by that happy, singing-flight,
I caught the stormy summons of the sea,
And dared the restless deeps that, day and night,
Surge with the life-song of humanity.

### THE STONE

"And will you cut a stone for him,
To set above his head?
And will you cut a stone for him—
A stone for him?" she said.

Three days before, a splintered rock
Had struck her lover dead—
Had struck him in the quarry dead,

Where, careless of the warning call,
He loitered, while the shot was fired—
A lively stripling, brave and tall,
And sure of all his heart desired . . .
A flash, a shock,
A rumbling fall . . .
And, broken 'neath the broken rock,
A lifeless heap, with face of clay;
And still as any stone he lay,
With eyes that saw the end of all.

I went to break the news to her;
And I could hear my own heart beat
With dread of what my lips might say
But, some poor fool had sped before;
And flinging wide her father's door,
Had blurted out the news to her,
Had struck her lover dead for her,
Had struck the girl's heart dead in her,
Had struck life lifeless, at a word,
And dropped it at her feet:
Then hurried on his witless way,
Scarce knowing she had heard.

And when I came, she stood alone,
A woman turned to stone:
And, though no word at all she said,
I knew that all was known.
Because her heart was dead,
She did not sigh nor moan,
His mother wept:
She could not weep.
Her lover slept:
She could not sleep.
Three days, three nights,
She did not stir:
Three days, three nights,
Were one to her,
Who never closed her eyes
From sunset to sunrise,
From dawn to evenfall:
Her tearless, staring eyes,
That seeing naught, saw all.

The fourth night when I came from work,
I found her at my door.
"And will you cut a stone for him?"
She said: and spoke no more:
But followed me, as I went in,
And sank upon a chair;
And fixed her gray eyes on my face,
With still, unseeing stare.
And, as she waited patiently,
I could not bear to feel

Those still, gray eyes that followed me,
Those eyes that plucked the heart from me,
Those eyes that sucked the breath from me
And curdled the warm blood in me,
Those eyes that cut me to the bone,
And pierced my marrow like cold steel.

And so I rose, and sought a stone;
And cut it, smooth and square:
And, as I worked, she sat and watched,
Beside me, in her chair.
Night after night, by candlelight,
I cut her lover's name:
Night after night, so still and white,
And like a ghost she came;
And sat beside me in her chair;
And watched with eyes aflame.

She eyed each stroke;
And hardly stirred:
She never spoke
A single word:
And not a sound or murmur broke
The quiet, save the mallet-stroke.

With still eyes ever on my hands,
With eyes that seemed to burn my hands,
My wincing, overwearied hands,
She watched, with bloodless lips apart,
And silent, indrawn breath:
And every stroke my chisel cut,
Death cut still deeper in her heart:
The two of us were chiseling,
Together, I and death.

And when at length the job was done,
And I had laid the mallet by,
As if, at last, her peace were won,
She breathed his name; and, with a sigh,
Passed slowly through the open door:
And never crossed my threshold more.

Next night I labored late, alone,
To cut her name upon the stone.

## SIGHT

By the lamplit stall I loitered, feasting my eyes
On colors ripe and rich for the heart's desire—
Tomatoes, redder than Krakatoa's fire,
Oranges like old sunsets over Tyre,
And apples golden-green as the glades of Paradise.

And as I lingered, lost in divine delight,
My heart thanked God for the goodly gift of sight
And all youth's lively senses keen and quick . . .
When suddenly, behind me in the night,
I heard the tapping of a blind man's stick.

# Alfred Noyes

ALFRED NOYES was born at Staffordshire, September 16, 1880, one of the few contemporary poets who have been fortunate enough to write a kind of poetry that is not only readable but extraordinarily saleable.

His first book, *The Loom of Years* (1902), was published when he was only 22 years old, and *Poems* (1904) emphasized the promise of this first publication. Swinburne, grown old and living in retirement, was so struck with Noyes's talent that he had the young poet out to read to him. Unfortunately, Noyes never developed his gifts as deeply as his admirers expected. His poetry, extremely straightforward and rhythmical, degenerated too often into sentimentalities and cheap tirades; the later work attempted to express programs and profundities far beyond Noyes's power.

What is most appealing about his best verse is its ease and heartiness; this singer's gift lies in the almost personal bond established between the poet and his public. It may be said that many people have such a good time reading his vivacious lines because Noyes had such a good time writing them. Rhyme in a thumping rhythm seems to be not merely his trade but his morning exercise. Noyes's own relish quickens the glees and catches like *Forty Singing Seamen* (1907), the lusty choruses in *Tales of the Mermaid Tavern* (1913), the seemingly inspired nonsense of the earlier *Forest of Wild Thyme* (1905).

The least popular work of Noyes is, as a unified product, his most remarkable performance. It is an epic in twelve books of blank verse, *Drake* (1908), a pageant of the sea and England's drama upon it. It is a spirited echo of the maritime Elizabethans, a vivid orchestral work interspersed with lyric passages and brisk songs. The companion volume, an attempted reconstruction of the literary phase of the same period, is less successful; but these *Tales of the Mermaid Tavern* (which introduce Shakespeare, Marlowe, Drayton, Raleigh, Ben Jonson, and other immortals) are colorful, if somewhat too insistently rollicking and smoothly lilting.

Noyes's eight volumes were assembled in 1913 and published in two books of *Collected Poems*. The third volume of his rapidly accumulating *Collected Poems* appeared in 1920, the fourth in 1927. In 1922 Noyes began *The Torch-Bearers*, "An Epic Trilogy," a sort of outline of man's accomplishment rendered in verse, which was cruelly parodied by E. V. Knox in "The Steam-Givers."

Besides his verse, Noyes has written several volumes of prose. *Some Aspects of Modern Poetry* (1924) is a critical study; *The Sun Cure* (1929) is a novel; both volumes are marred by Noyes's petulant and often irrelevant gibes at modern poetry.

Although most of his smooth-running rhymes seemed doomed to rush to an early death—are, in fact, already extinct—Noyes will remain a poet pleasant to read because of his "Sherwood," the lilt of "The Barrel-Organ," the galloping "The Highwayman" and a handful of other ballads.

### SHERWOOD

Sherwood in the twilight, is Robin Hood awake?
Gray and ghostly shadows are gliding through the brake;
Shadows of the dappled deer, dreaming of the morn,
Dreaming of a shadowy man that winds a shadowy horn.

Robin Hood is here again: all his merry thieves
Hear a ghostly bugle-note shivering through the leaves,
Calling as he used to call, faint and far away,
In Sherwood, in Sherwood, about the break of day.

Merry, merry England has kissed the lips of June:
All the wings of fairyland were here beneath the moon;
Like a flight of rose-leaves fluttering in a mist
Of opal and ruby and pearl and amethyst.

Merry, merry England is waking as of old,
With eyes of blither hazel and hair of brighter gold:
For Robin Hood is here again beneath the bursting spray
In Sherwood, in Sherwood, about the break of day.

Love is in the greenwood building him a house
Of wild rose and hawthorn and honeysuckle boughs;
Love is in the greenwood: dawn is in the skies;
And Marian is waiting with a glory in her eyes.

Hark! The dazzled laverock climbs the golden steep:
Marian is waiting: is Robin Hood asleep?
Round the fairy grass-rings frolic elf and fay,
In Sherwood, in Sherwood, about the break of day.

Oberon, Oberon, rake away the gold,
Rake away the red leaves, roll away the mold,
Rake away the gold leaves, roll away the red,
And wake Will Scarlet from his leafy forest bed.

Friar Tuck and Little John are riding down together
With quarter-staff and drinking-can and gray goose-feather;
The dead are coming back again; the years are rolled away
In Sherwood, in Sherwood, about the break of day.

Softly over Sherwood the south wind blows;
All the heart of England hid in every rose
Hears across the greenwood the sunny whisper leap,
Sherwood in the red dawn, is Robin Hood asleep?

Hark, the voice of England wakes him as of old
And, shattering the silence with a cry of brighter gold,
Bugles in the greenwood echo from the steep,
*Sherwood in the red dawn, is Robin Hood asleep?*

Where the deer are gliding down the shadowy glen
All across the glades of fern he calls his merry men;
Doublets of the Lincoln green glancing through the May,
In Sherwood, in Sherwood, about the break of day;

Calls them and they answer: from aisles of oak and ash
Rings the *Follow! Follow!* and the boughs begin to crash;
The ferns begin to flutter and the flowers begin to fly;
And through the crimson dawning the robber band goes by.

*Robin! Robin! Robin!* All his merry thieves
Answer as the bugle-note shivers through the leaves:
Calling as he used to call, faint and far away,
In Sherwood, in Sherwood, about the break of day.

### THE BARREL-ORGAN

There's a barrel-organ caroling across a golden street
    In the City as the sun sinks low;
And the music's not immortal; but the world has made it sweet
    And fulfilled it with the sunset glow;
And it pulses through the pleasures of the City and the pain
    That surround the singing organ like a large eternal light;
And they've given it a glory and a part to play again
    In the Symphony that rules the day and night.
And now it's marching onward through the realms of old romance,
    And trolling out a fond familiar tune,
And now it's roaring cannon down to fight the King of France,
    And now it's prattling softly to the moon.
And all around the organ there's a sea without a shore
    Of human joys and wonders and regrets;
To remember and to recompense the music evermore
    For what the cold machinery forgets . . .

        Yes; as the music changes,
            Like a prismatic glass,
        It takes the light and ranges
            Through all the moods that pass:
        Dissects the common carnival
            Of passions and regrets,
        And gives the world a glimpse of all
            The colors it forgets.

        And there *La Traviata* sighs
            Another sadder song;
        And there *Il Trovatore* cries
            A tale of deeper wrong;

And bolder knights to battle go
With sword and shield and lance,
Than ever here on earth below
Have whirled into—a dance!—

Go down to Kew in lilac-time, in lilac-time, in lilac-time;
Go down to Kew in lilac-time (it isn't far from London!)
And you shall wander hand in hand with Love in summer's wonderland;
Go down to Kew in lilac-time (it isn't far from London!)

The cherry-trees are seas of bloom and soft perfume and sweet perfume,
The cherry-trees are seas of bloom (and oh, so near to London!)
And there they say, when dawn is high and all the world's a blaze of sky
The cuckoo, though he's very shy, will sing a song for London.

The nightingale is rather rare and yet they say you'll hear him there
At Kew, at Kew in lilac-time (and oh, so near to London!)
The linnet and the throstle, too, and after dark the long halloo
And golden-eyed *tu-whit, tu-whoo* of owls that ogle London.

For Noah hardly knew a bird of any kind that isn't heard
At Kew, at Kew in lilac-time (and oh, so near to London!)
And when the rose begins to pout and all the chestnut spires are out
You'll hear the rest without a doubt, all chorusing for London:—

*Come down to Kew in lilac-time, in lilac-time, in lilac-time;*
*Come down to Kew in lilac-time (it isn't far from London!)*
*And you shall wander hand in hand with Love in summer's wonderland;*
*Come down to Kew in lilac-time (it isn't far from London!)*

And then the troubadour begins to thrill the golden street,
In the City as the sun sinks low;
And in all the gaudy busses there are scores of weary feet
Marking time, sweet time, with a dull mechanic beat,
And a thousand hearts are plunging to a love they'll never meet,
Through the meadows of the sunset, through the poppies and the wheat,
In the land where the dead dreams go.

Verdi, Verdi, when you wrote *Il Trovatore* did you dream
Of the City when the sun sinks low,
Of the organ and the monkey and the many-colored stream
On the Piccadilly pavement, of the myriad eyes that seem
To be litten for a moment with a wild Italian gleam
As *A che la morte* parodies the world's eternal theme
And pulses with the sunset-glow?

There's a thief, perhaps, that listens with a face of frozen stone
In the City as the sun sinks low;
There's a portly man of business with a balance of his own,
There's a clerk and there's a butcher of a soft reposeful tone,
And they're all of them returning to the heavens they have known:
They are crammed and jammed in busses and—they're each of them alone
In the land where the dead dreams go.

There's a laborer that listens to the voices of the dead
   In the City as the sun sinks low;
And his hand begins to tremble and his face is rather red
As he sees a loafer watching him and—there he turns his head
And stares into the sunset where his April love is fled,
For he hears her softly singing and his lonely soul is led
   Through the land where the dead dreams go . . .


There's a barrel-organ caroling across a golden street
   In the City as the sun sinks low;
Though the music's only Verdi there's a world to make it sweet
Just as yonder yellow sunset where the earth and heaven meet
Mellows all the sooty City! Hark, a hundred thousand feet
Are marching on to glory through the poppies and the wheat
   In the land where the dead dreams go.


      So it's Jeremiah, Jeremiah,
        What have you to say
      When you meet the garland girls
        Tripping on their way?


      All around my gala hat
        I wear a wreath of roses
      (A long and lonely year it is
        I've waited for the May!)
      If anyone should ask you,
        The reason why I wear it is—
      My own love, my true love, is coming home today.


And it's buy a bunch of violets for the lady
   (*It's lilac-time in London; it's lilac-time in London!*)
Buy a bunch of violets for the lady;
   While the sky burns blue above:


On the other side the street you'll find it shady
   (*It's lilac-time in London; it's lilac-time in London!*)
But buy a bunch of violets for the lady,
   And tell her she's your own true love.


There's a barrel-organ caroling across a golden street
   In the City as the sun sinks glittering and slow;
And the music's not immortal; but the world has made it sweet
And enriched it with the harmonies that make a song complete
In the deeper heavens of music where the night and morning meet,
   As it dies into the sunset glow;
And it pulses through the pleasures of the City and the pain
   That surround the singing organ like a large eternal light,
And they've given it a glory and a part to play again
   In the Symphony that rules the day and night.

And there, as the music changes,
 The song runs round again;
Once more it turns and ranges
 Through all its joy and pain:
Dissects the common carnival
 Of passions and regrets;
And the wheeling world remembers all
 The wheeling song forgets.

Once more *La Traviata* sighs
 Another sadder song:
Once more *Il Trovatore* cries
 A tale of deeper wrong;
Once more the knights to battle go
 With sword and shield and lance
Till once, once more, the shattered foe
 Has whirled into—a dance!

*Come down to Kew in lilac-time, in lilac-time, in lilac-time;*
 *Come down to Kew in lilac-time (it isn't far from London!)*
*And you shall wander hand in hand with Love in summer's wonderland,*
 *Come down to Kew in lilac-time (it isn't far from London!)*

### EPILOGUE

(*from "The Flower of Old Japan"*)

Carol, every violet has
Heaven for a looking-glass!

Every little valley lies
Under many-clouded skies;
Every little cottage stands
Girt about with boundless lands.
Every little glimmering pond
Claims the mighty shores beyond—
Shores no seaman ever hailed,
Seas no ship has ever sailed.

All the shores when day is done
Fade into the setting sun,
So the story tries to teach
More than can be told in speech.

Beauty is a fading flower,
Truth is but a wizard's tower,
Where a solemn death-bell tolls,
And a forest round it rolls.
We have come by curious ways
To the light that holds the days;
We have sought in haunts of fear
For that all-enfolding sphere:
And lo! it was not far, but near.
We have found, O foolish-fond,
The shore that has no shore beyond.
Deep in every heart it lies
With its untranscended skies;
For what heaven should bend above
Hearts that own the heaven of love?

Carol, Carol, we have come
Back to heaven, back to home.

# Padraic Colum

PADRAIC COLUM was born at Longford, Ireland (in the same county as Oliver Goldsmith), December 8, 1881, and was educated at the local schools. At twenty he was a member of the group that created the Irish National Theatre.

Colum began as a dramatist with *Broken Soil* (1904), *The Land* (1905), *Thomas Muskerry* (1910), and this early dramatic influence has colored much of his work; in fact, his best poetry is in the form of dramatic lyrics. *Wild Earth,* his most quoted collection of verse, first appeared in 1909, and an amplified edition of it was published in America in 1916. Colum himself had come to America (where he has lived ever since) shortly before that date; his *Dramatic Poems* appeared in 1922.

*Creatures* (1927), utterly different in theme from its predecessors, is held together by the same gift of condensation. Though Colum's animals are less obviously divine than his gods, his treatment of them is no less devotional. He combines an innocence of vision with wisdom of experience.

As a recorder, Colum has been equally successful as an autobiographer (*My Irish Year,* 1912), a folk-lorist (*Tales and Legends of Hawaii,* 1924, *The Bright Islands,* 1925) and a deservedly popular adapter of tales for children.

## THE PLOWER

Sunset and silence! A man: around him earth savage, earth broken;
Beside him two horses—a plow!

Earth savage, earth broken, the brutes, the dawn man there in the sunset,
And the Plow that is twin to the Sword, that is founder of cities!

"Brute-tamer, plow-maker, earth-breaker! Can'st hear?
  "There are ages between us.
"Is it praying you are as you stand there alone in the sunset?

"Surely our sky-born gods can be naught to you, earth-child and earth-master?
"Surely your thoughts are of Pan, or of Wotan, or Dana?

"Yet, why give thought to the gods? Has Pan led your brutes where they stumble?
"Has Dana numbed pain of the child-bed, or Wotan put hands to your plow?

"What matter your foolish reply! O man, standing lone and bowed earthward,
"Your task is a day near its close. Give thanks to the night-giving God."

✦

Slowly the darkness falls, the broken lands blend with the savage;
The brute-tamer stands by the brutes, a head's breadth only above them.

A head's breadth? Aye, but therein is hell's depth, and the height up to heaven,
And the thrones of the gods and their halls, their chariots, purples, and splendors.

## AN OLD WOMAN OF THE ROADS

O, to have a little house!
To own the hearth and stool and all!
The heaped-up sods upon the fire,
The pile of turf against the wall!

To have a clock with weights and chains
And pendulum swinging up and down!
A dresser filled with shining delph,
Speckled and white and blue and brown!

I could be busy all the day
Clearing and sweeping hearth and floor,
And fixing on their shelf again
My white and blue and speckled store!

I could be quiet there at night
Beside the fire and by myself,
Sure of a bed and loth to leave
The ticking clock and the shining delph!

Och! but I'm weary of mist and dark,
And roads where there's never a house nor
    bush,
And tired I am of bog and road,
And the crying wind and the lonesome hush!

And I am praying to God on high,
And I am praying Him night and day,
For a little house—a house of my own—
Out of the wind's and the rain's way.

## INTERIOR

The little moths are creeping
Across the cottage pane;
On the floor the chickens gather,
And they make talk and complain.

And she sits by the fire
Who has reared so many men;
Her voice is low like the chickens'
With the things she says again.

"The sons that come back do be restless,
They search for the thing to say;
Then they take thought like the swallows,
And the morrow brings them away.

"In the old, old days, upon Innish,
The fields were lucky and bright,
And if you lay down you'd be covered
By the grass of one soft night."

She speaks and the chickens gather,
And they make talk and complain,
While the little moths are creeping
Across the cottage pane.

## A DROVER

To Meath of the pastures,
From wet hills by the sea,
Through Leitrim and Longford,
Go my cattle and me.

I hear in the darkness
Their slipping and breathing—
I name them the by-ways
They're to pass without heeding;

Then the wet, winding roads,
Brown bogs with black water;
And my thoughts on white ships
And the King o' Spain's daughter.

Oh! farmer, strong farmer!
You can spend at the fair;
But your face you must turn
To your crops and your care.

And soldiers, red soldiers!
You've seen many lands;
But you walk two by two,
And by captain's commands.

Oh! the smell of the beasts,
The wet wind in the morn;
And the proud and hard earth
Never broken for corn;

And the crowds at the fair,
The herds loosened and blind,
Loud words and dark faces
And the wild blood behind.

(Oh! strong men, with your best
I would strive breast to breast,

I could quiet your herds
With my words, with my words.)

I will bring you my kine,
Where there's grass to the knee;
But you'll think of scant croppings
Harsh with salt of the sea.

## WILD ASS

The wild ass lounges, legs struck out
In vagrom unconcern:
The tombs of Achaemenian kings
Are for those hooves to spurn.

And all of rugged Tartary
Lies with him on the ground.
The Tartary that knows no awe
That has nor ban nor bound.

The wild horse from the herd is plucked
To bear a saddle's weight;
The boar is one keeps covert, and
The wolf runs with a mate.

But he's the solitary of space,
Curbless and unbeguiled;
The only being that bears a heart
Not recreant to the wild.

# Joseph Campbell

## (SEOSAMH MacCATHMHAOIL)

JOSEPH CAMPBELL was born in Belfast in 1881, and is not only a poet but an artist; he made all the illustrations for *The Rushlight* (1906), a volume of his own poems. Writing under the Gaelic form of his name, he has published half a dozen books of verse, the most striking of which is *The Mountainy Singer,* first published in Dublin in 1909. *Judgment* (1912), a play in two acts, was followed by a collection of racy poems, *Earth of Cualann* (1917).

### I AM THE MOUNTAINY SINGER

I am the mountainy singer—
The voice of the peasant's dream,
The cry of the wind on the wooded hill,
The leap of the fish in the stream.

Quiet and love I sing—
The carn on the mountain crest,
The *cailin* in her lover's arms,
The child at its mother's breast.

Beauty and peace I sing—
The fire on the open hearth,
The *cailleach* spinning at her wheel,
The plow in the broken earth.

Travail and pain I sing—
The bride on the childing bed,

The dark man laboring at his rhymes,
The ewe in the lambing shed.

Sorrow and death I sing—
The canker come on the corn,
The fisher lost in the mountain loch,
The cry at the mouth of morn.

No other life I sing,
For I am sprung of the stock
That broke the hilly land for bread,
And built the nest in the rock!

### THE OLD WOMAN

As a white candle
In a holy place,
So is the beauty
Of an aged face.

As the spent radiance
Of the winter sun,
So is a woman
With her travail done,

Her brood gone from her,
And her thoughts as still
As the waters
Under a ruined mill.

# John Freeman

JOHN FREEMAN, born in 1881 in London, published several volumes of pleasantly descriptive verse. His first volume appeared in 1909; since then, his two most distinctive books are *Stone Trees* (1916) and *Memories of Childhood* (1919). A collected edition of the poems from the previous volumes was published in 1920 under the title *Poems New and Old*. In the same year, Freeman was awarded the Hawthornden prize. He had written a great quantity of love lyrics, but Freeman's landscapes are more distinctive than his subjective pieces. Even his pastorals are too patterned, too perfunctory; instead of being rural they are merely suburban.

The best of Freeman's preceding eleven volumes of poems were gathered in *Collected Poems* (1928). He was also the author of several novels and studies, the most interesting of which is *Herman Melville* (1926). *English Portraits and Essays* appeared in 1924, a volume that promised a mature critical faculty, cut off by Freeman's sudden death in 1929.

### STONE TREES

Last night a sword-light in the sky
Flashed a swift terror on the dark.
In that sharp light the fields did lie
Naked and stone-like; each tree stood
Like a tranced woman, bound and stark.
    Far off the wood
With darkness ridged the riven dark.

And cows astonished stared with fear,
And sheep crept to the knees of cows,
And conies to their burrows slid,
And rooks were still in rigid boughs,
And all things else were still or hid.
    From all the wood
Came but the owl's hoot, ghostly, clear.

In that cold trance the earth was held
It seemed an age, or time was nought.
Sure never from that stone-like field
Sprang golden corn, nor from those chill
Gray granite trees was music wrought.
    In all the wood
Even the tall poplar hung stone still.

It seemed an age, or time was none . . .
Slowly the earth heaved out of sleep
And shivered, and the trees of stone
Bent and sighed in the gusty wind,
And rain swept as birds flocking sweep.
    Far off the wood
Rolled the slow thunders on the wind.

From all the wood came no brave bird,
No song broke through the close-fall'n night,
Nor any sound from cowering herd:
Only a dog's long lonely howl
When from the window poured pale light.
    And from the wood
The hoot came ghostly of the owl.

### THE FUGITIVE

In the hush of early even
The clouds came flocking over,
Till the last wind fell from heaven
    And no bird cried.

Darkly the clouds were flocking,
Shadows moved and deepened,
Then paused; the poplar's rocking
    Ceased; the light hung still

Like a painted thing, and deadly.
Then from the cloud's side flickered
Sharp lightning, thrusting madly
    At the cowering fields.

Thrice the fierce cloud lighten'd
Down the hill slow thunder trembled;
Day in her cave grew frightened,
    Crept away, and died.

### THE WAKERS

The joyous morning ran and kissed the grass
And drew his fingers through her sleeping hair,
    And cried, "Before thy flowers are well awake
    Rise, and the lingering darkness from thee shake.

"Before the daisy and the sorrel buy
Their brightness back from that close-folding night,
    Come, and the shadows from thy bosom shake,
    Awake from thy thick sleep, awake, awake!"

Then the grass of that mounded meadow stirred
Above the Roman bones that may not stir
    Though joyous morning whispered, shouted, sang:
    The grass stirred as that happy music rang.

O, what a wondrous rustling everywhere!
The steady shadows shook and thinned and died,
    The shining grass flashed brightness back for brightness,
    And sleep was gone, and there was heavenly lightness.

As if she had found wings, light as the wind,
The grass flew, bent with the wind, from east to west,
    Chased by one wild gray cloud, and flashing all
    Her dews for happiness to hear morning call. . . .

But even as I stepped out the brightness dimmed,
I saw the fading edge of all delight.
    The sober morning waked the drowsy herds,
    And there was the old scolding of the birds.

# Lascelles Abercrombie

L ASCELLES ABERCROMBIE was born in 1881, at Ashton-upon-Mersey, near Manchester.
He was educated at Malcolm College and Manchester University. After that, he
engaged in a variety of professions; he taught literature at the University in Liverpool, and in London.

Like Masefield, Abercrombie gained his reputation rapidly; unknown until 1909,
upon the publication of *Interludes and Poems,* he was recognized as one of the
true metaphysical poets of his period. *Emblems of Love* (1912), the ripest collection
of his dialogues, justified the enthusiasm of his admirers.

Many of Abercrombie's poems, the best of which are too long to quote, are founded on scriptural themes, but his blank verse is biblical neither in mood nor in manner. It is the undercurrent rather than the surface of his verse which moves with a strong religious conviction. Abercrombie's images are daring and brilliant; his lines, sometimes too closely packed, glow with an intensity that is spiritual and yet recognizably human.

As a dramatist, Abercrombie has achieved a series of literary but scarcely popular successes with *Deborah* (1914), *Four Short Plays* (1921), and *Phoenix* (1923), brilliantly written though not eminently actable pieces. His knotted, almost tortured, style presents many difficulties to the performers as well as to audiences; but, once the speech is mastered, a swift intellectuality and a dramatic sense are disclosed.

It is only the superficially dense style which keeps Abercrombie an unpopular, almost an unread, poet. Actually his diction, though thickened, is extraordinarily flexible; his characters, if overburdened with analysis, are vividly imagined; and, as Edward Thomas wrote, "the march or leap or stagger or hesitation of the syllables correspond to varying emotions with thrilling delicacy."

It seems a pity that the poet who conceived the ecstatic action of *The Sale of St. Thomas* (1911), the racing vigor of "Witchcraft: New Style," and the brilliant couplets of "Epilogue," should turn away from poetry. Since 1916, Abercrombie has concerned himself (with the exception of two plays) almost entirely with prose. Since 1914 he has written no less than six volumes about prosody and the technique of verse; *The Theory of Poetry* (1924) is one of the most illuminating books on the subject.

### SONG

#### (from "Judith")

Balkis was in her marble town,
And shadow over the world came down.
Whiteness of walls, towers and piers,
That all day dazzled eyes to tears,
Turned from being white-golden flame,
And like the deep-sea blue became.
Balkis into her garden went;
Her spirit was in discontent
Like a torch in restless air.
Joylessly she wandered there,
And saw her city's azure white
Lying under the great night,
Beautiful as the memory
Of a worshiping world would be
In the mind of a god, in the hour
When he must kill his outward power;
And, coming to a pool where trees
Grew in double greeneries,
Saw herself, as she went by
The water, walking beautifully,
And saw the stars shine in the glance
Of her eyes, and her own fair countenance

Passing, pale and wonderful,
Across the night that filled the pool.
And cruel was the grief that played
With the queen's spirit; and she said:
"What do I here, reigning alone?
For to be unloved is to be alone.
There is no man in all my land
Dare my longing understand;
The whole folk like a peasant bows
Lest its look should meet my brows
And be harmed by this beauty of mine.
I burn their brains as I were sign
Of God's beautiful anger sent
To master them with punishment
Of beauty that must pour distress
On hearts grown dark with ugliness.
But it is I am the punisht one.
Is there no man, is there none,
In whom my beauty will but move
The lust of a delighted love;
In whom some spirit of God so thrives
That we may wed our lonely lives?
Is there no man, is there none?"—
She said, "I will go to Solomon."

EPILOGUE

What shall we do for Love these days?
How shall we make an altar-blaze
To smite the horny eyes of men
With the renown of our Heaven,
And to the unbelievers prove
Our service to our dear god, Love?
What torches shall we lift above
The crowd that pushes through the mire,
To amaze the dark heads with strange fire?
I should think I were much to blame,
If never I held some fragrant flame
Above the noises of the world,
And openly 'mid men's hurrying stares,
Worshipt before the sacred fears
That are like flashing curtains furl'd
Across the presence of our lord Love.
Nay, would that I could fill the gaze
Of the whole earth with some great praise
Made in a marvel for men's eyes,
Some tower of glittering masonries,
Therein such a spirit flourishing
Men should see what my heart can sing:
All that Love hath done to me
Built into stone, a visible glee;
Marble carried to gleaming height
As moved aloft by inward delight;
Not as with toil of chisels hewn,
But seeming poised in a mighty tune.

For of all those who have been known
To lodge with our kind host, the sun,
I envy one for just one thing:
In Cordova of the Moors
There dwelt a passion-minded King,
Who set great bands of marble-hewers
To fashion his heart's thanksgiving
In a tall palace, shapen so
All the wondering world might know
The joy he had of his Moorish lass.
His love, that brighter and larger was
Than the starry places, into firm stone
He sent, as if the stone were glass
Fired and into beauty blown.
    Solemn and invented gravely
In its bulk the fabric stood,
Even as Love, that trusteth bravely
In its own exceeding good
To be better than the waste
Of time's devices; grandly spaced,

Seriously the fabric stood.
But over it all a pleasure went
Of carven delicate ornament,
Wreathing up like ravishment,
Mentioning in sculptures twined
The blitheness Love hath in his mind;
And like delighted senses were
The windows, and the columns there
Made the following sight to ache
As the heart that did them make.
Well I can see that shining song
Flowering there, the upward throng
Of porches, pillars and windowed walls,
Spires like piercing panpipe calls,
Up to the roof's snow-cloudy flight;
All glancing in the Spanish light
White as water of arctic tides,
Save an amber dazzle on sunny sides.
You had said, the radiant sheen
Of that palace might have been
A young god's fantasy, ere he came
His serious worlds and suns to frame;
Such an immortal passion
Quiver'd among the slim hewn stone.
And in the nights it seemed a jar
Cut in the substance of a star,
Wherein a wine, that will be poured
Some time for feasting Heaven, was stored.
    But within this fretted shell,
The wonder of Love made visible,
The King a private gentle mood
There placed, of pleasant quietude.
For right amidst there was a court,
Where always muskèd silences
Listened to water and to trees;
And herbage of all fragrant sort,—
Lavender, lad's love, rosemary,
Basil, tansy, centaury,—
Was the grass of that orchard, hid
Love's amazements all amid.
Jarring the air with rumor cool,
Small fountains played into a pool
With sound as soft as the barley's hiss
When its beard just sprouting is;
Whence a young stream, that trod on moss,
Prettily rippled the court across.
And in the pool's clear idleness,
Moving like dreams through happiness,
Shoals of small bright fishes were;
In and out weed-thickets bent
Perch and carp, and sauntering went

With mounching jaws and eyes a-stare;
Or on a lotus leaf would crawl,
A brinded loach to bask and sprawl,
Tasting the warm sun ere it dipt
Into the water; but quick as fear
Back his shining brown head slipt
To crouch on the gravel of his lair,
Where the cooled sunbeams broke in wrack,
Spilt shatter'd gold about his back.
　　So within that green-veiled air,
Within that white-walled quiet, where
Innocent water thought aloud,—
Childish prattle that must make
The wise sunlight with laughter shake
On the leafage overbowed,—
Often the King and his love-lass
Let the delicious hours pass.
All the outer world could see
Graved and sawn amazingly
Their love's delighted riotise,
Fixt in marble for all men's eyes;
But only these twain could abide
In the cool peace that withinside

Thrilling desire and passion dwelt;
They only knew the still meaning spelt
By Love's flaming script, which is
God's word written in ecstasies.
　　And where is now that palace gone,
All the magical skill'd stone,
All the dreaming towers wrought
By Love as if no more than thought
The unresisting marble was?
How could such a wonder pass?
Ah, it was but built in vain
Against the stupid horns of Rome,
That pusht down into the common loam
The loveliness that shone in Spain.
But we have raised it up again!
A loftier palace, fairer far,
Is ours, and one that fears no war.
Safe in marvelous walls we are;
Wondering sense like builded fires,
High amazement of desires,
Delight and certainty of love,
Closing around, roofing above
Our unapproacht and perfect hour
Within the splendors of love's power.

## WOMAN'S BEAUTY

### (from "Vashti")

What thing shall be held up to woman's beauty?
Where are the bounds of it? Yea, what is all
The world, but an awning scaffolded amid
The waste perilous Eternity, to lodge
This Heaven-wander'd princess, woman's beauty?
The East and West kneel down to thee, the North
And South; and all for thee their shoulders bear
The load of fourfold space. As yellow morn
Runs on the slippery waves of the spread sea,
Thy feet are on the griefs and joys of men
That shine to be thy causey. Out of tears
Indeed, and blitheness, murder and lust and love,
Whatever has been passionate in clay,
Thy flesh was tempered. Behold in thy body
The yearnings of all men measured and told,
Insatiate endless agonies of desire
Given thy flesh, the meaning of thy shape!
What beauty is there, but thou makest it?
How is earth good to look on, woods and fields,
The season's garden, and the courageous hills,
All this green raft of earth moored in the seas?
The manner of the sun to ride the air,

The stars God has imagined for the night?
What's this behind them that we cannot near,
Secret still on the point of being blabbed,
The ghost in the world that flies from being named?
Where do they get their beauty from, all these?
They do but glaze a lantern lit for man,
And woman's beauty is the flame therein.


### WITCHCRAFT: NEW STYLE

The sun drew off at last his piercing fires.
Over the stale warm air, dull as a pond
And moveless in the gray quieted street,
Blue magic of a summer evening glowed.
The sky, that had been dazzling stone all day,
Hollowed in smooth hard brightness, now dissolved
To infinite soft depth, and smoldered down
Low as the roofs, dark burning blue, and soared
Clear to that winking drop of liquid silver,
The first exquisite star. Now the half-light
Tidied away the dusty litter parching
Among the cobbles, veiled in the color of distance
Shabby slates and brickwork moldering, turned
The hunchback houses into patient things
Resting; and golden windows now began.

A little brisk gray slattern of a woman,
Pattering along in her loose-heeled clogs,
Pusht the brass-barred door of a public-house;
The spring went hard against her; hand and knee
Shoved their weak best. As the door poised ajar,
Hullabaloo of talking men burst out,
A pouring babble of inflamed palaver,
And overriding it and shouted down
High words, jeering or downright, broken like
Crests that leap and stumble in rushing water.
Just as the door went wide and she stept in,
"She cannot do it!" one was bawling out:
A glaring hulk of flesh with a bull's voice.
He fingered with his neckerchief, and stretcht
His throat to ease the anger of dispute,
Then spat to put a full stop to the matter.
The little woman waited, with one hand
Propping the door, and smiled at the loud man.
They saw her then; and the sight was enough
To gag the speech of every drinker there:
The din fell down like something chopt off short.
Blank they all wheeled towards her, with their mouths
Still gaping as though full of voiceless words.
She let the door slam to; and all at ease,

Amused, her smile wrinkling about her eyes,
Went forward; they made room for her quick enough.
Her chin just topt the counter; she gave in
Her bottle to the potboy, tuckt it back,
Full of bright tawny ale, under her arm,
Rapt down the coppers on the planisht zinc,
And turned: and no word spoken all the while.
    The first voice, in that silent crowd, was hers,
Her light snickering laugh, as she stood there
Pausing, scanning the sawdust at her feet.
Then she switcht round and faced the positive man
Whose strong "She cannot do it!" all still felt
Huskily shouting in their guilty ears.
"She can't, eh? She can't do it?"—Then she'd heard!
The man, inside his ruddy insolent flesh,
Had hoped she did not hear. His barrel chest
Gave a slight cringe, as though the glint of her eyes
Prickt him. But he stood up to her awkwardly bold,
One elbow on the counter, gripping his mug
Like a man holding on to a post for safety.

| | |
|---|---|
| *The Man* | You can't do what's not nature: nobody can. |
| *The Woman* | And louts like you have nature in your pocket? |
| *The Man* | I don't say that— |
| *The Woman* |                 If you kept saying naught, |
| | No one would guess the fool you are. |
| *Second Man* |                               Almost |
| | My very words! |
| *The Woman* |                   O you're the knowing man! |
| | The spark among the cinders! |
| *First Man* |                         You can't fetch |
| | A free man back, unless he wants to come. |
| *The Woman* | Nay, I'll be bound he doesn't want to come! |
| *Third Man* | And he won't come: he told me flat he wouldn't. |
| *The Woman* | Are you there too? |
| *Third Man* |                 And if he does come back |
| | It will be devilry brought him. |
| *The Woman* |                       I shall bring him;— |
| | Tonight. |
| *First Man* |       How will he come? |
| *The Woman* |                       Running: unless |
| | He's broke his leg, and then he'll have to come |
| | Crawling. But he will come. |
| *First Man* |                   How do you know |
| | What he may choose to do, three countries off? |
| *The Woman* | He choose? |
| *Third Man* |          You haven't got him on a lead. |
| *The Woman* | Haven't I though! |
| *Second Man* |            That's right: it's what I said. |
| *The Woman* | Aye, there are brains in your family. |

| | |
|---|---|
| *First Man* | You have |

Some sort of pull on him, to draw him home?

*The Woman*  You may say that: I have hold of his mind.
And I can slack it off or fetch it taut,
And make him dance a score of miles away
An answer to the least twangling thrum
I play on it. He thought he lurkt at last
Safely; and all the while, what has he been?
An eel on the end of a night-line; and it's time
I hauled him in. You'll see, tonight I'll land him.

*Third Man*  Bragging's a light job.

*The Woman*                          You daren't let me take
Your eyes in mine!—Haul, did I say? no need:
I give his mind a twitch, and up he comes
Tumbling home to me. Whatever work he's at,
He drops the thing he holds like redhot iron
And runs—runs till he falls down like a beast
Pole-axt, and grunts for breath; then up and on,
No matter does he know the road or not:
The strain I put on his mind will keep him going
Right as a homing-pigeon.

*First Man*                          Devilry
I call it.

*The Woman*          And you're welcome.

*Second Man*                          But the law
Should have a say here.

*The Woman*                          What, isn't he mine,
My own? There's naught but what I please about it.

*Third Man*  Why did you let him go?

*The Woman*                          To fetch him back!
For I enjoy this, mind. There's many a one
Would think to see me, There goes misery!
There's a queer starveling for you!—and I do
A thing that makes me like a saint in glory,
The life of me the sound of a great tune
Your flesh could never hear: I can send power
Delighting out of me! O, the mere thought
Has made my blood go smarting in my veins,
Such a flame glowing along it!—And all the same
I'll pay him out for sidling off from me.
But I'll have supper first.

When she was gone,
Their talk could scarcely raise itself again
Above a grumble. But at last a cry
Sharp-pitcht came startling in from the street: at once
Their moody talk exploded into flare
Of swearing hubbub, like gunpowder dropt
On embers; mugs were clapt down, out they bolted
Rowdily jostling, eager for the event.
All down the street the folk thronged out of doors,

But left a narrow track clear in the middle;
And there a man came running, a tall man
Running desperately and slowly, pounding
Like a machine, so evenly, so blindly;
And regularly his trotting body wagged.
Only one foot clattered upon the stones;
The other padded in his dogged stride:
The boot was gone, the sock hung frayed in shreds
About his ankle, the foot was blood and earth;
And never a limp, not the least flinch, to tell
The wounded pulp hit stone at every step.
His clothes were tattered and his rent skin showed,
Harrowed with thorns. His face was pale as putty,
Thrown far back; clots of drooping spittle foamed
On his mustache, and his hair hung in tails,
Mired with sweat; and sightless in their sockets
His eyeballs turned up white, as dull as pebbles.
Evenly and doggedly he trotted,
And as he went he moaned. Then out of sight
Round a corner he swerved, and out of hearing.
—"The law should have a say to that, by God!"

## James Stephens

JAMES STEPHENS was born in Dublin in February, 1882. His youth was difficult, his livelihood precarious. Stephens was "discovered" in an office and saved from clerical slavery by George Russell ("Æ"). Always a poet, many of Stephens's most poetic moments are in his highly colored prose. Yet, although the finest of his novels, *The Crock of Gold* (1912), contains more wild fantasy and quaint imagery than his verse, his *Insurrections* (1909) and *The Hill of Vision* (1912) reveal a rebellious spirit that is at once hotly ironic and coolly whimsical. *Green Branches* (1916) and *Reincarnations* (1918)—the latter being free adaptations from the Gaelic —are further persuasive volumes of his verse.

*Collected Poems* (1926) discloses two strongly differentiated personalities. There is the familiar and well-beloved Irish gamin, intimate with goats and gods, the playboy of the roads, deferential to rabbits and lesser folk, impudent to the universe. There is, also, the less popular but more sizeable poet, the thoughtful author of "The Crest Jewel," "In Waste Places," "The Main-Deep" with its surging rhythm held in a few syllables, and "A Prelude and a Song" which moves with the gentle solemnity of a river. Traces of Blake are in the later Stephens; the poet, discarding his light grotesquerie, becomes the seer. A less amusing singer is the result, but a more impassioned one. In youth Stephens delighted in gay mischiefs, pranking with unnatural phenomena; in maturity he is concerned with nothing less than elemental truths.

Both personalities combine in the prose fiction for which Stephens is famous.

*Deirdre* (1923) and *In the Land of Youth* (1924) continue the re-creations from the Irish folk- and fairy-tales. *Hunger* (1918), originally published under the pseudonym "James Esse," was incorporated in the somber collection of short stories *Etched in Moonlight* (1928) which, curiously enough, was poorly received in England but an enormous success in America. An edition of his *Irish Fairy Tales* was arranged for children.

*Strict Joy* (1931) is a small book containing a dozen new poems, yet its very range is characteristic. Stephens lightly runs the scale from badinage to mysticism and seldom strikes an uncertain note, never a false one.

Stephens's final characteristic is his delightful blend of incongruities—he successfully mingles the bizarre and the charming, the buoyant and the profound. No more vigorous imagination has come out of Ireland since J. M. Synge.

### THE SHELL

And then I pressed the shell
Close to my ear
And listened well,
And straightway like a bell
Came low and clear
The slow, sad murmur of the distant seas,
Whipped by an icy breeze
Upon a shore
Wind-swept and desolate.
It was a sunless strand that never bore
The footprint of a man,
Nor felt the weight
Since time began
Of any human quality or stir
Save what the dreary winds and waves incur.

And in the hush of waters was the sound
Of pebbles rolling round,
For ever rolling with a hollow sound.
And bubbling sea-weeds as the waters go
Swish to and fro
Their long, cold tentacles of slimy gray.
There was no day,
Nor ever came a night
Setting the stars alight
To wonder at the moon:
Was twilight only and the frightened croon,
Smitten to whimpers, of the dreary wind
And waves that journeyed blind—
And then I loosed my ear . . . O, it was sweet
To hear a cart go jolting down the street.

### WHAT THOMAS AN BUILE SAID IN A PUB

I saw God. Do you doubt it?
  Do you dare to doubt it?
I saw the Almighty Man. His hand
Was resting on a mountain, and
He looked upon the World and all about it:
I saw Him plainer than you see me now,
  You mustn't doubt it.

He was not satisfied;
  His look was all dissatisfied.
His beard swung on a wind far out of sight
Behind the world's curve, and there was light
Most fearful from His forehead, and He sighed,
"That star went always wrong, and from the start
  "I was dissatisfied."

He lifted up His hand—
    I say He heaved a dreadful hand
Over the spinning Earth. Then I said, "Stay,
You must not strike it, God; I'm in the way;
And I will never move from where I stand."
He said, "Dear child, I feared that you were dead,"
    And stayed His hand.


### TO THE FOUR COURTS, PLEASE

The driver rubbed at his nettly chin
With a huge, loose forefinger, crooked and black,
And his wobbly, violet lips sucked in,
And puffed out again and hung down slack:
One fang shone through his lop-sided smile,
In his little pouched eye flickered years of guile.

And the horse, poor beast, it was ribbed and forked,
And its ears hung down, and its eyes were old,
And its knees were knuckly, and as we talked
It swung the stiff neck that could scarcely hold
Its big, skinny head up—then I stepped in,
And the driver climbed to his seat with a grin.

God help the horse and the driver too,
And the people and beasts who have never a friend,
For the driver easily might have been you,
And the horse be me by a different end.
And nobody knows how their days will cease,
And the poor, when they're old, have little of peace.


### LITTLE THINGS

Little things that run and quail
And die in silence and despair;

Little things that fight and fail
And fall on earth and sea and air;

All trapped and frightened little things,
The mouse, the coney, hear our prayer.

As we forgive those done to us,
The lamb, the linnet, and the hare,

Forgive us all our trespasses,
Little creatures everywhere.

## THE RED-HAIRED MAN'S WIFE

I have taken that vow—
   And you were my friend
But yesterday—now
   All that's at an end,
And you are my husband, and claim me, and I must depend.

Yesterday I was free,
   Now you, as I stand,
Walk over to me
   And take hold of my hand.
You look at my lips, your eyes are too bold, your smile is too bland.

My old name is lost,
   My distinction of race:
Now the line has been crossed,
   Must I step to your pace?
Must I walk as you list, and obey and smile up in your face?

All the white and the red
   Of my cheeks you have won;
All the hair of my head,
   And my feet, tho' they run,
Are yours, and you own me and end me just as I begun.

Must I bow when you speak,
   Be silent and hear,
Inclining my cheek
   And incredulous ear
To your voice, and command, and behest, hold your lightest wish dear?

I am woman, but still
   Am alive, and can feel
Every intimate thrill
   That is woe or is weal.
I, aloof, and divided, apart, standing far, can I kneel?

If not, I shall know,
   I shall surely find out,
And your world will throw
   In disaster and rout;
I am woman and glory and beauty, I mystery, terror, and doubt.

I am separate still,
   I am I and not you:
And my mind and my will,
   As in secret they grew,
Still are secret, unreached and untouched and not subject to you.

### HATE

My enemy came nigh,
And I
Stared fiercely in his face.
My lips went writhing back in a grimace,
And stern I watched him with a narrow eye.
Then, as I turned away, my enemy,
That bitter heart and savage, said to me:
"Some day, when this is past,
When all the arrows that we have are cast,
We may ask one another why we hate,
And fail to find a story to relate.
It may seem to us then a mystery
That we could hate each other."

      Thus said he,
And did not turn away,
Waiting to hear what I might have to say.
But I fled quickly, fearing if I stayed
I might have kissed him as I would a maid.

### THE WATCHER

A rose for a young head,
A ring for a bride,
Joy for the homestead
Clean and wide—
 Who's that waiting
 In the rain outside?

A heart for an old friend,
A hand for the new:
Love can to earth lend
Heaven's hue—
 Who's that standing
 In the silver dew?

A smile for the parting,
A tear as they go,
God's sweethearting
Ends just so—
 Who's that watching
 Where the black winds blow?

He who is waiting
In the rain outside,
He who is standing
Where the dew drops wide,
He who is watching
In the wind must ride
 (Tho' the pale hands cling)
 With the rose
 And the ring
 And the bride,
  Must ride
With the red of the rose,
And the gold of the ring,
And the lips and the hair of the bride.

### RIGHTEOUS ANGER

The lanky hank of a she in the inn over there
Nearly killed me for asking the loan of a glass of beer:
May the devil grip the whey-faced slut by the hair,
And beat bad manners out of her skin for a year.

That parboiled imp, with the hardest jaw you will see
On virtue's path, and a voice that would rasp the dead,
Came roaring and raging the minute she looked at me,
And threw me out of the house on the back of my head!

If I asked her master he'd give me a cask a day;
But she with the beer at hand, not a gill would arrange!
May she marry a ghost and bear him a kitten and may
The High King of Glory permit her to get the mange.

### ODELL

My mind is sad and weary thinking how
 The griffins of the Gael went over the sea

From noble Eiré, and are fighting now
  In France and Flanders and in Germany.

If they, 'mid whom I sported without dread,
  Were home I would not mind what foe might do,
Or fear tax-man Odell would seize my bed
  To pay the hearth-rate that is overdue.

I pray to Him who, in the haughty hour
  Of Babel, threw confusion on each tongue,
That I may see our princes back in power,
  And see Odell, the tax-collector, hung.

### BLUE BLOOD

#### (*After O'Bruaidar*)

We thought at first, this man is a king for sure,
Or the branch of a mighty and ancient and famous lineage—
That silly, sulky, illiterate, black-avised boor
Who was hatched by foreign vulgarity under a hedge.

The good men of Clare were drinking his health in a flood,
And gazing with me in awe of the princely lad,
And asking each other from what bluest blueness of blood
His daddy was squeezed, and the pa of the da of his dad?

We waited there, gaping and wondering, anxiously,
Until he'd stop eating and let the glad tidings out,
And the slack-jawed booby proved to the hilt that he
Was lout, son of lout, by old lout, and was da to a lout!

| THE MAIN-DEEP | IN WASTE PLACES |
|---|---|
| The long rólling, | As a naked man I go |
| Steady-póuring, | Through the desert, sore afraid; |
| Deep-trenchéd | Holding high my head, although |
| Green billow: | I'm as frightened as a maid. |
| | |
| The wide-topped, | The lion crouches there! I saw |
| Unbróken, | In barren rocks his amber eye! |
| Green-glacid, | He parts the cactus with his paw! |
| Slow-sliding. | He stares at me as I go by! |
| | |
| Cold-flushing, | He would pad upon my trace |
| On—on—on— | If he thought I was afraid!. |
| Chill-rushing, | If he knew my hardy face |
| Hush-hushing, | Veils the terrors of a maid. |
| | |
| Hush—hushing. . . . | He rises in the night-time, and |
| | He stretches forth! He snuffs the air! |

He roars! He leaps along the sand!
He creeps! He watches everywhere!

His burning eyes, his eyes of bale
Through the darkness I can see!
He lashes fiercely with his tail!
He makes again to spring at me!

I am the lion, and his lair!
I am the fear that frightens me!
I am the desert of despair!
And the night of agony!

Night or day, whate'er befall,
I must walk that desert land,
Until I dare my fear and call
The lion out to lick my hand.

## GOOD AND BAD

Good and bad and right and wrong,
Wave the silly words away:
This is wisdom to be strong,
This is virtue to be gay:
Let us sing and dance until
We shall know the final art,
How to banish good and ill
With the laughter of the heart.

## THE OUTCAST

Shy and timid, Gloom to me
Said, I am lost! How shall I go?
There is no place for Misery,
Welcome for Woe!

And to him,
Desolate and fey,
My stricken heart
Found nought to say.

But soon: Be thou my Joy, I said:
Give me your hand, rest here your head:
Come to my home, and eat my bread,
And rest thee from annoy.

For I shall give thee all of mine,
Until my all be sealéd thine,
And thou shalt be, in little time,
A Child of Joy.

Now, on my heart, as on a throne,
Gloom, as heavy as a stone,
Sits, and I go dark till he
Is Joy, and gives Joy back to me.

## THE CREST JEWEL

### I

The leaf will wrinkle to decay
And crumble into dust away!

The rose, the lily, grow to eld,
And are, and are no more, beheld!

Nothing will stay! For, as the eye
Rests upon an object nigh,

It is not there to look upon!
It is mysteriously gone!

And, in its place, another thing
Apes its shape and fashioning!

### II

All that the sun will breathe today
The moon will lip and wear away

Tonight. And all will re-begin
Tomorrow as the dawn comes in.

Is no beginning, middle-trend
Or argument to that or end.

No cause and no effect, and no
Reason why it should be so.

Or why it might be otherwise
To other minds or other eyes.

### III

The soul can dream itself to be
Adrift upon an endless sea

Of day and night. The soul can seem
To be all things that it can dream!

Yet needs but look within to find
That which is steady in the wind,

That which the fire does not appal,
Which good and ill mourn not at all.

Which does not seek, or lack, or try.
And was not born, and cannot die!

IV

It has been writ in wisdom old—
This is the last word to be told:

—There is no dissolution! No
Creation! There are none in woe!

There is no teacher, teaching, taught!
Are none who long for, lack for aught!

Are none who pine for freedom! None
Are liberated under sun!

—And this is absolutely true
In Him who dreams in me and you.

## *James Joyce*

JAMES JOYCE was born in Dublin, February 2, 1882. He was educated at the Jesuit school at Clongowes Wood, Belvedere College and the Royal University of Dublin. He studied medicine in Paris (where he has lived since early manhood), discontinued his medical studies in the hope of becoming a professional singer, gave up singing to become a teacher in Berlitz Schools on the Continent, and published his first book in 1907.

This first was a volume of verse, *Chamber Music,* written in his early twenties, but not published in America until 1918. Admirers of Joyce point out that, even in his most difficult prose, he has never ceased being the poet. His work in prose has received international attention and almost universal notoriety. *Dubliners* (1914) and *A Portrait of the Artist as a Young Man* (1916) were received with respect and little disapproval. But with *Ulysses* (1922) Joyce became a storm-center. His appraisers trod no middle way: they either asserted, and loudly, that he was an unqualifiedly great genius, or insisted, even more vociferously, that he was an obscene madman, whose writings were subversive and properly banned by the censor. This is not the place to enter so controversial a problem. It may, however, be stated that there can be no question regarding the importance of *Ulysses* as a richly creative novel, an experimental art work, and as a document of the times.

*Pomes Penyeach* (1927) resembles Joyce's later style only in its title. It is delicate, certain, and lyrical throughout. Like the early *Chamber Music,* the verse is conventional in theme, orthodox in treatment, harmonically simple, and the very antithesis of everything for which Joyce is celebrated.

### I HEAR AN ARMY

I hear an army charging upon the land,
 And the thunder of horses plunging, foam about their knees:
Arrogant, in black armor, behind them stand,
 Disdaining the reins, with fluttering whips, the charioteers.

They cry unto the night their battle-name:
 I moan in sleep when I hear afar their whirling laughter.
They cleave the gloom of dreams, a blinding flame,
 Clanging, clanging upon the heart as upon an anvil.

They come shaking in triumph their long, green hair:
They come out of the sea and run shouting by the shore.
My heart, have you no wisdom thus to despair?
My love, my love, my love, why have you left me alone?

### ALL DAY I HEAR

All day I hear the noise of waters
  Making moan,
Sad as the sea-bird is when, going
  Forth alone,
He hears the winds cry to the waters'
  Monotone.

The gray winds, the cold winds are blowing
  Where I go.
I hear the noise of many waters
  Far below.
All day, all night, I hear them flowing
  To and fro.

### O SWEETHEART, HEAR YOU

O sweetheart, hear you
  Your lover's tale;
A man shall have sorrow
  When friends him fail.

For he shall know then
  Friends be untrue
And a little ashes
  Their words come to.

But one unto him
  Will softly move
And softly woo him
  In ways of love.

His hand is under
  Her smooth round breast;
So he who has sorrow
  Shall have rest.

### SONG

O, it was out by Donnycarney,
  When the bat flew from tree to tree,

My love and I did walk together,
  And sweet were the words she said to me.

Along with us the summer wind
  Went murmuring—O, happily!—
But softer than the breath of summer
  Was the kiss she gave to me.

### ON THE BEACH AT FONTANA

Wind whines and whines the shingle,
The crazy pierstakes groan;
A senile sea numbers each single
Slimesilvered stone.

From whining wind and colder
Gray sea I wrap him warm
And touch his trembling fineboned shoulder
And boyish arm.

Around us fear, descending
Darkness of fear above
And in my heart how deep unending
Ache of love!

### FLOOD

Goldbrown upon the sated flood
The rockvine clusters lift and sway,
Vast wings above the lambent waters brood
Of sullen day.

A waste of waters ruthlessly
Sways and uplifts its weedy mane
Where brooding day stares down upon the
  sea
In dull disdain.

Uplift and sway, O golden vine,
Your clustered fruits to love's full flood,
Lambent and vast and ruthless as in thine
Incertitude!

# *J. C. Squire*

JACK (JOHN) COLLINGS SQUIRE was born April 2, 1884, at Plymouth, of Devonian ancestry. He was educated at Blundell's and Cambridge University, and first became known as a remarkably adroit parodist. His *Imaginary Speeches* (1912) and *Tricks of the Trade* (1917) are amusing parodies and, what is more, excellent criticism. He first contributed to and then edited *The New Statesman,* and founded *The London Mercury* (a monthly of which he was editor) in November, 1919. Under the pseudonym "Solomon Eagle" he wrote a page of literary criticism every week for six years; many of these papers are collected in his volume, *Books in General* (1919).

His original poetry is intellectual, occasionally metaphysical, and always interesting in its variable rhythms. A collection of his best verse up to 1919 was published under the title, *Poems: First Series.* A subsequent *Poems: Second Series* appeared in 1921.

Squire's *Collected Parodies, American Poems and Others, Essays at Large* all appeared in 1923. Since that year Squire has published little original work, busying himself almost exclusively with editing and anthologizing. *Apes and Peacocks* (1930) is his shrewd collection of the burlesques and satires of other parodists.

### A HOUSE

Now very quietly, and rather mournfully,
 In clouds of hyacinth the sun retires,
And all the stubblefields that were so warm to him
 Keep but in memory their borrowed fires.

And I, the traveler, break, still unsatisfied,
 From that faint exquisite celestial strand,
And turn and see again the only dwelling-place
 In this wide wilderness of darkening land.

The house, that house, O now what change has come to it.
 Its crude red-brick façade, its roof of slate;
What imperceptible swift hand has given it
 A new, a wonderful, a queenly state?

No hand has altered it, that parallelogram,
 So inharmonious, so ill-arranged;
That hard blue roof in shape and color's what it was;
 No, it is not that any line has changed.

Only that loneliness is now accentuate
 And, as the dusk unveils the heaven's deep cave,
This small world's feebleness fills me with awe again,
 And all man's energies seem very brave.

And this mean edifice, which some dull architect
　　Built for an ignorant earth-turning hind,
Takes on the quality of that magnificent
　　Unshakable dauntlessness of human kind.

Darkness and stars will come, and long the night will be,
　　Yet imperturbable that house will rest,
Avoiding gallantly the stars' chill scrutiny,
　　Ignoring secrets in the midnight's breast.

Thunders may shudder it, and winds demoniac
　　May howl their menaces, and hail descend:
Yet it will bear with them, serenely, steadfastly,
　　Not even scornfully, and wait the end.

And all a universe of nameless messengers
　　From unknown distances may whisper fear,
And it will imitate immortal permanence,
　　And stare and stare ahead and scarcely hear.

It stood there yesterday; it will tomorrow, too,
　　When there is none to watch, no alien eyes
To watch its ugliness assume a majesty
　　From this great solitude of evening skies.

So lone, so very small, with worlds and worlds around,
　　While life remains to it prepared to outface
Whatever awful unconjectured mysteries
　　May hide and wait for it in time and space.

### SONNET

There was an Indian, who had known no change,
　　Who strayed content along a sunlit beach
Gathering shells. He heard a sudden strange
　　Commingled noise: looked up; and gasped for speech.
For in the bay, where nothing was before,
　　Moved on the sea, by magic, huge canoes,
With bellying cloths on poles, and not one oar,
　　And fluttering colored signs and clambering crews.

And he, in fear, this naked man alone,
　　His fallen hands forgetting all their shells,
His lips gone pale, knelt low behind a stone,
　　And stared, and saw, and did not understand,
Columbus's doom-burdened caravels
　　Slant to the shore, and all their seamen land.

A FRESH MORNING

Now am I a tin whistle
Through which Gods blows,
And I wish to God I were a trumpet
—But why, God only knows.

PROLOGUE: IN DARKNESS

With my sleeping belovèd huddled beside me, why do I lie awake,
Listening to the loud clock's hurry in the darkness, and feeling my heart's fierce
    ache
That beats one response to the brain's many questionings, and in solitude bears the
    weight
Of all the world's evil and misery and frustration, and the senseless pressure of fate?

Is it season of plowing and sowing, this long vigil, that so certainly it recurs?
Is this unsought return of a pain that was ended, is it here that a song first
    stirs?
Can it be that from this, when tonight's gone from memory, there will spring of a
    sudden, some time,
Like a silver lily breaking from black deadly waters, the thin-blown shape of a
    rhyme?

# *James Elroy Flecker*

ANOTHER remarkable poet whose early death was a blow to English literature was
James Elroy Flecker. Born in London, November 5, 1884, he studied at Trinity
College, Oxford, specialized in Oriental languages at Cambridge, and went to Con-
stantinople in the Consular Service in 1910. The fact that the remainder of his life
was spent in the East has a direct bearing on Flecker's work: his play *Hassan,* one
of the most powerful and brilliantly colored modern dramas, is the definite reflection
of his adopted Orientalism.

Possibly due to low vitality, Flecker found little to interest him but a reaction
against realism in verse, a delight in verbal craftsmanship, and a passion for technical perfection—especially the deliberate technique of the French Parnassians, whom
he worshiped. Flecker was opposed to any art that was emotional or that "taught"
anything. "The poet's business," he declared, "is not to save the soul of man, but to
make it worth saving." Flecker's desire to be objective rather than passionate was
scarcely consistent with his actual creation, even though he maintained that "the
Parnassians raised the technique of their art to a height which enabled them to
express the subtlest ideas in powerful and simple verse." Technique and manner
were his abstract gods.

The advent of the war began to make Flecker's verse more personal and romantic.
The tuberculosis that finally killed him at Davos Platz, Switzerland, January 3,
1915, forced him from an Olympian disinterest to a deep concern with life and

death. He passionately denied that he was weary of living "as the pallid poets are," and he was attempting higher flights of song when his singing ceased altogether.

Flecker's two notable volumes are *The Golden Journey to Samarkand* (1913) and *The Old Ships* (1915). *Collected Poems,* with an autobiographical introduction and notes by J. C. Squire, was published in 1917 and drew fresh attention to Flecker's half-classical, half-romantic, and always vivid style.

### THE OLD SHIPS

I have seen old ships sail like swans asleep
Beyond the village which men still call Tyre,
With leaden age o'ercargoed, dipping deep
For Famagusta and the hidden sun
That rings black Cyprus with a lake of fire;
And all those ships were certainly so old—
Who knows how oft with squat and noisy gun,
Questing brown slaves or Syrian oranges,
The pirate Genoese
Hell-raked them till they rolled
Blood, water, fruit and corpses up the hold.
But now through friendly seas they softly run,
Painted the mid-sea blue or shore-sea green,
Still patterned with the vine and grapes in gold.

But I have seen,
Pointing her shapely shadows from the dawn
An image tumbled on a rose-swept bay,
A drowsy ship of some yet older day;
And, wonder's breath indrawn,
Thought I—who knows—who knows—but in that same
(Fished up beyond Aeaea, patched up new
—Stern painted brighter blue—)
That talkative, bald-headed seaman came
(Twelve patient comrades sweating at the oar)
From Troy's doom-crimson shore,
And with great lies about his wooden horse
Set the crew laughing, and forgot his course.

It was so old a ship—who knows, who knows?
—And yet so beautiful, I watched in vain
To see the mast burst open with a rose,
And the whole deck put on its leaves again.

### STILLNESS

When the words rustle no more,
  And the last work's done,
When the bolt lies deep in the door,

And Fire, our Sun,
Falls on the dark-laned meadows of the floor;

When from the clock's last chime to the next chime
  Silence beats his drum,
And Space with gaunt gray eyes and her brother Time
  Wheeling and whispering come,
She with the mold of form and he with the loom of rhyme:

Then twittering out in the night my thought-birds flee,
  I am emptied of all my dreams:
I only hear Earth turning, only see
  Ether's long bankless streams,
And only know I should drown if you
  Laid not your hand on me.

### THE WAR SONG OF THE SARACENS

We are they who come faster than fate: we are they who ride early or late:
We storm at your ivory gate: Pale Kings of the Sunset, beware!
Not on silk nor in samet we lie, not in curtained solemnity die
Among women who chatter and cry, and children who mumble a prayer.
But we sleep by the ropes of the camp, and we rise with a shout, and we tramp
With the sun or the moon for a lamp, and the spray of the wind in our hair.

From the lands, where the elephants are, to the forts of Merou and Balghar,
Our steel we have brought and our star to shine on the ruins of Ruhm.
We have marched from the Indus to Spain, and, by God, we will go there again;
We have stood on the shore of the plain where the Waters of Destiny boom.
A mart of destruction we made at Jalúla where men were afraid,
For death was a difficult trade, and the sword was a broker of doom;

And the Spear was a Desert Physician who cured not a few of ambition,
And drave not a few to perdition with medicine bitter and strong;
And the shield was a grief to the fool and as bright as a desolate pool,
And as straight as the rock of Stamboul when their cavalry thundered along:
For the coward was drowned with the brave when our battle sheered up like a wave,
And the dead to the desert we gave, and the glory to God in our song.

### TENEBRIS INTERLUCENTEM

A linnet who had lost her way
Sang on a blackened bough in Hell,
Till all the ghosts remembered well
The trees, the wind, the golden day.

At last they knew that they had died
When they heard music in that land,
And someone there stole forth a hand
To draw a brother to his side.

### TO A POET A THOUSAND YEARS HENCE

I who am dead a thousand years,
  And wrote this sweet archaic song,
Send you my words for messengers
  The way I shall not pass along.

I care not if you bridge the seas,
  Or ride secure the cruel sky,
Or build consummate palaces
  Of metal or of masonry.

But have you wine and music still,
  And statues and a bright-eyed love,
And foolish thoughts of good and ill,
  And prayers to them who sit above?

How shall we conquer? Like a wind
  That falls at eve our fancies blow,
And old Maeonides the blind
  Said it three thousand years ago.

O friend unseen, unborn, unknown,
  Student of our sweet English tongue,
Read out my words at night, alone:
  I was a poet, I was young.

Since I can never see your face,
  And never shake you by the hand,
I send my soul through time and space
  To greet you. You will understand.

## THE TOWN WITHOUT A MARKET

There lies afar behind a western hill
The town without a Market, white and still;
For six feet long and not a third as high
Are those small habitations. There stood I,
Waiting to hear the citizens beneath
Murmur and sigh and speak through tongueless teeth.
When all the world lay burning in the sun
I heard their voices speak to me. Said one:
"Bright lights I loved and colors, I who find
That death is darkness, and has struck me blind."
Another cried: "I used to sing and play,
But here the world is silent, day by day."
And one: "On earth I could not see or hear,
But with my fingers touched what I was near,
And knew things round and soft, and brass from gold,
And dipped my hand in water, to feel cold,
And thought the grave would cure me, and was glad
When the time came to lose what joy I had."
Soon all the voices of a hundred dead
Shouted in wrath together. Someone said,
"I care not, but the girl was sweet to kiss
At evening in the meadows." "Hard it is,"
Another cried, "to hear no hunting horn.
Ah me! the horse, the hounds, and the great gray morn
When I rode out a-hunting." And one sighed,
"I did not see my son before I died."
A boy said, "I was strong and swift to run:
Now they have tied my feet; what have I done?"
A man, "But it was good to arm and fight
And storm their cities in the dead of night."
An old man said, "I read my books all day,
But death has taken all my books away."
And one, "The popes and prophets did not well
To cheat poor dead men with false hopes of hell.
Better the whips of fire that hiss and rend
Than painless void proceeding to no end."
I smiled to hear them restless, I who sought
Peace. For I had not loved, I had not fought,

And books are vanities, and manly strength
A gathered flower. God grants us peace at length!
I heard no more, and turned to leave their town
Before the chill came, and the sun went down.
Then rose a whisper, and I seemed to know
A timorous man, buried long years ago.
"On Earth I used to shape the Thing that seems.
Master of all men, give me back my dreams.
Give me the world that never failed me then,
The hills I made and peopled with tall men,
The palace that I built and called my home,
My cities which could break the pride of Rome,
The three queens hidden in the sacred tree,
And those white cloudy folk who sang to me,
O death, why hast thou covered me so deep?
I was thy sister's child, the friend of Sleep."

Then said my heart, Death takes and cannot give.
Dark with no dream is hateful: let me live!

## *Anna Wickham*

A NNA WICKHAM was born in Wimbledon, Surrey, in 1884. She went to Australia
at six, returned when she was twenty-one, studied for Opera in Paris with
De Reszke and suddenly, after a few years of marriage, became a poet. In a burst
of creative energy she wrote nine hundred poems in four years.

Her first two books (*The Contemplative Quarry,* 1915, and *The Man with a
Hammer,* 1916) were republished in America in one volume, *The Contemplative
Quarry* (1921). This was followed by *The Little Old House* (1922). Another volume, *The Noiseless Propeller,* was prepared, but its publication was postponed.
The most casual reading of Anna Wickham's work reveals the strength of her
candor. The poems could scarcely be put in the category of "charming" verse; they
are astringent and sometimes harsh, gnarled frequently by their own violences of
mood. But there is no disputing their incisiveness and integrity. Mrs. Wickham's
lines present the picture of woman struggling between dreams and domesticity;
they are acutely sensitive, restless, analytical. The very tone of her poetry reflects
the disturbed music and the nervous protests of her age.

Sometimes her verse tends toward introverted self-questioning, but usually it is
as just in phrase as it is fearless in thought. Much of her poetry is a poetry of the
senses, and in this she seems kin to D. H. Lawrence. But where Lawrence, lost and
suffering in the "mazes of the female mystery," is sexually tormented, Anna Wickham, unhampered in her sensuality, delights even in her torments. She turns upon
men for maintaining a traditional attitude, not to the real women of today, but to
creatures half-historical, half-illusory; she berates women for fostering this tendency,
thus weakening men and enchaining themselves.

> We, vital women, are no more content
> Bound, first to passion, then to sentiment.
> Of you, the masters, slaves in our poor eyes
> Who most are moved by women's tricks and lies,
> We ask our freedom. In good sooth,
> We only ask to know and speak the truth!

Yet Mrs. Wickham does more than "only ask to know and speak the truth." Her angers and revulsions cannot choke the lyric impulse. Time and again she makes songs that are sweet without being sentimental, almost perfect in their simple cadences.

For the most part she is torn between being the instrument of love and love itself; making, with a wry determination, an unhappy compromise between the conflicting claims of modernity and maternity. She is rarely objective; even such dramatic projections as "Meditation at Kew" and the acrid humor of "Nervous Prostration" are too bitter to be impersonal. Out of all her poems, the plangent as well as the powerful, rises this cry which is also an apologia:

> Let it be something for my song,
> If it is sometimes swift and strong.

"Self-Analysis," "Divorce," and "The Affinity" are this remarkable and unappreciated poet *in petto*. Divided between her desire for mastery and being mastered, for perfection and her distrust of it, she typifies the woman who has repudiated order but is frustrated in lawlessness; even her domesticity, which she celebrates, is, if not self-condemning, self-contradicting.

Although Mrs. Wickham has written longer poems, her terse, pungently flavored lyrics are most characteristic of her. She is a psychologist by intention, but a psychologist who has not forgotten how to sing. At her worst she offers an interesting exhibit of the age; at her best she displays a genius for the firm epithet and quick-thrusting phrase—and an unforgettable power of emotion.

### CREATRIX

Let us thank Almighty God
For the woman with the rod.
Who was ever and is now
Strong, essential as the plow.
She shall goad and she shall drive,
So to keep man's soul alive.
Amoris with her scented dress
Beckons, in pretty wantonness;
But the wife drives, nor can man tell
What hands so urge, what powers compel.

### SONG

I was so chill, and overworn, and sad,
To be a lady was the only joy I had.
I walked the street as silent as a mouse,
Buying fine clothes, and fittings for the
  house.

But since I saw my love
I wear a simple dress,
And happily I move
Forgetting weariness.

### SELF-ANALYSIS

The tumult of my fretted mind
Gives me expression of a kind;

But it is faulty, harsh, not plain—
My work has the incompetence of pain.

I am consumed with a slow fire,
For righteousness is my desire;
Towards that good goal I cannot whip my will,
I am a tired horse that jibs upon a hill.

I desire Virtue, though I love her not—
I have no faith in her when she is got:
I fear that she will bind and make me slave
And send me songless to the sullen grave.

I am like a man who fears to take a wife,
And frets his soul with wantons all his life.
With rich, unholy foods I stuff my maw;
When I am sick, then I believe in law.

I fear the whiteness of straight ways—
I think there is no color in unsullied days.
My silly sins I take for my heart's ease,
And know my beauty in the end disease.

Of old there were great heroes, strong in fight,
Who, tense and sinless, kept a fire alight:
God of our hope, in their great name,
Give me the straight and ordered flame!

### SEHNSUCHT

Because of body's hunger are we born,
And by contriving hunger are we fed;
Because of hunger is our work well done,
As so are songs well sung, and things well said.
Desire and longing are the whips of God—
God save us all from death when we are fed.

### WEAPONS

Up the crag
In the screaming wind,
Naked and bleeding
I fought blind.

Then at dawn
On the snowy height
I seized a spear
By the eastern light.

On I trudged
In the eye of the sun,

Past the cromlech
I found a gun.

Then I strayed
In the cities of men,
In the house of my Love
I found a pen!

### THE LAST ROUND

Clasp you the God within yourself
And hold it fast;
After all combats shall ye come
To this good fight at last.

God is a mighty wrestler
He battles in the night;
Not till the end shall it be known
What foe you fight.

When God in you is overthrown
He'll show a light
And claim the victor for his own
And crown the fight.

## TO A CRUCIFIX

O courteous Christ—Kind guest, most gracious host,
Which of these ugly things had pained you most
That silly priests repeat your words for gain
Or in your house hang symbols of your pain?

How had you withered at the servile breath
Spent in the praises of your common death,
Scorning these claims to honor and to pride
For such a death as multitudes have died.

Not in the cross was such indignity
As these acclaiming Christian ages see,
When you who lived for cure and for relief
Are most remembered for your wounds and grief.

## FRIEND CATO

When the master sits at ease
He joys in generalities;
In aphorisms concerning all things human,
But most of all concerning woman.
Saying, "Women are this or that.
Woman is round, or high, or square, or flat."

Sir, a shepherd knows his sheep apart,
And mothers know young babes by heart.
To taste no little shade of difference
Is sign of undiscerning sense.
Cato, in pity, hear our just demur,
Man to be critic, must be connoisseur.

## THE SONG-MAKER

I would live for a day and a night,
In the rigorous land where everything's right.
Then I would sit and make a song,
In the leisurely land where everything's wrong.

## DEDICATION OF THE COOK

If any ask why there's no great She-Poet,
Let him come live with me, and he will know it:
If I'd indite an ode or mend a sonnet,
I must go choose a dish or tie a bonnet;

For she who serves in forced virginity
Since I am wedded will not have me free;
And those new flowers my garden is so rich in
Must die for clammy odors of my kitchen.

Yet had I chosen Dian's barrenness
I'm not full woman, and I can't be less,
So could I state no certain truth for life,
Can I survive and be my good man's wife?

Yes! I will make the servant's cause my own
That she in pity leave me hours alone
So I will tend her mind and feed her wit
That she in time have her own joy of it;
And count it pride that not a sonnet's spoiled
Lacking her choice betwixt the baked and boiled.
So those young flowers my garden is so rich in
Will blossom from the ashes of my kitchen!

### MEDITATION AT KEW

Alas! for all the pretty women who marry dull men,
Go into the suburbs and never come out again,
Who lose their pretty faces, and dim their pretty eyes,
Because no one has skill or courage to organize.

What do these pretty women suffer when they marry?
They bear a boy who is like Uncle Harry,
A girl, who is like Aunt Eliza, and not new,
These old, dull races must breed true.

I would enclose a common in the sun,
And let the young wives out to laugh and run;
I would steal their dull clothes and go away,
And leave the pretty naked things to play.

Then I would make a contract with hard Fate
That they see all the men in the world and choose a mate,
And I would summon all the pipers in the town
That they dance with Love at a feast, and dance him down.

From the gay unions of choice
We'd have a race of splendid beauty, and of thrilling voice.
The World whips frank, gay love with rods,
But frankly, gayly shall we get the gods.

### THE AFFINITY

I have to thank God I'm a woman,
For in these ordered days a woman only
Is free to be very hungry, very lonely.

It is sad for Feminism, but still clear
That man, more often than woman, is pioneer.
If I would confide a new thought,
First to a man must it be brought.

Now, for our sins, it is my bitter fate
That such a man wills soon to be my mate,
And so of friendship is quick end:
When I have gained a love I lose a friend.

It is well within the order of things
That man should listen when his mate sings;
But the true male never yet walked
Who liked to listen when his mate talked.

I would be married to a full man,
As would all women since the world began;
But from a wealth of living I have proved
I must be silent, if I would be loved.

Now of my silence I have much wealth,
I have to do my thinking all by stealth.
My thoughts may never see the day;
My mind is like a catacomb where early Christians pray.

And of my silence I have much pain,
But of these pangs I have great gain;
For I must take to drugs or drink,
Or I must write the things I think.

If my sex would let me speak,
I would be very lazy and most weak;
I should speak only, and the things I spoke
Would fill the air awhile, and clear like smoke.

The things I think now I write down,
And some day I will show them to the Town.
When I am sad I make thought clear;
I can re-read it all next year.

I have to thank God I'm a woman,
For in these ordered days a woman only
Is free to be very hungry, very lonely.

### THE TIRED WOMAN

O my Lover, blind me,
Take your cords and bind me,
Then drive me through a silent land
With the compelling of your open hand!

There is too much of sound, too much for sight,
In thundrous lightnings of this night,
There is too much of freedom for my feet,
Bruised by the stones of this disordered street.

I know that there is sweetest rest for me,
In silent fields, and in captivity.
O Lover! drive me through a stilly land
With the compelling of your open hand.

### DIVORCE

A voice from the dark is calling me.
In the close house I nurse a fire.
Out in the dark, cold winds rush free,
To the rock heights of my desire.
I smother in the house in the valley below,
Let me out to the night, let me go, let me go!

Spirits that ride the sweeping blast,
Frozen in rigid tenderness,
Wait! For I leave the fire at last,
My little-love's warm loneliness.
I smother in the house in the valley below,
Let me out in the night, let me go, let me go!

High on the hills are beating drums,
Clear from a line of marching men
To the rock's edge the hero comes.
He calls me, and he calls again.
On the hill there is fighting, victory, or quick death,
In the house is the fire, which I fan with sick breath.
I smother in the house in the valley below,
Let me out in the dark, let me go, let me go!

### AFTER ANNUNCIATION

Rest, little Guest,
Beneath my breast.
Feed, sweet Seed,
At your need.

I took Love for my lord
And this is my reward,
My body is good earth,
That you, dear Plant, have birth.

### THE CHERRY-BLOSSOM WAND

I will pluck from my tree a cherry-blossom wand,
And carry it in my merciless hand,

So I will drive you, so bewitch your eyes,
With a beautiful thing that can never grow wise.

Light are the petals that fall from the bough,
And lighter the love that I offer you now;
In a spring day shall the tale be told
Of the beautiful things that will never grow old.

The blossoms shall fall in the night wind,
And I will leave you so, to be kind:
Eternal in beauty are short-lived flowers,
Eternal in beauty, these exquisite hours.

I will pluck from my tree a cherry-blossom wand,
And carry it in my merciless hand,
So I will drive you, so bewitch your eyes,
With a beautiful thing that shall never grow wise.

### SOUL'S LIBERTY

He who has lost soul's liberty
Concerns himself for ever with his property,
As, when the folk have lost both dance and song,
Women clean useless pots the whole day long.

Thank God for war and fire
To burn the silly objects of desire,
That from the ruin of a church thrown down
We see God clear and high above the town.

### TO MEN

*(Variation on Ella Wheeler Wilcox, after a poem of the same name)*

Sirs—though we fail you—let us live;
Be just, have pity, and forgive.
Think how poor Mother Eve was brought
To being as God's afterthought.

God had a vast expanse of clay
To fashion Adam's primal day;
Yet was the craftsman's limit shown
His image could not live alone.

Yet God supports eternal life
Without the comfort of a wife;
So it was proved e'er we began
God had miscalculated man.

And of his fault, he took a part
Formed woman's brain and woman's heart
Of Imperfection—vainly planned—
To love, to serve, to understand.

How can you wonder, if we stray
Through coward night and sloven day
When power in us can but reflect
God's wifelessness and man's defect.

Had lonely God when earth was new
Some blest remembrances of two,
He had not made one half of life
A shambles and a hell-stung strife.

✦

Do you remember, O my Dear,
The seventh night of our first year,
The night, when my first son was given
With ecstasy to tutor Heaven—

Had God loved thus, all Hell were blind
And famine, lust and murder kind.
Come, my co-adjutor, beloved smith,
Raise thou thy hammer—break the myth.

There is no marvel of creation
Exists beyond our full relation—
Yet God shall strengthen from his sins
To breed us new and breed us twins.

Thou bungling artificer, yet
Thou shalt be artist and beget
And on the form of Chaos lie
To wash the earth and raise the sky.

Not equal I, but counterpart
And in relation is my heart
Perfect with man's—as with his mind—
Mine is all strong to loose and bind.

Come then, my husband, here and rest
On my so well-remolded breast.
At morning we'll go out and see
How well God works for you and me.

### THE SINGER

If I had peace to sit and sing,
Then I could make a lovely thing;
But I am stung with goads and whips,
So I build songs like iron ships.

Let it be something for my song,
If it is sometimes swift and strong.

### ENVOI

God, thou great symmetry,
Who put a biting lust in me
From whence my sorrows spring,
For all the frittered days
That I have spent in shapeless ways,
Give me one perfect thing.

# D. H. Lawrence

D(AVID) H(ERBERT) LAWRENCE was born September 17, 1885, in the colliery town of Eastwood, a drab hamlet on the border between Derbyshire and Nottinghamshire. The son of workers, his novels return again and again to the rural and industrial backgrounds of his boyhood. Lawrence obtained a scholarship at the Nottingham High School and at sixteen became a pupil-teacher. After a short appointment in a London school, he abandoned teaching for literature. He traveled considerably in search of health and, during his last fifteen years, lived in Italy, New Mexico, and Southern France.

Even in his mid-twenties—in *The White Peacock* (1909), *Love Poems and Others* (1913) and, first of all, in *Sons and Lovers* (1913)—Lawrence pronounced the strain with which he was to be so closely identified. The two volumes of *Collected Poems* (1929) are autobiographically candid, completely characterizing. No one in his generation pursued the cry of sex so passionately, so painfully as D. H. Lawrence; and no one was more confused by it. A magnificently equipped craftsman, a writer *pur sang,* his gamut never extended. His novels, with two unimportant exceptions and, more explicitly, his poems are concerned with little else than the dark fire, the broken body, the struggle, death and resurrection of crucified flesh, the recurring cycle of fulfillment and frustration. This is Lawrence's theme, a theme which he varied with great skill, but one which he could neither leave nor fully control. It is not merely his passion, it is his obsession.

This is as far as Lawrence goes. And he could go no farther except in that limbo where sex and love are desperately confused. He could not separate his spirit from his loins; he was, at the same time, mentally detached and emotionally victimized.

His agony grew sharper, his solution vaguer. This, it seems, was the core of Lawrence's *malaise*. There is something about his excitation which is uncomfortably flagellant; his sudden heats and swift revulsions are too neurotic to evoke more than pity; hysteria, in many of the poems, is subdued but not silenced.

But there is something here beyond the sex-fearful, sex-fascinated being; something beyond the self-worshiping, self-deluded artist, and that is Lawrence's intensity. Whatever its faults, the pitch and register of his work is poetry. Impotence itself has power in his propulsive verse. A poet of sensibilities which are refined to the point of being always wounded, a recorder of kaleidoscopic images and sensory nuances, Lawrence at forty-four had made a permanent if painful contribution to literature. There are passages in his novels—especially in *The Rainbow* (1915) and *Women in Love* (1921)—that have the accent and the sweep of poetry; there are poems that fasten on the mind and will not be shaken off. It is rather a curious commentary that his objective or "fictional" poems are among his best. Nothing that he has written, none of his verse is more surely projected than the dramatic lyrics in dialect: "A Youth Mowing," "Violets," "Whether or Not," that remarkable sequence which a ruder Browning might have fathered and which is a completely rounded .tale, a poignantly condensed novel.

Lawrence is more the enmeshed self, less the detached poet in "A Young Wife," "Love on the Farm," "Wedding Morn," and the irritated fragments in *Pansies* (1929). Here speaks "the hot blood's blindfold art," chaotically, characteristically, but always eloquently.

After a struggle of many years, Lawrence succumbed to tuberculosis. His wish that he be taken to Arizona, either to die or to recuperate, could not be granted and he died March 2, 1930, at Nice, France. Immediately thereafter reappraisals set in: Lawrence was subjected to new examinations as poet, prophet, and pamphleteer. No less than four "intimate" biographers, including his wife, attempted the almost impossible task of presenting Lawrence as he seemed to the world and himself—and succeeded only in presenting him as he appeared to Mabel Dodge Luhan, Middleton Murry, Catherine Carswell, and Freda Lawrence. Horace Gregory was more critical in his study of Lawrence's symbols, estimating the man in relation to his work in *Pilgrim of the Apocalypse*. Lawrence's early stories were collected with a Memoir by David Garnett; posthumous and partly finished stories were issued for several years after his death. *Last Poems,* a volume of some three hundred pages with an introduction by Richard Aldington, appeared in 1933. The book consists of the greater part of two large manuscripts found among Lawrence's papers. It ranges from the sharp, snarling, and often trivial pensées, which Lawrence liked to call "Pansies," to long premonitory poems on death, poems which voice a new dignity.

Few writers had roused more violent and controversial issues; four of his books had been suppressed, a show of his paintings (an art to which Lawrence turned in his forties) was raided. Though he was unusually fecund, opposition kindled a bitter flame in him and his creative passion turned to propaganda. *The Psychology of the Unconscious* is a fantastic variation on Jung; *Studies in American Literature* is a poorly proportioned but provocative plea for the recognition of a native spirit; *Pornography and Obscenity* (1929) is a tract, an argument for the appreciation of the realities as against the hypocrisies of sexual morality.

But his polemical writing is, after all, the least of his work. In the best of his novels and poems he achieved a style that was dynamic, inflamed, savagely honest. A conscientious barbarian, he was, as Stuart Sherman wrote, "a revolutionist in favor of an individualistic, aristocratic barbarianism." He seldom wrote badly. True, his preoccupation was sex (he was described as "the novelist of the over- and the under-sexed"); he dealt almost entirely with the intensification or the perversion of the sexual instinct. But his deeper obsession, the "inner theme," was the possession and maintenance of masculine power and the understanding of men's and women's basic relations with each other. He clarified, though he did not altogether resolve, the complexities in two essays published in *We Need One Another* (1933). Here Lawrence pleaded for a relinquishing of the over-inflated ego and a realization of the sexes' spiritual dependence—"the great flow of the relationship goes on, undying, and this is the flow of living sex, the relation that lasts a lifetime, and of which sex-desire is only one vivid, most vivid, manifestation."

This conviction was fully expressed only toward the end of Lawrence's life; most of his writing lacks such clarity. One homily was apparent in all his works: The world has gone stale, feebly promiscuous, prettily fetid. Small spurts of lust instead of a long passion; talk instead of acts. The world has ceased to be masculine. Its discontent, like its nervous art, its soft-rotten culture, its middle-class *malaise,* is all the outcome of womanishness. Women, pretending to need us, have used us up; women have destroyed us with merciless softness. All we cherish has become effeminized, vitiated with the white poison of their approval and the black venom of their jealousy. Suffering from a "mind-perverted, will-perverted, ego-perverted love," the world will be happy only when man—overcivilized man—regains the free power and security which are the well-spring of emotional vitality. The defect in thinking is obvious. It is not "maleness" which troubles the artist but his consciousness of it. It is this lack of peace which Lawrence instinctively resented and which kept him enslaved to his narrow freedom. Coming up from that lower English world "where the good form and restraint of the public school tradition was a gag to be spat out once the speaker gained the strength of self-confidence," Lawrence, rising by self-improvement, could never resist improving others. In this he was, beneath his libertarian manner, the Puritan. "He came up," said Henry S. Canby, "when the bourgeois Victorian morality was losing its vigor, and he preached his new gospel of virility just as the Methodists preached revivalism to the Anglicans." His methods were extravagant, often exacerbated, but they were vitally his own. He had, above all, the faculty of making the reader revalue his own standards. Whatever status as an artist the future may assign him, there can be no question that he was a force.

A YOUTH MOWING

There are four men mowing down by the Isar;
I can hear the swish of the scythe-strokes, four
Sharp breaths taken; yea, and I
Am sorry for what's in store.

The first man out of the four that's mowing
Is mine, I claim him once and for all;
Though it's sorry I am, on his young feet, knowing
None of the trouble he's led to stall.

As he sees me bringing the dinner, he lifts
His head as proud as a deer that looks
Shoulder-deep out of the corn; and wipes
His scythe-blade bright, unhooks

The scythe-stone and over the stubble to me.
Lad, thou hast gotten a child in me,
Laddie, a man thou'lt ha'e to be,
Yea, though I'm sorry for thee.


### LIGHTNING

I felt the lurch and halt of her heart
  Next my breast, where my own heart was beating;
And I laughed to feel it plunge and bound,
And strange in my blood-swept ears was the sound
  Of the words I kept repeating,
Repeating with tightened arms, and the hot blood's blind-fold art.

Her breath flew warm against my neck,
  Warm as a flame in the close night air;
And the sense of her clinging flesh was sweet
Where her arms and my neck's blood-surge could meet.
  Holding her thus, did I care
That the black night hid her from me, blotted out every speck?

I leaned me forward to find her lips,
  And claim her utterly in a kiss,
When the lightning flew across her face,
And I saw her for the flaring space
  Of a second, afraid of the clips
Of my arms, inert with dread, wilted in fear of my kiss.

A moment, like a wavering spark,
  Her face lay there before my breast,
Pale love lost in a snow of fear,
And guarded by a glittering tear,
  And lips apart with dumb cries;
A moment, and she was taken again in the merciful dark.

I heard the thunder, and felt the rain,
  And my arms fell loose, and I was dumb.
Almost I hated her, she was so good,
Hated myself, and the place, and my blood,
  Which burned with rage, as I bade her come
Home, away home, ere the lightning floated forth again.

## SUSPENSE

The wind comes from the north
Blowing little flocks of birds
Like spray across the town,
And a train roaring forth
Rushes stampeding down
South, with flying curds
Of steam, from the darkening north.

Whither I turn and set
Like a needle steadfastly,
Waiting ever to get
The news that she is free;
But ever fixed, as yet,
To the lode of her agony.

## A YOUNG WIFE

The pain of loving you
Is almost more than I can bear.

I walk in fear of you.
The darkness starts up where
You stand, and the night comes through
Your eyes when you look at me.

Ah, never before did I see
The shadows that live in the sun!

Now every tall glad tree
Turns round its back to the sun
And looks down on the ground, to see
The shadow it used to shun.

At the foot of each glowing thing
A night lies looking up.

Oh, and I want to sing
And dance, but I can't lift up
My eyes from the shadows: dark
They lie spilt round the cup.

What is it?—Hark
The faint fine seethe in the air!

Like the seething sound in a shell!
It is death still seething where
The wild-flower shakes its bell
And the skylark twinkles blue—

The pain of loving you
Is almost more than I can bear.

## CHERRY ROBBERS

Under the long dark boughs, like jewels red
  In the hair of an Eastern girl
Hang strings of crimson cherries, as if had bled
  Blood-drops beneath each curl.

Under the glistening cherries, with folded wings
  Three dead birds lie:
Pale-breasted throstles and a blackbird, robberlings
  Stained with red dye.

Against the haystack a girl stands laughing at me,
  Cherries hung round her ears.
Offers me her scarlet fruit: I will see
  If she has any tears.

## A WINTER'S TALE

Yesterday the fields were only gray with scattered snow,
  And now the longest grass-leaves hardly emerge;
Yet her deep footsteps mark the snow, and go
  On toward the pines at the hill's white verge.

I cannot see her, since the mist's pale scarf
Obscures the dark wood and the dull orange sky;
But she's waiting, I know, impatient and cold, half
Sobs struggling into her frosty sigh.

Why does she come so promptly, when she must know
She's only the nearer to the inevitable farewell?
The hill is steep, on the snow my steps are slow—
Why does she come, when she knows what I have to tell?

## LOVE ON THE FARM

What large, dark hands are those at the window
Grasping in the golden light
Which weaves its way through the evening wind
  At my heart's delight?

Ah, only the leaves! But in the west
I see a redness suddenly come
Into the evening's anxious breast—
  'Tis the wound of love goes home!

The woodbine creeps abroad
Calling low to her lover:
  The sun-lit flirt who all the day
  Has poised above her lips in play
  And stolen kisses, shallow and gay
  Of pollen, now has gone away—
    She woos the moth with her sweet, low word;
And when above her his moth-wings hover
Then her bright breast she will uncover
And yield her honey-drop to her lover.

Into the yellow, evening glow
Saunters a man from the farm below;
Leans, and looks in at the low-built shed
Where the swallow has hung her marriage bed.
  The bird lies warm against the wall.
  She glances quick her startled eyes
  Towards him, then she turns away
  Her small head, making warm display
  Of red upon the throat. Her terrors sway
  Her out of the nest's warm, busy ball,
  Whose plaintive cry is heard as she flies
  In one blue stoop from out the sties
  Into the twilight's empty hall.

Oh, water-hen, beside the rushes,
Hide your quaintly scarlet blushes,
Still your quick tail, lie still as dead,
Till the distance folds over his ominous tread!

The rabbit presses back her ears,
Turns back her liquid, anguished eyes
And crouches low; then with wild spring
Spurts from the terror of his oncoming;
To be choked back, the wire ring
Her frantic effort throttling:
    Piteous brown ball of quivering fears!
Ah, soon in his large, hard hands she dies,
And swings all loose from the swing of his walk!
Yet calm and kindly are his eyes
And ready to open in brown surprise
Should I not answer to his talk
Or should he my tears surmise.

I hear his hand on the latch, and rise from my chair
Watching the door open; he flashes bare
His strong teeth in a smile, and flashes his eyes
In a smile like triumph upon me; then careless-wise
He flings the rabbit soft on the table board
And comes toward me: he! the uplifted sword
Of his hand against my bosom! and oh, the broad
Blade of his glance that asks me to applaud
His coming! With his hand he turns my face to him
And caresses me with his fingers that still smell grim
Of rabbit's fur! God, I am caught in a snare!
I know not what fine wire is round my throat;
I only know I let him finger there
My pulse of life, and let him nose like a stoat
Who sniffs with joy before he drinks the blood.

And down his mouth comes to my mouth! and down
His bright dark eyes come over me, like a hood
Upon my mind! his lips meet mine, and a flood
Of sweet fire sweeps across me, so I drown
Against him, die, and find death good.


PIANO

Softly, in the dusk, a woman is singing to me;
Taking me back down the vista of years, till I see
A child sitting under the piano, in the boom of the tingling strings
And pressing the small, poised feet of a mother who smiles as she sings.

In spite of myself, the insidious mastery of song
Betrays me back, till the heart of me weeps to belong
To the old Sunday evenings at home, with winter outside
And hymns in the cozy parlor, the tinkling piano our guide.

So now it is vain for the singer to burst into clamor
With the great black piano appassionato. The glamour
Of childish days is upon me, my manhood is cast
Down in the flood of remembrance, I weep like a child for the past.

## GREEN

The dawn was apple-green,
  The sky was green wine held up in the sun,
The moon was a golden petal between.

She opened her eyes, and green
  They shone, clear like flowers undone
For the first time, now for the first time seen.

## A WHITE BLOSSOM

A tiny moon as small and white as a single jasmine flower
Leans all alone above my window, on night's wintry bower,
Liquid as lime-tree blossom, soft as brilliant water or rain
She shines, the first white love of my youth, passionless and in vain.

## WEDDING MORN

The morning breaks like a pomegranate
  In a shining crack of red;
Ah, when tomorrow the dawn comes late
  Whitening across the bed
It will find me at the marriage gate
  And waiting while light is shed
On him who is sleeping satiate
  With a sunk, unconscious head.

And when the dawn comes creeping in,
  Cautiously I shall raise
Myself to watch the daylight win
  On my first of days,
As it shows him sleeping a sleep he got
  With me, as under my gaze
He grows distinct, and I see his hot
  Face freed of the wavering blaze.

Then I shall know which image of God
  My man is made toward;
And I shall see my sleeping rod
  Or my life's reward;
And I shall count the stamp and worth
  Of the man I've accepted as mine,
Shall see an image of heaven or of earth
  On his minted metal shine.

Oh, and I long to see him sleep
  In my power utterly;
So I shall know what I have to keep. . . .
  I long to see
My love, that spinning coin, laid still
  And plain at the side of me
For me to reckon—for surely he will
  Be wealth of life to me.

And then he will be mine, he will lie
  Revealed to me;
Patent and open beneath my eye
  He will sleep of me;
He will lie negligent, resign
  His truth to me, and I
Shall watch the dawn light up for me
  This fate of mine.

And as I watch the wan light shine
  On his sleep that is filled of me,
On his brow where the curved wisps clot and
    twine
  Carelessly,
On his lips where the light breaths come and
    go
  Unconsciously,
On his limbs in sleep at last laid low
  Helplessly,
I shall weep, oh, I shall weep, I know
  For joy or for misery.

### WHETHER OR NOT

#### I

Dunna thee tell me it's his'n, mother,
　Dunna thee, dunna thee!
—Oh, ay, he'll come ·an' tell thee his-sèn,
　Wench, wunna he?

Tha doesna mean ter say ter me, mother,
　He's gone wi' that—
—My gel, owt'll do for a man i' th' dark;
　Tha's got it flat!

But 'er's old, mother, 'er's twenty year
　Older nor him—
—Ay, an' yaller as a crowflower; an' yet i' th' dark
　Er'd do for Tim.

Tha niver believes it, does ter, mother?
　It's somebody's lies.
—Ax 'im thy-sèn, wench; a widder's lodger!
　It's no surprise.

#### II

A widow o' forty-five
Wi' a bitter, dirty skin,
To ha' 'ticed a lad o' twenty-five,
An' 'im to 'ave been took in!

A widow o' forty-five
As 'as sludged like a horse all 'er life
Till 'er's tough as whit-leather, to slive [1]
Atween a lad an' 'is wife!

A widow o' forty-five!
A glum old otchel, wi' long
Witch teeth, an' 'er hawk-eyes, as I've
Mistrusted all along!

An' me as 'as kept my-sèn
Shut like a daisy bud,
Clean an' new an' nice, so's when
He wed he'd ha'e summat good!

An' 'im as nice an' fresh
As any man i' th' force,
To ha' gone an' given his clean young flesh
To a woman that coarse!

#### III

You're stout to brave this snow, Miss Stainwright,
　Are you makin' Brinsley way?
—I'm off up th' line to Underwood
　Wi' a dress as is wanted today.

---

[1] To slive = to slip, to interfere.

Oh, are you goin' to Underwood?
 'Appen then you've 'eered!
—What's that as 'appen I've 'eered on, Missis?
 Speak up, you nedn't be feared.

Why, your young man an' Widow Naylor,
 'Er as 'e lodges wi'!
They say he's got 'er wi' childt; but there—
 It's nothing to do wi' me!

Though if it's true, they'll turn 'im out
 O' th' p'lice force, without fail;
An' if it's *not* true, you may back your life
 They'll listen to *her* tale.

—Well, I'm believin' no tale, Missis,
 I'm seein' for my-sèn.
An' when I know for sure, Missis,
 I'll talk *then*.

IV

Nay, robin red-breast, tha needna
 Sit noddin' thy head at me!
My breast's as red as thine, I reckon,
 Flayed red, if tha could but see.

Nay, yo' blessed pee-whips,
 Yo' needna scraight [1] at me!
I'm scraightin' my-sèn but arena goin'
 Ter let iv'rybody see.

Tha *art* smock-raveled, bunny,
 Larropin' neck an' crop
I' th' snow! but I's warrant thee
 *I'm* further ower th' top.

V

Now sithee theer at th' reelroad crossin'
Warmin' 'is-sèn at the stool o' fire
Under the tank as fills th' ingines,
If there isn't my dearly-beloved liar!

My constable, wi' 'is buttoned breast
As stout as the truth, my Sirs! an' 'is face
As bold as a robin! It's much he cares
For this nice old shame an' disgrace.

Oh, but 'e drops 'is flag when 'e sees me!
Yi, an' 'is face goes white! Oh, yes,
Tha can stare at me wi' thy fierce blue eyes;
Tha won't stare me out, I guess.

[1] Scraight = cry.

### VI

Whativer brings thee out so far
    In a' this depth o' snow?
—I'm takin' 'ome a weddin'-dress,
    If yer mun know.

Why, is there a weddin' at Underwood
    As tha ne'd trudge up 'ere?
—It's Widder Naylor's weddin'-dress,
    'Er'll be wantin' it, I 'ear.

*'Er* doesna want no weddin'-dress—
    —Why—? but what dost mean?
—Doesn't ter know what I mean, Timmy?
    Yi, tha must ha' bin 'ard ter wean!

Tha'rt a good-un at suckin'-in yet, Timmy!
    But tell me, isn't it true
As 'er'll be wantin' my weddin'-dress
    In a wik or two?

—Tha's no 'casions ter ha'e me on,
    Lizzie; what's done is done.
—*Done,* I should think so! An' might I ask
    When tha begun?

It's thee as 'as done it, as much as me,
    So there, an' I tell thee flat.
—Me gotten a childt ter thy landlady?
    —Tha's gotten thy answer pat.

As tha allus 'ast; but let me tell thee
    Hasna ter sent me whoam, when I
Was a'most burstin' mad o' my-sèn,
    An' walkin' in agony?

After I'd kissed thee at night, Lizzie,
    An' tha's laid against me, an' melted
Into me, melted right into me, Lizzie,
    Till I was verily swelted.

An' if my landlady seed me like it,
    An' if 'er clawkin' eyes
Went through me as the light went out,
    Is it any cause for surprise?

—No cause for surprise at all, my lad;
    After kissin' an' cuddlin' wi' me, tha could
Turn thy mouth on a woman like that!
    I hope it did thee good.

—Ay, it did; but afterwards
 I could ha' killed 'er.
—Afterwards! how many times afterwards
 Could ter ha' killed 'er?

Say no more, Liz, dunna thee;
 'Er's as good as thee.
—Then I'll say good-by to thee, Timothy;
 Take 'er i'stead o' me.

I'll ta'e thy word good-by, Liz,
 Though I shonna marry 'er.
Nor 'er nor nub'dy.—It is
 Very brave of you, Sir!

—T' childt maun ta'e its luck, it mun,
 An' 'er maun ta'e *'er* luck.
F'r I tell yer I h'arena marryin' none
 On yer; yo'n got what yer took!

—That's spoken like a man, Timmy,
 That's spoken like a man!
" 'E up an' fired 'is pistol,
 An' then away 'e ran!"

—I damn well shanna marry 'er,
 Nor yo', so chew it no more!
I'll chuck the flamin' lot o' you—
 —Yer nedn't 'ave swore!

### VII

There's 'is collar round th' candlestick,
An' there's the dark-blue tie I bought 'im!
An' these is the woman's kids 'es's so fond on,
An' 'ere comes the cat as caught 'im!

I dunno wheer 'is eyes was—a gret
Round-shouldered hag! My Sirs, to think
Of 'im stoopin' to 'er! You'd wonder 'e could
Throw 'imself down *that* sink!

I expect yer know who I am, Mrs. Naylor?
 Who y'are? yis, you're Lizzie Stainwright.
An' 'appen you'd guess then what I've come for?
 —'Appen I mightn't, 'appen I might.

Yer knowed as I was courtin' Tim Merfin?
 —Yis, I knowed 'e wor courtin' thee.
An' yet yer've bin carryin' on wi' 'im!
 —Ay, an' 'im wi' me.

Well, now yer've got ter pay for it.
    —If I han, what's that ter thee?
'E isn't goin' ter marry yer.
    —Tha wants 'im thy-sèn, I see.

It 'asn't nothin' to do with me.
    —Then what art colleyfoglin' for?
*I'm* not 'avin' your orts an' slarts.
    —Which on us said you wor?

But I want you to know 'e's not *marryin'* you.
    —Tha wants 'im thy-sèn too bad.
Though I'll see as 'e pays you, an' does what's right.
    —Tha'rt for doin' a lot wi' t' lad!

### VIII

To think I should 'ave ter 'affle an' caffle
    Wi' a woman, an' name 'er a price
For lettin' me marry the lad as I thought
    Ter marry wi' cabs an' rice!

But we'll go unbeknown ter th' registrar,
    An' give *'er* the money there is;
For I won't be beholden to such as 'er,
    I won't, or my name's not Liz.

### IX

Ta'e off thy duty stripes, Tim,
    An' come in 'ere wi' me;
Ta'e off thy p'liceman's helmet
    An' look at me.

I wish tha hadna done it, Tim,
    I do, an' that I do!
For whenever I look thee i' th' face, I s'll see
    Her face too.

I wish I could wesh 'er off'n thee;
    'Appen I can, if I try.
But tha'll ha'e ter promise ter be true ter me
    Till I die. . . .

### X

Twenty pounds o' thy own tha hast, an' fifty pound ha'e I;
Thine shall go ter pay the woman, an' wi' my bit we'll buy
All as we s'll want for furniture when tha leaves this place;
An' we'll be married at th' registrar—now lift thy face.

Lift thy face an' look at me, man! canna ter look at me?
Sorry I am for this business, an' sorry if ever I've driven thee
To do such a thing; though it's a poor tale, it is, that I'm bound to say,
Afore I can ta'e thee I've got a widder o' forty-five ter pay!

Dunna thee think but what I've loved thee; I've loved thee too well.
An' 'deed an' I wish as this tale o' thine wor niver my tale to tell!
Deed an' I wish I c'd 'a' stood at th' altar wi' thee an' bin proud o' thee!
That I could 'a' bin first woman ter thee, as tha'rt first man ter me!

But we maun ma'e the best on't. So now rouse up an' look at me.
Look up an' say tha'rt sorry tha did it; say tha'rt sorry for me.
They'll turn thee out o' th' force, I doubt me; if they do, we can see
If my father can get thee a job on t'bank. Say tha'rt sorry, Timmy!

### XI

Ay, I'm sorry, I'm sorry,
 But what o' that!
Ay, I'm sorry! Tha needna worry
 Nor fret thy fat.

I'm sorry for thee, I'm sorry f'r 'er,
 I'm sorry f'r us a'.
But what then? Tha wants me, does ter
 After a'?

Ah'n put my-sèn i' th' wrong, Liz,
 An' 'er as well.
An' tha'rt that right, tha knows; 'tis
 Other folks in hell.

Tha *art* so sure tha'rt right, Liz!
 That damned sure!
But 'ark thee 'ere, that widder woman
 's less graspin', if 'er's poor.

What 'er gen, 'er gen me
 Beout a thought.
'Er gen me summat; I shanna
 Say it wor nought.

I'm sorry for th' trouble, ay
 As comes on us a'.
But sorry for what I had? why
 I'm not, that's a'.

As for marryin', I shanna marry
 Neither on yer.
Ah've 'ad a' as I can carry
 From you an' from 'er.

So I s'll go an' leave yer,
 Both on yer,
I don't like yer, Liz, I want ter
 Get away from yer.

An' I don't really like 'er neither,
    Even though I've 'ad
More from 'er than from you; but either
    Of yer's too much for this lad.

Let me go! what's good o' talkin'?
    Let's a' ha' done.
Talk about love o' women!
    Ter me it's no fun.

I s'll say good-by, Liz, to yer,
    Yer too much i' th' right for me.
An' wi' 'er somehow it isn't right.
    So good-by, an' let's let be!


## AWARE

Slowly the moon is rising out of the ruddy haze,
Divesting herself of her golden shift, and so
Emerging white and exquisite; and I in amaze
See in the sky before me, a woman I did not know
I loved, but there she goes, and her beauty hurts my heart;
I follow her down the night, begging her not to depart.


## KISSES IN THE TRAIN

I saw the midlands
    Revolve through her hair;
The fields of autumn
    Stretching bare,
And sheep on the pasture
    Tossed back in a scare.

And still as ever
    The world went round,
My mouth on her pulsing
    Neck was found,
And my breast to her beating
    Breast was bound.

But my heart at the center
    Of all, in a swound
Was still as a pivot,
    As all the ground
On its prowling orbit
    Shifted round.

And still in my nostrils
    The scent of her flesh,

And still my wet mouth
    Sought her afresh;
And still one pulse
    Through the world did thresh.

And the world all whirling
    Around in joy
Like the dance of a dervish
    Did destroy
My sense—and my reason
    Spun like a toy.

But firm at the center
    My heart was found;
Her own to my perfect
    Heart-beat bound,
Like a magnet's keeper
    Closing the round.


## SPRING MORNING

Ah, through the open door
Is there an almond tree
Aflame with blossom!
    —Let us fight no more.

Among the pink and blue
Of the sky and the almond flowers
A sparrow flutters.
 —We have come through.

It is really spring!—See,
When he thinks himself alone
How he bullies the flowers.
 —You and me

How happy we'll be!—See him,
He clouts the tufts of flowers
In his impudence.
 —But, did you dream

It would be so bitter? Never mind
It is finished, the spring is here.
And we're going to be summer-happy
 And summer-kind.

We have died, we have slain and been slain.
We are not our old selves any more.
I feel new and eager
 To start again.

It is gorgeous to live and forget.
And to feel quite new.
See the bird in the flowers?—he's making
 A rare to-do!

He thinks the whole blue sky
Is much less than the bit of blue egg
He's got in his nest—we'll be happy
 You and I, I and you.

With nothing to fight any more—
In each other, at least.
See, how gorgeous the world is
 Outside the door!

### TREES IN THE GARDEN

Ah in the thunder air
how still the trees are!

And the lime-tree, lovely and tall, every leaf silent
hardly looses even a last breath of perfume.

And the ghostly, creamy colored little tree of leaves
white, ivory white among the rambling greens,
how evanescent, variegated elder, she hesitates on the green grass
as if, in another moment, she would disappear
with all her grace of foam!

And the larch that is only a column, it goes up too tall to see:
and the balsam-pines that are blue with the gray-blue blueness of things from the sea,
and the young copper beech, its leaves red-rosy at the ends
how still they are together, they stand so still
in the thunder air, all strangers to one another
as the green grass glows upwards, strangers in the garden.

# F. S. Flint

F(RANCIS) S(TEWART) FLINT was born in 1885 and, besides being a poet, is known as a skillful translator from the French. He was one of the first to form the Imagist group and his "History of Imagism," in *The Egoist* (May, 1915) shows that the movement had a much earlier origin than is commonly supposed. His youth was spent in a struggle to maintain existence. As he wrote in the Introduction to

*Otherworld,* "I am not a scholar in any sense; the chance of life has made me a wage-earner since I could read and write almost—so that when I invented the term 'unrhymed cadence' I was not aware that I was in the oldest of traditions, that Chaucer had spoken of it in his *House of Fame* or that Cynewulf had sung:

> Many varied voices voice I through my mouth.
> Cunning are the notes I sing, and incessantly I change them.
> Clear I cry and loud with the chant within my head;
> Holding to my tones, hiding not their sweetness,
> . . . when I burst forth with a cadenced song."

Flint himself was one of the most accomplished of the Imagist poets. His first volume, *In the Net of the Stars* (1909), anticipates the later experiments although most of it is formal in structure and is like its title, influenced by Yeats. Ford Madox Ford was quick to appreciate Flint's gift and printed his work in *The English Review. Cadences* appeared in 1915, *Otherworld* in 1920. The latter volume began with this statement: "There is only one art of writing and that is the art of poetry; and wherever you feel the warmth of human experience and imagination in any writing, there is poetry—whether it is in the form we call prose, or in rhyme and meter, or in the unrhymed cadence in which the greater part of this book is written."

Apart from his form, which is usually successful in registering racial memories, Flint's philosophy is apparent beneath a not so obvious music. It is regrettable that Flint has not pursued poetry, having discontinued it with *Otherworld.* Since 1920 he has busied himself with translating the works of modern French poets and essayists, especially Verhaeren and Jean de Bosschere.

### LONDON

London, my beautiful,
it is not the sunset
nor the pale green sky
shimmering through the curtain
of the silver birch,
nor the quietness;
it is not the hopping
of birds
upon the lawn,
nor the darkness
stealing over all things
that moves me.

But as the moon creeps slowly
over the tree-tops
among the stars,
I think of her
and the glow her passing
sheds on men.

London, my beautiful,
I will climb
into the branches
to the moonlit tree-tops,
that my blood may be cooled
by the wind.

### PLANE-TREE

O tardy plane-tree,
Was not the winter long enough?
The April sun
Has sprayed with green
The gray house behind the boughs
And burst the first lit
Golden lamps of the chestnut:
Its leaves fall limply
Away from the brown flower-buds;
He has dressed in pink
The black and naked almond-tree,

Bestrewn the pavement with red-tipped cat-
   kins,
And sent the sparrows to find
His pouting buds on every twig,
Excepting yours, O motley plane-tree,
Whom the motor-cars,
In scorn of your laziness,
Spurn with their dust.

### SADNESS

Spirit in me,
why are you so sad?
Is it that men are still but men
and know no other way?

Over the hills
go and find the golden-garlanded trees. . . .
Autumn has come. . . .
In the soft sadness of her mists,
you may discover
a memory of the joys
of summer past,
and there forget
what men are,
and think
what men may be.

### CHRYSANTHEMUMS

O golden-red and tall chrysanthemums,
you are the graceful soul of the china vase
wherein you stand
amid your leaves.

O quiet room,
you are the symbol of my patient heart.
O flowers of flame, O tall chrysanthemums,
my love who comes

will wave wide ripples of disquiet there,
and a great tide of the eternal sea
will rise at her approach,
and surge to song.

O quiet room, O flame chrysanthemums,
images of my heart and its proud love,
you have no presage of the power that comes
to fill with anguish the essential calm.

O calm wrought face, O sphinx behind the
   door,
her hand is on the latch.

### BEGGAR

In the gutter
piping his sadness
an old man stands,
bent and shriveled,
beard draggled,
eyes dead.

Huddled and mean,
shivering in threadbare clothes—
winds beat him,
hunger bites him,
forlorn, a whistle in his hands,
piping.

Hark! the strange quality
of his sorrowful music,
wind from an empty belly
wrought magically
into the wind,—

pattern of silver on bronze.

# Gerald Gould

G ERALD GOULD was born in 1885 at Scarborough, was educated at Magdalen College, Oxford, and was Fellow of Merton College from 1906 to 1916. Journalist
as well as author, he was associate editor of *The Daily Herald* from 1919 to 1921
and literary editor of *The Saturday Review* from 1922 to 1926.

   Gould began as a poet and, although he is the author of half a dozen books of
essays and sketches, remains a poet. Of his eight books of verse, the most interesting

are *The Happy Tree* (1919), *The Journey* (1920), and *Beauty, the Pilgrim* (1927). Extremely versatile, his smoothly running lines sometimes descend to mere facility; but a dignity of spirit underlines the best of Gould's lyrics. A comprehensive *Collected Poems* was published simultaneously in America and England in 1929.

### SONG

She whom I love will sit apart,
  And they whom love makes wise
May know the beauty in her heart
  By the beauty in her eyes.

Thoughts that in quietness confute
  The noisy world are hers,
Like music in a listening lute
  Whose strings no finger stirs.

And in her eyes the shadows move,
  Not glad nor sad, but strange
With those unchanging dreams that prove
  The littleness of change.

### MORTALITY

In the green quiet wood, where I was used,
  In summer, to a welcome calm and dark,
I found the threat of murder introduced
  By scars of white paint on the wrinkled
  bark.

How few old friends were to be spared! And
  now
  I see my friends with new eyes here in town
—Men as trees walking, and on every brow
  A pallid scar, and all to be cut down.

### TWILIGHT

The fields grow dim; the somber mills
Stand crucified against the skies;
Blue in the distance rise
The ancient hills.

The stars come softly, and the least
Last wind is dead as dead desires;

A swarm of silver spires
Fades in the East.

The heavy thoughts that dwelt with me
Slip from me soundless, as the dead
Sink to their quiet bed
Far out at sea.

The stars are empty of concern,
The earth is empty of unrest;
Almost the burning West
Has ceased to burn.

Gray rivers and gray roads, and dells
Having the darkness at their heart;
From valleys, far apart,
The noise of bells.

### THE HAPPY TREE

There was a bright and happy tree;
  The wind with music laced its boughs;
Thither across the houseless sea
  Came singing birds to house.

Men grudged the tree its happy eves,
  Its happy dawns of eager sound;
So that all crown and tower of leaves
  They leveled with the ground.

They made an upright of the stem,
  A cross-piece of a bough they made:
No shadow of their deed on them
  The fallen branches laid.

But blithely, since the year was young,
  When they a fitting hill did find,
There on the happy tree they hung
  The Saviour of mankind.

## Humbert Wolfe

H UMBERT WOLFE was born at Milan in Italy, January 5, 1885. As he himself declared, he "lost no time in crossing to Bradford in the West Riding of Yorkshire, which town he reached during the same year and remained there till he left it for Oxford some 18 years later. Wrote sporadic and increasingly unsatisfactory verse from the age of 16 till his appointment to the British Civil Service in 1909. This appointment naturally induced in him a more restrained outlook upon life and, beyond a few casual poems and a rejected novel, he had no literary output or recognition till after the War in 1919. In that year, he published *London Sonnets,* followed in the next year by *Shylock Reasons with Mr. Chesterton.* In 1923, he published *Circular Saws,* a collection of ambiguous aphorisms, and, in 1924, *Kensington Gardens,* a collection of short poems dealing with that delectable locality. It is to be anticipated (and feared) that his output will tend rapidly to increase."

That was in 1924. Between that year and 1935 Wolfe published some fourteen volumes, all, with two exceptions, in verse. The outstanding quality is neither the dexterous satire which Wolfe uses so incisively nor the grace and charm of which he is somewhat too fond, but a confusion of the two. The surface characteristics are modern, but modern only in certain tricks of typography and employment of "slant" or "suspended" rhymes. There is, above all, a fancy that delights to improvise on major themes which somehow slide into minor cadences. It is this contradiction which marks even the most definite of his volumes, an indetermination from which Wolfe seems unable to escape. It is as if the "pale musicianer" of whom he speaks had composed a robust theme—and arranged it as a pretty duet for dulcimer and *viola d'amore.*

Thus the poet cannot make up his mind whether to thrust sentimentally or sigh sardonically; whether to be a mimic Heine or a tragic Pierrot; whether to be the last of an old tradition of lyricists or the first of a new generation of ironists. As a result, he is all of these in quick succession, often, indeed, at the same time. *Humoresque* (1926), the least remarkable poetically, is the most rewarding as a study of this paradoxical ambidexterity. *The Unknown Goddess* (1925) wavers between earnestness and artificiality; "Iliad," as memorable a set of stanzas about poetry as was ever written, is followed by half a dozen fragilities composed of whipped cream and a spun-sugar *Weltschmerz.* In *News of the Devil* (1926) the barb of satire speeds with a savage purpose. *Cursory Rhymes* (1927), on the other hand, is a collection of verses to and for children in which the author begins by being unsure of his audience and ends by being unsure of himself; the note of naïveté seems forced, the archness calculated, the humor tricky and bookish. *This Blind Rose* (1929) and *Snow* (1931) again alternate Wolfe's not quite detached irony, his bitter-sweet overtones, the artificial idiom which surrenders, in spite of the author's weak struggle, to "the soft advances of the charmed senses." The poet admonishes himself:

> Yield to the easy hunger
> Of beauty no longer—

But, though the later poems show a gain in external discipline there is little evidence of a deepened consciousness or inner necessity.

Wolfe's two best volumes up to 1935 are the early *Kensington Gardens* (1924) and the larger *Requiem* (1927). In their very differences they are this poet, flower and essence, all compact. In the first, his fantasies enchant not only with their delicacy but with their inherent truth. The squirrel "like a small gray coffee-pot," the half-metal tulip "clean as a lady, cool as glass," the city financier with his "tableland of shiny hat," the "flushed example" of the rose with her "dazzling inch of scent"—all these are seen, felt, and communicated in such a way that the reader thrills with that emotion which is at the base of all enjoyment, the mingling of recognition and surprise. *Requiem* is the most reflective of all Wolfe's work and the nearest to a synthesis. This symphonic and almost fugual creation retains Wolfe's exactitude of epithet embodied in a graver music whose pattern cannot be so easily defined. It is, in spite of small lapses, a major achievement.

*Homage to Meleager* (1930) and *Others Abide* (1927) display Wolfe as the translator of many epigrams from the Greek, a task for which he was unusually capable. His quick ear and nimble technique fitted him exactly to render the shades of declamation and wit; James Stephens wrote, "It may reasonably be said that his versions supersede all others."

*X at Oberammergau* (1935) again attempts to construct a major poem upon minor effects. The theme is large as well as timely: The actor who plays the part of Christ in the Passion Play has fallen ill and a stranger has been drafted to assume the rôle. His presence, and something which emanates from his being, divides the village in two parties, one led by the actor who plays John supported by the two Marys, the other led by Judas under the guidance of the Nazi State Commissioner. The Gospel narrative from this point on is paralleled and, in spite of its modernization, moves swiftly to the foreseen tragic climax. Unfortunately Wolfe's treatment fails to meet the demands of his striking subject. Instead of building up a long unified poem he attempts a mosaic of narrative couplets, disintegrated choruses, and lyrics—many of them trivial—until the reader's attention is subdivided and distracted. Nevertheless, though the scenes are almost void of action, there is communicated a sense of bitter drama and irony.

### TULIP

Clean as a lady,
cool as glass,
fresh without fragrance
the tulip was.

The craftsman, who carved her
of metal, prayed:
"Live, oh thou lovely!"
Half metal she stayed.

### THRUSHES

The City Financier
walks in the gardens,

stiffly, because of
his pride and his burdens.

The daisies, looking
up, observe
only a self-
respecting curve.

The thrushes only
see a flat
table-land
of shiny hat.

He looks importantly
about him,
while all the spring
goes on without him.

### THE GRAY SQUIRREL

Like a small gray
coffee-pot,
sits the squirrel.
He is not

all he should be,
kills by dozens
trees, and eats
his red-brown cousins.

The keeper, on the
other hand
, who shot him, is
a Christian, and

loves his enemies,
which shows
the squirrel was not
one of those.

### LAMB

The old bellwether
looked at the lamb,
as a gentleman looks
when he mutters "Damn!"

"If you jump and frisk,
you little fool,
you'll only end
by losing your wool.

"When I was a lamb
I always would
behave as like a sheep
as I could."

"Did you!" the lamb
replied with a leap,
"I always thought
you were born a sheep."

The park-keeper said
to the boy on the fence,
"Let's have less
of your impudence!

"Off with you now,
and do as you're bade,
or you'll end in prison.
When I was a lad . . ."

### THE LILAC

Who thought of the lilac?
"I," dew said,
"I made up the lilac
out of my head."

"She made up the lilac!
Pooh!" thrilled a linnet,
and each dew-note had a
lilac in it.

### THE ROSE

Why should a man
, though six foot tall,
think he matters
at all, at all?

and, though he live
for seventy years,
does he suppose that
anyone cares?

Rather let me
to him propose
the flushed example
of the rose,

who, with her dazzling
inch of scent,
a summer's day
weighs imminent

upon the spirit
entranced, and goes
richer with that
than he with those.

### LABURNUM

Laburnum hangs
her golden fleece
through a thousand
lattices.

In the silken
flosses caught
struggles Spring,
the Argonaut.

## THINGS LOVELIER

You cannot dream
    Things lovelier
Than the first love
    I had of her.

Nor air is any
    By magic shaken
As her first breath in
    The first kiss taken.

And who, in dreaming,
    Understands
Her hands stretched like
    A blind man's hands?

Open, trembling,
    Wise they were—
You cannot dream
    Things lovelier.


## GREEN CANDLES

"There's someone at the door," said gold
    candlestick:
"Let her in quick, let her in quick!"
"There is a small hand groping at the handle.
Why don't you turn it?" asked green candle.

"Don't go, don't go," said the Heppelwhite
    chair,
"Lest you find a strange lady there."
"Yes, stay where you are," whispered the
    white wall:
"There is nobody there at all."

"I know her little foot," gray carpet said:
"Who but I should know her light tread?"
"She shall come in," answered the open door,
"And not," said the room, "go out any more."


## QUEEN VICTORIA

Queen Victoria's
statue is
the work of her
daughter Beatrice.

The shape's all wrong,
and the crown don't fit,

but--bless her old heart!
she was proud of it.


## LOVE IS A KEEPER OF SWANS

Love is a keeper of swans!
Helen! amid what dark wherries
are you steering the silver boat,
that for all the love of Paris,
and his lips against your throat,
passed out of Troy with windless vans?

And, fairest of Italians,
where do you glimmer, Beatrice?
What light of heaven stains your wings
with gold that were all fleur de lys?
And do you hear when Dante sings?
"Love is a keeper of swans."

Love is a keeper of swans.
Have you left the barren plain,
and stormed a gold-eagle's eyrie?
Queen-swan of the eagle strain,
what mountain has you, Mary?
And is its name, as ever, still romance?

And you, bright cynet of immortal Hans,
you need not join your sisters yet.
You have all time. Why should you hasten.
What though the lake with reeds be set,
one reed is murmuring, oh, listen!
"Love is a keeper of swans."


## MAN

The feathers in a fan
are not so frail as man;
the green embossèd leaf
than man is no more brief.
His life is not so loud
as the passing of a cloud;
his death is quieter
than harebells when they stir.
The years that have no form
and substance are as warm,
and space has hardly less
supreme an emptiness.
And yet man being frail
does on himself prevail,

and with a single thought
can bring the world to naught,
as being brief he still
bends to his fleeting will
all time and makes of it
the shadow of his wit.
Soundless in life and death

although he vanisheth,
the echo of a song
makes all the stars a gong.
Cold, void, and yet the grim
darkness is hot with him,
and space is but the span
of the long love of man.

### THE WATERS OF LIFE

When, hardly moving, you decorate night's hush
   with the slim pencil of your grace, retrieving
the clean flat stroke of some old Grecian brush
   that painted dancers fair beyond believing;

when, leaning back the harvest of your hair
   under the moon with beauty as still as hers,
your body's wonder writes upon the air
   the perfect cadence of consummate verse,

I think, if this upon the air be shaken,
   brief as a falling blossom, it can but be
that Time records, by beauty overtaken,
   in one gold instant, immortality,

and that the patterns you weave upon the night
   have such swift passion, such essential heat,
that all the painter sees, the poet can write,
   are but pale shadows of your dancing feet.

### THIS IS NOT DEATH

Lay aside phrases; speak as in the night
a child in terror might.
Confess that you are lonely, that you heard
some foot or hand that stirred,
that, holding your own breath, you almost hear
the midnight breath of Fear,
that tearless, soundless in your heart you pray:
"God! give me back the day!"
Yes! God can give it back, but not the one
that you have dreamed upon.
The black will turn to gray, the gray to blue
distance, but not for you,
and not for you the cheerful voice of men
will warm the heart again.
Nor will your friends or enemies intrude
upon that solitude
where only shadows drift and cross and pass,
seen sideways in your glass.

Make not complaint. For neither prayer nor tear
has its old power here.
This is not silence rounded by the deep
deliverance of sleep,
but by the empty spaces where the will
to wake again is still.
You chose, and you abide the choice, apart,
saying to your own heart:
"Beat if you must, though softly," to the brain:
"Must you imagine pain?"
And last of all say to the sobbing breath:
"No, fool, this is not death."

### ILIAD

False dreams, all false,
mad heart, were yours.
The word, and nought else,
in time endures.
Not you long after,
perished and mute,
will last, but the defter
viol and lute.
Sweetly they'll trouble
the listeners
with the cold dropped pebble
of painless verse.
Not you will be offered,
but the poet's false pain.
You have loved and suffered,
mad heart, in vain.
What love doth Helen
or Paris have
where they lie still in
a nameless grave?
Her beauty's a wraith,
and the boy Paris
muffles in death
his mouth's cold cherries.
Yes! these are less,
that were love's summer,
than one gold phrase
of old blind Homer.
Not Helen's wonder
nor Paris stirs,
but the bright, untender
hexameters.
And thus, all passion
is nothing made,
but a star to flash in
an Iliad.
Mad heart, you were wrong!
No love of yours,
but only what's sung,
when love's over, endures.

# Frances Cornford

FRANCES (DARWIN) CORNFORD, daughter of Sir Francis Darwin, the third son of Charles Darwin, was born in 1886 at Cambridge. She married Francis Macdonald Cornford, Fellow and Lecturer of Trinity College, Cambridge, in 1909.

Her first volume, *Poems* (1910), though unaffected, showed little trace of individuality. With *Spring Morning* (1915) a much more distinct personality expressed itself. Hers is a firmly realized, clean-edged verse, with a clarity of utterance which is also found in the more suggestive *Autumn Midnight* (1923). Her later verse in *Different Days* (1928) is no less spontaneous than the simple "A Wasted Day," the acute and onomatopoetic "The Watch," and the delightfully mocking triolet "To a Fat Lady Seen from the Train." It is, however, more measured; gravity has been added without the loss of charm. Whether grave or mocking Mrs. Cornford's tone maintains a quiet distinction.

In *Mountains and Molehills* (1935), with distinctive woodcuts by Gwen Raverat, Mrs. Cornford continues to write of the English countryside with a quaint difference, of thoughts in a night nursery, of a back view particular yet universal, of Cambridge autumns, of madmen and fairies—a seemingly heterogeneous set of variations on traditional themes. Yet Mrs. Cornford, somehow, imposes unity upon them, if only by virtue of making her subjects sing.

### THE COUNTRY BEDROOM

My room's a square and candle-lighted boat,
In the surrounding depths of night afloat.
My windows are the portholes, and the seas
The sound of rain on the dark apple-trees.

Sea-monster-like beneath, an old horse blows
A snort of darkness from his sleeping nose,
Below, among drowned daisies. Far off, hark!
Far off, one owl amidst the waves of dark.

### TO A FAT LADY SEEN FROM THE TRAIN

O why do you walk through the fields in gloves,
    Missing so much and so much?
O fat white woman whom nobody loves,
Why do you walk through the fields in gloves,
When the grass is soft as the breast of doves
    And shivering sweet to the touch?
O why do you walk through the fields in gloves,
    Missing so much and so much?

### THE WATCH

I wakened on my hot, hard bed;
Upon the pillow lay my head;
Beneath the pillow I could hear
My little watch was ticking clear.
I thought the throbbing of it went
Like my continual discontent;
I thought it said in every tick:
I am so sick, so sick, so sick:
O death, come quick, come quick, come
    quick,
Come quick, come quick, come quick, come
    quick. . . .

### A WASTED DAY

I spoiled the day;
    Hotly, in haste
All the calm hours
    I gashed and defaced.

Let me forget,
    Let me embark
—Sleep for my boat—
    And sail through the dark.

Till a new day
    Heaven shall send,
Whole as an apple,
    Kind as a friend.

## AT NIGHT

My brain is like the ravaged shores—the sand
Torn cruelly by footsteps from the land.
O hushing waves; O profound sea of sleep,
Send your curved ripples surely-lapping.
  Creep,
Pour on the scarrèd surface of my brain;
With your vast pity, wash it smooth again.

## THE UNBESEECHABLE

### (To be set to music)

"Time stands still
  With gazing on her face,"
Sang Dowland to his lute,
  Full of courtly grace.

Now that his musician's face
  And her face are dust,
Still I cry, Stand still:
  Still cry I must.

Stand still, Time,
  Hold, hold your pace;
Stiller stand than the smile
  On Pharaoh's face.

Stiller than December's frost
  That takes the heart with wonder,
Or the pause that comes between
  Lightning and thunder.

Time, stand still,
  Hush now your tread,
Stiller, stiller than a room
  Where lies the sheeted dead.

Where, though it's busy noon,
  Naught comes or goes;
Where the tree of endless peace
  To the ceiling grows.

O Time, Time—
  Stark and full of pain
Why drag me into space,
  A dog upon a chain?

I who would float with you,
  A ship sailing white,
Who cannot tell which power is hers,
  And which the wind's delight.

So my refreshèd soul
  Time would adore,
If for one moment's breath
  Time were no more.

But, with Dowland's broken lute
  And his forgotten rhyme,
Still I cry, Stand still,
  Stand still, Time.

## THE HILLS

Out of the complicated house, come I
To walk beneath the sky.
Here mud and stones and turf, here every-
    thing
Is mutely comforting.
Now hung upon the twigs and thorns appear
A host of lovely rain-drops cold and clear.
And on the bank
Or deep in brambly hedges dank
The small birds nip about, and say:
"Brothers, the Spring is not so far away!"
The hills like mother-giantesses old
Lie in the cold,
And with a complete patience, let
The cows come cropping on their bosoms wet,
And even tolerate that such as I
Should wander by
With paltry leathern heel which cannot harm
Their bodies' calm;
And, with a heart they cannot know, to bless
The enormous power of their peacefulness.

# T. E. Hulme

T E. HULME was born in 1886, and was educated at Cambridge, where he dis-
. tinguished himself in philosophy. Coming to London, he was soon established
as the intellectual stimulus if not the leader of a group of writers, painters, and
thinkers, all of whom paid posthumous tribute to his genius. Entering the War, he
was killed in action in 1917.

It is doubtful whether any writer of his generation considered theories of expression more seriously than Hulme. He distrusted the word *per se,* regarding it
as a thing with no inner reality. As Herbert Read says, "Against words he opposed
the *image* as a unit and the *analogy* as an instrument of thought. Poetry, in the
broad sense of imaginative literature, becomes the only kind of logic worthy of
consideration, and the art of poetry the only science of meaning. Thought, he
argued, was prior to its expression in language, being the simultaneous presentation to the mind of two different images; thought was the recognition of their
analogy. The poet is he who can awaken this analogy in the mind of the reader.
There can be no question of exact conveyance, because language is a feeble instrument. The poet only suggests, and his suggestion falls flat on a mind that is not in
some manner prepared for this sudden fertilization. But suggestion is not produced
by 'eye-blur': poetry is a mosaic of exactly defined words, and suggestion must not
be related to indefiniteness, but is the most exact conveyance possible of a vivid
visual image." Five of Hulme's image-built poems appeared at the end of Pound's
*Ripostes* (1915) gravely entitled "The Complete Poetical Works of T. E. Hulme."

After Hulme's death Herbert Read undertook the labor of deciphering and editing his manuscripts. Most of the material appeared under the title *Speculations* in
1924. A supplementary pamphlet, *Notes on Language and Style,* also collated by
Read, was published as one of the University of Washington Chapbooks in 1929.

## AUTUMN

A touch of cold in the Autumn night—
I walked abroad,
And saw the ruddy moon lean over a hedge
Like a red-faced farmer.
I did not speak, but nodded,
And round about were the wistful stars
With white faces like town children.

## CONVERSION

Lighthearted I walked into the valley wood
In the time of hyacinths,
Till beauty like a scented cloth
Cast over, stifled me. I was bound
Motionless and faint of breath
By loveliness that is her own eunuch.

Now pass I to the final river
Ignominiously, in a sack, without sound,
As any peeping Turk to the Bosphorus.

## THE EMBANKMENT

*(The fantasia of a fallen gentleman
on a cold, bitter night)*

Once, in finesse of fiddles found I ecstasy,
In the flash of gold heels on the hard pave-
ment.
Now see I
That warmth's the very stuff of poesy.
Oh, God, make small
The old star-eaten blanket of the sky,
That I may fold it round me and in comfort
lie.

## Siegfried Sassoon

SIEGFRIED (LORAINE) SASSOON was born September 8, 1886. He was educated at Marlborough and Clare College, Cambridge, and, during the War, was a captain in the Royal Welsh Fusiliers. He fought in France and Palestine; he won the Military Cross for bringing in wounded on the battlefield.

Sassoon's literary development seems as contradictory as it is curious. Descended from Persian Jews on his father's side, from a traditional English country family on his mother's, Sassoon's boyhood was spent alternating between fox- and rhyme-hunting. He was divided between a love of rugged activity and a fondness for pale, Dowsonesque lyrics. Several volumes ranging from parody to the verge of preciosity were issued anonymously and privately printed. The earliest book, *Poems* (1906), was published in Sassoon's twentieth year and is, according to its author, "mostly weak imitations of Tennyson, Swinburne, and Rossetti." A sense of their unreality drove him to a larger work, *The Daffodil Murderer* (1913), a poem which, beginning as a burlesque of Masefield, ended in serious self-expression.

By this time the poet had chaffed himself out of his juvenile admirations for Stephen Phillips and the Pre-Raphaelites, and strong feeling demanded a powerful expression. The war compelled it. With *The Old Huntsman* (1917) Sassoon came into his own idiom, taking his place immediately as "one of England's most brilliant rising stars." The first poem, a pseudo-Masefieldian monologue, was followed by a series of war poems, undisguised in their reality and bitterness. Every line of these quivering stanzas bore the mark of a sensitive and outraged nature; there was scarcely a phrase that did not protest against the "glorification" and false glamor of war.

*Counter-Attack* appeared in 1918. In this volume, Sassoon turned from ordered loveliness to the gigantic brutality of war. At heart a lyric idealist, the bloody years intensified and twisted his tenderness till what was stubborn and satiric in him forced its way to the top. In *Counter-Attack* Sassoon found his angry outlet. Most of these poems are choked with passion; many of them are torn out, roots and all, from the very core of an intense conviction. They rush on, not so much because of the poet's art but almost in spite of it. A suave utterance, a neatly-joined structure would be out of place and even inexcusable in such verses as the title-poem, "The Rear-Guard," "Base Details," "Does It Matter?"—verses that are composed of love and indignation. "Let no one ever," Robert Nichols in his preface quotes Sassoon as saying, "from henceforth say one word in any way countenancing war. It is dangerous even to speak of how here and there the individual may gain some hardship of soul by it. For war is hell, and those who institute it are criminals. Were there even anything to say for it, it should not be said; for its spiritual disasters far outweigh any of its advantages. . . ." Nichols adds his approval to these sentences, saying, "For myself, this is the truth. War does not ennoble, it degrades."

Early in 1920, Sassoon visited America. At the same time, he brought out his *Picture Show* (1920), a vigorous answer to those who feared that Sassoon had "written himself out" or had begun to burn away in his own fire. Had Rupert Brooke lived, he might have written many of these lacerated but somehow exalted lines. "The Dug-Out" and "Everyone Sang" are splendid examples of how much poignance and (in the latter) winged joy can be held in less than a dozen lines. Sassoon's three volumes are the most vital and unsparing records of the war we have had. They synthesize in poetry what Barbusse's *Under Fire* and Remarque's *All Quiet on the Western Front* spread out in panoramic prose or Sheriff's *Journey's End* compacted in his stripped tragedy.

*Recreations,* a privately distributed volume, printed at Christmas, 1923, for his friends, shows Sassoon in a more playfully intellectual vein. Another, even more strictly limited publication, *Lingual Exercises for Advanced Vocabularians,* was issued in 1925. Most of the contents of the two volumes appeared in *Satirical Poems* (1926). Less direct than his deeper notes, these poems display another interesting though not so compelling aspect of Sassoon's genius. *Poems of Pinchbeck Lyre* (1931), issued anonymously, is a revival of Sassoon's talent for parody; this small but bitter collection is a set of diabolical burlesques of Humbert Wolfe.

*The Heart's Journey* (1928) and *Vigils* (1935) represent a further maturing. They seem the work of another poet, but it is the essential Sassoon. Here is the distillation of the post-war years, of silence and sorrow, of long conflict and final unity. Here are the visionary ideals of youth sharpened and purified through pain; here is bitter knowledge saved from bitterness by the spirit of faith; here, in short, Sassoon's Songs of Innocence are mingled with his Songs of Experience. This spiritual autobiography reveals the old fire, but a fire subdued. It has dignity, a gentle ecstasy which places it in the line of great religious poetry. With almost monosyllabic simplicity of word and music, Sassoon shares the power of the mystic; he achieves a sense of identification with all things—be they inanimate objects like a lamp or a book, intangible concepts like music, or his fellowmen, living or dead—fusing every element in a rapt and universal love.

*Memoirs of a Fox-Hunting Man* (1928), first published anonymously, was awarded the two most coveted literary prizes in England: the Hawthornden Prize and the James Tait Black Memorial Prize in 1929. *Memoirs of an Infantry Officer,* its sequel, appeared in 1930; the details of active-service are fact, not invention. Here in a prose so straightforward as to seem bare, there is suffused a poetry, void of decoration, independent of diction, but implicit in Sassoon's tenderness and nobility. These volumes with the later verse give us the complete man, the mature and molded poet.

### DREAMERS

Soldiers are citizens of death's gray land,
  Drawing no dividend from time's tomorrows.
In the great hour of destiny they stand,
  Each with his feuds, and jealousies, and sorrows.
Soldiers are sworn to action; they must win
  Some flaming, fatal climax with their lives.
Soldiers are dreamers; when the guns begin
  They think of firelit homes, clean beds, and wives.

I see them in foul dug-outs, gnawed by rats,
  And in the ruined trenches, lashed with rain,

Dreaming of things they did with balls and bats,
    And mocked by hopeless longing to regain
Bank-holidays, and picture shows, and spats,
    And going to the office in the train.

### THE REAR-GUARD

Groping along the tunnel, step by step,
He winked his prying torch with patching glare
From side to side, and sniffed the unwholesome air.

Tins, boxes, bottles, shapes too vague to know,
A mirror smashed, the mattress from a bed;
And he, exploring fifty feet below
The rosy gloom of battle overhead.
Tripping, he grabbed the wall; saw someone lie
Humped at his feet, half-hidden by a rug,
And stooped to give the sleeper's arm a tug.
"I'm looking for headquarters." No reply.
"God blast your neck!" (For days he'd had no sleep.)
"Get up and guide me through this stinking place."
Savage, he kicked a soft, unanswering heap,
And flashed his beam across the livid face
Terribly glaring up, whose eyes yet wore
Agony dying hard ten days before;
And fists of fingers clutched a blackening wound.
Alone he staggered on until he found
Dawn's ghost that filtered down a shafted stair
To the dazed, muttering creatures underground
Who hear the boom of shells in muffled sound.
At last, with sweat of horror in his hair,
He climbed through darkness to the twilight air,
Unloading hell behind him step by step.

### BASE DETAILS

If I were fierce and bald and short of breath,
    I'd live with scarlet Majors at the Base,
And speed glum heroes up the line to death.
    You'd see me with my puffy petulant face,
Guzzling and gulping in the best hotel,
    Reading the Roll of Honor. "Poor young chap,"
I'd say—"I used to know his father well.
    Yes, we've lost heavily in this last scrap."
And when the war is done and youth stone dead,
I'd toddle safely home and die—in bed.

### ATTACK

At dawn the ridge emerges massed and dun
In the wild purple of the glowering sun

Smoldering through spouts of drifting smoke that shroud
The menacing scarred slope; and, one by one,
Tanks creep and topple forward to the wire.
The barrage roars and lifts. Then, clumsily bowed
With bombs and guns and shovels and battle-gear,
Men jostle and climb to meet the bristling fire.
Lines of gray, muttering faces, masked with fear,
They leave their trenches, going over the top,
While time ticks blank and busy on their wrists,
And hope, with furtive eyes and grappling fists,
Flounders in mud. O Jesu, make it stop!

### COUNTER-ATTACK

We'd gained our first objective hours before
While dawn broke like a face with blinking eyes,
Pallid, unshaved and thirsty, blind with smoke.
Things seemed all right at first. We held their line,
With bombers posted, Lewis guns well placed,
And clink of shovels deepening the shallow trench.
The place was rotten with dead; green clumsy legs
High-booted, sprawled and groveled along the saps;
And trunks, face downward in the sucking mud,
Wallowed like trodden sand-bags, loosely filled;
And naked, sodden buttocks, mats of hair,
Bulged, clotted heads, slept in the plastering slime.
And then the rain began—the jolly old rain!

A yawning soldier knelt against the bank,
Staring across the morning blear with fog;
He wondered when the Allemands would get busy;
And then, of course, they started with five-nines
Traversing, sure as fate, and never a dud.
Mute in the clamor of shells he watched them burst
Spouting dark earth and wire with gusts from hell,
While posturing giants dissolved in drifts of smoke.
He crouched and flinched, dizzy with galloping fear,
Sick for escape,—loathing the strangled horror
And butchered, frantic gestures of the dead.

An officer came blundering down the trench:
"Stand-to and man the fire-step!" On he went. . . .
Gasping and bawling, "Fire-step . . . counter-attack!"
Then the haze lifted. Bombing on the right
Down the old sap: machine guns on the left;
And stumbling figures looming out in front.
"O Christ, they're coming at us!" Bullets spat,
And he remembered his rifle . . . rapid fire . . .
And started blazing wildly . . . then a bang
Crumpled and spun him sideways, knocked him out
To grunt and wriggle: none heeded him; he choked

And fought the flapping veils of smothering gloom,
Lost in a blurred confusion of yells and groans. . . .
Down, and down, and down, he sank and drowned,
Bleeding to death. The counter-attack had failed.


### DOES IT MATTER?

Does it matter?—losing your leg? . . .
For people will always be kind,
And you need not show that you mind
When the others come in after hunting
To gobble their muffins and eggs.

Does it matter?—losing your sight? . . .
There's such splendid work for the blind;
And people will always be kind,
As you sit on the terrace remembering
And turning your face to the light.

Do they matter?—those dreams from the pit? . . .
You can drink and forget and be glad,
And people won't say that you're mad;
For they'll know that you've fought for your country,
And no one will worry a bit.


### THE DUG-OUT

Why do you lie with your legs ungainly huddled,
And one arm bent across your sullen, cold,
Exhausted face? It hurts my heart to watch you,
Deep-shadowed from the candle's guttering gold;
And you wonder why I shake you by the shoulder;
Drowsy, you mumble and sigh and turn your head. . . .
*You are too young to fall asleep for ever;*
*And when you sleep you remind me of the dead.*


### INVOCATION

Come down from heaven to meet me when my breath
Chokes, and through drumming shafts of stifling death
I stumble toward escape, to find the door
Opening on morn where I may breathe once more
Clear cock-crow airs across some valley dim
With whispering trees. While dawn along the rim
Of night's horizon flows in lakes of fire,
Come down from heaven's bright hill, my song's desire.

Belov'd and faithful, teach my soul to wake
In glades deep-ranked with flowers that gleam and shake

And flock your paths with wonder. In your gaze
Show me the vanquished vigil of my days.
Mute in that golden silence hung with green,
Come down from heaven and bring me in your eyes
Remembrance of all beauty that has been,
And stillness from the pools of Paradise.

### AFTERMATH

*Have you forgotten yet?* . . .
For the world's events have rumbled on since those gagged days,
Like traffic checked a while at the crossing of city ways:
And the haunted gap in your mind has filled with thoughts that flow
Like clouds in the lit heavens of life; and you're a man reprieved to go,
Taking your peaceful share of Time, with joy to spare.
*But the past is just the same,—and War's a bloody game.* . . .
*Have you forgotten yet?* . . .
*Look down, and swear by the slain of the War that you'll never forget.*

Do you remember the dark months you held the sector at Mametz,—
The nights you watched and wired and dug and piled sand-bags on parapets?
Do you remember the rats; and the stench
Of corpses rotting in front of the front-line trench,—
And dawn coming, dirty-white, and chill with a hopeless rain?
Do you ever stop and ask, "Is it all going to happen again?"

Do you remember that hour of din before the attack,—
And the anger, the blind compassion that seized and shook you then
As you peered at the doomed and haggard faces of your men?
Do you remember the stretcher-cases lurching back
With dying eyes and lolling heads, those ashen-gray
Masks of the lads who once were keen and kind and gay?

*Have you forgotten yet?* . . .
*Look up, and swear by the green of the Spring that you'll never forget!*

### EVERYONE SANG

Everyone suddenly burst out singing;
And I was filled with such delight
As prisoned birds must find in freedom
Winging wildly across the white
Orchards and dark green fields; on; on;
   and out of sight.

Everyone's voice was suddenly lifted,
And beauty came like the setting sun.
My heart was shaken with tears, and horror
Drifted away. . . . O, but everyone

Was a bird; and the song was wordless; the
    singing will never be done.

### FALLING ASLEEP

Voices moving about in the quiet house:
Thud of feet and a muffled shutting of doors:
Everyone yawning. Only the clocks are alert.

Out in the night there's autumn-smelling gloom
Crowded with whispering trees; across the park
A hollow cry of hounds like lonely bells:
And I know that the clouds are moving across the moon;
The low, red, rising moon. Now herons call
And wrangle by their pool; and hooting owls
Sail from the wood above pale stooks of oats.

Waiting for sleep, I drift from thoughts like these;
And where today was dream-like, build my dreams.
Music . . . there was a bright white room below,
And someone singing a song about a soldier,
One hour, two hours ago: and soon the song
Will be *"last night"*: but now the beauty swings
Across my brain, ghost of remembered chords
Which still can make such radiance in my dream
That I can watch the marching of my soldiers,
And count their faces; faces; sunlit faces.

Falling asleep . . . the herons, and the hounds. . . .
September in the darkness; and the world
I've known; all fading past me into peace.

### THE WISDOM OF THE WORLD

The wisdom of the world is this; to say, *"There is
No other wisdom but to gulp what time can give"* . . .
To guard no inward vision winged with mysteries;
To hear no voices haunt the hurrying hours we live;
To keep no faith with ghostly friends; never to know
Vigils of sorrow crowned when loveless passions fade . . .
From wisdom such as this to find my gloom I go,
Companioned by those powers who keep me unafraid.

### EVERYMAN

The weariness of life that has no will
    To climb the steepening hill:
The sickness of the soul for sleep, and to be still.

And then once more the impassioned pygmy fist
    Clenched cloudward and defiant;

The pride that would prevail, the doomed protagonist,
Grappling the ghostly giant.

Victim and venturer, turn by turn; and then
Set free to be again
Companion in repose with those who once were men.

### CONCLUSION

An image dance of change
Throngs my dim-sighted flesh,
To music's air-built mesh
Move thoughts forever strange.
I am so woven of sense
And subtlety uncharted
That I must vanish hence
Blind-souled and twilight-hearted.

Soon death the hooded lover
Shall touch my house of clay,
And life-lit eyes discover
That in the warbling gray
I have been early waking,
And while the dawn was breaking

Have stolen afield to find
That secrecy which quivers
Beyond the skies and rivers
And cities of the mind.

Till then my thought shall strive
That living I may not lose
The wonder of being alive,
Nor Time's least gift refuse.
For, though the end be night,
This wonder and this white
Astonishment of sight
Make hours of magic shine;
And heaven's a blaze and bloom
Of transience and divine
Inheritance of doom.

### PREHISTORIC BURIALS

These barrows of the century-darkened dead,—
Memorials of oblivion, these turfed tombs
Of muttering ancestries whose fires, once red,
Now burn for me beyond mysterious glooms,
  I pass them, day by day, while daylight fills
  My sense of sight on these time-haunted hills.

Could I but see those burials that began
Whole History,—flint and bronze and iron beginnings,—
When under the wide Wiltshire sky, crude man
Warred with his world and augured our world-winnings!
  Could I but enter that unholpen brain,
  Cabined and comfortless and insecure,
  Ruling some settlement on Salisbury Plain
  And offering blood to blind primeval powers,—
  Dim Caliban whose doom was to endure
  Earth's ignorant nullity made strange with flowers.

### LIMITATIONS

If you could crowd them into forty lines!
Yes; you can do it once you get a start:
All that you want is waiting in your head,
For long ago you've learnt it off by heart.

Begin: your mind's the room where you have slept,
(Don't pause for rhymes), till twilight woke you early.
The window stands wide-open, as it stood
When tree-tops loomed enchanted for a child
Hearing the dawn's first thrushes through the wood
Warbling (you know the words) serene and wild.

You've said it all before: you dreamed of Death,
A dim Apollo in the bird-voiced breeze
That drifts across the morning veiled with showers,
While golden weather shines among dark trees.

You've got your limitations; let them sing,
And all your life will waken with a cry:
Why should you halt when rapture's on the wing
And you've no limit but the cloud-flocked sky? . . .

But some chap shouts, "Here, stop it; that's been done!"
As God might holloa to the rising sun,
And then relent, because the glorying rays
Remind Him of green-glinting Eden days,
And Adam's trustful eyes as he looks up
From carving eagles on his beechwood cup.

Young Adam knew his job; he could condense
Life to an eagle from the unknown immense. . . .
Go on, whoever you are, your lines can be
A whisper in the music from the weirs
Of song that plunge and tumble toward the sea
That is the uncharted mercy of our tears.

✦

I told you it was easy! . . . Words are fools
Who follow blindly, once they get a lead.
But thoughts are kingfishers that haunt the pools
Of quiet; seldom-seen: and all you need
Is just that flash of joy above your dream.
So, when those forty platitudes are done,
You'll hear a bird-note calling from the stream
That wandered through your childhood; and the sun
Will strike old flaming wonder from the waters. . . .
And there'll be forty lines not yet begun.

### GRANDEUR OF GHOSTS

When I have heard small talk about great men
I climb to bed; light my two candles; then
Consider what was said; and put aside
What Such-a-one remarked and Someone-else replied.

They have spoken lightly of my deathless friends,
(Lamps for my gloom, hands guiding where I stumble,)
Quoting, for shallow conversational ends,
What Shelley shrilled, what Blake once wildly muttered. . . . .

How can they use such names and not be humble?
I have sat silent; angry at what they uttered.
The dead bequeathed them life; the dead have said
What these can only memorize and mumble.

## ALONE

*"When I'm alone"*—the words tripped off his tongue
As though to be alone were nothing strange.
*"When I was young,"* he said; *"when I was young. . . ."*

I thought of age, and loneliness, and change.
I thought how strange we grow when we're alone,
And how unlike the selves that meet and talk,
And blow the candles out, and say good night.
*Alone.*. . . . The word is life endured and known.
It is the stillness where our spirits walk
And all but inmost faith is overthrown.

## PRESENCES PERFECTED

I looked on that prophetic land
Where, manifested by their powers,
Presences perfected stand
Whom night and day no more command
With shine and shadow of earthly hours.

I saw them. Numberless they stood
Half-way toward heaven, that men might mark
The grandeur of their ghostlihood
Burning divinely on the dark.

Names had they none. Through spirit alone
They triumphed, the makers of mankind,
Whose robes like flames were round them blown
By winds which raved from the unknown
Erebus of earth's ancestral mind.

## ELECTED SILENCE

Where voices vanish into dream,
I have discovered, from the pride
Of temporal trophydoms, this theme,
That silence is the ultimate guide.

Allow me now much musing-space
To shape my secrecies alone:
Allow me life apart, whose heart
Translates instinctive tragi-tone.

How solitude can hear! O see
How stillness unreluctant stands
Enharmonized with cloud and tree . . .
O earth and heaven not made with hands!

## Rupert Brooke

Possibly the most famous of the younger Georgians, Rupert Brooke was born at Rugby August 3, 1887, where his father was assistant master at the school. As a youth, Brooke was fastidious, finicky in dress, but keenly interested in athletics; he played cricket, football, and tennis, and swam as well as most professionals. He was six feet tall, his finely molded head topped with a crown of loose hair of lively brown: "a golden young Apollo," said Edward Thomas. Another friend wrote, "To look at, he was part of the youth of the world." His beauty encouraged a naturally romantic disposition; his poems are a blend of delight in the splendor of actuality and disillusion in a loveliness that dies. The shadow of John Donne lies over many of his early and more than a few of his later pages, while the accent of Housman (*vide* "The Chilterns") prompts the conversational tone which Brooke adopted, extended, and popularized.

At first Brooke affected a tired sophistication not uncommon to the young poet of the times. However, the bored cynicisms, the fashionable ennuis were purged, when after several years of travel (he had been to Germany, Italy and Honolulu) the War came, turning Brooke away from

"A world grown old and cold and weary . . .
And half men, and their dirty songs and dreary,
And all the little emptiness of love."

Brooke enlisted with a relief that was like a rebirth; he sought new energy in the struggle "where the worst friend and enemy is but Death." After seeing service in Belgium, 1914, he spent the following winter in a training-camp in Dorsetshire and sailed with the British Mediterranean Expeditionary Force in February, 1915, to take part in the unfortunate Dardanelles Campaign.

Brooke never reached his destination. He died of blood-poison at Skyros in the Aegean, April 23, 1915. His early death was one of England's great literary losses; Lascelles Abercrombie, W. W. Gibson (with both of whom he had been associated on the quarterly, *New Numbers*), Walter De la Mare, Winston Spencer Churchill, and a host of others united to pay tribute to the most brilliant and passionate of the younger poets.

Brooke's sonnet-sequence, *1914* (from which "The Soldier" is taken), appeared with prophetic irony, a few weeks before his death. It contains the accents of immortality. "The Old Vicarage, Grantchester," "Heaven" and "Fish" are characteristic of the lighter and more playful side of Brooke's temperament. The metaphysician, not yet free of Donne, speaks in the mingled fancy and philosophy of "Dining-Room Tea," in several of the sonnets, and "Second Best." Both phases are combined in "The Great Lover," of which Abercrombie has written, "It is life he loves, and not in any abstract sense, but all the infinite little familiar details of life, remembered and catalogued with delightful zest."

Brooke published only two volumes during his lifetime. After his death, both volumes, with several posthumous poems, were issued as *Collected Poems of Rupert Brooke,* with a Memoir, in 1915. With a few exceptions, when Brooke yielded to the merely clever, his poetry is alert with the sparkle of his personality. It is the self-aware, self-examining mind that rules his emotions; his verse is a triumph of the intellectual imagination. "The theme of his poetry," says Walter De la Mare, "is the life of the mind, the senses, the feelings—life here and now. . . . His world stands out sharp and distinct, like the towers and pinnacles of a city under the light of a sunny sky." Brooke's delight was not in the shadows of revery and meditation, but in the swift play of ideas, in energetic action and reaction.

Thus Brooke was as thorough in his inconsistencies as in his sincerities. Impulse was his god—and his goad. He worshiped glamor and turned from it in revulsion, in a kind of sea- and beauty-sickness; he celebrated (in "Dust") the immortality of love and (in "Kindliness" and the sonnet already quoted) ridiculed its empty impermanence; turned from the intellect to sheer imagination—and abandoned fantasy for an ordered philosophy. His later work indicates that Brooke had tired of shifting extremes. It is impossible to predict what integration might have come with maturity. He was dead at twenty-seven.

### THE GREAT LOVER

I have been so great a lover: filled my days
So proudly with the splendor of Love's praise,
The pain, the calm, and the astonishment,
Desire illimitable, and still content,
And all dear names men use, to cheat despair,
For the perplexed and viewless streams that bear
Our hearts at random down the dark of life.
Now, ere the unthinking silence on that strife
Steals down, I would cheat drowsy Death so far,
My night shall be remembered for a star
That outshone all the suns of all men's days.
Shall I not crown them with immortal praise
Whom I have loved, who have given me, dared with me
High secrets, and in darkness knelt to see
The inenarrable godhead of delight?
Love is a flame:—we have beaconed the world's night.
A city:—and we have built it, these and I.
An emperor:—we have taught the world to die.
So, for their sakes I loved, ere I go hence,
And the high cause of Love's magnificence,

And to keep loyalties young, I'll write those names
Golden for ever, eagles, crying flames,
And set them as a banner, that men may know,
To dare the generations, burn, and blow
Out on the wind of Time, shining and streaming. . . .

These I have loved:
              White plates and cups, clean-gleaming,
Ringed with blue lines; and feathery, faëry dust;
Wet roofs, beneath the lamp-light; the strong crust
Of friendly bread; and many-tasting food;
Rainbows; and the blue bitter smoke of wood;
And radiant raindrops couching in cool flowers;
And flowers themselves, that sway through sunny hours,
Dreaming of moths that drink them under the moon;
Then, the cool kindliness of sheets, that soon
Smooth away trouble; and the rough male kiss
Of blankets; grainy wood; live hair that is
Shining and free; blue-massing clouds; the keen
Unpassioned beauty of a great machine;
The benison of hot water; furs to touch;
The good smell of old clothes; and other such—
The comfortable smell of friendly fingers,
Hair's fragrance, and the musty reek that lingers
About dead leaves and last year's ferns. . . .
                                    Dear names,
And thousand others throng to me! Royal flames;
Sweet water's dimpling laugh from tap or spring;
Holes in the ground; and voices that do sing:
Voices in laughter, too; and body's pain,
Soon turned to peace; and the deep-panting train;
Firm sands; the little dulling edge of foam
That browns and dwindles as the wave goes home;
And washen stones, gay for an hour; the cold
Graveness of iron; moist black earthen mold;
Sleep; and high places; footprints in the dew;
And oaks; and brown horse-chestnuts, glossy-new;
And new-peeled sticks; and shining pools on grass;—
All these have been my loves. And these shall pass,
Whatever passes not, in the great hour,
Nor all my passion, all my prayers, have power
To hold them with me through the gate of Death.
They'll play deserter, turn with the traitor breath,
Break the high bond we made, and sell Love's trust
And sacramental covenant to the dust.
—Oh, never a doubt but, somewhere, I shall wake,
And give what's left of love again, and make
New friends now strangers. . . .
                              But the best I've known
Stays here, and changes, breaks, grows old, is blown

About the winds of the world, and fades from brains
Of living men, and dies.
                    Nothing remains.

O dear my loves, O faithless, once again
This one last gift I give: that after men
Shall know, and later lovers, far-removed
Praise you, "All these were lovely"; say, "He loved."

## THE CHILTERNS

Your hands, my dear, adorable,
   Your lips of tenderness
—Oh, I've loved you faithfully and well,
   Three years, or a bit less.
   It wasn't a success.

Thank God, that's done! and I'll take the road,
   Quit of my youth and you,
The Roman road to Wendover
   By Tring and Lilley Hoo,
   As a free man may do.

For youth goes over, the joys that fly,
   The tears that follow fast;
And the dirtiest things we do must lie
   Forgotten at the last;
   Even love goes past.

What's left behind I shall not find,
   The splendor and the pain;
The splash of sun, the shouting wind,
   And the brave sting of rain,
   I may not meet again.

But the years, that take the best away,
   Give something in the end;
And a better friend than love have they,
   For none to mar or mend,
   That have themselves to friend.

I shall desire and I shall find
   The best of my desires;
The autumn road, the mellow wind
   That soothes the darkening shires.
   And laughter, and inn-fires.

White mist about the black hedgerows,
   The slumbering Midland plain,
The silence where the clover grows,
   And the dead leaves in the lane,
   Certainly, these remain.

And I shall find some girl perhaps,
   And a better one than you,
With eyes as wise, but kindlier,
   And lips as soft, but true.
   And I daresay she will do.

## THE HILL

Breathless, we flung us on the windy hill,
Laughed in the sun, and kissed the lovely grass.
You said, "Through glory and ecstasy we pass;
Wind, sun, and earth remain, the birds sing still,
When we are old, are old. . . ." "And when we die
All's over that is ours; and life burns on
Through other lovers, other lips," said I,
"Heart of my heart, our heaven is now, is won!"
"We are Earth's best, that learnt her lesson here.
Life is our cry. We have kept the faith!" we said;
"We shall go down with unreluctant tread
Rose-crowned into the darkness! . . ." Proud we were,
And laughed, that had such brave true things to say.
And then you suddenly cried, and turned away.

### DUST

When the white flame in us is gone,
  And we that lost the world's delight
Stiffen in darkness, left alone
  To crumble in our separate night;

When your swift hair is quiet in death,
  And through the lips corruption thrust
Has stilled the labor of my breath—
  When we are dust, when we are dust!—

Not dead, not undesirous yet,
  Still sentient, still unsatisfied,
We'll ride the air, and shine and flit,
  Around the places where we died,

And dance as dust before the sun,
  And light of foot, and unconfined,
Hurry from road to road, and run
  About the errands of the wind.

And every mote, on earth or air,
  Will speed and gleam down later days,
And like a secret pilgrim fare
  By eager and invisible ways,

Nor ever rest, nor ever lie,
  Till, beyond thinking, out of view,

One mote of all the dust that's I
  Shall meet one atom that was you.

Then in some garden hushed from wind,
  Warm in a sunset's afterglow,
The lovers in the flowers will find
  A sweet and strange unquiet grow

Upon the peace; and, past desiring,
  So high a beauty in the air,
And such a light, and such a quiring,
  And such a radiant ecstasy there,

They'll know not if it's fire, or dew,
  Or out of earth, or in the height,
Singing, or flame, or scent, or hue,
  Or two that pass, in light, to light,

Out of the garden higher, higher . . .
  But in that instant they shall learn
The shattering fury of our fire,
  And the weak passionless hearts will burn

And faint in that amazing glow,
  Until the darkness close above;
And they will know—poor fools, they'll
    know!—
  One moment, what it is to love.

### SONNET

Oh! Death will find me, long before I tire
  Of watching you; and swing me suddenly
Into the shade and loneliness and mire
  Of the last land! There, waiting patiently,

One day, I think, I'll feel a cool wind blowing,
  See a slow light across the Stygian tide,
And hear the Dead about me stir, unknowing,
  And tremble. And I shall know that you have died,

And watch you, a broad-browed and smiling dream,
  Pass, light as ever, through the lightless host,
Quietly ponder, start, and sway, and gleam—
  Most individual and bewildering ghost!—

And turn, and toss your brown delightful head
Amusedly, among the ancient Dead.

### THE SOLDIER

If I should die, think only this of me;
　That there's some corner of a foreign field
That is for ever England. There shall be
　In that rich earth a richer dust concealed;
A dust whom England bore, shaped, made aware,
　Gave, once, her flowers to love, her ways to roam,
A body of England's breathing English air,
　Washed by the rivers, blest by suns of home.

And think, this heart, all evil shed away,
　A pulse in the eternal mind, no less
　　Gives somewhere back the thoughts by England given;
Her sights and sounds; dreams happy as her day;
　And laughter, learnt of friends; and gentleness,
　　In hearts at peace, under an English heaven.

### HEAVEN

Fish (fly-replete, in depth of June
Dawdling away their wat'ry noon)
Ponder deep wisdom, dark or clear,
Each secret fishy hope or fear.
Fish say, they have their Stream and Pond;
But is there anything Beyond?
This life cannot be All, they swear,
For how unpleasant, if it were!
One may not doubt that, somehow, good
Shall come of Water and of Mud;
And, sure, the reverent eye must see
A Purpose in Liquidity.
We darkly know, by Faith we cry,
The future is not Wholly Dry.
Mud unto Mud!—Death eddies near—
Not here the appointed End, not here!

But somewhere, beyond Space and Time,
Is wetter water, slimier slime!
And there (they trust) there swimmeth One
Who swam ere rivers were begun,
Immense, of fishy form and mind,
Squamous, omnipotent and kind;
And under that Almighty Fin
The littlest fish may enter in.
Oh! never fly conceals a hook,
Fish say, in the Eternal Brook,
But more than mundane weeds are there,
And mud, celestially fair;
Fat caterpillars drift around,
And Paradisal grubs are found;
Unfading moths, immortal flies,
And the worm that never dies.
And in that Heaven of all their wish,
There shall be no more land, say fish.

### SECOND BEST

Here in the dark, O heart;
Alone with the enduring Earth, and Night,
And Silence, and the warm strange smell of clover;
Clear-visioned, though it break you; far apart
From the dead best, the dear and old delight;
Throw down your dreams of immortality,
O faithful, O foolish lover!
Here's peace for you, and surety; here the one
Wisdom—the truth!—"All day the good glad sun
Showers love and labor on you, wine and song;
The greenwood laughs, the wind blows, all day long

Till night." And night ends all things.
                                        Then shall be
No lamp relumed in heaven, no voices crying,
Or changing lights, or dreams and forms that hover!
(And, heart, for all your sighing,
That gladness and those tears, are over, over. . . .)

And has the truth brought no new hope at all,
Heart, that you're weeping yet for Paradise?
Do they still whisper, the old weary cries?
"'Mid youth and song, feasting and carnival,*
*Through laughter, through the roses, as of old*
*Comes Death, on shadowy and relentless feet,*
*Death, unappeasable by prayer or gold;*
*Death is the end, the end!"*
Proud, then, clear-eyed and laughing, go to greet
Death as a friend!

Exile of immortality, strongly wise,
Strain through the dark with undesirous eyes
To what may lie beyond it. Sets your star,
O heart, for ever! Yet, behind the night,
Waits for the great unborn, somewhere afar,
Some white tremendous daybreak. And the light,
Returning, shall give back the golden hours,
Ocean a windless level, Earth a lawn
Spacious and full of sunlit dancing-places,
And laughter, and music, and among the flowers,
The gay child-hearts of men, and the child-faces,
O heart, in the great dawn!

## THE BUSY HEART

Now that we've done our best and worst, and parted,
    I would fill my mind with thoughts that will not rend.
(O heart, I do not dare go empty-hearted)
    I'll think of Love in books, Love without end;
Women with child, content; and old men sleeping;
    And wet strong plowlands, scarred for certain grain;
And babes that weep, and so forget their weeping;
    And the young heavens, forgetful after rain;
And evening hush, broken by homing wings;
    And Song's nobility, and Wisdom holy,
That live, we dead. I would think of a thousand things,
    Lovely and durable, and taste them slowly,
One after one, like tasting a sweet food.
I have need to busy my heart with quietude.

## DINING-ROOM TEA

When you were there, and you, and you,
Happiness crowned the night; I too,
Laughing and looking, one of all,
I watched the quivering lamplight fall
On plate and flowers and pouring tea
And cup and cloth; and they and we
Flung all the dancing moments by
With jest and glitter. Lip and eye
Flashed on the glory, shone and cried,
Improvident, unmemoried;
And fitfully, and like a flame
The light of laughter went and came.
Proud in their careless transcience moved
The changing faces that I loved.

Till suddenly, and otherwhence,
I looked upon your innocence.
For lifted clear and still and strange
From the dark woven flow of change
Under a vast and starless sky
I saw the immortal moment lie.
One instant I, an instant, knew
As God knows all. And it and you,
I, above Time, oh, blind! could see
In witless immortality.

I saw the marble cup; the tea,
Hung on the air, an amber stream;
I saw the fire's unglittering gleam,
The painted flame, the frozen smoke.
No more the flooding lamplight broke
On flying eyes and lips and hair;
But lay, but slept unbroken there,
On stiller flesh, and body breathless,
And lips and laughter stayed and deathless,
And words on which no silence grew.
Light was more alive than you.

For suddenly, and otherwhence,
I looked on your magnificence.
I saw the stillness and the light,
And you, august, immortal, white,
Holy and strange; and every glint
Posture and jest and thought and tint
Freed from the mask of transiency,
Triumphant in eternity,
Immote, immortal.

                              Dazed at length
Human eyes grew, mortal strength
Wearied; and Time began to creep.
Change closed about me like a sleep.
Light glinted on the eyes I loved.
The cup was filled. The bodies moved.
The drifting petal came to ground.
The laughter chimed its perfect round,
The broken syllable was ended.
And I, so certain and so friended,
How could I cloud, or how distress,
The heaven of your unconsciousness?
Or shake at Time's sufficient spell,
Stammering of lights unutterable?
The eternal holiness of you,
The timeless end, you never knew,
The peace that lay, the light that shone.
You never knew that I had gone
A million miles away, and stayed
A million years. The laughter played
Unbroken round me; and the jest
Flashed on. And we that knew the best
Down wonderful hours grew happier yet.
I sang at heart, and talked, and ate,
And lived from laugh to laugh, I too,
When you were there, and you, and you.

## THE OLD VICARAGE, GRANTCHESTER

*(Café des Westens, Berlin. May, 1912)*

Just now the lilac is in bloom,
All before my little room;
And in my flower-beds, I think,
Smile the carnation and the pink;
And down the borders, well I know,
The poppy and the pansy blow . . .
Oh! there the chestnuts, summer through,
Beside the river make for you
A tunnel of green gloom, and sleep
Deeply above; and green and deep
The stream mysterious glides beneath,
Green as a dream and deep as death.
—Oh, damn! I know it! and I know
How the May fields all golden show,
And when the day is young and sweet,
Glide gloriously the bare feet
That run to bathe . . .
                              *Du lieber Gott!*
Here am I, sweating, sick, and hot,

And there the shadowed waters fresh
Leap up to embrace the naked flesh.
*Temperamentvoll* German Jews
Drink beer around;—and *there* the dews
Are soft beneath a morn of gold.
Here tulips bloom as they are told;
Unkempt about those hedges blows
An English unofficial rose;
And there the unregulated sun
Slopes down to rest when day is done,
And wakes a vague unpunctual star,
A slippered Hesper; and there are
Meads towards Haslingfield and Coton
Where *das Betreten's* not *verboten*.

εἴθε γενοίμην . . . would I were
In Grantchester, in Grantchester!—
Some, it may be, can get in touch
With Nature there, or Earth, or such.
And clever modern men have seen
A Faun a-peeping through the green,
And felt the Classics were not dead,
To glimpse a Naiad's reedy head,
Or hear the Goat-foot piping low; . . .
But these are things I do not know.
I only know that you may lie
Day long and watch the Cambridge sky,
And, flower-lulled in sleepy grass,
Hear the cool lapse of hours pass,
Until the centuries blend and blur
In Grantchester, in Grantchester. . . .
Still in the dawnlit waters cool
His ghostly Lordship swims his pool,
And tries the strokes, essays the tricks,
Long learnt on Hellespont, or Styx.
Dan Chaucer hears his river still
Chatter beneath a phantom mill.
Tennyson notes, with studious eye,
How Cambridge waters hurry by . . .
And in that garden, black and white,
Creep whispers through the grass all night;
And spectral dance, before the dawn,
A hundred vicars down the lawn;
Curates, long dust, will come and go
On lissom, clerical, printless toe;
And oft between the boughs is seen
The sly shade of a Rural Dean . . .
Till, at a shiver in the skies,
Vanishing with Satanic cries,
The prim ecclesiastical rout
Leaves but a startled sleeper-out,

Gray heavens, the first bird's drowsy calls,
The falling house that never falls.

God! I will pack, and take a train,
And get me to England once again!
For England's the one land, I know,
Where men with Splendid Hearts may go;
And Cambridgeshire, of all England,
The shire for Men who Understand;
And of *that* district I prefer
The lovely hamlet Grantchester.
For Cambridge people rarely smile,
Being urban, squat, and packed with guile;
And Royston men in the far South
Are black and fierce and strange of mouth;
At Over they fling oaths at one,
And worse than oaths at Trumpington,
And Ditton girls are mean and dirty,
And there's none in Harston under thirty,
And folks in Shelford and those parts
Have twisted lips and twisted hearts,
And Barton men make Cockney rhymes,
And Coton's full of nameless crimes,
And things are done you'd not believe
At Madingley on Christmas Eve.
Strong men have run for miles and miles,
When one from Cherry Hinton smiles,
Strong men have blanched, and shot their
    wives,
Rather than send them to St. Ives;
Strong men have cried like babes, bydam,
To hear what happened in Babraham.
But Grantchester! ah, Grantchester!
There's peace and holy quiet there,
Great clouds along pacific skies,
And men and women with straight eyes,
Lithe children lovelier than a dream,
A bosky wood, a slumb'rous stream,
And little kindly winds that creep
Round twilight corners, half asleep.
In Grantchester their skins are white;
They bathe by day, they bathe by night;
The women there do all they ought;
The men observe the Rules of Thought;
They love the Good; they worship Truth;
They laugh uproariously in youth;
(And when they get to feeling old,
They up and shoot themselves, I'm told) . . .

Ah God! to see the branches stir
Across the moon at Grantchester!

To smell the thrilling-sweet and rotten
Unforgettable, unforgotten
River-smell, and hear the breeze
Sobbing in the little trees.
Say, do the elm-clumps greatly stand
Still guardians of that holy land?
The chestnuts shade, in reverend dream,
The yet unacademic stream?
Is dawn a secret shy and cold
Anadyomene, silver-gold?
And sunset still a golden sea
From Haslingfield to Madingley?

And after, ere the night is born,
Do hares come out about the corn?
Oh, is the water sweet and cool,
Gentle and brown, above the pool?
And laughs the immortal river still
Under the mill, under the mill?
Say, is there Beauty yet to find?
And Certainty? And Quiet kind?
Deep meadows yet, for to forget
The lies, and truths, and pain? . . . oh! yet
Stands the Church clock at ten to three?
And is there honey still for tea?

# Joseph Plunkett

JOSEPH (MARY) PLUNKETT was born in Ireland in 1887 and devoted himself to the cause that compelled so many martyrs. He gave his hours and finally his life in an effort to establish the freedom of his country. He was one of the leaders of that group of Nationalists which included Macdonagh and Padraic Pearse. (See page 289.) Had he been allowed to develop his gifts as singer, there is no doubt that he would have added a luster to the roll of Irish poets. Even the two brief lyrics reprinted here show (*vide* "Poppies" in particular) that Plunkett possessed a subtle craftsmanship to express his tender mysticism.

After the Easter Week uprising in Dublin in 1916, Plunkett and his compatriots were arrested, tried, and executed.

### I SEE HIS BLOOD UPON THE ROSE

I see His blood upon the rose
And in the stars the glory of His eyes,
His body gleams amid eternal snows,
His tears fall from the skies.

I see His face in every flower;
The thunder and the singing of the birds
Are but His voice—and carven by His power,
Rocks are His written words.

All pathways by His feet are worn,
His strong heart stirs the ever-beating sea,
His crown of thorns is twined with every
  thorn,
His cross is every tree.

### POPPIES

O Sower of sorrow,
From the seed of your sowing
Tomorrow the mower
The wheat will be mowing.

O Reaper of ruth,
Mid the roots of your reaping
Springs the truth that in sleep
Bears the fruit of all sleeping.

O Binder of sheaves
That are loose for your binding,
Withered leaves you shall find
And shall lose after finding.

# Edwin Muir

EDWIN MUIR was born in Deerness, in the Orkney Islands, in 1887. He had practically no schooling in boyhood and none whatever after his fourteenth year, when his family moved to Glasgow and young Muir started work as a clerk. Although he is best known as a critic, Muir's first literary work to be published was in verse. Later, he contributed a series of prose aphorisms to *The New Age* which were published in book form under the title of *We Moderns* (1918).

In 1919, Muir became assistant editor of *The New Age*. Two years later, he gave up all editorial work, and went to Central Europe. It was while living in Austria that his *Latitudes* (1924), a collection of essays, attracted a greater audience than Muir had ever reached. Although his verse, *First Poems* (1926), is little known, it is Muir's favorite medium and reveals the same freshness of feeling as his prose.

Besides his poetry, Muir has established himself as one of the most sympathetic translators from the German, especially successful in the case of Hauptmann and Feuchtwanger. His first novel, *The Marionette,* appeared in 1927, his third and most important set of studies, *Transition,* in 1926.

*Variations on a Time Theme* (1934) is a meditation on this poet's favorite theme: the antimony of life and time. It contains, wrote Geoffrey Grigson, one of the most discerning of the younger critics, "some of the best poetry which he has written, metaphysical verse in which idea and emotion are fused like the contradictory components of a lens."

## THE ENCHANTED PRINCE

Here lying on the ancient mount,
  Through days grown stagnant and too rich,
My half-raised eyes keep sleepy count
  Of wild weeds springing in the ditch,

Of turf so quiet and so clean
  The sun's light seems more ancient there,
As if the softly slumbering green
  Had grown indifferent to the air.

And all worn smooth 'neath deadened years
  Which have forgotten that they roll,
Though at its secret term appears
  The lawful grass upon the knoll.

There lies the peace of ended toil
  Heavy and rich, too rich, as though
A race were mingled with the soil
  And could no more rise up and go.

A willow hangs above the vale,
  Here at my foot, and I have sight,
Through twisted branches dusty pale,
  Of distant hills in different light.

So inaccessible and so clear,
  The houses gleam on every hill!
The silent valley tumbles sheer,
  Like an abyss where time is still.

Yet here upon the enchanted mount
  I look out towards the farther heights,
And, lost far onward, strive to count
  Ambiguous shapes in shifting lights,

Till, where peaks battle in the haze,
  In mortal fight without a cry,
Upon unnameable things I gaze,
  And dragons rearing at the sky.

If now, turned back, I think again
  That all these lines which heaved and
    strove
Just now, were quiet earth, I fain
  Would perish of a boundless love. . . .

Here lying on the ancient mount,
  Through days grown stagnant and too rich,
My heart is dust, the while I count
  The wild weeds springing in the ditch.

### GRASS

The vague immutable contour of the earth—
This insubstantial phantom of green hills
Which ever falling away forever change,
Perpetual mirage hung beyond Time's reach—
Is grass, which sets the round world in our sight.
Grass standing thick and still in soundless vales
No eye has seen, or straggling into wastes,
Beat down but spared by winds which tear up oaks;
Green in the sun, and beneath smothering mists,
Where each moist blade sweats one clear glistening drop;
Grass growing below huge rocks and round lone graves;
Climbing, a tiny host, up mountainsides;
Hanging on mist-locked keeps above dun lakes;
Tossing on low small islets on the tide,
Soft meadows mid the currents of the sea,
Where the green glossy blades drink the blue wave;
Grass waiting in dark table-lands of snow;
O'er new-riven chasms weaving its light veil,
And quiet fields o'er fallen and jagged peaks:
The invulnerable vesture of the world.

# *Edith Sitwell*

EDITH SITWELL, daughter of Sir George and Lady Ida Sitwell, granddaughter of the Earl of Landesborough, was born at Scarborough, Yorkshire, in 1887. She was educated, as she puts it, "in secrecy" and in 1914 came to London, where she has lived ever since. A portrait of her, painted by Alvaro Guevara, hangs in the Tate Gallery. In her forties she occupied herself with prose, with a life of Pope, a history of Bath, and a critical anthology.

In 1916, she began the editing of *Wheels,* a determinedly modern anthology which outraged most of the conservative critics. Her own poems provided an even greater series of shocks. After a mild and undistinguished début—*The Mother and Other Poems* (1915)—Miss Sitwell published, in a succession so speedy as to seem little less than rapid-fire, *Clown's Houses* (1918), *The Wooden Pegasus* (1920), *Façade* (1922), *Bucolic Comedies* (1923).

In these volumes—particularly in the last two—Miss Sitwell limits her gamut; but, within her range, there is no poet quite like her. Her favorite instrument seems to be the xylophone, and it is amazing what effects she produces from its restricted timbre. Miss Sitwell is a virtuoso in the communication of a half-wooden, half-glassy tone which is seldom without brilliance. It has been objected that Miss Sitwell's poetry is artificial, and this may be true. But the criticism is not as devastating as it seems, for hers is obviously, and purposefully, an artificial world. It is a curious, semi-mechanical heaven and earth over which her keen eye ranges, a landscape in which Miss Sitwell sees, as none before her has seen, skies of paper, seas of wool, the "reynard-colored sun," the world "like a bare egg laid by the feathered air," the "coltish wind nuzzling the hand," trees "hissing like green geese," "barley-sugar children,"—she even hears Silence "like a slow-leaking tap." If Miss Sitwell's is nothing but a clock-work, conjuring-trick sort of poetry—and it is often more than that—there has rarely been so brilliant an exhibition of verbal legerdemain.

But, it must be reiterated, Miss Sitwell is more than an adroit juggler of startling phrases. Purely as a craftsman in nonsense, she has written some of the most delectable nonsense verses of the age; her grotesque nursery rhymes are, in their own genre, as memorable as De la Mare's. The secret of her serious poetry is scarcely more difficult to capture. After one's initial bewilderment (due chiefly to the galloping pace of her verse), the wit of her comments, her strange associations, the novel romanticism of an essentially feminine mind—all these lie ready to disclose themselves beneath the surface glitter.

Beginning with *The Sleeping Beauty* (1924) Miss Sitwell has essayed to humanize her hard, bright idiom. Here, as in the succeeding *Troy Park* (1925) and *Rustic Elegies* (1927), she achieves an intensity which her other work, for all its felicities, never expressed. Her poems approach reality, but this recorder is never content with representation. She delights to juxtapose actualities and impossibilities; assuming, in quick succession, an enigmatic mask, a bizarre clarity, shifting suddenly from patent absurdity to piercing sympathy. No longer reflecting life from the outside, she adds the note of compassion. She moves with care and sensitivity, charting the border between reality and insanity. She is Donne one moment, Lewis Carroll the next. To apply the term "mystic" to her will surprise only those who have never cared to see through the glassy surface of her verse. To such readers, Miss Sitwell will remain the artificer of a *papier-mâché* universe, a juggler amusing herself in a world where grass is shrill, fire furry, where rains hang like wooden stalactites, where the creaking air, combed seas, and spangled emotions are equally automatic.

In the later volumes her occupation with the human drama is far more apparent. Here man's hunger for beauty is no longer seen as a pitiful joke in a vegetable existence, but as an insatiate passion. The pictures become actually autobiographical; the touching "Colonel Fantock" reveals the poet in her simplest mood, and those who know her brothers Osbert and Sacheverell will have little difficulty identifying "Dagobert" and "Peregrine."

*Gold Coast Customs and Other Poems* (1930) repeats the pattern which Miss Sitwell's work has formed: a combination of contempt and nostalgia. The scorn is for a fatuous world she refuses to join, and the nostalgia is for the quiet, primitive world left in childhood. Her idiom, more than ever, is a building-up of repetitions and contrasting shocks with a lush music, lingering and illogical. If the luxuriance recalls the modern ballet, it is no accident, since this is the effect that the poet tries to achieve. It is stylized, opulent, and always original in movement.

It should be added that Miss Sitwell has written some of the best if slightly mad metaphysics of her day. In her incongruous collating of objects, colors, sensory distortions, she is a grown-up child, innocently absurd, accidentally wise, scattering her observations to a sometimes appreciative though often bewildered audience.

### AUBADE

Jane, Jane,
Tall as a crane,
The morning light creaks down again.

Comb your cockscomb-ragged hair;
Jane, Jane, come down the stair.

Each dull blunt wooden stalactite
Of rain creaks, hardened by the light,

Sounding like an overtone     •
From some lonely world unknown.

But the creaking empty light
Will never harden into sight,

Will never penetrate your brain
With overtones like the blunt rain.

The light would show (if it could harden)
Eternities of kitchen-garden,

Cockscomb flowers that none will pluck,
And wooden flowers that 'gin to cluck.

In the kitchen you must light
Flames as staring, red and white

As carrots or as turnips, shining
Where the cold dawn light lies whining.

Cockscomb hair on the cold wind
Hangs limp, turns the milk's weak mind. . . .

Jane, Jane,
Tall as a crane,
The morning light creaks down again!

### SIR BEELZEBUB

WHEN
Sir
Beelzebub called for his syllabub in the hotel in Hell
      Where Proserpine first fell,
Blue as the gendarmerie were the waves of the sea,

      (Rocking and shocking the bar-maid.)

Nobody comes to give him his rum but the
Rim of the sky hippopotamus-glum
Enhances the chances to bless with a benison
Alfred Lord Tennyson crossing the bar laid
With cold vegetation from pale deputations
Of temperance workers (all signed In Memoriam)
Hoping with glory to trip up the Laureate's feet,

      (Moving in classical meters). . . .

Like Balaclava, the lava came down from the
Roof, and the sea's blue wooden gendarmerie
Took them in charge while Beelzebub roared for his rum.

. . . None of them come!

### THE KING OF CHINA'S DAUGHTER

The King of China's daughter,
She never would love me
Though I hung my cap and bells upon
Her nutmeg tree.

For oranges and lemons,
The stars in bright blue air,
(I stole them long ago, my dear)
Were dangling there.
The Moon did give me silver pence,
The Sun did give me gold,

And both together softly blew
And made my porridge cold;
But the King of China's daughter
Pretended not to see,
When I hung my cap and bells upon
Her nutmeg tree.

## SOLO FOR EAR-TRUMPET

The carriage brushes through the bright
Leaves (violent jets from life to light).
Strong polished speed is plunging, heaves
Between the showers of bright hot leaves.
The window-glasses glaze our faces
And jar them to the very basis,—
But they could never put a polish
Upon my manners, or abolish
My most distinct disinclination
For calling on a rich relation!
In her house,—bulwark built between
The life man lives and visions seen,—
The sunlight hiccups white as chalk,
Grown drunk with emptiness of talk,
And silence hisses like a snake,
Invertebrate and rattling ache. . . .

Till suddenly, Eternity
Drowns all the houses like a sea,
And down the street the Trump of Doom
Blares,—barely shakes this drawing-room
Where raw-edged shadows sting forlorn
As dank dark nettles. Down the horn
Of her ear-trumpet I convey
The news that: "It is Judgment Day!"

"Speaker louder; I don't catch, my dear."
I roared: *"It is the Trump we hear!"*
"The *What?"*—"The .T R U M P !" . . .
   "I shall complain—
Those boy-scouts practicing again!"

## GARDENER JANUS CATCHES
## A NAIAD

Baskets of ripe fruit in air
The bird-songs seem suspended where

Between the hairy leaves trills dew
All tasting of fresh green anew.

Ma'am, I've heard your laughter flare
Through your waspish-gilded hair:

Feathered masks,
Pots of peas,—
Janus asks
Nought of these,
Creaking water
Brightly stripèd
Now I've caught her—
Shrieking biped.
Flute sounds jump
And turn together,
Changing clumps
Of glassy feather.
In among the
Pots of peas
Naiad changes—
Quick as these.

## SPINNING SONG

The miller's daughter
Combs her hair,
Like flocks of dove
As soft as vair. . . .

Oh, how those soft flocks flutter down
Over the empty grassy town.

Like a queen in a crown
Of gold light, she
Sits 'neath the shadows'
Flickering tree—

Till the old dame went the way she came,
Playing bobcherry with a candle-flame.

Now Min the cat
With her white velvet gloves
Watches where sat
The mouse with her loves—

(Old and malicious Mrs. Grundy
Whose washing day is from Monday to Monday.)

"Not a crumb," said Min,
"To a mouse I'll be giving.
For a mouse must spin
To earn her living."

So poor Mrs. Mouse and her three cross Aunts
Nibble snow that rustles like gold wheat plants.

And the miller's daughter
Combs her locks,
Like running water
Those dove-soft flocks;

And her mouth is sweet as a honey flower cold
But her heart is heavy as bags of gold.

The shadow-mice said
"We will line with down
From those doves, our bed
And our slippers and gown,

For everything comes to the shadows at last
If the spinning-wheel Time move slow or fast."

### PANOPE

How lovely are the tombs of the dead nymphs
On the heroic shore—the glittering plinths
Of jacynth . . . hyacinthine waves profound
Sigh of the beauty out of sight and sound

And many a golden foot that pressed the sand—
Panope walking like the pomp of waves
With plumaged helmet near the fountain caves
The panoply of suns on distant strand—

Is only now an arena for the worm,
Her golden flesh lies in the dust's frail storm

And beauty water-bright for long is laid
Deep in the empire of eternal shade—

Only the sighing waves know now the plinth
Of those deep tombs that were of hyacinth.

But still the echoes of that helmeted bright hair
Are like the pomp of tropic suns, the blare
That from the inaccessible horizon runs—
The eternal music of heroic suns
When their strong youth comes freshened from deep seas—
And the first music heard among the trees.


COLONEL FANTOCK

Thus spoke the lady underneath the tree:
I was a member of a family
Whose legend was of hunting—(all the rare
And unattainable brightness of the air)—
A race whose fabled skill in falconry
Was used on the small song-birds and a winged
And blinded Destiny. . . . I think that only
Winged ones know the highest eyrie is so lonely.

There in a land austere and elegant
The castle seemed an arabesque in music;
We moved in an hallucination born
Of silence, which like music gave us lotus
To ear, perfuming lips and our long eyelids
As we trailed over the sad summer grass
Or sat beneath a smooth and mournful tree.

And Time passed, suavely, imperceptibly.

But Dagobert and Peregrine and I
Were children then; we walked like shy gazelles
Among the music of thin flower-bells.
And life still held some promise,—never ask
Of what,—but life seemed less a stranger then
Than ever after in this cold existence.
I always was a little outside life,—
And so the things we touch could comfort me,
I loved the shy dreams we could hear and see—
For I was like one dead, like a small ghost,
A little cold air wandering and lost.

All day within the straw-roofed arabesque
Of the towered castle and the sleepy gardens wandered
We; those delicate paladins, the waves
Told us fantastic legends that we pondered.
And the soft leaves were breasted like a dove,
Crooning old mournful tales of untrue love.

When night came sounding like the growth of trees,
My great-grandmother bent to say good night,
And the enchanted moonlight seemed transformed
Into the silvery tinkling of an old

And gentle music-box that played a tune
Of Circean enchantments and far seas.
Her voice was lulling like the splash of these
When she had given me her good night kiss
There, in her lengthened shadow, I saw this
Old military ghost with mayfly whiskers,—
Poor harmless creature, blown by the cold wind,
Boasting of unseen, unreal victories
To a harsh unbelieving world unkind,—
For all the battles that this warrior fought
Were with cold poverty and helpless age—
His spoils were shelters from the winter's rage.
And so forever through his braggart voice,
Through all that martial trumpet's sound, his soul
Wept a little sound, so pitiful,
Knowing that he is outside life for ever
With no one that will warm or comfort him. . . .
He is not even dead, but Death's buffoon
On a bare stage, a shrunken pantaloon.—
His military banner never fell,
Nor his account of victories, the stories
Of old apocryphal misfortunes, glories
Which comforted his heart in later life
When he was the Napoleon of the schoolroom
And all the victories he gained were over
Little boys who would not learn to spell.

All day within the sweet and ancient gardens
He had my childish self for audience—
Whose body flat and strange, whose pale straight hair
Made me appear as though I had been drowned—
(We all have the remote air of a legend)—
And Dagobert my brother whose large strength,
Great body and grave beauty still reflect
The Angevin dead kings from whom we spring;
And sweet as the young tender winds that stir
In thickets where the earliest flower-bells sing
Upon the boughs, was his just character;
And Peregrine the youngest with a naïve
Shy grace like a faun's, whose slant eyes seemed
The warm green light beneath eternal boughs.
His hair was like the fronds of feathers, life
In him was changing ever, springing fresh
As the dark songs of birds . . . the furry warmth
And purring sound of fires was in his voice
Which never failed to warm and comfort me.

And there were haunted summers in Troy Park
When all the stillness budded into leaves;
We listened like Ophelia drowned in blond
And fluid hair, beneath stag-antlered trees;

Then in the ancient park the country-pleasant
Shadows fell as brown as any pheasant,
And Colonel Fantock seemed like one of these.
Sometimes for comfort in the castle kitchen
He drowsed, where with a sweet and velvet lip
The snapdragons within the fire
Of their red summer never tire.
And Colonel Fantock liked our company.
For us he wandered over each old lie,
Changing the flowering hawthorn full of bees
Into the silver helm of Hercules,
For us defended Troy from the top stair
Outside the nursery, when the calm full moon
Was like the sound within the growth of trees.
But then came one cruel day in deepest June
When pink flowers seemed a sweet Mozartian tune,
And Colonel Fantock pondered o'er a book.
A gay voice like a honeysuckle nook,—
So sweet,—said, "It is Colonel Fantock's age
Which makes him babble." . . . Blown by winter's rage
The poor old man then knew his creeping fate,
The darkening shadow that would take his sight
And hearing; and he thought of his saved pence
Which scarce would rent a grave . . . that youthful voice
Was a dark bell which ever clanged "Too late"—
A creeping shadow that would steal from him
Even the little boys who would not spell—
His only prisoners. . . . On that June day
Cold Death had taken his first citadel.

# *Arthur Waley*

ARTHUR WALEY was born in 1889 and was educated at Rugby School and King's
College, Cambridge. He entered the employ of the British Museum in 1913
and began the study of Chinese and Japanese. Five years later he was known as a
leading English authority on Chinese and Japanese literatures.

His first publication, *A Hundred and Seventy Chinese Poems* (1918, revised edition 1927), has taken its place as a standard work. *More Translations* (1919) and
*The Temple* (1923) affirm his admirers' contention that Waley is no mere competent adapter, but a poet in his own right. Whatever the Chinese original may be,
the re-creation is a separate work in which the craftsman reveals himself. In his
balanced imagery, his enameled phrases, his use but not abuse of color, Waley's own
poetic personality is imposed on the originals as certainly as Khayyám's Rubáiyát
was suffused with Fitzgerald. As Humbert Wolfe wrote in his foreword to the
pamphlet *Poems from the Chinese* published in The Augustan Books of English
Poetry in 1928, "We must address ourselves to these poems as though they had

been written by an Englishman of the twentieth century, and judge them on that basis. It is a severe test to apply to translations, but Mr. Waley emerges from it serenely victorious. Indeed, serenity is the keynote of all this work—the serenity of assured mastery in a difficult medium, but still more of outlook. The beauty with which these poems are inlaid is fundamentally a wise beauty, and the wisdom is as much in the shape of Mr. Waley's mind as in that of China."

Waley has also translated a quantity of Oriental prose, notably *The Tale of Genji*.

## FROM THE "BOOK OF ODES"

### Anon. (c. 1000 b.c.)

There grows an elm-tree on the hill,
And by the mere an alder-tree—
You have a coat, but do not wear it,
You have a gown, but do not trail it,
You have a horse, but do not ride it,
A coach, but do not drive it,
And so it will be when you are dead
And others can enjoy them!
There grows a gum-tree on the hill,
And by the mere a chestnut tree.
You have wine and food, why do you for-
get
Sometimes to play your lute,
Sometimes to laugh and sing,
Sometimes to steal new playtime from the
night?
Shall it be so when you are dead
And others have your house?

## HOT CAKE

### Shu Hsi (c. a.d. 281)

Winter has come; fierce is the cold;
In the sharp morning air new-risen we meet.
Rheum freezes in the nose;
Frost hangs about the chin.
For hollow bellies, for chattering teeth and
    shivering knees
What better than hot cake?
Soft as the down of spring,
Whiter than autumn wool!
Dense and swift the steam
Rises, swells and spreads.
Fragrance flies through the air,
Is scattered far and wide,
Steals down along the wind and wets
The covetous mouth of the passer-by.
Servants and grooms
Throw sidelong glances, munch the empty
    air.
They lick their lips who serve;
While lines of envious lackeys by the wall
Stand dryly swallowing.

## THE CRANES

### Po Chü-i (a.d. 830)

The western wind has blown but a few days;
Yet the first leaf already flies from the bough.
On the drying paths I walk in my thin shoes;
In the first cold I have donned my quilted coat.
Through shallow ditches the floods are clearing away;
Through sparse bamboos trickles a slanting light.
In the early dusk, down an alley of green moss,
The garden-boy is leading the cranes home.

# *W. J. Turner*

WALTER JAMES (REDFERN) TURNER was born in Melbourne, Australia, in 1889. He was educated at Scotch College, Melbourne, and, at seventeen, made the long journey to Europe. He studied in Germany and, shortly afterward, came to England, where, except for short intervals of travel, he has lived ever since.

His activities have been numerous. He was literary editor of *The Daily Herald,* dramatic critic of *The London Mercury,* and musical critic for three English weeklies. In the last rôle, his essays have been collected in three volumes, the first being *Music and Life* (1921). Later Turner made a reputation as an incisive dramatist with the imaginative *The Man Who Ate the Popomack* (1922) and the satiric *Smaragda's Lover* (1924).

But it is as a poet that Turner first attracted and still challenges attention. *The Hunter and other Poems* (1916) contains other matter besides the whimsical "Romance," which has been much quoted. *The Dark Fire* (1918) suggests if it does not sound depths; repressed passion adds a somber note to the fancies. Turner's subsequent volumes, *Paris and Helen* (1921), *In Time Like Glass* (1921) and *Landscape of Cytherea* (1923), suffer from an overproductive and uncritical ease, but many of the individual poems are on a level with the author's successful work. A dramatic poem, *The Seven Days of the Sun* (1925), was followed by the simpler, more persuasive *New Poems* (1928). A critical study of Beethoven was published in 1927.

*Pursuit of Psyche* (1931) and *Jack and Jill* (1934) came as a surprise to all except Turner's insistent admirers. *Jack and Jill* has a freshness of idea and a technical proficiency which command instant attention. *Pursuit of Psyche,* Turner's most ambitious project, concerns (as the title suggests) the search for the spirit through the varying forms of human desire. The ten cantos suffer from the lack of a fiery imagination which should unify the whole—the poem has organization without integration—but its parts are admirable. There are reminders of Abercrombie's *Emblems of Love* not only in the philosophy but in the phrasing. Beauty fills

> This common function of all living things
> With a pure value, vivid as the pact
> The rosebush makes with summer, or the wings
> The dove makes with the wind, or water when ice is still.

But Turner is, at the same time, more abstract and more lyrical than Abercrombie. The shorter poems are particularly convincing, and such pieces as "Talking with Soldiers," "The Music of a Tree," and "The Lion" pronounce an imagination altogether his own.

*Blow for Balloons* (1935), Turner's first novel, is a mixture of naïve egotism, penetration, poetry, and general literary sans-culottisme—a headlong fantasy, the best part of which is the author's account of his boyhood in Australia.

### ROMANCE

When I was but thirteen or so
  I went into a golden land,
Chimborazo, Cotopaxi
  Took me by the hand.

My father died, my brother too,
  They passed like fleeting dreams,
I stood where Popocatapetl
  In the sunlight gleams.

I dimly heard the master's voice
  And boys far-off at play,—
Chimborazo, Cotopaxi
  Had stolen me away.

I walked in a great golden dream
  To and fro from school—
Shining Popocatapetl
  The dusty streets did rule.

I walked home with a gold dark boy
  And never a word I'd say,
Chimborazo, Cotopaxi
  Had taken my speech away.

I gazed entranced upon his face
  Fairer than any flower—
O shining Popocatapetl,
  It was thy magic hour:

The houses, people, traffic seemed
  Thin fading dreams by day;
Chimborazo, Cotopaxi,
  They had stolen my soul away!

### SONG

Lovely hill-torrents are
  At cold winterfall;

Among the earth's silence, they
  Stonily call.

Gone Autumn's pageantry;
  Through woods all bare
With strange, locked voices
  Shining they stare!

### THE ROBBER

The Trees were taller than the night,
  And through my window square,
Earth-stupefied, great oranges
  Drowsed in the leaf-carved air.

Into that tree-top crowded dream
  A white arm stretched, and soon
Those green-gold oranges were plucked,
  Were sucked pale by the Moon.

And white and still that robber lay
  On the frail boughs asleep,
Eating the solid substance through
  In silence clear and deep.

Suddenly he went, and then
  The wood was dark as death:
Come back, O robber; robber, come;
  These gray trees are but breath:

These gray trees are but breath, the Night
  Is a wind-walled, dream-filled Hall!
But on the mirror of the air
  The wood wreathed dark and tall.

No movement and no sound there was
  Within that silent House.
Behind a cloud, the Robber laughed
  In a mad white carouse.

### TALKING WITH SOLDIERS

The mind of the people is like mud,
From which arise strange and beautiful things,
But mud is none the less mud,
Though it bear orchids and prophesying Kings,
Dreams, trees, and water's bright babblings.

It has found form and color and light,
The cold glimmer of the ice-wrapped Poles;

It has called a far-off glow: Arcturus,
And some pale weeds: lilies of the valley.

It has imagined Virgil, Helen and Cassandra,
The sack of Troy, and the weeping for Hector—
Rearing stark up 'mid all this beauty
In the thick, dull neck of Ajax.

There is a dark Pine in Lapland,
And the great, figured Horn of the Reindeer
Moving soundlessly across the snow,
Is its twin brother, double-dreamed,
In the mind of a far-off people.

It is strange that a little mud
Should echo with sounds, syllables, and letters,
Should rise up and call a mountain Popocatapetl,
And a green-leafed wood Oleander.

These are the ghosts of invisible things;
There is no Lapland, no Helen and no Hector,
And the Reindeer is a darkening of the brain,
And Oleander is but oleander.

Mary Magdalena and the vine Lachryma Christi
Were like ghosts up the ghost of Vesuvius,
As I sat and drank wine with the soldiers,
As I sat in the Inn on the mountain,
Watching the shadows in my mind.

The mind of the people is like mud:
Where are the imperishable things,
The ghosts that flicker in the brain—
Silent women, orchids, and prophesying Kings,
Dreams, trees, and water's bright babblings!

## THE LION

Strange spirit with inky hair,
   Tail tufted stiff in rage,
I saw with sudden stare
   Leap on the printed page.

The stillness of its roar
   From midnight deserts torn
Clove silence to the core
   Like the blare of a great horn.

I saw the sudden sky;
   Cities in crumbling sand;
The stars fall wheeling by;
   The lion roaring stand:

The stars fall wheeling by,
   Their silent, silver stain
Cold on his glittering eye,
   Cold on his carven mane.

The full-orbed Moon shone down,
   The silence was so loud,
From jaws wide-open thrown
   His voice hung like a cloud.

Earth shrank to blackest air;
   That spirit stiff in rage
Into some midnight lair
   Leapt from the printed page.

### THE MUSIC OF A TREE

Once, walking home, I passed beneath a Tree,
It filled the dark like stone statuary,
  It was so quiet and still,
  Its thick green leaves a hill
Of strange and faint earth-branching melody:

Over a wall it hung its leaf-starred wood,
And as I lonely there beneath it stood,
  In that sky-hollow street
  Where rang no human feet,
Sweet music flowed and filled me with its flood;

And all my weariness then fell away,
The houses were more lovely than by day;
  The Moon and that old Tree
  Sang there, and secretly,
With throbbing heart, tip-toe I stole away.

## Camilla Doyle

C AMILLA DOYLE was born at Cathedral Close, Norwich, where she has lived ever
since. Besides being a writer, Miss Doyle is well known as an artist and craftsman, having exhibited her paintings and furniture at various galleries.

Her *Poems* (1923) reveal the same sensitivity to line and motion as her drawings;
even so tiny a sketch as "The Rabbit" has the faithful economy of a Japanese print,
while "March" is a whimsical painting in the modern manner faintly suggestive of
Edward Thomas.

### THE RABBIT

All day this spring—the first he's known—
He lets himself be sideways blown
When the wind comes; he'll leap and
    pounce,
And try to rush two ways at once,
On feet that catch the very sound
Cascades make spattering to the ground.
  Though men with difficulty sing how
    soon
  They die, how seldom living they can
    thrive,
  He makes a little dancing-tune
    By only being alive;
No leaf that April winds blow off the tree
Falls and leaps round again so gay as he.

### MARCH

Green triangles have come on the ground,
  Green fretted things that we shall see
Grown to wild parsley soon. The hens
  Are talking news excitedly.

Big dimples stay in the sparrows' fluff,
  They preen with such fine energy.
The very dust's alert. His songs
  The blackbird stirs from memory—

The prettiest one he knew last year
  Is still a soft uncertainty.
The catkins drip like honey spilt,
  The cock crows twice as frequently.

And the wind rises, tossing back
    The spring: "You'll like it more," says he,
"For twisting aside, like the blackbird's song,
    And vexing you with 'Presently.' "

### THE MOON

How like a beckoning finger shows
The fair young moon that lately rose—
As though she called her thirty days
With bright deluding promises.

The answering waves at night, that took
Her silver livery, leap to crook

Themselves into her form as well,
And sink in tears because they fail.

Who'd think her beckoning finger were
A skeleton's, all white and bare?
For all her loveliness the moon
Is but a long-dead skeleton.

And if you doubt, all you that are
Fonder than waves of this bright star—
Wait but a little, at the full
We'll see her as a fleshless skull.

## Muriel Stuart

MURIEL STUART first attracted notice with "Christ at Carnival," a long poem which appeared in *The English Review* in 1915. This, later, became the title-poem of her first volume, published during the following year. More lyrical, however, are *The Cockpit of Idols and Other Poems* (1918) and *Poems* (1922), in both of which the verse suggests an imaginative power beneath smooth contours.

### THE SEED SHOP

Here in a quiet and dusty room they lie,
Faded as crumbled stone or shifting sand,
Forlorn as ashes, shriveled, scentless, dry—
Meadows and gardens running through my hand.

Dead that shall quicken at the call of Spring,
Sleepers to stir beneath June's magic kiss,
Though birds pass over, unremembering,
And no bee seek here roses that were his.

In this brown husk, a dale of hawthorn dreams;
A cedar in this narrow cell is thrust
That will drink deeply of a century's streams.
These lilies shall make summer on my dust.

Here in their safe and simple house of death,
Sealed in their shells, a million roses leap;
Here I can blow a garden with my breath,
And in my hand a forest lies asleep.

### COMMON FIRES

The fern and flame had fought and died together,
From fading frond the falling smoke crept gray,
The heath drew close her old brown shawl of heather,
And turned her face away.

Today the bee no bell of honey misses,
The birds are nesting where the bracken lies
Green, tranquil, deep, quiet as dreams or kisses
On weary lips and eyes.

The heath has drawn the blackened threads together;
My heart has closed her lips upon old pain;
But somewhere in my heart and in the heather,
No bud shall grow again.

# Theodore Maynard

THEODORE MAYNARD was born November 3, 1890, at Madras, India, where his parents were missionaries. His early education was in England, but he took his degree at Fordham University while teaching at its Graduate School. He came to America for the first time in 1909, intending to study for the Congregational ministry, but while "supplying" at a country church in Vermont preached a sermon which led to a call for his resignation. It was a sermon on fools, and the rustic congregation, suspecting personal implications, regarded it as heretical. Fortunately rebuffed in his ambition, Maynard returned to England in 1911, working his passage on a cattle-boat, and not long afterwards (having become a Catholic), tested unsuccessfully his vocation to the Dominican order. Seven months later he returned to the world, married, and took up journalism, writing for *The New Witness* under the editorship of the Chestertons and for other London periodicals. He came to the United States for the second time in 1920 to lecture, but remained to teach in California. In 1925 he moved to New York, and three years later was appointed head of the English Department at Georgetown University.

Maynard's first book, *Laughs and Whiffs of Song* (1915), was incorporated with two other small volumes and published in America as *Poems* in 1919. This collection, like *The Last Knight* (1920), was immature and imitative. Maynard, it is evident, had absorbed his influences, but had not gestated them. *Exile* (1928) is far better. The influence of Chesterton and other Catholic poets is not so apparent; Maynard's stanzas proceed from concepts and convictions which are his own.

In addition to his verse, Maynard has published a novel, two anthologies, and two collections of essays, one of which (*Our Best Poets,* 1922) is a partisan but provocative set of estimates.

### EXILE

Here where the season swiftly turns
Its great wheel forward while there burns
    Red in the redwood trees:
And while the eucalyptus climbs
Above the palm trees and the limes
    By Californian seas,

I think of England—and there wakes
Pain like wild roses in her brakes,
    A pain as dear as they,
That digs its roots in English earth,
And brings an English flower to birth
    Six thousand miles away.

The Downs are standing hugely drawn
Magnificent against the dawn,
    Deep black against the sky.
The first cock crows; the light leaps higher;
The Channel is a flood of fire
    And crimson suddenly.

And London, moving in her bed,
Hears on the eaves above her head
    The earlier sparrows stir.
A thin mist rises and the dew
Is thick on Hampstead and at Kew—
    The dawn has greeted her.

I ache in memory, yet I know
That if I ever homeward go
    I shall not ever find
In England's gentle tenderness
The rest I seek for which can bless
    My tired, unquiet mind.

For though I wander through all lands,
Seeking a house not built with hands
    For my eternal home,
No city in this world of men
Can claim me as a citizen
    From Babylon to Rome.

Not even London, where I burned
With bliss because in her I learned
    My faith, my love, my art;
Not even London, where I trod
Through crowded streets alone with God,
    And anguish in my heart;

Not even London, though she stands
To me with priestly praying hands
    In every dome and spire,

Can be the city of my quest,
Of infinite and final rest,
    The end of all desire.

But London, London has become
A heavenly symbol and the sum
    Of all the world can give.
And English air that was my breath
Remains my mortal life, till death
    Shall set me free to live.

The apple tree's an apple still
Here or upon an English hill;
    The moon among the boughs
Is the same moon, although it went
O'er ghostly orchards far in Kent
    When noon shone on my house.

But ah! some change had come to it
Beyond my exegetic wit:
    I know not what it was;
Not as the sailor on the spars
Among the Australasian stars
    Beholds the Southern Cross—

This map of heaven I know by rote.
But something struggles at my throat:
    And stirs my secret blood,
While a vague light, unearthly, strange
Glows through the lineaments of change
    On field and hill and wood.

The Roman poplars in their lines
Like Roman soldiers, Roman vines—
    These I had known of old.
And here in evidence the plain
And iron intellect of Spain,
    Her fury hot and cold.

But these are exiles, too, whose need
Has clung and stiffened round the Creed
    Which made them clear and strong.
Though far from Europe, here they keep
Her name remembered in their sleep,
    And in their classic song.

The apple tree remembers how
The blossoms burgeoned on her bough
    By little English streams;
And how the cider-drinking men
Were mighty with the sword and pen,
    And mightiest in their dreams.

The poplar and the olive know
How like an arrow from a bow
   The Roman road was shot;
How Roman law and Roman Pope
Brought order and outrageous hope
   To men who had them not.

✦

The giant masonry shall pass,
The palaces be mounds of grass—
   And yet not all in vain
That energy of brain and bone,
Though no stone on another stone
   Shall ever stand again.

I well may join the cry with them,
"If I forget Jerusalem . . ."
   I who shall not forget
My holy city, made more fair
By distance and the alien air
   Wherein my life is set.

If London come to empty loss,
And jackals wail at Charing Cross;
   And if at Westminster
The lizards crawl about each niche,
And she be poor who once was rich—
   I shall remember her.

For now I know with what in mind
The Abbey windows were designed,
   Her pavements were laid down;
And how her streets were meant to go
Beyond the steeple bells of Bow
   To the celestial Town.

And so beside the Golden Gate
A gate of purer gold I wait,
   A more resplendent wall

Than London's—daring now to lift
My voice to praise God's bitter gift,
   Exile, the best of all.

### THE WORLD'S MISER

I

A miser with an eager face
Sees that each roseleaf is in place.

He keeps beneath strong bolts and bars
The piercing beauty of the stars.

The colors of the dying day
He hoards as treasure—well He may!—

And saves with care (lest they be lost)
The dainty diagrams of frost.

He counts the hairs of every head,
And grieves to see a sparrow dead.

II

Among the yellow primroses
He holds His summer palaces,

And sets the grass about them all
To guard them as His spearmen small.

He fixes on each wayside stone
A mark to show it as His Own,

And knows when raindrops fall through air
Whether each single one be there,

That gathered into ponds and brooks
They may become His picture-books,

To shew in every spot and place
The living glory of His face.

# Isaac Rosenberg

ISAAC ROSENBERG was born at Bristol on November 25, 1890. At the age of seven his parents brought him to London; at fourteen he was compelled to leave school and work for his living. Later some friends interested themselves in the boy who had begun to show great talent as a writer and draftsman, and made it possible for the young Jew from the East End to attend the Slade School. After three years of art schooling, during which Rosenberg won prizes, ill health forced him to leave

England. In 1914, he went to South Africa, to a married sister in Capetown. It was there that he definitely decided to become a poet. He attempted to support himself by writing and lecturing, but his efforts were without success and, in less than a year, he was back in London. War had broken out. Sick and unhappy, Rosenberg enlisted in 1915. Early in 1916, he was sent to France, totally unfitted for military life. Nevertheless, his endurance was amazing; he hated war with all the force of his keen mind and disabled body, but he never whined. He was killed in action on April 1, 1918.

As a poet, Rosenberg is greater in promise than achievement. Most of the privately printed *Night and Day* (1912), although published at the age of twenty-two, was written in his 'teens. Even the succeeding *Youth* (1915) suffers from verbal awkwardness; a fear of falling into weak writing led him to complicate his images until they are, for the most part, turgid and overburdened. But in *Moses* (1916), and in the posthumous war-poems, the passionate young poet speaks in his own half-savage voice. Here and there a passage suggests Abercrombie, whom Rosenberg admired greatly; but the images are so fiercely fresh, the accent so personal, that there is no mistaking the strength and originality of Rosenberg's gift.

Rosenberg's three small books, as well as a quantity of uncollected verse including an unfinished play, were published in one volume, *Poems,* in 1922. Not the least remarkable feature of this unusual collection is the fact that the contents were selected and edited by Gordon Bottomley and the introductory memoir was supplied by Laurence Binyon.

### THE ONE LOST

I mingle with your bones;
You steal in subtle noose
This lighted dust Jehovah loans
And now I lose.

What will the Lender say
When I shall not be found,
Safe-sheltered at the Judgment Day,
Being in you bound?

He'll hunt through wards of Heaven,
Call to uncoffined earth,
"Where is this soul, unjudged, not given
Dole for good's dearth?"

And I, lying so safe
Within you, hearing all,
To have cheated God shall laugh,
Freed by your thrall.

### THE JEW

Moses, from whose loins I sprung,
Lit by a lamp in his blood

Ten immutable rules, a moon
For mutable lampless men.

The blond, the bronze, the ruddy,
With the same heaving blood,
Keep tide to the moon of Moses.
Then why do they sneer at me?

### THE DEAD HEROES

Flame out, you glorious skies,
Welcome our brave;
Kiss their exultant eyes;
Give what they gave.

Flash, mailèd seraphim,
Your burning spears;
New days to outflame their dim
Heroic years.

Thrills their baptismal tread
The bright proud air;
The embattled plumes outspread
Burn upwards there.

Flame out, flame out, O Song!
Star, ring to star!
Strong as our hurt is strong,
Our children are.

Their blood is England's heart;
By their dead hands,

It is their noble part
That England stands.

England—Time gave them thee;
They gave back this
To win Eternity
And claim God's kiss.

# Francis Ledwidge

FRANCIS LEDWIDGE was born in Slane, County Meath, Ireland, in 1891. His brief life was fitful and uncertain. He was, at various times, a miner, a grocer's clerk, a farmer, a scavenger, an experimenter in hypnotism, and, at the end, a soldier. He served as a lance-corporal on the Flanders front and was killed in July, 1917, at the age of twenty-six years.

Ledwidge's poetry is rich in nature-drawing; his lines palpitate with a thin but romantic charm. Obviously influenced by the sensuous imagery of Keats, his twilight-colored verse is unaffectedly melodious. He was—as is obvious by his choice of titles—fondest of dim hours and evening clouds in some "blue corner off the moon's highway."

Discovered and sponsored by Lord Dunsany, Ledwidge published two volumes during his lifetime: *Songs of the Fields* (1914) and *Songs of Peace* (1916). Both books (with posthumous *Last Songs*) were incorporated in *Complete Poems* (1919).

### EVENING CLOUDS

A little flock of clouds go down to rest
In some blue corner off the moon's highway,
With shepherd-winds that shook them in the West
To borrowed shapes of earth, in bright array,
Perhaps to weave a rainbow's gay festoons
Around the lonesome isle which Brooke has made
A little England full of lovely noons,
Or dot it with his country's mountain shade.

Ah, little wanderers, when you reach that isle [1]
Tell him, with dripping dew, they have not failed,
What he loved most; for late I roamed a while
Thro' English fields and down her rivers sailed;
And they remember him with beauty caught
From old desires of Oriental Spring
Heard in his heart with singing overwrought;
And still on Purley Common gooseboys sing.

[1] The island of Skyros where Rupert Brooke was buried.

### THE WIFE OF LLEW

And Gwydion said to Math, when it was Spring:
"Come now and let us make a wife for Llew."
And so they broke broad boughs yet moist with dew,
And in a shadow made a magic ring:
They took the violet and the meadow-sweet
To form her pretty face, and for her feet
They built a mound of daisies on a wing,
And for her voice they made a linnet sing
In the wide poppy blowing for her mouth.
And over all they chanted twenty hours.
And Llew came singing from the azure south
And bore away his wife of birds and flowers.

### A RAINY DAY IN APRIL

When the clouds shake their hyssops, and the rain
Like holy water falls upon the plain,
'Tis sweet to gaze upon the springing grain
    And see your harvest born.

And sweet the little breeze of melody
The blackbird puffs upon the budding tree,
While the wild poppy lights upon the lea
    And blazes 'mid the corn.

The skylark soars the freshening shower to hail,
And the meek daisy holds aloft her pail,
And Spring all radiant by the wayside pale
    Sets up her rock and reel.

See how she weaves her mantle fold on fold,
Hemming the woods and carpeting the wold.
Her warp is of the green, her woof the gold,
    The spinning world her wheel.

# Viola Meynell

VIOLA MEYNELL, daughter of Alice Meynell (see page 120), is the sister of Francis
Meynell. Her prose is less metaphysical than her poetry, but the short stories in
*Young Mrs. Cruse* as well as her novels are enriched with the same subtlety that
informs her verse.

*Verses* (1919) contained only fifteen poems, a book so slight that it almost escaped notice. These earlier poems were republished, with the addition of several
new ones, in *The Frozen Ocean* (1931), a book which was applauded by the poets
and neglected by the public. The reason for this is not far to seek: Miss Meynell's

mood is contemplative; her emotions are reserved; she is clairvoyant, but her communication is so quiet that the common reader, missing the common rhetoric, is reluctant to listen. It is as if she did not expect her poems to be heard, but overheard. The tone is restrained, the transpositions are gradual and sensitive. "She has inherited her mother's lucid mysticism," wrote Louise Bogan, "but escapes the faintly dry touch of literary air which Alice Meynell absorbed from the late nineteenth century. The form is frugal, undisturbed, candid as thoughtful speech. This candor reveals emotion brightly alive and clearly felt, emotion that is itself form: the kernel which builds outward from inner intensity every lyric capable of touching the heart and mind."

Such a poem as "Jonah and the Whale" seems a seventeenth century creation, a definite visualization and a daring conceit. "The Maid in the Rice-fields" and "A Girl" sound the note of romantic fervor. The first is particularly eloquent with its mounting invocation and terror of young love, a strain which the poet has amplified and stressed in her novels.

### JONAH AND THE WHALE

He sported round the watery world.
His rich oil was a gloomy waveless lake
Within the waves. Affrighted seamen hurled
Their weapons in his foaming wake.

One old corroding iron he bore
Which journeyed through his flesh but yet had not
Found out his life. Another lance he wore
Outside him pricking in a tender spot.

So distant were his parts that they
Sent but a dull faint message to his brain.
He knew not his own flesh, as great kings may
Not know the farther places where they reign.

His play made storm in a calm sea;
His very kindness slew what he might touch;
And wrecks lay scattered on his anger's lee.
The Moon rocked to and fro his watery couch.

His hunger cleared the sea. And where
He passed, the ocean's edge lifted its brim.
He skimmed the dim sea-floor to find if there
Some garden had its harvest ripe for him.

But in his sluggish brain no thought
Ever arose. His law was instinct blind.
No thought or gleam or vision ever brought
Light to the dark of his old dreamless mind.

Until one day sudden and strange
Half-hints of knowledge burst upon his sight.
Glimpses he had of Time, and Space, and Change,
And something greater than his might;

And terror's leap to imagine sin;
And blinding Truth half-bare unto his seeing.
It was the living man who had come in . . .
Jonah's thoughts flying through his being.


### THE MAID IN THE RICE-FIELDS

Until the day when thou and I are wed
        How shall my life be fed!
But first this rice that's newly sown
Must rise and multiply and be
A full crop in the granary
        Before thou art my own.

Last night I dreamt that I walked out at dusk
        And heard the first dry husk
Fall rustling from the ripened ear.
But now today I wake and weep
To see the fields no man may reap
        In the cold early year.

O passing clouds, have pity on my need,
        Water the thirsting seed;
O mighty sun, find out this plain,
Call up the stalk, hasten the leaf;
O bare fields, harken to my grief,
        Foster the holy grain.

Weeping, I stand above the seed and say
        Why do you hide away?
Do you fear the storm if you leave your rest?
I have taken the storm into my breast.
        Why do you still delay?
O if the cloud you wait to rain forbears,
        Here are a maiden's tears.
And if the sun you seek denies his dart,
        Behold my burning heart.


### A GIRL

Wherever she may turn her ravished eyes
Something so precious to her bosom lies,
She spends her fervent passion more and more,
Thinking such beauty has not been before.
The common virtue in things, to her excess,
Seems like some new undreamt-of loveliness.
Whatever allurement may her senses move
Her fair false judgment hurries to approve.
She clasps to her fond heart what's poor and mean,
For joy of some beguilement she has seen.
But all her sins of word and look and touch
God may forgive because she hath loved much.

# Francis Meynell

FRANCIS MEYNELL, son of Alice and Wilfred Meynell, was born in 1891. He was, he says, "fattened up to be a poet, but early decided better to print other people's good poems well than to have his own bad poems printed at all." After working as printer, journalist and politician, he founded The Nonesuch Press in 1923. Since that time the Press under his direction has brought out more than a hundred and fifty books of literary value, flawless in all details—typography, editing, choice of paper, binding and general composition.

Although he is better known as a master-printer, he has, Meynell himself to the contrary, published several excellent verses. His literary talents also found expression in the editing of George Herbert's *The Temple* (1927) and Thomas Beedome's *Select Poems* (1928), as well as in the authorship of *The Typography of Newspaper Advertisements* (1929).

### MAN AND BEAST

I am less patient than this horse
And it is fleeter far than I.
Its hair is silky, mine is coarse;
Grasses have shaped that larger eye,
While to feed me live things must die.

The birds make little darts in air,
And fishes little darts in water,
Old sheep a silver glory share,
Peacocks are peacocks everywhere . . .
Man lies awake, planning the slaughter.

What woman has this old cat's graces?
What boy can sing as the thrush sings?
For me, I'd rather not run races
With dragon-flies, nor thread the mazes
Of a smooth lawn with ants and things.

Yet horse and sheep tread leaf and stem
And bud and flower beneath their feet;
They sniff at Stars-of-Bethlehem
And buttercups are food to them—
No more than bitter food or sweet.

I, to whom air and waves are sealed,
I yet possess the human part.
O better beasts, you now must yield!
I name the cool stars of the field,
I have the flowers of heaven by heart.

### PERMANENCE

There is no power to change
    One act, one word.
We move in time: these range
    Immortal. I have heard

Egypt and her Antony,
    With their love first fulfilled
Cry out, and again cry—
    Nor ever are they stilled.

And Sheba I have seen
    Bare for her love her breast.
The silken Lesbian queen
    Leaves nothing unconfest.

Unspaced, untimed, held fast
    Are all things done or undone.
Eternity knows no haste—
    In Babylon, or London.

Though they have never moved
    These hundred hundred years,
Their rhythm when they loved
    Lives ever, and their tears.

When your love's flight shall falter,
    Shall fall like a wounded bird,
You too cannot alter
    The said or the unsaid word.

O passion of wisdom, this
    (Helen held it for such):
You cannot unkiss that kiss,
    You cannot untouch that touch.

# Richard Aldington

RICHARD ALDINGTON was born in England in 1892, and educated at Dover College and London University. His first poems were published in England in 1909; *Images Old and New* appeared in 1915. Aldington and "H. D." (the chief American Imagist) were conceded to be two of the foremost Imagist poets; their sensitive and clean-cut lines put to shame their scores of imitators. Both appeared, with four others, under Amy Lowell's *Aegis* in the three issues of *Some Imagist Poets,* published from 1915 to 1917.

Aldington's *War and Love* (1918) is somewhat more regular in pattern; the poems in this latter volume are less consciously programmatic but more searching. Recently, Aldington, in common with most of the *vers libristes,* has been writing in regular rhythms and fixed forms. *Images of Desire* (1919) was followed by *Exile and Other Poems* (1923) which contains whole sections of surprisingly archaic, pseudo-Elizabethan songs. *A Fool i' the Forest* (1925) is a return to Aldington's earlier manner with the addition of foreign dissonances. Though the influence of Eliot is obvious, this phantasmagoria is in many ways Aldington's most important work. Juxtaposing classic calm with the incongruities of a mechanical civilization, Aldington projects an agony unrelated to either ancient or modern backgrounds. This agony was amplified in Aldington's first novel, *Death of a Hero* (1929), a novel dealing with three generations, beginning in the snug little England of the Victorian Nineties; a work kaleidoscopic in effect and, as might be imagined, rich in musical variety. *Roads to Glory* (1931), *All Men Are Enemies* (1933), and *Women Must Work* (1934) are his decreasingly important books of prose. His *Collected Poems* was published in 1928.

Critics differ concerning Aldington's position as a poet; none disputes his eminence as a translator. Among his many translations (of which more than twenty were published prior to 1929) are *The Poems of Anyte of Tegea, The Poems of Meleager,* Cyrano de Bergerac's *Voyages to the Moon and the Sun, Letters of Voltaire and Frederick the Great.* He is also the editor and translator of *Latin Poems of the Renaissance, Eighteenth Century French Literature* and *Fifty Romance Lyric Poems.*

## IMAGES

### I

Like a gondola of green scented fruits
Drifting along the dank canals of Venice,
You, O exquisite one,
Have entered into my desolate city.

### II

The blue smoke leaps
Like swirling clouds of birds vanishing.
So my love leaps forth toward you,
Vanishes and is renewed.

### III

A rose-yellow moon in a pale sky
When the sunset is faint vermilion
In the mist among the tree-boughs
Art thou to me, my beloved.

### IV

A young beech tree on the edge of the forest
Stands still in the evening,
Yet shudders through all its leaves in the
    light air
And seems to fear the stars—
So are you still and so tremble.

### V

The red deer are high on the mountain,
They are beyond the last pine trees.
And my desires have run with them.

### VI

The flower which the wind has shaken
Is soon filled again with rain;
So does my heart fill slowly with tears,
O Foam-Driver, Wind-of-the-Vineyards,
Until you return.

## THE FAUN SEES SNOW FOR THE FIRST TIME

Zeus,
Brazen-thunder-hurler,
Cloud-whirler, son-of-Kronos,
Send vengeance on these Oreads
Who strew
White frozen flecks of mist and cloud
Over the brown trees and the tufted grass
Of the meadows, where the stream
Runs black through shining banks
Of bluish white.

Zeus,
Are the halls of heaven broken up
That you flake down upon me
Feather-strips of marble?

Dis and Styx!
When I stamp my hoof
The frozen-cloud specks jam into the cleft
So that I reel upon two slippery points. . . .

Fool, to stand here cursing
When I might be running!

## AT THE BRITISH MUSEUM

I turn the page and read:
"I dream of silent verses where the rhyme
Glides noiseless as an oar."

The heavy musty air, the black desks,
The bent heads and rustling noises
In the great dome
Vanish . . .
And
The sun hangs in the cobalt-blue sky,

The boat drifts over the lake shallows,
The fishes skim like umber shadows
          through undulating weeds,
The oleanders drop their rosy
          petals on the lawns,
And the swallows dive and swirl and whistle
About the cleft battlements of Can Grande'
   castle. . . .

## EVENING

The chimneys, rank on rank,
Cut the clear sky;
The moon,
With a rag of gauze about her loins,
Poses among them, an awkward Venus—

And here am I looking wantonly at her
Over the kitchen sink.

## VICARIOUS ATONEMENT

This is an old and very cruel god. . . .

We will endure;
We will try not to wince
When he crushes and rends us.

If indeed it is for your sakes,
If we perish or moan in torture,
Or stagger under sordid burdens
That you may live—
Then we can endure.

If our wasted blood
Makes bright the page
Of poets yet to be;
If this our tortured life
Save from destruction's nails
Gold words of a Greek long dead;
Then we can endure,
Then hope,
Then watch the sun rise
Without utter bitterness.

But, O thou old and very cruel god,
Take if thou canst this bitter cup from us.

## POSSESSION

I must possess you utterly
And utterly must you possess me;

So even if that dreamer's tale
Of heaven and hell be true
There shall be two spirits rived together
Either in whatever peace be heaven
Or in the icy whirlwind that is hell
For those who loved each other more than
  God—
So that the other spirits shall cry out:
"Ah! Look how the ancient love yet holds to
  them
That these two ghosts are never driven apart
But kiss with shadowy kisses and still take
Joy from the mingling of their misty limbs!"

AFTER TWO YEARS

She is all so slight
And tender and white

As a May morning.
She walks without hood
At dusk. It is good
    To hear her sing.

It is God's will
That I shall love her still
    As he loves Mary,
And night and day
I will go forth to pray
    That she love me.

She is as gold
Lovely, and far more cold.
    Do thou pray with me,
For if I win grace
To kiss twice her face
    God has done well to me.


# Stella Benson

STELLA BENSON was born in 1892 at Much Wenlock in Shropshire, her father being "a sort of squire down there," but, as she was a delicate child, she spent most of her girlhood in Switzerland and Southern France. After doing social work during the War, she paid her first visit to America in 1918. Ordered to a warm climate by her physician, she came to California and, having no funds, tried to support herself in San Francisco as lady's maid, bill-collector, and book-agent, but without success in any of these capacities. Later, she tutored at the University of California, returned to England by way of China, where she taught Chinese boys in an English church school, and during her travels in the Orient met her husband, J. C. O'Gorman Anderson. Her health was uncertain and her work was continually interrupted by spells of illness. She died in Hongai, Tongking, French Indo-China, December 7, 1933.

Stella Benson is generally known as a novelist of piquant charm. Her volume of verse, Twenty (1918), reveals more of herself than her more voluminous prose; it has all the insouciance of I Pose (1915), the delicacy of The Poor Man (1920) and the finesse of Pipers and a Dancer (1924).

Toward the end of her life her work grew increasingly more brilliant and sensitive; the short stories and sketches with their premonitory concern with death cannot easily be forgotten. Perhaps her finest extended work is Tobit Transplanted (1932), published in America under the simpering title The Faraway Bride, in which she shifted the Biblical background to modern Manchuria without violating either the spirit of the apocryphal tale or the actuality of the present setting and added a wealth of poetic understanding.

### WORDS

O words, O words, and shall you rule
The world? What is it but the tongue
That doth proclaim a man a fool,
So that his best songs go unsung,
So that his dreams are sent to school
And all die young.

There pass the traveling dreams, and these
My soul adores—my words condemn—
Oh, I would fall upon my knees
To kiss their golden garments' hem,
Yet words do lie in wait to seize
And murder them.

Tonight the swinging stars shall plumb
The silence of the sky. And herds
Of plumèd winds like huntsmen come
To hunt with dreams the restless birds.
Tonight the moon shall strike you dumb,
O words, O words. . . .

### FIVE SMOOTH STONES

It was young David, lord of sheep and cattle,
Pursued his fate, the April fields among,
Singing a song of solitary battle,
A loud mad song, for he was very young.

Vivid the air—and something more than vivid,—
Tall clouds were in the sky—and something more,—
The light horizon of the spring was livid
With a steel smile that showed the teeth of war.

It was young David mocked the Philistine.
It was young David laughed beside the river.
There came his mother—his and yours and mine—
With five smooth stones, and dropped them in his quiver.

You never saw so green-and-gold a fairy.
You never saw such very April eyes.
She sang him sorrow's song to make him wary.
She gave him five smooth stones to make him wise.

*The first stone is love, and that shall fail you.*
*The second stone is hate, and that shall fail you.*
*The third stone is knowledge, and that shall fail you.*
*The fourth stone is prayer, and that shall fail you.*
*The fifth stone shall not fail you.*

For what is love, O lovers of my tribe?
And what is love, O women of my day?
Love is a farthing piece, a bloody bribe
Pressed in the palm of God—and thrown away.

And what is hate, O fierce and unforgiving?
And what shall hate achieve, when all is said?
A silly joke that cannot reach the living,
A spitting in the faces of the dead.

And what is knowledge, O young man who tasted
The reddest fruit on that forbidden tree?
Knowledge is but a painful effort wasted,
A bitter drowning in a bitter sea.

And what is prayer, O waiters for the answer?
And what is prayer, O seekers of the cause?
Prayer is the weary soul of Herod's dancer,
Dancing before blind kings without applause.

The fifth stone is a magic stone, my David,
Made up of fear and failure, lies and loss.
Its heart is lead, and on its face is gravèd
A crooked cross, my son, a crooked cross.

It has no dignity to lend it value;
No purity—alas, it bears a stain.
You shall not give it gratitude, nor shall you
Recall it all your days, except with pain.

Oh, bless your blindness, glory in your groping!
Mock at your betters with an upward chin!
And when the moment has gone by for hoping,
Sling your fifth stone, O son of mine, and win.

Grief do I give you, grief and dreadful laughter;
Sackcloth for banner, ashes in your wine.
Go forth, go forth, nor ask me what comes after;
The fifth stone shall not fail you, son of mine.

*Go forth, go forth, and slay the Philistine.*

# V. Sackville-West

V(ITA) SACKVILLE-WEST, daughter of Baron Sackville of Knole Park, was born in
1892. Her ancestral home figures prominently in Virginia Woolf's *Orlando*
(1928). *Orlando,* that time-dissolving tour de force, is in fact an elaborate fantasia—
half poem, half parody—on the Sackvilles with Vita Sackville-West (to whom the
book is dedicated) scarcely disguised as the hero-heroine. The "plot" of Virginia
Woolf's fiction, with its magical telescoping of periods, places and passions, seems
to be suggested by one of the interludes in Miss Sackville-West's *The Land,* a
passage ending:

> Perilla, fly! Corinna, stay!
> In deserts of Bohemia,
> A wood near Athens, or the wood
> Where these grown oaks as saplings stood
> Three hundred English years gone by,
> "And yet I love her till I die."

V. Sackville-West has become well known in three capacities: as the wife of the
critic, biographer, and diplomat, Harold Nicolson; as a novelist; as a poet. It was
as a poet that she began, with *Poems of West and East* (1917). The volume failed
to attract attention and she turned to prose, publishing four novels and two volumes of short stories between 1919 and 1924. Of these *The Heir* (1922) received
the greatest commendation.

It was not until 1926 that her reputation as a poet was established. In that year
she published *The Land,* which was awarded the Hawthornden Prize in 1927. This,
with the earlier poems, was reprinted in a *Collected Poems* in 1935. *The Land* is
a long tribute to the English countryside, interspersed with lyrics. The movement
is slow; there is no narrative; the scheme is no more original than Thomson's *The
Seasons.* But while there is no novelty of theme or technique, there is an utterance
so sincere, a rapport with her material so intense, that they produce a keen if quiet
rapture. Here, without pomp, is penetration.

> The country habit has me by the heart,
> For he's bewitched forever who has seen,
> Not with his eyes but with his vision, Spring
> Flow down the woods and stipple leaves with sun,
> As each man knows the life that fits him best,
> The shape it makes in his soul, the tune, the tone . . .

This is a poetry that speaks for itself more clearly than any résumé. Whether
Miss Sackville-West writes about the sowing of crops, orchards, cider-making,
sheep-shearing, wood-flowers, or weeds, she knows, "as each man knows the life
that fits him best," the tone which fits the changing look of spring or winter landscapes. Truly the country habit has her by the heart.

WEED MONTH

(*from "The Land"*)

This is the month of weeds.
Kex, charlock, thistle,
Among the shorn bristle
Of stubble drop seeds.
This is the month of weeds.

Spurry, pimpernel, quitch,
Twine in the stubble,
Making for trouble;
With nettle in ditch,
Spurry, pimpernel, quitch.

Yet the field has a friend,
The nimble clover,

Custodian, lover,
Yare to defend.
The field has a friend.

Humble-bees boldly reach
Red clover's honey,
Paid in sweet money.
Hives-bees in vain beseech:
Honey is out of reach.

Now let the clover spread;
Nature it craveth;
Foemen it braveth,
Strangling them dead.
So let the clover spread.

FULL MOON

She was wearing the coral taffeta trousers
Someone had brought her from Ispahan,
And the little gold coat with pomegranate blossoms,
And the coral-hafted feather fan;
But she ran down a Kentish lane in the moonlight,
And skipped in the pool of the moon as she ran.

She cared not a rap for all the big planets,
For Betelgeuse or Aldebaran,
And all the big planets cared nothing for her,
That small impertinent charlatan;
But she climbed on a Kentish stile in the moonlight,
And laughed at the sky through the sticks of her fan.

A SAXON SONG

Tools with the comely names,
Mattock and scythe and spade,
Couth and bitter as flames,
Clean, and bowed in the blade,—
A man and his tools make a man and his trade.

Breadth of the English shires,
Hummock and kame and mead,
Tang of the reeking byres,[1]
Land of the English breed,—
A man and his land make a man and his creed.

Leisurely flocks and herds,
Cool-eyed cattle that come

[1] Byres = buildings, literally cow-sheds.

Mildly to wonted words,
Swine that in orchards roam,—
A man and his beasts make a man and his home.

Children sturdy and flaxen
Shouting in brotherly strife,
Like the land they are Saxon,
Sons of a man and his wife,—
For a man and his loves make a man and his life.

### WINTER SONG

*(from "The Land")*

Many have sung the summer's songs,
Many have sung the corn,
Many have sung white blossom too
That stars the naked thorn—
That stars the black and naked thorn
Against the chalky blue.

But I, crouched up beside the hearth,
Will sing the red and gray;
Red going-down of sun behind
Clubbed woods of winter's day;
Of winter's short and hodden [1] day
That seals the sober hind:

Seals him sagacious through the year
Since winter comes again:
Since harvest's but another toil
And sorrow through the grain
Mounts up, through swathes of ripest grain
The sorrow of the soil.

No lightness is there at their heart,
No joy in country folk;
Only a patience slow and grave
Beneath their labor's yoke,—
Beneath the earth's compelling yoke
That only serves its slave,

Since countryman forever holds
The winter's memory,

[1] Hodden = rustic-coarse, gray.

When he, before the planets' fires
Have faded from the sky,
From black, resplendent winter sky
Must go about his byres;

And whether to the reaper's whirr
That scythes the falling crops,
He travels round the widening wake
Between the corn and copse,
The stubble wake 'twixt corn and copse
Where gleaners ply the rake,

Or whether in his granary loft
He pours the winnowed sacks,
Or whether in his yard he routs
The vermin from the stacks,
The vermin from the staddled [2] stacks
With staves and stones and shouts,

Still, still through all the molten eves
Whether he reaps or hones,
Or counts the guerdon of his sweat,
Still to his inward bones,
His ancient, sage, sardonic bones,
The winter haunts him yet.

Winter and toil reward him still
While he his course shall go
According to his proven worth,
Until his faith shall know
The ultimate justice and the slow
Compassion of the earth.

[2] Staddled = upheld, supported.

# Osbert Sitwell

OSBERT SITWELL (brother of Sacheverell and Edith Sitwell) was born in London, December 6, 1892, was educated at Eton, and became an officer in the Grenadier Guards, with whom he served in France for various periods from 1914 to 1917. After contesting the 1918 election at Scarborough in the Liberal interests, he devoted himself to literature.

His first contributions appeared in *Wheels* (an annual anthology of a few of the younger radical writers, edited by his sister) and disclosed an ironic touch. That impression was strengthened by *Argonaut and Juggernaut* (1920), where Sitwell's cleverness and satire are intensified if not fused. His most remarkable though least satisfactory poems are his protests against smugness and hypocrisy. Osbert Sitwell's more conventional poetry has a freshness of movement and definiteness of outline. *Out of the Flame* (1923) reënforces this judgment. It is in two parts; a contrast, not a combination. There is the world of ideal beauty which the poet loves and the world of idle luxury which rouses his satirical hate. In spite of a certain wildness of aim, Sitwell rarely misses his mark.

For several years after 1923 this author distinguished himself in prose, registering a deep impression with the short stories in *Triple Fugue* (1924) and the novel *Before the Bombardment* (1926). *The Man Who Lost Himself* (1929) is the largest of his prose works; here he seems to shed all but the last drop of his spleen and has accomplished a fancifully philosophic tale in which poetry is instinct.

His subsequent volume of poetry presented him in a new and simpler vein. Sharing the nostalgia of his sister, Edith, he also returns to his childhood for much of the material in *England Reclaimed: A Book of Eclogues* (1927). Satire is still here, but it is satire softened with sympathy; if he laughs at such rustic figures as Mr. Goodbeare and Moping Fred, he smiles with Mr. and Mrs. Nutch, the Southerns, the gamekeepers, gardeners and the homely gentles of the countryside. The author aims at "recording a broad panorama, essentially English, but which seems now, by force of circumstance, to be slipping away into the past." He has evoked an atmosphere in which the landscape is alive, in which recollection is newly shaped by the imagination.

*Penny Foolish* (1935) assembles Sitwell's enthusiasms and irritations—English public school, games, and war being among the latter and the telephone among the former! Altogether there are seventy articles, ranging from satirical squibs to provocative essays.

### THE BLIND PEDDLER

I stand alone through each long day
Upon these pavers; cannot see
The wares spread out upon this tray
—For God has taken sight from me!

I've cursed the night
born. My peering eyes

Have sought for but one ray of light
To pierce the darkness. When the skies

Rain down their first sweet April showers
On budding branches; when the morn
Is sweet with breath of spring and flowers,
I've cursed the night when I was born.

But now I thank God, and am glad
For what I cannot see this day

—The young men cripples, old, and sad,
With faces burnt and torn away;

Or those who, growing rich and old,
Have battened on the slaughter,
Whose faces, gorged with blood and gold,
Are creased in purple laughter!

### FOUNTAINS

Proud fountains, wave your plumes,
Spread out your phoenix-wing,
Let the tired trees rejoice
Beneath your blossoming
(Tired trees, you whisper low).

High up, high up, above
These green and drooping sails,
A fluttering young wind
Hovers and dives, but fails
To steal a foaming feather.

Sail, like a crystal ship,
Above your sea of glass;
Then, with your quickening touch,
Transmute the things that pass
(Come down, cool wind, come down).

All humble things proclaim,
Within your magic net,
Their kinship to the Gods.
More strange and lovely yet
All lovely things become.

Dead, sculptured stone assumes
The life, from which it came;
The kingfisher is now
A moving tongue of flame,
A blue, live tongue of flame—

While birds, less proud of wing,
Crouch, in wind-ruffled shade,
Hide shyly, then pour out
Their jealous serenade;
. . . Close now your golden wings!

### ELEGY FOR MR. GOODBEARE

Do you remember Mr. Goodbeare, the carpenter,
Godfearing and bearded Mr. Goodbeare,
Who worked all day
At his carpenter's tray,
Do you remember Mr. Goodbeare?
Mr. Goodbeare, that Golconda of gleaming fable,
Lived, thin-ground between orchard and stable,
Pressed thus close against Alfred, his rival—
Mr. Goodbeare, who had never been away.

Do you remember Mr. Goodbeare,
Mr. Goodbeare, who never touched a cup?
Do you remember Mr. Goodbeare,
Who remembered a lot?
   Mr. Goodbeare could remember
     When things were properly kept up:
   Mr. Goodbeare could remember
     The christening and the coming-of-age:
   Mr. Goodbeare could remember
     The entire and roasted ox:
   Mr. Goodbeare could remember
     When the horses filled the stable,
And the port-wine-colored gentry rode after the tawny fox:
   Mr. Goodbeare could remember
     The old lady in her eagle rage,
      Which knew no bounds:

Mr. Goodbeare could remember
   When the escaped and hungering tiger
Flickered lithe and fierce through Foxton Wood,
When old Sir Nigel took his red-tongued, clamoring hounds,
And hunted it then and there,
   As a Gentleman Should.

Do you remember Mr. Goodbeare,
Mr. Goodbeare who never forgot?
Do you remember Mr. Goodbeare,
That wrinkled and golden apricot,
Dear, bearded, godfearing Mr. Goodbeare
Who remembered remembering such a lot?

Oh, do you remember, do you remember,
As I remember and deplore,
That day in drear and far-away December
When dear, godfearing, bearded Mr. Goodbeare
Could remember
No more?

# Robert Nichols

ROBERT (MALISE BOWYER) NICHOLS was born on the Isle of Wight in 1893. His first volume, *Invocations* (1915), was published while he was at the front, Nichols having joined the army as an undergraduate at Trinity College, Oxford. After serving one year as second lieutenant in the Royal Field Artillery, he was incapacitated by shell shock, and visited America in 1918-19 as a lecturer. His *Ardors and Endurances* (1917) is a representative early work of this poet, although *The Budded Branch* (1918) and *Aurelia* (1920) show an advance in power.

Since 1920, Nichols has devoted himself to drama and philosophic fiction, *Fantastica: The Smile of the Sphinx* (1921) and *Guilty Souls* (1922). The poet, theorist, and dramatist were fused in *Wings Over Europe* (1928), a play written in collaboration with Maurice Browne. Here the sheer force of Nichols' conviction has vitalized a drama in which there is no specious romantic element, in which no woman appears or is mentioned, in which the entire action transpires around a table in a room on Downing Street. The tension in which a struggle of ideas rises to a creative excitement could have been accomplished only by a poet.

*Fisbo* (1934) shows Nichols' gift for sustained poetic narrative. The medium is unhappily chosen—a Byronic satire cast in Pope-like couplets—but the writing is lively and the thrusts are deadly, even though one feels that Nichols is using an extra heavy wheel to break an already broken butterfly.

### FULFILLMENT

Was there love once? I have forgotten her.
  Was there grief once? Grief still is mine.
Other loves I have; men rough, but men who stir
  More joy, more grief than love of thee and thine.

Faces cheerful, full of whimsical mirth,
  Lined by the wind, burned by the sun;
Bodies enraptured by the abounding earth,
  As whose children, brothers we are and one.

And any moment may descend hot death
  To shatter limbs! pulp, tear, and blast
Belovèd soldiers who love rude life and breath
  Not less for dying faithful to the last.

O the fading eyes, the grimèd face turned bony,
  Open, black, gushing mouth, fallen head,
Failing pressure of a held hand shrunk and stony,
  O sudden spasm, release of the dead!

Was there love once? I have forgotten her.
  Was there grief once? Grief still is mine.
O loved, living, dying, heroic soldier,
  All, all my joy, my grief, my love are thine!

### THE PILGRIM

Put by the sun, my joyful soul,
We are for darkness that is whole;

Put by the wine, now for long years
We must be thirsty with salt tears;

Put by the rose, bind thou instead
The fiercest thorns about thy head;

Put by the courteous tire, we need
But the poor pilgrim's blackest weed;

Put by—albeit with tears—thy lute,
Sing but to God or else be mute.

Take leave of friends save such as dare
Thy love with loneliness to share.

It is full tide. Put by regret.
Turn, turn away. Forget. Forget.

Put by the sun, my lightless soul,
We are for darkness that is whole.

, TO ——

Asleep within the deadest hour of night
And turning with the earth, I was aware
How suddenly the eastern curve was bright,
As when the sun arises from his lair.
But not the sun arose: it was thy hair
Shaken up heaven in tossing leagues of light.

Since then I know that neither night nor day
May I escape thee, O my heavenly hell!
Awake, in dreams, thou springest to waylay;
And should I dare to die, I know full well
Whose voice would mock me in the mourning bell,
Whose face would greet me in hell's fiery way.

NEARER

Nearer and ever nearer . . .
My body, tired but tense,
Hovers 'twixt vague pleasure
And tremulous confidence.

Arms to have and to use them
And a soul to be made
Worthy, if not worthy;
If afraid, unafraid.

To endure for a little,
To endure and have done:
Men I love about me,
Over me the sun!

And should at last suddenly
Fly the speeding death,
The four great quarters of heaven
Receive this little breath.

# *Wilfred Owen*

WILFRED OWEN's biography is pitifully brief. He was born at Oswestry on the
          of March, 1893, was educated at the Birkenhead Institute, matriculated
               in 1910, obtained a private tutorship in 1913 near Bordeaux
          two years. In 1915, in spite of delicate health, he joined
          ved in France from 1916 to June, 1917, when he was in-
          en months later, he returned to the Western Front, was
          Cross for gallantry in October, and was killed while trying

to get his men across the Sambre Canal—with tragic irony—a week before the armistice, on November 4, 1918.

Owen's name was unknown to the world until his friend Siegfried Sassoon unearthed the contents of his posthumous volume, *Poems* (1920). It was evident at once that here was one of the most important contributions to the literature of the War, expressed by a poet whose courage was surpassed only by his integrity of mind and nobility of soul. The restrained passion as well as the pitiful outcries in Owen's poetry have a spiritual kinship with Sassoon's stark verses. They reflect that second stage of the War, when the glib patter wears thin and the easy patriotics have a sardonic sound in the dug-outs and trenches. "He never," writes Sassoon, "wrote his poems (as so many war poets did) to make the effect of a personal gesture. He pitied others; he did not pity himself."

In a scrap which serves as an unfinished preface, Owen wrote, "This book is not about heroes. English poetry is not yet fit to speak of them. Nor is it about deeds or lands, nor anything about glory, honor or dominion. . . .

except War.
Above all, this book is not concerned with Poetry,
The subject of it is War, and the pity of War.
The Poetry is in the pity."

"Strange Meeting," "Miners," and the poignant "Futility" illustrate, beneath their emotional content, Owen's great fondness for assonance. He was continually experimenting with devices to enrich or take the place of rhyme, testing alliterative consonants as substitutes for the prepared and often monotonous matching of vowels. Almost half of his volume is a record of such unique and surprisingly successful experiments. But it is the nobility, the profound sympathy, compassionate without ever becoming maudlin, that gives Owen's verse a place among the authentic poetry of his day. "Dulce et Decorum Est" is obviously a reaction against the "glory" of war; but it is bigger than its subject, something far beyond a protest, surpassing its program.

It is difficult to choose among Owen's few but compelling poems. "Apologia pro Poemate Meo," "Greater Love," "Anthem for Doomed Youth" and the rhymed suspensions already mentioned will live beyond the tragic events during which they were created. They influenced the post-war poets (*vide* C. Day Lewis' *A Hope for Poetry*) in theme as well as technique; time has already found a place for them.

A new and enlarged edition entitled *The Poems of Wilfred Owen* was published in 1931 with an introduction by Edmund Blunden. This complete collection included many poems hitherto unprinted, notably "The Unreturning," "Arms and the Boy"—both full of Owen's peculiar broken music—and "From My Diary," in which Owen added initial consonantal dissonances (Blunden calls them "pararhymes") to the usual end-rhymes. They emphasize that Owen's death at twentyfive was one of modern poetry's greatest losses.

FUTILITY

Move him into the sun—
Gently its touch awoke him once,

At home, whispering of fields unsown.
Always it woke him, even in France.
Until this morning and this snow.
If anything might rouse him now
The kind old sun will know.

Think how it wakes the seeds—
Woke, once, the clay of a cold star.
Are limbs so dear-achieved, are sides
Full-nerved,—still warm,—too hard to stir?
Was it for this the clay grew tall?
—Oh, what made fatuous sunbeams toil
To break earth's sleep at all?

### APOLOGIA PRO POEMATE MEO

I, too, saw God through mud—
    The mud that cracked on cheeks when wretches smiled.
    War brought more glory to their eyes than blood,
    And gave their laughs more glee than shakes a child.

Merry it was to laugh there—
    Where death becomes absurd and life absurder.
    For power was on us as we slashed bones bare
    Not to feel sickness or remorse of murder.

I, too, have dropped off fear—
    Behind the barrage, dead as my platoon,
    And sailed my spirit surging, light and clear,
    Past the entanglement where hopes lay strewn;

And witnessed exultation—
    Faces that used to curse me, scowl for scowl,
    Shine and lift up with passion of oblation,
    Seraphic for an hour, though they were foul.

I have made fellowships—
    Untold of happy lovers in old song.
    For love is not the binding of fair lips
    With the soft silk of eyes that look and long,

By Joy, whose ribbon slips,—
    But wound with war's hard wire whose stakes are strong;
    Bound with the bandage of the arm that drips;
    ⸱⸱ the welding of the rifle-thong.

    ⸱⸱ved much beauty
    ⸱⸱oarse oaths that kept our courage straight;
    ⸱⸱music in the silentness of duty;
    ⸱⸱peace where shell-storms spouted reddest spate.

Nevertheless, except you share
 With them in hell the sorrowful dark of hell,
 Whose world is but the trembling of a flare,
 And heaven but as the highway for a shell,

You shall not hear their mirth:
 You shall not come to think them well content
 By any jest of mine. These men are worth
 Your tears: You are not worth their merriment.


### ANTHEM FOR DOOMED YOUTH

What passing-bells for these who die as cattle?
Only the monstrous anger of the guns.
Only the stuttering rifles' rapid rattle
Can patter out their hasty orisons.
No mockeries for them; no prayers nor bells,
Nor any voice of mourning save the choirs,—
The shrill, demented choirs of wailing shells;
And bugles calling for them from sad shires.

What candles may be held to speed them all?
Not in the hands of boys, but in their eyes
Shall shine the holy glimmers of good-bys.
The pallor of girls' brows shall be their pall;
Their flowers the tenderness of patient minds,
And each slow dusk a drawing-down of blinds.


### DULCE ET DECORUM EST

Bent double, like old beggars under sacks,
Knock-kneed, coughing like hags, we cursed through sludge,
Till on the haunting flares we turned our backs,
And towards our distant rest began to trudge.
Men marched asleep. Many had lost their boots,
But limped on, blood-shod. All went lame, all blind;
Drunk with fatigue; deaf even to the hoots
Of gas-shells dropping softly behind.

Gas! Gas! Quick, boys!—An ecstasy of fumbling,
Fitting the clumsy helmets just in time,
But someone still was yelling out and stumbling
And flound'ring like a man in fire or lime.
Dim through the misty panes and thick green light,
As under a green sea, I saw him drowning.

In all my dreams before my helpless sight
He plunges at me, guttering, choking, drowning.

If in some smothering dreams, you too could pace
Behind the wagon that we flung him in,

And watch the white eyes wilting in his face,
His hanging face, like a devil's sick of sin,
If you could hear, at every jolt, the blood
Come gargling from the froth-corrupted lungs
Bitten as the cud
Of vile, incurable sores on innocent tongues,—
My friend, you would not tell with such high zest
To children ardent for some desperate glory,
The old lie: *Dulce et decorum est
Pro patria mori.*[1]

### FROM MY DIARY, JULY 1914

Leaves
 Murmuring by myriads in the shimmering trees.
Lives
 Wakening with wonder in the Pyrenees.
Birds
 Cheerily chirping in the early day.
Bards
 Singing of summer scything thro' the hay.
Bees
 Shaking the heavy dews from bloom and frond.
Boys
 Bursting the surface of the ebony pond.
Flashes
 Of swimmers carving thro' the sparkling cold.
Fleshes
 Gleaming with wetness to the morning gold.
A mead
 Bordered about with warbling water brooks.
A maid
 Laughing the love-laugh with me; proud of looks.
The heat
 Throbbing between the upland and the peak.
Her heart
 Quivering with passion to my pressed cheek.
Braiding
 Of floating flames across the mountain brow.
Brooding
 Of stillness; and a sighing of the bough.
Stirs
 Of leaflets in the gloom; soft petal-showers;
Stars
 Expanding with the starr'd nocturnal flowers.

### THE UNRETURNING

Suddenly night crushed out the day and hurled
Her remnants over cloud-peaks, thunder-walled.

---

[1] "It is sweet and dignified to die for one's country."

Then fell a stillness such as harks appalled
When far-gone dead return upon the world.

There watched I for the Dead; but no ghost woke.
Each one whom Life exiled I named and called.
But they were all too far, or dumbed, or thralled;
And never one fared back to me or spoke.

Then peered the indefinite unshapen dawn
With vacant gloaming, sad as half-lit minds,
The weak-limned hour when sick men's sighs are drained.
And while I wondered on their being withdrawn,
Gagged by the smothering wing which none unbinds,
I dreaded even a heaven with doors so chained.

## GREATER LOVE

Red lips are not so red
    As the stained stones kissed by the English dead.
Kindness of wooed and wooer
Seems shame to their love pure.
O Love, your eyes lose lure
    When I behold eyes blinded in my stead!

Your slender attitude
    Trembles not exquisite like limbs knife-skewed,
Rolling and rolling there
Where God seems not to care;
Till the fierce love they bear
    Cramps them in death's extreme decrepitude.

Your voice sings not so soft,—
    Though even as wind murmuring through raftered loft,—
Your dear voice is not clear,
Gentle, and evening clear,
As theirs whom none now hear
    Now earth has stopped their piteous mouths that coughed.

Heart, you were never hot,
    Nor large, nor full like hearts made great with shot;
And though your hand be pale,
Paler are all which trail
Your cross through flame and hail:
    Weep, you may weep, for you may touch them not.

## MINERS

    There was a whispering in my hearth,
      A sigh of the coal,
    Grown wistful of a former earth
      It might recall.

I listened for a tale of leaves
  And smothered ferns,
Proud forests, and the low sly lives
  Before the fawns.

My fire might show steam-phantoms simmer
  From Time's old caldron,
Before the birds made nests in summer,
  Or men had children.

But the coals were murmuring of their mine.
  And moans down there,
Of boys that slept wry sleep, and men
  Writhing for air.

I saw white bones in the cinder-shard,
  Bones without number.
For many hearts with coal are charred,
  And few remember.

I thought of all that worked dark pits
  Of war, and died
Digging the rock where Death reputes
  Peace lies indeed:

Comforted years will sit soft-chaired,
  In rooms of amber,
The years will stretch their hands, well cheered
  By our life's ember;

The centuries will burn rich loads
  With which we groaned,
Whose warmth shall lull their dreamy lids,
  While songs are crooned;
But they will not dream of us poor lads
  Lost in the ground.


### ARMS AND THE BOY

Let the boy try along this bayonet-blade
How cold steel is, and keen with hunger of blood;
Blue with all malice, like a madman's flash;
And thinly drawn with famishing for flesh.

Lend him to stroke these blind, blunt bullet-heads
Which long to nuzzle in the heart of lads,
Or give him cartridges of fine zinc teeth,
Sharp with the sharpness of grief and death.

For his teeth seem for laughing round an apple.
There lurk no claws behind his fingers supple;
And god will grow no talons at his heels,
Nor antlers through the thickness of his curls.

## STRANGE MEETING

It seemed that out of the battle I escaped
Down some profound dull tunnel, long since scooped
Through granites which Titanic wars had groined.
Yet also there encumbered sleepers groaned,
Too fast in thought or death to be bestirred.
Then, as I probed them, one sprang up, and stared
With piteous recognition in fixed eyes,
Lifting distressful hands as if to bless.
And by his smile, I knew that sullen hall.
With a thousand fears that vision's face was grained;
Yet no blood reached there from the upper ground,
And no guns thumped, or down the flues made moan.
"Strange, friend," I said, "here is no cause to mourn."
"None," said the other, "save the undone years,
The hopelessness. Whatever hope is yours,
Was my life also; I went hunting wild
After the wildest beauty in the world,
Which lies not calm in eyes, or braided hair,
But mocks the steady running of the hour,
And if it grieves, grieves richlier than here.
For by my glee might many men have laughed,
And of my weeping something has been left,
Which must die now. I mean the truth untold,
The pity of war, the pity war distilled.
Now men will go content with what we spoiled,
Or, discontent, boil bloody, and be spilled.
They will be swift with swiftness of the tigress,
None will break ranks, though nations trek from progress.
Courage was mine, and I had mystery,
Wisdom was mine, and I had mastery;
To miss the march of this retreating world
Into vain citadels that are not walled.
Then when much blood had clogged their chariot-wheels
I would go up and wash them from sweet wells,
Even with truths that lie too deep for taint.
I would have poured my spirit without stint
.But not through wounds; not on the cess of war.
Foreheads of men have bled where no wounds were.
I am the enemy you killed, my friend.
I knew you in this death; for so you frowned
Yesterday through me as you jabbed and killed.
I parried; but my hands were loath and cold.
Let us sleep now. . . ."

# *Frank Prewett*

FRANK PREWETT was born on a farm near Mount Forest, Ontario, Canada, of a pioneer family, August 24, 1893. He attended University College, Toronto, and joined the University Officers' Training Corps on the outbreak of war, but enlisted in the ranks shortly afterwards. He served, as he puts it, "uneventfully" at the Front. After peace was declared, he entered Oxford as an undergraduate, and subsequently lived as a farmer near Abingdon, Berkshire.

Prewett's first publication was a little volume, *Poems* (1920), which sounded an agreeable though not unusual note. *The Rural Scene* (1924) is far more personal. In his condensed simplicities, Prewett strikes the truly pastoral note. Bound to the soil by inheritance as well as by a natural affection, the poet never strains to achieve that *naïveté* which one so often finds in the work of many of the Georgians. His is the gift of spontaneous song; his is an instinctive expression of "the rural scene" with freshness and rarely a trace of affectation.

### OUT OF THE NIGHT

Out of the night they drop with troubled cries,
   Splitting the keen-tuned freezing air,
Lone travelers through the wind-cut skies
   Instinct-propelled to regions harsh and bare.

They settle with loud shuffling midst the snow;
   The pitiless cold hushes all things to peace;
And I reluctant silent homeward go,
   But leave my soul to chatter with the geese.

Oh, ye mysterious creatures swift and high
   That beat in angle-flights from land to land,
Whence came into your breasts your troubled cry
   And strange desire that gathers you like sand!

With the first streak of dawn they crane their necks,
   Cry out aloud, and rise upon the air,
Taking with them my soul, nor much it recks
   Towards what homeless wastes their flight may bear.

### WHEN CUCKOO FIRST

When cuckoo first the vale o'erflows
   With barks and bubble-blasts of sound,
And daisies white, or tinctured rose,
   Make a pleasanter sky the ground,
Then maids are trim and neatly seen
And youth strides godly under green.

Spring is a season we revive
　With the upthrusting hedgy things,
When yellowhammers courtship drive
　And old cock-pheasants busk their wings,
Then cows dream udder-deep in grass
　And hawk over hovers with eye of glass.

Cheevio-chee trills on the spray,
　He finds his life so good;
Oh, now be natural and gay
　Like the kind God meant we should,
For all things beautiful, sight and sound,
　Love made, and make love to abound.

### VOICES OF WOMEN

Met ye my love?
Ye might in France have met him;
He has a wooing smile,
Who sees cannot forget him!
Met ye my love?
—We shared full many a mile.

Saw ye my love?
In lands far-off he has been,
With his yellow-tinted hair;
In Egypt such ye have seen.
Ye knew my love?
—I was his brother there.

Heard ye my love?
My love ye must have heard,
For his voice when he will
Tinkles like cry of a bird;
Heard ye my love?
—We sang on a Grecian hill.

Behold your love,
And how shall I forget him,
His smile, his hair, his song?
Alas, no maid shall get him
For all her love,
Where he sleeps a million strong.

### SNOW-BUNTINGS

They come fluttering helpless to the ground
Like wreaths of wind-caught snow,
Uttering a plaintive, chirping sound,
And rise and fall, and know not where they go.

So small they are, with feathers ruffled blown,
Adrift between earth desolate and leaden sky;
Nor have they ever known
Any but frozen earth, and scudding clouds on high.

What hand doth guide these hapless creatures small
To sweet seeds that the withered grasses hold?—
The little children of men go hungry all,
And stiffen and cry with numbing cold.

In a sudden gust the flock are whirled away
Uttering a frightened, chirping cry,
And are lost like a wraith of departing day,
Adrift between earth desolate and leaden sky.

# Richard Church

RICHARD CHURCH was born in London in 1893 and began to write at the age of
eighteen, having by that time also obtained a permanent post in the Civil
Service. He wrote for the majority of the weeklies, particularly *The Spectator*.

His volume, *Philip* (1921), reveals the work of an artist extremely sensitive to
the implications behind the physical fact. Tentative though much of it may be, it
expresses a poet who, like a lesser Robert Frost, combines the power of sight with
insight.

Since 1922 Church has developed a more somber note. *Mood Without Measure*
(1927) is, as the title indicates, a transcript of emotion in free or cadenced verse
instead of meter. *Theme with Variations* (1928), though a smaller volume, has
larger implications. Never a popular poet, Church frequently succeeds in sounding,
in a subterranean music, currents deeper than surface agitations.

### THE LANTERN

She swings the lantern. Night around her
Swings out, swings in; the roadside falls.
Under her feet abysmal darkness sinks;
Then from the pit, to meet her feet,
Earth rises, somber stones and steady soil
Loom up, stare at the lantern, then . . .
Sink, sink again as it swings.

On she tramps, towering above the lantern,
All her daylight beauty lifted away,
Underlit, and drenched with the dye,
The smudgy gold of the drowsy beams from the lantern.
Over the light her hip turns smooth and strong,
Rolling the shadows to and fro on its breadth,

To and fro in rhythm as on she swings.—
The gaunt trees over her leap, and mope, and bow.—
And one deep breast, like the old moon lacking light,
Rides above, rimmed with a ghostly line,
Then waxes full as the lantern swings before.
Crowning this wild-lit moving life,
The aureoled hair glows gold, a smoke-veiled fire,
Flaming and changing, but ever her crown as she swings
On, swings on, steady and sure, while the earth and skies
Tumble and leap and prance and dance round the lantern.

The cows are milked; she is going home to her babe.

## FROM AN UPLAND VALLEY

In a high valley of the hills
Where the wind spun Earth
In a gust of mirth,
I saw the conflict of our wills:
You the wild
Unreconciled
Self-diviner, trustless; true
Only to the cruel self in you;
Cruel yet kind,
Harsh, tortured mind,
Worse than wanton, sweeter than faith;
I saw you, heard you, fought you—wraith!

There is no absence since you came
Into this vale we call
Life, where the winds fall
Like eagles on quarry, a piercing blame,
Then lulling to dear
Confidences, near
Whisperings, close, so intimate
There's hardly room for love or hate
To slip between.
For what has been,
Was past, is present, will future be,
One piercing agony, one joy for me.

And you, so swift, so sure, burnt clean
And sparse with your soul-inflicted pain,
What have you left to feel?
Could you see the trees kneel
As they kneel here beneath the storm,
Bowed with invisible alarm
Down to stones, grasses,
Sheep-runs, hare-passes,
Shuddering under the siffling wrath
That hisses through each gap and path;

Could you be near me
Would your mind sear me,
With such a wild exemplar by,
As this embrace of earth and sky?

I torture you, I who am still
Yours, shall be till death takes his fill
Of the brimmed lake
Whereat we slake
Our thirst, self poured on self, and run
Into such stillness under the sun
That light is pain,
And loss is gain
Refracted from that source of pleasure.
Oh, brood on this, dear heart, at leisure;
Absent, here,
Gone, but near,
Your passion is flame you cannot measure.

## PORTENT

There is no sound:
Only the quiet brittle of the fire
And flake-fall of ash:
Only the pursed drip,
Long drop, drip of water:
Only the sigh,
The high sigh of winter trees
As the east sifts through their branches:
Only the tramp, tramp,
And running to and fro of thoughts
Far away down the avenues of my mind:
Only that ominous gathering,
Distant murmur and cry,
Faint clash of steel:
Only that hoarse preparation
In the sleeping city of my brain.

## THE PURIFICATION

They have gone over, the god, the friend, the lover,
They have gone over.
It is growing gray now;
There comes the end of day now.

They were signs then, the stars were a glory for men,
They were signs then.
Those lights flare unseen now,
Things paltry and mean now.

They were true pleasure, the friendly trust, the praise without measure.
They were true pleasure.
Praise is an empty sound now.
Trust treads no firm ground now.

They were music, joy, and truth, the kisses she gave him in youth.
They were music, joy, and truth.
They are less beautiful now;
They are but dutiful now.

Aye, they have come to an end, the god, the lover, the friend;
They have come to an end.
The soul is alone now:
Strong, naked, full-grown now.

## Frank Kendon

FRANK KENDON was born in 1893 at Goudhurst, Kent, educated at St. John's College, Cambridge, and was in Egypt and Palestine during the War. Besides being a poet, he has been a schoolmaster and journalist, "a countryman by birth and youth, Londoner by necessity, poet by chance, business man by fate." Since 1929 he has been assistant editor of *John o' London's Weekly*.

Kendon's first appearance was in his section in *Poems by Four Authors* (1923). A full view of his characteristics is obtained in the succeeding *Poems and Sonnets* (1924) in which, without straining for idiomatic effect, Kendon achieves a personal distinction. He is particularly happy in his combinations of rhyme and assonance, or (as in "I spend my days vainly") in the variation of rhyming vowels and shifting consonantal sounds, sometimes referred to as "analyzed rhyme." The first two lyrics here reprinted are unusually adroit pieces of technique—and both are much more than mere technical exercises.

*Arguments and Emblems* (1925), a book of lyrics, was succeeded by *A Life and Death of Judas Iscariot* (1926). Critics disputed whether this or *Tristram* (1934) was Kendon's most important work in verse. The author agreed with those who considered the nourishment in *Tristram* of a finer product and better distilled, though "persons looking for a meal might find *Judas* more filling." *Tristram* is a narrative in ballad measure interchaptered with songs, a *tour de force* and a triumph over the time-worn subject matter. *The Cherry Minder* (1935) contains the best of his later lyrics.

Besides his verse Kendon has written *The Adventure of Poetry* (1932) and *The Small Years* (1930), an autobiography up to the age of ten, with an introduction by Walter De la Mare, the only book of Kendon's that had a large public success.

### I SPEND MY DAYS VAINLY

I spend my days vainly,
  Not in delight;
Though the world is elate
  And tastes her joys finely.

Here wrapped in slow musing
  Lies my dark mind,
To no music attuned
  Save its own, and despising

The lark for remoteness,
  The thrush for bold lying,
The soft wind for blowing,
  And the round sun for brightness.

O tarry for me, sweet;
  I shall stir, I shall wake!
And the melody you seek
  Shall be lovely, though late.

### THE KERNEL

Now that the flush of summer is gone,
And in the lane no flower is seen,
  No hedge in leaf,
No tree in gold or green;

Now that the golden fruit is stored,
And in the wood no song is heard,
  No merry stir
Of song from any bird;

Now that the uncompanioned wind
Blows cold across the naked land
  And, hung in black,
Bare trees like mourners stand;

Winter reveals through falling rain,
A strength which summer had left unseen:
  Beauty and peace
Which, but for tears, had been in vain,
Which, but for loss, had never been.

### THE IMMIGRANT

When Ruth was old
She'd take her children's children on her knee,
They never wearied to be told
Tales of her girlhood in a far country.

For though her eyes grew dim
Men said of her: "Her heart is always young,"
And Boaz, while she spoke of him,
Loved the faint accent of a foreign tongue.

### SO DEEP IS DEATH

So deep is death in silence lapped,
  So deep in sleep their spirits are
Who, out of tempest earth escaped,
  Lie down untroubled. Like a star
On the rich beds of evening skies
  Before the night has peopled heaven,
So deeply shut from love she lies,
  And her quick going is forgiven.

Come little Spring, come, give us heart;
  Come noisy Summer, sing and drowse;
If sense must now play double part,
  Come life again! She will not rouse;
She will not hear, nor laugh to hear,
  Whatever challenge wildness make;
Music is silence in her ear.
  Only her lovers lie awake.

# *Herbert Read*

HERBERT READ was born, December 4, 1893, at Muscoates Grange, Kirbymoorside, Yorkshire. He was educated at Crossley's School, Halifax, and at the University of Leeds. Commissioned in January 1915 to the Yorkshire Regiment, he fought in France and Belgium from 1915 to 1918, having been made a captain in 1917. He left the army in 1919, married, and became Assistant at the Victoria and Albert Museum.

Read's early work was experimental and unsatisfactory; his first volume, *Songs of Chaos* (1915), scarcely justified the title. *Naked Warriors* (1919), a much more vitalized work, suggested, somewhat remotely, what Siegfried Sassoon and Wilfred Owen had been saying directly. But Read's was no mere echo; his utterance, gnarled and contorted, formed vivid if unlovely lines. *Mutations of the Phoenix* (1923) is overweighted by a concern with style and by the influence of T. S. Eliot, although Read has his own distinct philosophy, intense and individualistic.

*Collected Poems 1913-1925* (1926) shows a poet in transition. Under the cloudy angers and distortions he seeks

> . . . some state of high serenity
> Beyond the range
> Of febrile senses.

But he attains neither serenity nor integration. Almost ten years later his *Poems 1914-1934* (1935) proves that Read is still striving for a solid poetic character, and striving vainly. His volume covers twenty years of original writing, yet the book seems little more than a mirror of recent poetic fashions, a cross between a retrospective anthology and a volume of humorless parodies. The opening "Eclogues" are leftovers from the Imagist ice-box; the "War Poems" are mannered, as might be expected of a poet who can, in 1935, append this note, "It is not my business as a poet to condemn war"—this in the face of the records left by such indubitable poets as Wilfred Owen, Edmund Blunden, Siegfried Sassoon, Robert Nichols, Isaac Rosenberg, and Robert Graves. "Satirical Verses," "Lyrical Poems" and "Longer Poems" are equally undistinguished. There are occasional interesting intellectual exercises, but the lyrical note is thin and, contrasted with such a savage wit as Auden, whose military images are imitated in "The Nuncio," the satire is feeble.

Read established himself as a critic with his *Reason and Romanticism* (1926), *English Prose Style* (1928), and *Phases of English Poetry* (1929). Besides editing T. E. Hulme's *Speculations* (see page 387) and writing a book on ceramics, Read is the author of a book of war sketches, *In Retreat,* published in 1925.

DEVICE

O that I might believe that time
Is but a measure thrown on things
That hold existence in a sphere
Intense alone, and always felt
In full reality! For then

I could evade despondency
By magnifying to my frame
The ecstatic beat that night and day
Pulses within the milk-white walls
Of mental sloth, eager to break
Into the radiant release
Of vision divine and precise.

—Time that is shrouded thought
Involving earth and life in doubt.

FROM "THE ANALYSIS OF LOVE"

Nature has perpetual tears
  In drooping boughs,
And everywhere inanimate death
  Is immemorial.

But I have naught that will express
  The grief I feel
When men and moods combine to show
  The end of this—

This mental ecstasy all spent
  In disuniting death;
And the years that spread
  Oblivion on our zest.

THE REFUGEES

Mute figures with bowed heads
They travel along the road:
Old women, incredibly old,
And a hand-cart of chattels.

They do not weep:
Eyes are too raw for tears.

Past them have hastened
Processions of retreating gun-teams,
Baggage-wagons and swift horsemen.
Now they struggle along
With the rearguard of a broken army.

We will hold the enemy towards nightfall
And they will move
Mutely into the dark behind us,
Only the creaking cart
Disturbing their sorrowful serenity.

TOURISTS IN A SACRED PLACE

A pallid rout stepping like phantoms
beneath the arching boughs,
have come with angel hands and wretched voices
to the valley and this choir of perished stones.

Valid was my anguish—as though a turbulent dove
had scattered the leafy silence.
Now in airless vistas, dim and blind my limbs will loiter
while the senses stray to vast defeats.

  A rocking bell
  peals in a gray tower.
  The sound has broken down the strong defenses
  of age and innocence.

  Cecily come with your virginal tremors,
  Cecily still the bell.
  Your tresses are wet from the rushing river,
  a green weed clings like a vein on your breast.

  Cecily, listen, the clangor is over
  now only the burden of bees in the clover.
  God and his angels have given you grace,
  and stamped your mission on your naiad face.

## Sylvia Townsend Warner

SYLVIA TOWNSEND WARNER was born December 1893 at Harrow on the Hill, Middlesex, where her father was a schoolmaster. From 1916 to 1926 she worked on the preparation of the critical edition of *Tudor Church Music,* a vast and learned compilation in ten volumes, of which she was one of four editors. Research work in the music of the fifteenth and sixteenth centuries was not only her occupation but her preoccupation, and it was not until 1922 that she started writing as a by-product.

Although she first attracted wide attention with the fanciful *Lolly Willowes: or The Loving Huntsman,* which was the first "book-of-the-month" in America in 1926, her literary début was made with a volume of verse, *The Espalier* (1925). There followed two more books of prose, quaintly misnamed novels by the publishers: *Mr. Fortune's Maggot* (1927) and *The True Heart* (1929). Three years after her first volume, her second book of poems appeared, *Time Importuned* (1928).

Although her work seems to fall into two categories, it actually forms a unified expression. The poems, objective, sharply characterized, compact with drama, are condensed stories; the novels are poetry from beginning to end. *Lolly Willowes* is a fantasy which alternates between the unashamedly tender and the lightly terrible. *Mr. Fortune's Maggot* adds compassionate understanding to extravaganza; fantasy turns here to philosophy whose motto implies surrender instead of possession in love. The title-story of *The Salutation* (1932) is a sequel to *Mr. Fortune's Maggot,* exquisite in style, tragic in effect. *The True Heart* is the simplest and the deepest of her larger works. Seemingly an idyll of Victorian England, it is really one of the oldest love stories, the classic tale of Psyche and Eros retold. Although no critic seems to have noted the fact, Miss Warner has supplied sufficient hints; "Sukey" is obviously an Anglicized Psyche; the mad Love, Eros, is the witless "Eric"; Venus is less than half-disguised as "Mrs. Seaborn."

Thus all of Miss Warner's work is a paradoxical union of subtlety and simplicity, with no sense of strain between these opposites. Each quality is equally characteristic of this author; if the mode tends toward increasing simplicity, it is as though the subtle brain were being counseled if not always controlled by the simple —and the true—heart.

The element which holds these contraries in so nice a balance is the rightness, the so-to-speak connoisseurship of Miss Warner's taste. She can be utterly exquisite when elegance dictates the mood; her coarseness is no less in place when theme and measure demand rudeness. Thus *Time Importuned* has the same sparse imagery and no little of the earth smell of which *The Espalier* is redolent, but the rustic note is not so broad; the rough country humor which underlines her bucolic comedies turns to rustic elegies without effort or affectation. "Nelly Trim," a poem which touches the ballad with nothing short of magnificence, finds its complement in "The Rival"; the neat incisiveness of "The Alarum" is matched by the bittersweetness of "Song."

Craftsmen will be quick to detect Miss Warner's innovations. She is particularly resourceful in her use of the unrhymed line; she is as adroit in her mingling of assonantal and dissonantal rhyme as Wilfred Owen and Humbert Wolfe. But it is unwise to place too much emphasis on technique. Each reader will discover a different quality on which to lay stress: the poet's marked accent; or her half-modern, half-archaic blend of naïveté and erudition; or the low-pitched but tart tone of voice, like a feminine Thomas Hardy. Every year seems to distill Miss Warner's gift nearer to its basic essence. "Modo and Alciphron," which has not yet appeared in book form, illustrates this quality in which *grotesquerie* and metaphysics so nimbly combine. "Killing No Murder" and "Building in Stone," two other uncollected poems, abandon by-play and raillery in their grave music and graver implications.

*Opus 7* (1931) is, in spite of its unimaginative title, a highly imaginative tale in precise couplets of one Rebecca Random who, with her "green thumb," has a way with flowers, but who has no love for them except as a means of supplying herself with gin. It is both a delicate and a diabolic long poem, realistic and revenant, musing and epigrammatic. It is as though the ghost of Pope had seized Miss Warner's pen and, allowing her to control her own fancy, had added a series of commentaries to prove that the proper student of mankind was woman. *Whether a Dove or Seagull* (1933) contains more than a hundred poems, half of which are by Miss Warner and half by her friend Valentine Ackland. The authors believed that by issuing their separate work under one cover the element of contrast would add to the pleasure of the reader; by withholding their signatures from the poems they attained the freshness as well as the provocation of anonymity. The book contains some of Miss Warner's finest poems.

Greatly gifted, she barely misses greatness. Ironic, critical, compassionate, her mind rules her emotions a fraction too well. She cannot quite give herself to a self-forgetting, world-forgetting ecstasy. Miss Warner is a philosopher, but never a labored one. She is one who walks, light-footed, a long road, singing her long thoughts to a light—though usually legato—measure.

### FOUR EPITAPHS

John Bird, a laborer, lies here,
Who served the earth for sixty year
With spade and mattock, drill and plow;
But never found it kind till now.

✦

I, an unwedded wandering dame,
For quiet into the country came:
Here, hailed it; but did not foretell
I'd stay so long and rest so well.

✦

I, Richard Kent, beneath these stones,
Sheltered my old and trembling bones;
But my best manhood, quick and brave,
Lies buried in another grave.

✦

Her grieving parents cradled here
Ann Monk, a gracious child and dear.
Lord, let this epitaph suffice:
Early to Bed and Early to Rise.

### COUNTRY THOUGHT

Idbury bells are ringing
And Westcote has just begun,
And down in the valley
Ring the bells of Bledington.

To hear all the church-bells
Ring-ringing together,
Chiming so pleasantly
As if nothing were the matter.

The notion might come
To some religious thinker,

That The Lord God Almighty
Is a traveling tinker,

Who travels through England
From north to south,
And sits him at the roadside
With a pipe in his mouth,

A-tinkling and a-tinkering
To mend up the souls
That week-day wickedness
Has worn into holes.

And yet there is not
One tinker, but Three—
One at Westcote, One at Bledington
And One at Idbury.

### NELLY TRIM

"Like men riding,
The mist from the sea
Drives down the valley
And baffles me."
"Enter, traveler,
Whoever you be."

By lamplight confronted
He staggered and peered;
Like a wet bramble
Was his beard.
"Sit down, stranger,
You look a-feared."

Shudders rent him
To the bone,
The wet ran off him
And speckled the stone.
"Dost bide here alone, maid?"
"Yes, alone."

As he sat down
In the chimney-nook
Over his shoulder
He cast a look,
As if the night
Were pursuing; she took

A handful of brash
To mend the fire,

He eyed her close
As the flame shot higher;
He spoke—and the cattle
Moved in the byre.

"Though you should heap
Your fire with wood,
'Twouldn't warm me
Nor do no good,
Unless you first warm me
As a maiden should."

With looks unwavering,
With breath unstirred,
She took off her clothes
Without a word,
And stood up naked
And white as a curd.

He breathed her to him
With famished sighs,
Against her bosom
He sheltered his eyes,
And warmed his hands
Between her thighs.

Strangely assembled
In the quiet room,
Alone alight
Amidst leagues of gloom,
So brave a bride,
So sad a groom;

And strange love-traffic
Between these two;
Nor mean, nor shamefaced—
As though they'd do
Something more solemn
Than they knew:

As though by this greeting
Which chance had willed
'Twixt him so silent
And her so stilled,
Some pledge or compact
Were fulfilled,

Made for all time
In times unknown,
'Twixt man and woman
Standing alone

In mirk night
By a tall stone.

His wayfaring terrors
All cast aside,
Brave now the bridegroom
Quitted the bride;
As he came, departing—
Undenied.

But once from darkness
Turned back his sight
To where in the doorway
She held a light:
"Good-by to you, maiden."
"Stranger, good night."

Long time has this woman
Been bedded alone.
The house where she slept
Lies stone on stone:
She'd not know her ash-tree,
So warped has it grown.

But yet this story
Is told of her
As a memorial;
And some aver
She'd comfort thus any
Poor traveler.

A wanton, you say—
Yet where's the spouse,
However true
To her marriage-vows,
To whom the lot
Of the earth-born allows

More than this?—
To comfort the care
Of a stranger, bound
She knows not where,
And afraid of the dark,
As his fathers were.

### THE ALARUM

With its rat's tooth the clock
Gnaws away delight.
Piece by piece, piece by piece
It will gnaw away tonight,

Till the coiled spring released
Rouses me with a hiss
To a day, to another night
Less happy than this.

And yet my own hands wound it
To keep watch while I slept;
For though they be with sorrow
Appointments must be kept.

### AFTER HE HAD GONE

After he had gone the wind rose,
Buffeting the house and rumbling in the chimney,
And I thought: It will roar against him like a lion
As onward he goes.

Seven miles before him, all told—
Chilled will be the lips I kissed so warm at parting,
Kissed in vain; for he's forth into the wind, and kisses
Won't keep out the cold.

Closer should I have kissed, fondlier prayed:
Pleasant is the room in the wakeful firelight,
And within is the bed, arrayed with peace and safety.
Would he had stayed!

## ELIZABETH

"Elizabeth the Beloved"—
So much says the stone
That is all with weather defaced,
With moss overgrown.

But if to husband or child,
Brother or sire, most dear
Is past deciphering;
This only is clear:

That once she was beloved,
Was Elizabeth,
And is now beloved no longer,
If it be not of Death.

## TRIUMPH OF SENSIBILITY

"Tiger, strolling at my side,
Why have you unbound the zone
Of your individual pride?
Why so meek did you come sneaking
After me as I walked alone?"

"Since the goat and since the deer
Wait the shattering death you wield
In a constancy of fear,
By your stripes, my strange disciple,
Am I also to be healed?"

"Woman, it was your tender heart
Did my bloody heart compel.
Master-mistress of my art,
Past my wit of wrath your pity,
Ruthless and inexorable.

"I hunt flesh by fallible sense;
You a more exquisite prey pursue
With a finer prescience,
And lap up another's unhappiness:
Woman, let me learn of you."

## SAD GREEN

The glass falls lower,
And lowers the wet sky,
And by a fire sit I
Hearing the lawn-mower

Nearing and waning—
Howbeit out of tune

The essential voice of June,
Patient and uncomplaining;

For though by frost and thunder
Summer be overthrown,
The grass plat must be mown
And the daisies kept under.

## SONG

She has left me, my pretty,
Like a fleeting of apple-blows
She has left her loving husband.
And who she has gone to
The Lord only knows.

She has left me, my pretty,
A needle in a shirt,
Her pink flannelette bedgown,
And a pair of pattens
Caked over with dirt.

I care not for the pattens,
Let 'em lie in the mold;
But the pretty pink bedgown
Will comfort my lumbago
When midnights are cold;

And the shirt I will wear it,
And the needle may bide.
Let it prick, let it rankle,
Let my flesh remember
How she lay against my side!

## SONG FROM THE BRIDE
## OF SMITHFIELD

A thousand guileless sheep have bled,
A thousand bullocks knelt in fear,
To daub my Henry's cheek with red
And round the curl above his ear.

And wounded calves hung up to drip
Have in slow sweats distilled for him
To dew that polishes his lip,
The inward balm that oils each limb.

In vain I spread my maiden arts,
In vain for Henry's love I pine.
He is too skilled in bleeding hearts
To turn this way and pity mine.

### THE RIVAL

The farmer's wife looked out of the dairy:
She saw her husband in the yard;
She said: "A woman's life is hard,
The chimney smokes, the churn's contrary."
    She said:
"I of all women am the most ill-starred.

"Five sons I've borne and seven daughters,
And the last of them is on my knee.
Finer children you could not see.
Twelve times I've put my neck in the halter:
    You'd think
So much might knit my husband's love to me.

"But no! Though I should serve him double
He keeps another love outdoors,
Who thieves his strength, who drains his
        stores,
Who haunts his mind with fret and trouble;
    I pray
God's curse may light on such expensive
        whores.

"I am grown old before my season,
Weather and care have worn me down;
Each year delves deeper in my frown,
I've lost my shape and for good reason:
    But she
Yearly puts on young looks like an Easter
        gown.

"And year by year she has betrayed him
With blight and mildew, rain and drought,
Smut, scab, and murrain, all the rout;
But he forgets the tricks she's played him
    When first
The fields give a good smell and the leaves
        put out.

"Aye, come the Spring, and the gulls keening,
Over her strumpet lap he'll ride,
Watching those wasteful fields and wide,
Where the darkened tilth will soon be green-
        ing,
    With looks
Fond and severe, as looks the groom on bride."

### KILLING NO MURDER

You, master of delays,
Need no artillery but days

One after one
Loosed off in blank against hope's garrison;
No art,
Save doing nothing, to undo a heart.

### MODO AND ALCIPHRON

In the Lybian desert I
Saw a hermit's carcass lie,
And a melancholy fiend
Over the battered bosom leaned.

Black as a widow dead for love,
Motionless he drooped above;
Only his tail from side to side
Switched the sand with narrow stride.

"Grievest thou, imp, to see thy spoil
Lie thus quenched on burning soil?
Rinsed the brain, and the loin's lust
Safely reconciled with dust?

"Or perchance thy mournful hide
Dreads how well the lash will chide
When Pope Satan makes thee skip
For a negligent stewardship?"

With a sullen silence he
Raised his head, and looked at me,
Looked me through, and looked away,
Nor for all that I could say

Looked again. Quoth I, I've matched
Patience with yours; and so I watched
The slow, sun-swollen daytime through
To mark what this strange fiend would do.

Cramped and cold I woke from sleep
To hear the fiend begin to weep.
Twinkling in starlight the tears ran
Along his beard, and he began:

"Dead is the holy Alciphron!
Modo's occupation's gone.
All my pretty joys are sped,
Gentle Alciphron is dead!

"Never was there saint so mild
And so easily beguiled;
'Twas pure pleasure to torment
Anything so innocent.

"Danced I, gleaming in a dress
Of nimble maiden nakedness,
His prompt heart with hastening beat
Drummed the measure for my feet,

"And his glances whipped me round,
Till toppling in a dizzy swound
With long recovery I would twine
About him like the conjugal vine,

"While my forked and flickering tongue,
Constant as summer lightning, hung
On the scant flesh that wrapped his bones,
Till sighs long-husbanded, chuckling groans,

"Vouched for the pleasures he endured;
By thorns such pleasures must be cured,
And when most thick the thin blood fell
I knew that I had pleased him well.

"Then at other times I'd sit
Praising his spiritual wit,
Assuring him how deftly he
Could comprehend the Trinity,

"Flesh Christ, with never a trespassing glide
To error on this or t'other side,
Show how original sin doth breed
Inherent in the genital seed,

"And every tinkling sophist quell,
Who questions that the troops of hell
Pester the saint upon his knees,
Actual and numerous as his fleas.

"But most of all 'twas my delight
To cajole him from the elected night
Wherewith the christian cowls his sense
From the allurement and offense

"Of a lost planet. I would be
Damnation singing from a tree
With voice more wildly ravishing
For being damned, or in a spring

"With chill adulteries surprise
Him parched; often I thieved his eyes
To love me in lizard, or in braid
Of sun begetting from a shade

"A spawn of dancing babies—all
Accursed as their original.
In many a salad I laid a snare
Of joy that he on such poor fare

"Fared well, or else on wafts of thyme
Into the warded brain would climb
Unchallenged, or tweaked him by the nose
With the remembrance of a rose.

"Thus did we wrestle, and never chaste
Turtles did rarer dalliance taste,
Thus mixed our opposites, as true
As plighted dock and nettle do,

"Thus to all time example gave
Of the mutual comfort saint should have
With devil, devil with saint, and thus
I clean forgot how envious

"In his unmated splendor sits
He, the Tyrant—"
                            As oak splits
Before the ax, and falls with loud
Indignant groan, so groaned, so bowed,

The fiend, and lay in silence long;
But once or twice against the throng
Of stars raised up a blackening fist;
Then mourned, as mourning from a mist:

"Alas, how faithless man can be
To a friend's eternity!
Into untiring malice doomed,
Virtue as long-breathed I presumed;

"With never a care save which art next
To ply I looked on time unvexed,
Nor, in this plenty of sand, did doubt
The tale of his was running out.

"So Alciphron grew old, though I
Knew it not. This gew-gawed sky
Its virgin hood of gray had on,
And light was scarce, when Alciphron

"Awoke, and laid his hand on me,
And stared east. *Haec dies,* said he,
*Quam fecit Dominus.* I too
Looked east, and saw a path run through

"The kindling cloud. It bruised my gaze
To meet the intolerable blaze,
The ostentatious Rose, the blare
And uproar of light which threatened there;

"But Alciphron beheld and smiled,
Crowing for pleasure like a child
Who views its promised sugarplum:
Then, with a crash which has left dumb

"All thunder since, about us came
A simpering angel in a flame,
Who seized upon redemption's prey,
And bore him, like a child, away.

"Thus, O woe, I'm left alone
With this unanswering flesh and bone.
All my pretty joys are sped,
Gentle Alciphron is dead!

"Nothing is left me of my joy
But this contemptuous broken toy.
Modo's occupation's gone,
Dead is the holy Alciphron!"

## THE ABSENCE

How happy I can be with my love away!
No care comes all day;
Like a dapple of clouds the hours pass by,
Time stares from the sky
But does not see me where I lie in the hay,
So still do I lie.

Like points of dew the stars well in the skies;
Taller the trees rise.
Dis-shadowed, unselved, I wander slow,
My thoughts flow and flow,
But whither tending I know not, nor need
   surmise,
So softly I go,

Till to my quiet bed I must undress—
Then I say, Alas!
That he whom, too anxious or too gay,
I torment all day
Can never know me in my harmlessness
While he is away.

## BUILDING IN STONE

God is still glorified—
To him the wakeful arch holds up in prayer,
Nightly dumb glass keeps vigil to declare
His East, and Eastertide;

The constant pavement lays
Its flatness for his feet, each pier acquaints
Neighbor, him housed; time-thumbed, forgotten saints
Do not forget to praise;

All parcels of the whole,
Each hidden, each revealed, each thrust and stress,
Antiphonally interlocked, confess
Him, stay, and him, control.

Whether upon the fens
Anchored, with all her canvas and all her shrouds,
Ely signal him to willows and clouds
And cattle, or whether Wren's

Unperturbed dome, above
The city roaring with mechanic throat
And climbing in layer on layer of Babel, float
Like an escaping dove,

Or whether in countryside
Stationed all humble and holy churches keep
Faith with the faith of those who lie asleep,
God is still glorified;

Since by the steadfastness
Of his most mute creation man conjures
—Man, so soon hushed—the silence which endures
To bear in mind, and bless.

# Aldous Huxley

ALDOUS (LEONARD) HUXLEY, grandson of Thomas Huxley, was born in 1894 at Godalming and educated at Eton and Balliol College, Oxford. From 1919 to 1921, he was on the editorial staff of *The Athenaeum* and, although he has recently devoted himself entirely to prose, his first publications were in verse; his three volumes, *The Burning Wheel* (1916), *The Defeat of Youth* (1918) and *Leda* (1920), are in that medium.

As a poet, Huxley is at least three writers. At times, he is a precise, rather academic picture-maker, rhyming his subjects in the broad, traditional manner. At other times—and far more frequently—he is a disillusioned ironist, a conscious imitator of Rimbaud and Laforgue, a sardonic *Pierrot lunaire*. (The latter vein is best illustrated by the poem "Male and Female Created He Them" and the bitter "Soles Occidere et Redire Possunt" in *Leda*.) More rarely, his poetry strikes the somber note which finds its fullest expression in the novel *Antic Hay* (1923), the note of tragic despair echoing in a vast emptiness. *Brief Candles* (1930) contains four brilliant and ruthless novelettes.

In 1928 Huxley published his largest and most uncomfortable novel, *Point-Counter-Point*. Its theme was futility, disillusion having already been the motivating power—or lack of power—in his short stories, *Limbo* (1920), *Mortal Coils* (1922), *Two or Three Graces* (1926). Active as a feuilletonist, his sketches sometimes attained the dignity of essays, three volumes of them being published since the initial *On the Margin* (1923).

*The Cicadas and other Poems* (1931) is more mannered—even more ill-mannered —than the preceding volumes of verse. The title-poem and one or two others break away from the tight pattern, and many of the shorter poems are lyric in impulse but they are songs accompanied by shrugs and the mood is unhappily nostalgic.

### SONG OF POPLARS

Shepherd, to yon tall poplars tune your flute:
Let them pierce keenly, subtly shrill,
The slow blue rumor of the hill;
Let the grass cry with an anguish of evening gold.
And the great sky be mute.

Then hearken how the poplar trees unfold
Their buds, yet close and gummed and blind,
In airy leafage of the mind,
Rustling in silvery whispers the twin-hued scales
That fade not nor grow old.

"Poplars and fountains and you cypress spires
Springing in dark and rusty flame,
Seek you aught that hath a name?
Or say, say: Are you all an upward agony
Of undefined desires?

"Say, are you happy in the golden march
Of sunlight all across the day?
Or do you watch the uncertain way
That leads the withering moon on cloudy stairs
Over the heaven's wide arch?

"Is it towards sorrow or towards joy you lift
The sharpness of your trembling spears?
Or do you seek, through the gray tears
That blur the sky, in the heart of the triumphing blue,
A deeper, calmer rift?"

So; I have tuned my music to the trees,
And there were voices, dim below
Their shrillness, voices swelling slow
In the blue murmur of hills, and a golden cry
And then vast silences.

### FIFTH PHILOSOPHER'S SONG

A million million spermatozoa,
    All of them alive:
Out of their cataclysm but one poor Noah
    Dare hope to survive.

And among that billion minus one
    Might have chanced to be
Shakespeare, another Newton, a new Donne—
    But the One was Me.

Shame to have ousted your betters thus,
    Taking ark while the others remained outside!
Better for all of us, forward Homunculus,
    If you'd quietly died!

### A SUNSET

Over against the triumph and the close—
    Amber and green and rose—
        Of this short day,

The pale ghost of the moon grows living-bright
  Once more, as the last light
    Ebbs slowly away.
Darkening the fringes of these western glories
  The black phantasmagories
    Of cloud advance
With noiseless footing—vague and villainous shapes,
  Wrapped in their ragged fustian capes,
    Of some grotesque romance.
But overhead where, like a pool between
  Dark rocks, the sky is green
    And clear and deep,
Floats windlessly a cloud, with curving breast
  Flushed by the fiery west,
    In god-like sleep . . .
And in my mind opens a sudden door
  That lets me see once more
    A little room
With night beyond the window, chill and damp,
  And one green-lighted lamp
    Tempering the gloom,
While here within, close to me, touching me
  (Even the memory
    Of my desire
Shakes me like fear), you sit with scattered hair;
  And all your body bare
    Before the fire
Is lapped about with rosy flame. . . . But still,
  Here on the lonely hill,
    I walk alone;
Silvery green is the moon's lamp overhead,
  The cloud sleeps warm and red,
    And you are gone.

# Charles Hamilton Sorley

CHARLES HAMILTON SORLEY, who promised great things, was born at Old Aberdeen in May, 1895. Son of Professor Sorley of Cambridge, he studied at Marlborough College and University College, Oxford. He was finishing his studies abroad and was on a walking-tour along the banks of the Moselle when war came. Sorley returned home to receive an immediate commission in the 7th Battalion of the Suffolk Regiment. In August, 1915, at the age of twenty, he was made a captain. On October 13, 1915, he was killed in action near Hulluch.

Jingoism, violent propaganda, falsely patriotic slogans could not obscure his piercing vision. "There is no such thing as a just war," he wrote. "What we are doing is casting out Satan by Satan." At nineteen, while he was training at Shorncliffe, he dared to write, "England—I am sick of the sound of the word. In training to fight for England, I am training to fight for that deliberate hypocrisy, that terrible middle-class sloth of outlook and appalling 'imaginative indolence' that has marked us out from generation to generation. . . . Indeed I think that after the War all brave men will renounce their country and confess that they are strangers and pilgrims on the earth." Such electrifying sentences, as well as his independent appreciations of Masefield, Richard Jefferies, and Thomas Hardy, are to be found in the posthumous *Letters of Charles Sorley* (1919). These letters perform the same service to Sorley the poet as the letters of Keats perform in rounding out that greater poet who also died at the beginning of manhood.

Sorley left but one book, *Marlborough and Other Poems,* a posthumous collection, edited by his father, published in 1916. The verse contained in it is sometimes rough but never rude. Although he admired Masefield, loveliness rather than liveliness was his aim. Restraint, tolerance, and a dignity unusual for a boy of twenty distinguish his verse. There is scarcely a line in Sorley's work which does not breathe the spirit of compelling exaltation.

Whether it blows with breezy youth in "The Song of the Ungirt Runners" or burns with steady ardor in the sonnets, his poetry is, in the fullest sense, radiant. What Sorley might have accomplished is apparent though indefinable. He died before he was twenty-one.

### TWO SONNETS

#### I

Saints have adored the lofty soul of you.
Poets have whitened at your high renown.
We stand among the many millions who
Do hourly wait to pass your pathway down.

You, so familiar, once were strange: we tried
To live as of your presence unaware.
But now in every road on every side
We see your straight and steadfast signpost there.

I think it like that signpost in my land
Hoary and tall, which pointed me to go
Upward, into the hills, on the right hand,
Where the mists swim and the winds shriek and blow,
A homeless land and friendless, but a land
I did not know and that I wished to know.

#### II

Such, such is Death: no triumph: no defeat:
Only an empty pail, a slate rubbed clean,
A merciful putting away of what has been.

And this we know: Death is not Life effete,
Life crushed, the broken pail. We who have seen
So marvelous things know well the end not yet.

Victor and vanquished are a-one in death:
Coward and brave: friend, foe. Ghosts do not say,
"Come, what was your record when you drew breath?"
But a big blot has hid each yesterday
So poor, so manifestly incomplete.
And your bright Promise, withered long and sped,
Is touched; stirs, rises, opens and grows sweet
And blossoms and is you, when you are dead.

### THE SONG OF THE UNGIRT RUNNERS

We swing ungirded hips,
And lightened are our eyes,
The rain is on our lips,
We do not run for prize.
We know not whom we trust
Nor whitherward we fare,
But we run because we must
    Through the great wide air.

The waters of the seas
Are troubled as by storm.
The tempest strips the trees
And does not leave them warm.
Does the tearing tempest pause?
Do the tree tops ask it why?
So we run without a cause
    'Neath the big bare sky.

The rain is on our lips,
We do not run for prize.
But the storm the water whips
And the wave howls to the skies.
The winds arise and strike it
And scatter it like sand,
And we run because we like it
    Through the broad bright land.

### TO GERMANY

You are blind like us. Your hurt no man designed,
And no man claimed the conquest of your land.
But gropers both, through fields of thought confined,
We stumble and we do not understand.
You only saw your future bigly planned,
And we the tapering paths of our own mind,
And in each other's dearest ways we stand,
And hiss and hate. And the blind fight the blind.

When it is peace, then we may view again
With new-won eyes each other's truer form

And wonder. Grown more loving-kind and warm
We'll grasp firm hands and laugh at the old pain,
When it is peace. But until peace, the storm,
The darkness and the thunder and the rain.


ROOKS

There where the rusty iron lies,
  The rooks are cawing all the day.
Perhaps no man, until he dies,
  Will understand them, what they say.

The evening makes the sky like clay.
  The slow wind waits for night to rise.
The world is half content. But they

Still trouble all the trees with cries,
  That know, and cannot put away,
The yearning to the soul that flies
  From day to night, from night to day.


ALL THE HILLS AND VALES

All the hills and vales along
Earth is bursting into song,
And the singers are the chaps
Who are going to die perhaps.
    O sing, marching men,
    Till the valleys ring again.
    Give your gladness to earth's keeping,
    So be glad, when you are sleeping.

Cast away regret and rue,
Think what you are marching to.
Little live, great pass.
Jesus Christ and Barabbas
Were found the same day.
This died, that went his way.
    So sing with joyful breath.
    For why, you are going to death.
    Teeming earth will surely store
    All the gladness that you pour.

Earth that never doubts nor fears,
Earth that knows of death, not tears,
Earth that bore with joyful ease
Hemlock for Socrates,
Earth that blossomed and was glad
'Neath the cross that Christ had,

Shall rejoice and blossom too
When the bullet reaches you.
   Wherefore, men marching
   On the road to death, sing!
   Pour your gladness on earth's head,
   So be merry, so be dead.

From the hills and valleys earth
Shouts back the sound of mirth,
Tramp of feet and lilt of song
Ringing all the road along.
Ringing, swinging, glad song-throwing,
Earth will echo still when foot
Lies numb and voice mute.
   On, marching men, on
   To the gates of death with song.
   Sow your gladness for earth's reaping,
   So you may be glad, though sleeping.
   Strew your gladness on earth's bed,
   So be merry, so be dead.

# Robert Graves

ROBERT (RANKE) GRAVES, son of the Irish poet and song-writer Alfred Percival Graves, was born July 26, 1895. He was educated at Charterhouse and Oxford, after which he joined the British Expeditionary Force and served three times in France, in the same regiment as Siegfried Sassoon. His activities were as numerous as incongruous. He won a prize at the Olympic games, lost his capital as an unsuccessful shopkeeper, was the biographer of Colonel T. E. Lawrence, and taught literature in Cairo.

Graves was one of the writers who, roused by the War and giving himself to his country, refused to glorify warfare or chant new hymns of hate. Like Sassoon, Graves reacted against the storm of fury and blood-lust, but, fortified by a lighter and more whimsical spirit, where Sassoon is violent, Graves is volatile; where Sassoon grew bitter, Graves was almost blithe in his irony.

An easy gayety rises from *Fairies and Fusiliers* (1917), a surprising and healing humor that is warmly individual. In *Country Sentiment* (1919) Graves turns to a more rustic simplicity. But a buoyant fancy ripples beneath the most archaic of his ballads and a quaintly original turn of mind saves them from their own echoes.

With *Country Sentiment,* Graves, so one was ready to believe, had established his characteristics. His gift was charming rather than startling, playful and lightly *macabre* rather than profound; qualities, which, while not those of a great poet, were distinctly those of an enjoyable one. The young poet seemed happy in his combinations (and mutations) of two traditionally English forms: the ballad and the Mother Goose rhyme. "A Frosty Night," "Star-Talk," "True Johnny," "It's a Queer Time," "Neglectful Edward," "I Wonder What It Feels Like to Be

Drowned?" are some of the measures written out of a surplus and careless fertility, with little effort, scarcely with thought, and with one eye winking at the Nursery.

But Thought, that enemy of the lyric impulse, spread her theory-spun snare for Graves and soon he was laboring in her toils. He began to analyze, pare, probe, to examine ways, means and the creative process—his own as well as others'. No less than seven volumes were devoted to interpretation and technique; *On English Poetry* (1922), *The Meaning of Dreams* (1924), *Poetic Unreason* (1925), *Contemporary Techniques of Poetry* (1925), *Another Future of Poetry* (1926), *A Survey of Modernist Poetry,* the last in collaboration with Laura Riding (1928). His volumes of verse during this period reflect changing preoccupations. *The Pier Glass* (1921), *Whipperginny* (1923), *Mock Beggar Hall* (1924), *Welchman's Hose* (1925), *The Marmosite's Miscellany,* issued pseudonymously as by "John Doyle" (1925), turn from fancy to philosophy, from philosophy to metaphysics, from Skelton to Freud.

One sees the kaleidoscopic shifts only too plainly in *Collected Poems 1914-1926* and *Poems—1929* (1929) where the whimsical vein and amatory moods run through war-verse and "poems of unrest and transition" to the heavily intellectual and awkwardly involved. The later Graves is scarcely the poet who once nonchalantly wrote:

> May sudden justice overtake
>   And snap the froward pen,
> That old and palsied poets shake
>   Against the minds of men.
>
> Blasphemers trusting to hold caught
>   In far-flung webs of ink
> The utmost ends of human thought
>   Till nothing's left to think.
>
> But may the gift of heavenly peace
>   And glory for all time
> Keep the boy Tom who, tending geese,
>   First made the nursery rhyme.

Thus the early Graves (*circa* 1916) seems to be admonishing—and with good reason—the mature but unstabilized experimentalist, who, some dozen years later, attempts the dislocations of James Joyce, echoes Gertrude Stein, and flounders in a morass of speculations. Graves began as one who had simplicity rather than acquired *simplesse*. He was a true innocent. By taking thought unsuited to his intuitive temperament he did not increase his stature. He lost innocence without gaining wisdom.

Much of this intellectual and emotional indecision is reflected in *Good-by to All That* (1930). In this exciting and candid autobiography, Graves (as is made plain by more than the title) waves a public farewell to his youth. Without bitterness or bravado, the poet, like his friends Sassoon and Blunden, describes the horror of an offensive, the drudgery of trench-life, the abuses of officialdom, intensifying his pages with a hatred of injustice in any form. Unlike his fellows, he is even more candid in revealing the stress of his personal—and highly private—encounters.

*Good-by to All That* may, as a reviewer implied, "suffer little from that instinctive good taste which is to the twentieth century the unpardonable sin," but, in its undeviating honesty, it rounds and completes not only the portrait of a poet but of a period.

Graves was always interested in reconstructed literature and history. He "condensed" Dickens' *David Copperfield* in 1933. In his fortieth year this penchant was reënforced by shrewdly selected and boldly interpreted research to compose his most popular book: *I, Claudius* (1934), a quasi-biography. It was followed within a year by the equally successful *Claudius the God.*

### NEGLECTFUL EDWARD

*Nancy*

Edward, back from the Indian Sea,
"What have you brought for Nancy?"

*Edward*

"A rope of pearls and a gold earring,
And a bird of the East that will not sing.
A carven tooth, a box with a key—"

*Nancy*

"God be praised you are back," says she,
"Have you nothing more for your Nancy?"

*Edward*

"Long as I sailed the Indian Sea
I gathered all for your fancy:
Toys and silk and jewels I bring,
And a bird of the East that will not sing:
What more can you want, dear girl, from me?"

*Nancy*

"God be praised you are back," said she,
"Have you nothing better for Nancy?"

*Edward*

"Safe and home from the Indian Sea,
And nothing to take your fancy?"

*Nancy*

"You can keep your pearls and your gold earring,
And your bird of the East that will not sing,
But, Ned, have you nothing more for me
Than heathenish gew-gaw toys?" says she,
"Have you nothing better for Nancy?"

### IT'S A QUEER TIME

It's hard to know if you're alive or dead
When steel and fire go roaring through your head.

One moment you'll be crouching at your gun
Traversing, mowing heaps down half in fun:
The next, you choke and clutch at your right breast—
No time to think—leave all—and off you go . . .
To Treasure Island where the Spice winds blow,
To lovely groves of mango, quince and lime—
Breathe no good-by, but ho, for the Red West!
       It's a queer time.

You're charging madly at them yelling "Fag!"
When somehow something gives and your feet drag.
You fall and strike your head; yet feel no pain
And find . . . you're digging tunnels through the hay
In the Big Barn, 'cause it's a rainy day.
Oh, springy hay, and lovely beams to climb!
You're back in the old sailor suit again.
       It's a queer time.

Or you'll be dozing safe in your dug-out—
A great roar—the trench shakes and falls about—
You're struggling, gasping, struggling, then . . . *hullo!*
Elsie comes tripping gayly down the trench,
Hanky to nose—that lyddite makes a stench—
Getting her pinafore all over grime.
Funny! because she died ten years ago!
       It's a queer time.

The trouble is, things happen much too quick;
Up jump the Boches, rifles thump and click,
You stagger, and the whole scene fades away:
Even good Christians don't like passing straight
From Tipperary or their Hymn of Hate
To Alleluiah-chanting, and the chime
Of golden harps . . . and . . . I'm not well today . . .
       It's a queer time.

### A PINCH OF SALT

When a dream is born in you
  With a sudden clamorous pain,
When you know the dream is true
  And lovely, with no flaw nor stain,
O then, be careful, or with sudden clutch
You'll hurt the delicate thing you prize so much.

Dreams are like a bird that mocks,
  Flirting the feathers of his tail.
When you seize at the salt box,
  Over the hedge you'll see him sail.
Old birds are neither caught with salt nor chaff:
They watch you from the apple bough and laugh.

Poet, never chase the dream.
  Laugh yourself, and turn away.
Mask your hunger; let it seem
  Small matter if he come or stay;
But when he nestles in your hand at last,
Close up your fingers tight and hold him fast.


### STAR-TALK

"Are you awake, Gemelli,
  This frosty night?"
"We'll be awake till revéille,
Which is Sunrise," say the Gemelli,
"It's no good trying to go to sleep:
If there's wine to be got we'll drink it deep,
  But sleep is gone tonight,
  But sleep is gone tonight."

"Are you cold too, poor Pleiads,
  This frosty night?"
"Yes, and so are the Hyads:
See us cuddle and hug," say the Pleiads,
"All six in a ring: it keeps us warm:
We huddle together like birds in a storm:
  It's bitter weather tonight,
  It's bitter weather tonight."

"What do you hunt, Orion,
  This starry night?"
"The Ram, the Bull and the Lion,
And the Great Bear," says Orion,
"With my starry quiver and beautiful belt
I am trying to find a good thick pelt
  To warm my shoulders tonight,
  To warm my shoulders tonight."

"Did you hear that, Great She-bear,
  This frosty night?"
"Yes, he's talking of stripping *me* bare
Of my own big fur," says the She-bear,
"I'm afraid of the man and his terrible arrow:
The thought of it chills my bones to the marrow,
  And the frost so cruel tonight!
  And the frost so cruel tonight!"

"How is your trade, Aquarius,
  This frosty night?"
"Complaints is many and various
And my feet are cold," says Aquarius,
"There's Venus objects to Dolphin-scales,
And Mars to Crab-spawn found in my pails,
  And the pump has frozen tonight,
  And the pump has frozen tonight."

### I WONDER WHAT IT FEELS LIKE TO BE DROWNED?

Look at my knees,
That island rising from the steamy seas!
The candle's a tall lightship; my two hands
Are boats and barges anchored to the sands,
With mighty cliffs all round;
They're full of wine and riches from far lands. . . .
*I wonder what it feels like to be drowned?*

I can make caves,
By lifting up the island and huge waves
And storms, and then with head and ears well under
Blow bubbles with a monstrous roar like thunder,
A bull-of-Bashan sound.
The seas run high and the boats split asunder . . .
*I wonder what it feels like to be drowned?*

The thin soap slips
And slithers like a shark under the ships.
My toes are on the soap-dish—that's the effect
Of my huge storms; an iron steamer's wrecked.
The soap slides round and round;
He's biting the old sailors, I expect. . . .
*I wonder what it feels like to be drowned?*

### ESCAPE

*(August 6, 1916. Officer Previously Reported Died of Wounds, Now Reported Wounded: Graves, Capt. R., Royal Welsh Fusiliers)*

. . . But I *was* dead, an hour or more:
I woke when I'd already passed the door
That Cerberus guards and half-way down the road
To Lethe, as an old Greek sign-post showed.
Above me, on my stretcher swinging by,
I saw new stars in the sub-terrene sky,
A Cross, a Rose in Bloom, a Cage with Bars,
And a barbed Arrow feathered with fine stars.
I felt the vapors of forgetfulness
Float in my nostrils: Oh, may Heaven bless
Dear Lady Proserpine, who saw me wake
And, stooping over me, for Henna's sake
Cleared my poor buzzing head and sent me back
Breathless, with leaping heart along the track.
After me roared and clattered angry hosts
Of demons, heroes, and policemen-ghosts.
"Life, life! I can't be dead, I won't be dead:
Damned if I'll die for anyone," I said . . .
Cerberus stands and grins above me now,
Wearing three heads, lion and lynx and sow.

"Quick, a revolver! but my Webley's gone,
Stolen . . . no bombs . . . no knife . . . (the crowd swarms on,
Bellows, hurls stones) . . . not even a honeyed sop . . .
Nothing . . . Good Cerberus . . . Good dog . . . But stop!
Stay! . . . A great luminous thought . . . I do believe
There's still some morphia that I bought on leave."
Then swiftly Cerberus' wide mouths I cram
With Army biscuit smeared with Tickler's jam;
And Sleep lurks in the luscious plum and apple.
He crunches, swallows, stiffens, seems to grapple
With the all-powerful poppy . . . then a snore,
A crash; the beast blocks up the corridor
With monstrous hairy carcase, red and dun—
Too late: for I've sped through.
                    O Life! O Sun!

## THE TRAVELER'S CURSE AFTER MISDIRECTION

### (*from the Welsh*)

May they wander stage by stage
Of the same vain pilgrimage,
Stumbling on, age after age,
Night and day, mile after mile,
At each and every step, a stile;
At each and every stile, withal,
May they catch their feet and fall;
At each and every fall they take,
May a bone within them break;
And may the bones that break within
Not be, for variation's sake,
Now rib, now thigh, now arm, now shin,
But always, without fail, THE NECK.

## SONG: ONE HARD LOOK

Small gnats that fly
In hot July
And lodge in sleeping ears,
Can rouse therein
A trumpet's din
With Day of Judgment fears.

Small mice at night
Can wake more fright
Than lions at midday.
A straw will crack
The camel's back;
There is no easier way.

One smile relieves
A heart that grieves
Though deadly sad it be,
And one hard look
Can close the book
That lovers love to see.

## A FROSTY NIGHT

*Mother*

Alice, dear, what ails you,
    Dazed and white and shaken?
Has the chill night numbed you?
    Is it fright you have taken?

*Alice*

Mother, I am very well,
    I felt never better,
Mother, do not hold me so,
    Let me write my letter.

*Mother*

Sweet, my dear, what ails you?

*Alice*

No, but I am well;
The night was cold and frosty,
    There's no more to tell.

*Mother*

Aye, the night was frosty,
    Coldly gaped the moon,
Yet the birds seemed twittering
    Through green boughs of June.

Soft and thick the snow lay,
  Stars danced in the sky.
Not all the lambs of May-day
  Skip so bold and high.

Your feet were dancing, Alice,
  Seemed to dance on air,
You looked a ghost or angel
  In the starlight there.

Your eyes were frosted starlight,
  Your heart fire and snow.
Who was it said, "I love you"?

        *Alice*
Mother, let me go!

## IN THE WILDERNESS

Christ of His gentleness
Thirsting and hungering,
Walked in the wilderness;
Soft words of grace He spoke
Unto lost desert-folk
That listened wondering.
He heard the bitterns call
From ruined palace-wall,
Answered them brotherly.
He held communion
With the she-pelican
Of lonely piety.
Basilisk, cockatrice,
Flocked to his homilies,
With mail of dread device,
With monstrous barbèd slings,
With eager dragon-eyes;
Great bats on leathern wings
And poor blind broken things,
Foul in their miseries.
And ever with Him went,
Of all His wanderings
Comrade, with ragged coat,
Gaunt ribs—poor innocent—
Bleeding foot, burning throat,
The guileless old scapegoat;
For forty nights and days
Followed in Jesus' ways,
Sure guard behind Him kept,
Tears like a lover wept.

## A FORCED MUSIC

Of Love he sang, full hearted one,
But when the song was done,
The King demanded more,
Aye, and commanded more.
The boy found nothing for encore,
Words, melodies—none,
Ashamed the song's glad rise and plaintive
    fall
Had so charmed King and Queen and all.

He sang the same verse once again
But urging less Love's pain.
With altered time and key
He showed variety,
Seemed to refresh the harmony
Of his only strain,
So still the glad rise and the plaintive fall
Could charm the King, the Queen and all.

He of his song then wearying ceased,
But was not yet released:
The Queen's request was "More,"
And her behest was "More."
He played of random notes some score,
Then suddenly let his twangling harp down
    fall
And fled in tears from King and Queen and
    all.

## LOST LOVE

His eyes are quickened so with grief,
He can watch a grass or leaf
Every instant grow; he can
Clearly through a flint wall see,
Or watch the startled spirit flee
From the throat of a dead man:
Across two counties he can hear,
And catch your words before you speak;
The woodlouse or the maggot's weak
Clamor rings in his sad ear;
And noise so slight it would surpass
Credence:—drinking sound of grass,
Worm-talk, clashing jaws of moth
Chumbling tiny holes in cloth:
The groan of ants who undertake
Gigantic loads for honor's sake,

Their sinews creak, their breath comes thin:
Whir of spiders when they spin,
And minute, whispering, mumbling sighs
Of idle grubs and flies.

This man is quickened so with grief,
He wanders god-like or like thief
Inside and out, below, above,
Without relief seeking lost love.

# Louis Golding

LOUIS GOLDING was born in Manchester, in November, 1895, and received his early education at Manchester Grammar School. War found him in 1914, taking him to Macedonia and France, where he was chiefly occupied with educational work in various armies. On his return to England in 1919, he published his first volume of poems, *Sorrow of War,* and in the same year pursued his studies at Oxford. A succeeding collection, *Shepherd Singing Ragtime* (1921), and a novel, *Forward from Babylon* (1921), appeared while he was still an undergraduate.

The two volumes of poems appeared in America as one book entitled *Prophet and Fool* (1923), displaying the author as a traditionally romantic poet, but one with a vigorous if not always controlled utterance. *Seacoast of Bohemia,* a satiric fantasy, followed in the same year. Then Golding traveled extensively through Europe and the Mediterranean and published two colorful volumes of travel, *Sunward* (1924) and *Sicilian Noon* (1925). *Day of Atonement* (1925) is a return to the somber and impressive background of *Forward from Babylon.*

Two lighter novels proved more popular than Golding's intenser work; *Store of Ladies* (1927) and *The Miracle Boy* (1928) provided him with a following in America and prepared the way for his welcome there. His adventures in Palestine were recorded in *Many Ways to Zion* (1928). His later novels took a more local turn: *Magnolia Street* (1933), *Five Silver Daughters* (1934), and *The Camberwell Beauty* (1935). Of these the first was both the best and the most popular.

## PLOWMAN AT THE PLOW

He, behind the straight plow, stands
Stalwart; firm shafts in firm hands.

Naught he cares for wars and naught
For the fierce disease of thought.

Only for the winds, the sheer
Naked impulse of the year,

Only for the soil which stares
Clean into God's face, he cares.

In the stark might of his deed
There is more than art or creed;

In his wrist more strength is hid
Than the monstrous Pyramid;

Stauncher than stern Everest
Be the muscles of his breast;

Not the Atlantic sweeps a flood
Potent as the plowman's blood.

He, his horse, his plowshare, these
Are the only verities.

Dawn to dusk, with God he stands,
The Earth poised on his broad hands.

## THE SINGER OF HIGH STATE

On hills too harsh for firs to climb,
 Where eagle dare not hatch her brood,
 On the sheer peak of Solitude,

With anvils of black granite crude
He beats austerities of rhyme.

Such godlike stuff his spirit drinks,
    He made great odes of tempest there.
    The steel-winged eagle, if he dare
    To cleave these tracts of frozen air,
Hearing such music, swoops and sinks.

Stark tumults, which no tense night awes,
    Of godly love and titan hate
    Down crags of song reverberate.
    Held by the Singer of High State,
Battalions of the midnight pause.

On hills uplift from Space and Time,
    On the sheer peak of Solitude,
    With stars to give his furnace food,
    On anvils of black granite crude
He beats austerities of rhyme.

### NIGHT ON THE FIELDS OF ENNA

*(Dove il sol tace.*—"Inferno")

    Grass there doth not
    Make reply faint as thought
    To the bird-like din
    Of the sun's cherubin.
    And the birds themselves do
    Blunder the branches through
    Till the earth's root stains
    With their knocked-out brains.

O the sun's silent and
Blood's on the land.
The birds die there
In the clotted air
And their wing-beats make no noise.
The four winds are lank lead
Suspended in a dead poise.
A scurf is on the mouth
Of west wind and south.
And the east and the north
Loll swollen tongues forth,
Into the blank immanence
Of the sun's silence.

Never Moloch and his peers,
Beelzebub, Ashtaroth,
So racked the cracked spheres
With the trumpets of their wrath
As this black hush hath rent
The collapsing firmament.

Dante, of thy charity
Restore sound unto sea,
Slake the winds their thirst.
Let the sun walk on
The split ramparts of this worst
Pandemonion.
Let the sun's cherubin,
Dante, once again begin
Their bird-like din.
Restore to birds their lost eyes,
To grass its little cries.

# L. A. G. Strong

LEONARD A. G. STRONG was born on March 8, 1896, in the parish of Plympton, in Devon. "One of his parents," Strong informed the editor some years ago, "is Irish, the other is half English and half Irish, so that he is fairly entitled to describe himself as a mongrel. He spent his childhood partly on Southern Dartmoor and partly on the borders between Dublin and Wicklow. From a preparatory school at Plymouth, he went with a scholarship to Brighton College, and thence, five years later, won an open Classical Scholarship at Wadham College, Oxford. Illness interrupting his career, he finally graduated in 1920 and taught at Summer Fields, a famous preparatory school near Oxford. Delicate health has confined him to a spectator's part in his favorite sports. Swimming is the only form of violent exercise he has been able to keep up—perhaps because, as legend has it, one of his ancestors, Teig Riarach O'Dowda, King of Connaught, captured and married a mermaid, thereby endowing his descendants with a taste for the sea!"

Strong is known in America chiefly through his *Dublin Days* (1921), a small volume of shrewd appraisals, in which satire nudges characterization. *The Lowery Road* (1923) depends for its effect less on humor and more on exaltation. Without sacrificing originality of speech, Strong summons the spirit of the English countryside in these terse Dartmoor lyrics. Besides the celebration of Strong's native Devon, the author has written poetry which is by no means local; his *Eight Poems,* privately distributed at Christmas 1923, show him capable of supporting himself in somewhat higher flights. Later Strong distinguished himself as a shrewd compiler of anthologies of magazine verse. His first novel, *Dewer Rides,* was published in America as one of *Paper Books* in 1929 and considerably enlarged his audience.

In 1930 Strong left Oxford and teaching, came down to London and there established himself as the author of a successful set of novels, the best of which (up to 1935) are *Dewer Rides, The Garden, The Brothers,* and *The Seven Arms.* A pamphlet of his later lyrics, *March Evening,* was issued in 1932, containing two of his gravest interpretations.

### OLD DAN'L

Out of his cottage to the sun
Bent double comes old Dan'l,
His chest all over cotton wool,
His back all over flannel.

"Winter will finish him," they've said
Each winter now for ten:
But come the first warm day of Spring
Old Dan'l's out again.

### ZEKE

Gnarly and bent and deaf's a pos',
Pore old Ezekiel Purvis
Goeth crippin' slowly up the 'ill
To the Commoonion Survis.

And tappy, tappy up the haisle
Goeth stick and brassy ferule:
And Passen [1] 'ath to stoopy down
An' 'oller in ees yerole.

### AN OLD WOMAN, OUTSIDE THE ABBEY THEATER

In this Theayter they has plays
   On us, and high-up people comes

[1] Parson.

And pays to see things playin' here
   They'd run like hell from in the slums.

### RUFUS PRAYS

In the darkening church
   Where but a few had stayed
At the Litany Desk
   The idiot knelt and prayed.

Rufus, stunted, uncouth,
   The one son of his mother.
"Eh, I'd sooner 'ave Rufie,"
   She said, "than many another:

" 'E's useful about the 'ouse,
   And so gentle as 'e can be.
An' 'e gets up early o' mornin's
   And makes me a cup o' tea."

The formal evensong
   Had passed over his head:
He sucked his thumb, and squinted,
   And dreamed, instead.

Now while the organ boomed
   To the few who still were there,
At the Litany Desk
   The idiot made his prayer:

"Gawd bless Mother,
  'N make Rufie a good lad:
Take Rufie to Heaven
  'N forgive him when 'e's bad.

" 'N early mornin's in Heaven
  'E'll make mother's tea,
'N a cup for the Lord Jesus
  'N a cup for Thee."

### THE MAD WOMAN OF PUNNET'S TOWN

A-swell within her billowed skirts
  Like a great ship with sails unfurled,
The mad woman goes gallantly
  Upon the ridges of her world.

With eagle nose and wisps of gray
  She strides upon the westward hills,
Swings her umbrella joyously
  And waves it to the waving mills.

Talking and chuckling as she goes
  Indifferent both to sun and rain,
With all that merry company:
  The singing children of her brain.

### LOWERY COT

This is the house where Jesse White
Run staring in one misty night,
And said he seed the Holy Ghost
Out to Lowery finger-post.

Said It rised up like a cloud
Muttering to Itself out loud,
And stood tremendous on the hill
While all the breathing world was still.

They put en shivering to bed,
And in three days the man was dead.
Gert solemn visions such as they
Be overstrong for mortal clay.

### THE DOOR

One in the boat cried out
  Pointing to land,
For the sun leaped clear of the mist

And a rainbow spanned
With one vast arch the mountain, the trees,
  and the sand.

The mountain stood like a huge
  Ghost in a cloud;
The startled trees were caught
  In a wavering crowd;
And the four in their glittering oilskins cried
  aloud

As that pure and soaring arch
  More marvelous grew,
And the sandhills stared beneath it
  Wild and new,
And down the unearthly beaches lamenting
  flew

Gull upon gull distraught
  Blown through that Door,
Handful on handful flung
  High over the shore.
Such desperate beauty they never had seen
  before.

### MARCH EVENING

This pool, the quiet sky,
  Is rippled with a chime.
Night gathers, and the cry
  Of lambs in the far fold
Comes to us as we climb:
  The moorland air is cold.

Ghost-pale the grass, and bare
  The bowlder-scattered crest.
A frightened rabbit starts—
  With quickening eyes and hearts
We turn about, and stare
  Into the open west.

The Cornish hills lie small,
  So huge the sky has grown.
We can look down on all
  Western and southern ground,
And see the Eddystone,
  Pricking the seaward pall,
Wink over Plymouth Sound.

Below us, dim and deep,
  Mist-hidden, murmuring,

The valley winds away:
Beneath its shadow Spring
Lies light asleep
In dreams of coming day,
With cuckoos on the wing
And steep banks blossoming.

Again the quiet sky
Is troubled with a chime
That spreads in rings of sound.
We sigh, and think, What rhyme
That man has ever bound
Can hold a sigh?

## Edmund Blunden

Edmund (c.) blunden was born in 1896, and educated at Queen's College, Oxford. During the War he served as lieutenant in the Royal Sussex Regiment. His bucolic poems were a direct revulsion from his experiences as a soldier. In 1916 he published three small volumes of pastorals which appeared as one book, *The Wagoner and other Poems,* in 1920. In the same year, he edited, with Alan Porter, *The Poems of John Clare,* most of the verses being deciphered from a mass of old manuscript. Two years later, he published *The Shepherd* (1922), which was awarded the Hawthornden Prize for that year. He was Professor of English Literature at Tokio University from 1924 to 1927.

The most casual glance at his volumes discloses that Blunden's use of the pastoral note is not, as it is with some of his contemporaries, a mere literary device. Here, the verse is gnarled and twisted as the bent trees of which he loves to write; there is rude country air in his lines and even the words have the smell of apple orchards. It has been objected that Blunden depends too often on unusual and obsolescent terms, but—as Robert Bridges wrote in a pamphlet on *The Dialectical Words in Blunden's Poems* (1921)—"his poetry cannot be imagined without them, and the strength and beauty of the effects must be estimated in his successes and not in his failures."

Blunden's subsequent poetry is milder; a softness but not a flabbiness of texture clothes *To Nature* (1923), *Masks of Time* (1925) and *Retreat* (1928). These verses, lacking the earthy flavor of the early poems, lose the spiciness that dialect confers, but they retain the contemplative quality of Blunden's mind and a dignity which inheres both in the tradition and in the man. *Near and Far* (1929), on the other hand, is composed of pretty trifles which did Blunden's reputation no good. The contents, betraying a monotonous solemnity, are, as Peter Quennell remarked, "a drowsy methodical grinding out of familiar tunes."

In spite of his attainments, Blunden remained known to only a small circle until 1929. In that year he published his large prose work, *Undertones of War,* which was received with instant enthusiasm in Europe and America and took its place among such vivid anti-militaristic documents as Remarque's *All Quiet on the Western Front,* Zweig's *The Case of Sergeant Grischa,* Hemingway's *A Farewell to Arms,* and E. E. Cummings' *The Enormous Room.*

*The Poems of Edmund Blunden* (1932) collects all the poetry written by Blunden between 1914 and 1930. Nature and war are the chief themes and, though one sometimes wishes for more abandon, no reader can be deaf to the admirable diction and the grave music, particularly in such poems as "A Country God" and the later "The Recovery."

(For the definitions appended to the following poems, thanks must be given to the late Robert Bridges, whose skill as etymologist can scarcely be overrated.)

### THE POOR MAN'S PIG

Already fallen plum-bloom stars the green
 And apple-boughs as knarred [1] as old toads' backs
Wear their small roses ere a rose is seen;
 The building-thrush watches old Job who stacks

The bright-peeled osiers on the sunny fence,
 The pent sow grunts to hear him stumping by,
And tries to push the bolt and scamper thence,
 But her ringed snout still keeps her to the sty.

Then out he lets her run; away she snorts
 In bundling gallop for the cottage door,
With hungry hubbub begging crusts and orts.[2]
 Then like a whirlwind bumping round once more;
Nuzzling the dog, making the pullets run,
 And sulky as a child when her play's done.

### A COUNTRY GOD

When groping farms are lanterned up
 And stolchy [3] plowlands hid in grief,
And glimmering byroads catch the drop
 That weeps from sprawling twig and leaf,
And heavy-hearted spins the wind
 Among the tattered flags of Mirth,—
Then who but I flit to and fro,
With shuddering speech, with mope and mow,
 And glass the eyes of earth?

Then haunt I by some moaning brook
 Where lank and snaky brambles swim,
Or where the hill pines swartly look
 I whirry [4] through the dark and hymn
A dull-voiced dirge and threnody,
 An echo of the sad world's drone
That now appals the friendly stars—
O wail for blind brave youth, whose wars
 Turn happiness to stone.

[1] *Knarred,* a word meaning "wrinkled," is a country-cousin to our "gnarled."
[2] *Orts* are fragments or scraps of refuse.
[3] *Stolchy* is such an excellent onomatopoetic word that it scarcely needs explanation. But there is an old English verb *stolch:* "to tread down in wet land or mud."
[4] *Whirry* is another sound-word, not to be confused with "worry." It means "to fly rapidly with noise"—a combination of "whir" and "hurry."

How rang the cavern-shades of old
　　To my melodious pipes, and then
My bright-haired bergomask patrolled
　　Each lawn and plot for laughter's din:
Never a sower flung broadcast,
　　No hedger brished [1] nor scythesman swung,
Nor maiden trod the purpling press,
But I was by to guard and bless
　　And for their solace sung.

But now the sower's hand is writhed
　　In livid death, the bright rhythm stolen,
The gold grain flatted and unscythed,
　　The boars in the vineyard, gnarled and sullen,
Havocking the grapes; and the pouncing wind
　　Spins the spattered leaves of the glen
In a mockery dance, death's hue-and-cry;
With all my murmurous pipes flung by
　　And summer not to come again.

### THE BARN

Rain-sunken roof, grown green and thin
For sparrows' nests and starlings' nests;
Disheveled eaves; unwieldy doors,
Cracked rusty pump, and oaken floors,
And idly-penciled names and jests
　　Upon the posts within.

The light pales at the spider's lust,
The wind tangs [2] through the shattered pane:
An empty hop-poke spreads across
The gaping frame to mend the loss
And keeps out sun as well as rain,
　　Mildewed with clammy dust.

The smell of apples stored in hay
And homely cattle-cake is there.
Use and disuse have come to terms,
The walls are hollowed out by worms,
But men's feet keep the mid-floor bare
　　And free from worse decay.

All merry noise of hens astir
Or sparrows squabbling on the roof
Comes to the barn's broad open door;

You hear upon the stable floor
Old hungry Dapple strike his hoof,
　　And the blue fan-tail's whir.

The barn is old, and very old,
But not a place of spectral fear.
Cobwebs and dust and speckling sun
Come to old buildings every one.
Long since they made their dwelling here,
　　And here you may behold

Nothing but simple wane and change;
Your tread will wake no ghost, your voice
Will fall on silence undeterred.
No phantom wailing will be heard,
Only the farm's blithe cheerful noise;
　　The barn is old, not strange.

### EASTERN TEMPEST

This flying angel's torrent cry
Will hurl the mountains through the sky!
A wind like fifty winds at once
Through the bedragoned kingdom runs,
And hissing rain slants icy stings
At many a wretch afield who clings

---

[1] *Brished* is country dialect for "brush"—principally used in connection with trimming trees and hedges.

[2] *Tangs*—an old term (differing from our word meaning "taste") denoting a barb or a sting. Blunden uses it here as a verb.

His cloak of straw, with glistening spines
Like a prodigious porcupine's.
The reptile grasses by his path
Wind sleek as unction from that Wrath
Which with its glassy claw uproots
The broad-leaved *kiri,* flays and loots
Torn and sprung sinews, leaves for dead
The young crops with the shining head,
While blotched blunt melons darkly dot
The slaughtered swathes like cannon-shot.
The lotus in the pond upheaves
Its sacred, slow, appealing leaves,
And many a bush with wrestling jerk
Defies the demon's murderous work—
Yet nature stares white-lipped, to read
In Chance's eye what desperate deed?
    A kinder god discerns, replies,
And stills the land's storm-shouts to sighs;
The clouds in massy folds apart
Disclose the day's bright bleeding heart,
Huge plumes and scarves black-tossing wide
As if a Kubla Khan had died!
From flame to flame the vision glows,
Till all the pools of heaven unclose
The lotus-light, the hue, the balm
Of wisdom infinitely calm.

## THE MIDNIGHT SKATERS

The hop-poles stand in cones,
    The icy pond lurks under,
The pole-tops touch the star-gods' thrones
    And sound the gulfs of wonder,
But not the tallest there, 'tis said,
Could fathom to this pond's black bed.

Then is not Death at watch
    Within those secret waters?
What wants he but to catch
    Earth's heedless sons and daughters?
With but a crystal parapet
Between, he has his engines set.

Then on, blood shouts, on, on,
    Twirl, wheel and whip above him,

Dance on this ball-floor thin and wan,
    Use him as though you love him;
Court him, elude him, reel and pass,
And let him hate you through the glass.

## THE RECOVERY

From the dark mood's control
    I free this man; there's light still in the
        West.
The most virtuous, chaste, melodious soul
    Never was better blest.

Here medicine for the mind
    Lies in a gilded shade; this feather stirs
And my faith lives; the touch of this tree's
        rind,—
    And temperate sense recurs.

No longer the loud pursuit
    Of self-made clamors dulls the ear; here
        dwell
Twilight societies, twig, fungus, root,
    Soundless, and speaking well.

Beneath the accustomed dome
    Of this chance-planted, many-centuried tree
The snake-marked earthy multitudes are
        come
    To breathe their hour like me.

The leaf comes curling down,
    Another and another, gleam on gleam;
Above, celestial leafage glistens on,
    Borne by time's blue stream.

The meadow-stream will serve
    For my refreshment; that high glory yields
Imaginings that slay; the safe paths curve
    Through unexalted fields

Like these, where now no more
    My early angels walk and call and fly,
But the mouse stays his nibbling, to explore
    My eye with his bright eye.

## *Sacheverell Sitwell*

S ACHEVERELL SITWELL, brother of Edith and Osbert Sitwell, was born in 1897 at
Scarborough and educated at Eton. As soon as he was of military age, he joined
the Grenadier Guards as second lieutenant. After the War he attended Balliol College, Oxford, for a short time, but came to London before completing his courses,
confining his activities to literature.

From the first, his poetry was experimental, but even the early *The People's
Palace* contained his gesture. *The Hundred and One Harlequins* (1922) and *The
Thirteenth Caesar* (1924) are less dependent on influences, although the accents of
such dissimilar poets as Vachel Lindsay and T. S. Eliot arise from his pages. Here
the youngest of the Sitwells displays a lively imagination, a delight in toying with
the subject as well as distorting it, a glittering, if sometimes too self-conscious,
cleverness.

His more recent work shows him milder in manner and idiom. Less distinctive
than his strepitant sister and brother, he seems to be developing a more traditional
vein. His larger efforts would seem to dispute this; "Canons of Giant Art" and
"Doctor Donne and Gargantua" are exercises in the approved modern manner. But
they are not the poet. Try as he will with all the resources of the brain, his art is
not in them. His art (and for that manner his heart) finds its response in unaffected
song, a group of twenty-five lyrics being the core of *The Cyder Feast* (1927). Apart
from a dissonance or two, an inverted image, a strained or dislocated adjective, these
horticultural verses might have been written in the eighteenth century.

It is curious to note how the more modern "modernists" turn their eyes not to
formless futurism, but to a precise past. Thus we find T. S. Eliot rediscovering
Dryden and Lancelot Andrewes, Humbert Wolfe looting the Greek Anthology,
Edith Sitwell turning from Gertrude Stein and Dr. Steiner to pen an introduction
to the didactic rhymes of Jane Taylor. And here, in *The Cyder Feast,* in the midst
of the "alchemy of dank leaves," one finds the youngest Sitwell writing "Four
Variations upon William Browne of Tavistock," "Variation on a Theme by Robert
Herrick," "Variation upon a Couplet of Alexander Pope," "An Adaptation from
John Milton." Moreover most of the poems not adapted or "varied" betray accents
of a period that is scarcely Sitwellian. "Tulip Tree" and "Kingcups" are two examples among many.

The irruption of a kind of architectural fancy is not unnatural in one who has
established himself as an ardent appraiser if not an authority on the genesis of the
rococo, embodied in his three volumes *Southern Baroque Art* (1924), *German
Baroque Art* (1927) and *The Gothick North* (1929).

### FOUNTAINS

This night is pure and clear as thrice refinèd silver.
Silence, the cape of Death, lies heavy
Round the bare shoulders of the hills.
Faint throbs and murmurs

At moments growing to a mutter, then subsiding,
Fill the night with mystery and panic.
The honey-tongued arguings of fountains
Stir the air with flutes and gentle voices.

The graven fountain-masks suffer and weep—
Curved with a smile, the poor mouths
Clutch at a half-remembered song
Striving to forget the agony of ever laughing,—
Laughing while they hear the secrets
Echoed from the depths of Earth beneath them.

This half-remembered song—
This flow of sad-restrainèd laughter
Jars with the jets of youthful water
Springing from the twisted masks,
For this is but the birth of water;
And singing joyfully
It springs upon the world
And wanders ceaselessly
Along its jeweled valleys to the sea,
Rattling like rolls of drums
The shells and pebbles down its bed.

The endless argument of water ceases,
A few drops fall heavily, splashing on the marble:
A Sultan with his treasures
Seeking to gain the goodwill of his love,
Pouring before her chains of crackling pearls
And weeping heavy jealous tears
Because she will not heed him.

### THE RED-GOLD RAIN

#### (Orange Tree by Day)

Sun and rain at work together
Ripened this for summer weather;
Sun gave it color tawny red
And rain its life as though it bled;
In the long days full of fire
Its fruit will cool us when we tire.
Against the house-wall does it grow
With smooth stem like a fountain's flow,
Dark are its leaves, a colder shade
Than ever rock or mountain made;
When the wind plays soft they sing,
For here the birds' songs never ring,
Quite still the fruit that in a golden shower
Will fall one day to flood this tower.

### "PSITTACHUS EOIS IMITATRIX ALES AB INDIS"—Ovid

The parrot's voice snaps out—
No good to contradict—
What he says he'll say again:
Dry facts, like biscuits,—

His voice and vivid colors
Of his breast and wings
Are immemorably old;
Old dowagers dressed in crimpèd satin
Boxed in their rooms
Like specimens beneath a glass
Inviolate—and never changing,
Their memory of emotions dead;
The ardor of their summers

Sprayed like camphor
On their silken parasols
Intissued in a cupboard.

Reflective, but with never a new thought
The parrot sways upon his ivory perch—
Then gravely turns a somersault
Through rings nailed in the roof—
Much as the sun performs his antics
As he climbs the aerial bridge
We only see
Through crystal prisms in a falling rain.

### TULIP TREE

Whose candles light the tulip tree?
What is this subtle alchemy,
That builds an altar in one night
And touches the green boughs with light?
Look at the shaped leaves below
And see the scissor-marks they show,
As if a tailor had cut fine
The marking of their every line!

These are no leaves of prudery
Hiding what all eyes should see;
No Adam and no Eve lie hid
Below this leafy coverlid:
The long limbs of that flower-hid girl
Would need no leaves to twist and curl,

The markings of that leaf-hid boy
Want no flowers to mar and cloy.

And so these cut leaves and their lights
Live only for the tulip-rites
At this altar of bright fires
Sweet-scented lest their ardor tires;
Leaf, and flower, and scent are all
Alive for this lit interval:
Between two winters are they born
To make great summer seem forlorn.

### KINGCUPS

When poetry walked the live, spring wood,
Hid, ghostlike, in the leaves' green hood
She came to a slant fence of sun,
Whose golden timbers, one by one,
Trod into a marsh's toils
And here she stayed her flowery spoils;
But pitying the marshes' plight
She shook her lap and wide and bright
Great kingcups to that waste she threw
Where nothing lived and nothing grew;
Now, where poetry passed, there stays
The light of suns, the fire of days,
And these cups for kings to hold
Make summer with their wide-eyed gold.

### THE RIVER GOD

Leap out, chill water, over reeds and brakes,
Flash bright your sword
Out of my hand that never shakes,
Your voice rings louder than my whispered word,
For my song is but a murmur down the wind and water
No louder than the leaves that make my chequered shade,
Cooling the bank on which I'm laid.
My urn I move not, lest the blade may break,
Its round lip no more dropping water,
When this, my river, at its source will die
And sinking through the sand will bare each daughter,
Born of this glassy world, though now they lie
On the green bank high above that falling flood,
And wait like snow for sun or rain to move them.
I could not help them, were my stream to stop,
Until it springs again from out my urn,
But now it floods the pool and wells up high,
Sparkling like the sun's gold eye,

While from this plenitude it flows away
And hides those nymphs again below its glass.
Heaped on the hills, till with the sun they flow,
Safe runs the river now made sure with snow,
Snow, as those nymphs cool, as white my locks,
Which, while they also fall, tell time like clocks.

# Richard Hughes

RICHARD HUGHES was born in 1900 of a Welsh family settled in England. Educated at Charterhouse School and Oriel College, Oxford, his first play, *The Sisters' Tragedy,* was produced in London in 1922 while Hughes was still an undergraduate. In the same year, his first volume of poems, *Gypsy-Night,* appeared and before he graduated he was poetry-critic to the London *Saturday Westminster* and contributor to leading periodicals. He traveled extensively in Europe, North Africa, and America, often on foot, and has, he confesses, "a slight amateur knowledge of Balkan revolutions and seamanship."

Hughes began his career as a poet although his reputation was made by two dramas. The first of these has been mentioned; the other, composed in his twenties, was a comedy praised by Shaw and selected with works of Chekhov and Pirandello as "one of the three most important productions in London in seven years."

*Gypsy-Night* (1922) marked the début of a poet with acute sensibility, a precocious apprehension emphasized by the short stories in *A Moment of Time* (1925). After a silence of three years, Hughes published his first full-length novel, *The Innocent Voyage* (1929), published in England as *A High Wind in Jamaica.* This tale is an accomplishment in an untried genre. Upon a basis of traditional melodrama, including pirates and kidnaping, Hughes has constructed a story wholly unexpected, an unromantic romance, where the psychological reënforces the fantastic and where the union of cut-throats and children is convincing, delicate and, at the same time, horrible. Modern writing has produced several techniques for dealing fancifully with the commonplace; Hughes has developed a realistic way of handling the extraordinary.

This gift of familiarizing the unusual is of paramount service to his poetry. Chekhov counseled writers to cease being insincere about the moon and say what they really felt about a rain-puddle. But, Hughes implies, one can also be faithful to subject and self, when writing about the moon, or the mad immortal unicorn, or the elephant-swallowing roc, or inditing meditative and ecstatic odes to vision, or transfixing the windlike passing of Time. Such subjects brighten the pages of *Confessio Juvenis* (1926) which, as its title indicates, collects Hughes' early work. But if it is a poet's eye which rolls toward these strangenesses, it is his mind which carries them off in a fine frenzy.

Besides three privately printed volumes, Hughes is the author of some seven books. His collected *Plays* were issued in 1928 and his edition of John Skelton's poems appeared in 1924.

### INVOCATION TO THE MUSE

Fair maiden, fair maiden,
 Come spin for me:
Come spin till you're laden
 Though hard it may be.

'Tis an honor and glory
 To be a king's maid,
Though (I'll not tell a story)
 You won't be well paid.
                          *Aetat. 6*

### TRAMP

*(The Bath Road, June)*

When a brass sun staggers above the sky,
When feet cleave to boots, and the tongue's dry,
And sharp dust goads the rolling eye
Come thoughts of wine and dancing thoughts of girls:
They shiver their white arms, and the head whirls,
And noon light is hid in their dark curls;
Then noon feet stumble, and head swims,
Till out shines the sun, and the thought dims;
And death, for blood, runs in the weak limbs.

To fall on flints in the shade of tall nettles
Gives easy sleep as a bed of rose petals,
And dust drifting from the highway
As light a coverlet as down may.
The myriad feet of many-sized flies
May not open those tired eyes.

But the first wind of night
Twitches the coverlet away quite:
The first wind and large first rain,
Flickers the dry pulse to life again,
Flickers the lids burning on the eyes:
Come sudden flashes of the slipping skies:
Hunger, oldest visionary,
Hides a devil in a tree,
Hints a glory in the clouds,
Fills the crooked air with crowds
Of ivory sightless demons singing—
Eyes start: straightens back:
Limbs stagger and crack:
But brain flies, brain soars
Up, where the Sky roars
Upon the backs of cherubim:
Brain rockets up to Him.

Body gives another twist
To the slack waist-band;
In agony clenches fist
Till the nails bite the hand.
Body floats light as air,
With rain in its sparse hair.

Brain returns; and he would tell
The things he has seen well:

But Body will not stir his lips:
So Mind and Body come to grips
And deadly each hates the other
As his treacherous blood-brother.

Yet no sight, no sound shows
How the struggle goes.

I sink at last faint in the wet gutter;
So many words to speak that the tongue cannot utter.

### LOVER'S REPLY TO GOOD ADVICE

Could you bid an acorn
When in earth it heaves
On Time's backward wing be borne
To forgotten leaves:
Could you quiet Noah's flood
To an essence rare,
Or bid the roaring wind
Confine in his lair:

Could round the iron shell
When the spark was in it
Hold gun-powder so well
That it never split:
Had you reins for the sun,
And curb and spur,
Held you God in a net
So He might not stir:

Then might you take this thing,
Then strangle it, kill:
By weighing, considering,
Conform it to will:
As man denied his Christ
Deny it, mock, betray—
But being Seed, Wind, God,
It bears all away.

ON TIME

Unhurried as a snake I saw Time glide
Out of the shape of his material frame:
I, who am part of Time's material name,
Saw that unhurried serpent quietly slide
Through a straight crack in his material side
Between a prince and a stone: flicker, and presently coil,
A small bright worm about a stalk of fennel;
While light stood still as spar, and smell
Spread like a fan, sound hung festooned, and toil
Rose balanced and patterned like a storied palace
Whose wild tons grapple in immovable grace;
While laughter sat on a rustic seat with tears
And watched the corn-sheaves lean across the plow:
Ah! then what wind across the nodding years!
What ecstasies upon the bough
Sang, like a fountain to its peers:
And in the meadows what deep-rooted men
Flowered their lovely faces in the grass,
Where death, like a butterfly of dark-colored glass,
Flitted and sipped, and sipped again!


BURIAL OF THE SPIRIT

OF A YOUNG POET

Dead hangs the fruit on that tall tree:
The lark in my cold hand is dead.
What meats his funeral stars decree
By their own light I've spread:
The bearded fog among the leaves
Too sad to move, excludes the air:
No bursting seed this stiff soil heaves,
Nor ever will again, when we have laid him there.

Then come, ye silent wheels of fire,
Ye birds among the tulip-trees,
And let your brilliancy conspire
In rings of visual threnodies:
And thou, heart-breaking nightingale
Who phoenix-like forever burnst
In thine own voice, oh Philomel
Let not thy tuneful flame now fail,
But burn in it this spirit pale
Which once was grand, but now to naught, to nothing-naught returns.

# Roy Campbell

ROY CAMPBELL was born in Durban, Natal, South Africa, in 1902. After marriage to Mary Garman in 1922, he became active—evidently too active—in South African affairs, for in 1926 he was compelled to come to England where he has since lived.

*The Flaming Terrapin* appeared in 1922. It was at once apparent that a poet of unusual vitality had come out of the Colonies. Campbell had chosen a huge theme and he had sufficient vigor to cope with it. The poem is a broad allegory: The ark of Noah plunges through terror and tempest carrying with it all of humanity. Unlike the Biblical vessel, this ark does not merely float; it is pulled along, swept to its goal by a tremendous saurian, blood brother to Leviathan, a Flaming Terrapin, which is the symbol of the all-suffering, all-surviving power of persistence. It is this monster, the life-force, which brings the ark to a richer Ararat.

So much for the theme. The reader, however, is scarcely aware of the philosophic content, for the lines sweep him on at such a pace that he is conscious of little except the momentum of the verse, the bright concatenation of figures, and a general sense of exuberance. The headlong speed may be accounted a vice, but Campbell's poetic vices and virtues are inseparable. Both proceed from prodigality; epithet and emotion rush forward in continual and creative excitement.

*The Wayzgoose* (1928) is a more local and less arousing work. Satirizing conditions in South Africa, it limits not only Campbell's audience but his own spirit, for this poet needs amplitude for his effects. The subsequent poetry is in the early, gustier vein with a new control. "Tristan Da Cunha" and "The Palm" display less alacrity and violence than *The Flaming Terrapin,* but contain much of its lavish energy. "The Palm" is particularly successful in its combinations of assonance and interior rhyming. In addition, the new poems have a condensed power which dignifies the sometimes too crashing effects in *Adamastor* (1930), the satirical "Charlotade," *The Georgiad* (1931), and *Flowering Reeds* (1933). The color is still sometimes too crude, the imagery too theatrical, but there can be little doubt of the poetic authority in this vigorous, even violent, work.

## ·THE ZEBRAS

From the dark woods that breathe of fallen showers,
Harnessed with level rays in golden reins,
The zebras draw the dawn across the plains
Wading knee-deep among the scarlet flowers.
The sunlight, zithering their flanks with fire,
Flashes between the shadows as they pass
Barred with electric tremors through the grass
Like wind along the gold strings of a lyre.

Into the flushed air snorting rosy plumes
That smolder round their feet in drifting fumes,

With dove-like voices call the distant fillies,
While round the herds the stallion wheels his flight,
Engine of beauty volted with delight,
To roll his mare among the trampled lilies.

### TRISTAN DA CUNHA

Snore in the foam: the night is vast and blind,
The blanket of the mist around your shoulders,
Sleep your old sleep of rock, snore in the wind,
Snore in the spray! The storm your slumber lulls,
His wings are folded on your nest of bowlders
As on their eggs the gray wings of your gulls.

No more as when, ten thousand years ago,
You hissed a giant cinder from the ocean—
Around your rocks you furl the shawling snow,
Half sunk in your own darkness, vast and grim,
And round you on the deep with surly motion
Pivot your league-long shadow as you swim.

Why should you haunt me thus,but that I know
My surly heart is in your own displayed,
Round whom such wastes in endless circuit flow,
Whose hours in such a gloomy compass run—
A dial with its league-long arm of shade
Slowly revolving to the moon and sun.

My heart has sunk, like your gray fissured crags,
By its own strength o'ertoppled and betrayed:
I too have burned the wind with fiery flags,
Who now am but a roost for empty words—
An island of the sea whose only trade
Is in the voyages of its wandering birds.

Did you not, when your strength became your pyre,
Deposed and tumbled from your flaming tower,
Awake in gloom from whence you sank in fire
To find Antaeus-like, more vastly grown,
A throne in your own darkness, and a power
Sheathed in the very coldness of your stone?

Your strength is that you have no hope or fear,
You march before the world without a crown:
The nations call you back, you do not hear:
The cities of the earth grow gray behind you,
You will be there when their great flames go down
And still the morning in the van will find you.

You march before the continents: you scout
In front of all the earth: alone you scale
The masthead of the world, a lorn look-out,

Waving the snowy flutter of your spray
And gazing back in infinite farewell
To suns that sink, and shores that fade away.

From your gray tower what long regrets you fling
To where, along the low horizon burning,
The great swan-breasted seraphs soar and sing,
And suns go down, and trailing splendors dwindle,
And sails on lonely errands unreturning,
Glow with a gold no sunrise can rekindle.

Turn to the Night, these flames are not for you
Whose steeple for the thunder swings its bells:
Gray Memnon, to the tempest only true,
Turn to the night, turn to the shadowing foam,
And let your voice, the saddest of farewells,
With sullen curfew toll the gray wings home.

The wind your mournful syren haunts the gloom:
The rocks, spray-clouded, are your signal-guns
Whose stony niter, puffed with flying spume,
Rolls forth in grim salute your broadside hollow,
Over the gorgeous burials of suns,
To sound the tocsin of the storms that follow.

Plunge forward; like a ship to battle hurled,
Slip the long cables of the failing light,
The level rays that moor you to the world:
Sheathed in your armor of eternal frost,
Plunge forward, in the thunder of the fight
To lose yourself as I would fain be lost.

Exiled, like you, and severed from my race
By the cold ocean of my own disdain,
Do I not freeze in such a wintry space,
Do I not travel through a storm as vast
And rise at times, victorious from the main,
To fly the sunrise at my shattered mast?

Your path is but a desert where you reap
Only the bitter knowledge of your soul,
You fish with nets of seaweed in the deep
As fruitlessly as I with nets of rhyme,
Yet forth you stride: yourself the way, the goal,
The surges are your strides, your path is time.

Hurled by what aim to what tremendous range!
A missile from the great sling of the past
Your passage leaves its track of death and change
And ruin on the world: you fly beyond,
Leaping the current of the ages vast
As lightly as a pebble skims a pond.

The years are undulations in your flight
Whose awful motion we can only guess:
Too swift for sense, too terrible for sight,
We only know how fast behind you darken
Our days like lonely beacons of distress:
We know that you stride on and will not hearken.

Now in the eastern sky the fairest planet
Pierces the dying wave with dangled spear,
And in the whirring hollows of your granite
That vaster Sea, to which you are a shell,
Sighs with a ghostly rumor like the drear
Moan of the nightwind in a hollow cell.

We shall not meet again: over the wave
Our ways divide, and yours is straight and endless—
But mine is short and crooked to the grave:
Yet what of these dark crowds, amid whose flow
I battle like a rock, aloof and friendless—
Are not their generations, vague and endless,
The waves, the strides, the feet on which I go?

FROM "THE FLAMING TERRAPIN"

## Part I

Maternal Earth stirs redly from beneath
Her blue sea-blanket and her quilt of sky,
A giant Anadyomene from the sheath
And chrysalis of darkness; till we spy
Her vast barbaric haunches, furred with trees,
Stretched on the continents, and see her hair
·Combed in a surf of fire along the breeze
To curl about the dim sierras, where
Faint snow-peaks catch the sun's far-swiveled beams:
And, tinder to his rays, the mountain-streams
Kindle, and volleying with a thunder-stroke
Out of their roaring gullies, burst in smoke
To shred themselves as fine as women's hair,
And hoop gay rainbows on the sunlit air.
Winnowed by radiant eagles, in whose quills
Sing the swift gales, and on whose waving plumes
Flashing sunbeams ignite—the towering hills
Yearn to the sun, rending the misty fumes
That clogged their peaks, and from each glistening spire
Fling to the winds their rosy fleece of fire.
Far out to sea the gales with savage sweep
Churning the water, waken drowsy fins
Huge fishes to propel from monstrous sleep,
That spout their pride as the red day begins,
"We are the great volcanoes of the deep!"

Now up from the intense creative Earth
Spring her strong sons: the thunder of their mirth
Vibrates upon the shining rocks and spills
In floods of rolling music on the hills.
Action and flesh cohere in one clean fusion
Of force with form: the very ethers breed
Wild harmonies of song: the frailest reed
Holds shackled thunder in its heart's seclusion.
And every stone that lines my lonely way,
Sad tongueless nightingale without a wing,
Seems on the point of rising up to sing
And donning scarlet for its dusty gray!

How often have I lost this fervent mood,
And gone down dingy thoroughfares to brood
On evils like my own from day to day;
"Life is a dusty corridor," I say,
"Shut at both ends." But far across the plain,
Old Ocean growls and tosses his gray mane,
Pawing the rocks in all his old unrest
Or lifting lazily on some white crest
His pale foam-feathers for the moon to burn—
Then to my veins I feel new sap return,
Strength tightens up my sinews long grown dull,
And in the old charred crater of the skull
Light strikes the slow somnambulistic mind
And sweeps her forth to ride the rushing wind,
And stamping on the hill-tops high in air,
To shake the golden bonfire of her hair.

This sudden strength that catches up men's souls
And rears them up like giants in the sky,
Giving them fins where the dark ocean rolls,
And wings of eagles when the whirlwinds fly,
Stands visible to me in its true self
(No spiritual essence of wing'd elf
Like Ariel on the empty winds to spin).
I see him as a mighty Terrapin,
Rafting whole islands on his stormy back,
Built of strong metals molten from the black
Roots of the inmost earth: a great machine,
Thoughtless and fearless, governing the clean
System of active things: the winds and currents
Are his primeval thoughts: the raging torrents
Are moods of his, and men who do great deeds
Are but the germs his awful fancy breeds.

For when the winds have ceased their ghostly speech
And the long waves roll moaning from the beach,
The Flaming Terrapin that towed the Ark
Rears up his hump of thunder on the dark,

And like a mountain, seamed with rocky scars,
Crinkles white rings, as from its ancient sleep
Into a foam of life he wakes the Deep.
His was the crest that from the angry sky
Tore down the hail: he made the bowlders fly
Like balls of paper, splintered icebergs, hurled
Lassoes of dismal smoke around the world,
And like a bunch of crisp and crackling straws,
Coughed the sharp lightning from his craggy jaws.
His was the eye that blinked beyond the hill
After the fury of the flood was done,
And breaching from the bottom, cold and still,
Leviathan reared up to greet the Sun.
Perched on the stars around him in the air,
White angels rinsed the moonlight from their hair,
And the drowned trees into new flowers unfurled
As it sank dreaming down upon the world.
As he rolled by, all evil things grew dim.
The Devil, who had scoffed, now slunk from him
And sat in Hell, dejected and alone,
Rasping starved teeth against an old dry bone.

Before the coral reared its sculptured fern
Or the pale shellfish, swinging in the waves
With pointed steeples, had begun to turn
The rocks to shadowy cities—from dark caves
The mixed and drowsy poisons of the sea
Mixed their corrosive strength with horny stones,
And coaxed new substances from them to be
The ponderous material of his bones.
The waves by slow erosion did their part
Shaping his heavy bonework from the mass,
And in that pillared temple grew a heart
That branched with mighty veins, through which to pass
His blood, that, filtering the tangled mesh,
Built walls of gristle, clogged each hollow gap
With concrete vigor, till through bone and flesh
Flowed the great currents of electric sap.
While thunder clanging from the cloudy rack
With elemental hammers fierce and red,
Tempered the heavy target of his back,
And forged the brazen anvil of his head.

Freed from the age-long agonies of birth
This living galleon oars himself along
And roars his triumph over all the earth
Until the sullen hills burst into song.
His beauty makes a summer through the land,
And where he crawls upon the solid ground,
Gigantic flowers, exploding from the sand,
Spread fans of blinding color all around.

His voice has roused the amorphous mud to life—
Dust thinks: and tired of spinning in the wind,
Stands up to be a man and feel the strife
Of brute-thoughts in the jungle of his mind.
Bellerophon, the primal cowboy, first
Heard that wild summons on the stillness burst,
As, from the dusty mesa leaping free,
He slewed his white-winged broncho out to sea,
And shaking loose his flaming coils of hair,
Shot whistling up the smooth blue roads of air:
As he rose up, the moon with slanted ray
Ruled for those rapid hoofs a shining way,
And streaming from their caves, the sirens came
Riding on seals to follow him: the flame
Of their moon-tinseled limbs had flushed the dim
Green depths, and as when winds in Autumn skim
Gold acres, rustling plume with fiery plume,
Their long hair flickered skyward in the gloom,
Tossed to the savage rhythms of their tune.
Till, far across the world, the rising moon
Heard, ghost-like, in the embered evening sky
Their singing fade into a husky sigh,
And splashed with stars and dashed with stinging spray
The dandy of the prairies rode away!

That voice on Samson's mighty sinews rang
As on a harp's tense chords: each fiber sang
In all his being: rippling their strings of fire,
His nerves and muscles, like a wondrous lyre,
Vibrated to that sound; and through his brain
Proud thoughts came surging in a gorgeous train.
He rose to action, slew the grumbling bear,
Hauled forth the flustered lion from its lair
And swung him yelping skyward by the tail:
Tigers he mauled, with tooth and ripping nail
Rending their straps of fire, and from his track
Slithering like quicksilver, pouring their black
And liquid coils before his pounding feet,
He drove the livid mambas of deceit.
Oppression, like a starved hyena, sneaked
From his loud steps: Tyranny, vulture-beaked,
Rose clapping iron wings, and in a cloud
Of smoke and terror, wove its own dark shroud,
As he strode by and in his tossing hair,
Rippled with sunshine, sang the morning air.

Like a great bell clanged in the winds of Time,
Linking the names of heroes chime by chime
That voice rolled on, and as it filled the night
Strong men rose up, thrilled with the huge delight

Of their own energy. Upon the snows
Of Ararat gigantic Noah rose,
Stiffened for fierce exertion, like the thong
That strings a bow before its arrow strong
Sings on the wind; and from his great fists hurled
Red thunderbolts to purify the world.

## THE PALM

Blistered and dry was the desert I trod
When out of the sky with the step of a god,
Victory-vanned with her feathers out-fanned,
The palm tree alighting my journey delayed
And spread me, inviting, her carpet of shade.
Vain were evasions, though urgent my quest,
And there as the guests of her lovely persuasions
To lie in the shade of her branches was best.
Like a fountain she played, spilling plume over plume in
A golden cascade for the winds to illumine,
Ascending in brilliance and falling in shade,
And spurning the ground with a tiptoe resilience
Danced to the sound of the music she made.
Her voice intervened on my shadowed seclusion
Like the whispered intrusion of seraph or fiend,
In its tone was the hiss of the serpent's wise tongue,
But soft as the kiss of a lover it stung—
"Unstrung is your lute? For despair are you silent?
Am I not an island in oceans as mute?
Around me the thorns of the desert take root;
Though I spring from the rock of a region accurst,
Yet fair is the daughter of hunger and thirst
Who sings like the water the valleys have nursed,
And rings her blue shadow as deep and as cool
As the heavens of azure that sleep on a pool.
And you, who so soon by the toil were undone,
Could you guess through what horrors my beauty had won
Ere I crested the noon as the bride of the sun?
The roots are my anchor struck fast in the hill,
The higher I hanker, the deeper they drill,
Through the red mortar their claws interlock
To ferret the water through warrens of rock.
Each inch of my glory was wrenched with a groan,
Corroded with fire from the base of my throne
And drawn like a wire from the heart of a stone:
Though I soar in the height with a shape of delight
Uplifting my stem like the string of a kite,
Yet still must each grade of my climbing be told
And still from the summit my measure I hold,
Sounding the azure with plummet of gold,
Partaking the strain of the heavenward pride
That soars me away from the earth I deride;

Though my stem be a rein that would tether me down
And fasten a chain on the height of my crown,
Yet through its tense nerve do I measure my might,
The strain of its curb is the strength of my flight:
And when by the hate of the hurricane blown
It doubles its forces with fibers that groan,
Exulting I ride in the tower of my pride
To feel that the strength of the blast is my own. . . .
Rest under my branches, breathe deep of my balm
From the hushed avalanches of fragrance and calm,
For suave is the silence that poises the palm.

The wings of the egrets are silken and fine,
But hushed with the secrets of Eden are mine:
Your spirit that grieves like the wind in my leaves
Shall be robbed of its care by those whispering thieves
To study my patience and hear, the day long,
The soft foliations of sand into song—
For bitter and cold though it rasp to my root,
Each atom of gold is the chance of a fruit,
The sap is the music, the stem is the flute,
And the leaves are the wings of the seraph I shape
Who dances, who springs in a golden escape,
Out of the dust and the drought of the plain,
To sing with the silver hosannahs of rain."

### AUTUMN

I love to see, when leaves depart,
The clear anatomy arrive,
Winter, the paragon of art,
That kills all forms of life and feeling
Save what is pure and will survive.

Already now the clanging chains
Of geese are harnessed to the moon:
Stripped are the great sun-clouding planes:
And the dark pines, their own revealing,
Let in the needles of the noon.

Strained by the gale the olives whiten
Like hoary wrestlers bent with toil
And, with the vines, their branches lighten
To brim our vats where summer lingers
In the red froth and sun-gold oil.

Soon on our hearth's reviving pyre
Their rotted stems will crumble up:
And like a ruby, panting fire,
The grape will redden on your fingers
Through the lit crystal of the cup.

ON SOME SOUTH AFRICAN NOVELISTS

You praise the firm restraint with which they write—
    I'm with you there, of course.
They use the snaffle and the curb all right;
    But where's the bloody horse?

# C. Day Lewis

C. (CECIL) DAY LEWIS was born April 27, 1904, at Ballintubber, Queens County,
Ireland. He was educated at Sherbourne School and Wadham College, Oxford,
where he became affiliated with Stephen Spender, W. H. Auden, and others of the
post-war group. He taught at the Junior School of Cheltenham College and wrote
with increasing rapidity and purpose.

There were two early publications (*Beechen Vigils* and *Country Comets*) which
were derivative and received little attention. *Transitional Poem* (1929) is Day Lewis'
first serious bid for notice. The early influences are not altogether discarded, but it
is immediately evident that a new and indubitably lyric voice is being sounded.
This is "nature poetry," but nature poetry sharply differentiated from the philo-
sophic-meditative manner of Wordsworth and the tired detachment of the Georgians. Day Lewis is no mere onlooker, he is a passionate participant; there is courage
as well as color in his lines, and even the awkward passages are redeemed by a
challenging vision.

That vision is amplified, sometimes distorted, and finally explicated in *From
Feathers to Iron* (1931) and *The Magnetic Mountain* (1933), both of which, with
*Transitional Poem,* were assembled in *Poems 1929-1933,* published in America in
1935. Since the three young English poets were printed almost simultaneously in
this country, Day Lewis was continually linked with Spender and Auden in the
public press. Actually the so-called "triumvirate" was composed of three different
types of poet. Auden is satirical, experimental, and often (except to those who understand his private parables) incomprehensible; Spender is rhapsodic, sometimes
sentimental, and usually forthright; Lewis is almost continuously lyrical and candid.
Although he, too, plays with internal rhyme and concealed assonance, he is less
concerned than Auden with craftsmanship; although he shares Spender's political
convictions, he does not lose himself, as Spender sometimes does, in rhetoric. Yet
if he is the most dependable he is the least original of the three. He has not yet
outgrown his influences; one does not have to read closely to recognize the accents
of Gerard Manley Hopkins, Wilfred Owen, T. S. Eliot, most of all W. H. Auden,
to all of whom C. Day Lewis pays credit. There are even moments (as in the poem
"You'll be leaving soon and it's up to you boys") which sound strangely like Robert
W. Service and Rudyard Kipling's "If" turned upside down. It should also be said
that his social sentiments have little to do with the final effect of his poetry; it is,
poetically speaking, unimportant that the author has chosen communism for his
faith rather than the more profitable fascism. He knows that in the end a poet is

measured by his poetry, not by his policies; that, although Southey was an ardent believer in the French Revolution, Southey means nothing to us, and readers of the *Ode on the Intimations of Immortality* do not care when or why Wordsworth ceased to be a liberal. But Day Lewis also knows that a poet must have a creed; and a belief in the dignity and possible brotherhood of man is certainly no more to be deplored than a belief in the sacredness of the Georgian Squirearchy and its incorporated nightingales. As a matter of record, the best of his poems are the least protesting ones.

This poet is still fluctuating between a tradition which he distrusts, but in which he is quite at home, and a conviction which his mind applauds but his imagination has not yet fully accepted. From the conflict no less than half a dozen serene, illuminating, and indignant lyrics are born, lyrics which will find their way into even the most cautious anthologies. It is his certainties, coming after a generation of negativism, which matter, not his arbitrary symbols of "kestrel," "airman" and "magnetic mountain" (for imagination, poet, and the coöperative commonwealth). It is not the fighting figures and stretched metaphors, straining under the demands of their author, but the athletic belief, the alert spirit, which breaks through to music spontaneous and bitter-sweet.

*A Time to Dance* (1935) emphasizes this. It apostrophizes the spirit

> For those who had the power,
> Unhesitating whether to kill or cure:
> Those who were not afraid
> To dam the estuary or start the forest fire:
> Whose hearts were filled
> With enthusiasm as with a constant wind. . . .
> There need be neither obituary nor wreath,
> Accomplices of death. . . .
> Their spirit shall be blowing out of the sunrise,
> Their veins our rivers, their bones our bread.

The title-poem, however, is something of a disappointment. It is ambitiously "symphonic," but its program is more impressive than the performance, and the last movement, a jumble of crude parodies, is awkward as humor, ineffective as satire. Far better are the lyrics which occupy the first half of *A Time to Dance;* the prevailing motif is "the conflict between the past and the future of the individual," particularly Day Lewis' statement of his own uncertain position.

Day Lewis has also written a book-length essay entitled *A Hope for Poetry,* which is by far the best analysis of post-war poetry that has yet appeared. It is more than a timely appraisal. Besides preparing a background for his own group and its "ancestors," the poet manages to say many things about the poetic art which reveal an unpretentious and clear authority.

### NEARING AGAIN THE LEGENDARY ISLE

> Nearing again the legendary isle
> Where sirens sang and mariners were skinned,
> We wonder now what was there to beguile
> That such stout fellows left their bones behind.

Those chorus-girls are surely past their prime,
Voices grow shrill and paint is wearing thin,
Lips that sealed up the sense from gnawing time
Now beg the favor with a graveyard grin.

We have no flesh to spare and they can't bite,
Hunger and sweat have stripped us to the bone;
A skeleton crew we toil upon the tide
And mock the theme-song meant to lure us on:

No need to stop the ears, avert the eyes
From purple rhetoric of evening skies.


## REST FROM LOVING AND BE LIVING

Rest from loving and be living.
Fallen is fallen past retrieving
The unique flyer dawn's dove
Arrowing down feathered with fire.

Cease denying, begin knowing.
Comes peace this way, here comes renewing
With dower of bird and bud, knocks
Loud on winter wall on death's door.

Here's no meaning but of morning.
Naught soon of night but stars remaining,
Sink lower, fade, as dark womb
Recedes creation will step clear.


## NOW SHE IS LIKE THE WHITE TREE-ROSE

Now she is like the white tree-rose
That takes a blessing from the sun:
Summer has filled her veins with light,
And her warm heart is washed with noon.

Or as a poplar, ceaselessly
Gives a soft answer to the wind:
Cool on the light her leaves lie sleeping,
Folding a column of sweet sound.

Powder the stars. Forbid the night
To wear those brilliants for a brooch
So soon, dark death, you may close down
The mines that made this beauty rich.

Her thoughts are pleiads, stooping low
O'er glades where nightingale has flown:
And like the luminous night around her
She has at heart a certain dawn.

## DO NOT EXPECT AGAIN A PHOENIX HOUR

Do not expect again a phoenix hour,
The triple-towered sky, and dove complaining,
Sudden the rain of gold and heart's first ease
Tranced under trees by the eldritch light of sundown.

By a blazed trail our joy will be returning:
One burning hour throws light a thousand ways,
And hot blood stays into familiar gestures.
The best years wait, the body's plenitude.

Consider then, my lover, this is the end
Of the lark's ascending, the hawk's unearthly hover:
Spring season is over soon and first heatwave;
Grave-browed with cloud ponders the huge horizon.

Draw up the dew. Swell with pacific violence.
Take shape in silence. Grow as the clouds grew.
Beautiful brood the cornlands, and you are heavy;
Leafy the boughs—they also hide big fruit.

## CHIEFLY TO MIND APPEARS

Chiefly to mind appears
That hour on Silverhowe
When evening's lid hung low
And the sky was about our ears.
Buoyed between fear and love
We watched in eastward form
The armadas of the storm
And sail superbly above;
So near, they'd split and founder
On the least jag of sense,
One false spark fire the immense
Broadside the confounding thunder.
They pass, give not a salvo,
And in their rainy wash
We hear the horizons crash
With monitors of woe.

Only at highest power
Can love and fear become
Their equilibrium,
And in that eminent hour
A virtue is made plain
Of passionate cleavage
Like the hills' cutting edge
When the sun sets to rain.
This is the single mind,

This is the star-solved equation
Of life with life's negation:
A deathless cell designed
To demonstrate death's act,
Which, the more surely it moves
To earth's influence, but proves
Itself the more intact.

## TEMPT ME NO MORE

Tempt me no more; for I
Have known the lightning's hour,
The poet's inward pride,
The certainty of power.

Bayonets are closing round.
I shrink; yet I must wring
A living from despair
And out of steel a song.

Though song, though breath be short,
I'll share not the disgrace
Of those that ran away
Or never left the base.

Comrades, my tongue can speak
No comfortable words;
Calls to a forlorn hope
Give work and not rewards.

Oh keep the sickle sharp
And follow still the plow:
Others may reap, though some
See not the winter through.

Father who endest all,
Pity our broken sleep;
For we lie down with tears
And waken but to weep.

And if our blood alone
Will melt this iron earth,
Take it. It is well spent
Easing a savior's birth.

### THE CONFLICT

I sang as one
Who on a tilting deck sings
To keep their courage up, though the wave
   hangs
That shall cut off their sun.

As storm-cocks sing,
Flinging their natural answer in the wind's
   teeth,
And care not if it is waste of breath
Or birth-carol of spring.

As ocean-flyer clings
To height, to the last drop of spirit driving on
While yet ahead is land to be won
And work for wings.

Singing I was at peace,
Above the clouds, outside the ring:
For sorrow finds a swift release in song
And pride its poise.

Yet living here,
As one between two massing powers I live
Whom neutrality cannot save
Nor occupation cheer.

None such shall be left alive:
The innocent wing is soon shot down,
And private stars fade in the blood-red dawn
Where two worlds strive.

The red advance of life
Contracts pride, calls out the common blood,
Beats song into a single blade,
Makes a depth-charge of grief.

Move then with new desires,
For where we used to build and love
Is no man's land, and only ghosts can live
Between two fires.

# Peter Quennell

PETER QUENNELL was born March 5, 1905, in Kent. He was educated at Berkhamstead Grammar School and at Balliol College, Oxford, where he spent two years, and where he was co-editor of *Oxford Poetry*. He made "the customary pilgrimages" to Greece and the Balkans, and since 1927 has lived in London.

*Poems* (1926) appeared before Quennell was twenty-one years old, four of the poems being "very early"—"Procne," for example, having been written at the age of sixteen. Quennell's verse is wholly unlike that of his living compatriots, although American readers will detect a similarity to the verbal elegances of Wallace Stevens. It is as near the abstract as verse can come and still depend on words. Here language flowers of itself, feeding automatically on its own air; image suggests image, and associations grow freely on seemingly unrelated suggestions. In "The Divers" and "Leviathan," among others, the poetry wanders far from common experience or recognizable emotions or, for that matter, its own subject. But it is never less than poetry. Although the figures flowing into each other have the uncertain, fluid outlines of dream pictures, the musical progression is clear.

It is as music, first of all, that Quennell's poetry succeeds. His accomplishment is the greater since, without the aid of rhyme or definite rhythm, he achieves melodies intangible but more original than lightly summoned tunes. The actors in his verse are vague, the happenings remote and unreal, yet the intent is never false, and the effect is a set of nicely adjusted modulations and strange harmonics. It is, in essence, a poetry of shock, but shock without eccentricity, smoothed and almost without surprise.

As an essayist, Quennell has developed slowly but with increasing surety. His *Baudelaire and the Symbolists* (1930) contains five essays outlining the stream which sprang from Baudelaire and which swayed not only French literature but determined in no inconsiderable degree the course of English poetry during and after the Eighteen Nineties.

Quennell made his most successful bid for popularity as biographer. Readers and reviewers united to praise the wit and vitality of his *Byron: The Years of Fame* published in 1935.

### PROCNE

So she became a bird and bird-like danced
On a long sloe-bough, treading the silver blossom
With a bird's lovely feet,
And shaken blossoms fell into the hands
Of sunlight, and he held them for a moment
And let them drop.
And in the autumn Procne came again
And leapt upon the crooked sloe-bough singing
And the dark berries winked like earth-dimmed beads,
As the branch swung beneath her dancing feet.

### THE DIVERS

Ah, look,
How sucking their last sweetness from the air
These divers run upon the pale sea verge;
An evening air so smooth my hand could round
And grope a circle of the hollow sky
Without a harshness or impediment.

Look now,
How they run cowering and each unknots
A rag, a girdle twisted on his loins,
Stands naked, quivered in the cool of night.

As boldest lovers will tire presently,
When dawn dries up a radiance on the limbs,
And lapse to common sleep,
To the deep tumult of habitual dreams,
Each sighing, with loosened limbs, as if regretfully,
Gives up his body to the foamless surge.

Water combs out his body, and he sinks
Beyond all form and sound.
Only the blood frets on,
Grown fearful, in a shallow dissonance.

Water strains on his hair and drums upon his flank,
Consumes his curious track
And straight or sinuous path
Dissolves as swift, impermanent as light.

Still his strange purpose drives him, like a beam,
Like the suspended shaft of cavern-piercing sun;
And, hardier still,
With wavering hands, divides the massive gloom,—
A vast caress through which he penetrates,
Or obscure death withdrawing
Veil upon veil,
Discovering new darkness and profounder terror.

"Consider you your loss,
For now what strength of foot or hand
Can take you by the narrow way you came
Through the clear darkness up again and up.
Watch a procession of the living days,
Where dawn and evening melt so soft together
As wine in water, or milk shed in water,
Filming and clouding into even dullness."

"Who weeps me now with pulse of noisy tears,
Who strikes the breast?
If I regret among the flowing weed,
My regret is
Not vocal, cannot pierce to hidden day,
Momentary, soon quenched, like a strangled flame."

### LEVIATHAN

#### (Second Section)

A music met Leviathan returning,
While the still troubled waters of his passage
Danct every island like a lily head.
Through all the shadowed throats of the wide forest
His unnumbered monster children rode to greet him
On horses winged and dappled over like flowers.

Now huddled waves had lulled their bursting foam
And slight clouds laid their breasts upon the sea;
The sullen winds, head downward from the sky,
Solicited his movement on their viols.

And the palm trees, heat weary,
Chafing smooth limbs within a rinded shell,
Spoke of his coming with soft acclamation,
Like watchers long grown tired, languid and sorry:

"Look, how he comes"—as faint as whispering deer—
"What storm and state he brings." Then louder voices,
The unchaste turtles crying out with pleasure,
And badgers from the earth
Sprawled upon the rocks with animal laughter.

"The Cretan bull ferrying across the sea
Bore home no richer load;
In the reed forest of Eurotas' bank
That quivering swan, clapping strong wings together,
With harsh, sweet voice called out no keener marriage."

Then shrill response, as seeming from the air,
Invoking joy, summoning desire:

"Hither desires,
Coming as thick and hot as the press and hurry of blood
Striking the apse of the brain,
Ranging abroad, carrying your torches high,
Running as light and remote as a scattered cast of pearls."

Then antic spirits from the tulip trees:

"We must have tumblers like a wheel of fire.
We must have dancers moving their suave hands:
The tumblers strung backward like a hoop
Until they thrust vermilioned cheeks between their knees.
And the intricacy
Of sweet involving gayety,
And wine to warm our innocence,
Music to sooth the prickled sense,
Sounding like water or like ringing glass."

The mitered Queen of Heaven stirred on her broad, low throne,
Setting the lattice just so much ajar
That wandering airs from earth should cool the room,
Peered down on more-than-Leda and smoothed her wrinkled snood,
Crying to her Father-Spouse—"Dear Lord, how sweet she looks."
The clumsy hierarchies,
Wearied by their continual task of praise,
Rested wide heifer eyes upon her fallen lids.
Islanded in stars,
Even the keen Intelligences turned away
From the mathematic splendor of the spheres' incessant rolling chime.

Himself, the Father moved,
Traditional and vast,
Remembering fresher years,
Might have inclined his steeply pinnacled head,
But his more zealous son,
As neat as Thammuz, with smooth, pallid cheeks,
Sensing an evil, shut the casement fast.

✦

But I, remembering Atlantis, wept,
Remembering her paths and unswept flowers,
Clean beaches, patterned by a light sea wrack,
And the ruined halcyon nests that came on shore.

Tears, in their freedom, cloud the eyes,
Drowsing the sense.
Honey and poppy equally mixed together,
They cannot drug away or curtain off with sleep
Such pitiless disharmony of shapes.

# John Lehmann

JOHN LEHMANN was born at Bourne End by the Thames in June, 1907, and educated at Eton as a King's scholar, and at Trinity College, Cambridge. A brother of Rosamund Lehmann, the novelist, he has been in the publishing business and has lived much in Central Europe. He has (so he concludes a brief unpublished biographical note) "an American mother and strong political views, and is very fond of water."

Lehmann's work first commanded attention upon the appearance of four poems in *New Signatures* (1932) with Stephen Spender, W. H. Auden, C. Day Lewis, and other young poets, an anthology which contrasted vividly, almost violently, with *New English Poems,* published at the same time and which had contributions by such well-known poets as Harold Monro, Humbert Wolfe, W. W. Gibson, W. H. Davies. *New Signatures* was by far the more exciting collection; it roused the reader—even if it only roused him to protest—partly because of its frank experimentations and partly because of its extremities, but chiefly because it attempted to restore vigor of utterance to English poetry. The imagery was taken from contemporary life and most of the contributors to the new venture revolted from the traditional detachment of the artist, expressing their sympathy, even their solidarity, with the great mass of humanity. Curiously, this close attachment was not expressed in forthright declarations as the editor maintained, "in a clear reaction against esoteric poetry," but in a recondite allusiveness and a set of arbitrary "modern" symbols.

Lehmann's poetry was, like much of his confrères', tangential. It attained its object by circumlocution and suggestion. Superficially simple, the poems concealed meanings that baffled alert intelligences. The very simplicity was deceptive, for the statements uttered in a straightforward conversational tone were rarely as direct as they seem. Lehmann's recent work is less symbolistic and more "representative." Experiment and accomplishment alternate in *The Noise of History* (1934), and such a poem as "Crimea Red," written after a visit to Russia, declares itself without dubiety, even without decoration. In the best of Lehmann's poetry there is combined a richness of feeling and a restraint of phrase.

### TO PENETRATE THAT ROOM

To penetrate that room is my desire,
The extreme attic of the mind, that lies
Just beyond the last bend in the corridor.
Writing I do it. Phrases, poems are keys.
Loving's another way (but not so sure).
A fire's in there, I think, there's truth at last
Deep in a lumber-chest. Sometimes I'm near,
But draughts puff out the matches, and I'm lost.
Sometimes I'm lucky, find a key to turn,
Open an inch or two,—but always then
A bell rings, someone calls, or cries of "fire"
Arrest my hand when nothing's known or seen,
And running down the stairs again I mourn.

### LOOKING WITHIN

Looking within, I find no hint of green.
They say Spring comes in countries over there
With much-desired sleek buds and burst of leaves,
Release of sap, new songs; but travel's hard,
For though we try the bridges or the pass
The frontiers of this state are closely guarded,
Raised rifles daunt, and the government persuades
All's best at home,—go, cultivate the fields.
Yet still no delicate blade divides the furrows,
The pitted earth is waterless, the trees
Point black and jagged that no leaves adorn.
No break to freedom yet, but talk in corners.
All's well? We ponder wary: this the life
Rulers would make believe is fixed and good?
Passing the palace gates we notice now
Cracked windows gaping, rain that lashes through.
Are coffers coinless? Is he dead, the King?
The regiments come drumming through the square
Neat as machines, impose on muttering crowds;
Yet still no tip of green peers up the furrows,
The pitted earth is waterless. . . .
                              Who whispers?
No break to freedom yet?—There's time, there's time,

The King, I tell you, rotted years ago,
Shot through the lung before the war was over,
Your ground is barren, the poison gas that soaked
Too deeply through the clods denies all life,
No corn, no rash weeds' loveliness revives
Under morning's lifting mist,—leave, quickly leave
The empty acres and the splintered trunks,
Shoulder the household gods, and take the train
Eastward to land where scattered grain gives root,
Quickly before the sentries take their aim
Lynx-eyed along the frontier, at the stations,
Before they post you *Traitor* on the walls,
Plant spies in ports, and wire the Flying Squad—
But you'll be hours in flight by then, you'll find
A farm beyond their writ, where naked trees
Like columns to uphold the new-built world
Show gummy buds of leaves aflame in sun,
As frosts of Winter yield, and furrowed earth
Assents to labor of young harvest ears.

### CRIMEA RED

Their masses whiten the shore,
As the green-splashed blue water turns to rose
And Ai-Petri creeps over the sun,
Tatars and Russians, Mongols, Turks,
Twirling Spring flowers through the twilight,
Rippling out laughter, ease.

Their singing rises,
As the smoke of the mountain fire,
From the balconies of white villas
Like sculptured blooms among the cypress-groves
Their fathers built for half-savage princes
Day-dreaming of culture.

They have come
From the factories of Moscow and Siberia,
The machine stamping and molten metal
The swelling womb of their world,
From the farms they till in common
Those giant steppes of the North Caucasus,
To this coast of vineyards and roses
To the pine-sweet clinics and palace rest-homes
Breathing the sea.

In the new phase of history,
After the years of the enemy warships
And their brothers hurled from these rocks,
After the first epic of creation
They are taking their ease,

Laughing with flowers from white balconies
Streaming in white by the shore,
Free at last of their Fathers' achievement
Their hands will shape for strength to come,
In tomorrow's sun returning
To roaring wheel and workshop and red harvest.

# Louis MacNeice

LOUIS MAC NEICE was born September 12, 1907, in the North of Ireland. His family, however, came from the West of Ireland, so he is not to be designated an Orangeman. He was at Oxford, Merton College, from 1926 to 1930, when he married and moved to Birmingham.

His first volume, *Blind Fireworks* (1929), is more than an exhibit of the usual juvenilia, but the author dismisses it with the assurance that none of it will survive. The influence of Edith Sitwell (obvious in "Cradle Song") is here, but an alert mind is fashioning an idiom of its own. In the succeeding *Poems* published in 1935, the imaginative power is apparent. Like his immediate contemporaries, Mac-Neice prefers to spice the piquant half-rhyme with the traditional full vowel; like Auden and Spender, he uses the strictly contemporary scene. Like them, also, he adapts, turns, and generally "heightens" the ordinary speech of the day. It is in such poems as "Sunday Morning," "Morning Sun" and "Birmingham" that MacNeice, in common with a few others, points to a revival of vitality, a reliance on contemporary life, however complicated and difficult it may be.

### CRADLE SONG

The clock's untiring fingers wind the wool of darkness
And we all lie alone, having long outgrown our cradles
(Sleep, sleep, Miriam)
And the flames like faded ladies always unheeded simper
And all is troubledness.

Soft the wool, dark the wool
Is gathered slowly, wholly up
Into a ball, all of it.

And yet in the back of the mind, lulled all else,
There is something unsleeping, un-tamperable-with,
Something that whines and scampers
And like the ladies in the grate will not sleep nor forget itself,
Clawing at the wool like a kitten.

The clock's fingers wind, wind the wool of Lethe,
(Sleep, sleep, Miriam)
It glides across the floor drawn by hidden fingers

And the beast droops his head
And the fire droops its flounces
And winks a final ogle out of the fading embers
But no one pays attention;

This is too much, the flames say, insulted,
We who were once the world's beauties and now
No one pays attention
No one remembers us.

Sleep, sleep, Miriam.
And as for this animal of yours
He must be cradled also.
That he may not unravel this handiwork of forgetfulness.
That he may not philander with the flames before they die.

The world like a cradle rises and falls
On a wave of confetti and funerals
And sordor and stinks and stupid faces
And the deity making bored grimaces.

Oh what a muddle he has made of the wool,
(God will tomorrow have his hands full),
You must muzzle your beast, you must fasten him
For the whole of life—the interim.

Through the interim we pass
Everyone under an alias
Till they gather the strands of us together
And wind us up for ever and ever.

### SUNDAY MORNING

Down the road someone is practicing scales,
The notes like little fishes vanish with a wink of tails,
Man's heart expands to tinker with his car
For this is Sunday morning, Fate's great bazaar,
Regard these means as ends, concentrate on this Now,
And you may grow to music or drive beyond Hindhead anyhow,
Take corners on two wheels until you go so fast
That you can clutch a fringe or two of the windy past,
That you can abstract this day and make it to the week of time
A small eternity, a sonnet self-contained in rhyme.

But listen, up the road, something gulps, the church spire
Opens its eight bells out, skulls' mouths which will not tire
To tell how there is no music or movement which secures
Escape from the weekday time. Which deadens and endures.

## MUSEUMS

Museums offer us, running from among the buses,
A centrally heated refuge, parquet floors and sarcophaguses,
Into whose tall fake porches we hurry without a sound
Like a beetle under a brick that lies, useless, on the ground.
Warmed and cajoled by the silence the cowed cypher revives,
Mirrors himself in the cases of pots, paces himself by marble lives,
Makes believe it was he that was the glory that was Rome,
Soft on his cheek the nimbus of other people's martyrdom,
And then returns to the street, his mind an arena where sprawls
Any number of consumptive Keatses and dying Gauls.

## MORNING SUN

Shuttles of trains going north, going south, drawing threads of blue
The shining of the lines of trams like swords
Thousands of posters asserting a monopoly of the good, the beautiful, the true
Crowds of people all in the vocative, you and you,
The haze of the morning shot with words.

Yellow sun comes white off the wet streets but bright
Chromium yellows in the gay sun's light
Filleted sun streaks the purple mist,
Everything is kissed and reticulated with sun
Scooped-up and cupped in the open fronts of shops
And bouncing on the traffic which never stops.

And the street fountain blown across the square
Rainbow-trellises the air and sunlight blazons
The red butcher's and scrolls of fish on marble slabs
Whistled bars of music crossing silver sprays
And horns of cars, touché, touché, rapiers' retort, a moving cage,
A turning page of shine and sound, the day's maze.

But when the sun goes out, the streets go cold, the hanging meat
And tiers of fish are colorless and merely dead
And the hoots of cars neurotically repeat and the tiptoed feet
Of women hurry and falter whose faces are dead
And I see in the air but not belonging there
The blown gray powder of the fountain gray as the ash
That forming on a cigarette covers the red.

## BIRMINGHAM

Smoke from the train-gulf hid by hoardings blunders upward, the brakes of cars
Pipe as the policeman pivoting round raises his flat hand, bars
With his figure of a monolith Pharaoh the queue of fidgety machines
(Chromium dogs on the bonnet, faces behind the triplex screens)
Behind him the streets run away between the proud glass of shops
Cubical scent-bottles artificial legs arctic foxes and electric mops

But beyond this center the slumward vista thins like a diagram:
There, unvisited, are Vulcan's forges who doesn't care a tinker's damn.

Splayed outwards through the suburbs houses, houses for rest
Seducingly rigged by the builder, half-timbered houses with lips pressed
So tightly and eyes staring at the traffic through bleary haws
And only a six-inch grip of the racing earth in their concrete claws;
In these houses men as in a dream pursue the Platonic Forms
With wireless and cairn terriers and gadgets approximating to the fickle norms
And endeavor to find God and score one over the neighbor
By climbing tentatively upward on jerry-built beauty and sweated labor.

The lunch hour: the shops empty, shopgirls' faces relax
Diaphanous as green glass empty as old almanacs
As incoherent with ticketed gewgaws tiered behind their heads
As the Burne-Jones windows in St. Philip's broken by crawling leads
Insipid color, patches of emotion, Saturday thrills—
(This theater is sprayed with "June")—the gutter take our old playbills,
Next week-end it is likely in the heart's funfair we shall pull
Strong enough on the handle to get back our money; or at any rate it is possible.

On shining lines the trams like vast sarcophagi move
Into the sky, plum after sunset, merging to duck's egg, barred with mauve
Zeppelin clouds, and pentecost-like the cars' headlights bud
Out from sideroads and the traffic signals, crème-de-menthe or bull's blood,
Tell one to stop, the engine gently breathing, or to go on
To where like black pipes of organs in the frayed and fading zone
Of the West the factory chimneys on sullen sentry will all night wait
To call, in the harsh morning, sleep-stupid faces through the daily gate.

# W. H. Auden

W. H. (WYSTAN HUGH) AUDEN was born in 1907, was at Oxford with Day Lewis and Spender, and went down from Christ Church in 1928, teaching near Malvern.

*Poems* (1930) and *The Orators* (1932) were published, together with the supplementary *Dance of Death,* in a one-volume American edition severely entitled *Poems* (1934). Printed in this country simultaneously with Stephen Spender, Auden was continually reviewed with Spender, and when it was learned that both poets had an Oxford education, poetic influences, and radical political policies in common, critics coupled them as though they were two parts of one poet, dangerous but distinguished Siamese twins. No understanding reader could have confused or coupled the two. Spender is a romantic and, in spite of a "modern" vocabulary, traditional poet; Auden is a satirical and experimental one. But contrasts are as misleading as comparisons, and Spender's work is considered separately on page 528. Auden has entirely different claims upon the reader.

The two most obvious features of Auden's poetry are its vitality and its obscurity. No contemporary poet has a greater natural command of language; he makes rhetoric out of banal jargon, and summons eloquence without raising his voice. This very eloquence is his undoing, for, having launched his poem brilliantly, he plunges too often into a sea of free association, private symbols, mad wit, and incoherent angers until Auden loses first the reader and, finally, himself. Yet, even in the most difficult longer poems, parts break through which require no key nor comment. "Paid on Both Sides" is typical; it is a thirty-page play (its author calls it a "charade") which has a collapsing civilization for its background and which, in its confusion of purpose and effects, baffles intelligences higher than the average. Yet every individual scene is dynamic; the sense of shock is communicated with a touch of horror; and passage after passage calls attention to Auden's technical gifts. Surpassing Spender in his use of shifting rhyme and other devices of sound, Auden is the most daring and successful experimenter (with the exception of MacLeish) since Wilfred Owen. A single reading will barely suggest the skill of Auden's metric and the integrity of his idiom, maintained through all the varying forms. He employs suspensions and "analyzed" rhyme with great freedom, mingles assonance with perfect rhyme, and explores the limbo between prose and verse, between music and mathematics. In the midst of the "Journal of an Airman"—a mélange of diagrams, technical signs, and general discontinuity—Auden casually inserts a perfectly disciplined sestina, possibly the strictest and most complicated of the antique forms.

Such procedure hints at a lack of integration; it points to willfullness and self-division, and it is not difficult to find both characteristics throughout Auden's work. He is a writer of many styles rather than a perfecter of one idiom. He adopts the structure of *The Waste Land,* the consonantal rhymes of Wilfred Owen, the interior monologue of Joyce. He even imitates Gerard Manley Hopkins' alliterative assonance and his onrushing syllables, imitates them to the point of parody:

> Which of you waking early and watching daybreak
> Will not hasten in heart, handsome, aware of wonder
> At light unleashed, advancing, a leader of movement,
> Breaking like surf on turf on road and roof . . .

or even more obviously and unapologetically:

> Me, March, you do with your movements master and rock
> With wing-whirl, whale-wallow, silent budding of cell. . . .

Self-divided, too, is Auden's philosophy. He is merciless in his mockery of "the old gang"; yet he is not convincingly on the "other side." He speaks for those who are bullied into war and exploited in peace, but he is not really one of them. Even his satire fails, for it is indiscriminate. In burlesquing his victims Auden sometimes becomes confused and identified with them, so that, as Day Lewis said, "instead of the relation between satirist and victim which alone can give significance to satire we get a series of figures of fun into each of whom the satirist temporarily disappears." There are pages which make a complete and immediate communication, and there are whole poems which exhibit a total indifference to whether or not they are understood.

It is doubtful if Auden's best qualities are revealed in the long, involved poems he prefers to write, poems which seem dictated by a savage *sur-realisme* and sheer irresponsibility. The odes and the shorter poems are more rewarding; they do not suffer from the arbitrariness and obliquity which prevent his technical mastery from reaching all but a few readers. Even in the poems which are least successful there is a vigor, a real virtuosity, of expression. In such poems as the "Ode; To My Pupils," with its militant figures and setting of imminent war, in such lyrics as "The strings' excitement" and "This lunar beauty," and the choruses in "Paid on Both Sides" with their morose and desperate overtones, there is an energy of statement, a swiftness of suggestion unmatched by any of Auden's contemporaries. If Auden does not become bogged in his own brilliance, if he relies on broader effects and plainer patterns, as he can well afford to do, he may well become the most effective, as he already is the most forceful, poet of his generation.

## CHORUS FROM A PLAY

Doom is dark and deeper than any sea-dingle:
Upon what man it fall
In spring, day-wishing flowers appearing,
Avalanche sliding, white snow from rock-face,
That he should leave his house;
No cloud-soft hands can hold him, restraint by women,
But ever that man goes
By place-keepers, by forest trees,
A stranger to strangers over undried sea,
Houses for fishes, suffocating water;
Or lonely on fell as chat,
By pot-holed becks
A bird stone-haunting, an unquiet bird.

There head falls forward, fatigued at evening,
And dreams of home:
Waving from window, spread of welcome,
Kissing of wife under single sheet;
But waking sees
Bird-flocks nameless to him, through doorway voices
Of new men making another love.

Save him from hostile capture
From sudden tiger's spring at corner:
Protect his house,
His anxious house where days are counted
From thunderbolt protect,
From gradual ruin spreading like a stain:
Converting number from vague to certain
Bring joy, bring day of his returning,
Lucky with day approaching, with leaning dawn.

## ODE; TO MY PUPILS

Though aware of our rank and alert to obey orders,
Watching with binoculars the movement of the grass for an ambush,
The pistol cocked, the code-word committed to memory;
      The youngest drummer
Knows all the peace-time stories like the oldest soldier,
      Though frontier-conscious,

About the tall white gods who landed from their open boat,
Skilled in the working of copper, appointing our feast-days,
Before the islands were submerged, when the weather was calm,
      The maned lion common,
An open wishing-well in every garden;
      When love came easy.

Perfectly certain, all of us, but not from the records,
Not from the unshaven agent who returned to the camp;
The pillar dug from the desert recorded only
      The sack of a city,
The agent clutching his side collapsed at our feet,
      "Sorry! They got me!"

Yes, they were living here once but do not now,
Yes, they are living still but do not here;
Lying awake after Lights Out a recruit may speak up:
      "Who told you all this?"
The tent-talk pauses a little till a veteran answers
      "Go to sleep, Sonny!"

Turning over he closes his eyes, and then in a moment
Sees the sun at midnight bright over cornfield and pasture,
Our hope. . . . Someone jostles him, fumbling for boots,
      Time to change guard:
Boy, the quarrel was before your time, the aggressor
      No one you know.

Your childish moments of awareness were all of our world,
At five you sprang, already a tiger in the garden,
At night your mother taught you to pray for our Daddy
      Far away fighting,
One morning you fell off a horse and your brother mocked you:
      "Just like a girl!"

You've got their names to live up to and questions won't help,
You've a very full program, first aid, gunnery, tactics,
The technique to master of raids and hand-to-hand fighting;
      Are you in training?
Are you taking care of yourself? are you sure of passing
      The endurance test?

Now we're due to parade on the square in front of the Cathedral,
When the bishop has blessed us, to file in after the choir-boys,
To stand with the wine-dark conquerors in the roped-off pews,
        Shout ourselves hoarse:
"They ran like hares; we have broken them up like fire-wood;
        They fought against God."

While in a great rift in the limestone miles away
At the same hour they gather, tethering their horse beside them;
A scarecrow prophet from a bowlder foresees our judgment,
        Their oppressors howling;
And the bitter psalm is caught by the gale from the rocks:
        "How long shall they flourish?"

What have we all been doing to have made from Fear
That laconic war-bitten captain addressing them now?
"Heart and head shall be keener, mood the more
        As our might lessens":
To have caused their shout "We will fight till we lie down beside
        The Lord we have loved."

There's Wrath who has learnt every trick of guerilla war-fare,
The shamming dead, the night-raid, the feinted retreat;
Envy their brilliant pamphleteer, to lying
        As husband true,
Expert Impersonator and linguist, proud of his power
        To hoodwink sentries.

Gluttony living alone, austerer than us,
Big simple greed, Acedia famed with them all
For her stamina, keeping the outposts, and somewhere Lust
        With his sapper's skill,
Muttering to his fuses in a tunnel "Could I meet here with Love,
        I would hug him to death."

There are faces there for which for a very long time
We've been on the look-out, though often at home we imagined,
Catching sight of a back or hearing a voice through a doorway,
        We had found them at last;
Put our arms round their necks and looked in their eyes and discovered
        We were unlucky.

And some of them, surely, we seem to have seen before:
Why, that girl who rode off on her bicycle one fine summer evening
And never returned, she's there; and the banker we'd noticed
        Worried for weeks;
Till he failed to arrive one morning and his room was empty,
        Gone with a suitcase.

They speak of things done on the frontier we were never told,
The hidden path to their squat Pictish tower

They will never reveal though kept without sleep, for their code is
        "Death to the squealer":
They are brave, yes, though our newspapers mention their bravery
        In inverted commas.

But careful; back to our lines; it is unsafe there,
Passports are issued no longer; that area is closed;
There's no fire in the waiting-room now at the climbers' Junction,
        And all this year
Work has been stopped on the power-house; the wind whistles under
        The half-built culverts.

Do you think that because you have heard that on Christmas Eve
In a quiet sector they walked about on the skyline,
Exchanged cigarettes, both learning the words for "I love you"
        In either language:
You can stroll across for a smoke and a chat any evening?
        Try it and see.

That rifle-sight you're designing; is it ready yet?
You're holding us up; the office is getting impatient;
The square munition-works out on the old allotments
        Needs stricter watching;
If you see any loiterers there you may shoot without warning,
        We must stop that leakage.

All leave is cancelled tonight; we must say good-by.
We entrain at once for the North; we shall see in the morning
The headlands we're doomed to attack; snow down to the tide-line:
        Though the bunting signals
"Indoors before it's too late; cut peat for your fires,"
        We shall lie out there.

## THE STRINGS' EXCITEMENT

The strings' excitement, the applauding drum
Are but the initiating ceremony
That out of cloud the ancestral face may
  come.

And never hear their subaltern mockery,
Graphiti-writers, moss-grown with whimsies,
Loquacious when the watercourse is dry.

It is your face I see, and morning's praise
Of you is ghost's approval of the choice,
Filtered through roots of the effacing grass.

Fear, taking me aside, would give advice
"To conquer her, the visible enemy,
It is enough to turn away the eyes."

Yet there's no peace in this assaulted city
But speeches at the corners, hope for news,
Outside the watchfires of a stronger army.

And all emotions to expression came,
Recovering the archaic imagery:
This longing for assurance takes the form

Of a hawk's vertical stooping from the sky;
These tears, salt for a disobedient dream,
The lunatic agitation of the sea;

While this despair with hardened eyeballs
  cries
"A Golden Age, a Silver . . . rather this,
Massive and taciturn years, the Age of Ice."

THIS LUNAR BEAUTY

This lunar beauty
Has no history
Is complete and early;
If beauty later
Bear any feature
It had a lover
And is another.

This like a dream
Keeps other time
And daytime is
The loss of this;

For time is inches
And the heart's changes
Where ghost has haunted
Lost and wanted.

But this was never
A ghost's endeavor
Nor finished this,
Was ghost at ease;
And till it pass
Love shall not near
The sweetness here
Nor sorrow take
His endless look.

ALWAYS THE FOLLOWING WIND

*Voice:*

Always the following wind of history
Of others' wisdom makes a buoyant air
Till we come suddenly on pockets where
Is nothing loud but us; where voices seem
Abrupt, untrained, competing with no lie
Our fathers shouted once. They taught us war,
To scamper after darlings, to climb hills,
To emigrate from weakness, find ourselves
The easy conquerors of empty bays:
But never told us this, left each to learn,
Hear something of that soon-arriving day
When to gaze longer and delighted on
A face or idea be impossible.
Could I have been some simpleton that lived
Before disaster sent his runners here;
Younger than worms, worms have too much to bear.
Yes, mineral were best: could I but see
These woods, these fields of green, this lively world
Sterile as moon.

*Chorus:*

The Spring unsettles sleeping partnerships,
Foundries improve their casting process, shops
Open a further wing on credit till
The winter. In summer boys grow tall
With running races on the froth-wet sand,
War is declared there, here a treaty signed;
Here a scum breaks up like a bomb, there troops
Deploy like birds. But proudest into traps
Have fallen. These gears which ran in oil for week
By week, needing no look, now will not work;
Those manors mortgaged twice to pay for love
Go to another.

O how shall man live
Whose thought is born, child of one farcical night,
To find him old? The body warm but not
By choice, he dreams of folk in dancing bunches,
Of tart wine spilt on home-made benches,
Where learns, one drawn apart, a secret will
Restore the dead; but comes thence to a wall.
Outside on frozen soil lie armies killed
Who seem familiar, but they are cold.
Now the most solid wish he tries to keep
His hands show through; he never will look up,
Say "I am good." On him misfortune falls
More than enough. Better where no one feels,
The out-of-sight, buried too deep for shafts.

### CHORUS

#### (from "Paid on Both Sides")

To throw away the key and walk away
Not abrupt exile, the neighbors asking why,
But following a line with left and right
An altered gradient at another rate
Learns more than maps upon the whitewashed wall
The hand put up to ask; and makes us well
Without confession of the ill. All pasts
Are single old past now, although some posts
Are forwarded, held looking on a new view;
The future shall fulfill a surer vow
Not smiling at queen over the glass rim
Nor making gunpowder in the top room,
Not swooping at the surface still like gulls
But with prolonged drowning shall develop gills.

But there are still to tempt; areas not seen
Because of blizzards or an erring sign
Whose guessed-at wonders would be worth alleging,
And lies about the cost of a night's lodging.
Travelers may sleep at inns but not attach,
They sleep one night together, not asked to touch;
Receive no normal welcome, not the pressed lip,
Children to lift, not the assuaging lap.
Crossing the pass descend the growing stream
Too tired to hear except the pulses' strum,
Reach villages to ask for a bed in
Rock shutting out the sky, the old life done.

### BALLAD

O what is that sound which so thrills the ear
Down in the valley drumming, drumming?

Only the scarlet soldiers, dear,
  The soldiers coming.

O what is that light I see flashing so clear
  Over the distance brightly, brightly?
Only the sun on their weapons, dear,
  As they step lightly.

O what are they doing with all that gear;
  What are they doing this morning, this morning?
Only the usual maneuvers, dear,
  Or perhaps a warning.

O why have they left the road down there;
  Why are they suddenly wheeling, wheeling?
Perhaps a change in the orders, dear;
  Why are you kneeling?

O haven't they stopped for the doctor's care;
  Haven't they reined their horses, their horses?
Why, they are none of them wounded, dear,
  None of these forces.

O is it the parson they want, with white hair;
  Is it the parson, is it, is it?
No, they are passing his gateway, dear,
  Without a visit.

O it must be the farmer who lives so near,
  It must be the farmer, so cunning, cunning;
They have passed the farm already, dear,
  And now they are running.

O where are you going? stay with me here.
  Were the vows you swore me deceiving, deceiving?
No, I promised to love you, my dear,
  But I must be leaving.

O it's broken the lock and splintered the door,
  O it's the gate where they're turning, turning;
Their feet are heavy on the floor
  And their eyes are burning.

## Stephen Spender

STEPHEN SPENDER. was born February 28, 1909, of mixed German, Jewish and English origins; his mother was Violet Schuster, his father was Harold Spender, the journalist. As a child he was especially interested in painting; at seventeen he supported himself by printing chemists' labels on his own press. At nineteen he attended University College, Oxford, but finding university training alien to his temperament, did not then complete his courses. After traveling abroad he returned to Oxford, and went down from University in 1931.

In his eighteenth year Spender himself set up and printed a paper-bound pamphlet of verse, *Nine Experiments* (1928), which is now unprocurable. Immature though much of it is, an individuality already declares itself. *Twenty Poems* (1930), printed while Spender was still an undergraduate, emphasizes his fecundity; it sounds, tentatively but distinctly, the note of passion so recognizable in the later verse. An imagination, and a fiery one, is at play in such early poems as "A Whim of Time," "Farewell in a Dream," "Winter Landscape" and "Epilogue."

*Poems,* published in England in 1933 and in America in 1934, reveals a complete poet. Maturity is manifest in every poem and a revolutionary fervor which caused the critics to compare Spender to Shelley. Some of the reviewers demurred at the unconcealed communism throughout, but the lyrical impulse was so great that Spender was hailed as one of the most significant voices of his day. The American edition of *Poems* is more inclusive than the English volume since it contains nine new poems, one of which is the moving "Van der Lubbe," written shortly after the Reichstag fire. Spender's subject matter is arresting—sometimes too arresting— for it directs too much attention on externals and leads to controversy about that which matters least in poetry. Spender himself is a little too conscious, even too belligerent, about his properties. Riding in a train, watching the world hasten away "like the quick spool of a film," he sees the grass, the cottage by the lake, the familiar symbols, "vivid but unreal."

> Real were iron lines, and, smashing the grass
> The cars in which we ride, and real our compelled time:
> Painted on enamel beneath the moving glass
> Unreal were cows, the wave-winged storks, the lime:
> These burned in a clear world from which we pass
> Like *rose* and *love* in a forgotten rhyme.

Oftener than not, Spender brought machinery over into poetry, accomplishing a fusion of modern imagery and traditional magic. He has not merely stated the superficial aspects of the machine age, he has assimilated and re-created the daily symbols of his environment. As early as 1928, while a remnant of the Georgians were still invoking literary laverocks, lonely lambs, and dependably deathless nightingales, Spender was writing, "Come let us praise the gasworks." And a few years later, the same unaffected accent expressed itself in simple, transparent delight:

> More beautiful and soft than any moth
> With burring furred antennae feeling its huge path
> Through dusk, the air-liner with shut-off engines
> Glides over suburbs and the sleeves set trailing tall
> To point the wind. Gently, broadly, she falls,
> Scarcely disturbing charted currents of air.

Spender is not always as direct as this. Inclined to sentimentality he overcompensates by forcing himself to the other extreme; distrusting the appearance of his simplicities he disguises them in strained metaphors and involved images. The result

is a blurring of vision and an ambiguity of communication. Too often the reader
has to guess at the very meaning of a line that begins clearly enough but ends in
a verbal fog. There is, however, no uncertainty about Spender's emotion. The emotion is always clear, warm, compelling. It is serious and straightforward, especially
in such poems as "The Express," "What I Expected," reaching a powerful climax
in "The Prisoners," "The Funeral" and the moving "An Elementary Classroom,"
which has not yet appeared in a volume. It is not so much Spender's choice of
opinions—though there is no doubt on which side he will fight—nor his disdain
for clichés of thought or phrase, but the integrity of his aim, the sheer thrust of
his seriousness and power of vision which makes this poet's work so vigorous and
exciting.

> Eye, gazelle, delicate wanderer,
> Drinker of horizon's fluid line;
> Ear that suspends on a chord
> The spirit drinking timelessness.

From such expressions of sensibility he proceeds to his chief concern:

> We have come at last to a country
> Where light equal, like shine from snow, strikes all faces,
> Here you may wonder
> How it was that works, money, interest, building, could ever hide
> The palpable and obvious love of man.

That is Spender's major theme: "The palpable and obvious love of man." In
spite of his occasional weaknesses, Spender has the power of animating facts and
figures, of opening up new territory, of turning abstractions into action. His passion
warms statistics and achieves an utterance which is intense, humorless, intimate and,
without parading its courage, noble.


### FAREWELL IN A DREAM

> Now shout into my dream. These trumpets snored
> Less golden by my side, when you were there. . .
> It is no reason now to think me coward
> That, being insulted by a gamekeeper,
> I hung my head, or looked into the air:
> Thrusting between the peaks without a word,
> Buttressed against the winds, or like a sword,
> Then you were undisputed conqueror.
>
> But dragged into this nightmare symphony
> Of drum and tempest surging in my head,
> Faced by these symbols of reality
> You showed as one most pitifully naked.
> I hailed your earth. Salute my Hades too.
> Since we must part, let's part as heroes do.

## STATISTICS

Lady, you think too much of speeds,
　Pulleys and cranes swing in your mind;
　The Woolworth Tower has made you blind
To Egypt and the pyramids.

Too much impressed by motor-cars
　You have a false historic sense.
　But I, perplexed at God's expense
Of electricity on stars,

From Brighton pier shall weigh the seas,
　And count the sands along the shore:
　Despise all moderns, thinking more
Of Shakespeare and Praxiteles.

## A WHIM OF TIME

A whim of time, the general arbiter,
Proclaims the love instead of death of friends.
Under the domed sky and athletic sun
The three stand naked, the new, bronzed German,
The young communist and myself, being English.
Yet to unwind the traveled sphere ten years
And two take arms, spring to a ghostly posture:
Or else roll on the thing a further ten
And the poor clerk with world-offended eyes
Builds with red hands his heaven; makes our bones
A necessary scaffolding to peace.

Now I suppose that the once-envious dead
Have learnt a strict philosophy of clay
After these centuries, to haunt us no longer
In the churchyard, or at the end of the lane,
Or howling at the edge of the city
Beyond the last bean-rows, near the new factory.
Our fathers enemies, yet lives no feud
Of prompting Hamlet on the kitchen stair,
There falls no shade across our blank of peace
Being together struck across the path
Or taper finger threatening solitude.

Our father's misery, the dead man's mercy,
The cynic's mystery, weaves a philosophy—
That history of man traced purely from dust
Is lipping skulls on the revolving rim
Or posture of slavery with the granite head bowed:
These, risen a moment, joined or separate,
Fall heavily, then are always separate.
A stratum scarce reckoned by geologers,
Sod lifted, turned, slapped back again with spade.

### EPILOGUE

Time is a thing
That does not pass through boredom and the wishing,
But must be fought with, rushed at, over-awed,
And threatened with a sword:

For that prodigious voyager, the Mind,
Another self doth find
At each hour's stage, and riven, hewn and wrought
Cannot foretell its port.

Let heart be done, shut close the whining eyes,
And work, or drink, or sleep, till life defies
Minute, month, hour and day
Which are harrowed, and beaten, and scared away.

### DISCOVERED IN MID-OCEAN

He will watch the hawk with an indifferent eye
            Or pitifully;
Nor on those eagles that so feared him, now
            Will strain his brow;
Weapons men use, stone, sling, and strong-thewed bow
            He will not know.

This aristocrat, superb of all instinct,
            With death close linked
Had paced the enormous cloud, almost had won
            War on the sun;
Till now like Icarus mid-ocean-drowned,
            Hands, wings, are found. . . .

### WHAT I EXPECTED

What I expected was
Thunder, fighting,
Long struggles with men
And climbing.
After continual straining
I should grow strong;
Then the rocks would shake
And I should rest long.

What I had not foreseen
Was the gradual day
Weakening the will
Leaking the brightness away,
The lack of good to touch
The fading of body and soul
Like smoke before wind
Corrupt, unsubstantial.

The wearing of Time,
And the watching of cripples pass
With limbs shaped like questions
In their odd twist,
The pulverous grief
Melting the bones with pity,
The sick falling from earth—
These, I could not foresee.

For I had expected always
Some brightness to hold in trust,
Some final innocence
To save from dust;
That, hanging solid,
Would dangle through all
Like the created poem
Or the dazzling crystal.

### THE PRISONERS

Far, far the least of all, in want,
Are these,
The prisoners
Turned massive with their vaults and dark with dark.

They raise no hands, which rest upon their knees,
But lean their solid eyes against the night,
Dimly they feel
Only the furniture they use in cells.

Their time is almost Death. The silted flow
Of years on years
Is marked by dawns
As faint as cracks on mud-flats of despair.

My pity moves amongst them like a breeze
On walls of stone
Fretting for summer leaves, or like a tune
On ears of stone.

Then, when I raise my hands to strike,
It is too late,
There are no chains that fall
Nor visionary liquid door
Melted with anger.

When have their lives been free from walls and dark
And airs that choke?
And where less prisoner to let my anger
Like a sun strike?

If I could follow them from room to womb
To plant some hope
Through the black silk of the big-bellied gown
There would I win.

No, no, no,
It is too late for anger,
Nothing prevails
But pity for the grief they cannot feel.

### WINTER LANDSCAPE

Come home with white gulls waving across gray
Fields. Evening. A daffodil West.
Somewhere in clefts of rock the birds hide, breast to breast.

I warm with fire. Curtain shrouds dying day.
Alone. By the glowing ember
I shut out the bleak-tombed evenings of November.

And breast to breast, those swans. Sheep huddle and press
Close. Each to each. Oh,
Is there no herd of men like beasts where man may go?

Come home at last; come, end of loneliness.
Sea. Evening. Daffodil West.
And our thin dying souls against Eternity pressed.


### THE FUNERAL

Death is another milestone on their way.
With laughter on their lips and with winds blowing round them
They record simply
How this one excelled all others in making driving-belts.

This is festivity, it is the time of statistics
When they record what one unit contributed:
They are glad as they lay him back in the earth
And thank him for what he gave them.

They walk home remembering the straining red flags,
And with pennons of song still fluttering through their blood
They speak of the world-state
With its towns like brain-centers and its pulsing arteries.

They think how one life hums, revolves and toils,
One cog in a golden and singing hive:
Like spark from fire, its task happily achieved,
It falls away quietly.

No more are they haunted by the individual grief
Nor the crocodile tears of European genius,
The decline of a culture
Mourned by scholars who dream of the ghosts of Greek boys.


### THE EXPRESS

After the first powerful plain manifesto
The black statement of pistons, without more fuss
But gliding like a queen, she leaves the station.
Without bowing and with restrained unconcern
She passes the houses which humbly crowd outside,
The gasworks and at last the heavy page
Of death, printed by gravestones in the cemetery.
Beyond the town there lies the open country
Where, gathering speed, she acquires mystery,
The luminous self-possession of ships on ocean.
It is now she begins to sing—at first quite low
Then loud, and at last with a jazzy madness—
The song of her whistle screaming at curves,
Of deafening tunnels, brakes, innumerable bolts.

And always light, aerial, underneath
Goes the elate meter of her wheels.
Steaming through metal landscape on her lines
She plunges new eras of wild happiness
Where speed throws up strange shapes, broad curves
And parallels clean like the steel of guns.
At last, further than Edinburgh or Rome,
Beyond the crest of the world, she reaches night
Where only a low streamline brightness
Of phosphorus on the tossing hills is white.
Ah, like a comet through flames she moves entranced
Wrapt in her music no bird song, no, nor bough
Breaking with honey buds, shall ever equal.


THE LANDSCAPE NEAR AN AERODROME

More beautiful and soft than any moth
With burring furred antennae feeling its huge path
Through dusk, the air-liner with shut-off engines
Glides over suburbs and the sleeves set trailing tall
To point the wind. Gently, broadly, she falls,
Scarcely disturbing charted currents of air.

Lulled by descent, the travelers across sea
And across feminine land indulging its easy limbs
In miles of softness, now let their eyes trained by watching
Penetrate through dusk the outskirts of this town
Here where industry shows a fraying edge.
Here they may see what is being done.

Beyond the winking masthead light
And the landing-ground, they observe the outposts
Of work: chimneys like lank black fingers
Or figures frightening and mad: and squat buildings
With their strange air behind trees, like women's faces
Shattered by grief. Here where few houses
Moan with faint light behind their blinds
They remark the unhomely sense of complaint, like a dog
Shut out and shivering at the foreign moon.

In the last sweep of love, they pass over fields
Behind the aerodrome, where boys play all day
Hacking dead grass: whose cries, like wild birds,
Settle upon the nearest roofs
But soon are hid under the loud city.

Then, as they land, they hear the tolling bell
Reaching across the landscape of hysteria
To where, larger than all the charcoaled batteries
And imaged towers against that dying sky,
Religion stands, the church blocking the sun.

AN ELEMENTARY SCHOOL CLASSROOM

Far far from gusty waves, these children's faces.
Like rootless weeds the torn hair round their paleness.
The tall girl with her weighed-down head. The paper-
seeming boy with rat's eyes. The stunted unlucky heir
Of twisted bones, reciting a father's gnarled disease,
His lesson from his desk. At back of the dim class
One unnoted, mild and young: his eyes live in a dream
Of squirrels' game, in tree room, other than this.

On sour cream walls, donations. Shakespeare's head
Cloudless at dawn, civilized dome riding all cities.
Belled, flowery, Tyrolese valley. Open-handed map
Awarding the explicit world, of every name but here.
To few, too few, these are real windows: world and words and waving
Leaves, to heal. For these young lives, guilty and dangerous
Is fantasy of travel. Surely, Shakespeare is wicked

To lives that wryly turn, under the structural Lie,
Toward smiles or hate? Amongst their heap, these children
Wear skins peeped through by bones, and spectacles of steel
With mended glass, like bottle bits in slag.
Tyrol is wicked; map's promising a fable:
All of their time and space are foggy slum,
So blot their maps with slums as big as doom.

Unless, dowager, governor, these pictures, in a room
Columned above childishness, like our day's future drift
Of smoke concealing war, are voices shouting
O that beauty has words and works which break
Through colored walls and towers. The children stand
As in a climbing mountain train. This lesson illustrates
The world green in their many valleys beneath:
The total summer heavy with their flowers.

# INDEXES

# INDEX OF AUTHORS

*References in parentheses are to editorial mentions.*

# INDEX OF TITLES